PROCEEDINGS OF THE TWENTY-SIXTH ANNUAL SYMPOSIUM ON

COMPUTATIONAL GEOMETRY

(SCG'10)

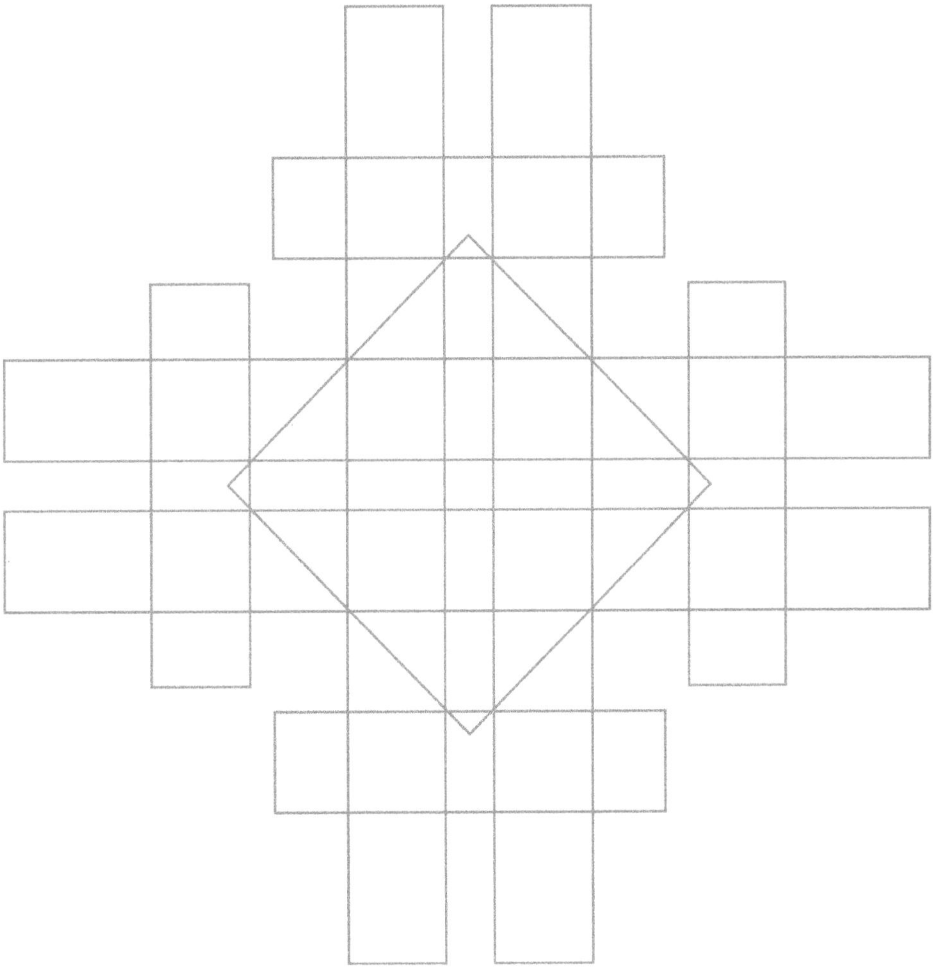

June 13–16, 2010
Snowbird, Utah, USA

Sponsored by ACM SIGACT & ACM SIGGRAPH

Association for
Computing Machinery

Advancing Computing as a Science & Profession

The Association for Computing Machinery
2 Penn Plaza, Suite 701
New York, New York 10121-0701

ISBN: 978-1-4503-0016-2

Additional copies may be ordered prepaid from:

ACM Order Department
PO Box 30777
New York, NY 10087-0777, USA

Phone: 1-800-342-6626 (USA and Canada)
+1-212-626-0500 (Global)
Fax: +1-212-944-1318
E-mail: acmhelp@acm.org
Hours of Operation: 8:30 am – 4:30 pm ET

ACM Order Number 429100

Printed in the USA

Foreword

This volume collects the research papers, short descriptions of the video presentations, and summaries of the two invited talks, that together constitute the technical proceedings of the *26th Annual Symposium on Computational Geometry (SoCG 2010),* held June 13-16, at Snowbird, Utah, USA.

A total of 145 papers were received in response to the call for papers. The program committee reviewed the submissions carefully, with a distributed effort that included expert input from both members of the program committee and a host of external reviewers (acknowledged herein); the substantial help provided by the external reviewers, under serious time constraints, is very gratefully acknowledged. The program committee deliberated electronically from January 25 to February 13; based on reviews and discussions, a total of 47 papers were selected for presentation at the symposium.

The on-line paper submission process, the review process, and the electronic discussion and decision process were all conducted with the aid of the free conference management system EasyChair.

The papers presented in these proceedings generally represent preliminary, often abstracted, results of ongoing research. We anticipate that most of these papers will eventually appear in a more fully developed form in refereed journals.

In addition to the technical papers, seven videos were received in response to the call for videos and multimedia submissions. Five videos were accepted by the video and multimedia committee for presentation at the symposium. The web proceedings showcase the revised videos at http://www.computational-geometry.org/SoCG-videos/socg10video/.

We thank all of the authors who submitted papers and videos. We are especially grateful to the members of the program committee and the video and multimedia committee for their dedication and very generous devotion of time and expertise.

SoCG 2010 is presented in cooperation with ACM SIGACT and SIGGRAPH, with local arrangements overseen by co-chairs Valerio Pascucci and Suresh Venkatasubramanian.

We hope that readers will find the contents of these proceedings interesting and thought-provoking, and that all those who attend will enjoy a vibrant and stimulating conference in the best tradition of SoCG.

David Kirkpatrick
Program Committee Chair
University of British Columbia

Joseph Mitchell
Video and Multimedia Committee Chair
SUNY Stony Brook

Table of Contents

Session 6A (Tuesday, June 15 • 9:00–10:15 am)

Session 6B (Tuesday, June 15 • 9:00–10:15 am)

Session 7A (Tuesday, June 15 • 10:45 am–12:00 pm)

Session 7B (Tuesday, June 15 • 10:45 am–12:00 pm)

Session 8A (Tuesday, June 15 • 3:00–4:20 pm)

SCG 2010 Symposium Organization

SoCG Steering Committee:

Jack Snoeyink, Chair (*University of North Carolina, USA*)
Mark de Berg, Secretary (*TU Eindhoven, The Netherlands*)
Joe Mitchell (*SUNY Stony Brook, USA*)
Günter Rote (*FU Berlin, Germany*)
Monique Teillaud (*INRIA Sophia Antipolis – Mediterranae, France*)

Program Committee:

Hee-Kap Ahn (*POSTECH, Korea*)
Nina Amenta (*University of California, Davis, USA*)
Tetsuo Asano (*JAIST, Japan*)
Sergey Bereg (*University of Texas at Dallas, USA*)
Therese Biedl (*University of Waterloo, Canada*)
Robert Bridson (*University of British Columbia, Canada*)
Erin Chambers (*Saint Louis University, USA*)
Hazel Everett (*University Nancy 2, France*)
Sándor Fekete (*Braunschweig University of Technology, Germany*)
Efi Fogel (*Tel Aviv University, Israel*)
David Kirkpatrick, Chair (*University of British Columbia, Canada*)
Valentin Polishchuk (*Helsinki Institute for Information Technology, Finland*)
Raimund Seidel (*Saarland University, Germany*)
Bettina Speckmann (*TU Eindhoven, The Netherlands*)
Csaba D. Tóth (*University of Calgary, Canada*)
Chee Yap (*Courant Institute, NYU, USA*)

Video and Multimedia Commitee:

Tamal Dey (*Ohio State University, USA*)
David Eppstein (*UC Irvine, USA*)
Jie Gao (*SUNY Stony Brook, USA*)
David Gu (*SUNY Stony Brook, USA*)
George Hart (*SUNY Stony Brook, USA*)
Joe Mitchell, Chair (*SUNY Stony Brook, USA*)
Jonathan Shewchuk (*UC Berkeley, USA*)
Monique Teillaud (*INRIA Sophia Antipolis – Mediterranae, France*)

Local Arrangements Committee:

Valerio Pascucci, Co-chair (*University of Utah, USA*)
Suresh Venkatasubramanian, Co-chair (*University of Utah, USA*)

Additional reviewers:

Mohammad Ali Abam
Peyman Afshani
Oswin Aichholzer
Dror Aiger
Helmut Alt
Victor Alvarez
Boris Aronov
Matti Åstrand
Franz Aurenhammer
Jonathan Backer
Sang Won Bae
Chandrajit Bajaj
Gill Barequet
Mark de Berg
Binay Bhattacharia
Christopher Bishop
Jean-Daniel Boissonnat
Glencora Borradaile
Prosenjit Bose
Kevin Buchin
Paz Carmi
Hamish Carr
Timothy Chan
Victor Chepoi
Yi-Jen Chiang
Bogdan Chlebus
Jinhee Chun
Sebastien Collette
Atlas F. Cook IV
Bastian Degener
Olivier Devillers
Luc Devroye
Tamal Dey
Ilias Diakonikolas
Vida Dujmovic
Adrian Dumitrescu
Christian Duncan
Laurent Dupont
Stephane Durocher
Jeff Edmonds
Alon Efrat
David Eppstein
Jeff Erickson
Will Evans
Esther Ezra
Danny Feldman
Robin Flatland
Stephan Foldes
Bernd Gärtner
Burkay Genc
Andrew Gillette
Marc Glisse
Xavier Goaoc
Mordecai J. Golin
Michael Goodrich
Chris Gray
Leonidas Guibas
Dan Halperin
Sariel Har-Peled
Masud Hasan
Herman Haverkort
Petr Hilneny
Andreas Holmsen
Ferran Hurtado
John Iacono
Piotr Indyk
Ali Jadbabaie
Minghui Jiang
Tiko Kameda
Tom Kamphans
Menelaos Karavelas
Matya Katz
Michael Kaufmann
Mark Keil
Barbara Kempkes
Michael Kerber
Mahdad Khatirinejad
Edward Kim
Jamie King
Rolf Klein
Christian Knauer
Stephen Kobourov
Vladlen Koltun
Matias Korman
Evangelos Kranakis
Robi Krauthgamer
Marc van Kreveld
Klaus Kriegel
Alexander Kroeller
Piyush Kumar
Sylvain Lazard
James Lee
Jon Lenchner
David Letscher

Additional reviewers (continued):

Vincenzo Liberatore
Beppe Liotta
Maarten Löffler
Alex Lopez-Ortiz
Anna Lubiw
Andrey Lukyanenko
Avner Magen
Pedro Machado Manhaes de Castro
Jirka Matousek
Henk Meijer
Facundo Memoli
Manor Mendel
Taneli Mielikainen
Gary Miller
Joe Mitchell
Bojan Mohar
Pat Morin
Dmitriy Morozov
David Mount
Nabil Mustafa
Amir Nayyeri
Yakov Nekrich
Raymond Ng
Martin Nöllenburg
Pavel Novotný
Yoshio Okamoto
Steve Oudot
Maks Ovsjanikov
Eli Packer
Igor Pak
Evanthia Papadopoulou
Amit Patel
Pablo Pérez-Lantero
Sylvain Petitjean
Jeff Phillips
Igor Potapov
Marc Pouget
Suneeta Ramaswami
Pedro A. Ramos
David Rappaport
Saurabh Ray
Iris Reinbacher
Marcel Roeloffzen
Günter Rote
Bardia Sadri
Stefan Schirra
Yevgeny Schreiber
André Schulz
Andre Schumacher
Michael Segal
Jeff Sember
Ophir Setter
R Sharathkumar
Don Sheehy
Vin de Silva
Michiel Smid
Shakhar Smorodinsky
Jack Snoeyink
Christian Sohler
Joachim Spoerhase
Frank van der Stappen
Daniel Stefankovic
Ileana Streinu
Xuehou Tan
Shin-ichi Tanigawa
Monique Teillaud
Takeshi Tokuyama
Ryuhei Uehara
Kevin Verbeek
Eric Colin de Verdiere
Antoine Vigneron
Kira Vyatkina
Uli Wagner
Charlie C L Wang
Christophe Weibel
Andreas Wiese
Steve Wismath
Emre Alper Yildirim
Hai Yu
Huizhen Yu
Yisong Yue
Mariette Yvenic
Binhai Zhu
Afra Zomorodian

SoCG 2010 Sponsors & Supporters

Sponsors:

SIGACT

ACMSIGGRAPH

Supporters:

SCI
www.sci.utah.edu

SCHOOL OF COMPUTING
THE UNIVERSITY OF UTAH

Optimal Partition Trees

Timothy M. Chan[*]
School of Computer Science
University of Waterloo
tmchan@uwaterloo.ca

ABSTRACT

We revisit one of the most fundamental classes of data structure problems in computational geometry: range searching. Back in SoCG'92, Matoušek gave a partition tree method for d-dimensional simplex range searching achieving $O(n)$ space and $O(n^{1-1/d})$ query time. Although this method is generally believed to be optimal, it is complicated and requires $O(n^{1+\varepsilon})$ preprocessing time for any fixed $\varepsilon > 0$. An earlier method by Matoušek (SoCG'91) requires $O(n \log n)$ preprocessing time but $O(n^{1-1/d} \log^{O(1)} n)$ query time. We give a new method that achieves simultaneously $O(n \log n)$ preprocessing time, $O(n)$ space, and $O(n^{1-1/d})$ query time with high probability. Our method has several advantages:

- It is conceptually simpler than Matoušek's SoCG'92 method. Our partition trees satisfy many ideal properties (e.g., constant degree, optimal crossing number at almost all layers, and disjointness of the children's cells at each node).
- It leads to more efficient multilevel partition trees, which are important in many data structural applications (each level adds at most one logarithmic factor to the space and query bounds, better than in all previous methods).
- A similar improvement applies to a shallow version of partition trees, yielding $O(n \log n)$ time, $O(n)$ space, and $O(n^{1-1/\lfloor d/2 \rfloor})$ query time for halfspace range emptiness in even dimensions $d \geq 4$.

Numerous consequences follow (e.g., improved results for computing spanning trees with low crossing number, ray shooting among line segments, intersection searching, exact nearest neighbor search, linear programming queries, finding extreme points, ...).

*This work has been supported by NSERC.

SCG'10, June 13–16, 2010, Snowbird, Utah, USA.

Categories and Subject Descriptors

F.2.2 [**Analysis of Algorithms and Problem Complexity**]: Nonnumerical Algorithms and Problems—*geometrical problems and computations*

General Terms

Algorithms, Theory

Keywords

Simplex range searching, halfspace range searching, geometric data structures

1. INTRODUCTION

Data structures for range searching [4, 7, 31, 34] are among the most important and most often used results within the computational geometry literature—countless papers applied such results and techniques to obtain the best theoretical computational bounds for a wide variety of geometric problems. However, to this day, some questions remain even concerning the most basic version of nonorthogonal range searching, simplex range searching. The purpose of this paper is to provide a (hopefully) final resolution to some of these lingering questions, by nailing down the best precise upper bounds.

History. Formally, in *simplex range searching*, we want to preprocess n (weighted) points in $\mathbb{R}^d$ so that we can quickly find (the sum of the weights of) all points inside a given query simplex. The dimension d is assumed to be a small constant. The problem not only is fundamental but has a remarkably rich history. We will confine the discussion of previous work to linear- or near-linear space data structures (otherwise, the number of results multiplies). The first published method was by Willard [38] in 1982, who gave a simple $O(n)$-space *partition tree* achieving $O(n^{0.792})$ query time in 2-d. This prompted researchers to look for data structures with the best exponent in the query time. Many subsequent results appeared; for example, in 2-d, Willard himself improved the exponent to about 0.774, which was further reduced to 0.695 by Edelsbrunner and Welzl [24]; in 3-d, F. Yao [40] obtained 0.936, Dobkin and Edelsbrunner [21] 0.916, Edelsbrunner and Huber [23] 0.909, and Yao *et al.* [41] 0.899; in higher dimensions, Yao and Yao [39] obtained $1 - \lceil \lg(2^d - 1) \rceil / d$; and so on. A significant advance was made in Haussler and Welzl's seminal paper [25], which introduced probabilistic techniques to computational geometry; they presented a partition tree with $O(n^{1-1/[d(d-1)+1]+\varepsilon})$ query time for any fixed $\varepsilon > 0$, greatly improving all results that came before, in all dimensions.

The right exponent turned out to be $1 - 1/d$. Four major papers described (near-)linear-space methods achieving the final near-$O(n^{1-1/d})$ query time:

1. Welzl (SoCG'88) and Chazelle and Welzl [19, 37] devised the key technique of *iterative reweighting*[1] to compute *spanning trees with low crossing number*. They obtained an elegant $O(n)$-space data structure where the answer to any query can be expressed using $O(n^{1-1/d} \log n)$ arithmetic (semigroup) operations on the weights (if subtractions on weights are allowed, the number of operations can be reduced to $O(n^{1-1/d}\alpha(n))$). Unfortunately, this combinatorial bound on the number of arithmetic operations does not bound the actual query time. Chazelle and Welzl obtained true "algorithmic" results only in 2-d, with $O(n)$ space and $O(\sqrt{n} \log n)$ query time, and in 3-d, with $O(n \log n)$ space and $O(n^{2/3} \log^2 n)$ query time. The preprocessing time of these data structures is also poor; in 2-d, one can get $O(n^{3/2} \log^{1/2} n)$ preprocessing time by a randomized algorithm [37], but improvement to a near-linear bound requires further ideas from subsequent papers. Despite these issues, their approach was a remarkable breakthrough and set up the right direction for subsequent methods to follow.

2. Next, Chazelle, Sharir, and Welzl (SoCG'90) [18] applied *cuttings* [16, 20] to get efficient data structures for simplex range searching. In the $O(n)$-space case, their method has query time $O(n^{1-1/d+\varepsilon})$ with $O(n^{1+\varepsilon})$ preprocessing time for any fixed $\varepsilon > 0$. Although this brings us closer to the ideal bounds in any dimension, this method seems inherently suboptimal by at least a logarithmic factor (the data structure requires multiple separate cuttings, so as to guarantee that for every query, at least one of the cuttings is "good").

3. Matoušek (SoCG'91) [27] combined the iterative reweighting technique with the use of cuttings to prove a new *simplicial partition theorem*. Applying the theorem in a recursive fashion gives an $O(n)$-space partition tree with $O(n^{1-1/d} \log^{O(1)} n)$ query time and $O(n \log n)$ preprocessing time.

   (The same paper also gives an alternative $O(n)$-space structure with query time $O(n^{1-1/d}(\log \log n)^{O(1)})$—or better still $O(n^{1-1/d}2^{O(\log^* n)})$ if subtractions of weights are allowed—but the preprocessing time increases to $O(n^{1+\varepsilon})$. This result is subsumed by the next result, so will be ignored here.)

4. Finally, Matoušek (SoCG'92) [30] combined iterative reweighting with the *hierarchical cuttings* of Chazelle [14] to obtain an $O(n)$-space partition tree with $O(n^{1-1/d})$ query time. The preprocessing time is $O(n^{1+\varepsilon})$. This method is considerably more complicated than Matoušek's previous partition-theorem-based method.

[1]Also called the "multiplicative weights update method" in some circles.

Among data structures that are ordinary (unaugmented) partition trees, it is not difficult to show that the query cost must be $\Omega(n^{1-1/d})$ in the worst case [19]. More generally, Chazelle [13] proved a lower bound of $\Omega(\sqrt{n})$ in 2-d and $\Omega(n^{1-1/d}/\log n)$ in higher dimensions, for any simplex range searching data structure under the semigroup arithmetic model (see [17] for another lower bound); the $\log n$ factor in the denominator could likely be an artifact of the proof.

Matoušek's final method thus seems to achieve asymptotically optimal query time. However, the story is not as neatly resolved as one would like. The main issue is preprocessing time: Matoušek's final method is suboptimal by an n^ε factor. This explains why in actual algorithmic applications of range searching results, where we care about preprocessing and query times combined, researchers usually abandon his final method and resort to his earlier partition-theorem method. Unfortunately, this is the reason why in algorithmic applications, we frequently see appearances of extra $\log^{O(1)} n$ factors in time bounds, with unspecified numbers of log factors.

Even in 2-d, no ideal data structure with $O(n \log n)$ preprocessing time, $O(n)$ space, and $O(\sqrt{n})$ query time has been found.

New results. In this paper, we give a new method that rederives Matoušek's final result of $O(n)$ space and $O(n^{1-1/d})$ query time for simplex range searching. Our new method is much simpler and easier to explain than Matoušek's final method (it is a little more involved than the partition-theorem method, but not considerably so). The partition tree satisfies many desirable properties not achieved by Matoušek's and, for example, eliminates essentially all the disadvantages mentioned in the next-to-last paragraph of his paper [30] (we use a single tree and have complete control over the crossing number at almost all layers of the tree). Our tree also satisfies properties not achieved by the partition-theorem method [27] (we use a constant-degree tree and cells do not overlap). In the 2-d case, we can even make our partition tree a BSP tree, like Willard's original partition tree. These properties in themselves are already interesting, in the author's opinion, but the approach has further major implications:

- Our method immediately yields improved results on *multilevel* versions of partition trees [7, 31], which are needed in applications that demand more sophisticated kinds of queries. With our method, each level costs at most *one* more logarithmic factor in space and at most *one* more logarithmic factor in the query time—this behavior is exactly what we want and, for example, is analogous to what we see in the classical multilevel data structure, the range tree [7, 35], which can be viewed as a d-level 1-dimensional partition tree.

  In contrast, Matoušek's final method is not applicable at all, precisely because of the disadvantages mentioned. Matoušek's final paper did explore multilevel results in detail but had to switch to a different method based on Chazelle, Sharir, and Welzl's cutting approach [18], now with hierarchical cuttings. This method costs *two* logarithmic factors in space and *one* logarithmic factor in the query time per level (see [30, Theorem 5.2]). Furthermore, the preprocessing time is huge. (An alternative version [30, Corollary 5.2] has $O(n^{1+\varepsilon})$ preprocessing time, but the space and query time increases by an unspecified number of extra logarithmic factors.) Matoušek's partition-theorem method in the multilevel setting is worse, giving extra $O(n^\varepsilon)$ (or more precisely $2^{O(\sqrt{\log n})}$) factors in space and query time per level [27].

For concrete applications, consider the problems of preprocessing n simplices in $\mathbb{R}^d$ so that we can (i) report all simplices containing a query point, or (ii) report all simplices contained inside a query simplex. These problems can be solved by a $(d+1)$-level partition tree. The previous method from [30] requires $O(n \log^{2d} n)$ space and $O(n^{1-1/d} \log^d n)$ query time. Our result reduces the space bound to $O(n \log^d n)$.

We get improved data structures for many other problems, even some traditional 2-d problems, e.g., counting the number of intersections of line segments with a query line segment, and performing ray shooting among a collection of line segments. (It is especially pleasurable to improve a few old results from Pankaj Agarwal's Ph.D. thesis [2].)

- That our method is simpler allows us to examine the preprocessing time more carefully. We show that with some extra effort, a variant of our method indeed accomplishes what we set out to find: a simplex range searching structure with $O(n \log n)$ preprocessing time, $O(n)$ space, and $O(n^{1-1/d})$ query time w.h.p.[2] The approach works in the multilevel setting as well, with one more logarithmic factor in the preprocessing time per level.

  The improved preprocessing time should immediately lead to improved time bounds for a whole array of algorithmic applications.

- We can also obtain new bounds for the *halfspace range emptiness/reporting* problem. Here, we want to decide whether a query halfspace contains any data point, or report all points inside a query halfspace. Matoušek [28] described a *shallow* version of his partition theorem to obtain a data structure with $O(n \log n)$ preprocessing time, $O(n \log \log n)$ space, and $O(n^{1-1/\lfloor d/2 \rfloor} \log^{O(1)} n + k)$ query time for any $d \geq 4$, where k denotes the output size in the reporting case. (The space was reduced to $O(n)$ by Ramos [36] for even d; see also [1] for $d = 3$.) The same paper by Matoušek also gave an alternative data structure with $O(n^{1+\varepsilon})$ preprocessing time, $O(n)$ space, and $O(n^{1-1/\lfloor d/2 \rfloor} 2^{O(\log^* n)})$ query time for halfspace range emptiness for any $d \geq 4$. Although it is conceivable that Matoušek's final method for simplex range searching with hierarchical cuttings could similarly be adapted to halfspace range emptiness for even d, to the best of the author's knowledge, no one has attempted to find out, perhaps daunted by the amount of technical details in the paper [30]. It is generally believed that the exponent $1 - 1/\lfloor d/2 \rfloor$ is tight, although a matching lower bound is currently not known.

  With our simpler method, we can derive the following, likely optimal result for even dimensions without too much extra trouble: there is a data structure for halfspace range emptiness with $O(n \log n)$ preprocessing time, $O(n)$ space, $O(n^{1-1/\lfloor d/2 \rfloor})$ query time w.h.p. for any even $d \geq 4$. The same bounds hold for halfspace range reporting when the output size k is small $(o(n^{1-1/\lfloor d/2 \rfloor} / \log^{\omega(1)} n))$.

  Halfspace range emptiness/reporting has its own long list of applications [29, 33, 12]. As a consequence, we get improved results for ray shooting and linear programming queries in intersections of halfspaces in even dimensions, exact nearest neighbor search in odd dimensions, and the computation of extreme points and convex hulls in even dimensions, to name just a few. (It is also nice to see improvements of results from the author's own Ph.D. thesis.)

Organization. The highlight of the paper is to be found in Section 3—in particular, the proof of Theorem 3.1—which describes the basic version of our new partition tree with $O(n)$ space and $O(n^{1-1/d})$ query time. This part is meant to be self-contained (except for the side remarks at the end), assuming only the background provided by Section 2. The rest of the paper—notably, Section 5 on getting $O(n \log n)$ preprocessing time—will get a bit more technical and incorporate additional known techniques, but mostly involves working out consequences of the basic new approach. Due to space constraints, results on halfspace range searching and various applications are deferred to the full version of the paper.

2. BACKGROUND

Let P be the given set of n points in $\mathbb{R}^d$, which we assume to be in general position (by standard perturbation techniques). For our purposes, we define a *partition tree* T to be any tree where each leaf stores at most a constant number of points, each point of P is stored in exactly one leaf, and each node v stores a cell $\Delta(v)$ which encloses the subset $P(v)$ of all points stored at the leaves underneath v. Throughout the paper, we take "cell" to mean a constant-size polyhedron, or to be more specific, a simplex. In general, the degree of a node is allowed to be nonconstant and the cells of the children of a node are allowed to overlap (although in our new basic method, we can guarantee constant degree and no overlaps of the cells). At each node v, we do not store any auxiliary information about $P(v)$, other than the sum of the weights in $P(v)$. Therefore, a partition tree is by our definition always an $O(n)$-space data structure.

We can answer a query for a simplex q by proceeding recursively, starting at the root. When visiting a node, we only have to recurse in children whose cells cross the boundary ∂q, since each cell completely outside q can be ignored, and each cell completely inside q can be dealt with directly using the information stored at the node (or, in the case of the reporting problem, directly reporting all points underneath the node). We can identify the children cells crossing ∂q trivially in time linear in the number of children (the degree). The total query time is then upper-bounded by the expression

$$\sum_{v \in T:\ \Delta(v) \cap \partial q \neq \emptyset} \deg(v), \qquad (1)$$

which we call the *query cost of* ∂q. (In the case of the reporting problem, we add an $O(k)$ term to the query time where

[2]Throughout the paper, the notation "w.h.p.(n)" (or "w.h.p." for short, if n is understood) means "with probability at least $1 - 1/n^{c_0}$" for an arbitrarily large constant c_0.

k is the output size.) Since the boundary ∂q has $O(1)$ facets contained in $O(1)$ hyperplanes, it suffices to asymptotically bound the maximum query cost of an arbitrary hyperplane, which we refer to as the *query cost of the tree T*.

It is known [19] that there are point sets where the query cost is $\Omega(n^{1-1/d})$ for any partition tree under the above definitions. We want to devise a worst-case optimal method to construct partition trees matching this lower bound.

We begin by mentioning Matoušek's simplicial partition theorem [27], to set the context. (We will not use this theorem anywhere, but will prove something stronger in Section 3.)

THEOREM 2.1. (Matoušek's Partition Theorem) *Let P be a set of n points in $\mathbb{R}^d$. Then for any t, we can partition P into t subsets P_i and find t cells Δ_i, with $\Delta_i \supset P_i$, such that each subset contains $\Theta(n/t)$ points and each hyperplane crosses at most $O(t^{1-1/d})$ cells.*

A recursive application of the above theorem immediately gives a partition tree where the query cost satisfies the recurrence $Q(n) \leq O(t^{1-1/d})Q(n/t) + O(t)$. If we set t to a sufficiently large constant, the recurrence has solution $Q(n) \leq O(n^{1-1/d+\varepsilon})$ for any constant $\varepsilon > 0$. If instead we set $t = n^\delta$ for a sufficiently small constant $\delta > 0$, the solution becomes $Q(n) \leq O(n^{1-1/d} \log^{O(1)} n)$. To avoid the extra n^ε or $\log^{O(1)} n$ factors, we need a more refined method, since each time we recurse using Theorem 2.1, the hidden constant in the crossing number bound "blows up".

Our new method is described in the next section, and is self-contained except for the use of two tools: a minor observation and an important lemma, both well-known and stated here without proofs.

First, we observe that in proving statements like Theorem 2.1, instead of considering an infinite number of possible hyperplanes, it suffices to work with a finite set of "test" hyperplanes. This type of observations was made in many of the previous papers [18, 19]; the particular version we need is a special case of one from [27]:

OBSERVATION 2.2. (Test Set) *Given a set P of n points in $\mathbb{R}^d$, we can construct a set H of $n^{O(1)}$ hyperplanes with the following property: For any collection of disjoint cells each containing at least one point of P, if the maximum number of cells crossed by a hyperplane in H is ℓ, then the maximum number of cells crossed by an arbitrary hyperplane is $O(\ell)$.*

For this version of the test-set observation, the proof is quite simple (briefly, we can just take H to be the $O(n^d)$ hyperplanes passing through d-tuples of points of P).

For the next lemma, we need a definition first. For a given set H of m hyperplanes, a *$(1/r)$-cutting* [15, 32, 34] is a collection of disjoint cells such that each cell Δ is crossed by at most m/r hyperplanes. Let $\mathcal{A}(H)$ denote the arrangement of H. We let H_Δ denote the subset of all hyperplanes of H that cross Δ.

LEMMA 2.3. (Cutting Lemma) *Let H be a set of m hyperplanes and Δ be any simplex in $\mathbb{R}^d$. For any r, we can find a $(1/r)$-cutting of H into $O(r^d)$ disjoint cells whose union is Δ.*

If the number of vertices in $\mathcal{A}(H)$ inside Δ is X, then the number of cells can be reduced to $O(X(r/m)^d + r^{d-1})$.

The first part of the lemma is standard and was first shown by Chazelle and Friedman [16]. The X-sensitive variant is also known; e.g., see [11, 14]. The proof is by random sampling.

To understand the intuitive significance of the cutting lemma, let H be a set of m test hyperplanes, $\Delta = \mathbb{R}^d$, and $r = t^{1/d}$. Then we get $O(t)$ cells each crossed by $O(m/t^{1/d})$ hyperplanes. The average number of points per cell is $O(n/t)$, and the average number of cells crossed by a test hyperplane is $O((t \cdot m/t^{1/d})/m) = O(t^{1-1/d})$. Thus, the cutting lemma "almost" implies the partition theorem. The challenge is to turn these average bounds into maximum bounds. For this purpose, Matoušek's proof of his partition theorem adopts an *iterative reweighting* strategy by Welzl [19, 37] (roughly, in each iteration, we apply the cutting lemma to a multiset of hyperplanes in H to find one good cell, then increase the multiplicities of the hyperplanes crossing the cell, and repeat).

3. THE BASIC METHOD

We now present our new method for simplex range searching with $O(n)$ space and $O(n^{1-1/d})$ query time. To keep the presentation simple, we defer discussion of preprocessing time to Section 5.

The key lies in the following theorem, where instead of constructing one partition of the point set from scratch as in Matoušek's partition theorem, we consider the problem of *refining* a given partition. As we will see, the main result will follow just by repeated applications of our theorem in a straightforward manner.

THEOREM 3.1. (Partition Refinement Theorem) *Let P be a set of at most n points and H be a set of m hyperplanes in $\mathbb{R}^d$. Suppose we are given t disjoint cells covering P, such that each cell contains at most $2n/t$ points of P and each hyperplane in H crosses at most ℓ cells. Then for any b, we can subdivide every cell into $O(b)$ disjoint subcells, such that each subcell contains at most $n/(bt)$ points of P, and each hyperplane in H crosses at most the following total number of subcells:*

$$O((bt)^{1-1/d} + b^{1-1/(d-1)}\ell + b \log t \log m). \qquad (2)$$

Note that the first term matches the bound from Matoušek's partition theorem for a partition into $O(bt)$ parts. In the second term, it is crucial that the coefficient $b^{1-1/(d-1)}$ is asymptotically smaller than $b^{1-1/d}$; this will ensure that repeated applications of the theorem do not cause a constant-factor blow-up, if we pick b to be sufficiently large. The third term will not matter much in the end, and is purposely not written in the tightest manner. The proof of the theorem (like Matoušek's) uses the cutting lemma repeatedly in conjunction with an iterated reweighting strategy as detailed below. The basic algorithm is quite elegant, in the author's opinion:

PROOF. We maintain a multiset $\widehat{H}$, initially containing C copies of each hyperplane in H. The value of C is not important (for conceptual purposes, we can set C to be a sufficiently large power of b, which will ensure that future multiplicities are always integers). The size $|\widehat{H}|$ of a multiset $\widehat{H}$ always refers to the sum of the multiplicities (the "weights") of the elements. Let $X_\Delta(\widehat{H})$ denote the number of vertices inside Δ defined by the hyperplanes in $\widehat{H}$ (the multiplicity of a vertex is the product of the multiplicities of its defining hyperplanes).

The algorithm. Let $\Delta_t, \dots, \Delta_1$ be the given cells in a random order. For $i = t, \dots, 1$ do:

1. Subdivide Δ_i into disjoint subcells by building a $(1/r)$-cutting of $\widehat{H}_{\Delta_i}$ inside Δ_i with
$$r := \min\left\{ |\widehat{H}_{\Delta_i}| \left(\frac{b}{X_{\Delta_i}(\widehat{H})} \right)^{1/d},\ b^{1/(d-1)} \right\}.$$
By Lemma 2.3, the number of subcells is $O(X_{\Delta_i}(\widehat{H})(r/|\widehat{H}_{\Delta_i}|)^d + r^{d-1}) = O(b)$.

2. Further subdivide each subcell, e.g., by using vertical cuts, to ensure that each subcell contains at most $n/(bt)$ points. At most $O(b)$ extra cuts are sufficient, so the number of subcells inside Δ_i remains $O(b)$.

3. For each hyperplane h, multiply the multiplicity of h in $\widehat{H}$ by $(1+1/b)^{\lambda_i(h)}$ where $\lambda_i(h)$ denotes the number of subcells inside Δ_i crossed by h.

Analysis. For a fixed hyperplane $h \in H$, let $\ell_i(h)$ be the number of cells in $\{\Delta_i, \dots, \Delta_1\}$ crossed by h. Since $\{\Delta_i, \dots, \Delta_1\}$ is a random subset of size i from a set of size t, we have $\ell_i(h) \le O(\ell i/t + \log(mt))$ w.h.p.(mt) by a Chernoff bound (a version for sampling without replacement). So, defining $\ell_i := \max_{h\in H} \ell_i(h)$, we have $\ell_i \le O(\ell i/t + \log(mt))$ w.h.p.(t).

In step 3, $\sum_{h\in\widehat{H}} \lambda_i(h) \le O(b|\widehat{H}_{\Delta_i}|/r)$, since each of the $O(b)$ subcells is crossed by at most $|\widehat{H}_{\Delta_i}|/r$ hyperplanes of $\widehat{H}_{\Delta_i}$. As $\lambda_i(h) \le O(b)$, step 3 increases $|\widehat{H}|$ by

$$\sum_{h\in\widehat{H}} [(1+1/b)^{\lambda_i(h)} - 1] \ \le\ O\left(\sum_{h\in\widehat{H}} \lambda_i(h)/b\right) \ \le\ O(|\widehat{H}_{\Delta_i}|/r) \ =\ O(\alpha_i)|\widehat{H}|$$

where $\alpha_i := \dfrac{|\widehat{H}_{\Delta_i}|}{r|\widehat{H}|} = O\left(\dfrac{1}{|\widehat{H}|}\left(\dfrac{X_{\Delta_i}(\widehat{H})}{b}\right)^{1/d} + \dfrac{|\widehat{H}_{\Delta_i}|}{b^{1/(d-1)}|\widehat{H}|} \right).$

Note that $\sum_{j=1}^{i} |\widehat{H}_{\Delta_j}| \le |\widehat{H}|\ell_i$ and $\sum_{j=1}^{n} X_{\Delta_j}(\widehat{H}) \le |\widehat{H}|^d$ by disjointness of the cells. Conditioned to a fixed choice of $\Delta_t, \dots, \Delta_{i+1}$, since Δ_i is a random element among the remaining i cells, we have $E[|\widehat{H}_{\Delta_i}|] \le |\widehat{H}|\ell_i/i$ and $E[X_{\Delta_i}(\widehat{H})] \le |\widehat{H}|^d/i$, and in particular, $E[X_{\Delta_i}(\widehat{H})^{1/d}] \le |\widehat{H}|/i^{1/d}$, so

$$E[\alpha_i] \ \le\ O\left(\frac{1}{(bi)^{1/d}} + \frac{\ell_i}{b^{1/(d-1)}i}\right).$$

Unconditionally, since $E[\ell_i] \le O(\ell i/t + \log(mt))$,

$$E[\alpha_i] \ \le\ O\left(\frac{1}{(bi)^{1/d}} + \frac{\ell}{b^{1/(d-1)}t} + \frac{\log(mt)}{b^{1/(d-1)}i}\right).$$

At the end, $|\widehat{H}| \le Cm\prod_{i=1}^{t}(1 + O(\alpha_i)) \le Cm\exp\left(O\left(\sum_{i=1}^{t}\alpha_i\right)\right)$, where

$$E\left[\sum_{i=1}^{t}\alpha_i\right] \ \le\ O\left(\frac{t^{1-1/d}}{b^{1/d}} + \frac{\ell}{b^{1/(d-1)}} + \frac{\log(mt)\log t}{b^{1/(d-1)}}\right).$$

Let $\lambda(h)$ be the total number of subcells crossed by h. Since the final multiplicity of h in $\widehat{H}$ is equal to $C(1 + 1/b)^{\lambda(h)} \le |\widehat{H}|$, it follows that $\max_{h\in H}\lambda(h) \le \log_{1+1/b}(|\widehat{H}|/C) \le O(b\log(|\widehat{H}|/C))$, which has expected value at most $O(b\log m + (bt)^{1-1/d} + b^{1-1/(d-1)}\ell + b^{1-1/(d-1)}\log(mt)\log t)$, which is upper-bounded by (2). □

THEOREM 3.2. *Given n points in $\mathbb{R}^d$, we can build a partition tree with query cost $O(n^{1-1/d})$.*

PROOF. In what follows, summations involving the variable t are over all t that are powers of 2. Let H be the test set from Observation 2.2 of size $m \le n^{O(1)}$. Initially, our partition tree consists of just a root cell containing all n points.

The algorithm. For $t = 2, 4, 8, \dots$ do:

> Let Π_t be the set of all current leaf cells Δ such that the number of points inside Δ is between n/t and $2n/t$; the number of such cells is at most t. Apply Theorem 3.1 to Π_t to get a set Π'_t of subcells where the number of points inside each subcell is at most $n/(bt)$. Make the $O(b)$ subcells of each cell $\Delta \in \Pi_t$ the children of Δ in our partition tree (Δ is no longer a leaf but its children now are).

Analysis. Let $\ell(t)$ denote the maximum number of cells of Π_t crossed by an arbitrary hyperplane. Let $\ell'(t)$ denote the maximum number of cells of Π'_t crossed by a hyperplane in H, which is bounded by (2). The maximum number of cells of Π_u crossed by a hyperplane in H is at most $\sum_{t:\ bt\le u}\ell'(t)$. By Observation 2.2, $\ell(u)$ is asymptotically bounded by the same expression. We obtain the following recurrence:

$$\ell(u) \ \le\ O\left(\sum_{t:\ bt\le u} [(bt)^{1-1/d} + b^{1-1/(d-1)}\ell(t) + b\log t\log n]\right). \quad (3)$$

Fix an arbitrarily small constant $\delta > 0$. Set b to be a sufficiently large constant depending on δ. It is a straightforward exercise to verify by induction that

$$\ell(u) \ \le\ c[u^{1-1/d} + u^{1-1/(d-1)+\delta}\log n]$$

for some constant c depending on δ and b. Note that the first term dominates when u exceeds $\log^{c'} n$ for some constant c', so we can write $\ell(u) \le O(u^{1-1/d} + \log^{O(1)} n)$. (For the induction proof, it is helpful to note that sums like $\sum_t (bt)^{1-1/d}$ form geometric series and are asymptotically bounded by their last term, as summations are over t's that are powers of 2.)

We conclude that the query cost is at most $O\left(\sum_{t\le n} b\,\ell(t)\right) \le O\left(\sum_{t\le n}[t^{1-1/d} + \log^{O(1)} n]\right) = O(n^{1-1/d})$. □

Remarks. To readers familar with the proof of Matoušek's partition theorem [27], we point out some differences with our proof of the partition refinement theorem. First, to ensure $\sum_j X_{\Delta_j}(\widehat{H}) \le |\widehat{H}|^d$, we need disjointness of cells, which forces us to choose multiple subcells from a cutting instead of one subcell per iteration. This in turn forces us to use a different multiplier $(1 + 1/b)$ instead of doubling. Unlike Theorem 2.1, Theorem 3.1 guarantees an upper but not a lower bound on size of each subset (certain versions of the test set observation, e.g., Observation 5.1, require such a lower bound), though this is not an issue in our proof of Theorem 3.2.

To those familiar with Matoušek's final method based on hierarchical cuttings [30], we note that our method share certain common ideas. Both apply iterative reweighting more "globally" to refine multiple cells simultaneously, as a way to avoid constant-factor blow-up in the partition-theorem method; and hierarchical cuttings originate from the same X-sensitive version of the cutting lemma. However, Matoušek's method uses a far more complicated weight/multiplicity function, because it tries to deal with different layers of the tree all at once; in contrast, our partition refinement theorem works with one layer at a time and leads to a simpler, more modular design. Matoušek's method also requires a special root of $O(n^{1/d}\log n)$ degree (whose children cells may overlap), and does not guarantee optimality for $\ell(t)$ except at the bottommost layer, whereas our method ensures optimality for almost all layers (except near the very top for very small t, which is not important). This will make a difference in the next section and in subsequent applications to multilevel data structures.

Random ordering is convenient but is not the most crucial part of the proof of Theorem 3.1: We can easily deterministically find a good cell Δ_i in each iteration if we do not care about the bound on ℓ_i. The naive bound $\ell_i \le \ell$ can still lead to a weaker version of Theorem 3.1 with an extra logarithmic factor in the second term of (2), and Theorem 3.2 can still be derived but with some extra effort. Alternatively, we can derandomize (hint: consider the potential function $\sum_{h\in\widehat{H}} 2^{c\ell_i(h)t/i}$).

In the 2-d case, our partition tree can be made into a BSP tree, since the cuttings produced by taking canonical triangulations of the arrangements of samples are easily realizable as binary plane partitions (our algorithm computes such cuttings for $r \le b^{O(1)}$ bounded by a constant).

4. ADDITIONAL PROPERTIES

We point out some implications that follow from our method. Define the *order-γ query cost* of ∂q to be $\sum_{v\in T:\ \Delta(v)\cap\partial q=\emptyset}\sum_{w \text{ child of } v}|P(w)|^\gamma$. Define the order-$\gamma$ query cost of T to be the maximum order-γ query cost of an arbitrary hyperplane. Our previous definition coincides with the case $\gamma = 0$. This extended definition is relevant in multilevel data structures where secondary data structures for $P(v)$ are stored at each node v (see Section 6 for more details). We have the following new result:

THEOREM 4.1. *Given n points in $\mathbb{R}^d$, we can build a partition tree with*

(i) *height $O(\log n)$ and order-$(1 - 1/d)$ query cost $O(n^{1-1/d}\log n)$;*

(ii) *height $O(\log\log n)$ and order-γ query cost $O(n^{1-1/d})$ for any fixed $\gamma < 1 - 1/d$.*

PROOF. (i) The same partition tree in the proof of Theorem 3.2 has order-$(1 - 1/d)$ query cost at most

$$O\left(\sum_{t\le n} b\left(\frac{n}{bt}\right)^{1-1/d}\ell(t)\right)$$
$$\le\ O\left(\sum_{t\le n}(n/t)^{1-1/d}\cdot[t^{1-1/d}+t^{1-1/(d-1)+\delta}\log n]\right)$$
$$=\ O(n^{1-1/d}\log n + n^{1-1/d}\log n)\ =\ O(n^{1-1/d}\log n).$$

(ii) To lower the height, we modify our partition tree T. Fix a sufficiently small constant $\varepsilon > 0$. We examine each node v of T in a top-down order, and whenever a child w of a node v has $|P(w)| > |P(v)|^{1-\varepsilon}$, we remove w by making w's children v's children. In the new tree T', every child w of a node v has $|P(w)| \le |P(v)|^{1-\varepsilon}$, so the height is $O(\log\log n)$. For each child w of v in T', w's parent in T has size at least $|P(v)|^{1-\varepsilon}$, so the degree of v in T' is at most $b|P(v)|^\varepsilon \le O((n/t)^\varepsilon)$ if $|P(v)| = \Theta(n/t)$. The order-γ query cost is at most

$$O\left(\sum_{t\le n}(n/t)^\varepsilon\left((n/t)^{1-\varepsilon}\right)^\gamma\ell(t)\right)$$
$$\le\ O\left(\sum_{t\le n}(n/t)^{\gamma+\varepsilon}\cdot[t^{1-1/d}+\log^{O(1)}n]\right)$$
$$=\ O(n^{1-1/d}+n^{\gamma+\varepsilon}\log^{O(1)}n)\ =\ O(n^{1-1/d}).$$

□

We have omitted the case $\gamma > 1 - 1/d$, because a simple recursive application of Matoušek's partition theorem already gives optimal order-γ query cost $O(n^\gamma)$ with height $O(\log\log n)$ in this case.

Next, define a *B-partial partition tree* for a point set P to be the same as in our earlier definition of a partition tree, except that a leaf now may contain up to B points. Define the *query cost* in the same manner, as in (1). Note the query cost of a partial partition tree upper-bounds the number of internal and leaf cells crossed by a hyperplane, but does not account for the cost of any auxiliary data structures we plan to store at the leaves. The following theorem is useful in applications that need space/time tradeoffs, where we can switch to a larger-space data structure with small query time at the leaves . The theorem is also self-evidently useful in the external memory model (hence, the choice of name "B"): we get improved external-memory range searching data structures [5] immediately as a byproduct.

THEOREM 4.2. *Given n points in $\mathbb{R}^d$ and $B < n/\log^{\omega(1)} n$, we can build a B-partial partition tree with size $O(n/B)$ and query cost $O(n/B)^{1-1/d}$.*

PROOF. Stop the algorithm in the proof of Theorem 3.2 when t reaches n/B. As a result, we get $O(bn/B)$ leaf cells, each containing at most B points. The maximum number of internal node cells crossed by an arbitrary hyperplane is at most $O(\sum_{t\le n/B}\ell(t)) = O(n/B)^{1-1/d}$. The maximum number of leaf cells crossed by an arbitrary hyperplane is at most b times this number. Recall that the tree has degree $O(b)$, which is a constant. □

5. PREPROCESSING TIME

In this section, we examine the issue of preprocessing time. Obtaining polynomial time is easy with our method, and it might be possible to lower the bound to $O(n^{1+\varepsilon})$ by using recursion, as was done in Matoušek's final method [30]. Instead of recursion, we show how to directly speed up the algorithm in Section 3. For now, we aim for $O(n \log^{O(1)} n)$ preprocessing time; later, we show how to improve it to $O(n \log n)$.

First, we need a better version of Observation 2.2 with a smaller number of test hyperplanes. The following observation was shown by Matoušek [27] (see also [34]).

OBSERVATION 5.1. (Test Set) *Given a set P of n points and any t, we can construct a set H_t of $O(t \log^{O(1)} N)$ test hyperplanes, in $O(t \log^{O(1)} N)$ time, satisfying the following property w.h.p.(N) for any $N \geq n$: For any collection of disjoint cells each containing at least n/t points of P, if the maximum number of cells crossed by a hyperplane in H_t is ℓ, then the maximum number of cells crossed by an arbitrary hyperplane is at most $O(\ell + t^{1-1/d})$.*

(Roughly interpreted, the proof involves drawing a random sample of $t^{1/d} \log N$ points and taking the $O(t \log^d N)$ hyperplanes through d-tuples of points in the sample; the time bound is clearly as stated. The $\log N$ factors can be removed with more work, using cuttings, but will not matter.)

In the proof of Theorem 3.2, we can take H to be the union of the test sets H_t from Observation 5.1 over all t (powers of 2); the total size is $m = O(n \log^{O(1)} N)$. This causes an extra term $O(u^{1-1/d})$ in the recurrence (3), but the solution is unaffected.

Regarding Lemma 2.3, we can use known cutting algorithms [16, 27, 14] to get running time $O(mr^{O(1)})$ (expected, or even worst-case).

To get the best time bound for Theorem 3.1, we need to modify the algorithm. The details become more involved, but there are two new main ideas:

- in step 1, we work with a sparser subset of $\widehat{H}$, by considering a random sample of $\widehat{H}$;
- more crucially, in step 3, we update the multiplicities less frequently, by considering a random sample of the subcells.

To prepare for the proof of the theorem below, we make two definitions, the first of which is standard: Given a (multi)set S, let a *p-sample* be a subset R generated by taking each (occurrence of an) element of S, and independently choosing to put the element in R with probability p. (Note that we can generate a p-sample in time linear in the output size rather than the size of S, by using a sequence of exponentially distributed random variables rather than 0-1 random variables.)

For a list $S = \langle s_1, \ldots, s_K \rangle$ and a sublist R of S, we say that R is a *generalized p-sample of S* if the events $E_i = \{s_i \in R\}$ are all independent. Note the subtle difference with the earlier definition: here, the list S (the elements s_i and the size K) is allowed to be random; it is acceptable for s_i to be dependent on $E_1, \ldots, E_{i-1}$, as long as we decide to choose whether to put s_i to R independently of $E_1, \ldots, E_{i-1}$ and s_i.

Properties enjoyed by standard random samples may not necessarily hold for generalized p-samples. However, the Chernoff bound is still clearly applicable to show that $|R \cap \{s_1, \ldots, s_k\}| \leq O(pk + \log N)$ and $k \leq O(1/p)(|R \cap \{s_1, \ldots, s_k\}| + \log N)$ for all $k \leq N$ w.h.p.(N). In particular, assuming $K \leq N$, we have $|R| \leq O(p|S| + \log N)$ and $|S| \leq O(1/p)(|R| + \log N)$ w.h.p.(N).

We now present a near-linear-time algorithm for the partition refinement theorem:

THEOREM 5.2. *In Theorem 3.1, given the subset of points inside each cell, we can construct a subdivision into subcells, together with the subset of points inside each subcell, in time*

$$O(bn + b^{O(1)}(m+t) \log^{O(1)} N),$$

such that the stated properties are satisfied, except that the crossing number bound is now $O((bt)^{1-1/d} + b^{1-1/(d-1)}\ell + b \log t \log N)$ w.h.p.(N) for any $N \geq mt$.

PROOF. *The algorithm.* Let $\Delta_t, \ldots, \Delta_1$ be the given cells in a random order. For $i = t, \ldots, 1$ do:

0. Let q be a power of 2 (with a negative integer exponent) closest to $\min\{\frac{(bi)^{1/d} \log N}{|\widehat{H}|}, \frac{b^{1/(d-1)} t \log N}{|\widehat{H}|\ell}, \frac{b^{1/(d-1)} i}{|\widehat{H}|}\}$. If q is different from its value in the previous iteration, then create a new q-sample $\widehat{R}$ of $\widehat{H}$.
1. Subdivide Δ_i into disjoint subcells by building a $(1/r)$-cutting of $\widehat{R}_{\Delta_i}$ inside Δ_i with
$$r := \min\left\{ |\widehat{R}_{\Delta_i}| \left(\frac{b}{X_{\Delta_i}(\widehat{R})} \right)^{1/d}, \ b^{1/(d-1)} \right\}.$$
By Lemma 2.3, the number of subcells is $O(b)$.
2. Further subdivide each subcell by using extra cuts to ensure that each subcell contains at most $n/(bt)$ points. The number of subcells inside Δ_i remains $O(b)$.
3. Take a p-sample ρ_i of the subcells of Δ_i with $p := \min\{\frac{b^{1/d} \log N}{t^{1-1/d}}, \frac{b^{1/(d-1)} \log N}{\ell}, \frac{b^{1/(d-1)}}{\log t}, 1\}$. If $\rho_i \neq \emptyset$, then
   (a) for each $h \in H_{\Delta_i}$, add new copies of h to $\widehat{H}$ so that the multiplicity of h in $\widehat{H}$ gets multiplied by $(1 + 1/b)^{|\rho_i(h)|}$, where $\rho_i(h)$ denotes the set of subcells in ρ_i crossed by h;
   (b) insert a q-sample of the newly added hyperplanes of $\widehat{H}$ to $\widehat{R}$.

Analysis of the crossing number. Let $\widehat{R}^{(q)}$ denote the set $\widehat{R}$ in the duration when the power of 2 closest to $\min\{\frac{(bi)^{1/d} \log N}{|\widehat{H}|}, \frac{b^{1/(d-1)} t \log N}{|\widehat{H}|\ell}, \frac{b^{1/(d-1)} i}{|\widehat{H}|}\}$ is equal to q. For any fixed q, observe that $\widehat{R}^{(q)}$ is a generalized q-sample of $\widehat{H}$ if we view the multiset $\widehat{H}$ as a list where the hyperplanes are listed in order they are added to $\widehat{H}$. Similarly, for any fixed simplex σ, $\widehat{R}^{(q)}_\sigma$ is a generalized q-sample of $\widehat{H}_\sigma$. Call two simplices σ_1 and σ_2 equivalent if $H_{\sigma_1} = H_{\sigma_2}$. The number of equivalence classes is polynomially bounded in N. Since $|\widehat{H}|$ is loosely upper-bounded by $Cm(1 + 1/b)^{O(bt)}$ at all times, the total number of different q's encountered is polynomially bounded in N. By the Chernoff bound, we can thus guarantee that the following holds at all times for all simplices σ and all q w.h.p.(N):

$$|\widehat{H}_\sigma| \le O(1/q)(|\widehat{R}^{(q)}_\sigma| + \log N) \text{ and } |\widehat{R}| \le O(q|\widehat{H}| + \log N).$$

After step 1, w.h.p., for each subcell σ, we have $|\widehat{H}_\sigma| \le O(1/q)(|\widehat{R}_\sigma| + \log N) \le O(1/q)(|\widehat{R}_{\Delta_i}|/r + \log N)$, implying that $\sum_{h\in\widehat{H}} |\rho_i(h)| \le |\rho_i| \cdot O(1/q)(|\widehat{R}_{\Delta_i}|/r + \log N)$. W.h.p., step 3(a) increases $|\widehat{H}|$ by the following amount:

$$\sum_{h\in\widehat{H}} [(1+1/b)^{|\rho_i(h)|} - 1] \;\le\; O\left(\sum_{h\in\widehat{H}} |\rho_i(h)|/b\right)$$
$$\le\; \frac{|\rho_i|}{bq} \cdot O(|\widehat{R}_{\Delta_i}|/r + \log N) \;\le\; \frac{|\rho_i|}{bq} \cdot O(\alpha_i|\widehat{R}| + \log N)$$
$$\text{where } \alpha_i := \frac{|\widehat{R}_{\Delta_i}|}{r|\widehat{R}|} = O\left(\frac{1}{|\widehat{R}|}\left(\frac{X_{\Delta_i}(\widehat{R})}{b}\right)^{1/d} + \frac{|\widehat{R}_{\Delta_i}|}{b^{1/(d-1)}|\widehat{R}|}\right)$$
$$\le\; \frac{|\rho_i|}{bq} \cdot O(\alpha_i q|\widehat{H}| + \log N) \;\le\; O(\beta_i)|\widehat{H}|$$
$$\text{where } \beta_i := \frac{|\rho_i|}{b}\left(\alpha_i + \frac{\log N}{q|\widehat{H}|}\right).$$

Let ℓ_i be as before. Conditioned to a fixed choice of $\Delta_t, \ldots, \Delta_{i+1}$ and $\widehat{R}$, we have $E[|\widehat{R}_{\Delta_i}|] \le |\widehat{R}|\ell_i/i$ and $E[X_{\Delta_i}(\widehat{R})] \le |\widehat{R}|^d/i$, so $E[\alpha_i] \le O(1/(bi)^{1/d} + \ell_i/(b^{1/(d-1)}i))$. Furthermore, $E[|\rho_i|] \le O(bp)$ conditioned to any fixed value of α_i, so $E[\beta_i] \le p \cdot O((1/(bi)^{1/d} + \ell_i/(b^{1/(d-1)}i) + (\log N)/(q|\widehat{H}|))$. Unconditionally, since $E[\ell_i] \le O(\ell i/t + \log N)$,

$$E[\beta_i] \;\le\; p \cdot O\left(\frac{1}{(bi)^{1/d}} + \frac{\ell}{b^{1/(d-1)}t} + \frac{\log N}{b^{1/(d-1)}i} + \frac{\log N}{q|\widehat{H}|}\right).$$

The last term disappears for our choice of q.

At the end, w.h.p., we can upper-bound $|\widehat{H}|$ by $Cm\prod_{i=1}^t (1 + O(\beta_i)) \le Cm \exp\left(O\left(\sum_{i=1}^t \beta_i\right)\right)$, where

$$E\left[\sum_{i=1}^t \beta_i\right] \;\le\; p \cdot O\left(\frac{t^{1-1/d}}{b^{1/d}} + \frac{\ell}{b^{1/(d-1)}} + \frac{\log N \log t}{b^{1/(d-1)}}\right),$$

which is $O(\log N)$ for our choice of p. By Markov's inequality, with probability $\Omega(1)$, we have $\sum_{i=1}^t \beta_i \le O(\log N)$ and $|\widehat{H}| \le CN^{O(1)}$. If not, we declare failure.

Let $\rho(h) = \bigcup_i \rho_i(h)$. Since the multiplicity of h in $\widehat{H}$ is $C(1 + 1/b)^{|\rho(h)|} \le |\widehat{H}|$, it follows that $\max_{h\in H} |\rho(h)| \le \log_{1+1/b}(|\widehat{H}|/C) \le O(b \log N)$ if algorithm does not fail. Observe that $\rho(h)$ is a generalized p-sample of the list $\lambda(h)$ of all subcells crossed by h, where the subcells are listed in the order they are created. Thus, w.h.p., we have $\max_{h\in H} |\lambda(h)| \le O((1/p)(|\rho(h)| + \log N)) \le O((b/p)\log N) \le O((bt)^{1-1/d} + b^{1-1/(d-1)}\ell + b^{1-1/(d-1)} \log t \log N + b \log N)$ if the algorithm does not fail.

Analysis of running time. Conditioned to a fixed choice of $\Delta_t, \ldots, \Delta_{i+1}$ and $\widehat{R}$, we have $E[|\widehat{R}_{\Delta_i}|] \le |\widehat{R}|\ell_i/i$. Unconditionally, $E[|\widehat{R}_{\Delta_i}|] \le (q|\widehat{H}| + \log N) \cdot O(\ell i/t + \log N)/i \le (b \log N)^{O(1)}$ for our choice of q. Assuming that $\widehat{R}_{\Delta_i}$ is available, step 1 takes time $|\widehat{R}_{\Delta_i}|r^{O(1)}$, which has expected value $(b \log N)^{O(1)}$. We don't need to compute $X_{\Delta_i}(\widehat{R})$, but rather we try different values of r (powers of 2) until we find a cutting with the right number of subcells. Thus, the expected cost over all iterations is $O(t)(b \log N)^{O(1)}$. By Markov's inequality, with probability $\Omega(1)$, this bound holds; if not, we declare failure.

In step 2, we can check the number of points per subcell by assigning points to subcells in $O(b)$ time per point, for a total cost of $O(bn)$. We can actually make the cost sublinear in n—namely, $O(t)(b \log N)^{O(1)}$—by replacing P by a $\frac{bt \log N}{n}$-sample Q of P. W.h.p., $|Q| = O(bt \log N)$, and for any simplex σ, $|Q \cap \sigma| \le |Q|/(bt)$ implies $|P \cap \sigma| \le O(n/(bt))$ by a Chernoff bound.

For step 3(a), we first need to compute the set H_{Δ_i}, i.e., report all hyperplanes of H intersecting a query cell Δ_i. In the dual, H becomes an m-point set and Δ_i becomes a constant-size polyhedron, and this subproblem reduces to simplex range searching. We can use existing data structures, e.g., [27], to get $O(m \log m)$ preprocessing time and $O(m^{1-1/d} \log^{O(1)} m + |H_{\Delta_i}|)$ query time. Since $\sum_i |H_{\Delta_i}| \le m\ell$ and the probability that $\rho_i \ne \emptyset$ is at most $O(bp)$, the total expected query time is $bp \cdot O(tm^{1-1/d} \log^{O(1)} m + m\ell) \le O(t^{1/d}m^{1-1/d} + m)(b \log N)^{O(1)} \le O(t + m)(b \log N)^{O(1)}$. Again, by Markov's inequality, with probability $\Omega(1)$, this bound holds; if not, we declare failure. We can compute $|\rho_i(h)|$ for each $h \in H_{\Delta_i}$ naively in time $O(b)$, which can be absorbed in the $b^{O(1)}$ factor.

Finally, we account for the total cost of all operations done to $\widehat{R}^{(q)}$: initialization in step 0, insertions in step 3(b), and computing $\widehat{R}^{(q)}_{\Delta_i}$ in step 1. Fix q. We continue inserting to $\widehat{R}^{(q)}$ only if $q \le 2\frac{(bt)^{1/d} \log N}{|\widehat{H}|}$. Thus, w.h.p., at all times, $|\widehat{R}^{(q)}| \le O(q|\widehat{H}| + \log N) \le O(t^{1/d})(b \log N)^{O(1)}$. Computing $\widehat{R}^{(q)}_{\Delta_i}$ reduces to simplex range searching again. This time, we use an existing data structure that has larger space but supports faster querying, with preprocessing time and total insertion time $O(|\widehat{R}^{(q)}|^d \log^{O(1)} |\widehat{R}^{(q)}|) = O(t)(b \log N)^{O(1)}$ w.h.p., and query time $O(\log^{O(1)} |\widehat{R}^{(q)}| + |\widehat{R}^{(q)}_{\Delta_i}|)$. (Insertions are supported by standard amortization techniques [10].) Since $|\widehat{H}| \le CN^{O(1)}$, the total number of different q's is $O(\log N)$, which can be absorbed in the $\log^{O(1)} N$ factor.

To summarize, our algorithm succeeds with probability $\Omega(1)$, and w.h.p. the stated bound holds if the algorithm does not fail. We can re-run the algorithm until success, with $O(\log N)$ number of trials w.h.p. The running time remains $O(m + t)(b \log N)^{O(1)}$. At the end, we can assign all the input points to subcells in $O(bn)$ additional time (this term can actually be reduced to $O(n \log b)$ with point location data structures). □

THEOREM 5.3. *We can build data structures in $O(n \log n)$ time achieving the bounds stated in Theorems 3.2, 4.1, and 4.2 w.h.p.(n).*

PROOF. Using Theorem 5.3, the algorithm in the proof of Theorem 3.2 can immediately be implemented in $O(n \log^{O(1)} n)$ time w.h.p.(n). To reduce the time bound further, we "bootstrap" as follows.

Build a B_0-partial partition tree with $O(n/B_0)$ size and $O(n/B_0)^{1-1/d}$ query cost, as in the proof of Theorem 4.2, with $B_0 = \log^c n$ for a sufficiently large constant c. Here, we take H to be the union of H_t for all $t \le n/B_0$, of total size $m = O((n/B_0)\log^{O(1)} n)$, and the time bound drops to $O(\sum_{t\leq n/B_0}[n + (n/B_0)\log^{O(1)} n]) = O(n\log n)$ for our choice of B_0. Using the preceding partition tree method with $P(B_0) = O(B_0 \log^{O(1)} B_0)$ and $Q(B_0) = O(B_0^{1-1/d})$ to handle the subproblems at the leaf cells, we then get a new partition tree with preprocessing time $O(n/B_0)P(B_0) + O(n\log n) = O(n\log n)$ and query time $O(n/B_0)^{1-1/d}Q(B_0) = O(n^{1-1/d})$.

The query bound is expected but can be made to hold w.h.p.(n): For a fixed query hyperplane, we are bounding a sum Z of independent random variables lying between 0 and $O(B_0)$ with $E[Z] \leq O(n^{1-1/d})$; by a Chernoff bound, w.h.p.(n), we have $Z \leq O(n^{1-1/d} + B_0 \log n) = O(n^{1-1/d})$. Observe that every cell in our construction are defined by a constant number of input points, so the number of possible cells, and hence the number of combinatorially different query hyperplanes, is polynomially bounded in n. Thus, the maximum query cost is indeed $O(n^{1-1/d})$ w.h.p.(n).

The same approach also works for Theorems 4.1 and 4.2. □

Note that the above result is Las Vegas, since the random choices made in the preprocessing algorithm only affect the query time, not the correctness of the query algorithm.

6. SOME APPLICATIONS

We briefly mention a few applications of our results; more can be found in the full paper.

Spanning trees with low crossing number. A series of papers [2, 9, 22, 26, 37] addressed the construction of spanning trees such that the maximum number of edges crossed by a hyperplane is small. This problem has direct applications to a number of geometric problems [3, 37]. We obtain the first $O(n \log n)$-time algorithm that attains asymptotically optimal worst-case crossing number. The result follows directly from Theorems 3.2 and 5.3: inside each cell in the partition tree, we just create a constant $(O(b))$ number of edges to connect the subsets at the children.

Corollary 6.1. *Given n points in $\mathbb{R}^d$, there is an $O(n \log n)$-time Monte Carlo algorithm to compute a spanning tree with the property that any hyperplane crosses at most $O(n^{1-1/d})$ tree edges w.h.p.(n). For $d = 2$, we can ensure that the output tree is planar.*

Multilevel data structures. Many query problems are solved using multilevel partition trees, where we build secondary data structures for each *canonical subset* and answer a query by identify relevant canonical subsets and querying their corresponding secondary structures. The corollary below encapsulates the main property of our partition tree for multilevel applications, and is a direct consequence of Theorems 4.1 and 5.3:

Corollary 6.2. *Given n points in $\mathbb{R}^d$,*

(i) *we can form $O(n)$ canonical subsets of total size $O(n \log n)$ in $O(n \log n)$ time, such that the subset of all points inside any query simplex can be reported as a union of disjoint canonical subsets C_i with $\sum_i |C_i|^{1-1/d} \leq O(n^{1-1/d} \log n)$ in time $O(n^{1-1/d} \log n)$ w.h.p.(n);*

(ii) *for any fixed $\gamma < 1 - 1/d$, we can form $O(n)$ canonical subsets of total size $O(n \log\log n)$ in $O(n \log n)$ time, such that the subset of all points inside any query simplex can be reported as a union of disjoint canonical subsets C_i with $\sum_i |C_i|^\gamma \leq O(n^{1-1/d})$ in time $O(n^{1-1/d})$ w.h.p.(n).*

For example, we can get the following results:

Corollary 6.3. *Given n line segments in the plane, there is a data structure with $O(n \log^3 n)$ preprocessing time and $O(n \log^2 n)$ space such that we can report the k intersections with a query line segment in $O(\sqrt{n} \log^2 n + k)$ expected time.*

Specifically, the above follows by applying Corollary 6.2(i) thrice. For another example, we get the following result by applying Corollary 6.2(i) $d+1$ times:

Corollary 6.4. *Given n simplices in $\mathbb{R}^d$, there is a data structure with $O(n \log^{d+1} n)$ preprocessing time and $O(n \log^d n)$ space, such that we can find all simplices containing a query point in $O(n^{1-1/d} \log^d n)$ expected time; and we can find all simplices contained inside a query simplex in $O(n^{1-1/d} \log^d n)$ expected time.*

7. CONCLUSIONS

The new results of this paper completely subsume most of the results from Matoušek's SoCG'92 paper [30], at least if randomized algorithms are acceptable (which are to most researchers nowadays). Although we have resolved some of the main open questions concerning upper bounds, there are still a few minor issues. For example, is it possible to eliminate the extra iterated logarithmic factor in Matoušek's algorithm for Hopcroft's problem [30]? For halfspace range reporting for even d, can one get $O(n)$ space and $O(n^{1-1/\lfloor d/2 \rfloor} + k)$ query time for all k? More importantly, for halfspace emptiness for odd d, can one get $O(n)$ space and $O(n^{1-1/\lfloor d/2 \rfloor})$ query time?

In the other direction, for simplex range searching, can one prove a tight $\Omega(n^{1-1/d})$ lower bound on the query time for linear-space data structures in, say, the semigroup model [13], without any extra logarithmic factor? Can one prove lower bounds showing in some sense that logarithmic-factor increase is necessary for multilevel partition trees, or that extra logarithmic factors are necessary in the query time in the case of large near-$O(n^{\lfloor d/2 \rfloor})$ space [30]? More importantly, can one prove near optimal lower bounds for halfspace range emptiness?

It seems plausible that our approach could be adapted to other kinds of partition trees for semialgebraic sets [8, 6] in some cases (where the complexity of arrangements or lower envelopes in $d-1$ dimensions is strictly less than in d dimensions). We do not know yet if our approach could lead to new results for dynamic partition trees that support insertions and deletions.

8. REFERENCES

[1] P. Afshani and T. M. Chan. Optimal halfspace range reporting in three dimensions. In *Proc. 20th ACM-SIAM Sympos. Discrete Algorithms*, pages 180–186, 2009.

[2] P. K. Agarwal. *Intersection and Decomposition Algorithms for Planar Arrangements.* Cambridge University Press, 1991.

[3] P. K. Agarwal. Ray shooting and other applications of spanning trees with low stabbing number. *SIAM J. Comput.*, 21:540–570, 1992.

[4] P. K. Agarwal. Range searching. In *CRC Handbook of Discrete and Computational Geometry* (J. Goodman and J. O'Rourke, eds.), CRC Press, New York, 2004.

[5] P. K. Agarwal, L. Arge, J. Erickson, P. G. Franciosa, and J. S. Vitter. Efficient searching with linear constraints. *J. Comput. Sys. Sci.*, 61:194–216, 2000.

[6] P. K. Agarwal, A. Efrat, and M. Sharir. Vertical decomposition of shallow levels in 3-dimensional arrangements and its applications. In *SIAM J. Comput.*, 29:912–953, 1999.

[7] P. K. Agarwal and J. Erickson. Geometric range searching and its relatives. In *Discrete and Computational Geometry: Ten Years Later* (B. Chazelle, J. E. Goodman, and R. Pollack, eds.), AMS Press, pages 1–56, 1999.

[8] P. K. Agarwal and J. Matoušek. On range searching with semialgebraic sets. *Discrete Comput. Geom.*, 11:393–418, 1994.

[9] P. K. Agarwal and M. Sharir. Applications of a new space-partitioning technique. *Discrete Comput. Geom.*, 9:11–38, 1993.

[10] J. Bentley and J. Saxe. Decomposable searching problems I: static-to-dynamic transformation. *J. Algorithms*, 1:301–358, 1980.

[11] M. de Berg and O. Schwarzkopf. Cuttings and applications. *Int. J. Comput. Geom. Appl.*, 5:343–355, 1995.

[12] T. M. Chan. Output-sensitive results on convex hulls, extreme points, and related problems. *Discrete Comput. Geom.*, 16:369–387, 1996.

[13] B. Chazelle. Lower bounds on the complexity of polytope range searching. *J. AMS*, 2:637–666, 1989.

[14] B. Chazelle. Cutting hyperplanes for divide-and-conquer. *Discrete Comput. Geom.*, 9:145–158, 1993.

[15] B. Chazelle. Cuttings. In *Handbook of Data Structures and Applications* (D. P. Mehta and S. Sahni, eds.), CRC Press, pages 25.1–25.10, 2005.

[16] B. Chazelle and J. Friedman. A deterministic view of random sampling and its use in geometry. *Combinatorica*, 10:229–249, 1990.

[17] B. Chazelle and B. Rosenberg. Simplex range reporting on a pointer machine. *Comput. Geom. Theory Appl.*, 5:237–247, 1996.

[18] B. Chazelle, M. Sharir, and E. Welzl. Quasi-optimal upper bounds for simplex range searching and new zone theorems. *Algorithmica*, 8:407–429, 1992.

[19] B. Chazelle and E. Welzl. Quasi-optimal range searching in space of finite VC-dimension. *Discrete Comput. Geom.*, 4:467–489, 1989.

[20] K. L. Clarkson and P. W. Shor. Applications of random sampling in computational geometry, II. *Discrete Comput. Geom.*, 4:387–421, 1989.

[21] D. Dobkin and H. Edelsbrunner. Organizing point sets in two and three dimensions. Report F130, Inst. Informationsverarb., Tech. Univ. Graz, Austria, 1984.

[22] H. Edelsbrunner, L. Guibas, J. Hershberger, R. Seidel, M. Sharir, J. Snoeyink, and E. Welzl. Implicitly representing arrangements of lines or segments. *Discrete Comput. Geom.*, 4:433–466, 1989.

[23] H. Edelsbrunner and F. Huber. Dissecting sets of points in two and three dimensions. Report F138, Inst. Informationsverarb., Tech. Univ. Graz, Austria, 1984.

[24] H. Edelsbrunner and E. Welzl. Halfplanar range search in linear space and $O(n^{0.695})$ query time. *Inform. Process. Lett.*, 23:289–293, 1986.

[25] D. Haussler and E. Welzl. Epsilon-nets and simplex range queries. *Discrete Comput. Geom.*, 2:127–151, 1987.

[26] J. Matoušek. Spanning trees with low crossing number. *Informatique Théorique et Applications*, 25:103–124, 1991.

[27] J. Matoušek. Efficient partition trees. *Discrete Comput. Geom.*, 8:315–334, 1992.

[28] J. Matoušek. Reporting points in halfspaces. *Comput. Geom. Theory Appl.*, 2:169–186, 1992.

[29] J. Matoušek. Linear optimization queries. *J. Algorithms*, 14:432–448, 1993. Also with O. Schwarzkopf in *Proc. 8th ACM Sympos. Comput. Geom.*, pages 16–25, 1992.

[30] J. Matoušek. Range searching with efficient hierarchical cuttings. *Discrete Comput. Geom.*, 10:157–182, 1993.

[31] J. Matoušek. Geometric range searching. *ACM Comput. Surv.*, 26:421–461, 1994.

[32] J. Matoušek. *Lectures on Discrete Geometry.* Springer-Verlag, 2002.

[33] J. Matoušek and O. Schwarzkopf. On ray shooting in convex polytopes. *Discrete Comput. Geom.*, 10:215–232, 1993.

[34] K. Mulmuley. *Computational Geometry: An Introduction Through Randomized Algorithms.* Prentice-Hall, Englewood Cliffs, N.J., 1994.

[35] F. P. Preparata and M. I. Shamos. *Computational Geometry: An Introduction.* Springer-Verlag, New York, 1985.

[36] E. Ramos. On range reporting, ray shooting, and k-level construction. In *Proc. 15th ACM Sympos. Comput. Geom.*, pages 390–399, 1999.

[37] E. Welzl. On spanning trees with low crossing numbers. In *Data Structures and Efficient Algorithms (B. Monien and T. Ottmann, eds.)*, Lect. Notes Comput. Sci., vol. 594, Springer-Verlag, pages 233–249, 1992.

[38] D. E. Willard. Polygon retrieval. *SIAM J. Comput.*, 11:149–165, 1982.

[39] A. C. Yao and F. F. Yao. A general approach to D-dimensional geometric queries. In *Proc. 17th ACM Sympos. Theory Comput.*, pages 163–168, 1985.

[40] F. F. Yao. A 3-space partition and its applications. In *Proc. 15th ACM Sympos. Theory Comput.*, pages 258–263, 1983.

[41] F. F. Yao, D. P. Dobkin, H. Edelsbrunner, and M. S. Paterson. Partitioning space for range queries. *SIAM J. Comput.*, 18:371–384, 1989.

Consistent Digital Line Segments

Tobias Christ
Institute of Theoretical Computer Science
ETH Zürich
Switzerland
tobias.christ@inf.ethz.ch

Dömötör Pálvölgyi
Department of Combinatorial Geometry
EPF Lausanne
Switzerland
dom@cs.elte.hu

Miloš Stojaković
Department of Mathematics and Informatics
University of Novi Sad
Serbia
milos.stojakovic@dmi.uns.ac.rs

ABSTRACT

We introduce a novel and general approach for digitalization of line segments in the plane that satisfies a set of axioms naturally arising from Euclidean axioms. In particular, we show how to derive such a system of digital segments from any total order on the integers. As a consequence, using a well-chosen total order, we manage to define a system of digital segments such that all digital segments are, in Hausdorff metric, optimally close to their corresponding Euclidean segments, thus giving an explicit construction that resolves the main question of [1].

Categories and Subject Descriptors

I.3.5 [**Computer Graphics**]: Computational Geometry and Object Modeling

General Terms

Theory

1. INTRODUCTION

One of the most fundamental challenges in digital geometry is to define a "good" digital representation of a geometric object. Of course, the meaning of the word "good" here heavily depends on particular conditions we may impose. Looking at the problem of digitalization in the plane, the goal is to find a set of points on the integer grid $\mathbb{Z}^2$ that approximates well a given object. The topology of the grid $\mathbb{Z}^2$ is commonly defined by the graph whose vertices are all the points of the grid, and each point is connected by an edge to each of the four points that are either horizontally or vertically adjacent to it.

Knowing that a straight line segment is one of the most basic geometric objects and a building block for many other objects, defining its digitalization in a satisfying manner is vital. Hence, it is no wonder that this has been a hot scientific topic in the last few decades, see [4] for a recent survey and [3], [2], and [6] for related work, dealing with the problem of representing objects in digital geometry without causing topological and combinatorial inconsistencies.

For any pair of points p and q in the grid $\mathbb{Z}^2$ we want to define the digital line segment $S(p,q)$ connecting them, that is, $\{p,q\} \subseteq S(p,q) \subseteq \mathbb{Z}^2$. Chun et al. in [1] put forward the following four axioms that arise naturally from properties of line segments in Euclidean geometry.

(S1) *Grid path property:* For all $p,q \in \mathbb{Z}^2$, $S(p,q)$ is the vertex set of a path from p to q in the grid graph.

(S2) *Symmetry property:* For all $p,q \in \mathbb{Z}^2$, we have $S(p,q) = S(q,p)$.

(S3) *Subsegment property:* For all $p,q \in \mathbb{Z}^2$ and every $r \in S(p,q)$, we have $S(p,r) \subseteq S(p,q)$.

(S4) *Prolongation property:* For all $p,q \in \mathbb{Z}^2$, there exists $r \in \mathbb{Z}^2$, such that $r \notin S(p,q)$ and $S(p,q) \subseteq S(p,r)$.

First, note that (S3) is not satisfied by the usual way a computer visualizes a segment. A natural definition of the digital straight segment between $p = (p_x, p_y)$ and $q = (q_x, q_y)$, where $p_x \le q_x$ and $0 \le q_y - p_y < q_x - p_x$ is

$$\left\{\left(x, \left\lfloor (x - p_x)\frac{q_y - p_y}{q_x - p_x} + p_y + 0.5 \right\rfloor\right) : p_x \le x \le q_x\right\}.$$

This does not satisfy (S1), but it could be easily fixed by a slight modification of the definition. Still, it also does not satisfy (S3), for example, for $p = (0,0), r = (1,0), q = (4,1)$, the subsegment from r to q is not contained in the segment from p to q.

Even though the set of axioms (S1)-(S4) seems rather natural, there are still some fairly exotic examples of digital segment systems that satisfy all four of them. For example, let us fix a double spiral $\mathcal{D}$ centered at an arbitrary point of $\mathbb{Z}^2$, traversing all the points of $\mathbb{Z}^2$. As it is a spanning path of the grid graph, we can set $S(p,q)$ to be the path between p and q on $\mathcal{D}$, for every $p,q \in \mathbb{Z}^2$. It is easy to verify that this system satisfies axioms (S1)-(S4).

Another condition was introduced in [1] to enforce the monotonicity of the segments, ruling out pathological examples like the one above. Here, we phrase this monotonicity axiom differently, but still, the system of axioms (S1)-(S5) remains equivalent to the one given in [1].

(S5) *Monotonicity property:* If both $p,q \in \mathbb{Z}^2$ lie on a line that is either horizontal or vertical, then the whole segment $S(p,q)$ belongs to this line.

SCG'10, June 13–16, 2010, Snowbird, Utah, USA.

We call a system of digital line segments that satisfies the system of axioms (S1)-(S5) a *consistent digital line segments system (CDS)*. It is straightforward to verify that every CDS also satisfies the following three conditions.

(C1) If the slope of the line going through p and q is non-negative, then the slope of the line going through any two points of $S(p,q)$ is non-negative. The same holds for non-positive slopes.

(C2) For all $p,q \in \mathbb{Z}^2$, the grid-parallel box spanned by points p and q contains $S(p,q)$.

(C3) If the intersection of two digital segments contains two points $p,q \in \mathbb{Z}^2$, then their intersection also contains the whole digital segment $S(p,q)$.

We give a simple example of a CDS, where segments follow the boundary of the grid-parallel box spanned by the endpoints. Let $p,q \in \mathbb{Z}^2$ be two points with coordinates $p = (p_x, p_y)$ and $q = (q_x, q_y)$. If $p_y \le q_y$, we define $S(p,q) = S(q,p) = \{(x, p_y) : \min\{p_x, q_x\} \le x \le \max\{p_x, q_x\}\} \cup \{(q_x, y) : p_y \le y \le q_y\}\}$. If $p_y > q_y$, we swap the points p and q, and define the segment as in the previous case.

It can be easily verified that this way we defined a CDS, but the digital segments in this system visually still do not resemble well the Euclidean segments.

One of the standard ways to measure how close a digital segment is to a Euclidean segment is to use the Hausdorff distance. We denote by $\overline{pq}$ the Euclidean segment between p and q, and by $|\overline{pq}|$ the Euclidean length of $\overline{pq}$. For two plane objects A and B, by $H(A,B)$ we denote their Hausdorff distance.

The main question raised in [1] was if it is possible to define a CDS such that a Euclidean segment and its digitalization have a reasonably small Hausdorff distance. More precisely, the goal is to find a CDS satisfying the following condition.

(H) *Small Hausdorff distance property:* For every $p,q \in \mathbb{Z}^2$, we have that $H(\overline{pq}, S(p,q)) = O(\log|\overline{pq}|)$.

Note that in the CDS example we gave, the Hausdorff distance between a Euclidean segment of length n and its digitalization can be as large as $n/\sqrt{2}$.

While this question was not resolved in [1], a clever construction of a system of digital rays *emanating from the origin of* $\mathbb{Z}^2$ that satisfy (S1)-(S5) and (H) was presented. Moreover, it was shown using Schmidt's theorem [5] that already for rays emanating from the origin, the log-bound imposed in condition (H) is the best bound we can hope for, directly implying the following theorem.

THEOREM 1. [1] *There exists a constant $c > 0$, such that for any CDS and any $d > 0$, there exist $p,q \in \mathbb{Z}^2$ with $|\overline{pq}| > d$, such that $H(\overline{pq}, S(p,q)) > c\log|\overline{pq}|$.*

In this paper, we introduce a novel and general approach for the construction of a CDS. Namely, for any total order $\prec$ on $\mathbb{Z}$, we show how to derive a CDS from $\prec$. (By total order we always mean a strict total order.) This process is described in Section 2. As a consequence, in Section 3, we manage to define a CDS that satisfies (H), deriving it from a specially chosen order on $\mathbb{Z}$, and thus giving the explicit construction that resolves the main question of [1].

THEOREM 2. *There is a CDS that satisfies condition (H).*

Note that Theorem 1 ensures that such a CDS is optimal up to a constant factor in terms of the Hausdorff distance from the Euclidean segments.

Finally, in Section 4, we make a step towards a characterization of CDSes, demonstrating their connection to total orders on $\mathbb{Z}$.

2. DIGITAL LINE SEGMENTS DERIVED FROM TOTAL ORDERS

Let $\prec$ be a total order on $\mathbb{Z}$. We are going to define a CDS $\mathcal{S}_\prec$, deriving it from $\prec$. Let $p,q \in \mathbb{Z}^2$, $p = (p_x, p_y)$ and $q = (q_x, q_y)$. If $p_x > q_x$, we swap p and q. Hence, from now on we may assume that $p_x \le q_x$.

If $p_y \le q_y$, then $S_\prec(p,q)$ is defined as follows. We start at the point $p = (p_x, p_y)$ and we repeatedly go either up or to the right, collecting the points from $\mathbb{Z}^2$, until we reach q. Note that the sum of the coordinates $x+y$ increases by 1 in each step. In total we have to make $q_x + q_y - p_x - p_y$ steps and in exactly $q_y - p_y$ of them we have to go up. The decision whether to go up or to the right is made as follows: if we are at the point (x,y) for which $x+y$ is among the $q_y - p_y$ greatest elements of the interval $[p_x+p_y, q_x+q_y-1]$ according to $\prec$, we go up, otherwise we go to the right. We will refer to this interval as the *segment interval.*

If $p_y > q_y$, that is, if p is the top-left and q the bottom-right corner of the grid-parallel box spanned by p and q, then we define $S_\prec(p,q)$ as the reflection of $S_\prec((-q_x, q_y), (-p_x, p_y))$ in the y-axis.

Example 1. Suppose $p = (0,0)$ and $q = (2,2)$. Their segment interval consists of four numbers, $0,1,2,3$. If $\prec$ is the natural order on $\mathbb{Z}$, then the two greatest elements of the segment interval are 2 and 3. Since $0+0$ is not one of these, at $(0,0)$ we go right, to $(1,0)$. At $(1,0)$ we again go to right, to $(2,0)$, from there to $(2,1)$ (since $2+0$ is one of the greater elements) and finally to $(2,2)$. In fact, it can be easily seen that using the natural order on $\mathbb{Z}$ we get the CDS mentioned in Section 1, the one that always follows the boundary of the box spanned by the endpoints.

THEOREM 3. *$\mathcal{S}_\prec$, defined as above, is a CDS.*

PROOF. The conditions (S1) and (S5) follow directly from the definition of $\mathcal{S}_\prec$. It remains to verify the axioms (S2), (S3), and (S4).

(S2): Let p,q be two points from $\mathbb{Z}^2$. If the first coordinates of p and q are different, then condition (S2) follows directly. Otherwise, p and q belong to the same vertical line, and from the construction we see that both $S_\prec(p,q)$ and $S_\prec(q,p)$ consist of all the points on that line between p and q.

(S3): For a contradiction, assume that there are points $p = (p_x, p_y)$, $q = (q_x, q_y)$ and $r = (r_x, r_y)$, with $r \in S_\prec(p,q)$, such that $S_\prec(p,r) \nsubseteq S_\prec(p,q)$. W.l.o.g. we may assume that $\overline{pq}$ has a non-negative slope.

Case 1. $p_x \le q_x$ and $p_y \le q_y$. We also have $p_x \le r_x$ and $p_y \le r_y$, and going on each of the segments $S_\prec(p,r)$ and $S_\prec(p,q)$ point-by-point starting from p, we move either up or right. By assumption, these two segments separate at some point (a,b) and then meet again, for the first time after this separation, at some other point (c,d), see Figure 1. One of the segments goes up at (a,b) and enters (c,d) horizontally

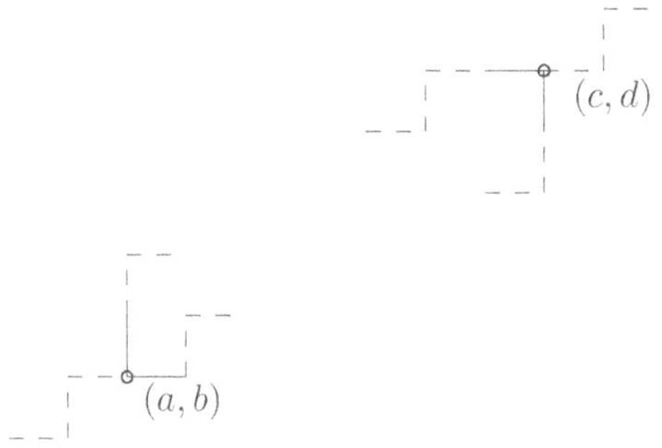

Figure 1: Two paths splitting up at (a, b) and meeting again at (c, d).

coming from the left, which implies that $a + b$ is among the greater numbers of the segment interval of this segment, while $c + d - 1$ is not, thus $c + d - 1 \prec a + b$. But the other segment goes horizontally at (a, b) and enters (c, d) vertically coming from below, which similarly implies $a + b \prec c + d - 1$, a contradiction.

Case 2. $q_x \leq p_x$ and $q_y \leq p_y$. We also have $q_x \leq r_x$ and $q_y \leq r_y$. By assumption, the two segments starting at q and r, $S_\prec(q, p)$ and $S_\prec(r, p)$, separate at some point (a, b) and then meet again, for the first time after this separation, at some other point (c, d). Using the same argument as before, we get a contradiction. Hence, (S3) holds.

(S4): To show that condition (S4) holds, consider the segment from $p = (p_x, p_y)$ to $q = (q_x, q_y)$. W.l.o.g. we can assume that $p_x \leq q_x$ and $p_y \leq q_y$. We distinguish two cases.

Case 1. If $q_x + q_y$ is among the $q_y - p_y + 1$ greatest numbers of $[p_x + p_y, q_x + q_y]$ according to $\prec$, then we can prolong the segment going one step vertically up, that is, the segment $S_\prec((p_x, p_y), (q_x, q_y + 1))$ contains the segment $S_\prec((p_x, p_y), (q_x, q_y))$ as a subsegment.

Case 2. If, on the other hand, $q_x + q_y$ is not among the $q_y - p_y$ greatest numbers of $[p_x + p_y, q_x + q_y]$, we can prolong the segment horizontally to the right, $S_\prec((p_x, p_y), (q_x, q_y)) \subset S_\prec((p_x, p_y), (q_x + 1, q_y))$.

Note that if $q_x + q_y$ is exactly the $(q_y - p_y + 1)^{th}$ number in $[p_x + p_y, q_x + q_y]$, then the conclusions of both cases are true, and indeed the rays emanating from (p_x, p_y) split at (q_x, q_y). $\square$

REMARK 4. *Even though our focus is on the digitalization of line segments, the present setup can be conveniently extended to a definition of digital lines. We say that a digital line is a path infinite in both directions in the $\mathbb{Z}^2$ base graph, such that the digital line segment between any two points on the digital line belongs to the digital line. It can be shown (using an argument similar to the proof of (S3) in Theorem 3) that there are no "touching" lines in $\mathcal{S}_\prec$. If two different lines have a common point, then they either cross (having a common segment), or they have a common half-line.*

3. SMALL HAUSDORFF DISTANCE

For integers k and $l \geq 2$, let $|k|_l$ denote the number of times k is divisible by l, that is,

$$|k|_l := \max\{m : l^m \mid k\}$$

and $|0|_l := \infty$.

We define a total order on $\mathbb{Z}$ as follows. Let $a \prec b$ if and only if there exists a non-negative integer i such that $|a - i|_2 < |b - i|_2$, and for all $j \in \{0, \ldots, i - 1\}$ we have $|a - j|_2 = |b - j|_2$. In plain words, for two integers a and b, we say that the one that contains a higher power of 2 as a divisor is greater under $\prec$. In case of a tie, we repeatedly subtract 1 from both a and b, until at some point one of them contains a higher power of 2 than the other. Thus, for example, $-1 \prec -5 \prec 3 \prec -3 \prec 5 \prec 1 \prec -2 \prec 6 \prec -6 \prec 2 \prec -4 \prec 4 \prec 0$. Note that if we take the elements of an interval of the form $(-2^n, 2^n)$ in $\prec$-decreasing order and we apply the function $0.5 - x2^{-n-1}$ to them, then we get the first few elements of the Van der Corput sequence [7].

We will prove that using this total order to define the system of digital line segments $\mathcal{S}_\prec$, as described in the previous section, we obtain a CDS which satisfies condition (H). In Figure 2 we give some examples of digital segments in this CDS, and Figure 3 shows the segments emanating from $(0, 0)$ to some neighboring points, as well as the segments from $(2, 3)$ to the neighboring points.

At first sight it may be surprising to observe that all the segments emanating from the origin in our construction coincide with the ones given in the construction of digital rays in [1]. However, it is not a coincidence, as the construction from [1] also relies on the same total order on integers.

For points $v, w \in \mathbb{R}^2$ and $A \subseteq \mathbb{R}^2$, let $d(v, w) = |v - w|$ and $d(v, A) = \inf_{a \in A} d(v, a)$ denote the usual Euclidean distances between two points, and between a point and a set. For $p, q, r, s \in \mathbb{Z}^2$, by $\overline{pqrs}$ we denote the union of Euclidean linear line segments from p to q, from q to r, and from r to s.

OBSERVATION 5. *For any $p, q \in \mathbb{Z}^2$, $H(S_\prec(p, q), \overline{pq}) = max\{d(r, \overline{pq}) : r \in S_\prec(p, q)\}$.*

We proceed by proving three statements that we will use to ultimately prove Theorem 2.

LEMMA 6. *If $p, q \in \mathbb{Z}^2$ and $r, s \in S_\prec(p, q)$. Then*

$$H(\overline{rs}, S_\prec(r, s)) \leq 2H(\overline{pq}, S_\prec(p, q)).$$

PROOF. We know that $d(r, \overline{pq}) \leq H(\overline{pq}, S_\prec(p, q)) =: h$ and $d(s, \overline{pq}) \leq h$, therefore $H(\overline{prsq}, \overline{pq}) \leq h$. Hence, for all $v \in \overline{pq}$, $d(v, \overline{prsq}) \leq h$. Let $t \in S_\prec(r, s) \subseteq S_\prec(p, q)$ and $v \in \overline{pq}$ be such that $d(t, v) = d(t, \overline{pq}) \leq h$. Using the triangle inequality we conclude $d(t, \overline{prsq}) \leq d(t, v) + d(v, \overline{prsq}) \leq 2h$. Because of (C2), we have $d(t, \overline{rs}) = d(t, \overline{prsq}) \leq 2h$, and therefore $H(S_\prec(r, s), \overline{rs}) \leq 2h$. $\square$

LEMMA 7. *Let $p, q, r, r' \in \mathbb{Z}^2$, such that $r_x - p_x = q_x - r'_x + \varepsilon$, $r_y - p_y = q_y - r'_y - \varepsilon$, with $\varepsilon \in \{0, 1, -1\}$, $r'_x = r_x$ and $r'_y = r_y + 1$. Then $H(\overline{pq}, \overline{prr'q}) \leq c = \sqrt{5}/2$.*

PROOF. Without loss of generality $p = (0, 0)$. We have

$$H(\overline{pq}, \overline{prr'q}) = \max\{d(r, \overline{pq}), d(r', \overline{pq})\}.$$

By assumption, $2r_x - \varepsilon = q_x$ and $2r_y + \varepsilon + 1 = q_y$. So we get

$$\begin{aligned} d(r, \overline{pq}) &= \frac{q_y r_x - q_x r_y}{\sqrt{q_x^2 + q_y^2}} \\ &= \frac{q_y \frac{q_x + \varepsilon}{2} - q_x \frac{q_y - \varepsilon - 1}{2}}{\sqrt{q_x^2 + q_y^2}} \\ &= \frac{1}{2\sqrt{q_x^2 + q_y^2}}(q_y \varepsilon + q_x \varepsilon + q_x). \end{aligned}$$

Similarly,

$$d(r', \overline{pq}) = \frac{1}{2\sqrt{q_x^2 + q_y^2}}(q_y \varepsilon + q_x \varepsilon - q_x).$$

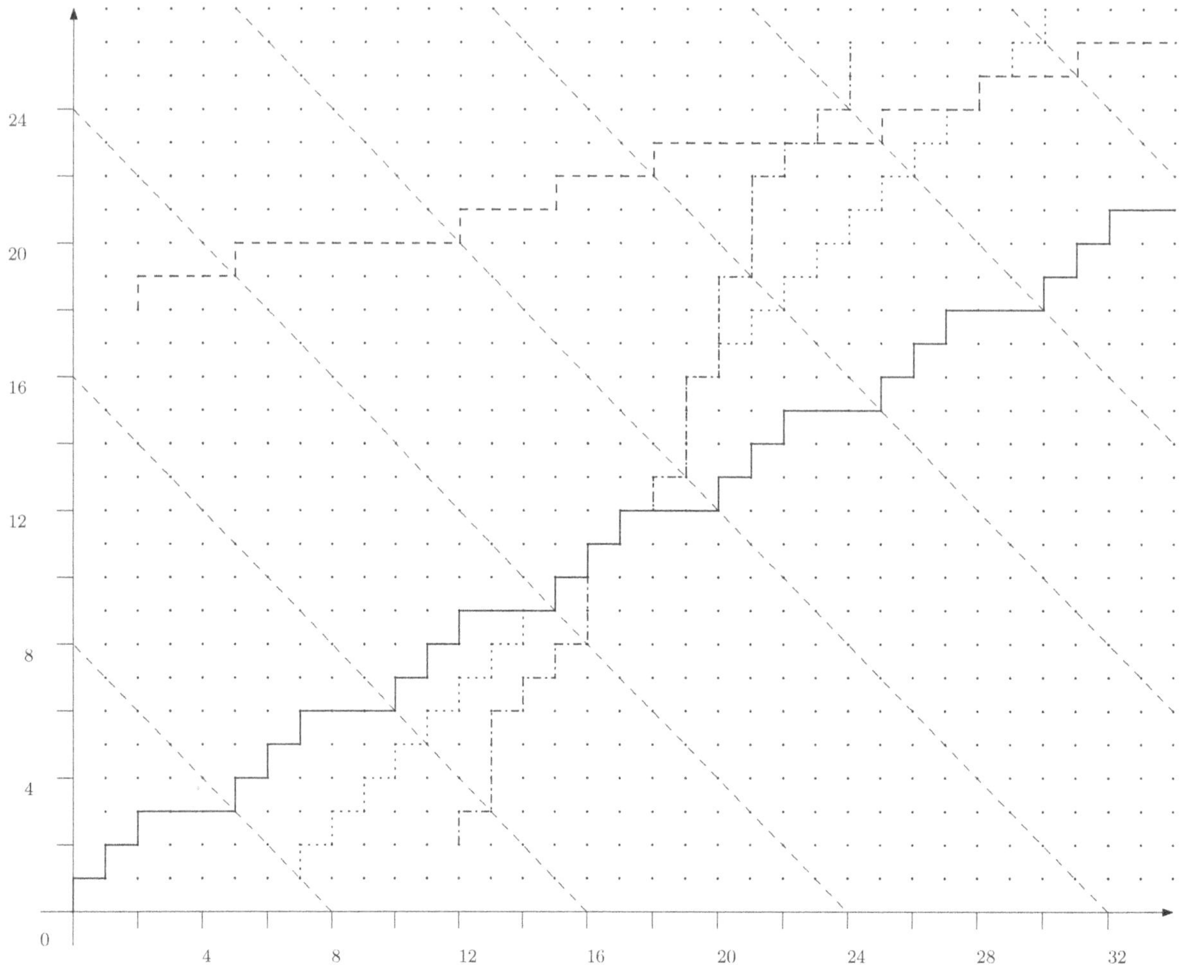

Figure 2: Some digital line segments.

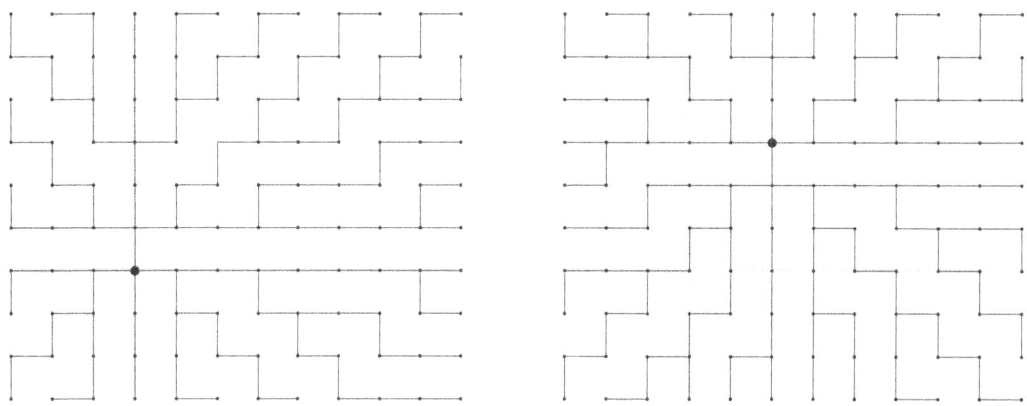

Figure 3: Digital line segments emanating from $(0,0)$ and from $(2,3)$.

Setting $x := q_x/q_y$, we observe

$$\begin{aligned} H(\overline{pq}, \overline{prr'q}) &\leq \frac{1}{2\sqrt{(xq_y)^2+q_y^2}}(q_y + 2xq_y) \\ &= \frac{x+1/2}{\sqrt{x^2+1}} \\ &\leq \sqrt{5}/2, \end{aligned}$$

as the function

$$f(x) = \frac{x+1/2}{\sqrt{x^2+1}}$$

attains its global maximum at $x = 2$. □

The following lemma is a statement about the order $\prec$ and will be the key ingredient of the proof of Theorem 2.

LEMMA 8. *Let $\{x \in \mathbb{Z} | A \leq x < B\}$ be an interval of integers with the following properties:*

(i) Its number of elements is $B - A = 2^{k+1} - 1$ for some number k.

(ii) $|(A + B - 1)/2|_2 \geq k$, and $|x|_2 < k$ for all $A \leq x < B$ such that $x \neq (A + B - 1)/2$.

Let $x_1 \prec x_2 \prec \ldots \prec x_{2^{k+1}-1}$ be the elements of the interval sorted in increasing order according to $\prec$.

Then elements from the left half and elements from the right half of the interval alternate, that is, if $x_i < (A + B - 1)/2$ for some $1 \leq i < 2^{k+1} - 1$, then $x_{i+1} \geq (A + B - 1)/2$, and vice versa.

PROOF. Define $M := (A + B - 1)/2$. Assume for a contradiction that there is an $1 \leq i < 2^{k+1} - 1$ such that both $x_i < M$ and $x_{i+1} < M$. First we look at the case $|A - 1|_2 < |M|_2$. Then, on one hand, $x_i \prec x_i + 2^k$, because $|x_i - j|_2 = |x_i + 2^k - j|_2$ for all $0 \leq j \leq x_i - A$ and $|x_i - j|_2 = |A - 1|_2 < |M|_2 = |x_i + 2^k - j|_2$ for $j = x_i - (A - 1)$. (We use the simple observation that if $|x|_2 < k$ then $|x + 2^k|_2 = |x|_2$.) But, on the other hand, $x_i + 2^k \prec x_{i+1}$, because there is a $0 \leq j_0 \leq x_i - A$ such that $|x_i + 2^k - j_0|_2 = |x_i - j_0|_2 < |x_{i+1} - j_0|_2$ and $|x_i + 2^k - j|_2 = |x_i - j|_2 = |x_{i+1} - j|_2$ for all $0 \leq j < j_0$. So $x_i \prec x_i + 2^k \prec x_{i+1}$, a contradiction.

In the case $|A - 1|_2 > |M|_2$, we can argue similarly that $x_i \prec x_{i+1} + 2^k \prec x_{i+1}$. (Note that equality never occurs, as $|A - 1|_2 = |M|_2$ implies $|(A - 1 + M)/2|_2 \geq |M|_2 \geq k$, but $|(A - 1 + M)/2|_2 < k$ by assumption.)

We have shown that if $x_i < M$, then $x_{i+1} \geq M$. Similarly we can show that $x_i > M$ implies $x_{i+1} \leq M$. So the elements to the left and to the right of M alternate. □

PROOF. (of Theorem 2) Let $p, q \in \mathbb{Z}^2$. We may assume that $p_x < q_x$ and $p_y < q_y$. We are going to prove that $H(\overline{pq}, S_\prec(p, q)) \leq 2c \log(p_x + p_y - q_x - q_y)$ for $c = \sqrt{5}/2$. Let $r \in S_\prec(p, q)$ be the point with the property that $r_x + r_y$ is the greatest element of the segment interval, that is, $r_x + r_y \succ s$ for all $s \in [p_x + p_y, q_x + q_y)$, $s \neq r_x + r_y$, see Figure 4 for an example. Now let s' be the second greatest element of the segment interval according to $\prec$. Define $k := |s'|_2 + 1$.

We can extend the segment $S_\prec(p, q)$ over both endpoints, moving both p and q such that $|p_x + p_y - 1|_2 \geq k$ and $|q_x + q_y|_2 \geq k$, that is, we extend the segment as far as we can, so that k, defined as above, remains unchanged. From Lemma 6 we get that by this extension we decreased the Hausdorff distance by at most a factor of 2. Now the segment interval contains exactly $2^{k+1} - 1$ elements and $r_x + r_y$ is the element in the very middle. We call such a segment *normalized.*

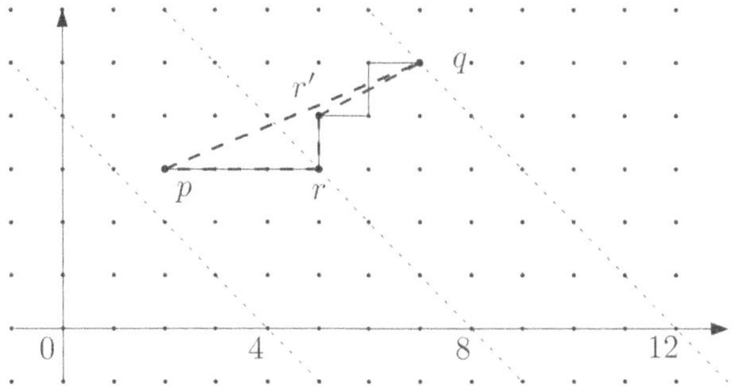

Figure 4: The digital line segment from $p = (2, 3)$ to $q = (7, 5)$, with the ordered segment interval $8 \succ 10 \succ 6 \succ 9 \succ 5 \succ 11 \succ 7$. The Euclidean segments $\overline{pq}$ and $\overline{prr'q}$ (dashed) can have Hausdorff distance at most c, as shown in Lemma 7.

We are going to proceed by induction on k to prove that for all normalized digital line segments $H(\overline{pq}, S_\prec(p, q)) \leq ck$ with $c = \sqrt{5}/2$. This will prove the theorem, as $k + 1 = \log(p_x + p_y - q_x - q_y + 1)$, the distance of the original segment (we started from) is at most $2ck = 2c(\log(p_x + p_y - q_x - q_y + 1) - 1) \leq 2c \log(p_x + p_y - q_x - q_y)$.

In the base case $k = 1$, the segment interval consists of 3 numbers, so $S_\prec(p, q)$ is a path of length 3 and by checking all possibilities we see that $H(\overline{pq}, S_\prec(p, q)) < c$.

If $k > 1$, the idea is to split the segment at r into two subsegments which are similar in some sense and apply induction. Let $r' = (r_x, r_y + 1)$ be the point that comes after r in the segment $S_\prec(p, q)$. (We know that we go up at r, because we go up at least once and $r_x + r_y$ is the greatest element of the segment interval). Consider the subsegments $S_\prec(p, r)$ and $S_\prec(r', q)$ and partition the segment interval accordingly. The key observation is that picking the elements of the interval according to $\prec$ starting with the greatest, we first get r, and then alternately the elements of the left and the right subsegment interval. This is shown in Lemma 8 setting $A = p_x + p_y$, $B = q_x + q_y$. Therefore, up to a difference of at most one, half of the $q_y - p_y - 1$ greatest elements (after $r_x + r_y$) belong to $[p_x + p_y, r_x + r_y)$ and half of them to $[r_x + r_y + 1, q_x + q_y)$. This implies that p, q, r, r' meet the conditions of Lemma 7, leading to $H(\overline{pq}, \overline{prr'q}) \leq c$. By the induction hypothesis we have $H(\overline{pr}, S_\prec(p, r)) \leq c(k - 1)$ and $H(\overline{r'q}, S_\prec(r', q)) \leq c(k - 1)$. Now $H(\overline{prr'q}, S_\prec(p, q)) = \max\{H(\overline{pr}, S_\prec(p, r)), H(\overline{r'q}, S_\prec(r', q))\} \leq c(k - 1)$. Using the triangle inequality we conclude $H(\overline{pq}, S_\prec(p, q)) \leq ck$. □

4. TOWARDS A CHARACTERIZATION

Now we approach the same problem from a different angle, taking arbitrary CDSes and trying to find some common patterns in their structure. Knowing that condition (C1) holds for all CDSes, it is easy to verify that we can analyze the segments with non-positive and non-negative slopes separately, as they are completely independent. More precisely, the union of any CDS on segments with non-positive slopes and another CDS on segments with non-negative slopes is automatically a CDS. Having this in mind, in this section we will proceed with the analysis of only one half of the CDS, namely, of segments with non-negative slope.

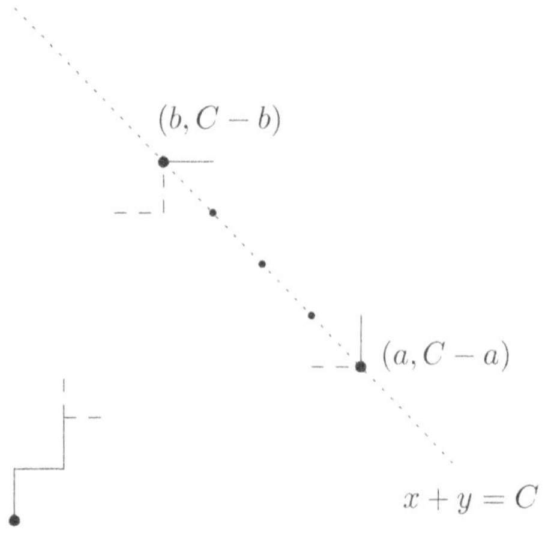

Figure 5: Two segments having p as their lower-left endpoint, one of them going up at $(a, C-a)$ and the other going right at $(b, C-b)$, with $a > b$.

We will show that, in a CDS, all the segments with non-negative slope emanating from one fixed point must be derived from a total order. However, as we will show later, these orders may differ for different points. Earlier, we used that these orders cannot be arbitrary when we proved Case 2 of (S3) in the proof of Theorem 3. When we defined $S_{\prec}(p, q)$ for $p_x \leq q_x$ in Section 2, we started from p and went towards q. Note that we could have done just the opposite, start from q and go towards p. This way we can define the rays emanating from p to both directions using only the total order that belongs to p.

PROPOSITION 9. *For any CDS and for any point $p = (p_x, p_y) \in \mathbb{Z}^2$, there is a total order $\prec_p$ that is uniquely defined on both $(-\infty, p_x + p_y - 1]$ and $[p_x + p_y, +\infty)$, such that the segments with non-negative slope emanating from p are derived from $\prec_p$ (in the way described in Section 2).*

PROOF. We fix a CDS $\mathcal{S}$ and a point p. The segments with non-negative slope with $p = (p_x, p_y)$ as their upper-right point will induce an order on the integers smaller than $p_x + p_y$, the segments for which p is the lower-left endpoint will induce an order on the rest of the integers. In the following we will just look at the latter type of segments.

First we will show that it cannot happen that for two segments with non-negative slope having p as their lower-left endpoint, one of them goes up at $(a, C-a)$ and the other goes right at $(b, C-b)$, for some C and $a > b$. Let us, for a contradiction, assume the opposite, see Figure 5. We look at the $a - b + 1$ segments between p and each of the points on the line $x + y = C$ between the points $(a, C-a)$ and $(b, C-b)$. It is possible to extend all of them through their upper-right endpoints, applying (S4). Note that each of the extended segments goes through a different point on the line $x + y = C$, and hence, because of condition (C3), no two of them can go through the same point on the line $x + y = C + 1$. But, there are only $a - b$ available points on the line $x + y = C + 1$ between the points $(a, C - a + 1)$ and $(b + 1, C - b)$, one less than the number of segments, a contradiction.

Now, we define the order $\prec_p$ in the following way. Whenever there is a segment in $\mathcal{S}$ starting at p going right at a point $(x, D - x)$ and going up at a point $(x', E - x')$ we set $D \prec_p E$. Assume that for some integers D and E we run into a conflict determining which one is greater in the order. That can happen only when there are two segments with non-negative slope having p as their lower-left endpoint, such that on the line $x + y = D$ one of them goes up, the other right, and then on $x + y = E$ they both go in different direction than at $x + y = D$. But then the situation described in the previous paragraph must occur on one of the two lines, a contradiction.

If $C \prec_p D$ and $D \prec_p E$, then we also have $C \prec_p E$ – we just take a segment starting from p that goes right at C and up at D, and (if necessary) extend it until it passes the line $x + y = E$. It must also go up at E because of $D \prec_p E$. This shows that $\prec_p$ is a partial order on $[p_x + p_y, +\infty)$.

It remains to prove that it is in fact a total order. That is, for any pair of integers $p_x + p_y \leq D < E$, either $D \prec_p E$ or $E \prec_p D$ holds. Consider a segment from p to some point q on the line $x + y = E$, such that this segment splits at q, that is, there are two extensions of the segment, one going up and another one going right. That segment exists since in the upper-right quadrant of p, the line $x + y = E + 1$ contains one more point than the line $x + y = E$. If we look at all the segments between p and the points on $x + y = E + 1$, the pigeonhole principle ensures that two of them will contain the same point q on the line $x + y = E$. Now the segment $S(p, q)$ crosses the line $x + y = D$ at some point q'. Depending on whether it goes up or right at the point q', either $E \prec_p D$ or $D \prec_p E$ holds. □

To see that these orders can differ for different points, consider the following example of a CDS, which we call the *waterline example* because of the special role of the x-axis. To connect two points with a segment, we do the following. Above the x-axis we go first right, then up, below the x-axis we go first up, then right, and when we have to traverse the x-axis, we go straight up to it, then travel on it to the right, and finally continue up, see Figure 6. It is easy to check that this construction satisfies all five axioms.

Now, if we consider a point $p = (a, b)$ below the waterline, $b < 0$, the induced total order $\prec_p$ on $[a + b, +\infty)$ is $a \prec_p a + 1 \prec_p \ldots \prec_p (+\infty) \prec_p a - 1 \prec_p a - 2 \prec_p \ldots \prec_p a + b$, and the order on $(-\infty, a+b-1]$ is $a+b-1 \prec_p a+b-2 \prec_p \ldots \prec_p -\infty$. If p is above the waterline, $b \geq 0$, the induced total orders are $a - 1 \prec a - 2 \prec \ldots \prec (-\infty) \prec a \prec a + 1 \prec \ldots \prec a + b - 1$ and $a + b \prec a + b + 1 \prec \ldots \prec +\infty$. Obviously, there is no total order on $\mathbb{Z}$ compatible with these orders for all possible choices of p.

The special role played by the x-axis in the waterline example can be fulfilled by any other monotone digital line with a positive slope; above the line we go right, then up, below the line we go up, then right, and whenever the line is hit, we follow it until either the x- or the y-coordinate matches that of the final destination, see Figure 7.

Acknowledgments

We are indebted to Jiří Matoušek, who posed this problem at the 7th Gremo Workshop on Open Problems - GWOP 2009. We would like to thank József Solymosi for participating in the fruitful discussions that led to the main result of this paper. Finally, we thank the organizers of GWOP 2009 for inviting us to the workshop and providing us with a gratifying working environment.

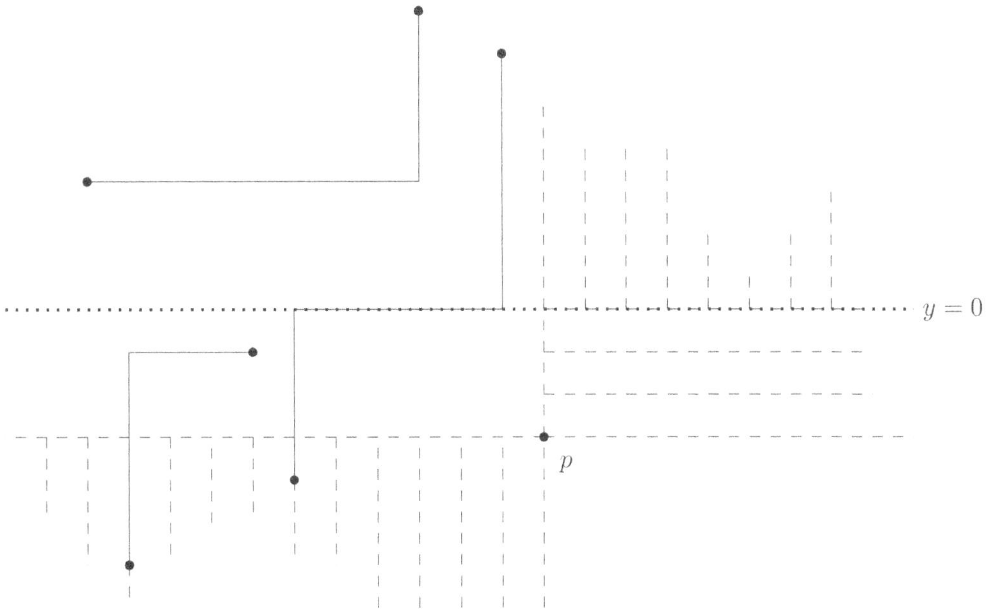

Figure 6: The waterline example: Examples of three characteristic segments, and the rays emanating from a point p, which is below the waterline

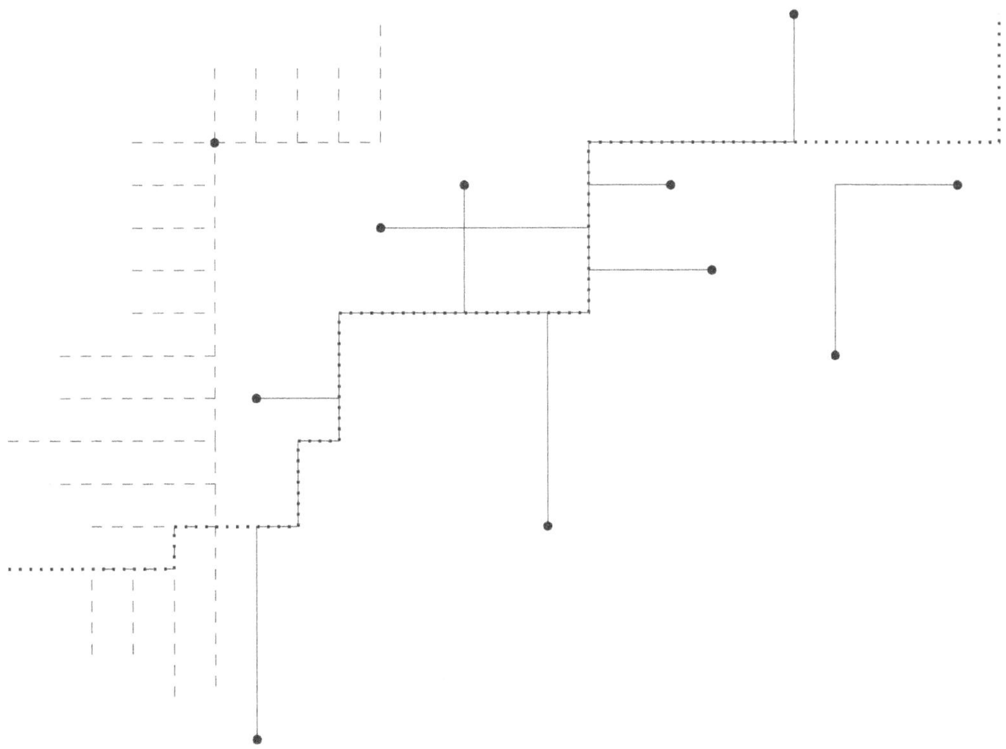

Figure 7: A more exotic example of a CDS with an arbitrary "special" line (bold and dotted).

5. REFERENCES

[1] J. Chun, M. Korman, M. Nöllenburg, and T. Tokuyama. Consistent digital rays. *Discrete Comput. Geom.*, 42(3):359–378, 2009.

[2] M. T. Goodrich, L. J. Guibas, J. Hershberger, and P. J. Tanenbaum. Snap rounding line segments efficiently in two and three dimensions, 1997.

[3] D. H. Greene and F. F. Yao. Finite-resolution computational geometry. In *SFCS '86: Proceedings of the 27th Annual Symposium on Foundations of Computer Science*, pages 143–152, Washington, DC, USA, 1986. IEEE Computer Society.

[4] R. Klette and A. Rosenfeld. Digital straightness – a review. *Discrete Appl. Math.*, 139(1-3):197–230, 2004.

[5] W. M. Schmidt. Irregularities of distribution. VII. *Acta Arith.*, 21:45–50, 1972.

[6] K. Sugihara. Robust geometric computation based on topological consistency. In V. N. Alexandrov, J. Dongarra, B. A. Juliano, R. S. Renner, and C. J. K. Tan, editors, *International Conference on Computational Science (1)*, volume 2073 of *Lecture Notes in Computer Science*, pages 12–26. Springer, 2001.

[7] J. van der Corput. Verteilungsfunktionen. I. Mitt. *Proc. Akad. Wet. Amsterdam*, 38:813–821, 1935.

The Geometry of Flocking

Bernard Chazelle*
Department of Computer Science
Princeton University
chazelle@cs.princeton.edu

ABSTRACT

The convergence time for flocking in the Vicsek-Cucker-Smale model is known to be bounded by a tower-of-twos of height linear in the number of birds. We improve the height to logarithmic, which matches the known lower bound. In the process, we introduce an intriguing geometric object, the *flight net*, and develop the idea of a *virtual agent*. These two concepts give us insight into early flocking behavior, which is still the most mysterious aspect of these dynamical systems.

Categories and Subject Descriptors

F.2.2 [**Nonnumerical Algorithms and Problems**]: Geometrical problems and computations

General Terms

Algorithms, Theory

Keywords

Bird flocking, Flight net, Multiagent agreement systems

1. INTRODUCTION

Beginning with Reynolds's pioneering work in the mid-eighties, bird flocking has generated voluminous literature, with a sudden flurry of interest in the last 5 years. There are several reasons for this: one is that computer simulations are inexplicably effective. Why? Many believe a deep scientific principle lies behind the answer. Another reason is that the problem can be approached fruitfully from many different angles: evolutionary ecology; statistical physics; dynamics; algebraic graph theory; computational geometry. A third reason is that no other consensus system boasts such a rich mathematical structure, combining algebra, analysis, and geometry in equal measures [1, 2, 3, 5, 6, 7, 9, 10, 11, 12, 13, 14, 15, 16, 17, 18, 19, 20]. Following the holonomic Vicsek-Cucker-Smale model, we express the dynamics of bird flocking as follows [1, 5, 20]:

$$\begin{cases} x(t) = x(t-1) + v(t); \\ v(t+1) = (P_t \otimes I_d)v(t). \end{cases} \quad (1)$$

The vectors $x(t), v(t)$ encode the positions and velocities of the n birds in dimension d (by stacking all the data into a vector of $\mathbb{Q}^{dn}$); P_t is the stochastic transition matrix of the flocking network G_t, which links any two birds within unit distance of each other. (The Kronecker product with the identity distributes the averaging over each coordinate.) A connected component of G_t is called a *flock*. Intuitively, each bird averages out its own velocity with those of its neighbors in G_t: all its neighbors weigh equally in the average except perhaps for itself; as usual, all nonzero entries in P_t are assumed to be at least $n^{-O(1)}$, as are the rational initial conditions—many more bits can be accommodated if so desired. Each P_t defines a reversible, aperiodic Markov chain; hence it is diagonalizable. Of course, there is no reason these matrices should commute and thus share a common eigenbasis. This difficulty arises in most distributed consensus systems. But there is another hurdle, specific to flocking: the averaging is kinetic but the network is positional; in other words, G_t is defined by integrating the velocities. It is hard to overstate the technical challenges arising from this "feature." This paper is almost self-contained, except for a few results we quote from [1]: While the network is invariant, a single flock drifts in space at constant speed with its birds subject to decaying oscillations. If π is the stationary distribution of P_t, then

$$x(t) = \underbrace{x(0)}_{start} + \underbrace{t((\mathbf{1}\pi^T)\otimes I_d)v(1)}_{linear\ drift} + \underbrace{(\Gamma_t \otimes I_d)v(1)}_{damped\ oscillator}, \quad (2)$$

where, as t goes to infinity, Γ_t converges to

$$-\mathbf{1}\pi^T + (I_n - P_t + \mathbf{1}\pi^T)^{-1}$$

at the rate of $e^{-t(1-\lambda)}$, where λ is the second largest eigenvalue of P_t. The general Landau-Odlyzko spectral gap [8] is sufficient for our purposes, which gives us a rate of $e^{-tn^{-O(1)}}$.

Our results. Let $2 \uparrow\uparrow n$ denote the tower-of-twos of height n. We proved [1] that n birds reach steady state (ie, G_t no longer changes) after $2 \uparrow\uparrow O(n)$ time.[1] We lower the

*This work was supported in part by NSF grants CCF-0634958 and NSF CCF-0832797.

SCG'10, June 13–16, 2010, Snowbird, Utah, USA.

[1]Hysteresis-free systems may never converge, so we assume that microscopic perturbations cannot break an edge. The rule is

height to $O(\log n)$. Specifically, we bound the convergence time by $2 \uparrow\uparrow 3.912 \log n$. (The exact constant is $1/\log x_0$, where x_0 is the unique real root of $x^5 - x^2 - 1$.) Surprisingly, there is a matching lower bound of $\log n$ on the height [2]. Up to a constant factor on the height, therefore, this establishes the exact worst-case complexity of flocking. The early behavior of any given bird can be quite arbitrary, as several birds can conspire to control the flight trajectory of another one at will. After a while, however, two birds that deviate by too large an angle can never meet again, regardless of what they and the other birds do. This *escape angle* is bounded by $n^{O(n)}(\log t)/t$.

We introduce two useful tools: the *flight net* and the *virtual agent*. The former traces the ancestry of a bird back in time: it is a geometric object made of convex polytopes; the second idea is that, even though any given bird can have a wild behavior, one can define a virtual bird whose motion is well-behaved. We believe that both concepts will play an important role in future work on collective motion.

2. THE VIRTUAL AGENT

We introduce a simple, powerful idea. Imagine that, at any time, exactly one bird holds a baton. The bird can pass the baton to any of its neighbors in the flocking network G_t. Is there a way of passing the baton that ensures that it almost follows a straight line? We prove that the answer is yes. The baton holder is called the *virtual bird*. By using virtuality we are able to bound the *escape angle*: that is the maximum angle at which two birds can fly away for a long time and still be able to get back together in a flock later. This plays a crucial role in bounding the convergence time.

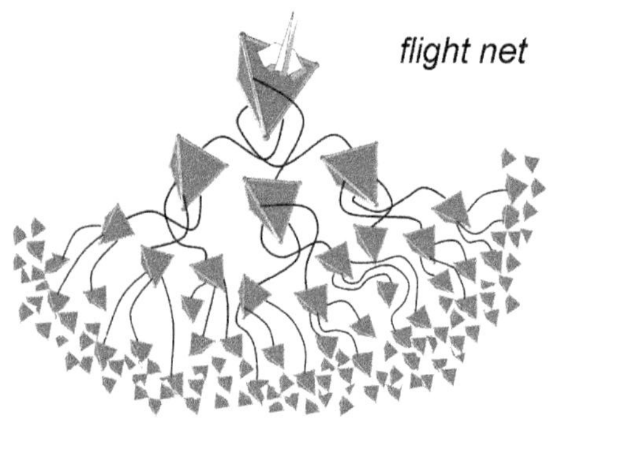

A word of intuition. The phase space of the dynamical system consists of positions and velocities. Both of these variables pull in opposite directions. Positions are expansive: in steady state separate flocks drift away from one another. But velocities form a dissipative system ($|\det P_t| < 1$). To reconcile the two, we introduce the *flight net*, which is a geometric trace of a bird's ancestry in time. It is a collection of convex polytopes which allows for a geometric reading of the averaging process occurring at each step. It is convenient to lift the birds into $\mathbb{R}^{d+1}$ by adding time as an extra dimension: $x(t) \mapsto (x_1(t), \ldots, x_d(t), t)^T$; $v(t) \mapsto (v_1(t), \ldots, v_d(t), 1)^T$. Since $\mathbf{1}$ is a right eigenvector, this lifting still satisfies the equation of motion. The *angular offset* $\angle(x_i(t), v_i(t))$, denoted by $\omega_i(t)$, plays an important role in the analysis. An obvious consequence of the velocity equation (1) is that

$$v_i(t) \in \text{conv}\{\, v_j(t-1) \mid (i,j) \in G_{t-1} \,\}.$$

By iterating in this fashion, we create the *flight net* $\mathcal{N}_i(t)$ of bird $\mathcal{B}_i$ at time $t > 0$. It is a connected collection of line segments (ie, a 1-skeleton): $\mathcal{N}_i(t) = \mathcal{N}_i(t, K_t)$, where K_t is a large integer parameter. Specifically, we set

$$K_t = \lceil n^{b_0} \log t \rceil \tag{3}$$

for a big enough constant b_0. Let K be an arbitrary positive integer; we define $\mathcal{N}_i(t, K)$ inductively as follows. The case $t = 1$ is straightforward: $\mathcal{N}_i(t, K)$ consists of the single line segment $x_i(0)x_i(1)$. Suppose that $t > 1$. We say that time s is *critical* if $s \le K$ or if, during the time interval $[s - K, s]$, there is a network switch, ie, the velocity of at least one flock is multiplied by $G_u \neq G_{u+1}$ for some u ($s - K \le u \le s$).

- If t is critical, then $\mathcal{N}_i(t, K)$ consists of the segment $x_i(t-1)x_i(t)$, together with the translates $\mathcal{N}_j(t-1, K) + x_i(t-1) - x_j(t-1)$, for all $(i,j) \in G_{t-1}$ and $j = i$.
- If t is noncritical, then $\mathcal{N}_i(t, K)$ consists of the segment $x_i(t-1)x_i(t)$, together with $\mathcal{N}_i(t-1, K)$.

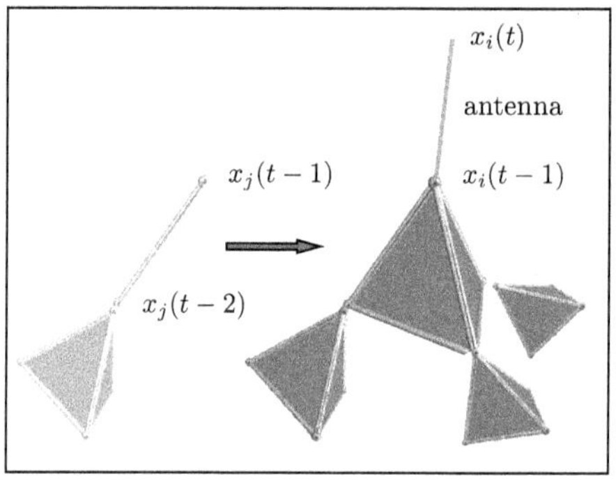

Every flight net has an *antenna* sitting on top, which is a line segment extending from $X_{d+1} = t-1$ to $X_{d+1} = t$ in the case of $\mathcal{N}_i(t, K)$. In the noncritical case, the antenna is connected on top of the previous one, ie, the one for $\mathcal{N}_i(t-1, K)$. Otherwise, we slide the time-$(t-1)$ flight nets of the adjacent birds so that their antennas join with the bottom vertex of the new antenna: this shift is called the *baton-passing drift*. The flight net allows us to prove the Escape Lemma, which implies that, as time goes by, it becomes increasingly easy to predict the velocity of a bird from its location, and vice versa. We begin with a simple observation. For any time $t > 0$, the $(d+1)$-dimensional vector $w_i(t) = \frac{1}{t} x_i(t)$ represents the constant velocity that bird $\mathcal{B}_i$ would need to have if it were to leave the origin at time 0 and be at position $x_i(t)$ at time t while flying in a fixed direction. We show that $\omega_i(t)$ cannot deviate too much from the *velocity offset* $\|v_i(t) - w_i(t)\|_2$. The law of sines easily implies that, for any $t > 0$,

$$n^{-O(1)} \|v_i(t) - w_i(t)\|_2 \le \omega_i(t) = O(\|v_i(t) - w_i(t)\|_2). \tag{4}$$

LEMMA 2.1. **(Escape Lemma)** *For any bird $\mathcal{B}_i$, $\omega_i(t) = \frac{\log t}{t} n^{O(n)}$ at any time $t > 1$.*

sound, as we can show that edges longer than $1 + o(1)$ will indeed break. We omit the proof, which is quite technical.

Proof Sketch. We may assume that t is large enough and $\omega_i(t) > 0$. The line passing through $x_i(t)$ in the direction of $v_i(t)$ intersects the hyperplane $X_{d+1} = 0$ in a point p at distance from the origin, $\|p\|_2 = \Omega(t\omega_i(t))$. Recall that the bird $\mathcal{B}_i$ started its journey at distance $n^{O(1)}$ from the origin. If it had flown in a straight line, then we would have $p = x_i(0)$, hence $\omega_i(t) = \frac{1}{t}n^{O(1)}$, and we would be done. Chances are the bird did not fly straight, however. If not, then we exhibit a virtual bird that (almost) does, at least in the sense that it does not get much closer to the origin at time 0 that a straightline flight would. The idea is to use the flight net to follow the trajectory of a virtual bird that closely mimics a straight flight from p to $x_i(t)$. We describe the *shadow path*. By (4), there exists a coordinate axis, say X_1, such that $0 < \omega_i(t) = O(v_i(t)_1 - w_i(t)_1)$. Note that we may have to reverse the sign of $v_i(t)_1 - w_i(t)_1$, but this is immaterial. The shadow path $x_i^{\mathrm{v}}(t), x_i^{\mathrm{v}}(t-1), \ldots, x_i^{\mathrm{v}}(0)$ describes the flight of the virtual bird $\mathcal{B}_i^{\mathrm{v}}$ backwards in time. The first two vertices are $x_i^{\mathrm{v}}(t) = x_i(t)$ and $x_i^{\mathrm{v}}(t-1) = x_i(t-1)$. This means the virtual bird flies down the topmost edge of $\mathcal{N}_i(t)$, ie, in the negative X_{d+1} direction. Next, the following rule applies for $s = t, t-1, \ldots, 2$:

- If s is noncritical, $\mathcal{N}_i(t)$ has a single edge $y_{s-2}y_{s-1}$, with $(y_{s-2})_{d+1} = s-2$. The virtual bird flies down $y_{s-2}y_{s-1}$ and we set $x_i^{\mathrm{v}}(s-2) = y_{s-2}$ accordingly.
- If s is critical, $\mathcal{N}_i(t)$ has one or several edges $y_{s-2}^k y_{s-1}$, with $(y_{s-2}^k)_{d+1} = s-2$. The virtual bird follows the edge with maximum X_1-extant, ie, the one that maximizes $(y_{s-1})_1 - (y_{s-2}^k)_1$. (Recall that, although neither y_{s-1} nor y_{s-2}^k might be the position of any actual bird, their difference $y_{s-1} - y_{s-2}^k$ is the velocity vector $v_j(s-1)$ of some $\mathcal{B}_j$.) We set $x_i^{\mathrm{v}}(s-2) = y_{s-2}^k$.

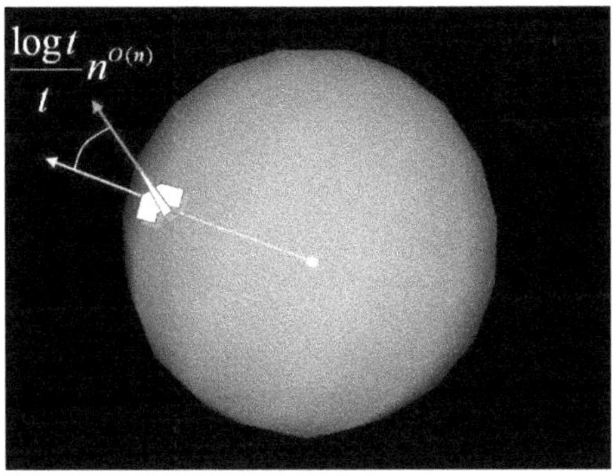

The virtual bird thus moves down the flight net back in time until it lands at $X_{d+1} = 0$. The resulting collection of $t+1$ vertices forms the shadow path of the virtual bird $\mathcal{B}_i^{\mathrm{v}}$ at time t. Naturally, we define the velocity of $\mathcal{B}_i^{\mathrm{v}}$ at time $s > 0$ as $v_i^{\mathrm{v}}(s) = x_i^{\mathrm{v}}(s) - x_i^{\mathrm{v}}(s-1)$. Note that $v_i^{\mathrm{v}}(t) = v_i(t)$. To prove that the shadow path does not stray far from the straightline flight from $x_i(t)$ to p, we focus on the difference $V_s = v_i^{\mathrm{v}}(s)_1 - w_i(t)_1$, for $s \geq 1$. If we could show that V_s is always nonnegative then, measured in projection along the X_1 axis, the virtual bird would fly back in time even further away from the origin that it would if it flew straight from $x_i(t)$ to the hyperplane $X_{d+1} = 0$ in the direction of $-v_i(t)$. Except for the fact that a virtual bird at time 0 may not share the location of any actual bird (an issue we will address later), this would entirely rescue our initial argument. We cannot quite ensure the nonnegativity of V_s, but we come close enough to serve our purposes.

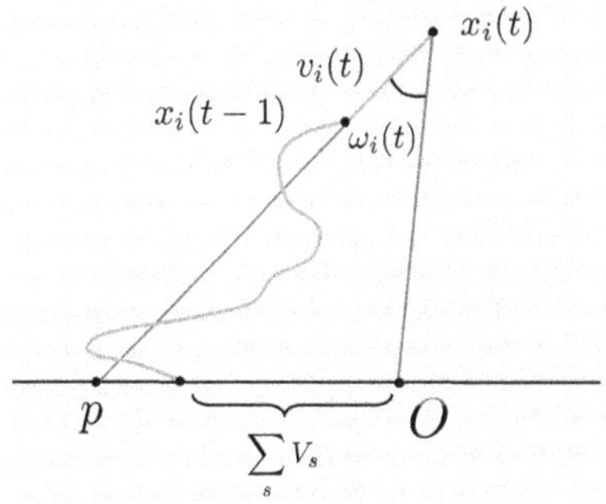

Consider an interval $[r, s]$ consisting entirely of noncritical times (hence $r > K_t$). The flock that contains the virtual bird $\mathcal{B}_i^{\mathrm{v}}$ is invariant between times $r - K_t$ and s; furthermore, $\mathcal{B}_i^{\mathrm{v}}$ has the same incarnation as some fixed $\mathcal{B}_j$ during the time period $[r-1, s]$. If $\chi(j)$ denotes the n-dimensional vector with all coordinates equal to 0, except for $\chi(j)_j = 1$, then

$$v_j(u) = ((\chi(j)^T P_t^{u-r+K_t}) \otimes I_d)v(r - K_t),$$

for $r - 1 \leq u \leq s$. We abuse notation and restrict the transition matrix P_t and $v(r - K_t)$ to the flock of $\mathcal{B}_j$ and not to all of $G_{r-K_t} = \cdots = G_s$. As in (2), we bound the Frobenius norm of the difference between P_t^s and its best rank-one ℓ_2-approximation: $\|P_t^s - \mathbf{1}\pi^T\|_F \leq e^{-sn^{-O(1)}+O(\log n)}$. It follows that

$$\begin{aligned}|v_j(u)_1 - ((\pi^T \otimes I_d)v(r - K_t))_1| \leq \|(((\chi(j)P_t^{u-r+K_t}) \otimes I_d) \\ - (\pi^T \otimes I_d))v(r-K_t)\|_2,\end{aligned}$$

which is at most

$$\begin{aligned}\sqrt{d}\,\|P_t^{u-r+K_t} - \mathbf{1}\pi^T\|_F \|v(r-K_t)\|_2 \\ \leq e^{-(u-r+K_t)n^{-O(1)}+O(\log n)}.\end{aligned}$$

We conclude that

$$\begin{aligned}|V_{r-1} - V_s| \leq |v_j(r-1)_1 - ((\pi^T \otimes I_d)v(r-K_t))_1| \\ + |v_j(s)_1 - ((\pi^T \otimes I_d)v(r-K_t))_1|\end{aligned}$$

which is at most

$$\leq e^{-K_t n^{-O(1)}+O(\log n)}.$$

Suppose now that $s > 1$ is critical; then $v_i^{\mathrm{v}}(s)$ is a convex combination of the vectors of the flight net joining $X_{d+1} = s-2$ to $X_{d+1} = s-1$. By construction, it follows that $v_i^{\mathrm{v}}(s-1)_1 \geq v_i^{\mathrm{v}}(s)_1$. Let $\mathfrak{C}$ be the number of critical times. For $1 \leq s \leq t$, $V_s \geq V_t - \mathfrak{C}e^{-K_t n^{-O(1)}+O(\log n)}$. Summing over all s,

$$\sum_{s=1}^{t} V_s \geq tV_t - (t-1)\mathfrak{C}e^{-K_t n^{-O(1)}+O(\log n)}.$$

By the bound above, $V_t = v_i^{\mathrm{v}}(t)_1 - w_i(t)_1 = \Omega(\omega_i(t))$; therefore,

$$\omega_i(t) = O(V_t) = \frac{O(1)}{t}\Big|\sum_{s=1}^{t} V_s\Big| + \mathfrak{C}e^{-K_t n^{-O(1)} + O(\log n)}. \quad (5)$$

A telescoping sum gives us

$$\sum_{s=1}^{t} V_s = \sum_{s=1}^{t} \{x_i^{\mathrm{v}}(s)_1 - x_i^{\mathrm{v}}(s-1)_1 - w_i(t)_1\} = -x_i^{\mathrm{v}}(0)_1.$$

Since $x_i^{\mathrm{v}}(0)_1$ is the position of a virtual bird at time 0, it is tempting to infer that it is also the position of some actual bird at that time; hence $|x_i^{\mathrm{v}}(0)_1| = n^{O(1)}$. This is not quite true because adding together the velocity vectors ignores the baton-passing drift, ie, the displacements caused by switching birds. At critical times, the virtual bird gets assigned a new physical bird that is adjacent to its currently assigned feathered creature. Recall how the net $\mathcal{N}_j(t-1, K)$ is translated by $x_i(t-1) - x_j(t-1)$. Since $(i,j) \in G_{t-1}$, this causes a displacement of at most 1. This highlights the role of the flight net as both a kinetic and a positional object. Summing them up, we find that $|x_i^{\mathrm{v}}(0)_1| \le \mathfrak{C} + n^{O(1)}$; hence

$$\Big|\sum_{s=1}^{t} V_s\Big| \le \mathfrak{C} + n^{O(1)}.$$

By (5), we can bound the number of critical times by $\mathfrak{C} \le K_t N(n) \le n^{O(n)} \log t$, where $N(n)$ is the maximum number of network switches. By interpreting the velocity component of the system as following a bidirectional agreement system, we can bound $N(n)$ by $n^{O(n)}$ [4]. □

The Escape Lemma has many interesting consequences. We mention two of them without proofs, the second one being fairly technical.

COROLLARY 2.2. *If two birds are adjacent in the flocking network at time $t > 1$, their distance prior to t always remains within $n^{O(n)} \log t$. The difference in stationary velocities between two distinct flocks joining into a common one at time t has Euclidean norm at most $\frac{\log t}{t} n^{O(n)}$. For some constant f_0, there is $t_f = n^{f_0 n}$ after which the flocking network G_t may gain new edges but never lose any.*

COROLLARY 2.3. *Consider two birds newly adjacent at time t. Assume that the flocks that contain them remain invariant during the period $[t_1, t-1]$, where $t_f < t_1 < t - 1$. If, at time $t-1$, the birds are in different flocks with distinct stationary velocities, then $t \le n^{O(t_1 n)}$; otherwise, $t \le t_1 2^{n^{O(1)}}$.*

3. THE LOGARITHMIC HEIGHT

Armed with the Escape Lemma, we now prove that the tower-of-twos has height $O(\log n)$. The tower-of-twos results from a curious phenomenon of *spectral shift*: roughly, when two flocks collide, the worst-case scenario is a shift in the energy spectrum which wipes out the two lowest modes and mixes the higher frequencies without cancelling them. Unfortunately, the spectral shift alone cannot yield an upper bound lower than linear on the tower's height. To prove a logarithmic bound, one must show that spectral shifts are such remarkable events they require balancing conditions that can be met only rarely. We model the sequence of flock merges after the fragmentation breakpoint t_f by a forest $\mathcal{F}$: each internal node a corresponds to a flock F_a of n_a birds formed at time $t_a > t_f$. If a is a leaf of $\mathcal{F}$, then its formation time t_a is at most t_f. A node with at least two children is called *branching*. A nonbranching node represents the addition of edges within the same flock. Our analysis will focus (wlog) on branching nodes with no more than two children. Let $L(t)$ denote the minimum value of n_a, the number of birds in F_a, over all branching nodes a such that $t_a \ge t$. The upper bound of $2 \uparrow\uparrow (3.912 \log n)$ on the convergence time follows from this lower bound:

LEMMA 3.1. *$L(t) \ge (1.1938)^{\log^* t - O(\log\log n)}$, where $x_0 \approx 1.1938$ is the unique real root of $x^5 - x^2 - 1$.*

The intuition. The proof involves a rather technical process of "residue clearing." To build intuition, we begin with a toy problem which illustrates the idea with none of the heavy flocking baggage. Consider an n-leaf binary tree whose nodes are associated with polynomials in $\mathbb{R}[X]$. Each leaf is assigned its own polynomial of degree 1. The polynomial p_v at an internal node v is defined recursively by combining those at the children u, w:

$$p_v = p_u \oplus p_w = p_u + p_w + (p_u - p_w)x^{2^{h(p_u - p_w)}},$$

where $h(p)$ is 0 if $x = 0$ is not a root of p and $h(p)$ is its multiplicity otherwise; in other words, it is the lowest degree among the (nonzero) monomials of p. How big can the degree of p_{root} be? It is immediate to achieve a degree that is a tower-of-twos of logarithmic height. Take a complete binary tree and assign the polynomial $(-1)^{l(v)}x$ to a leaf v, where $l(v)$ is the number of left turns from the root to the leaf. We verify by induction that the polynomials at level k are of the form $\pm c_k x^{d_k}$, where $d_1 = 1$ and, for $k > 1$,

$$c_k x^{d_k} = \pm 2c_{k-1} x^{d_{k-1} + 2^{d_{k-1}}}.$$

This shows that $d_k = d_{k-1} + 2^{d_{k-1}}$; hence the stated tower-of-twos of logarithmic height. Couldn't we increase the height by choosing a nonbalanced tree? The answer is no, but not for the obvious reason. The "obvious reason" would be that to go from a node u of degree d to a parent of degree 2^d requires not just one but two children u, v of degree d. Nice idea. Unfortunately, it is not true:

$$x^d \oplus 0 = x^d + x^{d+2^d}. \quad (6)$$

Note, however, that if we try to repeat this trick we get

$$(x^d + x^{d+2^d}) \oplus 0 = x^d(1 + x^{2^d})^2,$$

which increases the degree by only a constant factor. The reason for this is that during the exponential jump in (6) the polynomial inherited a *residue*, ie, the "low-degree" monomial x^d, which will hamper future growth until it is removed. But to do so requires another "big-degree" child. This residue-clearing task is what keeps the tower's height logarithmic. We prove this below.

THEOREM 3.2. *A tree of n nodes can produce only polynomials of degree at most $2 \uparrow\uparrow O(\log n)$.*

Proof. Let $L(d)$ be the minimum number of leaves needed to produce at the root a polynomial of degree at least d. We prove that

$$L(d) \geq 2^{\Omega(\log^* d)}, \tag{7}$$

from which the theorem follows. Let v be the root of the smallest n-leaf tree that achieves $d_v \geq d$, where d_v denotes the degree of p_v. Let u, w be the children of v, with $d_u \geq d_w$, and let y, z be the children of u with $d_y \geq d_z$. We assume that d is large enough, so all these nodes exist. Note that

$$d_v \leq d_u + 2^{d_u} \qquad \text{and} \qquad d_u \leq d_y + 2^{d_y}. \tag{8}$$

Assume that

$$\begin{cases} d_z, d_w < \log\log\log d_v; \\ d_y < \sqrt{d_u} < d_u < \sqrt{d_v}. \end{cases} \tag{9}$$

In view of (8), this shows that $d_u > d_w$ and $d_y > d_z$. This first inequality implies that $d_u + 2^{h(p_u - p_w)} = d$; therefore, by (9), $h(p_u - p_w) > \frac{1}{2}\log d_v$. In other words,

$$p_u = p_w + x^{\lceil (\log d_v)/2 \rceil} q_u\,, \tag{10}$$

for some polynomial $q_u \neq 0$. Repeating the same line of reasoning at node u, we derive the identity $d_y + 2^{h(p_y - p_z)} = d_u$ from the strict inequality $d_y > d_z$. It follows from (8, 9) that

$$d_z < \log\log\log d_v < \tfrac{1}{2}\log d_u < h(p_y - p_z) \leq \log d_u < \tfrac{1}{2}\log d_v.$$

This implies two things: first, by $d_z < h(p_y - p_z)$, the polynomial p_y has a monomial q of degree $h(p_y - p_z)$; second, that degree is strictly between $\log\log\log d_v$ and $\frac{1}{2}\log d_v$. A quick look at the formula

$$p_u = p_y + p_z + (p_y - p_z)x^{2^{h(p_y - p_z)}}$$

shows that p_u also contains q: indeed, by $d_z < h(p_y - p_z)$, it must be the case that $p_y + p_z$ contains the monomial q; on the other hand, the minimum degree in

$$(p_y - p_z)x^{2^{h(p_y - p_z)}}$$

exceeds $h(p_y - p_z)$. This proves the presence of q in p_u, which contradicts (10). This, in turn, means that (9) cannot hold. The monomial q of degree $h(p_y - p_z)$ is the *residue* that the big-number engine must clear before it can continue exponentiating degrees. Since $d_y > \frac{1}{2}\log\log d$, at least one of these two conditions applies for any large enough d:

$$L(d) \geq \begin{cases} L(\frac{1}{2}\log\log d) + L(\log\log\log d)\,; \\ L(d^{1/4}) + 1\,. \end{cases}$$

We use the monotonicity of L to reduce all the cases to the two above. The lower bound (7) follows by induction. □

Clearing residues.

Recall that $t_a > t_f$ is the time at which the flock F_a is formed at node a of $\mathcal{F}$ after t_f (see Corollary 2.2). If $\mathbf{m}_a = (\pi_a^T \otimes I_d)v_a(t_a)$ then

$$\|v_a(t) - (\mathbf{1}_{n_a} \otimes I_d)\mathbf{m}_a\|_2 \leq e^{-(t-t_a)n^{-O(1)} + O(\log n)}. \tag{11}$$

If $\ell(\mathbf{m}_a)$ denotes the bit length, then

$$\ell(\mathbf{m}_a) = O(t_a n \log n). \tag{12}$$

Consider a flock F_c associated with a branching node c of $\mathcal{F}$: let a and b be the two children of c in $\mathcal{F}$ (hence $n_c = n_a + n_b$) and assume that $t_a \geq t_b$ and that no node of the forest $\mathcal{F}$ has more than two children, ie, flocks merge only two at a time. By Corollary 2.2, the difference in stationary velocities between F_a and F_b satisfies

$$n^{-O(t_a n)} \leq \|\mathbf{m}_a - \mathbf{m}_b\|_2 \leq \tfrac{\log t_c}{t_c}\, n^{O(n)}. \tag{13}$$

It follows (with a little bit of work) that, whether $\mathbf{m}_a = \mathbf{m}_b$ or not, $t_c \leq n^{O(t_a n)}$.

Let $\mathcal{F}_o$ be the forest derived from $\mathcal{F}$ by removing all nonbranching internal nodes and merging the adjacent edges in the obvious way. Our assumption implies that each internal node of $\mathcal{F}_o$ has exactly two children. Let $a_0, \ldots, a_k$ ($k > 1$) be an ascending path in $\mathcal{F}_o$ and let b_i denote the unique sibling of a_i.

Lemma 3.3. *Assume that $2^{2^{t_f}} < \log\log\log t_{a_k} < t_{a_0}^4 < t_{a_1} < \log t_{a_k}$. Then, $t_{b_{i_0}} \geq \sqrt{\log\log t_{a_0}}$, for some $0 \leq i_0 < k$.*

The recurrence.

We set up a recurrence relation on $L(t)$ to prove the lower bound of Lemma 3.1. Let $t_0 = 2 \uparrow\uparrow \lfloor \log\log n \rfloor$. It is assumed that n is large enough. For $t \leq t_0$, we have the trivial lower bound $L(t) \geq 1$, so we may assume that $t > t_0$. The child b of a node c (both defined with respect to $\mathcal{F}_o$) is called *near* if $t_b > (\log t_c)^{2/3}$.

Lemma 3.4. *Any internal node c of $\mathcal{F}_o$ such that $t_c \geq 2^{2^{t_f}}$ has at least one near child.*

Proof. By the upper bound on t_c, we know that c has a child b_0 in the original forest $\mathcal{F}$ such that $t_c = n^{O(t_{b_0} n)}$. We exhibit a near child b for c. If b_0 is branching, set $b = b_0$; otherwise, set b to the nearest branching descendent of b_0. By Corollary 2.3, the formation times of any node in $\mathcal{F}$ and its nonbranching parent differ by at most a factor of $2^{n^{O(1)}}$. Since $\mathcal{F}$ has fewer than n^2 nodes and $t_c \geq 2^{2^{t_f}}$, with $t_f = n^{f_o n}$,

$$t_b \geq 2^{-n^{O(1)}} t_{b_0} \geq 2^{-n^{O(1)}} \log t_c > (\log t_c)^{2/3}.$$

□

Let c_0 be an arbitrary node of $\mathcal{F}_o$ such that

$$t_{c_0} \geq t > t_0 = 2 \uparrow\uparrow \lfloor \log\log n \rfloor. \tag{14}$$

By the previous lemma, we can follow a descending path in $\mathcal{F}_o$ of near children $c_0, c_1, \ldots, c_l$, where $t_{c_l} < 2^{2^{t_f}} \leq t_{c_{l+1}}$. Because t_0 is so much greater than t_{c_l}, the path has more than a constant number of nodes—in fact, at least on the order of $\log\log n$. For future use, we note that

$$2^{2^{t_f}} < \log\log\log t_{c_0}. \tag{15}$$

Lemma 3.5. *There exists $k > 1$ such that*

$$\log\log\log t_{c_0} < t_{c_k}^4 < t_{c_{k-1}} < \log t_{c_0}\,.$$

Proof. By (15) and Lemma 3.4, there exists some c_j in $\mathcal{F}_o$ such that $(\log\log t_{c_0})^{2/3} < t_{c_j} < \log t_{c_0}$. Suppose now that all the nodes c_i, for $i = j+1, j+2, \ldots, l$, satisfy $t_{c_i}^4 \geq t_{c_{i-1}}$.

Since there are most n nodes along the path from c_0 to c_l in $\mathcal{F}_o$, then, by (15) again,

$$2^{2^{t_f}} > t_{c_l} \geq t_{c_j}^{4^{-n}} > (\log\log t_{c_0})^{4^{-n-1}} > 2^{2^{2^{t_f/2}}}. \qquad (16)$$

This contradiction proves the existence of some node c_k ($j < k \leq l$) such that $t_{c_k}^4 < t_{c_{k-1}} < \log t_{c_0}$. The argument used in (16) shows that the smallest such k satisfies, via (15),

$$t_{c_{k-1}} \geq t_{c_j}^{4^{-n}} > (\log\log t_{c_0})^{4^{-n-1}} > 2^{2^{t_f}}.$$

Another application of the inequality above, $t_{c_{k-1}} > 2^{2^{t_f}}$, allows us to invoke Lemma 3.4. By virtue of t_{c_0} being so big (15) and c_k being a near child of c_{k-1} (by construction), $t_{c_k}^4 > \log\log\log t_{c_0}$. □

We now prove Lemma 3.1. Setting $a_i = c_{k-i}$ for $i = 0, \ldots, k$, together with (15), the lemma sets the conditions of Lemma 3.3. This shows that $t_{a_0} > (\log\log\log t_{a_k})^{1/4}$ and, conservatively,

$$t_{b_{i_0}} > (\log\log\log\log\log t_{a_k})^{1/3}.$$

Nodes a_0 and b_{i_0} are roots of disjoint subtrees, so the number of leaves below a_k is at least that of those below a_0 added to those below b_{i_0}. Since L is a monotone function and, by (14), a_k is an arbitrary node such that $t_{a_k} \geq t$,

$$L(t) \geq L((\log\log\log t)^{1/4}) + L((\log\log\log\log\log t)^{1/3}),$$

for $t > t_0 = 2 \uparrow\uparrow \lfloor \log\log n \rfloor$, and $L(t) \geq 1$ for $t \leq t_0$. We solve the recurrence without the exponents, and then show that ignoring them makes no asymptotic difference. Define $L^*(t) = 1$ for $t \leq t_0$ and, for any $t > t_0$,

$$L^*(t) = L^*(\log\log\log t) + L^*(\log\log\log\log\log t).$$

Given the bound we are aiming for, we can round off t down to the next tower-of-twos. If $L^*(t) = M(\sigma)$, where $\sigma = \log^* t$, we can rewrite the recurrence relation as

$$M(\sigma) = M(\sigma - 3) + M(\sigma - 5),$$

where $M(\sigma) = 1$ for $\sigma \leq \log^* t_0$. Quite clearly, $M(\sigma)$ upper-bounds the maximum number n_s of leaves in a binary tree $\mathcal{T}^*$ where: (i) each left edge is labeled 3 and each right edge 5; and (ii) the sum of the labels along any path is at most $s = \log^* t - \log^* t_0$. Note that $\mathcal{T}^*$ is binary: the constraint that each internal node should have exactly two nodes does not follow from the definition and is therefore added. We seek a lower bound of the form cx^s. This means that $x^s \geq x^{s-3} + x^{s-5}$, for $s \geq 5$ and $cx^s \leq 1$ else. The characteristic equation is $x^5 - x^2 - 1 = 0$. We choose the unique real root $x_0 \approx 1.19385$; this leads to $c = x_0^{-5}$. This shows that $n_s \geq x_0^{s-5}$; hence,

$$L^*(t) \geq x_0^{\log^* t - \log\log n - 5}.$$

It is obvious that the binary tree $\mathcal{T}$ associated with the recurrence for $L(t)$ embeds in $\mathcal{T}^*$ with the same root. We claim that it is not much smaller: specifically, no leaf in $\mathcal{T}$ has more than a constant number of descendents in $\mathcal{T}^*$. This implies immediately that

$$L(t) \geq x_0^{\log^* t - O(\log\log n)},$$

which proves Lemma 3.1. □

To prove our claim, we show that no path in $\mathcal{T}^*$ extends past its counterpart in $\mathcal{T}$ by more than a constant number of nodes. We model simultaneous, parallel walks down the trees as a collaborative game between two players, Bob and Alice, who take turns. Initially, both of them share the same value $t_A = t_B = t > t_0$. In one round, Bob modifies his current value by taking iterated logs. He is entitled to up to 5 logarithm iterations; in other words, he can set $t_B \leftarrow \log t_B$ or $t_B \leftarrow \log\log\log\log\log t_B$, or anything in-between. Alice mimics Bob's move but then completes it by taking a fractional power; for example, if Bob opts for, say, $\log\log t_B$, then Alice resets her value to $(\log\log t_A)^\alpha$, where α is a number between $\frac{1}{4}$ and 1. To summarize, Bob chooses the number of log iterations and Alice chooses α: they can change these parameters at each round. A player's *score* is the number of rounds before his or her value falls below (or at) t_0. Alice's score cannot be higher than Bob's, so the latter is expected to play the last rounds on his own.

The joint goal of the players is to maximize their score differential. Regardless of either player's strategy, we show that Bob's score never exceeds Alice's by more than a constant. This follows directly from the next two lemmas, whose proofs we postpone.

LEMMA 3.6. *The score differential is maximized when Bob always selects the single-iterated log rule and Alice follows suit with* $\alpha = \frac{1}{4}$*; in other words,* $t_B \leftarrow \log t_B$ *and* $t_A \leftarrow (\log t_A)^{1/4}$.

With the strategy of the lemma, Bob's score is $\log^* t - \log^* t_0$. Within an additive constant, Alice's score is at least the minimum h such that $c_h \geq t$, where c_i is defined by $c_0 = t_0^4$ and, for $i > 0$, $c_i = 2^{4c_{i-1}}$. To see why, note that, with the inverse of the function $z \mapsto (\log z)^{1/4}$ being $z \mapsto 2^{z^4}$, taking logarithms on both sides gives the recurrence on c_i.

LEMMA 3.7. *For* $t > t_0$,

$$\min\{\, h \mid c_h \geq t \,\} \geq \log^* t - \log^* t_0 - O(1).$$

This validates our claim that no path in $\mathcal{T}^*$ extends past its counterpart in $\mathcal{T}$ by more than a constant number of nodes. This fills in the missing part in the proof of Lemma 3.1 and establishes the upper bound on the convergence time claimed in §1.

Proof of Lemma 3.3. The flock F_c is associated with a branching node c of $\mathcal{F}$ and that a and b are its two children in $\mathcal{F}$; furthermore, $t_a \geq t_b$ and $t_a > t_f$, where $t_f = n^{f_0 n}$. Assume that the velocity vector of F_a at time t_a is of the form

$$v_a(t_a) = (\mathbf{1}_{n_a} \otimes I_d)\widetilde{\mathbf{m}}_a + (u_a \otimes I_d)\mu_a + \zeta_a\,, \qquad (17)$$

where $u_a \in \mathbb{R}^{n_a}$, $\mu_a \in \mathbb{R}^d$, and, for some real τ,

$$\begin{cases} 2^{t_f} \leq \tau \leq t_a^{1/3}; \\ \ell(\widetilde{\mathbf{m}}_a) = O(\log\log \tau); \\ \|u_a\|_\infty = 1 \;\;\&\;\; u_a \geq 0; \\ e^{-\tau n^{O(1)}} \leq \|\mu_a\|_2 \leq \frac{1}{\tau}; \\ \|\zeta_a\|_2 \leq e^{-\tau^2 n^{-O(1)} + n^{O(1)}}. \end{cases} \qquad (18)$$

Note that the d-dimensional rational vector $\widetilde{\mathbf{m}}_a$ is not defined as the stationary velocity $\mathbf{m}_a$ of F_a, though it plays essentially the same role. The term $(u_a \otimes I_d)\mu_a$ creates the *residue* $\|\mu_a\|_2$ of F_a. Unless F_b can "destroy" this residue when it joins with F_a, one should not expect the flock formation time to grow exponentially. The crux is then to show that only a flock F_b with many birds can perform such a task. The following result says that, if the flock F_b settles too early, its effect on the residue of F_a is negligible. The conditions on F_c stated below differ slightly from those for F_a to make them closed under composition. The lemma below also covers the case $n_b = 0$, when the transition from F_a to F_c is involves the addition of an edge within the same flock. (Here, too, we assume without loss of generality that these additions occur only one at a time within the same flock.) We postpone the proof of this result.

LEMMA 3.8. *If node b is well defined, then assume that* $t_b < \log\log\tau$. *Whether node b exists or not,*

$$v_c(t_c) = (\mathbf{1}_{n_c} \otimes I_d)\widetilde{\mathbf{m}}_a + (u_c \otimes I_d)\mu_c + \zeta_c\,,$$

where

$$\begin{cases} \|u_c\|_\infty = 1 \;\;\&\;\; u_c \geq 0\,; \\ \|\mu_a\|_2\, n^{-O(1)} \leq \|\mu_c\|_2 \leq \|\mu_a\|_2\,; \\ \|\zeta_c\|_2 \leq n\|\zeta_a\|_2 + e^{-\tau^2}. \end{cases}$$

Furthermore, if node b is well defined, then $\mathbf{m}_b = \widetilde{\mathbf{m}}_a \neq \mathbf{m}_a$.

Let's explain, at an intuitive level, the meaning of the three terms in the expression for $v_a(t_a)$, or equivalently $v_c(t_c)$: $\widetilde{\mathbf{m}}_a$ is a low-precision approximation of the stationary velocity $\mathbf{m}_a$; the vector $(u_a \otimes I_d)\mu_a$ creates the residue; the remainder ζ_a is an error term. The term $\widetilde{\mathbf{m}}_a$ is a low-resolution component of the velocity that any other flock F_b has to share if it is to create small angles with F_a (the key to high flock formation times) This component must be factored out from the analysis since it cannot play any role in engineering small angles. To create small angles with F_a, incoming flocks F_b must attack the residue vector $(u_a \otimes I_d)\mu_a$. Of course, they could potentially take turns doing so. Informally, one should read the inequalities of the lemma as a repeat of (18). The lemma states a closure property: unless F_b brings many bits to the table (via a formation time at least $\log\log\tau$), conditions (18) will still hold. These conditions prevent the creation of small angles between flocks, and hence of huge formation times. In other words, flocks that settle too early cannot hope to dislodge the residue $\|\mu_a\|_2$. The reason is that this residue is shielded in three ways: first, it is too big for the error term ζ_a to interfere with it—compare $e^{-\tau n^{O(1)}}$ with $e^{-\tau^2 n^{-O(1)} + n^{O(1)}}$; second, it is too small to be affected by $\widetilde{\mathbf{m}}_a$—compare $\frac{1}{\tau}$ with a rational over $O(\log\log\tau)$ bits; third, all of its coordinates have the same sign ($u_a \geq 0$), so taking averages among them cannot cause any cancellations. This form of "enduring" positivity is the most remarkable aspect of residues. By (18), the lemma's bounds imply that

$$e^{-\tau n^{O(1)}} \leq \|\mu_c\|_2 \leq \tfrac{1}{\tau} \quad \& \quad \|\zeta_c\|_2 \leq e^{-\tau^2 n^{-O(1)} + n^{O(1)}},$$

which brings us back to (18). If c has a parent c' and sibling b', then we can apply the lemma again. Note that composition will always be applied for the same value of τ, ie, one is that is not updated at each iteration. In other words, the first two lines of (18), unlike the last three, are global inequalities that do not change with each iteration. This closure property is not foolproof. First, of course, we need to ensure that $t_{b'} < \log\log\tau$. More important, we lose a polynomial factor at each iteration. So we may compose the lemma only $n^{O(1)}$ times if we are to avoid any visible loss in the bounds of (18). Since the forest has fewer than n^2 nodes, this means that, as long as its conditions are met, we can compose the lemma with ancestors of c to our heart's content and still get the full benefits of (18).

The provision that b might not be well defined allows us to handle nonbranching switch nodes with equal ease. Recall that $v_c(t_c)$ is the velocity leading to time t_c, ie, before the flock F_b has had a chance to infuence it. The provision in question might thus appear somewhat vacuous. Its power will come from allowing us to apply the lemma repeatedly with no concern whether a node has one of two children. A related observation is that nowhere shall we use the fact that t_a is the actual formation time of F_a. It could be replaced in (17) by any t'_a strictly between t_a and t_c. We thus trivially derive a "delayed" version of Lemma 3.8. We summarize its two features: (i) Lemma 3.8 can be composed iteratively as often as we need to; (ii) node a need not be an actual node of $\mathcal{F}$ but one introduced artificially along an edge of $\mathcal{F}$. The proof itself is somewhat technical. We have included its main components in the appendix following the bibliography. This concludes our discussion of Lemma 3.1.

4. REFERENCES

[1] Chazelle, B. *Natural algorithms*, Proc. 20th ACM-SIAM SODA 2009, 422–431.

[2] Chazelle, B. *The convergence of bird flocking*, arXiv:0905.4241v1, 2009.

[3] Chazelle, B. *Analytical tools for natural algorithms*, Proc. 1st Symposium on Innovations in Computer Science (2010), Beijing, 32–41.

[4] Chazelle, B. *A geometric approach to collective motion*, SoCG 2010.

[5] Cucker, F., Smale, S. *Emergent behavior in flocks*, IEEE Trans. Automatic Control 52 (2007), 852–862.

[6] Hendrickx, J.M., Blondel, V.D. *Convergence of different linear and non-linear Vicsek models*, Proc. 17th International Symposium on Mathematical Theory of Networks and Systems (MTNS2006), Kyoto (Japan), July 2006, 1229–1240.

[7] Ji, M., Egerstedt, M. *Distributed coordination control of multi-agent systems while preserving connectedness*, IEEE Transactions on Robotics 23 (2007), 693–703.

[8] Landau, H.J., Odlyzko, A.M. *Bounds for eigenvalues of certain stochastic matrices*, Linear algebra and Its Applications 38 (1981), 5–15.

[9] Li, S., Wang, H. *Multi-agent coordination using nearest neighbor rules: revisiting the Vicsek model*, 2004, arXiv:cs/0407021v2

[10] Lorenz, J. *A stabilization theorem for dynamics of continuous opinions*, Physica A: Statistical Mechanics and its Applications 355 (2005), 217–223.

[11] Moreau, L. *Stability of multiagent systems with time-dependent communication links*, IEEE Transactions on Automatic Control 50 (2005), 169–182.

[12] Moshtagh, N., Jadbabaie, A., Daniilidis, K. *Distributed geodesic control laws for flocking of nonholonomic agents*, Proc. 44th IEEE Conference on Decision and Control and European Control Conference 2005 (ECC-CDC'05), Seville, Spain.

[13] Olfati-Saber, R. *Flocking for multi-agent dynamic systems: algorithms and theory*, IEEE Transactions on Automatic Control 51 (2006), 401–420.

[14] Reynolds, C.W. *Flocks, herds, and schools: A distributed behavioral model*, Computer Graphics 21 (1987), 25–34.
[15] Shi, H., Wang, L., Chu, T. *Coordination of multiple dynamic agents with asymmetric interactions*, Proc. 2005 IEEE International Symposium on Intelligent Control, Cyprus (2005), 1423-Ű1428.
[16] Tahbaz-Salehi, A., Jadbabaie, A. *On recurrence of graph connectivity in Vicsek's model of motion coordination for mobile autonomous agents*, Proc. 2007 American Control Conference, New York, NY (2007), 699–704.
[17] Tanner, H.G., Jadbabaie, A., Pappas, G.J. *Stable flocking of mobile agents, Part I: fixed topology*, Proc. IEEE Conference on Decision and Control, Maui, Hawaii (2003), 2010–2015.
[18] Tanner, H.G., Jadbabaie, A., Pappas, G.J. *Stable flocking of mobile agents, Part II: dynamic topology*, Proc. IEEE Conference on Decision and Control, Maui, Hawaii (2003), 2016–2021.
[19] Tanner, H.G., Jadbabaie, A., Pappas, G.J. *Flocking in fixed and switching networks*, IEEE Trans. Automatic Control 52 (2007), 863–868.
[20] Vicsek, T., Czirók, A., Ben-Jacob, E., Cohen, I., Shochet, O. *Novel type of phase transition in a system of self-driven particles*, Physical Review Letters 75 (1995), 1226–1229.

5. APPENDIX

LEMMA 5.1. *Let $c_0, \ldots, c_l$ be an ascending path in $\mathcal{F}$ and let d_i be the sibling, if any, of c_i. Assume that c_0, possibly an artificial node, satisfies the conditions of node a in (18) and that $t_{d_i} < \log\log\tau$ for all d_i. Then,*

$$v_{c_i}(t_{c_i}) = (\mathbf{1}_{n_{c_i}} \otimes I_d)\widetilde{\mathbf{m}}_{c_i} + (u_{c_i} \otimes I_d)\mu_{c_i} + \zeta_{c_i}\,,$$

where

$$\begin{cases} \ell(\widetilde{\mathbf{m}}_{c_i}) = O(\log\log\tau); \\ \|u_{c_i}\|_\infty = 1 \ \ \&\ \ u_{c_i} \geq 0\,; \\ e^{-\tau n^{O(1)}} \leq \|\mu_{c_i}\|_2 \leq \frac{1}{\tau}\,; \\ \|\zeta_{c_i}\|_2 \leq e^{-\tau^2 n^{-O(1)} + n^{O(1)}}. \end{cases}$$

For all d_i, $\mathbf{m}_{d_i} = \widetilde{\mathbf{m}}_{c_i} \neq \mathbf{m}_{c_i}$.

We are now equipped with all the high-level tools we need to complete the proof of 3.3. Recall that $a_0, \ldots, a_k$ ($k > 1$) is an ascending path in $\mathcal{F}_o$ and b_i denotes the unique sibling of a_i. (Note that $a_0 \cdots a_k$ is a path in $\mathcal{F}_o$ whereas, in Lemma 5.1, $c_0 \cdots c_l$ is a path in $\mathcal{F}$.) Also,

$$2^{2^{t_f}} < \log\log\log t_{a_k} < t_{a_0}^4 < t_{a_1} < \log t_{a_k}.$$

Assume, by contradiction, that $t_{b_i} < \sqrt{\log\log t_{a_0}}$ for $i = 0, \ldots, k-1$. As we observed earlier, Corollary 2.3 ensures that the ratio between the formation times of any node in $\mathcal{F}$ and that of its nonbranching parent is at least $2^{-n^{O(1)}}$. Since there are fewer than n^2 switches, this implies that F_{a_0} can undergo switches only between t_{a_0} and $t_{a_0}2^{n^{O(1)}}$. Because $t_{a_1} > t_{a_0}^4 > 2^{2^{t_f}}$, this shows that the entire time interval $[\frac{1}{2}t_{a_1}, t_{a_1})$ is free of switches. Let a be the last node in $\mathcal{F}$ from a_0 to a_1 and let c_0 be the artificial parent of a corresponding to the flock F_a at time $t_{a_1} - 1$: we set $n_{c_0} = n_{a_0}$ and $t_{c_0} = t_{a_1} - 1$. The bound in (11) ensures that the oscillations in the flock F_{c_0} are heavily damped. Indeed,

$$v_{c_0}(t_{c_0}) = (\mathbf{1}_{n_{c_0}} \otimes I_d)\mathbf{m}_{c_0} + \zeta_{c_0}\,, \tag{19}$$

where, because of the magnitude of t_{a_1},

$$\|\zeta_{c_0}\|_2 \leq e^{-(t_{a_1}/2-1)n^{-O(1)}} \leq e^{-t_{a_1}n^{-O(1)}} \leq e^{-\tau^2}. \tag{20}$$

where $\tau = \frac{1}{2}t_{a_1}^{1/3}$. The rest of the sequence $\{c_i\}$ is now entirely specified. In particular, note that $c_1 = a_1$ and $d_0 = b_0$. By extension, $\mathbf{m}_{c_0} = \mathbf{m}_a$; so, by (13),

$$\|\mathbf{m}_{c_0} - \mathbf{m}_{b_0}\|_2 \leq \frac{\log t_{a_1}}{t_{a_1}} n^{O(n)} < \frac{1}{\tau}\,.$$

therefore, $\mathbf{m}_{c_0} = \mathbf{m}_{b_0} + \mu_{c_0}$, where

$$\|\mu_{c_0}\|_2 < \frac{1}{\tau}\,. \tag{21}$$

As we shall see, the presence of the square τ^2 in the exponent of (20) ensures that the oscillations of F_{c_0} are too small to interfere with the residue $\|\mu_{c_0}\|_2$. Writing $\widetilde{\mathbf{m}}_{c_0} = \mathbf{m}_{b_0}$, it follows from (19) that

$$v_{c_0}(t_{c_0}) = (\mathbf{1}_{n_{c_0}} \otimes I_d)\widetilde{\mathbf{m}}_{c_0} + (\mathbf{1}_{n_{c_0}} \otimes I_d)\mu_{c_0} + \zeta_{c_0}\,,$$

which matches (17), with $u_{c_0} = \mathbf{1}_{n_{c_0}}$. Since all the nodes d_i are of the form b_{j_i},

$$t_{d_i} < \sqrt{\log\log t_{a_0}} < \log\log\tau.$$

Thus, we will be able to apply Lemma 5.1 once we verify that all conditions in (18) are met:

- $[\,2^{t_f} \leq \tau \leq t_{c_0}^{1/3}\,]$: This follows from our setting $\tau = \frac{1}{2}(t_{c_0}+1)^{1/3}$ and our assumption that $t_{a_1} > 2^{2^{t_f}}$.
- $[\,\ell(\widetilde{\mathbf{m}}_{c_0}) = O(\log\log\tau)\,]$: Because $\tau > 2^{2^{t_f-2}}$,
  $$\sqrt{\log\log t_{a_0}}\, n\log n < (\log\log t_{a_0})^{2/3} = o(\log\log\tau).$$
  The desired bound follows from (12):
  $$\begin{aligned}\ell(\widetilde{\mathbf{m}}_{c_0}) = \ell(\mathbf{m}_{b_0}) &= O(t_{b_0} n\log n) \\ &= O(\sqrt{\log\log t_{a_0}}\, n\log n) < \log\log\tau.\end{aligned}$$
- $[\,e^{-\tau n^{O(1)}} \leq \|\mu_{c_0}\|_2 \leq \frac{1}{\tau}\,]$: The upper bound comes from (21). For the lower bound, note that $\mathbf{m}_{c_0} = \mathbf{m}_a$, with $t_a \leq t_{a_0}2^{n^{O(1)}}$. Another application of (12) shows that
  $$\ell(\mathbf{m}_{c_0}) = O(t_a n\log n) < t_{a_0}^{7/6} < \tau.$$
  We just saw that $\ell(\mathbf{m}_{b_0}) < \log\log\tau$, so $\mu_{c_0} = \mathbf{m}_{c_0} - \mathbf{m}_{b_0}$ is a d-dimensional vector with rational coordinates over fewer than 2τ bits. The lower bound follows from the fact that $\mu_{c_0} \neq 0$. By Corollary 2.3, the stationary velocities $\mathbf{m}_{c_0}$ and $\mathbf{m}_{b_0}$ cannot be equal, otherwise the two flocks F_a and F_{b_0} could not take so long to meet at time t_{a_1}. Indeed, the time elapsed would be at least $t_{a_1} - t_a$, (since $t_a > t_{b_0}$), which would greatly exceed the limit of $t_a 2^{n^{O(1)}}$ allowed.
- $[\,\|u_{c_0}\|_\infty = 1 \ \&\ u_{c_0} \geq 0 \ \&\ \|\zeta_{c_0}\|_2 \leq e^{-\tau^2 n^{-O(1)} + n^{O(1)}}\,]$: The bounds follow from (20) and $u_{c_0} = \mathbf{1}_{n_{a_0}}$.

Let c_l be the node a_k. By applying Lemma 5.1 at c_l, we find that $\mathbf{m}_{b_{k-1}} = \widetilde{\mathbf{m}}_{c_{l-1}}$. Applying the same lemma now at node c_{l-1} shows that

$$v_{c_{l-1}}(t_{c_{l-1}}) = (\mathbf{1}_{n_{c_{l-1}}} \otimes I_d)\widetilde{\mathbf{m}}_{c_{l-1}} + (u_{c_{l-1}} \otimes I_d)\mu_{c_{l-1}} + \zeta_{c_{l-1}}\,,$$

where

$$\begin{cases} \|\mu_{c_{l-1}}\|_2 \geq e^{-\tau n^{O(1)}} \\ \|u_{c_{l-1}}\|_\infty = 1 \ \ \& \ \ u_{c_{l-1}} \geq 0; \\ \|\zeta_{c_{l-1}}\|_2 \leq e^{-\tau^2 n^{-O(1)} + n^{O(1)}}. \end{cases}$$

The lemma also allows us to express the stationary velocity at c_{l-1}:

$$\begin{aligned} \mathbf{m}_{c_{l-1}} &= (\pi_{c_{l-1}}^T \otimes I_d) v_{c_{l-1}}(t_{c_{l-1}}) \\ &= (\pi_{c_{l-1}}^T \otimes I_d)((\mathbf{1}_{n_{c_{l-1}}} \otimes I_d)\widetilde{\mathbf{m}}_{c_{l-1}} \\ &\qquad + (u_{c_{l-1}} \otimes I_d)\mu_{c_{l-1}} + \zeta_{c_{l-1}}) \\ &= \mathbf{m}_{b_{k-1}} + (\pi_{c_{l-1}}^T u_{c_{l-1}} \otimes I_d)\mu_{c_{l-1}} + (\pi_{c_{l-1}}^T \otimes I_d)\zeta_{c_{l-1}}. \end{aligned}$$

By the triangle inequality, it follows that

$$\begin{aligned} \|\mathbf{m}_{c_{l-1}} - \mathbf{m}_{b_{k-1}}\|_2 &\geq \|(\pi_{c_{l-1}}^T u_{c_{l-1}} \otimes I_d)\mu_{c_{l-1}}\|_2 \\ &\qquad - \|(\pi_{c_{l-1}}^T \otimes I_d)\zeta_{c_{l-1}}\|_2 \\ &\geq \pi_{c_{l-1}}^T u_{c_{l-1}} \|\mu_{c_{l-1}}\|_2 \\ &\qquad - \|(\pi_{c_{l-1}}^T \otimes I_d)\|_F \|\zeta_{c_{l-1}}\|_2 \\ &\geq \min_i\{(\pi_{c_{l-1}})_i\} e^{-\tau n^{O(1)}} \\ &\qquad - \sqrt{d}\, e^{-\tau^2 n^{-O(1)} + n^{O(1)}} \\ &\geq e^{-\tau n^{O(1)}}. \end{aligned}$$

By (13),

$$\|\mathbf{m}_{c_{l-1}} - \mathbf{m}_{b_{k-1}}\|_2 \leq \frac{\log t_{a_k}}{t_{a_k}} n^{O(n)};$$

therefore, since $t_{a_k} > 2^{t_f} > n^{n^4}$,

$$t_{a_k} \leq \|\mathbf{m}_{c_{l-1}} - \mathbf{m}_{b_{k-1}}\|_2^{-2} \leq e^{\tau n^{O(1)}} \leq e^{\tau^{1.5}},$$

which contradicts our assumption that

$$\tau = \tfrac{1}{2} t_{a_1}^{1/3} < (\log t_{a_k})^{1/3}.$$

□

Proof of Lemma 3.8. Using the shorthand $u^a = P_a^{t_c - t_a} u_a$ and $\zeta^a = (P_a^{t_c - t_a} \otimes I_d)\zeta_a$, we express the velocity of the flock F_a at time t_c. From

$$v_a(t_c) = (P_a^{t_c - t_a} \otimes I_d) v_a(t_a),$$

we find that, by (17),

$$\begin{aligned} v_a(t_c) &= (P_a^{t_c - t_a} \otimes I_d)(\mathbf{1}_{n_a} \otimes I_d)\widetilde{\mathbf{m}}_a \\ &\qquad + (P_a^{t_c - t_a} \otimes I_d)(u_a \otimes I_d)\mu_a + \zeta^a \\ &= (\mathbf{1}_{n_a} \otimes I_d)\widetilde{\mathbf{m}}_a + (u^a \otimes I_d)\mu_a + \zeta^a. \end{aligned} \tag{22}$$

Because P_a is an averaging operator, $\|P_a^{t_c - t_a} u_a\|_\infty \leq \|u_a\|_\infty = 1$. The vector u_a is nonnegative, so

$$\begin{aligned} \|P_a^{t_c - t_a} u_a\|_\infty &\geq \tfrac{1}{n_a} \|P_a^{t_c - t_a} u_a\|_1 = \tfrac{1}{n_a} \mathbf{1}_{n_a}^T P_a^{t_c - t_a} u_a \\ &\geq \tfrac{1}{n_a} \pi_a^T P_a^{t_c - t_a} u_a \geq \tfrac{1}{n_a} \pi_a^T u_a \\ &\geq \tfrac{1}{n_a} \min_i\{(\pi_a)_i\} \|u_a\|_\infty \geq n^{-O(1)}. \end{aligned}$$

Similarly, by convexity,

$$\begin{aligned} \|(P_a^{t_c - t_a} \otimes I_d)\zeta_a\|_2 &\leq \sqrt{d n_a}\, \|(P_a^{t_c - t_a} \otimes I_d)\zeta_a\|_\infty \\ &\leq \sqrt{d n_a}\, \|\zeta_a\|_\infty \leq \sqrt{d n_a}\, \|\zeta_a\|_2; \end{aligned}$$

therefore,

$$\begin{cases} n^{-O(1)} \leq \|u^a\|_\infty \leq 1 \ \ \& \ \ u^a \geq 0; \\ \|\zeta^a\|_2 \leq n \|\zeta_a\|_2. \end{cases} \tag{23}$$

Case I. Node b is well defined and $t_b < \log\log\tau$: Since, by (18), $t_c > t_a \geq \tau^3 \geq 8^{t_f}$,

$$-(t_c - t_b) n^{-O(1)} \leq -\tau^2;$$

so, by applying (11) to the flock F_b, we find that

$$\|v_b(t_c) - (\mathbf{1}_{n_b} \otimes I_d)\mathbf{m}_b\|_2 \leq e^{-(t_c - t_b) n^{-O(1)}};$$

hence

$$v_b(t_c) = (\mathbf{1}_{n_b} \otimes I_d)\mathbf{m}_b + e^{-\tau^2} z_c,$$

where $\|z_c\|_2 \leq 1$. It follows from (22) that

$$\begin{aligned} v_c(t_c) = \begin{pmatrix} v_a(t_c) \\ v_b(t_c) \end{pmatrix} &= \begin{pmatrix} (\mathbf{1}_{n_a} \otimes I_d)\widetilde{\mathbf{m}}_a \\ (\mathbf{1}_{n_b} \otimes I_d)\mathbf{m}_b \end{pmatrix} + \begin{pmatrix} (u^a \otimes I_d)\mu_a \\ 0 \end{pmatrix} \\ &\qquad + \begin{pmatrix} \zeta^a \\ e^{-\tau^2} z_c \end{pmatrix} \\ &= \begin{pmatrix} (\mathbf{1}_{n_a} \otimes I_d)\widetilde{\mathbf{m}}_a \\ (\mathbf{1}_{n_b} \otimes I_d)\mathbf{m}_b \end{pmatrix} + \left\{ \begin{pmatrix} u^a \\ 0 \end{pmatrix} \otimes I_d \right\} \mu_a \\ &\qquad + \begin{pmatrix} \zeta^a \\ e^{-\tau^2} z_c \end{pmatrix}. \end{aligned} \tag{24}$$

By (17), the stationary velocity of F_a is equal to

$$\begin{aligned} \mathbf{m}_a &= (\pi_a^T \otimes I_d) v_a(t_a) \\ &= (\pi_a^T \otimes I_d)((\mathbf{1}_{n_a} \otimes I_d)\widetilde{\mathbf{m}}_a + (u_a \otimes I_d)\mu_a + \zeta_a) \\ &= \widetilde{\mathbf{m}}_a + (\pi_a^T u_a)\mu_a + (\pi_a^T \otimes I_d)\zeta_a. \end{aligned} \tag{25}$$

By the triangle inequality, it follows that

$$\begin{aligned} \|\mathbf{m}_a - \widetilde{\mathbf{m}}_a\|_2 &\geq \pi_a^T u_a \|\mu_a\|_2 - \|(\pi_a^T \otimes I_d)\|_F \|\zeta_a\|_2 \\ &\geq \min_i\{(\pi_a)_i\} e^{-\tau n^{O(1)}} - \sqrt{d}\, e^{-\tau^2 n^{-O(1)} + n^{O(1)}} \\ &\geq e^{-\tau n^{O(1)}}, \end{aligned}$$

which shows that

$$\mathbf{m}_a \neq \widetilde{\mathbf{m}}_a. \tag{26}$$

Note also that, by (25),

$$\begin{aligned} \|\widetilde{\mathbf{m}}_a - \mathbf{m}_b\|_2 &\leq \|\widetilde{\mathbf{m}}_a - \mathbf{m}_a\|_2 + \|\mathbf{m}_a - \mathbf{m}_b\|_2 \\ &\leq \pi_a^T u_a \|\mu_a\|_2 + \|\pi_a^T \otimes I_d\|_F \|\zeta_a\|_2 + \|\mathbf{m}_a - \mathbf{m}_b\|_2. \end{aligned}$$

We bound each term on the right-hand side: by (18) and Cauchy-Schwarz,

$$\pi_a^T u_a \|\mu_a\|_2 \leq \tfrac{1}{\tau} \|\pi_a\|_2 \|u_a\|_2 \leq \tfrac{1}{\tau} \sqrt{n_a}\, \|u_a\|_\infty \leq \tfrac{1}{\tau} \sqrt{n}.$$

By (13) and $t_c > \tau^3 \geq 8^{t_f}$,

$$\|\mathbf{m}_a - \mathbf{m}_b\|_2 \leq \tfrac{1}{\tau}.$$

Also, $\|\pi_a^T \otimes I_d\|_F = O(1)$ and, by (18), $\|\zeta_a\|_2 \leq e^{-\tau^2 n^{-O(1)} + n^{O(1)}}$; therefore

$$\|\widetilde{\mathbf{m}}_a - \mathbf{m}_b\|_2 < \sqrt{\tfrac{1}{\tau}}.$$

By (12), our assumption that $t_b < \log\log\tau$ implies that

$$\ell(\mathbf{m}_b) = O(n(\log n)\log\log\tau) < (\log\log\tau)^2.$$

Since, by (18), $\ell(\widetilde{\mathbf{m}}_a) = O(\log\log\tau)$, the squared distance $\|\widetilde{\mathbf{m}}_a - \mathbf{m}_b\|_2^2$ is a rational over $O(\log\log\tau)^2$ bits: being less than $1/\tau$ implies that it is actually zero; hence $\widetilde{\mathbf{m}}_a = \mathbf{m}_b$, as claimed in the lemma. We verify from (23) that

$$\mu_c \stackrel{\text{def}}{=} \mu_a\|u^a\|_\infty \qquad \text{and} \qquad u_c \stackrel{\text{def}}{=} \begin{pmatrix} u^a \\ 0 \end{pmatrix} \|u^a\|_\infty^{-1}$$

satisfy the conditions of the lemma. By (24),

$$v_c(t_c) = (\mathbf{1}_{n_c} \otimes I_d)\widetilde{\mathbf{m}}_a + (u_c \otimes I_d)\mu_c + \zeta_c\,,$$

where

$$\zeta_c = \begin{pmatrix} \zeta^a \\ e^{-\tau^2} z_c \end{pmatrix}.$$

By (23) and $\|z_c\|_2 \leq 1$, the lemma's condition on ζ_c is trivially satisfied.

Case II. Node b is not defined: We set $\zeta_c = \zeta^a$; $\mu_c = \mu_a\|u^a\|_\infty$; and $u_c = u^a\|u^a\|_\infty^{-1}$. This matches the identity (22) with the one claimed in the lemma. □

Proof of Lemma 3.6.

Suppose that Bob does not always follow the single-iterated log rule. We show how to force him to do so without decreasing the score differential. If Bob uses the rule $t_B \leftarrow \log\log t_B$, then Alice follows up with $t_A \leftarrow (\log\log t_A)^\alpha$. Let us break this round into two parts:

1. $t_B \leftarrow \log t_B$ and $t_A \leftarrow \log t_A$;
2. $t_B \leftarrow \log t_B$ and $t_A \leftarrow (\log t_A)^\alpha$.

We proceed similarly for higher log-iterations and apply the modification systematically. This transformation increases the scores of the players but it does not change their difference. Finally, we apply one last transformation to the new game, which is to convert all of Alice's moves into $t_A \leftarrow (\log t_A)^{1/4}$. This can only increase the score differential. □

Proof of Lemma 3.7.

Consider the two recurrence relations:

$$a_0(x) = b_0(x) = x,$$

and, for $h > 0$,

$$\begin{cases} a_h(x) = 2^{a_{h-1}(x)} \\ b_h(x) = 2^{b_{h-1}(x)} + 2. \end{cases}$$

Recall that c_h is defined by $c_0 = t_0^4$ and, for $h > 0$, $c_h = 2^{4c_{h-1}}$. We verify by induction that, for any $h > 0$,

$$c_h = 2^{2^{b_{h-1}(4\log t_0 + 2)}}.$$

To prove the inequality we seek,

$$\min\{\, h \mid c_h \geq t \,\} \geq \log^* t - \log^* t_0 - O(1),$$

where $t > t_0$, we may assume that $t > 2^{t_0}$, otherwise the result is trivial. The assumption implies that the minimum h is positive; therefore it suffices to prove that, for all $h \geq 0$,

$$b_h(4\log t_0 + 2) \leq a_h(4\log t_0 + 4). \tag{27}$$

We see by induction that, for all $h \geq 0$, $x \geq 2$, and $\varepsilon > 0$,

$$a_h(x) + \varepsilon \leq a_h(x + \varepsilon 2^{-h}). \tag{28}$$

The case $h = 0$ is obvious, so consider $h > 0$. Note that, for any $y \geq 2$,

$$2^y + \varepsilon \leq 2^{y + \varepsilon/2},$$

which follows from

$$\ln(1 + \varepsilon 2^{-y}) \leq \varepsilon 2^{-y} \leq \tfrac{\ln 2}{2}\varepsilon.$$

Since $a_{h-1}(x) \geq 2$, this shows that

$$\begin{aligned} a_h(x) + \varepsilon &= 2^{a_{h-1}(x)} + \varepsilon \leq 2^{a_{h-1}(x) + \varepsilon/2} \leq 2^{a_{h-1}(x + \varepsilon 2^{-h})} \\ &= a_h(x + \varepsilon 2^{-h}), \end{aligned}$$

which proves (28). Next, we show by induction that, for all $h \geq 0$ and $x \geq 2$,

$$b_h(x) \leq a_h(x + 2 - 2^{1-h}). \tag{29}$$

The case $h = 0$ again being obvious, assume that $h > 0$. By (28),

$$\begin{aligned} b_h(x) &= 2^{b_{h-1}(x)} + 2 \leq 2^{a_{h-1}(x + 2 - 2^{2-h})} + 2 \\ &\leq a_h(x + 2 - 2^{2-h}) + 2 \leq a_h(x + 2 - 2^{1-h}), \end{aligned}$$

which establishes (29); and hence (27). □

Tight Lower Bounds for Halfspace Range Searching

[Extended Abstract]

Sunil Arya[*]
Department of Computer Science and Engineering
The Hong Kong University of Science and Technology
Clear Water Bay, Kowloon, Hong Kong
arya@cse.ust.hk

David M. Mount[†]
Department of Computer Science and Institute for Advanced Computer Studies
University of Maryland
College Park, Maryland 20742
mount@cs.umd.edu

Jian Xia
Department of Computer Science and Engineering
The Hong Kong University of Science and Technology
Clear Water Bay, Kowloon, Hong Kong
piper@cse.ust.hk

ABSTRACT

We establish two new lower bounds for the halfspace range searching problem: Given a set of n points in $\mathbb{R}^d$, where each point is associated with a weight from a commutative semigroup, compute the semigroup sum of the weights of the points lying within any query halfspace. Letting m denote the space requirements, we prove a lower bound for general semigroups of $\widetilde{\Omega}(n^{1-1/(d+1)}/m^{1/(d+1)})$ and for integral semigroups of $\widetilde{\Omega}(n/m^{1/d})$.

Our lower bounds are proved in the semigroup arithmetic model. Neglecting logarithmic factors, our result for integral semigroups matches the best known upper bound due to Matoušek. Our result for general semigroups improves upon the best known lower bound due to Brönnimann, Chazelle, and Pach. Moreover, Fonseca and Mount have recently shown that, given uniformly distributed points, halfspace range queries over idempotent semigroups can be answered in $O(n^{1-1/(d+1)}/m^{1/(d+1)})$ time in the semigroup arithmetic model. As our lower bounds are established for uniformly distributed point sets, it follows that they also resolve the computational complexity of halfspace range searching over idempotent semigroups in this important special case.

Categories and Subject Descriptors

F.2.2 [**Analysis of Algorithms and Problem Complexity**]: Nonnumerical Algorithms and Problems—*Geometrical problems and computations*

[*]The work of the first and third author was supported by the Research Grants Council, Hong Kong, China under project number 610106.

[†]This author's work was supported in part by the National Science Foundation under grant CCR-0635099 and the Office of Naval Research under grant N00014-08-1-1015.

General Terms

Algorithms, Theory

Keywords

Range searching, lower bounds, idempotence

1. INTRODUCTION

Given a set of points P in $\mathbb{R}^d$, preprocess these points so that given any halfspace η, the number of points of P lying within η can be computed efficiently. This problem, called *halfspace range counting*, which is so simple to state, has proven to be among the most challenging problems in the field of computational geometry. It is arguably the most fundamental search problem in affine geometry and is a building block in a number of other search problems, such as simplex range searching and spherical range searching.

This problem is typically posed in a weighted setting. Each point is associated with a weight from a commutative semigroup, and the output of the query is the semigroup sum of the points lying within the halfspace. Semigroup properties can be exploited by the data structure and may affect the computational complexity of the problem. A semigroup is *idempotent* if $x + x = x$ for all semigroup elements x. It is *integral* if, for all nonzero semigroup elements x and all natural numbers $k \geqslant 2$, the k-fold sum $x + \cdots + x$ is not equal to x [11]. For example, $(\mathbb{R}, \min)$ and $(\{0,1\}, \vee)$ are both idempotent, and $(\mathbb{N}, +)$ is integral.

Idempotence is relevant because of the way that most range searching algorithms work. At preprocessing time the algorithm implicitly computes the semigroup sum of a number of suitably chosen subsets of P, which we call *generators* (also known as *canonical subsets*). To answer a query η, the algorithm determines an (ideally small) subset of generators whose union is equal to $P \cap \eta$ and then returns their total sum. If the semigroup is idempotent these subsets may overlap, but for integral semigroups they must be disjoint. Because of the constraint of disjointness, one would expect that range searching over integral semigroups should be harder than for idempotent semigroups.

This problem has an extensive history within computational geometry. Early work focused on data structures of linear size. A number of methods based on partition-trees were proposed, including methods by Willard [19], Edelsbrunner and Welzl [10], and Yao [21]. A major breakthrough was achieved by Haussler and Welzl [14], who applied the concepts of VC-dimension and ε-nets to obtain a data structure with query time $O(n^\alpha)$, where $\alpha \approx 1 - \frac{1}{d(d-1)+1}$. In a subsequent sequence of papers, a number of new techniques were introduced, resulting in linear-space (or nearly linear space) algorithms by Welzl [18], Chazelle and Welzl [8], Matoušek and Welzl [17], and Chazelle *et al.* [7]. This culminated in a solution by Matoušek [15], which achieves linear space and the optimal query time of $O(n^{1-\frac{1}{d}})$. Very recently, Chan [5] has shown that this same query time can be achieved with a conceptually simpler and more flexible approach based on partition trees. For further information, see the excellent surveys by Agarwal and Erickson [1] and Matoušek [16]. All of these results apply in the most general case of integral semigroups, and so apply to idempotent semigroups as well.

Given the relatively high query time, it is natural to consider space-time tradeoffs. By precomputing more generators, it should be possible to cover an arbitrary range by a smaller number of generators, and so achieve lower query times. Letting m denote the space requirements, where $n \leqslant m \leqslant n^d$, the best upper bound for halfspace range searching is due to Matoušek [15] and Chan [5], who have shown that using m units of space, queries can be answered in $O(n/m^{1/d})$ time. This bound holds in both the standard real RAM model as well as in the semigroup arithmetic model.

Lower bounds for this problem were established by Brönnimann, Chazelle, and Pach [4] in the semigroup arithmetic model. We refer to this paper throughout as BCP. They established a lower bound on the query time for general semigroups of $\widetilde{\Omega}(n^{1-\frac{d-1}{d(d+1)}}/m^{1/d})$ using m units of space. This bound holds for both idempotent and integral semigroups. The gap between the BCP lower bound and Matoušek's upper bound was investigated by Arya *et al.* [2], and the lower bound was strengthened to $\widetilde{\Omega}\left(n/m^{\frac{d+1}{d^2+1}}\right)$ for the special case of integral semigroups.

In this paper, we take a substantial step towards achieving the goal of resolving the complexity of halfspace range searching by reducing the gap between the upper and lower bounds to logarithmic factors. Because of the weakness of the semigroup arithmetic model (which considers only the number of generators needed to answer a query, and not the time to determine these generators), it is natural to ignore logarithmic factors and focus on polynomial factors of n and m. In particular, we establish the following two new lower bounds for halfspace range searching in the semigroup arithmetic model:

- We establish an improved lower bound for general semigroups of $\widetilde{\Omega}(n^{1-1/(d+1)}/m^{1/(d+1)})$.
- We establish an improved lower bound for integral semigroups of $\widetilde{\Omega}(n/m^{1/d})$.

The latter result relies on the assumption that the convex hulls of the generator subsets used to answer a query are disjoint. Although this assumption does not hold for Matoušek's data structure [15], which is based on hierarchical cuttings, it is satisfied by Chan's partition-tree construction [5]. (We conjecture that our bound holds even without this assumption.)

To understand the significance of these results, observe that, neglecting logarithmic factors, our lower bound for integral semigroups matches the best known upper bounds to date.

For general semigroups, it is useful to observe that, as with BCP, our lower bounds are established for uniformly distributed point sets. In contrast to many geometric problems, uniformly distributed point sets appear to represent a fairly hard case for halfspace range searching. Fonseca and Mount [9] recently showed that, given uniformly distributed points, halfspace range queries over idempotent semigroups can be answered in $O(n^{1-1/(d+1)}/m^{1/(d+1)})$ time in the semigroup arithmetic model. Thus, for the semigroup arithmetic model, our results resolve the computational complexity of halfspace range searching over idempotent semigroups in the case of uniformly distributed point sets.

2. TECHNIQUES

Our proofs are structurally similar to those in BCP. Their proof is based on a number of sophisticated geometric tools, such as the isoperimetric inequality, the slicing lemma, and Macbeath regions. In the BCP proof the generators used to answer a query are allowed to overlap. Arya *et al.* [2] showed how to enhance their proof, so it yields a better lower bound in the integral case, by exploiting the fact that the generators used to answer a query must be disjoint.

Our paper makes two key technical contributions. First, by building on the ideas in BCP, we design new slicing lemmas specifically tailored to the requirements of the idempotent and integral cases. Second, we describe a much better way of taking advantage of disjointness than given in [2], leading to a nearly optimal bound in the integral case.

Before discussing our contributions in more detail, we need to first briefly recall the essential ingredients of the BCP proof. We let $\mathbb{U} = [0,1]^d$ denote the unit hypercube in $\mathbb{R}^d$, and for any body K in $\mathbb{R}^d$, we let $\mu(K)$ denote its Lebesgue measure. We will assume some familiarity with the semigroup arithmetic model. (See Section 3 for more information about this model.) The data point instance used in the proof consists of a set of uniformly distributed points in $\mathbb{U}$. This makes it possible to relate the volume of a convex subset of $\mathbb{U}$ to the number of data points it contains.

The complexity of halfspace range searching arises from the difficulty of covering points close to the boundary of the query halfspace. To formalize this idea, they define a suitable set of query halfspaces and a suitable *region of interest* for each query halfspace, which is defined to be a thin slab close to the boundary of the halfspace. Recall that the goal in the arithmetic model is to relate the space (number of generators) to the query time (maximum number of generators needed to answer any query). In order to establish this relationship, a probability distribution is defined on the set of query ranges, and a lower bound is obtained by showing that if a generator covers a large number of points in the region of interest for some range, then it cannot be useful in this manner for many query ranges.

In order to achieve query time t, the storage scheme must have at most t generators that cover all the points of P that lie in the region of interest R_H associated with the query halfspace H. It is possible to define a generator's *usefulness* to H, based on the number of such points it covers. The analysis proceeds by establishing an upper bound on the expected usefulness of any generator. In turn, this implies a lower bound on the total number of generators needed to achieve the given query time.

Techniques are presented in the BCP paper for bounding the usefulness of a generator. They involve an *isoperimetric inequality* and a *slicing lemma*. Their isoperimetric inequality bounds the probability that a fixed convex body is contained within a random query slab, as a function of the volume of the convex body and the thickness of the slab. Since P is uniformly distributed, a generator G that is useful for some halfspace H enjoys the property that its convex hull K has a large volume of intersection with R_H. Their slicing lemma involves breaking the convex hull K of the generator into a small collection of convex bodies called *Macbeath regions*, all contained within K, which serve as witnesses to usefulness. In particular, if G is useful to H, then at least one of these bodies lies within the slab R_H, and it has volume at least $\Omega(\mu(K \cap R_H))$.

A critical quantity in the BCP analysis is the number of convex bodies into which we need to decompose the convex hull K of a generator in order to satisfy the aforementioned property. Define a *cap* to be the intersection of a convex body and a halfspace. We require that, for any cap C of K of sufficiently large volume and limited thickness, one of these bodies is contained within C and has volume $\Omega(\mu(C))$. BCP's slicing lemma produces a decomposition of K into convex bodies by considering only the volume condition on the caps. Our key observation is that many of the bodies produced by their slicing lemma are actually too thick to lie inside the caps that arise in their proof, and as a result the size of their decomposition is much larger than necessary. We develop a new slicing lemma that is sensitive to *both* the volume and the thickness of the caps, and, as a consequence, we are able to show that a much smaller number of bodies suffice. This approach leads to an improved lower bound in the case of idempotent (and hence general) semigroups.

We now discuss our ideas for the integral case. As mentioned earlier, Arya *et al.* [2] showed how to exploit the disjointness of the generators to improve the BCP lower bound. Their proof relies on the following simple but critical observation: because of disjointness, the total volume of the convex hulls of the generators used to answer a query must be $O(1)$. In turn, they show that this implies that, for a typical generator G used to answer a query H, the volume of intersection of its convex hull K with the slab R_H is at least $\Omega(\mu(K) \cdot \Delta_0)$, where Δ_0 denotes the slab thickness. They use this fact together with the BCP slicing lemma to derive an improved lower bound in the integral case. While this approach is perhaps the simplest way of incorporating disjointness into the BCP framework, it leads to a lower bound that falls short of Matoušek's upper bound [15].

In this paper, we close this gap by exploiting the disjointness of generators in a more sophisticated manner. More precisely, we show that, for a typical generator G used to answer a query H, the volume of intersection of its convex hull K with the slab R_H is at least $\widetilde{\Omega}(\mathrm{breadth}(K, H) \cdot \Delta_0)$, where $\mathrm{breadth}(K, H)$ denotes the maximum cross-sectional area of a surface formed by intersecting K with any hyperplane parallel to ∂H. In order to bound the usefulness of generators based on this new criterion, we need to develop a slicing lemma specifically tailored to it. In contrast with both the BCP framework and the aforementioned work by Arya *et al.* [2], in which each convex hull of a generator is decomposed into a polynomial number of bodies, our slicing lemma decomposes each hull into only a polylogarithmic number of pieces. This improvement turns out to be critical and allows us to obtain a lower bound in the integral case that matches Matoušek's upper bound, up to logarithmic factors.

3. PRELIMINARIES

Before presenting our results we begin with some general definitions and assumptions. Throughout we assume that the dimension d is a fixed constant greater than 1. Unless otherwise stated, we will use the term "constant" to refer to any fixed quantity, which may depend on d but not on n. To avoid specifying many real-valued constants that arise in our analyses, we will often hide them using asymptotic notation. For positive real x, we use the notation $O(x)$ (resp., $\Omega(x)$) to mean a quantity whose value is at most (resp., at least) cx for an appropriately chosen constant c. We use the notation $\widetilde{\Omega}(x)$ in place of $\Omega(x)$ to ignore factors depending logarithmically on n. It will also be convenient in our analysis to use the notations $\preceq$ (resp., $\succeq$) to denote less than (resp., greater than) up to constant factors.

Let $(S, +)$ be a commutative semigroup. Let P be a set of n points in $\mathbb{R}^d$, and let $w : P \to S$ be a function that assigns a semigroup value in S to each point in P. For any subset G of P, we define its weight $w(G) = \sum_{p \in G} w(p)$, where the summation is taken over the semigroup. Let $\mathcal{Q}$ denote the set of query ranges in the range space. In the range searching problem, we are required to preprocess P so that for any query range $\eta \in \mathcal{Q}$, we can efficiently compute $w(P \cap \eta)$.

Our lower bound proofs are in the *semigroup arithmetic model* [12, 20]. We briefly recall some of the basic elements of this model for online range searching problems. Lower bounds in this model assume that the semigroup is *faithful*, meaning that any two identically equal linear forms have the same set of variables [6]. For example, $(\mathbb{N}, +)$, $(\mathbb{R}, \min)$, and $(\{0, 1\}, \vee)$ are faithful, but $(\{0, 1\}, + \bmod 2)$ is not. Given a set $\{x_1, \ldots, x_n\}$ of n variables over S, a *generator* $G(x_1, \ldots, x_n)$ is a linear form $\sum_{i=1}^{n} \alpha_i x_i$, where the values α_i are nonnegative integers, not all zero. A *storage scheme* is a set of generators $\{G_1, \ldots, G_m\}$ satisfying the following property. For any query range $\eta \in \mathcal{Q}$, there exists a set $I_\eta \subseteq \{1, \ldots, m\}$ and a set of labeled nonnegative integers $\{\beta_i : i \in I_\eta\}$ such that

$$w(P \cap \eta) = \sum_{i \in I_\eta} \beta_i G_i(w(p_1), \ldots, w(p_n)),$$

for *any* weight function w. The *query time* for η is defined to be the size of smallest such set I_η. In this model the *space* is the number of generators in the storage scheme. Intuitively, the generators correspond to partial sums that have been precomputed in the data structure. The query time in the semigroup arithmetic model counts the minimum number of semigroup operations on these generators needed to answer a query. The time for auxiliary operations, such as determining which generators to use, is ignored.

For our purposes, it will be convenient to identify a generator with the subset of P corresponding to the variables in the linear form with positive integer coefficients. Given an idempotent semigroup, the time to answer a query η is the size of the smallest set of generators whose union is $P \cap \eta$. More formally, let $\mathcal{G}$ be any storage scheme consisting of m generators. For any range $\eta \in \mathcal{Q}$, define $A_\eta \subseteq \mathcal{G}$ to be the smallest subset of generators of $\mathcal{G}$ such that $\bigcup_{G \in A_\eta} G = P \cap \eta$. The worst-case query time for a storage scheme $\mathcal{G}$ is the maximum of $|A_\eta|$ over all ranges $\eta \in \mathcal{Q}$. Given a space bound m, the worst-case query time complexity in the semigroup arithmetic model is the minimum worst-case query time over all storage schemes $\mathcal{G}$ of size m [6]. We can adapt this to integral semigroups by adding the restriction that, when taking unions in answering a query, the generators, viewed as subsets of P, are pairwise disjoint.

Let us define some other terms that will be used throughout the chapter. Consider a compact (closed and bounded) convex body K, a halfspace H, and a vector u orthogonal to ∂H. The *width* of K in the direction u, denoted $\mathrm{width}(K, u)$, is defined to be the orthogonal distance between the two supporting hyperplanes for K that are orthogonal to u. The *breadth* of K orthogonal to u, denoted $\mathrm{breadth}(K, u)$, is defined to be the maximum cross-sectional area of K orthogonal to u. Note that for our purposes, width is always a one-dimensional measure, while breadth is a $(d-1)$-dimensional measure. As a convenience, we also define $\mathrm{width}(K, H) = \mathrm{width}(K, u)$ and $\mathrm{breadth}(K, H) = \mathrm{breadth}(K, u)$.

The closed region in $\mathbb{R}^d$ bounded by two parallel $(d-1)$-dimensional hyperplanes is called a *slab*, and its *width* (or *thickness*) is the orthogonal distance between these hyperplanes. Let $\Delta > 0$ be a real parameter. Given any hyperplane J, let $S^\Delta(J)$ denote the slab consisting of points in $\mathbb{R}^d$ whose distance from J is at most Δ. This slab has width 2Δ. Given a halfspace H, let ∂H denote its bounding hyperplane. For any halfspace H, let $S^\Delta(H) = S^\Delta(\partial H) \cap H$ denote the slab consisting of points in H that are within distance Δ of the bounding hyperplane of H.

Consider a compact, convex body K and a halfspace H that has a nonempty intersection with K. Let u be a vector orthogonal to ∂H. The intersection $C = K \cap H$ is called the *cap* of K generated by H. We refer to u, the vector orthogonal to ∂H, as the *defining direction* of cap C. The *width* (or *thickness*) of a cap, denoted $\mathrm{width}(C)$, is defined to be the width of C along its defining direction u.

4. LOWER BOUND

The main results of this chapter are summarized in the following theorem. Our first result for general semigroups improves the lower bound of Brönnimann, Chazelle, and Pach [4]. Moreover, since our bounds are established for uniformly distributed points, Fonseca and Mount's result mentioned in the introduction implies that this result is almost optimal for this distribution and idempotent semigroups. Our second result is almost optimal in the worst-case for integral semigroups in light of Matoušek's upper bound [15].

THEOREM 4.1. *Let $d \geqslant 2$ be a fixed dimension. Consider a range space consisting of all halfspaces and a weight function over any faithful semigroup. Then for all sufficiently large n, using $m \geqslant n$ units of storage,*

(i) For general (and hence idempotent) semigroups, the worst-case query time in the semigroup arithmetic model is at least

$$\Omega\left(\frac{n^{1-\frac{1}{d+1}}}{m^{\frac{1}{d+1}}} \cdot \frac{1}{\log^{1-\frac{1}{d+1}} n}\right) = \widetilde{\Omega}\left(\frac{n^{1-\frac{1}{d+1}}}{m^{\frac{1}{d+1}}}\right).$$

(ii) If the semigroup is integral, then under the assumption that convex hulls of the generators used to answer a query are disjoint, the query time is at least

$$\Omega\left(\frac{n}{m^{\frac{1}{d}}} \cdot \frac{1}{\log^{1+\frac{2}{d}} n}\right) = \widetilde{\Omega}\left(\frac{n}{m^{\frac{1}{d}}}\right).$$

4.1 New Slicing Lemmas

In this section, we establish our new slicing lemmas tailored to the requirements of the idempotent and integral cases. We will need the following lemma, involving important convex bodies called *Macbeath regions*, to help us in that task. This lemma is an easy consequence of Lemma 2.7 in BCP. Recall that for any body K in $\mathbb{R}^d$, we let $\mu(K)$ denote its Lebesgue measure.

LEMMA 4.1. *Consider a compact convex body $K \subset \mathbb{R}^d$ and a parameter $0 < v \leqslant \mu(K)$. There exists a collection of pairwise disjoint convex bodies $K_1, K_2, \ldots \subseteq K$ satisfying the following properties:*

(i) $\mu(K_i) = \Omega(v)$ for all i.

(ii) Let H be a halfspace, and let C be the cap $K \cap H$. If $\mu(C) \geqslant v$, then there exists j such that $K_j \subseteq C$.

Using the above lemma, we now prove our slicing lemma that will be useful in the idempotent case. It differs from the one given in BCP in that it incorporates a condition on the cap width and, thereby, produces a smaller number of convex bodies in cases of interest.

LEMMA 4.2. *Consider a compact convex body $K \subset \mathbb{R}^d$ of surface area $O(1)$, and two parameters $v > 0$ and $\Delta > 0$. There exists a collection of $O(\Delta/v)$ convex bodies $K_1, K_2, \ldots \subseteq K$ satisfying the following property: Let H be a halfspace and let C be the cap $K \cap H$. If $\mathrm{width}(C) \leqslant \Delta$ and $\mu(C) \geqslant v$, then there exists j such that $K_j \subseteq C$ and $\mu(K_j) = \Omega(\mu(C))$.*

PROOF. Let $K_\Delta \subseteq K$ denote the region consisting of points in K that are within distance Δ of K's boundary. Observe that $\mu(K_\Delta) = O(\Delta)$ since the surface area of K is $O(1)$.

Consider the set $\mathcal{C}$ consisting of caps C formed by intersecting K with any halfspace, such that C satisfies the properties $\mathrm{width}(C) \leqslant \Delta$ and $\mu(C) \geqslant v$. We partition the set $\mathcal{C}$ into groups based on the volume of the caps as follows. For $i > 0$, let $\mathcal{C}_i$ be the subset of $\mathcal{C}$ consisting of caps whose volume lies between $2^{i-1}v$ and $2^i v$. We claim that there exists a collection of $O(\Delta/(2^{i-1}v))$ convex bodies satisfying the properties mentioned in the lemma with respect to the caps in $\mathcal{C}_i$. The lemma then follows immediately from this claim by summing over all i.

To prove the claim, we apply Lemma 4.1, setting the parameter v in that lemma to $2^{i-1}v$. Clearly, this yields a collection $\mathcal{K}_i$ of pairwise disjoint convex bodies, each contained within K and having volume $\Omega(2^{i-1}v)$. Further, for any cap $C \in \mathcal{C}_i$, one of these bodies is contained within C and has volume $\Omega(\mu(C))$ (because the volume of each body is $\Omega(2^{i-1}v)$ and $\mu(C) \leqslant 2^i v$). Thus, the collection $\mathcal{K}_i$ satisfies all the required properties with respect to the caps in $\mathcal{C}_i$. However, the number of bodies in $\mathcal{K}_i$ may be too large. We fix this by eliminating any convex body in $\mathcal{K}_i$ that is not contained in K_Δ. Since the caps in $\mathcal{C}_i$ have width at most Δ, such a body is in any case of no use in satisfying a

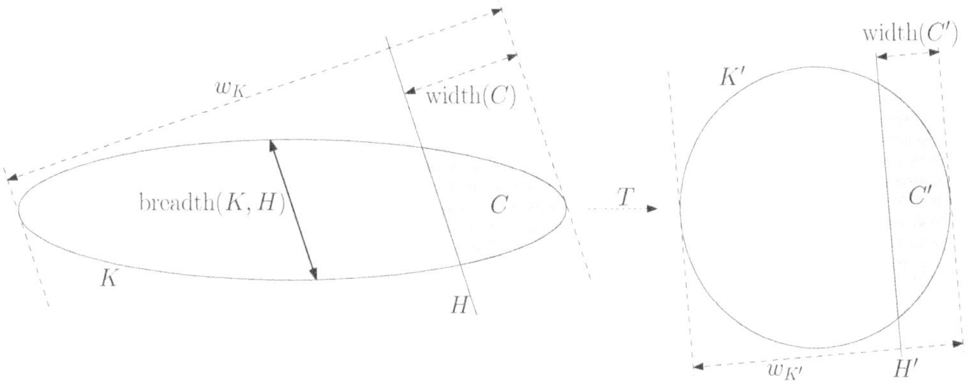

Figure 1: Proof of Lemma 4.4.

cap of $\mathcal{C}_i$. Thus, the resulting collection continues to satisfy all the desired properties. Finally, since the bodies in $\mathcal{K}_i$ are pairwise disjoint and are all contained in K_Δ, we have $|\mathcal{K}_i| = O(\mu(K_\Delta)/(2^{i-1}v)) = O(\Delta/(2^{i-1}v))$. This completes the proof of the claim and the lemma. □

Before presenting our slicing lemma that will be useful for integral semigroups, we need to introduce a standard notion of fatness. A convex body $K \subset \mathbb{R}^d$ is said to be *α-fat*, for some $\alpha \geqslant 1$, if there exist two concentric balls B^+ and B^- such that $B^- \subseteq K \subseteq B^+$, and the ratio between the radius of B^+ and B^- is at most α. Further, we say that K is *fat* if α is a constant depending only on d. The following well-known result states that any convex body can be transformed by a volume-preserving affine transformation into a fat convex body (see e.g. [13]).

LEMMA 4.3. *Given any compact convex body $K \subset \mathbb{R}^d$, there exists a volume-preserving affine transform T such that $T(K)$ is fat.*

The next lemma considers the effect of the above fattening transformation on the width of caps. We will find it useful in proving the slicing lemma.

LEMMA 4.4. *Consider any compact convex body $K \subset \mathbb{R}^d$ of unit volume. Let H be a halfspace and let C denote the cap $K \cap H$. Let $K' = T(K)$ and $H' = T(H)$, where T is the transformation of Lemma 4.3. Let $C' = K' \cap H'$. Then* $\mathrm{width}(C') = \Theta(\mathrm{breadth}(K, H) \cdot \mathrm{width}(C))$.

PROOF. Let w_K denote the width of K along the defining direction of C and $w_{K'}$ denote the width of K' along the defining direction of C'. (See Figure 1.) A straightforward geometric argument implies that $\mu(K) = \Theta(\mathrm{breadth}(K, H) \cdot w_K)$. Since $\mu(K) = 1$, we have $w_K = \Theta(1/\mathrm{breadth}(K, H))$. By Lemma 4.3, K' is fat and $\mu(K') = 1$. It follows that the width of K' in any direction is $\Theta(1)$. In particular, we have $w_{K'} = \Theta(1)$. Thus $w_{K'}/w_K = \Theta(\mathrm{breadth}(K, H))$. By standard properties of affine transformations, we obtain $\mathrm{width}(C')/\mathrm{width}(C) = w_{K'}/w_K$. Thus $\mathrm{width}(C')/\mathrm{width}(C) = \Theta(\mathrm{breadth}(K, H))$, as desired. □

We are now ready to prove the slicing lemma that will be applied in the integral case.

LEMMA 4.5. *Consider an α-fat compact convex body $K \subset \mathbb{R}^d$ and two parameters $\beta \geqslant 1$ and $\Delta > 0$. There exists a collection of $O(\beta \log \alpha)$ convex bodies $K_1, K_2, \ldots \subseteq K$ satisfying the following property: Let H be a halfspace and let C denote the cap $K \cap H$. If* $\mathrm{width}(C) \leqslant \Delta$ *and* $\mu(C) \geqslant \mathrm{breadth}(K, H) \cdot \Delta/\beta$, *then there exists j such that $K_j \subseteq C$ and $\mu(K_j) = \Omega(\mu(C'))$.*

PROOF. Without loss of generality, we may assume that K has unit volume. (It is easy to check that it suffices to prove the lemma for K under this condition.) Consider the set $\mathcal{C}$ consisting of caps C formed by intersecting K with some halfspace H, such that C satisfies the properties $\mathrm{width}(C) \leqslant \Delta$ and $\mu(C) \geqslant \mathrm{breadth}(K, H) \cdot \Delta/\beta$. We partition the set $\mathcal{C}$ into groups such that for all caps in a group, the breadth of K orthogonal to the defining direction of the cap differs by a factor of at most 2. Since K is α-fat, it is clear that the ratio between the largest and smallest value of the breadth of K over all possible directions cannot exceed α^{d-1}, and thus we can obtain a partitioning with at most $O(\log \alpha)$ groups.

Let us focus on one such group of caps, for which the breadth of K orthogonal to the defining direction of any cap in it is between b and $2b$. We will show that there exists a collection of $O(\beta)$ convex bodies satisfying the properties mentioned in the lemma with respect to all the caps in this group. Since the total number of groups is $O(\log \alpha)$, the lemma will then directly follow from this.

Let $C = K \cap H$ denote any cap in this group. From the conditions in the lemma, we have $\mu(C) \geqslant \mathrm{breadth}(K, H) \cdot \Delta/\beta \geqslant b\Delta/\beta$ and $\mathrm{width}(C) \leqslant \Delta$. Let $K' = T(K)$ and $H' = T(H)$, where T is the transformation of Lemma 4.3. Let $C' = K' \cap H'$. Since T is volume-preserving, we have $\mu(C') = \mu(C) \geqslant b\Delta/\beta$. By Lemma 4.4, we have $\mathrm{width}(C') = \Theta(\mathrm{breadth}(K, H) \cdot \mathrm{width}(C))$. Since $\mathrm{width}(C) \leqslant \Delta$ and $\mathrm{breadth}(K, H) \leqslant 2b$, we obtain $\mathrm{width}(C') = O(b\Delta)$.

Note that the surface area of K' is $O(1)$. We invoke Lemma 4.2 on K', setting the parameter Δ (upper bound on cap width) to a suitable constant times $b\Delta$, and parameter v (lower bound on cap volume) to $b\Delta/\beta$. We obtain a collection of $O((b\Delta)/(b\Delta/\beta)) = O(\beta)$ convex bodies in K', such that one of these bodies is inside any cap C' of K' corresponding to a cap C of K in the group under consideration, and its volume is $\Omega(\mu(C'))$. It follows that the set of bodies in the original space corresponding to these bodies satisfy all the desired properties with respect to the caps in the group. This completes the proof of the lemma. □

4.2 Lower Bound: The Idempotent Case

We begin with the proof of Theorem 4.1(i), namely the lower bound in the idempotent case. As mentioned earlier, our proof in this case is a simple adaptation of the one in BCP, differing only in its use of a more suitable slicing lemma. We present details for the sake of completeness.

Let P be a set of n points in the unit hypercube $\mathbb{U} = [0,1]^d$. Let K be any convex body contained within $\mathbb{U}$ and let $k = |P \cap K|$. We say that P is *scattered* if the following two properties hold for some constant $a > 1$:

(i) If $\mu(K) \geqslant a \log n/n$, then $k \geqslant (n/a)\mu(K)$.

(ii) If $k \geqslant \log n$, then $k \leqslant an\mu(K)$.

Intuitively, scattered point sets behave like uniformly distributed points in the sense that the volume of a convex body is related to the number of points it contains. The following lemma asserts the existence of such point sets. It is proved in [3] and is a simple variant of Lemma 2.1 in BCP.

LEMMA 4.6. *A random set of n points sampled uniformly and independently in $\mathbb{U}$ is scattered with probability $1-o(1)$.*

The data set P in the proof consists of a scattered set of n points in $\mathbb{U}$. We next describe the set of query ranges. Let O denote the origin of the coordinate system in $\mathbb{R}^d$. Let q be any point in $\mathbb{R}^d \setminus \{O\}$. Let H_q denote the halfspace containing the origin, whose bounding hyperplane passes through q and is orthogonal to segment $\overline{Oq}$. Let B be the ball of radius $1/4$ whose center coincides with the center of $\mathbb{U}$. We define the query set $\mathcal{Q}$ to be the set of halfspaces $\{H_q | q \in B\}$.

Next, we define a probability measure over the set of queries. As in BCP, define the measure of any set $\mathcal{H}$ of halfspaces as follows:

$$\int_{\mathcal{H}} dH_q = \int_{H_q \in \mathcal{H}} \frac{dx_1 \wedge \cdots \wedge dx_d}{\|q\|^{d-1}},$$

where $q = (x_1, \ldots, x_d)$. The choice of this measure is based on the fact that it is invariant under rigid motions [6]. It is easy to see that the measure of the query set $\mathcal{Q}$ is $\Theta(1)$. Therefore, restricted to the set $\mathcal{Q}$, we can interpret this measure as a probability density by dividing it by the total measure of $\mathcal{Q}$. In our analysis, we will assume that a query halfspace is selected from $\mathcal{Q}$ according to this probability density (we will say that the halfspace is *random* over $\mathcal{Q}$). Given any query halfspace $H \in \mathcal{Q}$, we have that for a suitable constant c_1 and any sufficiently small Δ (say $\Delta \leqslant 1/4$), $\mu(S^{\Delta}(H) \cap \mathbb{U}) \geqslant c_1\Delta$.

The following isoperimetric inequality, which was proved by Chazelle [6], bounds the probability that a random slab encloses a given convex body. We restate it slightly for convenience.

LEMMA 4.7. *Let $K \subseteq \mathbb{U}$ be any compact convex body, let H be a random halfspace of $\mathcal{Q}$, and let $\Delta > 0$ be a real parameter. Then*

$$\mu(K) \cdot \Pr\Big[K \subseteq S^{\Delta}(H)\Big] = O(\Delta^{d+1}).$$

Let $\mathcal{G}$ be any set of $m \geqslant n$ generators for P. Let $t = t(n,m)$ denote the worst-case query time in the semigroup arithmetic model over all the ranges of $\mathcal{Q}$. We will establish a lower bound on t, assuming that n is sufficiently large.

In BCP it is observed that the complexity of halfspace range searching stems from the difficulty of covering points that lie close to the boundary of the halfspace. To formalize the idea, for each halfspace $H \in \mathcal{Q}$, define a *region of interest* $R_H \subseteq H$ to be $S^{\Delta_0}(H)$, where $\Delta_0 = c_0 t \log n/n$ for a suitable constant c_0.

Let Φ denote the expected number of points of P in the region of interest R_H. That is,

$$\Phi = \mathrm{E}\Big[|P \cap R_H|\Big].$$

We will compute lower and upper bounds on Φ, which together will provide the desired lower bound on the query time t. We may assume that $t = O(n/\log^2 n)$, since otherwise Theorem 4.1 holds trivially.

We claim that, for a suitable choice of c_0, $|P \cap R_H| \geqslant 8t \log n$ for all $H \in \mathcal{Q}$. By the property of query halfspaces mentioned above, we have $\mu(R_H \cap \mathbb{U}) \geqslant c_1\Delta_0 = c_1(c_0 t \log n/n)$, if $c_0 t \log n/n \leqslant 1/4$. Since $t = O(n/\log^2 n)$, this condition holds for sufficiently large n. Setting $c_0 = 8a/c_1$, where a is the constant used in the scattered set properties, we have $\mu(R_H \cap \mathbb{U}) \geqslant 8at \log n/n$. Since $t \geqslant 1$, we can apply property (i) of scattered point sets to obtain $|P \cap R_H| = |P \cap R_H \cap \mathbb{U}| \geqslant (n/a)\mu(R_H) \geqslant 8t \log n$, as desired. The following lower bound on Φ is now immediate.

LEMMA 4.8. *Φ is at least $\Omega(t \log n)$.*

Next we compute an upper bound on Φ. Towards this end, it is helpful to focus on those generators that are most efficient in covering the region of interest R_H. Intuitively, in order to achieve a query time of t, a typical generator should cover a fraction of roughly $\Omega(1/t)$ of the points in R_H. This suggests the following definition. We say that a generator $G \in \mathcal{G}$ is *absolutely fat* with respect to a query $H \in \mathcal{Q}$ if $|G \cap R_H| > \log n$ and $G \subseteq H$. The following lemma, implicit in the BCP proof, shows that a constant fraction of the points in R_H are covered by such generators.

LEMMA 4.9. *For any query $H \in \mathcal{Q}$, a constant fraction of the points of P lying within R_H are covered by generators of $\mathcal{G}$ that are absolutely fat with respect to H.*

PROOF. Given $H \in \mathcal{Q}$, consider the set $A_H \subseteq \mathcal{G}$ of generators that allow us to answer query H within time t. Clearly, $|A_H| \leqslant t$. Let A_H^1 denote the subset of A_H consisting of generators that are not absolutely fat with respect to H. Observe that the generators in the set A_H^1 cover at most $t \log n$ points of $P \cap R_H$ (because there are at most t such generators and each covers at most $\log n$ points of $P \cap R_H$). Recalling that $|P \cap R_H|$ is at least $8t \log n$, it follows that at least $7/8$ of the points of $P \cap R_H$ are covered by the generators in $A_H \setminus A_H^1$. As all these generators are absolutely fat with respect to H, the lemma follows. □

Consider any $G \in \mathcal{G}$ and $H \in \mathcal{Q}$. We define the *usefulness* of G with respect to H to be $|G \cap R_H|$ if G is absolutely fat with respect to H, and 0 otherwise. We denote this quantity by $u(G,H)$. Further, we define the *usefulness* of G, denoted $u(G)$, to be the expectation of $u(G,H)$, where the average is taken over the query distribution.

The above lemma implies that,

$$|P \cap R_H| \preceq \sum_{G \in \mathcal{G}} u(G,H).$$

Therefore,

$$\begin{aligned}\Phi &= \mathrm{E}\Big[|P \cap R_H|\Big] \preceq \mathrm{E}\Big[\sum_{G\in\mathcal{G}} u(G,H)\Big] \\ &= \sum_{G\in\mathcal{G}} \mathrm{E}\Big[u(G,H)\Big] = \sum_{G\in\mathcal{G}} u(G).\end{aligned}$$

In the remainder, we compute an upper bound on $u(G, H)$, and hence on $u(G)$, with the help of our version of the slicing lemma and Chazelle's isoperimetric inequality. This will then allow us to upper bound Φ by using the above equation.

LEMMA 4.10. *Consider any $G \in \mathcal{G}$ and $H \in \mathcal{Q}$ such that G is absolutely fat with respect to H. Let $K = \mathrm{conv}(G)$. Then $|G\cap R_H| \preceq n\,\mu(K\cap R_H)$ and $\mu(K\cap R_H) = \Omega(\log n/n)$.*

PROOF. By the definition of absolute fatness, $|G \cap R_H| > \log n$. Clearly, $|P \cap K \cap R_H| \geqslant |G \cap R_H|$. Therefore $|P \cap K \cap R_H| > \log n$. Applying property (ii) of scattered point sets, we have $|P \cap K \cap R_H| \preceq n\,\mu(K \cap R_H)$. Putting these inequalities together, the lemma follows. □

Let G, H, K be as in the above lemma. Since G is absolutely fat with respect to H, by definition, $G \subseteq H$, and so $K \cap R_H$ is a cap of K. Clearly, this cap has width at most $\Delta_0 = O(t \log n/n)$, and its volume, by the above lemma, is $\Omega(\log n/n)$. Also, since $K \subseteq \mathbb{U}$, its surface area is $O(1)$. We apply our slicing lemma (Lemma 4.2) to K, setting v to a suitable constant times $\log n/n$ and Δ to Δ_0. We obtain a collection of $O(\Delta/v) = O(t)$ convex bodies $K_1, K_2, \ldots \subseteq K$ such that one of these bodies lies inside $K \cap R_H$ and has volume $\Omega(K \cap R_H)$. Thus,

$$\mu(K \cap R_H) \preceq \sum_i \mu(K_i) \cdot \mathrm{I}\Big[K_i \subseteq R_H\Big],$$

where $\mathrm{I}[K_i \subseteq R_H]$ is an indicator random variable that takes the value 1 if $K_i \subseteq R_H$ and 0 otherwise. Applying Lemma 4.10, we obtain

$$u(G,H) = |G\cap R_H| \preceq n\mu(K\cap R_H) \preceq n \sum_i \mu(K_i)\cdot \mathrm{I}\Big[K_i \subseteq R_H\Big].$$

Since $u(G, H) = 0$, if G is not absolutely fat with respect to H, it follows that the inequality

$$u(G,H) \preceq n \sum_i \mu(K_i) \cdot \mathrm{I}\Big[K_i \subseteq R_H\Big]$$

holds for all $G \in \mathcal{G}$ and $H \in \mathcal{Q}$. Taking expectation on both sides, we obtain

$$u(G) \preceq n \sum_i \mu(K_i) \cdot \Pr\Big[K_i \subseteq R_H\Big] \preceq n\, t \Delta_0^{d+1},$$

where we have used Lemma 4.7 (Chazelle's isoperimetric inequality) and the $O(t)$ bound on the number of convex bodies derived from our slicing lemma.

Recalling that $\Phi \preceq \sum_{G\in\mathcal{G}} u(G)$ and the total number of generators is $|\mathcal{G}| = m$, we obtain

$$\Phi = O(m\, n\, t \Delta_0^{d+1}).$$

Combining this with the lower bound of $\Omega(t \log n)$ on Φ derived earlier, substituting $\Delta_0 = O(t \log n/n)$, we obtain

$$t \log n \preceq m\, n\, t \left(\frac{t \log n}{n}\right)^{d+1},$$

which can be simplified to

$$t^{d+1} \succeq \frac{n^d}{m} \cdot \frac{1}{\log^d n}.$$

Therefore,

$$t = \Omega\left(\frac{n^{\frac{d}{d+1}}}{m^{\frac{1}{d+1}}} \cdot \frac{1}{\log^{\frac{d}{d+1}} n}\right) = \widetilde{\Omega}\left(\frac{n^{1-\frac{1}{d+1}}}{m^{\frac{1}{d+1}}}\right).$$

This completes the proof of Theorem 4.1(i).

4.3 Lower Bound: The Integral Case

In this section we prove part (ii) of Theorem 4.1. As mentioned earlier, throughout this section we assume that the convex hulls of the generators used to answer a query are disjoint. This assumption does not seem to be too restrictive. As mentioned earlier, although it does not hold for Matoušek's data structure [15], it is satisfied by Chan's partition-tree structure [5].

Our proof is structurally similar to that of Arya *et al.* [2], who first showed how to enhance the BCP framework to take advantage of disjointness. The key difference is that we use a different formulation for capturing disjointness, which enables us to obtain better bounds. We now present the details.

We define the data set P, query set $\mathcal{Q}$, worst-case query time t, region of interest R_H for each halfspace $H \in \mathcal{Q}$, set of generators $\mathcal{G}$, and Φ, exactly as in the idempotent case. To simplify the notation, for any generator G, we use $\mathrm{breadth}(G, H)$ to denote the quantity $\mathrm{breadth}(\mathrm{conv}(G), H)$. As before, we can establish a lower bound of $\Omega(t \log n)$ on Φ. A key aspect of our strategy is to use a different notion of generator *usefulness*. Towards this end, define a generator $G \in \mathcal{G}$ to be *relatively fat* with respect to a query $H \in \mathcal{Q}$ if $|G \cap R_H| \geqslant (\mathrm{breadth}(G, H) \cdot \Delta_0 \cdot n)/(c \log n)$, for a suitable constant c to be specified later. Further, define generator G to be *fat* with respect to query H if G is absolutely fat with respect to H and either (i) $G \subset R_H$ or (ii) G is relatively fat with respect to H. We can now strengthen Lemma 4.9 for the integral case as follows.

LEMMA 4.11. *Assume that the convex hulls of the generators used to answer a query are disjoint. For any query $H \in \mathcal{Q}$, a constant fraction of the points of P lying within R_H are covered by generators of $\mathcal{G}$ that are fat with respect to H.*

The proof of Lemma 4.11 relies on the following important geometric observation.

LEMMA 4.12. *Consider a halfspace $H \in \mathcal{Q}$ and any subset $\mathcal{G}_H \subseteq \mathcal{G}$ consisting of generators whose convex hulls are disjoint. Further, suppose that each generator $G \in \mathcal{G}_H$ satisfies the following properties: (i) $G \subset H$, (ii) $G \cap S^{\Delta_0/2}(H) \neq \emptyset$, and (iii) $G \not\subset S^{\Delta_0}(H)$. Then $\sum_{G\in\mathcal{G}_H} \mathrm{breadth}(G, H) = O(\log n)$.*

PROOF. For the sake of illustration, assume that ∂H is "horizontal" and H is the halfspace consisting of points "below" ∂H. Let J_0 denote the hyperplane parallel to ∂H and at distance $\Delta_0/2$ below it. Further, for $i \geqslant 1$, let J_i denote the hyperplane parallel to J_0 and at distance $2^{i-3}\Delta_0$ below it. (See Figure 2.) Note that the number of hyperplanes in the set $\{J_i : i \geqslant 0\}$ that intersect $\mathbb{U} = [0, 1]^d$ is $O(\log(1/\Delta_0)) = O(\log n)$.

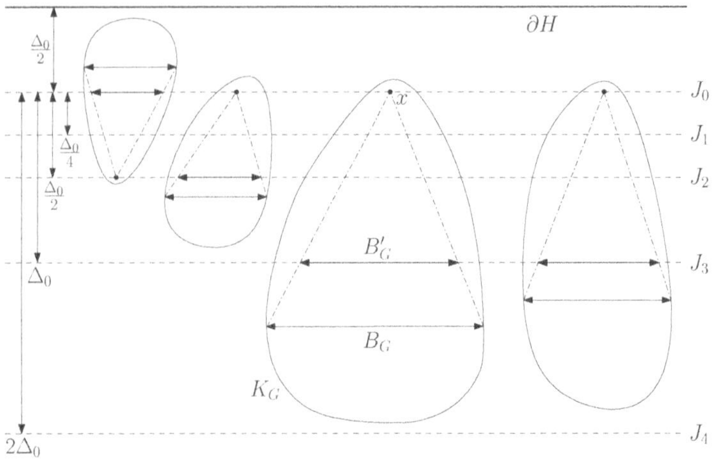

Figure 2: Proof of Lemma 4.12.

Let G be any generator of $\mathcal{G}_H$. Let $K_G = \text{conv}(G)$, $b_G = \text{breadth}(G, H)$, and let B_G be the cross-section that defines b_G (note area of B_G is b_G). Let $\mathcal{G}'_H$ be the subset of $\mathcal{G}_H$ consisting of generators G such that B_G lies below J_1. It will suffice to show that $\sum_{G \in \mathcal{G}'_H} b_G = O(\log n)$, because a similar reasoning will show that $\sum b_G = O(1)$, where the sum is over generators $G \in \mathcal{G}_H$ such that B_G lies above J_1.

Consider any generator $G \in \mathcal{G}'_H$. Observe that K_G intersects both J_0 and J_2, since $G \cap S^{\Delta_0/2}(H) \neq \emptyset$ (Property (ii)) and $G \not\subset S^{\Delta_0}(H)$ (Property (iii)). Suppose that B_G lies between the hyperplanes J_i and J_{i+1}, for some $i \geqslant 1$. Consider the pyramid formed by joining any fixed point x in $K_G \cap J_0$ to all the points in the base B_G. Let B'_G be the surface formed by intersecting this pyramid with the plane J_i. It follows from convexity that $B'_G \subseteq K_G$. Also, since the distance of x from J_i is at least half the distance of x from J_{i+1}, it follows that the area of B'_G is $\Omega(b_G)$.

Finally, observe that since the convex hulls of the generators of $\mathcal{G}_H$, and hence $\mathcal{G}'_H$, are disjoint, it follows that the associated set of surface patches $\{B'_G : G \in \mathcal{G}'_H\}$ are also disjoint. Since these patches lie on the portions of the hyperplanes $J_i, i \geqslant 1$, that lie inside $\mathbb{U}$, and the number of these hyperplanes that intersect $\mathbb{U}$ is $O(\log n)$, it follows that $\sum_{G \in \mathcal{G}'_H} b_G = O(\log n)$. This completes the proof. □

We can now prove Lemma 4.11 by using the above observation. The proof relies crucially on showing that, among the set of generators used to answer query H, the ones that are neither contained in R_H nor relatively fat do not cover more than a constant fraction of the points of $P \cap S^{\Delta_0/2}(H)$. It can be shown that the convex hulls of such generators intersect both bounding hyperplanes of the slab $S^{\Delta}(H) \setminus S^{\Delta_0/2}(H)$. We show that the convex hull disjointness assumption implies that the sum of the breadths associated with these generators is at most $O(\log n)$. Recall that generators that are not relatively fat cover "few" points in R_H relative to their associated breadths. Using these two facts then allows us to obtain the desired bound on the number of points covered by these generators.

Proof. (of Lemma 4.11) Given $H \in \mathcal{Q}$, consider the set $A_H \subseteq \mathcal{G}$ of generators that allow us to answer the query H within time t. Clearly, $|A_H| \leqslant t$. Consider the slab $S^{\Delta_0/2}(H)$. Note that $S^{\Delta_0/2}(H) \subset S^{\Delta_0}(H) = R_H$. Just as we showed $|P \cap R_H| \geqslant 8t \log n$ (after Lemma 4.7), we can show that $|P \cap S^{\Delta_0/2}(H)| \geqslant 4t \log n$. Applying property (ii) of scattered point sets, we can easily show that $|P \cap R_H| = O(t \log n)$. We claim that the generators of A_H that are not fat cover at most $2t \log n$ points of $P \cap S^{\Delta_0/2}(H)$. (Here and throughout this proof, fatness, absolute fatness, and relative fatness of generators are understood to be with respect to H.) Clearly this would prove the lemma as it would imply that the fat generators of A_H cover at least $2t \log n$ points of $P \cap S^{\Delta_0/2}(H)$, and hence a constant fraction of the points of $P \cap R_H$.

To see the claim, consider the subset $A'_H \subseteq A_H$ consisting of generators that are not fat and cover some point of $P \cap S^{\Delta_0/2}(H)$. Let A^1_H denote the subset of A'_H consisting of generators that are not absolutely fat. By definition, each such generator covers at most $\log n$ points of $P \cap R_H$. Therefore, the generators of A^1_H cover at most $t \log n$ points of $P \cap R_H$, and hence of $P \cap S^{\Delta_0/2}(H)$.

Let $A^2_H = A'_H \setminus A^1_H$. Since any generator $G \in A^2_H$ is absolutely fat but not fat, and covers some point of $P \cap S^{\Delta_0/2}(H)$, it is easy to see that it satisfies the following:

(i) $G \subset H$,
(ii) $G \cap S^{\Delta_0/2}(H) \neq \emptyset$,
(iii) $G \not\subset R_H$, and
(iv) G is not relatively fat (i.e., $|G \cap R_H| < (\text{breadth}(G, H) \cdot \Delta_0 \cdot n)/(c \log n)$).

Also, by the statement of the lemma, the convex hulls of the generators in A^2_H are disjoint. Clearly, the generators of A^2_H satisfy all the preconditions of Lemma 4.12, and therefore $\sum_{G \in A^2_H} \text{breadth}(G, H) = O(\log n)$. Since the generators of A^2_H are not relatively fat, it follows that the number of points of $P \cap S^{\Delta_0/2}(H)$ covered by these generators is at most

$$\sum_{G \in A^2_H} |G \cap R_H| \leqslant \sum_{G \in A^2_H} \frac{\text{breadth}(G, H) \cdot \Delta_0 \cdot n}{c \log n} = \frac{\Delta_0 n}{c \log n} \sum_{G \in A^2_H} \text{breadth}(G, H).$$

We know that $\sum_{G \in A_H^2} \text{breadth}(G, H) = O(\log n)$ and $\Delta_0 = O(t \log n/n)$, and so by choosing the constant c (in the definition of relatively fat generators) to be sufficiently large, we can ensure that the generators of A_H^2 cover at most $t \log n$ points of $P \cap S^{\Delta_0/2}(H)$. Combining the contributions from the generators of A_H^1 and A_H^2, it follows that the generators of A'_H together cover at most $2t \log n$ points of $P \cap S^{\Delta_0/2}(H)$. This completes the proof. □

Next we define a notion of generator usefulness based on the above lemma, which will help us derive the lower bounds. Consider any $G \in \mathcal{G}$ and $H \in \mathcal{Q}$. We define the *usefulness* of G with respect to H, denoted $u(G, H)$, as in the idempotent case, except that we use "fatness" in place of "absolute fatness". As before, let $u(G) = \mathrm{E}[u(G, H)]$. Arguing as before, but using Lemma 4.11 in place of Lemma 4.9, we obtain $\Phi \leqslant \sum_{G \in \mathcal{G}} u(G)$.

Consider any $G \in \mathcal{G}$ and $H \in \mathcal{Q}$ such that G is fat with respect to H. Let $K = \text{conv}(G)$. If $G \subset R_H$ then by Lemma 4.10,

$$u(G, H) = |G \cap R_H| \preceq n\,\mu(K \cap R_H) = n\mu(K).$$

Otherwise, G must be relatively fat with respect to H. In this case, applying Lemma 4.10, we have

$$\mu(K \cap R_H) \succeq \frac{|G \cap R_H|}{n} \geqslant \frac{\text{breadth}(G, H) \cdot \Delta_0}{c \log n}.$$

Thus, $K \cap R_H$ is a cap of K of width at most Δ_0 and volume $\Omega\left((\text{breadth}(G, H) \cdot \Delta_0)/\log n\right)$. Also, since $K \subseteq \mathbb{U}$ and, by Lemma 4.10, $\mu(K) \geqslant \mu(K \cap R_H) = \Omega(\log n/n)$, it is easy to show that K is α-fat for $\alpha = O(n/\log n)$. We apply our slicing lemma (Lemma 4.5) to K, setting β to a suitable constant times $\log n$ and Δ to Δ_0. We obtain a collection of $O(\beta \log \alpha) = O(\log^2 n)$ convex bodies $K_1, K_2, \ldots \subseteq K$ such that one of these bodies lies inside $K \cap R_H$ and has volume $\Omega(K \cap R_H)$. Arguing as before, we obtain

$$u(G, H) \preceq n \sum_i \mu(K_i) \cdot \mathrm{I}\Big[K_i \subseteq R_H\Big].$$

By definition, $u(G, H) = 0$ if G is not fat with respect to H. Combining all the cases, we have

$$u(G, H) \preceq n \left(\mu(K) \cdot \mathrm{I}\Big[K \subseteq R_H\Big] + \sum_i \mu(K_i) \cdot \mathrm{I}\Big[K_i \subseteq R_H\Big] \right).$$

Taking expectation on both sides and arguing as before we obtain $u(G) \preceq n \log^2(n) \Delta_0^{d+1}$, which yields

$$\Phi = O\left(mn \log^2(n) \Delta_0^{d+1}\right).$$

Combining this with the $\Omega(t \log n)$ lower bound on Φ, we can now easily complete the proof of Theorem 4.1(ii).

5. REFERENCES

[1] P. K. Agarwal and J. Erickson. Geometric range searching and its relatives. In B. Chazelle, J. E. Goodman, and R. Pollack, editors, *Advances in Discrete and Computational Geometry*, volume 223 of *Contemporary Mathematics*, pages 1–56. American Mathematical Society, Providence, RI, 1999.

[2] S. Arya, T. Malamatos, and D. M. Mount. On the importance of idempotence. In *Proc. 38th Annu. ACM Sympos. Theory Comput.*, pages 564–573, 2006.

[3] S. Arya, T. Malamatos, and D. M. Mount. The effect of corners on the complexity of approximate range searching. *Discrete Comput. Geom.*, 41(3):398–443, 2009.

[4] H. Brönnimann, B. Chazelle, and J. Pach. How hard is halfspace range searching? *Discrete Comput. Geom.*, 10:143–155, 1993.

[5] T. M. Chan. Optimal partition trees. In *Proc. 26th Annu. ACM Sympos. Comput. Geom.*, 2010. To appear.

[6] B. Chazelle. Lower bounds on the complexity of polytope range searching. *J. Amer. Math. Soc.*, 2:637–666, 1989.

[7] B. Chazelle, M. Sharir, and E. Welzl. Quasi-optimal upper bounds for simplex range searching and new zone theorems. *Algorithmica*, 8:407–429, 1992.

[8] B. Chazelle and E. Welzl. Quasi-optimal range searching in spaces of finite VC-dimension. *Discrete Comput. Geom.*, 4(5):467–489, 1989.

[9] G. D. da Fonseca and D. M. Mount. Approximate range searching: The absolute model. *Comput. Geom. Theory Appl.*, 43(4):434–444, 2009.

[10] H. Edelsbrunner and E. Welzl. Halfplanar range search in linear space and $O(n^{0.695})$ query time. *Inf. Process. Lett.*, 23(6):289–293, 1986.

[11] J. Erickson. Space-time tradeoffs for emptiness queries. *SIAM J. Comput.*, 29:1968–1996, 2000.

[12] M. L. Fredman. Lower bounds on the complexity of some optimal data structures. *SIAM J. Comput.*, 10:1–10, 1981.

[13] M. Grötschel, L. Lovász, and A. Schrijver. *Geometric Algorithms and Combinatorial Optimization*, volume 2 of *Algorithms and Combinatorics*. Springer-Verlag, 2nd edition, 1993.

[14] D. Haussler and E. Welzl. Epsilon-nets and simplex range queries. *Discrete Comput. Geom.*, 2:127–151, 1987.

[15] J. Matoušek. Range searching with efficient hierarchical cuttings. *Discrete Comput. Geom.*, 10(2):157–182, 1993.

[16] J. Matoušek. Geometric range searching. *ACM Comput. Surv.*, 26:421–461, 1994.

[17] J. Matoušek and E. Welzl. Good splitters for counting points in triangles. In *Proc. 5th Annu. ACM Sympos. Comput. Geom.*, pages 124–130, 1989.

[18] E. Welzl. Partition trees for triangle counting and other range searching problems. In *Proc. 4th Annu. ACM Sympos. Comput. Geom.*, pages 23–33, 1988.

[19] D. E. Willard. Polygon retrieval. *SIAM J. Comput.*, 11:149–165, 1982.

[20] A. C. Yao. On the complexity of maintaining partial sums. *SIAM J. Comput.*, 14:277–288, 1985.

[21] F. F. Yao. A 3-space partition and its applications. In *Proc. 15th Annu. ACM Sympos. Theory Comput.*, pages 258–263, 1983.

Invited Talk

Discrete Geometric Structures for Architecture

Helmut Pottmann
King Abdullah University of Science and Technology
Thuwal, Saudi Arabia
helmut.pottmann@kaust.edu.sa

Abstract

The emergence of freeform structures in contemporary architecture raises numerous challenging research problems, most of which are related to the actual fabrication and are a rich source of research topics in geometry and geometric computing. The talk will provide an overview of recent progress in this field, with a particular focus on discrete geometric structures. Most of these result from practical requirements on segmenting a freeform shape into planar panels and on the physical realization of supporting beams and nodes.

A study of quadrilateral meshes with planar faces reveals beautiful relations to discrete differential geometry. In particular, we discuss meshes which discretize the network of principal curvature lines. Conical meshes are among these meshes; they possess conical offset meshes at a constant face/face distance, which in turn leads to a supporting beam layout with so-called torsion free nodes. This work can be generalized to a variety of multilayer structures and laid the ground for an adapted curvature theory for these meshes. There are also efforts on segmenting surfaces into planar hexagonal panels. Though these are less constrained than planar quadrilateral panels, this problem is still waiting for an elegant solution.

Inspired by freeform designs in architecture which involve circles and spheres, we present a new kind of triangle mesh whose faces' in-circles form a packing, i.e., the in-circles of two triangles with a common edge have the same contact point on that edge. These "circle packing (CP) meshes" exhibit an aesthetic balance of shape and size of their faces. They are closely tied to sphere packings on surfaces and to various remarkable structures and patterns which are of interest in art, architecture, and design. CP meshes constitute a new link between architectural freeform design and computational conformal geometry.

Recently, certain timber structures motivated us to study discrete patterns of geodesics on surfaces. This topic is closely related to the classical geometry of webs. There are numerous open problems in the geometry of webs, in particular when one asks for webs formed by special types of curves, as preferred in applications such as architecture.

Categories & Subject Descriptors: [Computer Graphics]: Computational Geometry and Object Modeling—Geometric algorithms, languages, and systems; I.3.5 [Computer Graphics]: Computational Geometry and Object Modeling—Curve, surface, solid, and object representations

General Terms: Algorithms, Design.

Bio

The speaker is the director of the Geometric Modeling and Scientific Visualization Center at KAUST, Saudi Arabia. He received his PhD in Mathematics from Vienna University of Technology. His research focus is on Applied Geometry and Geometric Computing.

SCG'10, June 13–16, 2010, Snowbird, Utah, USA.
ACM 978-1-4503-0016-2/10/06.

Better Bounds on the Union Complexity of Locally Fat Objects

Mark de Berg*
Department of Computer Science, TU Eindhoven
PO Box 513, 5600 MB Eindhoven, the Netherlands
mdberg@win.tue.nl

ABSTRACT

We prove that the union complexity of a set of n constant-complexity locally fat objects (which can be curved and/or non-convex) in the plane is $O(\lambda_{t+2}(n)\log n)$, where t is the maximum number of times the boundaries of any two objects intersect. This improves the previously best known bound by a logarithmic factor.

Categories and Subject Descriptors

F.2 [**Theory of Computation**]: Analysis of Algorithms and Problem Complexity

General Terms

Algorithms, Theory.

Keywords

Combinatorial geometry, union complexity, fat objects.

1. INTRODUCTION

When analyzing the running time of a geometric algorithm, it is often crucial to obtain a bound on the combinatorial complexity of a certain geometric structure. In particular, in many cases one needs a bound on the complexity of the *union* of a collection of objects in $\mathbb{R}^d$. In general, the maximum complexity of the union of n constant-complexity objects can be as high as $\Theta(n^d)$. In many special cases, however, the union complexity is significantly smaller—see the recent survey by Agarwal *et al.* [2] for an overview of the results and the applications of union-complexity bounds.

In this paper we study the union complexity of so-called *fat objects* in the plane. Two early results in this area are by Kedem *et al.* [11], who proved that the union complexity of n disks is $O(n)$, and by Alt *et al.* [1] and Efrat *et al.* [6], who proved that the union complexity of n fat wedges—wedges whose interior angle is bounded from below by a constant—is $O(n)$. Later Matoušek *et al.* [12] considered the case of *δ-fat triangles*: triangles all of whose angles are at least δ for some constant δ. They proved that the union complexity of n δ-fat triangles is $O(n \log\log n)$; see also the paper by Pach and Tardos [13] for a proof of the same bound, but with a better dependency on the fatness factor δ.

The work by Matoušek *et al.* [12] has been generalized in various ways. For instance, several papers deal with fat objects in 3- or higher-dimensional space; see the recent paper by Ezra and Sharir [10] and the references therein. Other papers still deal with the planar case, but consider more general objects than triangles. The main challenge here is to prove near-linear bounds on the union complexity of n fat objects that are curved and/or non-convex. The first such result was obtained by Efrat and Sharir [7], who showed that the union complexity of fat *convex* objects with curved boundaries is $O(n^{1+\varepsilon})$, for any fixed $\varepsilon > 0$. Efrat and Katz [8] proved that the union complexity of so-called κ-curved objects is $O(\lambda_{t+2}(n))$; here t is the maximum number of times the boundaries of any two objects intersect, and $\lambda_{t+2}(n)$ is the maximum length of an $(n, t+2)$ Davenport-Schinzel sequence [14]. Unfortunately, the class of κ-curved objects is rather restricted, since it does not allow convex vertices; in particular, fat triangles are not κ-curved. The first general result for fat, curved objects—where the objects can be non-convex and also have convex vertices—was obtained by Efrat [5]. He proved that the union complexity of n so-called (α,β)-covered objects is $O(\lambda_{t+2}(n)\log^2 n \log\log n)$. Recently this was further generalized and slightly improved by De Berg [4], who showed that the union complexity of n so-called *locally γ-fat objects* is $O(\lambda_{t+2}(n)\log^2 n)$. The class of locally γ-fat objects—see Section 2 for a formal definition—is the most general class of fat objects for which near-linear union-bounds are known, and it is also the class we will consider in this paper.

The known lower bounds on the union complexity are $\Omega(n\alpha(n))$ for fat triangles, and $O(\lambda_{t+2}(n))$ for curved fat objects. These bounds are obtained by starting with an upper envelope of segments (or curves) of the given complexity, and then extending each segment (curve) downward so that it becomes a fat triangle (fat curved object). It is conjectured that these lower bounds are tight. For fat triangles the gap between the upper and lower bound is only a factor $O((\log\log n)/\alpha(n))$. For fat curved objects, however, the gap is a factor $O(\log^2 n)$. In this paper we decrease the gap by a logarithmic factor: we show that the union complexity of n locally γ-fat objects is $O(\lambda_{t+2}(n)\log n)$.

*MdB was supported by the Netherlands' Organisation for Scientific Research (NWO) under project no. 639.023.301.

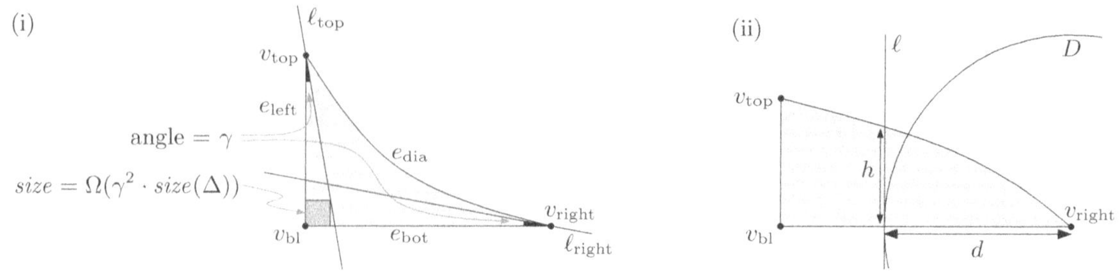

Figure 1: Illustration for the proof of Lemma 4.

2. PRELIMINARIES

Let F be a collection of n compact (that is, bounded and closed) objects in the plane. We assume each object has constant complexity; in particular we assume the boundary of each object consists of $O(1)$ algebraic curves of constant maximum degree. Hence, any two object boundaries intersect at most t times, for some constant t. The union of F is denoted by $\mathcal{U}(F)$ and its complexity by $|\mathcal{U}(F)|$. In the sequel, whenever we refer to a *vertex* of the union of some collection of objects we mean a union vertex that is the intersection of two object boundaries. The number of such union vertices gives an upper bound on the union complexity, up to an additive $O(n)$ factor, so we will focus on bounding the number of union vertices.

Before we give the definition of local fatness, we need some notation. The diameter of an object o is denoted by $diam(o)$. The size of an object o, denoted $size(o)$, is defined as the maximum edge length of its axis-aligned bounding box. The Euclidean distance between two objects o_1 and o_2 is denoted by $dist(o_1, o_2)$. Finally, $area(o)$ denotes the area of an object o and $length(s)$ denotes the length of a segment s. Now consider an object o and a disk D whose center lies inside o. If o is non-convex then $D \cap o$ can consist of several connected components. We define $D \sqcap o$ to be the connected component that contains the center of D.

Definition 1. **[4]** *Let o be an object in the plane and γ a parameter with $0 \leqslant \gamma \leqslant 1$. We say that o is* locally γ-fat *if, for any disk D whose center lies in o and that does not fully contain o in its interior, we have $area(D \sqcap o) \geqslant \gamma \cdot area(D)$.*

This definition is similar to the fatness definition of Van der Stappen *et al.* [15, 16], except that we use $area(D \sqcap o)$ instead of $area(D \cap o)$. For convex objects, where $D \sqcap o = D \cap o$, the definitions are identical. For non-convex objects, local fatness is a stronger condition than fatness. This stronger condition is necessary, as there are sets of n objects that are fat under the definition of Van der Stappen (but not locally fat) whose union complexity is $\Theta(n^2)$ [4].

We shall make extensive use of the Merging Lemma [4], which bounds the union complexity of a set $F_1 \cup F_2$ of locally fat objects in terms of the union complexities of F_1 and F_2. In fact, we will need a slightly more general version, which bounds the union complexity of $F_1 \cup F_2$ inside a region R in terms of the union complexities of F_1 and F_2 inside R. It immediately follows from the proof of the Merging Lemma that this more general version holds as well.

Merging Lemma [4] *Let F_1 and F_2 be two sets of locally γ-fat objects and let R be a constant-complexity region in the plane. Then*

$$|\mathcal{U}(F_1 \cup F_2) \cap R| = O\left((1/\gamma) \cdot (|\mathcal{U}(F_1) \cap R| + |\mathcal{U}(F_2) \cap R|)\right).$$

The first step in our proof is similar to the previous paper [4]: we reduce the problem to the case of simpler, canonical objects. More precisely, we reduce the problem to bounding the union complexity of so-called γ-triangles, which are defined as follows.

Definition 2. *A* γ-triangle *is a locally γ-fat planar object Δ bounded from below by a horizontal straight edge, bounded from the left by a vertical straight edge, and bounded from the right and from the top by a smooth xy-monotone Jordan arc without inflection points. These three edges are called the* bottom edge, left edge, *and* diagonal edge *of Δ, respectively.*

Like for the objects in our initial set F, we assume that the boundaries (and, in particular, the diagonal edges) of any two γ-triangles intersect at most t times. The next lemma states that in order to bound the maximum union complexity of a set of locally γ-fat objects, it is sufficient to bound the maximum union complexity of a set of γ-triangles.

Lemma 3. *Let $U_\gamma(n)$ denote the maximum union complexity of any set of n γ-triangles. Then the maximum union complexity of any set of n locally γ-fat objects is $O((1/\gamma^2) \cdot U_\gamma(n/\gamma^2))$.*

Proof. Our γ-triangles are essentially the same as the so-called canonical quasi-triangles used in the previous paper [4]; the only difference is that we require the angle between the left and bottom edge to be $\pi/2$, whereas in a set of canonical quasi-triangles this angle is a fixed constant close to π. A set of canonical quasi-triangles can be transformed to a set of γ-triangles by a shear transformation, so the lemma follows from the corresponding lemma for canonical quasi-triangles. The formal proof of this fact is given in Appendix A. □

We will need the following geometric properties of γ-triangles.

Lemma 4. *Let Δ be a γ-triangle. Then we have:*

(i) Δ contains a square of size $\Omega(\gamma^2 \cdot size(\Delta))$ whose bottom-left corner coincides with the bottom-left corner of Δ.

(ii) Let ℓ be a vertical line intersecting a γ-triangle Δ and whose distance to Δ's right vertex is d, or a horizontal line intersecting Δ whose distance to Δ's top vertex is d. Then $length(\ell \cap \Delta) \geqslant \gamma\pi d$.

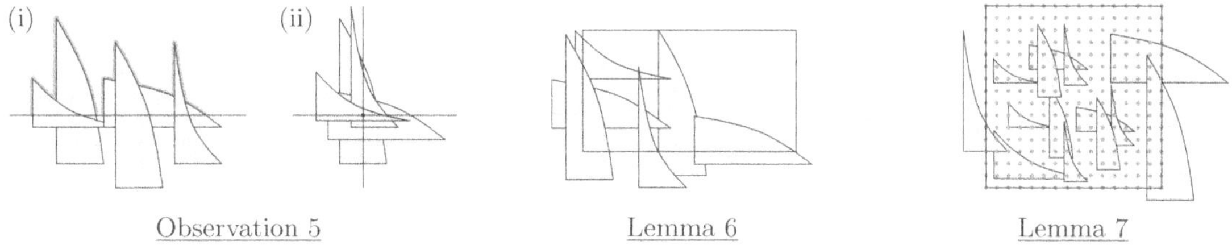

Figure 2: Illustrations for the observation and lemmas in Subsection 3.1.

PROOF. Let v_{top}, v_{right}, and v_{bl} be the top vertex, right vertex, and bottom-left vertex of Δ, and let e_{left}, e_{bot}, and e_{dia} be its left edge, bottom edge, and diagonal edge; see Fig. 1(i).

To prove (i), let ℓ_{top} be the line through v_{top} and intersecting Δ that makes an angle γ with e_{left}. This line intersects e_{bot} (otherwise Δ would not be locally γ-fat) and the segment from v_{top} to this intersection point is completely contained in Δ. Similarly, the line ℓ_{right} through v_{right} intersecting Δ and making an angle γ with e_{bot} intersects e_{left}, and up to the intersection point it is contained in Δ. Hence, the area A enclosed by ℓ_{top}, ℓ_{right}, e_{bot}, and e_{left} is contained in Δ. Now assume without loss of generality that the shorter of e_{left} and e_{bot} has length 1. Since Δ is locally γ-fat this implies that $size(\Delta)$, which equals the length of the longer of the two edges, is $O(1/\gamma)$. Using elementary geometry one can verify that the square σ of side length $\frac{1}{2}\tan\gamma$ whose bottom-left corner is v_{bl} is contained in A. Since $\tan\gamma = \Theta(\gamma)$ for γ sufficiently small, this implies that $size(\sigma) = \Omega(\gamma^2 \cdot size(\Delta))$. This proves (i).

To prove (ii), let ℓ be the vertical line intersecting Δ whose distance from v_{right} is d, and let $h := length(\ell \cap \Delta)$. (The proof for the horizontal line at distance d from v_{top} is similar.) Let D be the disk centered at v_{right} and of radius d—see Fig. 1(ii). Because Δ is xy-monotone, we have $area(D \cap \Delta) < hd$. On the other hand, since Δ is locally γ-fat we have $area(D \cap \Delta) \geqslant \gamma \cdot area(D) = \gamma\pi d^2$. Hence, $h > \gamma\pi d$, as claimed. □

3. THE UNION OF γ-TRIANGLES

In this section we prove bounds on the union complexity of a set of n γ-triangles. Lemma 3 will then give us the desired result. With a slight abuse of notation, we will use F to denote the set of γ-triangles. We scale the whole scene so that F is contained in the unit square.

3.1 Some easy cases

We start with some special cases, which are illustrated in Fig. 2. The bounds for these cases will serve as building blocks in the general case. For a horizontal line ℓ, let ℓ^+ denote the half-plane above ℓ and let ℓ^- denote the half-plane below ℓ. Similarly, for a vertical line ℓ, let ℓ^+ denote the half-plane to the right of ℓ and let ℓ^- denote the half-plane to the left of ℓ.

OBSERVATION 5. *Let F be a set of γ-triangles.*

(i) Let ℓ be a horizontal or vertical line such that the bottom-left vertex of each $\Delta \in F$ lies in ℓ^-. Then $|\mathcal{U}(F) \cap \ell^+| = O(\lambda_{t+2}(n))$.

(ii) If there is a point q stabbing all γ-triangles in F, then $|\mathcal{U}(F)| = O(\lambda_{t+2}(n))$.

PROOF. To prove (i) we use the fact that γ-triangles are x-monotone. Hence, if ℓ is horizontal then $\mathcal{U}(F) \cap \ell^+$ is bounded by the upper envelope of the diagonal edges of the γ-triangles in F (and by parts of their left edges), and so $|\mathcal{U}(F) \cap \ell^+| = O(\lambda_{t+2}(n))$ [14]. Since γ-triangles are also y-monotone, a similar proof applies in case ℓ is vertical.

To prove (ii), let ℓ_{hor} and ℓ_{vert} be the horizontal and vertical line through q, respectively. Then $|\mathcal{U}(F) \cap \ell^+_{hor}| = O(\lambda_{t+2}(n))$ and $|\mathcal{U}(F) \cap \ell^+_{vert}| = O(\lambda_{t+2}(n))$ by part (i). Since $\Delta \cap \ell^-_{hor} \cap \ell^-_{vert}$ is a rectangle with q as its top-right vertex for each $\Delta \in F$, we have $|\mathcal{U}(F) \cap \ell^-_{hor} \cap \ell^-_{vert}| = O(n)$, thus proving (ii). □

LEMMA 6. *Let R be a rectangle and F be a set of n γ-triangles whose bottom-left vertex lies outside R. Then $|\mathcal{U}(F) \cap R| = O((1/\gamma) \cdot \lambda_{t+2}(n))$.*

PROOF. Let $F_{bot} \subset F$ be the subset of γ-triangles whose bottom-left vertex lies below the line containing R's bottom edge, and let $F_{left} \subset F$ be the subset of γ-triangles whose bottom-left vertex lies to the left of the line containing R's left edge. Since all γ-triangles in F have their bottom-left vertex outside R, the subsets F_{bot} and F_{left} together contain all γ-triangles intersecting R. By Observation 5(i), we have $|\mathcal{U}(F_{bot}) \cap R| = O(\lambda_{t+2}(n))$ and $|\mathcal{U}(F_{left}) \cap R| = O(\lambda_{t+2}(n))$. Hence, by the Merging Lemma, $|\mathcal{U}(F_{bot} \cup F_{left}) \cap R| = O((1/\gamma) \cdot \lambda_{t+2}(n))$. □

LEMMA 7. *Let F be a set of n γ-triangles intersecting a square σ such that $size(\Delta) \geqslant c \cdot size(\sigma)$ for all $\Delta \in F$, where $c \leqslant 1$ is some constant. Then $|\mathcal{U}(F) \cap \sigma| = O((1/c^2\gamma^5) \cdot \lambda_{t+2}(n))$.*

PROOF. Let $F_{bot} \subset F$ be the subset of γ-triangles whose bottom-left vertex lies below the line through σ's bottom edge, and let $F_{left} \subset F$ be the subset of γ-triangles whose bottom-left vertex lies to the left of the line through σ's left edge. By Observation 5(i), we have $|\mathcal{U}(F_{bot}) \cap R| = O(\lambda_{t+2}(|F_{bot}|))$ and $|\mathcal{U}(F_{left}) \cap R| = O(\lambda_{t+2}(|F_{left}|))$.

The γ-triangles in $F_\sigma := F \setminus (F_{bot} \cup F_{left})$ all have their bottom-left vertex inside σ. By Lemma 4(i), for each γ-triangle Δ there is a square of size $\Omega(\gamma^2 \cdot size(\Delta)) = \Omega(c\gamma^2 \cdot size(\sigma))$ that is contained in Δ and whose bottom-left vertex is the bottom-left vertex of Δ. Hence, we can put a set Q of $O((1/c\gamma^2)^2)$ grid points inside σ, such that each γ-triangle $\Delta \in F_\sigma$ is stabbed by at least one grid point. We assign each $\Delta \in F_\sigma$ to one of the grid points stabbing it. For a grid point q, let F_q denote the set of γ-triangles assigned to it. By Observation 5(ii), we have $|\mathcal{U}(F_q)| = O(\lambda_{t+2}(|F_q|))$.

So far, we have not accounted for vertices of $\mathcal{U}(F) \cap \sigma$ that are generated by γ-triangles from two different subsets

F_1, F_2, where F_1 (and similarly F_2) can be F_{bot} or F_{left} or some subset F_q. By the Merging Lemma, the number of vertices generated by a pair F_1, F_2 is $O((1/\gamma) \cdot (|\mathcal{U}(F_1)| + |\mathcal{U}(F_2)|))$. Note that each of the subsets F_{bot}, F_{left}, F_q is involved in $|Q|+1$ pairs. Hence, the overall number of union vertices is

$$O\left(\frac{1}{\gamma} \cdot |Q| \cdot \left(\lambda_{t+2}(|F_{\text{bot}}|) + \lambda_{t+2}(|F_{\text{left}}|) + \sum_{q \in Q} \lambda_{t+2}(|F_q|)\right)\right)$$
$$= O\left(\frac{1}{c^2\gamma^5} \cdot \lambda_{t+2}(n)\right).$$

□

3.2 The global approach: counting with a skip quadtree

We will use a hierarchical counting scheme, based on a tree structure storing the γ-triangles. The γ-triangles associated with each node of the tree will be classified as either "large" or "small", and we will only need to deal with large-large and large-small interactions. Similar counting schemes have been used before, usually with a segment tree as underlying tree structure. We will use a skip quadtree, as explained next.

Let V be the set of vertices of the γ-triangles in F. We assume without loss of generality that no two vertices coincide. Let $\mathcal{T}$ be a skip quadtree [9] for V. In fact, since we only use the tree in a combinatorial argument, we do not need the full power of a skip quadtree. In Appendix B we describe a simplified version of the skip quadtree that is sufficient for our purposes. Here we only list the properties we will use.

For an integer s, let G_s denote the grid whose cells have size $2^{-s} \times 2^{-s}$ and for which the origin O is a grid point. A *canonical square* is any cell of one of the grids G_s. A *canonical donut* is the set-theoretic difference of a canonical square σ_{out} and a canonical square σ_{in} with $\sigma_{\text{in}} \subset \sigma_{\text{out}}$. The properties we need from the skip quadtree $\mathcal{T}$ are the following.

- Each node ν in $\mathcal{T}$ corresponds to a region in the plane, denoted by *region*(ν), which is either a canonical square or a canonical donut. The region corresponding to the root of $\mathcal{T}$ is the smallest canonical square containing all the vertices from V, and the regions corresponding to the children of any node ν form a partition of *region*(ν).
- Each node has constant degree, and the depth of $\mathcal{T}$ is $O(\log n)$.
- Each leaf region contains at most one vertex from V.

We define a γ-triangle Δ to be *small* at a node ν in $\mathcal{T}$ if *region*(ν) contains a vertex of Δ. The set of all γ-triangles that are small at ν is denoted by $F_S(\nu)$. A γ-triangle Δ is defined to be *large* at ν if Δ is small at the parent of ν but not at ν itself. The set of γ-triangles that are large at a node ν is denoted by $F_L(\nu)$. Let $F(\nu) := F_L(\nu) \cup F_S(\nu)$. A vertex of $\mathcal{U}(F(\nu))$ is called a *large-large vertex* if it is induced by two γ-triangles from $F_L(\nu)$, it is called a *large-small vertex* if it is induced by a γ-triangle from $F_L(\nu)$ and a γ-triangle from $F_S(\nu)$, and it is called a *small-small vertex* if it is induced by two γ-triangles from $F_S(\nu)$.

The following lemma—note that part (i) implies we do not need to count small-small vertices—is standard, but we include its proof for completeness.

LEMMA 8. *Let $\mathcal{T}$ be a skip quadtree for the set V of vertices of the γ-triangles in F.*

(i) For every vertex v of the union $\mathcal{U}(F)$ there is a node ν in $\mathcal{T}$ such that v is a large-large vertex or a large-small vertex of $\mathcal{U}(F(\nu))$ inside region(ν).

(ii) $\sum_{\nu \in \mathcal{T}} |F(\nu)| = O(n \log n)$.

PROOF. To prove (i), consider a union vertex v defined by γ-triangles Δ_1 and Δ_2. Descend down $\mathcal{T}$, always going to the child whose region contains v. Let ν be the first node where one of the γ-triangles Δ_1 and Δ_2, say Δ_1, becomes large. Such a node must exist, because any γ-triangle is small at the root of $\mathcal{T}$ and at most one γ-triangle is small at any leaf. Since ν is the first node where one of the two γ-triangles becomes large, Δ_2 is either still small or it has just become large as well. In the first case v is a large-small vertex at ν, and in the second case v is a large-large vertex.

To prove (ii), we observe that for any $\Delta \in F(\nu)$, at least of one Δ's vertices is contained in the region of ν's parent. Since the depth of $\mathcal{T}$ is $O(\log n)$, any vertex is contained in $O(\log n)$ regions. Because the degree of the nodes is $O(1)$, this proves (ii). □

3.3 Getting rid of difficult cases: randomly shifting the origin

Given a node ν, our task is to bound the number of large-large and large-small vertices of $\mathcal{U}(F(\nu))$ inside *region*(ν). As it turns out, large-small vertices involving a small γ-triangle located close to the boundary of *region*(ν) are hard to handle. We get rid of this problem using a probabilistic argument: we randomly shift the origin—note that the origin determines the canonical squares used in the quadtree construction—and then argue that we can simply ignore the problematic γ-triangles. (The trick of randomly shifting the origin when constructing a quadtree is also used, for instance, in Arora's famous TSP algorithm [3].) Next we give the details of this shifting approach; in Subsection 3.4 we will then show how to bound the number of large-large and large-small vertices.

Recall that we have scaled the scene such that the set F of γ-triangles lies inside the unit square $[0,1]^2$. We pick a point O in the square $[-1,0]^2$ uniformly at random, which we designate to be the origin of our new coordinate system. The grids G_s and, hence, the canonical squares, are defined with respect to this random origin O. Next we define which γ-triangles we will ignore. (There is nothing special about the threshold value τ in the definition below; the chosen value is just large enough to make to it work.)

DEFINITION 9. *Let $\Delta \in F$ be a γ-triangle. Let $\tau = 32$. We say that Δ is* ignorable *in a grid G_s if*

(i) size(Δ) $\leqslant 2^{-s}/\tau$, and
(ii) there is a grid line ℓ such that dist(Δ, ℓ) $\leqslant$ size(Δ).

We say that Δ is ignorable if there is an integer s such that Δ is ignorable in the grid G_s.

Intuitively, a γ-triangle Δ is ignorable if there is a grid G_s whose cells are large with respect to Δ (condition (i)) and in which Δ lies close to a grid line (condition (ii)). Recall that the origin of our coordinate system, which determines the exact placement of the grids G_s, is chosen uniformly at random in $[-1,0]^2$.

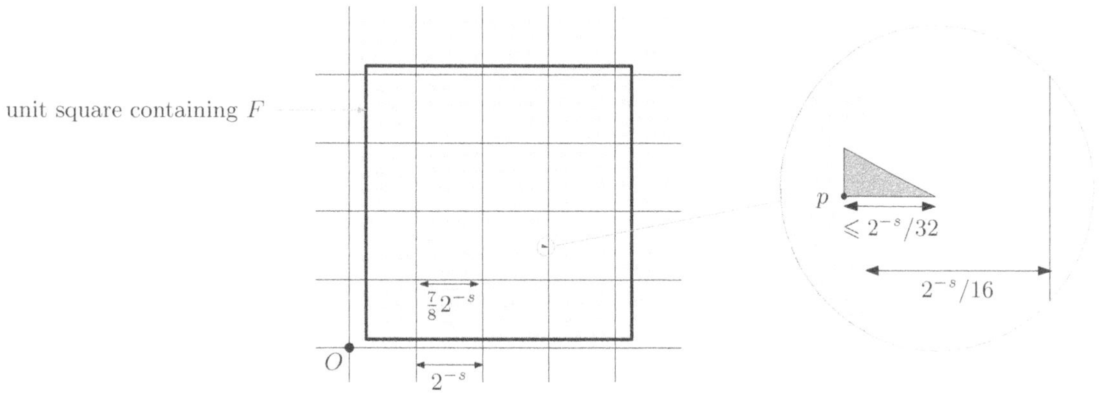

Figure 3: Illustration for the proof of Lemma 10.

LEMMA 10. *For any γ-triangle $\Delta \in F$ we have*

$$\Pr[\Delta \text{ is ignorable}] < 1/4.$$

PROOF. Let s be the largest integer such that $size(\Delta) \leqslant 2^{-s}/\tau$. Clearly Δ is ignorable if and only if it is ignorable in G_s. Let p be the lower left corner of Δ. Since the origin O was chosen randomly, p is likely to end up roughly in the middle of a grid cell of G_s. More precisely, if we place a square of side length $(7/8) \cdot 2^{-s}$ in the middle of each cell, as shown in Fig. 3, then p ends up in one of these squares with probability $(7/8)^2 > 3/4$. Hence,

$$\Pr\left[\text{ (distance from } p \text{ to any grid line in } G_s) \leqslant \frac{2^{-s}}{16}\right] < \frac{1}{4}.$$

It remains to observe that if the distance from p to any grid line ℓ is greater than $2^{-s}/16$, then the distance from Δ to ℓ cannot be too small either:

$$\begin{aligned} dist(\Delta, \ell) &\geqslant dist(p, \ell) - size(\Delta) \\ &> \tfrac{2^{-s}}{16} - size(\Delta) \\ &\geqslant \tfrac{\tau \cdot size(\Delta)}{16} - size(\Delta) \\ &= size(\Delta). \end{aligned}$$

Hence, Δ cannot be ignorable if the distance from p to any grid line is more than $2^{-s}/16$, so

$$\begin{aligned} &\Pr[\Delta \text{ is ignorable}] \\ &\leqslant \Pr\left[\text{ (distance from } p \text{ to any grid line in } G_s) \leqslant \tfrac{2^{-s}}{16}\right] \\ &< \tfrac{1}{4}, \end{aligned}$$

which proves the lemma. □

Let F^* denote the set F with all ignorable γ-triangles removed. Lemma 10 allows us to use a bound on the number of vertices of $\mathcal{U}(F^*)$ as an asymptotic bound on the number of vertices of $\mathcal{U}(F)$. Indeed, consider a vertex v of $\mathcal{U}(F)$ defined by γ-triangles Δ_1 and Δ_2. Since the probability that Δ_1 is removed is at most 1/4 and the same holds for Δ_2, the probability that v shows up as a vertex of $\mathcal{U}(F^*)$ is at least 1/2. Hence, $\mathrm{E}[|\mathcal{U}(F^*)|] \geqslant |\mathcal{U}(F)|/2$. Thus our strategy is this: we pick a random origin O, remove all ignorable γ-triangles from F to obtain a set F^*, construct a skip quadtree $\mathcal{T}$ for the vertices of the γ-triangles in F^*, and then count the large-large and large-small vertices at each node in $\mathcal{T}$. By the above arguments, the worst-case upper bound on $|\mathcal{U}(F^*)|$ thus obtained bounds $|\mathcal{U}(F)|$ up to a factor 2.

3.4 Counting large-large and large-small vertices

Consider a node ν in $\mathcal{T}$. Let $L := F^*_L(\nu)$ and $S := F^*_S(\nu)$ denote the set of large and small γ-triangles at ν, respectively. Recall that $region(\nu)$ is either a canonical square or a canonical donut. In the remainder we assume that $region(\nu)$ is a canonical donut. The case of a canonical square is strictly simpler; the only difference is that some of the cases cannot occur. Let σ_{out} and σ_{in} denote the canonical squares such that $region(\nu) = \sigma_{\text{out}} \setminus \sigma_{\text{in}}$.

LEMMA 11. *The number of large-large vertices of $\mathcal{U}(L \cup S)$ inside $region(\nu)$ is $O((1/\gamma) \cdot \lambda_{t+2}(|L|))$.*

PROOF. We will bound the number of vertices of $\mathcal{U}(L)$ inside $region(\nu)$, which is an upper bound on the number of large-large vertices of $\mathcal{U}(L \cup S)$ inside $region(\nu)$. Since $region(\nu)$ is the set-theoretic difference of two squares, it can be partitioned into four rectangles. Moreover, the γ-triangles from L are large, so they do not have a vertex inside these rectangles. It now follows from Lemma 6 that $|\mathcal{U}(L) \cap region(\nu)| = O((1/\gamma) \cdot \lambda_{t+2}(|L|))$. □

It remains to count the large-small vertices of $\mathcal{U}(L \cup S)$ inside $region(\nu)$. First, we further subdivide the set S of small γ-triangles into two subsets: a subset S^+ of γ-triangles whose size is more than $size(\sigma_{\text{out}})/32$ and a subset S^- of γ-triangles whose size is at most $size(\sigma_{\text{out}})/32$. Bounding the number of large-small vertices involving a γ-triangle in S^+ is easy.

LEMMA 12. *The number of large-small vertices involving a γ-triangle from S^+ is $O((1/\gamma^5) \cdot \lambda_{t+2}(|L| + |S|)$.*

PROOF. Any large-small vertex of $\mathcal{U}(L \cup S)$ involving a γ-triangle from S^+ is also a vertex of $\mathcal{U}(L \cup S^+)$. All γ-triangles in $L \cup S^+$ intersect σ_{out} and have size at least $size(\sigma_{\text{out}})/32$. The lemma thus follows from Lemma 7. □

We proceed to count the large-small vertices involving a γ-triangle from S^-. From now on we refer to the γ-triangles in S^- as *tiny*, and we refer to the vertices they induce with large triangles as *large-tiny* vertices. Our proof for this case

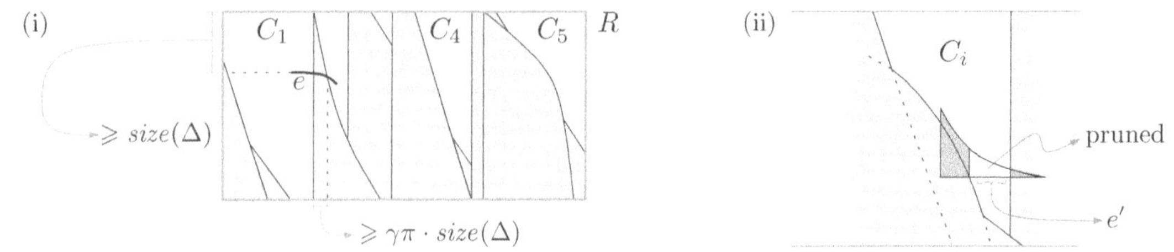

Figure 4: Illustrations for the proof of Lemma 13.

is based on the following lemma, which uses the fact that we have removed the ignorable γ-triangles.

LEMMA 13. *Let σ be a canonical square and R a rectangle whose top-right vertex coincides with the top-right-vertex of σ. Let T_{large} be a set γ-triangles without a vertex inside R, called the large γ-triangles. Let T_{tiny} be a set of γ-triangles whose size is at most $size(\sigma)/32$, called the tiny γ-triangles. Then the number of large-tiny vertices of $\mathcal{U}(T_{\text{large}} \cup T_{\text{tiny}})$ inside R is $O(\lambda_{t+2}(|T_{\text{large}}| + (1/\gamma) \cdot |T_{\text{tiny}}|))$.*

PROOF. Since large γ-triangles do not have a vertex inside R, any large γ-triangle intersecting R completely crosses R from left to right, or it completely crosses R from bottom to top, or it contains the bottom-left corner of R. We show how to count the number of large-tiny vertices induced by large γ-triangles of the latter two types. We call them *bottom-to-top γ-triangles*; note that a γ-triangle containing the bottom-left corner of R is also considered a bottom-to-top γ-triangle. The number of large-tiny vertices induced by γ-triangles of the first type (the left-to-right γ-triangles) can be counted in a similar way.

The union of the bottom-to-top γ-triangles is x-monotone inside R. As shown in Fig. 4(i) its complement consists of a number of maximally connected regions C_i, each bounded from the right by a left edge of some γ-triangle (or by the right edge of R) and bounded from the left by one or more diagonal edges (or by the left edge of R). We first argue that any tiny γ-triangle Δ_{tiny} intersects at most $O(1/\gamma)$ regions C_i, and then analyze what happens inside these regions.

Since Δ_{tiny} is tiny and not ignorable, it lies completely inside σ. Hence, Δ_{tiny} intersects a complement region C_i if and only if its diagonal edge intersects the region. Now imagine traversing the diagonal edge e of Δ_{tiny} from left to right. Consider the moment that e hits the left edge of a large γ-triangle Δ_{large}. Then before e can enter into the next complement region it must leave Δ_{large} through the diagonal edge of Δ_{large}. The fact that Δ_{tiny} is not ignorable means that the distance from Δ_{tiny} to the top edge of σ is at least $size(\Delta_{\text{tiny}})$. Since σ and R share their top-right corner, this means that the distance from Δ_{tiny} to the top edge of R is at least $size(\Delta_{\text{tiny}})$ as well. By Lemma 4(ii) this implies that the horizontal span of $e \cap \Delta_{\text{large}}$ is at least $\gamma\pi \cdot size(\Delta_{\text{tiny}})$—see Fig. 4(i). The number of complement regions intersected by Δ_{tiny} is therefore $O(1/\gamma)$.

It remains to analyze what happens inside the complement regions C_i. Consider a tiny γ-triangle Δ_{tiny} intersecting such a region C_i. Notice that both the left edge and the bottom edge of Δ_{tiny} intersect the boundary of C_i at most twice. Let e' be the part of the bottom edge of Δ_{tiny} inside C_i. We prune the part of Δ_{tiny} above e', as in Fig. 4(ii). This is allowed since it cannot be involved in any large-tiny intersection. Now observe that the lower boundary of the part of C_i not covered by a pruned tiny γ-triangle is bounded by an upper envelope.

Thus we can argue as follows. After pruning, we have a collection of $O(|T_{\text{tiny}}|/\gamma)$ pieces of tiny γ-triangles and at most $|T_{\text{large}}|$ large top-to-bottom γ-triangles. The large-tiny vertices that we need to count are vertices of the upper envelope of the diagonal edges of these (pieces of) γ-triangles. The number of such vertices is bounded by $O(\lambda_{t+2}(|T_{\text{large}}| + |T_{\text{tiny}}|/\gamma))$. □

Now let R_{top} denote the part of σ_{out} above the line through the top edge of σ_{in}; see Fig. 5(i). The number of large-tiny vertices inside R_{top} can be counted by applying Lemma 13 with $\sigma = \sigma_{\text{out}}$, and $R = R_{\text{top}}$, and $T_{\text{large}} = L$, and $T_{\text{tiny}} = S^-$. The number of large-tiny vertices inside R_{right}, the part of σ_{out} to the right of the line through the right edge of σ_{in}, can be counted similarly. We get the following corollary.

LEMMA 14. *The number of large-tiny vertices inside $R_{\text{top}} \cup R_{\text{right}}$ is $O(\lambda_{t+2}(|L| + (1/\gamma) \cdot |S^-|))$.*

It remains to bound the number of large-tiny vertices inside the L-shaped region A, defined as $A := region(\nu) \setminus (R_{\text{top}} \cup R_{\text{right}})$ and depicted in Fig. 5(ii).

LEMMA 15. *The number of large-tiny vertices inside A is $O((1/\gamma^6) \cdot \lambda_{t+2}(|L| + |S^-|))$.*

PROOF. We partition L into several subsets, and we analyze the large-tiny vertices inside A induced by each subset separately. The partitioning is based on which vertices of the γ-triangles lie inside σ_{in}; see Fig. 5(ii).

L_1: the set of large γ-triangles that do not have a vertex in σ_{in}. These γ-triangles do not have a vertex in σ_{out}. Hence, we can apply Lemma 13 with $\sigma = R = \sigma_{\text{out}}$, and $T_{\text{large}} = L_1$, and $T_{\text{tiny}} = S^-$ to conclude that the number of large-tiny vertices they induce inside σ_{out} is $O(\lambda_{t+2}(|L_1| + |S^-|/\gamma))$. Trivially, this also bounds the number of vertices they induce inside A.

L_2: the set of large γ-triangles that have their bottom-left vertex inside σ_{in}. These γ-triangles do not intersect A, so we need not take them into account.

L_3: the set of large γ-triangles that have their right vertex in σ_{in}. Clearly the intersection of any γ-triangle in L_3 with A is confined to the rectangular region lying to the left of σ_{in}; see Fig. 5(iii), where this region is shown in grey. We partition this region into squares of the same size as σ_{in}. Let $\sigma_1, \sigma_2, \ldots$ denote these squares, numbered from right to left. Note that each σ_i is a canonical square.

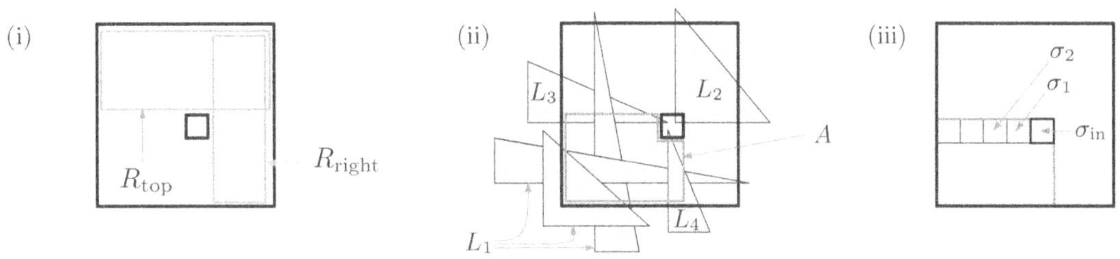

Figure 5: (i) The rectangles $R_{\rm top}$ and $R_{\rm right}$ (shown slightly smaller than their actual sizes). (ii) Different types of large γ-triangles. (iii) Partitioning the region left of $\sigma_{\rm in}$ into squares.

First we consider the squares σ_i with $i \leqslant \lceil \frac{1}{\gamma\pi} \rceil$. Let σ_i be such a square. For all the γ-triangles $\Delta_{\rm tiny}$ intersecting σ_i such that $size(\Delta_{\rm tiny}) \geqslant size(\sigma_i)/32$, we can apply Lemma 7 to conclude that they generate at most $O((1/\gamma^5) \cdot \lambda_{t+2}(|L| + |S^-|))$ large-tiny union vertices with L_3. (Note that the γ-triangles from L_3 have size at least $size(\sigma_i)$.) For the γ-triangles $\Delta_{\rm tiny}$ intersecting σ_i such that $size(\Delta_{\rm tiny}) < size(\sigma_i)/32$, we can apply Lemma 13 with $\sigma = R = \sigma_i$, and $T_{\rm large} = L_3$, and $T_{\rm tiny} = S^-$ to conclude that the number of large-tiny vertices for this case is $O(\lambda_{t+2}(|L_3| + (1/\gamma) \cdot |S^-|)$. Thus, the number of large-tiny vertices over the cells σ_i with $i \leqslant \lceil \frac{1}{\gamma\pi} \rceil$ is $O((1/\gamma^6) \cdot \lambda_{t+2}(|L_3| + |S^-|))$ in total.

It remains to deal with the squares σ_i with $i > \lceil \frac{1}{\gamma\pi} \rceil$, if any such squares exist. Let B be the union of these squares. Observe that for any γ-triangle $\Delta_{\rm large} \in L_3$, the distance between its rightmost vertex and the right boundary edge of B is at least $\lceil \frac{1}{\gamma\pi} \rceil \cdot size(\sigma_{\rm in})$. It then follows from Lemma 4(ii) that $\Delta_{\rm large}$ contains the top-right vertex of B. This implies that the intersection of $\Delta_{\rm large}$ with B is a rectangle. In fact, the intersection of $\mathcal{U}(L_3)$ with B is a rectangle and so each tiny γ-triangle generates at most one union vertex with $\mathcal{U}(L_3)$ inside B.

Overall, the number of large-tiny vertices involving L_3 is thus $O((1/\gamma^6) \cdot \lambda_{t+2}(|L_3| + |S^-|))$.

L_4: the set of large γ-triangles that have their top-left vertex in $\sigma_{\rm in}$. Symmetric to L_3. □

Putting everything together we obtain our final result.

THEOREM 16. *The union complexity of any set F of n locally γ-fat objects of constant complexity is $O((1/\gamma^8) \cdot \lambda_{t+2}(n) \log n)$, where t is the maximum number of intersections between any two boundary curves of the objects in F.*

PROOF. First consider F^*, the set of γ-triangles with the ignorable γ-triangles removed. Lemma 8(i) implies that to bound $|\mathcal{U}(F^*)|$, it suffices to count the large-large and large-small vertices at each node ν in $\mathcal{T}$. By Lemma 11 the number of large-large vertices at ν is $O((1/\gamma) \cdot \lambda_{t+2}(|F^*(\nu)|)$ and by Lemmas 12, 14, and 15 the number of large-small vertices is $O((1/\gamma^6) \cdot \lambda_{t+2}(|F^*(\nu)|)$. Using Lemma 8(ii), we get that $|\mathcal{U}(F^*)|$ is bounded by

$$\sum_{\nu \in \mathcal{T}} O\left((1/\gamma^6) \cdot \lambda_{t+2}(|F^*(\nu)|)\right) = O\left((1/\gamma^6) \cdot \lambda_{t+2}(n) \log n\right).$$

As argued in Section 3.3, this also gives an upper bound on $|\mathcal{U}(F)|$, the union-complexity of a set of n γ-triangles. Using Lemma 3 we obtain our final result. □

4. CONCLUSION

We have shown that the union complexity of n locally fat objects is $O(\lambda_{t+2}(n) \log n)$, a logarithmic factor away from the conjectured bound. The logarithmic factor is inherent to our hierarchical counting scheme; to improve the bound, a more direct approach is needed. We believe the next step should perhaps be to return to the case of fat triangles, and try to prove a tight bound there. Whether any of the techniques or insights from the present paper will be of any help in this undertaking remains to be seen.

5. REFERENCES

[1] H. Alt, R. Fleischer, M. Kaufmann, K. Mehlhorn, S. Näher, S. Schirra and C. Uhrig. Approximate motion planning and the complexity of the boundary of the union of simple geometric figures. *Algorithmica* 8:391–406 (1992).

[2] P.K. Agarwal, J. Pach and M. Sharir. State of the union (of geometric objects): A Review. In: J. Goodman, J. Pach, and R. Pollack (eds.), *Computational Geometry: Twenty Years Later*, American Mathematical Society, pages 9–48, 2008.

[3] S. Arora. Polynomial time approximation schemes for Euclidean traveling salesman and other geometric problems. *J. ACM* 45: 753–782 (1998).

[4] M. de Berg. Improved bounds for the union complexity of fat objects. *Discr. Comput. Geom.* 20:127–140 (2008).

[5] A. Efrat. The complexity of the union of (α, β)-covered objects. *SIAM J. Comput.* 34:775–787 (2005).

[6] A. Efrat, G. Rote and M. Sharir. On the union of fat wedges and separating a collection of segments by a line. *Comput. Geom. Theory Appl.* 3: 277–288 (1993).

[7] A. Efrat and M. Sharir. The complexity of the union of fat objects in the plane. In *Proc. 13th ACM Symp. Comput. Geom.*, pages 104–112, 1997.

[8] A. Efrat and M. Katz. On the union of κ-curved objects. In *Proc. 14th ACM Symp. Comput. Geom.*, pages 206–213, 1998.

[9] D. Eppstein, M.T. Goodrich, and J.Z. Sun. Skip quadtrees: Dynamic data structures for multidimensional point sets. *Int. J. Comput. Geom. Appl.* 18:131–160 (2008).

[10] E. Ezra and M. Sharir. Almost tight bound for the union of fat tetrahedra in three dimensions. In *Proc. 48th IEEE Symp. Found. Comput. Sci.*, pages 525–535, 2007.

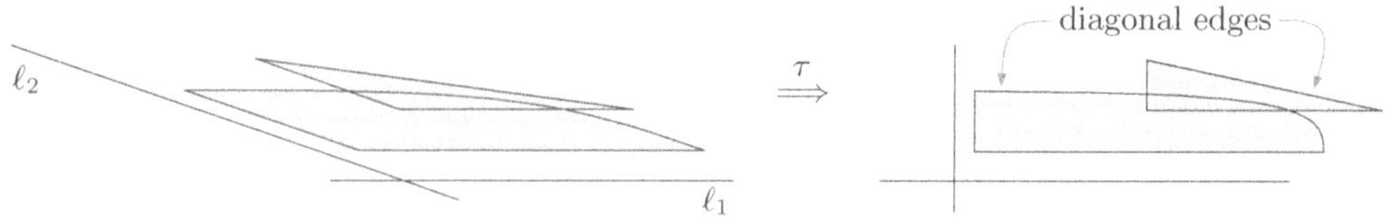

Figure 6: The shear transformation.

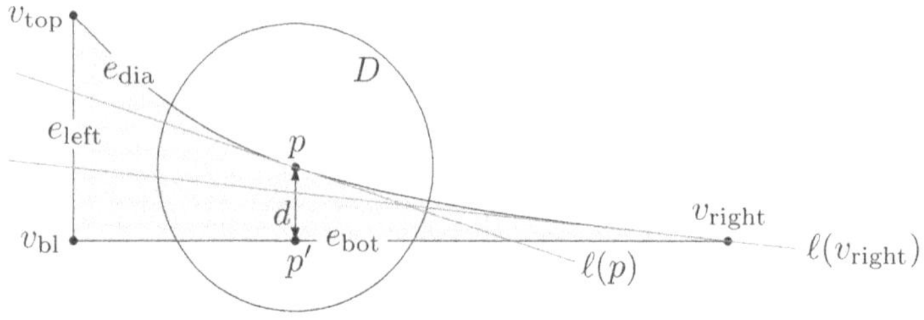

Figure 7: The case where $\tau(\Delta)$ is non-convex.

[11] K. Kedem, R. Livne, J. Pach, and M. Sharir. On the union of Jordan regions and collision-free translational motion amidst polygonal obstacles in the plane. *Discr. Comput. Geom.* 1:59–71 (1986).

[12] J. Matoušek, J. Pach, M. Sharir, S. Sifrony, and E. Welzl. Fat triangles determine linearly many holes. *SIAM J. Comput.* 23:154-169 (1994).

[13] J. Pach and G. Tardos. On the boundary complexity of the union of fat triangles. *SIAM J. Comput.* 31: 1745–1760 (2002).

[14] M. Sharir and P.K. Agarwal. *Davenport-Schinzel sequences and their geometric applications.* Cambridge University Press, 1995.

[15] A.F. van der Stappen. *Motion planning amidst fat obstacles.* Ph.D. thesis, Utrecht University, 1994.

[16] A.F. van der Stappen, D. Halperin, and M.H. Overmars. The complexity of the free space for a robot moving amidst fat obstacles. *Comput. Geom. Theory Appl.* 3:353–373 (1993).

Appendix A: Proof of Lemma 3

LEMMA 3. *Let $U_\gamma(n)$ denote the maximum union complexity of any set of n γ-triangles. Then the maximum union complexity of any set of n locally γ-fat objects is $O((1/\gamma^2) \cdot U_\gamma(n/\gamma^2))$.*

PROOF. As remarked in the main text, Lemma 3 follows from a corresponding lemma—below stated as Lemma A.1—for so-called quasi-triangles [4]. Next we prove that the result for quasi-triangles indeed implies Lemma 3.

A *quasi-triangle* is an object Δ bounded by two straight edges and one smooth Jordan arc without inflection points. Now consider a set Q of quasi-triangles with the following properties. Let γ^* be a parameter.

(a) There are two fixed lines, ℓ_1 and ℓ_2, such that each quasi-triangle in Q has an edge parallel to ℓ_1 and an edge parallel to ℓ_2 and they all lie to the same side of these edges. Moreover, the internal angle between these edges is between $\pi - 7\gamma^*$ and $\pi - \gamma^*$.

(b) The tangent line at any point of the Jordan arc makes an angle of at least γ^* with the edges of Δ, and the tangent direction along σ does not vary by more than γ^*. Note that this property implies that any line parallel to one of the two edges of a quasi-triangle from Q intersects its Jordan arc at most once.

LEMMA A.1 [4]. *Let $U_\gamma(n)$ denote the maximum union complexity of any set Q of n quasi-triangles satisfying properties (a) and (b) with $\gamma^* = \gamma\pi/20$. Then the maximum union complexity of a set of locally γ-fat objects is $O((1/\gamma^2) \cdot U_\gamma(n/\gamma^2))$.*

Now consider a set Q of quasi-triangles satisfying properties (a) and (b) with $\gamma^* = \gamma\pi/20$. Such quasi-triangles are γ'-fat for some $\gamma' = \Omega(\gamma)$ [4]. We assume without loss of generality that the line ℓ_1 is parallel to the x-axis, and that the quasi-triangles lie above their horizontal edge. Assume further that the quasi-triangles lie to the right of the edge parallel to ℓ_2. We now apply a shear transformation τ that makes ℓ_2 vertical—see Fig. 6. Clearly, this transformation does not change the union complexity. By Lemma A.1, to prove Lemma 3 it is now sufficient to show that the shear transformation results in a set of $\overline{\gamma}$-triangles, for some $\overline{\gamma} = \Omega(\gamma)$.

Let Δ be a quasi-triangle satisfying properties (a) and (b). Property (b) immediately implies that the diagonal edge of $\tau(\Delta)$ is xy-monotone. Moreover, the diagonal edge of $\tau(\Delta)$ does not have inflection points, because the same is true for quasi-triangles. It remains to show that $\tau(\Delta)$ is locally fat. More precisely, we need to show that $\tau(\Delta)$ is locally $\overline{\gamma}$-fat, for some $\overline{\gamma} = \Omega(\gamma)$.

Let v_{top}, v_{right} and v_{bl} be the top, right, and bottom left vertex of Δ, respectively, and let e_{left}, e_{bot}, and e_{dia} denote the left, bottom, and diagonal edge of Δ—see Fig. 7.

First assume Δ is convex—note that Δ is convex if and only $\tau(\Delta)$ is convex. We will use the fact [15] that the fatness of a convex object o is equal to $area(o)/(\pi \cdot diam(o)^2)$. Now we observe that v_{top} and v_{right} are opposite corners of the bounding box of Δ, before and after the transformation. Hence, $v_{\text{top}}v_{\text{right}}$ determines the diameters Δ and $\tau(\Delta)$. Since the angle at v_{bl} is greater than $\pi/2$ before the transformation and equal to $\pi/2$ after the transformation, it follows that $diam(\tau(\Delta)) < diam(\Delta)$. Since the area is not

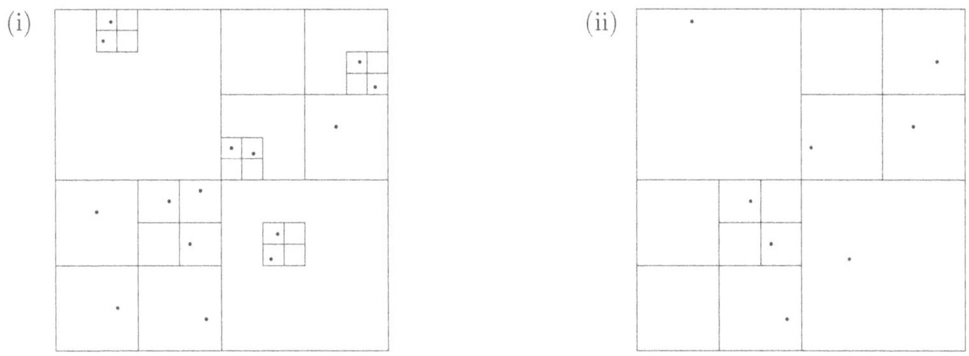

Figure 8: (i) A compressed-quadtree subdivision for a set V of points. (ii) A compressed-quadtree subdivision for a subset of V.

changed by the transformation we can conclude that $\tau(\Delta)$ is fatter than Δ; in particular, $\tau(\Delta)$ is $\Omega(\gamma)$-fat.

Now assume that Δ and, hence, $\tau(\Delta)$, is not convex. Let D be a disk with center p, such that $p \in \tau(\Delta)$ and D does not fully contain $\tau(\Delta)$ in its interior—see Fig. 7. We may assume that p lies on the boundary of $\tau(\Delta)$, because the so-called boundary fatness of an object (the fatness if we restrict our attention to disks whose center lies on the boundary of the object) is within a constant factor of the normal fatness [17]. We assume $p \in e_{\text{dia}}$; the cases where $p \in e_{\text{left}}$ or $p \in e_{\text{bot}}$ are easier. Assume without loss of generality that $length(e_{\text{bot}}) \geqslant length(e_{\text{left}})$.

Let $\ell(v_{\text{right}})$ be the line tangent to e_{dia} at v_{right}. In Δ the angle of $\ell(v_{\text{right}})$ with e_{bot} is at least γ^*, and this is also true in $\tau(\Delta)$; in fact, the shear transformation only increases this angle. Similarly we can argue that the angles that $\ell(p)$, the tangent line at p, makes with e_{bot} and e_{left} are at least γ^*. Finally, let $d := dist(p, e_{\text{bot}})$. We distinguish two cases.

- If $radius(D) \leqslant 2d$, then we argue as follows. Let t be the triangle bounded by $\ell(p)$, e_{left}, and e_{bot}. The triangle t is $\Omega(\gamma)$-fat. If D does not completely contain t in its interior, then this implies that $area(D \cap t) = \Omega(\gamma \cdot area(D))$. Since $t \subset \tau(\Delta)$, this shows that $area(D \cap \tau(\Delta)) = \Omega(\gamma \cdot area(D))$, as required. If $t \subset D$ we also get $area(D \cap \tau(\Delta)) = \Omega(\gamma \cdot area(D))$, because $radius(D) \leqslant 2d$ implies that D cannot be much larger than t.

- If $radius(D) > 2d$, then we can argue as follows. Let p' be the point on e_{bot} closest to p. Let t' be the triangle bounded by $\ell(v_{\text{right}})$, e_{left}, and e_{bot}. The triangle t' is $\Omega(\gamma)$-fat. Let D' be the disk centered at p' of radius $radius(D) - d$. Note that $D' \subset D$ and $radius(D') \geqslant radius(D)/2$. Since t' is $\Omega(\gamma)$-fat and D' cannot be much larger than t', we can argue that $area(D \cap t') = \Omega(\gamma \cdot area(D))$ which is sufficient since $t' \subset \tau(\Delta)$.

We conclude that $\tau(\Delta)$ is $\overline{\gamma}$-fat for some $\overline{\gamma} = \Omega(\gamma)$, which proves Lemma 3. □

Appendix B: The skip quadtree

For an integer s, let G_s denote the grid whose cells have size $2^{-s} \times 2^{-s}$ and for which the origin O is a grid point. A *canonical square* is any cell of one of the grids G_s. Let V be a set of n points contained in a canonical square σ. A *compressed-quadtree subdivision* for V inside σ is obtained by a recursive process, as follows—see also Fig. 8(i).

- If $n \leqslant 1$ then the subdivision just consists of the single square σ.
- If $n > 1$ and there are points from V in more than one quadrant of σ, then the subdivision is obtained as follows: split σ into its four quadrants $\sigma_1, \ldots, \sigma_4$ and, for each quadrant σ_i, recursively construct a compressed-quadtree subdivision for $V \cap \sigma_i$ inside σ_i.
- If $n > 1$ and all points from V lie in the same quadrant of σ, then the subdivision is defined as follows. Let σ_{in} be the smallest canonical square containing V. The subdivision is now obtained by splitting σ into a donut $\sigma \setminus \sigma_{\text{in}}$ and an inner square σ_{in}, and recursively constructing a compressed-quadtree subdivision for V inside σ_{in}.

Now consider a sequence of subsets $V_0 \subset V_1 \subset \cdots \subset V_k$, where V_0 contains a single point and $V_k = V$. Let Q_i be a compressed-quadtree subdivision for V_i. Observe that since $V_i \subset V_{i+1}$, the subdivision Q_i is a refinement of Q_i: each region in Q_i is contained in a single *parent region* in Q_{i+1}. Fig. 8(ii) illustrates this. Thus we can represent the set of subdivisions Q_i as a tree structure $\mathcal{T}$ in which the nodes at level i represent the regions in Q_i.

The *skip quadtree* introduced by Eppstein *et al.* [9] is essentially such a tree structure $\mathcal{T}$, where V_i is obtained from V_{i+1} by selecting every point in V_{i+1} with probability $\frac{1}{2}$. This way the expected depth of $\mathcal{T}$ is $O(\log n)$ and the expected degree of the nodes is $O(1)$. (Eppstein *et al.* also have a deterministic version of their skip quadtree.) Since we do not need our structure to be dynamic, we can do something simpler. First, we define an order $\prec$ on the points in V, as follows. For any two points p, q we consider the canonical square with p and q in different quadrants, and we order p and q according to the quadrants they lie in. For example, if we define

north-west quadrant $\prec$ north-east quadrant $\prec$ south-west quadrant $\prec$ south-east quadrant

then we obtain the so-called Z-order. Now we obtain V_i from V_{i+1} by deleting every second point in $\prec$-order. Obviously the depth of the resulting tree $\mathcal{T}$, which we still call a skip quadtree for convenience, is $O(\log n)$. Moreover, the degree of any node in the tree is at most five.

On the Complexity of Sets of Free Lines and Line Segments Among Balls in Three Dimensions

Marc Glisse
INRIA Saclay Île de France
Orsay, France
marc.glisse@inria.fr

Sylvain Lazard
INRIA Nancy Grand Est, LORIA laboratory
Nancy, France
sylvain.lazard@inria.fr

ABSTRACT

We present two new fundamental lower bounds on the worst-case combinatorial complexity of sets of free lines and sets of maximal free line segments in the presence of balls in three dimensions.

We first prove that the set of maximal non-occluded line segments among n disjoint *unit* balls has complexity $\Omega(n^4)$, which matches the trivial $O(n^4)$ upper bound. This improves the trivial $\Omega(n^2)$ bound and also the $\Omega(n^3)$ lower bound for the restricted setting of arbitrary-size balls [Devillers and Ramos, 2001]. This result settles, negatively, the natural conjecture that this set of line segments, or, equivalently, the visibility complex, has smaller worst-case complexity for disjoint fat objects than for skinny triangles.

We also prove an $\Omega(n^3)$ lower bound on the complexity of the set of non-occluded lines among n balls of arbitrary radii, improving on the trivial $\Omega(n^2)$ bound. This new bound almost matches the recent $O(n^{3+\varepsilon})$ upper bound [Rubin, 2010].

Categories and Subject Descriptors

F.2.2 [**Theory of Computation**]: Analysis of Algorithms and Problem Complexity—*Geometrical problems and computations*

General Terms

Theory

Keywords

3D visibility, visibility complex, free lines, free segments, balls

1. INTRODUCTION

Given a set of objects in $\mathbb{R}^3$, a line is said to be *free* if it does not intersect the interior of any object (we assume here that all objects have a non-empty interior). A *maximal free line segment* is a (possibly infinite) segment that does not intersect the interior of any object and is not contained in any other segment satisfying the same property. We are interested here in the worst-case combinatorial complexity of sets of free lines, and sets of maximal free line segments.

Free lines and line segments play an important role in several topics in computational and combinatorial geometry. In particular, they play a central role in 3D visibility problems, such as the problem of determining the occlusion between two objects in a three-dimensional scene. In many applications, visibility computations are well-known to account for a significant portion of the total computation cost. Consequently, a large body of research is devoted to speeding up visibility computations through the use of data structures (see [14] for a survey). One such structure, the visibility complex [15, 23], encodes visibility relations by, roughly speaking, partitioning the set of maximal free line segments into connected components of segments tangent to the same set of objects. The vertices of this structure correspond, generically, to the maximal free line segments that are tangent to four objects in the scene, and the total number of faces, from dimension zero to four, is exactly the combinatorial complexity of the space of maximal free line segments. The space of free lines in the presence of balls is also closely related, as noted by Agarwal et al. [1], to motion planning of a line among balls, or, equivalently, of a cylindrical robot (of infinite length) moving among points or balls. This is also related to computing largest empty cylinders among points in three dimensions, ray shooting, and other problems in geometric optimization.

Previous work.

For scenes where the objects are n triangles, the worst-case complexity of the space of free lines (or lines, for short) or maximal free line segments (or segments, for short) can easily be seen to be $\Theta(n^4)$ [8]. When the triangles form a terrain, the same bound of $\Theta(n^4)$ holds for segments [9] and a near-cubic lower bound was proved for lines by Halperin and Sharir [17] and Pellegrini [22]. De Berg et al. [10] showed an $\Omega(n^3)$ lower bound and an almost matching $O(n^2\lambda_4(n))$ upper bound[1] on the complexity of the set of free lines among n disjoint homothetic polytopes (*i.e.*, convex polyhedra) of constant complexity. The lower bound of $\Omega(n^3)$ also applies to the set of free segments, because any lower bound on the

[1]Recall that $\lambda_4(n)$ denotes an almost linear function equal to the maximum length of an $(n, 4)$-Davenport-Schinzel sequence [3].

	Free lines		Free line segments	
Triangles	$\Theta(n^4)$		$\Theta(n^4)$	
Polyhedral terrain	$\Omega(n^3 2^{c\sqrt{\log n}})$	$O(n^4)$	$\Theta(n^4)$	
k disjoint homoth. polytopes	$\Omega(k^3)$	$O(k^2\lambda_4(k))$	$\Omega(k^3)$	$O(k^4)$
k polytopes of total size n	$\Omega(n^2 + nk^3)$	$O(n^2k^2)$	$\Theta(n^2k^2)$	
Unit balls	$\Omega(n^2)$	$O(n^{3+\varepsilon})$	$\mathbf{\Theta(n^4)}$	
Arbitrary balls	$\mathbf{\Omega(n^3)}$	$O(n^{3+\varepsilon})$	$\mathbf{\Theta(n^4)}$	

Table 1: Known bounds on the worst-case combinatorial complexity of sets of free lines and maximal free line segments (results presented in this paper are shown in bold).

complexity of the set of free lines trivially holds for segments as well.

When the triangles are organized into k polytopes of total complexity n, with $k \ll n$, better bounds can be obtained. For the case of disjoint polytopes in general position, Efrat et al. [16] proved a worst-case bound of $O(n^2k^2)$ on the complexity of the set of free segments. When the k polytopes may intersect, Brönnimann et al. [5] proved, independently, the tight bound of $\Theta(n^2k^2)$; their lower bound holds for disjoint polytopes, and their upper bound extends to polytopes in degenerate configurations. Any upper bound on the complexity of the set of segments trivially holds for lines as well. Thus, for free lines among k polytopes of total complexity n, the upper bound of $O(n^2k^2)$ holds. However, the best known lower bound is $\Omega(n^2 + nk^3)$, in which $\Omega(n^2)$ follows from the bound of $\Omega(n^2k^2)$ on maximal free line segments for $k = 4$, and $\Omega(nk^3)$ can be obtained by slightly modifying the lower-bound construction [12](Th.9) proving that the umbra cast on a plane by one segment light source in the presence of k disjoint polytopes of total complexity n can have $\Omega(nk^2)$ connected components (one simply has to consider k perturbed copies of the segment light source).

Much less is known for curved objects. For n *unit* balls, Agarwal et al. [1] proved an upper bound of $O(n^{3+\varepsilon})$, for any $\varepsilon > 0$, on the complexity of the space of free lines. Rubin [24] recently extended this result to balls of *arbitrary* radii. Devillers et al. [13] showed a simple bound of $\Omega(n^2)$ on the number of vertices of this free space (note that a trivial $\Omega(n^2)$ bound on the complexity of the whole space is obtained by considering sparsely distributed balls on two parallel planes). For n balls of *arbitrary* radii, Devillers and Ramos (personal communication 2001, see also [13]) showed an $\Omega(n^3)$ lower bound on the complexity of the set of free line segments and the trivial upper bound of $O(n^4)$ holds.

Our results.

Our main contribution is a tight worst-case bound of $\Theta(n^4)$ on the space of maximal free line segments among unit balls, or, equivalently, on the visibility complex of unit balls. This bound improves the trivial bound of $\Omega(n^2)$ for unit balls and also the $\Omega(n^3)$ lower bound for balls of arbitrary radii. This result is particularly surprising because it was natural to conjecture that the visibility complex of fat objects of similar size had a lower worst-case complexity than that for thin triangles. Our result settles negatively this conjecture, and shows exactly the opposite, that is, that fatness and similarity, alone, do not reduce the worst-case complexity of that structure.

Our second result is a worst-case lower bound of $\Omega(n^3)$ on the complexity of the space of free lines among balls of arbitrary radii. This bound improves the trivial $\Omega(n^2)$ bound and almost matches the $O(n^{3+\varepsilon})$ upper bound recently proved by Rubin [24].

The complexity results discussed so far are summarized in Table 1.

Related work.

The complexity of the space of maximal free line segments has also been studied in a random setting. Devillers et al. [13] proved that, in the presence of uniformly distributed unit balls, this structure has complexity $\Theta(n)$.

Related literature on free lines and line segments among objects fall in various categories. One deals with characterizing sets of lines tangent to four objects, such as balls or triangles, possibly in degenerate configuration (see [4, 6, 7, 19, 20, 21]). Another related line of research focuses on sets of lines that intersect objects and, in particular, on the complexity of the space of line transversals to a set of objects. For n balls, Agarwal, et al. [2] showed an $\Omega(n^3)$ lower bound and a $O(n^{3+\varepsilon})$ upper bound. For k polytopes of total complexity n, Kaplan et al. [18] recently proved a $O(n^2k^{1+\varepsilon})$ upper bound.

Paper organization.

We prove in Section 2 the $\Omega(n^3)$ lower bound on the complexity of the space of free lines among n balls. In Section 3, we prove the bound of $\Theta(n^4)$ on the space of maximal free line segments among n unit balls.

We will describe our lower-bound constructions using a Cartesian coordinate system (x, y, z). In this coordinate system, we denote by M_x, M_y and M_z the coordinates of a point M (or also the coordinates of the center of a ball M).

2. FREE LINES TANGENT TO BALLS

We prove here the following result.

THEOREM 1. *The combinatorial complexity of the space of free lines among n disjoint balls is $\Omega(n^3)$ in the worst case.*

We prove Theorem 1 with a lower-bound construction. For convenience, our construction involves $3n + 3$ balls instead of just n, which does not affect the asymptotic complexities.

Refer to Figure 1. We define a set $\mathcal{S}$ of disjoint balls that consists of the following three subsets of $n + 1$ balls.

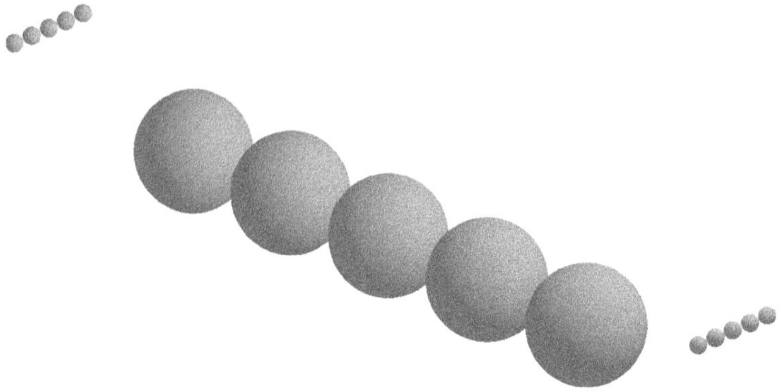

(a) 3D view.

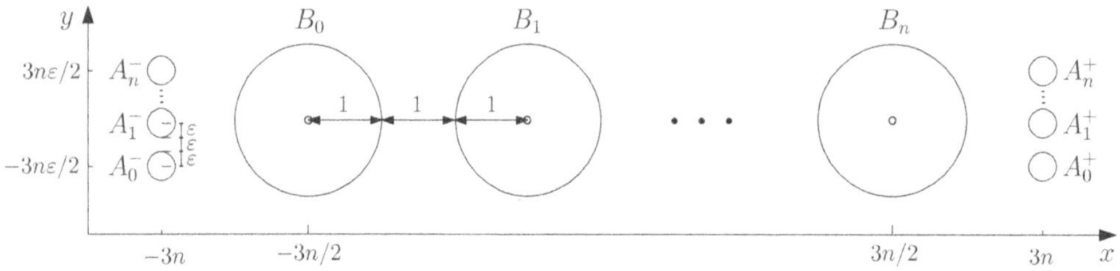

(b) Projection on the xy-plane.

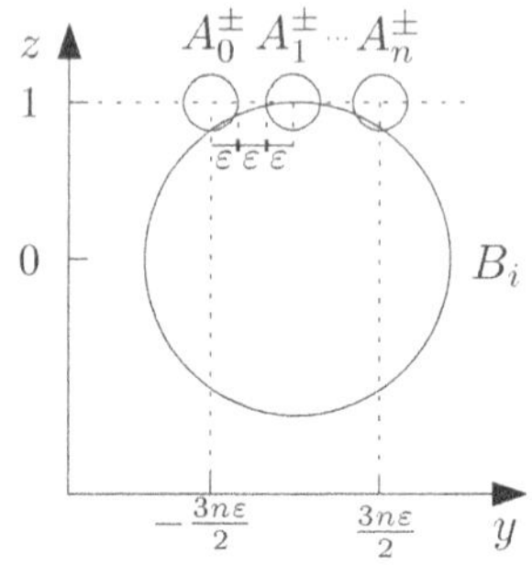

(c) Projection on the yz-plane.

Figure 1: Illustration of our construction for Theorem 1.

We consider first a set of unit balls $\mathcal{B} = \{B_0 \dots B_n\}$ whose centers are aligned along the x-axis with coordinates $(3(i - n/2), 0, 0)$. We then consider two sets of balls, $\mathcal{A}^- = \{A_0^- \dots A_n^-\}$ and $\mathcal{A}^+ = \{A_0^+ \dots A_n^+\}$, of sufficiently small radius ε and whose centers are aligned on two lines parallel to the y-axis in the plane $z = 1$. As we will see in Lemma 4, we require $\varepsilon < \frac{1}{5400n^2}$. The center of A_i^- has coordinates $(-3n, 3(i - n/2)\varepsilon, 1)$, and A_i^+ is its reflection with respect to the yz-plane.

We prove Theorem 1 by proving the following bound. A line tangent to a set of balls is said to be *isolated* if it cannot be moved continuously while remaining tangent to these balls.

PROPOSITION 2. *There are $\Omega(n^3)$ isolated free lines tangent to any four of the balls of $\mathcal{S}$.*

The idea of the proof is as follows. Consider only two consecutive balls B_i and B_{i+1}. We study the lines that are tangent to them close to their north poles (*i.e.,* their points with maximum z-coordinate). These lines are almost in the horizontal plane $z = 1$. Now, in this plane, the balls in $\mathcal{A}^-$ and $\mathcal{A}^+$ form two sets of gates which decompose the set of free lines in $\Omega(n^2)$ connected components defined by the gates the line goes through. On the boundary of each such component, there are lines tangent to one ball of $\mathcal{A}^-$ and one of $\mathcal{A}^+$. There are thus $\Omega(n^2)$ free lines tangent to one ball of $\mathcal{A}^-$, one of $\mathcal{A}^+$, and two consecutive balls of $\mathcal{B}$. Since this can be done for any two consecutive balls of $\mathcal{B}$, there are $\Omega(n^3)$ free lines tangent to four balls. Moreover, since the centers of these balls are not aligned, these tangents are isolated [4].

We now give a formal proof of Proposition 2. The first step of the proof is to prove the following technical lemma which formalizes the fact that the considered tangent lines to two consecutive balls in $\mathcal{B}$ lie *almost* in the horizontal plane through their north poles.

Let $\tilde{B}_0$ and $\tilde{B}_1$ be two unit balls centered at $(0, 0, 0)$ and $(3, 0, 0)$ and let L be a line tangent to $\tilde{B}_0$ and $\tilde{B}_1$ respectively at $M_0 = (x_0, y_0, z_0)$ and $M_1 = (x_1, y_1, z_1)$ in their northern hemispheres (that is, such that z_0 and z_1 are positive). Lemma 3 states, roughly speaking, that, as the y-coordinates of M_0 and M_1 go to 0, the z-coordinates converge *quadratically* to 1.

LEMMA 3. *If $|y_0|$ and $|y_1|$ are smaller than some constant $m < 1/25$ and $|y_1 - y_0|$ is smaller than some constant α, then z_0 and z_1 are larger than $1 - 100m^2$ and $|z_1 - z_0|$ is smaller than $110m\alpha$.*

PROOF. We first argue that the result is intuitively clear by showing that it would be straightforward if, instead of balls, we had discs parallel to the yz-plane. Writing that M_i is on $\tilde{B}_i$ gives $x_0^2 + y_0^2 + z_0^2 = 1$ and $(x_1 - 3)^2 + y_1^2 + z_1^2 = 1$. Considering discs instead of balls (that is $x_0 = 0$ and $x_1 = 3$) gives $|z_i| = \sqrt{1 - y_i^2} \geqslant \sqrt{1 - m^2} \geqslant 1 - m^2 > 1 - 100m^2$. Furthermore, the difference of the two equations gives $|z_1 - z_0| = \frac{|y_1 + y_0||y_1 - y_0|}{|z_1 + z_0|} < \frac{2m \cdot \alpha}{2(1 - m^2)}$ which is less that $2m\alpha$ because $\frac{1}{2(1-m^2)} < 1$ since $m < 1/25$.

Since the balls are not discs, we need a few more steps. Consider the vertical plane Π that contains L and refer to

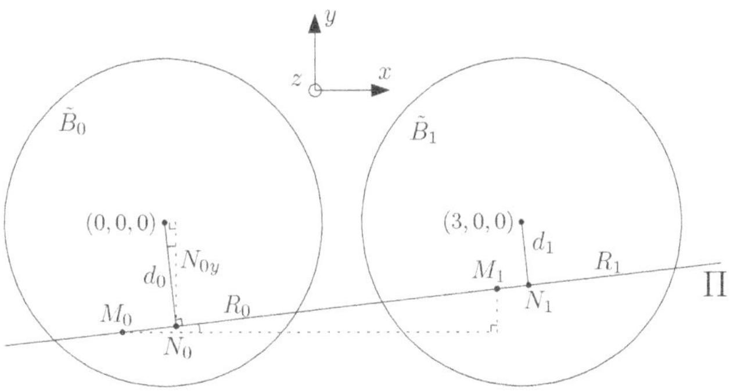

Figure 2: For the proof of Lemma 3: balls $\tilde{B}_0$ and $\tilde{B}_1$ viewed from above.

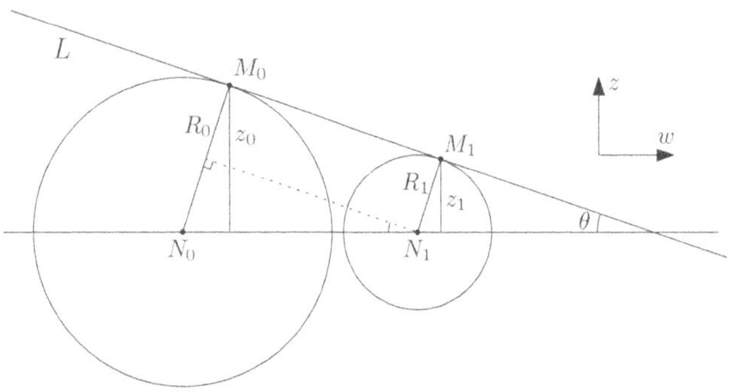

Figure 3: For the proof of Lemma 3: intersection of balls $\tilde{B}_0$ with plane Π.

Figure 2. Plane Π cuts the two spheres in two circles of centers N_0 and N_1 and radii R_0 and R_1. Let d_i denote the signed distance from the center of $\tilde{B}_i$ to Π (that is to N_i) such that d_i has the same sign as N_{iy}.

First, we prove that $|N_{0y}|$ and $|N_{1y}|$ are smaller than or equal to $5m$. In projection on the xy-plane, since M_0 and M_1 are on L, the absolute value of the slope of the projection of L is $\frac{|y_1-y_0|}{|x_1-x_0|} \leqslant 2m$ since $|y_1 - y_0| \leqslant 2m$ and $|x_1 - x_0| \geqslant 1$. Now, N_i is in Π so its projection on the xy-plane is on the projection of L. Since $|N_{ix} - x_i| \leqslant 2$ (M_i and N_i are in the same unit ball), $|N_{iy} - y_i| \leqslant 2 \cdot 2m$ and thus $|N_{iy}| \leqslant |y_i| + 4m \leqslant 5m$.

Second, we prove that $|d_i| \leqslant 10m$ and $|d_1 - d_0| < 10\alpha$. Notice that, since the two angles shown on Figure 2 are equal, they have the same cosine, that is

$$N_{iy}/d_i = (x_1 - x_0)/\sqrt{(x_1 - x_0)^2 + (y_1 - y_0)^2}.$$

Since $x_1 - x_0 \geqslant 1 > 0$ and $m < 1/25$, the right-hand expression can be rewritten as

$$\frac{1}{\sqrt{1 + \left(\frac{y_1-y_0}{x_1-x_0}\right)^2}} \geqslant \frac{1}{\sqrt{1+4m^2}} > \frac{1}{2}.$$

We thus have $d_i = \chi N_{iy}$ with $0 < \chi < 2$. This implies that $|d_i| < 2|N_{iy}| \leqslant 10m$ and $|d_1 - d_0| = \chi|N_{1y} - N_{0y}| < 2|N_{1y} - N_{0y}|$. Once again, the projections of M_0, M_1, N_0 and N_1 on the xy-plane are aligned, so the slope of the projection of L is $(N_{1y} - N_{0y})/(N_{1x} - N_{0x}) = (y_1 - y_0)/(x_1 - x_0)$. Since M_i and N_i lie in ball $\tilde{B}_i$, $|N_{1x} - N_{0x}| \leqslant 5$ and $|x_1 - x_0| > 1$ and, since $|y_1 - y_0| < \alpha$, we have $|N_{1y} - N_{0y}| < 5\alpha$. Hence $|d_1 - d_0| < 10\alpha$.

Third, we prove that $R_i \geqslant \sqrt{1-(10m)^2}$ and $|R_1 - R_0| \leqslant 110m\alpha$. The radii of the intersection circles satisfy $d_i^2 + R_i^2 = 1$. This implies that $R_i \geqslant \sqrt{1-(10m)^2}$. Also, $(R_1 - R_0)(R_1 + R_0) = -(d_1 - d_0)(d_1 + d_0)$, so

$$|R_1 - R_0| \leqslant 10\alpha \frac{20m}{2\sqrt{1-(10m)^2}} < 110m\alpha$$

because $1/\sqrt{1-(10m)^2} < 1.1$ since $m < 1/25$.

We now work in the plane Π, using a Cartesian coordinate system (w, z) (see Figure 3). Let θ be the (unsigned) angle between L and the w-axis. We have $z_i = R_i \cos\theta$. Therefore, $z_1 - z_0 = (R_1 - R_0)\cos\theta$ and $|z_1 - z_0| \leqslant |R_1 - R_0| < 110m\alpha$, which is the second inequality of the lemma.

Consider now the line in Π parallel to L through N_1 if $R_1 \leqslant R_0$ and through N_0 otherwise, as shown on Figure 3. Remember that the distance between N_0 and N_1 is at least 1 and note that we can assume without loss of generality that $\alpha \leqslant 2m$ since $|y_1 - y_0| < 2m$ and when $\alpha \geqslant 2m$, Lemma 3 is a trivial consequence of the case $\alpha = 2m$. We have that $\sin\theta = |R_1 - R_0|/||N_1 - N_0|| < 110m\alpha \leqslant 220m^2 < 10m$. Hence $\cos\theta > \sqrt{1-(10m)^2}$. We have already proved that $R_i \geqslant \sqrt{1-(10m)^2}$. Therefore $z_i = R_i\cos\theta > 1 - 100m^2$ which concludes the proof. □

We now prove that, roughly speaking, a line tangent to two consecutive balls of $\mathcal{B}$ near their north poles intersects each of the convex hulls of $\mathcal{A}^-$ and of $\mathcal{A}^+$ and thus that the balls of $\mathcal{A}^\pm$ play the role of gates as discussed earlier.

Let L be a line tangent to B_i and B_{i+1} ($0 \leqslant i \leqslant n-1$) at some points with positive z-coordinate and let L^+ and L^- be the points of intersection of L with the planes $x = 3n$ and $x = -3n$, respectively (see Figure 4).

LEMMA 4. *If $|L_y^+|$ and $|L_y^-|$ are smaller than $3n\varepsilon/2$ with $\varepsilon < \frac{1}{5400n^2}$, then $|L_z^+ - 1|$ and $|L_z^- - 1|$ are smaller than $\varepsilon/2$.*

PROOF. Let P and Q denote the tangency points of L on B_i and B_{i+1} (refer to Figure 4). L^-, P, Q and L^+ are aligned in this order on L, and $|L_y^+|$ and $|L_y^-|$ are both smaller than $3n\varepsilon/2$, so $|P_y|$ and $|Q_y|$ are smaller than $3n\varepsilon/2$. Furthermore, the slope of the projection of L in the xy-plane is $\frac{L_y^+ - L_y^-}{L_x^+ - L_x^-} = \frac{Q_y - P_y}{Q_x - P_x}$ and, by hypothesis, $|L_y^+ - L_y^-| \leqslant 3n\varepsilon$, $L_x^+ - L_x^- = 6n$ and $|Q_x - P_x| \leqslant 5$, so $|Q_y - P_y| \leqslant 5\varepsilon/2$. We can now apply Lemma 3 because $|P_y|$ and $|Q_y|$ are both smaller than $m = 3n\varepsilon/2$ which is smaller than $1/25$ since $\varepsilon < 1/5400n^2$ and $|Q_y - P_y| \leqslant 5\varepsilon/2$. We thus get $|Q_z - P_z| < 110\frac{3n\varepsilon}{2}\frac{5\varepsilon}{2} = 110\frac{15}{4}n\varepsilon^2$ and $Q_z > 1 - 100(\frac{3n\varepsilon}{2})^2$. Moreover, since $Q_z \leqslant 1$, we have $|Q_z - 1| < 100(\frac{3n\varepsilon}{2})^2$.

L^-, P, Q and L^+ are still aligned on L and we now consider the slope of the projection of L on the xz-plane: $\frac{L_z^+ - Q_z}{L_x^+ - Q_x} = \frac{Q_z - P_z}{Q_x - P_x}$. By construction, $|L_x^+ - Q_x| < 6n$ and $Q_x - P_x \geqslant 1$ so

$$|L_z^+ - 1| - |Q_z - 1| \leqslant |L_z^+ - Q_z| < 6n|Q_z - P_z| < 6 \cdot 110\frac{15}{4}n^2\varepsilon^2.$$

Moreover, since $|Q_z - 1| < 100\frac{9}{4}n^2\varepsilon^2$ and $100\frac{9}{4} + 6 \cdot 110\frac{15}{4} = 2700$, we have $|L_z^+ - 1| < 2700n^2\varepsilon^2 < \varepsilon/2$ since $\varepsilon < \frac{1}{5400n^2}$. The same holds for $|L_z^- - 1|$. □

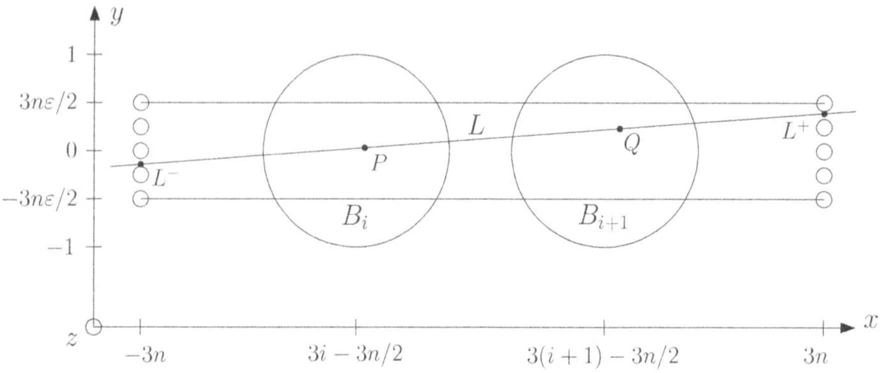

Figure 4: A line L for Lemma 4.

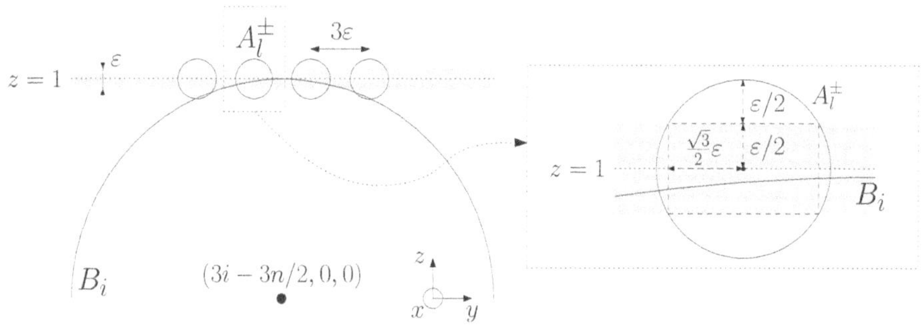

Figure 5: For the proof of Proposition 2: lines L intersect planes $x = \pm 3n$ in the shaded region.

We can now prove that there are $\Omega(n^3)$ isolated free lines tangent to any four of the balls of $\mathcal{S}$.

PROOF OF PROPOSITION 2. We prove the proposition by showing that any pair of consecutive balls B_i, B_{i+1} ($0 \leqslant i < n$) and any two balls A_j^- and A_k^+ ($j, k \in \{0, \dots, n\}$) admit at least one common tangent free line.

Notice first that any line tangent to B_i and B_{i+1} cannot intersect the interior of any ball B_j and thus can only be occluded by a ball in $\mathcal{A}^\pm$.

In the xy-plane, consider the two segments S^+ and S^- defined by $x = \pm 3n$ and $-3n\varepsilon/2 < y < 3n\varepsilon/2$ (see Figure 4); as in Lemma 4, we assume $\varepsilon < \frac{1}{5400n^2}$. Any pair of points, one on each of these two segments, defines uniquely a line L that lies in the vertical plane containing these two points and such that L is tangent to B_i and B_{i+1} at points in their northern hemispheres (at points with positive z coordinates). We parameterize these lines by the y-coordinates, u and v, of the two points on S^- and S^+, respectively, defining the line. In the following, u and v are thus restricted to the interval $[-3n\varepsilon/2, 3n\varepsilon/2]$.

Using this parameterization, we consider the set of lines $L(u,v)$ (or, for simplicity, L) represented as a square in the (u,v)-parameter space. As in the proof of Lemma 4, let $L^\pm$ denote the point of intersection of L and plane $x = \pm 3n$ (note that $u = L_y^-$ and $v = L_y^+$) and recall that the y-coordinate of the center of ball A_j^- is denoted A_{jy}^-.

We first show that there exist nonempty intervals $I_j \subset J_j$ of u such that (see Figure 6) the intervals J_j are pairwise disjoint and for all v: (i) for all $u \in I_j$, $L(u,v)$ intersects ball A_j^-, (ii) for all $u \notin J_j$, $L(u,v)$ does not intersect ball A_j^-. The same result will also hold by exchanging the role of u and v and of the A_j^- and A_j^+.

Refer to Figure 5. By Lemma 4, $|L_z^- - 1| < \varepsilon/2$. It follows that $|L_y^- - A_{jy}^-| \leqslant \frac{\sqrt{3}}{2}\varepsilon$ implies that L intersects A_j^- since the square distance between L^- and the center of A_j^- is less than or equal to $(\frac{1}{2}\varepsilon)^2 + (\frac{\sqrt{3}}{2}\varepsilon)^2 = \varepsilon^2$. Hence, any line $L(u,v)$ such that $u = L_y^-$ is in $I_j = [A_{jy}^- - \frac{\sqrt{3}}{2}\varepsilon, A_{jy}^- + \frac{\sqrt{3}}{2}\varepsilon]$ intersects ball A_j^-.

We now show that any line $L(u,v)$ that intersects A_j^- satisfies $u \in J_j = [A_{jy}^- - \frac{5}{4}\varepsilon, A_{jy}^- + \frac{5}{4}\varepsilon]$. The slope of the projection of line L onto the xy-plane is (in absolute value) $\frac{|L_y^+ - L_y^-|}{|L_x^+ - L_x^-|} \leqslant \frac{3n\varepsilon}{6n} = \frac{\varepsilon}{2}$ (see Figure 4) which is less than $\frac{1}{8}$ since $\varepsilon < \frac{1}{5400n^2}$. Thus, the y-coordinate of points on L varies by at most $\frac{\varepsilon}{4}$ in the slab $-3n - \varepsilon \leqslant x \leqslant -3n + \varepsilon$. If L intersects A_j^-, one point of L in this slab has its y-coordinate in $[A_{jy}^- - \varepsilon, A_{jy}^- + \varepsilon]$, hence $u = L_y^- \in J_j$.

We now partition the set of lines L in parameter space (u,v) as follows (see Figure 6): the dark grey region is the set of (u,v) such that u or v is in some I_j; the white region is the set of (u,v) such that neither u nor v belongs to $\bigcup_j J_j$; the light grey region is the complement of the dark grey and white regions in $[\frac{-3n\varepsilon}{2}, \frac{3n\varepsilon}{2}]^2$.

Finally, consider a line $L(u,v)$ for (u,v) in a connected component of the white region bounded by the u-strips J_j and J_{j+1} and by the v-strips J_k and J_{k+1} (the hatched region in Figure 6). By the above properties of intervals I_j and J_j, if we decrease u (resp. increase u), the line $L(u,v)$ while

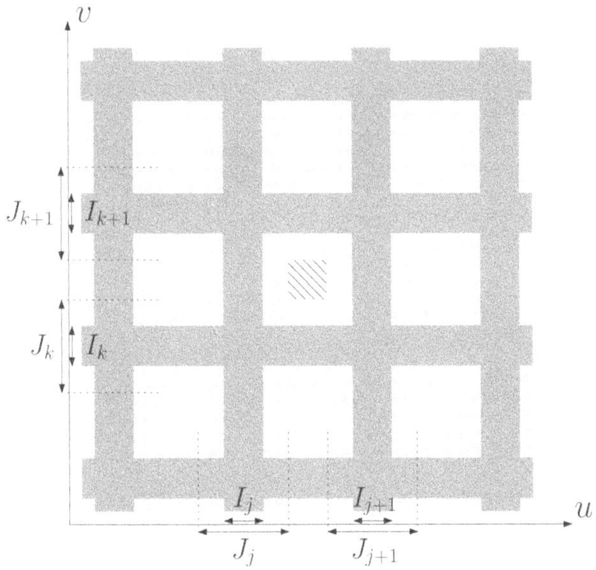

Figure 6: For the proof of Proposition 2: A line parameterized by a point (u, v) in the dark grey region intersects a ball in $\mathcal{A}^{\pm}$. If (u, v) lies in the white region, the line intersects no ball in $\mathcal{A}^{\pm}$.

remaining free becomes, at some point in the grey region, tangent to A_j^- (resp. A_{j+1}^-). Similarly, while $L(u, v)$ remains free and tangent to A_j^- or A_{j+1}^-, if we decrease (resp. increase) v (u may vary slightly in order to maintain the tangency), $L(u, v)$ becomes, at some point, tangent to A_k^+ (resp. A_{k+1}^+). In other words, in parameter space (u, v), the white cell is contained in a connected component of the set of free lines $L(u, v)$ which is bounded by lines $L(u, v)$ that are tangent to A_j^-, A_{j+1}^-, A_k^+, or A_{k+1}^+; moreover, the vertices of the boundary of the cell correspond to lines $L(u, v)$ that are tangent to A_j^- or A_{j+1}^- and to A_k^+ or A_{k+1}^+.

Hence, any two consecutive balls B_i and B_{i+1} $(0 \leqslant i < n)$ and any two balls A_j^- and A_k^+ $(j, k \in \{0, \ldots, n\})$ admit at least one common tangent free line. This concludes the proof because any four balls with nonaligned centers admit finitely many common tangents [4]. □

REMARK. Although our construction admits $\Omega(n^3)$ isolated free lines tangent to four balls, many four-tuples of balls are aligned and thus have infinitely many common tangents. Perturbing all the balls by a sufficiently small amount would easily ensure that all the four-tuples of balls admit finitely many common tangents while all the $\Omega(n^3)$ isolated free lines remain free and tangent to their respective balls.

3. FREE LINE SEGMENTS TANGENT TO UNIT BALLS

We prove here the following theorem.

THEOREM 5. *The combinatorial complexity of the space of maximal free line segments among n disjoint unit balls is $\Theta(n^4)$ in the worst case.*

First notice that the $O(n^4)$ upper bound is trivial. We prove the lower bound by giving a construction. Refer to Figure 7. We define a set $\mathcal{S}$ of disjoint balls that consists of the four subsets $\mathcal{A}^{\pm}, \mathcal{B}^{\pm}$ of n or $n+1$ balls each. We consider first a set of unit balls $\mathcal{A}^- = \{A_1^- \ldots A_n^-\}$ whose centers are almost aligned on the x-axis, except that each ball is slightly higher than the one in front of it (looking from $x = +\infty$). The center of A_i^- has coordinates $(-M - 3i, 0, i\varepsilon)$ for some large M and some small positive ε. The set $\mathcal{B}^- = \{B_0^- \ldots B_n^-\}$ consists of unit balls whose centers lie on a helix of axis the x-axis; in particular, the centers project onto the yz-plane on a circle centered at the origin and of radius slightly smaller than 2. Note that the purpose of this helix is to ensure that the balls are disjoint; if we allowed intersecting balls, we could simply place all these centers on a circle in the plane $x = -M$. The center of B_i^- has coordinates $(-M + 3i, (2 - \eta)\sin(\alpha_i), (2 - \eta)\cos(\alpha_i))$ where $\alpha_i = \alpha(-\frac{1}{2} + \frac{i}{n})$, α is a positive constant and η is a small positive constant. Finally, the sets $\mathcal{A}^+$ and $\mathcal{B}^+$ are the mirror images of $\mathcal{A}^-$ and $\mathcal{B}^-$, respectively, with respect to the yz-plane. An appropriate set of constants is: $\alpha = \frac{\pi}{4}$, $\eta = \frac{1}{160n^2}$, $\varepsilon = \frac{1}{160n^3}$ and $M = cn^3$ for a sufficiently large fixed constant c.

We prove Theorem 5 by proving the following bound on the balls of $\mathcal{S}$, where a line segment tangent to a set of balls is said to be *isolated* if it cannot be moved continuously while remaining tangent to these balls.

PROPOSITION 6. *There are $\Theta(n^4)$ isolated free line segments tangent to any four of the balls of $\mathcal{S}$.*

The idea of the lower-bound construction is as follows. Consider the affine transformation changing x into x/M which flattens the spheres into ellipsoids. When M tends to infinity, the scene changes (as it depends on M) and the transformed scene tends to two flat versions of Figure 7(b) on the planes $x = \pm 1$, facing each other. Joining the $\Theta(n^2)$ intersections on each side defines $\Theta(n^4)$ free line segments tangent to 4 of the discs. We prove that, for M sufficiently large, the free line segments tangent to 4 of the ellipsoids still exist. Moreover, each of the free line segments tangent to four ellipsoids remains free and tangent to four balls by the inverse affine transformation.

In order to ensure that the set of balls looks like Figure 7(b), η and ε need to be small enough so that, when viewed in the $-x$ direction, the boundary of A_i^- is visible between B_j^- and B_{j+1}^-. Furthermore, M needs to be large enough so that the view of $\mathcal{A}^-$ and $\mathcal{B}^-$ remains combinatorially the same from any point of $\mathcal{A}^+$ and $\mathcal{B}^+$.

We now give a formal proof of Proposition 6 by first showing that if four balls, taken respectively in $\mathcal{A}^-$, $\mathcal{B}^-$, $\mathcal{B}^+$, $\mathcal{A}^+$, admit a common tangent line, then this line contains a free segment that still touches the four balls.

LEMMA 7. *If four balls $A_i^-, B_j^-, B_k^+, A_l^+$ admit a (possibly occluded) common tangent line L, then L contains a free segment tangent to the four balls.*

PROOF. We parameterize line L by its two points of intersection $P^{\pm}$ with planes $x = \pm M$ (this is possible because L does not lie in a vertical plane). Let $\tilde{A}_i^{\pm}$ and $\tilde{B}_j^{\pm}$ be the two discs obtained by projecting balls $A_i^{\pm}$ and $B_j^{\pm}$ onto plane $x = \pm M$.

We first show that any two points on line L and in the slab $-M - 3n - 1 \leqslant x \leqslant -M + 3n + 1$ (which contains all balls $A_1^-, \ldots, A_n^-$ and $B_0^-, \ldots, B_n^-$) project onto plane $x = -M$ in two points that are at distance less than $\frac{1}{320n^2}$. Consider

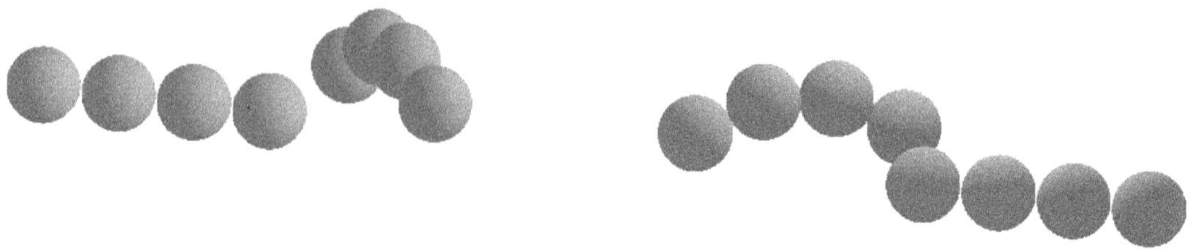

(a) 3D view.

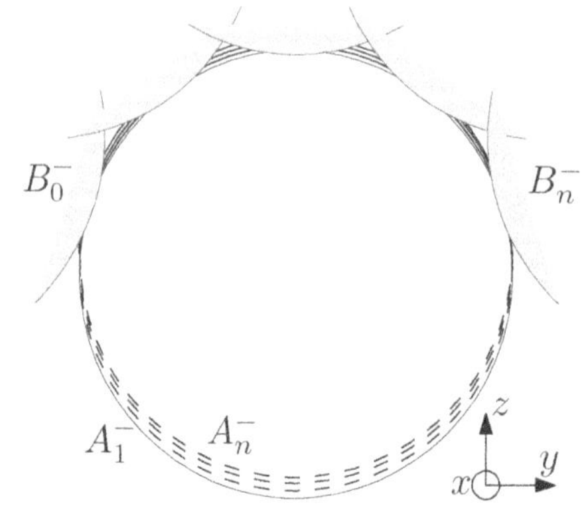

(b) Balls in $\mathcal{A}^-$ and $\mathcal{B}^-$ viewed in the $-x$-direction.

Figure 7: Illustration of our construction for Theorem 5.

any plane parallel to the x-axis and a Cartesian coordinate system (x, w) in that plane. The slope of the projection of L in that plane is less (in absolute value) than $2/M$; indeed, the line L goes through a point on A_i^- and a point on A_l^+ and, between these two points, the minimum variation in x is $2M + 2 > 2M$, and the maximum variation in w is $2(1+n\varepsilon) < 4$ because it is at most the sum of the distances between the x-axis and each of these points; each of these distances is at most 1 plus the distance from the ball center to the x-axis, which is at most $n\varepsilon$; furthermore, $2(1+n\varepsilon) < 4$ since $|\varepsilon| < \frac{1}{n}$ by assumption. Thus, the w-coordinate of points on L and in the slab $-M-3n-1 \leqslant x \leqslant -M+3n+1$ varies by at most $\frac{2}{M}(6n+2) \leqslant \frac{13n}{M}$ (for $n \geqslant 4$) which is less than $\frac{1}{320n^2}$ since $M = cn^3 > 13 \cdot 320n^3$ for some sufficiently large constant c.

We now prove that line L does not intersect the interior of balls $B_0^-, \ldots, B_n^-$ and $A_1^-, \ldots, A_{i-1}^-$. Suppose first, for a contradiction, that L intersects the interior of a ball B_u^- at a point Q_u, for some $u \neq j$. This point projects onto plane $x = -M$ in a point $\tilde{Q}_u$ strictly inside disc $\tilde{B}_u^-$. By the above argument, this point $\tilde{Q}_u$ is at distance at most $\frac{1}{320n^2}$ from discs $\tilde{A}_i^-$ and $\tilde{B}_j^-$ (since $\tilde{Q}_u$ is at distance at most $\frac{1}{320n^2}$ from the projections of the two points of tangency between L and balls A_i^- and B_j^-). We obtain a contradiction by showing that the three discs $\tilde{A}_i^-$, $\tilde{B}_j^-$ and $\tilde{B}_u^-$, each enlarged by $\frac{1}{320n^2}$, do not have a common intersection. Note that it is sufficient to consider $u = j+1$ because the centers of discs $\tilde{B}_u^-$ are ordered on a half-circle of radius larger than 1 (see Figure 8(a)) and the intersection of the enlarged versions of $\tilde{B}_j^-$ and $\tilde{B}_u^-$ is thus contained in the intersection of the enlarged versions of $\tilde{B}_j^-$ and $\tilde{B}_{j\pm1}^-$.

Refer to Figure 8(a) and denote by $\tilde{A}_i^{-\prime}$, $\tilde{B}_j^{-\prime}$ and $\tilde{B}_{j+1}^{-\prime}$ the discs $\tilde{A}_i^-$, $\tilde{B}_j^-$ and $\tilde{B}_{j+1}^-$ enlarged by $\frac{1}{320n^2}$. We prove that they have empty common intersection by showing that the rightmost point (*i.e*, with maximum y-coordinate) of intersection, Q, of the boundary of discs $\tilde{A}_i^{-\prime}$ and $\tilde{B}_j^{-\prime}$ lies outside $\tilde{B}_{j+1}^{-\prime}$. This is done by showing that the angle $\gamma = \angle(C_{\tilde{B}_j^-} C_{\tilde{A}_i^-} Q)$ is less than half the angle δ where $\delta = \angle(C_{\tilde{B}_j^-} C_{\tilde{A}_i^-} C_{\tilde{B}_{j+1}^-}) = \frac{\alpha}{n}$ and $C_{\tilde{A}_i^-}$ and $C_{\tilde{B}_j^-}$ denote the centers of the discs $\tilde{A}_i^-$ and $\tilde{B}_j^-$. Let d denote the distance between $C_{\tilde{A}_i^-}$ and $C_{\tilde{B}_j^-}$. The triangle inequality on triangle $O^- C_{\tilde{A}_i^-} C_{\tilde{B}_j^-}$ (where O^- denotes the projection of the origin O on the plane $x = -M$) gives $2 - \eta \leqslant d + i\varepsilon$ or also $(\frac{d}{2})^2 \geqslant (1 - \frac{\eta + i\varepsilon}{2})^2$ (since $1 - \frac{\eta+i\varepsilon}{2} = 1 - \frac{1}{320n^2} - \frac{i}{320n^3} \geqslant 1 - \frac{1}{160n^2} > 0$).

On the other hand, $\sin\gamma = \frac{\sqrt{(1+\frac{1}{320n^2})^2 - (\frac{d}{2})^2}}{1+\frac{1}{320n^2}}$ and, since $\arcsin z < 2z$ for $z > 0$, we have

$$\begin{aligned}\gamma &< 2\frac{\sqrt{(1+\frac{1}{320n^2})^2 - (1-\frac{\eta+i\varepsilon}{2})^2}}{1+\frac{1}{320n^2}} \\ &< 2\sqrt{\left(1+\frac{1}{320n^2}\right)^2 - \left(1-\frac{\eta+i\varepsilon}{2}\right)^2} \\ &< 2\sqrt{\frac{1}{160n^2} + \frac{1}{320^2n^4} + \eta + n\varepsilon} < 2\sqrt{\frac{1}{80n^2} + \eta + n\varepsilon}.\end{aligned}$$

We have by assumption that $\eta = \frac{1}{160n^2}$, $\varepsilon = \frac{1}{160n^3}$ and $\alpha^2 = \frac{\pi^2}{4^2} \approx 0.62 > \frac{4}{10}$, thus $\gamma < 2\sqrt{\frac{1}{40n^2}} < 2\sqrt{\frac{\alpha^2}{16n^2}} = \frac{\alpha}{2n}$ which

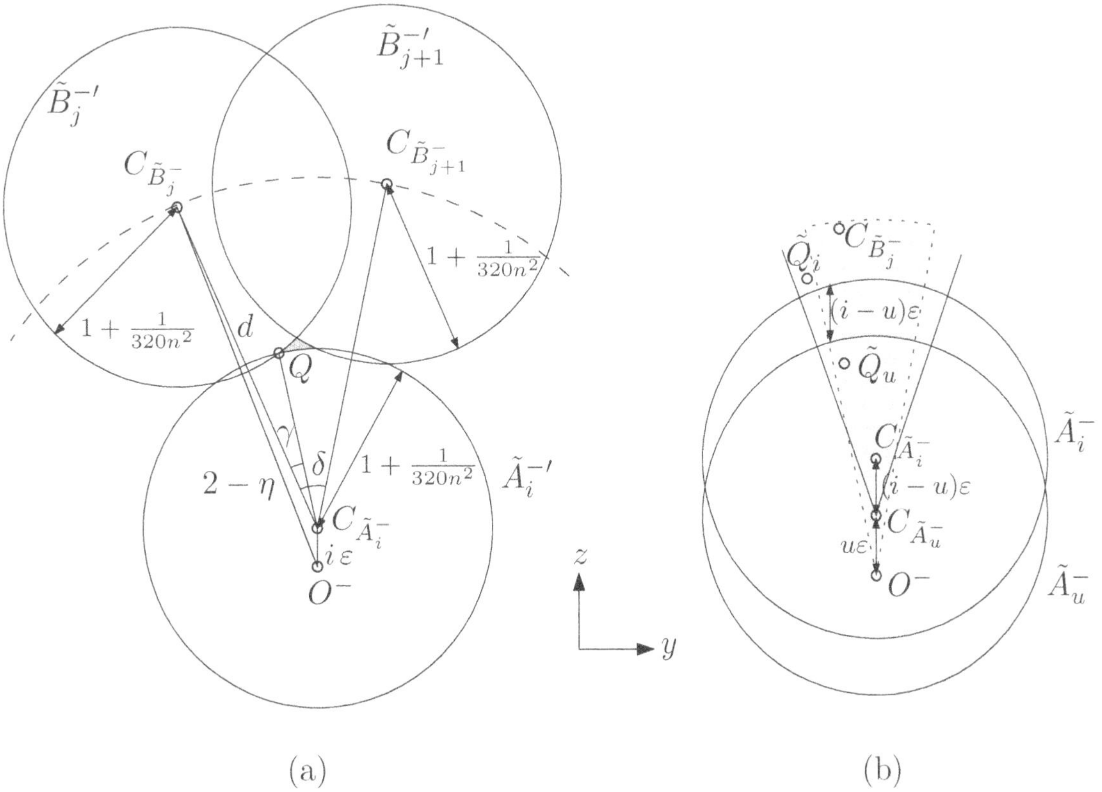

Figure 8: For the proof of Lemma 7: in the plane $x=-M$, (a) discs $\tilde{A}_i^{-\prime}$, $\tilde{B}_j^{-\prime}$, $\tilde{B}_{j+1}^{-\prime}$ and (b) discs $\tilde{A}_i^-$ and $\tilde{A}_u^-$.

concludes the proof that L does not intersect the interior of balls $B_0^-,\ldots,B_n^-$.

We now show that L does not intersect the interior of balls $A_1^-,\ldots,A_{i-1}^-$. Recall that the slope of the projection of L onto any plane parallel to the x-axis is at most $\frac{2}{M}$. Suppose for a contradiction that L intersects A_u^-, $u<i$, at a point Q_u and let Q_i be the intersection of L with plane $x=-M-3i$ containing the center of ball A_i^-. The x-coordinates of Q_u and Q_i differ by at most $(-M-3u+1)-(-M-3i-1)=3(i-u)+2\leqslant 5(i-u)$ (since $1\leqslant i-u$). The distance between the projections, $\tilde{Q}_u$ and $\tilde{Q}_i$, of Q_u and Q_i onto plane $x=-M$ is thus at most $\frac{2}{M}5(i-u)$.

We now show that, for n large enough, these two points $\tilde{Q}_u$ and $\tilde{Q}_i$ lie at distance at least $c_0(i-u)\varepsilon$ for some constant c_0 independent of M. This will give that $c_0(i-u)\varepsilon\leqslant\frac{10(i-u)}{M}$, hence $\frac{c_0}{160n^3}\leqslant\frac{10}{cn^3}$ which yields a contradiction for c large enough.

Refer to Figure 8(b). First note that, for n large enough, $\tilde{Q}_u$ and $\tilde{Q}_i$ lie inside the wedge of angle $\frac{\pi}{3}$ (or any angle strictly larger than $\frac{\pi}{4}$) centered at $C_{\tilde{A}_u^-}$ (and of axis parallel to the z-axis in plane $x=-M$). Indeed, similarly as before, $\tilde{Q}_i$ lies within distance $\frac{1}{320n^2}$ of $\tilde{Q}_u$ which lies in the intersection of the two enlarged discs $\tilde{A}_i^{-\prime}$ and $\tilde{B}_j^{-\prime}$. The center of $\tilde{B}_j^{-\prime}$ lies in a wedge of angle $\frac{\pi}{4}$ centered at O^- (and of axis parallel to the z-axis in plane $x=-M$). The claim follows from the fact that, when n goes to infinity, the two apexes converge toward each other and the distance between centers of the two enlarged discs ($\tilde{A}_i^{-\prime}$ and $\tilde{B}_j^{-\prime}$) converges to 2 (from below). Now, since $\tilde{Q}_u$ and $\tilde{Q}_i$ lie inside this wedge and, by definition, $\tilde{Q}_u$ lies inside disc $\tilde{A}_u^-$ and $\tilde{Q}_i$ lies outside disc $\tilde{A}_i^-$, we get that $\tilde{Q}_u$ and $\tilde{Q}_i$ are at distance at least $c_0(i-u)\varepsilon$ for some constant c_0.

We have thus proved that line L does not intersect the interior of balls $B_0^-,\ldots,B_n^-$ and $A_1^-,\ldots,A_{i-1}^-$. We obtain similarly that L does not intersect the interior of balls $B_0^+,\ldots,B_n^+$ and $A_1^+,\ldots,A_{l-1}^+$. We thus proved that line L may only intersect the interior of balls $A_{i+1}^-,\ldots,A_n^-$ and $A_{l+1}^+,\ldots,A_n^+$. The slab $-M-3i-\frac{3}{2}<x<M+3l+\frac{3}{2}$ contains none of these balls and contains all the other balls, hence the part of the line L in that slab is tangent to A_i^-,B_j^-,B_k^+,A_l^+ and is free. □

It remains to show that any four balls A_i^-,B_j^-,B_k^+,A_l^+ admit a (possibly occluded) common tangent line.

Proof of Proposition 6. We have proved in the proof of Lemma 7, that (with the notation introduced in that proof) any triple of enlarged discs $\tilde{A}_i^{-\prime}$, $\tilde{B}_j^{-\prime}$ and $\tilde{B}_{j+1}^{-\prime}$ have an empty intersection.

Denote by $\tilde{A}_i^{-\prime\prime}$, $\tilde{B}_j^{-\prime\prime}$ and $\tilde{B}_{j+1}^{-\prime\prime}$ the discs $\tilde{A}_i^-$, $\tilde{B}_j^-$ and $\tilde{B}_{j+1}^-$ shrunk by $\frac{1}{320n^2}$. We notice that these discs intersect pairwise. $\tilde{B}_j^{-\prime\prime}$ and $\tilde{B}_{j+1}^{-\prime\prime}$ are obviously close enough so that they intersect. For $\tilde{A}_i^{-\prime\prime}$ and $\tilde{B}_j^{-\prime\prime}$ (the third pair is similar), this is a simple consequence of the fact that $\eta\geqslant 2\frac{1}{320n^2}$.

Hence, any three discs $\tilde{A}_i^-$, $\tilde{B}_j^-$ and $\tilde{B}_{j+1}^-$ define a nonempty region $R_{i,j}^-$ (that is, the bounded component of the intersection of the complement of their enlarged versions)

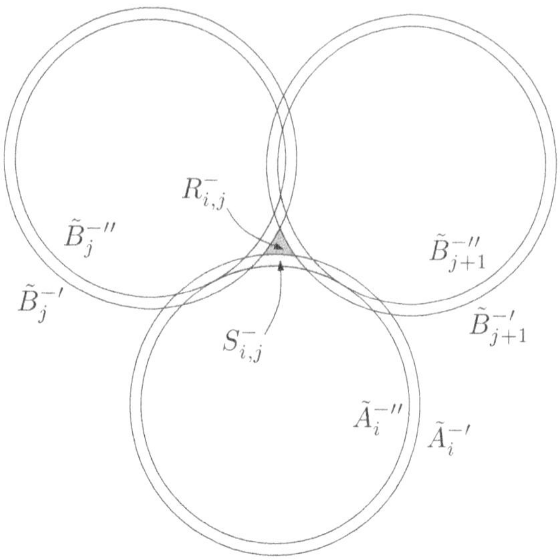

Figure 9: For the proof of Proposition 6.

shown in grey in Figures 8(a) and 9 and a bounded region $S^-_{i,j}$ (that is, the bounded component of the intersection of the complement of their shrunk versions) shown in light grey in Figure 9 that contains $R^-_{i,j}$.

We define similarly regions $R^+_{k,l}$ and $S^+_{k,l}$ in the plane $x = M$. For any i, j, k, l, any line through the two regions $R^-_{i,j}$ and $R^+_{k,l}$ does not intersect A^-_i, A^+_l nor any ball of $\mathcal{B}^{\pm}$. Moving the line continuously, it is impossible to make it escape the set of lines that intersect $S^-_{i,j}$ and $S^+_{k,l}$ without the line intersecting one of A^-_i, B^-_j, B^-_{j+1}, B^+_k , B^+_{k+1} and A^+_l. Using an argument similar to the one illustrated by Figure 6, we start with a line that intersects $R^-_{i,j}$ and $R^+_{k,l}$ and move it down until it is tangent to A^-_i or A^+_l, we then rotate it around the center of that ball in a vertical plane until it is tangent to the other one. We can then move it while it remains tangent to A^-_i and A^+_l until it is tangent to B^-_j and B^+_k. □

4. CONCLUSION

We proved a $\Theta(n^4)$ bound on the worst-case combinatorial complexity of the space of maximal free line segments among n balls of unit or arbitrary radii. This closes the problem of bounding the complexity of this space for balls and it improves on the previously known $\Omega(n^3)$ lower bound for balls of arbitrary radii and on the trivial $\Omega(n^2)$ bound for unit balls. This result also settles negatively the natural conjecture that this space of free line segments has smaller worst-case complexity for disjoint fat objects than for skinny triangles.

We also proved an $\Omega(n^3)$ lower bound on the worst-case combinatorial complexity of the space of free lines among n balls of arbitrary radii, improving over the trivial $\Omega(n^2)$ bound. This bound almost matches the upper bound of $O(n^{3+\varepsilon})$ from [24] and essentially closes the problem of determining tight worst-case bounds on the complexity of the space of free lines among balls of *arbitrary* radii. On the other hand, the case of *unit* balls (Problem 61 of The Open Problems Project [11]) remains open with a complexity between $\Omega(n^2)$ and $O(n^{3+\varepsilon})$.

Acknowledgments

The authors wish to thank Olivier Devillers and Jeff Erickson for fruitful discussions on this topic.

5. REFERENCES

[1] P. K. Agarwal, B. Aronov, V. Koltun, and M. Sharir. Lines avoiding unit balls in three dimensions. *Discrete Comput. Geom.*, 34(2):231–250, 2005.

[2] P. K. Agarwal, B. Aronov, and M. Sharir. Line transversals of balls and smallest enclosing cylinders in three dimensions. *Discrete and Computational Geometry*, 21:373–388, 1999.

[3] P. K. Agarwal and M. Sharir. Davenport-Schinzel sequences and their geometric applications. In J.-R. Sack and J. Urrutia, editors, *Handbook of Computational Geometry*. North-Holland, 1998.

[4] C. Borcea, X. Goaoc, S. Lazard, and S. Petitjean. Common tangents to spheres in $\mathbb{R}^3$. *Discrete and Computational Geometry*, 35(2):287–300, 2006.

[5] H. Brönnimann, O. Devillers, V. Dujmovic, H. Everett, M. Glisse, X. Goaoc, S. Lazard, H. Na, and S. Whitesides. Lines and free line segments tangent to arbitrary three-dimensional convex polyhedra. *SIAM Journal on Computing*, 37(2):522–551, 2007.

[6] H. Brönnimann, O. Devillers, S. Lazard, and F. Sottile. Lines tangent to four triangles in three-dimensional space. *Discrete and Computational Geometry*, 37(3):369–380, 2007.

[7] H. Brönnimann, H. Everett, S. Lazard, F. Sottile, and S. Whitesides. Transversals to line segments in three-dimensional space. *Discrete and Computational Geometry*, 34(3):381–390, 2005.

[8] B. Chazelle, H. Edelsbrunner, L. Guibas, M. Sharir, and J. Stolfi. Lines in space: combinatorics and algorithms. *Algorithmica*, 15:428–447, 1996.

[9] R. Cole and M. Sharir. Visibility problems for polyhedral terrains. *Journal of Symbolic Computation*, 7(1):11–30, 1989.

[10] M. de Berg, H. Everett, and L. Guibas. The union of moving polygonal pseudodiscs – combinatorial bounds and applications. *Computational Geometry: Theory and Applications*, 11:69–82, 1998.

[11] E. Demaine, J. Mitchell, and J. O'Rourke. The Open Problems Project – problem 61. `http://maven.smith.edu/~orourke/TOPP/P61.html`.

[12] J. Demouth, O. Devillers, H. Everett, M. Glisse, S. Lazard, and R. Seidel. On the complexity of umbra and penumbra. *Computational Geometry: Theory and Applications*, 42(8):758–771, 2009.

[13] O. Devillers, V. Dujmovic, H. Everett, X. Goaoc, S. Lazard, H.-S. Na, and S. Petitjean. The expected number of 3D visibility events is linear. *SIAM Journal on Computing*, 32(6):1586–1620, 2003.

[14] F. Durand. A multidisciplinary survey of visibility, 2000. ACM Siggraph course notes, Visibility, Problems, Techniques, and Applications. `http://people.csail.mit.edu/fredo/PUBLI/surv.pdf`.

[15] F. Durand, G. Drettakis, and C. Puech. The 3D

visibility complex. *ACM Transactions on Graphics*, 21(2):176–206, 2002.

[16] A. Efrat, L. J. Guibas, O. A. Hall-Holt, and L. Zhang. On incremental rendering of silhouette maps of a polyhedral scene. *Computational Geometry, Theory and Applications*, 38(3):129–138, 2007.

[17] D. Halperin and M. Sharir. New bounds for lower envelopes in three dimensions, with applications to visibility in terrains. *Discrete and Computational Geometry*, 12:313–326, 1994.

[18] H. Kaplan, N. Rubin, and M. Sharir. Line transversals of convex polyhedra in $\mathbb{R}^3$. In *20th Annual ACM-SIAM Symposium on Discrete Algorithms - SODA'09*, pages 170–179, 2009.

[19] I. Macdonald, J. Pach, and T. Theobald. Common tangents to four unit balls in $\mathbb{R}^3$. *Discrete and Computational Geometry*, 26(1):1–17, 2001.

[20] G. Megyesi and F. Sottile. The envelope of lines meeting a fixed line and tangent to two spheres. *Discrete and Computational Geometry*, 33(4):617–644, 2005.

[21] G. Megyesi, F. Sottile, and T. Theobald. Common transversals and tangents to two lines and two quadrics in $\mathbb{P}^3$. *Discrete and Computational Geometry*, 30(4):543–571, 2003.

[22] M. Pellegrini. On lines missing polyhedral sets in 3-space. *Discrete and Computational Geometry*, 12:203–221, 1994.

[23] M. Pocchiola and G. Vegter. The visibility complex. *Internat. J. Comput. Geom. Appl.*, 6(3):279–308, 1996.

[24] N. Rubin. Lines avoiding balls in three dimensions revisited. In *26th Annual ACM Symposium on Computational Geometry - SCG'10*, 2010.

Lines Avoiding Balls in Three Dimensions Revisited*

Natan Rubin
The Blavatnik School of Computer Science
Tel Aviv University
Tel Aviv 69978, Israel
rubinnat@post.tau.ac.il

ABSTRACT

Let $\mathcal{B}$ be a collection of n arbitrary balls in $\mathbb{R}^3$. We establish an almost-tight upper bound of $O(n^{3+\varepsilon})$, for any $\varepsilon > 0$, on the complexity of the space $\mathcal{F}(\mathcal{B})$ of all the lines that avoid all the members of $\mathcal{B}$. In particular, we prove that the balls of $\mathcal{B}$ admit $O(n^{3+\varepsilon})$ free isolated tangents, for any $\varepsilon > 0$. This generalizes the result of Agarwal *et al.* [1], who established this bound only for *congruent* balls, and solves an open problem posed in that paper. Our bound almost meets the recent lower bound of $\Omega(n^3)$ of Glisse and Lazard [6].

Our approach is constructive and yields an algorithm that computes a discrete representation of the boundary of $\mathcal{F}(B)$ in $O(n^{3+\varepsilon})$ time, for any $\varepsilon > 0$.

Categories and Subject Descriptors

F.2.2 [**Analysis of algorithms and problem complexity**]: Nonnumerical algorithms and problems—*Geometrical problems and computations*; G.2.1 [**Discrete mathematics**]: Combinatorics—*Counting problems*

General Terms

Algorithms, Theory

Keywords

Free lines, lines in space, tangency surfaces, arrangements, combinatorial complexity

1. INTRODUCTION

Let $\mathcal{B}$ be a collection of n arbitrary balls in 3-space. We show that the combinatorial complexity of the space $\mathcal{F}(\mathcal{B})$ of all lines that *miss* all the balls of $\mathcal{B}$, also referred to as *free* lines, is $O(n^{3+\varepsilon})$, for any $\varepsilon > 0$. See below for a more formal statement of the result. This result is related to several topics in computational and combinatorial geometry, including ray shooting and visibility in space, motion planning, the theory of arrangements, and the theory of transversals. Our result extends the result established by Agarwal *et al.* [1] for the case of unit (or congruent) balls, and solves an open problem posed in their paper. See [1] for a more detailed discussion of the problem.

Isolated free lines. A line in $\mathbb{R}^3$ is *isolated* (with respect to $\mathcal{B}$) if it is tangent to one or more balls in $\mathcal{B}$ and cannot be continuously moved without missing or penetrating into one of its tangent balls. Since lines in $\mathbb{R}^3$ have *four* degrees of freedom, they are naturally represented by points in $\mathbb{R}^4$, so that each ball $B \in \mathcal{B}$ defines an algebraic surface σ_B in $\mathbb{R}^4$ which is the locus of all (points representing) lines tangent to B. Since any line on the boundary of $\mathcal{F}(\mathcal{B})$ is necessarily tangent to some $B \in \mathcal{B}$, the boundary of $\mathcal{F}(\mathcal{B})$ is contained in the union of the surfaces σ_B, for $B \in \mathcal{B}$. In fact, as is easily seen, $\mathcal{F}(\mathcal{B})$ is the union of some of the cells of the arrangement $\mathcal{A}$ of the surfaces σ_B, and its boundary is the union of the lower-dimensional faces of $\mathcal{A}$ bounding those cells.

The combinatorial complexity of $\mathcal{F}(\mathcal{B})$ is defined as the number of faces of $\mathcal{A}$, of all dimensions, contained in $\partial\mathcal{F}(\mathcal{B})$. For simplicity of exposition, we will assume *general position* of the balls in $\mathcal{B}$, meaning that (i) the set of lines tangent to any k balls in $\mathcal{B}$, for $1 \le k \le 4$, corresponds to a $(4-k)$-dimensional surface in the parametric space $\mathbb{R}^4$, (ii) no line is tangent to any five distinct balls in $\mathcal{B}$, (iii) any plane is tangent to at most three balls in $\mathcal{B}$, and (iv) any point is contained in the boundaries of at most three balls in $\mathcal{B}$. This envolves no loss of generality because we can apply a sufficiently small random perturbation to the balls, putting them in general position, without losing more than an (expected) constant fraction of the faces of $\partial\mathcal{F}(\mathcal{B})$; see Section 7.3.1 of [13] for similar arguments.

The lower-dimensional faces of $\partial\mathcal{F}(\mathcal{B})$ represent lines tangent to two or more balls of $\mathcal{B}$. Since we are in four (parametric) dimensions, it is easy to see that the number of such faces is at most proportional to n^3 plus the number of boundary *vertices*, each of which is a common intersection of four of the surfaces σ_B, and represents a line which is tangent to the four corresponding balls (and misses all the other balls). Thus, any boundary vertex of $\mathcal{F}(\mathcal{B})$ corresponds to an isolated tangent line which misses the rest of the balls. Most of this paper is therefore devoted to proving a nearly-cubic bound on the number of isolated free tangent lines.

*Work on this paper has been partially supported by Grants 155/05, 975/06 and 338/09 from the Israel Science Fund. It is part of the author's Ph.D. Dissertation, prepared under the supervision of Haim Kaplan and Micha Sharir.

Transversals and free lines. The tangency surface σ_B of each ball $B \in \mathcal{B}$ encloses the set σ_B^+ of all lines which stab (intersect) B. Thus, the space of all free lines corresponds to the complement of $\bigcup_{B\in\mathcal{B}} \sigma_B^+$, and each isolated free tangent line corresponds to a boundary vertex of $\bigcup_{B\in\mathcal{B}} \sigma_B^+$. In contrast, the *intersection* $\bigcap_{B\in\mathcal{B}} \sigma_B^+$ corresponds to the *transversal space* $\mathcal{T}(\mathcal{B})$ of all line transversals of $\mathcal{B}$, which is, in a sense, antithetical to $\mathcal{F}(\mathcal{B})$. The complexity of $\mathcal{T}(\mathcal{B})$ has been extensively studied in the past two decades; see [14] for a comprehensive survey. Specifically, the above 4-dimensional representation, with a careful choice of parameters, allows us to represent $\mathcal{T}(\mathcal{B})$ as a certain *sandwich region* in $\mathbb{R}^4$, enclosed between an upper envelope of one collection of surfaces and a lower envelope of another collection (where these surfaces are portions of the tangency surfaces σ_B); see [8, 13]. Thus, the nearly-cubic bound on the complexity of such sandwich regions, as established in [9], immediately leads to a nearly-cubic bound on the complexity of $\mathcal{T}(\mathcal{B})$ for any collection $\mathcal{B}$ of simply-shaped convex sets (formally, of *constant description complexity*; see [9]) in $\mathbb{R}^3$. Unfortunately, unlike the transversal space $\mathcal{T}(\mathcal{B})$, the space $\mathcal{F}(\mathcal{B})$ of free lines cannot be conveniently represented as a sandwich region in $\mathbb{R}^4$, which makes the general bound of [9] inapplicable. For example, if $\mathcal{B}$ consists of n triangles, the complexity of $\mathcal{T}(\mathcal{B})$ can be as large as $\Theta(n^4)$ [11].

Our results: overview and organization. Assuming general position of $\mathcal{B}$, it suffices to bound the number of isolated free tangent lines ℓ which are tangent to exactly four balls $B_i \in \mathcal{B}$, for $0 \le i \le 3$. Following the approach of [8], we bound the number of such lines ℓ for which one of the corresponding balls B_i is a fixed ball $B_0 \in \mathcal{B}$, and repeat the analysis for each choice of B_0. More precisely, let h be a plane containing ℓ and crossing each of the balls $B_0, \ldots, B_3$. Then, inside h, ℓ is tangent to the four disks $B_i \cap h$, $0 \le i \le 3$. We charge ℓ to the ball B_i for which the disk $B_i \cap h$ has the smallest radius for at least a constant portion of such planes h. (Specifically, the angular measure of the set of normals to these planes is at least 1/6 of the full circle of orientations orthogonal to ℓ.) For each ball $B_0 \in \mathcal{B}$ we derive a bound of $O(n^{2+\varepsilon})$, for any $\varepsilon > 0$, on the number of isolated free tangent lines which are charged to B_0. This immediately implies the asserted bound of $O(n^{3+\varepsilon})$, for any $\varepsilon > 0$, on the number of free isolated tangent lines.

We thus reduce our study to the space of lines tangent to some fixed ball $B_0 \in \mathcal{B}$ and avoiding the interiors of all balls in $\mathcal{B} \setminus \{B_0\}$. The advantage of this reduction is that the restricted space $\mathcal{L} = \mathcal{L}(B_0)$ of lines tangent to B_0 has only three degrees of freedom, and corresponds to a three-dimensional manifold in $\mathbb{R}^4$ (see [7, 8] for similar arguments). The space $\mathcal{F}(\mathcal{B} \setminus \{B_0\}) \cap \mathcal{L}$ of free lines within $\mathcal{L}$ is again described as the complement of $\bigcup_{B\in\mathcal{B}\setminus\{B_0\}} [\sigma_B^+ \cap \mathcal{L}]$. Clearly, each isolated free tangent line charged to B_0 corresponds to a vertex of the three-dimensional set $\mathcal{F}(\mathcal{B} \setminus \{B_0\}) \cap \mathcal{L}$ (but not vice versa; not all these vertices are necessarily charged to B_0). The task at hand, for a fixed B_0, is to bound the complexity of the union of the regions $\sigma_B^+ \cap \mathcal{L}$, for $B \in \mathcal{B} \setminus \{B_0\}$, in the 3-dimensional space $\mathcal{L}$. A recent work of Ezra [4] deals with a similar problem, and shows that the complexity of the union of n arbitrary cylinders in $\mathbb{R}^3$ is $O(n^{2+\varepsilon})$, for any $\varepsilon > 0$. As it turns out, we can adapt the analysis technique of [4] and apply it to our setup. The adaptation requires some care, because of the more envolved geometry in our setup, but the overall resulting scheme is similar (and even somewhat simplified).

In Section 2 we formally describe how to charge an isolated free tangent line to at least one of the balls in $\mathcal{B}$ it is tangent to. We then describe a convenient way to represent lines tangent to the chosen ball B_0, and establish several essential geometric properties of the space $\mathcal{L}$ of such lines. In Section 3 we derive a near quadratic bound on the number of isolated free tangent lines charged to any fixed ball B_0. In Section 4 we describe an algorithm that computes $\mathcal{F}(\mathcal{B})$ in nearly-cubic time, and give some concluding remarks and directions for future research.

2. CHARGING FREE TANGENT LINES TO A FIXED BALL

Charging isolated free tangent lines to balls in $\mathcal{B}$. Let us assume general position of $\mathcal{B}$, which, as discussed above, implies that each isolated free tangent line is tangent to exactly four balls in $\mathcal{B}$. Let B_0 be a fixed ball in $\mathcal{B}$. Without loss of generality we assume that B_0 is centered at the origin and has unit radius. For each free isolated line ℓ tangent to B_0 and to some three other balls $B_1, B_2, B_3 \in \mathcal{B}$, we charge ℓ to B_0 if the set of all planes h containing ℓ, such that $B_0 \cap h$ has radius *smaller* than or equal to the radii of $B_i \cap h$, for all $1 \le i \le 3$, contains a double wedge of angle at least $\pi/6$; see Figure 1 (left) for an illustration.

LEMMA 1. *Each isolated free tangent line is charged to at least one of the four balls in $\mathcal{B}$ it is tangent to.*

PROOF. Parametrize the (oriented) planes containing ℓ by Π_θ, where $0 \le \theta \le 2\pi$ measures the angle between the normal to the plane and some fixed plane normal. Let B_i, $0 \le i \le 3$, denote the four balls tangent to ℓ. For each $0 \le i \le 3$ and $0 \le \theta \le 2\pi$ we define $r_i(\theta)$ to be the radius of the circle $B_i \cap \Pi_\theta$. See Figure 1 (right) for an illustration. We claim that, for any pair $i < j$, $r_i(\theta) = r_j(\theta)$ has two solutions, up to antipodality (clearly, if θ is a solution so is $\theta + \pi$). To see this, project ℓ, B_i and B_j onto some plane orthogonal to ℓ. The respective projections B_i^*, B_j^* of B_i, B_j are two discs whose boundaries meet at the point ℓ^* to which ℓ projects; see Figure 1 (right). Each plane Π_θ projects to a line Π_θ^* through ℓ^*, and $r_i(\theta)$ is half the chord $\Pi_\theta^* \cap B_i^*$, and similarly for B_j. Hence we have $r_i(\theta) = \frac{1}{2}R_i|\cos(\theta - \alpha_i)|$, where R_i is the radius of B_i and α_i is the angle at which Π_θ^* intersects B_i^* in a diameter, and similarly for $r_j(\theta)$. This implies that $r_i(\theta) = r_j(\theta)$ when $R_i \cos(\theta - \alpha_i) = R_j \cos(\theta - \alpha_j)$ or $R_i \cos(\theta - \alpha_i) = -R_j \cos(\theta - \alpha_j)$, and each of these equations has a unique solution in the range $(0, \pi)$ and an antipodal solution in $(\pi, 2\pi)$. This implies the claim.

Hence, in the range $(0, \pi)$, these four functions behave as pseudo-parabolas, and therefore their minimization diagram consists of at most $\lambda_2(4) = 7$ arcs[1], delimited by 6 breakpoints; see [13]. Hence, over $(0, 2\pi)$ the diagram consists of at most 12 arcs, which appear in antipodal pairs. Hence, there must exist such a pair for which the angular extent of each arc in the pair is at least $2\pi/12 = \pi/6$. By definition, we can charge ℓ to the ball B_i which attains the lower envelope at this pair of arcs. □

In Section 3, we prove the following theorem.

[1] In general, $\lambda_s(n)$ denotes the maximum length of a Davenport-Schinzel sequence or order s on n symbols. For the special case $s = 2$ we have $\lambda_2(n) = 2n - 1$; see [13].

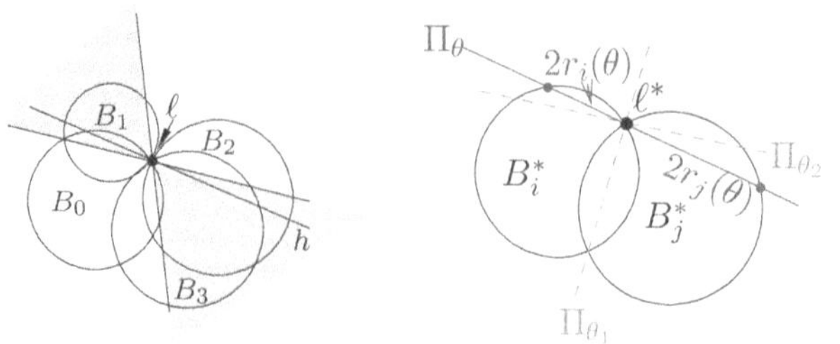

Figure 1: Left: Charging an isolated free tangent line ℓ to a tangent ball B_0; the angle of the shaded double wedge is $\geq \pi/6$. Right: The projections B_i^*, B_j^* of balls B_i, B_j, for $0 \leq i < j \leq 3$, and the respective functions $r_i(\theta), r_j(\theta)$–the equation $r_i(\theta) = r_j(\theta)$ has two solutions, θ_1 and θ_2, up to untipodality.

THEOREM 2. *Let $\mathcal{B}$ be a collection of n arbitrarily balls in $\mathbb{R}^3$ in general position. Then each ball $B \in \mathcal{B}$ is charged by at most $O(n^{2+\varepsilon})$ isolated free tangent lines, for any $\varepsilon > 0$.*

As an immediate corollary of Lemma 1 and Theorem 2, we obtain the following main result of the paper.

THEOREM 3. *Let $\mathcal{B}$ be a collection of n arbitrary balls in $\mathbb{R}^3$ in general position. Then $\mathcal{B}$ admits $O(n^{3+\varepsilon})$ isolated free tangent lines, for any $\varepsilon > 0$.*

As mentioned, a recent construction of Glisse and Lazard [6] gives a set $\mathcal{B}$ of n balls (in general position) with $\Omega(n^3)$ isolated free tangent lines, thus making the bound in Theorem 3 almost tight in the worst case.

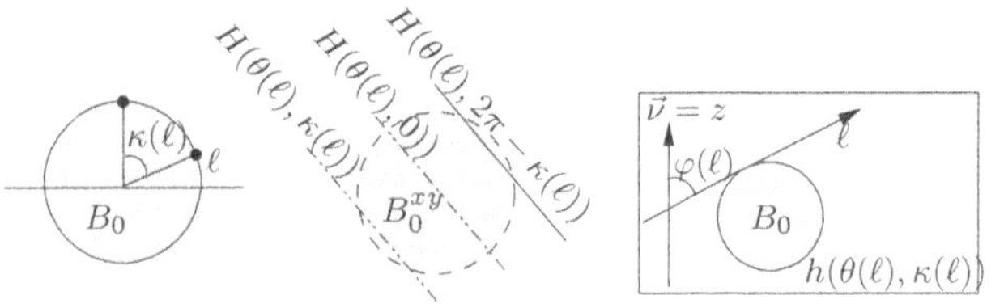

Figure 2: Representing $\ell \in \mathcal{L}$ by $(\theta(\ell), \kappa(\ell), \varphi(\ell))$. Three views: ℓ-parallel projection (left), xy-projection (middle), and inside the plane $h(\theta(\ell), \kappa(\ell))$ (right).

Lines tangent to a fixed ball. In preparation for the proof of Theorem 2, we introduce the following notations. Fix a ball $B_0 \in \mathcal{B}$ and let $\mathcal{L} = \mathcal{L}(B_0)$ denote the space of all lines that are tangent to B_0. Lines in $\mathcal{L}$ have *three* degrees of freedom, and we parametrize them as follows. The representation is with respect to a fixed choice of a *reference direction* $\vec{\nu} \in \mathbb{S}^2$; we will later choose different reference directions, and thereby obtain different parametrizations of $\mathcal{L}$. We first consider the *standard* representation, which uses the standard xyz-coordinate frame, in which $\vec{\nu}$ is the positive z-direction. We then represent each *oriented* line $\ell \in \mathcal{L}$ by the triple $(\theta(\ell), \kappa(\ell), \varphi(\ell))$, where $(\theta(\ell), \varphi(\ell)) \in \mathbb{S}^2$ is the representation in spherical coordinates of the orientation of ℓ, and $\kappa(\ell) \in (0, 2\pi)$ represents the point $\ell \cap B_0$ on the great circle of B_0 orthogonal to the direction $(\theta(\ell), \varphi(\ell))$. Here we set $\kappa(\ell) = 0$ for the line touching the great circle at its highest point (in the $\vec{\nu}$-direction), and let it increase in the counterclockwise direction, with respect to the orientation of ℓ. The $\vec{\nu}$-parallel (vertical) plane through the line ℓ with $\kappa(\ell) = 0$ passes through the center of B_0. Note that each line $\ell \in \mathcal{L}$ with a fixed $\theta(\ell) = \theta \in (0, 2\pi)$ lies in one of the $\vec{\nu}$-parallel planes making an angle θ with the x-axis in our coordinate frame. Similarly, all lines with a fixed $(\theta(\ell), \kappa(\ell)) = (\theta, \kappa)$ lie in a single $\vec{\nu}$-parallel plane, $h(\theta, \kappa)$, of this kind so that $\varphi(\ell) \in (0, \pi)$ describes the angle that ℓ makes with the $\vec{\nu}$-parallel axis inside $h(\theta, \kappa)$. As φ varies from 0 to π, the line ℓ turns around the upper semicircle, if $-\pi/2 \leq \kappa \leq \pi/2$, or the lower semicircle, if $\pi/2 \leq \kappa \leq 3\pi/2$, of the disk $h(\theta, \kappa) \cap B_0$. See Figure 2 (right) for an illustration.

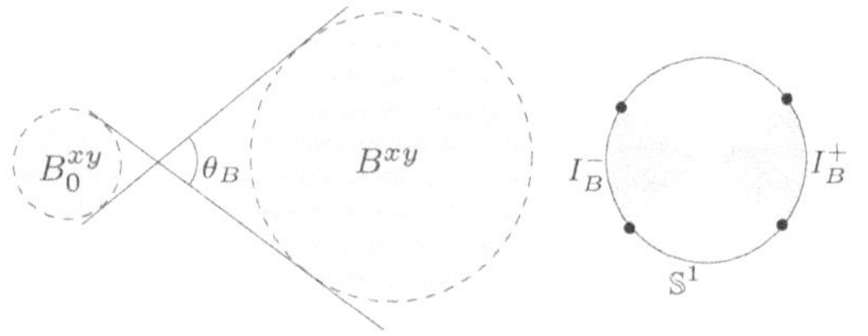

Figure 3: The θ-span of B is equal to the angle between the two vertical inner tangent planes to B_0 and B.

θ-span. Let $B \in \mathcal{B} \setminus \{B_0\}$ be a ball such that the xy-projections of B_0 and B are disjoint. Let I_B^+ and I_B^- be the pair of antipodal arcs on $\mathbb{S}^1$ such that $I_B^+ \cup I_B^-$ is the set of all $\theta \in \mathbb{S}^1$ for which there is at least one line $\ell \in \mathcal{L}$, with $\theta(\ell) = \theta$, which stabs B. Define the *θ-span* of B to be the angular extent θ_B of I_B^+ (or of I_B^-). Clearly, θ_B is equal to the angle between the two vertical planes that are common tangents to B_0 and B and separate the two balls. See Figure 3 for an illustration. If the xy-projections of B_0 and B intersect, we either set θ_B to be π, when B is not contained in B_0, or, otherwise, ignore B (within the analysis pertaining to the fixed ball B_0), since no $\ell \in \mathcal{L}$ can be tangent to B.

Choosing a *good* reference direction. In the remainder of this paper, $(\theta, \kappa, \varphi)$ denotes the *standard* coordinate frame of $\mathcal{L}$, i.e., the one corresponding, as above, to the reference direction $(0, 0, 1)$ and to the real x- and y-axes complementing the frame.

In the course of the proof of Theorem 2 we assign to each isolated free line $\ell \in \mathcal{L}$, charged to B_0, another reference direction $\vec{\nu}$, which is chosen from a certain set of $O(1)$ candidate directions on $\mathbb{S}^2$. An appropriate choice of $\vec{\nu}$ defines a *new* coordinate frame $(\theta', \kappa', \varphi')$ in which the point $(\theta'(\ell), \kappa'(\ell), \varphi'(\ell))$ becomes a vertex on the boundary of a sandwich region enclosed between an upper envelope of one collection of $\theta'\kappa'$-monotone portions of the tangency surfaces of the balls of $\mathcal{B} \setminus \{B_0\}$, and a lower envelope of another such collection.

Specifically, we fix some sufficiently small constant $\delta > 0$. Let $B \in \mathcal{B} \setminus \{B_0\}$ be a ball with θ-span θ_B, and let $\ell \in \mathcal{L}$ be a line tangent to B. Let $\vec{\nu} \in \mathbb{S}^2$ be a reference direction, and let $(\theta', \kappa', \varphi')$ be the coordinate frame of $\mathcal{L}$ which corresponds to $\vec{\nu}$. [2] For each $-\varphi'(\ell) \leq \Delta \leq \pi - \varphi'(\ell)$ let $\ell(\Delta)$ denote the line whose $(\theta', \kappa', \varphi')$-coordinates are $(\theta'(\ell), \kappa'(\ell), \varphi'(\ell) + \Delta)$. Observe that $\ell(0) = \ell$ and that all such lines $\ell(\Delta)$ lie in the $\vec{\nu}$-parallel plane through ℓ; let us denote this plane by $H(\ell, \vec{\nu})$. Keeping θ', κ' fixed and varying Δ causes the line $\ell(\Delta)$ to rotate around the disk $B_0 \cap H(\ell, \vec{\nu})$. An appropriate choice of the direction of the rotation (either clockwise or counterclockwise, starting from $\ell(0) = \ell$) will cause $\ell(\Delta)$ to penetrate into the interior of B

[2] The choice of the other two $\vec{\nu}$-orthogonal axes of the frame is arbitrary; see the remark below.

as soon as it starts moving away from ℓ. We keep rotating $\ell(\Delta)$ in this direction until either it stops penetrating B and becomes tangent to it again, or it becomes parallel to the $\vec{\nu}$-axis and $\varphi'(\ell)+\Delta$ becomes equal to either 0 or π. Letting $\tilde{\ell}$ denote the final position of ℓ, we say that the direction $\vec{\nu}$ is *good* for the pair (ℓ, B) if either $|\theta(\ell) - \theta(\tilde{\ell})| > \delta\theta_B$ or $\varphi'(\tilde{\ell}) \in \{0, \pi\}$.

Remark: Note that the other tangent, $\tilde{\ell}$, is fully determined by the choice of $\vec{\nu}$. Hence the choice of the two $\vec{\nu}$-orthogonal coordinates which, together with $\vec{\nu}$, form the new coordinate system in $\mathbb{R}^3$, is immaterial for the definition of a good direction.

Figure 4: Left: Choosing a good reference direction $\vec{\nu}$. All lines $\ell \in \mathcal{L}$ that have same (θ', κ')-coordinates as ℓ, lie in the plane $H(\ell, \vec{\nu})$. Right: As the line $\ell(\Delta)$ rotates in the plane $H(\ell, \vec{\nu})$, its direction moves along the $\vec{\nu}$-orthogonal great circle C_H.

We say that the reference direction $\vec{\nu}$ is *good* for an isolated free tangent line $\ell \in \mathcal{L}$ tangent to B_0 and to some three other balls B_i, $1 \le i \le 3$, so that ℓ is charged to B_0, if $\vec{\nu}$ is good *for each of the pairs* (ℓ, B_i), $1 \le i \le 3$. The following technical theorem provides the main geometric infrastructure for our analysis.

THEOREM 4. *Let η be a sufficiently small positive constant and let $\ell \in \mathcal{L}$ be an isolated free line charged to B_0, which is tangent to B_0 and to three other balls B_i, $1 \le i \le 3$, so that the center c_i of B_i lies at distance d_i from the center c_0 of B_0, for $i = 1, 2, 3$. Suppose that for each $1 \le i \le 3$ the angle between c_0c_i and the z-axis is at least $\sin^{-1}\eta$. Then there is a spherical cap $C \subset \mathbb{S}^2$ of radius 1/100, say, such that all directions $\vec{\nu} \in C$ are* ***good reference directions*** *for ℓ (with a constant δ that depends on η; specifically, we can choose $\delta = \Theta(\eta^3)$).*

Clearly, the set of good directions also contains the spherical cap antipodal to C.

PROOF. We start with the set $\mathbb{S}^2$ and gradually reduce the set of directions under consideration, until we end up with a subset of $\mathbb{S}^2$ all of whose directions $\vec{\nu}$ are good for ℓ, which still contains a spherical cap of radius 1/100.

Since ℓ is charged to B_0, Lemma 1 implies the existence of a double wedge W_0 of planes through ℓ, of angle $\ge \pi/6$ with the following property: For any plane $H \subset W_0$, the disk $B_0 \cap H$ has radius smaller than that of $B_i \cap H$, for all $1 \le i \le 3$. We restrict ourselves to the directions $\vec{\nu} \in \mathbb{S}^2$ for which the corresponding plane $H(\ell, \vec{\nu})$ is contained in W_0. On the unit sphere $\mathbb{S}^2$, those directions form a spherical double wedge bounded by the two great circles parallel to the planes bounding W_0; see Figure 5. Thus, restricting $\vec{\nu}$ to lie in this double wedge, we ensure that the radius of $B_0 \cap H(\ell, \vec{\nu})$ is smaller than the radii of the disks $B_i \cap H(\ell, \vec{\nu})$, for $1 \le i \le 3$.

We next ensure that for each $1 \le i \le 3$ the disk $B_i \cap H(\ell, \vec{\nu})$ has radius at least ηr_i, where r_i denotes the radius

Figure 5: The constructed set of good directions is contained in a spherical double wedge W bounded by the two great circles parallel to the planes bounding W_0.

of B_i. Let H_i denote the plane that is tangent to B_i at the point $\ell \cap B_i$, and let C_i denote the H_i-parallel great circle on $\mathbb{S}^2$. Clearly, for each $0 \le i \le 3$ the disk $H(\ell, \vec{\nu}) \cap B_i$ has radius $r_i \sin\alpha$, where α is the dihedral angle between $H(\ell, \vec{\nu})$ and H_i. Note that α is greater than or equal to the angle between $\vec{\nu}$ and H_i. This follows from the easily established fact that the dihedral angle between the planes maximizes the angle between a vector on one plane and the other plane; see Figure 6 (left).

Thus, in order to ensure that the radius of $B_i \cap H(\ell, \vec{\nu})$ is greater than ηr_i it is sufficient to remove all directions $\vec{\nu}$ which lie in the strip of width[3] $2\sin^{-1}\eta = O(\eta)$ around C_i, for each $1 \le i \le 3$.

Finally, we exclude all directions $\vec{\nu}$ which make an angle of at most $\sin^{-1}\eta$ with the z-parallel plane $H^{\perp} = H(\ell, (0,0,1))$ that contains ℓ. All the removed directions lie in a strip of width $2\sin^{-1}\eta$ around the $H^{\perp}$-parallel great circle in $\mathbb{S}^2$. Each remaining direction $\vec{\nu}$ makes an angle of at least $\sin^{-1}\eta$ with $H^{\perp}$ (and, in particular, with the z-axis).

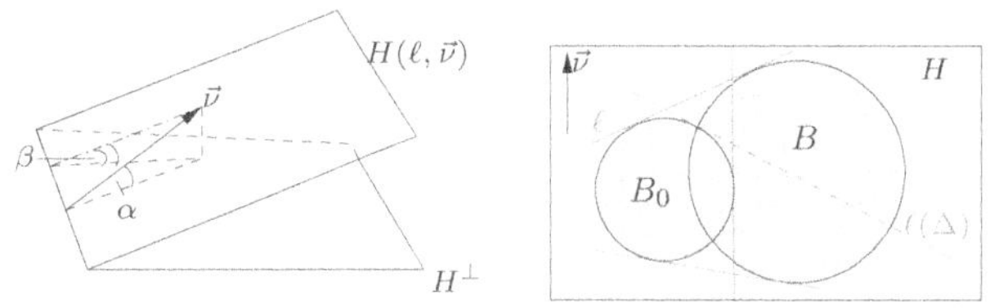

Figure 6: Left: The dihedral angle α between a pair of planes H_1, H_2 is greater than or equal to the angle β between a vector $\vec{\nu}$ in H_1 and H_2. Right: The case when $B_0 \cap H$ intersects $B_i \cap H$: The line $\ell(\Delta)$ must rotate by an angle greater than π (while intersecting B) before it becomes tangent to B_i again.

Clearly, by choosing η sufficiently small, the set of all unremoved reference directions $\vec{\nu} \in \mathbb{S}^2$ contains a spherical cap C of radius 1/100. We next claim that any surviving reference direction (and in particular any direction $\vec{\nu} \in C$) is good for ℓ. Recall that this is equivalent to showing that $\vec{\nu}$ is good for each of the pairs (ℓ, B_i), for $1 \le i \le 3$.

To establish the claim, fix the ball B_i, for some $1 \le i \le 3$, and a reference direction, $\vec{\nu} \in C$. Let $(\theta', \kappa', \varphi')$ be the coordinate frame that corresponds to $\vec{\nu}$, and let $H = H(\ell, \vec{\nu})$ denote the $\vec{\nu}$-parallel plane through ℓ. Suppose, without loss of generality, that the rotated line $\ell(\Delta)$ penetrates the interior of B_i for arbitrarily small $\Delta > 0$. If $\ell(\Delta)$ stabs B_i for all $0 \le \Delta \le \pi - \varphi'(\ell)$ then $\vec{\nu}$ is good for (ℓ, B_i) by definition. Thus, we may assume that for some $0 \le \Delta \le \pi - \varphi'(\ell)$ the line $\ell(\Delta)$ becomes tangent to B_i again, and leaves it

[3]We use the inequality $\sin^{-1}\eta < 2\eta$, say, for η sufficiently small, and choose η in the statement of the theorem to satisfy this inequality.

immediately afterwards. In particular, this, and the fact that $r(B_i \cap H) > r(B_0 \cap H)$, implies that $B_0 \cap H$ is disjoint from $B_i \cap H$. Otherwise, ℓ is a common outer tangent to $B_0 \cap H$ and $B_i \cap H$, and $\ell(\Delta)$ must rotate around B_0 by an angle greater than π, while intersecting B_i, before it becomes tangent to B_i again, so it must become $\vec{\nu}$-parallel before leaving B_i; see Figure 6 (right).

Assume then that $B_0 \cap H$ and $B_i \cap H$ are disjoint, and let Δ_{end} be the smallest $0 \le \Delta \le \pi - \varphi'(\ell)$ such that $\ell(\Delta)$ misses the interior of B_i, and put $\tilde{\ell} = \ell(\Delta_{end})$. In the plane $H = H(\ell, \vec{\nu})$, the line $\tilde{\ell}$ is another common tangent to the disks $B_0 \cap H$ and $B_i \cap H$, and makes an angle of Δ_{end} with ℓ; see Figure 7 (left). Note that one of $\ell, \tilde{\ell}$ is an outer tangent and the other is a common inner tangent to these two disks.

We need to show that $|\theta(\tilde{\ell}) - \theta(\ell)| > \delta\theta_{B_i}$, for an appropriate constant $\delta > 0$ (which will depend on η). This is done in three steps. First, we show that $\Delta_{end} > \eta r_i/d_i$. Then we prove that θ_{B_i} is at most $O(r_i/(\eta d_i))$. Finally, we show that $|\theta(\tilde{\ell}) - \theta(\ell)|$ is $\Omega(\eta\Delta_{end})$. The combination of these three inequalities would then imply that $|\theta(\tilde{\ell}) - \theta(\ell)| > \delta\theta_{B_i}$, with $\delta = \Omega(\eta^3)$. We proceed to establish the three claims:

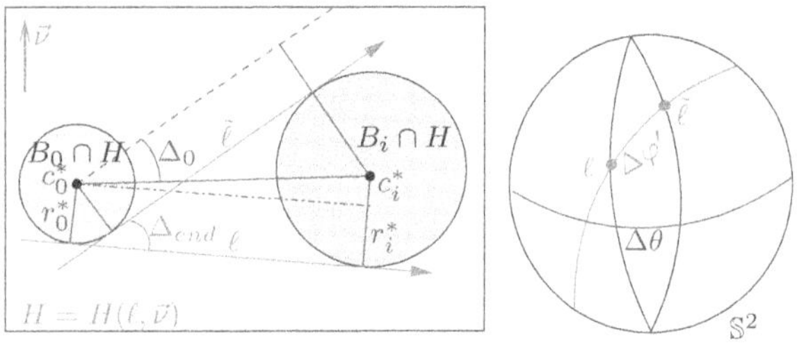

Figure 7: Left: The lines ℓ and $\tilde{\ell} = \ell(\Delta_{end})$. Right: The θ-interval $\Delta\theta = (\theta(\ell), \theta(\tilde{\ell}))$.

Claim 1: $\Delta_{end} > \eta r_i/d_i$.

PROOF. Refer to Figure 7 (left), depicting the cross-section of B_0 and B_i within $H = H(\ell, \vec{\nu})$. Denote the center of $B_0 \cap H$ by c_0^* and its radius by r_0^*. Similarly, denote the center of $B_i \cap H$ by c_i^* and its radius by r_i^*. We have $c_0^*c_i^* \le d_i$ and $r_0^* \le r_i^*$. We also have $r_i^* \ge \eta r_i$, by construction of $\vec{\nu}$. Draw through c_0^* lines parallel to the two tangents $\ell, \tilde{\ell}$. One of $\ell, \tilde{\ell}$ is a common inner tangent to $B_0 \cap H, B_i \cap H$, say it is $\tilde{\ell}$. Denote by Δ_0 the angle between $c_0^*c_i^*$ and the line through c_0^* parallel to $\tilde{\ell}$; see Figure 7 (left). The angle between the two new lines (parallel to $\ell, \tilde{\ell}$) is equal to Δ_{end}, and since $r_0^* \le r_i^*$, it is greater than Δ_0. Hence[4]

$$\Delta_{end} \ge \Delta_0 = \sin^{-1}\frac{r_0^* + r_i^*}{|c_0^*c_i^*|} \ge \sin^{-1}\frac{r_0^* + r_i^*}{d_i} \ge \sin^{-1}\frac{\eta r_i}{d_i} > \frac{\eta r_i}{d_i}.$$

In this argument we assume that $B_0 \cap H$ and $B_i \cap H$ are disjoint, so $\tilde{\ell}$ exists, which is indeed what the current analysis has been assuming. □

Claim 2: $\theta_{B_i} = O(r_i/(\eta d_i))$.

PROOF. Here we project B_0 and B_i on the xy-plane. Referring to Figure 8 (left), it is easily seen that the distance $\hat{d}_i$ between the centers of the projection disks of B_0 and B_i is at most d_i. On the other hand, the angle between c_0c_i and the z-axis is at least $\sin^{-1}\eta$, by assumption, so we have $\hat{d}_i \ge \eta d_i$. Moreover, the radii of the projection disks are clearly r_0 and r_i, respectively.

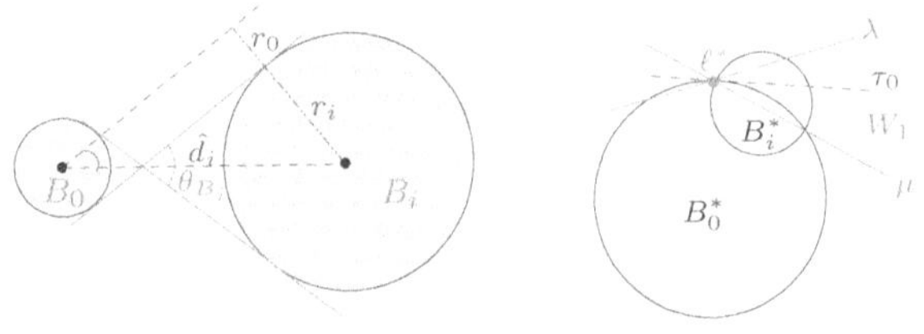

Figure 8: Left: If the xy-projections of the two balls are disjoint then $\sin\theta_{B_i}/2 = (r_0 + r_i)/\hat{d}_i$. Right: Proving that B_0 has radius at most $14r_i$.

We claim that r_0 cannot be much bigger than r_i. Specifically, we show that $r_0 \le 14r_i$. Indeed, recall that ℓ is charged to B_0, so there exists a double wedge W_0 bounded by two planes passing through ℓ and forming a dihedral angle of at least $\pi/6$, such that, for every plane H contained in W_0, $r(B_0 \cap H) \le r(B_i \cap H)$. Project W_0, B_0, B_i and ℓ on some plane orthogonal to ℓ. In the projection, B_0 and B_i are mapped to two respective disks B_0^*, B_i^*, so that their boundaries meet at the point ℓ^* into which ℓ projects; see Figure 8 (right).

Suppose to the contrary that $r_0 > 14r_i$. Draw a line λ through ℓ^* which makes equal and openly disjoint chords within B_0^* and B_i^*. Draw another line μ by connecting ℓ^* to the other intersection point of ∂B_0^* and ∂B_i^*. Let τ_0 denote the tangent to B_0^* at ℓ^*. One of the double wedges, W_1, delimited by λ and μ consists of lines which mark in B_0^* a smaller chord than the chord marked in B_i^* and W_1 has to contain τ_0, because the "chord" it makes in B_0^* is of length 0; see Figure 8 (right). The length of each of the two chords $\lambda \cap B_0^*, \mu \cap B_0^*$ is at most the diameter of B_i^*, namely at most $2r_i$. Therefore, the angles β_1, β_2 between these chords and the tangent τ_0, which are half the respective central angles subtended by these chords at the center of B_0^*, are small. Specifically, we have $\sin\beta_1, \sin\beta_2 \le r_i/r_0 < 1/14$. Hence the angular size of W_1 is $\beta_1 + \beta_2 < \pi/6$. However, W_1, when lifted back to 3-space, is exactly the wedge W_0 with the property that $r(B_0 \cap H) < r(B_i \cap H)$ for every plane H in W_0. By assumption, the dihedral angle of W_0 is at least $\pi/6$, a contradiction that shows that $r_0 \le 14r_i$.

If the xy-projections of B_0 and B_i are disjoint, as depicted in Figure 8 (left), we have

$$\sin\frac{\theta_{B_i}}{2} = \frac{r_0 + r_i}{\hat{d}_i} \le \frac{r_0 + r_i}{\eta d_i} \le \frac{15r_i}{\eta d_i},$$

implying that $\theta_{B_i} = O(r_i/(\eta d_i))$.

If the xy-projections of B_0 and B_i intersect, then $\theta_{B_i} = \pi = \Theta(1)$ and $\hat{d}_i \le r_i + r_0 \le 15r_i$. The claim now follows since

$$\frac{r_i}{\eta d_i} \ge \frac{r_i}{\hat{d}_i} \ge \frac{r_i}{15r_i} \ge \frac{1}{15}.$$

□

In the full version [12] we establish the following thrid claim.

Claim 3: $|\theta(\tilde{\ell}) - \theta(\ell)| = \Omega(\eta\Delta_{end})$.

As noted, the three claims just proved complete the proof of Theorem 4. □

[4]The last inequality in the following derivation follows from the inequality $\sin x < x$ for $x > 0$.

Remarks:

(1) In Theorem 4 we assume that ℓ is charged to B_0, which allows us to focus on the directions $\vec{\nu}$ for which the cross-section of B_0 by $H(\ell, \vec{\nu})$ is smaller than those of B_i, for $1 \le i \le 3$. We critically use this restriction to handle the case where the cross-sections $B_0 \cap H(\ell, \vec{\nu})$ and $B_i \cap H(\ell, \vec{\nu})$ intersect (see Figure 6 (right)). It is unclear whether the theorem still holds if we replace this assumption by a simpler one (e.g., that $r_0 < r_i$, for all $1 \le i \le 3$).

(2) The technical assumption in Theorem 4 about the angles between the vectors c_0c_i and the z-axis can be removed by using a constant number of different standard frames. Put differently, the definition of a good reference direction depends on the standard coordinate frame, and each isolated free tangent line ℓ may need to use a different standard frame (out of $O(1)$ possible ones) to deduce the existence of a large set of good directions for ℓ.

(3) An additional pruning step makes each $\vec{\nu} \in C$ satisfy that the angle between c_0c_i and the $\vec{\nu}$-direction is at least $\sin^{-1}\eta$, for each $1 \le i \le 3$. This is done by pruning all directions $\vec{\nu} \in \mathbb{S}^2$ that make angle at most $\sin^{-1}\eta$ with c_0c_i, for $1 \le i \le 3$. Clearly, all of the pruned directions belong to the union of six spherical caps of radius $\sin^{-1}\eta$ on $\mathbb{S}^2$, so we can still assume that, for sufficiently small $\eta > 0$, the set of remaining directions contains a spherical cap of radius $1/100$. (The usefulness of this note will become clear when we prove Lemma 9.)

(4) In some steps of the analysis in Section 3 we will need to assume that $\vec{\nu}$ is a good reference direction for a free tangent line ℓ, in the strong sense that $\vec{\nu}$ is a direction surviving the pruning steps of our construction.

3. THE NUMBER OF LINES CHARGED TO A FIXED BALL

In this section we prove Theorem 2. Let $\eta > 0$ be a fixed constant as in Theorem 4. We restrict our task to bounding the number of isolated free lines tangent to B_0 and to some three other balls B_i, for $1 \le i \le 3$, which are charged to B_0. We denote by d_{B_i} the distance of the center c_{B_i} of B_i from the center c_0 of B_0, and assume that the angle between $c_0c_{B_i}$ and the z-axis is at least $\sin^{-1}\eta$, for each $1 \le i \le 3$. Assuming η is small enough, as remarked above, this restriction involves no loss of generality, since we can choose a constant number of directions for the z-axis such that any isolated free tangent line $\ell \in \mathcal{L}$ satisfies these inequalities for at least one of these directions. Therefore, we henceforth assume that the angle between $c_0c_{B_i}$ and the z-axis is at least $\sin^{-1}\eta$, for every $B \in \mathcal{B} \setminus \{B_0\}$.

In addition, we may assume, without loss of generality, that, for each $B \in \mathcal{B} \setminus \{B_0\}$, there is at least one isolated free line in $\mathcal{L}$ which is tangent to B and charged to B_0.

Notation. Recall from Section 2 that each ball $B \in \mathcal{B} \setminus \{B_0\}$ defines a pair of mutually antipodal circular arcs I_B^+ and I_B^- on $\mathbb{S}^1$ of angular extent θ_B each. Let $\Delta \subset \mathbb{S}^1$ be a circular arc of angular extent $\theta_\Delta < \pi$. We say that a ball $B \in \mathcal{B}$, having θ-extent θ_B, is *wide* (resp., *narrow*) *in* Δ if Δ intersects $I_B^+ \cup I_B^-$, and $\theta_\Delta < \theta_B$ (resp., $\theta_\Delta \ge \theta_B$); see Figure 10 (left).

Let $\ell \in \mathcal{L}$ be an isolated free tangent line with $\theta(\ell) \in \Delta$, which is tangent to B_0 and to some three other balls $B_i \in \mathcal{B} \setminus \{B_0\}$, $1 \le i \le 3$, and which is charged to B_0. Clearly, for each $1 \le i \le 3$ the ball B_i is either wide or narrow in Δ. We classify ℓ as a *free WWW-line* in Δ, if all three balls B_i, $1 \le i \le 3$, are wide in Δ. We classify ℓ as a free *WWN-line (resp., WNN-line, NNN-line)* in Δ, if exactly one (resp., two, three) balls among B_i, $1 \le i \le 3$, are narrow in Δ.

To establish the asserted nearly-quadratic bound on the number of isolated free tangent lines that are charged to B_0, we will analyze separately the number of isolated free tangents of each type. The overall analysis involves a three-level recursion scheme which resembles (and is actually simpler than) the one described in [4]; see also [5].

Overall recursion. Let r be a sufficiently large constant (which will be determined later). In each step, we are given a circular arc $\Delta_0 \subset \mathbb{S}^1$ and a set $\mathcal{B}_N^{\Delta_0}$ of n narrow balls in Δ_0, and our task is to bound the number of isolated free tangents in $\{B_0\} \cup \mathcal{B}_N^{\Delta_0}$ which (belong to $\mathcal{L}$ and) are charged to B_0. (Here n denotes the size of the current subproblem rather than that of the overall initial scenario.) For this, we decompose Δ_0 into at most $2r$ subarcs Δ, each containing at most n/r endpoints of the arcs I_B^+, I_B^-, for $B \in \mathcal{B}_N^{\Delta_0}$, and each of extent smaller than π. At the first recursive step, Δ_0 is equal to $\mathbb{S}^1$, and $\mathcal{B}_N^{\Delta_0}$ is equal to $\mathcal{B} \setminus \{B_0\}$. (Here, and only here, the angular extent of Δ_0 is larger than π, but this will not affect the analysis.) As $\mathbb{S}^1$ is progressively cut into subarcs Δ, progressively more narrow balls become wide in these arcs, and the size of the subsets $\mathcal{B}_N^{\Delta}$ keeps decreasing. In fact, in a single recursive partition of an arc, a ball can remain narrow in at most two of the subarcs. During each step of recursion we immediately dispose of any *new* free WWW-, WWN-, and WNN- lines within each subarc Δ (which were free NNN-lines in the parent arc Δ_0), and continue to bound recursively the number of the remaining free NNN-lines. The recursion bottoms out when $n < r$. In this case the number of remaining isolated free tangent lines within the current arc Δ_0 can be crudely upper bounded by $O(r^4) = O(1)$.

We show below that the overall number of isolated free tangent lines of types WWW, WWN, and WNN, in a fixed subarc Δ_0, is $O(n^{2+\varepsilon})$, for any $\varepsilon > 0$. Assume for the moment that we have these bounds. Let $F(\Delta_0, \mathcal{B}_N^{\Delta_0})$ denote the number of isolated free tangent lines $\ell \in \mathcal{L}$ which are tangent to B_0 and to some triple of balls in $\mathcal{B}_N^{\Delta_0}$ and which are charged to B_0, and let $F(n)$ denote the maximum value of $F(\Delta_0, \mathcal{B}_N^{\Delta_0})$, over all possible choices of B_0, a circular arc Δ_0, and a collection $\mathcal{B}_N^{\Delta_0}$ of n narrow balls in Δ_0. Then $F(n)$ satisfies the following recurrence:

$$F(n) \le \begin{cases} 2rF(n/r) + O(n^{2+\varepsilon_0}), & n \ge r, \\ O(1), & n < r, \end{cases} \tag{1}$$

where $r > 0$ is a sufficiently large constant, $\varepsilon_0 > 0$ is an arbitrarily small constant, and the constants of proportionality in the non-recursive terms depend on r and ε_0. Clearly, for any $\varepsilon > 0$, choosing r sufficiently large and ε_0 sufficiently small (as functions of ε), yields the solution $F(n) = O(n^{2+\varepsilon})$, where the constant of proportionality depends on ε.

In what follows, we derive nearly-quadratic bounds on the number of free WWW-lines, WWN-lines, and WNN-lines within a fixed subarc Δ of Δ_0. By Theorem 4, there exists a set $\mathcal{D}$ of $O(1)$ directions on $\mathbb{S}^2$, so that for each free isolated tangent line ℓ in $\mathcal{L}$ (which is charged to B_0) there exists $\vec{\nu} \in \mathcal{D}$ which is a good reference direction for ℓ. (For example, we can choose a collection of $O(1)$ directions that hits every spherical cap of radius $1/100$. Recall that we may also assume (by applying the foregoing analysis to a constant number of choices of the z-direction) that the extra condition on the orientations of the vectors c_0c_B is satisfied for all balls $B \in \mathcal{B} \setminus \{B_0\}$.) Therefore, it is sufficient to fix a reference direction $\vec{\nu} \in \mathcal{D}$, and to bound the number of isolated free tangent lines of the above types, for which $\vec{\nu}$ is a good reference direction. Let $(\theta', \kappa', \varphi')$ denote the coordinate frame of $\mathcal{L}$ induced by $\vec{\nu}$, and let $(\theta, \kappa, \varphi)$ continue to denote the *standard* coordinate frame induced by the vertical direction $(0,0,1)$. Let δ be the constant from Theorem 4. We partition the fixed arc Δ into $\lceil 1/\delta \rceil$ subarcs $\Delta' \subset \Delta$, each of angular extent[5] $\theta_{\Delta'} \le \delta\theta_\Delta$. In what follows, we also fix a subarc Δ', and consider only lines $\ell \in \mathcal{L}$ with $\theta(\ell) \in \Delta'$.

Informally, the analysis proceeds as follows. We first derive a near-quadratic bound on the number of WWW-lines using a direct, non-recursive argument. Then we derive a recurrence for the number of WWN-lines, in which we use the bound on WWW-lines, and show that it also yields a near-quadratic bound. Then we derive another recurrence for the number of WWN-lines, which uses the bounds obtained in the two preceeding steps. This recurrence too yields a near-quadratic bound. All these bounds are then plugged into the analysis given above, thereby obtaining an overall near-quadratic bound.

The number of free WWW-lines. Fix the arcs $\Delta' \subset \Delta \subset \Delta_0$ (and the reference direction $\vec{\nu}$), as above, and denote by $\mathcal{B}_W^\Delta$ and $\mathcal{B}_N^\Delta$ the subsets of $\mathcal{B}_N^{\Delta_0}$ consisting of balls which are respectively wide and narrow in Δ. Working in the $\theta'\kappa'\varphi'$-coordinate frame of $\mathcal{L}$, we wish to represent each free WWW-line $\ell \in \mathcal{L}$ (which is charged to B_0 and satisfies $\theta(\ell) \in \Delta'$) as a vertex in a certain 3-dimensional *sandwich region* [13], below the *lower envelope* of some collection Γ^+ of at most n $\theta'\kappa'$-monotone surfaces, and above the *upper envelope* of another collection Γ^- of at most n $\theta'\kappa'$-monotone surfaces, where each surface consists of points representing common tangents to B_0 and to some other ball $B \in \mathcal{B}_W^\Delta$. Using the bounds in [3], this will yield the bound $O(n^{2+\varepsilon})$ on the number of free WWW-lines.

Definition. A line $\ell \in \mathcal{L}$ is a *positive* (resp., *negative*) tangent to $B \in \mathcal{B} \setminus \{B_0\}$ if an infinitesimally small increase (resp., descrease) in its φ'-coordinate, while keeping the $\theta'\kappa'$-coordinates fixed, causes ℓ to penetrate the interior of B. See Figure 9 (left).

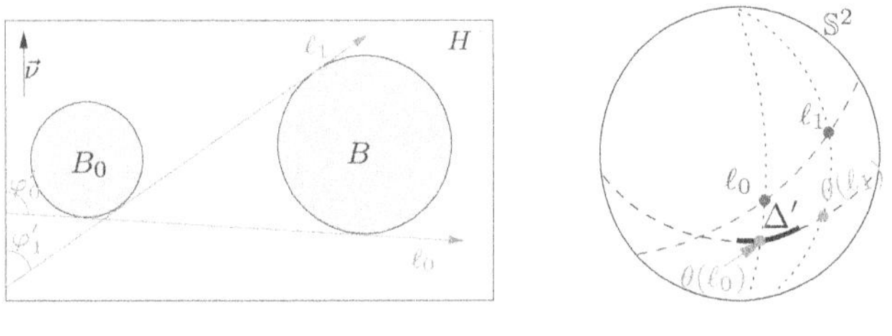

Figure 9: Left: The lines ℓ_0 and ℓ_1, sharing the same $\theta'\kappa'$-coordinates and the same plane $H = H(\ell_0, \vec{\nu}) = H(\ell_1, \vec{\nu})$, are respectively negative and positive tangents to B. Right: The point $\theta(\ell_1)$ lies outside Δ', implying that B is stabbed by all lines ℓ with $\theta'\kappa'\varphi'$-coordinates $(\theta'_0, \kappa'_0, \xi)$, such that $\xi \le \varphi'_0$ and $\theta(\ell) \in \Delta'$.

For each $B \in \mathcal{B}_W^\Delta$ let σ_B^+ (resp., σ_B^-) denote the surface patch consisting of all points representing (in the $\theta'\kappa'\varphi'$-frame) lines $\ell \in \mathcal{L}$ which are positive (resp., negative) tangents to B and satisfy the following additional conditions: (i) $\theta(\ell) \in \Delta'$, and (ii) $\vec{\nu}$ is a good reference direction for (ℓ, B). See Figure 9 (left). As is easily verified, after appropriate reparametrization, each surface patch σ_B^+, σ_B^- has *constant description complexity* (that is, it is defined as a Boolean combination of a constant number of polynomial equalities and inequalities, of constant maximum degree; see, e.g., [13]). The collection Γ^+ (resp., Γ^-) is the set of all (non-empty) surface patches of the form σ_B^+ (resp., σ_B^-), over $B \in \mathcal{B}_W^\Delta$.

The following lemma guarantees that for each ball $B \in \mathcal{B}_W^\Delta$ the surface patches $\sigma_B^+ \in \Gamma^+$ and $\sigma_B^- \in \Gamma^-$ defined above are $\theta'\kappa'$-monotone and lie respectively above and below the set of all free lines $\ell \in \mathcal{L}$ with $\theta(\ell) \in \Delta'$.

Lemma 5. *Let B be a ball in $\mathcal{B}_W^\Delta$ and let $(\theta'_0, \kappa'_0, \varphi'_0)$ be a point on the surface patch $\sigma_B^+ \in \Gamma^+$ (resp., $\sigma_B^- \in \Gamma^-$). Then B is stabbed by all lines $\ell \in \mathcal{L}$ with $\theta'\kappa'\varphi'$-coordinates $(\theta'_0, \kappa'_0, \xi)$, such that $\xi > \varphi'_0$ (resp., $\xi < \varphi'_0$) and $\theta(\ell) \in \Delta'$.*

Proof. We establish the claim only for $(\theta'_0, \kappa'_0, \varphi'_0)$ lying on σ_B^+; the argument for σ_B^- is symmetric. Suppose B is missed by some line with coordinates $(\theta'_0, \kappa'_0, \xi)$, where $\xi > \varphi'_0$, and let φ'_1 be the infimum of all such ξ. Let ℓ_0 and ℓ_1 be the lines with respective coordinates $(\theta'_0, \kappa'_0, \varphi'_0)$ and $(\theta'_0, \kappa'_0, \varphi'_1)$. Then ℓ_0 is a positive tangent and ℓ_1 is a negative tangent to B. Since $\vec{\nu}$ is good for (ℓ_0, B), we have $|\theta(\ell_0) - \theta(\ell_1)| \ge \delta\theta_B > \delta\theta_\Delta \ge \theta_{\Delta'}$. Thus, $\theta(\ell_1)$ lies outside Δ'. [6]

Note that the lines $\ell \in \mathcal{L}$ with coordinates $(\theta'_0, \kappa'_0, \xi)$ stab B for all $\varphi'_0 \le \xi \le \varphi'_1$. Now, referring to Figure 9 (right), we observe that as we rotate ℓ around B_0 by increasing $\varphi'(\ell) = \xi$ from φ'_0 to φ'_1, the value $\theta(\ell)$ either monotonically increases or monotonically decreases.[7] Let ℓ be a line as in the lemma. Since $\theta(\ell_1)$ is outside Δ', the condition that $\theta(\ell) \in \Delta'$ ensures that $\varphi'(\ell) \le \varphi'_1 = \varphi'(\ell_1)$, implying that ℓ stabs B; see Figure 9 (right). $\Box$

We next argue that each free WWW-line $\ell \in \mathcal{L}$, such that ℓ is charged to B_0, $\theta(\ell) \in \Delta'$, and $\vec{\nu}$ is a good direction for ℓ, corresponds to a vertex on the sandwich region below the lower envelope of Γ^+ and above the upper envelope of Γ^-. Indeed, any such line ℓ is tangent to B_0, and to some three other balls $B_1, B_2, B_3 \in \mathcal{B}_W^\Delta$, such that $\vec{\nu}$ is good for (ℓ, B_i), for each $1 \le i \le 3$. Therefore, $(\theta'(\ell), \kappa'(\ell), \varphi'(\ell))$ belongs to one of $\sigma_{B_i}^+, \sigma_{B_i}^-$ for each $1 \le i \le 3$. Moreover, by Lemma 5, $(\theta'(\ell), \kappa'(\ell), \varphi'(\ell))$ lies above all the other surfaces σ_B^- and below all the other surfaces σ_B^+, for $B \in \mathcal{B}_W^\Delta$. Hence ℓ corresponds to a vertex of the sandwich region, as claimed.

It follows that the number of free WWW-tangents $\ell \in \mathcal{L}$ which are charged to B_0, and satisfy the above conditions, is bounded by the number of boundary vertices of the above sandwich region. As already discussed, since each of Γ^+, Γ^- consists of $O(n)$ surface patches of constant description complexity, it follows from [3] (see also [9]) that the number of such vertices is $O(n^{2+\varepsilon})$, for any $\varepsilon > 0$. Thus, we have shown the following.

Theorem 6. *Let Δ be a circular arc on $\mathbb{S}^1$ and let $\mathcal{B}_W^\Delta$ be a collection of n wide balls in Δ. Then $\{B_0\} \cup \mathcal{B}_W^\Delta$ admits*

[5] Without loss of generality, we assume that $\delta < 1/2$, which ensures that Δ' has θ-span at most π.

[6] The intersection between Δ' and $(\theta(\ell_0), \theta(\ell_1))$ is connected since $\theta_{\Delta'}, \theta_B < \pi$. (This condition has to be verified only at the top level of recursion; it holds trivially at deeper levels.)

[7] This follows since the direction vector of ℓ moves along the $H(\ell, \vec{\nu})$-parallel great circle on $\mathbb{S}^2$.

at most $O(n^{2+\varepsilon})$ free isolated tangent lines that are charged to B_0, for any $\varepsilon > 0$.

The number of free WWN-lines. We continue to follow the setup assumed in the preceding analysis. That is, we have fixed arcs $\Delta' \subseteq \Delta \subseteq \Delta_0$ on $\mathbb{S}^1$, a fixed reference direction $\vec{\nu} \in \mathcal{D}$, and two sets $\mathcal{B}_W^\Delta, \mathcal{B}_N^\Delta$ of balls which are, respectively, wide and narrow in Δ. Put $m = |\mathcal{B}_W^\Delta|$ and $n = |\mathcal{B}_N^\Delta|$. We only consider free WWN-lines ℓ charged to B_0 and tangent to two balls in $\mathcal{B}_W^\Delta$ and to one ball in $\mathcal{B}_N^\Delta$, so that $\theta(\ell) \in \Delta'$, and $\vec{\nu}$ is a good reference direction for ℓ.

For each $B \in \mathcal{B}\setminus\{B_0\}$, in analogy to the definition of the θ-span, let $I_B'^{+}$ and $I_B'^{-}$ denote the pair of mutually antipodal circular arcs whose union forms the set of all θ'-values of lines $\ell \in \mathcal{L}$ that stab B. Accordingly, we define the θ'-span θ'_B of each $B \in \mathcal{B} \setminus \{B_0\}$ as the angular extent of each one of the arcs $I_B'^{+}, I_B'^{-}$. (As in the case of the θ-span, if the $\vec{\nu}$-orthogonal projections of B_0 and B intersect each other, we either set θ'_B to be π, if B is not contained in B_0, or, otherwise, ignore B, since no $\ell \in \mathcal{L}$ can be tangent to B. See Section 2 for more details.) Our analysis relies on the following technical lemma. By definition, the θ-span of a narrow ball is smaller than that of a wide ball. The lemma shows that this is also true, up to a constant factor, for the θ'-spans of the two balls. It actually establishes a slightly more general result.

LEMMA 7. *Let $B_W, B_N \in \mathcal{B} \setminus \{B_0\}$, such that $\theta_{B_N} \le \theta_{B_W}$. Then $\theta'_{B_N} = O(\theta'_{B_W}/\eta^2)$.*

PROOF. Let r_{B_W}, r_{B_N} be the respective radii of B_W, B_N, and let d_{B_W}, d_{B_N} be the respective distances of their centers, c_{B_W}, c_{B_N}, from c_0. The fact that the angle between $c_0c_{B_W}$ and the z-axis is at least $\sin^{-1}\eta$, together with Claim 2 of Section 2 (applied to B_W), imply that

$$\theta_{B_W} = O(\min\{r_{B_W}/(\eta d_{B_W}), 1\}). \qquad (2)$$

We also have that

$$\theta_{B_W} \ge \theta_{B_N} = \Omega(\min\{r_{B_N}/d_{B_N}, 1\}). \qquad (3)$$

Indeed, if the xy-projections of B_0, B_N intersect then $\theta_{B_N} = \Theta(1)$; otherwise we refer to Figure 8 (with B_N instead of B_i) and observe that $\sin\theta_{B_N} = (r_0 + r_{B_N})/\hat{d}_{B_N} \ge r_{B_N}/d_{B_N}$.

The combination of (2) and (3) implies that

$$\min\{r_{B_N}/d_{B_N}, 1\} = O(\min\{r_{B_W}/(\eta d_{B_W}), 1\}). \qquad (4)$$

Similarly to (2), the fact that the angle between $c_0c_{B_N}$ and $\vec{\nu}$ is $\ge \sin^{-1}\eta$ implies that $\theta'_{B_N} = O(\min\{r_{B_N}/(\eta d_{B_N}), 1\})$. Thus, (4) implies that $\theta'_{B_N} = O(\min\{r_{B_W}/(\eta^2 d_{B_W}), 1\})$. Similarly to (3), we can show that $\theta'_{B_W} = \Omega(\min\{r_{B_W}/d_{B_W}, 1\})$, implying finally that $\theta'_{B_N} = O(\theta'_{B_W}/\eta^2)$. $\square$

For each ball $B \in \mathcal{B}_W^\Delta$ we construct the $\theta'\kappa'$-monotone surface patches σ_B^+, σ_B^-, as defined above, and let Γ^+, Γ^- denote the corresponding collections of these patches. (Recall that these patches are defined for the fixed pair of arcs $\Delta' \subseteq \Delta$.)

We fix a sufficiently large constant parameter $r \ge 0$ and apply a secondary recursive decomposition of the problem, where the arc $\Delta' \subset \Delta$ is kept fixed and the decomposition is of the $\theta'\kappa'$-domain. To do so, we extend the notions of wideness and narrowness to $\theta'\kappa'$-regions (rather than θ-ranges), as follows. Let τ be any (connected) region within the $\theta'\kappa'$-domain, and let θ'_τ denote the angular extent of the θ'-projection of τ. We call a ball $B \in \mathcal{B} \setminus \{B_0\}$ *wide* (resp., *narrow*) *in* τ if (i) B is stabbed by at least one line $\ell \in \mathcal{L}$ having $(\theta'(\ell), \kappa'(\ell)) \in \tau$, and (ii) B has θ'-span θ'_B larger than (resp., at most) θ'_τ. To distinguish between the two notions of wideness/narrowness, we refer to balls which are wide/narrow in the earlier sense as θ-wide or θ-narrow, and to balls which are wide/narrow in the new sense as θ'-wide or θ'-narrow, respectively.

At each recursive step we are given a (parent) pseudo-trapezoidal (and connected) region τ_0 in the $\theta'\kappa'$-domain, a set $\mathcal{B}_N^{\tau_0}$ of n balls that are θ-narrow in Δ and θ'-narrow in τ_0, and a set $\mathcal{B}_W^{\tau_0}$ of m balls that are θ-wide in Δ and contribute a surface patch to $\Gamma^+ \cup \Gamma^-$ which appears on the boundary of $\mathcal{F}(\mathcal{B})$ over τ_0. The subsets of Γ^+, Γ^- consisting of these patches are denoted by $\Gamma_{\tau_0}^+, \Gamma_{\tau_0}^-$, respectively. Our goal is to bound the number of free lines $\ell \in \mathcal{L}$ such that $(\theta'(\ell), \kappa'(\ell)) \in \tau_0$, ℓ is tangent to two balls of $\mathcal{B}_W^{\tau_0}$ and to one ball in $\mathcal{B}_N^{\tau_0}$. Initially, τ_0 is the entire $\theta'\kappa'$-domain, and $\mathcal{B}_N^{\tau_0} = \mathcal{B}_N^\Delta$; all these balls are indeed θ-narrow in Δ and θ'-narrow in τ_0.

The parent region τ_0 is decomposed into $O(r^{2+\varepsilon})$ connected pseudo-trapezoidal cells τ, for any $\varepsilon > 0$, satisfying the following properties:

(i) At most m/r surface patches of $\Gamma_{\tau_0}^+ \cup \Gamma_{\tau_0}^-$ appear on the boundary of $\mathcal{F}(\mathcal{B})$ over τ. We denote the set of all balls generating those patches by $\mathcal{B}_W^\tau$. Observe that any free WWN-line $\ell \in \mathcal{L}$, having $(\theta'(\ell), \kappa'(\ell)) \in \tau$, is tangent to two balls from $\mathcal{B}_W^\tau$.

(ii) At most n/r balls from $\mathcal{B}_N^{\tau_0}$ remain θ'-narrow in τ. Let us denote the set of these balls as $\mathcal{B}_N^\tau$.

In more detail, our decomposition scheme is defined in two stages. First, we sample, randomly and uniformly, a collection of $br\log r$ surface patches from $\Gamma_{\tau_0}^+ \cup \Gamma_{\tau_0}^-$, for a sufficiently large constant $b > 0$, and treat each sampled patch as a partially defined function over the $\theta'\kappa'$-domain. Denote by $\mathcal{M}^+$ (resp., $\mathcal{M}^-$) the portions within τ_0 of the minimization (resp., maximization) diagram of the surfaces sampled from Γ^+ (resp., Γ^-). Let $\mathcal{M}$ be the decomposition of τ_0 obtained by partitioning the overlay of $\mathcal{M}^+$ and $\mathcal{M}^-$ into pseudo-trapezoidal cells (of constant description complexity). The analysis in [3, 9] implies that $\mathcal{M}$ consists of $O(r^{2+\varepsilon})$ cells, for any $\varepsilon > 0$. Let τ be any fixed (pseudo-trapezoidal) cell in $\mathcal{M}$, and let Γ_τ^+ (resp., Γ_τ^-) denote the set of patches from $\Gamma_{\tau_0}^+$ (resp., $\Gamma_{\tau_0}^-$) that appear over τ on the boundary of the sandwich region below the lower envelope of $\Gamma_{\tau_0}^+$ and above the upper envelope of $\Gamma_{\tau_0}^-$.

The ε-net theory (see, e.g., [13]) guarantees that, for $b > 0$ sufficiently large, we have $|\Gamma_\tau^+| \le m/(2r)$ and $|\Gamma_\tau^-| \le m/(2r)$ (that is, τ satisfies condition (i)), with probability close to 1. This guarantees, with high probability, that $|\mathcal{B}_W^\tau| \le m/r$, for any child subcell τ of τ_0. We assume that our sample does indeed satisfy this property.

We further refine $\mathcal{M}$ as follows. We partition the θ'-projection of τ_0 into $O(r)$ circular arcs, each containing at most n/r endpoints of the arcs $I_B'^{+}, I_B'^{-}$, for $B \in \mathcal{B}_N^\Delta$. We obtain a strip decomposition of the $\theta'\kappa'$-domain by lifting each of the above circular arcs into a κ'-parallel strip. Let $\mathcal{M}'$ denote the overlay of $\mathcal{M}$ with the resulting strip decomposition. See Figure 10 (right). Clearly, each cell $\tau \in \mathcal{M}'$ satisfies $|\mathcal{B}_N^\tau| \le n/r$, so the cells of $\mathcal{M}'$ satisfy both (i) and (ii).

The following lemma has been proved, in a different, albeit

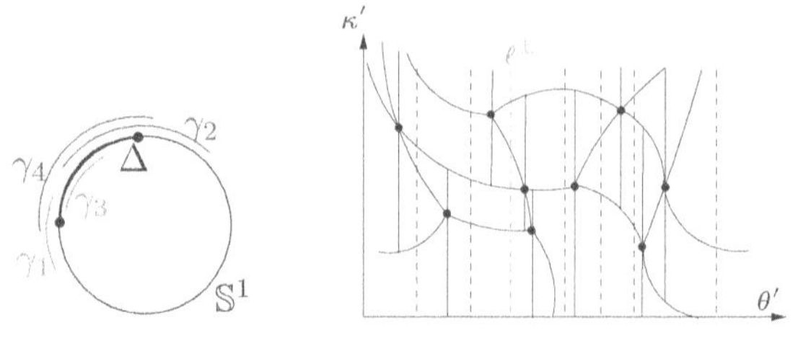

Figure 10: Left: The circular arcs γ_1 and γ_3 are narrow with respect to $\Delta \subset \mathbb{S}^1$, while the arcs γ_2 and γ_4 are wide. Right: The pseudo-trapezoidal decomposition $\mathcal{M}'$ (at the first level of recursion, where τ_0 is the whole $\theta'\kappa'$-domain). The edges of $\mathcal{M}$ are drawn solid, and the strip decomposition is drawn dashed.

very similar context, in [4]. For the sake of completeness, we give a sketch of its proof for the setup considered here.

LEMMA 8. *The decomposition $\mathcal{M}'$ consists of $O(r^{2+\varepsilon})$ pseudo-trapezoidal cells, for any $\varepsilon > 0$.*

PROOF. As the complexity of $\mathcal{M}$ is $O(r^{2+\varepsilon})$, for any $\varepsilon > 0$, it is sufficient to bound the number of vertices v in $\mathcal{M}'$ that are formed by the intersection between the edges of $\mathcal{M}$ and the κ'-parallel lines of the strip decomposition. Fix such a line $\ell^{\perp}$. Let $\tilde{\Gamma}^+$ (resp., $\tilde{\Gamma}^-$) denote the collection of $O(r \log r)$ arcs, each of which is formed by intersecting some patch of Γ^+ (resp., Γ^-) with the φ'-parallel ("vertical") plane through $\ell^{\perp}$. Then each vertex v of $\mathcal{M}'$ of the above kind is the $\theta'\kappa'$-projection of a vertex of the sandwich region which is enclosed between the lower envelope of $\tilde{\Gamma}^+$ and the upper envelope of $\tilde{\Gamma}^-$. The number of such vertices v is $O(\lambda_s(r) \log r)$, for an appropriate constant parameter s, for any fixed $\ell^{\perp}$ (see also [13]). The bound now follows by repeating this argument to each of the $O(r)$ lines $\ell^{\perp}$. $\square$

As the $\theta'\kappa'$-domain is progressively cut into subcells τ, more and more balls of $\mathcal{B}_N^{\Delta}$ become θ'-wide in τ, while the size of $\mathcal{B}_N^{\tau}$ and $\mathcal{B}_W^{\tau}$ keeps decreasing. During each step of the recursion we immediately dispose of any free WWN-lines tangent to the new θ'-wide balls from $\mathcal{B}_N^{\Delta}$ (that is, balls that were θ'-narrow in the parent cell τ_0 of τ). The number of these lines is bounded by the following lemma.

LEMMA 9. *Let Δ be a circular arc on $\mathbb{S}^1$, and let τ be a (connected) region in the $\theta'\kappa'$-domain. Let $\mathcal{B}_W^{\tau} \subset \mathcal{B} \setminus \{B_0\}$ be a collection of m balls which are θ-wide in Δ, and let $\mathcal{B}_N^{\tau} \subset \mathcal{B} \setminus \{B_0\}$ be another collection of n balls which are θ-narrow in Δ and θ'-wide in τ. Then the number of free lines $\ell \in \mathcal{L}$ which are charged to B_0 and satisfy: (i) $(\theta'(\ell), \kappa'(\ell)) \in \tau$, (ii) ℓ is tangent to two balls from $\mathcal{B}_W^{\tau}$ and to one ball from $\mathcal{B}_N^{\tau}$, and (iii) $\vec{\nu}$ is a good direction for ℓ, is $O((n+m)m^{1+\varepsilon})$, for any $\varepsilon > 0$.*

PROOF. We partition the set of all balls $B \in \mathcal{B}_N^{\tau}$ into $O(\lceil n/m \rceil)$ sets of size $O(m)$ each. For each resulting set $\mathcal{B}'$ we establish the bound $O(m^{2+\varepsilon})$, for any $\varepsilon > 0$, on the number of free WWN-lines $\ell \in \mathcal{L}$ as in the lemma, which are tangent to two balls from $\mathcal{B}_W^{\Delta}$, and to one from $\mathcal{B}'$. Summing over all subsets $\mathcal{B}'$, and observing that all lines under consideration are counted in this sum, the bound asserted in the lemma follows.

Fix a subset $\mathcal{B}'$. Each ball $\hat{B} \in \mathcal{B}'$ satisfies $\theta'_{\hat{B}} \geq \theta'_{\tau}$. On the other hand, each ball $B \in \mathcal{B}_W^{\tau} \subset \mathcal{B}_W^{\Delta}$ satisfies $\theta_B \geq \theta_{\Delta} \geq \theta_{\hat{B}}$, and thus, by Lemma 7, we have $\theta'_B = \Omega(\eta^2 \theta'_{\hat{B}})$. Hence $\theta'_B = \Omega(\eta^2 \theta'_{\tau})$, for every $B \in \mathcal{B}_W^{\tau}$.

We partition τ, by κ'-parallel lines, into c/η^2 pseudo-trapezoidal subcells $\mu \subset \tau$, where c is a sufficiently large constant, such that $\theta'_{\mu} = O(\eta^2 \theta'_{\tau})$, for every μ. Then, with an appropriate choice of c, for each $B \in \mathcal{B}_W^{\tau} \cup \mathcal{B}'$, either B is θ'-wide in μ, or $I_B'^{+} \cup I_B'^{-}$ is disjoint from the θ'-projection Δ'_{μ} of μ. Balls of the second kind can be ignored because they do not induce any free lines with $(\theta'(\ell), \kappa'(\ell)) \in \mu$. We now apply Theorem 6 to the set $\mathcal{B}_W^{\tau} \cup \mathcal{B}'$ (and the arc $\Delta'_{\mu} \subset \mathbb{S}^1$). In this application we regard $\vec{\nu}$ as the positive z-direction. Then the balls of $\mathcal{B}_W^{\tau} \cup \mathcal{B}'$ are wide, in the original sense, with respect to Δ'_{μ}. In this new setting, Theorem 6 implies that the number of free lines in $\mathcal{L}$, charged to B_0 and admitted by the balls of $\mathcal{B}' \cup \mathcal{B}_W^{\tau}$, such that $(\theta'(\ell), \kappa'(\ell)) \in \mu$ (and hence $\theta'(\ell) \in \Delta'_{\mu}$), and $\vec{\nu}$ is good for ℓ, is $O(m^{2+\varepsilon})$, for any $\varepsilon > 0$.

Recall that in order to apply Theorem 6 in the new context, we must assume that, for every $B \in \mathcal{B}_W^{\tau} \cup \mathcal{B}'$, the angle between $c_0 c_B$ and the $\vec{\nu}$-direction is at least $\sin^{-1} \eta$. This assumption can be made because of the additional pruning step imposed on the set of good directions in Section 2 (see Remark 3 at the end of that section), and because $\vec{\nu}$ is assumed to be a good direction, belonging to the set constructed in the pruning procedure of Section 2, for all isolated free lines $\ell \in \mathcal{L}$ counted by the current lemma. This allows us to consider in $\mathcal{B}_W^{\tau} \cup \mathcal{B}'$ only the balls $B \in \mathcal{B} \setminus \{B_0\}$ for which the angle between $c_0 c_B$ and the $\vec{\nu}$-direction is at least $\sin^{-1} \eta$. $\square$

We now return to the "global" subproblem involving a fixed arc Δ (and a subarc Δ') $\subseteq \mathbb{S}^1$. Let $F_1(n, m)$ denote the maximum number of free WWN-lines $\ell \in \mathcal{L}$ charged to B_0 and tangent to one ball from $\mathcal{B}_N^{\Delta}$ and two balls from $\mathcal{B}_W^{\Delta}$, such that $\vec{\nu}$ is a good direction for ℓ, over all possible collections $\mathcal{B}_W^{\Delta} \subset \mathcal{B} \setminus \{B_0\}$ and $\mathcal{B}_N^{\Delta} \subset \mathcal{B} \setminus \{B_0\}$ of m (resp., n) θ-wide (resp., θ-narrow) balls in Δ. Then $F_1(n, m)$ satisfies the following recurrence.

$$F_1(n,m) = \begin{cases} O(r^{2+\varepsilon_0}) F_1(\frac{n}{r}, \frac{m}{r}) + O((n+m)m^{1+\varepsilon_0}), & \min\{n,m\} \geq r, \\ O(n+m^2), & \min\{n,m\} < r, \end{cases} \quad (5)$$

where $r > 0$ is a sufficiently large constant, $\varepsilon_0 > 0$ is an arbitrarily small constant, and the constants of proportionality depend on ε_0, and, in the two non-recursive terms, also on r. (The second bound is the trivial bound $O(nm^2)$, specialized for the case $\min\{m, n\} < r$) The recurrence solves to $F_1(n, m) = O((n+m)m^{1+\varepsilon})$, for any $\varepsilon > \varepsilon_0$. Hence, the bound holds for any $\varepsilon > 0$, by choosing a smaller value for ε_0. Thus, summing over all good directions and subarcs Δ', we obtain the following theorem.

THEOREM 10. *The number of free WWN-lines of $\mathcal{L}$ (which are charged to B_0) in Δ, with respect to a set $\mathcal{B}_W^{\Delta}$ of m θ-wide balls and a set $\mathcal{B}_N^{\Delta}$ of n θ-narrow balls, is $O((n+m)m^{1+\varepsilon})$, for any $\varepsilon > 0$.*

The number of free WNN-lines. As in the case of free WWN-lines, we assume a fixed choice the θ-arcs $\Delta' \subseteq \Delta \subseteq \mathbb{S}^1$, and of the direction $\vec{\nu} \in \mathbb{S}^2$, and only consider free WWN-lines ℓ charged to B_0 and tangent to two balls in $\mathcal{B}_W^{\Delta}$ and to one ball in $\mathcal{B}_N^{\Delta}$, so that $\theta(\ell) \in \Delta'$, and $\vec{\nu}$ is a good reference direction for ℓ. To bound the number of such lines we use the same recursive decomposition of the $\theta'\kappa'$-domain as in the case WWN-lines. At each step of this recursion we consider a fixed pseudo-trapezoid τ and dispose of all WNN-lines that are tangent to one ball of $\mathcal{B}_W^\tau \subseteq \mathcal{B}_W^\Delta$, to ball of $\mathcal{B}_N^\tau$ which is θ'-wide in τ, and to one ball of $\mathcal{B}_N^\tau$ which is either θ'-wide or θ'-narrow in τ.

To bound the number of free WNN-lines disposed of at each recursion step (in terms of $|\mathcal{B}_N^\tau|$ and $|\mathcal{B}_W^\tau|$), we establish in the full version [12] a stronger variant of Lemma 9 whose proof uses Theorem 10 instead of Theorem 6. This yields a recursion formula on the number of free WNN-lines, as above, whose solution implies the following theorem; see the full version [12] for more details.

THEOREM 11. *The number of free WNN-lines of $\mathcal{L}$ (which are charged to B_0) in Δ, with respect to a set $\mathcal{B}_W^\Delta$ of m θ-wide balls and a set $\mathcal{B}_N^\Delta$ of n θ-narrow balls, is $O((n+m)n^{1+\varepsilon})$, for any $\varepsilon > 0$.*

Returning to the overall recursion scheme, we apply Theorems 6, 10, and 11 to bound the overall number of new free WWW-, WWN-, and WNN-lines that are disposed of while processing a single θ-arc $\Delta \subset \mathbb{S}^1$. Let n denote the number of balls $B \in \mathcal{B} \setminus \{B_0\}$ which are θ-narrow at the parent arc Δ_0 of Δ. Then $|\mathcal{B}_W^\Delta| + |\mathcal{B}_N^\Delta| \le n$, and the preceding analysis implies that the number of lines disposed of at Δ is $O(n^{2+\varepsilon})$, for any $\varepsilon > 0$. Hence, the number of isolated free tangent lines of $\mathcal{L}$ admitted by $\mathcal{B}$, which are charged to B_0, is bounded by the function $F(n)$ satisfying the recurrence (1). As we have shown, $F(n) = O(n^{2+\varepsilon})$, for any $\varepsilon > 0$. This completes the proof of Theorem 2, and thus also of the main Theorem 3. □

4. DISCUSSION

Finding free lines. Unlike the analysis of [1], our proof of Theorem 3 is constructive, and leads to an deterministic algorithm which finds all isolated free lines (and, hence, the boundary description of the free space $\mathcal{F}(\mathcal{B})$) in $O(n^{3+\varepsilon})$ time, for any $\varepsilon > 0$. For each ball $B_0 \in B$, we compute in $O(n^{2+\varepsilon})$ time, for any $\varepsilon > 0$, a superset $A_{\mathcal{L}}$ of isolated tangent lines in $\mathcal{L} = \mathcal{L}(B_0)$ which contains all isolated free lines charged to B_0, by closely following the recursion in Section 3; see the full version [12] for more details. We can then use the data structure of [10] which supports ray shooting amid the spheres of $\mathcal{B}$ in polylogarithmic time, and requires $O(n^{3+\varepsilon})$ storage and preprocessing time, for any $\varepsilon > 0$, to find all free lines in $A_{\mathcal{L}}$.

Union of geometric objects and free lines. Our analysis works through reduction to the problem of bounding the number of vertices on the boundary of the union of a certain kind of regions in parametric 3-space. Hence, a side interpretation of our result is that it provides yet another class of objects in 3-space whose union has near-quadratic complexity, adding to the growing body of such instances studied in the past decade (see [2] for a comprehensive survey.)

Overlays of minimization diagrams in $\mathbb{R}^2$ and in $\mathbb{R}^3$. The analysis of [1], for the case of unit balls, uses an upper bound of $O(n^{3+\varepsilon})$, for any $\varepsilon > 0$, on the complexity of the overlay of two minimization diagrams in $\mathbb{R}^3$, whose proof in [9] requires a fairly intricate analysis. In contrast, our (more general) result only needs the simpler bound of $O(n^{2+\varepsilon})$, for any $\varepsilon > 0$, on the complexity of the overlay of two minimization diagrams in $\mathbb{R}^2$, given in [3].

Open problems. The construction of [6] suggests that our bound on the number of isolated free tangents to a collection of n arbitrary balls is nearly tight in the worst case. However, this is still open for *unit* balls, because the construction of [6] uses balls of different radii, whereas the best known lower bound for unit balls, as given in [1], is only $\Omega(n^2)$.

In addition, the problem of bounding the maximum number of isolated free lines tangent to a fixed ball of $B_0 \in \mathcal{B}$ is still open, since the near-quadratic bound of Theorem 2 pertains only to the number of such lines that are *charged* to B_0.

Acknowledgements. I would like to thank my advisor Micha Sharir for helpful discussions concerning the results of the paper, and, in particular, for his invaluable help in the proof of Theorem 4 and in the preparation of the paper. I would also like to thank the anonymous referees for valuable suggestions that helped to improve the presentation.

5. REFERENCES

[1] P. K. Agarwal, B. Aronov, V. Koltun and M. Sharir, On lines avoiding unit balls in three dimensions, *Discrete Comput. Geom.* 34 (2005), 231–250.

[2] P. K. Agarwal, J. Pach, M. Sharir, State of the union–of geometric objects, In *Surveys in Discrete and Computational Geometry Twenty Years Later* (J. E. Goodman et al., eds.), Contemporary Mathematics, AMS, Providence, RI, vol. 453, AMS, Providence, RI, 2008, pp. 9–48.

[3] P. K. Agarwal, O. Schwarzkopf and M. Sharir, The overlay of lower envelopes in 3-space and its applications, *Discrete Comput. Geom.* 15 (1996), 1–13.

[4] E. Ezra, On the union of cylinders in three dimensions, *Proc. 43rd Annu. IEEE Symp. on Foundations of Computer Science* (2008), 179–188.

[5] E. Ezra and M. Sharir, Counting and representing intersections among triangles in three dimensions, *Comput. Geom. Theory Appl.* 32 (2005), 196–215.

[6] M. Glisse and S. Lazard, On the complexity of sets of free lines and line segments among balls in three dimensions, this proceedings. See also `http://geometrica.saclay.inria.fr/team/Marc.Glisse/tmp/scg35-glisse.pdf`

[7] H. Kaplan, N. Rubin and M. Sharir, Linear data structures for fast ray-shooting amidst convex polyhedra, *Algorithmica* 55 (2) (2009), 283–310.

[8] H. Kaplan, N. Rubin and M. Sharir, Line transversals of convex polyhedra in $\mathbb{R}^3$, *Proc. 19th Annu. ACM-SIAM Symp. on Discrete Algorithms* (2009), 170–179. Also *SIAM. J. Comput., to appear.*

[9] V. Koltun and M. Sharir, The partition technique for overlays of envelopes, *SIAM J. Comput.* 32(4) (2003), 841–863.

[10] S. Mohaban and M. Sharir, Ray shooting amidst spheres in 3 dimensions and related problems, *SIAM J. Comput.* 26 (1997), 654–674.

[11] M. Pellegrini, On lines missing polyhedral sets in 3-space, *Discrete Comput. Geom.* 12 (1994), 203–221.

[12] N. Rubin, Lines avoiding balls in three dimensions revisited, `http://www.cs.tau.ac.il/~rubinnat/AvoidingLines.pdf`.

[13] M. Sharir and P. K. Agarwal, *Davenport-Schinzel Sequences and Their Geometric Applications,* Cambridge University Press, Cambridge-New York-Melbourne, 1995.

[14] R. Wenger, Helly-type theorems and geometric transversals, in *Handbook of Discrete and Computational Geometry*, 2nd Edition (J.E. Goodman and J. O'Rourke, Eds.), Chapman & Hall/CRC Press, 2004, pp. 73–96.

Adding One Edge to Planar Graphs Makes Crossing Number Hard*

Sergio Cabello
Department of Mathematics
IMFM and FMF, University of Ljubljana
Slovenia
sergio.cabello@fmf.uni-lj.si

Bojan Mohar†
Department of Mathematics
Simon Fraser University
Burnaby, B.C. V5A 1S6
mohar@sfu.ca

ABSTRACT

A graph is *near-planar* if it can be obtained from a planar graph by adding an edge. We show that it is NP-hard to compute the crossing number of near-planar graphs. The main idea in the reduction is to consider the problem of simultaneously drawing two planar graphs inside a disk, with some of its vertices fixed at the boundary of the disk. This approach can be used to prove hardness of some other geometric problems. As an interesting consequence we obtain a new, geometric proof of NP-completeness of the crossing number problem, even when restricted to cubic graphs. This resolves a question of Hliněný.

Categories and Subject Descriptors

F.2.2 [**Analysis of Algorithms and Problem Complexity**]: Nonnumerical algorithms and problems—*Geometric problems and computations; Computations on discrete structures*; G.2.2 [**Discrete Mathematics**]: Graph theory—*Graph algorithms*

General Terms

Algorithms, Theory

Keywords

Topological graph theory, planar graphs, crossing number, NP-hard, graph drawing, graph embedding

1. INTRODUCTION

A *drawing* of a graph G in the plane is a representation of G where vertices are represented by distinct points of $\mathbb{R}^2$, edges are represented by simple polygonal arcs in $\mathbb{R}^2$ joining points that correspond to their endvertices, and the interior of every arc representing an edge contains no points representing the vertices of G. A *crossing* of a drawing $\mathcal{D}$ is a pair $(\{e, e'\}, p)$, where e and e' are distinct edges and $p \in \mathbb{R}^2$ is a point that belongs to the interiors of both arcs representing e and e' in the drawing $\mathcal{D}$. The number of crossings of a drawing $\mathcal{D}$ is denoted by $\mathtt{cr}(\mathcal{D})$ and is called the *crossing number* of the drawing. The *crossing number* $\mathtt{cr}(G)$ of a graph G is the minimum $\mathtt{cr}(\mathcal{D})$ taken over all drawings $\mathcal{D}$ of G. A drawing $\mathcal{D}$ with $\mathtt{cr}(\mathcal{D}) = 0$ is called an *embedding* of G.

A graph is *near-planar* if it can be obtained from a planar graph G by adding an extra edge xy between vertices x and y of G. We denote such near-planar graph by $G + xy$. (The term *almost planar* has also been used for the same concept [10, 13].) Near-planarity is a very weak relaxation of planarity, and hence it is natural to study the crossing number of near-planar graphs. Graphs embeddable in the torus and apex graphs are a superfamily of near-planar graphs. We show that it is NP-hard to compute the crossing number of near-planar graphs. This result is not only surprising but also fundamental. It provides evidence that computing crossing numbers is an extremely challenging task, even for the simplest families of non-planar graphs.

Our reduction is based on considering the following optimization problem: draw two planar graphs inside a disk with some of its vertices at prescribed positions of the boundary, so as to minimize the number of crossings in the drawing. We show that this problem is NP-hard using a reduction from satisfiability (SAT). The reduction is inspired by the work of Werner [16], although the details in our proof are essentially different. We can then use a technique from [13] to provide NP-hardness of computing the crossing number of near-planar graphs.

Our approach can be used to prove hardness of some other geometric problems. As an interesting consequence we obtain a new, geometric proof of NP-completeness of the crossing number problem, even when restricted to cubic graphs. Hardness of the crossing number problem for cubic graphs was established by Hliněný [9], who asked if one can prove this result by a reduction from an NP-complete geometric problem instead of the LINEAR ARRANGEMENT problem used in his proof.

Related work. It has been known for quite some time that it is NP-hard to compute crossing numbers of graphs. Pre-

*Research partially supported by the Slovenian Research Agency, program P1-0297, by an NSERC Discovery Grant, and by the Canada Research Chair Program.

†On leave from IMFM & FMF, Department of Mathematics, University of Ljubljana, 1000 Ljubljana, Slovenia.

SCG'10, June 13–16, 2010, Snowbird, Utah, USA.

vious proofs involved reductions from the problem LINEAR ARRANGEMENT [6, 9, 14]. The spirit of our reduction is completely different from previous proofs and hence of interest in its own right. In particular, we provide an alternative proof that computing crossing numbers is NP-hard (even when restricted to cubic graphs). Our NP-hardness proof is more complicated, but it provides the additional bonus of having control over the structure of the graph and henceforth working for near-planar graphs.

The study of crossing numbers for near-planar graphs was initiated by Riskin [15], who showed that if G is a planar 3-connected cubic graph, then the crossing number of $G + xy$ is equal to the length of a shortest path in the geometric dual graph of the planar subgraph $G - x - y$. A consequence of his result it that the crossing number of a 3-connected cubic near-planar graph can be computed in polynomial time. Riskin asked if a similar result holds in more general situations. This was disproved by Mohar [13] and Gutwenger, Mutzel, and Weiskircher [8]. In fact, the result cannot be extended even assuming 5-connectivity.

For near-planar graphs of maximum degree Δ, Hliněný and Salazar [10] provided a Δ-approximation algorithm for the crossing number. Later, we [2] improved the approximation factor of this algorithm to $\lfloor \Delta/2 \rfloor$ using combinatorial bounds that relate the crossing number of $G + xy$ to the number of vertex-disjoint and edge-disjoint cycles in G that separate x and y. This separation has to be defined in a certain strong sense over all planar embeddings of G. Approximation algorithms for the crossing number have been provided for some superfamilies of near-planar graphs [3, 4, 11]. However, it should be noted that it was not known if computing the crossing number in any of those families is NP-hard. Combinatorial bounds have also been studied in [1, 5].

Our previous paper [2] contained a closely related result: namely, we showed that computing the crossing number of near-planar graphs is NP-hard for *weighted* graphs. Unfortunately, our reduction was from PARTITION, and hence required weights that are not polynomially bounded in the size of the graph. Moreover, the planarizing edge xy needed large weight, so $G + xy$ could not be transformed into an unweighted near-planar graph. See the discussion below. In this paper we use completely different techniques.

Kawarabayashi and Reed [12], improving upon a result of Grohe [7], have shown that for each constant k_0 there is a linear-time algorithm that decides if the crossing number of an input graph is at most k_0. Hence, it is clear that in our reduction the crossing number has to be an increasing function in the number of vertices.

Weighted vs. unweighted edges. Our discussion will be simplified by using weighted edges. When each edge e of G has a weight $w_e \in \mathbb{N}$, the crossing number of a drawing $\mathcal{D}$ is defined as $\sum w_e \cdot w_{e'}$, the sum taken over all crossings $(\{e, e'\}, p)$ in $\mathcal{D}$. The crossing number of G is then defined again as the minimum $\mathtt{cr}(\mathcal{D})$ taken over all drawings $\mathcal{D}$ of G.

Let G be a weighted graph. Consider the unweighted graph H_G with $V(H_G) = V(G)$, in which there are w_{uv} subdivided "parallel" edges between u and v in H_G, for each edge $uv \in E(G)$. It is easy to see that $\mathtt{cr}(H_G) = \mathtt{cr}(G)$. If the weights of G are polynomially bounded in $|V(G)|$, then H_G can be constructed in polynomial time. Hence, in our reduction it will be enough to describe a weighted planar graph G whose weights are polynomially bounded, and then describe which extra edge xy we add. The resulting unweighted near-planar graph is $H_G + xy$. The additional edge xy that we add must have unit weight, as otherwise the resulting graph H_{G+xy} would not be near-planar.

Anchored graphs. The main idea in our proof is considering a concept of anchored graphs, and studying the corresponding crossing numbers. We are not aware of any previous work considering this concept.

An *anchored graph* is a triple (G, A_G, π_G), where G is a graph, A_G is a subset of vertices of G, and π_G is a circular ordering of A_G. For reasons that will become evident soon, we call the vertices A_G *anchors*. With a slight abuse of notation, we will sometimes use G to denote an anchored graph when the anchor set A_G and the ordering π_G are implicit.

Let $\Omega \subseteq \mathbb{R}^2$ be a topological disk whose boundary is a closed polygonal line. An *anchored drawing* of an anchored graph (G, A_G, π_G) is a drawing of G in Ω such that the vertices of A_G are represented by points on the boundary of the disk Ω, and the ordering of the anchors A_G along the boundary of Ω is π_G. An anchored drawing without crossings is an *anchored embedding*. An *anchored planar graph* is an anchored graph that has an anchored embedding. The *anchored crossing number* $\mathtt{acr}(G, A_G, \pi_G)$, or simply $\mathtt{acr}(G)$, of an anchored graph G is the minimum number of crossings over all anchored drawings of G.

Let (G, A_G, π_G) be an anchored graph. Any subgraph H of G naturally defines the *anchored subgraph* (H, A_H, π_H), where $A_H = A_G \cap V(H)$ and π_H is the restriction of π_G to the vertices in A_H. We say that an anchored graph (G, A_G, π_G) can be *decomposed into two anchored graphs* if there are anchored subgraphs (R, A_R, π_R) and (B, A_B, π_B) such that $R \cup B = G$ and $E(R) \cap E(B) = \emptyset$. The decomposition is *vertex-disjoint* when $V(R) \cap V(B) = \emptyset$. For helping the exposition we will refer to R as "red" graph and to B as "blue" graph.

2. ANCHORED CROSSING NUMBER IN A DISK

The problem of minimizing the number of crossings in drawings of anchored graphs is of independent interest. In this section we show that computing the crossing number of anchored graphs is hard even in a very special case when the anchored graph is decomposed into two vertex-disjoint planar anchored subgraphs.

THEOREM 1. *Computing the anchored crossing number of anchored graphs is NP-hard, even if the input graph is decomposed into two vertex-disjoint planar anchored subgraphs (and the decomposition is part of the input).*

The rest of this section is devoted the proof of Theorem 1. We will use the notation $[m] = \{0, 1, \ldots, m\}$. The reduction will be from the decision problem of satisfiability:

> SAT.
> *Input:* A set of n variables $x_1, \ldots, x_n$ and a set of m disjunctive clauses $C_1, \ldots, C_m$. *Output:* Can we assign boolean values T/F to the variables such that the formula $C_1 \wedge \cdots \wedge C_m$ is satisfied?

Consider an instance I to SAT. Henceforth, we will use n to denote the number of variables and use m to denote the number of clauses. Let $w = 30nm$. It is convenient to think of w as a sufficiently large weight to make the reduction work. Let $k = (6nm + 6n + 2m + 1)w^3 - m(w^2 + w - 1)$. The upper bound $k < (6nm + 6n + 2m + 1)w^3 \leq 15nmw^3 < (w^2 - 1)^2$ will be useful in our discussion.

We next provide an overview of our reduction. Our aim at this point is to provide intuition. An example showing how the whole reduction works is given in Figure 1. It may help getting the global picture through the discussion. We will describe an anchored *blue* planar graph $B = B(I)$ and an anchored *red* planar graph $R = R(I)$. The graphs B and R will be vertex-disjoint. We will then construct an anchored graph $G = G(I)$ that has a decomposition into R and B; the graph G is determined by R, B and by specifying the circular ordering of the anchors $A_B \cup A_R$. It will turn out from the construction that the anchored crossing number of G is at least k, and that it is equal to k if and only if the instance I can be satisfied.

The blue graph B has a grid-like structure. In an optimal drawing there are no blue-blue crossings. The weights of the blue edges are used to encode the clauses of the instance I. The red graph has the following structure. For each variable x_i there is a pair of 'vertical paths' in the red graph; they connect anchor $r(x_i)$ to anchor $r'(x_i)$ in Figure 1. The construction will enforce that in an optimal drawing such a pair will be drawn either to the left or to the right of the middle line, i.e. either in the gray or in the black region as shown in the left part of Figure 3. Each such option correspond to an assignment of the variable as T or F. For each clause C_j there is a 'horizontal path'; it connects anchor $r_{(0,j)}$ to anchor $r_{(2n+1,j)}$ in Figure 1. Such path must cross a 'horizontal line' of the blue grid once. The number of crossings with such horizontal path depends on where it crosses the 'blue line', and tells if the clause is satisfied with the assignment of the variables or not.

We next proceed with the formal proof. The blue graph $B = B(I)$ is constructed as follows; see Figure 2:

(i) Take a grid-like graph with vertices $b_{(\alpha,\beta)}$, $(\alpha, \beta) \in [2n+2] \times [2m+3]$, and an edge between vertices $b_{(\alpha,\beta)}$ and $b_{(\alpha',\beta')}$ if and only if $|\alpha - \alpha'| + |\beta - \beta'| = 1$.

(ii) Remove the vertices $b_{(2i,0)}$ and $b_{(2i,2m+3)}$ for each $i \in [n+1]$.

(iii) Define as anchors the vertices $b_{(2i+1,0)}$ and $b_{(2i+1,2m+3)}$ for each $i \in [n]$, and the vertices $b_{(0,\beta)}$ and $b_{(2n+2,\beta)}$ for each $\beta \in [2m+2] \setminus \{0\}$.

(iv) Remove the edges between any two anchors.

(v) The weights of the edges are defined as follows:

- each edge adjacent to an anchor has weight w^4;
- if the literal x_i appears in clause C_j, then the edge $b_{(2i-1,2j)}b_{(2i,2j)}$ has weight $w^2 - 1$;
- if the literal $\neg x_i$ appears in clause C_j, then the edge $b_{(2i,2j)}b_{(2i+1,2j)}$ has weight $w^2 - 1$;
- the edge $b_{(2i-1,2m+2)}b_{(2i,2m+2)}$ has weight $w^2 + |\{j \mid \text{literal } x_i \text{ appears in } C_j\}|$;
- the edge $b_{(2i,2m+2)}b_{(2i+1,2m+2)}$ has weight $w^2 + |\{j \mid \text{literal } \neg x_i \text{ appears in } C_j\}|$;
- all other edges have weight w^2.

Note that each edge in the blue graph B has weight at least $w^2 - 1$. Hence, independently of the red graph R to be defined below, a drawing of B with crossing number at most $k < (w^2 - 1)^2$ has to be an embedding of B. Henceforth, we will assume that B is anchored embedded. Note that the graph B has a unique combinatorial embedding with anchors because of 3-connectivity. For each variable x_i, we define two *columns*; see Figure 3. The column C_i^T is the region of the disk enclosed between the curves

$$b_{(2i-1,0)}b_{(2i-1,1)}\cdots b_{(2i-1,2m+3)} \quad \text{and}$$
$$b_{(2i+1,0)}b_{(2i+1,1)}b_{(2i,1)}b_{(2i,2)}\cdots$$
$$\cdots b_{(2i,2m+2)}b_{(2i+1,2m+2)}b_{(2i+1,2m+3)},$$

and the column C_i^F is the region of the disk enclosed between the curves

$$b_{(2i+1,0)}b_{(2i+1,1)}\cdots b_{(2i+1,2m+3)} \quad \text{and}$$
$$b_{(2i-1,0)}b_{(2i-1,1)}b_{(2i,1)}b_{(2i,2)}\cdots$$
$$\cdots b_{(2i,2m+2)}b_{(2i-1,2m+2)}b_{(2i-1,2m+3)}.$$

The blue edges of the form $b_{(\alpha,\beta)}b_{(\alpha+1,\beta)}$ are called *horizontal*. The blue edges of the form $b_{(\alpha,\beta)}b_{(\alpha,\beta+1)}$ are called *vertical*. The weights of the horizontal edges $b_{(2i-1,2j)}b_{(2i,2j)}$ and $b_{(2i-1,2m+2)}b_{(2i,2m+2)}$ contained in the column C_i^T have been chosen so that they add up to $2(m+1)w^2$: each time we have a -1 in the weight of $b_{(2i-1,2j)}b_{(2i,2j)}$ we have a $+1$ in the weight of $b_{(2i-1,2m+2)}b_{(2i,2m+2)}$. The same holds for the column C_i^F.

For each clause C_j, we define two *rows*; see Figure 3. The *upper row* U_j is the region of the disk enclosed between the curves

$$b_{(0,2j)}b_{(1,2j)}\cdots b_{(2n+2,2j)} \quad \text{and}$$
$$b_{(0,2j+1)}b_{(1,2j+1)}\cdots b_{(2n+2,2j+1)},$$

and the *lower row* L_j is the region of the disk enclosed between the curves

$$b_{(0,2j-1)}b_{(1,2j-1)}\cdots b_{(2n+2,2j-1)} \quad \text{and}$$
$$b_{(0,2j)}b_{(1,2j)}\cdots b_{(2n+2,2j)}.$$

There is an additional row, called *enforcing row* and denoted by R_{enf}, which is the region of the disk enclosed between the curves

$$b_{(0,2m+1)}b_{(1,2m+1)}\cdots b_{(2n+2,2m+1)} \quad \text{and}$$
$$b_{(0,2m+2)}b_{(1,2m+2)}\cdots b_{(2n+2,2m+2)}.$$

The role of the enforcing row R_{enf} is to reduce the number of possible drawings to a well-structured subset of drawings. We will use the columns and the rows as some sort of coordinate system to tell where some red vertices go. For example, we may refer to the face $C_i^T \cap L_j$.

The red graph $R = R(I)$ is constructed as follows; see Figure 4:

(i) Take a grid-like graph with vertices $r_{(\alpha,\beta)}$, $(\alpha, \beta) \in [2n+1] \times [m+2]$, and an edge between vertices $r_{(\alpha,\beta)}$ and $r_{(\alpha',\beta')}$ if and only if $|\alpha - \alpha'| + |\beta - \beta'| = 1$.

(ii) Remove the four vertices $r_{(0,0)}$, $r_{(0,m+2)}$, $r_{(2n+1,0)}$, and $r_{(2n+1,m+2)}$.

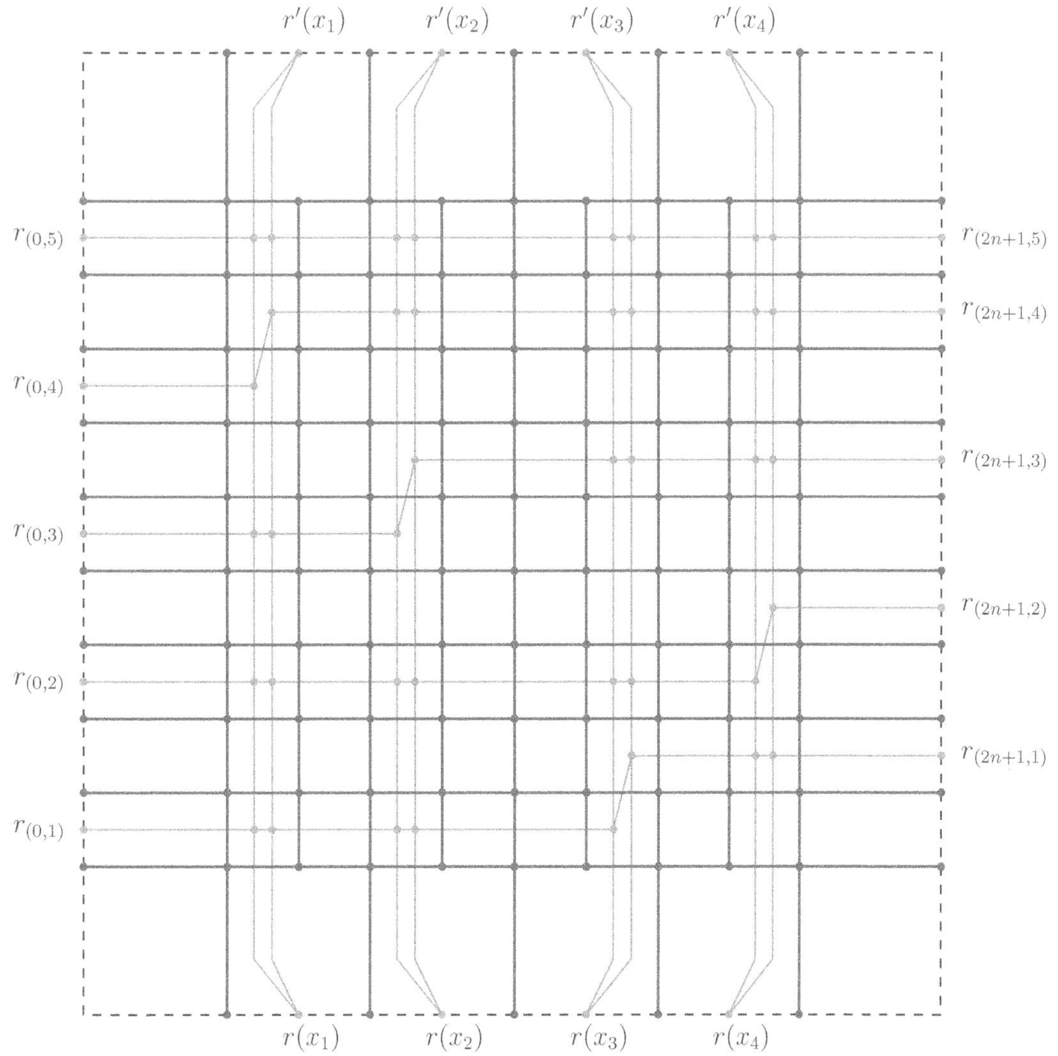

Figure 1: Example of the resulting reduction for the formula on 4 variables x_1, x_2, x_3, x_4 and clauses $\neg x_1 \vee \neg x_3 \vee x_4$, $\neg x_2 \vee \neg x_4$, $x_2 \vee \neg x_3$, $x_1 \vee x_2$. The optimal drawing in the figure corresponds to the boolean assignment $x_1 = x_2 = T$ and $x_3 = x_4 = F$.

(iii) For each variable x_i, identify the vertices $r_{(2i-1,0)}$ and $r_{(2i,0)}$ into a new vertex called $r(x_i)$, and identify the vertices $r_{(2i-1,m+2)}$ and $r_{(2i,m+2)}$ into a new vertex called $r'(x_i)$. For each variable x_i, the vertices $r(x_i)$ and $r'(x_i)$ are anchors for R. The vertices $r_{(0,j)}$ and $r_{(2n+1,j)}$ are also anchors for R, for every $j \in [m+1] \setminus \{0\}$.

(iv) Remove the edges between any two anchors.

(v) The weights of the edges are defined as follows:

- for each variable x_i the edge $r_{(2i-1,m+1)}r_{(2i,m+1)}$ has weight w^4;
- for each variable x_i and each clause C_j the edge $r_{(2i-1,j)}r_{(2i,j)}$ has weight $w-1$;
- all other edges have weight w.

For each variable x_i the following two *vertical paths* are important:

$$r(x_i)r_{(2i-1,1)}r_{(2i-1,2)} \dots r_{(2i-1,m+1)}r'(x_i) \quad \text{and}$$
$$r(x_i)r_{(2i,1)}r_{(2i,2)} \dots r_{(2i,m+1)}r'(x_i).$$

We will use V_i to denote their union. For each clause C_j, we will consider the *horizontal path* H_j defined by

$$r_{(0,j)}r_{(1,j)} \dots r_{(2n+1,j)}.$$

We also define the *horizontal enforcing path* H_{enf} as

$$r_{(0,m+1)}r_{(1,m+1)} \dots r_{(2n+1,m+1)}.$$

The role of the horizontal enforcing path H_{enf} will be to reduce the number of possible drawings to a well-structured subset of drawings.

It is important to note that the paths

$$V_1, V_2, \dots, V_n, H_1, H_2 \dots, H_m, H_{\text{enf}}$$

form a partition of the edge set of the red graph R. Hence, we can add the number of crossings that each of them con-

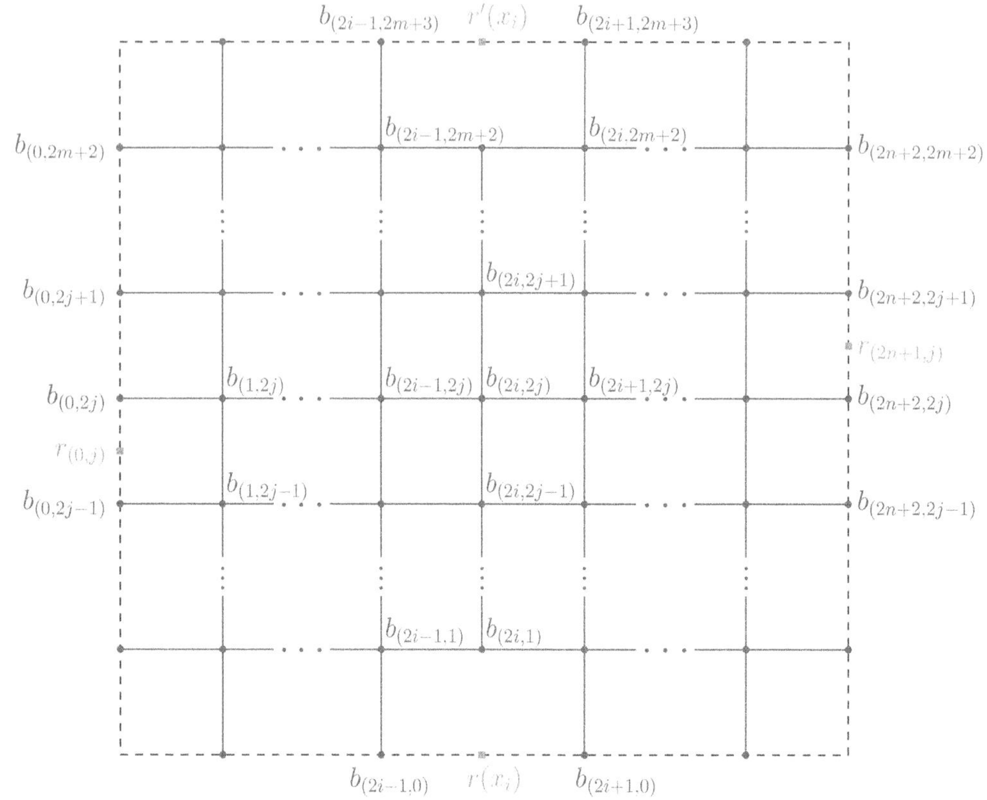

Figure 2: The graph $B = B(I)$. Anchors of the red graph are included to show the cyclic ordering of $A_B \cup A_R$.

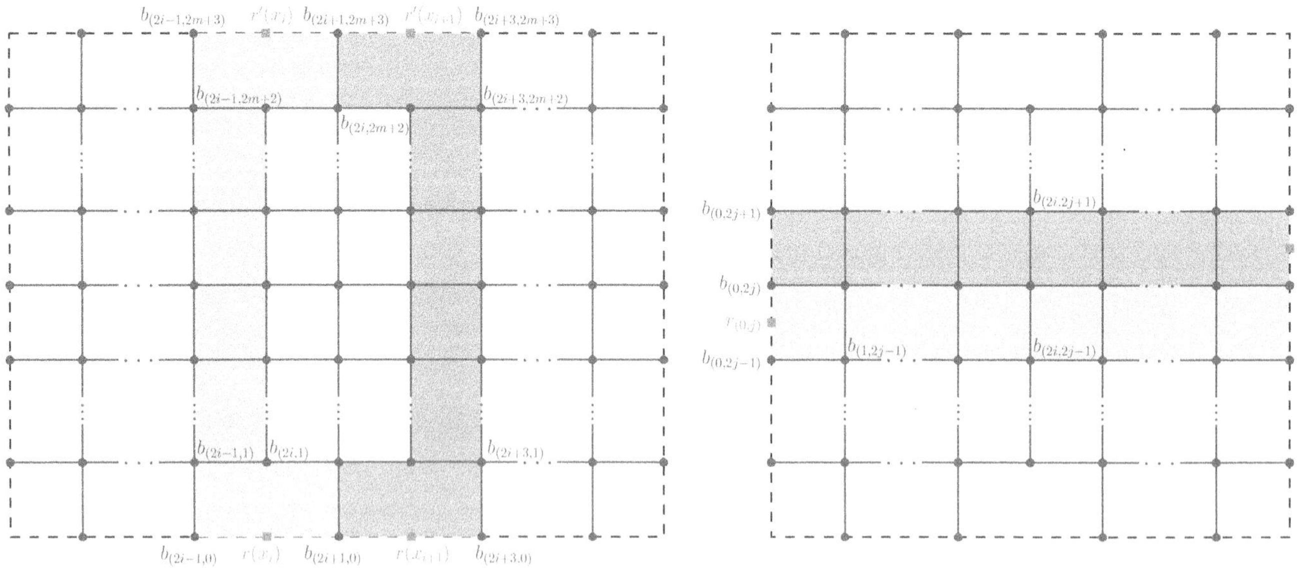

Figure 3: Left: columns C_i^T (lighter shading) and C_{i+1}^F (darker shading). Right: the upper row U_j (darker shading) and the lower row L_j (lighter shading).

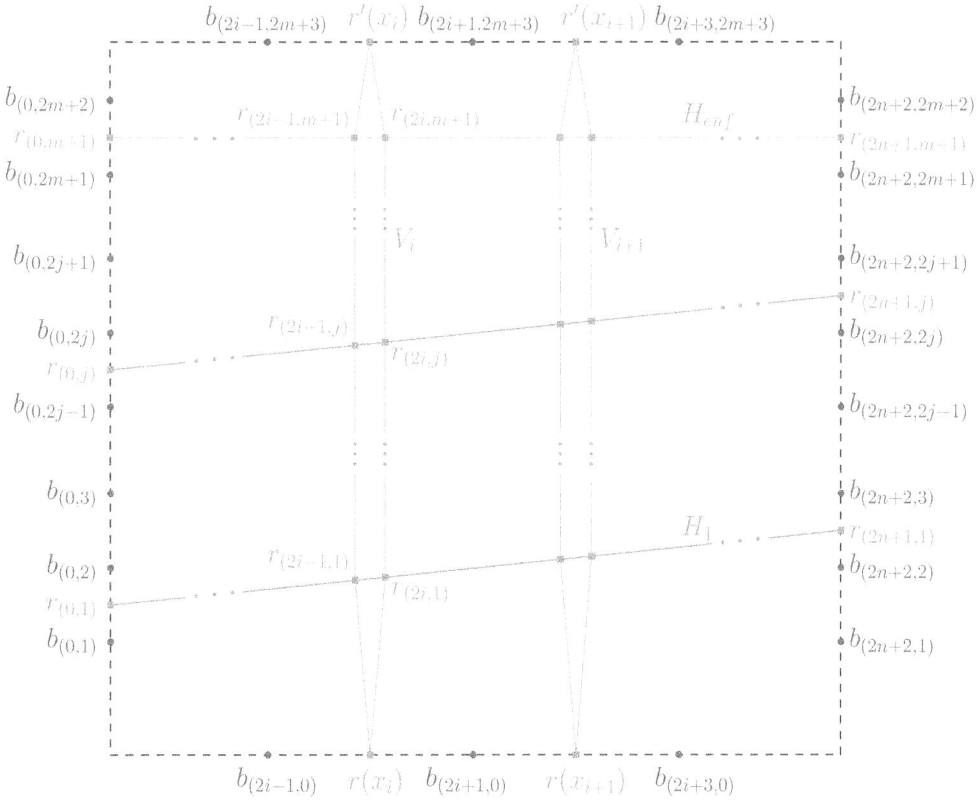

Figure 4: The graph $R = R(I)$. Anchors of the blue graph are also included to show the cyclic order of $A_B \cup A_R$.

tributes separately to obtain the crossing number of a drawing. Note also, that the intersection of a vertical pair of paths V_i and a horizontal path H_j (or H_{enf}) always consists of two vertices.

Let $G = G(I)$ be the anchored graph obtained by joining the red graph R and the blue graph B. The (clockwise) circular ordering of the anchors along the boundary of the disk as follows:

- For each clause C_j we have the sequence of anchors

  $$b_{(0,2j-1)},\ r_{(0,j)},\ b_{(0,2j)},\ b_{(0,2j+1)},$$

  and the sequence

  $$b_{(2n+2,2j+2)},\ b_{(2n+2,2j+1)},\ r_{(2n+1,j)},\ b_{(2n+2,2j)}.$$

  Hence, the anchor $r_{(0,j)}$ is in the lower row L_j and anchor $r_{(2n+1,j)}$ is in the upper row U_j.

- For each variable x_i, the anchor $r(x_i)$ is between anchors $b_{(2i-1,0)}$ and $b_{(2i+1,0)}$, and the anchor $r'(x_i)$ is between $b_{(2i-1,2m+3)}$ and $b_{(2i+1,2m+3)}$. Hence, $r(x_i)$ and $r'(x_i)$ are in both columns C_i^T and C_i^F.

- Anchor $r_{(0,m+1)}$ is between $b_{(0,2m+1)}$ and $b_{(0,2m+2)}$, anchor $r_{(2n+1,m+1)}$ is between anchors $b_{(2n+2,2m+2)}$ and $b_{(2n+2,2m+1)}$. Hence, anchors $r_{(0,m+1)}$ and $r_{(2n+1,m+1)}$ are in the enforcing row R_{enf}.

- Anchor $b_{(0,1)}$ comes immediately after $b_{(1,0)}$, anchor $b_{(1,2m+3)}$ comes immediately after $b_{(0,2m+2)}$, anchor $b_{(2n+2,2m+2)}$ comes immediately after $b_{(2n+1,2m+3)}$, anchor $b_{(2n+1,0)}$ comes immediately after $b_{(2n+2,1)}$.

This finishes the description of the graph G. We first show the easy direction of the proof, which will also give an idea of how the reduction works. Recall that we have defined $k = (6nm + 6n + 2m + 1)w^3 - m(w^2 + w - 1)$.

LEMMA 1. *If the instance I is satisfiable, then there is an anchored drawing of G with k crossings.*

PROOF. We draw the blue graph B without crossings. The corresponding embedding is unique. The red graph R is also going to be drawn without crossings. Hence, it is enough to describe in which face of B is each red vertex and (when not obvious) where the red edges cross the blue edges. See Figure 1 for a particular example. Let $b_i \in \{T, F\}$ be an assignment for each variable x_i of I that satisfies all clauses. We draw the two red vertical paths of V_i inside the column $C_i^{b_i}$. For each clause C_j we proceed as follows. Let x_t, where $t = t(j)$, be a variable whose value b_t makes the clause C_j true. We then draw the horizontal path H_j as follows: the subpath of H_j between $r_{(0,j)}$ and $r_{(2t-1,j)}$ is drawn in the lower row L_j, the edge $r_{(2t-1,j)}r_{(2t,j)}$ crosses from L_j to U_j through the blue edge in $L_j \cap U_j \cap C_t^{b_t}$, and the subpath of H_j between $r_{(2t,j)}$ and $r_{(2n+1,j)}$ is drawn in the upper row U_j. The path H_{enf} is drawn inside the row R_{enf}. Note that this description implicitly assigns to each non-anchor vertex of R a face of B. The drawing can be extended to a planar embedding of R in such a way that no red edge crosses twice any blue edge.

Let us now compute the crossing number of the drawing we have described. There are no monochromatic crossings in the construction; hence we only need to count the red-blue crossings. Each of the two paths in V_i contributes $2(m +$

$1)w^3$ to the crossing number of the drawing: edges in V_i have weight w, and each path in V_i crosses all the horizontal blue edges contained in $C_i^{b_i}$, whose weights add to $2(m+1)w^2$. Each horizontal path H_j contributes $(2n+1)w^3+(w-1)(w^2-1)$ to the crossing number of the drawing: the edges on the horizontal path H_j connecting V_i to V_{i+1} have weight w and cross $2n+1$ blue vertical edges whose weight is w^2; there is only one red edge in H_j, namely $r_{(2t(j)-1,j)}r_{(2t(j),j)}$ with weight $w-1$, that crosses the boundary between rows L_i and U_i, namely at the edge of $L_j \cap U_j \cap C_t^{b_t}$ with weight w^2-1 because the corresponding literal x_i or $\neg x_i$ makes C_j satisfied. The horizontal path H_{enf} contributes $(2n+1)w^3$ to the crossing number of the drawing: the edges of H_j connecting V_i to V_{i+1} have weight w and cross $2n+1$ blue edges whose weight is w^2.

The crossing number of the drawing is thus

$$n \cdot 2 \cdot 2(m+1)w^3 + m \cdot \big((2n+1)w^3 + (w-1)(w^2-1)\big) + (2n+1)w^3$$

which is

$$(6nm + 6n + 2m + 1)w^3 - m(w^2+w-1) = k.$$

□

We next have to show the reverse implication: if the anchored crossing number of G is at most k, then the formula I is satisfiable. Henceforth, let us assume for the rest of this section that $\texttt{acr}(G) \leq k$, and let us fix an anchored drawing $\mathcal{D}$ of G with at most k crossings. As mentioned before, $\mathcal{D}$ cannot have any blue-blue crossing because otherwise $\texttt{cr}(\mathcal{D}) > k$. In principle, $\mathcal{D}$ could contain red-red crossings; we will show below that in fact this is not possible, and hence all crossings are red-blue. It will be convenient to look at the number of red-blue crossings without taking into account the weights. We refer to such crossings as *unweighted crossings*. Simple arithmetic shows the following two properties.

LEMMA 2. *The drawing $\mathcal{D}$ has at most $6nm+6n+2m+1$ unweighted red-blue crossings.*

LEMMA 3. (i) *For each clause C_j, the horizontal path H_j is inside the rows $U_j \cup L_j$ and crosses precisely $2n+2$ blue edges.*

(ii) *The horizontal path H_{enf} is drawn inside the row R_{enf}.*

(iii) *For each variable x_i, both vertical paths of V_i are inside the column C_i^T or both are inside the column C_i^F.*

LEMMA 4. *If $\texttt{cr}(\mathcal{D}) \leq k$, then the instance I is satisfiable. Moreover, the restriction of the drawing $\mathcal{D}$ to R or to B is an embedding.*

PROOF. By Lemma 3, in the drawing $\mathcal{D}$ both paths in V_i are contained either in C_i^T or C_i^F. Consider the assignment where variable x_i gets value $b_i = T$ if the two paths of V_i are contained in C_i^T, and $b_i = F$ otherwise. We will show that this assignment satisfies the formula $C_1 \wedge \cdots \wedge C_m$ of the instance I.

We will use in our analysis the properties of $\mathcal{D}$ obtained in Lemma 3. For a red subgraph X, let $\texttt{cr}(X)$ denote the crossing number of the subdrawing of $\mathcal{D}$ induced by X and the blue graph B.

All the edges in V_i have weight w. The weights of the horizontal blue edges contained in $C_i^{b_i}$ add to $2(m+1)w^2$. Furthermore, note that each of those blue horizontal edges is crossed by each of the two paths in V_i. Therefore we have $\texttt{cr}(V_i) = 2 \cdot (2m+2)w^3$, and thus $\texttt{cr}(\bigcup_i V_i) = (4nm+4n)w^3$. We next look at H_{enf}. All the edges from the path H_{enf} have weight w or w^4, and hence only edges from H_{enf} with weight w may cross the vertical blue edges contained in the row R_{enf}. Inside the row R_{enf} there are $2n+1$ vertical blue edges of weight w^2, and thus $\texttt{cr}(H_{\text{enf}}) = (2n+1)w^3$. Since $cr(\mathcal{D}) \leq k$ and the paths $V_1, \ldots, V_n, H_1, \ldots H_m, H_{\text{enf}}$ form an edge-disjoint partition of the edges of R, we have $\texttt{cr}(\bigcup_j H_j) + \texttt{cr}(\bigcup_i V_i) + \texttt{cr}(H_{\text{enf}}) \leq k$, and therefore

$$\texttt{cr}(\bigcup_j H_j) \leq k - (4nm+2n)w^3 - (2n+1)w^3 \qquad (1)$$

$$= m\big((2n+2)w^3 - (w^2+w-1)\big). \qquad (2)$$

The edges of H_j have weight w, if they connect a vertex in $V_i \cap H_j$ to a vertex in $V_{i+1} \cap H_j$ for some i, or weight $w-1$ if they connect both vertices of $V_i \cap H_j$ for some j. Because of Lemma 3, the edges with weight $w-1$ are always within the column $C_i^{b_i}$ for some i. This means that the boundary any column C_i^T or C_i^F, which has weight w^2, is always crossed by a red edge of H_j with weight w. Let ∂_j denote the boundary between the lower row L_j and the upper row U_j. This boundary ∂_j must also be crossed by an edge of H_j, and that crossing contributes weight at least $(w-1)(w^2-1)$ to $\texttt{cr}(H_j)$. We conclude that

$$\texttt{cr}(H_j) \geq (2n+1) \cdot w \cdot w^2 + (w-1)(w^2-1)$$
$$= (2n+2)w^3 - (w^2+w-1),$$

with equality if and only if the crossing between H_j and ∂_j contributes exactly $(w-1)(w^2-1)$ to the crossing number. Combining with equations (1)–(2), we see that

$$\texttt{cr}(H_j) = (2n+2)w^3 - (w^2+w-1) \qquad (3)$$

for each clause C_j. Therefore, the boundary ∂_j must be crossed at a blue edge $b_{(t,j)}b_{(t+1,j)}$ of weight w^2-1 by a red edge $r_{(2i-1,j)}r_{(2i,j)}$ of weight $w-1$. It may be that $t = 2i-1$ or $t = 2i$. Consider first the case when $t = 2i-1$. By the construction of the blue graph B, the edge $b_{(t,j)}b_{(t+1,j)}$ has weight w^2-1 because the literal x_i appears in the clause C_j of I. Moreover, the endpoints of $r_{(2i-1,j)}r_{(2i,j)}$ must be in the column C_i^T since they are part of the vertical paths V_i. Hence, the clause C_j is satisfied by the assignment $x_i = b_i = T$ we defined at the beginning of the proof. The case when $t = 2i$ is alike, but in this case the literal $\neg x_i$ appears in the clause C_j of I, and we took the assignment $x_i = b_i = F$.

Finally, note that our analysis shows that in $\mathcal{D}$ there are exactly k red-blue crossings, and therefore there cannot be any red-red crossings. Hence the restriction of the drawing $\mathcal{D}$ to the red graph is an embedding. □

Note that the graph G can be constructed in polynomial time and that it has weights that are polynomially bounded in n and m. Thus, in polynomial time we can replace in G each edge e by w_e parallel edges that are subdivided once, and the resulting graph has the same anchored crossing number as G; see the discussion in the introduction. Then Theorem 1 follows from Lemmas 1 and 4.

3. HARDNESS OF CROSSING NUMBER FOR NEAR-PLANAR GRAPHS

THEOREM 2. *Computing the crossing number of near-planar graphs is NP-hard.*

PROOF. Consider an (unweighted) anchored graph G that is decomposed into two planar anchored graphs R and B that are vertex-disjoint. Let m denote the number of edges of G.

Consider the weighted graph G', without anchors, obtained from G as follows: we start with G and assign weight $2m$ to each of its edges. For every two consecutive anchors a and a' of G in the cyclic ordering π_G, we introduce in G' an edge aa' with weight $5m^4$. The set of added edges defines a cycle, which we denote by C. Finally, we choose an arbitrary vertex r of R that is not an anchor, an arbitrary vertex b of B that is not an anchor, and add the edge rb to G' with unit weight. (If all vertices of R are anchors we just subdivide an edge and take r as the new vertex. A similar procedure can be done with B.) This completes the description of G'.

Firstly, we show that G' is a near-planar graph. The graph $G'-rb$ consists of the cycle C connecting consecutive anchors of G, and two planar anchored graphs R and B. We can thus embed $G'-xy$ taking an embedding of C in $\mathbb{R}^2$, embedding R in the disk bounded by C in $\mathbb{R}^2$, and embedding B in the exterior of the disk. Note that the embeddings of R and B exist because they are planar anchored graphs. Since the weight of the edge rb of G' is one, it follows that G' is a near-planar graph, even when replacing each edge distinct from rb by the corresponding number of subdivided parallel edges.

We claim that $\texttt{acr}(G) = \lfloor \texttt{cr}(G')/(4m^2) \rfloor$. Consider an optimal anchored drawing $\mathcal{D}$ of G in a topological disk Ω with $\texttt{cr}(\mathcal{D}) = \texttt{acr}(G)$. We then extend the drawing $\mathcal{D}$ to obtain a drawing $\mathcal{D}'$ of G' as follows. Pushing the interior of the edges inside Ω, we may assume that $\mathcal{D}$ touches the boundary $\partial\Omega$ of Ω only at the anchors. We then draw the edges aa' of G' between consecutive anchors along the boundary of the disk Ω. Finally, we draw the edge rb so as to minimize the number of crossings it contributes. Each crossing of $\mathcal{D}$ contributes $(2m)^2$ crossings to $\mathcal{D}'$. The edge rb can cross each edge of G' at most once in the drawing $\mathcal{D}'$ because of optimality of $\mathcal{D}'$ and the drawing of rb. Therefore $\texttt{cr}(\mathcal{D}') \leq \texttt{cr}(\mathcal{D}) \cdot 4m^2 + 2m^2$, and thus

$$\begin{aligned}\lfloor \texttt{cr}(G')/4m^2 \rfloor &\leq \lfloor \texttt{cr}(\mathcal{D}')/4m^2 \rfloor \\ &\leq \lfloor \texttt{acr}(G) + 1/2m^2 \rfloor \\ &= \texttt{acr}(G).\end{aligned}$$

Let $\mathcal{D}'$ be a drawing of G' in the plane such that no edge crosses itself and no two edges cross more than once. If the cycle C is embedded and no edge of C is involved in a crossing, then each pair of edges not in C can cross at most once, and hence $\texttt{cr}(D')$ is upper bounded by $\binom{m}{2}2m \cdot 2m + 1 \cdot m \cdot 2m < 5m^4$. If the restriction of $\mathcal{D}'$ to C is not an embedding or some edge of C participates in a crossing, then $\texttt{cr}(D') \geq 5m^4$. It follows that in every optimal drawing $\mathcal{D}'$ of G', the cycle C is embedded and no edge crosses C.

Consider now an optimal drawing $\mathcal{D}'$ of G' with $\texttt{cr}(\mathcal{D}') = \texttt{cr}(G')$. Let Ω be the disk bounded by the image of C in $\mathcal{D}'$. Since no edge of G' can cross an edge of C, the drawing $\mathcal{D}'$ is contained in the closure of Ω. If in $\mathcal{D}'$ we remove the image of C and the image of the edge rb, then we obtain an anchored drawing of G, which we shall denote by $\mathcal{D}$. Note that $\texttt{cr}(\mathcal{D})$ is equal to $\texttt{cr}(\mathcal{D}')$ minus the number of crossings contributed by rb and scaled down by $(2m)^2$ because of the weights introduced in G'. We thus have

$$\texttt{acr}(G) \leq \texttt{acr}(\mathcal{D}) \leq \texttt{cr}(\mathcal{D}')/(4m^2) = \texttt{cr}(G')/(4m^2),$$

and we may take the floor on the right-hand side because the value is an integer. This finishes the proof of the claim $\texttt{acr}(G) = \lfloor \texttt{cr}(G')/4m^2 \rfloor$.

The graph G' can be constructed from G in polynomial time. Moreover, since the weights of G' are polynomially bounded, we can also replace each edge by parallel subdivided edges to obtain an unweighted graph $H_{G'}$, as described in the introduction, that satisfies $\texttt{cr}(G') = \texttt{cr}(H_{G'})$. Since the graph $H_{G'}$ is near-planar and $\texttt{acr}(G) = \lfloor \texttt{cr}(H_{G'})/4m^2 \rfloor$, the result follows. $\square$

Extensions.

Our NP-hardness proof in Section 2 has the following additional property: we know the local rotation of the edges around each vertex in any optimal anchored drawing. This essentially follows from Lemma 4 because R and B have a unique anchored embedding. Hence, it is NP-hard to compute the *anchored* crossing number restricted to drawings that have a prescribed local rotation system in each vertex. We can also make the anchored crossing number with rotation systems to be the usual crossing number with rotation systems by taking large enough weight on the edges of the cycle C connecting the anchors, as we did in the proof of Theorem 2. Hence, it follows that computing the crossing number for graphs with prescribed rotation systems is NP-hard. This has been shown recently in [14] using a reduction from LINEAR ARRANGEMENT. It is then possible to replace each vertex by a 3-regular grid where the edges are attached preserving the local rotation; the techniques is detailed in [14]. Hence, we provide an alternative, geometric proof that crossing number of cubic graphs is NP-hard. This settles a question of Hliněný [9], who asked if one can prove this result by a reduction from an NP-complete problem with geometric flavor, instead of reducing from LINEAR ARRANGEMENT.

Acknowledgments

We thank the anonymous reviewers for several helpful suggestions.

4. REFERENCES

[1] K. J. Böröczky, J. Pach, and G. Tóth. Planar crossing numbers of graphs embeddable in another surface. *Int. J. Found. Comput. Sci.*, 17(5):1005–1016, 2006.

[2] S. Cabello and B. Mohar. Crossing and weighted crossing number of near-planar graphs. *Algorithmica*, accepted. Available at `http://dx.doi.org/10.1007/s00453-009-9357-5`. Preliminary version in Graph Drawing 2008.

[3] M. Chimani and P. Hliněný. Approximating the crossing number of graphs embeddable in any orientable surface. In *Proc. SODA 2010*, to appear.

[4] M. Chimani, P. Hliněný, and P. Mutzel. Vertex insertion approximates the crossing number for apex graphs. Manuscript available at `http:`

//www.fi.muni.cz/~hlineny/Research/papers/. Preliminary version in Graph Drawing 2008.

[5] H. Djidjev and I. Vrto. Planar crossing numbers of genus g graphs. In *ICALP 2006*, volume 4051 of *LNCS*, pages 419–430, 2006.

[6] M. R. Garey and D. S. Johnson. Crossing number is NP-complete. *SIAM J. Alg. Discr. Meth.*, 4:312–316, 1983.

[7] M. Grohe. Computing crossing numbers in quadratic time. In *Proc. STOC 2001*, pages 231–236, 2001.

[8] C. Gutwenger, P. Mutzel, and R. Weiskircher. Inserting an edge into a planar graph. *Algorithmica*, 41:289–308, 2005.

[9] P. Hlinený. Crossing number is hard for cubic graphs. *J. Comb. Theory, Ser. B*, 96(4):455–471, 2006.

[10] P. Hlinený and G. Salazar. On the crossing number of almost planar graphs. In M. Kaufmann and D. Wagner, editors, *GD 2006*, volume 4372 of *LNCS*, pages 162–173. Springer, 2007.

[11] P. Hliněný and G. Salazar. Approximating the crossing number of toroidal graphs. In T. Tokuyama, editor, *ISAAC 2007*, volume 4835 of *LNCS*, pages 148–159, 2007.

[12] K.-I. Kawarabayashi and B. Reed. Computing crossing number in linear time. In *Proc. STOC 2007*, pages 382–390, 2007.

[13] B. Mohar. On the crossing number of almost planar graphs. *Informatica*, 30:301–303, 2006.

[14] M. J. Pelsmajer, M. Schaefer, and D. Štefankovic. Crossing number of graphs with rotation systems. *Algorithmica*, accepted. Available at http://dx.doi.org/10.1007/s00453-009-9343-y.

[15] A. Riskin. The crossing number of a cubic plane polyhedral map plus an edge. *Studia Sci. Math. Hungar.*, 31:405–413, 1996.

[16] S. Werner. On the complexity of the planar edge-disjoint paths problem with terminals on the outer boundary. *Combinatorica*, 29(1):121–126, 2009.

Planar Visibility: Testing and Counting

Joachim Gudmundsson
NICTA, Sydney
joachim.gudmundsson@nicta.com.au

Pat Morin
Carleton University, Canada
morin@scs.carleton.ca

ABSTRACT

In this paper we consider query versions of visibility testing and visibility counting. Let S be a set of n disjoint line segments in $\mathbb{R}^2$ and let s be an element of S. Visibility testing is to preprocess S so that we can quickly determine if s is visible from a query point q. Visibility counting involves preprocessing S so that one can quickly estimate the number of segments in S visible from a query point q.

We present several data structures for the two query problems. The structures build upon a result by O'Rourke and Suri (1984) who showed that the subset, $V_S(s)$, of $\mathbb{R}^2$ that is weakly visible from a segment s can be represented as the union of a set, $C_S(s)$, of $O(n^2)$ triangles, even though the complexity of $V_S(s)$ can be $\Omega(n^4)$. We define a variant of their covering, give efficient output-sensitive algorithms for computing it, and prove additional properties needed to obtain approximation bounds. Some of our bounds rely on a new combinatorial result that relates the number of segments of S visible from a point p to the number of triangles in $\bigcup_{s\in S} C_S(s)$ that contain p.

Categories and Subject Descriptors

F.2.2 [**Analysis of Algorithms and problem complexity**]: Nonnumerical Algorithms and Problems—*Geometrical problems and computations*

General Terms

Algorithms, Theory

Keywords

geometric data structures, visibility

1. INTRODUCTION

Let S be a set of n closed line segments whose interiors are pairwise disjoint. Two points $p, q \in \mathbb{R}^2$ are (mutually) *visible* with respect to S if the open line segment pq does not intersect any element of S. A segment $s \in S$ is *visible* (with respect to S) from a point p if there exists a point $q \in s$ such that p and q are visible. If two objects (points, segments) A and B are visible (w.r.t. S), then we say that A and B *see* each other (w.r.t. S). In this paper we consider the following two problems:

PROBLEM 1. *(Visibility testing) Given a query point p and a segment $s \in S$, determine if p sees s.*

PROBLEM 2. *(Visibility counting) Given a query point p, report the number of segments of S visible from p.*

For a point $p \in \mathbb{R}^2$, the *visibility region* or *visibility polygon* of p (w.r.t. S) is defined as (see Figure 1.a):

$$V_S(p) = \{q \in \mathbb{R}^2 : p \text{ and } q \text{ are visible (w.r.t. } S)\} .$$

The visibility region of a point is star-shaped, has p in its kernel, and has size $O(n)$. It can be computed in $O(n \log n)$ time by sorting the endpoints of segments in S radially around p and then processing these in order using a binary search tree that orders segments by the order of their intersections with a ray emanating from p [3, 17]. (Equivalently, one can compute the lower-envelope of S in the polar coordinate system whose origin is p.) Because $V_S(p)$ is star-shaped with p in its kernel it is easy to determine if a query point q is contained in $V_S(p)$ in $O(\log n)$ time using binary search. In this way, one can consider $V_S(p)$ as an $O(n)$ sized data structure that can test, in $O(\log n)$ time, if a query point q sees p.

For a segment $s \in S$, the *visibility region* of s (w.r.t. S)

$$V_S(s) = \bigcup_{q\in s} V_S(q) = \{p \in \mathbb{R}^2 : s \text{ and } p \text{ are visible (w.r.t. } S)\}$$

is the set of points in $\mathbb{R}^2$ that see (at least some of) s, see Figure 1.b. Unlike the visibility region of a point, the visibility region of a segment is a complicated structure. For a segment s, $V_S(s)$ can have combinatorial complexity $\Omega(n^4)$ and $\mathbb{R}^2 \setminus V_S(s)$ can have $\Omega(n^4)$ connected components [15, Figure 8.13][9, Lemma 12], see also Figure 2.

More troublesome than the worst-case complexity of $V_S(s)$ is that there exist sets S of n line segments where, for most of the elements $s \in S$, the complexity of $V_S(s)$ is $\Omega(n^2)$. Therefore, explicitly computing $V_S(s)$ and preprocessing it for point location does not yield a particularly space-efficient data structure for testing if a query point p sees s, even if s is a "typical" (as opposed to worst-case) element of S.

In this paper we propose efficient data structures that use an old result of Suri and O'Rourke [17] which shows that

SCG'10, June 13–16, 2010, Snowbird, Utah, USA.

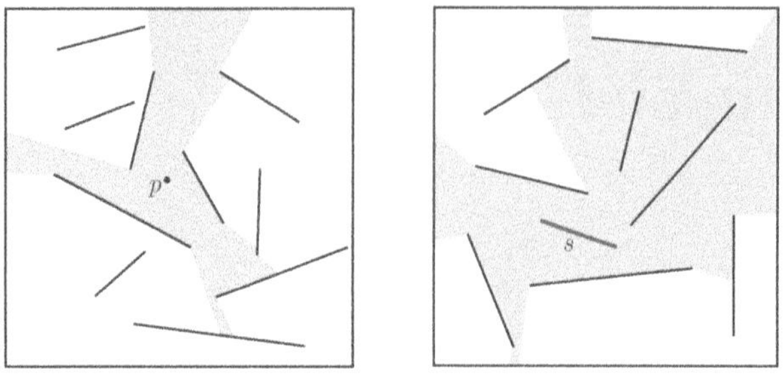

Figure 1: (a) The visibility region for a point and (b) The visibility region of a line segment.

$V_S(s)$ can be represented as a set of $O(n^2)$ triangles whose union is $V_S(s)$. We define a variant of their covering, give efficient algorithms for computing it, and prove additional properties of the covering. In particular, we define a covering $C_S(s)$ of $V_S(s)$ by triangles. We prove that for a randomly chosen $s \in S$, the expected size of $C_S(s)$ is $O(n)$. This, of course, implies that $|\bigcup_{s\in S} C_S(s)| = O(n^2)$. Additionally, if we define $C(S) = \bigcup_{s\in S} C_S(s)$, then we prove that the number of triangles of $C(S)$ containing any point p is a 2-approximation to the number of segments of S visible from p.

Applications of these results include efficient data structures for testing if a query point is contained in $V_S(s)$ as well as efficient data structures for estimating the number of points of S visible from a query point. In order to express our results more precisely, we need some further definitions.

1.1 Visibility Graphs and Extended Visibility Graphs

The *visibility graph* $VG(S)$ is a graph whose vertices are the $2n$ endpoints of the segments in S and in which the edge pq exists if and only if the open line segment with endpoints p and q does not intersect any (closed) segment in S. (see Figure 3.a). It is well-known that the number of edges m of $VG(S)$ is in $O(n^2)$. Ghosh and Mount [11] give an optimal $O(n \log n + m)$ time algorithm to compute the visibility graph of a set of n disjoint line segments. Here, and throughout the remainder of the paper, $m = m(S)$ is the number of edges of $VG(S)$.

Assume, w.l.o.g., that no segment in S is vertical, so we can say that a point p is *above* a segment $s \in S$ if p is above the line that contains s. Assume, furthermore, that S contains four segments that define a rectangle that contains all the elements of S in its interior. The first assumption can be ensured by performing a symbolic rotation of S. The second assumption is only used to ensure that all visibility regions that we discuss are bounded.

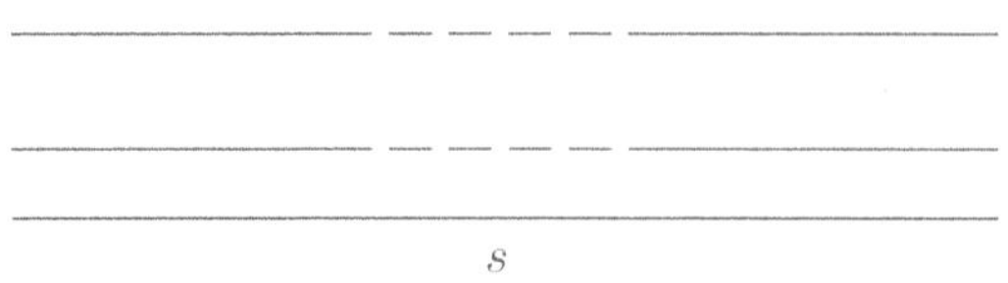

Figure 2: An example of a set S where $V_S(s)$ has complexity $\Omega(n^4)$. The $O(n)$ segments in the center define $\Omega(n^2)$ visibility graph edges whose extensions intersect in $\Omega(n^4)$ points.

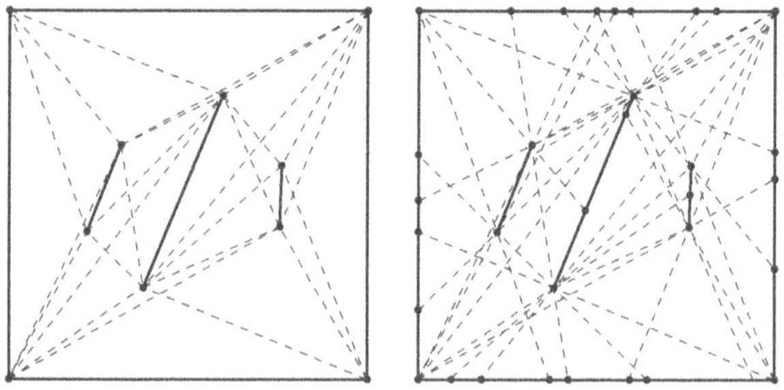

(a) (b)

Figure 3: The visibility graph and the extended visibility graph of a set of seven line segments. (Segments are bold, graph edges are dashed.)

The *extended visibility graph* $EVG(S)$ is obtained by adding $2m$ edges and at most $2m$ vertices to $VG(S)$ as follows (see Figure 3.b): For each (directed) edge uv in $VG(S)$, extend a segment e_{uv} from v in the direction $\overrightarrow{uv}$ until it intersects an element of S at some point w. If not already present, then add the vertex w to $EVG(S)$ and add the edge vw to $EVG(S)$. The extended visibility graph can be computed in $O(n \log n + m)$ time using the visibility graph algorithm by Ghosh and Mount [11].

The union of the edges of $EVG(S)$ and the segments in S form a 1-dimensional set whose removal disconnects $\mathbb{R}^2$ into a set of 2-dimensional regions. This set of 2-d regions is known as the *visibility space partition*, $VSP(S)$ of S. The regions of $VSP(S)$ are important because for any region $R \in VSP(S)$ and for any $p, q \in R$ the set of segments of S visible from p is equal to the set of segments of S visible from q. The region of $VSP(S)$ that contains p determines all the combinatorial information about $V_S(p)$.

Note that $VSP(S)$ is defined by $O(n^2)$ lines, rays, and segments and therefore has worst-case complexity $O(n^4)$.

1.2 Previous Work

There is a plethora of work on visibility in the plane. This section discusses only some of the work most relevant to the current paper.

The visibility space partition is bounded by a subset of the $O(n^2)$ lines induced by pairs of endpoints in S. The $VSP(S)$ has complexity $O(m^2)$ where m is the number of edges in $VG(S)$ and can be computed in $O(m^2)$ time after constructing $VG(S)$ using standard algorithms.

By preprocessing $VSP(S)$ with a point location structure and augmenting the regions of S with appropriate information, one obtains an $O(m^2)$ size data structure that can answer visibility testing queries and visibility counting queries in $O(\log n)$ time.

If the segments of S are the edges of a simple polygon then Bose *et al.* [4] and Guibas *et al.* [12] show that the complexity of $VSP(S)$ is only $O(n^3)$. In this case, this immediately solves the two problems using a structure of size $O(n^3)$. Aronov *et al.* [2] give a data structure that reduces the space to $O(n^2)$ but increases the $O(\log n)$ query time term to $O(\log^2 n)$, again for the case where segments of S are the edges of a simple polygon.

Pocchiola and Vegter [16] give an $O(m)$ space data structure, the *visibility complex*, that can compute the visibility polygon $V_S(p)$ from any query point p in $O(m_p \log n)$ time, where m_p is the complexity of $V_S(p)$. When the segments of S define a polygon with h holes then Zarei and Ghodsi [18] give an $O(n^3)$ space data structure that can compute $V_S(p)$ for any query point p in $O(\min\{h, m_p\} \log n + m_p)$ time. This improves the query time of Pocchiola and Vegter when $h = o(m_p)$.

Motivated by the computer graphics problem of estimating *a priori* the savings to be had by applying a visibility culling algorithm, Fischer *et al.* [9, 10] give approximation algorithms for Problem 2. They present two approximation data structures for visibility counting. One structure uses a (r/m)-cutting [14, Section 4.5] of the $EVG(S)$ to obtain a data structure of size $O((m/r)^2)$ that answers queries in $O(\log n)$ time and approximates the visibility count up to an absolute error of r. Another structure uses random sampling to obtain a data structure of size $(m^2 \log^{O(1)} n)/\ell$, that has query time $\ell \log^{O(1)} n$, and that approximates the visibility count up to an absolute error of δn for any constant $\delta > 0$. (Note that δ affects the leading constants of both the query time and space requirements.)

1.3 New Results

In the current paper we revisit O'Rourke and Suri's proof that, for any $s \in S$, there exists a set $C_S(s)$ of $O(m_s)$ triangles whose union is $V_S(s)$, where m_s is the number of edges of $EVG(S)$ incident on s. We show that this covering has the additional property that if we take the $O(m)$ size set $C(S) = \bigcup_{s \in S} C_S(s)$ of triangles, then the number of triangles containing any point $p \in \mathbb{R}^2$ is a 2-approximation to the number of segments of s that are visible from p.[1]

These triangle-covering results have several applications that are obtained by storing the resulting triangles in a layered partition tree. Here, and throughout the remainder of the paper, $\epsilon > 0$ is a constant that can be made arbitrarily small. To reduce clutter, we use the notation $O_\epsilon(f(n)) = O(f(n)n^\epsilon)$.

1.3.1 Visibility testing

By storing the elements of $C_S(s)$ in a partition tree, we obtain, for any k with $m_s \leq k \leq m_s^2$, an $O(k)$ space data structure that can test, in $O_\epsilon(m_s/\sqrt{k})$ time, if a query point p is contained in $V_S(s)$. Barring a major breakthrough on Hopcroft's Problem [7], this result is likely only a factor of $O(n^\epsilon)$ from the optimal. See Section 3.1.

For comparison, the best previously described structure for this problem, as used within the results of Fischer *et al.* [9, 10], has size $O(m_s^2/\ell)$ and answers queries in $O(\ell \log n)$ time, where $\ell \geq 1$ is a space/time tradeoff parameter of the data structure. Taking $\ell = \sqrt{n}$ yields a space of $O(m_s^{3/2})$ and a query time of $O(\sqrt{m_s} \log n)$. On the other hand, taking $k = m_s^{3/2}$ in our data structure yields an $O(m_s^{3/2})$ space data structure with query time $O_\epsilon(m_s^{1/4})$.

1.3.2 Visibility Counting — Relative Approximation

By putting all the triangles of $C(S)$ into a partition tree, we obtain a data structure that can 2-approximate the number of segments of S visible from any query point. For any k with $m \leq k \leq m^2$, this structure has size $O(k)$ and answers queries in time $O(m/\sqrt{k})$. The structure returns a visibility count m'_p that satisfies $m_p \leq m'_p \leq 2m_p$. See Section 3.2.

1.3.3 Visibility Counting — Absolute Approximation

By using a selective random sampling of the segments in S, we obtain a data structure of size $O_\epsilon((cm/n)(cn)^\alpha) = O_\epsilon(n^{1+\alpha})$ that approximates the number of segments of S visible from any query point in time $O_\epsilon(c(m/n)^{(1/2)(1-\alpha)}) = O_\epsilon(cn^{(1/2)(1-\alpha)})$, for any given constants $c, \delta > 0$ and $0 \leq \alpha \leq 1$. With probability at least $1 - n^{\Omega(\delta^2 cn/m_p)}$, the structure returns a value m''_p such that $m_p - c/n - \delta n \leq m''_p \leq m_p + \delta n$. This data structure is described in Section 3.3.1.

Using random sampling in a different manner, we obtain a space versus query time tradeoff. For any k with $m/n \leq k \leq (m/n)^2$, we obtain a structure of size $O_\epsilon(k)$ and query time $O_\epsilon(m/(n\sqrt{k}))$. This structure returns a visibility count m''_p that satisfies $m_p - \delta n \leq m''_p \leq 2m_p + \delta n$. The details can be found in Section 3.3.2.

These results compare favourably with those of Fischer *et al.* [9, 10]. Their cutting-based data structure, with parameter $r = \delta n$, gives an absolute error of δn, uses space $O((m/n)^2)$ and has a query time of $O(\log n)$. Their random sampling-based data structure, with parameter $\ell = \sqrt{n}$, gives a data structure of size $(m^2 \log^{O(1)} n)/\sqrt{n}$ with query time $\sqrt{n} \log^{O(1)} n$.

The remainder of the paper is organized as follows: Section 2 proves results on covering visibility regions with triangles. Section 3 applies these results to obtain new results on visibility testing and counting. Section 4 summarizes and concludes with open problems.

2. COVERING $V_S(S)$

In this section we give an algorithm for covering the visibility region $V_S(s)$ with a set $C_S(s)$ of triangles. The resulting covering is similar to the covering given by Suri and O'Rourke [17], the main difference being around the triangles adjacent to the endpoints of s. However, our exposition, and our algorithm for computing $C(S)$ are more s-centric. This leads to efficient output-sensitive algorithms for constructing $C_S(s)$, rather than the worst-case optimal $O(n^2)$ algorithm obtained by Suri and O'Rourke [17]. The number of triangles used in $C_S(s)$ is bounded by $O(m_s)$ where m_s is the number of edges of $EVG(S)$ that are incident to s.

We will show how to cover the portion $V_S^+(s) \subseteq V_S(s)$ in the halfplane bounded from below by the supporting line of s with a set $C_S^+(s)$ of triangles. The complementary part $V_S^-(s) = V_S(s) \setminus V_S^+(s)$ can be covered with a set $C_S^-(s)$ using a symmetric algorithm.

The covering algorithm works by sweeping a point p from left to right along the segment s. Events in this sweep occur at the vertices $p_1, \ldots, p_{m'_s}$ of $VSP(S)$ incident on s, in their left to right order, so that p_1 and $p_{m'_s}$ are the left and right endpoints, respectively, of s.

Let e be an edge of $V_S^+(p)$ that is collinear with p and such that the interior of $V_S^+(p)$ is to the right of e. We call such an edge an *active edge* of $V_S^+(p)$. Active edges are important because, as p moves to the right, they uncover regions of $\mathbb{R}^2$ which may not have been previously visible. See Figure 4.a.

Let q be the lower endpoint of an active edge e and note that q is an endpoint of some segment in S. Consider what happens to e as the viewpoint p moves left to right along s,

[1] In fact, O'Rourke and Suri's covering is a 3-approximation. The modified version in this paper is a 2-approximation.

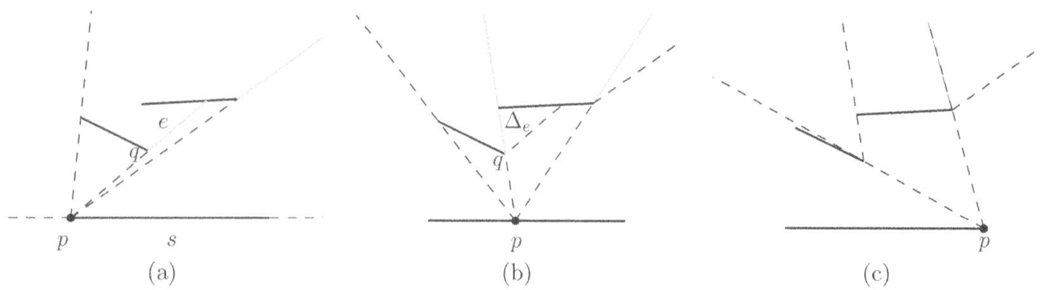

Figure 4: The algorithm for covering $V_S^+(s)$ with triangles processes the events at (a) p_1, (b) p_2 and (c) p_3. Active edges are shown in orange and triangles in the covering are shown at the time they are added to the covering.

but does not cross any edge of $EVG(S)$ collinear with q. As p moves left to right, the edge e remains collinear with p and q and sweeps over a triangle Δ_e whose lowest vertex is q. This continues until the point p reaches an edge of $VSP(S)$ incident on q. See Figure 4.b.

Algorithmically, the cover $C_S^+(s)$ is constructed as follows: Initially $p = p_1$ is the left endpoint of S. We compute the visibility polygon $V_S^+(p)$, whose boundary is a sequence of $2m_p = O(n)$ edges that alternate between subsegments of the elements of S and segments collinear with p and an endpoint of an element of S. This polygon can be covered in a natural way with m_p non-overlapping triangles, each of which has p as a vertex (see Figure 4.a). These m_p triangles are added to $C_S^+(s)$. After computing $V_S^+(p)$ we identify its active edges, and with each active edge e we store the value $\text{start}(e) = p_1$.

Next, we sweep p from left to right, pausing at the vertices $p_2, \ldots, p_{m'_s}$ as we go. Upon reaching a vertex p_i, we process the edges of $EVG(S)$ incident on p_i one at a time.[2] Let e' be an edge of $EVG(S)$ incident on p_i. If e' is collinear with an active edge e of $V_S^+(p)$ then we generate a new triangle Δ_e for $C_S^+(s)$. The lowest vertex of Δ_e is the lower endpoint q of e. Δ_e is bounded by two lines ℓ_1, ℓ_2, both of which contain q, and where ℓ_1 contains p_i and ℓ_2 contains $\text{start}(e)$. The third side of Δ_e is bounded by the segment in S incident on e and furthest from p_i. See Figure 4.b.

The visibility polygon $V_S^+(p)$ is updated in the neighbourhood of e, which possibly creates up to two new active edges incident to q. Each new active edge f is marked as active and we set $\text{start}(f) = p_i$. The exact nature of this update depends on the relative locations of the two segments that define e'. The three possible cases are illustrated in Figure 7.

Note that an important event, but which requires no special handling, occurs at the right endpoint of s when $p{=}p_{m_s}$. In this case, each active edge of $V_S^+(p)$ generates a triangle that is added to the set $C_S^+(s)$. See Figure 4.c.

We now prove the correctness, construction time and approximation bound of the above algorithm.

LEMMA 1. *Let $C_S^+(s)$ be the set of triangles generated by the above algorithm. Then $\cup C_S^+(s) = V_S^+(s)$ and $|C_S^+(s)| \leq m_s$ where m_s is the number of edges of $VSP(S)$ incident on s.*

[2]For segments in sufficiently general position, p_i, $1 < i < m_s$ will be incident to only one edge of $EVG(S)$, but the covering algorithm does not require this.

PROOF. To prove the bound on the size, first observe that the initial visibility polygon $V_S^+(p_1)$ has size that is bounded by the degree of p_1 in $VSP(S)$. Furthermore, at each event point p_i, $i > 1$, the number of triangles added to $C_S^+(s)$ is at most the number of edges of $VSP(S)$ incident to p_i. Therefore, the total number of triangles in $C_S^+(s)$ is at most the number of edges of $VSP(S)$ incident on s.

The fact that $\cup C_S^+(s) \subseteq V_S^+(s)$ follows immediately from the easily verifiable fact that each triangle added to $C_S^+(s)$ contains only points visible from some point on $p \in s$. In particular, for any point r in the triangle Δ_e that is added to $V_S^+(s)$ when processing p_i, there is a point q in the subsegment of s between $\text{start}(e)$ and p_i that sees r.

To prove that $C_S^+(s)$ covers $V_S^+(s)$, consider a point $r \in V_S^+(s)$. If r is visible from p_1 then r is contained in one of the triangles added during the initialization of the algorithm. Otherwise, there exists some point $p' \in s$ with minimum x-coordinate such that r is visible from p'. It follows that p' and r are collinear with a vertex q of some segment $s' \in S$ and that q is on the segment $p'r$ (see Figure 5.a). Then q is an endpoint of an active edge e of $V_S^+(p')$ with $\text{start}(e)$ to the left of p'. Since every active edge eventually adds a triangle to $C_S^+(s)$, there is some p_i to the right of p' that adds a triangle Δ_e to $C_S^+(s)$ that contains r (see Figure 5.b). Since this is true for every point $r \in V_S^+(s)$, we conclude that $\cup C_S^+(s) \supseteq V_S^+(s)$, and hence $\cup C_S^+(s) = V_S^+(s)$. □

LEMMA 2. *Let S be a set of n disjoint line segments. The covering $C_S(s)$ can be computed in*

1. *$O(m_s)$ time if we are given $EVG(S)$ or*
2. *$O_\epsilon(n + (m_s n)^{2/3})$ otherwise.*

PROOF. Part 1 of the lemma is clear. The algorithm for constructing $C_S(s)$ processes the edges of $EVG(S)$ incident

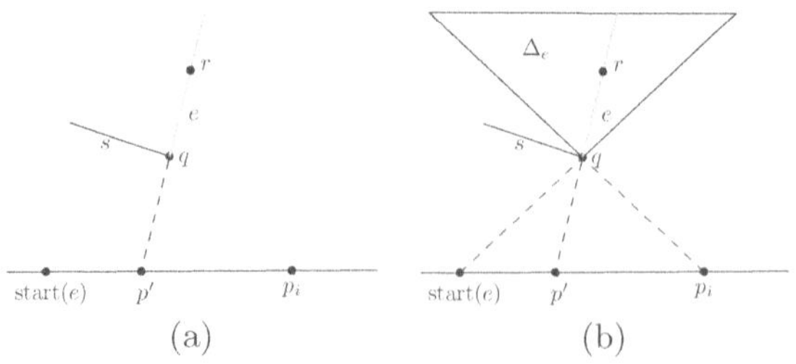

Figure 5: Proving that $C_S^+(s)$ covers $V_S^+(s)$.

on s in the order in which they appear. These m_s edges can be easily extracted from $EVG(S)$ in the order in which they appear and processing each edge takes $O(1)$ time.

Part 2 of the lemma requires some use of a geometric range searching structure for answering ray-sweeping queries. Let q and q' be two points that are visible, with q' on some segment $s'' \in S$. A *ray-sweeping query* asks to determine the first endpoint of a segment in S that is intersected by qq' as the point q' moves towards the left endpoint of s''.

A ray-sweeping query is an optimization problem. It's corresponding decision problem is a *triangle interference query*, which asks to determine if a query triangle Δ with vertices q, q' and $q'' \in s''$ intersects any segment of S. Because q and q' are visible and q' and q'' are both on s'', it is not hard to see that if Δ does intersect some segment in S, then Δ contains an endpoint of a segment in S. That is, a triangle interference query can be solved using a triangular range searching structure built on the endpoints of segments in S.

Triangular range searching is a well studied problem, and a number of solutions exist that give $O_\epsilon(k)$ space structures with $O_\epsilon(n/\sqrt{k})$ query time, for any k with $n \le k \le n^2$ [1, Section 4]. Using one of these structures and applying Chan's randomized optimization technique [5, Theorem 3.2] yields a data structure for ray-sweeping queries with the same preprocessing, space, and query time bounds.

To construct $C_S(s)$ we use essentially the same sweeping algorithm used to define $C_S(s)$ except that ray-sweeping queries are used to compute the algorithm's events on the fly. The algorithm uses a priority queue Q to order and process these event points in left to right order. To initialize the algorithm, we construct the visibility polygon $V_S(p = p_1)$ in $O(n \log n)$ time using a radial sweep [3, 17]. Next, each active edge of $V_S(p)$ is identified and processed.

Anytime (during initialization or later) that an active edge $e = qq'$ is created, the algorithm performs a ray-sweeping query with the segment qq' and a ray sweeping query with the edge $q'p$ (see Figure 6). The results of these two queries determine an event point $p' \in s$ to the right of p at which time the edge e contributes a triangle Δ_e to s. This event point p' is enqueued in Q. It is not hard to verify that this algorithm computes the same set of triangles $C_S(s)$ as the original algorithm and that the number of ray-sweeping queries performed is $O(m_s)$ (at most two queries are performed for each triangle added to $C_S(s)$).

Therefore, the algorithm can be implemented to run in $O_\epsilon(k + m_s n/\sqrt{k})$ for any $n \le k \le n^2$. Given the value of m_s in advance, setting $k = (m_s n)^{2/3}$ would yield the stated time bound. However, even without knowing m_s in advance we can begin by estimating the value of m_s as $m'_s = 2$ and doubling our estimate (and rebuilding the ray-sweeping structure) if we discover that $m_s > m'_s$. This doubling strategy yields the overall time bound of $O_\epsilon(n + (m_s n)^{2/3})$, as required. □

Next we show that, in a global sense, the number of triangles containing a point $p \in \mathbb{R}^2$ gives a 2-approximation to the number of segments of S that are visible from p.

Lemma 3. *Let $C(S) = \bigcup_{s \in S} C_S(s)$ and let p be any point in $\mathbb{R}^2$ that is not on the boundary of any triangle in $C(S)$. If m_p is the number of segments in S (partially) visible from p and m'_p is the number of triangles in $C(S)$ that contain p, then $m_p \le m'_p \le 2m_p$.*

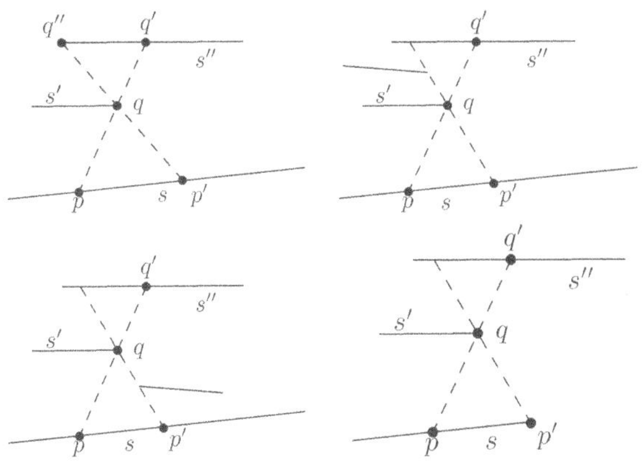

Figure 6: The four cases that can occur when using a ray-sweeping query to determine the point p' at which active edge $e = qq'$ contributes a triangle to $C_S(s)$.

Proof. Let $C_p \subseteq C(S)$ be the set of triangles in $C(S)$ that contain p, and let $S_p \subseteq S$ be the set of segments in S that are (partially) visible from p. Our goal is to show that $|S_p| \le |C_p| \le 2|S_p|$. The lower bound on $m'_p = |C_p|$ is trivial: For every segment $s \in S_p$, $V_S(s)$ contains p, so, by Lemma 1, $C_S(s)$ contributes at least one triangle to C_p.

To prove the upper bound, we describe a mapping $f : C_p \to S_p$ that is *2-to-1*; for every $s \in S_p$, there exists at most two triangles $\Delta \in C_p$ such that $f(\Delta) = s$. The existence of f then proves the upper bound.

Let $\Delta \in C_p$ be some triangle that contains p and suppose that $\Delta \in C_S(s)$ for some $s \in S$ that is, without loss of generality, below p. If Δ is incident on s (Figure 8.a) then Δ was added to $C_S(s)$ as part of $V_S(p)$ where p was the left endpoint of s. In this case, we set $f(\Delta) = s$. Otherwise, Δ was created when sweeping s with p and some active edge e of $V_S(p)$ generated Δ (Figure 8.b). The vertex q of Δ that is closest to s is incident on a segment $s' \in S$. In this case $f(\Delta) = s'$.

We now argue that f is 2-to-1. Let $s \in S$ be some segment and suppose, without loss of generality, that p is above s. Consider a triangle $\Delta \in f^{-1}(s)$ and observe that, by the definition of f, Δ has a vertex that is an endpoint of s.

Note that there is at most one triangle in $C_S(s) \cap C_p$ that maps to s, and this triangle exists precisely if p is visible from the left endpoint of s. All that remains to show is that

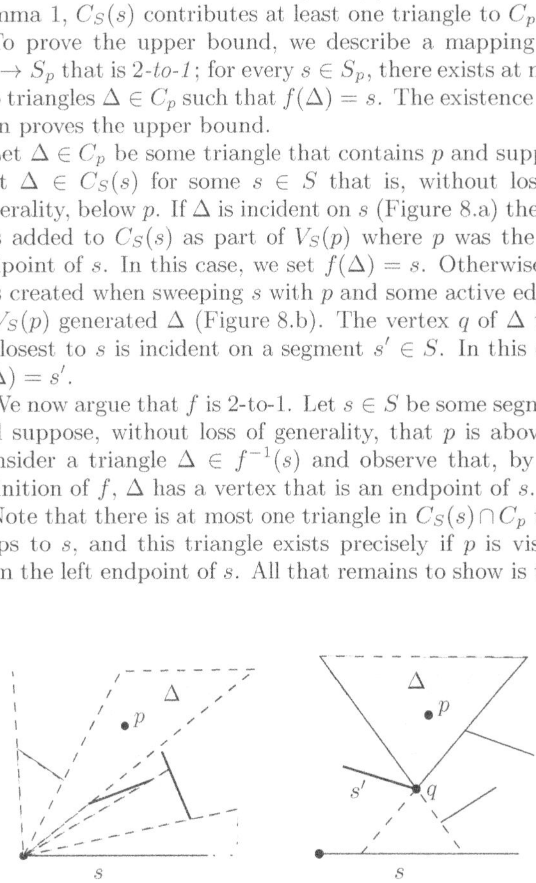

(a) $f(\Delta) = s$ (b) $f(\Delta) = s'$

Figure 8: f takes Δ onto (a) s and (b) s'.

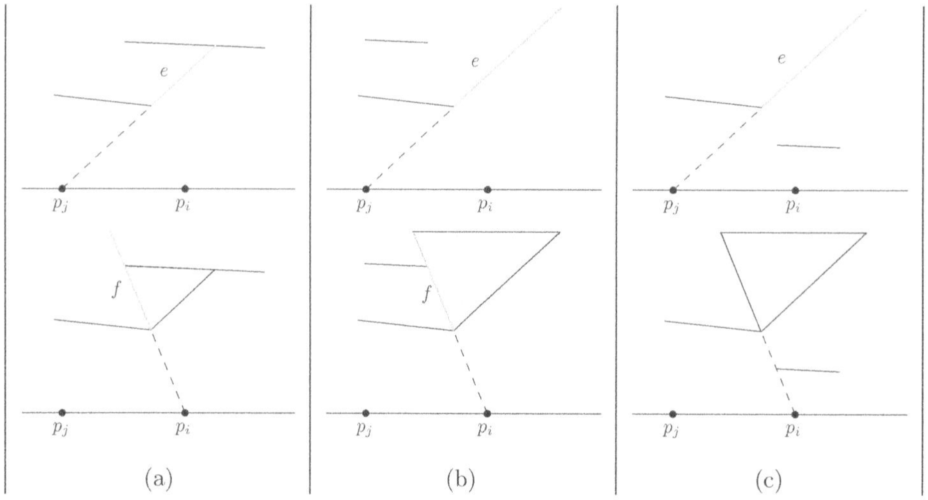

Figure 7: The three cases that occur when processing an edge of $EVG(S)$ incident on p_i. Here, $\text{start}(e) = p_j$.

there is at most one additional segment $s' \in S$, $s' \neq s$ such that $C_S(s')$ contains a triangle Δ with $f(\Delta) = s$.

Let Δ be such a triangle and suppose that Δ is incident to the endpoint q of s. Refer to Figure 9. The triangle Δ was generated by an active edge when processing s'. In particular, there is a subsegment $p_j p_i \subseteq s'$ such that an active edge e of $V_S^+(p)$ sweeps over Δ when p travels from p_j to p_i. (Note, $p_j = \text{start}(e)$.) This implies that p_i and p_j are below s. Since p travels from left to right along e, this implies that q is the right endpoint of s because, otherwise, e would not be an active edge of $V_S^+(p)$.

Thus far, we have established that at most one triangle in $f^{-1}(s)$ is incident to the left endpoint of s. To see that at most one triangle (Δ, discussed above) is incident to the right endpoint of s, suppose by way of contradiction that there are two such triangles Δ and Δ' with $\Delta \in C_S(s')$ and $\Delta' \in C_S(s'')$. Consider the line ℓ through p and q. Observe that ℓ intersects both s and s', in two points r and r', respectively. But this is not possible since then one of r or r' does not see the endpoint q. $\square$

Remark:.

The condition, in Lemma 3, that p is not on the boundary of any triangle in $C_S(s)$ is unnecessary if we take a little extra care. In particular, the mapping f actually maps triangles to the endpoints of segments. The set $C_S(v)$ of triangles mapped to a particular endpoint v all have v as a vertex and no two triangles in $C_S(v)$ share an interior point. This means that we can define each triangle in $C_S(v)$ to either include or exclude some of its edges or vertices so that the triangles are disjoint but their union remains unchanged. This yields a set of (partially open) triangles $C'(S)$ for which Lemma 3 holds for any point $p \in \mathbb{R}^2$.

3. APPLICATIONS

In this section, we consider applications of Lemma 1 and Lemma 3 to some visibility testing and counting problems. These applications rely on data structures for *triangle inclusion counting*: Given a set T of triangles, we want to preprocess T into a data structure for counting the number of triangles in T that contain a query point p.

The tools needed to perform these queries are well-known, but finding the relevant structures and techniques, and applying them correctly, can take some time. Therefore, we review the data structure here and point out the relevant references.

Let Δ be a triangle. Δ is the intersection of at most 4 halfplanes bounded by four lines $h(\Delta) = (u_1, u_2, d_1, d_2)$ where u_1 and u_2 bound Δ from below and d_1 and d_2 bound Δ from above. Given a triangle Δ we have either $u_1 = u_2$ or $d_1 = d_2$. By the standard duality mapping [6, Section 8.2] the four lines in $h(\Delta)$ map to four points u_1^*, u_2^*, d_1^* and d_2^*. A point $p \in \mathbb{R}^2$ maps to a line p^* in the dual plane. The point p is contained in Δ if and only if the line p^* is above (or on) u_1^* and u_2^* and below (or on) d_1^* and d_2^*. Let $h^*(\Delta) = (u_1^*, u_2^*, d_1^*, d_2^*)$.

A triangle inclusion counting structure for T stores the 8-dimensional point-set

$$h^*(T) = \{h^*(\Delta) : \Delta \in T\} \ .$$

Given a query point p, we want to count the number of points $(a, b, c, d) \in h^*(T)$ that satisfy the four requirements:

1. a is above p^*, and
2. b is above p^*, and
3. c is below p^*, and
4. d is below p^*.

Counting the number of points in $h^*(T)$ that satisfy any one of these requirements is a halfplane range counting problem. Data structures for halfplane range counting are plentiful, and there are several data structures known that use $O_\epsilon(k)$ space and have query time $O_\epsilon(n/\sqrt{k})$ [1, Section 4]. Several of these structures (for example, Matoušek's efficient partition trees [13]) are hierarchical structures that are efficient and r-convergent (see Agarwal and Erickson [1, Section 5] for definitions of hierarchical, efficient, and r-convergent). This implies [1, Theorem 10] that there exists a 4-layer structure that uses $O_\epsilon(k)$ space and preprocessing time and that, in time $O_\epsilon(n/\sqrt{k})$, can count the number of elements in $h^*(T)$ that satisfy the constraints 1–4 for any query point p^*.

Translating this back into primal space we obtain the data structure we need:

THEOREM 1 ([1, 13]). *Let T be a set of n triangles. For any k with $n \leq k \leq n^2$, there exists a data structure of size $O_\epsilon(k)$ that can be constructed in time $O_\epsilon(k)$ and that can count the number of triangles containing a query point p in $O_\epsilon(n/\sqrt{k})$ time.*

3.1 Visibility Testing

Our first application follows immediately by storing the triangles of Lemma 1 in the data structure of Theorem 1. This yields our first result:

THEOREM 2. *Let S be a set of n disjoint line segments and let $s \in S$ be a special segment. For any $m_s \leq k \leq m_s^2$, there exists a data structure of size $O_\epsilon(k)$ that can test, in $O_\epsilon(m_s/\sqrt{k})$ time, if any query point p is contained in $V_S(s)$. The data structure can be constructed in*

1. *$O_\epsilon(k)$ time if we are given $EVG(S)$ or*
2. *$O_\epsilon(n + (m_s n)^{2/3} + k)$ time otherwise.*

Next we argue that, barring a breakthrough on Hopcroft's Problem [7], Theorem 2 is near-optimal. *Hopcroft's Problem* takes as input a set L of n lines and a set P of n points and asks if any point in P is contained in any line in L. Currently, the most efficient methods of solving Hopcroft's Problem have running times in $\Omega(n^{4/3})$. Furthermore, $\Omega(n^{4/3})$ is a lower bound for Hopcroft's Problem in a restricted model of computation that can model all known algorithms for the problem [7].

Given the set L, we can compute the leftmost intersection point between any pair of lines by sorting the lines by slope and checking the intersection points between consecutive pairs of lines. Assume, without loss of generality, that this leftmost intersection point has x-coordinate equal to 0. Using infinitesimal gaps between segments,[3] we can easily construct a set of $3n + O(1)$ segments $s_0, \ldots, s_{3n+O(1)}$ such that a query point p whose x-coordinate is greater than 0 is visible from s_0 if and only if p lies on one of the lines in L (see Figure 10). For a query point p with x-coordinate smaller than 0 we can test if p is contained in any line of L in $O(\log n)$ time by storing the lines of L sorted by slope and using binary search.

Therefore, by the above discussion, setting $k = n^{4/3}$ and using Theorem 2 we can use this data structure to solve Hopcroft's Problem in $O_\epsilon(n^{4/3})$ time. Furthermore, the existence of a data structure for testing if $V_S(s)$ contains a query point p that could be constructed in $o(n^{4/3})$ time and whose query time is $o(n^{1/3})$ would give a $o(n^{4/3})$ time algorithm for Hopcroft's Problem.

[3]The use of infinitesimals in lower bounds is justified by Erickson's results [8].

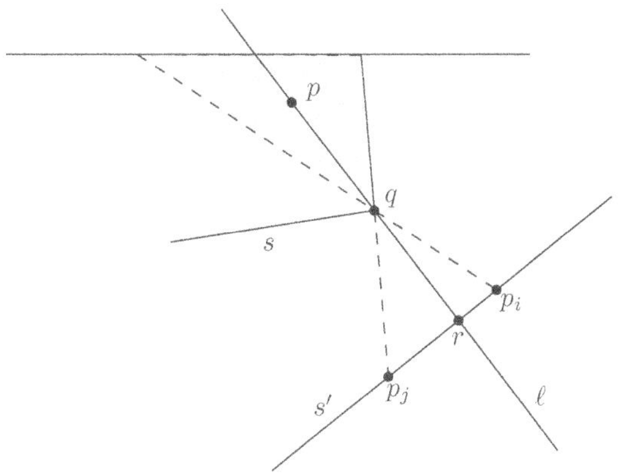

Figure 9: At most one triangle in $f^{-1}(s)$ is incident to the right endpoint of S.

3.2 Visibility Counting – Relative Approximation

Next we consider Fischer *et al.*'s problem of approximate visibility counting [9, 10]. We want to preprocess the segments in S, so that for any query point p we can quickly approximate the number of segments in S that are visible from p.

We begin with an easy corollary obtained by computing $C(S)$ using Lemma 2 and putting all the triangles of $C(S)$ into the data structure of Theorem 1. The resulting structure guarantees a relative approximation of the visibility count for all values of m_p:

COROLLARY 1. *Let S be a set of n disjoint line segments whose visibility graph has m edges, and let $0 < \alpha < 1$ be real valued parameters. There exists a data structure D that can approximate the number of segments of S visible from any query point p such that:*

1. *D has size $O_\epsilon(m^{1+\alpha}) = O_\epsilon(n^{2(1+\alpha)})$,*
2. *D can be constructed in time $O_\epsilon(m^{1+\alpha}) = O_\epsilon(n^{2(1+\alpha)})$,*
3. *D can perform a query in $O_\epsilon(m^{(1/2)(1-\alpha)}) = O_\epsilon(n^{1-\alpha})$ time, and*
4. *when querying D with a point p that sees m_p points of S, D returns a value m'_p that satisfies $m_p \leq m'_p \leq 2m_p$.*

3.3 Visibility Counting – Absolute Approximation

Although Corollary 1 offers a good approximation guarantee, the space requirement is too large. In the worst case, when $m = \Omega(n^2)$, a data structure of size $\omega(n^2)$ is required in order to achieve a sublinear query time.

Fischer *et al.* [9, 10] argue that, for the computer graphics application they consider, an absolute approximation is sufficient. In their application, there is a function $f(n)$ such that, for $m_p \ll f(n)$ it is more efficient to run a visibility

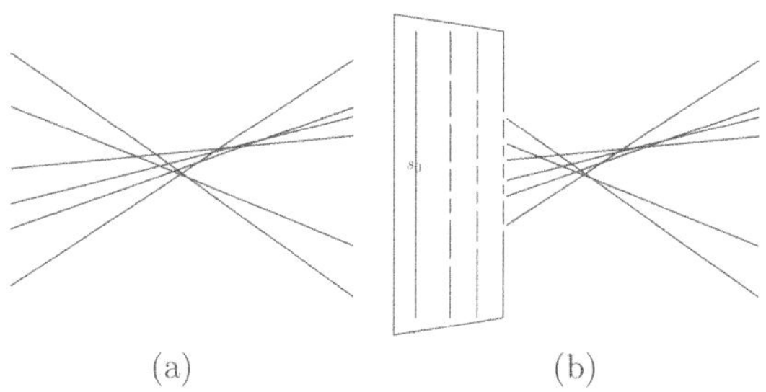

Figure 10: A set L of lines (a) and a set of $3n + O(1)$ segments where testing if a point is in $V_S(s_0)$ helps to determine if the point is contained in any line of L.

culling algorithm before rendering the view from p but for $f(n) \ll m_p$ it is preferable to simply send all elements of S to the graphics hardware for rendering. For $m_p \approx f(n)$ neither strategy has a clear advantage. If we define $a \ll b$ as $a < b - \delta n$ then we see that an algorithm that can approximate m_p with an additive error of at most δn is sufficient for this application.

We present two different data structures that offer this kind of approximation guarantee. These two structures offer different tradeoffs in terms of accuracy and query time.

3.3.1 *Solution 1: Sampling from S*

The data structure of Theorem 2 combined with a careful random sampling of the elements of S provides our first solution. We create a Bernoulli sample $S'' \subseteq S$ by choosing each element independently with probability $(c \log n)/n$, where $c \geq 1$ is a parameter of the data structure that controls the accuracy of the approximation. For each sample $s \in S''$, we construct the data structure of Theorem 2 with the value $k = m_s^{1+\alpha}$ for some parameter $0 \leq \alpha \leq 1$ that controls the space/query-time tradeoff. If, during the construction of this data structure, it turns out that $m_s > 4cn$, then discard s from S''. Notice that this algorithm is effectively drawing a Bernoulli sample from the set $S' = \{s \in S : m_s \leq 4cn\}$ and that, since $2m = \sum_{s \in S} m_s \leq 4n^2$, there are at most n/c elements in S that are not in S'. Suppose p is visible from m_p elements of S and m'_p elements of S'. Then, by the above discussion, we have $m_p - n/c \leq m'_p \leq m_p$. Let $m''_p = (n/(c \log n)) \cdot |\{s \in S'' : p \in V_S(s)\}|$. The quantity m''_p is an unbiased estimator of m'_p and, using Chernoff's bounds, we readily establish that

$$\Pr\{|m''_p - m'_p| \geq \delta n\} \leq n^{-\Omega(\delta^2 cn/m'_p)} \leq n^{-\Omega(\delta^2 cn/m_p)}$$

for any $\delta > 0$. Combining this with the previous equation gives

$$\Pr\{|m''_p - m_p| \geq \delta n + n/c\} \leq n^{-\Omega(\delta^2 cn/m_p)}.$$

This establishes the accuracy of the data structure. What remains is to analyze the query time, space, and construction time.

Query time. A query computes m''_s by performing a query in each of the data structures built on the elements of S''. The expected contribution of an element $s \in S'$ to the query time is therefore

$$\left(\frac{c \log n}{n}\right) \cdot O_\epsilon\left(m_s^{(1/2)(1-\alpha)}\right)$$

since it contributes $O_\epsilon(m_s/\sqrt{k}) = O_\epsilon(m_s^{(1/2)(1-\alpha)})$ to the query time if it is chosen to take part in S'' and it contributes nothing otherwise. Summing this over all s, we get a total expected query time of at most

$$\left(\frac{c \log n}{n}\right) \times \sum_{s \in S'} O_\epsilon\left(m_s^{(1/2)(1-\alpha)}\right) = O_\epsilon(c(m/n)^{(1/2)(1-\alpha)})$$

where the last step follows since $f(x) = x^{(1/2)(1-\alpha)}$ is a concave function and $\sum_{s \in S'} m_s = O(m)$.

Space. Arguing as above, the expected amount of space that an element $s \in S'$ contributes to this data structure is

$$\left(\frac{c \log n}{n}\right) \cdot O_\epsilon\left(m_s^{1+\alpha}\right).$$

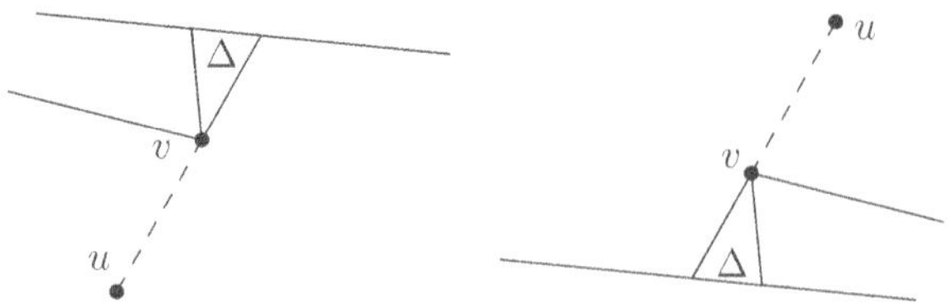

Figure 11: The two cases in which the ordered pair (u, v) generates the triangle Δ.

Therefore, the total expected amount of space used by the structure is

$$\left(\frac{c \log n}{n}\right) \cdot \sum_{s \in S'} O_\epsilon\left(m_s^{1+\alpha}\right) = O_\epsilon((cm/n)(cn)^\alpha) \quad (1)$$

which follows by maximizing the sum $\sum_{s \in S'} m_s^{1+\alpha}$ using the facts that $\sum_{s \in S'} m_s = O(m)$ and that any individual $s \in S'$ has $m_s \leq 4cn$.

Preprocessing time. The preprocessing phase requires computing $C_S(s)$ for each sample element $s \in S''$ and constructing a layered partition tree for the elements of $C_S(s)$. Constructing the partition tree takes $O_\epsilon(m_s^{1+\alpha})$ time, so, as above, the total expected cost of constructing the partition trees for all elements in S'' is $O_\epsilon((cm/n)(cn)^\alpha)$.

Computing $C_S(s)$, using Lemma 2 takes $O_\epsilon((m_s n)^{2/3})$ time. Since $f(x) = (xn)^{2/3}$ is a concave function, the total expected time to compute $C_S(s)$ for each $s \in S''$ is $O_\epsilon(cm^{2/3})$.

THEOREM 3. *Let S be a set of n disjoint line segments whose visibility graph has m edges and let $c > 1$ and $0<\alpha<1$ be real valued parameters. There exists a data structure D that can approximate the number of segments of S visible from any query point p such that:*

1. *D has expected size $O_\epsilon((cm/n)(cn)^\alpha) = O_\epsilon((cn)^{1+\alpha})$,*
2. *D can be constructed in $O_\epsilon(cm^{2/3} + (cm/n)(cn)^\alpha) = O_\epsilon(cn^{4/3} + (cn)^{1+\alpha})$ expected time,*
3. *D can perform a counting query in expected time $O_\epsilon(c(m/n)^{(1/2)(1-\alpha)}) = O_\epsilon(cn^{(1/2)(1-\alpha)})$, and*
4. *for any $\delta > 0$, when querying D with a query for a point p that sees m_p points of S, D returns a value m''_p that satisfies $m_p - n/c - \delta n \leq m''_p \leq m_p + \delta n$ with probability at least $1 - n^{-\Omega(\delta^2 cn/m_p)}$.*

Example: For any constant δ there exists a value $c = c(\delta)$ such that taking $\alpha = 4/3$ gives a data structure of size $O_\epsilon((m/n)n^{1/3}) = O_\epsilon(n^{4/3})$ with query time $O_\epsilon((m/n)^{1/3}) = O_\epsilon(n^{1/3})$ and the structure approximates m_p for any p with an absolute error of at most δn w.h.p..

As this example shows, the structure of Theorem 3 is quite efficient for constant values of δ. Unfortunately, the theorem becomes weaker when using subconstant values of δ. This is because, to obtain meaningful error bounds, we require $c = \Omega(1/\delta)$ and the running time of the query algorithm grows linearly with c.

3.3.2 *Solution 2: Sampling C(S)*

Next we consider a different data structure that is also based on random sampling. Rather than sample segments of S, we instead sample triangles of $C(S)$ and use Lemma 3 to bound the quality of the approximation. This results in a more efficient space/accuracy tradeoff than that provided by Theorem 3. The cost of this savings in space is that we obtain a relative approximation bound when m_p is large and an absolute approximation bound when m_p is small. For the application proposed by Fischer et al. [9, 10] this is an acceptable approximation bound.

Consider the set $C(S)$ of triangles described in Lemma 3. For any point $p \in \mathbb{R}^2$, the number, m'_p, of triangles in $C(S)$ that contain p is a 2-approximation of the number, m_p, of segments in S that are visible from p. In particular

$$m_p \leq m'_p \leq 2m_p \ . \tag{2}$$

Our strategy is to approximate m'_p by sampling elements of $C(S)$. The easiest way to proceed would be to select a Bernoulli sample by sampling each element of $C(S)$ independently with probability $(c \log n)/n$. This would require enumerating the elements of $C(S)$, of which there are $\Theta(m)$, yielding a construction time that is $\Omega(n^2)$ in the worst case. Instead, we use a different sampling strategy based on the rejection method that avoids computing $C(S)$.

Sampling $C(S)$. Our goal is to obtain a random multiset $C''(S) \subseteq C(S)$ of size roughly $c(m/n) \log n$. To achieve this, we repeat the following procedure $4cn \log n$ times: We select two points u and v at random, with replacement, from the $2n$ endpoints of S. Note that there are $4n^2$ ways of doing this. Next, using $O(1)$ ray sweeping queries, we determine if q is a vertex of some triangle $\Delta \in C(S)$ that has an edge collinear with $\overrightarrow{uv}$ and that lies to the left of $\overrightarrow{uv}$ (see Figure 11). Note that, for any $\Delta \in C(S)$, there is exactly one pair (u, v) for which this is true.[4] Therefore, if this test is affirmative then Δ is an element drawn uniformly at random from $C(S)$ and we add it to our sample $C''(S)$. The probability that we increase the size of $C''(S)$ this way is $m_S/(4n^2)$, where $m_S = |C(S)| = O(m)$.

Space, preprocessing time, and query time. To compute $C''(S)$ efficiently we use the ray-sweeping data structure described in the proof of Lemma 2. Each sampling step requires $O(1)$ ray-sweeping queries, which can be done in $O_\epsilon(n/\sqrt{\ell})$ time after $O_\epsilon(\ell)$ preprocessing. Thus, the expected time required to build the ray-sweeping data structure and perform $4cn \log n$ sampling steps is

$$O_\epsilon(\ell + (cn \log n)(n/\sqrt{\ell}) = O_\epsilon(c^{2/3} n^{4/3})$$

for $\ell = c^{2/3} n^{4/3}$.

Each sampling step adds an element to $C''(S)$ with probability $m_S/(4n^2)$. So, the number of samples in $C''(S)$ is a binomial random variable with parameters $4cn \log n$ and $m_S/(4n^2)$ and the expected size of $C''(S)$ is therefore $c(m_S/n) \log n$. Using Chernoff's Bounds, we find that the probability that the size of $C''(S)$ exceeds $ac(m_S/n) \log n$ is at most $n^{-\Omega(a)}$ for any $a > 1$. This concentration result ensures that when building the data structure of Theorem 1 on the elements of $C''(S)$ the expected size, preprocessing time, and query time of the resulting structure are $O_\epsilon(k)$, $O_\epsilon(k)$, and $O_\epsilon((m/n)/\sqrt{k})$, respectively, for any $m/n \leq k \leq (m/n)^2$.

[4]The pair (u, v) generates the triangle Δ precisely if u is below v and v is the right endpoint of its segment or u is above v and v is the left endpoint of its segment.

To summarize, for any k with $m/n \leq k \leq (m/n)^2$, the above sampling procedure runs in $O_\epsilon(c^{2/3} n^{4/3} + k)$ expected time and produces a data structure of $O_\epsilon(k)$ expected size, that can answer queries in $O_\epsilon((m/n)/\sqrt{k})$ expected time. All that remains is to calibrate and check the accuracy of the results provided by the data structure.

Estimating m'_p. Recall that our goal is to estimate m'_p, the number of elements of $C(S)$ that contain the query point p, as m'_p is a 2-approximation to the number of segments of S visible from p. Let

$$m''_p = (n/(c \log n)) \cdot |\{\Delta \in C''(S) : p \in \Delta\}| \ .$$

(Note that computing m''_p does not require knowing the value $m_S = |C(S)|$.) Each step of the sampling procedure finds an element $\Delta \in C(S)$ such that $p \in \Delta$ with probability exactly $m'_p/(4n^2)$. Since the sampling procedure runs for $4cn \log n$ steps, this implies that the number of triangles in $C''(S)$ that contain p is a binomial random variable with parameters $4cn \log n$ and $m'_p/(4n^2)$. Therefore,

$$\mathbf{E}[m''_p] = (n/(c \log n))(4cn \log n)(m'_p/4n^2) = m'_p \ .$$

That is, m''_p is an unbiased estimator of m'_p. Furthermore, applying Chernoff's bounds to the underlying binomial random variable we find that

$$\Pr\{|m''_p - m'_p| \geq \delta n\} \leq n^{-\Omega(\delta^2 cn/m_p)}$$

for any $\delta > 0$. Combining this with Equation (2) we obtain

$$\Pr\{m_p - \delta n \leq m''_p \leq 2m_p + \delta n\} \geq 1 - n^{-\Omega(\delta^2 cn/m_p)} \ .$$

This establishes the accuracy of the data structure and completes the proof of our last theorem:

THEOREM 4. *Let S be a set of n disjoint line segments whose visibility graph has m edges and let $c > 1$ and $0<\alpha<1$ be real valued parameters. There exists a data structure D that can approximate the number of segments of S visible from any query point p such that:*

1. *D has expected size $O_\epsilon((cm/n)^{1+\alpha}) = O_\epsilon((cn)^{1+\alpha})$,*
2. *D can be constructed in time $O_\epsilon(c^{2/3} n^{4/3} + (cn)^{1+\alpha})$,*
3. *D can perform a counting query in time $O_\epsilon((cm/n)^{(1/2)(1-\alpha)}) = O_\epsilon((cn)^{(1/2)(1-\alpha)})$, and*
4. *for any $\delta > 0$, when querying D with a point p that sees m_p points of S, D returns a value m''_p that satisfies $m_p - \delta n \leq m''_p \leq 2m_p + \delta n$ with probability at least $1 - n^{-\Omega(\delta^2 cn/m_p)}$.*

Example. Taking $c = dn^{1/3}$, for a large constant d, and α=0, we get a data structure of size $O_\epsilon(n^{4/3})$ that can be constructed in time $O_\epsilon(n^{14/9})$ and that can effectively distinguish between viewpoints p where $m_p \ll n^{2/3}$ and viewpoints p where $m_p \gg n^{2/3}$ in $O_\epsilon(n^{2/3})$ time.

4. SUMMARY AND CONCLUSIONS

Many open questions remain. The data structure for testing if a point is in $V_S(s)$ for a segment S (Theorem 2) is near-optimal, at least assuming an $\Omega(n^{4/3})$ lower-bound for Hopcroft's Problem. However, it is difficult to say if the data structures for approximate visibility counting are close to optimal. Our solutions reduce visibility counting to the problem of computing the depth of a query point in an arrangement of $O((m/n) \log n)$ (Theorem 3 and Theorem 4) or $O(m)$ (Corollary 1) triangles. In both cases, it would be sufficient to give a relative approximation for the depth of the query point. Unfortunately, without some additional assumptions (such as fatness) about the triangles, there is currently no good solution to this problem.

The results in the current paper consider the problem of *planar* visibility counting, where S is a set of disjoint line segments in $\mathbb{R}^2$. Of course, modern virtual environments are often 3-dimensional. Many of these environments are just barely 3-dimensional in the sense that they consist of a constant number of 2-dimensional layers that can be handled using the data structures presented in the current paper. However, ultimately we would like to develop data structures that store a set S of disjoint triangles in $\mathbb{R}^3$ and can approximately count the number of elements of S (at least partly) visible from a query point $p \in \mathbb{R}^3$.

Acknowledgements

This work was done while the second author was a visiting researcher at NICTA and the University of Sydney. The author is grateful for the hospitality and funding provided by both institutions. NICTA is funded through the Australian Government's Backing Australia's Ability initiative, in part through the Australian Research Council.

5. REFERENCES

[1] P. K. Agarwal and J. Erickson. Geometric range searching and its relatives. In B. Chazelle, J. E. Goodman, and R. Pollack, editors, *Advances in Discrete and Computational Geometry*, volume 223 of *Contemporary Mathematics*, pages 1–56. American Mathematical Society Press, 1999.

[2] B. Aronov, L. J. Guibas, M. Teichmann, and L. Zhang. Visibility queries and maintenance in simple polygons. *Discrete & Computational Geometry*, 27(4):461–483, 2002.

[3] T. Asano. An efficient algorithm for finding the visibility polygon for a polygonal region with holes. *IEICE Transactions*, E68-E:557–589, 1985.

[4] P. Bose, A. Lubiw, and J. I. Munro. Efficient visibility queries in simple polygons. *Computational Geometry Theory and Applications*, 23(3):313–335, 2002.

[5] T. M. Chan. Geometric applications of a randomized optimization technique. *Discrete & Computational Geometry*, 22(4):547–567, 1999.

[6] M. de Berg, O. Cheong, M. van Kreveld, and M. Overmars. *Computational Geometry Algorithms and Applications*. Springer, third edition, 2008.

[7] J. Erickson. New lower bounds for Hopcroft's problem. *Discrete & Computational Geometry*, 16(4):389–418, 1996.

[8] J. Erickson. Lower bounds for linear satisfiability problems. *Chicago Journal of Theoretical Computer Science*, 1999, 1999.

[9] M. Fischer, M. Hilbig, C. Jähn, F. Meyer auf der Heide, and M. Ziegler. Planar visibility counting. *CoRR*, abs/0810.0052, 2008.

[10] M. Fischer, M. Hilbig, C. Jähn, F. Meyer auf der Heide, and M. Ziegler. Planar visibility counting. In *Proceedings of the 25th European Workshop on Computational Geometry (EuroCG 2009)*, pages 203–206, 2009.

[11] S. K. Ghosh and D. Mount. An output sensitive algorithm for computing visibility graphs. *SIAM Journal on Computing*, 20:888–910, 1991.

[12] L. J. Guibas, R. Motwani, and P. Raghavan. The robot localization problem. *SIAM Journal on Computing*, 26(4):1120–1138, 1997.

[13] J. Matoušek. Efficient partition trees. *Discrete & Computational Geometry*, 8:315–334, 1992.

[14] J. Matoušek. *Lectures on Discrete Geometry*, volume 212 of *Springer Graduate Texts in Mathematic*. Springer, 2002.

[15] J. O'Rourke. *Art Gallery Theorems and Applications*. Oxford University Press, 1987.

[16] M. Pocchiola and G. Vegter. The visibility complex. *International Journal of Computational Geometry and Applications*, 6(3):279–308, 1996.

[17] S. Suri and J. O'Rourke. Worst-case optimal algorithms for constructing visibility polygons with holes. In *Proceedings of the Second Annual Symposium on Computational Geometry (SCG 1984)*, pages 14–23, 1984.

[18] A. Zarei and M Ghodsi. Efficient computation of query point visibility in polygons with holes. In *Proceedings of the 21st Annual ACM Symposium on Computational Geometry (SCG 2005)*, 2005.

The 2-Center Problem in Three Dimensions*

Pankaj K. Agarwal
Duke University

Rinat Ben Avraham
Tel Aviv University

Micha Sharir
Tel Aviv University and
New York University

ABSTRACT

Let P be a set of n points in $\mathbb{R}^3$. The *2-center problem* for P is to find two congruent balls of the minimum radius whose union covers P. We present two randomized algorithms for computing a 2-center of P. The first algorithm runs in $O(n^3 \log^8 n)$ expected time, and the second algorithm runs in $O(n^2 \log^8 n/(1-r^*/r_0)^3)$ expected time, where r^* is the radius of the 2-center of P and r_0 is the radius of the smallest enclosing ball of P. The second algorithm is faster than the first one as long as r^* is not very close to r_0, which is equivalent to the condition of the centers of the two balls in the 2-center of P not being very close to each other.

Categories and Subject Descriptors

F.2.2 [**Analysis of algorithms and problem complexity**]: Nonnumerical algorithms and problems—*Geometrical problems and computations*; I.5.3 [**Pattern recognition**]: Clustering—*algorithms*

General Terms

Algorithms, Theory

Keywords

2-center problem, facility location, geometric optimization, intersection of congruent balls, spherical polytopes, multi-dimensional parametric searching

*Work on this paper by Pankaj K. Agarwal and Micha Sharir has been supported by Grant 2006/194 from the U.S.-Israeli Binational Science Foundation. Work by Pankaj Agarwal is also supported by NSF under grants CNS-05-40347, CCF-06 -35000, IIS-07-13498, and CCF-09-40671, by ARO grants W911NF-07-1-0376 and W911NF-08-1-0452, by an NIH grant 1P50-GM-08183-01, and by a DOE grant OEG-P200A070505 Work by Micha Sharir has also been supported by NSF Grants CCF-05-14079 and CCF-08-30272, by Grants 155/05 and 338/09 from the Israel Science Fund, and by the Hermann Minkowski–MINERVA Center for Geometry at Tel Aviv University.

1. INTRODUCTION

Background. Let $P = \{p_1, \ldots, p_n\}$ be a set of n points in $\mathbb{R}^3$. The *2-center problem* for P is to find two congruent balls of the minimum radius whose union covers P. This is a special case of the general p-center problem in $\mathbb{R}^d$, which calls for covering a set P of n points in $\mathbb{R}^d$ by p congruent balls of the minimum radius. If p is part of the input, the problem is known to be NP-complete [28] even for $d = 2$, so the complexity of the algorithms for solving the p-center problem, for any fixed p, is expected to increase exponentially with p. Agarwal and Procopiuc showed that the p-center problem in $\mathbb{R}^d$ can be solved in $n^{O(p^{1-1/d})}$ time [3], improving upon a naive $n^{O(p)}$-solution. At the other extreme end, the 1-center problem (also known as the smallest enclosing ball problem) is known to be an LP-Type problem, and can thus be solved in $O(n)$ randomized expected time in any fixed dimension, and also in deterministic linear time [16, 26, 27]. Faster approximate solutions to the general p-center problem have also been proposed [3, 5, 6].

If d is not fixed, the 2-center problem in $\mathbb{R}^d$ is NP-Complete [29]. The 2-center problem in $\mathbb{R}^2$ has a relatively rich history, mostly in the past two decades. Hershberger and Suri [22] showed that the decision problem of determining whether P can be covered by two disks of a given radius r, can be solved in $O(n^2 \log n)$ time. This has led to several nearly-quadratic algorithms [4, 19, 23] that solve the optimization problem, the best of which, due to Jaromczyk and Kowaluk [23], runs in $O(n^2 \log n)$ deterministic time. Sharir [33] considerably improved these bounds and obtained a deterministic algorithm with $O(n \log^9 n)$ running time. His algorithm combines several geometric techniques, including parametric searching, searching in monotone matrices, and dynamic maintenance of planar configurations. Chan [13] (following an improvement by Eppstein [20]) improved the running time to $O(n \log^2 n \log^2 \log n)$.

The only earlier work on the 2-center problem in $\mathbb{R}^3$ we are aware of is by Agarwal *et al.* [2], which presents an algorithm with $O(n^{3+\varepsilon})$ running time, for any $\varepsilon > 0$. It uses a rather complicated data structure for dynamically maintaining upper and lower envelopes of bivariate functions.

Our results. We present two randomized algorithms for the 2-center problem in $\mathbb{R}^3$. We first present an algorithm whose expected running time is $O(n^3 \log^8 n)$. It is conceptually a natural generalization of the earlier algorithms for the planar 2-center problem [4, 19, 23]; its implementation however is considerably more involved. The second algorithm runs in $O(n^2 \log^8 n/(1-r^*/r_0)^3)$ expected time, where r^* is the radius of the 2-center and r_0 is the radius of the smallest enclosing ball of P. This is based on some of the ideas in Sharir's planar algorithm [33], but requires several new ideas. As in the previous algorithms, we first present algorithms for the decision problem: given $r > 0$, determine whether P can be covered by two balls of radius r. We then combine it with an adaption of Chan's randomized optimization technique [12] to obtain a solution for the optimization problem. The asymptotic expected running time of the optimization algorithm is the same as that of the decision procedure.

The paper is organized as follows. Section 2 briefly sketches our two solutions. Section 3 presents the near-cubic algorithm, and Section 4 presents the improved algorithm.

2. SKETCHES OF THE SOLUTIONS

The near-cubic algorithm. To solve the decision problem, in the less efficient but conceptually simpler manner, we use a standard point-plane duality, and replace each point $p \in P$ by a dual plane p^*, and each plane h by a dual point h^*, such that the above-below relations between points and planes are preserved. We note that if P can be covered by two balls B_1, B_2 (not necessarily congruent), then there exists a plane h (containing the circle $\partial B_1 \cap \partial B_2$, if they intersect at all, or separating B_1 and B_2 otherwise) separating P into two subsets P_1, P_2, such that $P_1 \subset B_1$ and $P_2 \subset B_2$. We therefore construct the arrangement $\mathcal{A}$ of the set $\{p^* \mid p \in P\}$ of dual planes. It has $O(n^3)$ cells, and each cell τ has the property that, for any point $w \in \tau$, its primal plane w^* separates P into two subsets of points, P_τ^+ and P_τ^-, which are the same for every $w \in \tau$, and depend only on τ. We thus perform a traversal of $\mathcal{A}$, which proceeds from each visited cell to a neighbor cell. When we visit a cell τ, we check whether the subsets P_τ^+ and P_τ^- can be covered by two balls of radius r, respectively. To do so, we maintain dynamically the intersection of the sets $\{B_r(p) \mid p \in P_\tau^+\}$, $\{B_r(p) \mid p \in P_\tau^-\}$, where $B_r(p)$ is the ball of radius r centered at p, and observe that (a) any point in the first (resp., second) intersection can serve as the center of a ball of radius r which contains P_τ^+ (resp., P_τ^-), and (b) no ball of radius r can cover P_τ^+ (resp., P_τ^-) if the corresponding intersection is empty. Moreover, when we cross from a cell τ to a neighbor cell τ', P_τ^+ changes by the insertion or deletion of a single point, and P_τ^- undergoes the opposite change, so each of the sets of balls $\{B_r(p) \mid p \in P_\tau^+\}$, $\{B_r(p) \mid p \in P_\tau^-\}$ changes by the deletion or insertion of a single ball. As we know the sequence of updates in advance, maintaining dynamically the intersection of either of these sets of balls is done in an offline manner. Still, the actual implementation is fairly complicated. It is performed performed using a variant of the multi-dimensional parametric searching technique of Matoušek [25] (see also [11, 18, 30]), which we spell out in some detail in Section 3.

The main algorithm uses a segment tree to represent the sets P_τ^+ (and another segment tree for the sets P_τ^-). Roughly, viewing the traversal of $\mathcal{A}$ as a sequence Σ of cells, each ball $B_r(p)$ has a *life-span* (in P_τ^+), which is a union of contiguous maximal subsequences of cells τ, in which $p \in P_\tau^+$, and a complementary life-span in P_τ^-. We store these (connected portions of the) life-spans as segments in the segment tree. Each leaf of the tree represents a cell τ of $\mathcal{A}$, and the balls stored at the nodes on the path to the leaf are exactly those, whose centers belong to the set P_τ^+ (or P_τ^-). By precomputing the intersection of the balls stored at each node of the tree, we can express each of the intersections $\bigcap\{B_r(p) \mid p \in P_\tau^+\}$ and $\bigcap\{B_r(p) \mid p \in P_\tau^-\}$, for each cell τ, as the intersection of a logarithmic number of precomputed intersections (see also [19]). We show that such an intersection can be tested for emptiness in $O(\log^8 n)$ time. This in turn allows us to execute the decision procedure with a total cost of $O(n^3 \log^8 n)$. We then return to the original optimization problem and apply a variant of Chan's randomization technique [12] to solve the optimization problem by a small number of calls to the decision problem, obtaining an overall algorithm with $O(n^3 \log^8 n)$ *expected* running time.[1]

The improved solution. The above algorithm runs in nearly cubic time because it has to traverse the entire arrangement $\mathcal{A}$, which is of complexity $O(n^3)$. In Section 4 we improve this bound by traversing only portions of $\mathcal{A}$, adapting some of the ideas in Sharir's improved solution for the planar problem [33]. Specifically, Sharir's algorithm solves the decision problem (for a given radius r) in three steps, treating separately three subcases, in which the centers c_1, c_2 of the two covering balls are, respectively, far apart ($|c_1c_2| > 3r$), at medium distance apart ($r < |c_1c_2| \le 3r$) and near each other ($|c_1c_2| \le r$). We base our solution on the techniques used in the first two cases. The first case is easy to generalize to $\mathbb{R}^3$, almost "as is". The generalization of the second case is considerably more involved. More precisely, letting $B_r(p)$ denote the disk of radius r centered at a point p, Sharir's algorithm guesses a constant number of lines l, one of which separates the centers c_1, c_2 of the respective solution disks D_1, D_2, so that the set P_L of the points to the left of l is contained in D_1. We then compute the intersection $K(P_L) = \bigcap_{p \in P_L} B_r(p)$, and intersect each $\partial B_r(p)$, for $p \in P_R = P \setminus P_L$ (the subset of points to the right of l), with $\partial K(P_L)$. It is easily seen that $\partial K(P_L)$ has linear complexity and that each circle $\partial B_r(p)$, for $p \in P_R$, intersects it at two points (at most). This produces $O(n)$ critical points (vertices and intersection points) on $\partial K(P_L)$ and $O(n)$ arcs in between. As argued in [33], it suffices to search these points and arcs for possible locations of the center of D_1 (and dynamically test whether the balls centered at the uncovered points have nonempty intersection).

Generalizing this approach to $\mathbb{R}^3$, we need to guess a separating plane λ, to retrieve the subset $P_L \subseteq P$ of points to the left of λ, to compute $\partial K(P_L)$ (which, fortunately, still has only linear complexity), to intersect $\partial B_r(p)$, for each $p \in P_R$, with $\partial K(P_L)$, and to form the arrangement of the resulting intersection curves. Each cell of this arrangement is a candidate for the location of the center of the left covering ball B_1.

However, the complexity of the resulting arrangement M_K on $\partial K(P_L)$ might potentially be cubic. We therefore compute only a portion M of M_K, which suffices for our purposes, and prove that its complexity is only $O(n^2)$. In addition, we can extend the solution for any positive separation between the centers of the covering balls. Specifically, our decision procedure assumes that $|c_1c_2| \ge \beta r$, for some pre-specified $\beta > 0$, and solves the decision version of the problem in $O((1/\beta^3)n^2 \log^8 n)$ time. We show that $\beta = 2(r_0/r - 1)$, where r_0 is the radius of the smallest enclosing ball of P, is a valid choice for β.

To solve the optimization problem, we conduct a search on the optimal radius r^*, using our decision procedure, starting from small values of r and going up, halving the gap between r and r_0 at each step[2], until the first time we reach a value $r > r^*$. Then we use a variant of Chan's technique [12], combined with our decision procedure, to find the exact value of r^*. The way the search is conducted guarantees that its cost does not exceed the bound $O((1/\beta^3)n^2 \log^8 n)$, for the separation parameter β for r^*. Hence, we obtain a randomized algorithm that solves the 2-center problem for any positive separation of c_1 and c_2, and runs in $O(n^2 \log^8 n/(1-r^*/r_0)^3)$ expected time.

[1]The earlier algorithm in [2] follows the same general approach, but uses an even more complicated, and slightly less efficient machinery for dynamic emptiness testing of the intersection of congruent balls.

[2]We have to act in this manner to make sure that we do not call the decision procedure with values of r, which are too close to r_0, thereby losing control over the running time.

Due to lack of space, some details are omitted in this extended abstract. Full details can be found in [1].

3. A NEARLY CUBIC ALGORITHM

The decision procedure. In this section we give details of the implementation of our less efficient solution, many of which are applicable in the improved solution. Recall from the description in the introduction that the decision procedure, on a given radius r, constructs two segment trees T^+, T^-, on the life-spans of the balls $B_r(p)$, for $p \in P$ (with respect to the tour of the dual arrangement $\mathcal{A}$). Each leaf is a cell τ of $\mathcal{A}$, and the balls, whose centers belong to P_τ^+ (resp., P_τ^-), are those stored at nodes on the path from the root to τ in T^+ (resp., T^-).

For each node u of T^+, let S_u denote the intersection of all the balls (of radius r) stored at u. We refer to each S_u as a *spherical polytope*; see [7, 8, 9] for (unrelated) studies of spherical polytopes. We compute each S_u in $O(|S_u| \log |S_u|)$ deterministic time, using the algorithm by Brönnimann et al. [10] (see also [17, 31]). Since the arrangement $\mathcal{A}$ consists of $O(n^3)$ cells, standard properties of segment trees imply that the two trees require $O(n^3 \log n)$ storage (see below for more details) and $O(n^3 \log^2 n)$ preproccessing time.

Intersection of spherical polytopes. Let $\mathcal{S} = \{S_1, \ldots, S_t\}$ be the set of $t = O(\log n)$ spherical polytopes stored at the nodes of a path from the root to a leaf of T^+ or of T^-. Each S_i is the intersection of some n_i balls, and $\sum_{i=1}^{t} n_i \leq n$. Our current goal is to determine, in polylogarithmic time, whether the intersection K of the spherical polytopes in $\mathcal{S}$ is nonempty. If this is the case for at least one path of T^+ and for the same path in T^- then $r^* \leq r$, and otherwise $r^* > r$. We describe this step in detail next, and then show how to adjust this solution to also discriminate between the cases $r^* < r$ and $r^* = r$.

As is well known, each ball b participating in the intersection S_i contributes at most one (connected) face to ∂S_i (see [31]). The vertices and edges of S_i are the intersections of two or three bounding spheres, respectively (for degenerate values of r, one vertex might be incident to four spheres). To simplify the forthcoming analysis, we assume that the points of P are in general position, meaning that no five of them are co-spherical, and that the radii of the balls determined by quadruples of points of P are all distinct. Hence S_i is a planar (or, rather, spherical) map with at most $|S_i|$ faces, which implies that the complexity of ∂S_i is $O(|S_i|)$. Consequently, the storage in each node u of T^+ (or T^-) is $O(|S_u|)$, so, as mentioned above, the total storage for T^+ (and for T^-) is $O(n^3 \log n)$.

We solve this problem by employing a technique similar to the multi-dimensional parametric searching technique of Matoušek [25] (see also [2, 11, 18, 30]). We solve in succession the following three subproblems, $\Pi_0(q)$, where q is a point in the xy-plane, $\Pi_1(l)$, where l is a y-parallel line in the xy-plane, and Π_2, over the entire xy-plane. In the latter problem we wish to to determine whether the xy-projection K^* of K is nonempty. During the execution of the algorithm for solving Π_2, we call recursively the algorithm for solving $\Pi_1(l)$, for certain y-parallel lines $l \subset \mathbb{R}^2$, and we wish to determine whether K^* meets l. If so, then Π_2 is solved directly (with a positive answer). Otherwise, we wish to determine which side of l, within $\mathbb{R}^2$, can meet K^* (since K^* is convex, there can exist at most one such side). The recursion bottoms out at certain points q, on which we run $\Pi_0(q)$ and determine whether K^* contains q. If so, then $\Pi_1(l)$ is solved directly (with a positive answer). Otherwise, we determine which side of q, within l, can meet K^*, and continue the search accordingly.

Our solutions to the subproblems Π_k, $0 \leq k \leq 2$, are based on generic simulations of the standard point-location machinery of Sarnak and Tarjan [32]. In each of the subproblems, if we find a point in $f \cap K^*$, for the respective point, line, or plane f, we know that $K \neq \emptyset$ and stop right away. If $f \cap K^* = \emptyset$, we want to "prove" it, by returning a small set of *witness balls* $b_1, \ldots, b_y$, where, for each j, b_j is one of the balls that participates in some spherical polytope S_i (so $b_j \supseteq S_i$), so that their intersection $K_0 = \bigcap_{j=1}^{y} b_j$ satisfies $f \cap K_0^* = \emptyset$ (where, as above, K_0^* is the xy-projection of K_0). If $K_0 = \emptyset$ then $K = \emptyset$ too and we stop. Otherwise, K_0 determines the side of f (within $\mathbb{R}^2$ if f is a line, or within the line l if f is a point) that might meet K^*; the opposite side is asserted at this point to be disjoint from K^*. We use this information to perform binary search (or, more precisely, parametric search) to locate K^* within the flat, from which we have recursed into f. The execution of the algorithm for solving Π_2 will therefore either find a point in K or determine that $K = \emptyset$, because it has collected a polylogarithmic number of witness balls, whose intersection, which has to contain K, is found to be empty.

Solving $\Pi_0(q)$ for a point q. Here we have a point $q \in \mathbb{R}^2$ and we wish to determine whether $q \in K^*$. We preprocess each of the t spherical polytopes S_i into a point-location structure. We first partition ∂S_i into its upper portion $\partial S_i{}^+$ and lower portion $\partial S_i{}^-$. We project vertically each of $\partial S_i{}^+$ and $\partial S_i{}^-$ onto the xy-plane and obtain two respective planar maps M_i^+ and M_i^- (see Figure 1). For each face ζ of each map we store the ball b that created it; that is, ζ is the projection of the (unique) face of ∂S_i that lies on ∂b. The xy-projection S_i^* of S_i is equal to both projections of $\partial S_i^+, \partial S_i^-$, and is bounded by a convex curve E^* that is the concatenation of the xy-projections of certain edges of S_i and of portions of horizontal equators of some of its balls.

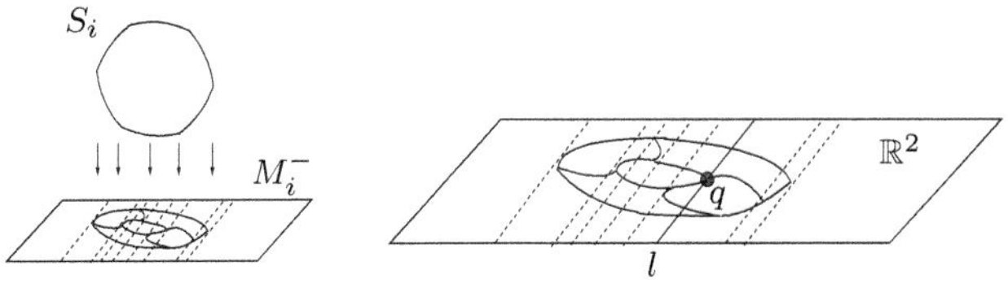

Figure 1. Projecting $\partial S_i{}^-$ vertically onto the xy-plane (left), and the point location structure for the resulting map M_i^- (right).

In order to locate a point in S_i we use the standard point-location algorithm of Sarnak and Tarjan [32]. That is, we divide each planar map into slabs by parallel lines (to the y-axis) through each of the endpoints (and locally x-extremal points) of the arcs obtained by projecting the edges of ∂S_i, including the new equatorial arcs. Using the persistent search structure of [32], the total storage is linear in n_i and the preprocessing cost is $O(n_i \log n_i)$, where n_i is the number of balls forming S_i. To locate a point q_0 in M_i^+ (or in M_i^-), we first find the slab in the x-structure that contains q_0, and then find the two curves between which q_0 lies in the y-structure.[3]

To determine whether $q \in S_i^*$, we locate the face ζ^+ (resp., ζ^-) of the map M_i^+ (resp., M_i^-) that contains q, as just described. Each of these faces can be a 2-face, an edge or a vertex. We therefore retrieve a set $\mathcal{B}_i^+$ (resp., $\mathcal{B}_i^-$) of the one, two, or three or four balls associated (respectively) with the 2-face, edge or vertex containing q. (We omit here the construction of witness balls when the faces ζ^+ and ζ^- are not associated with any ball, that is, $q \notin S_i^*$.)

Let $\mathcal{B}_i$ denote the set $\mathcal{B}_i^+ \cup \mathcal{B}_i^-$. We observe that $q \in S_i^*$ if and only if the z-vertical line λ_q through q intersects S_i. Moreover, we

[3] All these standard details are presented to make more precise the infrastructure used by the higher-dimensional routines Π_1 and Π_2.

have, by construction, $\lambda_q \cap S_i = \lambda_q \cap (\bigcap_i \mathcal{B}_i)$. Hence $q \in S_i^*$ if and only if $s_i := \lambda_q \cap (\bigcap_i \mathcal{B}_i) \neq \emptyset$. We compute the line segment s_i in $O(1)$ time, and repeat this step for each $i = 1, \ldots, t$. We then have $K_0 := \lambda_q \cap K = \bigcap_{i=1}^t s_i$, so it suffices to compute this intersection (in $O(t)$ time) and test whether it is nonempty. If K_0 is nonempty, then we have found a point q' in K. Otherwise, we return the set $\mathcal{B}_0 = \bigcup\{\mathcal{B}_i \mid 1 \leq i \leq t\}$ of up to $8 \log n$ balls as witness balls for the higher-dimensional step (involving the y-parallel line containing q).

The time complexity for solving $\Pi_0(q)$ is $O(\log^2 n)$, since it takes $O(\log n)$ time to compute, for each of the $O(\log n)$ spherical polytopes S_i, the intersection $\lambda_q \cap S_i$.

Solving $\Pi_1(l)$ for a line l. Here we have a y-parallel line $l \subset \mathbb{R}^2$ and we wish to determine whether K^* meets l. We first locate l in each of the planar maps M_i^+ and M_i^- of each S_i, and find the slabs ψ_i^+ and ψ_i^-, which contain l (in some cases l is the bounding line of two slabs ψ_i' and ψ_i'' of M_i^+ or of M_i^-, so we retrieve both slabs). We then simulate the binary search through the y-structure of each of the obtained slabs separately. In each step of the search, within some fixed slab ψ_0, we consider an arc γ of the y-structure, and determine whether K^* meets l above or below γ (within $\mathbb{R}^2$), assuming $K^* \cap l \neq \emptyset$. To this end, we find the intersection point $q_0 = l \cap \gamma$, and run the algorithm for solving $\Pi_0(q_0)$ (see Figure 2(left)). If $q_0 \in K^*$, then we have found a point q' in K, and we immediately stop. Otherwise, we have a set $\mathcal{B}_0$ of up to $8 \log n$ balls returned by the algorithm for solving $\Pi_0(q_0)$. We test whether the xy-projection K_0^* of $\bigcap \mathcal{B}_0$ intersects l. If $K_0^* \cap l = \emptyset$, then (due to the convexity of K) we know which side of l (within $\mathbb{R}^2$) meets K^*, and we return $\mathcal{B}_0$ as a set of witness balls for the higher-dimensional (planar) step. Otherwise (again due to the convexity of K), we know which side of γ, within l, meets K^*, and we continue the search through the y-structure of ψ_0 on this side. We continue the search in this manner, until, for each S_i, we obtain an interval ξ_i of l between two consecutive arcs of the y-structure of ψ_0, which meets K^* (assuming $l \cap K^* \neq \emptyset$). Let Ξ denote the collection of all these intervals. Clearly, $l \cap K^* \subseteq \bigcap \Xi$. We find the lowest endpoint E^- among the top endpoints of the intervals in Ξ and the highest endpoint E^+ among the bottom endpoints of the intervals in Ξ, and test whether E^- is above E^+. If so, we consider the set $\mathcal{B}_1$ of up to $16 \log n$ witness balls returned by the algorithms for solving $\Pi_0(E^-)$ and $\Pi_0(E^+)$. If the xy-projection K_1^* of $\bigcap \mathcal{B}_1$ intersects l, then K^* meets l and we stop immediately, for we have found that K is nonempty. Otherwise, we know which side of l (within $\mathbb{R}^2$) can meet K^*, and we return $\mathcal{B}_1$ as a set of witness balls for the higher (planar) recursive level. If E^- is not above E^+, then $K^* \cap l = \emptyset$ and we return $\mathcal{B}_1$ as a set of witness balls for the higher (planar) recursive level as well.[4]

The time complexity for solving $\Pi_1(l)$ is $O(\log^4 n)$, since for each of the $O(\log n)$ spherical polytopes S_i we run a binary search through the y-structure of at most two slabs of each of the maps M_i^+ and M_i^-, and in each of the binary search steps, we run the algorithm for solving $\Pi_0(q_0)$ for some point q_0. The other substeps take less time.

Solving Π_2. We next consider the main problem Π_2, where we want to determine whether $K^* \neq \emptyset$ (i.e., whether $K \neq \emptyset$). We use parametric searching, in which we run the point location algorithm that we used for solving Π_0, in the following generic manner.

In the first stage of the generic point location, we run a binary search through the slabs of each of the planar maps M_i^+ and M_i^-, for $i = 1, \ldots, t$. In each step of the search through any of the maps, we take a line l_0 delimiting two consecutive slabs of the map, and run the algorithm for solving $\Pi_1(l_0)$, thereby deciding on which side of l_0 to continue the search. At the end of this stage, unless we have already found a point in K or determined that K is empty, we obtain a single slab in each map that contains K^*. Let ψ denote the intersection of these slabs, which must therefore contain K^* (unless K is empty).

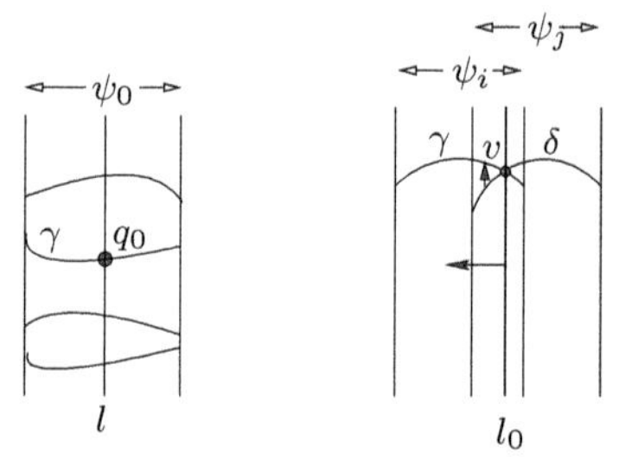

Figure 2. Left: The line l on which we run $\Pi_1(l)$. The point q_0 on which we run $\Pi_0(q_0)$ is the intersection point of l with some arc γ. Right: Comparing $\gamma \cap K^*$ with δ. The outcome of $\Pi_1(l_0)$ determines (a) the side of δ in which the search in ψ_j should continue, and (b) the portion of γ which can still meet K^*.

In the next stage of the generic point location, we consider each map M_i^+ or M_i^- (for simplicity we refer to it just as M_i) separately, and run a binary search through the y-structure of its slab ψ_i that contains ψ. In each step of the search we consider an arc γ of the y-structure, and determine which side of γ (within the slab ψ), can meet K^*, assuming that $\psi \cap K^* \neq \emptyset$; if $\gamma \cap K^* \neq \emptyset$ we will detect it and stop right away. The logic of our search is as follows. We act under the assumption that $\gamma \cap K^* \neq \emptyset$, and try to locate a point of $\gamma \cap K^*$ in each of the other maps. Suppose, to simplify the description, that we managed to locate the entire γ in a single face of each of the other maps M_j^+ and M_j^-. This yields a set $\mathcal{B}$ of $O(t)$ balls, so that a point $v \in \gamma$ lies in K^* if and only if it lies in the xy-projection K_0^* of $\bigcap \mathcal{B}$. We then test whether γ intersects K_0^*. If so, we have found a point in K and stop right away. Suppose then that $K_0^* \cap \gamma = \emptyset$. If $K_0^* \cap \psi = \emptyset$ then K must be empty, because we already know that $K^* \subset \psi$. If $K_0^* \cap \psi \neq \emptyset$, then we know on which side of γ to continue the binary search in ψ_i.

In general, though, γ might split between several cells of a map M_j, where M_j denotes one of the maps M_j^+ or M_j^-. This forces us to narrow the search to a subarc of γ, in the following manner. We run a binary search through the y-structure of the corresponding slab ψ_j of M_j, which contains ψ, and repeat it for each of the maps M_j. In each step of the search, we need to compare γ (or, more precisely, some point in $\gamma \cap K^*$) with some arc δ of ψ_j, which we do as follows. If γ lies, within ψ, completely on one side of δ, we continue the binary search in ψ_j on that side of δ. If γ intersects δ, we pick an intersection point v of γ and δ, pass a y-parallel line $l_0 \subset \mathbb{R}^2$ through v, and run the non-generic version of the algorithm to solve $\Pi_1(l_0)$. (See Figure 2(right).) As before, if $l_0 \cap K^* \neq \emptyset$ we detect this and stop. Otherwise, we know which of the two portions of γ, delimited by v, can intersect K^*. We repeat this step for each of the at most four intersection points of γ and δ (observing that these are elliptic arcs), and obtain a connected portion γ' of γ, delimited by two consecutive intersection points, whose relative interior lies completely above or below δ, so that $\gamma \cap K^*$, if nonempty, lies in γ'. This allows us to resolve the

[4] With some care, the number of witness balls can be significantly reduced. We do not go into this improvement, because handling the witness balls is an inexpensive step, whose cost is subsumed by the cost of the other steps of the algorithms.

generic comparison with δ, and continue the binary search through ψ_j.

When these searches terminate, we end up with a 2-face in each M_j, in which $\gamma \cap K^*$ lies, and we reach the scenario described in a preceding paragraph. As explained there, we can now either determine that $K \neq \emptyset$, or that $K = \emptyset$, or else we know which side of γ, within ψ_i (or, rather, within ψ) can contain K^*, and we continue the binary search through ψ_i on that side.

When the binary search through ψ_i terminates, we have a 2-face ζ_i of M_i, where K^* must lie, and we retrieve the ball b_i corresponding to ζ_i. We repeat this step to each of the maps M_i^+ and M_i^- of each of the t spherical polytopes S_i, and obtain a set $\mathcal{B}_1$ of $2t$ balls. In addition, the searches through the maps M_i^+ and M_i^- may have trimmed ψ to a narrower strip ψ', and have produced a set $\mathcal{B}_2$ of witness balls, so that the xy-projection of their intersection lies inside ψ'. $\mathcal{B}_2$ may consist of a total of $O(t^3 \log^2 n)$ witness balls, as is easy to verify. In addition, the second-level searches produce an additional collection $\mathcal{B}'_2$, consisting of balls corresponding to faces of the maps M_j^+ and M_j^-, in which the second-level searches have ended; their overall number is $O(t^2 \log n)$. Put $K_2 = \bigcap(\mathcal{B}_1 \cup \mathcal{B}_2 \cup \mathcal{B}'_2)$. Hence $K \neq \emptyset$ if and only if $K_2 \neq \emptyset$.

Finally, consider the running time of the procedure. It is easily seen to be subsumed by the cost of the second stage, where we run a binary search through the y-structure of each slab ψ_i, and in each of its steps we have to run another binary search over the corresponding slabs ψ_j of all the other maps. Since each comparison that we make involves the execution of the algorithm to solve $\Pi_1(l_0)$, for an appropriate line l_0, the time complexity for this stage is $O(\log^8 n)$.

Hence, the overall cost of the decision procedure is $O(n^3 \log^8 n)$.

Detecting equality $r^* = r$. As described so far, the decision procedure discriminates between the cases $r^* \leq r$ and $r^* > r$. To detect the case $r^* = r$, we note that if both $K(P_\tau^+)$ and $K(P_\tau^-)$ are non-degenerate (i.e., contain more than one point), then we can shrink the covering balls of P and find two balls of radius smaller than r that still cover P (that is, $r^* < r$). Hence, if for all separations of P to P_τ^+ and P_τ^- (i.e., for all cells of $\mathcal{A}$), that admit a solution for the decision procedure (with the given r), at least one of the intersections $K(P_\tau^+)$ or $K(P_\tau^-)$ is degenerate, then P cannot be covered by two balls of radius smaller than r. It follows that if at least one such separation exists then $r = r^*$. This affects the execution of the decision procedure in an obvious way: Stop when obtaining a solution for which both $K(P_\tau^+)$ and $K(P_\tau^-)$ are nonempty and non-degenerate, and report that $r^* < r$. Otherwise, test all cells τ. If at least one degenerate solution is found, report that $r^* = r$, and otherwise $r^* > r$. To detect whether the intersection K of t spherical polytopes is degenerate, we modify the algorithm for detecting whether K is nonempty, as follows. Each step in the decision procedure which detects that $K \neq \emptyset$ obtains a specific point w that belongs to K. Moreover, w belongs to the intersection K_1 of polylogarithmically many witness balls, and does not lie on the boundary of any other ball. This is because each of the procedures Π_0, Π_1, or Π_2 locates the xy-projection w^* of w (which, for Π_1 and Π_2 is a generic, unknown point in K) in each of the maps $M_i^+, M_i^-, i = 1, \ldots, t$, and the collection of the witness balls gathered during the various steps of the searches contains all the balls that participate in the corresponding spherical polytopes S_i on whose boundary w can lie. Thus, when we terminate with a point $w \in K$, we find, among the polylogarithmically many witness balls, the at most four balls whose boundaries contain w (recall our general position assumption), and test whether their intersection is the singleton $\{w\}$. It is easily checked that this is equivalent to the condition that K is degenerate.

Solving the optimization problem. We now combine our decision procedure with the randomized optimization technique of Chan [12], to obtain an algorithm for the optimization problem, which runs in $O(n^3 \log^8 n)$ *expected* time. Our application of Chan's technique, described next, is somewhat non-standard, because each recursive step has also to handle global data, which it inherits from its ancestors.

Chan's technique, in its "purely recursive" form, takes an optimization problem that has to compute an optimum value $w(P)$ on an input set P. The technique replaces P by several subsets $P_1, \ldots, P_s$, such that $w(P) = \min\{w(P_1), \ldots, w(P_s)\}$, and $|P_i| \leq \alpha|P|$ for each i (here $\alpha < 1$ and s are constants). It then processes the subproblems P_i in a *random* order, and computes $\min_i w(P_i)$ by comparing each $w(P_i)$ to the minimum w collected so far, and by replacing w by $w(P_i)$ if the latter is smaller.[5] Comparisons are performed by the decision procedure, and updates of w are computed recursively. The crux of this technique is that the expected number of recursive calls (in a single recursive step) is only $O(\log s)$, and this (combined with some additional enhancements, which we omit here) suffices to make the expected cost of the whole procedure asymptotically the same as the cost of the decision procedure, for *any* values of s and α. Technically, if the cost $D(n)$ of the decision procedure is $\Omega(n^\gamma)$, where γ is some fixed positive constant, the expected running time is $O(D(n))$ provided that

$$(\ln s + 1)\alpha^\gamma < 1. \quad (1)$$

However, even when (1) does not hold "as is", Chan's technique enforces it by compressing l levels of the recursion into a single level, for l sufficiently large, so its expected cost is still $O(D(n))$. See [12] for details.

To apply Chan's technique to our decision procedure, we pass to the dual space, where each point $p \in P$ is mapped to a plane p^*, as done in the decision procedure. We obtain the set $P^* = \{p^* \mid p \in P\}$ of dual planes, and we consider its arrangement $\mathcal{A} = \mathcal{A}(P^*)$, where each cell τ in $\mathcal{A}$ represents an equivalence class of planes in the original space, which separate P into the same two subsets of points P_τ^+, P_τ^-.

To decompose the optimization problem into subproblems, as required by Chan's technique, we construct a $(1/\varrho)$-*cutting* for $\mathcal{A}(P^*)$, for a specific constant value of ϱ, that we will fix later (see [14, 15, 24] for details concerning cuttings), and obtain $O(\varrho^3)$ simplices, such that the interior of each of them is intersected by at most n/ϱ planes of P^*. Each simplex Δ_i corresponds to one subproblem and contains some (possibly only portions of) cells $\tau_1, \ldots, \tau_k$ of the arrangement $\mathcal{A}$. All these subproblems have in common the sets $(P^*)_{\Delta_i}^+$, $(P^*)_{\Delta_i}^-$, consisting, respectively, of all the planes that pass fully above Δ_i and those that pass fully below Δ_i. (These sets are dual to respective subsets $P_{\Delta_i}^+, P_{\Delta_i}^-$ of P, where $P_{\Delta_i}^+$ is contained in all the sets $P_{\tau_j}^+$, for the cells τ_j, that meet Δ_i, and symmetrically for $P_{\Delta_i}^-$.) Note that most of the dual planes belong to $(P^*)_{\Delta_i}^+ \cup (P^*)_{\Delta_i}^-$; the "undecided" planes are those that cross the interior of Δ_i, and their number is at most n/ϱ. We denote the set of these planes as $(P^*)_{\Delta_i}^0$ (and the set of their primal points as $P_{\Delta_i}^0$).

To apply Chan's technique, we construct two segment trees on the arrangement of $(P^*)_{\Delta_i}^0$, as described above. Consider one of these segment trees, T^+, that maintains the set of balls $\mathcal{B}^+ = \{B_r(p) \mid p \in P_{\tau_j}^+\}$. Each cell τ_j in Δ_i is represented by a

[5] So the value of w keeps shrinking.

leaf of T^+. Each ball is represented as a collection of disjoint life-spans, with respect to a fixed tour of the cells of $\mathcal{A}((P^*)^0_{\Delta_i})$, which are stored as segments in T^+, as described earlier. In addition, we compute the intersection of the balls centered at the points of $P^+_{\Delta_i}$, in $O(n \log n)$ time, and store it at the root of T^+. Note that, as we go down the recursion, we keep adding planes to $(P^*)^+_{\Delta_i}$, that is, points to $P^+_{\Delta_i}$, and the actual set $P^+_{\Delta_i}$ of points dual to the planes above the current Δ_i is the union of logarithmically many subsets, each obtained at one of the ancestor levels of the recursion, including the current step. As we go down the recursion, Chan's technique keeps 'shrinking' the radius of the balls. Hence, each time we have to solve a decision subproblem, we compute the intersection of the balls centered at the points of $P^+_{\Delta_i}$ from scratch. We build a second segment tree T^- that maintains the balls of $\mathcal{B}^- = \{B_r(p) \mid p \in P^-_{\tau_j}\}$, in a fully analogous manner. The running time so far (of the decision procedure) is $O(n \log n + m^3 \log^2 m)$, where m is the number of planes in $(P^*)^0_{\Delta_i}$ and n is the size of the initial input set P.

To solve the decision procedure for a given subproblem associated with a simplex Δ_i, we test, by going over all the root-to-leaf paths in T^+ and T^-, whether there exists a cell τ (overlapping Δ_i), for which the intersections of the spherical polytopes on the two respective paths in T^+ and T^- are nonempty (and, if nonempty, whether one of them is degenerate). The overall cost of this step, iterating over the $O(m^3)$ cells of $\mathcal{A}((P^*)^0_{\Delta_i})$ and applying the procedure for intersecting spherical polytopes, as described above, is $O(m^3 \log^8 n)$.

The solution at the bottom of the recursion, where only $O(1)$ points of P are "undecided" can be performed in $O(n)$ time in a straightforward manner, which we omit here.

As stated earlier, the (expected) cost of applying Chan's technique to a decision procedure is asymptotically the same as that of the decision procedure. Here, however, we need to overcome some subtle issues, involving the "global" parameter n (appearing in the global sets $P^+_{\Delta_i}, P^-_{\Delta_i}$, which are passed down the recursion), which is involved in the recursive subproblems. What "saves" us is the fact that the dependence of the running time of the decision procedure on n is only $O(n \log n)$. This allows us to obtain the following recurrence for the expected running time $T(m, n)$ of a recursive step in Chan's procedure, involving m "local" points and n "global" points.

$$T(m,n) \leq \begin{cases} \log(c\varrho^3)T(m/\varrho, n) & \\ +O(m^3 \log^8 n + n \log n), & \text{for } m \geq \varrho, \\ & \\ O(n), & \text{for } m < \varrho, \end{cases} \quad (2)$$

where c is an appropriate absolute constant (so that $c\varrho^3$ bounds the number of cells of the cutting), and ϱ is chosen to be a sufficiently large constant. It is fairly routine (and we omit the details) to show that the recurrence (2) yields the overall bound $O(n^3 \log^8 n)$ on the expected cost of the initial problem; i.e., $T(n,n) = O(n^3 \log^8 n)$.

We thus obtain the following intermediate result.

THEOREM 1. *Let P be a set of n points in $\mathbb{R}^3$. A 2-center for P can be computed in $O(n^3 \log^8 n)$ randomized expected time.*

4. AN IMPROVED ALGORITHM

An improved decision procedure Γ. Consider the decision problem, where we are given a radius r and a parameter $\beta > 0$, and have to determine whether P can be covered by two balls of radius r, such that the distance between their centers c_1, c_2 is at least βr. By this we mean that there is no placement of two balls of radius r, which cover P, such that the distance between their centers is smaller than βr; see Figure 3(left).

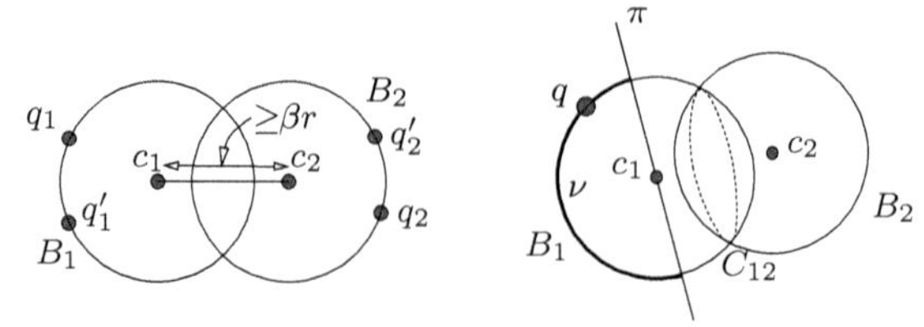

Figure 3. Left: The points q_1, q'_1, q_2, q'_2 prevent $|c_1c_2|$ from getting smaller. Right: The plane π passes through c_1 and is disjoint from C_{12}. The hemisphere ν delimited by π, which lies on the side of π not containing C_{12}, must contain a point q of P.

This assumption is easily seen to imply the following property: Let C_{12} denote the intersection circle of ∂B_1 and ∂B_2. Then any hemisphere ν of ∂B_1, such that (a) the plane π through c_1 delimiting ν is disjoint from C_{12}, and (b) ν and C_{12} lie on different sides of π, must contain a point q of P, for otherwise we could have brought B_1 and B_2 closer together by moving c_1 in the normal direction of π, into the halfspace containing c_2 (and C_{12}). See Figure 3(right).

The procedure tests for the existence of a solution under the following two complementary assumptions: (i) $|c_1c_2| \geq 3r$, and (ii) $\beta r \leq |c_1c_2| < 3r$, for the specified $\beta > 0$.

We first assume that the distance between c_1 and c_2 is at least $3r$. We fix a set D of $O(1)$ orientations (on the unit sphere $\mathbb{S}^2$) with the property that for each orientation $u \in \mathbb{S}^2$ there exists $v \in D$, such that the angle between u and v is at most $1°$, say. For each $v \in D$ we rotate the coordinate frame so that v becomes the x-axis. In one of these orientations the line connecting c_1 and c_2, with c_1 lying to the left of c_2, will form an angle of at most one degree with the x-axis. In this case $x(c_2) - x(c_1)$ will be at least $|c_1c_2| \cos 1° \geq 3r \cos 1° \approx 2.99r$, so we can separate B_1 from B_2 by a plane parallel to the yz-plane.

We sort the points by their x-coordinates (for each fixed choice of v), and try all $O(n)$ partitions of P into subsets P_L, P_R, so that all the points of P_L lie to the left of all points of P_R. For each such partition, we compute the smallest enclosing balls of P_L and of P_R, in linear (deterministic or randomized expected) time [16, 26, 27]. If both radii are at most r, we have found a solution to the decision problem. With this implementation, the cost of handling this case is $O(n^2)$, which is subsumed in the cost of handling the following main case.

We now focus on the second case, $\beta r \leq |c_1c_2| < 3r$, which is more difficult. The algorithm is composed of many components, and we describe each of them in detail.

Guessing orientations and separating planes. We again choose a set D of canonical orientations, so that the maximum angular deviation of any direction u from its closest direction in D is an appropriate multiple α of β. The connection between α and β is given by the following reasoning. Fix a direction $v \in D$ so that the angle between the orientation of c_1c_2 and v is at most α. Rotate the coordinate frame so that v becomes the x-axis. As above, let C_{12} denote the intersection circle of ∂B_1 and ∂B_2 (assuming that the balls intersect). Let v_1 be the leftmost point of C_{12} (in the x-direction); see Figure 4(left). If B_1 and B_2 are disjoint (which only happens when $|c_1c_2| > 2r$) we define v_1 to be the leftmost point of B_2. To determine the value of α, we note that (in complete analogy with Sharir's algorithm in the plane [33]) our procedure will try to find a yz-parallel plane, which separates c_1 from v_1. For this, we want to ensure that $x(v_1) - x(c_1) > \beta r/4$, say, to leave enough room for guessing such a separating plane. Let θ denote the angle $\sphericalangle v_1 c_1 c_2$ (see Figure 4(right)). Using the triangle inequality on angles, the angle between $\overrightarrow{c_1 v_1}$ and the x-axis is at most $\theta + \alpha$, so $x(v_1) - x(c_1) \geq r\cos(\theta + \alpha)$. Hence, to ensure the above separation, we need to choose α, such that $\cos(\theta + \alpha) > \beta/4$. Since $|c_1 c_2| \geq \beta r$, we have $\cos\theta \geq \beta/2$. Hence, it suffices to choose α, such that

$$\alpha \leq \cos^{-1}\frac{\beta}{4} - \cos^{-1}\frac{\beta}{2} = \sin^{-1}\frac{\beta}{2} - \sin^{-1}\frac{\beta}{4} = \Theta(\beta).$$

With this constraint on α, the size of D is $\Theta\left(1/\alpha^2\right) = \Theta\left(1/\beta^2\right)$.

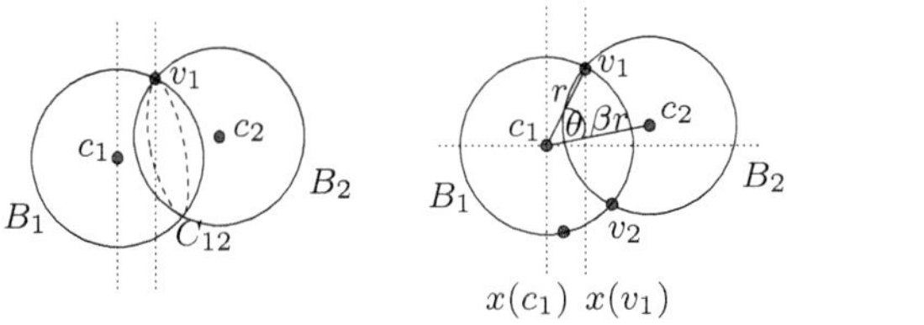

Figure 4. Left: The case $\beta r \leq |c_1 c_2| < 3r$. Right: $x(v_1) - x(c_1) \geq r\cos(\theta + \alpha)$.

Since the difference between the largest and smallest x-coordinates of points of P is at most $5r$, we can find a plane λ, parallel to the yz-plane, which separates v_1 from c_1, by drawing $O(1/\beta)$ yz-parallel planes, with horizontal separation of $\beta r/4$. Thus, the total number of guesses that we make (an orientation in D and a separating plane) is $O(1/\beta^3)$. The following description pertains to a correct guess, in which the properties that we require are satisfied.

Reducing to a 2-dimensional search. By the property noted above, the left hemisphere ν_{λ_0} of ∂B_1, delimited by the yz-parallel plane λ_0 through c_1, must pass through at least one point q of P (see Figure 5(left)).

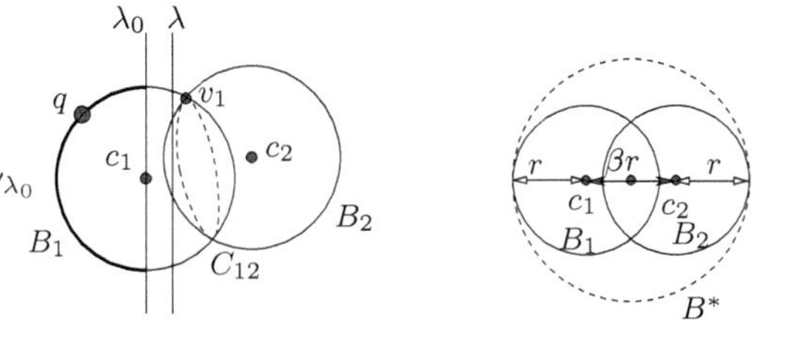

Figure 5. Left: The separating plane λ and its parallel copy λ_0 through c_1. The hemisphere ν_{λ_0} of ∂B_1 to the left of λ_0 must contain a point q of P. Right: The smallest enclosing ball B^* of $B_1 \cup B_2$.

Let P_L denote the subset of points of P lying to the left of λ. Then P_L must be fully contained in B_1 and contain q. We compute the intersection $K(P_L) = \bigcap\{B_r(p) \mid p \in P_L\}$ in $O(n \log n)$ time [10]. If $K(P_L)$ is empty, then P_L cannot be covered by a ball of radius r and we determine that the currently assumed configuration does not yield a positive solution for the decision problem. Otherwise, since $P_L \subseteq B_1$, c_1 must lie in $K(P_L)$. Moreover, since $q \in P_L$ lies on the *left* portion of ∂B_1, c_1 must lie on the *right* portion of the boundary of $K(P_L)$. Finally, since c_1 lies to the left of λ, only the portion σ_L of the right part of $\partial K(P_L)$ to the left of λ has to be considered. If $K(P_L)$ is disjoint from λ then σ_L is just the right portion of $\partial K(P_L)$. Otherwise, σ_L has a "hole", bounded by $\partial K(P_L) \cap \lambda$, which is a convex piecewise-circular curve, being the boundary of the intersection of the disks $B_r(p) \cap \lambda$, for $p \in P_L$.

For each $p \in P_R = P \setminus P_L$, we intersect $\partial B_r(p)$ with σ_L and obtain a curve γ_p on σ_L; this curve bounds the portion of the unique face of $\partial K(P_L \cup \{p\})$ within σ_L. Let M denote the arrangement formed on σ_L by the curves γ_p, for $p \in P_R$, and by the arcs of σ_L. Apriori, M might have cubic complexity, if many of the $O(n^2)$ pairs of curves γ_a, γ_b, for $a, b \in P_R$, traverse a linear number of common faces of σ_L, and intersect each other on many of these faces, in an overall linear number of points. Equivalently, the "danger" is that the intersection circle C_{ab} of a corresponding pair of spheres $\partial B_r(a), \partial B_r(b)$, for $a, b \in P_R$, could intersect a linear number of faces of σ_L (and each of these intersections is also an intersection point of γ_a and γ_b).

Complexity of M. In the assumed configuration, we claim that this cubic behavior is impossible — C_{ab} can meet only a constant number of faces of σ_L. Consequently, the overall complexity of M is only quadratic. This crucial claim follows from the observation that, for C_{ab} to intersect many faces of σ_L, it must have many short arcs, each delimited by two points on σ_L and lying outside $K(P_L)$. The main geometric insight, which rules out this possibility, and leads to our improved algorithm, is given in the following lemma.

LEMMA 2. *Let λ be a yz-parallel plane, which separates v_1 from c_1. Let $P_L \subseteq P$ be the subset of points of P to the left of λ, and let $P_R = P \setminus P_L$. Let C_{ab} denote the intersection circle of $\partial B_r(a), \partial B_r(b)$, for some pair of points $a, b \in P_R$, and let $q \in P_L$. If the arc $\omega = C_{ab} \setminus B_r(q)$ is smaller than a semicircle of C_{ab}, then at least one of its endpoints must lie to the right of λ.*

PROOF. The situation is depicted in Figure 6. To slightly simplify the analysis, and without loss of generality, assume that $r = 1$. Let h be the plane passing through a, b and q. Let c_{ab} denote the midpoint of ab, and let w denote the center of the circumscribing circle Q of $\triangle qab$. Denote the distance $|ab|$ by $2x$, and the radius of Q by y (so $|wp_1| = |wp_2| = |wq| = y$). Note that c_{ab} and w lie in h and that $y \geq x$. Observe that c_{ab} is the center of the intersection circle C_{ab} of $\partial B_r(a)$ and $\partial B_r(b)$. See Figure 6(a).

The intersection points z, z' of C_{ab} and $\partial B_r(q)$ are the intersection points of the three spheres $\partial B_r(a)$, $\partial B_r(b)$, and $\partial B_r(q)$. They lie on the line ℓ passing through w and orthogonal to h, at equal distances $\sqrt{1-y^2}$ from w. See Figure 6(b). (If $y > 1$ then z and z' do not exist, in which case C_{ab} does not intersect $\partial B_r(q)$; in what follows we assume that $y \leq 1$.) Hence, within C_{ab}, zz' is a chord of length $2\sqrt{1-y^2}$. In the assumed setup, z and z' delimit a short arc ω of C_{ab}, which lies outside $B_r(q)$, so points on the arc are (equally) closer to a and b than to q.

Hence, the projection of the arc ω onto h is a small interval ww', which lies on the bisector of ab in the direction that gets away from q; that is, it lies on the Voronoi edge of ab in the diagram $\mathrm{Vor}(\{a, b, q\})$ within h. See Figure 6(c). Moreover, c_{ab} also lies on the bisector, but it has to lie on the other side of w, or else the smaller arc ω would have to lie inside $B_r(q)$. That is, c_{ab} has to be closer to q than to a and b. Since λ separates a and b from q, it also separates c_{ab} from q. Moreover, the preceding arguments are easily seen to imply that wq crosses ab (as in Figure 6(a)), which implies that λ also separates q and w, so w has to lie to the right of λ. Since z and z' lie on two sides of w on the line ℓ, at least one of them has to lie on the same side of λ as w (i.e., to the right of λ). This completes the proof. ☐

Let $a, b \in P_R$ and consider those arcs of C_{ab} which lie outside $K(P_L)$ but their endpoints lie on σ_L. Clearly, all these arcs are

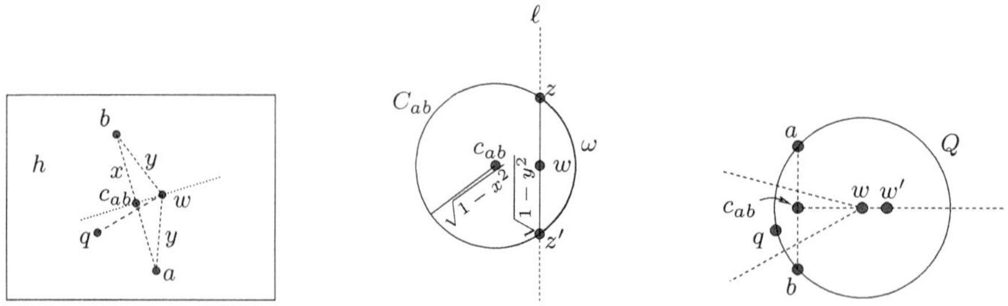

(a) (b) (c)

Figure 6. The setup in Lemma 2: (a) the setup within the plane h; (b) the setup within C_{ab}; (c) ww' lies on the bisector of ab in the direction that gets away from q.

pairwise disjoint. At most one such arc can be larger than a semicircle. Let ω be an arc of this kind which is smaller than a semicircle, and let $q \in P_L$ be such that one endpoint of ω lies on $\partial B_r(q)$. Then $\omega' = C_{ab} \setminus B_r(q)$ is contained in ω and therefore is also smaller than a semicircle. By Lemma 2, exactly one endpoint of ω' lies to the right of λ (the other endpoint lies on σ_L). Note that C_{ab} cannot have more than two such short arcs lying outside $K(P_L)$, since, due to the convexity of C_{ab}, only two arcs of C_{ab} can have their two endpoints lying on opposite sides of λ. Hence the number of arcs of C_{ab} under consideration is at most 3, implying that γ_a and γ_b intersect at most three times, and thus the complexity of M is $O(n^2)$, as asserted.

Constructing and searching M. We compute M in $O(n^2 \log n)$ time (see the full version [1] for the straightforward details). We next perform a traversal of the cells of M in a manner similar to the one used in the preceding section, via a tour, which proceeds from each visited cell to an adjacent one. For each cell τ that we visit, we place the center c_1 of B_1 in τ, and maintain dynamically the subset P_τ^+ of points of P not covered by B_1. (Here, unlike the algorithm of Section 3, the complementary set P_τ^- is automatically covered by B_1 and there is no need to test it.) As before, when we move from one cell τ to an adjacent cell τ_1, $P_{\tau_1}^+$ gains one point or loses one point. This implies that this tour generates only $O(n^2)$ connected life-spans of the points of P, where a life-span of a point p is a maximal connected interval of the tour, in which p belongs to P_τ^+. We can thus use a segment tree T_M to store these life-spans, as before. Each leaf u of T_M represents a cell τ of M, and the balls not containing τ are those with life-spans that are stored at the nodes on the path from the root to u. Arguing exactly as in Section 3, we can compute T_M in overall $O(n^2 \log^2 n)$ time, and the total storage used by T_M is $O(n^2 \log n)$.

As in the previous algorithm, we next test, for each leaf u of T_M, whether the spherical polytopes along the path from the root to u have non-empty intersection. We do this using the parametric search technique described in Section 3, which takes $O(\log^8 n)$ time for each path, for a total of $O(n^2 \log^8 n)$. More precisely, as above, we also need to distinguish between $r = r^*$ and $r > r^*$. We therefore stop only when both the intersection along the path and the cell of σ_L corresponding to u are non-degenerate, and then report that $r^* < r$. Otherwise, we continue running the above procedure over all paths of T_M, and repeat it for each of the $O(1/\beta^3)$ combinations of an orientation v and a separating plane λ. If we find at least one (degenerate) solution, we report that $r^* = r$, and otherwise conclude that $r^* > r$. Hence, the cost of handling Case 2, and thus also the overall cost of the decision procedure, is $O((1/\beta^3)n^2 \log^8 n)$.

Solving the optimization problem. We now combine the decision procedure Γ described above with the randomized optimization technique of Chan [12] (as briefly described in Section 3), to obtain a solution for the optimization problem.

The decision procedure Γ, on a specified radius r, relies on an apriori knowledge of a lower bound β for the separation ratio $|c_1c_2|/r$. To supply such a β, let r_0 denote the radius of the smallest enclosing ball of P, and observe that if there exist two balls B_1, B_2 of radius r covering P then the smallest ball B^* enclosing $B_1 \cup B_2$ must be at least as large as the smallest enclosing ball of P, so its radius must be at least r_0. Since this radius is $(1 + \beta/2)r$ (see Figure 5(right)), we have $(1 + \beta/2)r \geq r_0$ or $\beta \geq 2(r_0/r - 1)$. The running time is thus

$$O\left(\frac{1}{\beta^3} n^2 \log^8 n\right) = O\left(\frac{1}{(1 - r/r_0)^3} n^2 \log^8 n\right).$$

We consider the interval $(0, r_0)$, which contains r^*, and run an "exponential search" through it, calling Γ with the values $r_i = r_0\left(1 - 1/2^i\right)$, for $i = 1, 2, \ldots$, in order, until the first time we reach a value $r' = r_i \geq r^*$. Note that $1 - r'/r_0 = 1/2^i$ and $1/2^i < 1 - r^*/r_0 < 1/2^{i-1}$, so our lower bound estimates for the separation ratio β at r' and at r^* differ by at most a factor of 2, so the cost of running Γ at r' is asymptotically the same as at r^*. Moreover, since the (constants of proportionality in the) running time bounds on the executions of Γ at $r_1, \ldots, r_i$ form a geometric sequence, the overall cost of the exponential search is also asymptotically the same as the cost of running Γ at r^*. We then run Chan's technique, with r' as the initial minimum radius obtained so far. Hence, from now on, each call to Γ made by Chan's technique will cost asymptotically no more than the cost of calling Γ with r' (which is asymptotically the same as calling Γ with r^*).

Combining Chan's technique with the decision procedure Γ. To apply Chan's technique with our decision procedure, we use the same cutting-based decomposition as in Section 3. Consider the application of Γ to a subproblem represented by a simplex Δ_i of the cutting. The presence of "global" points (those dual to planes passing above or below Δ_i) forces us, as in Section 3, to modify each of the two cases considered in Γ.

Case 1: $|c_1c_2| \geq 3r$. The set $P_{\Delta_i}^-$ of points dual to the planes of $(P^*)_{\Delta_i}^-$ is fully contained in one of the solution balls, say B_1, and the set $P_{\Delta_i}^+$ of points dual to the planes of $(P^*)_{\Delta_i}^+$ is fully contained in the other ball B_2. The task at hand is to decide how to divide the set $P^0_{\Delta_i}$ of the dual points of the planes in $(P^*)^0_{\Delta_i}$ between B_1 and B_2. As is done in Case 1 of the "pure" decision procedure, we rotate the coordinate axes, in a constant number of ways. For each orientation we sort only the points in $P^0_{\Delta_i}$ by their x-coordinates, consider all $O(m)$ partitions of $P^0_{\Delta_i}$ into a left subset P_L and a right subset P_R, and, for each partition, compute the smallest enclosing balls of $P_L \cup P^+_{\Delta_i}$ and of $P_R \cup P^-_{\Delta_i}$. If the radii of these balls are both at most r, we have a solution to the decision procedure. The overall cost of running this step is $O(mn)$, which is subsumed in the cost of handling the second case.

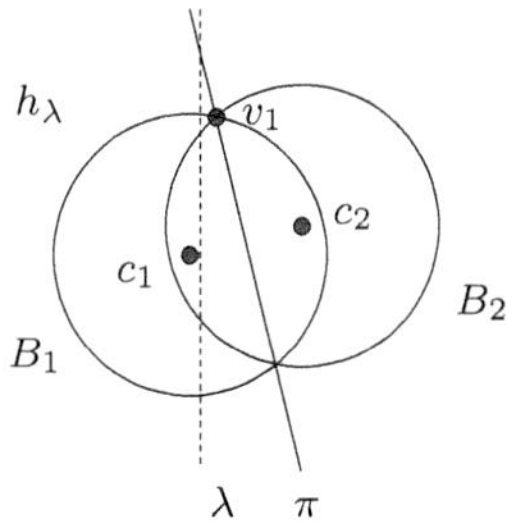

Figure 7. h_λ does not contain any point of $P^+_{\Delta_i}$.

Case 2: $\beta r \le |c_1c_2| < 3r$. (Relevant only when $\beta < 3$.) We again rotate the coordinate axes, in $O\left(1/\beta^2\right)$ ways (in the same manner as in Case 2 of the "pure" decision procedure), and draw $O(1/\beta)$ yz-parallel planes, such that, at the correct orientation, one of these planes, λ, separates c_1 from v_1 (if there is a solution for r). We assume, without loss of generality, that $P^-_{\Delta_i} \subseteq B_1$, and that $P^+_{\Delta_i} \subseteq B_2$. Recall also that the points in the left halfspace h_λ bounded by λ are all contained in B_1. Moreover, the plane π containing the intersection circle C_{12} is dual to a point π^*, which has to separate $(P^*)^+_{\Delta_i}$ from $(P^*)^-_{\Delta_i}$. Hence, all the points of $P^+_{\Delta_i}$ have to lie on the other side of π, and in B_2, which is easily seen to imply that none of them can lie in h_λ. See Figure 7. We thus verify that $P^+_{\Delta_i} \cap h_\lambda = \emptyset$, aborting otherwise the guess of λ. (Note that, in contrast, points of $P^-_{\Delta_i}$ can also lie to the right of λ.)

We now have a subset $P_L \subseteq P^0_{\Delta_i}$ of $O(m)$ points to the left of λ, which are assumed, together with the points of $P^-_{\Delta_i}$, to be contained in B_1. Note however that, for Lemma 2 to hold, we have to define σ_L only in terms of the points to the left of λ. Therefore, we compute the surface $\sigma'_L = \partial K(P_L \cup (P^-_{\Delta_i} \cap h_\lambda)) \cap h_\lambda$ and search on it for a placement of the center c_1 of B_1. However, since the remaining points of $P^-_{\Delta_i}$ are also assumed to belong to B_1, we need to consider only the portion of σ'_L inside $\bigcap\{B_r(p) \mid p \in P^-_{\Delta_i} \setminus h_\lambda\}$. Let σ''_L denote this portion. It is easy to compute σ''_L in $O(n \log n)$ time (details omitted). So far, the cost of the decision procedure also depends (cheaply — see below) on the initial input size n, but the saving in this setup comes from the fact that it suffices to intersect the $O(m)$ spheres $\partial B_r(p)$, for $p \in P^0_{\Delta_i} \setminus h_\lambda$, with σ''_L to obtain the map M, since only the points of $P^0_{\Delta_i}$ are "undecided". (The points of $P^+_{\Delta_i}$ are always placed in B_2 — see below.)

Note that σ''_L need not to be connected, but we can nevertheless visit all the cells of M in a single connected tour (possibly with repetitions), by "hopping" from one connected component of σ''_L to another via the (connected) network of edges of σ'_L. As is easy to check, the overall length of the tour is $O(m^2 + mn) = O(mn)$. We thus build a segment tree $T = T_M$ to maintain the subset P^+_τ of points of P not covered by B_1. Building T and searching through its paths is done as in Case 2 of the pure decision procedure, except for several easy modifications, such as precomputing $K(P^+_{\Delta_i})$, storing this spherical polytope at the root of the segment tree, and including it in the intersections along each path of the tree. We omit the further details, which can be found in [1].

Running time. For each cell of M we run the procedure described in Section 3 for determining whether the intersection of the corresponding spherical polytopes is non-degenerate. Therefore, solving each subproblem requires $O(mn \log^8 n)$ time. The $O(mn \log n)$ time required to build M, the $O(n \log n)$ time required to construct the intersection of the balls in $\{B_r(p) \mid p \in P^+_{\Delta_i}\}$, and the $O(mn)$ cost of Case 1, are all subsumed in that cost. Repeating this for each of the $O(1/\beta^3)$ guesses of an orientation and a separating plane, results in $O\left((1/\beta^3)mn \log^8 n\right)$ time. When the recursion bottoms out, we handle it the same way as in Section 3.

The expected cost of solving the optimization problem using Chan's technique is asymptotically the same as that of the decision procedure. To see this, we need to overcome some subtleties in the application of the original analysis of Chan, similar to those in the less efficient algorithm. Arguing similarly, we obtain the following recurrence for the maximum expected cost $T(m, n)$ of solving a recursive subproblem involving m "local" points, where n is the number of initial input points in P.

$$T(m,n) \le \begin{cases} \log(c\varrho^3)T(m/\varrho, n) & \\ +O\left((1/\beta^3)mn \log^8 n\right), & \text{for } m \ge \varrho, \\ & \\ O(n), & \text{for } m < \varrho, \end{cases} \qquad (3)$$

where c is an appropriate absolute constant (as in Section 3), ϱ is the parameter of the cutting, chosen to be a sufficiently large constant, and $\beta = 2(r_0/r' - 1)$, where r' is the value of r at which the initial exponential search is terminated.

It can be shown, rather easily (and we omit the details), that the recurrence (3) yields the overall bound $O\left((1/\beta^3)n^2 \log^8 n\right)$ on the expected cost of the initial problem; i.e.,

$$T(n,n) = O\left((1/\beta^3)n^2 \log^8 n\right).$$

We thus finally obtain our main result:

THEOREM 3. *Let P be a set of n points in $\mathbb{R}^3$. A 2-center for P can be computed in $O((n^2 \log^8 n/(1 - r^*/r_0)^3)$ randomized expected time, where r^* is the radius of the 2-center for P and r_0 is the radius of the smallest enclosing ball of P.*

5. CONCLUSIONS

In this paper we presented two algorithms for computing the 2-center of a set of points in $\mathbb{R}^3$. The first algorithm takes near-cubic time, and the second one takes near-quadratic time provided that the two centers are not too close to each other. An obvious open problem is to design an algorithm for the 2-center problem that runs in near-quadratic time on all point sets in $\mathbb{R}^3$. Another interesting question is whether the 2-center problem in $\mathbb{R}^3$ is n^2-*hard* (see [21] for details), which would suggest that a near-quadratic algorithm is (almost) the best possible for this problem.

References

[1] P. K. Agarwal, R. Ben Avraham and M. Sharir, The 2-center problem in three dimensions, `http://www.cs.tau.ac.il/~rinatbel/2center_in_3d.pdf`

[2] P. K. Agarwal, A. Efrat and M. Sharir, Vertical decomposition of shallow levels in 3-dimensional arrangements and its applications, *SIAM J. Comput.* 29 (2000), 912–953.

[3] P. K. Agarwal and C. M. Procopiuc, Exact and approximation algorithms for clustering, *Algorithmica* 33 (2002), 201–226.

[4] P. K. Agarwal and M. Sharir, Planar geometric location problems, *Algorithmica* 11 (1994), 185–195.

[5] M. Bădoiu, S. Har-Peled and P. Indyk, Approximate clustering via core-sets, *Proc. 34th ACM Sympos. Theory Comput.* (2002), 250–257.

[6] M. Bern and D. Eppstein, Approximation algorithms for geometric problems, In D. S. Hochbaum, editor, *Approximation algorithms for NP-Hard problems,* PWS Publishing Company, 1997.

[7] K. Bezdek and R. Connelly, The Kneser-Poulsen conjecture for spherical polytopes, *Discrete Comput. Geom.* 32 (2004), 101–106.

[8] K. Bezdek, Z. Langi, M. Naszódi and P. Papez, Ball polyhedra, *Discrete Comput. Geom.* 38 (2007), 201–230.

[9] K. Bezdek and M. Naszódi, Rigidity of ball-polyhedra in euclidean 3-space, *European J. Combin.* 27 (2006), 255–268.

[10] H. Brönnimann, B. Chazelle and J. Matoušek, Product range spaces, sensitive sampling, and derandomization, *SIAM J. Comput.* 28 (1999), 1552–1575.

[11] T. M. Chan, An optimal randomized algorithm for maximum Tukey depth, *Proc. 15th ACM-SIAM Sympos. Discrete Algorithms* (2004), 430–436.

[12] T. M. Chan, Geometric applications of a randomized optimization technique, *Discrete Comput. Geom.* 22 (1999), 547–567.

[13] T. M. Chan, More planar two-center algorithms, *Comput. Geom. Theory Appl.* 13 (1999), 189–198.

[14] B. Chazelle, Cutting hyperplanes for divide-and-conquer, *Discrete Comput. Geom.* 9 (1993), 145–158.

[15] B. Chazelle, and J. Friedman, A deterministic view of random sampling and its use in geometry, *Combinatorica* 10 (1990), 229–249.

[16] B. Chazelle and J. Matoušek, On linear-time deterministic algorithms for optimization problems in fixed dimension, *J. Algorithms* 21 (1996), 579–597.

[17] K. L. Clarkson and P. W. Shor, Applications of random sampling in computational geometry, II, *Discrete Comput. Geom.* 4 (1989), 387–421.

[18] E. Cohen and N. Megiddo Strongly polynomial-time and NC algorithms for detecting cycles in dynamic graphs, *J. ACM* 40 (1993), 791–830.

[19] D. Eppstein, Dynamic three-dimensional linear programming, *ORSA J. Computing* 4 (1992), 360–368.

[20] D. Eppstein, Faster construction of planar two-centers, *Proc. 8th ACM-SIAM Sympos. Discrete Algorithms* (1997), 131–138.

[21] A. Gajentaan and M. H. Overmars, On a class of $O(n^2)$ problems in computational geometry, *Comput. Geom. Theory Appl.* 5(3) (1995), 165–185.

[22] J. Hershberger and S. Suri, Finding tailored partitions, *J. Algorithms* 12 (1991), 431–463.

[23] J. Jaromczyk and M. Kowaluk, An efficient algorithm for the euclidean two-center problem, *Proc. 10th ACM Sympos. Comput. Geom.* (1994), 303–311.

[24] J. Matoušek, Cutting hyperplane arrangements, *Discrete Comput. Geom.* 6 (1991), 385–406.

[25] J. Matoušek, Linear optimization queries, *J. Algorithms* 14 (3) (1993), 432–448.

[26] N. Megiddo, Linear programming in linear time when the dimension is fixed, *J. ACM* 31 (1984), 114–127.

[27] N. Megiddo, Linear time algorithms for linear programming in $\mathbb{R}^3$ and related problems, *SIAM J. Comput.* 12 (1983), 759–776.

[28] N. Megiddo and K. Supowit, On the complexity of some common geometric location problems, *SIAM J. Comput.* 13 (1984), 1182–1196.

[29] N. Megiddo, On the complexity of some geometric problems in unbounded dimension, *J. Symbolic Comput.* 10 (1990), 327–334.

[30] C. H. Norton, S. A. Plotkin and E. Tardos, Using separation algorithms in fixed dimension, *J. Algorithms* 13 (1992), 79–98.

[31] E. A. Ramos, Intersection of unit-balls and diameter of a point set in $\mathbb{R}^3$, *Comput. Geom. Theory Appl.* 8 (1997), 57–65.

[32] N. Sarnak and R. E. Tarjan, Planar point location using persistent search trees, *Comm. ACM* 29 (7) (1986), 669–679.

[33] M. Sharir, A near linear algorithm for the planar 2-center problem, *Discrete Comput. Geom.* 18 (1997), 125–134.

Linkless and Flat Embeddings in 3-Space and the Unknot Problem

[Extended Abstract] *

Ken-ichi Kawarabayashi[†]
National Institute of Informatics
2-1-2 Hitotsubashi, Chiyoda-ku
Tokyo, Japan
k_keniti@nii.ac.jp

Stephan Kreutzer[‡]
Oxford University Computing Laboratory
Wolfson Building, Parks Road
Oxford, UK
kreutzer@comlab.ox.ac.uk

Bojan Mohar[§]
Department of Mathematics
Simon Fraser University
Burnaby, B.C., Canada
mohar@sfu.ca

ABSTRACT

We consider piecewise linear embeddings of graphs in 3-space $\mathbb{R}^3$. Such an embbeding is *linkless* if every pair of disjoint cycles forms a trivial link (in the sense of knot theory). Robertson, Seymour and Thomas [47] showed that a graph has a linkless embedding in $\mathbb{R}^3$ if, and only if, it does not contain as a minor any of seven graphs in Petersen's family (graphs obtained from K_6 by a series of $Y\Delta$ and ΔY operations). They also showed that a graph is linklessly embeddable in $\mathbb{R}^3$ if, and only if, it admits a *flat embedding* into $\mathbb{R}^3$, i.e. an embedding such that for every cycle C of G there exists a closed 2-disk $D \subseteq \mathbb{R}^3$ with $D \cap G = \partial D = C$. Clearly, every flat embeddings is linkless, but the converse is not true. We first consider the following algorithmic problem associated with embeddings in $\mathbb{R}^3$:

Flat Embedding: For a given graph G, either detect one of Petersen's family graphs as a minor in G or return a flat (and hence linkless) embedding in $\mathbb{R}^3$.

The first outcome is a certificate that G has no linkless and no flat embeddings. Our first main result is to give an $O(n^2)$ algorithm for this problem. While there is a known polynomial-time algorithm for constructing linkless embeddings [20], this is the first polynomial time algorithm for constructing flat embeddings in 3-space and we thereby settle a problem proposed by Lovász [29]. We also consider the following classical problem in topology.

The Unknot Problem: Decide if a given knot is trivial or not.

This is a fundamental problem in knot theory and low dimensional topology, whose time complexity is unresolved. It has been extensively studied by researchers working in computational geometry. A related problem is:

The Link Problem: Decide if two given knots form a link.

Hass, Lagarias and Pippenger [16] observed that a polynomial time algorithm for the link problem yields a polynomial time algorithm for the unknot problem. We relate the link problem to the following problem that was proposed independently by Lovász and by Robertson et al.

Conjecture. (Lovász [29]; Robertson, Seymour and Thomas [48]) *There is a polynomial time algorithm to decide whether a given embedding of a graph in the 3-space is linkless.*

Affirming this conjecture would clearly yield a polynomial-time solution for the link problem. We prove that the converse is also true by providing a polynomial-time solution for the above conjecture, if we are given a polynomial time oracle for the link problem.

General Terms

Algorithm, Theory

Categories and Subject Descriptors

G.2 [**Discrete Math**]: Combinatorics; G.2.2 [**Graph Theory**]: Combinatorics—*Graph algorithms, Computations on discrete structures*

Keywords

Linkless embedding, knot, unknot, flat embedding.

*A full version of this paper is available at `http://reseach.nii.ac.jp/~k_keniti/flatlink.pdf`

[†]Research partly supported by Japan Society for the Promotion of Science, Grant-in-Aid for Scientific Research, by C and C Foundation, by Kayamori Foundation and by Inoue Research Award for Young Scientists.

[‡]Research partly supported by DFG grant KR 2898/1-3.

[§]Supported in part by the ARRS, Research Program P1-0297, by an NSERC Discovery Grant, and by the Canada Research Chair Program. On leave from Department of Mathematics, University of Ljubljana, Slovenia.

SCG'10, June 13–16, 2010, Snowbird, Utah, USA.

1. INTRODUCTION

1.1 Embedding graphs in 3-space

A seminal result of Hopcroft and Tarjan [19] from 1974 is that there is a linear time algorithm for testing planarity of graphs. This is just one of a host of results on embedding graphs in surfaces. These problems are of both practical and theoretical interest. The practical issues arise, for instance, in problems concerning VLSI, and also in several other applications of "nearly" planar networks, as planar graphs and graphs embedded in low genus surfaces can be handled more easily. Theoretical interest comes from the importance of the genus parameter of graphs and from the fact that graphs of bounded genus naturally generalize the family of planar graphs and share many important properties with them. Recently, some apparently new and nontrivial linear time algorithms concerning graph embeddings have appeared [21, 22]. In addition, Mohar [33, 34] gave a linear time algorithm for testing embeddability of graphs in an arbitrary surface and constructing an embedding, if one exists. This is one of the deepest results in this area, and it generalizes linear time algorithms for testing planarity and constructing a planar embedding if one exists [5, 19, 54]. This algorithm is further simplified in [23].

In [41], Robertson and Seymour proved that for any fixed graph H there is a cubic-time algorithm for testing whether H is a minor of a given graph G. This implies that there is an $O(n^3)$ algorithm for deciding membership in any minor-closed family of graphs, because by their seminal result in [42], such a family can be characterized by a finite collection of excluded minors. However, this theorem is not explicit. More precisely, the graph minor theorem is not constructive; in general, we do not know how to obtain an excluded minor characterization of a given minor-closed family of graphs. In addition, Robertson and Seymour's algorithm solves the decision problem but it is not apparent how to construct, e.g., an embedding from their algorithm.

In this paper, we consider *embeddings of graphs* in $\mathbb{R}^3$, where all embeddings are piecewise linear. There are many minor-closed families of graphs that arise in the study of topological problems. An illustrative example is the class of linklessly embeddable graphs. We call a pair of vertex disjoint cycles drawn in $\mathbb{R}^3$ *un-linked* if there is a 2-dimensional disk[1] in $\mathbb{R}^3$ that contains the first cycle and is disjoint from the other one. Otherwise, the two cycles are *linked*. Intuitively, if two cycles in $\mathbb{R}^3$ are linked, we can not contract one into a single point without cutting the other. By a *linkless embedding* we mean an embedding of a graph in $\mathbb{R}^3$ in such a way that no two vertex-disjoint cycles are linked. Linkless embeddings were first studied by Conway and Gordon [9]. An algorithmic problem concerning linkless embeddings is studied by Motwani, Raghunathan and Saran [36], who gave a partial result for linkless embeddings and its algorithmic applications.

Robertson, Seymour and Thomas [47] proved that G is linklessly embeddable in the 3-space if, and only if, G does not have any graph in the Petersen family as a minor. By the *Petersen family* we mean the graphs that can be obtained from K_6 by a series of $Y\Delta$ and ΔY operations. See Figure 1 for drawings of these graphs on the projective plane; note that the third one, $K_{4,4} - e$, cannot be embedded in the projective plane. In the same paper [47] it is shown that a graph is linklessly embeddable in $\mathbb{R}^3$ if, and only if, it admits a *flat embedding* in $\mathbb{R}^3$, i.e. an embedding such that for every cycle C of G, there exists a closed 2-dimensional disk $D \subseteq \mathbb{R}^3$ with $D \cap G = \partial D = C$. Clearly, every flat embedding is linkless, but the converse is not true. In many ways flat embeddings are nicer to work with and in this paper we will work with flat rather than linkless embeddings.

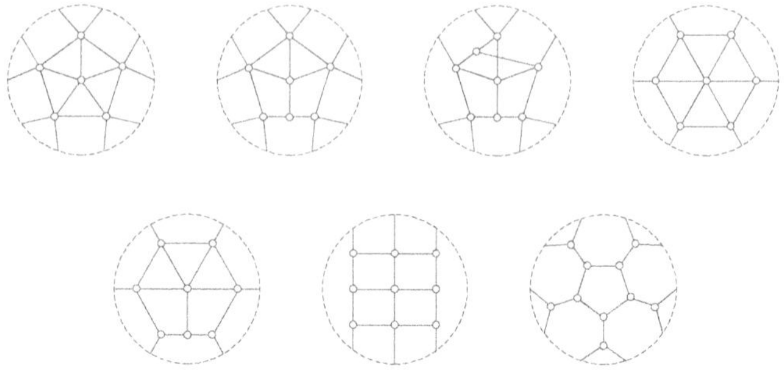

Figure 1: Petersen's family

Linkless embeddings have drawn attention of many researchers. Besides those working on knot theory, many researchers working in discrete mathematics are also interested in this topic. For example, Lovász and Schrijver [30, 31] proved that two well-known invariants given by Colin de Verdière [6, 7, 8] are closely related to linklessly embeddable graphs. The invariants are based on spectral properties of matrices associated with a graph G.

Flat embeddings in the 3-space are a generalization of embeddings in the plane. These two embedding problems share an interesting property. The famous theorem by Whitney which says that every 3-connected planar graph has a unique planar embedding, can be generalized to the flat embedding case, i.e., every flatly embeddable 4-connected graph G has an "essentially unique" flat embedding in $\mathbb{R}^3$, see [47]. Here, "essentially unique" means embeddings up to ambient isotopy, which we define later. In [29], Lovász conjectured that there is a polynomial time algorithm for the following problem:

Flat and Linkless Embedding
Input: A graph G.
Output: Either (1) detect one of Petersen's family graphs as a minor in G or (2) return a flat (and hence linkless) embedding of G in $\mathbb{R}^3$.

Let us observe that if the output is (1), then we have one of the excluded minors for linklessly embeddable graphs and hence this is a certificate that G has no linkless (and no flat) embeddings. As mentioned above, by Robertson and Seymour's results [41], we can test whether or not an input graph has one of Petersen's family graphs as a minor, but if it does not contain any of them, that algorithm does not give the second conclusion. In [20], van der Holst gives the first polynomial-time algorithm for deciding whether a given graph has a linkless embedding. In this paper we give a different algorithm for computing linkless embeddings which runs in quadratic time. Furthermore, our algorithm not only computes linkless embeddings but flat embeddings of linklessly embeddable graphs. As far as we are aware, no polynomial-time algorithm for constructing flat embeddings

[1] In this paper, by a 2-dimensional disk we always mean a 2-dimensional topological disk.

was known prior to our work. See below for a more detailed comparison of our algorithm and van der Holst's.

1.2 Testing linklessness of an embedding

We also consider some classical problems in knot theory and low dimensional topology, specifically the topology of 1-dimensional curves in the 3-space, with the objective of determining their computational complexity. Historically, determining whether a given knot is trivial or not is one of the central questions in low dimensional topology. The problem of finding an algorithm to decide about triviality of a knot was posed already by Dehn [11]. Let us formulate the problem in the following way:

The unknot problem
Input: A cycle C of order n and an embedding of C in $\mathbb{R}^3$.
Output: Decide whether or not C is knotted.

This problem has been extensively studied by researchers working on computational geometry as well. Let us observe that topologists study this problem at several levels, with varying meanings given to the terms *embedded* and *deformed*. The level that is most appropriate for studying computational questions is that of *piecewise-linear* embeddings. At this level, a closed curve is embedded in $\mathbb{R}^3$ as a simple non-self-intersecting polygonal curve, which is composed of finitely many straight line segments.

The first algorithm for the unknot problem was given by Haken [17]. But as observed by Hass, Lagarias and Pippenger [16], the algorithm clearly does not run in polynomial time. In fact, the question of how easy or difficult it might be to recognize the unknot was in the air immediately following Haken's 1954 announcement that the problem was decidable (the paper was published in 1961, see [17]). It is stated explicitly as an open question by Welsh in [53]. He actually traces the general idea of looking for efficient procedure for solving this problem back farther than Haken, to Tait.

As mentioned above, Hass, Lagarias and Pippenger [16] observed that Haken's algorithm runs in time $2^{O(n^2)}$. They also proved that the unknot problem is in co-NP, and conjectured that it is in NP $\cap$ co-NP. Some recent progress was made in [1, 18]. In particular, the result in [18] predicts that the unknot problem would be in P.

We now consider the following problem:

The link problem
Input: Two cycles C_1, C_2 of order n and an embedding of $C_1 \cup C_2$ in $\mathbb{R}^3$.
Output: Decide whether or not $C_1 \cup C_2$ forms a link in $\mathbb{R}^3$.

Hass, Lagarias and Pippenger [16] observed that a polynomial time algorithm for the link problem yields a polynomial time algorithm for the unknot problem.

More than 15 years ago, the following conjecture was made independently by Lovász [29], and Robertson, Seymour and Thomas [48].

CONJECTURE 1.1. *There is a polynomial time algorithm to decide for a given graph G and its embedding in the 3-space, whether or not this embedding is linkesss.*

Let us observe that Conjecture 1.1 clearly implies a polynomial time solution for the link problem. As pointed out by Robertson, Seymour and Thomas, there is an algorithm to test whether or not a given embedding of a graph G is linkless, using the results in [47, 49], but this does not give a polynomial time algorithm.

In this paper, we shall prove that Conjecture 1.1 is actually equivalent to polynomial-time solvability of the link problem, see Theorem 1.3 below.

1.3 Our results

Our first contribution in this paper is to give a polynomial-time algorithm for the flat and linkless embedding problem, which proves the conjecture by Lovász [29] mentioned above.

THEOREM 1.2. *There is an $O(n^2)$-time algorithm for the flat and linkless embedding problem.*

Clearly, every flat embedding is linkless but the converse is false, as a graph that consists of one vertex with two loops shows. However, Robertson, Seymour and Thomas proved that a graph admits a linkless embedding in $\mathbb{R}^3$ if, and only if, it admits a flat embedding. In [20], van der Holst gives a polynomial-time algorithm to construct a linkless embedding if one exists. Our algorithm is different from van der Holst's algorithm in several respects:

1. Our algorithm finds a flat embedding in $\mathbb{R}^3$, while the algorithm from [20] finds linkless embeddings that are not necessarily flat.
2. We improve on the time complexity as van der Holst's algorithm needs at least $\Omega(n^5)$ steps whereas ours runs in $O(n^2)$.
3. In order to give a polynomial time algorithm for the linkless embedding problem, [20] uses deep results of Robertson and Seymour [41] algorithmically, while our algorithm does not. To be precise, the proof of correctness for our algorithm relies on several results from [41] (recently, a shorter proof is found in [25]), but the algorithm itself does not use Robertson and Seymour's algorithm. So together with the arguments in [25, 41], our full proof can be given within 50 pages (in contrast with this, Robertson and Seymour's algorithm needs more than 300 pages for the correctness of the algorithm).
4. The algorithm and the proof method in [20] are very algebraic and are completely different from our paper, which is more combinatorial and geometric.

There are many NP-hard problems which can be solved in polynomial time (often, even linear time) when considering planar graphs or "nearly" planar graphs. Even for problems that remain NP-hard on planar graphs, we often have efficient approximation algorithms, e.g., INDEPENDENT SET, TSP, Weighted TSP, VERTEX COVER, DOMINATION SET, etc. [3, 15, 26, 28]. We expect that most of these fast algorithms for planar graphs can be generalized to linklessly embeddable graphs as well, using our algorithm in Theorem 1.2 and a flat embedding. In addition, linklessly embeddable graphs have an interesting property for the well-known feedback arc set problem. Seymour [51] proved that the minimum size of a feedback arc set in an eulerian linklessly embeddable digraph (i.e, the underlying undirected graph is linklessly embeddable) is equal to the maximum number of arc-disjoint directed cycles. This result can be compared to the well-known result by Lucchesi and Younger [32], who proved that the same conclusion holds for any directed planar graph. The proof given in [51] implies that, given a flat embedding of a given Eulerian digraph G, there is a polynomial time algorithm to find the minimum size of a feedback arc set, which gives rise to the maximum number of arc-disjoint directed cycles. Thus by Theorem 1.2, we can find such sets in polynomial time for any Eulerian linklessly embeddable graph.

Our second main result is an oracle algorithm that shows that Conjecture 1.1 is equivalent to polynomial-time solvability of the unknot problem.

THEOREM 1.3. *There is an oracle polynomial-time algorithm to decide whether a given embedding of a graph in the 3-space is linkless by using an oracle for the link problem.*

1.4 Overview of our algorithms

We first sketch the algorithm for Theorem 1.2. At a high level of description, our algorithm for Theorem 1.2 proceeds as follows: the algorithm first iteratively reduces the size of the input graph until it is 4-connected and reaches a graph of bounded tree-width. Then the algorithm solves the problem on this graph of bounded tree-width.

Bounded tree-width case. This second step needs two deep results in [47]. The first ingredient is that any Kuratowski graph, i.e, a subdivision of K_5 or $K_{3,3}$, has a unique flat embedding in the 3-space $\mathbb{R}^3$, where uniqueness means "up to an ambient isotopy". The second ingredient is that if G is 4-connected and has a flat embedding in $\mathbb{R}^3$, then G has a unique flat embedding. By combining these two results, we get the following strong fact:

> Fix a flat embedding of a Kuratowski subgraph K of a 4-connected graph G in $\mathbb{R}^3$. Then the rest of the graph is uniquely attached to K, if G has a flat embedding.

In general, this fact is not enough to derive a polynomial time algorithm for constructing flat embeddings. However, if the tree-width of a 4-connected graph is bounded, we can construct a flat embedding in polynomial time (even in linear time) using dynamic programming, whenever one exists.

Reduction step. For the reduction step, the algorithm uses the excluded grid theorem [13, 37, 39, 44]: if the tree-with of G is big enough, G contains a huge grid minor. By combining the results in [41] and [24], if an input graph does not contain a K_6-minor, then, after deleting at most one vertex, we can find a grid minor which is planarly drawn, i.e., up to 3-separations, the grid minor induces a planar embedding. In fact, if there is a separation (A, B) of order at most three in this planarly drawn grid, then this gives us a reduction (for details, we refer to Section 3). Otherwise, this grid minor induces a 2-cell embedding in a plane (and hence it is a planar subgraph).

A deep theorem in [41] tells us that every vertex "deep inside" this grid minor is irrelevant with respect to all excluded minors in the Petersen family (A shorter proof of this fact is given in [25]). In addition we will prove that such a vertex does not affect our flat embedding in the 3-space. Hence, we can remove this vertex without affecting flat embeddability of G. Note that the difficulty here is only in the proof of the existence of this vertex. Once we have proved that there is an irrelevant vertex, algorithmically such a vertex can easily be found in linear time. This concludes the reduction step for the proof of Theorem 1.2.

We now sketch the proof of Theorem 1.3. Suppose an embedding σ of a given graph G in $\mathbb{R}^3$ is given. In order to prove Theorem 1.3, we have to deal with the following two technical difficulties.

(a) We need to test, for any cycle, whether or not the embedding induced by this cycle is unknotted.

(b) We need to test, for any two disjoint cycles, whether or not the embedding induced by these two disjoint cycles contains a link.

Assuming the embedding induced by each cycle in G is unknotted and the embedding induced by any two disjoint cycles does not contain a link, it is possible to prove that σ is linkless.

Task (a) can be completed in polynomial time, having a (polynomial-time) oracle for the unknot problem, which, as explained above, can be obtained from an oracle for the link problem (see [16]). Also task (b) can also be completed in polynomial time, having a (polynomial-time) oracle for the link problem.

So by considering all the cycles in G, and then testing (a) and (b) for them, we can figure out whether or not σ is linkless. But the problem here is that G may contain exponentially many cycles. So, to obtain a polynomial time algorithm for Theorem 1.3, we cannot look at all cycles.

In order to overcome this problem, we first test whether or not G has small tree-width. If G has small tree-width, it can be shown that we only have to look at polynomially many disjoint cycles to test (a) and (b) for them.

So, suppose G has large tree-width. Then G contains a huge grid minor. As described above, after deleting at most one vertex, we can find a grid minor T which is planarly drawn, i.e, up to 3-separations, T induces a planar embedding.

We now construct an optimal flat embedding by Theorem 1.2. In this optimal flat embedding, the embedding induced by T must be an embedding in the sphere. So, our first task is to figure out whether or not the embedding induced by T satisfies this property. To do so, we need to figure out all faces in a planar embedding σ' of T. As it turns out, to test whether or not the embedding induced by the grid minor T is linkless, we only need to test (a) and (b) for all faces of σ'. Since there are linearly many faces in the graph induced by T, we can test, in polynomial time, whether or not the embedding induced by T is linkless.

The following two facts are our key observations:

1. Let G, T be as above, and suppose an embedding of G in $\mathbb{R}^3$ is given. If the embeddings induced by $G - T$ and by T are linkless, then there is a polynomial time algorithm to test whether or not σ is linkless.

2. If one of the embeddings induced by $G - T$ and by T is not linkless, then σ is not linkless either.

These two observations imply that it remains to look at the embedding induced by $G - T$. Thus this allows us to make a reduction. We just recurse the algorithm to $G - T$. Due to space restrictions we refer to the full version of this paper for a proof of Theorem 1.3.

1.5 Basic definitions

Before proceeding, we review basic definitions. For basic graph theory notions, we refer the reader to the book by Diestel [12], for topological graph theory we refer to the monograph by Mohar and Thomassen [35].

A *separation* of a graph G is a pair (A, B) of subgraphs of G with $A \cup B = G$ such that there is no edge between $A - B$ and $B - A$. The *order* of the separation is $|V(A) \cap V(B)|$. If (A, B) is a separation of G of order k, we write A^+ for the graph obtained from A by adding edges joining every pair of nonadjacent vertices in $V(A) \cap V(B)$. We define B^+ analogously.

A *tree-decomposition* of a graph G is a pair (T, B), where T is a tree and B is a family $\{B_t \mid t \in V(T)\}$ of vertex sets $B_t \subseteq V(G)$, such that the following two properties hold:

1. $\bigcup_{t\in V(T)} B_t = V(G)$, and every edge of G has both ends in some B_t.
2. If $t, t', t'' \in V(T)$ and t' lies on the path in T between t and t'', then $B_t \cap B_{t''} \subseteq B_{t'}$.

The *width* of a tree-decomposition (T, B) is $\max\{|B_t| : t \in V(T)\} - 1$. The *tree-width* of G is defined as the minimum width taken over all tree-decompositions of G. Let (T, B) be a tree-decomposition of a graph G. By fixing a root r of T we give T an orientation. For $t \in V(T)$ we define T_t to be the subtree of T rooted at t, i.e., the subtree of T induced by the set of nodes $s \in V(T)$ such that the unique path from s to r contains t. We define $B(T_t) := \bigcup_{s\in V(T_t)} B_s$.

One of the most important results about graphs, whose tree-width is large, is the existence of a large grid minor or, equivalently, a large wall. Let us recall that an *r-wall* or a *wall of height r* is a graph which is isomorphic to a subdivision of the graph W_r with vertex set $V(W_r) = \{(i, j) \mid 1 \leq i \leq r,\ 1 \leq j \leq r\}$ in which two vertices (i, j) and (i', j') are adjacent if, and only if, one of the following possibilities holds: (1) $i' = i$ and $j' \in \{j - 1, j + 1\}$ or (2) $j' = j$ and $i' = i + (-1)^{i+j}$. We can also define an $(a \times b)$-wall in a natural way, so that the r-wall is the same as the $(r \times r)$-wall. It is easy to see that if a graph G contains an $(a \times b)$-wall as a subgraph, then it has an $(\lfloor \frac{1}{2}a \rfloor \times b)$-grid minor, and conversely, if G has an $(a \times b)$-grid minor, then it contains an $(a \times b)$-wall. Let us recall that the $(a \times b)$-grid is the Cartesian product of paths, $P_a \square P_b$. An (8×5)-wall is shown in Figure 2.

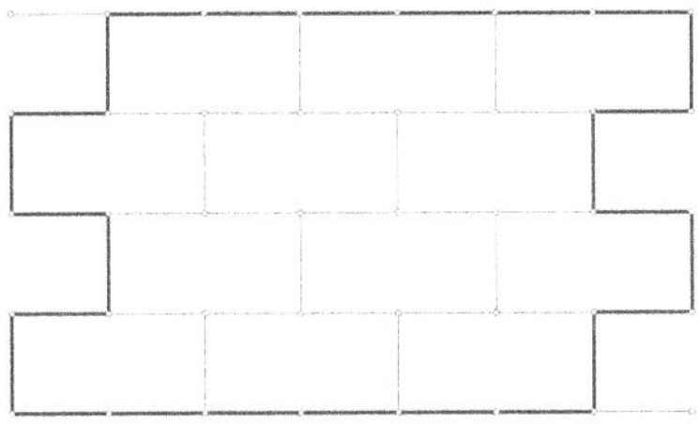

Figure 2: An (8×5)-wall and its outer cycle

THEOREM 1.4. *There is a computable function $f : \mathbb{N} \to \mathbb{N}$ such that if a graph G has tree-width at least $f(r)$, then G contains an r-wall.*

The best known upper bound for $f(r)$ is given in [13, 37, 44]. It is 20^{2r^5}. The best known lower bound is $\Theta(r^2 \log r)$, see [44].

2. FLATLY AND LINKLESSLY EMBEDDABLE GRAPHS

In this section we recall some results about linklessly embeddable graphs used later on. Due to space restrictions, we can only state the most relevant results and almost no background.

2.1 Construction of flat embeddings

Recall that a piecewise-linear embedding of a graph in the 3-space $\mathbb{R}^3$ is *flat* if every cycle of the graph bounds a 2-dimensional disk disjoint from the rest of the graph. If C, C' are disjoint simple closed curves in $\mathbb{R}^3$, then their *linking number* is the number of times (modulo 2) that C crosses C' in a regular projection of $C \cup C'$ onto some hyperplane. It is easy to see that the linking number (modulo 2) is the same for every such projection. Hereafter, all linking numbers discussed in this paper will be mod 2. The proof of the following result is easy and the details are left to the reader.

LEMMA 2.1. *Let G be a graph, and σ be an embedding of G in $\mathbb{R}^3$. Let C_1, C_2 be disjoint cycles in G, and let P be a path in G that is disjoint from $C_1 \cup C_2$, except that its endvertices are in $V(C_1)$. Let C_1', C_1'' be the two cycles in $V(C_1 \cup P)$ with $V(C_1') \cap V(C_1'') = V(P)$. If the linking number of C_1, C_2 is nonzero, then also one of the linking numbers of C_1', C_2 or C_1'', C_2 is nonzero.*

Let v be a vertex of degree 3 in a graph G, with its three neighbors v_1, v_2, v_3. Let H be a graph obtained from $G - v$ by adding three new edges v_1v_2, v_2v_3, v_3v_1. We say that H is obtained from G by a $Y\Delta$ change (at v), and G is obtained from H by a ΔY change (at v_1, v_2, v_3). If G' can be obtained from G by a series of $Y\Delta$ or ΔY changes, we say that G and G' are *$Y\Delta$-equivalent*. The *Petersen family* is the set of the seven graphs (up to isomorphism) that are $Y\Delta$-equivalent to K_6. One of these is the Petersen graph. The following result was proved in [47].

THEOREM 2.2. *Let G be a graph obtained from H by a ΔY operation. Then G has a flat embedding in $\mathbb{R}^3$ if, and only if, H has.*

It is easy to see that degree 1 vertices can be deleted and degree 2 vertices can be suppressed without affecting linkless embeddability. Thus it follows from Theorem 2.2 that we may assume that each vertex has degree at least 4. Furthermore, concerning vertices of degree 4, we have the following.

LEMMA 2.3. *Suppose that a graph G contains an edge uv, where $\deg_G(u) = 4$ and $\deg_G(v) = 5$. Suppose, moreover, that $N(u) = (N(v) \cup \{v\}) - \{u, a\}$ for some vertex a in $N(v)$. Then there is a separation (A, B) of order four such that $B - A$ consists of u and v only, and G has a flat embedding in $\mathbb{R}^3$ if, and only if, for every vertex $b \in N(v) - \{u, a\}$, the graph G' obtained from G by contracting the edge ub has a flat embedding.*

We sketch the proof of Lemma 2.3. If G' has a flat embedding in 3-space $\mathbb{R}^3$, then $A \cap B \cup \{v\} - \{a\}$ is contained in a disk. Then we can easily put the vertex u back to this disk so that the resulting embedding of G (that extends the flat embedding of G') is still flat.

The following is (6.5) in [47]. Recall from above the definition of the graphs A^+, B^+ for a separation (A, B) of a graph G.

THEOREM 2.4. *Suppose G has a separation (G_1, G_2) with $|V(G_1) \cap V(G_2)| \leq 4$. Suppose furthermore, G contains both G_1^+ and G_2^+ as a minor. Then G has a flat embedding in 3-space $\mathbb{R}^3$ if, and only if, both G_1^+ and G_2^+ have one.*

2.2 Spatial embeddings of 4-connected graphs

The aim of this section is to show that 4-connected linklessly embeddable graphs essentially have a unique flat embedding in 3-space $\mathbb{R}^3$. The following results are proved in [47] along with its companion papers [45, 46]. Readers not familiar with these results may wish to consider the survey [48] which contains many of the results needed below. We refer to the graphs K_5 and $K_{3,3}$ as the *Kuratowski graphs*. A *Kuratowski subgraph* of a graph G is a subgraph of G isomorphic to a subdivision of a Kuratowski graph. For embeddings ϕ_1, ϕ_2 of a graph G we write $\phi_1 \cong_{a.i.} \phi_2$ to denote that they are ambient isotopic. Let us recall that ϕ_1 and ϕ_2 are *ambient isotopic*, if there exists an orientation preserving homeomorphism $\mathbb{R}^3 \to \mathbb{R}^3$ mapping ϕ_1 onto ϕ_2.

LEMMA 2.5. *1. Any two flat embeddings of a planar graph in $\mathbb{R}^3$ are ambient isotopic.*

2. The graphs K_5 and $K_{3,3}$ have exactly two non-ambient isotopic flat embeddings.

3. Let ϕ_1, ϕ_2 be two flat embeddings of a graph G which are not ambient isotopic. Then there is a Kuratowski subgraph H of G for which $\phi_{1|H}$ and $\phi_{2|H}$ are not ambient isotopic. Here $\phi_{i|H}$ denotes the restriction of ϕ_i to H.

We now define a neighbourhood relation between Kuratowski subgraphs of a graph G. Let $H_1, H_2 \subseteq G$ be Kuratowski subgraphs of G such that $H_1 \neq H_2$. H_1 and H_2 are *1-adjacent* if there exists a path $P \subseteq G$ and an $i \in \{1, 2\}$ such that P has only its endpoints in common with H_i and such that $H_{3-i} \subseteq H_i \cup P$.

H_1 and H_2 are *2-adjacent* if there are distinct vertices $v_1, \ldots, v_7 \in V(G)$ and pairwise internally vertex disjoint paths $L_{i,j}$, for $(i,j) \in \{1, \ldots, 4\} \times \{5,6,7\} \cup \{(3,4)\}$ linking v_i and v_j such that $H_1 = \bigcup\{L_{i,j} \mid (i,j) \in \{2,3,4\} \times \{5,6,7\}\}$ and $H_2 = \bigcup\{L_{i,j} \mid (i,j) \in \{1,3,4\} \times \{5,6,7\}\}$. The path $L_{3,4}$ is not used here but is required to exist. Note that if H_1, H_2 are 2-adjacent then they are both isomorphic to subdivisions of $K_{3,3}$. H_1 and H_2 are *adjacent* if they are 1- or 2-adjacent. Let H, H' be Kuratowski subgraphs of G. We say that H and H' *communicate* if there are Kuratowski subgraphs $H = H_1, \ldots, H_k = H'$ of G such that H_i and H_{i+1} are adjacent for all $1 \leq i < k$.

LEMMA 2.6. *1. Let ϕ_1, ϕ_2 be flat embeddings of G and let H, H' be adjacent Kuratowski subgraphs of G. If $\phi_{1|H} \cong_{a.i.} \phi_{2|H}$ then $\phi_{1|H'} \cong_{a.i.} \phi_{2|H'}$.*

2. If G is 4-connected, then all pairs H, H' of Kuratowski subgraphs of G communicate.

3. If ϕ, ϕ' are flat embeddings of a 4-connected graph G, then $\phi \cong_{a.i.} \phi'$ or $\phi \cong_{a.i.} -\phi'$.

Note that *(iii)* follows easily from *(i)* and *(ii)* and the previous lemma. For the purpose of this paper this suggests the following algorithm for computing a flat embedding of a graph G. We first choose a Kuratowski subgraph H of G and compute a flat embedding of H. We then choose an adjacent Kuratowski subgraph H' of G and extend the flat embedding of H to $H \cup H' \cup L$ (where $L = L_{3,4}$ is the additional path in the case of 2-adjacency, and $L = \emptyset$ in case of 1-adjacency). This is essentially unique. For, suppose there were two non-ambient-isotopic flat embeddings ϕ_1, ϕ_2 of $H \cup H' \cup L$ extending the embedding of H. As ϕ_1, ϕ_2 agree (up to ambient isotopy) on H, and H and H' are adjacent in $H \cup H' \cup L$, Part 1 of Lemma 2.6 implies that they also agree on H'. But then, by Part 3 of Lemma 2.5, as they agree on all Kuratowski subgraphs, ϕ_1, ϕ_2 agree on $H \cup H' \cup L$. Note that Part 1 of Lemma 2.6 and Part 3 of Lemma 2.5 do not require the graph to be 4-connected.

However, if G is 4-connected, then by starting from one Kuratowski subgraph whose embedding we fix and iteratively proceeding to adjacent Kuratowski subgraphs, we can embed all Kuratowski subgraphs of G. This embedding then has a unique extension to the complete graph. We will employ this idea in Section 4 below.

3. BOUNDING THE TREE-WIDTH

In this section we will present the reduction step of the general algorithm for solving the Linkless Embedding problem presented in Section 5 below. Let us observe that by Theorem 2.2 and Lemma 2.3 (and remarks just after Lemma 2.3), we may assume that every vertex in a given graph G has minimum degree at least 4, and any vertex of degree 4 does not satisfy the assumption of Lemma 2.3.

Let us define that the *nails* of a wall are the vertices of degree three within it. The *perimeter* of a wall W, denoted $per(W)$, is the unique face in this embedding which contains more than 6 nails. The *bricks* of a wall are the faces containing 6 nails. As walls are essentially 3-connected, Whitney's theorem implies that any wall has a unique planar embedding. For any wall W in H, there is a unique component U of $H - per(W)$ containing $W - per(W)$. The *compass* of W, denoted $comp(W)$, consists of the graph with vertex set $V(U) \cup V(per(W))$ and edge set $E(U) \cup E(per(W)) \cup \{xy | x \in V(U), y \in V(per(W))\}$, where $xy \in E(G)$. A *subwall* W' of a wall W is a wall which is a subgraph of W. A h-subwall of W is *proper* if it consists of h consecutive bricks from each of h consecutive rows of W. The *exterior* of W' is $W - W'$. A proper subwall is *dividing* if its compass is disjoint from its exterior. We say a proper subwall W' is dividing in a subgraph H of F if $W' \subseteq H$ and the compass of W' in H is disjoint from $(W - W') \cap H$.

A wall is *planarly drawn* if its compass does not contain two vertex disjoint paths connecting the diagonally opposite corners. Note that if the compass of W has a planar embedding whose infinite face is bounded by the perimeter of W then W is clearly planarly drawn.

Seymour [50], Thomassen [52], and others have characterized that if the wall W is planarly drawn, then its compass $comp(W)$ can be embedded into a plane, up to 3-separations, such that its perimeter $per(W)$ is the outer face boundary.

It is easy to see that any subwall of a planarly drawn wall must be both planarly drawn and dividing. Furthermore, if x and y are two vertices of a planarly drawn wall W and there is a path between them which is internally disjoint from W then either x and y are both on $per(W)$ or some brick contains both of them. Robertson and Seymour [41] proved:

THEOREM 3.1. *For every pair of integers l and t there exist integers $w(l,t) > w'(l,t) > max(l,t)$ such that the following holds. Let K be a graph of order t. If the tree-width of a graph H is at least $w(l,t)$, and H has no K-minor, then there is a wall W of height $w'(l,t)$, and for some subset X of less than $\binom{t}{2}$ vertices of H there are t^{10} disjoint proper subwalls W' (of the wall W) of height l, which are disjoint from X and are planarly drawn and dividing in $H - X$. In addition, any of these disjoint proper subwalls of height l has face-distance at least t^{10} from any other in the wall W.*

In fact, we can give the explicit bound for $w(l,t)$. Combining the best known bound for the grid theorem in [44], the proof of Theorem 3.1 in [41] implies that $w(l,t) \leq 10^{10^{10^q}}$, where $q = l^t$.

A vertex v in G is called *irrelevant* with respect to a given minor M in G if G has an M-minor if, and only if, $G - v$ has. The following result was proved in [41] (a shorter proof was given in [25]).

THEOREM 3.2. *There is a computable function $f : \mathbb{N} \rightarrow \mathbb{N}$ satisfying the following: let $l \geq f(t)$ and let $H, W, X, K, w(l,t)$, $w'(l,t)$ be as in Theorem 3.1. Let W' be one of the proper subwalls (of the wall W) of height l which is disjoint from X, and is planarly drawn and dividing in $H - X$. Suppose furthermore that the comp(W') has a 2-cell embedding in a plane with per(W') in the outer face boundary. Then the unique vertex v which has distance exactly $l/2$ from the per(W') in the wall W' is irrelevant with respect to a K-minor.*

We now give an algorithmic result of Theorems 3.1 and 3.2 in [41].

THEOREM 3.3. *Let $t, l, f, w'(l,t)$ be as in Theorem 3.2. There is an $O(m)$ time algorithm, where m is the number of edges, which, given H, W, K as in Theorem 3.2 (thus the wall W is of height $w'(t,l)$), constructs one of the following.*

1. *A K-minor in H, or*
2. *for some subset X of less than $\binom{t}{2}$ vertices of H there are t^{10} disjoint proper subwalls W' (of the wall W) of height l, which are disjoint from X, and are dividing in $H - X$. In addition, any of these disjoint proper subwalls of height l has face-distance at least t^{10} from any other in the wall W.*

It is easy to see that if G has at least $2^t|V(G)|$ edges, then one can easily find a K_t-minor in linear time (see [38]). If we can find a K_6-minor in a given graph G in linear time, we are done. So a flatly embeddable graph G has at most $2^6|V(G)|$ edges, which, hereafter, we assume. Thus the time complexity of Theorem 3.3 can be improved to $O(n)$, where n is the number of vertices of an input graph.

If $K = K_6$ in Theorem 3.1, then the following stronger version of Theorem 3.1 is proved in [24].

THEOREM 3.4. *Let $f(t)$ be as in Theorem 3.2 with $t = 6$. For any $l \geq f(6)$, there are integers $w(l) > w'(l)$ satisfying the following: If the tree-width of a graph H is at least $w(l)$, then there is a wall W of height $w'(l)$, and one of the following holds: (1) a K_6-minor in H, or (2) for some subset X of at most one vertex of H, there are at least 10 disjoint proper subwalls W' (of the wall W) of height l, which are disjoint from X and dividing in $H - X$. In addition, any of these disjoint proper subwalls of height l has face-distance at least 2 from any other in the wall W. Moreover,*

(a) *if $|X| = 0$ and three of the disjoint proper subwalls of height l are not planarly drawn, then H has a K_6-minor, and*

(b) *if $|X| = 1$ and there is a proper subwall of height l that is not planarly drawn, then H has a K_6-minor.*

Furthermore, given the wall W, there is a linear time algorithm to compute one of 1 and 2 above.

Note that the last algorithmic conclusion follows from planarity testing [5, 19, 54].

We now prove the following result for the linkless embedding case. Recall from the beginning of this section that we assume that a graph G has minimum degree at least 4.

THEOREM 3.5. *There is a constant f satisfying the following: Let G be a given input graph with minimum degree 4, and $W, w(l), w'(l)$ be as in Theorem 3.4 with $l \geq f$. Then one of the following holds:*

1. *G has a K_6-minor, or*
2. *for some subset X of at most one vertex of G, there is a proper subwall W' (of the wall W) of height l, which is disjoint from X and dividing in $G - X$, and has a 2-cell embedding with per(W') in the outer face boundary in $G - X$. Moreover, the unique vertex v which has distance exactly $l/2$ from the per(W') in the wall W' is irrelevant with respect to a K-minor, where K is any graph in the Petersen family. Furthermore, no matter how we give a flat embedding of the graph $G - v$ in 3-space $\mathbb{R}^3$, the embedding of $G - v$ can be changed so that, after putting the vertex v back to the resulting embedding, the resulting embedding of G is flat, or*
3. *either there is a reduction as in Lemma 2.3, or there is a separation (A, B) of order at most three in $G - X$ such that $V(A) \cap V(B)$ only involves the vertices in the comp(W) in $G - X$, and B contains all the vertices of the per(W). Moreover, if the second happens, G contains both $(A \cup X)^+$ and $(B \cup X)^+$ as minors. Hence it follows that this separation $(A \cup X, B \cup X)$ is a reduction as in Theorem 2.4. Note that it is a separation of order at most 4 in G.*

Due to space restrictions we refer to the full version of this paper for a proof of Theorem 3.5 and the following main result of this section.

THEOREM 3.6. *Let $G, W, f, l, w(l), w'(l)$ be as in Theorem 3.5. Suppose the wall W is given. Then there is an $O(n)$ time algorithm, where n is the number of vertices of G, to construct one of the following:*

1. *one of the graphs in the Petersen family in G as a minor, or*
2. *for some subset X of at most one vertex of G there is a proper subwall W' (of the wall W) of height l, which is disjoint from X, dividing in $G - X$, and has a 2-cell embedding with per(W') in the outer face boundary in $G - X$. Moreover, we can find an irrelevant vertex as in the second conclusion of Theorem 3.5, or*

3. *either there is a reduction as in Lemma 2.3, or there is a separation (A, B) of order at most three in $G - X$ such that $V(A) \cap V(B)$ only involves the vertices in the comp(W) in $G - X$, and B contains all the vertices of the per(W'). Moreover, if the second happens, G contains both $(A \cup X)^+$ and $(B \cup X)^+$ as minors. Hence it follows that this separation $(A \cup X, B \cup X)$ is a reduction as in Theorem 2.4. Note that it is a separation of order at most 4 in G.*

4. LINKLESS EMBEDDINGS ON GRAPH CLASSES OF BOUNDED TREE-WIDTH

In this section we present a linear time algorithm for the linkless embedding problem on graph classes of bounded tree-width. The algorithm is based on various results about flat embeddings presented in Section 2.2. We first consider the case of 4-connected graphs.

LEMMA 4.1. *There is an algorithm which for a given 4-connected graph G either returns a flat embedding of G or produces a minor $H \preceq G$ of the Petersen family, in time $f(\text{tw}(G)) \cdot |G|$, for some computable function $f : \mathbb{N} \rightarrow \mathbb{N}$.*

PROOF. Due to space restrictions we only prove the existence of an $f(\text{tw}(G)) \cdot |G|^2$-algorithm here (which is enough for the application in Section 5). With some further effort this can be improved to linear time. Details of the linear time algorithm can be found in the full version of this paper.

Given G, we first test in linear time (for instance using Courcelle's theorem [10]) if any graph in the Petersen family is a minor of G. If no such minor is found, we compute a flat embedding of G. The lemmas outlined in Section 2.2 and the discussion at the end of that section suggest the following simple algorithm for constructing a flat embedding of a 4-connected graph in $\mathbb{R}^3$.

1. If G is planar, compute the unique embedding of G into $\mathbb{R}^3$. Otherwise, choose a Kuratowski subgraph of G and embed it flat into $\mathbb{R}^3$.

2. While there is a Kuratowski subgraph K of G that is not yet embedded, compute two adjacent Kuratowski subgraphs H, H' so that H is already embedded but at least one edge of H' is not yet embedded. As discussed in Section 2.2, there is a unique way of extending the embedding of H to an embedding of $H \cup H'$ which can easily be computed.

3. Once all Kuratowski subgraphs are embedded, the rest of the graph is planar and, by Lemma 3, there is an essentially unique extension to an embedding of G.

We claim that this algorithm can be implemented to run in time $f(\text{tw}(G)) \cdot |G|^2$, where f is a computable function $f : \mathbb{N} \rightarrow \mathbb{N}$. Given a 4-connected graph G, first use Bodlaender's algorithm [4] to compute an optimal tree-decomposition of G in time $g(\text{tw}(G)) \cdot |G|$, where $g : \mathbb{N} \rightarrow \mathbb{N}$ is some computable function. Using a planarity algorithm [5, 19, 54], we can find the Kuratowski subgraph K of G required in step 1 in linear time or conclude that G is planar, in which case we can easily compute the unique embedding into $\mathbb{R}^3$. Towards the second step, note that the while loop can take at most $||G||$ iterations as each iteration embeds at least one new vertex or edge. In each iteration we have to find the two Kuratowski subgraphs H and H'. This can easily be done in linear time, either by dynamic programming or by realizing that the condition "H, H' are Kuratowski subgraphs of which H is already embedded and H' is not" has a straightforward definition in monadic second-order logic (MSO). It follows from a result by Arnborg, Lagergren and Seese [2] that given the MSO-definition, the graphs H, H' can be computed in time $h(\text{tw}(G)) \cdot ||G||$. As for all graphs $||G|| \leq \text{tw}(G) \cdot |G|$, the result follows. □

We are now ready to present the complete linear time algorithm for computing flat embeddings of linklessly embeddable graphs of bounded tree-width.

LEMMA 4.2. *There is an algorithm which, on input G, solves the* Flat and Linkless Embedding *problem for G in time $f(\text{tw}(G)) \cdot |G|$, for some computable function $f : \mathbb{N} \rightarrow \mathbb{N}$.*

Due to space restrictions, we only sketch the proof here. A complete proof can be found in the full version of this paper. Let G be given. Using Bodlaender's algorithm [4], we first compute a tree-decomposition of G of width $\text{tw}(G)$ in time $g(\text{tw}(G)) \cdot |G|$. The next step is to test if any graph of the Petersen family is a minor of G. This can be done in time $g'(\text{tw}(G)) \cdot |G|$. If G contains a Petersen family minor, we can conclude that G has no linkless embeddings and return the minor. Otherwise, we split the graph into its 4-connected components using dynamic programming over the tree-decomposition. After some preprocessing in which we use $Y\Delta$-transformations to ensure that 3-separations are joined at triangles, we then use Lemma 4.1 to find flat embeddings of 4-connected components. The individual embeddings can then be glued together along the disks bounding 3-separations.

5. ALGORITHM

Finally, we are ready to present the complete algorithm.

Flat and Linkless Embedding

Input: A graph G.

Output: Either detect one of Petersen's family graphs as a minor in G or return a flat (and hence also linkless) embedding of G in $\mathbb{R}^3$.

Running time: $O(n^2)$.

Description: Initially, we delete all vertices of degree at most 1. Also, if there is a vertex v of degree 2, then we just contract vu, where u is one of the two neighbors of v. Thus we may assume that minimum degree is at least 3.

Step 1. If there is a vertex v of degree 3, then we perform $Y\Delta$ operation at v. We repeat doing this as long as there are some vertices of degree 3. Hereafter, we may assume that the minimum degree of the resulting graph G is at least 4.

Step 2. Test if the tree-width of the current graph G is small or not, say smaller than some value f, where f comes from Theorem 3.5. This can be done in linear time by the algorithm of Bodlaender [4]. If the tree-width is at least f, then go to Step 3. Otherwise we use the algorithm described in Lemma 4.2 to compute a flat embedding in linear time or certify that no such embedding exist by computing a minor of G in the Petersen family.

Step 3. It is easy to see that if the current graph G has at least $2^6|V(G)|$ edges, then one can easily find a K_6-minor in linear time (see [38]). So we may assume that the current graph G has at most $2^6|V(G)|$ edges.

At this moment, the tree-width of the current graph G is at least f. Use the algorithm of Bodlaender [4] (or the algorithm of Robertson and Seymour [41]) to construct a wall W of height at least $w'(l)$, where $w'(l)$ is as in Theorem 3.4. Perform the algorithm of Theorem 3.6 to find a separation or reduction as in the third conclusion of Theorem 3.6, or an irrelevant vertex v, or a minor of a graph in the Petersen family. If the third outcome occurs, then output the minor. If the second one happens, then we recurse this algorithm to $G - v$. If the first one happens, then we reduce the size of the the current graph G as in the proof of Theorem 3.6. This completes the description of the algorithm. □

The correctness of Steps 2 and 3 follow from Sections 3 and 4. It is easy to see that degree 1 vertices can be deleted and degree 2 vertices can be contracted. Thus the correctness of Step 1 follows.

The time complexity of the algorithm can be estimated as follows. All individual steps in the above algorithm can be done in linear time. Applying the recursion results in another factor of n. Thus the time complexity is $O(n^2)$.

Acknowledgments. Part of this work was done while all the authors participated the workshop "Graph Minors" at BIRS (Banff International Research Stations) in October 2008.

6. REFERENCES

[1] I. Agol, J. Hass, and W. Thurston, The computational complexity of knot genus and spanning area. *Trans. Amer. Math. Soc.* **358** (2006), 3821–3850. Also, *Proc. 34th ACM Symposium on Theory of Computing (STOC'02)*, 761–766.

[2] S. Arnborg, J. Lagergren, and D. Seese, Easy problems for tree-decomposable graphs, *Journal of Algorithms* **12(2)** (1991), 308–340.

[3] B. S. Baker, Approximation algorithms for NP-complete problems on planar graphs, *J. ACM*, **41** (1994), 153–180.

[4] H. L. Bodlaender, A linear-time algorithm for finding tree-decomposition of small treewidth, *SIAM J. Comput.* **25** (1996), 1305–1317.

[5] N. Chiba, T. Nishizeki, S. Abe and T. Ozawa, A linear time algorithm for embedding planar graphs using PQ-trees, *J. Comput. System Sci.* **30** (1985), 54–76.

[6] Y. Colin de Verdière, Sur un nouvel invariant des graphes et un critère de planarité, *J. Combin. Theory, Ser. B* **50** (1990), 11–21.

[7] Y. Colin de Verdière, Multiplicities of eigenvalues and tree-width of graphs, *J. Combin. Theory, Ser. B* **74** (1998), 121–146.

[8] Y. Colin de Verdière, On a new graph invariant and a criterion of planarity, in Graph Structure Theory, N. Robertson and P. Seymour, editors, Contemp. Math. 147, pp. 137–147, Amer. Math. Soc., Providence, RI, 1993.

[9] J. H. Conway and C. McA. Gordon, Knots and links in spatial graphs, *J. Graph Theory*, **7** (1983), 445–453.

[10] B. Courcelle, Graph rewriting: An algebraic and logic approach. In. J. van Leeuwen, Editor, *Handbook of Theoretical Computer Science*, **2**, 194–242, Elsevier Sicenence Publishers, (1990).

[11] M. Dehn, Über die Topologie des dreidimensional Raumes, *Math. Annalen*, **69** (1910), 137–168.

[12] R. Diestel, Graph Theory, 2nd Edition, Springer, 2000.

[13] R. Diestel, K. Yu. Gorbunov, T. R. Jensen, and C. Thomassen, Highly connected sets and the excluded grid theorem, *J. Combin. Theory Ser. B* **75** (1999), 61–73.

[14] D. Eppstein, Subgraph isomorphism in planar graphs and related problems, *J. Graph Algor. Appl.*, **3** (1999), 1–27.

[15] M. Grigni, E. Koutsoupias, and C. Papadimitriou, An approximation scheme for planar graphs TSP, *Proc. 36th Symposium on Foundations of Computer Science, (FOCS'95)*, 640–646, (1995).

[16] J. Hass, J. Lagarias and N. Pippenger, The computational complexity of knot and link problems, *J. ACM* **46** (1999), 185–211. Also, *Proc. 38th Annual Symposium on Foundations of Computer Science (FOCS'97)*, 172–181.

[17] W. Haken, Theorie der Normalflachen: Ein Isotopiekriterium für den Kreisknoten, *Acta Math.* **105** (1961), 245–375.

[18] M. Hara, S. Tani and M. Yamamoto, Unknotting is in AM ∩ co-AM, *Proc. 16th Annual ACM-SIAM Symposium on Discrete Algorithms (SODA'05)*, 359–364.

[19] J. E. Hopcroft and R. Tarjan, Efficient planarity testing, *J. ACM* **21** (1974), 549–568.

[20] H. van der Holst, A polynomial-time algorithm to find a linkless embedding of a graph, *J. Combin. Theory, Series B, 99 (2009), 512-530.*

[21] K. Kawarabayashi and B. Reed, Computing crossing number in linear time, *Proc. 39th ACM Symposium on Theory of Computing (STOC'07)*, 382–390.

[22] K. Kawarabayashi and B. Mohar, Graph and Map Isomorphism and all polyhedral embeddings in linear time, *Proc. 40th ACM Symposium on Theory of Computing (STOC'08)*, 471–480.

[23] K. Kawarabayashi, B. Mohar and B. Reed, A simpler linear time algorithm for embedding graphs on a surface and for bounded tree-width graphs, *Proc. 49th Annual Symposium on Foundations of Computer Science (FOCS'08)*, 771–780.

[24] K. Kawarabayashi, S. Norine, R. Thomas and P. Wollan, K_6 minors in large 6-connected graphs, *submitted.* Available at `http://www.math.princeton.edu/~snorin/papers/k6large.pdf`.

[25] K. Kawarabayashi and P. Wollan, A shorter proof of the graph minor algorithm – the uniquely linkage theorem –, *to appaer in Proc. 42nd ACM Symposium on Theory of Computing (STOC'10).*

[26] P. N. Klein, A linear time approximation scheme for TSP for planar wieghted graphs, *Proc. 46th Symposium on Foundations of Computer Science (FOCS'05)*, 146–155, (2005).

[27] C. Kuratowski Sur le problème des courbes gauches en topologie *Fund. Math.* **15** (1930), 271–283.

[28] R.J. Lipton and R. E. Tarjan, Applications of a planar separator theorem, *Siam J. Comput.*, **9** (1980), 615–627.

[29] L. Lovász, Steinitz representations, 2000, http://www.cs.elte.hu/~lovasz/klee.ppt

[30] L. Lovász and A. Schrijver, On the null space of a Colin de Verdière matrix, *Ann. Inst. Fourier (Grenoble)* **49** (1999), 1017–1026.

[31] L. Lovász and A. Schrijver, A Borsuk theorem for antipodal links and a spectral characterization of linklessly embeddable graphs, *Proc. Amer. Math. Soc.* **126** (1998), 1275–1285.

[32] C.L. Lucchesi and D. H. Younger, A minimax theorem for directed graphs, *J. London Math. Soc.* **17** (1978), 369–374.

[33] B. Mohar, Embedding graphs in an arbitrary surface in linear time, In *Proc. 28th ACM Symposium on Theory of Computing (STOC'96)*, 392–397.

[34] B. Mohar, A linear time algorithm for embedding graphs in an arbitrary surface, *SIAM J. Discrete Math.* **12** (1999) 6–26.

[35] B. Mohar and C. Thomassen, Graphs on Surfaces, Johns Hopkins University Press, Baltimore, MD, 2001.

[36] R. Motwani, A. Raghunathan and H. Saran, Constructive results from graph minors: Linkless embeddings, *Proc. 29th Annual Symposium on Foundations of Computer Science (FOCS'88)*, 398–409.

[37] B. Reed, Tree width and tangles: a new connectivity measure and some applications, in *"Surveys in Combinatorics, 1997 (London)"*, London Math. Soc. Lecture Note Ser. **241**, Cambridge Univ. Press, Cambridge, 1997, pp. 87–162.

[38] B. Reed and D. Wood, A linear time algorithm to find a separator in a graph with an excluded minor, *submitted.*

[39] N. Robertson and P. D. Seymour, Graph minors. V. Excluding a planar graph, *J. Combin. Theory Ser. B* **41** (1986), 92–114.

[40] N. Robertson, P. D. Seymour, Graph Minors. IX. Disjoint crossed paths, *J. Combin. Theory Ser. B* **49**, (1990) 40–77.

[41] N. Robertson and P. D. Seymour, Graph minors. XIII. The disjoint paths problem, *J. Combin. Theory Ser. B* **63** (1995), 65–110.

[42] N. Robertson and P. D. Seymour, Graph minors. XX. Wagner's Conjecture, *J. Combin. Theory Ser. B* **92** (2004), 325–357.

[43] N. Robertson, P. D. Seymour, and R. Thomas, Hadwiger's conjecture for K_6-free graphs, *Combinatorica* **13** (1993), 279–361.

[44] N. Robertson, P. D. Seymour and R. Thomas, Quickly excluding a planar graph, *J. Combin. Theory Ser. B* **62** (1994), 323–348.

[45] N. Robertson, P. D. Seymour, and R. Thomas, Kuratowski chains, *J. Combin. Theory Ser. B* **64** (1995), 127–154.

[46] N. Robertson, P. D. Seymour and R. Thomas, Petersen family minors, *J. Combin. Theory Ser. B* **64** (1995), 155–184.

[47] N. Robertson, P. D. Seymour and R. Thomas, Sach's linkless embedding conjecture, *J. Combin. Theory Ser. B* **64** (1995), 185–227.

[48] N. Robertson, P. D. Seymour and R. Thomas, A survey of linkless embeddings, *Contemporary Mathematics* **147** (1993), 125–136.

[49] M. Scharlemann and A. Thompson, Detecting unknotted graphs in 3-space, *J. Diff. Geometry* **34** (1991), 539–560.

[50] P. Seymour, Disjoint paths in graphs, *Discrete Math.* **29** (1980), 293–309.

[51] P. D. Seymour, Packing circuits in eulerian digraphs, *Combinatorica* **16**, (1996), 223–231.

[52] C. Thomassen, 2-linked graph, *European Journal of Combinatorics* **1** (1980), 371–378.

[53] D. J. A. Welsh, The complexity of knots. In *Quo Vadis, Graph Theory?* J. Gimbel, J. Kennedy and L.V. Quintoo eds. *Analls of Discrete Mathematics* **55** (1993), 159–172.

[54] S. G. Williamson, Depth-first search and Kuratowski subgraphs, *J. ACM* **31** (1984), 681–693.

[55] Y.-Q. Wu, On planarity of graphs in 3-manifolds, *Comment. Math. Helv.* **67** (1992) 635–647.

Visualizing 3D Euler Spirals

Gur Harary
Department of Electrical Engineering
Technion
gur@tx.technion.ac.il

Ayellet Tal
Department of Electrical Engineering
Technion
ayellet@ee.technion.ac.il

ABSTRACT

This video describes a new type of 3D curves, which generalizes the family of 2D Euler spirals. They are defined as the curves having both their curvature and their torsion evolve linearly along the curve. The utility of these spirals for curve completion applications is demonstrated. This video accompanies the paper presented in [4].

Categories and Subject Descriptors

I.3 [**Computer Graphics**]: Computational Geometry and Object Modeling—*Curve, surface, solid, and object representations*

General Terms

Algorithms, Design

Keywords

Euler spirals, 3D curves

1. 3D EULER SPIRALS

This video visually describes the 3D Euler spirals presented in [4] and their application to shape completion. Our curves can be considered as an extension to three dimensions of the planar Euler spirals. A 2D Euler spiral is the curve whose curvature evolves linearly with arc-length. A 3D Euler spiral is defined as the curve having both its curvature and its torsion evolve linearly along the curve (Figure 1):

$$\begin{aligned}\kappa(s) &= \kappa_0 + \gamma s,\\ \tau(s) &= \tau_0 + \delta s.\end{aligned}$$

Figure 1: A 3D Euler spiral

SCG'10, June 13–16, 2010, Snowbird, Utah, USA.
ACM 978-1-4503-0016-2/10/06.

It is proved that the suggested curve satisfies some desirable properties – ones that have been claimed to produce visually-pleasing curves [6]. In particular, our curves hold the following properties:

1. Invariance to similarity transformations (translation, rotation, and scaling).
2. Symmetry: The curve leaving the point $\mathbf{x}_0$ with tangent $\vec{T}_0$ and reaching the point $\mathbf{x}_f$ with tangent $\vec{T}_f$, coincides with the curve leaving the point $\mathbf{x}_f$ with tangent $-\vec{T}_f$ and reaching the point $\mathbf{x}_0$ with tangent $-\vec{T}_0$.
3. Extensibility: For every point $\mathbf{x}_m \in \mathcal{C}$ between points $\mathbf{x}_0$ and $\mathbf{x}_f$, the curves $\mathcal{C}_1$ between $\mathbf{x}_0$ and $\mathbf{x}_m$ and $\mathcal{C}_2$ between $\mathbf{x}_m$ and $\mathbf{x}_f$ coincide with $\mathcal{C}$, each in its own section.
4. Smoothness: The tangent is defined at every point, i.e., $\frac{\partial \mathcal{C}}{\partial s}$ is finite. (In fact, our curves are C^∞-smooth.)
5. Roundness: If $\mathcal{C}$ interpolates two point-tangent pairs lying on a circle, then $\mathcal{C}$ is a circle.

2. 3D CURVE COMPLETION

3D curve features convey important information about the shape. They are used as shape features, as strokes for sketch-based interaction, in non-photo realistic rendering, and in a variety of mesh analysis algorithms. However, it is often the case that curves appear incomplete due to either missing parts of the model, or due to the failure of edge detection algorithms. In these cases, we would like to complete the curves.

Shape completion has been an important task in computational geometry with applications to CAD and computer graphics [1, 2, 9]. While most of the work has focused on completing or repairing polyhedra and CAD models, we focus on completing curves in three dimensions.

We assume we are given two points and their associated tangents: $\left(\mathbf{x}_0, \vec{T}_0\right)$ and $\left(\mathbf{x}_f, \vec{T}_f\right)$. Our goal is to find the parameters $\kappa_0, \tau_0, \gamma, \delta, L \in \mathbb{R}$ that define the 3D Euler spiral that starts at $\mathbf{x}_0$ and $\vec{T}_0$ and minimizes both the difference between the curve's position at $s = L$ and $\mathbf{x}_f$, and the difference between the curve's tangent at $s = L$ and $\vec{T}_f$.

We propose a gradient-descent algorithm to perform this task. A major consideration in this approach is the initialization. Our algorithm is initialized using a planar Euler spiral. We define the plane for which three out of the four boundary conditions hold: $\mathbf{x}_0$, $\mathbf{x}_f$, and $\vec{T}_0$. The resulting

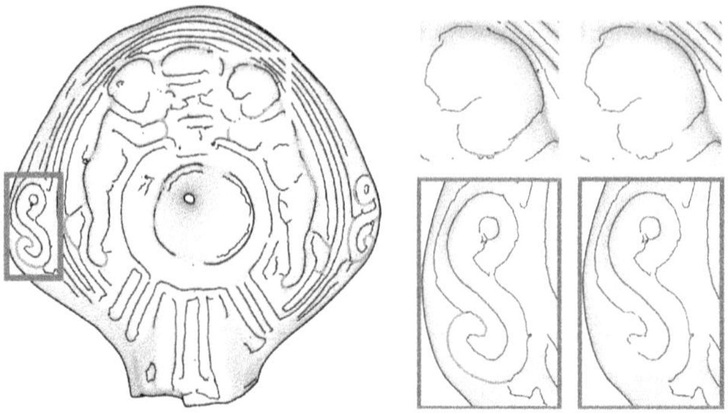

(a) Curve completion (b) Zoom-in

Figure 2: Fixing the curves detected by [7]. Our curves (red) manage to capture the "S" shape, in contrast to the automatically-scaled Hermite splines (green).

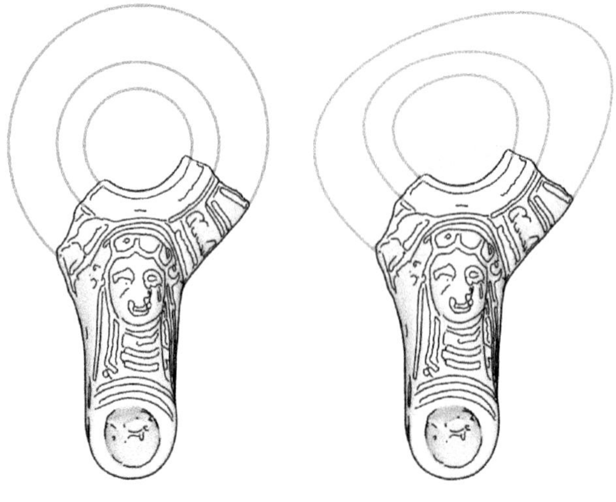

(a) Our completion (b) Hermite completion

Figure 3: 3D Euler spirals (red) complete the curves on a broken Hellenistic oil lamp – curves that would most likely be drawn if the model were complete. The scale of the Hermite splines is determined manually (magenta), since the automatically-scaled splines (green) are inferior due to the large ratio between the length of the curve and the size of the model. Note the perfect circular arcs of our curves.

planar Euler spiral interpolates $\vec{T}_0$ at $\mathbf{x}_0$ and the projection of $\vec{T}_f$ onto the plane at $\mathbf{x}_f$. The parameters of this 2D spiral κ_0, γ, L are used to initialize our curves. Since it lies on a plane, the torsion's parameters are initialized to zero ($\tau_0 = 0$, $\delta = 0$).

Applications: Our 3D Euler spirals are utilized in two completion applications. In the first application, the entire model is given together with the curves on its surface. These curves are generated using algorithms for curve detection on surfaces, such as valleys and ridges [10], suggestive contours [3], apparent ridges [5], demarcating curves [7], and relief edges [8]. These algorithms often fail to detect curves on "weak" surface patches. Therefore, an algorithm for curve completion is needed. We show that our curves can be utilized for this task (Figure 2). Since our curves are not constrained to lie on any surface, the produced 3D Euler curves are projected to the surface. This is done by projecting each point on the curve to its closest point onto the surface.

The second application is the completion of partial objects in archaeology. Though archaeological artifacts are often found broken, the user is interested in drawing the curves that would be drawn if the entire model were given. Traditionally, the archaeological artist draws the artifact manually, "completing" the broken pieces. Instead, our curves can be drawn and viewed in 3D along with the scanned model (Figure 3).

Our curves are compared to Hermite splines and are shown to outperform them in the context of completion applications. For instance, they better capture the "S" shapes in curves (Figure 2) and circular arcs (Figure 3), which are prevalent in many real-life objects.

Video production: The algorithm was implemented in Matlab and C and ran on a 2Ghz Intel Core 2 Duo-processor laptop with 2Gb of memory. The video was produced using VirtualDub and Adobe Premiere Pro CS4.

3. REFERENCES

[1] G. Barequet and S. Kumar. Repairing CAD models. In *IEEE Visualization*, 1997.

[2] G. Barequet and M. Sharir. Filling gaps in the boundary of a polyhedron. *Computer Aided Geometric Design*, 12(2):207–229, 1995.

[3] D. DeCarlo, A. Finkelstein, S. Rusinkiewicz, and A. Santella. Suggestive contours for conveying shape. *ACM Trans. Graph.*, 22(3):848–855, 2003.

[4] G. Harary and A. Tal. 3D Euler spirals for 3D curve completion. In *ACM Symposium on Computational Geometry*, 2010.

[5] T. Judd, F. Durand, and E. Adelson. Apparent ridges for line drawing. *ACM Trans. Graph.*, 26(3):19:1–7, 2007.

[6] D. Knuth. Mathematical typography. *American Mathematical Society*, 1(2):337–372, 1979.

[7] M. Kolomenkin, I. Shimshoni, and A. Tal. Demarcating curves for shape illustration. *ACM Trans. Graph.*, 27(5):157:1–9, 2008.

[8] M. Kolomenkin, I. Shimshoni, and A. Tal. On edge detection on surfaces. In *IEEE Conference on Computer Vision and Pattern Recognition (CVPR)*, pages 2767–2774, 2009.

[9] A. Sharf, M. Alexa, and D. Cohen-Or. Context-based surface completion. *ACM Trans. Graph.*, 23(3):878–887, 2004.

[10] S. Yoshizawa, A. Belyaev, and H. P. Seidel. Fast and robust detection of crest lines on meshes. In *ACM Symposium on Solid and Physical Modeling*, pages 227–232, 2005.

Shape Approximation Using k-Order alpha-Hulls

Dmitry N. Krasnoshchekov
krasnd@idg.chph.ras.ru
Institute for Dynamics of the Geospheres
Russian Academy of Sciences
Leninsky pr. 38 korp. 1, Moscow 119334 Russia

Valentin Polishchuk Arto Vihavainen
firstname.lastname@cs.helsinki.fi
Helsinki Institute for Information Technology
CS Department, University of Helsinki
P. O. Box 68, FI-00014, Finland

ABSTRACT

This video illustrates the notion of the *k-order* α-hull of a planar point set – a generalization of the α-hull and the k-hull.

Categories and Subject Descriptors

F.2.2 [**Analysis of Algorithms and Problem Complexity**]: Nonnumerical Algorithms and Problems—*Geometrical problems and computations*; I.3.5 [**Computer Graphics**]: Computational Geometry and Object Modeling—*Geometric algorithms, languages, and systems*

General Terms

Algorithms

1. DEFINITIONS

Let $S \subset \mathbb{R}^2$ be a set of points in the plane. Assume that no 3 points of S lie on a line, and that no 4 points are cocircular.

DEFINITION 1.1. *The* convex hull *of S is the complement of the union of all halfplanes that contain no points of S.*

Let α be a positive number.

DEFINITION 1.2. *[1] The* α-hull *of S is the complement of the union of all radius-α disks that contain no points of S. The α-shape of S is a graph whose vertices are points in S, with an edge between points $p, q \in S$ whenever there exists a radius-α disk that has p, q on its boundary and has no points of S in its interior.*

Let k be a non-negative integer.

DEFINITION 1.3. *[2] The k-hull of S is the complement of the union of all halfplanes that contain at most k points of S.*

DEFINITION 1.4. *The* k-order α-hull *of S is the complement of the union of all radius-α disks that contain at most k points of S.*

The k-order α-hull is the generalization of both the α-hull and the k-hull. The α-hull is the k-order α-hull for $k = 0$; the k-hull is the k-order α-hull for $\alpha = \infty$.

SCG'10, June 13–16, 2010, Snowbird, Utah, USA.
ACM 978-1-4503-0016-2/10/06.

DEFINITION 1.5. *The* k-order *α-shape of S is a graph whose vertices are points in S, with an edge between points $p, q \in S$ whenever there exists a radius-α disk that has p, q on its boundary and has k points of S in its interior.*

2. DESCRIPTION OF VIDEO

Individual frames were created with the Java application coded by the authors; the k-order α-shapes were computed with a brute-force algorithm. The frames were assembled into a movie using AVI-Mux GUI. Sound was recorded using Ardour. The video was compressed with VirtualDubMod.

The video opens by recapping the definitions of the convex hull, α-hull, α-shape and k-hull. It explains that the convex hull of S defines, in a sense, the "shape" of S. The convex hull may give only a crude approximation of the shape; the need for a finer shape reconstruction is satisfied with the α-hull and α-shape. The video animates how the α-hull and α-shape of a point set change with α.

We next show the k-hull. In particular, we animate how k-hull gets "in and out" of S, serving as level set for the halfplane depth function.

In the middle of the video, we define the k-order α-hull and show the connection between the convex hull, α-hull, k-hull, and k-order α-hull. We animate how the k-order α-hull and k-order α-shape depend on k (Fig. 1).

We then highlight the use of k-order α-shape in robust shape reconstruction. A point set with 2 outliers is shown. The α-shape is missing an important feature of the shape of the set – the hole. Using k-order α-shape with $k > 0$ brings the hole back (Fig. 2).

Finally, we demonstrate how the k-order α-shape with $\alpha < \infty$ helps to identify level sets for a depth function of multivariate data – a setting in which the k-hull fails (Fig. 3).

The video finishes with the invitation to play with our Java applet for the k-order versions of graphs on planar point sets. The address of the applet is `http://www.cs.helsinki.fi/group/compgeom/applets/shapes/` or `http://tinyurl.com/k-order-graphs` .

Acknowledgments. This work is partially supported by Academy of Finland grant 118653 (ALGODAN).

3. REFERENCES

[1] H. Edelsbrunner, D. G. Kirkpatrick, and R. Seidel. On the shape of a set of points in the plane. *IEEE Trans. Inform. Theory*, IT-29:551–559, 1983.

[2] R. Cole, M. Sharir, and C. K. Yap. On k-hulls and related problems. *SIJCOMP*, 16(1):61–77, 1987.

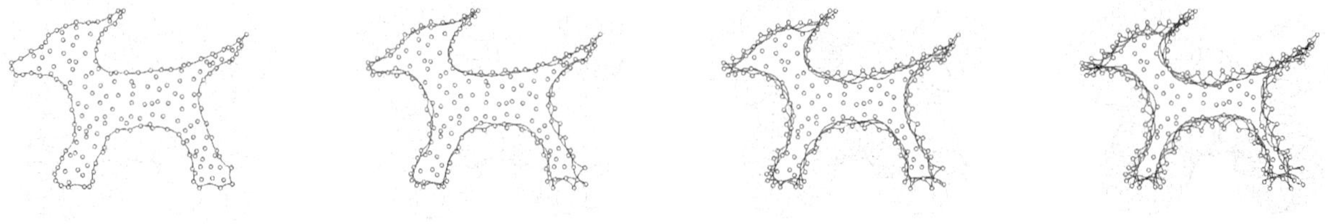

Figure 1: The k-order α-hull for $k = 0, 1, 2, 3$.

Figure 2: k-order α-shape ignores the outliers. From left to right: An α-shape. Two outliers change the picture. k-order α-shape with $k = 1, 2$ brings it back.

Figure 3: The points come in clusters. Left: The 4-hull (4-depth contour) oversmoothes the data; the points in the center of the picture are incorrectly classified as being deep inside S. Right: 4-order α-hull (for a suitable $\alpha < \infty$) better fits the data, independently identifying 4-depth contours within each cluster.

Constructing Reeb Graphs using Cylinder Maps

Harish Doraiswamy
Department of Computer Science and Automation
Indian Institute of Science
Bangalore 560012, India
harishd@csa.iisc.ernet.in

Aneesh Sood
Department of Computer Science and Automation
Indian Institute of Science
Bangalore 560012, India
aneesh.sood@gmail.com

Vijay Natarajan
Department of Computer Science and Automation
Supercomputer Education and Research Centre
Indian Institute of Science
Bangalore 560012, India
vijayn@csa.iisc.ernet.in

ABSTRACT

The Reeb graph of a scalar function represents the evolution of the topology of its level sets. In this video, we describe a near-optimal output-sensitive algorithm for computing the Reeb graph of scalar functions defined over manifolds. Key to the simplicity and efficiency of the algorithm is an alternate definition of the Reeb graph that considers equivalence classes of level sets instead of individual level sets. The algorithm works in two steps. The first step locates all critical points of the function in the domain. Arcs in the Reeb graph are computed in the second step using a simple search procedure that works on a small subset of the domain that corresponds to a pair of critical points. The algorithm is also able to handle non-manifold domains.

Categories and Subject Descriptors: I.3.5 [Computational Geometry and Object Modeling]: Geometric algorithms, languages, and systems

General Terms: Algorithms

1. INTRODUCTION

The Reeb graph of a scalar function is obtained by mapping each connected component of its level sets to a point. Level set components that contain critical points of the function map to nodes of the graph. The abstract representation of level-set topology within the Reeb graph enables development of simple and efficient methods for modeling objects and visualizing scientific data. They serve as an effective user interface for selecting meaningful level sets [1] and for designing transfer functions for volume rendering [8].

In this video, we illustrate an efficient two-step algorithm[†] for computing the Reeb graph of a piecewise-linear (PL) function in $O(n+l+t\log t)$ time, where n is the number of triangles in the input mesh, t is the number of critical points of the function, and l is the size (number of edges) of all critical level sets. For a comparison of our algorithm with existing approaches we refer the reader to the paper where we proposed the algorithm [4].

2. BACKGROUND

Let $\mathbb{M}^d$ denote a d-manifold with or without boundary. A smooth, real-valued function $f : \mathbb{M}^d \rightarrow \mathbb{R}$ is called a *Morse function* if it satisfies the following conditions [3]:

1. All critical points of f are non-degenerate and lie in the interior of $\mathbb{M}^d$.
2. All critical points of the restriction of f to the boundary of $\mathbb{M}^d$ are non-degenerate.
3. All critical values are distinct *i.e.*, $f(p) \neq f(q)$ for all critical points $p \neq q$.

The above conditions typically do not hold in practice for PL functions. However, simulated perturbation of the function [5, Section 1.4] ensures that no two critical values are equal. A total order on the vertices helps in consistently identifying the vertex with the higher function value between a pair of vertices.

Critical points and level sets. Critical points of a smooth function are exactly where the gradient becomes zero. Critical points of a PL function are located at vertices of the mesh [2].

The preimage of a real value is called a *level set*. The level set of a regular value is a $(d-1)$-manifold with or without boundary, possibly containing multiple connected components. We are interested in the evolution of level sets against increasing function value. Significant topological changes occur at critical points, whereas topology of the level set is preserved across regular points [6].

The *link* of a vertex consists of all vertices adjacent to it and the induced edges, triangles, and higher-order simplices. Adjacent vertices with lower function value and their induced simplices constitute the *lower link*, whereas the adjacent vertices with higher function value and their induced simplices constitute the *upper link*. In the context of Reeb graphs, we are only interested in critical points that modify the number of level set components. So, it is sufficient to count the number of connected components of the lower / upper link for identifying these critical points. Given a critical point c_i, call the level set $f^{-1}(f(c_i))$ as a *critical level set*.

Reeb graph. The *Reeb graph* of f is obtained by contracting each connected component of a level set to a point [7]. The Reeb graph expresses the evolution of connected components of level sets as a graph whose nodes correspond to critical points of the function. Nodes corresponding to minima and maxima have degree one. A node that corresponds to a saddle has degree three if the saddle merges / splits level set components. Genus modifying saddles do not alter the number of level set components. They are optionally included into the Reeb graph as degree two nodes.

The above description of the Reeb graph focuses on the mapping between individual level set components and nodes or points within arcs of the graph. We propose the use of an alternate but equivalent mapping, where nodes are mapped to components of critical level sets, and each arc is mapped to a *cylinder*, which is a collection of regular level set components that are topologically equivalent to each other. The advantage of our proposed alternate map is that a

[†]The algorithm is described in a paper that appeared in the Proceedings of the International Symposium on Algorithms and Computation [4].

SCG'10, June 13–16, 2010, Snowbird, Utah, USA.
ACM 978-1-4503-0016-2/10/06.

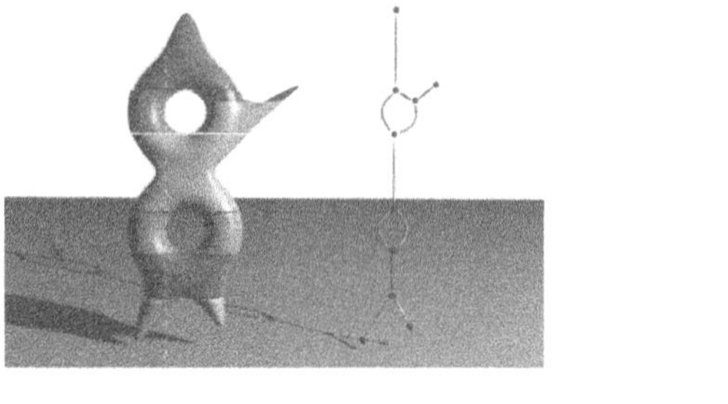

Figure 1: Reeb graph of the height function defined on a solid 2-torus. Reeb graph tracks the topology of level sets.

simple and efficient algorithm to compute the Reeb graph follows immediately from the mapping.

3. THE REEB GRAPH ALGORITHM

We now describe an algorithm [4] that computes the Reeb graph of a PL function f defined on a 3-manifold. We assume that the input manifold is represented by a triangulated mesh, the function is sampled at vertices, and linearly interpolated within each simplex.

The algorithm follows from the alternate mapping described in the previous section. It consists of two steps:

1. Locating critical points in the domain and sorting them based on function value.
2. Identifying pairs of critical points that define cylinders and inserting the corresponding arcs in the Reeb graph.

The link of a vertex in a 3-manifold is a triangulation of a sphere. The vertex is *regular* if it has exactly one lower link component and one upper link component. All other vertices are *critical*. A critical point is a *maximum* if the upper link is empty and a *minimum* if the lower link is empty. Else, it is classified as a saddle. We perform a breadth first search over the link to count the number of components of the upper and lower links.

Level set and cylinder representation. The 3-manifold is represented by a tetrahedral mesh. A level set of the input scalar function is generically a surface that is represented by a collection of triangles. However, the algorithm requires only the 2-skeleton (vertices, edges, and triangles) representation of the domain and the 1-skeleton (vertices and edges) representation of level sets. This is because the 1-skeleton captures the connectivity of level sets, which is exactly what we aim to abstract into the Reeb graph. Edges in a level set of f lie within unique triangles in the domain. So, a level set is represented by a collection of triangles in the input mesh. Cylinders are also represented as a collection of mesh triangles. Specifically, the cylinder bounded by two critical level set components is represented by triangles that contain the intermediate level set components.

Connecting the critical points. We compute arcs in the Reeb graph by tracing paths within each cylinder. Let $\{c_1, c_2, \ldots, c_t\}$ be the ordered set of critical points with function values $\{f_1, f_2, \ldots, f_t\}$ and $f_x < f_y$ whenever $x < y$. Let L_i denote the set of triangles containing the components of the critical level set $f^{-1}(f_i)$ that is modified by c_i. The ith iteration of the algorithm connects c_i with a set of critical points c_p $(f_p > f_i)$.

Each component of the upper link corresponds to a potential new arc in the Reeb graph that connects c_i with a higher critical point. We trace the cylinders bounded below by a level set component of c_i in the ith iteration of the algorithm. Starting from a triangle incident on an upper link component of c_i, we march to an adjacent triangle that is incident on a vertex with a higher function value. This traversal is equivalent to tracing a path within a cylinder. We continue the traversal until we reach a triangle that contains an edge of the level set $f^{-1}(f_{i+1})$. We insert an arc into the Reeb graph between nodes corresponding to c_i and c_{i+1} if this triangle is part of the critical level set L_{i+1}. If the triangle does not belong to L_{i+1}, we continue the traversal until it reaches a higher critical level set. If a search initiated from two components of the upper link of c_i reaches the same component of a critical level set, then c_i is declared a genus modifying saddle and the Reeb graph remains unaffected. We obtain the Reeb graph of f once all critical points are processed.

Discussion. Tracking the connected components of the level set requires only a 1-skeleton representation, which can be extracted from the 2-skeleton of the input mesh. So, the algorithm works directly on the 2-skeleton representation of d-manifolds ($d \geq 2$). In the case of non-manifolds, we relax the definition of critical points to include all vertices that modify the topology of the level set. Candidate critical points are again located by counting the number of connected components of the lower and upper link.

Our algorithm in the worst case has an $O(n + l + t \log t)$ running time, where n is the number of triangles in the input, t is the number of critical points of the input PL function and l is the total size of all critical level sets. Though it is possible in theory that $l = O(n^2)$, we notice that l is usually $O(n)$ in practice.

4. ABOUT THE VIDEO

The video animates the various stages of our algorithm for computing the Reeb graph of the height function defined on a solid 2-torus shown in Figure 1. Models were created and rendered using *Blender* (http://www.blender.org) and our implementation of the algorithm. The volume rendered images showing Reeb graphs for various datasets was created using *VTK* (http://www.vtk.org). The video was edited using Blender.

Acknowledgements. Harish Doraiswamy is supported by Infosys Technologies Ltd., Bangalore, under the Infosys Fellowship Award. This work was supported by the Department of Science and Technology, India, under Grant SR/S3/EECE/048/2007.

5. REFERENCES

[1] C. L. Bajaj, V. Pascucci, and D. R. Schikore. The contour spectrum. In *Proc. IEEE Conf. Visualization*, pages 167–173, 1997.

[2] T. F. Banchoff. Critical points and curvature for embedded polyhedral surfaces. *Am. Math. Monthly*, 77:475–485, 1970.

[3] K. Cole-McLaughlin, H. Edelsbrunner, J. Harer, V. Natarajan, and V. Pascucci. Loops in Reeb graphs of 2-manifolds. *Disc. Comput. Geom.*, 32(2):231–244, 2004.

[4] H. Doraiswamy and V. Natarajan. Efficient output-sensitive construction of Reeb graphs. In *Proc. Intl. Symp. Algorithms and Computation*, pages 557–568, 2008.

[5] H. Edelsbrunner. *Geometry and Topology for Mesh Generation*. Cambridge Univ. Press, England, 2001.

[6] Y. Matsumoto. *An Introduction to Morse Theory*. Amer. Math. Soc., 2002. Translated from Japanese by K. Hudson and M. Saito.

[7] G. Reeb. Sur les points singuliers d'une forme de pfaff complètement intégrable ou d'une fonction numérique. *Comptes Rendus de L'Académie ses Séances, Paris*, 222:847–849, 1946.

[8] G. H. Weber, S. E. Dillard, H. Carr, V. Pascucci, and B. Hamann. Topology-controlled volume rendering. *IEEE Trans. Vis. Comput. Graph.*, 13(2):330–341, 2007.

Convexification of Polygons by Length Preserving Transformations

Adrian Dumitrescu*
Dept. of Computer Science
Univ. of Wisconsin-Milwaukee
WI 53201-0784, USA
ad@cs.uwm.edu

Evan Hilscher†
Dept. of Computer Science
Univ. of Wisconsin-Milwaukee
WI 53201-0784, USA
hilscher@uwm.edu

ABSTRACT

A length preserving transformation of a polygon is any transformation of its vertices that preserves the lengths of the edges. In the video segment we will demonstrate three types of length preserving transformations: pocket flips, flipturns, and pops. We present sequences of such operations and study their power (or weakness) in the attempt of convexifying simple polygons.

Categories and Subject Descriptors

G.2.3 [**Discrete Mathematics**]: Applications

General Terms

Algorithms, Theory

Keywords

Discrete geometry, polygon convexification, edge-length preserving transformation.

1. INTRODUCTION

Consider a polygon $P = \{p_1, \ldots, p_n\}$ in the plane, that could be simple or self-intersecting. A *pop* operation is the reflection of a vertex, say p_i, with respect to the line through its adjacent vertices p_{i-1} and p_{i+1} (as usual indexes are taken modulo n, i.e., $p_{n+1} = p_1$) [4]. Observe that for the operation to be well-defined we need that p_{i-1} and p_{i+1} are distinct. This operation belongs to the larger class of edge-length preserving transformations, when applied to polygons [4, 12, 13, 14]. It seems to have been used for the first time by Millet. If instead of reflecting p_i with respect to the line through its adjacent vertices p_{i-1} and p_{i+1}, the reflection is executed with respect to the midpoint of p_{i-1} and p_{i+1}, the operation is called a *popturn*; see [3, 4]. Observe that both the pop and the popturn are single-vertex operations.

Each is an instance of a "flip", defined informally, which has been studied at length. The most common variant of flip is the *pocket flip* (or just *flip*), first considered by Erdös [9]. Another variant is the *flipturn*, first considered by Kazarinoff, and later by Joss and Shannon; see [6, 11] for an account of their results. In contrast with pops and popturns, both the flip and the flipturn may involve multiple vertices. The inverse of a pocket flip, called *deflation*, has been also considered. Interestingly enough, with deflations, there exist examples that can perform this operation forever [10]. We briefly describe pocket flips and pocket flipturns next.

Consider a simple polygon. A *pocket* is a region exterior to the polygon but interior to its convex hull, bounded by a subchain of the polygon edges and the pocket *lid*, the edge of the convex hull connecting the endpoints of that subchain; see e.g., [7, p. 74]. Observe that any non-convex polygon has at least one pocket. A *flip* of a pocket consists of reflecting the pocket about the line through the pocket lid. Instead, a *flipturn* of a pocket consists of reflecting the pocket about the midpoint of the pocket lid. Observe that if P is simple and non-convex, the polygons resulting after a pocket flip, or a pocket flipturn are again simple. It is known that within both of these variants, convexification can be achieved. More precisely: given a simple polygon, it can be convexified by a finite sequence of pocket flips [6]. Similarly, it can be convexified by a finite sequence of pocket flipturns [11]. Moreover, the first result continues to hold for self-intersecting polygons, under broad assumptions, see [6]. While the convexifying sequence can be arbitrarily long for pocket flips (i.e., irrespective of n, the number of vertices), a quadratic number of operations always suffices in the case of flipturns [1, 2, 5]. There is an extensive bibliography pertaining to these subjects [7]. See also [6, 8] and the references therein. More results on edge-length preserving transformations and chord stretching can be found in [4, 12, 13, 14].

Regarding pop operations, Thurston gave an example of a simple polygon that becomes self-intersecting with any pop, see [7, p.81]. Ballinger and Thurston showed (according to [7, p. 81]) that almost any simple polygon can be convexified by pops if self-intersection is permitted; however no proof has been published. Until recently, it has remained an open problem whether there exist polygons that cannot be convexified by pops [7, Open Problem 5.3]. We have shown [8] that such polygons do indeed exist, from both classes, simple or self-intersecting, thereby answering the above open problem in its full generality.

Specifically, for every even $n \geq 6$, we define a family $\mathcal{A}_n$ of *alternating polygons* with n vertices, and show that any polygon from this family cannot be convexified by pop operations. This family contains simple, as well as non-simple (i.e., self-intersecting) polygons, as desired. It is interesting

*Supported in part by NSF CAREER grant CCF-0444188.
†Supported by NSF CAREER grant CCF-0444188.

SCG'10, June 13–16, 2010, Snowbird, Utah, USA.
ACM 978-1-4503-0016-2/10/06.

that this family is closed under pop operations: any pop operation applied to a polygon in $\mathcal{A}_n$, at any vertex, yields a polygon in $\mathcal{A}_n$. A sequence of pops executed on an alternating simple polygon with 6 vertices appears in Fig. 1. A key fact regarding alternating polygons is that for $k \geq 3$, no polygon in the family A_{2k} is convex. As a consequence, any polygon in this family is non-convexifiable by pop operations.

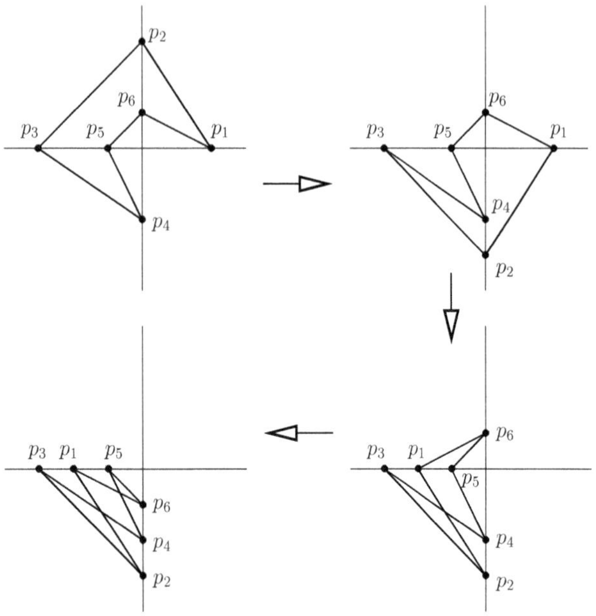

Figure 1: Sequence of three pops executed on vertices p_2, p_1, and p_6 of $\{p_1, p_2, p_3, p_4, p_5, p_6\}$.

2. THE VIDEO

The video presents operations from the class of edge-length preserving transformations, as they apply to polygons, such as pocket flips, pocket flipturns and pops. The video consists of three segments, each devoted to one of the above operations. While for pocket flips and pocket flipturns, the desired goal of convexification can be always achieved in a finite number of steps (sooner or later), pops cannot always succeed in this endeavor.

1. The first part introduces pocket flips and illustrates a family of quadrilaterals constructed by Joss and Shannon which require arbitrarily many pocket flips for convexification [11].

2. The second part introduces pocket flipturns and illustrates the quadratic lower bound on the length of the longest flipturn sequence in terms of the number of vertices [5].

3. The last part introduces the pop operation, and shows Thurston's example of a simple polygon that becomes self-intersecting with any pop. It then illustrates an instance from our class of alternating polygons that is non-convexifiable by pop operations.

Video location. The accompanying video is available for download[1].

[1] `https://pantherfile.uwm.edu/hilscher/public/lpt`

3. REFERENCES

[1] H.-K. Ahn, P. Bose, J. Czyzowicz, N. Hanusse, E. Kranakis, and P. Morin: Flipping your lid, *Geombinatorics*, **10(2)** (2000), 57–63.

[2] O. Aichholzer, C. Cortés, E. D. Demaine, V. Dujmović, J. Erickson, H. Meijer, M. Overmars, B. Balop, S. Ramaswami, and G. Toussaint: Flipturning polygons, *Discrete & Computational Geometry*, **28** (2002), 231–253.

[3] G. Aloupis, B. Ballinger, P. Bose, M. Damian, E. D. Demaine, M. L. Demaine, R. Flatland, F. Hurtado, S. Langerman, J. O'Rourke, P. Taslakian, and G. Toussaint: Vertex pops and popturns, *Proceedings of the 19th Canadian Conference on Computational Geometry*, (CCCG 2007), Ottawa, pp. 137–140.

[4] B. Ballinger: *Length-Preserving Transformations on Polygons*, PhD Thesis, University of California, Davis, 2003.

[5] T. Biedl: Polygons needing many flipturns, *Discrete & Computational Geometry*, **35** (2006), 131–141.

[6] E. D. Demaine, B. Gassend, J. O'Rourke, and G. Toussaint: Polygons Flip Finitely... Right?, *Contemporary Mathematics*, **453** (2006), 231–255.

[7] E. D. Demaine and J. O'Rourke: *Geometric Folding Algorithms: Linkages, Origami, Polyhedra*, Cambridge Univ. Press, Cambridge, 2007.

[8] A. Dumitrescu and E. Hilscher: On convexification of polygons by pops, manuscript, 2009, `http://arxiv.org/abs/0911.4146`.

[9] P. Erdös: Problem number 3763, *American Mathematical Monthly*, **42(10)** (1935), 627.

[10] T. Fevens, A. Hernandez, A. Mesa, P. Morin, M. Soss, and G. Toussaint: Simple polygons with an infinite sequence of deflations, *Beiträge zur Algebra und Geometrie*, **42** (2001), 307–311.

[11] B. Grünbaum: How to convexify a polygon, *Geombinatorics*, **5** (1995), 24–30.

[12] S.A. Robertson and B. Wegner: Full and partial inflation of plane curves, *Intuitive Geometry, Colloquia Math. Soc. János Bolyai*, vol. 63, North-Holland 1994, pp. 389–401.

[13] G. Sallee: Stretching chords of space curves, *Geometriae Dedicata*, **2** (1973), 311–315.

[14] J. Stratzen and J. Brooks: A chord stretching map of a convex loop is an isometry, *Geometriae Dedicata*, **41** (1992), 51–62.

Geometric Methods for Multi-Agent Collision Avoidance

Video: http://gamma.cs.unc.edu/CA/SoCG.mov

Stephen J. Guy, Jur van den Berg, Ming C. Lin, and Dinesh Manocha
Dept. of Computer Science, University of North Carolina at Chapel Hill
Chapel Hill, NC, USA
sjguy@cs.unc.edu,berg@cs.unc.edu,lin@cs.unc.edu,dm@cs.unc.edu

ABSTRACT

We present an approach to *reciprocal collision avoidance*, where multiple mobile agents must avoid collisions with each other while moving in a common workspace. Each agent acts fully independently, and does not communicate with others. Yet our approach guarantees that all agents will be collision-free for at least a fixed amount of time. Our approach provides a *sufficient* condition for collision-free motion. Given the agent's objective, the optimal collision-free action can be computed very efficiently, as it is the solution to a two-dimensional linear program. We show our approach on dense and complex simulation scenarios involving thousands of agents at fast real-time running times.

Categories and Subject Descriptors

I.2.11 [**Distributed Artificial Intelligence**]: Multiagent systems; I.6.8 [**Simulation and Modeling**]: Animation

General Terms

Algorithms, Performance, Theory

Keywords

crowd simulation, multi-agent motion planning, collision avoidance, virtual agents, robotics

1. INTRODUCTION

Collision avoidance is an important and fundamental problem in areas such as robotics and animation. The problem can generally be defined in the context of an autonomous entity (henceforth agent) navigating in an environment with obstacles and other agents. For the purpose of animation and robotics, the problem can be conceptually viewed as a continuous cycle of sensing and acting. With an agent sensing its current surrounding then choosing a collision free velocity as it's action.

The problem of collision avoidance has been well studied for one agent avoiding static or moving obstacles [2]. Here we address the problem of *reciprocal collision avoidance*, where collisions need to be avoided with other agents that also actively attempt to avoid collisions. This problem has important applications in a broad range of areas including robotics (multi-robot navigation, operating swarms of robots), graphics and VR (crowd simulation, AI for non-player characters), biology (studying flocks of birds and fish), and (air) traffic control. We present a fast method that computes actions for many robots, each having different objectives. The actions are computed for each agent independently, without communication among agents or central coordination. Yet, we prove that our method guarantees collision-free motion for each of the agents.

SCG'10, June 13–16, 2010, Snowbird, Utah, USA.
ACM 978-1-4503-0016-2/10/06.

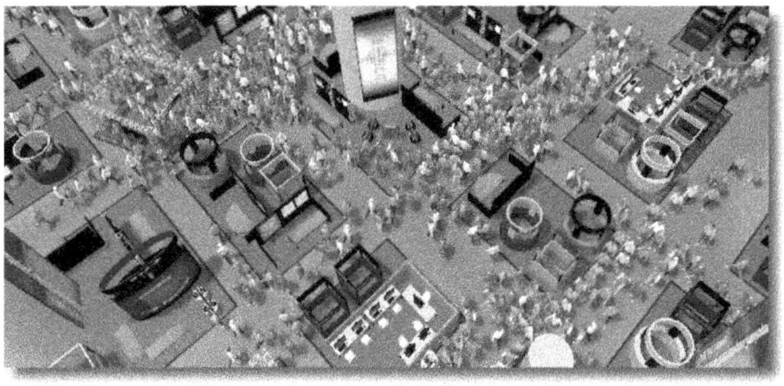

Figure 1: Crowd Simulation driven by our navigation technique. 1,000 agents are simulated and rendered at 60FPS.

Overview: Our approach is *velocity-based* [1]. That means that the agents take into account the observed velocity of other agents in order to avoid collisions with them, and also that the agents selects its own velocity from its two-dimensional *velocity space* in which certain regions are marked as 'forbidden' because of the presence of other agents. Our method, which we call "optimal reciprocal collision avoidance", infers a half-plane (in velocity-space) of velocities that are allowed to be selected in order to guarantee avoiding collisions with another agent.

2. PROBLEM DEFINITION

The problem we discuss in this paper is formally defined as follows. Let there be a set of n agents sharing an environment. For simplicity we assume the agents are disc-shaped and move in the plane $\mathbb{R}^2$ (the definitions and algorithms we present in this paper can easily be extended to translating polygons, and also to higher dimensions). Each agent A has a current position $\mathbf{p}_A$ (the center of its disc), a current velocity $\mathbf{v}_A$ and a radius r_A. These parameters are part of the agent's external state, i.e. we assume that they can be observed by other agents. Furthermore, each agent has a maximum speed $v_A^{\max}$ and a preferred velocity $\mathbf{v}_A^{\text{pref}}$, which is the velocity the agent would assume had no other agents been in its way (for instance a velocity directed towards the

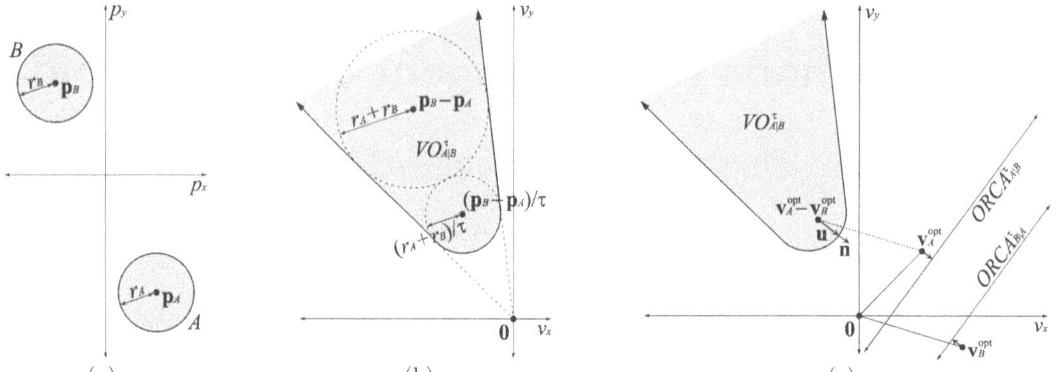

Figure 2: Velocity obstacle $VO^{\tau}_{A|B}$ (shown gray in (b)) for the configuration of agents A and B shown in (a). The velocity obstacle $VO^{\tau}_{A|B}$ can geometrically be interpreted as a truncated cone with its apex at the origin (in velocity space) and its legs tangent to the disc of radius $r_A + r_B$ centered at $\mathbf{p}_B - \mathbf{p}_A$. The amount of truncation depends on the value of τ; the cone is truncated by an arc of a disc of radius $(r_A + r_B)/\tau$ centered at $(\mathbf{p}_B - \mathbf{p}_A)/\tau$. The velocity obstacle shown in (b) is for $\tau = 2$. C - The set $ORCA^{\tau}_{A|B}$ of permitted velocities for A with B is a half-plane delimited by the line perpendicular to u through the point $\mathbf{v}_A^{\mathrm{opt}} + \frac{1}{2}\mathbf{u}$, where u is the vector from $\mathbf{v}_A^{\mathrm{opt}} - \mathbf{v}_B^{\mathrm{opt}}$ to the closest point on the boundary of $VO^{\tau}_{A|B}$.

agent's goal with a magnitude equal to the agent's preferred speed).

Notation: For two agents A and B, the velocity obstacle $VO^{\tau}_{A|B}$ is the set of all *relative* velocities of A with respect to B that will result in a collision between A and B at some moment before time τ [1]. Formally, let $D(\mathbf{p}, r)$ denote an open disc of radius r centered at $\mathbf{p}$: $D(\mathbf{p}, r) = \{\mathbf{q} \mid \|\mathbf{q} - \mathbf{p}\| < r\}$, then:

$$VO^{\tau}_{A|B} = \{\mathbf{v} \mid \exists t \in [0, \tau] :: t\mathbf{v} \in D(\mathbf{p}_B - \mathbf{p}_A, r_A + r_B)\} \quad (1)$$

The geometric interpretation of velocity obstacles is shown in Fig. 2(b). Note that $VO^{\tau}_{A|B}$ and $VO^{\tau}_{B|A}$ are *symmetric.*

We call a pair of sets V_A and V_B of velocities for A and B *reciprocally collision-avoiding* if $V_A \subseteq CA^{\tau}_{A|B}(V_B)$ and $V_B \subseteq CA^{\tau}_{B|A}(V_A)$. If $V_A = CA^{\tau}_{A|B}(V_B)$ and $V_B = CA^{\tau}_{B|A}(V_A)$, we call V_A and V_B *reciprocally maximal.*

3. RECIPROCAL COLLISION AVOIDANCE

Given the definitions above, we would like to choose sets of *permitted* velocities V_A for A and V_B for B such that $CA^{\tau}_{A|B}(V_B) = V_A$ and $CA^{\tau}_{B|A}(V_A) = V_B$, i.e. they are reciprocally collision-avoiding and reciprocally maximal and guarantee that A and B are collision-free for at least τ time.

We can geometrically construct $ORCA^{\tau}_{A|B}$ and $ORCA^{\tau}_{B|A}$ as follows. Let us assume that A and B adopt velocities $\mathbf{v}_A^{\mathrm{opt}}$ and $\mathbf{v}_B^{\mathrm{opt}}$, respectively, and let us assume that that causes A and B to be on collision course, i.e. $\mathbf{v}_A^{\mathrm{opt}} - \mathbf{v}_B^{\mathrm{opt}} \in VO^{\tau}_{A|B}$. Let $\mathbf{u}$ be the vector from $\mathbf{v}_A^{\mathrm{opt}} - \mathbf{v}_B^{\mathrm{opt}}$ to the closest point on the boundary of the velocity obstacle (see Fig. 2(c)):

$$\mathbf{u} = (\operatorname*{arg\,min}_{\mathbf{v} \in \partial VO^{\tau}_{A|B}} \|\mathbf{v} - (\mathbf{v}_A^{\mathrm{opt}} - \mathbf{v}_B^{\mathrm{opt}})\|) - (\mathbf{v}_A^{\mathrm{opt}} - \mathbf{v}_B^{\mathrm{opt}}), \quad (2)$$

and let $\mathbf{n}$ be the outward normal of the boundary of $VO^{\tau}_{A|B}$ at point $(\mathbf{v}_A^{\mathrm{opt}} - \mathbf{v}_B^{\mathrm{opt}}) + \mathbf{u}$. Then, $\mathbf{u}$ is the smallest change required to the relative velocity of A and B to avert collision within τ time. To "share the responsibility" of avoiding collisions among the agents in a fair way, agent A adapts its velocity by (at least) $\frac{1}{2}\mathbf{u}$ and assumes that B takes care of the other half. Hence, the set $ORCA^{\tau}_{A|B}$ of permitted velocities for A is the *half-plane* pointing in the direction of $\mathbf{n}$ starting at the point $\mathbf{v}_A^{\mathrm{opt}} + \frac{1}{2}\mathbf{u}$. More formally:

$$ORCA^{\tau}_{A|B} = \{\mathbf{v} \mid (\mathbf{v} - (\mathbf{v}_A^{\mathrm{opt}} + \frac{1}{2}\mathbf{u})) \cdot \mathbf{n} \geq 0\}. \quad (3)$$

The set $ORCA^{\tau}_{B|A}$ for B is defined symmetrically (Fig. 2(c)).

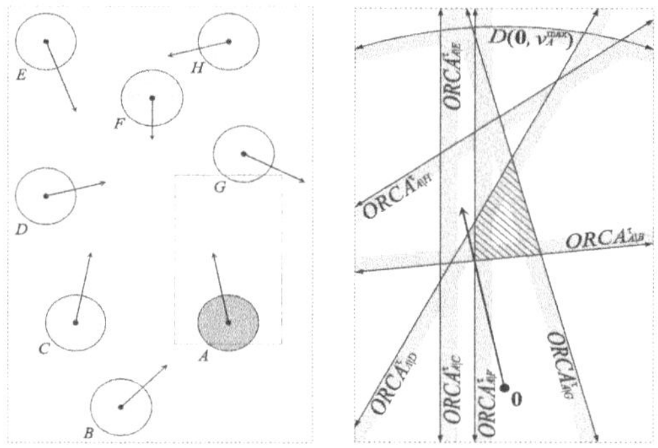

Figure 3: (a) A configuration with eight agents. Their current velocities are shown using arrows. (b) The half-planes of permitted velocities for agent A induced by each of the other agents with $\tau = 2$, permissible velocities shown in dashed region

Multi-agent Navigation: To navigate among multiple agents, each neighboring agents generates a new *ORCA* constraint. The union of these constraints creates a permissible region. We choose the velocity in the permissible region closest to the desired velocity. As each *ORCA* constraint is linear in velocity space, we can efficiently optimize for the closest velocity using linear programming. For more details, we refer the reader to [3]. Results can be found in the accompanying video to this abstract.

Acknowledgements: This research is supported in part by ARO Contract W911NF-04-1-0088, DARPA/RDECOM Contract WR91CRB-08-C-0137, NSF awards 0636208, 0917040 and 0904990 and Intel.

4. REFERENCES

[1] P. Fiorini and Z. Shiller. Motion planning in dynamic environments using velocity obstacles. In *IJRR*, 1998.

[2] S. M. LaValle. *Planning Algorithms*. Cambridge University Press, 2006.

[3] J. van den Berg, S. J. Guy, M. Lin, and D. Manocha. Reciprocal n-body collision avoidance. In *ISRR*, 2009.

A Geometric Approach to Collective Motion

Bernard Chazelle*
Department of Computer Science
Princeton University
chazelle@cs.princeton.edu

ABSTRACT

We introduce the *total s-energy* of a multiagent system and bound its maximum asymptotic value. This gives us a new analytical device to study the convergence rate of bidirectional agreement dynamics. We use it to bound the convergence rate of dynamical systems for synchronization, flocking, opinion dynamics, and social epistemology.

Categories and Subject Descriptors

F.2.2 [**Nonnumerical Algorithms and Problems**]: Geometrical problems and computations

General Terms

Algorithms, Theory

Keywords

Agreement dynamics, Collective motion, Total s-energy

1. INTRODUCTION

We introduce an analytical device for the study of multiagent agreement systems. The *total s-energy* of an infinite sequence of graphs $(G_t \mid t \geq 0)$ embedded in Euclidean d-space is a Dirichlet series that encodes all of the edge lengths. If $x_i(t)$ denotes the position in $\mathbb{R}^d$ of the i-th node of G_t, then the *total s-energy* is defined as:

$$E(s) = \sum_{t \geq 0} \sum_{(i,j) \in G_t} \|x_i(t) - x_j(t)\|_2^s . \qquad (1)$$

The definition generalizes both the graph Laplacian and the Riesz s-energy of points on a sphere. One not insignificant difference is that the total s-energy may diverge everywhere. Despite this inauspicious start, it reveals itself to be a powerful analytical device for bidirectional agreement systems. We prove that, for such systems, the total s-energy converges precisely for $s > 0$; we also establish asymptotic bounds for $0 < s \leq 1$. Intuitively, the total s-energy draws its power from its ability to handle products of stochastic matrices *without looking inside the matrices*. The proofs are purely algorithmic and combinatorial, and make no use of algebraic graph theory. For example, we can use the total s-energy to rederive standard mixing bounds for reversible Markov chains without using eigenvalues. We give several applications of the total s-energy to dynamical systems. In particular, we bound the convergence rate of classical systems in synchronization, flocking, opinion dynamics, and social epistemology. This work illustrates the benefits of viewing dynamical systems as *natural algorithms* [5].

*This work was supported in part by NSF grants CCF-0634958 and NSF CCF-0832797.

SCG'10, June 13–16, 2010, Snowbird, Utah, USA.

1.1 Multiagent Dynamics

Moreau [29] introduced an elegant geometric framework for multiagent agreement, general enough to model dynamical systems for flocking, schooling, synchronization, rendezvous, gossip, opinion dynamics, etc. He established qualitative convergence criteria but no quantitative results. The total s-energy attempts to fill this gap.

Bidirectional Agreement Systems

The model is a quantitative version of Moreau's. It consists of n agents located at the points $x_1(t), \ldots, x_n(t)$ in $\mathbb{R}^d$ at any time $t \geq 0$, together with an infinite sequence of undirected n-node graphs G_0, G_1, G_2, etc. We assume that $n \geq 2$ and that d is an arbitrary positive constant. These graphs represent the various configurations of a communication network changing over time, at $t = 0, 1, 2$, etc. By padding the sequence with n-node edge-free graphs, if necessary, we can always assume that it is infinite. The nodes are in one-to-one correspondence with the agents and have self-loops. The neighbors of i form the set $N_i(t) = \{ j \mid (i,j) \in G_t \}$, which includes i. At time t, each agent i moves anywhere within the convex hull

$$C_i(t) = \text{conv}\{ x_j(t) \mid j \in N_i(t) \},$$

but not too close to the boundary. To formalize this notion, first we pick a point $\omega_i(t)$ centrally located within $C_i(t)$. It is a classical result of convex geometry that $C_i(t)$ can be sandwiched between two concentric ellipsoids centered at a point $\omega_i(t)$, the *Löwner-John center*, so that the outer ellipsoid is a copy of the inner one scaled up by a factor of at most d [27]. Fix a parameter $0 < \rho \leq 1$. At time t, the next position of agent i is subject to the constraint:

$$x_i(t+1) \in (1-\rho)C_i(t) + \rho\,\omega_i(t). \tag{2}$$

Informally, this forces agent i to stay within a slightly shrunken version of its neighbors' convex hull (Figure 1). Note that the freedom of an agent increases as ρ decreases; when $\rho = 1$, the system becomes deterministic. For this reason, ρ can always be made smaller than any suitable constant, an assumption we make for technical convenience. All the agents are updated in parallel at each step $t = 0, 1, 2$, etc. Since the sequence (G_t) is infinite, this updating process goes on forever. We show that it always converges, regardless of the graph sequence, and we bound how long it takes (§1.3). Since agents may never stop moving, convergence needs to be defined rigorously: intuitively, each agent must stay arbitrarily close to a fixed point.

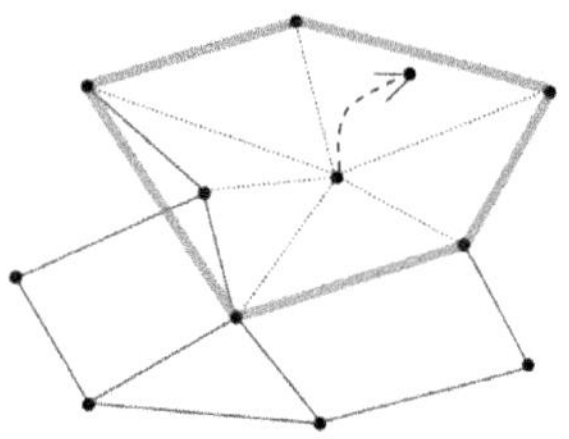

Figure 1: The agent can move anywhere inside the pentagon but may not touch the thick boundary.

The model defines a *bidirectional agreement system.* We conclude the presentation with a few general remarks. The model is affine-invariant, meaning that the dynamics commutes with affine transformations. There is considerable nondeterminism in both the choice of communication graphs and the motion of the agents, which are best thought of as left in the hands of an adversary. In real-life applications, the adversary is typically replaced by a feedback loop: the merit of an adversarial approach is to widen the applicability of the results. We choose the Löwner-John center to direct the shrinking as a matter of convenience; in fact, we switch to the mass center to deal with reversible systems because it is easier. In general, we could pick any point in the relative interior of the hull. As for the convex hull, that, too, is a matter of choice. We could just as well use the smallest enclosing box instead; we do not because we prefer coordinate-free models. (See [1, 24] for generalizations of Moreau's model to different shapes.) Not everything is up for grabs, however. For example, the condition $\rho > 0$ is essential. Without it, a 2-agent system with a single edge could see the agents swap places forever without ever converging. The system forms a line segment that can shrink by as little as a factor of $1-\rho$ at each step and thus wait as much as $\Omega(1/\rho)$ time before being reduced by a half. We should therefore expect any convergence bound to grow inversely with ρ.

The model extends naturally to directed graphs but convergence is then no longer guaranteed. We can see why by using a fixed 3-node graph G_t for all t: besides the obligatory self-loops, G_t has exactly two directed edges, (a, b) and (a, c). If a is positioned in the middle of the segment bc, it can oscillate around its initial position forever while b and c stay in place, thus preventing convergence under any reasonable definition of the term. It is a characteristic trait of bidirectionality that edges will eventually shrink to nothing. Nonbidirectional systems lack this feature, which is why their total s-energy is not always bounded.

Much of the previous work on agreement systems has been concerned with conditions for consensus (ie, with all agents coming together). Various connectivity assumptions have been identified to ensure that all the agents converge to the same point, beginning with the pioneering work of [37, 38] and then [1, 4, 15, 16, 20, 29, 30]. For example, all pairs of agents might be required to communicate infinitely often. Bounds on the convergence rate have been obtained under such restrictions [4, 30] or for certain closed-loop systems [6, 26]. The convergence of bidirectional agreement systems can be derived from the techniques in [15, 23, 29]. Bounding the convergence time for unrestricted systems, the focus of this paper, has been left open.

The Fixed-Agent Agreement Model

A simple yet useful observation is that we can fix one agent i if we so desire. The model is unchanged except for the fact that the updating rule is not applied to agent i. We simulate the evolution of the system by means of a standard bidirectional $(2n-1)$-agent system that obeys rule (2). The idea is to create the point reflection of the $n-1$ mobile agents about the fixed agent i (Figure 2). This creates a bidirectional system of $2n-1$ agents. Every mobile agent (and its reflected copy) mimics the behavior of its counterpart in the original n-agent system, while respecting (2). Fixing i is also compatible with (2) because the fixed agent now lies at the mass center of its neighbors: the convex hull $C_i(t)$ formed by the neighbors of agent i is centrally symmetric with respect to it, so the fixed agent's position itself can be used as the Löwner-John center and thus need not move, irrespective of the value of ρ. To summarize, any n-agent agreement system with one fixed agent can be simulated with a $(2n-1)$-agent bidirectional agreement system with the same value of ρ and at most twice the diameter. We apply this result to truth-seeking systems (see §2.2).

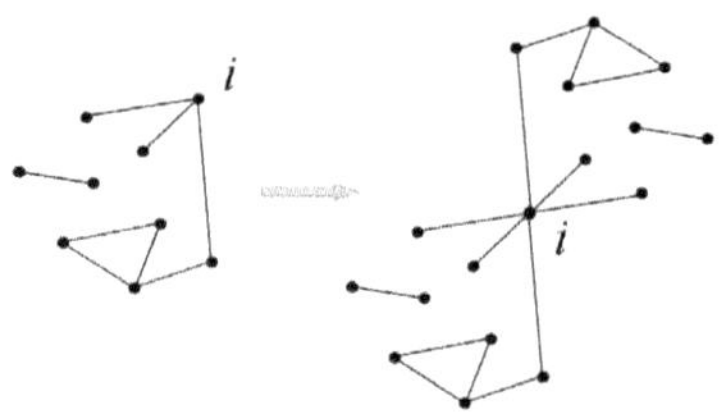

Figure 2: Reflecting the system about the agent i that we wish to fix.

Why Not Stochastic Matrices?

It is customary to model agreement systems by using products of (row)-stochastic matrices. This paper suggests an alternative. The philosophy behind the total s-energy is to focus on the phase space of the system so as to exploit the geometry of the agents. This means moving away from the space of transformations acting on the agents; in other words, the idea is to focus on the vectors, not on the matrices. There are several benefits to draw from this approach.

One of them is greater generality. We explain why. First, a simple observation: Consider a Cartesian system of reference and let $y_i(t)$ denote the first coordinate of agent i at time t. Fix t, i and let y_l (resp. y_r) denotes the minimum (resp. maximum) of $y_j(t)$ over all $j \in N_i(t)$; note that the indices l and r both depend on t, i. Since the Löwner-John center $\omega_i(t)$ is the center of an ellipsoid inside $C_i(t)$ that contains $C_i(t)$ after scaling up by a factor of d, we find that

$$\Big(1 - \frac{\rho}{2d}\Big) y_l + \frac{\rho}{2d} y_r \leq y_i(t+1) \leq \frac{\rho}{2d} y_l + \Big(1 - \frac{\rho}{2d}\Big) y_r \,. \quad (3)$$

These conditions are necessary in general and also sufficient if $d = 1$. Let us now reverse our perspective and, instead of (2), assume that the dynamics of the agents is given by

$$x_i(t+1) = \sum_{j=1}^{n} p_{ij}(t) x_j(t), \quad (4)$$

where $(p_{ij}(t))$ forms a stochastic matrix. When can we say that the $y_i(t)$'s form an agreement system? First, we need a communication graph G_t: we define it simply by including the edge (i, j) if $p_{ij}(t) > 0$; we also add a self-loop at i, whether $p_{ii}(t)$ is positive or not. This, in turn, defines $N_i(t)$ in the usual way. In one dimension, what plays the role of the convex hull $C_i(t)$ is the interval $[y_l, y_r]$; likewise, the Löwner-John center is now the midpoint $\frac{1}{2}(y_l + y_r)$. Setting $d = 1$ in (3), the system $y_i(t)$ obeys the dynamics of a one-dimensional bidirectional agreement system with parameter ρ as long as the following two conditions are satisfied: for all t,

$$\begin{cases} \textit{Mutual confidence}\text{: No pair } p_{ij}(t), p_{ji}(t) \text{ has one zero;} \\ \textit{No extreme influence}\text{: For all } i, \min\{\, p_{il}(t),\, p_{ir}(t)\,\} \geq \rho/2 \,. \end{cases} \quad (5)$$

Condition (5) is weaker than the usual set of three constraints found in the literature [15, 23], which, besides mutual confidence, include: *self-confidence* (nonzero diagonal entries) and *nonvanishing confidence* (lower bound on all nonzero entries). Our model does not need these two assumptions. In particular, we need lower bounds on only two entries per matrix row.

Our agent-based perspective, as opposed to one matrix-based, allows us to get by with weaker conditions, ignore coefficients of ergodicity altogether, including eigenvalues, and handle more general situations. Previous work [5, 23] highlighted the importance of self-confidence for the convergence of agreement systems. Our results refine this picture. Note that (5) implies self-confidence only when agent i is extreme among its neighbors. The moral of the story is that to reach harmony in a group it is fine to be influenced, even extremely so ($p_{ij}(t) = 1$), by non-extreme positions, but one should not be extremely influenced by extreme positions (y_l or y_r). Note that in the case of a two-agent system this maxim coincides with the need for self-confidence.

A quick remark about nonlinearity: viewing the evolution of the agents as a composition of linear transformations might suggest (wrongly) that the model is linear. To apply our model to any concrete situation often involves replacing the adversarial choice of communication graphs by a specific sequence defined typically through a feedback loop. Specifically, $p_{ij}(t)$ is actually $p_{ij}(t, S_t)$, where S_t encodes all previous positions of the agents. Any perturbation in the positions at time t might produce an entirely different set of matrices, so the system may be highly nonlinear.

Reversible Agreement Systems

We mention an important special case, which captures the notion of *reversibility*. Assume that each G_t is connected and, for each i, fix a parameter q_i between $|N_i(t)|$ and $\frac{1}{\rho}|N_i(t)|$ for all $t \geq 0$. (This is always possible if G_t is independent of t or if $\rho < 1/n$.) Let m_i be the mass center of $C_i(t)$, ie,

$$m_i(t) = \frac{1}{|N_i(t)|} \sum_{j \in N_i(t)} x_j(t).$$

We define $\alpha_i(t) = |N_i(t)|/q_i$ and note that $\rho \leq \alpha_i(t) \leq 1$. This allows us to specify the next position of agent i by

$$x_i(t+1) = x_i(t) + \alpha_i(t)(m_i(t) - x_i(t)).$$

This fits within the previous model because agent i moves toward $m_i(t)$ in a straight line by a distance at least a fraction $\alpha_i(t) \geq \rho$ of its original value, with $m_i(t)$ now playing the role of $\omega_i(t)$; this is the only case in this paper where $\omega_i(t)$ is not set to the Löwner-John center. We call this model a *reversible agreement system*. It is a strict generalization of reversible Markov chains. The maximum total s-energy drops significantly to become polynomial in the number of agents. The agents obey the dynamics (4), written in vector notation as

$$x_i(t+1) = \sum_{j \in N_i(t)} p_{ij}(t) x_j(t),$$

where

$$p_{ij}(t) = \begin{cases} 1 - \alpha_i(t) + 1/q_i & \text{if } i = j; \\ 1/q_i & \text{if } i \neq j \in N_i(t); \\ 0 & \text{else.} \end{cases} \quad (6)$$

We take note of the identity $q_i p_{ij}(t) = q_j p_{ji}(t)$. This is the standard balanced condition of a reversible Markov chain, with (q_i) in the role of the stationary distribution (up to scaling). Indeed, we easily verify that the sum $\sum_i q_i x_i(t)$ is independent of t. We bound the convergence time of reversible systems in §1.3.

1.2 The Total s-Energy

Recall our definition of the total s-energy (1):

$$E(s) = \sum_{t \geq 0} \sum_{(i,j) \in G_t} \|x_i(t) - x_j(t)\|_2^s \,,$$

where $x_i(t)$ is the position in $\mathbb{R}^d$ of the i-th node of G_t. There is no obvious reason why this sum should *ever* converge, so we treat it as a formal series for the time being. We prove that the series converges for any $s > 0$ and we bound its maximum value, $E_n(s)$, over all moves and graph sequences for n agents. We assume unit initial diameter throughout: $D = \operatorname{diam}\{x_1(0), \ldots, x_n(0)\} = 1$. For nonunit diameter, the total s-energy obeys the power-law $D^s E_n(s)$, which is why we may focus on the case $D = 1$. All the bounds below hold for any ρ ($0 < \rho < 1$) smaller than a suitable constant. The bounds are new, except for the case $s < 1$, which we established in [7].

THEOREM 1.1. *The maximal total s-energy of an n-agent bidirectional agreement system with unit initial diameter satisfies*

$$E_n(s) \leq \begin{cases} \rho^{-O(n)} & \textit{if } s = 1; \\ s^{1-n}\rho^{-n^2-O(1)} & \textit{if } 0 < s < 1. \end{cases}$$

There is a lower bound of $\rho^{-\lfloor n/2 \rfloor}$ on the 1*-energy and of $s^{1-n}\rho^{-\Omega(n)}$ on $E_n(s)$ for any $s \leq s_0$ and any fixed $s_0 < 1$.*

THEOREM 1.2., *The maximal total s-energy of an n-agent reversible agreement system with unit initial diameter satisfies, for all $s > 0$,*

$$E_n(s) \leq \frac{1}{s}\Big(\frac{n}{\rho}\Big)^{O(s+1)}.$$

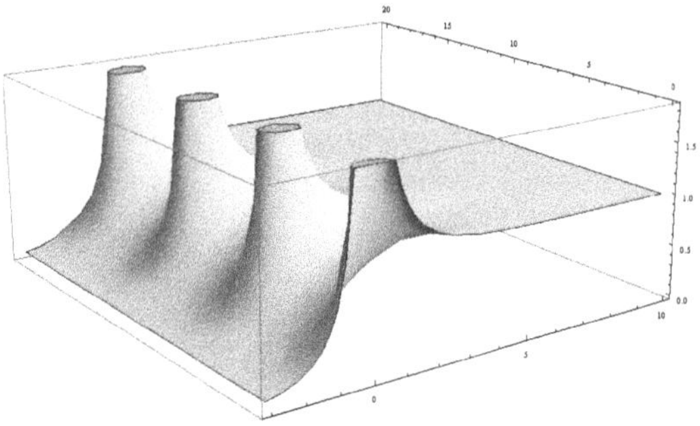

Figure 3: By analytic continuation, the maximum total s-energy of a two-agent system is a meromorphic function over the whole complex plane; the function is depicted in absolute value.

We proceed with general remarks about the function $E(s)$. All the terms in the series are nonnegative; therefore, we can assume they can be rearranged in decreasing order. This allows us to express the total s-energy as a general Dirichlet series:

$$E(s) = \sum_{k \geq 1} n_k e^{-\lambda_k s}, \tag{7}$$

where $\lambda_k = -\ln d_k$ and n_k is the number of edges of length d_k. It is easily seen that $E(s)$ is the Laplace transform of a sum of scaled Dirac delta functions centered at $x = \lambda_k$. This implies that the total s-energy can be inverted and, hence, provides a lossless encoding of the edge lengths. We show that $E(s)$ converges for any real $s > 0$. By the theory of Dirichlet series [12], it follows that $E(s)$ is uniformly convergent over any finite region $\mathcal{D}$ of the complex plane within $\Re(s) \geq r$, for any $r > 0$; furthermore, the series defines an analytic function over $\mathcal{D}$. It is not hard to determine the maximum s-energy of a 2-agent system with unit initial diameter. For $\rho = 1 - 1/e$ and $s = x + iy$, it satisfies (Figure 3):

$$|E(s)| = 1/\sqrt{1 - 2e^{-x}\cos y + e^{-2x}}\,.$$

The singularities are the simple poles $s = 2\pi ik$, for all k. The total s-energy can be continued meromorphically over the whole complex plane. We conjecture that the same holds true for $E_n(s)$ in general. Note that this is clearly false for *nonmaximal* s-energies: for example, the function $\sum_k e^{-sk!}$ is a valid total s-energy, but its singularities form a dense subset of its line of convergence (the imaginary axis): hence an impassable barrier for any analytic continuation into $\Re(s) < 0$.

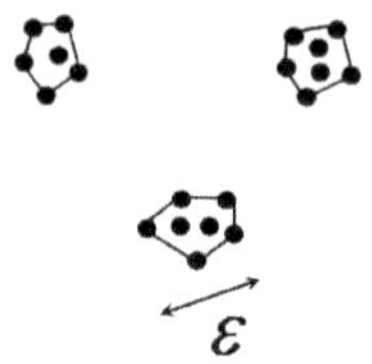

Figure 4: Convergence is reached when the agents fall within groups with disjoint convex hulls of diameter at most ε and no further interaction takes place between the groups. One cannot infer ε-convergence from the picture alone: it is required that no future edge of G_t should ever connect distinct clusters.

1.3 Convergence

Given $0 < \varepsilon < \frac{1}{2}$, we say that a step t is *trivial* (where ε is understood) if G_t has no edges or all of them are of length at most ε. The *communication count* C_ε is defined as the total number of nontrivial steps. As we shall see, this number is always finite. It is immediate from the definition, for example, that the convex hull of the n agents forms a downward-nested sequence over time: the convex hull at time $t+1$ lies within the convex hull at time t. (By abuse of notation, we identify the agents with their positions.) This suggests the following definition of convergence. The system is said to *ε-converge* if the n agents can be partitioned at some time t into subsets with disjoint convex hulls, each one of diameter at most ε, so that no edge in $G_{t'}$ ever joins two of these subsets for any $t' \geq t$ (Figure 4). *Consensus* refers to the case of a one-set partition. Informally, convergence means that, visually, the system appears frozen for good. Because of the model's high nondeterminism—both the graph sequence and the specific moves are left in adversarial hands—the convergence time can be fairly meaningless: indeed, the adversary can always delay convergence arbitrarily by throwing in as many copies of the n-node edge-free graph as it pleases. As we shall see, however, there are special cases where C_ε is an accurate bound on the convergence time. The communication count and the convergence rate are related in the following manner:

THEOREM 1.3. *For any $0 < \varepsilon < 1/2$, an n-agent bidirectional agreement system εn-converges by the time its last nontrivial step has elapsed. If the communication network remains connected at all times, then the system εn-converges to consensus within C_ε time.*

THEOREM 1.4. *For any $0 < \varepsilon < 1/2$, the maximum communication count $C_\varepsilon(n)$ of any n-agent bidirectional agree-*

ment system with unit initial diameter satisfies

$$\Omega(\rho^{-\lfloor n/2\rfloor}\log\tfrac{1}{\varepsilon}) \le C_\varepsilon(n) \le \min\Big\{\tfrac{1}{\varepsilon}\,\rho^{-O(n)},\ (\log\tfrac{1}{\varepsilon})^{n-1}\rho^{-n^2-O(1)}\Big\}.$$

If the initial diameter D is not 1, then we must replace ε by ε/D in the bounds for $C_\varepsilon(n)$. We easily check that the bound is tight as long as ε is not unreasonably small (ie, $1/\varepsilon$ is not superexponential).

COROLLARY 1.5. *If $\varepsilon \ge \rho^{O(n)}$, then $C_\varepsilon(n) = \rho^{-\Theta(n)}$.*

In the upper bounds of the theorem and its corollary we can replace $C_\varepsilon(n)$ by "maximum number of nontrivial steps before the system ε-converges." Indeed, Theorem 1.3 shows that ε-convergence is reached after at most $C_{\varepsilon/n}$ steps have witnessed edges longer than ε/n; furthermore, substituting ε/n for ε does not change the asymptotic bounds.

THEOREM 1.6. *For any $0 < \varepsilon < 1/2$, an n-agent reversible agreement system ε-converges to consensus in time $(\frac{n}{\rho})^{O(1)}\log\frac{1}{\varepsilon}$.*

The theorem implies the polynomial mixing time of lazy random walks in connected graphs. This classical result, of course, can be derived by using standard bounds on spectral gaps. What makes the use of the total s-energy intriguing is that it makes agreement dynamics amenable to algorithmic proofs. This largely obviates the need for algebraic graph theory and eigenvalue bounds. The communication count is related to the total s-energy via the obvious inequality:

$$C_\varepsilon \le \varepsilon^{-s}E(s).$$

In view of this relation, the three upper bounds in Theorems 1.4 and 1.6 follow directly from those in Theorems 1.1 and 1.2: simply set $s=1$, $s=(n-1)/\ln\frac{1}{\varepsilon}$, and $s = 1/\ln\frac{1}{\varepsilon}$, respectively. Note that the second assignment can be assumed to satisfy $s<1$, since it only concerns the case where $\frac{1}{\varepsilon}\rho^{-O(n)}$ is the dominant bound in the min expression of Theorem 1.4. From the third assignment we find that $C_\varepsilon(n) = (\frac{n}{\rho})^{O(1)}\log\frac{1}{\varepsilon}$. We have the same asymptotic upper bound on $C_{\varepsilon/n}(n)$; since reversibility implies connectivity, Theorem 1.6 follows from Theorem 1.3.

Communication and Consensus

Moreau showed that if some agent communicates with all others infinitely often then the system evolves to consensus [29]. We provide a quantitative version of this fact. Agent i is said to communicate with agent j if there exists a sequence of times $t_0 < \cdots < t_k$ and agents $i_1,\ldots,i_k$ such that the edges $(i,i_1),(i_1,i_2),\ldots,(i_{k-1},i_k),(i_k,j)$ belong to $G_{t_0},G_{t_1},\ldots,G_{t_k}$. We may have $i_j = i_{j+1}$, in which case the relevant edge is a self-loop. Two agents i and j *communicate with each other* if i communicates with j or the other way around. Communication is not a symmetric relation but almost. Indeed, if i communicates with j at least $n-1$ times during nonoverlapping time intervals, then agent j must communicate with i at least once. To see why, observe that, until j communicates with i, whenever i communicates with j, the set of agents with whom j communicates increases by at least one compared with the previous communication. Indeed, because of self-loops, this set cannot decrease. Moreover, any further communication from i to j must penetrate that set, hence involve an edge with exactly one endpoint in it; this can happen at most $n-1$ times.

If any two agents at distance greater than ε always communicate in the future, the system ε-converges to consensus. This follows directly from this result:

THEOREM 1.7. *Given any $0 < \varepsilon < 1/2$, consider two agents who always communicate at some point in the period following a separation by ε or more. The agents are then guaranteed to be at most ε apart when the system ε-converges. The total number of communications between them, counting only one after each such separation, is bounded by*

$$\min\Big\{\tfrac{1}{\varepsilon}\,\rho^{-O(n)},\ (\log\tfrac{1}{\varepsilon})^{n-1}\rho^{-n^2-O(1)}\Big\}.$$

2. APPLICATIONS

Moreau [29] illustrated the versatility of his multiagent agreement framework by applying it to several classical dynamical systems. Likewise, we highlight the relevance of the total s-energy by focusing on four specific examples: opinion dynamics; social epistemology; synchronization; and flocking.

2.1 Opinion Dynamics

The Hegselmann-Krause opinion dynamics model [13] is a sociological framework for tracking opinion polarization in a population. In its d-dimensional version, the *bounded-confidence model*, as it is often called, sets a parameter $0<\delta<1$ and, at time 0, specifies the opinions of n agents as n points in the unit cube $[0,1]^d$. We assume that d is a constant. At time $t = 0,1,\ldots,\infty$, each opinion x moves to the position given by the average of every opinion in the Euclidean ball centered at x of radius δ. Viewed as a multiagent agreement system, G_t consists of n nodes (the agents) with edges joining any two of them within distance δ of each other. The time transition is specified by

$$x_i(t+1) = \frac{1}{|N_i(t)|}\sum_{j\in N_i(t)} x_j(t), \tag{8}$$

where $N_i(t)$ is the set of neighbors of node i in G_t, which includes i itself. The system is known to converge [2, 18, 22, 23]. Theorem 1.4 allows us to bound how long it takes to reach equilibrium. Consider a Cartesian coordinate system. In view of (5, 8), we may set $p_{ij}(t) = 1/|N_i(t)|$ and $\rho = 2/n$ to make the opinion dynamics system along each coordinate axis conform to a one-dimensional multiagent agreement model (2). We can assume that the diameter D along each axis is at most δn. Indeed, by convexity, if along any coordinate axis the n opinions have diameter greater than δn, then they can be split into two subsets with no mutual interaction now and forever. Set $\varepsilon = \delta/2$ and let t_ε be the smallest t such that G_t consists only of edges in $\mathbb{R}^d$ of length at most ε. During the first $dC_{\varepsilon/\sqrt{d}}(n)+1$ steps, it must be the case that, at some time t, the graph G_t contains only edges of length at most ε. By Theorem 1.4, therefore

$$t_\varepsilon \le d^{3/2} \frac{D}{\varepsilon} n^{O(n)} = n^{O(n)}. \tag{9}$$

Each connected component of G_{t_ε} is a complete graph. To see why, observe that if opinion x is adjacent to y in G_{t_ε} and the same is true of y and z, then x and y are at a distance at most $2\varepsilon = \delta$, hence are connected and therefore at distance at most ε at time t_ε. This "transitive-closure" argument proves our claim. This implies that the opinions within any connected component end up at the same position at time $t_\varepsilon + 1$. Of course, when two opinions are joined together they can never get separated. The argument is now easy to complete. Either G_{t_ε} consists entirely of isolated nodes, in which case the system is frozen in place, or it consists of complete subgraphs that collapse into single points. The number of distinct opinions decreases by at least one, so this process can be repeated at most $n-2$ times. By (9), this proves that Hegselmann-Krause opinion dynamics converges in $n^{O(n)}$ time. We summarize our result:

THEOREM 2.1. *Any initial configuration of n opinions in the bounded-confidence model with equal-weight averaging converges to a fixed configuration in $n^{O(n)}$ time.*

Martinez et al [26] have established a polynomial bound for the one-dimensional case, $d = 1$. While extending their proof to higher dimensions might be difficult, a polynomial bound could well hold in any given dimension. See [3] for a comprehensive text on multiagent dynamics where such problems arise.

2.2 Truth-Seeking Systems

In their pioneering work on computer-aided social epistemology, Hegselmann and Krause considered a variant of the bounded-confidence model assuming a *cognitive division of labor* [14]. The idea is to take the previous model and fix one agent, *the truth,* while keeping the $n-1$ others mobile. A *truth seeker* is a mobile agent joined to the truth in every G_t. All the other mobile agents are *ignorant,* meaning that they never connect to the truth via an edge, although they might indirectly communicate with it via a path. Any two mobile agents are joined in G_t whenever their distance is less than δ. Again, we assume the points are in Euclidean d-space, so distance is understood in the ℓ_2 sense. Hegselmann and Krause [14] showed that, if all the mobile agents are truth seekers, they eventually reach consensus with the truth. Kurz and Rambau [19] proved that the presence of ignorant agents cannot prevent the truth seekers from converging toward the truth. The proof is quite technical and the authors leave open the higher-dimensional case. We generalize their results to higher dimension and bound the convergence rate. Our approach, based on total s-energies, is entirely different.

THEOREM 2.2. *Any initial configuration of n opinions in the truth-seeking model converges, with all the truth seekers coalescing around the truth. If, in addition, we assume that the initial coordinates of each opinion as well as the radius δ are encoded as $O(n)$-bit rationals then, after $n^{O(n)}$ time, all the truth seekers lie within a ball of radius 2^{-cn^n} centered at the truth, for any arbitrarily large constant $c > 0$. Ignorant agents either lie in that ball or are frozen in place forever. This holds in any fixed dimension.*

2.3 Kuramoto Synchronization

The *Kuramoto model* is a general framework for nonlinear coupled oscillators, with a dazzling array of applications: circadian neurons, chirping crickets, microwave oscillators, yeast cell suspensions, pacemaker cells in the heart, etc. Winfree's pioneering work on the subject led Kuramoto to formulate the standard sync model for coupled oscillators [35, 41]. The system consists of n oscillators: the i-th one has phase θ_i and natural frequency ω_i. In its original formulation, the model is a mean-field approximation that assumes all-pair coupling. A more realistic assumption is to use a time-varying network to model communications. Considerable work has been done on this problem; see [11, 17, 21, 25, 28, 31, 32, 40, 43] for a small sample. Further research introduced a time-1 discretization of the continuous model [25, 29, 33, 36]. Assuming all oscillators share the same natural frequency, a fixed phase shift yields the dynamics:

$$\theta_i(t+1) = \theta_i(t) + \frac{K\Delta T}{|N_i(t)|} \sum_{j \in N_i(t)} \sin(\theta_j(t) - \theta_i(t)),$$

where $|N_i(t)|$ is the degree of i in the communication graph G_t, which, as always, counts the self-loop at i (Figure 5). As in [29], we also assume that all the agents start in the same open half-circle. By shifting the origin, we express this condition as, $\alpha - \pi/2 \le \theta_i(0) \le \pi/2$, for some arbitrarily small positive constant α. This implies that

$$\sin(\theta_j(0) - \theta_i(0)) = a_{ij}(\theta_j(0) - \theta_i(0)),$$

for $\alpha/4 \le a_{ij} \le 1$. By (5); therefore, to make the dynamics conform to a bidirectional multiagent agreement system at time 0, it suffices to enforce the constraints:

$$\frac{2n\rho}{\alpha} \le K\Delta T \le 1 - \frac{\rho}{2}.$$

Choosing $\rho = b\alpha/n$ for a small enough constant $b > 0$, we note that the constraints are roughly equivalent to $0 < K\Delta T < 1$. By convexity, the angles at time 1 remain within $[\alpha - \pi/2, \pi/2]$; therefore, our previous argument can be repeated to show that the synchronization dynamics fits within the bidirectional agreement model. Invoking Corollary 1.5 to bound the number of nontrivial steps for any ε not too small, ie, $\varepsilon \ge n^{-O(n)}$, we observe that the system ε-converges within $n^{O(n)}$ nontrivial steps. If all the communication graphs have bounded degree, then the bound becomes $2^{O(n)}$. We note that the actual convergence time cannot be bounded unless we make further assumptions on the communication network. Our bound on the number of nontrivial steps is, indeed, independent of the adversarial choice of the communication graphs. Only in the case of closed-loop systems can we hope to bound the convergence time.

THEOREM 2.3. *Any Kuramoto synchronization system with n agents initialized in an open half-circle ε-converges after $n^{O(n)}$ nontrivial steps, for any $\varepsilon > n^{-cn}$ and any constant $c > 0$.*

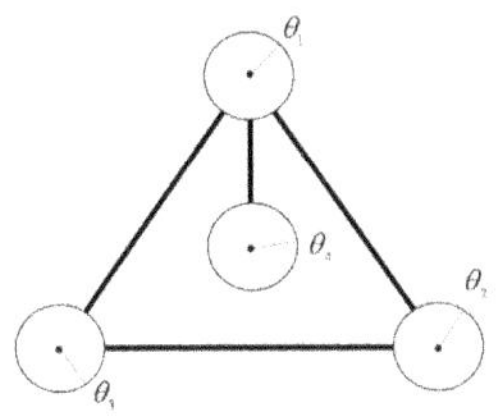

Figure 5: Four coupled oscillators connected by four edges.

2.4 Flocking

Mathematically, bird flocking appears more complex than the previous agreement systems because the communication network is specified not by the variables the system seeks to "agree upon" but by their integrals. Specifically, the graphs G_t are a function of the birds' *positions* while the agreement dynamics averages their *velocities*. For this reason, attempts to solve the problem has called upon a vast array of analytical techniques from algebraic graph theory, computational geometry, combinatorics, control theory, statistical mechanics, etc. Many models have been studied in the literature but most of them are variants of the following [5, 10, 16, 39]: given the initial conditions $y(0)$ and $y(1)$, for any $t > 0$,

$$\begin{cases} y(t) = y(t-1) + v(t); \\ v(t+1) = (P(t) \otimes I_3)v(t). \end{cases} \tag{10}$$

See our paper [8] in these proceedings for an explanation of the notation. We improve the bound of $n^{O(n^2)}$ that we proved in [7].

THEOREM 2.4. *The velocities of n birds ε-converge after $n^{O(n)}$ nontrivial steps, for any $\varepsilon > n^{-cn}$ and any constant $c > 0$.*

an agreement system with parameter ρ' onto a line, by (3), we get a wingshift system satisfying

$$a_{\ell(i)} + \frac{\rho'}{2d}(a_{r(i)} - a_{\ell(i)}) \leq b_i \leq a_{r(i)} - \frac{\rho'}{2d}(a_{r(i)} - a_{\ell(i)}),$$

hence a wingshift system with $\rho = \rho'/(2d)$. In other words, projecting a bidirectional agreement system onto a line gives us a wingshift system for a value of ρ a fraction $1/(2d)$ of what it is in the original agreement system.

The need for $\rho > 0$ is obvious. Indeed, consider the case $n = 2$, $a_1 = 0$ and $a_2 = 1$, with $l(1) = l(2) = 1$ and $r(1) = r(2) = 2$: each agent may move toward the other at a speed of ρ, and even more slowly in subsequent steps, which means that any upper bound on the communication count must grow at least inversely proportional to ρ. Rule 1 says that the interval $[\ell(i), r(i)]$ should contain all agents j pointing to i. This is also necessary. Consider three agents $a_1 = 0$, $a_2 = \frac{1}{2}$, $a_3 = 1$, with $\ell(1) = r(1) = \ell(2) = 1$ and $r(2) = \ell(3) = r(3) = 3$. Agents 1 and 3 are stuck in place while agent 2 can move about almost anywhere: again, convergence cannot be assured. Intuitively, iterating the functions ℓ and r in alternation should produce an outward-growing spiral ending in a cycle. Specifically, if we follow the path $i, r(i), l(r(i)), r(l(r(i)))$, etc, we spiral around i along edges of nondecreasing length until we eventually fall into a two-edge cycle of the form $l(r(j)) = j$. The *wingshift graph* consists of the nodes $1, \ldots, n$ and the directed edges $(i, \ell(i))$ and $(i, r(i))$.

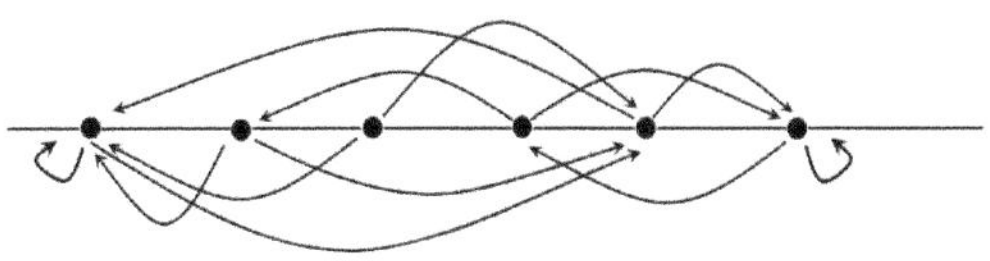

Figure 6: A six-node wingshift graph.

3. THE TOTAL 1-ENERGY

Because of space constraints, we only sketch the upper bound of Theorem 1.1 $s = 1$. To do that, we introduce a *wingshift system*. Since we will focus on a single transition at a time, we write a_i, b_i instead of $x_i(t), x_i(t+1)$ for notational convenience, and we relabel the agents so that $0 \leq a_1 \leq \cdots \leq a_n \leq 1$. Given $a_1, \ldots, a_n$, the agents move to their next positions $b_1, \ldots, b_n$ nondeterministically and then repeat this process endlessly in the manner described below. Let $\ell(i)$ and $r(i)$ be indices satisfying the following inequalities:

RULE 1: $1 \leq \ell(i) \leq i \leq r(i) \leq n$ and $(\ell \circ r)(i) \leq i \leq (r \circ \ell)(i)$;
RULE 2: $a_{\ell(i)} + \delta_i \leq b_i \leq a_{r(i)} - \delta_i$, where $\delta_i = \rho(a_{r(i)} - a_{\ell(i)})$.

Each agent i picks an *associate* to its left and one to its right, $\ell(i)$ and $r(i)$, respectively. It then shifts anywhere in the interval $[a_{\ell(i)}, a_{r(i)}]$, though keeping away from the endpoints by a small distance δ_i. This provides a strict generalization of the one-dimensional projection of a bidirectional agreement system, so any upper bound for a wingshift system will translate into an upper bound for agreement systems. We use the notation ρ by analogy with agreement systems in $\mathbb{R}^d$ but there is a slight difference. If we project

By analogy, we define the total 1-energy of the wingshift system as $V = \sum_{t \geq 0} V_t$, where

$$V_t = \sum_{i=1}^{n} (a_{r(i)} - a_{\ell(i)}).$$

We need some notation to describe rightward paths in the wingshift graph: $r(i, 0) = i$ and $r(i, k) = r(r(i, k-1))$ for $k > 0$. We define the distance between an agent and its right associate, $\Delta_i = a_{r(i)} - a_i$. When traversing a rightward path $i, r(i,1), r(i,2)$, etc, a sudden drop in Δ_k is of particular interest; so we define

$$k_i = \min \left\{ k \geq 1 \,|\, \Delta_{r(i,k)} \leq \tfrac{\rho}{2} \Delta_{r(i,k-1)} \right\}.$$

Since, for k large enough, $r(i, k) = r(i, k+1)$, a drop by a factor of at least $\rho/2$ is certain to occur and thus k_i is always well defined (even if $r(i) = i$, in which case $k_i = 1$). We now show that $r(i, k_i)$, which we call a *stopper*, must move left by an amount proportional to Δ_i. What makes this result interesting is that it points to some obligatory motion that the system must undergo; in other words, staying in place is not an option, unless the system consists entirely of self-loops.

Lemma 3.1. *For any agent i, its stopper $s = r(i, k_i)$ satisfies $a_s - b_s \geq (1+\rho)(\frac{\rho}{2})^{k_i}\Delta_i$.*

We bound V by tallying the *total motion* of the system, $M = \sum_{t\geq 0} M_t$, where $M_t = \sum_{i=1}^n |a_i - b_i|$. Recall that a_i and b_i are the positions of agent i at times t and $t+1$, respectively.

Lemma 3.2. *If V and M are finite, then $V \leq n2^n\rho^{1-n}M$.*

By symmetry, we can assume that at least half of the contribution to M is provided by rightward motions, ie, $M \leq 2\sum_{t,i}\{ b_i - a_i \,|\, b_i > a_i \}$. Thus we can conveniently ignore all leftward travel. We use an amortization technique that involves assigning a *credit account* to each agent and requiring them to spend an amount equal to the distance they travel to the right. We also have a bank where credits can be deposited, withdrawn, or borrowed. In the end, we will ensure that bank loans do not exceed deposits, so that the initial credit accounts provide an upper bound on $\frac{1}{2}M$. The power of the method is that agents can trade credits among one another.

Let $rk(a_i)$ be the rank of agent i. Initially, the agents are labeled from left to right, $a_1 \leq \cdots \leq a_n$, so that $rk(a_i) = i$; ties are broken arbitrarily. When agent i is moved from a_i to b_i, the ranks are updated in the obvious way; ties are broken by minimizing the number of agents whose ranks are changed. We call this *lazy tie-breaking*. We denote by $a_i(t)$ the position of agent i at time t. We often use a_i for $a_i(0)$. For convenience, we use a continuous time scale between 0 and 1, with $a_i(0) = a_i$ and $a_i(1) = b_i$. The notation $rk(a_i(t))$ refers to the current rank of agent i within the set of all agents at time t. We schedule the motion of each agent i from a_i to b_i one at a time in a specific fashion described below.

Invariant: The credit account of each agent i is supplied at time t with at least $a_i(t)\alpha^{rk(a_i(t))}$ credits, where $\alpha = 9/\rho$.

The cost of a right shift $a_i \to b_i$ ($a_i < b_i$) is $b_i - a_i$ plus whatever is needed to update the agents' accounts. Note that moving agent i to the right affects not only its own account but also those of the agents it passes over, whose ranks decrease by one, and who may therefore release credits and deposit them into the bank. The cost attached to shifting agent i is paid for by borrowing from the bank, a loan that will be paid back later by the stopper $r(i, k_i)$, ie, not by the borrower. To explain how this works, we partition the set of all agents into equivalence classes consisting of all the agents i with the same stopper $s = r(i, k_i)$. We define the set P_s of the immediate predecessors of s, in the wingshift graph, that claim s as their stopper; the set H_j^s consists of all the nodes that lead to $j \in P_s$: in other words, for any stopper s,

$$\begin{cases} P_s &= \{\, j \neq s \,|\, r(j) = s \text{ and } k_j = 1\,\}; \\ H_j^s &= \{\, i \neq j \,|\, r(i, k_i - 1) = j \text{ and } j \in P_s\,\}. \end{cases}$$

Note that some P_s or H_j^s might be empty. First, for each stopper s from right to left, we move all the right-shifting agents in each H_j^s and pass on the cost to agent j. Second, we move each such agent j to b_j, charging the bank for the cost. Finally, we move the stopper s to the left and use the credits released to pay back the bank. All remaining left moves, which are self-paying, are then carried out.

- For each stopper s in decreasing rank order, do:
  - **[1]** For each agent $j \in P_s$ ordered by nonincreasing value of $\max\{a_j, b_j\}$, do:
    - **[1.1]** Move from a_i to b_i any agent $i \in H_j^s$ such that $a_i < b_i$. Charge agent j for all the costs.
    - **[1.2]** If $a_j < b_j$ then move agent j from a_j to b_j. In both cases, borrow from bank to cover all charges incurred by agent j.
  - **[2]** Move agent s left from a_s to b_s. Use released credits to clear all outstanding bank loans.
- Move from a_i to b_i any agent such that $b_i < a_i$.

Step [1]. Fix s. We process each agent $j \in P_s$ in the order $j_1, \ldots, j_\nu$ such that $c_{j_1} \geq \cdots \geq c_{j_\nu}$, where $c_k = \max\{a_k, b_k\}$. We resolve ties in decreasing rank order of a_k; in other words, if $c_{j_k} = c_{j_l}$ and $rk(a_{j_k}(t)) > rk(a_{j_l}(t))$, then we process j_k before j_l (where t is the time before step [1]). Recall that lazy tie-breaking ensures that each agent has a distinct rank at any time. Fix $j = j_l$. The execution of step [1.1] occurs in the period denoted by $[t_{l,1}, t_{l,2})$, while that of step [1.2] takes place during $[t_{l,2}, t_{l+1,1})$. No agent moves left in step [1]. Agents of H_j^s may right-shift during $[t_{l,1}, t_{l,2})$ but agent j itself remains in place in that time interval. The sets H_j^s are disjoint over all j, s, so no agent in H_j^s has moved prior to $t_{l,1}$. But couldn't a stopper in H_j^s have moved left in earlier executions of step [2]? No. The reason is that we process stoppers from right to left.

Step [1.1]. Consider the motion of an agent $i \in H_j^s$ ($j = j_l$) during the period $[t_{l,1}, t_{l,2})$; the order in which we schedule the processing of these agents is immaterial. We use summation by parts to do the accounting. Picture a slow, continuous motion. An infinitesimal motion δ at any time requires $(\alpha^q + 1)\delta$ credits, with q the current rank of agent i: $\alpha^q\delta$ to maintain the credit invariant and δ to pay for the actual move. Whenever i passes over another agent m because a_i reaches a value $x = a_m$ along the way and $b_i > x$, we switch the identities of agents i and m. This is done only for accounting purposes in the analysis of step [1.1]. This way, agent m can then proceed to the right to complete the journey of agent i if need be. Further swaps may then occur before the motion $a_i \to b_i$ is over. The benefit of this perspective is that the ranks of the new, so-called *virtual*, agents no longer change: only their positions do. Instead of tallying the individual costs of each right shift $a_i \to b_i$, we simply add up the costs of the fixed-ranked virtual agents.

We apply this idea to step [1.1]. Each one of the n virtual agents has a distinct rank k at time $t_{l,1}$. Processing H_j^s may move some of them to the right (perhaps more than once in fact), so let $D_k \geq 0$ be the total distance traveled by that rank-k virtual agent v_k while processing H_j^s. Any shift in v_k at time $t \in [t_{l,1}, t_{l,2})$ implies the existence of an interval $[a_i, b_i] \subset [a_i, a_{r(i)})$, where $i \in H_j^s$, that contains the position of v_k at time t. Being in H_j^s or P_s, the $k_i - 1$ agents $r(i), r(i,2), \ldots, r(i, k_i - 1) = j$ did not move between during $[0, t_{l,1})$. They may have moved to the right between $t_{l,1}$ and t but they always remained between v_k and a_j: the reason is that, by definition, v_k cannot overtake any agent, while no agent in H_j^s can right-shift past a_j. As we mentioned earlier, they cannot have moved left either. It follows that $k_i \le rk(a_j(t)) - k + 1$. (Note that $a_j(t) = a_j$ but $rk(a_j(t))$ may be different from the original rank of a_j. There might be several a_i's that qualify for a given v_k: we choose the smallest one. We derive an upper bound on the distance traveled by v_k in the time interval $[t_{l,1}, t_{l,2})$. For any k, there exist i and $t \in [t_{l,1}, t_{l,2})$ such that

$$D_k \le a_j - a_i = \sum_{l=0}^{k_i-2} \Delta_{r(i,l)} \le 2\Delta_j \Big(\frac{\rho}{2}\Big)^{k - rk(a_j(t))}.$$

Summing over all virtual agents v_k allows us to bound the number A_l of credits that agent $j = j_l$ needs to cover the costs incurred in processing H_j^s in time period $[t_{l,1}, t_{l,2})$. No agent of H_j^s can move to the right of j during $[t, t_{l,2})$ and, of course, none can pass j from right to left in that time interval; therefore, $rk(a_j(t)) = rk(a_j(t_{l,2}))$ and agent j_l is charged

$$A_l = \sum_{k=1}^{rk(a_j(t_{l,2}))-1} (\alpha^k + 1) D_k \le \Delta_j \alpha^{rk(a_j(t_{l,2}))}, \tag{11}$$

where, we recall, $\alpha = 9/\rho$ and $t_{l,2}$ is the time at which step [1.1] ends for fixed s and $j = j_l$.

Step [1.2]. We keep the values of s and $j = j_l \in P_s$ set above. By Lemma 3.1, the scheduling of stoppers implies that s has not moved yet. Recall that, by definition of $j_l \in P_s$, we have $k_{j_l} = 1$ and $s = r(j_l)$. Define $x_l = a_s - \frac{1}{2}\rho\Delta_{j_l}$. By definition, $j_l \ne s$; therefore $\Delta_{j_l} > 0$; by Rule 2, the larger of a_{j_l} and b_{j_l} does not exceed $a_s - \rho\Delta_{j_l} < x_l$. Applying Lemma 3.1 to agent j_l shows that, in step [2], the stopper s will move left past x_l, as, indeed, $b_s = b_{r(j_l, k_{j_l})} = b_{r(j_l,1)} \le a_s - \frac{1}{2}(1+\rho)\rho\Delta_{j_l} < x_l$. Summarizing these bounds,

$$\begin{cases} \max\{a_{j_l}, b_{j_l}\} < x_l \quad \text{for each } l\,; \\ b_s < \min\{x_l \mid 1 \le l \le \nu\}. \end{cases} \tag{12}$$

We introduce $\sigma_l = \min\{rk(a_i(t_{l,2})) \mid x_l \le a_i(t_{l,2}) \text{ and } 1 \le i \le n\}$. Informally, σ_l would be the rank of x_l, were it an agent, measured once we are done handling $H_{j_l}^s$ in step [1.1]. Since $a_s(t_{l,2}) = a_s > x_l$, the agent of rank σ_l exists and is unique. Furthermore, by (12), it will not change even if agent j_l is shifted to b_{j_l} during $[t_{l,2}, t_{l+1,1})$ in step [1.2]. We define μ_l inductively by $\mu_1 = \sigma_1$ and $\mu_l = \min\{\sigma_l, \mu_{l-1} - 1\}$, for $1 < l \le \nu$. We show that agent j_l needs to borrow no more than B_l credits from the bank, where

$$B_l = |x_l - a_s| \Big(1 - \frac{1}{\alpha}\Big)\alpha^{\mu_l}. \tag{13}$$

The key fact driving our analysis is that

$$\mu_l \ge rk(a_{j_l}(t_{l+1,1})) + 1\,. \tag{14}$$

We prove this by induction, beginning with the case $l = 1$. By (12), $x_l > \max\{a_{j_l}, b_{j_l}\} = a_{j_l}(t_{l+1,1})$. (Recall that $t_{l+1,1}$ is the time agent j_l is moved to b_{j_l} if it is to the right.) This shows that agent j_l cannot reach across to the right of x_l; therefore, the agent i of rank σ_l at time $t_{l,2}$ still has that same rank at time $t_{l+1,1}$. Since $a_i(t_{l+1,1}) = a_i(t_{l,2}) \ge x_l > a_{j_l}(t_{l+1,1})$, it then follows that

$$\mu_l = \sigma_l = rk(a_i(t_{l,2})) = rk(a_i(t_{l+1,1})) > rk(a_{j_l}(t_{l+1,1}))\,;$$

hence (14). Suppose now that $l > 1$. The argument we just gave can be repeated verbatim for the case $\mu_l = \sigma_l$, so we can assume that $\sigma_l > \mu_{l-1} - 1$, and that $\mu_l = \mu_{l-1} - 1$. Agents j_l are processed by nonincreasing value of $\max\{a_{j_l}, b_{j_l}\}$. By lazy tie-breaking, the value of $rk(a_{j_l}(t_{l+1,1}))$ strictly decreases as l goes from 1 to ν. (This is not simply a result of agent j_l landing to the left of agent j_{l-1}, but also of the absence of leftward motion. Indeed, the strict monotonicity of $rk(a_{j_l}(t_{l+1,1}))$ is a claim about ranks at different times.) This immediately implies (14) by induction. We can show that agent j_l is charged $A'_l \le 3\alpha^{rk(a_{j_l}(t_{l+1,1}))}\Delta_{j_l}$. By (13, 14) and $\alpha = 9/\rho$,

$$B_l \ge \frac{\rho}{2}\Big(1 - \frac{1}{\alpha}\Big)\alpha^{rk(a_{j_l}(t_{l+1,1}))+1}\Delta_{j_l} \ge \frac{\alpha\rho}{6}\Big(1 - \frac{1}{\alpha}\Big)A'_l \ge A'_l\,,$$

which proves that agent j_l has enough credits borrowed from the bank to pay for step [1.2].

Step [2]. We need to tally the release of credits at time $t_{\nu+1,1}$ and show there are at least $B_1 + \cdots + B_\nu$ of them. Turning once again to the summation-by-parts argument, we track the leftward motion of s and rewrite the sum as an integral,

$$\sum_{l=1}^{\nu} B_l = -\int_{a_s}^{b_s} \sum_{l=1}^{\nu} (\alpha^{\mu_l} - \alpha^{\mu_l - 1}) I_l(u)\, du,$$

where $I_l(u) = 1$ if $x_l \le u \le a_s$ and 0 otherwise. At time $t_{\nu+1,1}$, the stopper s proceeds to the left continuously until it reaches b_s. Since leftward travel costs nothing, an infinitesimal motion δ at position u releases $\delta\alpha^{q(u)}$ credits, where $q(u)$ is the lowest rank of any agent (at time $t_{\nu+1,1}$) at or to the right of u. (Note that $q(u)$ compares the moving agent s against a snapshot of the agents taken at the beginning of step [2].) We can also express the release as the integral $R = -\int_{a_s}^{b_s} \alpha^{q(u)}\, du$. It suffices to prove that

$$\alpha^{q(u)} \ge \sum_{l=1}^{\nu} (\alpha^{\mu_l} - \alpha^{\mu_l - 1}) I_l(u). \tag{15}$$

If $l_1 < \cdots < l_k$ are the indices l such that $I_l(u) = 1$ then, by the strict monotonicity of μ_l,

$$\sum_{l=1}^{\nu} (\alpha^{\mu_l} - \alpha^{\mu_l - 1}) I_l(u) = \sum_{j=1}^{k} (\alpha^{\mu_{l_j}} - \alpha^{\mu_{l_j} - 1}) \le \alpha^{\mu_{l_1}}.$$

Because of the ordering of j_l, by (12), the rank of agent j_l remains unchanged between $t_{l,2}$ and $t_{\nu+1,1}$, so we could replace $t_{l,2}$ by $t_{\nu+1,1}$ in the definition of σ_l and get the same value of σ_l. This shows that μ_{l_1}, being at most σ_{l_1}, does not exceed the rank of the smallest-ranked $a_i(t_{\nu+1,1}) \ge x_{l_1}$. Since $I_{l_1}(u) = 1$, we have $u \ge x_{l_1}$; hence $q(u) \ge \mu_{l_1}$ and (15). This establishes the soundness of our credit invariant: allocating each agent i at time 0 with $a_i \alpha^{rk(a_i)}$ credits is sufficient to pay for all the costs, while maintaining the credit invariant. Since each $a_i \le 1$, this implies that

$$\tfrac{1}{2}M \le \sum_{i=1}^{n} a_i \alpha^{rk(a_i)} \le \sum_{i=1}^{n} \alpha^i < 2\Big(\frac{9}{\rho}\Big)^n.$$

In view of Lemma 3.2, this proves the upper bound of Theorem 1.1 for $s = 1$ and arbitrary d. □

4. REFERENCES

[1] Angeli, D., Bliman, P.-A. *Stability of leaderless multi-agent systems: extension of a result by Moreau*, Mathematics of Control, Signals & Systems 18 (2006), 293–322.

[2] Blondel, V.D., Hendrickx, J.M., Tsitsiklis, J.N. *On Krause's multi-agent consensus model with state-dependent connectivity*, IEEE Transactions on Automatic Control 54, 11 (2009), 2586–2597.

[3] Bullo, F., Cortés, J., Martinez, S., Distributed Control of Robotic Networks, Applied Mathematics Series, Princeton University Press, 2009.

[4] Cao, M., Spielman, D.A. Morse, A.S. *A lower bound on convergence of a distributed network consensus algorithm*, 44th IEEE Conference on Decision and Control, and the European Control Conference 2005, Seville, Spain, 2005.

[5] Chazelle, B. *Natural algorithms*, Proc. 20th Annual ACM-SIAM SODA 2009, 422–431.

[6] Chazelle, B. *The convergence of bird flocking*, arXiv:0905.4241v1, 2009.

[7] Chazelle, B. *Analytical tools for natural algorithms*, Proc. 1st Symposium on Innovations in Computer Science (2010), Beijing, 32–41.

[8] Chazelle, B. *The geometry of flocking*, SoCG 2010.

[9] Condon, A., Hernek, D. *Random walks on colored graphs*, Random Structures and Algorithms 5 (1994), 285–303.

[10] Cucker, F., Smale, S. *Emergent behavior in flocks*, IEEE Trans. Automatic Control 52 (2007), 852–862.

[11] Earl, M.G., Strogatz, S.H. *Synchronization in oscillator networks with delayed coupling: a stability criterion*, Phys. Rev. E, 67 (2003), 036204(1–4).

[12] Hardy, G.H., Riesz, M. The General Theory of Dirichlet's Series, Cambridge University Press, 1915.

[13] Hegselmann, R., Krause, U. *Opinion dynamics and bounded confidence models, analysis, and simulation*, J. Artificial Societies and Social Simulation 5, 3 (2002).

[14] Hegselmann R, Krause U. *Truth and cognitive division of labor: first steps towards a computer aided social epistemology*, J. Artificial Societies and Social Simulation 9 (2006).

[15] Hendrickx, J.M., Blondel, V.D. *Convergence of different linear and non-linear Vicsek models*, Proc. 17th International Symposium on Mathematical Theory of Networks and Systems (MTNS2006), Kyoto (Japan), July 2006, 1229–1240.

[16] Jadbabaie, A., Lin, J., Morse, A.S. *Coordination of groups of mobile autonomous agents using nearest neighbor rules*, IEEE Trans. Automatic Control 48 (2003), 988–1001.

[17] Jadbabaie, A., Motee, N., Barahona, M. *On the stability of the Kuramoto model of coupled nonlinear oscillators*, Proc. American Control Conference 5 (2004), 4296–4301.

[18] Krause, U. *A discrete nonlinear and non-autonomous model of consensus formation*, Communications in Difference Equations (2000), 227Ű236.

[19] Kurz, S., Rambau, J. *On the Hegselmann-Krause conjecture in opinion dynamics*, Journal of Difference Equations and Applications (2009).

[20] Li, S., Wang, H. *Multi-agent coordination using nearest neighbor rules: revisiting the Vicsek model*, 2004, arXiv:cs/0407021v2

[21] Li, C., Xu, H., Liao, X., Yu, J. *Synchronization in small-world oscillator networks with coupling delays*, Physica A 335 (2004), 359–364.

[22] Lorenz, J. *Multidimensional opinion dynamics when confidence changes*, Economic Complexity, Aix-en-Provence, May 2003.

[23] Lorenz, J. *A stabilization theorem for dynamics of continuous opinions*, Physica A: Statistical Mechanics and its Applications 355 (2005), 217–223.

[24] Lorenz, D., Lorenz, J. *Convergence to consensus by general averaging*, in R. Bru and S. Romero-Vivo (eds), Positive Systems (2009), LNCS Springer 91–99.

[25] Martinez, S. *A convergence result for multiagent systems subject to noise*, Proc. American Control Conference (2009), St. Louis, Missouri.

[26] Martinez, S., Bullo, F., Cortés, J., Frazzoli, E. *On synchronous robotic networks – Part II: Time complexity of rendezvous and deployment algorithms*, IEEE Transactions on Automatic Control 52 (2007), 2214–2226.

[27] Matoušek, J. Lectures on Discrete Geometry, Graduate Texts in Mathematics, Vol. 212, Springer, 2002.

[28] McGraw, P.N., Menzinger, M. *Analysis of nonlinear synchronization dynamics of oscillator networks by Laplacian spectral methods*, Phys. Rev. E 75 (2007), 027104(1–4).

[29] Moreau, L. *Stability of multiagent systems with time-dependent communication links*, IEEE Transactions on Automatic Control 50 (2005), 169–182.

[30] Olshevsky, A., Tsitsiklis, J.N. *Convergence speed in distributed consensus and averaging*, SIAM Journal on Control and Optimization 48 (2009), 33–55.

[31] Papachristodoulou, A., Jadbabaie, A. *Synchonization in oscillator networks: switching topologies and non-homogeneous delays*, Proc. IEEE CDC-ECC (2005), 5692–5697.

[32] Papachristodoulou, A., Jadbabaie, A. *Synchonization in oscillator networks with heterogeneous delays, switching topologies and nonlinear dynamics*, Proc. IEEE CDC-ECC (2006), 4307–4312.

[33] Scardovi, L., Sarlette, A., Sepulchre, R. *Synchronization and balancing on the N-torus*, Systems & Control Letters 56 (2007), 335–341.

[34] Seneta, E. Non-Negative Matrices and Markov Chains, Springer, 2nd ed., 2006.

[35] Strogatz, S.H. *From Kuramoto to Crawford: exploring the onset of synchronization in populations of coupled oscillators*, Physica D 143 (2000), 1–20.

[36] Triplett, B.I., Klein, D.J., Morgansen, K.A. *Discrete time Kuramoto models with delay*, Proc. Networked Embedded Sensing and Control Workshop, Lecture Notes in Control and Information Sciences, Springer, 2005.

[37] Tsitsiklis, J.N., *Problems in decentralized decision making and computation*, PhD thesis, MIT, 1984.

[38] Tsitsiklis, J.N., Bertsekas, D.P., Athans, M. *Distributed asynchronous deterministic and stochastic gradient optimization algorithms*, IEEE Transactions on Automatic Control 31 (1986), 803–812.

[39] Vicsek, T., Czirók, A., Ben-Jacob, E., Cohen, I., Shochet, O. *Novel type of phase transition in a system of self-driven particles*, Physical Review Letters 75 (1995), 1226–1229.

[40] Wang, Q., Duan, Z., Chen, G., Feng, Z. *Synchronization in a class of weighted complex networks with coupling delays*, Physica A 387 (2008), 5616–5622.

[41] Winfree, A.T. *Biological rhythms and the behavior of populations of coupled oscillators*, J. Theoret. Bio. 16, 1 (1967), 15–42.

[42] Yap C. *Fundamental Problems of Algorithmic Algebra*, Oxford University Press, Inc., New York, NY, 2000.

[43] Zanette, D.H. *Propagation of small perturbations in synchronized oscillator networks*, Europhys. Lett. 68 (2004), 356.

Kinetic Stable Delaunay Graphs

Pankaj K. Agarwal
Duke University

Jie Gao
SUNY Stony Brook

Leonidas J. Guibas
Stanford University

Haim Kaplan
Tel Aviv University

Vladlen Koltun
Stanford University

Natan Rubin
Tel Aviv University

Micha Sharir
Tel Aviv University and
New York University

ABSTRACT

The best known upper bound on the number of topological changes in the Delaunay triangulation of a set of moving points in $\mathbb{R}^2$ is (nearly) cubic, even if each point is moving with a fixed velocity. We introduce the notion of a *stable Delaunay graph* (SDG in short), a dynamic subgraph of the Delaunay triangulation, that is less volatile in the sense that it undergoes fewer topological changes and yet retains many useful properties of the full Delaunay triangulation. SDG is defined in terms of a parameter $\alpha > 0$, and consists of Delaunay edges pq for which the (equal) angles at which p and q see the corresponding Voronoi edge e_{pq} are at least α. We prove several interesting properties of SDG and describe two kinetic data structures for maintaining it. Both structures use $O^*(n)$ storage. They process $O^*(n^2)$ events during the motion, each in $O^*(1)$ time, provided that the points of P move along algebraic trajectories of bounded degree; the $O^*(\cdot)$ notation hides multiplicative factors that are polynomial in $1/\alpha$ and polylogarithmic in n. The first structure is simpler but the dependency on $1/\alpha$ in its performance is higher.

Categories and Subject Descriptors

F.2.2 [**Analysis of algorithms and problem complexity**]: Nonnumerical algorithms and problems—*Geometrical problems and computations*; G.2.1 [**Discrete mathematics**]: Combinatorics—*Combinatorial algorithms*

General Terms

Algorithms, Theory

Keywords

Delaunay triangulation, Voronoi diagram, kinetic data structures

1. INTRODUCTION

Delaunay triangulation and Voronoi diagram. Let P be a (finite) set of points in $\mathbb{R}^2$. Let $\mathrm{VD}(P)$ and $\mathrm{DT}(P)$ denote the Voronoi diagram and Delaunay triangulation of P, respectively. For a point $p \in P$, let $\mathrm{Vor}(p)$ denote the Voronoi cell of p. The Delaunay triangulation $\mathrm{DT} = \mathrm{DT}(P)$ consists of all triangles whose circumcircles do not contain points of P in their interior. Its edges form the *Delaunay graph*, which is the straight-edge dual graph of the Voronoi diagram of P. That is, pq is an edge of the Delaunay graph if and only if $\mathrm{Vor}(p)$ and $\mathrm{Vor}(q)$ share an edge, which we denote by e_{pq}. This is equivalent to the existence of a circle passing through p and q that does not contain any point of P in its interior—any circle centered at a point on e_{pq} and passing through p and q is such a circle. Delaunay triangulations and Voronoi diagrams are fundamental to much of computational geometry and its applications. See [6, 11] for a survey and a textbook on these structures.

In many applications of Delaunay/Voronoi methods (e.g., mesh generation and kinetic collision detection) the points are moving continuously, so these diagrams need to be efficiently updated as motion occurs. Even though the motion of the nodes is continuous, the combinatorial and topological structure of the Voronoi and Delaunay diagrams change only at discrete times when certain critical events occur. Their evolution under motion can be studied within the framework of *kinetic data structures* (KDS in short) of Basch *et al.* [7, 12, 13], a general methodology for designing efficient algorithms for maintaining such combinatorial attributes of mobile data.

For the purpose of kinetic maintenance, Delaunay triangulations are nice structures, because, as mentioned above, they admit local certifications associated with individual triangles. This makes it simple to maintain DT under point motion: an update is necessary only when one of these empty circumcircle conditions fails—this corresponds to co-circularities of certain subsets of four points. Whenever such an event happens, a single edge flip easily restores Delaunayhood. Estimating the number of such events, however, has been elusive—the problem of bounding the number of combinatorial changes in DT for points moving with constant velocities has been in the computational geometry lore for many years.

Let n be the number of moving points in P. We assume that each point moves along an algebraic trajectory of fixed degree (see Section 2 for a more formal definition). Guibas et al. [14] showed a roughly cubic upper bound of $O(n^2\lambda_s(n))$ on the number of discrete (also known as *topological*) changes in DT, where $\lambda_s(n)$ is the maximum length of an (n, s)-Davenport-Schinzel sequence [21], and s is a constant depending on the motions of the points. A substantial gap exists between this upper bound and a quadratic lower bound [21].

It is thus desirable to find approaches for maintaining a substantial portion of DT that *provably* experiences only a nearly quadratic

SCG'10, June 13–16, 2010, Snowbird, Utah, USA.

number of discrete changes, that is reasonably easy to define and maintain, and that retains useful properties for further applications.

Polygonal distance functions. If the "unit ball" of our underlying norm is *polygonal* then things improve considerably. In more detail, let Q be a convex polygon with a constant number, k, of edges. It induces a *convex distance function*

$$d_Q(x, y) = \min\{\lambda \mid y \in x + \lambda Q\};$$

d_Q is a metric if Q is centrally symmetric with respect to the origin.

We can define the Q-Voronoi diagram of a set P of points in the plane in the usual way, as the partitioning of the plane into Voronoi cells, so that the cell $\mathrm{Vor}^{\diamond}(p)$ of a point p is $\{x \in \mathbb{R}^2 \mid d_Q(x,p) = \min_{p' \in P} d_Q(x,p')\}$. Assuming that the points of P are in general position with respect to Q, these cells are nonempty, have pairwise disjoint interiors, and cover the plane.

As in the Euclidean case, the Q-Voronoi diagram of P has its dual representation, which we refer to as the *Q-Delaunay triangulation* $\mathrm{DT}^{\diamond}(P) = \mathrm{DT}^{\diamond}$. A triple of points in P define a triangle in $\mathrm{DT}^{\diamond}$ if and only if they lie on the boundary of some homothetic copy of Q that does not contain any point of P in its interior. Assuming that P is in general position, these Q-Delaunay triangles form a triangulation of a certain simply-connected polygonal region that is contained in the convex hull of P. Unlike the Euclidean case, it does not always coincide with the convex hull (see Figures 3 and 11 for examples). See Chew and Drysdale [9] and Leven and Sharir [18] for analysis of Voronoi and Delaunay diagrams of this kind.

For kinetic maintenance, polygonal Delaunay triangulations are "better" than Euclidean Delaunay triangulations because, as shown by Chew [8], when the points of P move (in the algebraic sense assumed above), the number of topological changes in the Q-Delaunay triangulation is only nearly quadratic in n. One of the major observations in this paper is that the *stable portions* of the Euclidean Delaunay triangulation and the Q-Delaunay triangulation are closely related.

Stable Delaunay edges. We introduce the notion of *α-stable Delaunay edges*, for a fixed parameter $\alpha > 0$, defined as follows. Let pq be a Delaunay edge under the Euclidean norm, and let $\triangle pqr^+$ and $\triangle pqr^-$ be the two Delaunay triangles incident to pq. Then pq is called *α-stable* if its opposite angles in these triangles satisfy $\angle pr^+q + \angle pr^-q < \pi - \alpha$. (The case where pq lies on the convex hull of P is treated as if one of r^+, r^- lies at infinity, so that the corresponding angle $\angle pr^+q$ or $\angle pr^-q$ is equal to 0.) An equivalent and more useful definition, in terms of the dual Voronoi diagram, is that pq is α-stable if the equal angles at which p and q see their common Voronoi edge e_{pq} are at least α. See Figure 1 (left).

A justification for calling such edges stable lies in the following observation: If a Delaunay edge pq is α-stable then it remains in DT during any continuous motion of P for which every angle $\angle prq$, for $r \in P \setminus \{p,q\}$, changes by at most $\alpha/2$. This is clear because at the time pq is α-stable we have $\angle pr^+q + \angle pr^-q < \pi - \alpha$ for *any* pair of points r^+, r^- lying on opposite sides of the line ℓ supporting pq, so, if each of these angles change by at most $\alpha/2$ we still have $\angle pr^+q + \angle pr^-q \le \pi$, which is easily seen to imply that pq remains an edge of DT. (This argument also covers the cases when a point crosses ℓ from side to side.) Hence, as long as the "small angle change" condition holds, stable Delaunay edges remain a "long time" in the triangulation.

Informally speaking, the non-stable edges pq of DT are those for p and q are almost co-circular with their two common Delaunay neighbors r^+, r^-, and hence more likely to get flipped "soon".

Overview of our results. Let $\alpha > 0$ be a fixed parameter. In this paper we show how to maintain a subgraph of the full Delaunay triangulation DT, which we call a *$(c\alpha, \alpha)$-stable Delaunay graph* (SDG in short), so that (i) every edge of SDG is α-stable, and (ii) every $c\alpha$-stable edge of DT belongs to SDG, where $c > 1$ is some (small) absolute constant. Note that SDG is not uniquely defined, even when c is fixed.

In Section 2, we introduce several useful definitions and show that the number of discrete changes in the SDGs that we consider is nearly quadratic. What this analysis also implies is that if the true bound for kinetic changes in a Delaunay triangulation is close to cubic, then the overhelming majority of these changes involve edges which never become stable and just flicker in and out of the diagram by co-circularity with their two Delaunay neighbors.

In Sections 3 and 4 we show that SDG can be maintained by a kinetic data structure that uses only near-linear storage (in the terminology of [7], it is *compact*), encounters only a nearly quadratic number of critical events (it is *efficient*), and processes each event in polylogarithmic time (it is *responsive*). For the second data structure described in Section 4, each point appears at any time in only polylogarithmically many places in the structure (it is *local*).

The scheme described in Section 3 is based on a useful and interesting "equivalence" connection between the (Euclidean) SDG and a suitably defined "stable" version of the Delaunay triangulation of P under the "polygonal" norm whose unit ball Q is a regular k-gon, for $k = \Theta(1/\alpha)$. As noted above, Voronoi and Delaunay structures under polygonal norms are particularly favorable for kinetic maintenance because of Chew's result [8], showing that the number of topological changes in $\mathrm{DT}^{\diamond}(P)$ is $O^*(n^2k^4)$; the $O^*(\cdot)$ notation hides a factor that depends sub-polynomially on both n and k. In other words, the scheme simply maintains the "polygonal" diagram $\mathrm{DT}^{\diamond}(P)$ in its entirety, and selects from it those edges that are also stable edges if the Euclidean diagram DT.

The major disadvantage of the solution in Section 3 is the rather high (proportional to $\Theta(1/\alpha^4)$) dependence on $1/\alpha (\approx k)$ of the bound on the number of topological changes. We do not know whether the upper bound $O^*(n^2k^4)$ on the number of topological changes in $\mathrm{DT}^{\diamond}(P)$ is nearly tight (in its dependence on k). To remedy this, we present in Section 4 an alternative scheme for maintaining stable (Euclidean) Delaunay edges. The scheme is reminiscent of the kinetic schemes used in [2] for maintaining closest pairs and nearest neighbors. It extracts $O^*(n)$ pairs of points of P that are candidates for being stable Delaunay edges. Each point $p \in P$ then runs $O(1/\alpha)$ *kinetic and dynamic tournaments* involving the other points in its candidate pairs. Roughly, these tournaments correspond to shooting $O(1/\alpha)$ rays from P in fixed directions and finding along each ray the nearest point equally distant from p and from some other candidate point q. We show that pq is a stable Delaunay edge if and only if q wins many consecutive tournaments of p (or p wins many consecutive tournaments of q). A careful analysis shows that the number of events that this scheme processes (and the overall processing time) is only $O^*(n^2/\alpha^2)$.

Section 5 reviews several useful properties of stable Delaunay graphs. In particular, we show that at any given time the stable subgraph contains at least $\left[1 - \frac{3}{2(\pi/\alpha - 2)}\right] n$ Delaunay edges, i.e., at least about one third of the maximum possible number of edges. In addition, we show that at any moment the SDG contains the closest pair, the so-called *β-skeleton* of P, for $\beta = 1 + \Omega(\alpha^2)$ (see [5, 17]), and the *crust* of a sufficiently densely sampled point set along a smooth curve (see [4, 5]). We also extend the connection in Section 3 to arbitrary distance functions d_Q whose unit ball Q is sufficiently close (in the Hausdorff sense) to the Euclidean one (i.e., the unit disk). Completing $\mathrm{DT}^{\diamond}(P)$ into a triangulation of the entire hull is an interesting challenge that we are currently exploring in a companion paper [16].

2. PRELIMINARIES

Stable edges in Voronoi diagrams. Let $\{u_0, \ldots, u_{k-1}\} \subset \mathbb{S}^1$ be a set of $k = \Theta(1/\alpha)$ equally spaced directions in $\mathbb{R}^2$. For concreteness take $u_i = (\cos(2\pi i/k), -\sin(2\pi i/k))$, $0 \le i < k$ (so our directions u_i go clockwise as i increases).[1] For a point $p \in P$ and a (unit) vector u let $u[p]$ denote the ray $\{p+\lambda u \mid \lambda \ge 0\}$ that emanates from p in direction u. For a pair of points $p, q \in P$ let b_{pq} denote the perpendicular bisector of p and q. If b_{pq} intersects $u_i[p]$, then the expression

$$\varphi_i[p,q] = \frac{\|q-p\|^2}{2\langle q-p, u_i\rangle} \qquad (1)$$

is the distance between p and the intersection point of b_{pq} with $u_i[p]$. If b_{pq} does not intersect $u_i[p]$ we define $\varphi_i[p,q] = \infty$. The point q minimizes $\varphi_i[p,q']$, among all points q' for which $b_{pq'}$ intersects $u_i[p]$, if and only if the intersection between b_{pq} and $u_i[p]$ lies on the Voronoi edge e_{pq}. We call q the *neighbor of p in direction u_i*, and denote it by $N_i(p)$; see Figure 1 (right).

The *(angular) extent* of a Voronoi edge e_{pq} of two points $p, q \in P$ is the angle at which it is seen from either p or q (these two angles are equal). For a given angle $\alpha \le \pi$, e_{pq} is called *α-long* (resp., *α-short*) if the extent of e_{pq} is at least (resp., smaller than) α. We also say that $pq \in \mathrm{DT}(P)$ is *α-long* (resp., *α-short*) if e_{pq} is *α-long* (resp., *α-short*). As noted in the introduction, these notions can also be defined (equivalently) in terms of the angles in the Delaunay triangulation: A Delaunay edge pq is α-long if and only if $\angle pr^+q + \angle pr^-q \le \pi - \alpha$, where $\triangle pr^+q$ and $\triangle pr^-q$ are the two Delaunay triangles incident to pq. See Figure 1(left).

Given parameters $\alpha' > \alpha > 0$, we seek to construct (and maintain under motion) an *(α', α)-stable Delaunay graph* (or *stable Delaunay graph*, for brevity, which we abbreviate as SDG) of P, which is any subgraph G of $\mathrm{DT}(P)$ with the following properties:

(S1) Every α'-long edge of $\mathrm{DT}(P)$ is an edge of G.

(S2) Every edge of G is an α-long edge of $\mathrm{DT}(P)$.

An (α', α)-stable Delaunay graph need not be unique. In what follows, α' will always be some fixed (and reasonably small) multiple of α.

Kinetic tournaments. Kinetic tournaments were first studied by Basch *et al.* [7], for kinetically maintaining the lowest point in a set P of n points moving on some vertical line, say the y-axis, so that their trajectories are algebraic of bounded degree, as above. We also want the tournament to be dynamic, so that we can insert and delete points into/from it. This can be achieved by maintaining the tournament as a heap, stored as a a *weight-balanced* $(BB(\alpha))$ *tree* [20] (and [19]). Omitting all further details, which can be found in [2] (and in the full version [1]), we state:

THEOREM 2.1 (AGARWAL *et al.* [2]). *A sequence of m insertions and deletions into a kinetic tournament, whose maximum size at any time is n (assuming $m \ge n$), when implemented as a weight-balanced tree, generates at most $O(m\beta_{r+2}(n)\log n)$ events, with a total processing cost of $O(m\beta_{r+2}(n)\log^2 n)$. Here r is the maximum number of times a pair of points intersect, and $\beta_{r+2}(n) = \lambda_{r+2}(n)/n$. Processing an update or a tournament event takes $O(\log^2 n)$ worst-case time. A dynamic kinetic tournament on n elements can be constructed in $O(n)$ time.*

[1] The index arithmetic is modulo k, i.e., $u_i = u_{i+k}$.

Maintenance of an SDG. Let $P = \{p_1, \ldots, p_n\}$ be a set of points moving in $\mathbb{R}^2$. Let $p_i(t) = (x_i(t), y_i(t))$ denote the position of p_i at time t. We call the motion of P *algebraic* if each $x_i(\cdot), y_i(\cdot)$ is a polynomial, and the *degree* of motion of P is the maximum degree of these polynomials. Throughout this paper we assume that the motion of P is algebraic and that its degree is bounded by a constant. In this subsection we present a simple technique for maintaining a $(2\alpha, \alpha)$-stable Delaunay graph. Unfortunately this algorithm requires quadratic space. It is based on the following easy observation (see Figure 1 (right)), where k is an integer, and the unit vectors (directions) $u_0, \ldots, u_{k-1}$ are as defined earlier.

LEMMA 2.2. *Let $\alpha = 2\pi/k$. (i) If the extent of e_{pq} is larger than 2α then there are two consecutive directions u_i, u_{i+1}, such that q is the neighbor of p in directions u_i and u_{i+1}.*
(ii) If there are two consecutive directions u_i, u_{i+1}, such that q is the neighbor of p in both directions u_i and u_{i+1}, then the extent of e_{pq} is at least α.

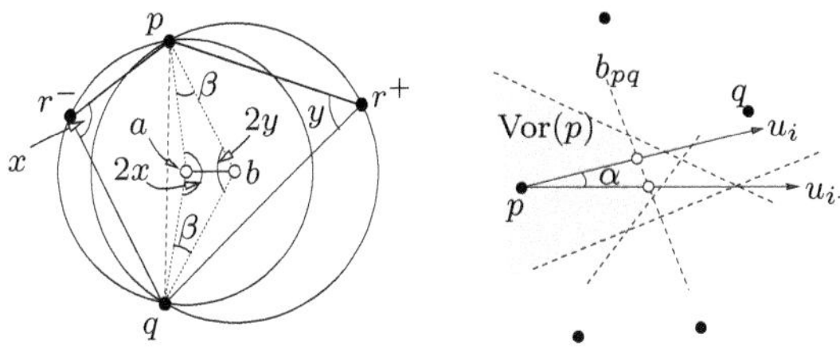

Figure 1. Left: The points p and q see their common Voronoi edge ab at (equal) angles β. This is equivalent to the angle condition $x + y = \pi - \beta$ for the two adjacent Delaunay triangles. Right: q is the neighbor of p in the directions u_i and u_{i+1}, so the Voronoi edge e_{pq} is α-long.

The algorithm maintains Delaunay edges pq such that there are two consecutive directions u_i and u_{i+1} along which q is the neighbor of p. For each point p and direction u_i we get a set of at most $n-1$ piecewise continuous functions of time, $\varphi_i[p,q]$, one for each point $q \ne p$, as defined in (1). (Recall that $\varphi_i[p,q] = \infty$ when $u_i[p]$ does not intersect b_{pq}.) By assumption on the motion of P, for each p and q, the domain in which $\varphi_i[p,q](t)$ is defined consists of a constant number of intervals.

For each point p, and ray $u_i[p]$, consider each function $\varphi_i[p,q]$ as the trajectory of a point moving along the ray and corresponding to q. The algorithm maintains these points in a dynamic and kinetic tournament $K_i(p)$ (see Theorem 2.1) that keeps track of the minimum of $\{\varphi_i[p,q](t)\}_{q\ne p}$ over time. For each pair of points p and q such that q wins in two consecutive tournaments, $K_i(p)$ and $K_{i+1}(p)$, of p, it keeps the edge pq in the stable Delaunay graph. It is trivial to update this graph as a by-product of the updates of the various tournaments. The analysis of this data structure is straightforward using Theorem 2.1, and yields the following result.

THEOREM 2.3. *Let P be a set of n moving points in $\mathbb{R}^2$ under algebraic motion of bounded degree, let k be an integer, and let $\alpha = 2\pi/k$. A $(2\alpha, \alpha)$-stable Delaunay graph of P can be maintained using $O(kn^2)$ storage and processing $O(kn^2\beta_{r+2}(n)\log n)$ events, for a total cost of $O(kn^2\beta_{r+2}(n)\log^2 n)$ time. The processing of each event takes $O(\log^2 n)$ worst-case time. Here r is a constant that depends on the degree of motion of P.*

3. AN SDG BASED ON POLYGONAL VD

Let $Q = Q_k$ be a regular k-gon for some even $k = 2s$, circumscribed by the unit disk, and let $\alpha = \pi/s$ (this is the angle at which the center of Q sees an edge). Let $\mathrm{VD}^\diamond(P)$ and $\mathrm{DT}^\diamond(P)$ denote the Q-Voronoi diagram and the dual Q-Delaunay triangulation of P, respectively. In this section we show that the set of edges of $\mathrm{VD}^\diamond(P)$ with sufficiently many *breakpoints* form a (β, β')-stable (Euclidean) Delaunay graph for appropriate multiples β, β' of α. Thus, by kinetically maintaining $\mathrm{VD}^\diamond(P)$ (in its entirety), we shall get "for free" a KDS for keeping track of a stable portion of the Euclidean DT.

3.1 Properties of $\mathrm{VD}^\diamond(P)$

We first review the properties of the (stationary) $\mathrm{VD}^\diamond(P)$ and $\mathrm{DT}^\diamond(P)$. Then we consider the kinetic version of these diagrams, as the points of P move, and review Chew's proof [8] that the number of topological changes in these diagrams, over time, is only nearly quadratic in n. Finally, we present a straightforward kinetic data structure for maintaining $\mathrm{DT}^\diamond(P)$ under motion that uses linear storage, and that processes a nearly quadratic number of events, each in $O(\log n)$ time. Although later on we will take Q to be a regular k-gon, the analysis in this subsection is more general, and we only assume here that Q is an arbitrary convex k-gon.

Stationary Q-diagrams. The *bisector* $b^\diamond_{pq}$ between two points p and q, with respect to $d_Q(\cdot,\cdot)$, is the locus of all placements of the center of any homothetic copy Q' of Q that touches p and q. Q' can be classified according to the pair of its edges, e_1 and e_2, that touch p and q, respectively. If we slide Q' so that its center moves along $b^\diamond_{pq}$ (and its size expands or shrinks to keep it touching p and q), and the contact edges, e_1 and e_2, remain fixed, the center traces a straight segment. The bisector is a concatenation of $O(k)$ such segments. They meet at *breakpoints*, which are placements of the center of a copy Q' that touches p and q and one of the contact points is a vertex of Q; see Figure 2. We call such a placement a *corner contact* at the appropriate point. Note that a corner contact where some vertex w of (a copy Q' of) Q touches p has the property that the center of Q' lies on the fixed ray emanating from p and parallel to the directed segment from w to the center of Q.

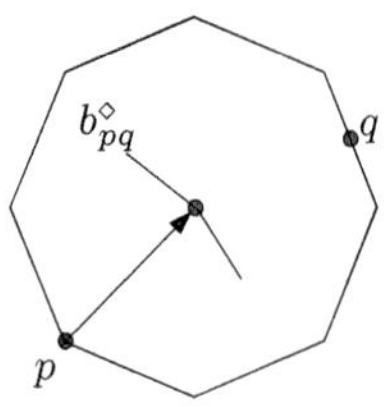

Figure 2. Each breakpoint on $b^\diamond_{pq}$ corresponds to a corner contact of Q at one of the points p, q, so that ∂Q also touches the other point.

A well known property of Q-bisectors and Voronoi edges is that two bisectors $b^\diamond_{pq_1}, b^\diamond_{pq_2}$, can intersect at most once (again, assuming general position) [15], so every Q-Voronoi edge $e^\diamond_{pq}$ is connected. Equivalently, this asserts that there exists at most one homothetic placement of Q at which it touches p, q_1, and q_2.

Another useful property of bisectors and Delaunay edges, in the special case where Q is a regular k-gon, which will be used in the next subsection, is that the breakpoints along a bisector $b^\diamond_{pq}$ alternate between corner contacts at p and corner contacts at q. The proof is omitted here.

Consider next an edge pq of $\mathrm{DT}^\diamond(P)$. Its dual Voronoi edge $e^\diamond_{pq}$ is a portion of the bisector $b^\diamond_{pq}$, and consists of those center placements along $b^\diamond_{pq}$ for which the corresponding copy Q' has an *empty interior* (i.e., its interior is disjoint from P). Following the notation of Chew [8], we call pq a *corner edge* if $e^\diamond_{pq}$ contains a breakpoint (i.e., a placement with a corner contact); otherwise it is a *non-corner edge*, and is therefore a straight segment.

Kinetic Q-diagrams. Consider next what happens to $\mathrm{VD}^\diamond(P)$ and $\mathrm{DT}^\diamond(P)$ as the points of P move continuously with time. In this case $\mathrm{VD}^\diamond(P)$ changes continuously, but undergoes topological changes at certain critical times, called *events*. There are two kinds of events:

(i) [FLIP EVENT.] A Voronoi edge $e^\diamond_{pq}$ shrinks to a point, disappears, and is "flipped" into a newly emerging Voronoi edge $e^\diamond_{p'q'}$.

(ii) [CORNER EVENT.] An endpoint of some Voronoi edge $e^\diamond_{pq}$ becomes a breakpoint (a corner placement). Immediately after this time $e^\diamond_{pq}$ either gains a new straight segment, or loses such a segment.

Some comments are in order:

(a) A flip event occurs when the four points p, q, p', q' become "cocircular": there is an empty homothetic copy Q' of Q that touches all four points.

(b) Only non-corner edges can participate in a flip event, as both the vanishing edge $e^\diamond_{pq}$ and the newly emerging edge $e^\diamond_{p'q'}$ do not have breakpoints near the event.

(c) A flip event entails a discrete change in the Delaunay triangulation, whereas a corner event does not. Still we will keep track of both kinds of events.

We first bound the number of corner events.

LEMMA 3.1. *Let P be a set of n points in $\mathbb{R}^2$ under algebraic motion of bounded degree, and let Q be a convex k-gon. The number of corner events in $\mathrm{DT}^\diamond(P)$ is $O(k^2 n\lambda_r(n))$, where r is a constant that depends on the degree of motion of P.*

PROOF. Fix a point p and a vertex w of Q, and consider all the corner events in which w touches p. As noted above, at any such event the center c of Q lies on a ray γ emanating from p at a fixed direction. For each other point $q \in P \setminus \{p\}$, let $\varphi^\diamond_\gamma[p,q]$ denote the distance, at time t, from p along γ to the center of a copy of Q that touches p (at w) and q. The value $\min_q \varphi^\diamond_\gamma[p,q](t)$ represents the intersection of $\partial\,\mathrm{Vor}^\diamond(p)$ with γ at time t, where $\mathrm{Vor}^\diamond(p)$ is the Voronoi cell of p in $\mathrm{VD}^\diamond(P)$. The point q that attains the minimum defines the Voronoi edge $e^\diamond_{pq}$ (or vertex if the minimum is attained by more than one point q) that intersects γ.

In other words, we have a collection of $n-1$ partially defined functions $\varphi^\diamond_\gamma[p,q]$, and the breakpoints of their lower envelope represent the corner events that involve the contact of w with p. By our assumption on the motion of P, each function $\varphi^\diamond_\gamma[p,q]$ is piecewise algebraic, with $O(k)$ pieces. Each piece encodes a continuous contact of q with a specific edge of Q', and has constant description complexity. Hence (see, e.g., [21, Corollary 1.6]) the complexity of the envelope is at most $O(k\lambda_r(n))$, for an appropriate constant r. Repeating the analysis for each point p and each vertex w of Q, the lemma follows. $\square$

Consider next flip events. As noted, each flip event involves a placement of an empty homothetic copy Q' of Q that touches simultaneously four points p_1, p_2, p_3, p_4 of P, in this counterclockwise order along $\partial Q'$, so that the Voronoi edge $e^\diamond_{p_1p_3}$, which is a non-corner edge before the event, shrinks to a point and is replaced by the non-corner edge $e^\diamond_{p_2p_4}$. Let e_i denote the edge of Q' that touches p_i, for $i = 1, 2, 3, 4$.

We fix the quadruple of edges e_1, e_2, e_3, e_4, bound the number of flip events involving a quadruple contact with these edges, and sum the bound over all $O(k^4)$ choices of four edges of Q. For a fixed quadruple of edges e_1, e_2, e_3, e_4, we replace Q by the convex hull Q_0 of these edges, and note that any flip event involving these edges is also a flip event for Q_0. We therefore restrict our attention to Q_0, which is a convex k_0-gon, for some $k_0 \leq 8$.

The number of flip events for a fixed Q_0 is bounded by extending and adapting the analysis of Chew [8]. Basically, we surround a non-corner edge by $O(1)$ nearby corner edges, and argue that, as long as none of them undergoes a corner event, only $O(1)$ flip events can occur in the "middle" edge. This allows us to charge a flip event to a corner event so that each corner event is charged only $O(1)$ times. See [8] and the full version [1] for details. Repeating this to each quadruple of edges of Q, we thus obtain:

THEOREM 3.2. *Let P be a set of n moving points in $\mathbb{R}^2$ under algebraic motion of bounded degree, and let Q be a convex k-gon. The number of topological changes in $\mathrm{VD}^\diamond(P)$ with respect to Q is $O(k^4 n\lambda_r(n))$, where r is a constant that depends on the degree of motion of P.*

Kinetic maintenance of $\mathbf{VD^\diamond(P)}$ and $\mathbf{DT^\diamond(P)}$. As already mentioned, it is a fairly trivial task to maintain $\mathrm{DT}^\diamond(P)$ and $\mathrm{VD}^\diamond(P)$ kinetically, as the points of P move. All we need to do is to assert the correctness of the present triangulation by a collection of local certificates, one for each edge of the diagram, where the certificate of an edge asserts that the two homothetic placements Q^-, Q^+ of Q that circumscribe the two respective adjacent Q-Delaunay triangles $\triangle pqr^-, \triangle pqr^+$, are such that Q^- does not contain r^+ and Q^+ does not contain r^-. The failure time of this certificate is the first time (if one exists) at which p, q, r^-, and r^+ become Q-co-circular—they all lie on the boundary of a common homothetic copy of Q. If pq is an edge of the periphery of $\mathrm{DT}^\diamond(P)$, so that $\triangle pqr^+$ exists but $\triangle pqr^-$ does not, then Q^- is a limiting wedge bounded by rays supporting two consecutive edges of (a copy of) Q, one passing through p and one through q (see Figure 3). The failure time of the corresponding certificate is the first time (if any) at which r^+ also lies on the boundary of that wedge. This corresponds to a flip event.

We maintain the breakpoints using "sub-certificates", each of which asserts that Q^-, say, touches each of p, q, r^- at a respective specific edge (and similarly for Q^+). The failure time of this sub-certificate is the first failure time when one of p, q or r^- touches Q^- at a vertex. In this case we have a corner event—two of the adjacent Voronoi edges terminate at a corner placement. Note that the failure time of each sub-certificate can be computed in $O(1)$ time. Moreover, for a fixed collection of valid sub-certificates, the failure time of an initial certificate (asserting non-co-circularity) can also be computed in $O(1)$ time (provided that it fails before the failures of the corresponding sub-certificates), because we know the four edges of Q^- involved in the contacts.

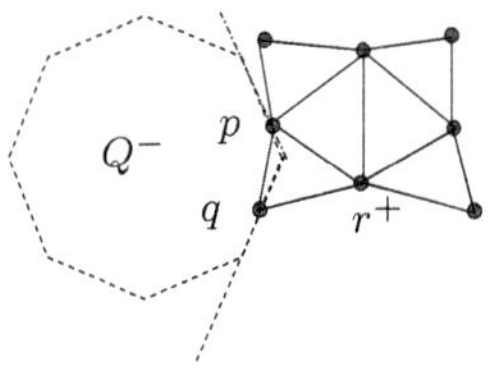

Figure 3. If r^- does not exist then Q^- is a limiting wedge bounded by rays supporting two consecutive edges of (a copy of) Q.

We therefore maintain an event queue that stores and updates all the active failure times (there are only $O(n)$ of them—the bound is independent of k). When a sub-certificate fails we do not change $\mathrm{DT}^\diamond(P)$, but only update the corresponding Voronoi edge, by adding or removing a segment and a breakpoint, and by replacing the sub-certificate by a new one; we also update the real certificate associated with the edge, because one of the contact edges has changed. When a real certificate fails we update $\mathrm{DT}^\diamond(P)$ and construct $O(1)$ new sub-certificates and certificates. Altogether, each update of the diagram takes $O(\log n)$ time. We thus have

THEOREM 3.3. *Let P be a set of n moving points in $\mathbb{R}^2$ under algebraic motion of bounded degree, and let Q be a convex k-gon. $\mathrm{DT}^\diamond(P)$ and $\mathrm{VD}^\diamond(P)$ can be maintained using $O(n)$ storage and $O(\log n)$ update time, so that $O(k^4 n\lambda_r(n))$ events are processed, where r is a constant that depends on the degree of motion of P.*

3.2 Stable Delaunay edges in $\mathrm{DT}^\diamond(\mathrm{P})$

We now restrict Q to be a regular k-gon. Let $v_0, \ldots, v_{k-1}$ be the vertices of Q arranged in a clockwise direction, with v_0 the leftmost. We call a homothetic copy of Q whose vertex v_j touches a point p, a *v_j-placement of Q at p*. Let u_j be the direction of the vector that connects v_j with the center of Q, for each $0 \leq j < k$ (as in Section 2). See Figure 4 (left).

We follow the machinery in the proof of Lemma 3.1. That is, for any pair $p, q \in P$ let $\varphi_j^\diamond[p,q]$ denote the distance from p to the point $u_j[p] \cap b_{pq}^\diamond$; we put $\varphi_j^\diamond[p,q] = \infty$ if $u_j[p]$ does not intersect $b_{pq}^\diamond$. If $\varphi_j^\diamond[p,q] < \infty$ then the point $b_{pq}^\diamond \cap u_j[p]$ is the center of the v_j-placement Q' of Q at p that also touches q. The value $\varphi_j^\diamond[q,p]$ is equal to the circumradius of Q'. See Figure 4 (middle).

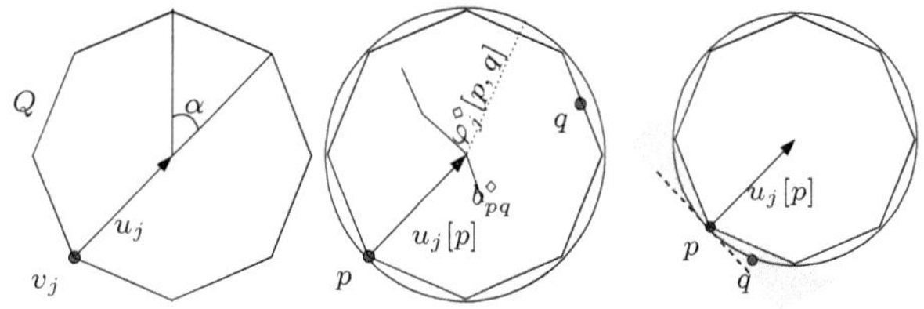

Figure 4. Left: u_j is the direction of the vector connecting vertex v_j to the center of Q. Middle: The function $\varphi_j^\diamond[p,q]$ is equal to the radius of the circle that circumscribes the v_j-placement of Q at p that also touches q. Right: The case when $\varphi_j^\diamond[p,q] = \infty$ while $\varphi_j[p,q] < \infty$. In this case q must lie in one of the shaded wedges.

The *neighbor* $N_j^\diamond[p]$ of p in direction u_j is defined to be the point $q \in P \setminus \{p\}$ that minimizes $\varphi_j^\diamond[p,q]$. Clearly, for any $p, q \in P$ we have $N_j^\diamond[p] = q$ if and only if there is an empty v_j-placement Q' of Q at p so that q touches one of its edges.

Remark: Note that, in the Euclidean case, we have $\varphi_j[p,q] < \infty$ if and only if the angle between $\overline{pq}$ and $u_j[p]$ is at most $\pi/2$. In contrast, $\varphi_j^\diamond[p,q] < \infty$ if and only if the angle between $\overline{pq}$ and $u_j[p]$ is at most $\pi/2 - \pi/k = \pi/2 - \alpha/2$. Moreover, we have $\varphi_j[p,q] \leq \varphi_j^\diamond[p,q]$. Therefore, $\varphi_j^\diamond[p,q] < \infty$ always implies $\varphi_j[p,q] < \infty$, but not vice versa; see Figure 4 (right).

LEMMA 3.4. *Let $p, q \in P$ be a pair of points such that $N_j(p) = q$ for $h \geq 3$ consecutive indices, say $0 \leq j < h$. Then for each of these indices, except possibly for the first and the last one, we also have $N_j^\diamond[p] = q$.*

PROOF. Let w_1 (resp., w_2) be the point at which the ray $u_0[p]$ (resp., $u_{h-1}[p]$) hits the edge e_{pq} in $\mathrm{VD}(P)$. (By assumption, both points exist.) Let D_1 and D_2 be the disks centered at w_1 and w_2, respectively, and touching p and q. By definition, neither of these disks contains a point of P in its interior. The angle between the

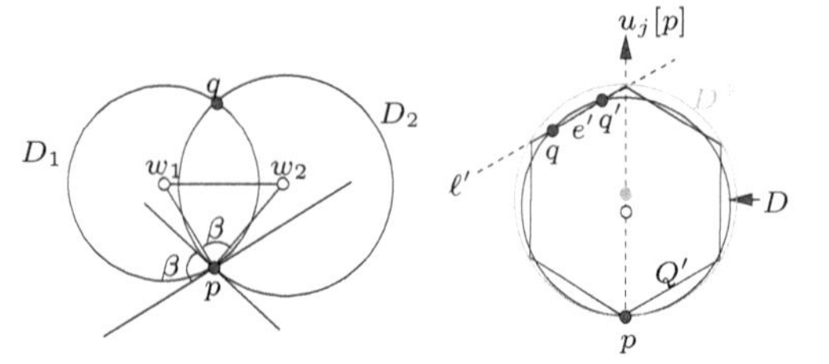

Figure 5. Left: The angle between the tangents to D_1 and D_2 is equal to $\angle w_1 p w_2 = \beta = (h-1)\alpha$. Right: The line ℓ' crosses D in a chord qq' which is fully contained in e' (right).

tangents to D_1 and D_2 at p or at q (these angles are equal) is $\beta = (h-1)\alpha$; see Figure 5 (left).

Fix an arbitrary index $1 \le j \le h-2$, so $u_j[p]$ intersects e_{pq} and forms an angle of at least α with each of pw_1, pw_2. Let Q' be the v_j-placement of Q at p that touches q. The existence of such a placement follows from the preceding remark. We claim that $Q' \subset D_1 \cup D_2$. Establishing this property for every $1 \le j \le h-2$ will complete the proof of the lemma. Let e' be the edge of Q' passing through q. Let D be the disk whose center lies on $u_j[p]$ and which passes through p and q, and let D^+ be the circumscribing disk of Q'. Since $q \in \partial D$ and is interior to D^+, and since D and D^+ are centered on the same ray $u_j[q]$ and pass through p, it follows that $D \subset D^+$. See Figure 5 (right). The line ℓ' containing e' crosses D in a chord qq' that is fully contained in e'. The angle between the tangent to D at q and the chord qq' is equal to the angle at which p sees qq'. This is smaller than the angle at which p sees e', which in turn is equal to $\alpha/2$.

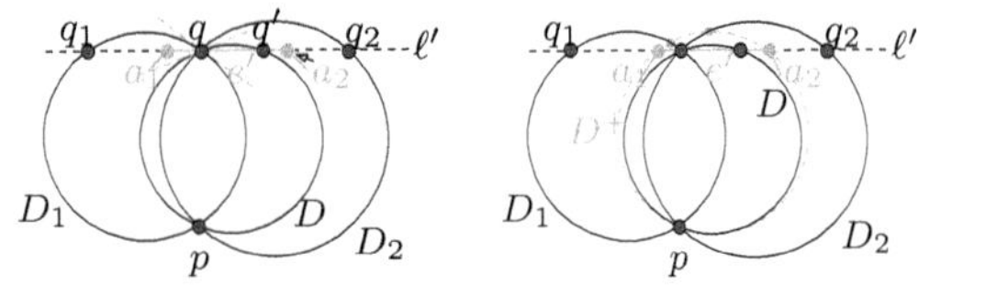

Figure 6. Left: The line ℓ' forms an angle of at least $\alpha/2$ with each of the tangents to D_1, D_2 at q. Right: The edge $e' = a_1a_2$ of Q' is fully contained in $D_1 \cup D_2$.

Arguing as in the analysis of D_1 and D_2, the tangent to D at q forms an angle of at least α with each of the tangents to D_1, D_2 at q, and hence e' forms an angle of at least $\alpha/2$ with each of these tangents; see Figure 6 (left). The line ℓ' marks two chords q_1q, qq_2 within the respective disks D_1, D_2. We claim that e' is fully contained in their union q_1q_2. Indeed, the angle q_1pq is equal to the angle between ℓ' and the tangent to D_1 at q, so $\angle q_1pq \ge \alpha/2$. On the other hand, the angle at which p sees e' is $\alpha/2$, which is smaller. This, and the symmetic argument involving D_2, are easily seen to imply the claim.

Now consider the circumscribing disk D^+ of Q'. Denote the endpoints of e' as a_1 and a_2, where a_1 lies in q_1q and a_2 lies in qq_2. Since the ray $\overline{pa_1}$ hits ∂D^+ before hitting D_1, and the ray $\overline{pq}$ hits these circles in the reverse order, it follows that the second intersection of ∂D_1 and ∂D^+ (other than p) must lie on a ray from p which lies between the rays $\overline{pa_1}, \overline{pq}$ and thus crosses e'. See Figure 6 (right). Symmetrically, the second intersection point of ∂D_2 and ∂D^+ also lies on a ray which crosses e'.

It follows that the arc of ∂D^+ delimited by these intersections and containing p is fully contained in $D_1 \cup D_2$. Hence all the vertices of Q' (which lie on this arc) lie in $D_1 \cup D_2$. This, combined with the argument in the preceding paragraphs, is easily seen to imply that $Q' \subseteq D_1 \cup D_2$, so its interior does not contain points of P, which in turn implies that $N_j^\diamond[p] = q$. As noted, this completes the proof of the lemma. □

Since Q-Voronoi edges are connected, Lemma 3.4 implies that $e_{pq}^\diamond$ is "long", in the sense that it contains at least $h-2$ breakpoints that represent corner placements at p, interleaved (as promised in Section 3.1) with at least $h-3$ corner placements at q. This property is easily seen to hold also under the weaker assumptions that: (i) for the first and the last indices $j = 0, h-1$, the point $N_j[p]$ either is equal to q or is undefined, and (ii) for the rest of the indices j we have $N_j[p] = q$ and $\varphi_j^\diamond[p,q] < \infty$ (i.e., the v_j-placement of Q at p that touches q exists). In this relaxed setting, it is now possible that any of the two points w_1, w_2 lies at infinity, in which case the corresponding disk D_1 or D_2 degenerates into a halfplane. This stronger version of Lemma 3.4 is used in the proof of the converse Lemma 3.5, asserting that every edge $e_{pq}^\diamond$ in $\mathrm{VD}^\diamond(P)$ with sufficiently many breakpoints has a stable counterpart e_{pq} in $\mathrm{VD}(P)$.

LEMMA 3.5. *Let $p, q \in P$ be a pair of points such that $N_j^\diamond[p] = q$ for at least three consecutive indices $j \in \{0, \ldots, k-1\}$. Then for each of these indices, except possibly for the first and the last one, we have $N_j[p] = q$.*

PROOF. Again, assume with no loss of generality that $N_j^\diamond[p] = q$ for $0 \le j \le h-1$, with $h \ge 3$. Suppose to the contrary that, for some $1 \le j \le h-2$, we have $N_j[p] \ne q$. Since $N_j^\diamond[p] = q$ by assumption, we have $\varphi_j[p,q] \le \varphi_j^\diamond[p,q] < \infty$, so there exists $r \in P$ for which $\varphi_j[p,r] < \varphi_j[p,q]$. Assume with no loss of generality that r lies to the left of the line from p to q, so that $\varphi_{j-1}[p,r] < \varphi_{j-1}[p,q] < \infty$, which follows because (i) $N_{j-1}^\diamond[p] = q$ by assumption, so $\varphi_{j-1}^\diamond[p,q] < \infty$, and (ii) $\varphi_{j-1}[p,q] \le \varphi_{j-1}^\diamond[p,q]$. See Figure 7 (left). Similarly, we get that either $\varphi_{j-2}[p,r] < \varphi_{j-2}[p,q] < \infty$ or $\varphi_{j-2}[p,r] \le \varphi_{j-2}[p,q] = \infty$ (where the latter can occur only for $j = 1$). Now applying (the extended version of) Lemma 3.4 to the point set $\{p,q,r\}$ and to the index set $\{j-2, j-1, j\}$, we get that $\varphi_{j-1}^\diamond[p,r] < \varphi_{j-1}^\diamond[p,q]$. But this contradicts the fact that $N_{j-1}^\diamond[p] = q$. □

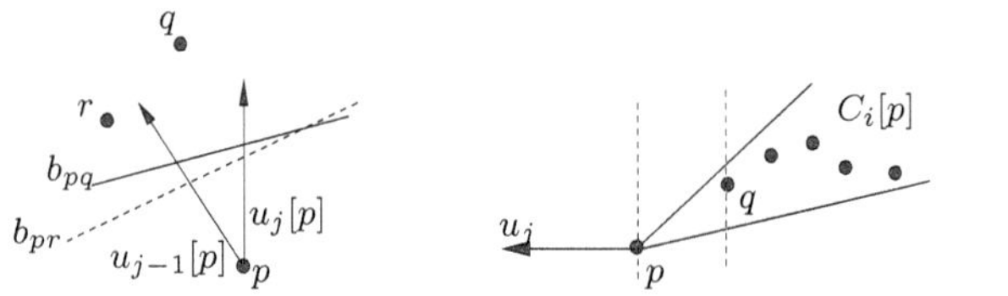

Figure 7. Left: Proof of Lemma 3.5. If $N_j[p] \ne q$ because some r, lying to the left of the line from p to r, satisfies $\varphi_j[p,r] < \varphi_j[p,q]$. Since $\varphi_{j-1}[p,q] < \varphi_{j-1}^\diamond[p,q] < \infty$, we have $\varphi_{j-1}[p,r] < \varphi_{j-1}[p,q]$. Right: q is j-extremal for p.

Maintaining an SDG using $\mathrm{VD}^\diamond(\mathbf{P})$. Lemmas 3.4 and 3.5 together imply that SDG can be maintained using the fairly straightforward kinetic algorithm for maintaining the whole $\mathrm{VD}^\diamond(P)$, provided by Theorem 3.3. We use $\mathrm{VD}^\diamond(P)$ to maintain the graph G on P, whose edges are all the pairs $(p,q) \in P \times P$ such that p and q define an edge $e_{pq}^\diamond$ in $\mathrm{VD}^\diamond(P)$ that contains at least seven breakpoints. As shown in Theorem 3.3, this can be done with $O(n)$ storage, $O(\log n)$ update time, and $O(k^4 n \lambda_r(n))$ updates (for an appropriate r). We claim that G is a $(6\alpha, \alpha)$-SDG in the Euclidean norm.

Indeed, if two points $p, q \in P$ define a 6α-long edge e_{pq} in $\mathrm{VD}(P)$ then this edge stabs at least six rays $u_j[p]$ emanating from p, and at least six rays $u_j[q]$ emanating from q. Thus, according to Lemma 3.4, $\mathrm{VD}^\diamond(P)$ contains the edge $e^\diamond_{pq}$ with at least four breakpoints corresponding to corner placements of Q at p that touch q, and at least four breakpoints corresponding to corner placements of Q at q that touch p. Therefore, $e^\diamond_{pq}$ contains at least 8 breakpoints, so $(p, q) \in \mathsf{G}$.

For the second part, if $p, q \in P$ define an edge $e^\diamond_{pq}$ in $\mathrm{VD}^\diamond(P)$ with at least 7 breakpoints then, by the interleaving property of breakpoints, we may assume, without loss of generality, that at least four of these breakpoints correspond to P-empty corner placements of Q at p that touch q. Thus, Lemma 3.5 implies that $\mathrm{VD}(P)$ contains the edge e_{pq}, and that this edge is hit by at least two consecutive rays $u_j[p]$. But then, as observed in Lemma 2.2, the edge e_{pq} is α-long in $\mathrm{VD}(P)$. We thus obtain the main result of this section.

THEOREM 3.6. *Let P be a set of n moving points in $\mathbb{R}^2$ under algebraic motion of bounded degree, and let $\alpha \geq 0$ be a parameter. A $(6\alpha, \alpha)$-stable Delaunay graph of P can be maintained by a KDS of linear size that processes $O(n\lambda_r(n)/\alpha^4)$ events, where r is a constant that depends on the degree of motion of P, and that updates the SDG at each event in $O(\log n)$ time.*

4. A FASTER DATA STRUCTURE

The data structure of Theorem 3.6 requires $O(n)$ storage but the best bound we have on the number of events it may encounter is $O^*(n^2/\alpha^4)$, which is much larger than the number of events encountered by the data structure of Theorem 2.3. In this section we present an alternative data structure that requires $O^*(n/\alpha^2)$ space and $O^*(n^2/\alpha^2)$ overall processing time. The algorithm is *local*, and it processes each event in $O^*(1/\alpha)$ time.

Notation. We use the directions u_i and the associated quantities $N_i[p]$ and $\varphi_i[p, q]$ defined in Section 2. We assume that k is even, and write, as in Section 2, $k = 2s$. We denote by C_i the cone (or wedge) with apex at the origin that is bounded by u_i and u_{i+1}. Note that C_i and $C_{i\pm s}$ are antipodal. As before, for a vector u, we denote by $u[x]$ the ray emanating from x in direction u. Similarly, for a cone C we denote by $C[x]$ the translation of C that places its apex at x. Let $0 \leq \beta \leq \pi/2$ be an angle. For a direction $u \in \mathbb{S}^1$ and for two points $p, q \in P$, we say that the edge $e_{pq} \in \mathrm{VD}(P)$ is *β-long around the ray $u[q]$* if p is the Voronoi neighbor of q in all directions in the range $[u-\beta, u+\beta]$, i.e., for all $v \in [u-\beta, u+\beta]$, the ray $v[q]$ intersects e_{pq}. The *β-cone around $u[q]$* is the cone whose apex is q and each of its bounding rays makes an angle of β with $u[q]$.

j-extremal points. Let $p, q \in P$, let i be the index such that $q \in C_i[p]$, and let u_j be a direction such that $\langle u_j, x\rangle \leq 0$ for all $x \in C_i$. We say that q is *j-extremal* for p if $q = \arg\max\{\langle p', u_j\rangle \mid p' \in C_i[p] \cap P \setminus \{p\}\}$. That is, q is the nearest point to p in this cone, in the $(-u_j)$-direction. Clearly, a point p has at most s j-extremal points, one for every admissible cone $C_i[p]$, for any fixed j. See Figure 7 (right).

For $0 \leq i < k$, let C'_i denote the extended cone that is the union of the seven consecutive cones $C_{i-3}, \ldots, C_{i+3}$. Let $p, q \in P$, let i be the index such that $q \in C_i[p]$, and let u_j be a direction such that $\langle u_j, x\rangle \leq 0$ for all $x \in C'_i$. We say that the point $q \in P$ is *strongly j-extremal* for p if $q = \arg\max\{\langle p', u_j\rangle \mid p' \in C'_i[p] \cap P \setminus \{p\}\}$.

We say that a pair $(p, q) \in P \times P$ is (strongly) (j, ℓ)-extremal, for some $0 \leq j, \ell \leq k-1$, if p is (strongly) ℓ-extremal for q and q is (strongly) j-extremal for p.

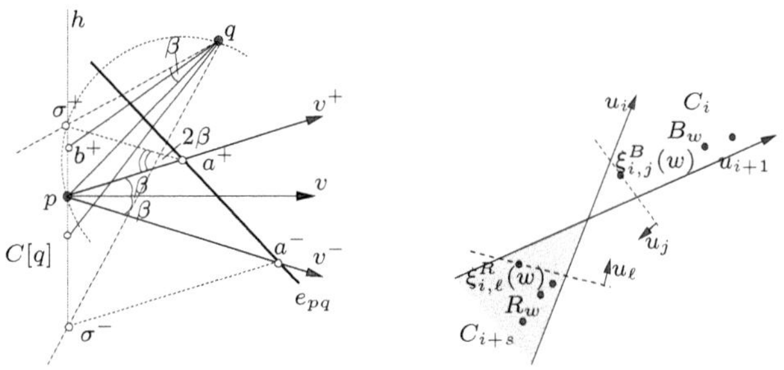

Figure 8. Left: Illustration of the setup in Lemma 4.1: the edge e_{pq} is β-long around $v[p]$, and the "tip" $\triangle\sigma^+q\sigma^-$ of the cone $C[q]$ is empty. Right: The points $\xi^R_{i,\ell}(w), \xi^B_{i,j}(w)$ for an appropriate node w.

LEMMA 4.1. *Let $p, q \in P$, and let v be a direction such that the edge e_{pq} appears in $\mathrm{VD}(P)$ and is β-long around the ray $v[p]$. Let $C[q]$ be the β-cone around the ray from q through p. Then $\langle p, v\rangle \geq \langle p', v\rangle$ for all $p' \in P \cap C[q] \setminus \{q\}$.*

PROOF. Refer to Figure 8 (left). Without loss of generality, we assume that v is the $(+x)$-direction and that q lies above the x-axis and to the right of p. (In this case the slope of the bisector b_{pq} is negative.) Let v^+ (resp., v^-) be the direction that makes a counterclockwise (resp., clockwise) angle of β with v. Let a^+ (resp., a^-) be the intersection of e_{pq} with $v^+[p]$ (resp., with $v^-[p]$); by assumption, both points exist. Let h be the vertical line passing through p. Let σ^+ (resp., σ^-) be the intersection point of h with the ray emanating from a^+ (resp., a^-) in the direction opposite to v^- (resp., v^+); see Figure 8 (left).

Note that $\angle pa^+\sigma^+ = 2\beta$, and that $\|a^+\sigma^+\| = \|pa^+\| = \|qa^+\|$, i.e., a^+ is the circumcenter of $\triangle p\sigma^+q$. Therefore $\angle\sigma^+qp = \frac{1}{2}\angle\sigma^+a^+p = \beta$. That is, σ^+ is the intersection of the upper ray of $C[q]$ with h. Similarly, σ^- is the intersection of the lower ray of $C[q]$ with h. Moreover, if there exists a point $x \in P$ properly inside the triangle $\triangle pq\sigma^+$ then $\|a^+x\| < \|a^+p\|$, contradicting the fact that a^+ is on e_{pq}. So the interior of $\triangle pq\sigma^+$ (including the edges pq, σ^+q) is disjoint from P. Similarly, by a symmetric argument, no points of P lie inside $\triangle pq\sigma^-$ or on its edges pq, σ^-q. Hence, the portion of $C[q]$ to the right of p is openly disjoint from P, and therefore p is a rightmost point of P (extreme in the v direction) inside $C[q]$. $\square$

COROLLARY 4.2. *Let $p, q \in P$. (i) If the edge e_{pq} is 3α-long in $\mathrm{VD}(P)$ then there are $0 \leq j, \ell < k$ for which (p, q) is a (j, ℓ)-extremal pair. (ii) If the edge e_{pq} is 9α-long in $\mathrm{VD}(P)$ then there are $0 \leq j, \ell < k$ for which (p, q) is a strongly (j, ℓ)-extremal pair.*

PROOF. To prove part (i), choose $0 \leq j, \ell < k$, such that e_{pq} is α-long around each of $u_\ell[p]$ and $u_j[q]$. By Lemma 4.1, p is u_ℓ-extremal in the α-cone $C[q]$ around the ray from q through p. Let i be the index such that $p \in C_i[q]$. Since the opening angle of $C[q]$ is 2α, it follows that $C_i[q] \subseteq C[q]$, so p is ℓ-extremal with respect to q, and, symmetrically, q is j-extremal with respect to p. To prove part (ii) choose $0 \leq j, \ell < k$, such that e_{pq} is 4α-long around each of $u_\ell[p]$ and $u_j[q]$ and apply Lemma 4.1 as in the proof of part (i). $\square$

The stable Delaunay graph. We kinetically maintain a $(9\alpha, \alpha)$-stable Delaunay graph, whose precise definition is given below, using a data-structure which is based on a collection of 2-dimensional orthogonal range trees similar to the ones used in [2].

Fix $0 \leq i < s$, and choose a "sheared" coordinate frame in which the rays u_i and u_{i+1} form the x- and y-axes, respectively.

That is, in this coordinate frame, $q \in C_i[p]$ if and only if q lies in the upper-right quadrant anchored at p.

We define a 2-dimensional range tree $\mathcal{T}_i$ consisting of a *primary* balanced binary search tree with the points of P stored at its leaves ordered by their x-coordinates, and of secondary trees, introduced below. Each internal node v of the primary tree of $\mathcal{T}_i$ is associated with the *canonical subset* P_v of all points that are stored at the leaves of the subtree rooted at v. A point $p \in P_v$ is said to be *red (resp., blue) in* P_v if it is stored at the subtree rooted at the left (resp., right) child of v in $\mathcal{T}_i$. For each primary node v we maintain a secondary balanced binary search tree $\mathcal{T}_i^v$, whose leaves store the points of P_v ordered by their y-coordinates. We refer to a node w in a secondary tree $\mathcal{T}_i^v$ as a *secondary node* w *of* $\mathcal{T}_i$.

Each node w of a secondary tree $\mathcal{T}_i^v$ is associated with a canonical subset $P_w \subseteq P_v$ of points stored at the leaves of the subtree of $\mathcal{T}_i^v$ rooted at w. We also associate with w the sets $R_w \subset P_w$ and $B_w \subset P_w$ of points residing in the *left* (resp., *right*) *subtree* of w and are red (resp., blue) in P_v. It is easy to verify that the sum of the sizes of the sets R_w and B_w over all secondary nodes of $\mathcal{T}_i$ is $O(n \log^2 n)$.

For each secondary node $w \in \mathcal{T}_i$ and each $0 \le j < k$ we maintain the points

$$\xi_{i,j}^R(w) = \arg\max_{p \in R_w} \langle p, u_j \rangle, \quad \xi_{i,j}^B(w) = \arg\max_{p \in B_w} \langle p, u_j \rangle,$$

provided that both R_w, B_w are not empty. See Figure 8 (right). It is straightforward to show that if (p, q) is a (j, ℓ)-extremal pair, so that $q \in C_i[p]$, then there is a secondary node $w \in \mathcal{T}_i$ for which $q = \xi_{i,j}^B(w)$ and $p = \xi_{i,\ell}^R(w)$.

For each $p \in P$ we define a set $\mathcal{N}[p]$ containing all points $q \in P$ for which (p, q) is a (j, ℓ)-extremal pair, for some pair of indices $0 \le j, \ell < k$. Specifically, for each $0 \le i < s$, and each secondary node $w \in \mathcal{T}_i$ such that $p = \xi_{i,\ell}^R(w)$ for some $0 \le \ell < k$, we include in $\mathcal{N}[p]$ all the points q such that $q = \xi_{i,j}^B(w)$ for some $0 \le j < k$. Similarly, for each $0 \le i < s$, and each secondary node $w \in \mathcal{T}_i$ such that $p = \xi_{i,\ell}^B(w)$ for some $0 \le \ell < k$ we include in $\mathcal{N}[p]$ all the points q such that $q = \xi_{i,j}^R(w)$ for some $0 \le j < k$.

For each $0 \le i < s$, any point $p \in P$ belongs to $O(\log^2 n)$ sets R_w and B_w, so the size of $\mathcal{N}[p]$ is bounded by $O(s^2 \log^2 n)$. Indeed, p may be coupled with up to $k = 2s$ neighbors at each of the $O(s \log^2 n)$ nodes containing it.

For each point $p \in P$ and $0 \le \ell < k$ we maintain all points in $\mathcal{N}[p]$ in a kinetic and dynamic tournament $\mathcal{D}_\ell[p]$ whose winner q minimizes the directional distance $\varphi_\ell[p, q]$, as given in (1). That is, the winner in $\mathcal{D}_\ell[p]$ is $N_\ell[p]$ in the Voronoi diagram of $\{p\} \cup \mathcal{N}[p]$.

We are now ready to define the stable Delaunay graph G that we maintain. For each pair of points $p, q \in P$ we add the edge (p, q) to G if the following hold.

(G1) There is an index $0 \le \ell \le k - 1$ such that q wins the 8 consecutive tournaments $\mathcal{D}_\ell[p], \ldots, \mathcal{D}_{\ell+7}[p]$.

(G2) The point p is strongly $(\ell + 3)$-extremal and strongly $(\ell + 4)$-extremal for q.

In the full version of the paper [1] we prove that G is $(9\alpha, \alpha)$-stable. We also show how to kinetically maintain (a refined version of) G efficiently, and establish the following theorem.

THEOREM 4.3. *Let P be a set of n moving points in $\mathbb{R}^2$ under algebraic motion of bounded degree, and let $\alpha > 0$ be a parameter. A $(9\alpha, \alpha)$-SDG of P can be maintained using a data structure that requires $O((n/\alpha^2) \log n)$ space and encounters two types of events: swap events and tournament events. There are $O(n^2/\alpha)$ swap events, each processed in $O(\log^4(n)/\alpha)$ time. There are*

$$O((n/\alpha)^2 \beta_{r+2}(\log(n)/\alpha) \log^2 n \log(\log(n)/\alpha))$$

tournament events, which are handled in a total of

$$O((n/\alpha)^2 \beta_{r+2}(\log(n)/\alpha) \log^2 n \log^2(\log(n)/\alpha))$$

processing time. The worst-case processing time of a tournament event is $O(\log^2(\log(n)/\alpha))$.

Remark: Comparing this algorithm with the space-inefficient one of Section 2, we note that they both use the same kind of tournaments, but here much fewer pairs of points ($O^*(n/\alpha^2)$ instead of $O(n^2/\alpha)$) participate in the tournaments. The price we have to pay is that the test for an edge pq to be stable is more involved. Moreover, keeping track of the subset of pairs that participate in the tournaments requires additional work, which is facilitated by the range trees $\mathcal{T}_i$.

5. PROPERTIES OF SDG

We conclude the paper by establishing some of the properties of stable Delaunay graphs.

Near co-circularities do not show up in an SDG. Consider a critical event during the kinetic maintenance of the full Delaunay triangulation, in which four points a, b, c, d become co-circular, in this order along their circumcircle, with this circle being empty. Just before the critical event, the Delaunay triangulation involved two triangles, say, abc, acd. The Voronoi edge e_{ac} shrinks to a point (namely, to the circumcenter of $abcd$ at the critical event), and, after the critical co-circularity, is replaced by the Voronoi edge e_{bd}, which expands from the circumcenter as time progresses.

Our algorithm will detect the possibility of such an event before the criticality occurs, when e_{ac} becomes α-short (or even before this happens). It will then remove this edge from the stable subgraph, so the actual co-circularity will not be recorded. The new edge e_{bd} will then be detected by the algorithm only when it becomes sufficiently long (if at all), and will then enter the stable Delaunay graph. In short, critical co-circularities do not arise *at all* in our scheme.

As noted in the introduction, a Delaunay edge ab is just about to become α-short or α-long when the sum of the opposite angles in its two adjacent Delaunay triangles is $\pi - \alpha$ (see Figure 1 (left)). This shows that changes in the stable Delaunay graph occur when the "co-circularity defect" of a nearly co-circular quadruple (i.e., the difference between π and the sum of opposite angles in the quadrilateral spanned by the quadruple) is between α and $c\alpha$, where c is the constant used in our definitions in Section 3 or Section 4. Note that a degenerate case of co-circularity is a collinearity on the convex hull. Such collinearities also do not show up in the stable Delaunay graph. A hull collinearity between three nodes a, b, c is detected before it happens, when (or before) the corresponding Voronoi edge becomes α-short, in which case the angle $\angle acb$, where c is the middle point the (near-)collinearity becomes $\pi - \alpha$ (see Figure 9 (left)). Therefore a hull edge is removed if the Delaunay triangle is almost collinear. The edge re-appears when its corresponding Voronoi edge is long enough, as before.

SDGs are not too sparse. Consider the Voronoi cell $\mathrm{Vor}(p)$ of a point p, and suppose that p has only one α-long edge e_{pq}. Since the angle at which p sees e_{pq} is at most π, the sum of the angles at which p sees the other edges is at least π, so $\mathrm{Vor}(p)$ has at least π/α α-short edges. Let m_1 denote the number of points p with this property. Then the sum of their degrees in $\mathrm{DT}(P)$ is at least $m_1(\pi/\alpha + 1)$. Similarly, if m_0 points do not have any α-long

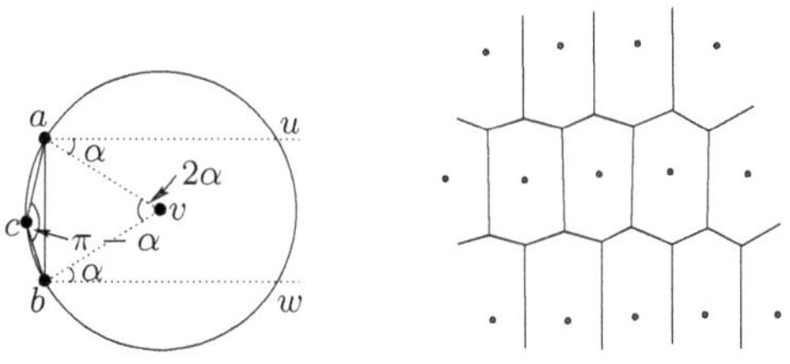

Figure 9. Left: The near collinearity that corresponds to a Voronoi edge becoming α-short. Right: If the points of P lie on a sufficiently spaced shifted grid then the number of α-long edges in $\mathrm{VD}(P)$ (the vertical ones) is close to n.

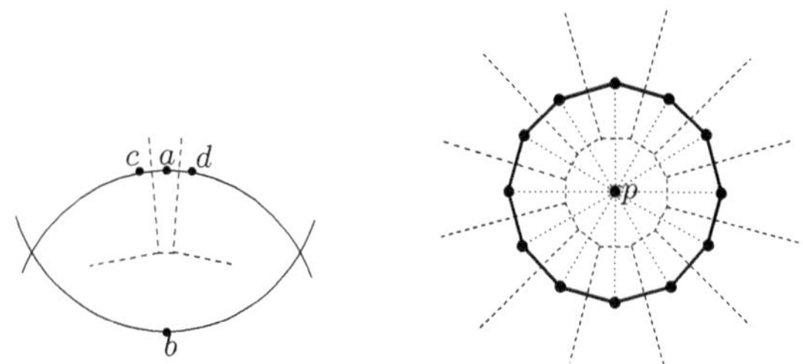

Figure 10. Two constructions with an appropriate choice of α. Left: ab is an edge of the relative neighborhood graph but not of SDG. Right: A wheel-like configuration that disconnects p in the stable Delaunay graph. The Voronoi diagram is drawn with dashed-dotted lines, the stable Delaunay edges are drawn as solid, and the remaining Delaunay edges as dotted edges. The points of the "wheel" need not be co-circular.

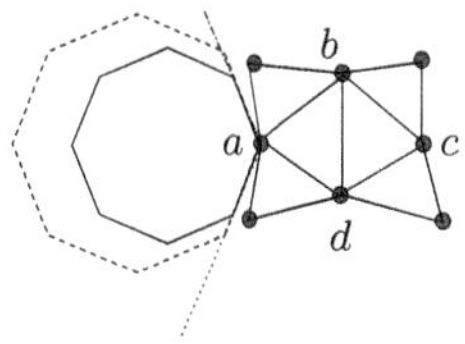

Figure 11. The triangulation $\mathrm{DT}^\diamond(P)$ of an 8-point set P. The points a, b, c, d, which do not lie on the convex hull of P, still lie on the boundary of the union of the triangles of $\mathrm{DT}^\diamond(P)$ because, for each of these points we can place an arbitrary large homothetic interior-empty copy of Q which touches that point.

Voronoi edge, then the sum of their degrees is at least $2\pi m_0/\alpha$. Any other point has degree at least 3 in $\mathrm{DT}(P)$ and has at least two α-long Voronoi edges. So the number of α-long edges is at least (recall that each α-long edge is counted twice)

$$n - m_1 - m_0 + m_1/2 = n - (m_1 + 2m_0)/2. \qquad (2)$$

Let h denote the number of hull vertices. Since the sum of the degrees is $6n - 2h - 6$, we get

$$3(n-h-m_1-m_0)+2h+m_1\left(\frac{\pi}{\alpha}+1\right)+2m_0\frac{\pi}{\alpha} \le 6n-2h-6,$$

implying that

$$m_1 + 2m_0 \le \frac{3n}{\pi/\alpha - 2}.$$

Plugging this inequality in (2), we concludet that the number of α-long edges is at least

$$n\left[1 - \frac{3}{2(\pi/\alpha - 2)}\right].$$

As α decreases, the number of edges in the SDG is always at least a quantity that gets closer to n. This is nearly tight, since there exist n-point sets for which the number of stable edges is only roughly n, see Figure 9 (right).

Closest pairs, crusts, β-skeleta, and the SDG. Let $\beta \ge 1$, and P a set of n points in the plane. The *β-skeleton* of P is a graph on P that consists of all the edges pq such that the union of the two disks of radius $(\beta/2)d(p,q)$, touching p and q, does not contain any point of $P \setminus \{p,q\}$. See, e.g., [5, 17] for properties of the β-skeleton, and for its applications in surface reconstruction. We show that the edges of the β-skeleton are α-stable in $\mathrm{DT}(P)$, provided $\beta \ge 1 + \Omega(\alpha^2)$. A similar argument shows that the stable Delaunay graph contains the closest pair in $P(t)$ as well as the crust of a set of points sampled sufficiently densely along a 1-dimensional curve (see [4, 5] for the definition of crusts and their applications in surface reconstruction). See the full version of the paper [1] for the proofs of these claims.

In contrast, stable Delaunay graphs need not contain all the edges of several other important subgraphs of the Delaunay triangulation, including the Euclidean minimum spanning tree, the Gabriel graph, the relative neighborhood graph, and the all-nearest-neighbors graph. An illustration for the relative neighborhood graph is given in Figure 10 (left). As a matter of fact, the stable Delaunay graph need not even be connected, as is illustrated in Figure 10 (right).

Completing SDG into a triangulation. As argued above, the Delaunay edges that are missing in the stable subgraph correspond to nearly co-circular quadruples of points, or to nearly collinear triples of points near the boundary of the convex hull. Arguably, these missing edges carry little information, because they may "flicker" in and out of the Delaunay triangulation even when the points move just slightly (so that all angles determined by the triples of points change only slightly). Nevertheless, in many applications it is desirable (or essential) to complete the stable subgraph into *some* triangulation, preferrably one that is also stable in the combinatorial sense—it undergoes only nearly quadratically many topological changes.

By the analysis in Section 3 we can achieve part of this goal by maintaining the full Delaunay triangulation $\mathrm{DT}^\diamond(P)$ under the polygonal norm induced by the regular k-gon Q_k. This diagram experiences only a nearly quadratic number of topological changes, is easy to maintain, and contains all the stable Euclidean Delaunay edges, for an appropriate choice of $k \approx 1/\alpha$. Moreover, the union of its triangles is simply connected — it has no holes. Unfortunately, in general it is not a triangulation of the entire convex hull of P, as illustrated in Figure 11.

For the time being, we leave it as an open problem to come up with a simple and "stable" scheme for filling the gaps between the triangles of $\mathrm{DT}^\diamond(P)$ and the edges of the convex hull. It might be possible to extend the kinetic triangulation scheme developed in [16] to kinetically maintain a triangulation of "fringes" between $\mathrm{DT}^\diamond(P)$ and the convex hull of P.

Of course, if we only want to maintain a triangulation of P that experiences only a nearly quadratically many topological changes, then we can use the scheme in [16], or the earlier, somewhat more involved scheme in [3]. However, if we want to keep the triangulation "as Delaunay as possible", we should include in it the stable portion of DT, and then the efficient completion of it, as mentioned above, becomes an issue.

Nearly Euclidean norms and some of their properties. One way of interpreting the results of Section 3 is that the stability of Delaunay edges is preserved, in an appropriately defined sense, if we replace the Euclidean norm by the polygonal norm induced by the regular k-gon Q_k (for $k \approx 1/\alpha$). That is, stable edges in one Delaunay triangulation are also edges of the other triangulation, and are stable there too. Here we note that there is nothing special about Q_k: The same property holds if we replace the Euclidean norm by any sufficiently close norm (or convex distance function [9]).

Specifically, let Q be a closed convex set in the plane that is contained in the unit disk D_0 and contains the disk $D_0' = (\cos\alpha)D_0$ that is concentric with D_0 and scaled by the factor $\cos\alpha$. This is equivalent to requiring that the Hausdorff distance $H(Q, D_0)$ between Q and D_0 be at most $1 - \cos\alpha$. We define the center of Q to coincide with the common center of D_0 and D_0'.

Q induces a convex distance function d_Q, defined by $d_Q(x, y) = \min\{\lambda \mid y \in x + \lambda Q\}$. Consider the Voronoi diagram $\mathrm{Vor}^Q(P)$ of P induced by d_Q, and the corresponding Delaunay triangulation $\mathrm{DT}^Q(P)$. We omit here the detailed analysis of the structure of these diagrams, which is similar to that for the norm induced by Q_k, as presented in Section 3. See also [8, 9] for more details. Call an edge e_{pq} of $\mathrm{Vor}^Q(P)$ α-stable if the following property holds: Let u and v be the endpoints of e_{pq}, and let Q_u, Q_v be the two homothetic copies of Q that are centered at u, v, respectively, and touch p and q. Then we require that the angle between the supporting lines at q (for simplicity, assume that Q is smooth; otherwise, the condition should hold for any pair of supporting lines at p or at q) to Q_u and Q_v at p is at least α, and that the same holds at q. In this case we refer to the edge pq of $\mathrm{DT}^Q(P)$ as α-stable.

Note that Q_k-stability was (implicitly) defined in a different manner in Section 3, based on the number of breakpoints of the corresponding Voronoi edges. Nevertheless, it is easy to verify that the two definitions are essentially identical. In the full version of the paper [1] we show:

THEOREM 5.1. *Let P, α, and Q be as above. Then (i) every 4α-stable edge of the Euclidean Delaunay triangulation is an α-stable edge of $\mathrm{DT}^Q(P)$. (ii) Conversely, every 4α-stable edge of $\mathrm{DT}^Q(P)$ is also an α-stable edge in the Euclidean norm.*

The proof follows the analysis in Section 3, and adapts it to handle the more general situation that arises here, requiring the derivation of several additional geometric properties of Q-stable edges.

There are many interesting open problems that arise here. One of the main problems is to bound the number of topological changes in $\mathrm{DT}^Q(P)$ under algebraic motion of bounded degree of the points of P, and to extend the class of sets Q for which a near quadratic bound on the number of these changes can be established.

References

[1] P. K. Agarwal, J. Gao, L. Guibas, H. Kaplan, V. Koltun, N. Rubin and M. Sharir, Kinetic stable Delaunay graphs, `http://www.cs.tau.ac.il/~rubinnat/StableF.pdf`.

[2] P. K. Agarwal, H. Kaplan and M. Sharir, Kinetic and dynamic data structures for closest pair and all nearest neighbors, *ACM Trans. Algorithms* 5 (1) (2008), Art. 4.

[3] P. K. Agarwal, Y. Wang and H. Yu, A 2D kinetic triangulation with near-quadratic topological changes, *Discrete Comput. Geom.* 36 (2006), 573–592.

[4] N. Amenta and M. Bern, Surface reconstruction by Voronoi filtering, *Discrete Comput. Geom.*, 22 (1999), 481–504.

[5] N. Amenta, M. W. Bern and D. Eppstein, The crust and beta-skeleton: combinatorial curve reconstruction, *Graphic. Models and Image Processing* 60 (2) (1998), 125–135.

[6] F. Aurenhammer and R. Klein, Voronoi diagrams, in *Handbook of Computational Geometry*, J.-R. Sack and J. Urrutia, Eds., Elsevier, Amsterdam, 2000, pages 201–290.

[7] J. Basch, L. J. Guibas and J. Hershberger, Data structures for mobile data, *J. Algorithms* 31 (1) (1999), 1–28.

[8] L. P. Chew, Near-quadratic bounds for the L_1 Voronoi diagram of moving points, *Comput. Geom. Theory Appl.* 7 (1997), 73–80.

[9] L. P. Chew and R. L. Drysdale, Voronoi diagrams based on convex distance functions, *Proc. First Annu. ACM Sympos. Comput. Geom.*, 1985, pp. 235–244.

[10] B. Delaunay, Sur la sphère vide. A la memoire de Georges Voronoi, *Izv. Akad. Nauk SSSR, Otdelenie Matematicheskih i Estestvennyh Nauk* 7 (1934), 793–800.

[11] H. Edelsbrunner, *Geometry and Topology for Mesh Generation*, Cambridge University Press, Cambride, 2001.

[12] L. J. Guibas, Modeling motion, In J. E. Goodman and J. O'Rourke, editors, *Handbook of Discrete and Computational Geometry*. CRC Press, Inc., Boca Raton, FL, USA, second edition, 2004, pages 1117–1134.

[13] L. J. Guibas, Kinetic data structures — a state of the art report, In P. K. Agarwal, L. E. Kavraki and M. Mason, editors, *Proc. Workshop Algorithmic Found. Robot.*, pages 191–209. A. K. Peters, Wellesley, MA, 1998.

[14] L. J. Guibas, J. S. B. Mitchell and T. Roos, Voronoi diagrams of moving points in the plane, *Proc. 17th Internat. Workshop Graph-Theoret. Concepts Comput. Sci.*, volume 570 of *Lecture Notes Comput. Sci.*, pages 113–125. Springer-Verlag, 1992.

[15] C. Icking, R. Klein, N.-M. Lê and L. Ma, Convex distance functions in 3-space are different, Fundam. Inform. 22 (4) (1995), 331–352.

[16] H. Kaplan, N. Rubin and M. Sharir, A kinetic triangulation scheme for moving points in the plane, this proceedings.

[17] D. Kirkpatrick and J. D. Radke, A framework for computational morphology, *Computational Geometry* (G. Toussaint, ed.), North-Holland (1985), 217–248.

[18] D. Leven and M. Sharir, Planning a purely translational motion for a convex object in two–dimensional space using generalized Voronoi diagrams, *Discrete Comput. Geom.* 2 (1987), 9–31.

[19] K. Mehlhorn, *Data Structures and Algorithms 1: Sorting and Searching*, Springer Verlag, Berlin 1984.

[20] J. Nievergelt and E. M. Reingold, Binary search trees of bounded balance, *SIAM J. Comput.* 2 (1973), 33–43.

[21] M. Sharir and P. K. Agarwal, *Davenport-Schinzel Sequences and Their Geometric Applications*, Cambridge University Press, New York, 1995.

Acknowledgements. Pankaj Agarwal was supported by NSF under grants CNS-05-40347, CCF-06 -35000, CCF-09-40671 and DEB-04-25465, by ARO grants W911NF-07-1-0376 and W911NF-08-1-0452, by an NIH grant 1P50-GM-08183-01, by a DOE grant OEG-P200A070505, and by a grant from the U.S.–Israel Binational Science Foundation. Leo Guibas was supported by NSF grants CCR-0204486, ITR-0086013, ITR-0205671, ARO grant DAAD19-03-1-0331, as well as by the Bio-X consortium at Stanford. Haim Kaplan and Natan Rubin were partially supported by Grant 2006/204 from the U.S. - Israel Binational Science Foundation, project number 2006204, and by the Israel Science Foundation grant no. 975-06. Micha Sharir and Natan Rubin were supported by NSF Grants CCF-05-14079 and CCF-08-30272, by Grant 338/09 from Israel Science Fund, and by the Hermann Minkowski–MINERVA Center for Geometry at Tel Aviv University.

A Kinetic Triangulation Scheme for Moving Points in the Plane*

Haim Kaplan
School of Computer Science
Tel Aviv University
Tel Aviv 69978, Israel
haimk@post.tau.ac.il

Natan Rubin
School of Computer Science
Tel Aviv University
Tel Aviv 69978, Israel
rubinnat@post.tau.ac.il

Micha Sharir
School of Computer Science
Tel Aviv University
Tel Aviv 69978 Israel
michas@post.tau.ac.il

ABSTRACT

We present a simple randomized scheme for triangulating a set P of n points in the plane, and construct a kinetic data structure which maintains the triangulation as the points of P move continuously along piecewise algebraic trajectories of constant description complexity. Our triangulation scheme experiences an expected number of $O(n^2\beta_{s+2}(n)\log^2 n)$ discrete changes, and handles them in a manner that satisfies all the standard requirements from a kinetic data structure: compactness, efficiency, locality and responsiveness. Here s is the maximum number of times where any specific triple of points of P can become collinear, $\beta_{s+2}(q) = \lambda_{s+2}(q)/q$, and $\lambda_{s+2}(q)$ is the maximum length of Davenport-Schinzel sequences of order $s+2$ on n symbols. Thus, compared to the previous solution of Agarwal et al. [4], we achieve a (slightly) improved bound on the number of discrete changes in the triangulation. In addition, we believe that our scheme is simpler to implement and analyze.

Categories and Subject Descriptors

F.2.2 [**Analysis of algorithms and problem complexity**]: Nonnumerical algorithms and problems—*Geometrical problems and computations*; G.2.1 [**Discrete mathematics**]: Combinatorics—*Combinatorial algorithms*

General Terms

Algorithms, Theory

*Work by Haim Kaplan and Natan Rubin was partially supported by Grant 975/06 from the Israel Science Fund. Work by Micha Sharir and Natan Rubin was partially supported by by Grants 155/05 and 338/09 from the Israel Science Fund. Work by Haim Kaplan was also supported by Grant 2006-204 from the U.S. - Israel Binational Science Foundation. Work by Micha Sharir was also supported by NSF Grant CCF-08-30272, by grant 2006-194 from the U.S.-Israeli Binational Science Foundation, and by the Hermann Minkowski–MINERVA Center for Geometry at Tel Aviv University.

Keywords

Triangulation, Moving points, Kinetic data structures

1. INTRODUCTION

Let $P(t) = \{p_1(t), \ldots, p_n(t)\}$ be a set of n moving points in the plane. We assume that the motions of the points are simple, in the sense that the trajectory of each point is a piecewise-algebraic curve of *constant description complexity*, meaning that it can be described as a Boolean combination of a constant number of polynomial equalities and inequalities of constant maximum degree.

Our goal is to devise a reasonably simple scheme for triangulating $P(t)$ at any fixed time t, and to maintain the triangulation as the points move. That is, we wish to partition the convex hull $\mathcal{CH}(P)$ of P into pairwise openly disjoint triangles whose vertices are the points of P, so that the interior of each triangle is empty—it does not contain any point of P. The scheme has to be *kinetic*, so that we can keep track of the discrete combinatorial changes that the triangulation undergoes as the points move, and update the triangulation so that it continues to conform to the underlying scheme. (That is, at any given time t the maintained triangulation coincides with the one that would result in applying the static scheme to $P(t)$.)

The study of triangulations plays a central role in computational geometry because of their numerous applications in such areas as computer graphics, physical simulation, collision detection, and geographic information systems [8, 13]. With the advancement in technology, many applications, for instance, video games, virtual reality, dynamic simulations, and robotics, call for maintaining a triangulation as the points move. For example, the arbitrary Eulerian-Lagrangian method [12] provides a way to integrate the motion of fluids and solids within a moving finite-element mesh.

In $\mathbb{R}^2$, the Delaunay triangulation $DT(P)$ of P produces well-shaped triangles, and thus is a good candidate for such a triangulation scheme. The problem, though, is that the best known upper bound on the number of discrete changes in $DT(P(t))$, as a function of time t, is only nearly cubic in n; see [2, 14, 15, 21]. While it is strongly believed that the maximum possible number of discrete changes that $DT(P(t))$ can experience is only nearly quadratic in n, this is one of the hardest open problems in computational and combinatorial geometry (as recognized, e.g., in [11]). Until this conjecture is established, one seeks alternative triangulation schemes with a provable *nearly-quadratic* upper bound on the number of discrete changes. (This is best possible, since the convex hull itself can change $\Omega(n^2)$ times during a simple motion of the points of P; see [21].) Moreover, the scheme should be sufficiently simple to define, to implement, and (as a secondary aesthetic virtue) to analyze. Finally, the scheme should satisfy the four basic properties of kinetic data structures [7] detailed below.

Agarwal et al. [4] have recently presented such a randomized scheme which experiences $O(n^2 2^{\sqrt{\log n \log\log n}})$ discrete changes. Their scheme, however, is fairly complicated, and its analysis is also rather involved. It uses a hierarchy of subsets $\emptyset = R_0 \subseteq R_1 \subseteq \cdots \subseteq R_w = P$, where each set R_{i-1}, for $1 \le i \le w$, is a random sample of roughly $|R_i|^{1-1/i} \log n$ points of R_i. The algorithm maintains an entire hierarchy of triangulations $\emptyset = \mathcal{T}_0 \subseteq \mathcal{T}_1 \subseteq \cdots \subseteq \mathcal{T}_w = \mathcal{T}$, where each $\mathcal{T}_i$ is a triangulation of R_i; it is a refinement of $\mathcal{T}_{i-1}$ which is obtained by a suitable variant of the *fan triangulation*, introduced in [1].

Kinetic data structures. The *Kinetic data structure* (KDS) framework, introduced by Basch et al. [7], proposes an algorithmic approach, together with several quality criteria, for maintaining certain geometric configurations determined by a set of objects, each moving along a trajectory whose graph, as a function of time, is a piecewise-algebraic curve (in space-time) of constant description complexity. See [3, 7, 16] and references therein for more details.

Typically, a KDS operates by maintaining a set of *certificates*. As long as they are all valid, the structure being maintained is guaranteed to be valid too. Each certificate has a (first future) failure time, and we store these critical times in an event priority queue. When a certificate fails, we repair the KDS, update, if needed, the geometric structure that we maintain, generate new certificates and insert their failure times into the queue.

Generally, a good KDS is expected to possess the following four properties: (i) *Compactness*, meaning that the storage that it requires is larger only by a polylogarithmic factor than the space required for the structure being maintained. (ii) *Efficiency*, meaning that the number of events that it processes (i.e., failure times of the certificates) is larger only by a polylogarithmic factor than the maximum possible number of discrete changes in the structure being maintained. (iii) *Responsiveness*, meaning that repairing the KDS at a certificate failure event takes only polylogarithmic time. (iv) *Locality*, meaning that each input object is stored at only a polylogarithmic number of places in the KDS, so that an expected change in the motion of a single object can be processed efficiently. See [5, 7] for more details.

Therefore, a good KDS for kinetic triangulation in $\mathbb{R}^2$ should have only nearly linear storage, process only a nearly-quadratic number of events, each in polylogarithmic time, and each moving point should be stored at only a polylogarithmic number of places in the KDS.

Our result. In Section 2, we present a simple triangulation scheme for a set P of n moving points in the plane. For the sake of efficient kinetization we make the scheme randomized, and assume a (natural) model in which the flight plans of the moving points are independent of the randomization used by the algorithm. The basic idea of the (static) triangulation is quite simple (some details are glossed over in this informal overview): We sort the points of P by their x-coordinates, split P at a (random) point p into a left portion P_L and a right portion P_R, compute recursively the upper convex hulls of $P_L \cup \{p\}$ and of $P_R \cup \{p\}$, and merge them into the upper convex hull of the whole set P.

This process results in a *pseudo-triangulation* of the portion of the convex hull of P lying above the x-monotone polygonal chain $\mathcal{C}(P)$ connecting the points of P in their x-order. Each pseudo-triangle is x-monotone, and consists of an upper *base* and of a left and right lower concave chains, meeting at its bottom *apex*. See Figure 1 for an illustration. A symmetric process is applied to the portion of the hull below $\mathcal{C}(P)$, by computing recursively lower convex hulls of the respective subsets of P. (In particular, we obtain a hierarchical representation of $\mathcal{CH}(P)$, similar to the one of Overmars and van Leeuwen [19]; see also [5]. See [1, 6, 22] for additional applications of hierarchical pseudo-triangulations to kinetic problems.)

To obtain a proper triangulation of (the convex hull of) P, we partition each pseudo-triangle τ into triangles. We accomplish this by chords drawn from its vertices in the order of their random priorities; see Section 2 for details.

In Section 3, we prove that the expected number of events that can arise during the motion is $O(n^2 \beta_{s+2}(n) \log n)$ (with s and β as defined in the abstract), and that the expected number of discrete (also called topological) changes caused in our triangulation by each such event is bounded by $O(\log n)$.

In Section 4, we show how to maintain this triangulation, as the points of P move, using a kinetic data structure that satisfies the criteria of [7], as listed above. There are several kinds of critical events we need to watch for, in which pairs of points are swapped in the x-order or triples of points become collinear. We process each event of the former type in $O(\log^2 n)$ expected time, and each event of the latter type in $O(\log n)$ expected time, for a total of $O(n^2 \beta_{s+2}(n) \log^2 n)$ (expected) processing time. Our implementation encodes the pseudo-triangulation as a *treap* on P [20].

The upper bounds that we obtain on the number of discrete events, and on their overall processing time, are slightly better than those of the scheme in [4], and we believe that our scheme is simpler (and more "explicit") than that of [4].

2. THE STATIC TRIANGULATION

In this section we describe a simple scheme for constructing a static triangulation $\mathcal{T}(P)$ of $\mathcal{CH}(P)$. We fix a random permutation π of the points of P. For each $p \in P$ we denote its rank in π as $\mathsf{priority}(p)$. Let $\mathcal{C}(P)$ denote, as above, the x-monotone polygonal chain which connects the points of P in their x-order, assuming that no two points of P have the same x-coordinate. (In degenerate cases, which will arise at discrete instances during the motion of the points of P, $\mathcal{C}(P)$ connects the points in the lexicographical order of their coordinates.) Since the two points of P with extreme x-coordinates are vertices of $\mathcal{CH}(P)$, $\mathcal{C}(P)$ partitions $\mathcal{CH}(P)$ into two components, $\mathcal{CH}^+(P)$ and $\mathcal{CH}^-(P)$, lying respectively above and below $\mathcal{C}(P)$. With no loss of generality, we only describe a triangulation $\mathcal{T}^+(P)$ of $\mathcal{CH}^+(P)$, and obtain the triangulation $\mathcal{T}^-(P)$ of $\mathcal{CH}^-(P)$ in a fully symmetric fashion. The overall triangulation $\mathcal{T}(P)$ is the union of $\mathcal{T}^+(P)$ and $\mathcal{T}^-(P)$.

A static pseudo-triangulation of $\mathcal{CH}^+(P)$. We first construct a *pseudo-triangulation* of $\mathcal{CH}^+(P)$ and then refine it into a triangulation by partitioning each pseudo-triangle into triangles.

Each pseudo-triangle τ that we construct consists of a

left tail, a middle *funnel*, and a *right tail* (any of these substructures may be empty; the tails were not mentioned in the overview in the introduction). The funnel is an x-monotone simple polygon, whose boundary consists of an upper *base*, which is the segment connecting its leftmost and rightmost vertices, and of a left and right lower concave *chains*, which are denoted respectively as $\mathcal{L}(\tau)$ and $\mathcal{R}(\tau)$. The point in which $\mathcal{L}(\tau)$ and $\mathcal{R}(\tau)$ meet is called the *apex* of τ and denoted by $\mathsf{apex}(\tau)$. The left chain $\mathcal{L}(\tau)$ extends from the left endpoint of the base to $\mathsf{apex}(\tau)$, and the right chain extends from $\mathsf{apex}(\tau)$ to the right endpoint of the base; see Figure 1. In addition, τ may have a left tail[1] $\mathcal{L}^-(\tau)$ and a right tail $\mathcal{R}^+(\tau)$, so that $\mathcal{L}^-(\tau)$ is an x-monotone polygonal chain which extends from the left vertex of the funnel to the left, till the *left endpoint* $\mathsf{left}(\tau)$ of τ, so that $\mathcal{L}^-(\tau) \cup \mathcal{L}(\tau)$ is a concave chain, and symmetrically for $\mathcal{R}^+(\tau)$, which extends to the right till the *right endpoint* $\mathsf{right}(\tau)$ of τ. Again, see Figure 1. We con-

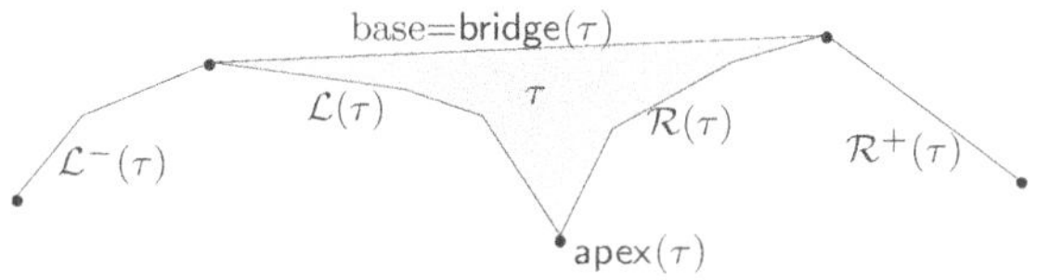

Figure 1: A single pseudo-triangle τ in our pseudo-triangulation of $\mathcal{CH}^+(P)$. In addition to its funnel (drawn shaded), τ has two tails $\mathcal{L}^-(\tau), \mathcal{R}^+(\tau)$.

struct the pseudo-triangulation of $\mathcal{CH}^+(P)$ recursively. At each step of the recursion we have some subset $Q \subseteq P$ of points which are consecutive in the x-order of P, and we construct a pseudo-triangulation $\mathcal{PT}^+(Q)$ of $\mathcal{CH}^+(Q)$. At the topmost level of the recursion we have $Q = P$. The construction of $\mathcal{PT}^+(Q)$ proceeds as follows; see Figure 2. Let $\mathsf{left}(Q)$ (resp., $\mathsf{right}(Q)$) denote the point of Q with the minimal (resp., maximal) x-coordinate, and let $\mathsf{mid}(Q)$ be the point p of $Q \setminus \{\mathsf{left}(Q), \mathsf{right}(Q)\}$ with the minimum value of $\mathsf{priority}(p)$. Set $Q_L = \{p \in Q \mid x(p) \le x(\mathsf{mid}(Q))\}$, $Q_R = \{p \in Q \mid x(p) \ge x(\mathsf{mid}(Q))\}$ (so $\mathsf{mid}(Q)$ belongs to both sets). We add to $\mathcal{PT}^+(Q)$ the following pseudo-triangle τ. The base of τ is the portion of the upper common tangent to $\mathcal{CH}^+(Q_L)$ and $\mathcal{CH}^+(Q_R)$ between the points of tangency. We call this base the *bridge* of τ and denote it by $\mathsf{bridge}(\tau)$. The left (resp., right) chain $\mathcal{L}(\tau)$ (resp., $\mathcal{R}(\tau)$) is the portion of the upper hull of Q_L (resp., Q_R) below $\mathsf{bridge}(\tau)$. We take $\mathcal{L}^-(\tau)$ to be the portion of the upper hull of Q_L to the left of $\mathcal{L}(\tau)$, and define $\mathcal{R}^+(\tau)$ symmetrically as the portion of the upper hull of Q_R to the right of $\mathcal{R}(\tau)$. The points $\mathsf{left}(Q)$ and $\mathsf{right}(Q)$ become the respective *endpoints* $\mathsf{left}(\tau)$, $\mathsf{right}(\tau)$ of τ. We also have $\mathsf{apex}(\tau) = \mathsf{mid}(Q)$ which belongs, by definition, to both chains. (The funnel of τ may be empty, if $\mathsf{mid}(Q)$ is a vertex of the upper hull of Q. In this case we can think of the funnel of τ as the singleton $\mathsf{apex}(\tau) = \mathsf{mid}(Q)$, and τ consists of the two tails $\mathcal{L}^-(\tau), \mathcal{R}^+(\tau)$, meeting at $\mathsf{mid}(Q)$, and forming together a common concave chain. Similarly, a pseudo-triangle may have an empty left tail and/or empty right tail.)

We then recursively pseudo-triangulate each of $\mathcal{CH}^+(Q_L)$, $\mathcal{CH}^+(Q_R)$. The recursion terminates when $|Q| \le 3$ (by con-

[1]These tailed pseudo-triangles are a special case of so-called *geodesic triangles* introduced in [9].

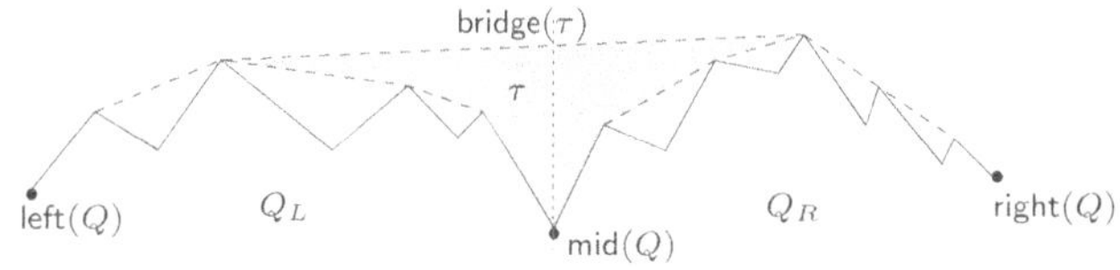

Figure 2: The recursive pseudo-triangulation of $\mathcal{CH}^+(Q)$. We add to $\mathcal{PT}^+(Q)$ the pseudo-triangle τ (whose funnel is drawn shaded), with endpoints $\mathsf{left}(\tau) = \mathsf{left}(Q), \mathsf{right}(\tau) = \mathsf{right}(Q)$, and $\mathsf{apex}(\tau) = \mathsf{mid}(Q)$, and then recursively construct $\mathcal{PT}^+(Q_L), \mathcal{PT}^+(Q_R)$.

struction, $|Q| \ge 2$). If $|Q| = 3$ then we output a single pseudo-triangle τ, which is either a triangle, when the midpoint lies below the segment connecting the endpoints, or, in the opposite case, consists of the two segments $\mathcal{L}^-(\tau) = \mathsf{left}(\tau)\mathsf{apex}(\tau)$ and $\mathcal{R}^+(\tau) = \mathsf{apex}(\tau)\mathsf{right}(\tau)$. If $|Q| = 2$, no pseudo-triangle is output. In this case $\mathcal{CH}^+(Q)$ is a single edge of the chain $\mathcal{C}(P)$.

Consider a pseudo-triangle τ such that $\mathsf{left}(\tau)$ is not the leftmost point of P and $\mathsf{right}(\tau)$ is not the rightmost point of P. Then one can show that the triple $(\mathsf{left}(\tau), \mathsf{right}(\tau), \mathsf{apex}(\tau))$ have the smallest priorities among all points whose x-coordinate is between $x(\mathsf{left}(\tau))$ and $x(\mathsf{right}(\tau))$, inclusive (see Lemma 2.1 below). To make this true for all pseudo-triangles, we augment the initial point set P with two dummy points $p_{-\infty} = (-\infty, -\infty)$ and $p_\infty = (\infty, -\infty)$, and assign to them priorities -1 and 0. The upper hull of the augmented point set is obtained from the upper hull of P by adding two vertical downward-directed rays at the leftmost and rightmost points of P. Hence, any triangulation of $\mathcal{CH}^+(P)$ is also a triangulation of $\mathcal{CH}^+(P \cup \{p_{-\infty}, p_\infty\})$, and vice versa. In the rest of the paper denote by P the augmented point set.

LEMMA 2.1. *Let a, b, and c be three points in P, such that $x(a) < x(b) < x(c)$. Then $\mathcal{PT}^+(P)$ contains a pseudo-triangle τ having endpoints $\mathsf{left}(\tau) = a$, $\mathsf{right}(\tau) = c$, and $\mathsf{apex}(\tau) = b$, if and only if*
(i) $\mathsf{priority}(b) > \max\{\mathsf{priority}(a), \mathsf{priority}(c)\}$, *and*
(ii) all points $p \in P$, such that $x(a) < x(p) < x(c)$ satisfy $\mathsf{priority}(p) \ge \mathsf{priority}(b)$.

PROOF. To prove the "only if" part we proceed by induction on our recursive construction. Recall that at each recursive step we process some subset $Q \subseteq P$ whose points are consecutive in the x-order of P, and add to $\mathcal{PT}^+(P)$ a pseudo-triangle τ with $\mathsf{left}(\tau) = \mathsf{left}(Q)$, $\mathsf{right}(\tau) = \mathsf{right}(Q)$, and $\mathsf{apex}(\tau) = \mathsf{mid}(Q)$. To establish both asserted conditions (i) and (ii) for τ, it is sufficient to observe that each point p, such that $x(\mathsf{left}(Q)) < x(p) < x(\mathsf{right}(Q))$, satisfies $\mathsf{priority}(p) > \max\{\mathsf{priority}(\mathsf{left}(Q)), \mathsf{priority}(\mathsf{right}(Q))\}$. Indeed, the desired property holds initially for P by our choice of the artificial points $p_{-\infty}$ and p_∞ and their priorities. Assuming that this holds when we process some subset Q, and using the fact that $\mathsf{mid}(Q)$ is the point with smallest priority in the range $x(\mathsf{left}(Q)) < x(p) < x(\mathsf{right}(Q))$, the claim also holds for Q_L and Q_R.

For the "if" part, we observe that for every choice of $b \in P$ there is exactly one choice of a and c in P so that the triple (a, b, c) satisfies (i) and (ii), and every point $b \in P$ is an apex of exactly one pseudo-triangle of $\mathcal{PT}^+(P)$ (and the apex of each pseudo-triangle is distinct from each of p_∞ and $p_{-\infty}$).

The latter is easy to establish by induction on the increasing order of the priorities of the points. This, combined with the arguments in the "only if" part, completes the proof. □

The pseudo-triangulation tree. The pseudo-triangulation $\mathcal{PT}^+(P)$ can be represented by a binary tree in which every node v represents a pseudo-triangle $\tau_v \in \mathcal{PT}^+(P)$, and stores the point $p_v = \mathsf{apex}(\tau_v)$. The inorder of the tree is the increasing x-order of the apices (i.e., the points of P). The subtree rooted at v represents the recursive pseudo-triangulation of $\mathcal{CH}^+(P_v \cup \{\mathsf{left}(\tau_v), \mathsf{right}(\tau_v)\})$, where $P_v \subseteq P$ denotes the set of points stored at the nodes of the subtree rooted at v. Note that $\mathsf{left}(\tau_v)$ and $\mathsf{right}(\tau_v)$ are not stored at this subtree—they are the next points to the left and to the right of the points of P_v. Abusing the notation slightly, we denote by $\mathcal{PT}^+(P)$ both the pseudo-triangulation $\mathcal{PT}^+(P)$ and the tree representing it.

Remark: Let v be a node in $\mathcal{PT}^+(P)$, so that $\mathsf{left}(\tau_v) \neq p_{-\infty}$. Then $\mathsf{left}(\tau_v)$ is stored at the lowest ancestor of v whose right subree contains v. If $\mathsf{left}(\tau_v) = p_{-\infty}$ then v belongs to the path from the root of $\mathcal{PT}^+(P)$ to the leftmost leaf. Symmetric properties hold for $\mathsf{right}(\tau_v)$. We have:

LEMMA 2.2. *The tree representing $\mathcal{PT}^+(P)$ is a treap on $P \setminus \{p_{-\infty}, p_\infty\}$. That is, $\mathcal{PT}^+(P)$ is a heap with respect to the priorities, and a search tree with respect to the x-coordinates of the points.*

Triangulating a fixed pseudo-triangle. Let τ be a pseudo-triangle of $\mathcal{PT}^+(P)$. Assume that the funnel of τ is not empty, and is not already a triangle. We say that two vertices p, q of the funnel of τ, where p belongs to $\mathcal{L}(\tau)$ and q belongs to $\mathcal{R}(\tau)$, are *visible* from each other if pq does not intersect $\partial\tau$ (except at its endpoints); in this case pq lies inside the funnel of τ. Denote by $\nu(p)$ the rightmost point on the right chain which is visible from p. Note that either $\nu(p)$ is the rightmost vertex of τ or $p\nu(p)$ is an upper tangent to $\mathcal{R}(\tau)$. Symmetic definition and properties hold for points q on $\mathcal{R}(\tau)$. This definition also applies when p is the leftmost vertex of $\mathcal{L}(\tau)$ and when q the rightmost vertex of $\mathcal{R}(\tau)$ (the endpoints of $\mathsf{bridge}(\tau)$), in which case $\nu(p) = q$ and $\nu(q) = p$. See Figure 3 (left).

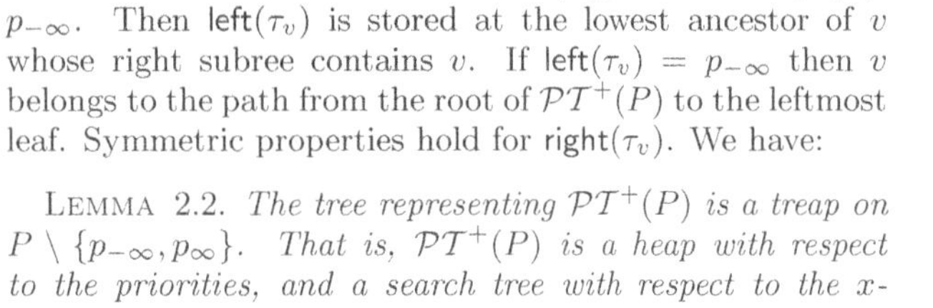

Figure 3: Left: The first step of triangulating a single pseudo-triangle $\tau \in \mathcal{PT}^+(P)$. Right: During the recursive construction of $\mathcal{T}(\tau)$ every non-corner vertex p of the funnel of τ generates exactly one edge $e_p = p\nu^*(p)$, thus recursively splitting some sub-pseudo-triangle τ_p (drawn shaded). Note that in this figure $\nu^*(p) \neq \nu(p)$, which is the left endpoint of $\mathsf{bridge}(\tau)$.

The triangulation $\mathcal{T}(\tau)$ of τ is obtained by recursively splitting τ by chords into sub-pseudo-triangles, in the following manner. Choose the minimum priority vertex q of the funnel of τ, other than the leftmost and the rightmost vertices and the apex. Assume, without loss of generality, that q lies on $\mathcal{L}(\tau)$. See Figure 3 (left). The segment $q\nu(q)$ splits τ into two sub-pseudo-triangles τ^+ and τ^-. The pseudo-triangle τ^+ has q as an apex and the same base as τ. Its left chain is the portion of $\mathcal{L}(\tau)$ from q to the left, and its right chain is the concatenation of $q\nu(q)$ with the portion of $\mathcal{R}(\tau)$ to the right of $\nu(q)$. The pseudo-triangle τ^- has $q\nu(q)$ as its base, the same apex as τ, and its left and right chains are the portions of $\mathcal{L}(\tau)$ and $\mathcal{R}(\tau)$ delimited respectively by q and by $\nu(q)$. A symmetric situation arises when $q \in \mathcal{R}(\tau)$. We add the edge $q\nu(q)$ to $\mathcal{T}(\tau)$, and recursively triangulate each of τ^+ and τ^-. We say that the edge $q\nu(q)$ in $\mathcal{T}(\tau)$ is *generated* by q. In the further recursive steps, we redefine $\nu(p)$, for vertices p of each of these sub-pseudo-triangles, restricting the visibility to only within the respective pseudo-triangle. Note that for any two vertices p, q that lie on the same chain of τ, the segments $p\nu(p)$ and $q\nu(q)$ do not intersect. Therefore, if $\nu(p)$ changes after a recursive call then it must change to a vertex of the base of the corresponding sub-pseudo-triangle. See Figure 3 (right). The recursion bottoms out when the interior of τ is a triangle. Note also that all the chords in $\mathcal{T}(\tau)$ cross the vertical ray above $\mathsf{apex}(\tau)$, and so they are totally ordered in the vertical direction.

Properties of $\mathcal{T}(\tau)$. Every vertex p of the funnel of τ, other than the leftmost and the rightmost vertices and the apex, generates exactly one edge e_p during the whole recursive process. (For example, in Figure 3 (left), the vertex $\nu(q)$ will not generate an edge in τ^-, since it is an endpoint of that funnel, but will still generate an edge within τ^+, or within some recursive sub-pseudo-triangle of τ^+.) We denote by τ_p the sub-pseudo-triangle in which e_p is generated, and by $\nu^*(p)$ the other endpoint of e_p. Note that $\nu^*(p)$ is either the original $\nu(p)$ or an endpoint of the base of τ_p.

3. NUMBER OF DISCRETE CHANGES

In this section we bound the overall expected number of discrete changes that $\mathcal{T}(P(t))$ experiences as the points of P move along (continuous) pseudo-algebraic trajectories of constant description complexity. The analysis is with respect to a fixed random permutation π of P drawn ahead of the motion, so that the motion is "oblivious" to the choice of π. Thus, even though the x-order of the points may change during the motion, each point retains its initial priority, and the permutation π is still a random permutation of P, with respect to the x-order of these points, at any fixed t.

Discrete changes in $\mathcal{PT}^+(P)$. For a fixed time instance $t \in \mathbb{R}$, each pseudo-triangle $\tau \in \mathcal{PT}^+(P(t))$ is defined by its endpoints $\mathsf{left}(\tau)$, $\mathsf{right}(\tau)$, and by its apex $\mathsf{apex}(\tau)$. Given such a triple of points, they define a valid pseudo-triangle at time t if and only if they, and the points in-between in the x-order, satisfy the conditions of Lemma 2.1 (at time t). Thus, as long as the x-order of the points does not change, $\mathcal{PT}^+(P(t))$ does not change either. That is, it consists of a fixed set of pseudo-triangles, each defined by a fixed triple of points. However, the geometric structure of a pseudo-triangle may change during such a time interval, and we will bound the number of these changes separately. Changes in $\mathcal{PT}^+(P(t))$ occur only at discrete times when the x-order of some pair of points in $P(t)$ changes; we refer to these changes as *x-swap events*.

We assume that each pseudo-triangle τ is present in $\mathcal{PT}^+(P(t))$ at a maximal connected time interval $I(\tau)$, which is associated with τ. That is, pseudo-triangles with the same triple left(τ), right(τ), and apex(τ) that appear in $\mathcal{PT}^+(P(t))$ at disjoint time intervals, are considered distinct. We emphasize that all the other features of τ, such as bridge(τ), the chains $\mathcal{L}(\tau)$ and $\mathcal{R}(\tau)$, and the triangulation $\mathcal{T}(\tau)$ of its funnel, may undergo discrete changes during the time interval $I(\tau)$. A pseudo-triangle τ is created or destroyed only at a swap event when a point $p \in P$ with priority(p) < priority(apex(τ)) crosses one of the vertical lines through its endpoints left(τ) and right(τ) (of course, this also subsumes the cases where priority(p) is smaller than that of an endpoint of τ), or when the x-order of the points in the triple defining τ changes. In the former case, if priority(p) > max{priority(left(τ)), priority(right(τ))} then τ is replaced by another pseudo-triangle τ' with the same endpoints left(τ') = left(τ), right(τ') = right(τ) but with p as a new apex.

If priority(p) < max{priority(left(τ)), priority(right(τ))} then p replaces the endpoint it was swapped with. Thus, each pseudo-triangle τ in our kinetic pseudo-triangulation $\mathcal{PT}^+(P(t))$ is *defined* by at most five points: left(τ), right(τ), apex(τ), and at most two additional points which determine, by swaps with the endpoints of τ, the endpoints of the lifespan $I(\tau)$ of τ in $\mathcal{PT}^+(P(t))$.

Discrete changes in $\mathcal{T}(\tau)$. Fix a pseudo-triangle $\tau \in \mathcal{PT}^+(P(t))$. For a fixed time instance $t \in I(\tau)$, the combinatorial structure of the triangulation $\mathcal{T}(\tau)$ of τ depends only on the discrete structure of the boundary of the funnel of τ (i.e., the ordered sequences of the points along the chains $\mathcal{L}(\tau)$, $\mathcal{R}(\tau)$, and the base bridge(τ)) and the visibility points $\nu(p)$ of all the vertices of the funnel of τ, excluding apex(τ) (of course, it also depends on π). Therefore, as the points of P move during the time interval $I(\tau)$, $\mathcal{T}(\tau)$ can change combinatorially only at events where the boundary or visibility structure of τ changes. These events fall into the following three types:

(i) *Envelope events*, which occur at instances when one of the chains $\mathcal{L}(\tau)$, $\mathcal{R}(\tau)$ contains three collinear vertices; see Figure 4 (right). This happens when a vertex (which is not an endpoint of bridge(τ)) is added to or removed from one of the chains bounding τ. We denote the total number of such events during the period $I(\tau)$ by E_τ.

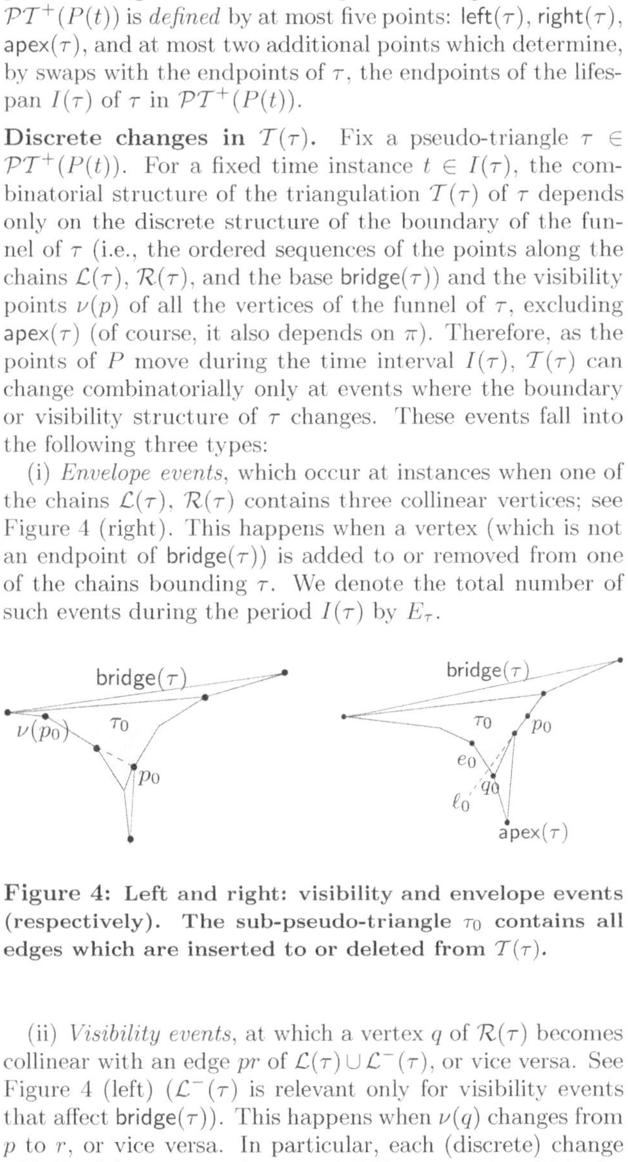

Figure 4: Left and right: visibility and envelope events (respectively). The sub-pseudo-triangle τ_0 contains all edges which are inserted to or deleted from $\mathcal{T}(\tau)$.

(ii) *Visibility events*, at which a vertex q of $\mathcal{R}(\tau)$ becomes collinear with an edge pr of $\mathcal{L}(\tau) \cup \mathcal{L}^-(\tau)$, or vice versa. See Figure 4 (left) ($\mathcal{L}^-(\tau)$ is relevant only for visibility events that affect bridge(τ)). This happens when $\nu(q)$ changes from p to r, or vice versa. In particular, each (discrete) change of bridge(τ) corresponds to a visibility event in which the bridge becomes collinear with an edge of $\mathcal{L}^-(\tau) \cup \mathcal{L}(\tau)$ or of $\mathcal{R}(\tau) \cup \mathcal{R}^+(\tau)$ that is incident to the respective endpoint of the bridge. We denote the total number of visibility events during $I(\tau)$ by V_τ.

A special case of this event occurs when bridge(τ) is created (resp., destroyed), so that right before (resp., after) the event, the funnel of τ is empty. Note that immediately after (resp., before) the creation (resp., destruction) of bridge(τ), the funnel of τ is a triangle.

(iii) *Swap events*, at which some point $p \in P$, satisfying priority(p) > priority(apex(τ)), crosses one of the vertical lines through left(τ), right(τ) or apex(τ). Note that a single swap event of this kind may cause massive discrete changes, of highly unlocal nature, in the chains $\mathcal{L}(\tau)$, $\mathcal{R}(\tau)$, in the visibility pointers $\nu(q)$ of the vertices of τ, and in bridge(τ). See Figure 5 (left) for an illustration.

Note that a swap between any other pair of points p, q within the x-range of τ can be ingnored in the present analysis, since the lower of the two points cannot belong to the funnel of τ at the time of swap.

Assuming general position of the trajectories of the points, the above events occur at distinct time instances (except that the same event may show up, in different forms, in several pseudo-triangles).

A visibility event happens when $\nu(p)$ changes for some point p; we then say that p is *involved* in the visibility event. An envelope event happens when a point p joins or leaves one of the chains $\mathcal{L}(\tau)$, $\mathcal{R}(\tau)$; we then say that p is *involved* in the envelope event.

LEMMA 3.1. *The only point p for which $\nu(p)$ changes in an envelope event is the point p involved in the event.*

PROOF. The lemma follows since at the moment following (resp., preceding) the appearance of p on (resp., disappearance from) its chain, say $\mathcal{L}(\tau)$, its two incident edges are almost collinear. Thus, all vertices q on the opposite chain satisfy $\nu(q) \neq p$ both before and after the event, and $\nu(q)$ is not affected by the event. □

The number of changes in $\mathcal{T}(\tau)$. We define P_τ as the set of points $p \in P$, other than apex(τ), that appear on $\mathcal{C}(P)$ between left(τ) and right(τ), at any time during the life span $I(\tau)$, and put $N_\tau = |P_\tau|$. (Note that the points of P_τ may enter or leave the interval between left(τ) and right(τ) in the middle of $I(\tau)$, at x-swaps with either left(τ) or right(τ).) As noted above, every point $p \in P_\tau$ satisfies priority(p) > priority(apex(τ)). Clearly, our triangulation undergoes $O(N_\tau)$ swap events during $I(\tau)$ (recall that we only consider swaps with left(τ), right(τ) or apex(τ)), and each of them leads to $O(N_\tau)$ edge insertions and deletions to $\mathcal{T}(\tau)$ (the maximum number of edges in the whole triangulation $\mathcal{T}(\tau)$), for a total of $O(N_\tau^2)$ such updates. We next bound the number of discrete changes in $\mathcal{T}(\tau)$ caused by events of the remaining two types.

Fix a set of at most five points that can potentially define a pseudo-triangle for some set of priorities. This set has an associated time interval $[t_1, t_2]$, and consists of three points a, b, and c, such that, at all times $t_1 < t < t_2$, $x(a(t)) < x(b(t)) < x(c(t))$, and of two additional points d_1 and d_2 (each of which could be equal to b), so that the x-coordinate of d_i swaps with either a or c at times t_i, for $i = 1, 2$. For some drawings of the random priorities, τ appears as a pseudo-triangle, and for other drawings it does not. For τ to appear in $\mathcal{PT}^+(P)$, the priorities of a = left(τ) and c = right(τ) should be smaller than the priority of b = apex(τ). The priorities of d_1 and d_2 have to be at most the priority of $b = \mathsf{apex}(\tau)$, and the priorities of all other points in P_τ should be larger than the priority of b. The probability of this to happen, assuming a, b, c, d_1, d_2 are all distinct, is easily seen to be $O(1/N_\tau^5)$ (for $N_\tau > 0$).

When we condition on drawings in which τ indeed appears in $\mathcal{PT}^+(P)$, the following holds.

THEOREM 3.2. *Let τ be a pseudo-triangle in the kinetic triangulation $\mathcal{PT}^+(P(t))$. Then the expected number of discrete changes in the triangulation $\mathcal{T}(\tau)$ of τ, caused by any single envelope or visibility event which happens during the period $I(\tau)$, and conditioned on τ appearing in $\mathcal{PT}^+(P)$, is $O(\log N_\tau) = O(\log n)$.*

PROOF. Clearly, the chords of $\mathcal{T}(\tau)$ (the additional edges which partition τ into triangles) admit a total vertical order, because they all cross the vertical line through $\mathsf{apex}(\tau)$. Consider a time instance $t_0 \in \mathbb{R}$ when an envelope or a visibility event occurs, and let $p_0 \in \mathcal{L}(\tau) \cup \mathcal{R}(\tau)$ be the point involved in the event. Let t_0^- (resp., t_0^+) be the time right before (resp., after) the event. Note that p_0 cannot be the apex of τ (unless the funnel of τ is already, or is going to become, a triangle). Note also that p_0 is not a vertex of $\mathsf{bridge}(\tau)$, neither at t_0^+ nor at t_0^-, unless p_0 is involved in a visibility event which changes $\mathsf{bridge}(\tau)$. In the latter case, $\mathcal{T}(\tau)$ gains or loses its topmost triangle at time t_0 and there are no other changes in the triangulation. We may therefore assume that $\mathsf{bridge}(\tau)$ does not change at time t_0, and that p_0 is not a vertex of $\mathsf{bridge}(\tau)$.

With no loss of generality, we assume that p_0 is a vertex of $\mathcal{R}(\tau)$ at time t_0^+, and treat the remaining cases symmetrically (for a visibility event, p_0 belongs to $\mathcal{R}(\tau)$ also at time t_0^-). Consider the triangulation $\mathcal{T}(\tau)$ at time t_0^+ (that we would have obtained if we were to reconstruct $\mathcal{T}^+(P)$ statically at time t_0^+). Let τ_0 be the sub-pseudo-triangle of τ within which the edge $p_0\nu^*(p_0)$ is generated during the construction of $\mathcal{T}^+(P)$ (see Figure 4 (right)). Note that the event at time t_0 leaves unchanged the visibility vertex $\nu(p)$ of each vertex p in τ other than p_0. Indeed, this follows from Lemma 3.1 for envelope events and is obvious for visibility events, using our assumption that $\mathsf{bridge}(\tau)$ does not change. The recursive construction of $\mathcal{T}(\tau)$ is easily seen to imply that τ_0 appears as a sub-pseudo-triangle in the construction also at time t_0^-. Indeed, an easy inductive argument on the order of the ranks of the funnel vertices implies that the modified visibility vertices $\nu^*(p)$, and the resulting chords $p\nu^*(p)$, also do not change, up to the point where τ_0 is constructed. Right after this step, the chord from p_0 is drawn, so the rest of the construction of $\mathcal{T}(\tau)$ might change completely, but only within τ_0. Hence, τ_0 contains every edge which is inserted to or deleted from $\mathcal{T}(\tau)$ at time t_0. Therefore, the number of changes in $\mathcal{T}(\tau)$ is bounded by $O(W_0)$, where W_0 denotes the number of vertices of τ_0 at the time of the event.

Note that W_0 is a random variable depending (only) on the permutation $\pi(P_\tau)$ of P_τ, which is obtained by restricting π to P_τ. Recall that we condition the analysis on permutations π such that τ indeed appears in $\mathcal{PT}^+(P)$. In these permutations, the points of P_τ have to follow all the (at most) five points defining τ, but as long as they obey this restriction they can appear in any order. It follows that, in our conditional probability subspace, the restriction of π to P_τ is a random permutation of P_τ.

To bound the expected value of W_0, we fix an arbitrary threshold $k \geq 10$ and prove that the event $\{W_0 > k\}$ occurs with probability at most $O(1/k)$. The expected value of W_0 is then bounded by

$$\sum_{i=0}^{\log N_\tau} 2^{i+1} \mathsf{Pr}\left\{W_0 > 2^i\right\} = O\left(\sum_{i=0}^{\log N_\tau} 1\right) = O(\log N_\tau). \qquad (1)$$

To show that $\mathsf{Pr}\{W_0 > k\} = O(1/k)$, we proceed through the following cases. In each case, except for the last one, we find a set S_0 of $\Omega(k)$ points which does not depend on $\pi(P_\tau)$, so that all its elements must appear in $\pi(P_\tau)$ after p_0. This readily implies the asserted bound. The last case is more involved but it is still based on the same general idea.

Visibility event. If $\nu^*(p_0)$ is a vertex of the base of τ_0, both at time t_0^- and at time t_0^+, then $\mathcal{T}(\tau)$ does not change combinatorially at time t_0. Otherwise, as follows from the discussion in Section 2, all three vertices that become collinear in the event appear in τ_0, both before and after the event, which implies that $\nu(p_0) = \nu^*(p_0)$ at both times t_0^- and t_0^+.

Suppose $W_0 > k$. If τ_0 contains at least $k/2$ vertices of $\mathcal{R}(\tau)$, then it also contains a sequence S_0 of $k/4 - 1$ consecutive vertices of $\mathcal{R}(\tau)$ either immediately to the left or immediately to the right of p_0. Otherwise, τ_0 contains $\nu(p_0)$ together with at least $k/2 - 1$ other vertices of $\mathcal{L}(\tau)$, so it must contain a sequence S_0 of $k/4 - 1$ consecutive vertices of $\mathcal{L}(\tau)$ lying either immediately to the left or immediately to the right of $\nu(p_0)$. In both cases, the key observation is that S_0 does not depend on $\pi(P_\tau)$, and that p_0 precedes all the vertices of S_0 in $\pi(P_\tau)$ (except possibly for one extremal vertex which is a corner of τ_0). As noted above, this establishes the asserted bound.

Envelope event. Again, suppose that $W_0 > k$. If τ_0 contains at least $k/2$ vertices of $\mathcal{R}(\tau)$, the bound follows by exactly the same argument as in the case of a visibility event. Otherwise, if τ_0 contains $\mathsf{apex}(\tau)$ we set S_0 to be the first $k/2 - 2$ points of $\mathcal{L}(\tau)$ to the left of $\mathsf{apex}(\tau)$. Again, S_0 does not depend on $\pi(P_\tau)$, and all its elements must appear in $\pi(P_\tau)$ after p_0, so the bound follows.

We therefore assume that τ_0 contains at most $k/2$ vertices of $\mathcal{R}(\tau)$, and that its apex q_0 is distinct from $\mathsf{apex}(\tau)$. Thus, the edge $q_0\nu^*(q_0)$ that q_0 generates is the lowest edge of τ_0 which is a chord of τ. We argue that $\nu^*(q_0) = \nu(q_0)$ (before and after t_0; the definition of τ_0 implies that q_0 precedes p_0 in $\pi(P_\tau)$). Indeed, otherwise, by the definition of $\mathcal{T}(\tau)$, $\nu^*(q_0)$ is a vertex of the base of τ_0, which happens only if one of the chains of τ_0 consists of the single edge $q_0\nu^*(q_0)$. Since $p_0 \in \mathcal{R}(\tau)$ and is involved in an envelope event, the edge $q_0\nu^*(q_0)$ must be the only edge of the left chain of τ_0, which contradicts the fact that $\mathcal{L}(\tau)$ must contain at least $k/2$ vertices of τ_0 (for $k \geq 10$). We distinguish between the following two cases.

(i) $q_0 \in \mathcal{L}(\tau)$ (as depicted in Figure 4 (right)). Then the entire left chain of τ_0 is contained in $\mathcal{L}(\tau)$. Let ℓ_0 be the line passing through p_0 and the other two vertices of $\mathcal{R}(\tau)$ participating in the envelope event, and let e_0 be the edge of $\mathcal{L}(\tau)$ intersected by ℓ. Clearly, e_0 is contained in τ_0, because otherwise $\mathcal{R}(\tau_0)$ is not convex. If τ_0 contains $k/4 - 1$ consecutive vertices of $\mathcal{L}(\tau)$ which lie immediately to the left e_0, we set S_0 to be the set of these points, except for the leftmost one (which may be the endpoint of the base of τ_0). Otherwise we set S_0 to be the set of $k/4 - 2$ points lying on $\mathcal{L}(\tau)$ to the right of e_0. Since the definition of e_0 does not depend on $\pi(P_\tau)$, so S_0 also does not depend on $\pi(P_\tau)$.

(ii) $q_0 \in \mathcal{R}(\tau)$ (as depicted in Figure 5 (right)). In this case we define at most $k/2$ sets, each consisting of $\Omega(1/k)$ points and independent of $\pi(P_\tau)$, such that the points in at least one of these sets appear after both p_0 and q_0 in $\pi(P_\tau)$. We fix q_0 on $\mathcal{R}(\tau)$ to the left of p_0 and define S_{q_0} as the set of $k/2-2$ consecutive vertices of $\mathcal{L}(\tau)$ which appear at time t_0 (along $\mathcal{L}(\tau)$) immediately to the left of $\nu^*(q_0) = \nu(q_0)$. By the current assumptions, if q_0 is indeed the apex of τ_0 then all points $q \in S_{q_0}$ belong to τ_0 and, hence, satisfy $\mathsf{priority}(q) > \mathsf{priority}(p_0) > \mathsf{priority}(q_0)$. Since q_0 is fixed, S_{q_0} is also fixed and is independent of $\pi(P_\tau)$. Hence, the above event happens with probability $O(1/k^2)$. Moreover, q_0 is one of the at most $k/2$ vertices of $\mathcal{R}(\tau)$ that lie to the left of p_0. Hence, by the probability union bound, the total probability of this scenario (over all the appropriate vertices $q_0 \in \mathcal{R}(\tau)$) is $O(1/k)$.

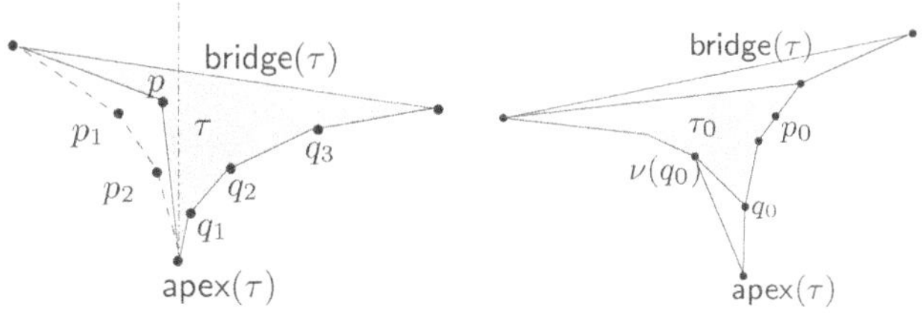

Figure 5: Left: Swap event. The funnel of τ immediately before the x-swap between p and $\mathsf{apex}(\tau)$, which causes the vertices p_1 and p_2 to appear on $\mathcal{L}(\tau)$, and the vertices q_1, q_2, q_3 to disappear from $\mathcal{R}(\tau)$. Right: Envelope event. The case in which q_0 lies on $\mathcal{R}(\tau)$.

We have proved for any $k \geq 10$ that $\mathsf{Pr}\,(W_0 > k) = O(1/k)$. This implies Equation (1) and completes the proof of Theorem 3.2. $\square$

COROLLARY 3.3. *Let τ be a pseudo-triangle in the kinetic pseudo-triangulation $\mathcal{PT}^+(P(t))$. Then the expected number of edge insertions and deletions to $\mathcal{T}(\tau)$ during the period $I(\tau)$, conditioned upon the event that τ appears in $\mathcal{PT}^+(P)$, is $O((E_\tau + V_\tau)\log N_\tau + N_\tau^2)$.*

For a fixed pseudo-triangle τ (including the choice of the connected life span $I(\tau)$), V_τ and E_τ are 2-valued random variables: They are 0 if τ does not appear in $\mathcal{PT}^+(P)$, and assume a fixed "deterministic" value if τ does appear. The following theorem gives an upper bound on these values.

THEOREM 3.4. *For each pseudo-triangle τ we have $V_\tau = O(N_\tau^2\beta_{s+2}(N_\tau))$ and $E_\tau = O(N_\tau^2\beta_{s+2}(N_\tau))$, where s is the maximum number of times at which any fixed triple of points of P becomes collinear.*

PROOF. We show the bound for visibility events. The bound for envelope events is known (see [1, 5]) and can be proved similarly.

We fix a point $p \in P_\tau$ and count the number of visibility events where p is a vertex of $\mathcal{L}(\tau)$ which is collinear with an edge of $\mathcal{R}(\tau)$. To do so, we define, for each $q \in P'_\tau = P_\tau \cup \{\mathsf{right}(\tau)\} \setminus \{p\}$, a partially defined function $\varphi_{p,q}(t)$ which measures the angle between pq and the y-axis, and whose domain consists of all $t \in \mathbb{R}$ at which $x(\mathsf{left}(\tau)) \leq x(p) \leq x(\mathsf{apex}(\tau)) \leq x(q) \leq x(\mathsf{right}(\tau))$. Clearly, each visibility event under consideration corresponds to a breakpoint of the lower envelope of $\{\varphi_{p,q}\}_{q\in P'_\tau}$. Since any pair $\varphi_{p,q_1}, \varphi_{p,q_2}$ of these functions can intersect in at most s points (these are times at which p, q_1, and q_2 are collinear), and for each q the domain of $\varphi_{p,q}(t)$ consists of a constant number of intervals (delimited by times at which either p or q swap with $\mathsf{left}(\tau), \mathsf{right}(\tau)$, or $\mathsf{apex}(\tau)$), it follows that the number of breakpoints is $O(N_\tau\beta_{s+2}(N_\tau))$ [21]. A symmetric argument holds for the number of visibility events where p is a vertex of $\mathcal{R}(\tau)$ which is collinear with an edge of $\mathcal{L}(\tau)$. Repeating this analysis for each $p \in P$ yields the asserted overall bound. $\square$

Fix a pseudo-triangle τ. Conditioned on priorities that cause τ to appear in $\mathcal{PT}^+(P(t))$, Corollary 3.3 and Theorem 3.4 imply that the expected number of discrete changes in $\mathcal{T}(\tau)$ is $O(N_\tau^2\beta_{s+2}(N_\tau)\log N_\tau)$. Let $\mathsf{Pr}(\tau)$ be the probability that τ indeed appears in $\mathcal{PT}^+(P(t))$. Then the total expected number of discrete changes in $\mathcal{PT}^+(P(t))$ is

$$O\left(\sum_\tau \mathsf{Pr}(\tau)N_\tau^2\beta_{s+2}(N_\tau)\log N_\tau\right) =$$
$$O\left(\beta_{s+2}(n)\log n \sum_\tau \mathsf{Pr}(\tau)N_\tau^2\right).$$

LEMMA 3.5. *$\sum_\tau \mathsf{Pr}(\tau)N_\tau^2 = O(n^2\log n)$, where the sum is over all (possible sets of $1 \leq h \leq 5$ points defining) possible pseudo-triangles τ.*

PROOF. Without loss of generality, we only consider pseudo-triangles τ with $N_\tau > 0$, which are defined by five distinct points of $P \setminus \{p_{-\infty}, p_\infty\}$. (Pseudo-triangles defined by fewer than 5 distinct points, or those whose defining 5-tuple includes $p_{-\infty}$ and/or p_∞ are analyzed similarly, replacing the exponent 5 by the appropriate $1 \leq h \leq 4$.) Thus, as already noted, $\mathsf{Pr}(\tau) = O(1/N_\tau^5)$, because τ appears in $\mathcal{PT}^+(P(t))$ if and only if the priorities of the five points that define τ are smaller than the priorities of all other points in P_τ (and $\mathsf{apex}(\tau)$ has the largest priority among the defining points). Therefore $\sum_\tau \mathsf{Pr}(\tau)N_\tau^2 = O\left(\sum_\tau 1/N_\tau^3\right)$.

In what follows, we call N_τ the *level* of τ. Let $M_k(n)$ (resp. $M_{\leq k}(n)$) denote the maximum number of pseudo-triangles of level k (resp., of level at most k), defined by 5 points, in a set of n moving points. We claim that $M_{\leq k}(n) = O(n^2k^3)$. To see this, consider all the pseudo-triangles τ (defined by five points) whose birth time is determined by a fixed x-swap event occurring at some time t_0, between some pair of points $a, b \in P$. Assume without loss of generality that $a = \mathsf{left}(\tau)$. Then $\mathsf{apex}(\tau)$ and $\mathsf{right}(\tau)$ are among the $k+2$ points whose x-coordinates lie at time t_0 immediately to the right of $x(a) = x(b)$. Similarly, the fifth point, which is responsible for the destruction of τ, is one of the first $k+1$ points whose x-coordinates enter the interval between $x(\mathsf{left}(\tau)) = x(a)$ and $x(\mathsf{right}(\tau))$. Thus, each of the $O(n^2)$ x-swap events defines the creation time of at most $O(k^3)$ pseudo-triangles of level at most k, which readily implies the asserted bound on $M_{\leq k}(n)$. We thus have

$$\sum_\tau \mathsf{Pr}(\tau)N_\tau^2 = O\left(\sum_\tau 1/N_\tau^3\right) = O\left(\sum_{k\geq 1} M_k(n)/k^3\right)$$
$$= O\left(\sum_{k\geq 1} M_{\leq k}(n)/k^4\right) = O\left(\sum_{k\geq 1} n^2/k\right) = O(n^2\log n). \quad \square$$

The combination of Corollary 3.3, Theorem 3.4, and Lemma 3.5 implies the following summary theorem.

THEOREM 3.6. *The total expected number of discrete changes in the kinetic triangulation $\mathcal{T}(P(t))$ is $O(n^2\beta_{s+2}(n)\log^2 n)$.*

4. KINETIC MAINTENANCE OF $\mathcal{T}(P)$

In this section we describe a kinetic data structure which supports efficient maintenance of $\mathcal{T}^+(P(t))$ under motion. The structure satisfies[2] the standard requirements of *efficiency, compactness, responsiveness*, and *locality*, as reviewed in the introduction.

The static structure. We store the pseudo-triangulation tree $\mathcal{PT}^+(P)$ as a treap over P, as described in Theorem 2.2, whose inorder is the x-order of the points and where the heap order is according to their random priorities. Each node v in $\mathcal{PT}^+(P)$ corresponds to the pseudo-triangle τ_v whose apex is the point stored at v. We also store at v, as auxiliary data, the endpoints $\mathsf{left}(\tau_v)$ and $\mathsf{right}(\tau_v)$, which are inherited from appropriate ancestors of v.

In addition, we also store at v the combinatorial description of the funnel of τ_v, and of its triangulation $\mathcal{T}(\tau_v)$. This includes $\mathsf{bridge}(\tau_v)$, two ordered lists storing the vertices of $\mathcal{L}(\tau_v)$, and $\mathcal{R}(\tau_v)$ in their left-to-right order, and the list of the chords of $\mathcal{T}(\tau_v)$, sorted in their vertical order (i.e., the order of their intersections with the vertical line through $\mathsf{apex}(\tau_v)$). We represent any sorted list of vertices or edges[3] as a balanced binary tree supporting each of the operations search, split, and concatenate, in $O(\log n)$ time [23]. To facilitate efficient kinetic maintenance of $\mathcal{T}^+(P(t))$, we also store the vertices of the upper hull of P, in their left-to-right order in a balanced search tree. Note that each edge of the triangulation (not on $\mathcal{C}(P)$) appears twice in our structure, once as $\mathsf{bridge}(\tau_v)$ for some pseudo triangle τ_v, and once on $\mathcal{L}(\tau_w)$ or $\mathcal{R}(\tau_w)$ for some ancestor w of v or on the convex hull of P.

THEOREM 4.1. *Let P be a set of n points in the plane. The pseudo-triangulation tree $\mathcal{PT}^+(P)$, augmented with the auxiliary data items, as above, uses $O(n)$ space, and it can be initialized in $O(n\log n)$ time.*

PROOF. The asserted bound on the overall storage follows from the easy observation that $\mathcal{PT}^+(P)$ contains $O(n)$ nodes, and every point $p \in P$ appears as a non-corner vertex on at most one chain $\mathcal{L}(\tau_v)$, $\mathcal{R}(\tau_v)$, over all nodes v of $\mathcal{PT}^+(P)$.

We construct the pseudo-triangulation tree $\mathcal{PT}^+(P)$ (excluding the auxiliary items $\mathsf{bridge}(\tau_v)$, $\mathcal{L}(\tau_v)$, $\mathcal{R}(\tau_v)$ and the chords of $\mathcal{T}(\tau_v)$) in a single *top-down* pass, which implements the recursive construction given in Section 2. Clearly, this can be done in $O(n)$ time, after an initial sorting of the points of P, by their x-coordinates and by their priorities; sorting the points takes $O(n\log n)$ time.

We next compute the items $\mathcal{L}(\tau_v)$, $\mathcal{R}(\tau_v)$, and $\mathsf{bridge}(\tau_v)$ stored at the nodes v of $\mathcal{PT}^+(P)$, by a single *bottom-up* traversal of $\mathcal{PT}^+(P)$, which computes for every node v the upper hull $\mathcal{U}(v)$ of the set $P_v \cup \{\mathsf{left}(\tau_v), \mathsf{right}(\tau_v)\}$. When we process a new non-leaf node v, we have already visited its respective left and right children v_ℓ and v_r, so their hulls $\mathcal{U}(v_\ell)$ and $\mathcal{U}(v_r)$ are already available. We compute $\mathsf{bridge}(\tau_v)$ in $O(\log n)$ time by a simultaneous binary seach over $\mathcal{U}(v_\ell)$ and $\mathcal{U}(v_r)$, in the manner described in [19]. Then we use $\mathsf{bridge}(\tau_v)$ to split $\mathcal{U}(v_\ell)$ (resp., $\mathcal{U}(v_r)$) into $\mathcal{L}^-(\tau_v)$ and $\mathcal{L}(\tau_v)$ (resp., $\mathcal{R}(\tau_v)$ and $\mathcal{R}^+(\tau_v)$). We store explicitly the chains $\mathcal{L}(\tau_v)$ $\mathcal{R}(\tau_v)$ at v, and compute $\mathcal{U}(v)$ by concatenating the three edge lists $\mathcal{L}^-(\tau)$, $\{\mathsf{bridge}(\tau)\}$, and $\mathcal{R}^+(\tau)$, in a similar manner to that described in [5]. Overall, we spend $O(\log n)$ time at each node of $\mathcal{PT}^+(P)$, for a total of $O(n\log n)$ time.

Finally, for each node v in $\mathcal{PT}^+(P)$, we compute the list of chords of $\mathcal{T}(\tau_v)$ using the recursive mechanism described in Section 2. Recall that every non-corner vertex p of the funnel of τ_v generates exactly one edge e_p which recursively splits the unique sub-pseudo-triangle τ_p of τ_v. We process the non-corner vertices of $\mathcal{T}(\tau_v)$ in the increasing order of their priorities, and store the previously generated edges in a list, in the order of their intersections with the vertical line through $\mathsf{apex}(\tau_v)$.

It takes $O(\log n)$ time to process a non-corner vertex p of τ_v, for a total of $O(n\log n)$ time. Indeed, we can determine the corners of τ_p in $O(\log n)$ time, by a binary search over the list of the previously generated edges. In addition, we can determine $\nu(p)$ by a binary search over the appropriate chain $\mathcal{L}(\tau_v)$ or $\mathcal{R}(\tau_v)$, and then obtain $\nu^*(p)$ in $O(1)$ additional time. □

The kinetic certificates. To ensure the validity of $\mathcal{PT}^+(P)$ and its triangulation $\mathcal{T}^+(P)$, we use three types of *certificates*, denoted as CT, CE and CV. Each certificate is a predicate on a constant number of points. As long as all the certificates remain true, the validity of $\mathcal{PT}^+(P)$ and $\mathcal{T}^+(P)$ is ensured. Each certificate contributes a critical event to the global event priority queue $\mathcal{Q}$, which is the first future time at which the certificate becomes invalid (if there is such a time).

CT-***certificates.*** To ensure the validity of the tree $\mathcal{PT}^+(P)$ (ignoring the auxiliary data), each pair of points $p, q \in P$ with consecutive x-coordinates contributes a CT-certificate asserting that the order of $x(p)$ and $x(q)$ remains unchanged. This certificate fails at the first future moment of an x-swap between p and q. According to Lemma 2.1, CT-certificates (together with the chosen priorities) are sufficient to ensure the validity of the "bare" tree $\mathcal{PT}^+(P)$.

CE-***certificates.*** For each node v in $\mathcal{PT}^+(P)$, the edge $\mathsf{bridge}(\tau_v) = pq$ contributes a CE-certificate ensuring that the (current) neighbors of p and q on $\mathcal{L}^-(\tau_v) \cup \mathcal{L}(\tau_v)$ and $\mathcal{R}(\tau_v) \cup \mathcal{R}^+(\tau_v)$ remain below the line through p and q. This certificate involves[4] at most six points and fails at the first future time of collinearity between p, q, and one of their four neighbor vertices on $\mathcal{L}^-(\tau_v) \cup \mathcal{L}(\tau_v)$ and on $\mathcal{R}(\tau_v) \cup \mathcal{R}^+(\tau_v)$.

So far, we have ensured the validity of the tree $\mathcal{PT}^+(P)$ and of the edges $\mathsf{bridge}(\tau_v)$ stored at its nodes v. Moreover, the validity of all the chains $\mathcal{L}(\tau_v), \mathcal{R}(\tau_v)$ is also ensured because each one of their edges either belongs to $\mathcal{C}(P)$ or appears as $\mathsf{bridge}(\tau_w)$ at some descendant w of v. Here a collinearity between three consecutive points on $\mathcal{L}(\tau_v)$ or on $\mathcal{R}(\tau_v)$ (an envelope event) will be detected as a change in $\mathsf{bridge}(\tau_w)$, for the appropriate descendant w. Similarly, the

[2]As in [5], all properties (except for compactness) hold *in expectation*, with respect to the random permutation π.

[3]Note that we do not store explicitly the tails $\mathcal{L}^-(\tau), \mathcal{R}^+(\tau)$, because the overall storage that they would require could be too large, as they can be shared by many pseudo-triangles.

[4]If $\mathsf{bridge}(\tau_v)$ does not exist then we have an even simpler certificate which fails when the two edges of $\mathcal{L}^-(\tau_v), \mathcal{R}^+(\tau_v)$ incident to $\mathsf{apex}(\tau_v)$ become collinear.

validity of the upper hull of P follows since each of its edges either belongs to $\mathcal{C}(P)$ or appears as $\mathsf{bridge}(\tau_v)$ at some node v. See [5] and [19] for more details.

CV-***certificates.*** It only remains to ensure the validity of the triangulations $\mathcal{T}(\tau_v)$, over all nodes $v \in \mathcal{PT}^+(P)$. For this we need the third type of certificates, denoted by CV. Fix a node v in $\mathcal{PT}^+(P)$. Every internal point p of $\mathcal{L}(\tau_v)$ or $\mathcal{R}(\tau_v)$ contributes a CV certificate ensuring the validity of $\nu(p)$. This certificate involves p, $\nu(p)$, and the two points adjacent to $\nu(p)$ on its chain. It fails when one of the points adjacent to $\nu(p)$ becomes collinear with p and $\nu(p)$.

Clearly, all of the above certificates use $O(n)$ storage, and can be initialized, including the construction of the event queue Q of their first failure times, by the algorithm of Theorem 4.1, without increasing its overall assymptotic running time, i.e., in $O(n \log n)$ time.

Handing critical events. We next describe the repair operations required when an event, at which some certificate fails, happens.

CT-***certificates.*** Failure of a CT-certificate occurs at an x-swap. That is, the order of the x-coordinates of two consecutive points along $\mathcal{C}(P)$ switches, at some time $t = t_0$.

With no loss of generality we assume that $\mathsf{priority}(p) < \mathsf{priority}(q)$, implying that $q(t_0^-)$ is a descendant of $p(t_0^-)$, where t_0^-, t_0^+ denote the time just before and just after t_0, respectively. To update $\mathcal{PT}^+(P(t_0^+))$ we reconstruct from scratch the subtree rooted at the node v containing p, and recompute the kinetic certificates associated with its nodes and the points that they contain. We remove the failure times of the expired certificates from $\mathcal{Q}$, and insert the new ones. All this can be done in $O(n_v \log n_v)$ time using the algorithm of Theorem 4.1, where $n_v = |P_v|$. We prove that $\mathbb{E}\{n_v\} = O(\log n)$ by applying a simplified version of the analysis used in Theorem 3.2. As above, it suffices to show that $\Pr\{n_v > k\} \le 4/k$, for any $k \ge 1$. Indeed, $n_v > k$ implies that either each of the $k/2$ points w whose x-coordinates immediately precede $x(p)$ or each of the $k/2$ points w whose x-coordinates immediately follow $x(p)$ at time t_0 satisfies $\mathsf{priority}(p) < \mathsf{priority}(w)$. This happens[5] with probability at most $4/k$. Thus, we can reconstruct the subtree rooted at v in $O(\log n \log\log n)$ expected time.

As can easily be checked, if neither p nor q is the leftmost or the rightmost point of P (excluding the points at infinity which we added) then no further updates outside the subtree of v are needed, and no additional certificates need to be created or destroyed. (That is because $\mathsf{left}(\tau_v) \ne p_{-\infty}$ and $\mathsf{right}(\tau_v) \ne p_\infty$, so the upper hull $\mathcal{U}(v)$ contains at most one of p, q, and it does not change as a result of the swap.) We next describe the necessary modifications in the setting, depicted in Figure 6, in which case we assume that (i) p and q are the two points with the smallest x-coordinates, (ii) $x(q(t_0^-)) > x(p(t_0^-))$, and (iii) the y-coordinate of p is larger than at q when they swap; the other cases are treated symmetrically. The x-swap between p and q causes q to appear on the upper hull of P. We add q to the upper hull in $O(\log n)$ time. Similarly, q becomes part of the tail $\mathcal{L}^-(\tau_w)$ of every ancestor w of v (both w and v lie on the leftmost path of the treap). If w is such an ancestor whose bridge is incident to p (from the right), then we have to incorporate q into the certificate of $\mathsf{bridge}(\tau_w)$, and possibly replace its old failure time in $\mathcal{Q}$ with a new one. Since the expected number of ancestors w of v, in the treap $\mathcal{PT}^+(P)$, is $O(\log n)$ (see, e.g., [20]), any swap event can be processed in $O(\log^2 n)$ expected time.

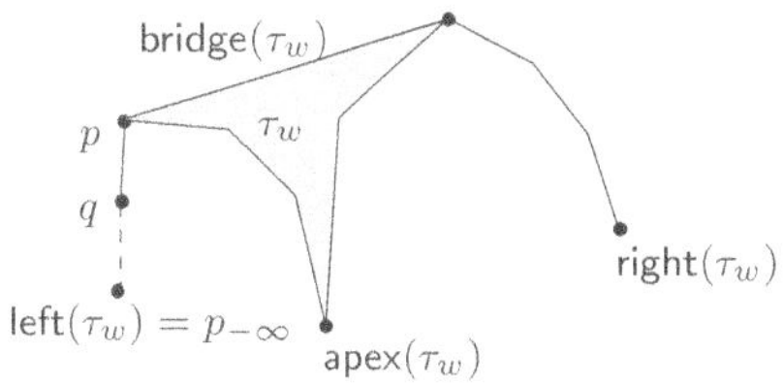

Figure 6: The view after a swap event between a pair of points p, q with the smallest x-coordinates stored in the left subtree of a node w, whose CE-certificate has to be updated.

CE-***certificates.*** Consider a time t_0 when a CE-certificate at some node v fails. We assume without loss of generality that at time t_0 the leftmost vertex p of $\mathcal{L}(\tau_v)$ becomes collinear with the leftmost edge qr of $\mathcal{R}^+(\tau_v)$ (so that $\mathsf{bridge}(\tau_v)$ was pq before the event and is pr afterwards), and treat the remaining cases symmetrically. As a result of this event, the edge pr replaces pq as $\mathsf{bridge}(\tau_v)$, the edge qr is added to the end of $\mathcal{R}(\tau_v)$, and the triangulation $\mathcal{T}(\tau_v)$ gains the new triangle $\triangle pqr$. We need $O(\log n)$ time to update the edge lists of $\mathcal{R}(\tau_v)$ and $\mathcal{T}(\tau_v)$, and to compute the CV-certificate of q (which ceases to be the endpoint of $R(\tau_v)$) and add its failure time to $\mathcal{Q}$. (Note that the CV-certificate of q is part of the former CE-certificate at v.)

To recompute the new certificate of $\mathsf{bridge}(\tau_v)$, we have to determine the next edge rr^+ of $\mathcal{R}^+(\tau_v)$ that is incident to r from the right. This edge is either stored in one of the lists $\mathcal{L}(\tau_w)$ or $\mathcal{R}(\tau_w)$ at some ancestor w of v, or it belongs to the upper hull of P. See Figure 7 (top). We find rr^+ by doing a binary search on the lists $\mathcal{L}(\tau_w)$ and $\mathcal{R}(\tau_w)$ for the ancestors w of v, and if necessary also on the convex hull of P.

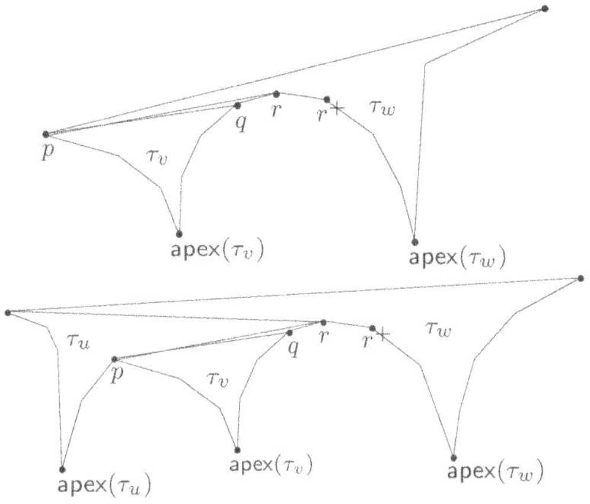

Figure 7: Failure of the CE-certificate at v (shown at time t_0^+ right after the event). Top: The case where the ancestor w that stores rr^+ coincides with the ancestor u that has lost q. Bottom: The case where u is distinct from w.

If pq and qr were part of the upper hull at time t_0^-, we

[5] We emphasize again that arguments of this kind are based on the assumption that the motion of the points is oblivious to the choice of priorities.

replace them by a single edge pr, in $O(\log n)$ time. Otherwise, v has some ancestor u such that pq and qr are stored in the edge list of $\mathcal{L}(\tau_u)$ or $\mathcal{R}(\tau_u)$. (There is exactly one such ancestor u, which is equal to w unless r is incident to $\mathsf{bridge}(\tau_u)$; see Figure 7. In the terminology of Section 3, τ_u experiences an envelope event at time t_0.) We find u in $O(\log^2 n)$ expected time by searching the edge lists stored at all ancestor nodes of v, whose expected number is bounded by $O(\log n)$. We then replace pq and qr by pr in the edge list of the respective chain $\mathcal{L}(\tau_u)$ or $\mathcal{R}(\tau_u)$, and remove from $\mathcal{Q}$ the failure time of the CV-certificate of q (within τ_u). Moreover, we have to retriangulate a suitable sub-pseudo-triangle τ_0 of τ_u whose boundary, according to Theorem 3.2, has expected complexity $O(\log n)$ (see also Figure 5). To do so, we determine τ_0 by searching the edge list of $\mathcal{T}(\tau_u)$, and then recursively triangulate it, as described in the proof of Theorem 4.1. All this can be done in $O(\log^2 n)$ expected time. Therefore, we can process any CE-certificate failure in $O(\log^2 n)$ expected time.

CV-***certificates.*** We finally consider the case when a visibility event, involving some point p within the funnel of τ_v, for some node v of $\mathcal{PT}^+(P)$, causes the failure of the corresponding CV-certificate at some time t_0. Since the failed certificate is associated with an internal vertex of $\mathcal{L}(\tau_v)$ or $\mathcal{R}(\tau_v)$, all the necessary updates are local to the funnel of τ_v, and to its triangulation $\mathcal{T}(\tau_v)$. We update the CV-certificate of p and insert its new failure time to $\mathcal{Q}$, in $O(\log n)$ time (the new neighbor of $\nu(p)$ is easily obtained in $O(\log n)$ from the respective edge list). In addition, we may have to determine and re-triangulate a suitable sub-pseudo-triangle τ_0 of τ_v, whose boundary has expected complexity $O(\log n)$ (see Theorem 3.2). An in the case of a failure of a CE-certificate, this can be done in $O(\log^2 n)$ expected time, by searching the edge list of $\mathcal{T}(\tau_v)$.

We thus obtain our main theorem.

THEOREM 4.2. *Let $P(t)$ be a collection of n moving points, as above. We can maintain the triangulation $\mathcal{T}(P(t))$ under motion in a kinetic data structure of linear size, which processes an expected number of $O(n^2\beta_{s+2}(n)\log n)$ events, each in $O(\log^2 n)$ expected time, where s is the maximum number of times at which any single triple of points of $P(t)$ can become collinear.*

Enforcing locality. As implied by Theorem 4.2, the proposed data structure for maintaining $\mathcal{T}(P)$ is compact, efficient, and responsive (where the last two properties hold in expectation). To make it also local (in expectation), it is sufficient to ensure that at any moment of time the expected number of kinetic certificates involving any single point is $O(\log n)$. Clearly, each point is associated with at most two CT-certificates. Since the expected depth of $\mathcal{PT}^+(P)$ is $O(\log n)$ and each pseudo-triangle of $\mathcal{PT}^+(P)$ defines a single CE-certificate, each point participates in an expected number of $O(\log n)$ CE-certificates. We can also achieve this for CV-certificates by slightly modifying their definition; see the full version [17] for details.

5. REFERENCES

[1] P. K. Agarwal, J. Basch, L. J. Guibas, J. Hershberger and L. Zhang, Deformable free-space tilings for kinetic collision detection, *Internat. J. Robotics Research* 21 (2002), 179–197.

[2] P. K. Agarwal, J. Gao, L. Guibas, H. Kaplan, V. Koltun, N. Rubin and M. Sharir, Kinetic stable Delaunay graphs, this proceedings.

[3] P. K. Agarwal, H. Kaplan and M. Sharir, Kinetic and dynamic data structures for closest pairs and nearest neighbors, *ACM Trans. Algorithms* 5 (2008), Article 4 (37 pp.)

[4] P. K. Agarwal, Y. Wang and H. Yu, A 2D kinetic triangulation with near-quadratic topological changes, *Discrete Comput. Geom.* 36 (2006), 573–592.

[5] G. Alexandron, H. Kaplan and M. Sharir, Kinetic and dynamic data structures for convex hulls and upper envelopes, *Comput. Geom. Theory Appls.* 36 (2007), 144–158.

[6] J. Basch, J. Erickson, L. J. Guibas, J. Hershberger and L. Zhang, Kinetic collision detection between two simple polygons, *Comput. Geom. Theory Appls.* 27 (3) (2004), 211–235.

[7] J. Basch, L. J. Guibas and J. Hershberger, Data structures for mobile data, *J. Algorithms* 31 (1999), 1–28.

[8] M. W. Bern and D. Eppstein, Mesh generation and optimal triangulation, in: Computing in Euclidean Geometry (D.-Z. Du and F. K.-M. Hwang, eds.), World Scientific, 2nd edition, 1995, pp. 47–123.

[9] B. Chazelle, H. Edelsbrunner, M. Grigni, L.J. Guibas, J. Hershberger, M. Sharir and J. Snoeyink, Ray shooting in polygons using geodesic triangulations, *Algorithmica* 12 (1994), 54–68.

[10] K. Clarkson and P. Shor, Applications of random sampling in computational geometry, II, *Discrete Comput. Geom.* 4 (1989), 387–421.

[11] E. D. Demaine, J. S. B. Mitchell and J. O'Rourke, The Open Problems Project, `http://www.cs.smith.edu/~orourke/TOPP/`.

[12] J. Donea, Arbitrary Lagrangian-Eulerian finite element methods, in: *Computational Methods for Transient Analysis* (T. B. Belytschk and T. J. R. Hughes, eds.), North-Holland, Elsevier, 1983, pp. 474–516.

[13] H. Edelsbrunner, Triangulations and meshes in computational geometry, *Acta Numerica* 9 (2000), 133–213.

[14] J.-J. Fu and R. C. T. Lee, Voronoi diagrams of moving points in the plane, *Internat. J. Comput. Geom. Appl.* 1 (1994), 23–32.

[15] L. Guibas, J. Mitchell and T. Roos, Voronoi diagrams of moving points in the plane, *Proc. 17th Internat. Workshop Graph-Theoret. Concepts Computer Science*, Lecture Notes in Comp. Sci., vol. 570, Springer-Verlag, 1991, pp. 113–125.

[16] L. Guibas, Kinetic data structures: A state of the art report. *Robotics: the Algorithmic Perspective* (WAFR 1998), 191–209, A.K. Peters, Natick, MA, 1998.

[17] H. Kaplan, N. Rubin and M. Sharir, A kinetic triangulation scheme for moving points in the plane, `http://www.cs.tau.ac.il/~rubinnat/KTriang.pdf`.

[18] D. Leven and M. Sharir, Planning a purely translational motion for a convex object in two-dimensional space using generalized Voronoi diagrams, *Discrete Comput. Geom.* 2 (1987), 9–31.

[19] M. H. Overmars and J. van Leeuwen, Maintenance of configurations in the plane, *J. Comput. Syst. Sci.* 23 (2) (1981), 166–204.

[20] R. Seidel and C. R. Aragon, Randomized search trees, *Algorithmica* 16 (1996), 464–497.

[21] M. Sharir and P. K. Agarwal, *Davenport-Schinzel sequences and their geometric applications*, Cambridge University Press, New York, 1995.

[22] D. Kirkpatrick, J. Snoeyink and B. Speckmann, Kinetic collision detection for simple polygons, *Internat. J. Comput. Geom. Appl.* 12 (1-2) (2002), 3–27.

[23] R. E. Tarjan, *Data Structures and Network Algorithms*, Society for Industrial and Applied Mathematics, Philadelphia, 1983.

Output-Sensitive Algorithm for the Edge-Width of an Embedded Graph*

Sergio Cabello
Department of Mathematics, IMFM
Department of Mathematics, FMF
University of Ljubljana, Slovenia
sergio.cabello@fmf.uni-lj.si

Éric Colin de Verdière
Laboratoire d'informatique
École normale supérieure
CNRS, Paris, France
Eric.Colin.de.Verdiere@ens.fr

Francis Lazarus
GIPSA-Lab, CNRS, Grenoble, France
Francis.Lazarus@gipsa-lab.grenoble-inp.fr

ABSTRACT

Let G be an *unweighted* graph of complexity n cellularly embedded in a surface (orientable or not) of genus g. We describe improved algorithms to compute (the length of) a shortest non-contractible and a shortest non-separating cycle of G.

If k is an integer, we can compute such a non-trivial cycle with length at most k in $O(gnk)$ time, or correctly report that no such cycle exists. In particular, on a fixed surface, we can test in linear time whether the edge-width or face-width of a graph is bounded from above by a constant. This also implies an output-sensitive algorithm to compute a shortest non-trivial cycle that runs in $O(gnk)$ time, where k is the length of the cycle.

Categories and Subject Descriptors: F.2.2 [Analysis of Algorithms and Problem Complexity]: Nonnumerical algorithms and problems—*Computations on discrete structures; Geometric problems and computations*; G.2.2 [Discrete Mathematics]: Graph theory—*Graph algorithms; path and circuit problems*; I.3.5 [Computer Graphics]: Computational geometry and object modeling—*Geometric algorithms, languages, and systems*

General Terms: Algorithms, Performance, Theory

Keywords: Topological graph theory, computational topology, edge-width, face-width, surface, embedded graph

*Research partially supported by the Slovenian Research Agency, program P1-0297 and project BI-FR/09-10-PROTEUS-014, funded by the French Ministry of Foreign and European Affairs.

1. INTRODUCTION

Let Σ be a surface (orientable or not) of genus g with b boundaries. Let G be an (unweighted, undirected) graph embedded on Σ of *complexity* n (this is the total number of vertices and edges of G), where all the faces of G are disks. In this paper, we are interested in the *edge-width* and *face-width* of G, which roughly measure how G "locally looks planar". Specifically, the *edge-width* of G is the minimum number of edges in a non-contractible cycle of G [2, 23]. The *face-width* of G (also known as *representativity*) is the minimum number of points in the image of G that are contained in a non-contractible curve on Σ [24]. There are also the corresponding concepts of non-separating edge-width and non-separating face-width, where the requirement of being non-contractible is strengthened into being non-separating.

This paper gives improved algorithms to compute these parameters. Before describing our new results in detail, we present some motivations and related works.

Topological Graph Theory. Edge-width and face-width were introduced in the field of topological graph theory (see Mohar and Thomassen [22, Chapter 5] for a survey). Graph embeddings with large face-width share many properties with planar graphs; we list a selection of them. Every graph embedded in a surface with sufficiently large face-width or edge-width, that depends on the surface, is 5-choosable and thus 5-colorable [27, 9]. Every graph with large face-width can be made planar by cutting along cycles that are far apart from each other [28]. A given graph is a minor of every graph of face-width k embedded on the same surface, when k is sufficiently large [23]. Finally, for any fixed surface there exists a constant bounding the number of embeddings with face-width at least 3 that any 3-connected graph may have [21, 16], thus extending Whitney's result for planar graphs to arbitrary surfaces.

Related Algorithmic Results. The computational aspects of the edge-width and face-width have also been studied. The face-width of G is half the edge-width of the *vertex-face incidence graph* of G, and similarly for the non-separating edge-width; therefore, the problem boils down to computing a shortest *non-trivial* cycle on an embedded graph, where non-trivial means either non-contractible or non-separating. Such cycles are the fundamental tool to perform surgery on embedded graphs. The first algorithm, by Thomassen [26], finds a shortest non-trivial cycle in cubic time. In essence, for each vertex of G, the algorithm computes a breadth-first search (BFS) tree T rooted at that vertex, and, for every non-tree edge e, tests whether the cycle formed by T and e is non-trivial; finally, the shortest such cycle is returned. In particular, the shortest non-trivial cycle has no repeated vertex.

Other papers on this topic study the computation of shortest non-trivial cycles in the more general situation of (non-negatively) *weighted* graphs. Erickson and Har-Peled [11] extend Thomassen's algorithm to this setting and decrease its complexity to $O(n^2 \log n)$, by interleaving Dijkstra's algorithm with tests for triviality. This is the best current result, and an algorithm with subquadratic running time would give rise to a subquadratic-time algorithm to find the girth of sparse graphs [5]. Some other papers study the problem parameterized by the genus [6, 19]. The best known algorithm by Cabello and Chambers [3] computes the shortest non-contractible (resp. non-separating) cycle on an orientable surface in $O((g+b)g^2 n \log n)$ (resp. $O(g^3 n \log n)$). As a consequence, the (possibly non-separating) edge-width and face-width of a graph in a fixed orientable surface can be computed in $O(n \log n)$ time. In a companion paper [4], we also consider the more general scenario of finding shortest non-trivial cycles in *directed* graphs.

Kawarabayashi and Mohar (private communication) point out that their results in [16] imply that the *face-width* k of a graph can be computed in $2^{O(gk)}n$ time, assuming that $k \geq 3$. This approach relies on graph minors, and in particular, the relations between the face-width and tree-width of embedded graphs. Their algorithm has an exponential dependency on the genus and the face-width, it uses an unknown (but computable) list of minimal graphs, and it does not extend to the problem of computing the edge-width.

A Faster Algorithm. A natural question arises: are there faster algorithms to compute these parameters, i.e., to find shortest non-trivial cycles in the restricted setting of *unweighted* graphs? All known algorithms for this purpose use shortest path trees, which are computed in $O(n \log n)$ time. However, for unweighted graphs, any BFS tree is a shortest path tree. While a BFS tree can be computed in linear time, current results are also relying on the minimum cut problem in planar graphs [19] or on dynamic trees [3], and require an extra logarithmic factor that is independent from the shortest path tree computation. The $O(n^2 \log n)$ time algorithm by Erickson and Har-Peled [11, Lemma 5.2] immediately gives an $O(n^2)$ time algorithm for the non-contractible case, but in the non-separating case, the complexity is still $O(n^2 \log n)$, because the extra logarithmic factor appears in their recurrence, independently of the shortest path tree computation.

The problem of computing the edge-width and face-width efficiently is an ingredient of several algorithms. In particular, the following problem has been raised in recent papers [16, 17, 18]: Let g_0, k_0 be constants. Is there an algorithm to decide in linear time if the edge-width (or face-width) of a given graph embedded in a surface of genus g_0 is bounded by k_0? Previous results imply that this problem can be solved in $O(n \log n)$ time. We solve it in $O(n)$ time:

Our Results

THEOREM 1. *Let G be an unweighted graph of complexity n cellularly embedded on a surface Σ (orientable or not) of genus g with b boundaries. Given an integer k, we can decide in $O((g+b)nk)$ time (resp. $O(gnk)$ time) if the edge-width (resp. non-separating edge-width) of G is at most k. If it is the case, we can also obtain a shortest non-contractible (resp. non-separating) cycle in G.*

Incidentally, we give alternate algorithms to find shortest non-trivial loops and cycles (possibly in weighted graphs). Our algorithms are (arguably) simpler to implement than those by Erickson and Har-Peled [11, Lemma 5.2]; some ideas of the proof are inspired from the paper by Erickson and Whittlesey to compute shortest homotopy generators [12]. Compared to Erickson and Har-Peled [11], our algorithms are faster by a logarithmic factor for the non-separating case in unweighted graphs, and have the same asymptotic running-time otherwise:

THEOREM 2. *Let G be an unweighted graph of complexity n cellularly embedded on a surface Σ (orientable or not, possibly with boundary). We can compute a shortest non-contractible or non-separating loop through a given basepoint in G in $O(n)$ time.*

By running the algorithm of Theorem 1 for exponentially increasing values of k, and combining with the result of Theorem 2, we obtain:

COROLLARY 1. *Let G be an unweighted graph of complexity n cellularly embedded on a surface Σ (orientable or not) of genus g with b boundaries. If k denotes the edge-width or the face-width of G, we can compute k in $O(n \min\{(g+b)k, n\})$ time. Similarly, if k denotes the non-separating edge-width or the non-separating face-width of G, we can compute k in $O(n \min\{gk, n\})$ time. The algorithm also computes a shortest cycle of the corresponding type (non-contractible or non-separating, in G or in its vertex-face incidence graph).*

For finding shortest non-contractible cycles the best time complexity known so far was $O(n \min\{(g+b)g^2 \log n, n\})$, while for finding shortest non-separating cycles the best time complexity was $O(n \log n \min\{g^3, n\})$. Furthermore, our algorithms are quite simple and do not require heavy data structures like self-adjusting top trees (needed by Cabello and Chambers [3]).

Our output-sensitive complexity can be combined with combinatorial bounds on the edge-width and face-width that are known. Hutchinson [15] showed that a triangulation with m vertices in an orientable surface without boundary has edge-width $O(\sqrt{m/g} \log g)$ if $g \leq m$ and $O(\log g)$ if $g > m$. This result can be extended to non-orientable surfaces, and the same bound applies to the face-width of arbitrary embedded graphs [6, Lemma 13 and Theorem 14]. Therefore, our algorithm implies that the edge-width of a triangulation and the face-width of an arbitrary graph in a surface (orientable or not) without boundary can be computed in $O(n^{3/2} g^{1/2} \log g)$ time, provided that $g \leq n$. This time bound is subquadratic unless $g \log^2 g = \Omega(n)$.

Applications. In topological graph theory there are several results of the following form: for any fixed surface Σ there exists a constant $c = c(\Sigma, \Pi)$ such that any graph embedded in Σ with face-width (or edge-width) at least c has property Π. See for example [27, 9, 28, 23, 21], and [22, Chapter 5]. Our results provide a linear-time algorithm to test if the hypotheses of those results are fulfilled.

Computing the edge-width or the face-width has been explicitly used as subroutine for computing crossing number of graphs [17], for graph isomorphism of graphs that admit polyhedral embeddings [16], and for finding certain induced cycles in embedded graphs [18]. In these papers, the authors make a detour computing a 2-approximation of the edge-width using ideas of Erickson and Har-Peled [11, Lemma 5.6]. Using a 2-approximation instead of the real edge-width affects exponentially the running time; however, this is hidden in the O-notation because the authors consider a fixed surface.

Also, there is a closed formula telling the orientable genus of a graph that can be embedded in the projective plane. Indeed, Fiedler et al. [13] have shown that a graph G that can be embedded in the projective plane with face-width $k \neq 2$ has orientable genus $\lfloor k/2 \rfloor$. Our results imply an algorithm to compute the orientable genus $g(G)$ of such graphs in $O(g(G)n)$ time.

The techniques we use in this paper to prove Theorem 2 are also useful in our companion paper [4], where we obtain efficient algorithms that find shortest non-trivial cycles in a more general setting than previously studied, namely, for *directed* weighted graphs on surfaces.

Overview of the Algorithm. Our main algorithm, to obtain Theorem 1, consists of two steps: (1) We first compute a set of vertices K such that any non-trivial cycle has to use some vertex of K. (2) For every vertex s in K, we compute the shortest non-trivial cycle passing through s in the graph induced by the vertices at distance at most $k/2$ from s. The key idea in our approach is to find an efficient way to carry Step (2) simultaneously for several basepoints that are far apart on the surface. This idea, in turn, requires to choose K in Step (1) adequately. This strategy also requires to be able to test in constant time whether a cycle with a special structure is trivial; we introduce a technique for this purpose, which implies Theorem 2, of independent interest.

After some preliminaries (Section 2), we prove Theorem 2 in Section 3. Then, reusing a large part of that section, we prove our main result, Theorem 1, in Section 4. Finally, Corollary 1 is deduced.

2. BACKGROUND AND TERMINOLOGY

2.1 Graph Theory

All the considered graphs may have loop edges and multiple edges. We sometimes denote by xy an edge with endpoints x and y: even if this notation is ambiguous in presence of multiple edges, it will always be clear from the context which edge is considered. A *walk* in a graph is a sequence of edges $e_1, \ldots, e_m$ with the property that the target of e_i is the source of e_{i+1}, for $i = 1, \ldots, m-1$; such a walk is *closed* if the target of e_m is the source of e_1. A *path* is a walk without repeated vertices; a *cycle* is a closed walk without repeated vertices. A *loop* with basepoint s is a closed walk with a distinguished occurrence of vertex s. We denote by $V(G)$ and $E(G)$ the set of vertices and edges of a graph G, respectively. For a subset $X \subseteq V(G)$, we use $G[X]$ to denote the subgraph of G induced by X. For an edge e of G, we denote by $G - e$ the graph G without that edge.

Suppose G is connected; consider a spanning tree T of G. For any vertex s and any edge uv of G, we denote by $\tau(T, s, uv)$ the loop consisting of the path in T from s to u, the edge uv, and the path in T from v to s. We also denote by $\tau(T, uv)$ the closed walk consisting of the edge uv and the path in T between u and v. Note that $\tau(T, uv)$ is a cycle, if uv is not in T.

2.2 Surfaces

We review some basic topology of surfaces. See any of the books by Hatcher [14], Massey [20], or Stillwell [25] for a comprehensive treatment.

A *surface* (or 2-manifold) Σ possibly with boundary is a compact, connected, topological space where each point has a neighborhood homeomorphic either to the plane or to the closed half-plane; the points without neighborhood homeomorphic to the plane comprise the *boundary* of Σ. A surface is *non-orientable* if it contains a subset homeomorphic to the Möbius band, and *orientable* otherwise. Here and in the sequel, surfaces are considered up to homeomorphism; in particular, a *disk* is just a surface homeomorphic to the standard unit disk in $\mathbb{R}^2$.

An orientable surface is homeomorphic to a sphere where g disjoint disks are removed, a handle (a torus with one boundary component) is attached to each of the remaining g circles, and then b disjoint disks are removed, for unique integers $g, b \geq 0$. A non-orientable surface is homeomorphic to a sphere where g disjoint disks are removed, a Möbius band is attached to each of the remaining g circles, and then b disjoint disks are removed, for unique integers $g \geq 1$ and $b \geq 0$. In both cases, g is called the *genus* of the surface. For simplicity, we define the *reduced genus* $\bar{g}$ to be $2g$, if Σ is orientable, and g, otherwise. $\overline{\Sigma}$ denotes the surface without boundary obtained by attaching a disk to each boundary component of Σ.

2.3 Graph Embeddings

An *embedding* of a graph G in a surface Σ is a drawing of G on Σ without crossings. More precisely, the vertices of G are mapped to distinct points of the interior Σ; each edge is mapped to a path in the interior of Σ, such that the endpoints of the path agree with the points assigned to the vertices of that edge. Moreover, all the paths must be without intersection or self-intersection except, of course, at common endpoints. We sometimes identify a graph G with its embedding on Σ. The *faces* of G are the connected components of the complement of the image of G in Σ.

In this paper, G is *cellularly embedded* on Σ if the faces of G on $\overline{\Sigma}$ are (homeomorphic to) open disks. In particular, each face of a cellular embedding on Σ is homeomorphic to an open disk with zero, one, or more disjoint open disks removed; the boundaries of these open disks belong to the boundary of Σ. For a cellularly embedded graph G with V vertices, E edges, and F faces, *Euler's formula* states that $V - E + F = 2 - \bar{g}$.

We assume that the embedding is represented in a suitable way, like for example the *gem representation*, using the incidence graph of *flags* (vertex-edge-face incidences) discussed by Eppstein [10], or rotation systems [22]. For orientable surfaces, one can also use the DCEL that is customary in Computational Geometry (see, e.g., de Berg et al. [8]). More precisely, we store the embedding of G on $\overline{\Sigma}$, and mark within each face of the embedding the number of boundary components of Σ it contains.

If G is a graph embedded on Σ without isolated vertices, we will denote by $\Sigma \backslash\!\backslash G$ the surface with boundary obtained after cutting Σ along G. Note that $\Sigma \backslash\!\backslash G$ is a surface with boundary. In contrast, $\Sigma \setminus G$ is a set operation where we remove from Σ the points in (the image of the embedding of) G. In particular, if G is cellularly embedded, $\overline{\Sigma} \backslash\!\backslash G$ is a union of closed disks, whereas $\overline{\Sigma} \setminus G$ is a union of open disks.

We say that G *separates* Σ if $\Sigma \backslash\!\backslash G$ (equivalently $\Sigma \setminus G$) has at least two connected components.

2.4 Homotopy and Homology

Let G be a graph embedded on Σ. Homotopy and homology are two equivalence relations on the set of loops in G with a given basepoint. Here, we stick to a concise description of these notions and refer to one of the aforementioned books for a more formal and detailed treatment.

Let us fix a common basepoint for all loops considered in this section. Two loops in G are *homotopic* if one can be deformed continuously to the other on the surface, keeping the basepoint fixed during the deformation. It turns out that the equivalence classes, called *homotopy classes*, form a group, where the multiplication in the group corresponds to the concatenation of the loops. The zero element is the set of loops that are homotopic to the constant loop; such loops are called *contractible*, or *homotopically trivial*. An important characterization is that a simple loop is contractible if and only if it bounds a disk on the surface.

Homology is a coarser equivalence relation than homotopy. The homology group is the abelianization of the homotopy group. A loop in G is *null-homologous*, or *homologically trivial*, if it belongs to the zero homology class. We also have a nice characterization for simple loops: a simple loop is null-homologous on $\overline{\Sigma}$ if and only if it separates $\overline{\Sigma}$ (or, equivalently, Σ). As in previous papers, when we write "separating on Σ", we really mean "null-homologous on $\overline{\Sigma}$": these two notions coincide for simple loops, and the latter is also defined for non-simple loops, which turns out to be useful. Therefore, contractible implies separating, even for non-simple loops.

If G is cellularly embedded on Σ, then G contains non-contractible cycles except when Σ is the sphere or the disk. Also, G contains non-separating cycles except when $\overline{\Sigma}$ is the sphere.

When considering the problem of finding a shortest non-contractible loops or cycles, we assume every face of G contains at most one boundary of Σ. This is possible since several boundary components of Σ in one face of G can be replaced with one single boundary component without changing the contractibility character of the loops in G. When considering the computation of shortest non-separating loops or cycles, we assume our input surface Σ has no boundary. This is valid since a cycle is separating in Σ if and only if it is separating in $\overline{\Sigma}$.

Henceforth, we use the term *non-trivial* as a shorthand for non-contractible or non-separating.

2.5 Duality

Let G be a graph cellularly embedded in Σ. Its *dual graph*, denoted by G^*, has for vertices the set of faces of Σ and for edges the set of edges (dual to) $E(G)$: two faces are adjacent if they share an edge of G. The edge dual to e is denoted by e^*, and it connects the two faces adjacent to e in the embedding. The dual graph G^* has a natural embedding in Σ: each vertex f^* of G^*, corresponding to face f of G, is assigned to a point p_f of the interior of the face f; for each edge uv of G, incident to faces f and f', the dual edge $(uv)^*$ is assigned a curve that connects the points p_f and $p_{f'}$ and crosses G precisely at the edge uv. For our discussion, it is convenient to make the following assumptions: for every face f of G containing a boundary component (which is unique in that face by our assumption of Section 2.4) the point p_f belongs to that boundary component, and we add to G^* a loop edge, whose image is the boundary component. (Such loop edges correspond to no edge of the primal graph G.) For a set of edges $A \subseteq E(G)$, we use the notation $A^* = \{e^* \mid e \in A\}$.

2.6 Deformation retract

A subspace A of a topological space X is a *deformation retract* of X if there is a continuous map $F : X \times [0, 1] \to X$ such that for every x in X and a in A, we have $F(x, 0) = x$, $F(x, 1) \in A$, and $F(a, 1) = a$.

It is known that if A is a deformation retract of X, then X and A have the same *homotopy type*. The (quite intuitive) consequence that will be useful to us is that, under this condition, A and X have the same number of connected components, and A has a non-contractible loop if and only if X has a non-contractible loop.

3. SHORTEST NON-TRIVIAL LOOPS

In this section, we prove Theorem 2; the tools developed here will be useful for the proof of Theorem 1 as well.

As already noted, for the non-contractible case, Theorem 2 follows directly from Erickson and Har-Peled [11, Lemma 5.2] by replacing Dijkstra's algorithm with a breadth-first search. For the non-separating case, this result is new and improves upon previous papers [11, 6, 3] in the case of unweighted graphs. The ideas are closely related to Erickson and Whittlesey's algorithm to compute a shortest system of loops [12] (specifically, a shortest non-separating loop is the first loop computed by their greedy algorithm, although they do not compute it in linear time). The idea of computing shortest non-trivial loops using this method appears in one of the authors' course notes [7].

Let T be an arbitrary spanning tree of G; let C^* be the subgraph of G^* with the same vertex set as G^* and edge set $E(G^*) \setminus E(T)^*$. (In particular, C^* contains every loop edge of G^* in a boundary component of Σ.)

LEMMA 1. *C^* is a cut graph of Σ; that is, $\Sigma \setminus C^*$ is (homeomorphic to) an open disk.*

PROOF. $\Sigma \setminus C^*$ can be obtained by taking all faces of G^* (which are open disks) and gluing them in a tree-like fashion

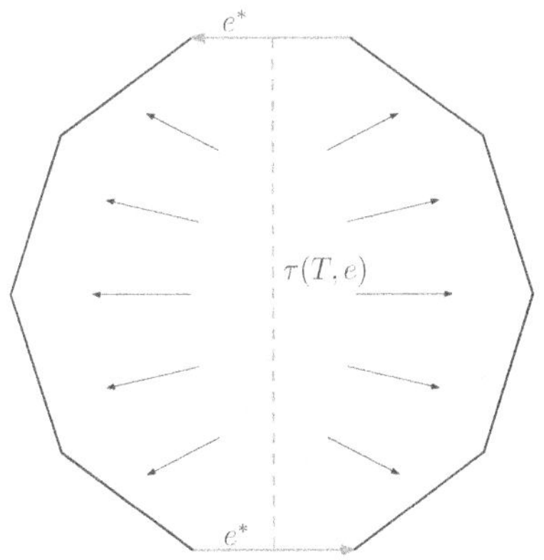

Figure 1. The retraction in the proof of Lemma 2. The boundary of the disk is the boundary of $\Sigma \backslash\backslash C^*$.

according to the tree T, i.e., along the edges of $E(T)^*$. Since attaching disks in this way gives a disk, we obtain that $\Sigma \backslash\backslash C^*$ is a disk. □

The following lemma was also noted and used by Erickson and Whittlesey [12, Section 3.4].

LEMMA 2. *Let $e \in E(G) \setminus E(T)$. Then $C^* - e^*$ is a deformation retract of $\Sigma \setminus \tau(T, e)$.*

PROOF. The cycle $\tau(T, e)$ cuts C^* at exactly one point. Therefore this cycle corresponds to a path intersecting the boundary of the closed disk $\Sigma \backslash\backslash C^*$ exactly at its endpoints. (See Figure 1.) Both halves of the disk retract to the corresponding portion of the boundary of the disk. Therefore, $\Sigma \backslash\backslash \tau(T, e)$ retracts to $C^* \backslash\backslash (e^* \cap \tau(T, e))$. This in turn retracts to $C^* - e^*$. □

COROLLARY 2. *Let $e \in E(G) \setminus E(T)$. The cycle $\tau(T, e)$ is separating on Σ if and only if $C^* - e^*$ is not connected. The cycle $\tau(T, e)$ is contractible if and only if $C^* - e^*$ has a connected component that is a tree (possibly reduced to a single vertex).*

PROOF. The cycle $\tau(T, e)$ is separating if and only if $\Sigma \setminus \tau(T, e)$ is not connected; by Lemma 2, this holds if and only if $C^* - e^*$ is not connected.

$\tau(T, e)$ is contractible if and only if one component of $\Sigma \setminus \tau(T, e)$ is a disk, i.e., has no non-contractible loop. By Lemma 2, this holds if and only if one component of $C^* - e^*$ has no non-contractible loop, i.e., is a tree. □

A cycle $\tau(T, e)$ is of one of the following three topological types: contractible, non-contractible but separating, and non-separating. We can partition the edges e^* of C^* into three sets, depending on the corresponding type of $\tau(T, e)$. Figure 2 illustrates this classification.

For later use, it will be convenient to use $E_{\text{non-con}}(T)$ (resp. $E_{\text{non-sep}}(T)$) for the set of edges e in $E(G) \setminus E(T)$ such that $\tau(T, e)$ is non-contractible (resp. non-separating). As before, we use $E_{\text{non-triv}}(T)$ as an ambiguous term to refer to $E_{\text{non-con}}(T)$ or $E_{\text{non-sep}}(T)$ as needed.

LEMMA 3. *The sets $E_{\text{non-con}}(T)$ and $E_{\text{non-sep}}(T)$ can be computed in $O(n)$ time.*

PROOF. We construct the cut graph C^* in linear time. By Corollary 2, $E_{\text{non-con}}(T)$ can be obtained by the following procedure: starting with C^*, we repeatedly remove edges with an incident vertex of degree one; the edge set of the resulting graph is then exactly $E_{\text{non-con}}(T)^*$. To obtain $E_{\text{non-sep}}(T)$, note that, by Corollary 2, $E_{\text{non-sep}}(T)^*$ is precisely the set of non-bridge edges in C^*. The computation of the bridge edges of a graph in linear time using depth-first search is part of the folklore (see Aho et al. [1, Section 5.3] for the similar problem of determining biconnected components). □

Let s be an arbitrary vertex of G. We have the following structural result on shortest non-trivial loops based at s.

LEMMA 4. *Assume T is a BFS tree from root s. Every shortest loop among the loops $\tau(T, s, e)$, where $e \in E_{\text{non-triv}}$, is a shortest non-trivial loop through s.*

PROOF. A proof appears in Thomassen [26] in a more general setting. We provide an ad hoc short proof. Let ℓ be a non-trivial loop with basepoint s. We show that some non-trivial loop $\tau(T, s, e)$ is no longer than ℓ. Let $e_1, e_2, \ldots, e_k$ be the edges of ℓ, in the same order as they appear along ℓ. Since ℓ is homotopic in Σ (and therefore also homologous in $\overline{\Sigma}$) to the concatenation of loops $\tau(T, s, e_1) \cdot \tau(T, s, e_2) \cdots \tau(T, s, e_k)$, at least one of the loops $\tau(T, s, e_i)$ is non-trivial. However, $\tau(T, s, e_i)$ is a shortest loop through s that contains e_i because T is a BFS tree, whence $\tau(T, s, e_i)$ is no longer than ℓ. Furthermore, e_i cannot belong to T, for otherwise the loop $\tau(T, s, e_i)$ would be contractible (and separating). □

We conclude the proof of Theorem 2.

PROOF OF THEOREM 2. We construct a BFS tree T of G from s in linear time. We attach to each vertex u of G a label $d(u)$ equal to its distance from s. We then compute $E_{\text{non-triv}}(T)$, again in linear time, using Lemma 3. Among the edges e of $E_{\text{non-triv}}(T)$, we select an edge e_0 minimizing the length of $\tau(T, s, e)$, or equivalently, minimizing the sum $d(u) + d(v)$ where u and v are the endpoints of e. Finally, we report the loop $\tau(T, s, e_0)$. The procedure takes linear time; its correctness follows from Lemma 4 and from the fact that $\tau(T, e)$ is non-trivial if and only if $\tau(T, s, e)$ is non-trivial. □

Our algorithm trivially extends to the weighted case, at the expense of a logarithmic factor, by replacing the BFS with a shortest path tree computation.

Also, the same ideas yield algorithms to compute shortest loops with an odd number of edges and shortest one-sided loops (which reverse the orientation of the surface, when it is non-orientable). Lemma 4 extends immediately to these two problems. To compute a shortest loop with an odd number of edges, it suffices to store, on each vertex of G, the parity of the number of edges to the root; then $\tau(T, s, e)$ has an odd number of edges if and only if the parities of the vertices of G incident with e are the same. To compute a shortest one-sided loop, it suffices to choose local orientations of the surface at each vertex that are consistent across each edge of T; then $\tau(T, s, e)$ is one-sided if and only if the orientations of the two vertices of G incident with e do not match across edge e. The results of the next section extend to the problem of finding shortest one-sided cycles, but do *not* extend to the problem of finding a shortest cycle with an odd number of edges.

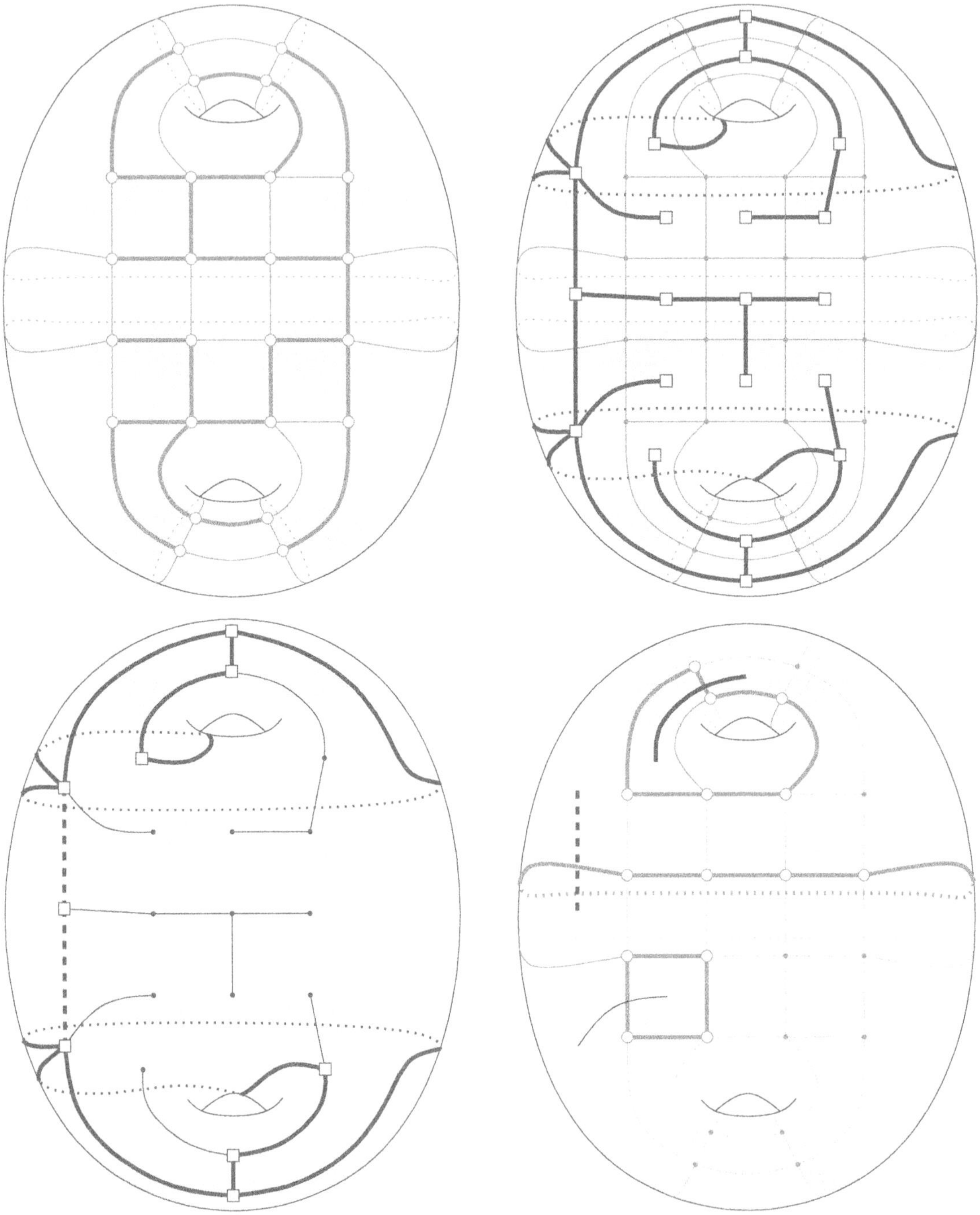

Figure 2. Top left: A graph G embedded in a double torus with a spanning tree T marked with bolder edges. Top right: The cut graph C^* is marked with bold edges; thinner edges are from the primal graph. Bottom left: classification of the edges of C^*. The bold solid edges are $E_{\text{non-sep}}(T)^*$; the bold dashed edges are $(E_{\text{non-con}}(T) \setminus E_{\text{non-sep}}(T))^*$; the thin edges are $E(C^*) \setminus E_{\text{non-con}}(T)^*$. The dotted parts of edges do not provide any information about their type. Bottom right: examples of the loop $\tau(T, e)$ in bold for different types of $e^* \in C^*$.

4. SHORTEST NON-TRIVIAL CYCLES

We now prove Theorem 1. The following result will be our tool to work with several sources simultaneously.

LEMMA 5. *Let $V_1, \ldots, V_t$ be subsets of $V(G)$ that are pairwise disjoint, let $s_1, \ldots, s_t$ be vertices with $s_i \in V_i$ for each i, and let $\mathbb{L}_i$ be the set of non-trivial loops through s_i contained in $G[V_i]$. In $O(n)$ time we can find a shortest loop in $\bigcup_i \mathbb{L}_i$, or correctly report that $\bigcup_i \mathbb{L}_i$ is empty.*

PROOF. We first describe the algorithm interlaced with an analysis of its running time, and then discuss its correctness.

For each i, we construct a BFS tree T_i with root s_i of the component of $G[V_i]$ that contains s_i. To each vertex u of G, we attach two labels, $c(u)$ and $d(u)$. The label $c(u)$ has value i if u is in the same connected component of $G[V_i]$ as s_i, and has value 0 otherwise. The label $d(u)$ is the distance between u and $s_{c(u)}$ if $c(u) \geq 1$, and undefined if $c(u) = 0$. Since the sets $V_1, \ldots, V_t$ are disjoint, the labels $c(u)$ and $d(u)$ are uniquely defined. These labels can be computed in $O(n)$ time using the BFS trees $T_1, \ldots, T_t$.

We then extend the forest $T_1, \ldots, T_t$ to a spanning tree T of G. This can also be done in linear time. Next, we compute $E_{\text{non-triv}}(T)$ using Lemma 3. Let $\tilde{E}$ be the subset of the edges $uv \in E_{\text{non-triv}}(T)$ such that $c(u) = c(v)$ and this number is non-zero. If $\tilde{E}$ is empty, we report that $\bigcup_i \mathbb{L}_i$ is empty. Otherwise, we compute

$$xy = \arg\min\{d(u) + d(v) \mid uv \in \tilde{E}\}$$

and return the loop $\tau(T, s_{c(x)}, xy)$. The construction of $E_{\text{non-triv}}(T)$ and $\tilde{E}$ takes linear time, and we spend additional constant time per edge in $\tilde{E}$ to find the edge xy. This concludes the description of the algorithm.

We now show the correctness of the algorithm. Let E_i be the set of edges uv in $E(G)$ with endpoints in T_i, i.e., such that $c(u) = c(v) = i$. Also, let $E_{\text{non-triv}}(T_i)$ be the subset of the edges e in E_i such that $\tau(T_i, s_i, e)$ is non-trivial.

By the same arguments as in the proof of Lemma 4, if $\mathbb{L}_i$ is not empty, then it contains a shortest loop of the form $\tau(T_i, s_i, e)$ for some edge e in E_i. As a consequence, a shortest non-trivial loop in $\mathbb{L}_i$ is given by $\tau(T_i, s_i, e)$ where

$$e = \arg\min\{d(u) + d(v) \mid uv \in E_{\text{non-triv}}(T_i)\}.$$

For any edge e in E_i, it holds that $\tau(T_i, s_i, e) = \tau(T, s_i, e)$ and $\tau(T_i, e) = \tau(T, e)$. It follows that

$$E_{\text{non-triv}}(T_i) = E_{\text{non-triv}}(T) \cap E_i,$$

whence $\tilde{E} = \bigcup_i E_{\text{non-triv}}(T_i)$. The correctness of the algorithm directly follows. □

Henceforth, let s be an arbitrary but fixed vertex of G.

LEMMA 6. *In $O(n)$ time, we can compute a set K of vertices of G such that every non-trivial cycle in G intersects K, satisfying the following property: For every integer i, the number of vertices of K at distance exactly i from s is at most $2\bar{g} + b$ for the non-contractible case, and $2\bar{g}$ for the non-separating case.*

PROOF. Assume first that Σ has no boundary (this is the only relevant situation in the non-separating case). We use the tree-cotree decomposition of Eppstein [10]. Consider a BFS tree T from the vertex s. Let $(T')^*$ be an arbitrary spanning tree of $G^* - E(T)^*$. Thus T and T' are edge-disjoint in G; we let X be the remaining edges of G. It follows from Euler's formula that X has $\bar{g}$ edges.

Figure 3. Detail of the graph $\hat{G}$ cellularly embedded in $\hat{\Sigma}$, as constructed in the proof of Lemma 6. We attach a handle to each boundary component and add two loop edges to obtain a cellular embedding.

Consider the set of loops $\mathbb{L} = \{\tau(T, s, e) \mid e \in X\}$: their union $\bigcup \mathbb{L}$ is a cut graph. Indeed, $\Sigma \setminus (T \cup X)$ is a set of faces connected according to the dual tree T', hence a disk. But $\bigcup \mathbb{L}$ is obtained from $T \cup X$ by iteratively removing a degree one vertex with its incident edge, and this operation preserves the fact that the complement is a disk. Let K be the set of vertices in $\mathbb{L}$. Since $\bigcup \mathbb{L}$ is a cut graph, each non-trivial closed walk must intersect K. Moreover, since T is a BFS, each loop in $\tau(T, s, e)$ has at most two vertices at distance i from s, for any integer i. It follows that, for every integer i, the set K contains at most $2|X| = 2\bar{g}$ vertices at distance i from s.

K can be computed in linear time, as we describe next. Computing a BFS tree T from s, the spanning tree in the dual graph, and computing the set of edges X takes linear time. We mark in T the vertex s and the endpoints of the edges in X. By definition of the loops in $\mathbb{L}$, the set K is the set of vertices of the minimal subtree of T that includes the marked vertices. This subtree is obtained in linear time by recursively removing unmarked degree one vertices.

It remains to consider the case where we want to compute a shortest non-contractible cycle on a surface Σ with boundary. In this case we attach a handle to every boundary component of Σ, obtaining a surface $\hat{\Sigma}$ without boundary. To make G cellular on $\hat{\Sigma}$, we just have to add two loop edges per boundary component of Σ; see Figure 3. Let $\hat{G}$ be the new graph. Then we apply the previous construction to this new graph. We obtain a set $\hat{K}$ that intersects every cycle of $\hat{G}$ that is non-trivial on $\hat{\Sigma}$; furthermore, $\hat{K}$ has at most $2\bar{g} + b$ vertices at distance i from the source s. (The two loop edges e_1 and e_2 defining a handle contribute to a single shortest path to K, namely, the shortest path from s to the common endpoint of e_1 and e_2.) Hence $\hat{K}$ intersects also every cycle in G that is non-trivial in $\hat{\Sigma}$. Furthermore, the distances from s in G and $\hat{G}$ are the same, because we only added loop edges, so $\hat{K}$ still has at most $2\bar{g} + b$ vertices at distance i from s. To conclude, note that a cycle is contractible in $\hat{\Sigma}$ if and only if it is contractible in Σ. So we can take $K = \hat{K}$. □

We are now ready to give the proof of Theorem 1.

PROOF OF THEOREM 1. We start by computing the set K of vertices as in Lemma 6. It then suffices to compute a shortest non-trivial loop based at some vertex in K, or to determine that every such loop has length larger than k.

Let S_i be the set of vertices in K at distance exactly i from s ($0 \leq i \leq n$). Each S_i has cardinality at most $2\bar{g} + b$ (non-contractible case) or $2\bar{g}$ (non-separating case). For simplicity, in the remaining part of the proof, we only consider the non-contractible case; the non-separating case is the same, except that we can replace $2\bar{g} + b$ by $2\bar{g}$.

For each j, $0 \leq j \leq k$, we put the elements of

$$S_j, S_{(k+1)+j}, S_{2(k+1)+j}, \ldots$$

into at most $2\bar{g} + b$ batches, each containing at most one element from each of these S_i. In total, we have a partition of K into $O((g+b)k)$ batches such that any two vertices in the same batch are at distance at least $k+1$ from each other (because an element in S_i and an element in S_j are at distance at least $|i-j|$ from each other by the triangle inequality).

Now, consider a single batch $\{s_1, \ldots, s_t\}$. For each i, let V_i be the set of vertices at distance at most $k/2$ from s_i; the V_i's are pairwise disjoint. We can thus apply Lemma 5: if there exists a non-trivial loop based at some s_i that has length at most k, we obtain the shortest such loop.

We apply this operation for every batch; thus we computed, for each vertex of K, the shortest loop based at that vertex, unless that loop has length larger than k. If the shortest of the resulting loops has length at most k, this is the output of the algorithm. Otherwise (or if no loop has been found), we report that no non-trivial loop with length at most k exists.

The set K and the $O((g+b)k)$ batches can be computed in $O(n)$ time. Then the $O(n)$ time algorithm of Lemma 5 is applied once for each of the $O((g+b)k)$ batches; thus the total running time is $O((g+b)nk)$. □

5. END OF PROOF

There only remains to prove Corollary 1. This combines the results of Theorems 1 and 2.

Proof of Corollary 1. The edge-width can be computed applying Theorem 1 with $k = 2^0, 2^1, 2^2, \ldots, 2^i, \ldots$ until a non-contractible cycle is found. The total cost is

$$O((g+b)n(2^{\lceil \log k \rceil + 1})) = O((g+b)nk),$$

where k is the edge-width. On the other hand, we can compute the edge-width in $O(n^2)$ time using Theorem 2, by choosing each vertex in turn to be the basepoint. Running both algorithms in parallel gives us the claimed complexity of $O(n \min\{(g+b)k, n\})$ for the edge-width. The same arguments, with $g+b$ replaced by g, yield the result for the non-separating edge-width.

For the face-width computations, let Γ be the *vertex-face incidence graph* of G (also called *radial graph*): this is a bipartite multigraph embedded on Σ whose vertices are the vertices and faces of G; there is an edge in Γ between a vertex v of G and a face f of G per incidence between v and f in G. Then, the face-width of G equals half of the edge-width of Γ [22, Proposition 5.5.4], which we can compute in the same asymptotic time by the first paragraph, since the complexity of Γ is linear in the complexity of G. □

Acknowledgment. We thank Jeff Erickson for pointing out reference [15] and its implications.

References

[1] A. V. Aho, J. E. Hopcroft, and J. D. Ullman. *The design and analysis of computer programs.* Addison-Wesley, 1974.

[2] M. O. Albertson and J. P. Hutchinson. The independence ratio and genus of a graph. *Transactions of the American Mathematical Society*, 226:161–173, 1977.

[3] S. Cabello and E. W. Chambers. Multiple source shortest paths in a genus g graph. In *Proceedings of the 18th Annual ACM-SIAM Symposium on Discrete Algorithms (SODA)*, pages 89–97, 2007.

[4] S. Cabello, É. Colin de Verdière, and F. Lazarus. Finding shortest non-trivial cycles in directed graphs on surfaces. In *These Proceedings*, 2010.

[5] S. Cabello, M. DeVos, J. Erickson, and B. Mohar. Finding one tight cycle. *ACM Transactions on Algorithms*, 2010. To appear. Preliminary version in SODA'08.

[6] S. Cabello and B. Mohar. Finding shortest non-separating and non-contractible cycles for topologically embedded graphs. *Discrete & Computational Geometry*, 37(2):213–235, 2007.

[7] É. Colin de Verdière. Algorithms for graphs on surfaces. Course notes, available at `http://www.di.ens.fr/~colin/cours/algo-graphs-surfaces.pdf`, 2008.

[8] M. de Berg, M. van Kreveld, M. Overmars, and O. Schwarzkopf. *Computational Geometry: Algorithms and Applications.* Springer-Verlag, Berlin, 1997.

[9] M. DeVos, K.-i. Kawarabayashi, and B. Mohar. Locally planar graphs are 5-choosable. *J. Comb. Theory Ser. B*, 98(6):1215–1232, 2008.

[10] D. Eppstein. Dynamic generators of topologically embedded graphs. In *Proceedings of the 14th Annual ACM-SIAM Symposium on Discrete Algorithms (SODA)*, pages 599–608, 2003.

[11] J. Erickson and S. Har-Peled. Optimally cutting a surface into a disk. *Discrete & Computational Geometry*, 31(1):37–59, 2004.

[12] J. Erickson and K. Whittlesey. Greedy optimal homotopy and homology generators. In *Proceedings of the 16th Annual ACM-SIAM Symposium on Discrete Algorithms (SODA)*, pages 1038–1046, 2005.

[13] J. R. Fiedler, J. P. Huneke, R. B. Richter, and N. Robertson. Computing the orientable genus of projective graphs. *J. Graph Theory*, 20(3):297–308, 1995.

[14] A. Hatcher. *Algebraic topology.* Cambridge University Press, 2002. Available at `http://www.math.cornell.edu/~hatcher/`.

[15] J. P. Hutchinson. On short noncontractible cycles in embedded graphs. *SIAM Journal on Discrete Mathematics*, 1(2):185–192, 1988.

[16] K.-i. Kawarabayashi and B. Mohar. Graph and map isomorphism and all polyhedral embeddings in linear time. In *Proceedings of the 40th Annual ACM Symposium on Theory of Computing (STOC)*, pages 471–480, 2008.

[17] K.-i. Kawarabayashi and B. Reed. Computing crossing number in linear time. In *Proceedings of the 39th Annual ACM Symposium on Theory of Computing (STOC)*, pages 382–390, 2007.

[18] Y. Kobayashi and K.-i. Kawarabayashi. Algorithms for finding an induced cycle in planar graphs and bounded genus graphs. In *Proceedings of the 20th Annual ACM-SIAM Symposium on Discrete Algorithms (SODA)*, pages 1146–1155, 2009.

[19] M. Kutz. Computing shortest non-trivial cycles on orientable surfaces of bounded genus in almost linear time. In *Proceedings of the 22nd Annual ACM Symposium on Computational Geometry (SOCG)*, pages 430–438, 2006.

[20] W. S. Massey. *Algebraic Topology: An Introduction*, volume 56 of *Graduate Texts in Mathematics*. Springer-Verlag, 1977.

[21] B. Mohar and N. Robertson. Flexibility of polyhedral embeddings of graphs in surfaces. *J. Comb. Theory Ser. B*, 83(1):38–57, 2001.

[22] B. Mohar and C. Thomassen. *Graphs on surfaces*. Johns Hopkins Studies in the Mathematical Sciences. Johns Hopkins University Press, 2001.

[23] N. Robertson and P. D. Seymour. Graph minors. VII. Disjoint paths on a surface. *Journal of Combinatorial Theory, Series B*, 45:212–254, 1988.

[24] N. Robertson and R. P. Vitray. Representativity of surface embeddings. In B. Korte, L. Lovász, and Prömel, editors, *Paths, flows, and VLSI-layout*, pages 293–328. Springer-Verlag, Berlin, 1990.

[25] J. Stillwell. *Classical topology and combinatorial group theory*. Springer-Verlag, New York, 1980.

[26] C. Thomassen. Embeddings of graphs with no short noncontractible cycles. *Journal of Combinatorial Theory, Series B*, 48(2):155–177, 1990.

[27] C. Thomassen. Five-coloring maps on surfaces. *J. Comb. Theory Ser. B*, 59(1):89–105, 1993.

[28] X. Yu. Disjoint paths, planarizing cycles, and spanning walks. *Transactions of the American Mathematical Society*, 349:1333–1358, 1997.

Finding Shortest Non-Trivial Cycles in Directed Graphs on Surfaces*

Sergio Cabello
Department of Mathematics, IMFM
Department of Mathematics, FMF
University of Ljubljana, Slovenia
sergio.cabello@fmf.uni-lj.si

Éric Colin de Verdière
Laboratoire d'informatique
École normale supérieure
CNRS, Paris, France
Eric.Colin.de.Verdiere@ens.fr

Francis Lazarus
GIPSA-Lab, CNRS, Grenoble, France
Francis.Lazarus@gipsa-lab.grenoble-inp.fr

ABSTRACT

Let D be a weighted directed graph cellularly embedded in a surface of genus g, orientable or not, possibly with boundary. We describe algorithms to compute a shortest non-contractible and a shortest surface non-separating cycle in D. This generalizes previous results that only dealt with *undirected* graphs.

Our first algorithm computes such cycles in $O(n^2 \log n)$ time, where n is the total number of vertices and edges of D, thus matching the complexity of the best known algorithm in the undirected case. It revisits and extends Thomassen's *3-path condition*; the technique applies to other families of cycles as well.

We also give an algorithm with subquadratic complexity in the complexity of the input graph, if g is fixed. Specifically, we can solve the problem in $O(\sqrt{g}\, n^{3/2} \log n)$ time, using a divide-and-conquer technique that simplifies the graph while preserving the topological properties of its cycles. A variant runs in $O(ng \log g + n \log^2 n)$ for graphs of bounded treewidth.

Categories and Subject Descriptors: F.2.2 [Analysis of Algorithms and Problem Complexity]: Nonnumerical algorithms and problems—*Computations on discrete structures; Geometric problems and computations*; G.2.2 [Discrete Mathematics]: Graph theory—*Graph algorithms; path and circuit problems*; I.3.5 [Computer Graphics]: Computational geometry and object modeling—*Geometric algorithms, languages, and systems*

General Terms: Algorithms, Performance, Theory

*Research partially supported by the Slovenian Research Agency, program P1-0297 and project BI-FR/09-10-PROTEUS-014, funded by the French Ministry of Foreign and European Affairs.

Keywords: Computational topology, topological graph theory, surface, embedded graph, non-contractible cycle, non-separating cycle, directed graph

1. INTRODUCTION

Graphs embedded in the plane have been studied in depth. For several computational problems, we know algorithms for planar graphs that are faster than a generic algorithm for arbitrary graphs: shortest paths, minimum spanning trees, (sub)graph isomorphism, maximum flow, minimum cut, etc. For some NP-hard problems we can obtain approximation schemes when restricted to planar graphs. Most of, if not all, these algorithms ultimately rely on topological properties of the plane and on the Jordan curve theorem.

Graphs embedded on surfaces are a natural generalization of planar graphs that have attracted much attention. From a theoretical perspective, they play a prominent role in particular in the graph minor theory developed by Robertson and Seymour (see e.g. Mohar and Thomassen [27]). From an applied perspective, efficient algorithms are needed to process non-planar surfaces: texture mapping, topological denoising, remeshing, and visualization (see e.g. the discussion in Erickson and Har-Peled [16]). In particular, when the embedded graph is weighted, the computation of shortest cycles satisfying some prescribed topological properties has been studied in a series of papers (see references below).

Considering digraphs (directed graphs) embedded in a surface is a natural next step in this area. This setting remains largely unexplored; except for the case of planar graphs, we are only aware of the following results. The data structures of Cabello and Chambers [3] to represent distances from the vertices of a face in an embedded graph can be easily extended to digraphs. Chambers et al. give an algorithm to compute maximum flows in undirected surface-embedded graphs, and claim their approach extends to the directed case [9, Conclusion]. Erickson has recently shown that the best known algorithm to compute maximum s-t flows in planar directed graphs [2] does not extend to directed graphs on the torus [15, Section 3].

In this paper, we study the problem of finding shortest non-contractible or non-separating cycles in weighted digraphs embedded on surfaces. Like in previous works, we assume that the weights of a graph or digraph are always non-negative.

This is the same as looking for shortest non-trivial closed walks (where *trivial* means either contractible or separating), since (as we will see shortly) shortest non-trivial closed walks are simple cycles; that is, they do not repeat any vertex. However, in contrast to the undirected case, shortest non-trivial walks through a given vertex may have several self-crossings.

Background on Shortest Non-Trivial Cycles. In the directed setting, the only case where the problem of computing shortest non-trivial walks is solved is the annulus [23]. In contrast, in the undirected setting, the problem for general surfaces has been largely explored; one reason is that cutting along such a cycle is the simplest way of simplifying the topology of a surface. Additionally, this is the basic ingredient for several more complex algorithms.

Thomassen [31] shows that shortest non-trivial cycles in undirected graphs can be found in near-cubic time (see also Mohar and Thomassen [27, Chapter 4]). The approach actually works for certain families of cycles that satisfy the so-called *3-path condition*, which we revisit later in this paper. Erickson and Har-Peled [16] provide an algorithm to find shortest non-trivial cycles in near-quadratic time; this is the best current result. Cabello and Mohar [5] propose considering the problem parameterized by the genus. Kutz [25] propose an algorithm for orientable surfaces with running time $O(g^{O(g)} n \log n)$, subsequently improved to $O(g^3 n \log n)$ by Cabello and Chambers [3]. In our companion paper [4] we consider the restricted scenario of *unweighted*, undirected graphs, and show that a shortest non-trivial cycle can be found in $O(gnk)$ time, where k is the length of the output cycle. Here and in the sequel, n is the number of vertices and edges of the graph, assumed to be cellularly embedded on the surface (i.e., each face of the graph is a disk).

Many other more complex algorithms need to cut the surface along shortest non-trivial cycles (possibly through a given vertex) as a subroutine [17, 10, 8, 7].

Several authors also considered computing shortest cycles with different topological properties, such as *splitting cycles* [8] and *essential cycles* [18]. The techniques of the present paper do not apply to these problems.

Overview of our Results. In Section 3, we first revisit the concept of 3-path condition given by Thomassen [31]. Specifically, we extend this notion to a family $\mathbb{L}$ of closed loops based at a given vertex s in a digraph. Note that the loops need not be simple and that the graph is directed and needs not be embedded. In an imprecise sense, it is convenient to think of the elements of $\mathbb{L}$ as "trivial" loops. This concept captures and extends the families of topologically trivial loops we want to study for embedded graphs. We provide a generic algorithm to find a shortest loop based at s *outside* the family $\mathbb{L}$. The algorithm basically produces a candidate family of loops that should contain a shortest desired loop, and calls an oracle for each loop to decide membership in $\mathbb{L}$. This algorithm is extended in Section 4 to the computation of a shortest closed walk (without fixing a basepoint)

We then move, in Section 5, to the particular case of topologically non-trivial loops. Here we use techniques from our companion paper [4] to determine in amortized constant time whether a given candidate loop based at s belongs to $\mathbb{L}$. This leads to an algorithm that finds the shortest non-trivial loop through s in $O(n \log n)$ time, and (repeating the procedure for each vertex) a shortest non-trivial cycle in $O(n^2 \log n)$ time, thus matching the complexity of the best known algorithm solving this problem in the undirected case.

In Section 6, we next turn our attention to the case where the genus is small, and give an algorithm that finds a shortest non-trivial cycle in $O(\sqrt{g} n^{3/2} \log n)$ time. The algorithm is based on a technique we could name *topologically preserving divide-and-conquer*. The idea is to use small separators in the graph to divide the problem into balanced subproblems, but each subproblem is kept in the original surface to avoid changing the topological character of the closed walks. The idea is reminiscent of the numerous algorithms for planar graphs that divide-and-conquer using a cycle separator; see for example [29, 6, 19, 24]. However, in these cases, the preservation of the topology is implicit. We believe that our new approach is very natural and could be useful for other problems as well. For graphs with bounded treewidth, which admit constant-size separators, this strategy also leads to an $O(ng \log g + n \log^2 n)$-time algorithm. We also give an $O(bn \log n)$-time algorithm for the special case where $g = 0$.

2. PRELIMINARIES

We introduce the background material used in this paper. A large part of it was also presented in our companion paper [4], but we repeat it for completeness.

2.1 Graph Theory Definitions and Notations

Graphs considered in this paper may have parallel edges and loop edges. We recall some usual definitions related to walks in graphs; we want to emphasize that all walks considered here are *oriented*. Specifically, let G be a (directed or undirected) graph. We denote the vertex set of G by $V(G)$ and the edge set of G by $E(G)$.

A *walk* is a sequence of edges $e_1, \ldots, e_m$ with the property that the target of e_i is the source of e_{i+1}, for $i = 1, \ldots, m-1$. A *cycle* in G is an oriented closed walk without repeated vertices; a cycle has no distinguished vertex. In contrast, a *loop* based at a vertex s of G is an oriented closed walk with a distinguished occurrence of s. If every oriented edge of G has a non-negative *weight*, the *weight* of a closed walk or loop is the sum of the lengths of the corresponding oriented edges (counted with multiplicity).

Given two vertices x and y of G, we denote by xy the edge oriented from x to y in G. In presence of parallel edges or loop edges, this notation is ambiguous, but it will always be clear from the context which edge xy is meant. The weight of the oriented edge xy is denoted by $\ell(xy)$.

Given walks α and β, we denote by α^{-1} the reversal of α, and by $\alpha \cdot \beta$ the concatenation of α and β. Furthermore, $\ell(\alpha)$ denotes the length of α. For any vertices x, y of G, we use $d_G(x, y)$ to denote the minimum length of the walks from x to y in G. We emphasize that $d_G(\cdot, \cdot)$ is not a distance in general (it does not necessarily satisfy symmetry); nevertheless, we still use the words "length" (as a synonym for "weight") and "shortest".

2.2 Topological Background

We review some basic topology of surfaces, which will be needed only after Section 5 on. See any of the books by

Hatcher [21], Massey [26], or Stillwell [30] for a comprehensive treatment.

A *surface* (or 2-manifold) Σ possibly with boundary is a compact, connected, topological space where each point has a neighborhood homeomorphic either to the plane or to the closed half-plane; the points without neighborhood homeomorphic to the plane comprise the *boundary* of Σ. A surface is *non-orientable* if it contains a subset homeomorphic to the Möbius band, and *orientable* otherwise. Here and in the sequel, surfaces are considered up to homeomorphism; in particular, a *disk* is just a surface homeomorphic to the standard unit disk in $\mathbb{R}^2$.

An orientable surface is homeomorphic to a sphere where g disjoint disks are removed, a handle (a torus with one boundary component) is attached to each of the remaining g circles, and then b disjoint disks are removed, for unique integers $g, b \geq 0$. A non-orientable surface is homeomorphic to a sphere where g disjoint disks are removed, a Möbius band is attached to each of the remaining g circles, and then b disjoint disks are removed, for unique integers $g \geq 1$ and $b \geq 0$. In both cases, g is called the *genus* of the surface. $\overline{\Sigma}$ denotes the surface without boundary obtained by attaching a disk to each boundary component of Σ.

An *embedding* of a graph G (viewed as an undirected graph) in a surface Σ is a drawing of G on Σ without crossings. More formally, the vertices of G are mapped to distinct points of the interior of Σ; each edge is mapped to a path in the interior of Σ, such that the endpoints of the path agree with the points assigned to the vertices of that edge. Moreover, all the paths must be without intersection or self-intersection except, of course, at common endpoints. We sometimes identify a graph G with its embedding on Σ. The *faces* of G are the connected components of the complement of the image of G.

We only consider *cellular embeddings* of a graph. By this, we mean that $\overline{\Sigma}$ minus the image of the graph is a union of disks. In particular, each face of a cellular embedding on Σ is homeomorphic to an open disk with zero, one, or more disjoint open disks removed; the boundaries of these open disks belong to the boundary of Σ.

Let G be a graph cellularly embedded on Σ, with V vertices, E edges, and F faces; then *Euler's formula* states that $V - E + F = 2 - 2g$ if Σ is orientable, and $V - E + F = 2 - g$ if Σ is non-orientable. In particular, $E = O(V + F + g)$. To simplify our complexity results, we sometimes introduce $n = V + E$; by Euler's formula, we have $g = O(n)$.

We assume that the embedding is represented in a suitable way, like for example the *gem representation*, using the incidence graph of *flags* (vertex-edge-face incidences) discussed by Eppstein [14], or rotation systems [27]. For orientable surfaces, one can also use the DCEL that is customary in Computational Geometry (see, e.g., de Berg et al. [12]). More precisely, we store the embedding of G on $\overline{\Sigma}$, and mark within each face of the embedding the number of boundary components of Σ it contains.

Homotopy and homology are standard topological notions, which will not be formally defined here. Intuitively, two paths or loops are *homotopic* if one can be deformed continuously on the surface to become the other, keeping the endpoints fixed during the deformation. A loop is *contractible*, or *homotopically trivial*, if it is homotopic to the constant loop with the same basepoint. If α and β are contractible loops with the same basepoint, then so are α^{-1} and $\alpha \cdot \beta$. Similar properties hold for *null-homologous*, or *homologically trivial*, loops[1]. Let us only mention that homotopically trivial implies homologically trivial. Moreover, a closed walk or loop without repeated vertices is null-homologous on $\overline{\Sigma}$ if and only if its image is *separating*, that is, it splits Σ into two connected components.

In every cellular embedding there is a non-contractible loop (based at an arbitrary vertex), except if Σ is the sphere or the disk. Every cellular embedding has a non-separating loop (based at an arbitrary vertex), except if $\overline{\Sigma}$ is the sphere.

2.3 Reduction to an Undirected Graph with Asymmetric Weights

Let D be a directed graph (not necessarily embedded), where each arc has a non-negative *length*. Our goal is to compute shortest loops or cycles in D satisfying some given property. We first transform D into an *undirected* graph G with *asymmetric* lengths. Specifically, G is the undirected version of D; each oriented edge of G corresponds:

- either to an arc of D with some length ℓ. In this case, the length of that oriented edge is ℓ;
- or to the reversal of an arc of D. In this case, the length of that oriented edge is a "very large" (symbolically infinite) number M.[2]

If there is a loop or cycle satisfying the desired property in D, one such loop or cycle has length strictly smaller than M. As a consequence, to compute shortest loops or cycles in D, it suffices to compute them in G; if the length of the resulting loop or cycle is at least M, then no such loop or cycle with that desired property exists in D; otherwise, that loop or cycle is a shortest desired loop or cycle in D.

For simplicity, we will assume throughout the paper that there is a *unique shortest path* between any pair of vertices of G. Clearly, this assumption does not hold in general; just consider the case when all edges have unit length. However, Erickson and Har-Peled [16] point out that this condition can be enforced with high probability via the Isolation Lemma [28, Chapter 12]: if we add to the length of each oriented edge xy a value $r_{xy} \cdot \varepsilon$, where ε is a formal infinitesimal and r_{xy} is chosen uniformly at random from a large enough set, then all shortest paths are unique with high probability.[3] It is possible to get rid of this probabilistic assumption using a more technical definition of "length" that makes the discussion more dense. In Appendix A, we introduce this alternative definition of length and explain in detail how to get rid of the assumption on unique shortest paths.

---

[1]In this paper, homology is considered with respect to any ring or field.

[2]Alternatively and more formally, lengths could be now considered as vectors in $\mathbb{R}^2_+$, which are added componentwise and compared lexicographically; every oriented edge of G corresponding to an arc of D of length k would have length $(0, k)$, and the reversal of such an edge would have length $(1, 0)$, that is, "infinitely larger" than the weight of the arcs of D.

[3]Alternatively and more formally, the lengths are now vectors in $\mathbb{R}^3_+$, added componentwise and compared lexicographically; the first two components are as above, and the third one contains the number r_{xy}.

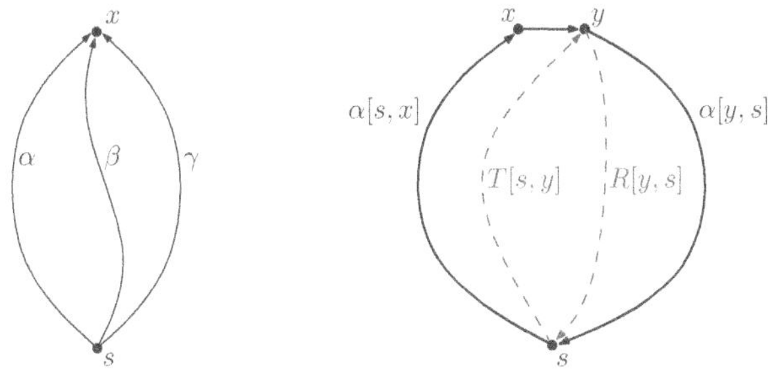

Figure 1. Left: Illustration of the 3-path condition. Right: Scenario in the proof of Lemma 1.

3. COMPUTING SHORTEST NON-TRIVIAL LOOPS

In this section and in Section 4, we consider the problem of computing the shortest loop or cycle in an undirected graph with asymmetric weights among a given family satisfying a certain property, the *3-path condition*. This property can be expressed without reference to an embedding of the graph, so here and in the following section, our graph needs not be embedded.

Our primary goal is to compute shortest non-trivial cycles. This will be done by taking each vertex s of the input graph, computing a shortest non-trivial loop based at s, and returning the shortest such loop. So, in this section, we focus on computing shortest non-trivial *loops*.

3.1 The 3-Path Condition

Let G be an undirected graph. A family of *loops* $\mathbb{L}$ in G based at some vertex s satisfies the *3-path condition* when the following two conditions are satisfied:

invariant under reversal: if $\alpha \in \mathbb{L}$, then $\alpha^{-1} \in \mathbb{L}$;

sum of zeros is zero: if α, β, γ are s-to-x walks in G (for some vertex x) such that $\alpha \cdot \beta^{-1}$ and $\beta \cdot \gamma^{-1}$ are in $\mathbb{L}$, then $\alpha \cdot \gamma^{-1}$ is also in $\mathbb{L}$.

Figure 1, left, illustrates the condition "sums of zero is zero". Some remarks on the definition may be convenient. Firstly, a clarification for the reader familiar with the work of Thomassen [31]: although the spirit of our definition is similar as that of Thomassen, we have exchanged the role of the family $\mathbb{L}$ and its complement. We believe that our presentation is more convenient, and is motivated by the following: the loops of $\mathbb{L}$ behave like the "trivial elements in a certain group", while the loops outside $\mathbb{L}$ behave like the "non-trivial elements". The main property of 3-path condition basically tells that the sum of two zero elements must be zero. Our aim is to find a shortest loop outside $\mathbb{L}$, that is, a shortest "non-trivial element".

Secondly, we may mention some families of loops based at s that satisfy the 3-path condition: the family of contractible loops, the family of null-homologous loops, the family of loops with an even number of edges, and the family of two-sided loops [27, Section 4.3]. We will be discussing the problem of finding a shortest loop in the *complement* of such families.

3.2 Properties

Let $\overline{\mathbb{L}}$ be the family of loops based at s that are *not* in $\mathbb{L}$. Our objective is to find a shortest element in $\overline{\mathbb{L}}$.

Let T be the shortest path tree in G from the source s. (Recall that we assume that shortest paths are unique.) Similarly, let R be the reversed shortest path tree in G to the sink s; that is, R corresponds to a shortest path tree from s in the graph G' obtained by exchanging the lengths $\ell(xy)$ and $\ell(yx)$ of each edge xy. Hence, for any vertex x of G, we have $d_G(s,x) = d_T(s,x)$ and $d_G(x,s) = d_R(x,s)$.

For a vertex x, we will use $T[s,x]$ to denote the unique s-to-x path in T, and $T[x,s]$ for the reversal of that path. Similarly, we will use $R[x,s]$ to denote the unique x-to-s path in R, and $R[s,x]$ for the reversal of that path. (So, the only relations among $\ell(T[s,x])$, $\ell(T[x,s])$, $\ell(R[s,x])$, and $\ell(R[x,s])$ that hold in general are $\ell(T[s,x]) < \ell(R[s,x])$ and $\ell(R[x,s]) < \ell(T[x,s])$.)

For any (oriented) loop α based at s and passing through vertex x, let $\alpha[s,x]$ denote the subwalk of α that goes from s to x, and $\alpha[x,s]$ be the complementary part of α.[4]

For any oriented edge $xy \in E(G) \setminus E(T)$, let $\mathrm{loop}_{T,R}(xy)$ denote the loop $T[s,x] \cdot xy \cdot R[y,s]$. Let $\mathbb{M}$ be the family of loops of the form $\mathrm{loop}_{T,R}(xy)$ that are in $\overline{\mathbb{L}}$:

$$\mathbb{M} = \{\mathrm{loop}_{T,R}(xy) \mid xy \in E(G) \setminus E(T)\} \cap \overline{\mathbb{L}}.$$

LEMMA 1. *If $\overline{\mathbb{L}}$ is non-empty, then a shortest element of $\mathbb{M}$ is a shortest element of $\overline{\mathbb{L}}$.*

PROOF. Assume that $\overline{\mathbb{L}}$ is non-empty, and let α be a shortest loop in $\overline{\mathbb{L}}$. Let x be the last vertex in the loop α as we start walking from s that satisfies $\alpha[s,x] = T[s,x]$. Let y be the next vertex in α after x. See Figure 1, right. The loop $\mathrm{loop}_{T,R}(xy) = \alpha[s,y] \cdot R[y,s]$ is no longer than α. To prove the lemma, it is thus enough to show that $\mathrm{loop}_{T,R}(xy)$ is in $\overline{\mathbb{L}}$, hence in $\mathbb{M}$. By uniqueness of shortest paths, $T[s,y]$ is strictly shorter than $\alpha[s,y]$. It follows that the loops $T[s,y] \cdot R[y,s]$ and $T[s,y] \cdot \alpha[y,s]$ are strictly shorter than α, hence in $\mathbb{L}$. By invariance under reversal $R[y,s]^{-1} \cdot T[s,y]^{-1}$ is also in $\mathbb{L}$, and we can apply the 3-path condition to the s-to-y walks $R[y,s]^{-1}, T[s,y]$, and $\alpha[y,s]^{-1}$ to deduce that $R[y,s]^{-1} \cdot \alpha[y,s]$ is in $\mathbb{L}$. If $\mathrm{loop}_{T,R}(xy)$ was also in $\mathbb{L}$ we would conclude, applying the 3-path condition to $\alpha[s,y]$, $R[y,s]^{-1}$, and $\alpha[y,s]^{-1}$, that $\alpha = \alpha[s,y] \cdot \alpha[y,s]$ is also in $\mathbb{L}$, and thus we would reach a contradiction. □

For each oriented edge $xy \in E(G) \setminus E(T)$, let $\mathrm{loop}_T(xy)$ denote the loop $T[s,x] \cdot xy \cdot T[y,s]$. For the topological problems that we will study below, it is convenient to introduce the following family of loops based at s:

$$\mathbb{N} = \{\mathrm{loop}_{T,R}(xy) \mid xy \in E(G) \setminus E(T), \mathrm{loop}_T(xy) \in \overline{\mathbb{L}}\}. \quad (1)$$

Note that we decide to include a loop in $\mathbb{N}$ by checking membership in $\overline{\mathbb{L}}$ of a different loop. The reason for this becomes apparent in the proof of the following lemma. A motivation to consider $\mathbb{N}$ is that, for certain topological properties to be considered below, we can manipulate $\mathbb{N}$ faster than $\mathbb{M}$ (see Section 5).

[4]More formally, x should be an *occurrence* of a vertex in the loop α, if α passes several times through that vertex; otherwise the definition is ambiguous. We omit this precision in the sequel, since the occurrence we are considering will always be clear from the context.

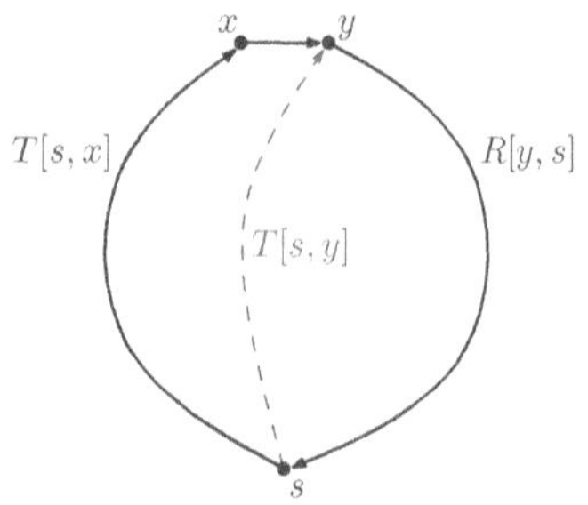

Figure 2. Scenario in the proof of Lemma 2.

LEMMA 2. *If $\overline{\mathbb{L}}$ is non-empty, then a shortest element of $\mathbb{N}$ is a shortest element of $\overline{\mathbb{L}}$.*

PROOF. Assume that $\overline{\mathbb{L}}$ is non-empty. By Lemma 1 the family $\overline{\mathbb{L}}$ has a shortest element of the form $\alpha = \text{loop}_{T,R}(xy)$ for some edge $xy \in E(G) \setminus E(T)$. We first prove that α belongs to $\mathbb{N}$, or equivalently, that $\text{loop}_T(xy) \in \overline{\mathbb{L}}$. See Figure 2. Since $T[s,y] \cdot R[y,s]$ is strictly shorter than α, it belongs to $\mathbb{L}$. If $\text{loop}_T(xy)$ was also in $\mathbb{L}$, then we could apply the 3-path condition to the s-to-y walks $T[s,x] \cdot xy$, $T[s,y]$, and $R[y,s]^{-1}$, and we would conclude that α is also in $\mathbb{L}$, which contradicts our choice of α. Thus the loop α is in $\mathbb{N}$.

Let β be a shortest element in $\mathbb{N}$; we can write β as $\text{loop}_{T,R}(xy)$ for some edge $xy \in E(G) \setminus E(T)$ such that $\text{loop}_T(xy) \in \overline{\mathbb{L}}$. There remains to prove that β belongs to $\overline{\mathbb{L}}$. See Figure 2. By the preceding paragraph β is no longer than α. Since $T[s,y] \cdot R[y,s]$ is strictly shorter than β, hence than α, it must be in $\mathbb{L}$. If β was also in $\mathbb{L}$, we could apply the 3-path condition to the s-to-y walks $T[s,x] \cdot xy$, $R[y,s]^{-1}$, and $T[s,y]$ to deduce that $\text{loop}_T(xy)$ is in $\mathbb{L}$, and reach a contradiction. Thus β is in $\overline{\mathbb{L}}$, and since it is no longer than α, it is a shortest element of $\overline{\mathbb{L}}$. □

The previous two lemmas show that finding a shortest element in $\mathbb{M}$ or in $\mathbb{N}$ is enough to find a shortest element in $\overline{\mathbb{L}}$. However, it should be pointed out that the role of $\mathbb{N}$ is surprising. In particular, $\mathbb{N}$ can contain loops from $\mathbb{L}$. We only know that the shortest one is in $\overline{\mathbb{L}}$. In general, it does not hold that $\mathbb{N} \subseteq \mathbb{M}$ or $\mathbb{M} \subseteq \mathbb{N}$. They just agree in having the same shortest element.

3.3 Algorithm

THEOREM 1. *Let G be an undirected graph with asymmetric weights, V vertices, and E edges, and let s be one of its vertices. Let $\mathbb{L}$ be a family of loops in G that satisfies the 3-path condition. Assume that there is an oracle that decides in time $\tau(k)$ if a loop with k edges is in $\mathbb{L}$. Then we can find a shortest loop based at s not in $\mathbb{L}$, or correctly report that no such loop exists, in time $O(E\tau(E) + V \log V)$.*

PROOF. The algorithm is as follows. Firstly, we construct a shortest path tree T and a reversed shortest path tree R for vertex s. Secondly, for each oriented edge xy, we construct explicitly the closed walk $\text{loop}_{T,R}(xy)$, check its membership in $\mathbb{L}$, and select the shortest one among the ones not in $\mathbb{L}$ (unless all of them are in $\mathbb{L}$, in which case we report that no such loop exists).

Correctness is clear by Lemma 1. As for the running time, note that T and R can be constructed in time $O(E+V \log V)$ time, using Dijkstra's algorithm [13] speeded up with Fibonacci heaps [20]. Once the trees T and R are available, we can preprocess the graph such that any distance query from or to vertex s takes $O(1)$ time. For each oriented edge xy, we need time $O(1+\tau(E)) = O(\tau(E))$ to compute the length of $\text{loop}_{T,R}(xy)$ and to check membership in $\mathbb{L}$. The result follows. □

4. COMPUTING SHORTEST NON-TRIVIAL CYCLES

Let G be an undirected graph. A family of *closed walks* $\mathbb{W}$ in G satisfies the *3-path condition* when the following two conditions are satisfied (recall that, by definition, closed walks have no distinguished basepoint, in contrast to loops):

invariant under reversal: if $\alpha \in \mathbb{W}$, then $\alpha^{-1} \in \mathbb{W}$;

sum of zeros is zero: if α, β, γ are x-to-y walks in G (for some arbitrary vertices x and y) such that $\alpha \cdot \beta^{-1}$ and $\beta \cdot \gamma^{-1}$ are in $\mathbb{W}$, then $\alpha \cdot \gamma^{-1}$ is also in $\mathbb{W}$.

In particular, if G is embedded on a surface, the families of contractible, null-homologous, even, and two-sided closed walks satisfy this condition.

LEMMA 3. *A shortest closed walk not in $\mathbb{W}$ is a cycle.*

PROOF. Let α be a shortest element not in $\mathbb{W}$ and assume, for the sake of contradiction, that α is not a cycle. Let x be a vertex that is visited twice by the walk α. Let β_1 be a closed subwalk of α between the first and the second appearance of x in α. Let β_2 be the closed walk between the second and the first appearance of x in α. By construction it holds that $\alpha = \beta_1 \cdot \beta_2$. Since β_1 and β_2 are strictly shorter than α, they must belong to $\mathbb{W}$. However, by the 3-path condition applied to the paths β_1, the constant walk consisting of the single vertex x, and β_2^{-1}, it follows that the path $\beta_1 \cdot (\beta_2^{-1})^{-1} = \alpha$ is also in $\mathbb{W}$. This is a contradiction with the choice of α. □

THEOREM 2. *Let G be an undirected graph with asymmetric weights, V vertices, and E edges. Let $\mathbb{W}$ be a family of closed walks in G that satisfies the 3-path condition. Assume that there is an oracle that decides in time $\tau(k)$ if a closed walk with k edges is in $\mathbb{W}$. Then in time $O(VE\tau(E) + V^2 \log V)$ we can find a shortest closed walk not in $\mathbb{W}$ (actually, this is a cycle by Lemma 3), or correctly report that no such walk exists.*

PROOF. We run the algorithm of Theorem 1, taking for s each vertex in turn, and return the shortest closed walk found. This is valid since the family of loops in $\mathbb{W}$ with a given basepoint satisfies the 3-path condition for loops. □

5. COMPUTING SHORTEST NON-TRIVIAL LOOPS AND CYCLES ON SURFACES

Let Σ be a compact surface, orientable or not, with genus g and b boundaries. Let G be a graph cellularly embedded on Σ. In this section, we present improved algorithms to compute a shortest non-contractible or non-separating loop or closed walk in G. Let $\mathbb{L}$ denote either the family of contractible loops or the family of non-separating loops based at some vertex s of G; this family satisfies the 3-path condition.

5.1 Computing Shortest Non-Trivial Loops on Surfaces

Recall the definition of $\mathbb{N}$ given in Equation (1). We want to find the oriented edges that define a loop in $\mathbb{N}$. This is equivalent to the problem of deciding if $\text{loop}_T(xy)$ is in $\mathbb{L}$. For this purpose, we can regard T as an undirected graph, and decide if $\text{loop}_T(xy)$ is in $\mathbb{L}$. This can be done efficiently using a characterization from our companion paper [4].

PROPOSITION 1. *In $O(E+V\log V)$ time, we can compute the shortest path tree T and determine the set of edges xy of $E(G) \setminus E(T)$ such that $\text{loop}_T(xy)$ is contractible (resp. separating).*

PROOF. The techniques are very similar to our companion paper [4, Section 3]; we briefly indicate the general strategy for completeness.

In this proof we will need the the *dual graph* G^*: it has for vertices the (dual) set of faces of G, for edges the (dual) set of edges of G, and two faces are adjacent if they share an edge of G. The edge dual to e is denoted by e^*, and it connects the two faces adjacent to e in the embedding. Furthermore, for every face f of G containing a boundary component, we add to G^* a loop edge. Such loop edges correspond to no edge of the primal graph G.)

We compute the shortest path tree T in $O(n \log n)$ time using Dijkstra's algorithm. Let C^* be the subgraph of G^* with the same vertex set as G^* and edge set $E(G^*) \setminus \{e^* \mid e \in E(T)\}$. The graph C^* can be constructed in linear time. Note that $\text{loop}_T(e)$ is non-contractible or non-separating if and only if $\text{cycle}_T(e)$ is non-contractible or non-separating, respectively.

In our companion paper [4], Corollary 2, we show the following characterization: The cycle $\text{cycle}_T(e)$ is non-separating if and only if C^*-e^* is connected. The cycle $\text{cycle}_T(e)$ is contractible if and only if $C^* - e^*$ has a connected component that is a tree (possibly reduced to a single vertex)

Therefore, the set of dual edges e^* such that $\text{loop}_T(e)$ is non-contractible can be obtained in linear time from the set of edges of C^* by repeatedly removing edges with an incident vertex of degree one. To obtain the set of edges e such that $\text{loop}_T(e)$ is non-separating, note that its dual set is precisely the set of non-bridge edges in C^*. The computation of the bridge edges of a graph in linear time using depth-first search is part of the folklore. □

THEOREM 3. *Let G be an undirected graph with asymmetric weights, V vertices, and E edges, that is cellularly embedded on Σ. Let s be one of its vertices. In time $O(E+V\log V)$ we can find a shortest non-contractible, respectively non-separating, loop based at s.*

PROOF. By Lemma 2, it suffices to compute the shortest element in $\mathbb{N}$; that is, the shortest $\text{loop}_{T,R}(xy)$ such that $xy \in E(G) \setminus E(T)$ and $\text{loop}_T(xy) \in \overline{\mathbb{L}}$. Proposition 1 allows to list the edges xy such that $\text{loop}_T(xy) \in \overline{\mathbb{L}}$ in $O(E + V \log V)$ time. For each xy, the length of $\text{loop}_{T,R}(xy)$ can be computed in constant time. Hence, we can find the shortest element of $\mathbb{N}$ in $O(E + V \log V)$ time. □

5.2 Computing Shortest Non-Trivial Cycles on Surfaces

THEOREM 4. *Let G be an undirected graph with asymmetric weights, V vertices, and E edges, that is cellularly embedded on Σ. In $O(E+Vg+V^2\log V)$ time, we can find a shortest non-contractible (resp. non-separating) closed walk; this is also a shortest non-contractible (resp. non-separating) cycle.*

PROOF. The algorithm consists essentially in applying V times Theorem 3, choosing each vertex in turn to be the basepoint. However, this gives a running-time of $O(VE + V^2 \log V)$. To decrease this to $O(E+Vg+V^2\log V)$, we use Proposition 2 below (which allows only for a slight improvement here, but will be used crucially in Section 6). This proposition says that, after $O(E)$ pre- and post-processing, we may assume $E = O(V + g)$. So the complexity of the algorithm is now $O(E + V(V+g) + V^2 \log V)$, as claimed.

The output of the algorithm is a cycle by Lemma 3. □

PROPOSITION 2. *Assume we want to compute a shortest non-contractible or non-separating cycle in G. With $O(E)$ time pre-processing and post-processing, it is sufficient to compute the shortest such cycle on another graph G' with V vertices and $E' = \Theta(V+g)$ edges, cellularly embedded on a surface Σ', such that Σ and Σ' have the same orientability character, the same genus, and the number of boundaries of Σ' is at most the number of boundaries of Σ.*

PROOF. We focus on the non-separating case first. In this case, we may assume $b = 0$, since attaching a disk to each boundary component does not change the separability character of a cycle. We will choose $\Sigma' = \Sigma$.

Whenever one face has degree one, we may remove the incident loop edge, which is contractible. Whenever one face has degree two, we may replace the two homotopic edges e_1 and e_2, with endpoints x and y, by an edge e with the same endpoints (removing the face in-between). The weight of e, oriented from x to y, is the minimum of the two weights of the edges of e_1 and e_2 from x to y, and similarly for the weights from y to x.

In linear time, we removed all the faces with degree one or two. The shortest cycle in G' within a given homotopy class corresponds to a shortest cycle in G within that homotopy class. So the shortest non-separating cycle in G' corresponds to the shortest non-separating cycle in G; recovering the cycle in G from the cycle in G' takes $O(E)$ time.

Clearly, G' has the same number V of vertices as G; let E' and F' be its number of edges and faces. The bound $V + g = O(E')$ comes from Euler's formula. The reverse bound follows from $F' \leq 2E'/3$ (by double-counting the incidences between the edges and the faces) and $E' = V + F' + O(g)$ (by Euler's formula).

For the non-contractible case, the same algorithm works, but we cannot assume anymore that the surface has no boundary, so this proof only gives us $E' = O(V + g + b)$. We next show that a slightly more complicated argument still gives us $E' = O(V + g)$, as claimed. Recall that our representation of the embedded graph G on the surface $\overline{\Sigma}$ is obtained by attaching disks to each boundary component of Σ, and recording, in each face of G, the number of boundaries inside it. (Actually, the exact number is irrelevant as far as contractibility is concerned; only the presence or absence of boundaries matter.)

The strategy is as in the non-separating case, except that we may remove some non-contractible cycles during the simplification from G to G'. So our algorithm maintains (1) an embedded graph G', such that every non-contractible cycle in G' corresponds to a non-contractible cycle in G of the same length, and (2) a non-contractible cycle α in G. The invariant is that the shortest non-contractible cycle in G either is α or corresponds to the shortest non-contractible cycle in G'. Initially, $G' = G$ and α is undefined.

Assume one face f (of the embedded graph G on $\overline{\Sigma}$) has degree one. If it contains no boundary component of Σ, we can remove it as before. Otherwise, the loop edge β incident to it is non-contractible; we remove β and the corresponding face f, and mark the other face incident to β as containing boundaries. Also, we let α be the shortest cycle among the current α and β.

Assume one face has degree two, and contains no boundary component of Σ. Then as before, we may remove that face, and replace both incident edges by a single edge e with appropriate weights: the weight of e, oriented from x to y, is the minimum of the two weights of the edges of e_1 and e_2, oriented from x to y, and similarly for the opposite orientation.

Assume that four edges e_1, e_2, e_3, and e_4 have the same endpoints and form three faces of degree two, whose boundaries are e_ie_{i+1} ($i = 1, 2, 3$). Then, assuming the previous step has been applied as much as possible, each face contains (at least) one boundary component of Σ. The shortest non-contractible cycle in G might be contained in $e_2 \cup e_3$, so we let α be the shortest cycle among the current α, $e_2 \cdot e_3^{-1}$, and $e_2^{-1} \cdot e_3$. Otherwise, since it has no repeated vertices, it uses at most one of e_2 and e_3, and at most once, so we may remove the face between e_2 and e_3, merging e_2 and e_3 into a single edge e with appropriate weights. This is valid since *any* cycle without repeated vertices using e_2 or e_3 is non-contractible, so the shortest one uses whichever is cheaper.

The pre-processing and post-processing steps can be implemented to run in $O(E)$ time. The new graph G' has V vertices; let E' and F' be its number of edges and faces. It remains to prove that $E' = \Theta(V + g)$. Again, the only non-trivial inequality is $E' = O(V + g)$. Let G'' be the graph G' where we iteratively remove every edge incident to a face of degree two; it has V vertices; let E'' be its number of edges. Then G'' contains no face of degree one or two, so we have $E'' = O(V + g)$ as before. Furthermore, transforming G' into G'' removes at most two thirds of the edges, by the preceding paragraph. So $E' = O(E'')$, which concludes. □

6. IMPROVED ALGORITHM FOR SMALL GENUS OR CONSTANT TREEWIDTH

Let Σ be a surface (orientable or not) with genus g and b boundaries. In this section, we improve the result of the previous section: we obtain algorithms with running time $O(\sqrt{g}\, n^{3/2} \log n)$ to compute a shortest non-contractible or non-separating cycle on Σ. The same technique yields near-linear-time algorithms for graphs with bounded treewidth, because they admit small separators.

6.1 Small Genus

THEOREM 5. *Let G be an undirected graph with asymmetric weights, V vertices, and E edges, that is cellularly embedded on Σ. We can compute a shortest non-contractible or non-separating cycle in G in $O(E + Vg \log g + \sqrt{g}\, V^{3/2} \log V)$ time.*

The proof uses *topology-preserving divide-and-conquer*: we compute a separator of the embedded graph, and recurse on two instances in which a different part of the graph is simplified, but the topology of the surface is preserved. Figure 3 illustrates this strategy.

LEMMA 4. *Let H be a non-empty subgraph of G. In $O(E)$ time, we can contract some edges of $E(G) \setminus E(H)$ such that the resulting graph is cellularly embedded on Σ and contains only vertices of H.*

PROOF. The strategy is to compute an initially empty set F of edges of $E(G) \setminus E(H)$ such that contracting all of them does not change the topology of the surface and removes all vertices of $G \setminus H$.

For every component K of the graph induced by the vertices in $G \setminus H$, we compute a spanning tree T of K. This tree must be incident to at least one edge with a vertex in H; otherwise the embedding G would not be cellular. Let e be one such edge; we add the edges of T and the edge e to the set F.

The union of the edges in F and their incident vertices is a forest (any cycle using only these edges would enter and leave at least one tree T, which is connected to the remaining part of F by at most one edge). So we can perform the contraction of the edges of F topologically, on the embedding G. After this operation, the new graph contains only vertices of H.

The contraction of all the edges of F can be done in $O(E)$ time. Note that, after the contraction of F, we can update the pointers from each vertex-edge-face incidence to its incident vertex in $O(E)$ total time. □

PROOF OF THEOREM 5. By Proposition 2, using $O(E)$ pre-processing and post-processing time, we may assume that $E = \Theta(V + g)$. If $V = O(g)$, we just compute the optimal solution using Theorem 4. Thus, it only remains to consider the case $V = \Omega(g)$, which implies $E = \Theta(V)$. The rest of the proof discusses this case. We describe the algorithm for non-separating cycles; the same argument applies to non-contractible cycles.

In $O(V)$ time, we find a graph separator X for G of size $O(\sqrt{gV})$ [14, Theorem 5]; that is, X is a set of $O(\sqrt{gV})$ vertices such that $G - X$ is the disjoint union of two subgraphs H_1 and H_2, each with at most $2V/3$ vertices. Now, by Theorem 3, we can compute the shortest non-separating loop α_0 passing through any of the vertices in X, in $O(\sqrt{gV}\,(V + g + V \log V)) = O(\sqrt{gV}\, V \log V)$ time.[5] In $O(V)$ time, we simplify the embedding G to a cellular embedding G_1 that contains H_1 and has the same vertex set as H_1 (Lemma 4), and put infinite weights on the edges not in H_1. We can recursively compute a shortest non-separating cycle α_1 in G_1 (the pre-processing and post-processing step of Proposition 2 takes $O(V)$ time). Similarly, we simplify G to a cellular embedding G_2 that contains H_2 and has the same vertex set as H_2, and compute a shortest non-separating cycle α_2 in G_2. The shortest of α_0, α_1, and α_2 is a shortest non-separating cycle in G.

[5] An additional property of the separator X is that the graph $G - X$ is the union of connected planar graphs. However, the embedding of such connected component in Σ is not contained in a disk, but in a sphere with (possibly multiple) punctures, and thus may contain non-trivial cycles.

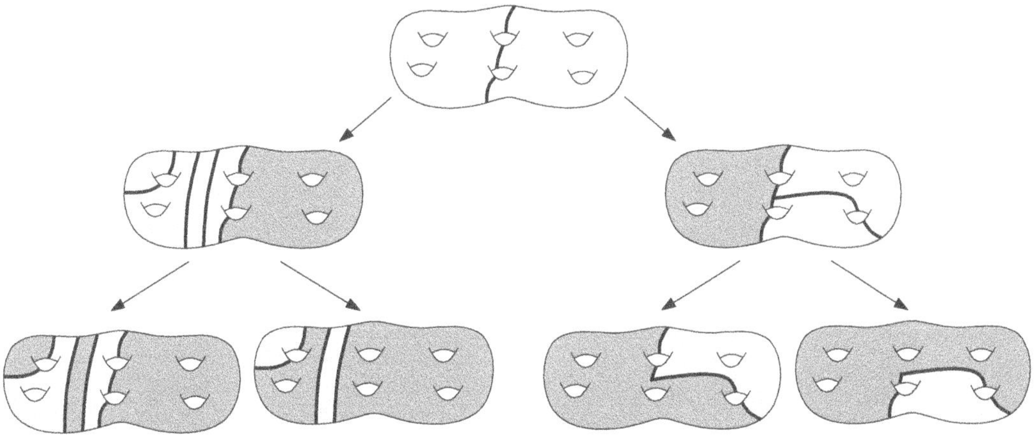

Figure 3. Topologically preserving divide and conquer. The light part of the surface represents the graph. The darker part represents faces without vertices. The bold curves represent the separator of the graph.

We stop the recursion when the number of vertices is $\Theta(g)$ (hence the number of edges is $\Theta(g)$). In this base case, we compute the shortest non-separating cycle using Theorem 4. This costs $O(g^2 \log g)$ time for each subproblem. Note that there are $O(V/g)$ base subproblems because every vertex of G is found in at most one base subproblem, so the total time spent in these base cases is $O(Vg \log g)$.

Let $T(V)$ be the total time spent in the recursive calls, without counting the base subproblems, for an input with V vertices. We have

$$T(V) \le O(\sqrt{gV}\, V \log V) + \max\{T(V_1) + T(V_2)\},$$

where the maximum is taken over values V_1, V_2 that satisfy

$$V_1 + V_2 \le V \text{ and } 0 \le V_1, V_2 \le 2V/3.$$

This solves to $T(V) = O(\sqrt{g}\, V^{3/2} \log V)$. Including the $O(E)$ pre- and post-processing time, and also the time for the base subproblems, this gives a total running time of $O(E + Vg \log g + \sqrt{g}\, V^{3/2} \log V)$. □

6.2 Constant Treewidth

Similarly, we get an improvement when the treewidth is constant:

THEOREM 6. *Let G be an undirected graph with asymmetric weights and V vertices that is cellularly embedded on Σ. Assume G has treewidth at most k_0, where k_0 is a constant. We can compute the shortest non-contractible or non-separating cycle in G in $O(Vg \log g + V \log^2 V)$.*

PROOF. The proof is the same as that of Theorem 5. The only difference is that, for graphs of bounded treewidth, it holds $E = O(V)$ and we can compute separators of constant size in linear time [1]. The recurrence is now

$$T(V) \le O(V \log V) + \max\{T(V_1) + T(V_2)\},$$

where the maximum is taken over values V_1, V_2 that satisfy

$$V_1 + V_2 \le V \text{ and } 0 \le V_1, V_2 \le 2V/3.$$

This solves to $T(V) = O(V \log^2 V)$. Adding the $O(E) = O(V)$ time pre- and post-processing and the $O(Vg \log g)$ term for the base cases yields the result. □

6.3 Improved Algorithm for Genus Zero

In the case of a sphere with boundaries (orientable, $g = 0$), if b is fixed, we can get an almost linear dependence on the complexity of the input graph. In this case, since every cycle is separating, only the non-contractible case is relevant.

THEOREM 7. *Assume Σ is a sphere with b boundaries. Let G be an undirected graph with asymmetric weights and E edges that is cellularly embedded on Σ. We can compute the shortest non-contractible cycle in G in $O(bE \log E)$ time.*

PROOF. Let $B_1, \ldots, B_b$ be the boundary components of Σ. A cycle on Σ is non-contractible if and only if it separates B_1 from another boundary component of Σ. Let $i \in \{2, \ldots, b\}$. We now prove that computing the shortest cycle that has B_1 on its left and B_i on its right is possible in $O(E \log E)$ time, which concludes.

We view G as an undirected plane graph. Let G^* be its dual graph with respect to the sphere without boundary obtained after attaching a disk to every boundary component; for each k, let B_k^* be the vertex of G^* corresponding to B_k. If e is an *oriented* edge of G, then e^* is the dual edge of G^* oriented so that e^* crosses e from left to right. Let X be a set of oriented edges of G. Then X contains the oriented edges of some cycle with B_1 on its left and B_i on its right if and only if every path from B_1^* to B_i^* in G^* uses an oriented edge in X^* [11, Lemma 7.2].

In $O(E \log E)$, we compute a minimum cut on G^* from B_1^* to B_i^*, where the capacity of a dual oriented edge is the length of its primal oriented edge; this can be done either using the algorithm by Janiga and Koubek [23], speeded up with the linear time shortest path algorithm by Henzinger et al. [22], or by computing a maximum flow [2, 15] and using the max-flow min-cut theorem. If all lengths are non-zero (which can be assumed by putting infinitesimally small lengths if necessary), this gives an inclusionwise minimum cut of smallest capacity, hence, by the preceding paragraph, a shortest cycle having B_1 on its left and B_i on its right. □

References

[1] H. L. Bodlaender. A partial k-arboretum of graphs with bounded treewidth. *Theor. Comput. Sci.*, 209(1-2):1–45, 1998.

[2] G. Borradaile and Ph. Klein. An $O(n \log n)$ algorithm for maximum st-flow in a directed planar graph. *Journal of the ACM*, 56(2), 2009.

[3] S. Cabello and E. W. Chambers. Multiple source shortest paths in a genus g graph. In *Proceedings of the 18th Annual ACM-SIAM Symposium on Discrete Algorithms (SODA)*, pages 89–97, 2007.

[4] S. Cabello, É. Colin de Verdière, and F. Lazarus. Output-sensitive algorithm for the edge-width of an embedded graph. In *These Proceedings*, 2010.

[5] S. Cabello and B. Mohar. Finding shortest non-separating and non-contractible cycles for topologically embedded graphs. *Discrete & Computational Geometry*, 37(2):213–235, 2007.

[6] P. Chalermsook, J. Fakcharoenphol, and D. Nanongkai. A deterministic near-linear time algorithm for finding minimum cuts in planar graphs. In *Proceedings of the 15th Annual ACM-SIAM Symposium on Discrete Algorithms (SODA)*, pages 828–829, 2004.

[7] E. Chambers, J. Erickson, and A. Nayyeri. Minimum cuts and shortest homologous cycles. In *Proceedings of the 25th Annual ACM Symposium on Computational Geometry (SOCG)*, pages 377–385, 2009.

[8] E. W. Chambers, É. Colin de Verdière, J. Erickson, F. Lazarus, and K. Whittlesey. Splitting (complicated) surfaces is hard. *Computational Geometry: Theory and Applications*, 41(1–2):94–110, 2008.

[9] E. W. Chambers, J. Erickson, and A. Nayyeri. Homology flows, cohomology cuts. In *Proceedings of the 41st annual ACM Symposium on Theory of Computing (STOC)*, pages 273–282, 2009.

[10] É. Colin de Verdière and J. Erickson. Tightening non-simple paths and cycles on surfaces. In *Proceedings of the 17th ACM-SIAM Symposium on Discrete Algorithms (SODA)*, pages 192–201, jan 2006.

[11] É. Colin de Verdière and A. Schrijver. Shortest vertex-disjoint two-face paths in planar graphs. *ACM Transactions on Algorithms*, To appear. Preliminary version in STACS'08.

[12] M. de Berg, M. van Kreveld, M. Overmars, and O. Schwarzkopf. *Computational Geometry: Algorithms and Applications*. Springer-Verlag, Berlin, 1997.

[13] E. W. Dijkstra. A note on two problems in connexion with graphs. *Numerische Mathematik*, 1:269–271, 1959.

[14] D. Eppstein. Dynamic generators of topologically embedded graphs. In *Proceedings of the 14th Annual ACM-SIAM Symposium on Discrete Algorithms (SODA)*, pages 599–608, 2003.

[15] J. Erickson. Maximum flows and parametric shortest paths in planar graphs. In *Proceedings of the 21st Annual ACM-SIAM Symposium on Discrete Algorithms (SODA)*, 2010. To appear.

[16] J. Erickson and S. Har-Peled. Optimally cutting a surface into a disk. *Discrete & Computational Geometry*, 31(1):37–59, 2004.

[17] J. Erickson and K. Whittlesey. Greedy optimal homotopy and homology generators. In *Proceedings of the 16th Annual ACM-SIAM Symposium on Discrete Algorithms (SODA)*, pages 1038–1046, 2005.

[18] J. Erickson and P. Worah. Computing the shortest essential cycle. *Discrete & Computational Geometry*, 2010. To appear.

[19] J. Fakcharoenphol and S. Rao. Planar graphs, negative weight edges, shortest paths, and near linear time. *J. Comput. Syst. Sci.*, 72(5):868–889, 2006.

[20] M. L. Fredman and R. E. Tarjan. Fibonacci heaps and their uses in improved netweok optimization algorithms. *Journal of the ACM*, 34:596–615, 1987.

[21] A. Hatcher. *Algebraic topology*. Cambridge University Press, 2002. Available at `http://www.math.cornell.edu/~hatcher/`.

[22] M. R. Henzinger, Ph. Klein, S. Rao, and S. Subramanian. Faster shortest-path algorithms for planar graphs. *Journal of Computer and System Sciences*, 55(1, part 1):3–23, 1997.

[23] L. Janiga and V. Koubek. Minimum cut in directed planar networks. *Kybernetica*, 28(1):37–49, 1992.

[24] P. N. Klein, S. Mozes, and O. Weimann. Shortest paths in directed planar graphs with negative lengths: a linear-space $O(n \log^2 n)$-time algorithm. *ACM Transactions on Algorithms*, To appear. Preliminary version in SODA'09.

[25] M. Kutz. Computing shortest non-trivial cycles on orientable surfaces of bounded genus in almost linear time. In *Proceedings of the 22nd Annual ACM Symposium on Computational Geometry (SOCG)*, pages 430–438, 2006.

[26] W. S. Massey. *Algebraic Topology: An Introduction*, volume 56 of *Graduate Texts in Mathematics*. Springer-Verlag, 1977.

[27] B. Mohar and C. Thomassen. *Graphs on surfaces*. Johns Hopkins Studies in the Mathematical Sciences. John Hopkins University Press, 2001.

[28] R. Motwani and P. Raghavan. *Randomized algorithms*. Press Syndicate of the University of Cambridge, 1995.

[29] J. H. Reif. Minimum $s-t$ cut of a planar undirected network in $O(n \log^2(n))$ time. *SIAM Journal on Computing*, 12(1):71–81, 1983.

[30] J. Stillwell. *Classical topology and combinatorial group theory*. Springer-Verlag, New York, 1980.

[31] C. Thomassen. Embeddings of graphs with no short noncontractible cycles. *Journal of Combinatorial Theory, Series B*, 48(2):155–177, 1990.

APPENDIX

A. WITHOUT UNIQUE SHORTEST PATHS

Throughout the paper we have assumed for simplicity that there is a unique shortest path between any pair of vertices. In this section, we explain how to remove this assumption while keeping the same running times. In practice, this assumption was only used in the proofs of Lemmas 1 and 2, for which we now provide alternative proofs without assuming uniqueness of shortest paths. Without loss of generality we can assume that all the edges have positive weights. Indeed, we can add an infinitesimal positive weight to edges of zero weight[6]. This does not change the order of the lengths of paths in the graph.

[6] More formally, we can consider weights as ordered pairs in the semigroup product $\mathbb{R}_+ \times \mathbb{Z}_+$; an edge of weight w is given the weight pair $(0, 1)$ if $w = 0$ and $(w, 0)$ otherwise.

We first introduce a composite definition of length, denoted by λ-length. Let s be the vertex for which we want to compute a shortest non-trivial loop. Fix a shortest path tree T in G from the source s and also a reversed shortest path tree R in G to the sink s. For any loop α through s we define $\lambda_T(\alpha)$ to be the length of the longest segment of α starting from s and contained in T. Finally, let us define the λ-length of α to be the couple $\lambda(\alpha) = (\ell(\alpha), -\lambda_T(\alpha))$. For the rest of this section, the length of two loops through s will be compared using the lexicographic order under $\lambda(\cdot)$. Thus, α is λ-*shorter* than another loop β through s if $\lambda(\alpha) \preceq \lambda(\beta)$. This means that to obtain a λ-shortest loop through s we want first to minimize the length of the loop, then to maximize the length of the segment starting from s and contained in T. We can now give a proof of Lemma 1.

PROOF OF LEMMA 1. Assume that $\overline{\mathbb{L}}$ is non-empty, and let α be a λ-shortest loop in $\overline{\mathbb{L}}$. Let x be the last vertex in α as we start walking from s that satisfies $\alpha[s,x] = T[s,x]$. Let y be the next vertex in α after x. By definition of the λ-length, we have $\mathrm{loop}_{T,R}(xy) \preceq \alpha$, where $\mathrm{loop}_{T,R}(xy) = \alpha[s,y] \cdot R[y,s]$. To prove the lemma, it is thus enough to show that $\mathrm{loop}_{T,R}(xy)$ is in $\overline{\mathbb{L}}$, hence in $\mathbb{M}$. We next note the following.

- The loop $\beta = T[s,y] \cdot R[y,s]$ is in $\mathbb{L}$. Indeed, either $\ell(\beta) < \ell(\alpha)$ or $\ell(\beta) = \ell(\alpha)$ and $\ell(T[s,x]) < \ell(T[s,y])$. In both cases $\lambda(\beta) \prec \lambda(\alpha)$, and β cannot be in $\overline{\mathbb{L}}$.
- The loop $T[s,y] \cdot \alpha[y,s]$ is in $\mathbb{L}$. The same argument as above applies.

We can now conclude exactly as in the first proof of this lemma. By invariance under reversal $\beta^{-1} = R[y,s]^{-1} \cdot T[s,y]^{-1}$ is also in $\mathbb{L}$, and we can apply the 3-path condition to the s-to-y walks $R[y,s]^{-1}, T[s,y]$, and $\alpha[y,s]^{-1}$ to deduce that $R[y,s]^{-1} \cdot \alpha[y,s]$ is in $\mathbb{L}$. If $\mathrm{loop}_{T,R}(xy)$ was also in $\mathbb{L}$ we would conclude, applying the 3-path condition to $\alpha[s,y]$, $R[y,s]^{-1}$, and $\alpha[y,s]^{-1}$, that $\alpha = \alpha[s,y] \cdot \alpha[y,s]$ is also in $\mathbb{L}$, a contradiction. □

We replace Lemma 2 by the following version, which uses λ-length.

LEMMA 5. *If $\overline{\mathbb{L}}$ is non-empty, then a λ-shortest element of $\mathbb{N}$ is a shortest element of $\overline{\mathbb{L}}$.*

PROOF. Assume $\overline{\mathbb{L}}$ is non-empty; by the refined proof of Lemma 1, $\overline{\mathbb{L}}$ has a λ-shortest element of the form $\alpha = \mathrm{loop}_{T,R}(xy)$ for some edge $xy \in E(G) \setminus E(T)$. We first prove that α belongs to $\mathbb{N}$, or equivalently, that $\mathrm{loop}_T(xy) \in \overline{\mathbb{L}}$. The loop $T[s,y] \cdot R[y,s]$ is in $\mathbb{L}$. Indeed, as in the above refined proof we have $\lambda(T[s,y] \cdot R[y,s]) \prec \lambda(\alpha)$ while α is λ-minimal in $\overline{\mathbb{L}}$. If $\mathrm{loop}_T(xy)$ was also in $\mathbb{L}$, then we could apply the 3-path condition to the s-to-y walks $T[s,x] \cdot xy$, $T[s,y]$, and $R[y,s]^{-1}$, and conclude that α is also in $\mathbb{L}$, a contradiction.

Let β be a λ-shortest element in $\mathbb{N}$; we can write β as $\mathrm{loop}_{T,R}(x'y')$ for some edge $x'y' \in E(G) \setminus E(T)$ such that $\mathrm{loop}_T(x'y') \in \overline{\mathbb{L}}$. There remains to prove that β belongs to $\overline{\mathbb{L}}$. By the preceding paragraph $\lambda(\beta) \preceq \lambda(\alpha)$. By the same reasoning as above $\lambda(T[s,y'] \cdot R[y',s]) \prec \lambda(\beta)$. Hence, $T[s,y'] \cdot R[y',s]$ is strictly λ-shorter than α, so it must be in $\mathbb{L}$. If β was also in $\mathbb{L}$, we could apply the 3-path condition to the s-to-y' walks $T[s,x'] \cdot x'y'$, $R[y',s]^{-1}$, and $T[s,y']$ to deduce that $\mathrm{loop}_T(x'y')$ is in $\mathbb{L}$, again a contradiction. □

The rest of the discussion in Section 3 goes through unchanged.

Approximating Loops in a Shortest Homology Basis from Point Data

Tamal K. Dey
Department of Computer Science and Engineering, The Ohio State University
Columbus, OH 43210, USA
tamaldey@cse.ohio-state.edu

Jian Sun
Department of Computer Science, Princeton University
Princeton, NJ 08544, USA
jiansun@cs.princeton.edu

Yusu Wang
Department of Computer Science and Engineering, The Ohio State University
Columbus, OH 43210, USA
yusu@cse.ohio-state.edu

ABSTRACT

Inference of topological and geometric attributes of a hidden manifold from its point data is a fundamental problem arising in many scientific studies and engineering applications. In this paper we present an algorithm to compute a set of loops from a point data that presumably sample a smooth manifold $M \subset \mathbb{R}^d$. These loops approximate a *shortest* basis of the one dimensional homology group $\mathsf{H}_1(M)$ over coefficients in finite field $\mathbb{Z}_2$. Previous results addressed the issue of computing the rank of the homology groups from point data, but there is no result on approximating the shortest basis of a manifold from its point sample. In arriving our result, we also present a polynomial time algorithm for computing a shortest basis of $\mathsf{H}_1(\mathcal{K})$ for any finite *simplicial complex* $\mathcal{K}$ whose edges have non-negative weights.

Categories and Subject Descriptors

F.2.2 [**Analysis of Algorithms and Problem Complexity**]: Nonnumerical Algorithms and Problems—*Geometrical problems and computations*

General Terms

Algorithms, Theory

Keywords

Topology, homology basis, Rips complex, point cloud

1. INTRODUCTION

Inference of unknown structures from point data is a fundamental problem in many areas of science and engineering that has motivated wide spread research [1, 13, 22, 24, 25, 26]. Typically, this data is assumed to be sampled from a manifold sitting in a high dimensional space whose geometric and topological properties are to be derived from the data. In this work, we are particularly interested in computing a set of loops from data which not only captures the topology but is also aware of the geometry of the sampled manifold. Specifically, we aim to approximate a shortest basis of the one dimensional homology group from the data.

Recently, a few algorithms for computing homology groups from point data have been developed. One approach would be to reconstruct the sampled space from its point data [4, 7, 12] and then apply known techniques for homology computations on triangulations [21]. However, this option is not very attractive since a full-blown reconstruction with known techniques requires costly computations with Delaunay triangulations in high dimensions. Chazal and Oudot [8] showed how one can use less constrained data structures such as Rips, Čech, and witness complexes to infer the rank of the homology groups by leveraging persistence algorithms [19, 26]. Among these, the Rips complexes are the easiest to compute though they consume more space than the others, an issue which has started to be addressed [17].

All of the works mentioned above focus on computing the Betti numbers, the rank of the homology groups. Although the persistence algorithms [19, 26] also provide representative cycles of a homology basis, they remain oblivious to the geometry of the manifold. As a result, these cycles do not have nice geometric properties. A natural question to pose is that if the loops of the one dimensional homology group are associated with a length under some metric, can one approximate/compute a shortest set of loops that generate the homology group in polynomial time? This question has been answered in affirmative for the special case of surfaces when they are represented with triangulations [20]. In fact, considerable progress has been made for this special case on various versions of the problem. We cannot apply these techniques, mainly because we deal with point data instead of an input triangulation. Also, these works either consider a surface [5, 6, 15, 20] instead of a manifold of arbitrary dimension in an Euclidean space, or use a local measure other than the lengths of the generators in a basis [9].

Our main result is an algorithm that can compute a set of loops from a Rips complex of the given data and a proof that the lengths of the computed loops approximate those of a shortest basis of the one dimensional homology group of the sampled manifold. In arriving at this result, we also show how to compute a shortest basis for the one dimensional homology group of any finite *simplicial complex* whose edges have non-negative weights. Given that computing a shortest basis for k-dimensional homology groups of a simplicial complex over $\mathbb{Z}_2$ coefficients is NP-hard for $k \geq 2$ (Chen and Freedman [11]), this result settles the open case for $k = 1$.

SCG'10, June 13–16, 2010, Snowbird, Utah, USA.

1.1 Background and notations

We use the concepts of homology groups, Čech and Rips complexes from algebraic topology and geodesics from differential geometry. We briefly discuss them and introduce relevant notations here; the readers can obtain the details from any standard book on the topics such as [18, 21].

Homology groups and generators: A homology group of a topological space $\mathbb{T}$ encodes its topological connectivity. We use $\mathsf{H}_k(\mathbb{T})$ to denote its k-dimensional homology group over the coefficients in $\mathbb{Z}_2$. Since $\mathbb{Z}_2$ is a field, $\mathsf{H}_k(\mathbb{T})$ is a vector space of dimension k and hence admits a basis of size k. We are concerned with the 1-dimensional homology groups $\mathsf{H}_1(\mathbb{T})$. The elements of $\mathsf{H}_1(\mathbb{T})$ are equivalent classes $[g]$ of 1-dimensional cycles g, also called *loops*. A set $\{[g_1], \ldots, [g_k]\}$ generating $\mathsf{H}_1(\mathbb{T})$ is called its basis where $k = rank(\mathsf{H}_1(\mathbb{T}))$. Simplifying the notation, we say $\{g_1, \ldots, g_a\}$ generates $\mathsf{H}_1(\mathbb{T})$ if $\{[g_1], \ldots, [g_a]\}$ generates $\mathsf{H}_1(\mathbb{T})$ and is a basis if $a = rank(\mathsf{H}_1(\mathbb{T}))$. We assume that each loop g in $\mathbb{T}$ is associated with a non-negative weight $w(g)$. If $\mathbb{T}$ is a simplicial complex, the loops are restricted to its 1-skeleton and $w(g)$ is defined to be the sum of edge weights in g which are assumed to be non-negative. If $\mathbb{T}$ is a Riemannian manifold, the weights on loops are taken as their lengths in the Riemannian metric. The weights of the loops define the length of a *set* of loops $G = \{g_1, \ldots, g_a\}$ as $\mathrm{Len}(G) = \Sigma_{i=1}^{a} w(g_i)$. A *shortest set of generators* or a *shortest basis* of $\mathsf{H}_1(\mathbb{T})$ is a basis G of $\mathsf{H}_1(\mathbb{T})$ where $\mathrm{Len}(G)$ is minimal over all bases.

Complexes: Let $B(p, r)$ denote an open Euclidean d-ball centered at p with radius r. For a point set $P \subset \mathbb{R}^d$, and a real $r > 0$, the Čech complex $\mathcal{C}^r(P)$ is a simplicial complex where a simplex $\sigma \in \mathcal{C}^r(P)$ if and only if $\mathrm{Vert}(\sigma)$, the vertices of σ, are in P and are the centers of d-balls of radius $r/2$ which have a non-empty common intersection, that is, $\cap_{p \in \mathrm{Vert}(\sigma)} B(p, r/2) \neq \emptyset$. Instead of common intersection, if we only require pairwise intersection among the d-balls, we get the Rips complex $\mathcal{R}^r(P)$. It is well known that the two complexes are related by a nesting property:

Proposition 1.1 *For any finite set $P \subset \mathbb{R}^d$ and any $r \geq 0$, one has $\mathcal{C}^r(P) \subseteq \mathcal{R}^r(P) \subseteq \mathcal{C}^{2r}(P)$.*

Geodesics: The vertex set P of the simplicial complexes we consider is a dense sample of a smooth compact manifold $M \subset \mathbb{R}^d$ without boundary. Assume that M is isometrically embedded, that is, M inherits the metric from $\mathbb{R}^d$. For two points $p, q \in M$, a *geodesic* is a curve connecting p and q in M whose acceleration has no component in the tangent spaces of M. Two points may have more than one geodesic among which the ones with the minimum length are called *minimizing geodesics*. Since M is compact, any two points admit a minimizing geodesic. The lengths of minimizing geodesics induce a distance metric $d_M : M \times M \to \mathbb{R}$ where $d_M(p, q)$ is the length of a minimizing geodesic between p and q. Clearly, $d(p, q) \leq d_M(p, q)$ where $d(p, q)$ is the Euclidean distance. If $d(p, q)$ is small, Proposition 1.2 asserts that there is an upper bound on $d_M(p, q)$ in terms of $d(p, q)$. Our proof extends a result in [2] where Belkin et al. show the same result on a surface in $\mathbb{R}^3$. The *reach* $\rho(M)$ is defined as the minimum distance between M and its medial axis.

Proposition 1.2 *If $d(p, q) \leq \rho(M)/2$, one has*

$$d_M(p, q) \leq \left(1 + \frac{4d^2(p, q)}{3\rho^2(M)}\right) d(p, q).$$

PROOF. Let $\gamma(t)$ be a minimizing geodesic between p and q parameterized by length and set $l = d_M(p, q)$. By Proposition 6.3 in [24] we have that $l \leq 2d(p, q)$. Let $u_t = \dot{\gamma}(t)$ be the *unit* tangent vector of γ at t. We have $t = d_M(p, \gamma(t))$.

Let $B : T_{\gamma(t)} \times T_{\gamma(t)} \to T^{\perp}_{\gamma(t)}$ be the second fundamental form associated with the manifold M. Since γ is a geodesic, $du_t/dt = B(u_t, u_t) = \ddot{\gamma}(t)$. Write $\rho = \rho(M)$ and $d = d(p, q)$ for convenience. From Proposition 6.1 in [24], we have

$$\|\ddot{\gamma}(t)\| \leq 1/\rho$$

since the norm of the second fundamental form is bounded by $1/\rho$ in all directions, and thus $\|du_t/dt\| \leq 1/\rho$. Hence we have that

$$\|u_t - u_p\| = \left\|\int_{[0,t]} du_y\right\| \leq \int_{[0,t]} \frac{1}{\rho} dy = \frac{t}{\rho}$$
$$\Rightarrow \quad \sin\frac{\angle(u_p, u_t)}{2} \leq \frac{t}{2\rho}.$$

Furthermore, let $u \cdot v$ denote the dot-product between vectors u and v. Then we have that

$$\begin{aligned}\int_{[0,l]} u_t \cdot u_p \, dt &= \int_{[0,l]} \cos\angle(u_t, u_p) \, dt \\ &= \int_{[0,l]} \left(1 - 2\sin^2\frac{\angle(u_t, u_p)}{2}\right) dt \\ &\geq \int_{[0,l]} \left(1 - \frac{t^2}{2\rho^2}\right) dt = l - \frac{l^3}{6\rho^2}\end{aligned}$$

On the other hand, observe that $\int_{[0,l]} u_t \cdot u_p \, dt$ measures the length of the (signed) projection of γ along the direction u_p. That is,

$$\int_{[0,l]} u_t \cdot u_p \, dl_t = (q - p) \cdot u_p.$$

Hence we have that

$$\begin{aligned} & d = \|p - q\| \geq (q - p) \cdot u_p \geq l - \tfrac{l^3}{6\rho^2} \\ \Rightarrow \quad & l \leq d + \tfrac{l^3}{6\rho^2} \leq d + \tfrac{4d^3}{3\rho^2}.\end{aligned}$$

The last inequality follows from the fact that $l \leq 2d$. This proves the lemma. □

Convexity radius and sampling: For a point $p \in M$, the set of all points q with $d_M(p, q) < r$ form p's *geodesic ball* $B_M(p, r)$ of radius r. It is known that there is a positive real r_p for each point $p \in M$ so that $B_M(p, r)$ is *convex* for $r \leq r_p$. It means that, for $r \leq r_p$, any two points in $B_M(p, r)$ admit a *unique* minimizing geodesic that lies in $B_M(p, r)$. The *convexity radius* of M is $\rho_c(M) = \inf_{p \in M} r_p$. We use Euclidean distances to define the sampling density. We say a discrete set $P \subset M$ is an ε-sample[1] of M if $B(x, \varepsilon) \cap P \neq \emptyset$ for each point $x \in M$.

1.2 Main results

We compute a set of loops $G = \{g_1, \ldots, g_k\}$ from an ε-sample P of M whose total length is within a factor of the total length of a shortest basis in $\mathsf{H}_1(M)$. The factor depends on ε, $\rho(M)$, and an input parameter $r > 0$.

Theorem 1.3 *Let $M \subset \mathbb{R}^d$ be a smooth, closed manifold with ℓ as the length of a shortest basis of $\mathsf{H}_1(M)$. Given an ε-sample*

[1] Here ε-sample is not defined relative to reach or feature size as commonly done in reconstruction literature [1, 7, 12].

$P \subset M$ *of* n *points and* $4\varepsilon \le r \le \min\{\frac{1}{2}\sqrt{\frac{3}{5}}\rho(M), \rho_c(M)\}$, *one can compute a set of loops* G *in* $\mathbb{R}^d$ *where:*

i.

$$\frac{1}{1+\frac{4r^2}{3\rho^2(M)}}\ell \le \mathrm{Len}(G) \le (1+\frac{4\varepsilon}{r})\ell.$$

ii. Treating G *as a 1-complex, there is a map* $h\colon G \to M$ *so that* $h(G)$ *is basis of* $\mathsf{H}_1(M)$ *and the Hausdorff distance between the underlying space of* g *and* $h(g)$ *is at most* $r/2$ *for each* $g \in G$.

iii. The loops in G *can be computed in* $O(n(n+n_e)^2(n_e+n_t))$ *time where* n_e *and* n_t *are the numbers of edges and triangles respectively in the Rips complex* $\mathcal{R}^{2r}(P)$.

The above result suggests that $\lim_{\frac{\varepsilon}{r},r\to 0}\mathrm{Len}(G) \to \ell$. To make $\frac{\varepsilon}{r}$ and r simultaneously approach 0, one may take $r = O(\sqrt{\varepsilon})$ and let $\varepsilon \to 0$. We note that $n_e = O(n^2)$ and $n_t = O(n^3)$ giving an $O(n^8)$ worst-case complexity for the algorithm. However, if $r = \Theta(\varepsilon)$ and points in P have $\Omega(\varepsilon)$ pairwise distance, n_e and n_t reduce to $O(n)$ by a result of [8]. In this case we get a time complexity of $O(n^4)$. In arriving at Theorem 1.3, we also prove the following result which is of independent interest.

Theorem 1.4 *Let* $\mathcal{K}$ *be a finite simplicial complex with non-negative weights on edges. A shortest basis for* $\mathsf{H}_1(\mathcal{K})$ *can be computed in* $O(n^4)$ *time where* n *is the size of* $\mathcal{K}$.

2. ALGORITHM DESCRIPTION

The algorithm that we propose proceeds as follows. We compute a Rips complex $\mathcal{R}^{2r}(P)$ out of the given point cloud $P \subset M$. Next, we compute the rank k of $\mathsf{H}_1(M)$ by considering the persistent homology group

$$\mathsf{H}_1^{r,2r}(\mathcal{R}(P)) = \text{image } \iota_*$$

where the inclusion $\iota : \mathcal{R}^r(P) \hookrightarrow \mathcal{R}^{2r}(P)$ induces the homomorphism $\iota_* : \mathsf{H}_1(\mathcal{R}^r(P)) \to \mathsf{H}_1(\mathcal{R}^{2r}(P))$. As a homology group over $\mathbb{Z}_2$, $\mathsf{H}_1^{r,2r}(\mathcal{R}(P))$ is a vector space and it is known that the rank of $\mathsf{H}_1^{r,2r}(\mathcal{R}(P))$ coincides with that of $\mathsf{H}_1(M)$ for appropriate r.

A basis of $\mathsf{H}_1^{r,2r}(\mathcal{R}(P))$ is formed by the classes of a maximal set of loops in $\mathcal{R}^r(P)$ whose classes remain independent in $\mathsf{H}_1(\mathcal{R}^{2r}(P))$ under the map ι_*. We show that a shortest basis of $\mathsf{H}_1^{r,2r}(\mathcal{R}(P))$ approximates a shortest basis of $\mathsf{H}_1(M)$. Therefore, we aim to compute a shortest basis of $\mathsf{H}_1^{r,2r}(\mathcal{R}(P))$ from $\mathcal{R}^r(P)$ and $\mathcal{R}^{2r}(P)$. To accomplish this, the algorithm augments $\mathcal{R}^{2r}(P)$ by putting a weight $w(e)$ on each edge $e \in \mathcal{R}^{2r}(P)$. The weights are of two types: either they are the lengths of the edges, or a very large value W which is larger than k times the total weight of $\mathcal{R}^r(P)$. Precisely we set

$$w(e) = \begin{cases} \text{length of } e & \text{if } e \in \mathcal{R}^r(P) \\ W & \text{if } e \in \mathcal{R}^{2r}(P) \setminus \mathcal{R}^r(P). \end{cases}$$

Let the complex $\mathcal{R}^{2r}(P)$ augmented with weights be denoted as $\mathcal{R}^{2r+}(P)$. A shortest basis of $\mathsf{H}_1(\mathcal{R}^{2r+}(P))$ does not necessarily form a shortest basis of $\mathsf{H}_1^{r,2r}(\mathcal{R}(P))$. However, the first k loops sorted according to lengths in a shortest basis of $\mathsf{H}_1(\mathcal{R}^{2r+}(P))$ form a shortest basis of $\mathsf{H}_1^{r,2r}(\mathcal{R}(P))$. We give an algorithm to compute a shortest basis for any simplicial complex which we apply to $\mathcal{R}^{2r+}(P)$.

Since we are interested in computing the generators of the first homology group, it is sufficient to consider all simplices up to dimension two, that is, only vertices, edges, and triangles in the simplicial complexes that we deal with. Henceforth, we assume that all complexes that we consider have simplices up to dimension two.

2.1 Computing loops

We will prove later that a shortest basis for $\mathsf{H}_1^{r,2r}(\mathcal{R}(P))$ indeed approximates a shortest basis for $\mathsf{H}_1(M)$. The algorithm SHORTLOOP computes them.

Algorithm 1 SHORTLOOP (P, r)

1: Compute the Rips complex $\mathcal{R}^{2r}(P)$ and a weighted complex $\mathcal{R}^{2r+}(P)$ from it as described.
2: Compute the rank k of $\mathsf{H}_1^{r,2r}(\mathcal{R}(P))$ by the persistence algorithm.
3: Compute a shortest basis for $\mathsf{H}_1(\mathcal{R}^{2r+}(P))$.
4: Return the first k smallest loops from this shortest basis.

Theorem 2.1 *The algorithm* SHORTLOOP(P, r) *computes a shortest basis for the persistent homology group* $\mathsf{H}_1^{r,2r}(\mathcal{R}(P))$.

PROOF. Let $g_1, \ldots, g_a$ be the set of generators sorted according to the non-decreasing lengths which are computed in step 3. They generate $\mathsf{H}_1(\mathcal{R}^{2r+}(P))$. Out of these generators the algorithm outputs the first k generators $g_1, \ldots, g_k$. Since k is the rank of $\mathsf{H}_1^{r,2r}(P)$ there are k independent generators in $\mathsf{H}_1(\mathcal{R}^r(P))$ which remain independent in $\mathsf{H}_1(\mathcal{R}^{2r+}(P))$. We claim that the loops $g_1, \ldots, g_k$ reside in $\mathcal{R}^r(P)$. For if they do not, the sum of their lengths would be more than W which is k times larger than the total weight of $\mathcal{R}^r(P)$. Then, we can argue that any independent set of k loops from $\mathcal{R}^r(P)$ which remain independent in $\mathsf{H}_1(\mathcal{R}^{2r+}(P))$ can replace $g_1, \ldots, g_k$ to have a smaller length so that $g_1, \ldots, g_a$ could not be a shortest basis of $\mathsf{H}_1(\mathcal{R}^{2r+}(P))$.

The above argument implies that $g_1, \ldots, g_k$ is a basis of $\mathsf{H}_1^{r,2r}(P)$. If it is not a shortest basis, it can be replaced by a shorter one so that again we would have a basis of $\mathsf{H}_1(\mathcal{R}^{2r+}(P))$ which is shorter than the one computed. This is a contradiction. □

It remains to show how to compute a shortest basis of $\mathsf{H}_1(\mathcal{R}^{2r+}(P))$ in step 3 of SHORTLOOP.

2.2 Shortest basis

Let $\mathcal{K}$ be any finite simplicial complex embedded in $\mathbb{R}^d$ whose edges have non-negative weights. To compute a shortest basis for $\mathsf{H}_1(\mathcal{K})$ we make use of the fact that $\mathsf{H}_1(\mathcal{K})$ is a vector space as we restrict ourselves to $\mathbb{Z}_2$ coefficients. For such cases, Erickson and Whittlesey [20] observed that if a set of loops $\mathcal{L}$ in $\mathcal{K}$ contains a shortest basis, then the greedy set G chosen from $\mathcal{L}$ is a shortest basis. The greedy set G of $\mathcal{L}$ is an *ordered* set of loops $\{g_1, \ldots g_k\}$, $k = rank\, \mathsf{H}_1(\mathcal{K})$, satisfying the following condition. The first element g_1 is the shortest loop in $\mathcal{L}$ which is nontrivial in $\mathsf{H}_1(\mathcal{K})$. Suppose $g_1, \ldots, g_i$ have already been defined in the set G. The next chosen loop g_{i+1} is the shortest loop in $\mathcal{L}$ which is independent of $g_1, \ldots, g_i$, that is, $[g_{i+1}]$ cannot be written as a linear combination of $[g_1], \ldots, [g_i]$. The check for independence is a costly step in this greedy algorithm which we aim to reduce. We construct a set of *canonical* loops which contains a basis of $\mathsf{H}_1(\mathcal{K})$. This set is pruned by a persistence based algorithm before applying the greedy algorithm.

2.2.1 Canonical loops

We start with citing a result of Erickson and Whittlesey [20]. A simple cycle L is *tight* if it contains a shortest path between every pair of points in L.

Proposition 2.2 *With non-negative weights, every loop in a shortest basis of* $\mathsf{H}_1(\mathcal{K})$ *is tight.*

To collect all tight loops, we consider the canonical loops defined as follows. Let T be a *shortest path tree* in $\mathcal{K}$ rooted at p. Notice that we are not assuming T to be unique, but it is fixed once computed. For any two nodes $q_1, q_2 \in P$, let $\Pi_T(q_1, q_2)$ denote the unique path from q_1 to q_2 in T. Let E_T be the set of edges in T. Given a non-tree edge $e = (q_1, q_2) \in E \setminus E_T$, define the *canonical loop* of e with respect to p, $c_p(e)$ in short, as the loop formed by concatenating $\Pi_T(p, q_1)$, e, and $\Pi_T(q_2, p)$, that is,

$$c_p(e) = \Pi_T(p, q_1) \circ e \circ \Pi_T(q_2, p).$$

Let C_p be the set of all canonical loops with respect to p, i.e., $C_p = \{c_p(e) : e \in E \setminus E_T\}$. Then we have the following easy consequence.

Proposition 2.3 $\cup_{p \in P} C_p$ *contains all tight loops.*

Therefore $\cup_{p \in P} C_p$ is a set of loops from which the greedy set can be selected. However, $\cup_{p \in P} C_p$ can be a very large set containing possibly many trivial loops which result into many unnecessary independence checks. To remedy this, we identify the greedy set G_p of C_p and choose the greedy set from the union $\cup_{p \in P} G_p$ instead of $\cup_{p \in P} C_p$. It turns out that G_p can be computed by a persistence based algorithm thereby avoiding explicit independence checks.

If the lengths of the loops in C_p are distinct, the greedy set G_p is unique. However, in presence of equal length loops we need a mechanism to break ties. For this we introduce the notion of *canonical order*. We assign a unique number $\nu(e)$ between 1 to m to each non-tree edge e if there are m of them. For any two non-tree edges e and e', let $e < e'$ if and only if either $\mathrm{Len}(c_p(e)) < \mathrm{Len}(c_p(e'))$, or $\mathrm{Len}(c_p(e)) = \mathrm{Len}(c_p(e'))$ and $\nu(e) < \nu(e')$. The total order imposed by '<' provides the canonical order

$$e_1 < e_2 < \ldots < e_m.$$

Based on this canonical order, we form the greedy set G_p of C_p as described in the beginning of Section 2.2.

Below we argue that $\cup_{p \in P} G_p$ is good for our purpose and each set G_p can be computed based on the persistence algorithm.

Proposition 2.4 *The greedy set chosen from* $\cup_{p \in P} G_p$ *is a shortest basis of* $\mathsf{H}_1(\mathcal{K})$.

PROOF. We show that $\cup_{p \in P} G_p$ contains a shortest basis of $\mathsf{H}_1(\mathcal{K})$. Then, the proposition follows by the argument as delineated at the beginning of section 2.2.

Consider all canonical loops $\cup_{p \in P} C_p$. Sort them in non-decreasing order of their lengths. If two loops have equal lengths and if there are points $p_i \in P$ for which both of them are in C_{p_i}, break the tie using the canonical order applied to the canonical loops for any such one point. Otherwise, break the tie arbitrarily. Based on this order let G be the greedy set from $\cup_{p \in P} C_p$. Proposition 2.2 and Proposition 2.3 imply that $\cup_{p \in P} C_p$ contains a shortest basis of $\mathsf{H}_1(\mathcal{K})$ and thus G is a shortest basis. Consider any loop L in G. It is a canonical loop with respect to some $q \in P$ for which all loops appearing before L in the canonical order precede it in the sorted sequence. The loop L is independent of the loops in $\cup_{p \in P} C_p$ appearing before L, in particular independent of the loops in C_q appearing before L in the canonical order, which means $L \in G_q$. Therefore $\cup_{p \in P} G_p$ contains a shortest basis G of $\mathsf{H}_1(\mathcal{K})$. The proposition follows. □

Motivated by the above observations, we formulate an algorithm CANONGEN that computes the greedy set G_p of C_p. We note that, very recently, Chen and Freedman [9] proposed a similar algorithm which computes an *approximation* of a shortest basis of a simplicial complex rather than an optimal one.

Algorithm 2 CANONGEN $(p, \mathcal{K})$

1: Construct a shortest path tree T in $\mathcal{K}$ with p as the root. Let E_T denote the set of tree edges.
2: For each non-tree edge $e = (q_1, q_2) \in E \setminus E_T$, let $c_p(e)$ be the canonical loop of e.
3: Perform the persistence algorithm based on the following filtration of $\mathcal{K}$: all the vertices in $P = \mathrm{Vert}(\mathcal{K})$, followed by all tree edges in T, followed by non-tree edges in the *canonical order*, and followed by all the triangles in $\mathcal{K}$. There are $k = \mathrm{rank}(H_1(\mathcal{K}))$ number of edges unpaired after the algorithm, and each of them is necessarily a non-tree edge. Return the set of canonical loops associated with them.

Proposition 2.5 CANONGEN $(p, \mathcal{K})$ *outputs the greedy set* G_p *chosen from* C_p.

PROOF. Let $\{e_1, e_2 \cdots, e_m\}$ be the set of non-tree edges for the shortest path tree T listed in the canonical order. Let

$$G_p = \{c_p(e_1^*), c_p(e_2^*), \cdots, c_p(e_k^*)\}.$$

It suffices to show that $\{e_1^*, e_2^* \cdots, e_k^*\}$ is the set of unpaired edges. Observe that for any e_i^*, $c_p(e_i^*)$ is independent of any subset of $\{c_p(e_j) : e_j < e_i^*\}$.

We prove the proposition by contradiction. Assume some e_i^* gets paired by a triangle t in the persistence algorithm. Let $\mathcal{K}_t$ denote the complex in the filtration right before t is added. Let $f : \mathcal{K}_t \hookrightarrow \mathcal{K}$ be the inclusion map; it induces a homomorphism $f_* = \mathsf{H}_1(\mathcal{K}_t) \to \mathsf{H}_1(\mathcal{K})$. Let $[L]_t$ denote the homology class in $\mathcal{K}_t$ carried by the loop L. The boundary ∂t uniquely determines a subset of unpaired positive edges $e_1' < \cdots < e_s'$ in $\mathcal{K}_t$ such that $[\partial t]_t = [c_p(e_1')]_t + \cdots + [c_p(e_s')]_t$. The persistence algorithm [19] picks the youngest one from this subset to pair with t, i.e., $e_i^* = e_s'$. On the other hand, we have

$$\begin{aligned}
&[c_p(e_1')] + \cdots + [c_p(e_{s-1}')] + [c_p(e_i^*)] \\
&= f_*([c_p(e_1')]_t + \cdots + [c_p(e_{s-1}')]_t + [c_p(e_i^*)]_t) \\
&= f_*([\partial t]_t) = 0
\end{aligned}$$

which means that $c_p(e_i^*)$ is dependent on a subset of $\{c_p(e_j) : e_j < e_i^*\}$. We reach a contradiction. □

All previous results put together provide a greedy algorithm for computing a shortest basis of $\mathsf{H}_1(\mathcal{K})$.

2.2.2 Checking independence

In step 7 of SPGEN we need to determine if a generator g is independent of all generators $g_1', \ldots, g_s'$ so far selected in G. Suppose we obtain g from running persistence algorithm on a shortest path tree based filtration for a point p in step 3 of CANONGEN. At the end of this persistence algorithm we must have gotten an

Algorithm 3 SPGEN ($\mathcal{K}$)

1: For each $p \in P = \text{Vert}(\mathcal{K})$ compute G_p :=CANONGEN $(p,\mathcal{K})$. Let $k = |G_p|$.
2: Sort all loops in $\cup_p G_p$ by their lengths in the increasing order. Let $g_1, \ldots, g_{k|P|}$ be this sorted list.
3: Initialize $G := \{g_1\}$.
4: **for** $i := 2$ to $k|P|$, **do**
5:    **if** $|G| = k$, **then**
6:       Exit the for loop.
7:    **else if** g_i is independent of all loops in G, **then**
8:       Add g_i to G.
9:    **end if**
10: **end for**
11: Return G.

unpaired edge, say e, where $c_p(e) = g$. To determine if g is independent of all generators selected so far we adopt a sealing technique proposed in [9]. We fill $g'_1 \ldots g'_s$ with triangles. The filling is done only combinatorially by choosing a dummy vertex, say v, and adding triangles vv_iv_{i+1} for each edge v_iv_{i+1} of the loops to be filled. Let $\mathcal{K}'$ be the new complex after adding these triangles and their edges to $\mathcal{K}$. In effect, these triangles and edges destroy the generators $g'_1, \ldots, g'_s$ from $\mathcal{K}$. They destroy the generator g as well if and only if g is dependent on $g'_1, \ldots, g'_s$. Since we are sealing according to the greedy order, the proof of Lemma 4.4 in [9] applies to establish this fact. Whether g is rendered trivial or not can be determined as follows. We continue the persistence algorithm corresponding to the vertex p with the addition of the simplices in $\mathcal{K}' \setminus \mathcal{K}$ and check if e is now paired or not.

Let n_v, n_e, and n_t denote the number of vertices, edges, and triangles respectively in $\mathcal{K}$. Notice that we add at most n_e edges and triangles for sealing since the dummy vertex is added to at most n_e edges to create new triangles in $\mathcal{K}'$.

2.3 Time complexity

First, we analyze the time complexity of CANONGEN. Shortest path tree computation in step 1 of CANONGEN takes $O(n_v \log n_v + n_e)$ time. The persistence algorithm for CANONGEN can be implemented using matrix reductions [14] in time $O((n_v + n_e)^2(n_e + n_t))$. This is because there are $n_v + n_e$ rows in this matrix and each insertion of $n_e + n_t$ simplices can be implemented in $O(n_v + n_e)$ column operations each taking $O(n_v + n_e)$ time. Therefore, CANONGEN takes $O(n_v \log n_v + (n_v + n_e)^2(n_e + n_t))$ time.

Step 1 of SPGEN calls CANONGEN n_v times. Therefore, step 1 of SPGEN takes $O(n_v^2 \log n_v + n_v(n_v + n_e)^2(n_e + n_t))$ time. Step 2 of SPGEN can be performed in $O(n_v k \log n_v k)$ time where $k = O(n_e)$ is the rank of $\mathsf{H}_1(\mathcal{K})$. The time complexity for independence check in step 7 is dominated by the persistence algorithm which is continued on $\mathcal{K}$ to accommodate simplices in $\mathcal{K}'$. Since we add $O(n_e)$ new simplices in $\mathcal{K}'$, it has the same asymptotic complexity as for running the persistence algorithm on $\mathcal{K}$. We conclude that SPGEN spends $O(n_v(n_v + n_e)^2(n_e + n_t))$ time in total. If we take $n = |\mathcal{K}|$, this gives an $O(n^4)$ time complexity.

Now, we analyze the time complexity of SHORTLOOP which is the main algorithm. Let n_e and n_t be the number of edges and triangles in $\mathcal{R}^{2r}(P)$ created out of n points. Step 1 takes at most $O(n + n_e + n_t)$ time since we only compute edges and triangles of $\mathcal{R}^{2r}(P)$ out of n points. Accounting for the persistence algorithm in step 2 and the time complexity of step 3 we get that SHORTLOOP takes

$$O(n(n + n_e)^2(n_e + n_t)) \text{ time.}$$

The procedure SPGEN($\mathcal{K}$) computes canonical sets G_p which is ensured by Proposition 2.5. Then, it forms a greedy set from these canonical sets which is a shortest basis for $\mathsf{H}_1(\mathcal{K})$ by Proposition 2.4. This and the time analysis for SPGEN establish Theorem 1.4.

3. APPROXIMATION FOR M

The algorithm SPGEN is used in SHORTLOOP to produce a shortest basis for the persistent homology group $\mathsf{H}_1^{r,2r}(\mathcal{R}(P))$. Proposition 3.5 in this section shows that a shortest basis of $\mathsf{H}_1^{r,2r}(\mathcal{R}(P))$ coincides with a shortest basis in $\mathsf{H}_1(\mathcal{C}^r(P))$. Therefore, if we show that a shortest basis in $\mathsf{H}_1(\mathcal{C}^r(P))$ approximates a shortest basis in $\mathsf{H}_1(M)$, we have the approximation result of Theoerm 1.3.

3.1 Connecting M, Čech complex, and Rips complex

First, we note the following result established in [24] which connects M with the union of the balls $P^r = \cup_{p \in P} B(p, r)$.

Proposition 3.1 *Let $P \subset M$ be an ε-sample. If $2\varepsilon \le r \le \sqrt{\frac{3}{5}}\rho(M)$, there is a deformation retraction from P^r to M so that the corresponding retraction $t : P^r \to M$ has $t(B) \subset B$ for any ball $B \in \{B(p,r)\}_{p \in P}$.*

Recall that $\mathcal{C}^{2r}(P)$ is the nerve of the cover $\{B(p,r)\}_{p \in P}$ of the space P^r. By a result of Leray [23], it is known that P^r and $\mathcal{C}^{2r}(P)$ are homotopy equivalent. The next proposition follows from examining the specific equivalence maps used to prove the Nerve Lemma in Hatcher [21]. In particular, the simplices of the Čech complex are mapped to a subset of the union of the balls centered at their vertices, see Appendix for its proof.

Proposition 3.2 *There exists a homotopy equivalence $f : \mathcal{C}^{2r}(P) \to P^r$ such that for each simplex $\sigma \in \mathcal{C}^{2r}(P)$, one has $f(\sigma) \subset \cup_{p \in \text{Vert}(\sigma)} B(p,r)$ and $f(p) = p$ for any $p \in P$.*

The two propositions above together provide the connection between M and the Čech complex:

Proposition 3.3 *Let $P \subset M$ be an ε-sample. If $2\varepsilon \le r \le \sqrt{\frac{3}{5}}\rho(M)$, there is a homotopy equivalence map $h = t \circ f : \mathcal{C}^{2r}(P) \to M$ such that $h(\sigma) \subset M \cap (\cup_{p \in \text{Vert}(\sigma)} B(p,r))$ and $h(p) = p$ for any $p \in P$.*

Now we establish a connection between Čech complex and Rips complexes which helps proving Proposition 3.5.

Proposition 3.4 *Let $P \subset M$ be an ε-sample. Then, for $4\varepsilon \le r \le \frac{1}{2}\sqrt{\frac{3}{5}}\rho(M)$, we have the following isomorphisms*

$$\mathsf{H}_1^{r,2r}(\mathcal{R}(P)) \approx \mathsf{H}_1(\mathcal{C}^r(P)) \overset{j_{1*}}{\approx} \mathsf{H}_1(\mathcal{C}^{2r}(P)) \overset{j_{2*}}{\approx} \mathsf{H}_1(\mathcal{C}^{4r}(P)),$$

where j_{1*} and j_{2*} are induced by the inclusion maps j_1 and j_2 respectively. Moreover, if

$$\mathcal{C}^r(P) \overset{i_1}{\hookrightarrow} \mathcal{R}^r(P)) \overset{i_2}{\hookrightarrow} \mathcal{C}^{2r}(P)) \overset{i_3}{\hookrightarrow} \mathcal{R}^{2r}(P)) \overset{i_4}{\hookrightarrow} \mathcal{C}^{4r}(P),$$

then $j_1 = i_2 \circ i_1$, and $j_2 = i_4 \circ i_3$ and $\mathsf{H}_1^{r,2r}(\mathcal{R}(P)) = image\ (\iota_*)$ where $\iota_* : \mathsf{H}_1(\mathcal{R}^r(P)) \to \mathsf{H}_1(\mathcal{R}^{2r}(P))$ is induced by the inclusion $\iota = i_3 \circ i_2$.

PROOF. Based on Proposition 3.3, it can be proved by following the idea in [8] of intertwined Čech and Rips complexes. □

By definition the set of edges in $\mathcal{C}^r(P)$ is same as the set of edges in $\mathcal{R}^r(P)$. This means a set of loops in $\mathcal{R}^r(P)$ also forms a set of loops in $\mathcal{C}^r(P)$. In light of Proposition 3.4, this implies:

Proposition 3.5 *Let $P \subset M$ be an ε-sample and $4\varepsilon \leq r \leq \frac{1}{2}\sqrt{\frac{3}{5}}\rho(M)$. Then $\mathsf{H}_1^{r,2r}(\mathcal{R}(P))$ and $\mathsf{H}_1(M)$ are isomorphic and a basis for $\mathsf{H}_1^{r,2r}(\mathcal{R}(P))$ is shortest if and only if it is shortest for $\mathsf{H}_1(\mathcal{C}^r(P))$.*

PROOF. From Proposition 3.3 and Proposition 3.4, we have the following isomorphisms:

$$\mathsf{H}_1^{r,2r}(\mathcal{R}(P)) \approx \mathsf{H}_1(\mathcal{C}^r(P)) \approx \mathsf{H}_1(M).$$

Let $A = \{a_1, \cdots, a_k\}$ be a shortest basis for $\mathsf{H}_1^{r,2r}(\mathcal{R}(P))$. Each a_i is a loop in $\mathcal{R}^r(P)$ and hence in $\mathcal{C}^r(P)$. Obviously A is a basis of $\mathsf{H}_1(\mathcal{C}^r(P))$ as the inclusion map from $\mathcal{C}^r(P)$ to $\mathcal{R}^r(P)$ induces a homomorphism. Thus, a shortest basis for $\mathsf{H}_1(\mathcal{C}^r(P))$ must be no longer than that of $\mathsf{H}_1^{r,2r}(\mathcal{R}(P))$. Similarly if $A = \{a_1, \cdots, a_k\}$ is a shortest basis of $\mathsf{H}_1(\mathcal{C}^r(P))$, then each a_i must be in $\mathcal{R}^r(P)$ and survive in $\mathcal{R}^{2r}(P)$ as it must survive in $\mathcal{C}^{4r}(P)$. Thus A is a basis for $\mathsf{H}_1^{r,2r}(\mathcal{R}(P))$ and hence a shortest basis of $\mathsf{H}_1^{r,2r}(\mathcal{R}(P))$ is no longer than that of $\mathsf{H}_1(\mathcal{C}^r(P))$. This proves the proposition. □

3.2 Bounding the lengths

Our idea is to argue that a shortest basis of $\mathsf{H}_1(\mathcal{C}^r(P))$ can be pulled back to a basis of $\mathsf{H}_1(M)$ by the map h of Proposition 3.3. We argue that the lengths of the generators cannot change too much in the process.

Let g be any closed curve in M. Following [3], we define a procedure to approximate g by a loop $\hat{g}$ in the 1-skeleton of $\mathcal{C}^r(P)$. This procedure called *Decomposition method* is not part of our algorithm, but is used in our argument about length approximations of loops in M.

Decomposition method.

If $\ell = \text{Len}(g) > r - 2\varepsilon > 0$, we can write $\ell = \ell_0 + (\ell_1 + \ell_1 + \ldots + \ell_1) + \ell_0$ where $\ell_1 = r - 2\varepsilon$ and $r - 2\varepsilon > \ell_0 \geq (r - 2\varepsilon)/2$. Starting from an arbitrary point, say x, split g into pieces whose lengths coincide with the decomposition of ℓ. This produces a sequence of points $x = x_0, x_1, \ldots, x_m = x$ along g which divide it according to the lengths constraints. Because of our sampling condition, each point x_i has a point $p_i \in P$ within ε distance. We define a loop $\hat{g} = \{p_0 p_1 \ldots p_m\}$ with consecutive points joined by line segments. Proposition 3.6 shows that $\hat{g}$ resides in the 1-skeleton of $\mathcal{C}^r(P)$.

Proposition 3.6 *Given a closed curve g on M with* $\text{Len}(g) > r - 2\varepsilon > 0$, Decomposition method *finds a loop $\hat{g}$ from the 1-skeleton of $\mathcal{C}^r(P)$ such that:* $\text{Len}(\hat{g}) \leq \frac{r}{r-2\varepsilon}\text{Len}(g)$.

PROOF. From the construction and sampling condition, it follows that, for $1 \leq i \leq m - 2$,

$$\begin{aligned} d(p_i, p_{i+1}) &\leq d(x_i, p_i) + d(x_i, x_{i+1}) + d(x_{i+1}, p_{i+1}) \\ &< 2\varepsilon + \ell_1 = r = \frac{r}{(r - 2\varepsilon)}\ell_1 \end{aligned}$$

Similarly,

$$d(p_0, p_1) \leq \frac{r}{r - 2\varepsilon}\ell_0 \text{ and } d(p_{m-1}, p_0) \leq \frac{r}{r - 2\varepsilon}\ell_0.$$

Since $\frac{r}{r-2\varepsilon}\ell_0 < r$, each edge $p_i p_{i+1}$ belongs to $\mathcal{C}^r(P)$. Therefore, we obtain a loop $\hat{g} = p_0 p_1 \ldots p_m$ in the 1-skeleton of $\mathcal{C}^r(P)$ whose length satisfies:

$$\text{Len}(\hat{g}) = \Sigma_{i=0}^{m-1} d(p_i, p_{i+1}) \leq \frac{r}{r - 2\varepsilon}\text{Len}(g).$$

□

Consider a basis of $\mathsf{H}_1(M)$ where each generator is a closed geodesic on M. For a smooth, compact manifold such a basis always exists by a well known result in differential geometry [18]. Let $G = \{g_1, \ldots, g_k\}$ be this set of geodesic loops. By Proposition 3.6, we claim that there is a set of loops $\hat{G} = \{\hat{g}_1, \ldots, \hat{g}_k\}$ in $\mathcal{C}^r(P)$ whose length is within a small factor of the length of G. However, we need to show that $\hat{G}$ indeed generates $\mathsf{H}_1(\mathcal{C}^r(P))$. We show this by mapping each $\hat{g}_j \in \hat{G}$ to M by the homotopy equivalence h (Proposition 3.3) and arguing that $[h(\hat{g}_j)] = [g_j]$ in $\mathsf{H}_1(M)$. Since h is a homotopy equivalence map, it follows that the isomorphism $h^* : \mathsf{H}_1(\mathcal{C}^r(P)) \to \mathsf{H}_1(M)$ maps the class $[\hat{g}_j]$ to $[g_j]$. This implies that $\hat{G}$ generates $\mathsf{H}_1(\mathcal{C}^r(P))$.

To prove that $h(\hat{g}_j)$ is a representative of the class $[g_j]$, we consider a tubular neighborhood of g_j of radius r which is smaller than the convexity radius $\rho_c(M)$. Then, we show that each segment $p_i p_{i+1}$ of $\hat{g}_j$ is mapped to a curve $h(p_i p_{i+1})$ which lies within this tubular neighborhood. Because of this containment, $h(p_i p_{i+1})$ must be homotopic to a geodesic segment of g_j. All these homotopies together provide a homotopy between $h(g_j)$ and g_j. First we show that the tubular neighborhood of a segment of g_j that we consider is indeed simply connected.

Proposition 3.7 *Let $\gamma = \gamma(p, q)$ be a minimizing geodesic between two points $p, q \in M$. Consider its tubular neighborhood $\text{Tub}_s(\gamma)$ on M that consists of the points on M within a geodesic distance s from γ, i.e., $\text{Tub}_s(\gamma) = \{x \in M : \min_{y \in \gamma} d_M(x, y) < s\}$. Then if $s < \rho_c(M)$, $\text{Tub}_s(\gamma)$ is contractible, in particular, $\text{Tub}_s(\gamma)$ is simply connected.*

PROOF. We show that $\text{Tub}_s(\gamma)$ deformation retracts to γ. For any point $x \in \text{Tub}_s(\gamma)$, consider an open geodesic ball B of radius s. We claim that $\gamma \cap B$ has a unique point x_m which is at a minimum geodesic distance from x. Suppose not, that is, there is another minimum x'_m. The geodesic segement $\gamma(x_m, x'_m)$ on γ goes outside the open geodesic ball $B' = B_M(x, d_M(x, x_m))$. Since $s < \rho_c(M)$, B' has a radius less than the convexity radius. It follows that there is a unique minimizing geodesic between x_m and x'_m lying in B'. Then, we have two distinct minimizing geodesics between x_m and x'_m, one lying in B' and another going outside B' though both of which lie in B. This is impossible since B also has a radius less than the convexity radius.

Consider the retraction map $t : \text{Tub}_s(\gamma) \to \gamma$ where $t(x) = x_m$. One can construct a deformation retraction that deforms the identity on $\text{Tub}_s(\gamma)$ to t by moving each point x along the minimizing geodesic path that connect x to x_m in γ. □

Proposition 3.8 *Let $P \subset M$ be an ε-sample and $4\varepsilon \leq r \leq \min\{\frac{1}{2}\rho(M), \rho_c(M)\}$. If $\hat{g}$ is the loop on $\mathcal{C}^r(P)$ constructed from a geodesic loop g in M by* Decomposition method, *then $[h(\hat{g})] = [g]$ where h is the homotopy equivalence defined in Proposition 3.3.*

PROOF. Since g is a geodesic loop, it follows from standard results in differential geometry [18] that $\text{Len}(g) > 2\rho_c(M)$. Thus $\hat{g}$ can be constructed from a geodesic loop g using *Decomposition method*. Each vertex p_i of $\hat{g}$ is within an ε Euclidean distance from the point x_i in g. Next, notice that, since $\mathcal{C}^r(P)$ uses balls of radius $r/2$, the stated range of r satisfies the condition of Proposition 3.3.

By Proposition 3.3, for any point y on the segment p_ip_{i+1}, $h(y)$ is within $r/2$ Euclidean distance to either p_i or p_{i+1}. This implies that $h(y)$ is within $r/2+\varepsilon$ Euclidean distance, and hence, by Proposition 1.2, within r geodesic distance to either x_i or x_{i+1}. In addition, since the sub-curve of the geodesic loop g between x_i and x_{i+1}, denoted $\gamma(x_i, x_{i+1})$, is of length $\ell_1 = r - 2\varepsilon < \rho_c(M)$, $\gamma(x_i, x_{i+1})$ is a minimizing geodesic between x_i and x_{i+1}. Therefore $h(p_ip_{i+1}) \in \mathrm{Tub}_r(\gamma(x_i, x_{i+1}))$ In particular, there are minimizing geodesics $\gamma(x_i, h(p_i))$ and $\gamma(x_{i+1}, h(p_{i+1}))$ that reside in $\mathrm{Tub}_r(\gamma(x_i, x_{i+1}))$.

Consider the loop formed by the three geodesic segments $\gamma(x_i, x_{i+1})$, $\gamma(x_i, h(p_i))$, $\gamma(x_{i+1}, h(p_{i+1}))$, and the curve $h(p_ip_{i+1})$. From Proposition 3.7, this cycle is contractible in M as it resides in $\mathrm{Tub}_r(\gamma(x_i, x_{i+1}))$. In fact, there is a homotopy H_i that takes $h(p_ip_{i+1})$ to $\gamma(x_i, x_{i+1})$ while H_i keeps $h(p_i)$ and $h(p_{i+1})$ on the geodesics $\gamma(x_i, p_i)$ and $\gamma(x_{i+1}, p_{i+1})$ respectively. We can combine all homotopies H_i for $0 \le i \le m$ to define a homotopy between $h(\hat{g})$ and g. It follows that $[h(\hat{g})] = [g]$. □

Proposition 3.9 *Let $P \subset M$ be an ε-sample and $4\varepsilon \le r \le \min\{\frac{1}{2}\rho(M), \rho_c(M)\}$. If $G = \{g_1, \ldots, g_k\}$ and $G' = \{g_1', \ldots, g_k'\}$ are the generators of a shortest basis of $\mathsf{H}_1(M)$ and $\mathsf{H}_1(\mathcal{C}^r(P))$ respectively, then we have* $\mathrm{Len}(G') \le (1 + \frac{4\varepsilon}{r})\mathrm{Len}(G)$.

PROOF. It is obvious that any g_i must be a geodesic loop. Let $\hat{g}_i$ be the loop constructed by *Decomposition method* in the 1-skeleton of $\mathcal{C}^r(P)$. Thus, we have a set $\hat{G} = \{\hat{g}_1, \cdots, \hat{g}_k\}$. By Proposition 3.8, there is a homotopy equivalence $h : \mathcal{C}^r(P) \to M$ so that $[h(\hat{g}_j)] = [g_i]$, which means that $\hat{G}$ is also a basis of $\mathsf{H}_1(\mathcal{C}^r(P))$. By Proposition 3.6,

$$\mathrm{Len}(G') \le \mathrm{Len}(\hat{G}) \le \frac{r}{r - 2\varepsilon}\mathrm{Len}(G) \le (1 + \frac{4\varepsilon}{r})\mathrm{Len}(G).$$

□

We now consider the opposite direction, and provide a lower bound for the total length of a shortest basis of $\mathsf{H}_1(\mathcal{C}^r(P))$ in terms of the length of a shortest basis of $\mathsf{H}_1(M)$.

Proposition 3.10 *Let $P \subset M$ be an ε-sample and $4\varepsilon \le r \le \min\{\frac{1}{2}\rho(M), \rho_c(M)\}$. Let G and G' be defined as in Proposition 3.9. We have* $\mathrm{Len}G \le (1 + \frac{4r^2}{3\rho^2(M)})\mathrm{Len}(G')$. *Moreover, there exists a map $h\colon G' \to M$ so that $h(G')$ is a basis of $\mathsf{H}_1(M)$ and the Hausdorff distance between each loop $g \in G'$ and $h(g')$ is at most $\frac{r}{2}$.*

PROOF. We construct a set of loops in M from G'. First, we show that the length of these loops is at most $(1 + \frac{4r^2}{3\rho^2(M)})$ times the length of G'. Next, we show that the constructed loops generate $\mathsf{H}_1(M)$.

For each loop $g' \in G'$, we construct $\bar{g}$ as follows. The vertices and edges of g' are the vertices and edges of $\mathcal{C}^r(P)$. For an edge $e = pq \in g'$, $p, q \in P$ thus $p, q \in M$. We connect p and q by a minimizing geodesic $\gamma(p, q)$ on M, and map e to this geodesic. Mapping each edge in g' on M, we obtain $\bar{g}$. Thus we obtain a set $\bar{G} = \{\bar{g}_1, \cdots, \bar{g}_k\}$. By Proposition 1.2, $d_M(p, q) \le (1 + \frac{4d^2(p,q)}{3\rho^2(M)})d(p, q) \le (1 + \frac{4r^2}{3\rho^2(M)})d(p, q)$. Hence the length bound follows.

We now show that the set $\bar{G}$ is a basis for M. Consider mapping $g_j' \in G'$ to M by the equivalence map h. Each edge $e = pq \in g_j'$ is mapped to a curve $h(pq)$. From Proposition 3.3, we have that $h(p) = p$ and $h(q) = q$ and each point of $h(pq)$ is within $r/2$ Euclidean distance and hence r geodesic distance to either p or q. This implies that $h(pq) \subset \mathrm{Tub}_r(\gamma(p, q))$. Then, by using similar argument as in Proposition 3.7, we claim that $\gamma(p, q)$ and $h(pq)$ are homotopic. Combining all homotopies for each edge of g_j', we get that $h(g_j')$ is homotopic to $\bar{g}_j$. Since h is a homotopy equivalence, $h(G')$ and hence $\bar{G} = \{\bar{g}_1, \ldots, \bar{g}_k\}$ are a basis of $\mathsf{H}_1(M)$. Therefore,

$$\mathrm{Len}(G) \le \mathrm{Len}(\bar{G}) \le (1 + \frac{4r^2}{3\rho^2(M)})\mathrm{Len}(G').$$

The loops in $h(G')$ form a basis of $\mathsf{H}_1(M)$ and each loop $g' \in G'$ has a Hausdorff distance of $r/2$ with $h(g')$ satisfying the last claim. □

Thanks to Proposition 3.5, shortest bases in $\mathcal{C}^r(P)$ and $\mathsf{H}_1^{r,2r}(\mathcal{R}(P))$ are same for an appropriate range of r.

Theorem 3.11 *Let $P \subset M$ be an ε-sample and r be a real positive with $4\varepsilon \le r \le \min\{\frac{1}{2}\sqrt{\frac{3}{5}}\rho(M), \rho_c(M)\}$. Let G and G' be a shortest basis of $\mathsf{H}_1(M)$ and $\mathsf{H}_1^{r,2r}(\mathcal{R}(P))$ respectively. We have*

i. $\frac{1}{1+\frac{4r^2}{3\rho^2(M)}}\mathrm{Len}(G) \le \mathrm{Len}(G') \le (1 + \frac{4\varepsilon}{r})\mathrm{Len}(G)$.

ii. There is a map $h : G' \to M$ so that $h(G')$ is a basis of $\mathsf{H}_1(M)$ and the Hausdorff distance between the underlying space of g' and $h(g')$ is at most $r/2$ for each $g' \in G'$.

Theorem 1.3 follows from Theorem 3.11, Theorem 2.1, and the time complexity analysis in section 2.3.

4. CONCLUSIONS

We have given a polynomial time algorithm for approximating a shortest basis of the first homology group of a smooth manifold from a point data. We have also presented an algorithm to compute a shortest basis for the first homology of any finite simplicial complex.

We use Rips complexes for computations and use Čech complexes for analysis. One may observe that Čech complexes can be used directly in the algorithm. Since we know that $\mathcal{C}^r(P)$ is homotopy equivalent to M for an appropriate range of r, we can compute a shortest basis for $\mathsf{H}_1(\mathcal{C}^r(P))$ which can be shown to approximate a shortest basis for $\mathsf{H}_1(M)$ using our analysis. In technical terms, this will get rid of the weighting in step 1 and also step 4 of SHORTLOOP algorithm, and make Theorem 2.1 and Proposition 3.5 redundant. Although the time complexity does not get affected in the worst-case sense, computing the triangles for Čech complexes becomes harder numerically in high dimensions than those for the Rips complexes. This is why we chose to describe an algorithm using the Rips complexes.

Computing a shortest basis for other homology groups under $\mathbb{Z}_2$ has been shown to be NP-hard by Chen and Freedman [11]. A related topic that has been addressed in the literature is the problem of homology localization which asks for computing a shortest cycle in a given homology class. The problem has been shown to be NP-hard for a large number of cases [6, 11] under $\mathbb{Z}_2$ coefficient. Interestingly, it is shown in [16] that the problem is polynomial time solvable for a class of spaces when the homology is defined with $\mathbb{Z}$ instead of $\mathbb{Z}_2$. Does similar disparity exist for the shortest basis problem between different coefficient rings?

Acknowledgments. We acknowledge the helpful comments of Steve Oudot on an earlier draft of this paper. We also acknowledge

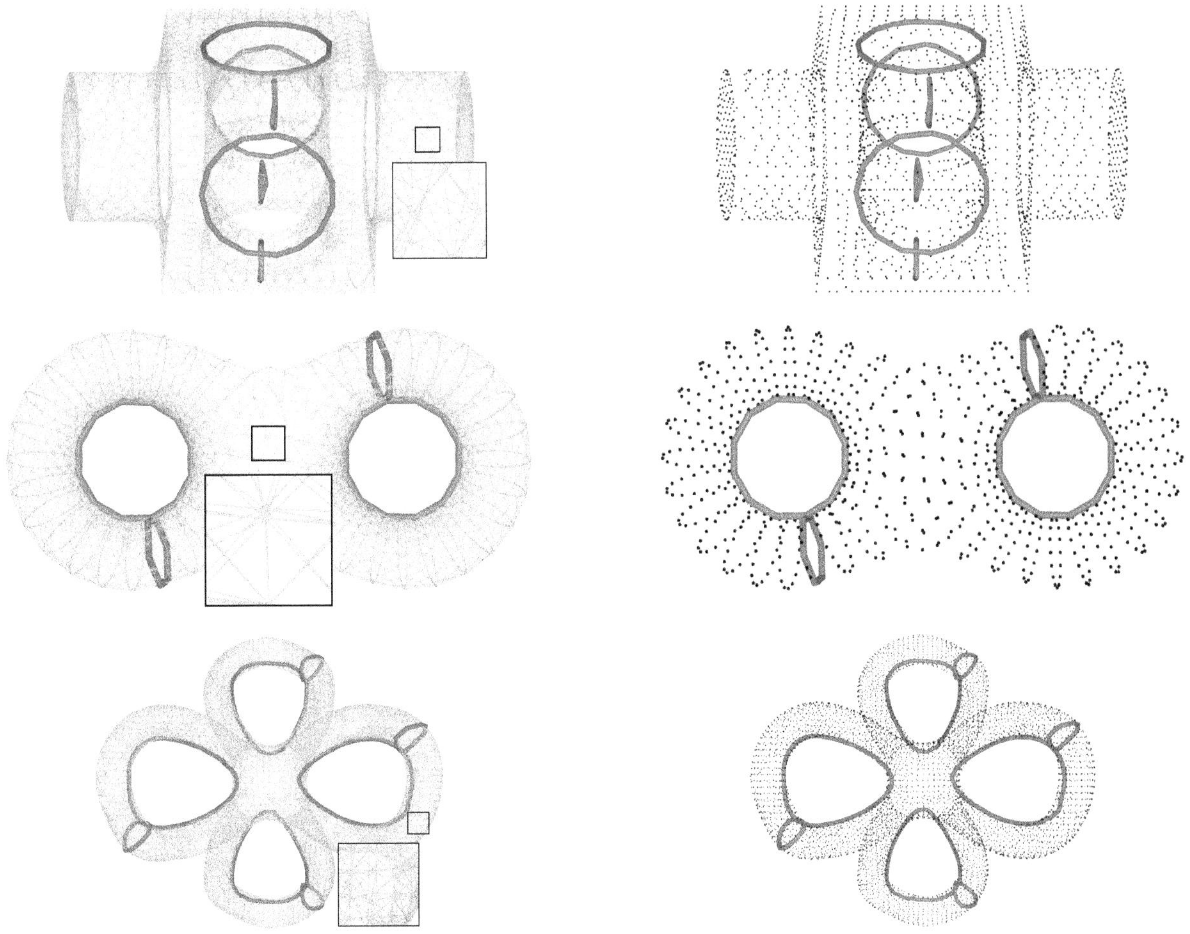

Figure 1: Loops in a shortest homology basis computed in Rips complexes (left column) constructed out of point data (right column).

Oleksiy Busaryev who implemented SHORTLOOP and produced the pictures in Figure 1. Tamal Dey acknowledges the support of NSF grants CCF-0830467 and CCF-0915996, Jian Sun acknowledges the support of NSF grant ITR 0205671 and DARPA grant HR0011-05-1-0007, and Yusu Wang acknowledges the support of NSF grants CCF-0747082 and DBI-0750891 .

5. REFERENCES

[1] N. Amenta and M. Bern. Surface reconstruction by Voronoi filtering. *Discrete Comput. Geom.* **22** (1999), 481–504.

[2] M. Belkin, J. Sun, and Y. Wang. Discrete Laplace operator for meshed surfaces. *24th. Ann. Sympos. Comput. Geom.* (2008), 278–287.

[3] M. Bernstein, V. de Silva, J. Langford, and J. Tenenbaum. Graph approximations to geodesics on embedded manifolds. *Tech Report*, Dept. Psychology, Stanford University, USA, 2000. Available at http://isomap.stanford.edu/BdSLT.pdf

[4] J.-D. Boissonnat, L. J. Guibas, and S. Y. Oudot. Manifold reconstruction in arbitrary dimensions using witness complexes. *Proc. 23rd Ann. Sympos. Comput. Geom.* (2007), 194–203.

[5] E. W. Chambers, J. Erickson, and A. Nayyeri. Homology flows, cohomology cuts. *41st Ann. ACM Sympos. Theory Comput.* (2009), 273–282.

[6] E. W. Chambers, J. Erickson, and A. Nayyeri. Minimum cuts and shortest homologous cycles. *25th Ann. Sympos. Comput. Geom.* (2009), 377–385.

[7] F. Chazal and A. Lieutier. Topology guaranteeing manifold reconstruction using distance function to noisy data. *Proc. 22nd Ann. Sympos. Comput. Geom.* (2006), 112–118.

[8] F. Chazal and S. Oudot. Towards persistence-based reconstruction in Euclidean spaces. *Proc. 24th Ann. Sympos. Comput. Geom.* (2008), 232–241.

[9] C. Chen and D. Freedman. Measuring and localizing homology classes. arXiv:0705.3061v2[cs.CG] (2007).

[10] C. Chen and D. Freedman. Quantifying homology classes. *Proc. 25th Ann. Sympos. Theoretical Aspects Comput. Sci.* (2009), 168–190.

[11] C. Chen and D. Freedman. Hardness results for homology localization. *ACM/SIAM Sympos. Discrete Algorithms* (2010), 1594–1604.

[12] S.-W. Cheng, T. K. Dey, and E. A. Ramos. Manifold reconstruction from point samples. *Proc. 16th Sympos. Discrete Algorithms* (2005), 1018–1027.

[13] D. Cohen-Steiner, H. Edelsbrunner, and J. Harer. Stability of persistence diagrams. *Discrete Comput. Geom.* **37** (2007), 103-120.

[14] D. Cohen-Steiner, H. Edelsbrunner, and D. Morozov. Vines

and vineyards by updating persistence in linear time. *Proc. 22nd Ann. Sympos. Comput. Geom.* (2006), 119–134.

[15] É. Colin de Verdière and J. Erickson. Tightening non-simple paths and cycles on surfaces. *Proc. ACM-SIAM Sympos. Discrete Algorithms* (2006), 192–201.

[16] T. K. Dey, A. Hirani, and B. Krishnamoorthy. Optimal homologous cycles, total unimodularity, and linear programming. *Proc. 42nd ACM Sympos. Theory Computing* (2010), to appear.

[17] T. K. Dey and K. Li. Cut locus and topology from surface point data. *25th Ann. Sympos. Comput. Geom.*(2009), 125–134.

[18] M. P. do Carmo. Riemannian geometry. Birkhäuser, Boston, 1992.

[19] H. Edelsbrunner, D. Letscher, and A. Zomorodian. Topological persistence and simplification. *Discrete Comput. Geom.* **28** (2002), 511–533.

[20] J. Erickson and K. Whittlesey. Greedy optimal homotopy and homology generators. *Proc. ACM-SIAM Sympos. Discrete Algorithms* (2005), 1038–1046.

[21] A. Hatcher. Algebraic Topology. Cambridge U. Press, New York, 2002.

[22] I. T. Jollife. Principal Component Analysis. Springer series in statistics, Springer, NY, 2002.

[23] J. Leray. Sur la forme des espaces topologiques et sur les points fixes des représentations. *J. Math. Pure Appl.* **24** (1945), 95–167.

[24] P. Niyogi, S. Smale, and S. Weinberger. Finding the homology of submanifolds with high confidence from random samples. *Discrete Comput. Geom.* **39** (2008), 419–441.

[25] J. B. Tenenbaum, V. de Silva, and J. C. Langford. A global geometric framework for nonlinear dimensionality reduction. *Science* **290** (2000), 2319–2323.

[26] A. Zomorodian and G. Carlsson. Computing persistent homology. *Discrete Comput. Geom.* **33** (2005), 249–274.

Appendix

Proof of Proposition 3.2.

PROOF. The proof is based on that of Nerve Lemma in [21] (Chapter 4.G). Let Γ be the barycentric subdivision of $\mathcal{C}^{2r}(P)$. Taking the definitions of the maps Δp, Δq, and the space ΔP^r from Hatcher [21], we consider the following sequence

$$\mathcal{C}^{2r}(P) \overset{h}{\leftrightarrow} \Gamma \underset{\Delta p}{\overset{\Delta q}{\rightleftarrows}} \Delta P^r \overset{\pi}{\to} P^r. \tag{1}$$

We prove the proposition by showing $f = \pi \circ \Delta q \circ h$ which is a homotopy equivalence. We first introduce the concept of mapping cylinder. For a map $f : X \to Y$, the mapping cylinder M_f is the quotient space of the disjoint union $(X \times I) \bigsqcup Y$ with $(x, 1)$ identified with $f(x) \in Y$, denoted $M_f = X \bigsqcup_f Y$, see Figure 2(a).

It is obvious that M_f deformation retracts to Y. It is also well-known that f is a homotopy equivalence map if and only if M_f deformation retracts to X, see Figure 2(b), where the map $g = e_X \circ i_Y$ is a homotopy equivalence map from Y to X.

We are now ready to explain each map in the composition of the map f. Γ is the barycentric subdivision of $\mathcal{C}^{2r}(P)$. Thus h is an identity map between the underlying spaces of $\mathcal{C}^{2r}(P)$ and Γ. Index the points in $P = \{p_i\}_{i=1}^{m}$ arbitrarily. Let $B_i = B(p_i, r)$. To facilitate the argument, label the vertices in Γ using B_i's and

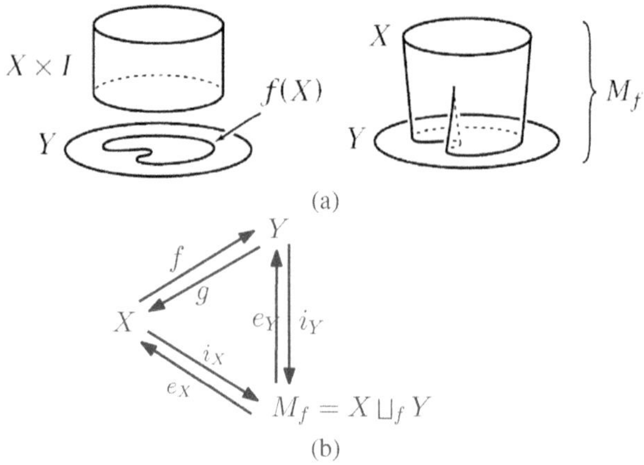

Figure 2: (a) the mapping cylinder $M_f = X \bigsqcup_f Y$ (courtesy of Hatcher [21]); (b) the maps among X, Y and M_f

their finite intersections, see Figure 3. Each edge (one simplex) in Γ is associated with an inclusion map, which induces a sequence of inclusion maps over a simplex of any dimension in Γ.

ΔP^r can be realized using the concept of mapping cylinder, see the top right most picture in Figure 3. The sequence of inclusion maps associated with each simplex in Γ

$$\begin{aligned}(B_{i_0} \cap \cdots \cap B_{i_n}) &\hookrightarrow (B_{i_0} \cap \cdots \cap B_{i_{n-1}}) \\ &\hookrightarrow \cdots \hookrightarrow (B_{i_0} \cap \cdots \cap B_{i_{n-k}}),\end{aligned}$$

induces an iterated mapping cylinder. ΔP^r is obtained by gluing these iterated mapping cylinders over all simplices in Γ, see [21] for details. There is a canonical projection $\Delta p : \Delta P^r \to \Gamma$ induced by projecting each finite intersection to its corresponding vertex in Γ. Consider the mapping cylinder $M_{\Delta p}$. The Nerve Lemma is proved in [21] by showing $M_{\Delta p}$ deformation retracts to ΔP^r. In fact, the deformation retraction described in [21] maps a simplex $\Delta^k \in \Gamma$ to the part of ΔP^r defined over the same Δ^k, namely $\Delta q = e_{\Delta P^r} \circ i_\Gamma$ is a homotopy equivalence and maps a simplex $\Delta^k \in \Gamma$ into the iterated mapping cylinder defined by the sequence of inclusion map associated with Δ^k.

On the other hand, ΔP^r can also be considered as the quotient space of the disjoint union of all the products $B_{i_0} \cap \cdots \cap B_{i_n} \times \Delta^n$, as the subscripts range over set of $n+1$ distinct indices and any $n \geq 0$, with the identifications over the faces of Δ^n using inclusions $B_{i_0} \cap \cdots \cap B_{i_n} \hookrightarrow B_{i_0} \cap \cdots \cap \hat{B}_{i_j} \cap \cdots \cap B_{i_n}$ where ^ means the corresponding term is missing. From this viewpoint, any point $x \in P^r$ has a fiber $\pi^{-1}(x)$ in ΔP^r defined as follows. $\pi^{-1}(x) = \{\sum_i t_i x_i\}$ where $\sum_i t_i = 1$ and $t^i \geq 0$, and x_i is a copy of x in B_i for those B_i containing x. see the bottom left most picture in Figure 3. It is easy to see that P^r can be embedded into ΔP^r as a section of ΔP^r, in particular π is a homotopy equivalence. Thus f is a homotopy equivalence.

Observe that each point y in an iterated mapping cylinder over some simplex $\Delta^k = (B_{i_0} \cap \cdots \cap B_{i_n}, \cdots, B_{i_0} \cap \cdots \cap B_{i_{n-k}})$ in Γ is in the fiber $\pi^{-1}(x)$ for some x in B_{i_0}. In other words, if Δ^k is in the closure of the star of a point $p \in P$ in Γ, then any point y in the iterated mapping cylinder over Δ^k is in the fiber of a point $x \in B(p, r)$. Now consider a simplex $\sigma \in \mathcal{C}^{2r}(P)$. Any simplex in its barycentric subdivision much be in the closure of the star of some vertex of σ. Thus σ, under the map $\Delta_q \circ h$, is mapped into the union of the iterated mapping cylinders defined over the simplices

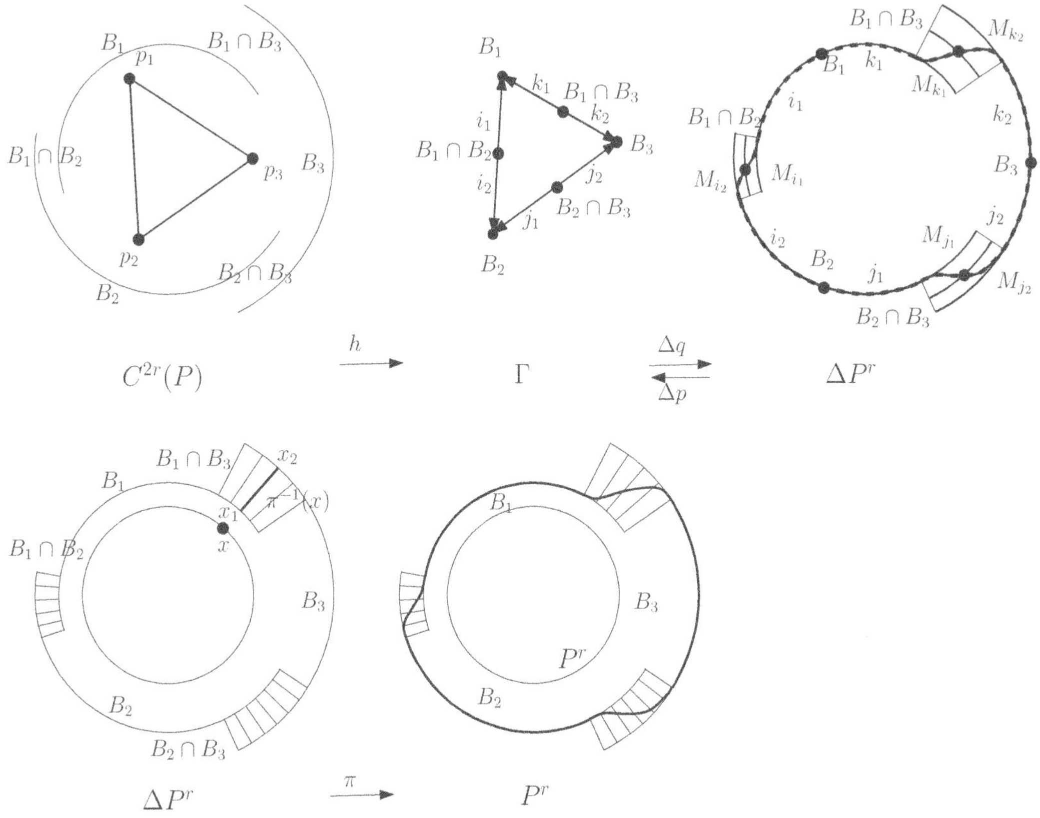

Figure 3: Illustration of the maps and the spaces involved in Eq. 1.

in the barycentric subdivision of σ, and its image, under the map π, is further mapped into $\cup_{p \in \mathrm{Vert}(\sigma)} B(p, r)$.

In addition, it is clear that the map f can fix each vertex in $\mathcal{C}^{2r}(P)$. This proves the proposition. $\square$

A Traveller's Problem

Florian Berger
berger@cs.uni-bonn.de

Rolf Klein
rolf.klein@uni-bonn.de

University of Bonn
Institute of Computer Science I
D-53117 Bonn, Germany

ABSTRACT

A traveller is planning a tour from some start position, s, to a goal position g in d-dimensional space. Transportation is provided by n carriers. Each carrier is a convex object that results from intersecting finitely many closed linear subspaces; it moves at constant speed along a line. Different carriers may be assigned different velocity vectors. While using carrier C, the traveller can walk at innate speed $v \geq 0$ in any direction, like a passenger on board a vessel. Whenever his current position on C is simultaneously contained in some other carrier C', the traveller can change from C to C', and continue his tour by C'.

Given initial positions of the carriers and of s and g, is the traveller able to reach g starting from s? If so, what minimum travel time can be achieved?

We provide the following answers. For a situation similar to the "Frogger" game, where the traveller has to cross a river on which n consecutive rectangular barges move at m different speeds, we provide an $O(n \log m)$ solution. In dimension 8 and higher, Traveller's Problem is undecidable, even for innate speed zero. An interesting case is in dimension 2. We prove that the problem is NP-hard, even if all carriers are vertical line segments. It turns out that an s-to-g path of finite duration may require an infinite number of carrier changes. Despite this difficulty, we can show that the two-dimensional problem is decidable. In addition, we provide a pseudo-polynomial approximation algorithm.

Categories and Subject Descriptors

F.2.2 [**Analysis of Algorithms and Problem Complexity**]: Nonnumerical Algorithms and Problems—*geometrical problems and computations*

General Terms

Algorithms, Theory

Keywords

Affine mappings, computational geometry, continuous Dijkstra, frogger, motion planning, NP-hardness, partition, pseudo-polynomial approximation, undecidability

1. INTRODUCTION

Motion planning in dynamic environments is one of the challenging problems in computational geometry. A classical, and important question is how to avoid collision with obstacles that move in time; see [2] for an example. In this paper we take a different view and consider a situation where moving objects can be used as a means of transportation.

A *carrier* in dimension d is a non-empty intersection of finitely many closed linear subspaces. Thus, in dimension 2, a carrier can be a point, a line segment, a half-line, a line, a possibly unbounded convex polygon, or the plane itself. Each carrier is assigned its own velocity vector, causing it to move linearly at constant speed. The *traveller* is modeled as a point, p. At time $t = 0$, his journey begins at a start point, s, which is located on some carrier C_s. Like a passenger on board a cruiser, traveller p will be moved along with C_s. In addition, he can walk on C_s (and any other carrier) at maximum speed v, called *innate speed* for short, as long as he does not fall off. If, at some time $t > 0$, traveller p is located in the intersection of C_s and some other carrier, C, he may decide to change from C_s to C, and continue his journey by C from time t on. In this model, the carrier change does not require any time duration > 0. The traveller's ultimate goal is to reach a goal point, g, located on some carrier C_g.

We observe that our definition of changing the carrier allows for the following implementations. First, the traveller can change if located at some point where two carriers touch each other, since such touch point belongs to either carrier. Second, we could introduce a special carrier C_0 that equals the whole plane and does not move. Then the traveller could, in our model, get off his current carrier anytime and wait for another carrier to arrive or, if $v > 0$, walk some distance in the plane, and board another carrier. In this model, start point s and goal point g could also be located in the plane, instead of being fixed to moving carriers.

In general it is not clear if g can be reached from s at all. Thus, we are interested in the following questions.

- Given initial positions for the carriers at time $t = 0$, is it possible for the traveller to reach g when starting from s?

- If so, what is the quickest way to get there, using only the carriers for transportation?

This model could be generalized in many ways. Instead of the quickest way, one could ask for the journey that minimizes the traveller's walking. Using a carrier could incur a cost; then a cheapest s-to-g path would be of interest. Moreover, there is some affinity to the highway systems on which city Voronoi diagrams [1, 5, 3] are based. We could model a straight, unbounded highway lane by a line that moves in axial direction. The same holds for navigation in currents near the shore [6]. However, our model differs from these settings in that carriers can move in arbitrary directions, independent of their shapes.

In this paper, we restrict ourselves to the simple model introduced above, and study the question of finding a quickest connection. A formal problem description is given in Section 2. As a warm-up example, we consider, in Section 3, a special case that resembles the well-known "Frogger" game. Our traveller wants to cross a river whose banks are modeled by two static lines containing s and g. The only other carriers are n rectangular barges that move up- or downstream at m different speeds, such that tracks of neighboring barges touch; see Figure 1. As with Frogger, the traveller can move on each carrier at maximum L_1 speed v. Using the continuous Dijkstra paradigm [9], we give an algorithm with running time $O(n \log m)$ that finds the quickest path from s to g (or establishes that no such path exists).

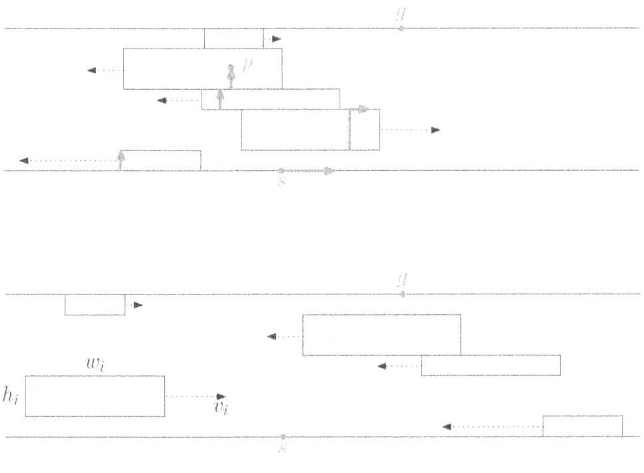

Figure 1: Barges on a river.

The ease of this solution is owed to the special situation. In Section 4 we show that the general Traveller's Problem is undecidable in dimension 8 or higher, employing a recent result on affine mappings [4].

Of all smaller dimensions, the case of the Euclidean plane is of particular interest. In Section 5 we provide the following results. First, we show the problem to be NP-hard, even if all carriers are vertical line segments. Not even a constant factor approximation is possible, unless P=NP.

Bounding the problem's complexity from above is made difficult by the following fact. Even for small problem instances an infinite number of carrier changes may be necessary to reach g in finite time; see Figure 5 for an example. Despite this complication, we can show that, in dimension two, Traveller's Problem is decidable if carriers are lines or line segments.

By discretising time and space, we finally provide a pseudo-polynomial approximation algorithm for the case of bounded, but otherwise arbitrary, convex carriers in the plane. To this end, we relax our original model by increasing the traveller's innate speed by ε and the carriers' extensions in all directions by μ. If an s-to-g path of duration $\leq W$ exists in the original model, then, in the relaxed model, a slightly longer journey can be computed in time

$$O\left(n \ L\log(L) \ W \ \frac{G}{H}\right)$$

where L denotes the total number of edges of the n carriers, G equals the maximum carrier diameter squared times the maximum speed to the 5th power, and $H = \varepsilon^4\mu^3$.

2. PROBLEM DESCRIPTION

An instance of *Traveller's Problem* consists of:

- a dimension d and a metric *dist* on $\mathbb{R}^d$
- a finite set C of carriers, $|C| = n$
- for each $c \in C$, a (possibly unbounded) convex polyhedron $R_0(c)$ in $\mathbb{R}^d$ corresponding to c at time $t = 0$
- for each $c \in C$, a velocity vector d_c
- the traveller's start location s at time $t = 0$
- the goal location g at time $t = 0$ and the velocity vector d_g of the goal
- the traveller's maximum innate speed v

A *feasible traveller path* (I, f, A, g) is given by:

- a closed and bounded interval I
- a continuous map $f : I \to \mathbb{R}^d$
- a set $A \subset I$ which is countable and closed, accordingly all connected components of $I \setminus A$ are open intervals
- a map $g : I \setminus A \to C$ which is constant on each connected component of $I \setminus A$

such that:

- If (a, a') is a connected component of $I \setminus A$ and $g(t) = c \forall t \in (a, a')$, then $\forall t \in (a, a')$:
  - $dist(f(t), f(a) + (t-a)d_c) \leq (t-a)v$, and
  - $f(t) \in R_0(c) + td_c$.

For $I = [0, T]$, the path is said to connect the start location with the goal location, if $f(0) = p$ and $f(T) = g + Td_g$.

Given an instance of Traveller's Problem, the task is to find a feasible traveller path of minimum travel time T which connects the start location with the goal location (or to determine that no such path exists).

3. CROSSING A RIVER

In this Section we consider a special case of the two-dimensional Traveller's Problem with the L_1-metric as *dist*. Imagine a river whose banks are realized, in our model, as two horizontal line-shaped carriers that do not move. On the river, n rectangular barges are sailing horizontally, at individual speeds and in both directions; see Figure 1. The ith barge in bottom-up order, B_i, is of width w_i, height h_i, and speed v_i. The strips defined by B_i and B_{i+1} touch each other; B_1 and B_n touch the lower resp. the upper lines, where start point s resp. goal point g are located. The traveller cannot swim. But, as in the well-known "Frogger" game, he can walk on the barges in X- or Y-direction at maximum innate speed $v = 1$. Also, where two barges touch, he can jump from one to the next.

Starting from s at time $t = 0$, is the traveller able to reach g? If so, what is the earliest possible arrival time? Clearly, this is a special case of the Traveller's Problem defined in Section 2.

THEOREM 1. *Suppose that the n barges are running at m different speeds. Then Traveller's Problem can, in this case, be solved in time $O(n \log m)$.*

PROOF. Using the continuous Dijkstra technique [9], we compute for $i = 1, 2, \ldots, n$ the traveller's earliest possible arrival time at each point of the upper edge of B_i. By an idea of [8], this information can easily be obtained by geometric reasoning.

In XT-coordinates we define a strip, S_i, of width w_i and slope $1/v_i$, that represents the motion of B_i's upper and lower horizontal edges in T-time and X-space. In Figure 2 (i), both p and p' are mapped to the same point $p'_t = p_t$ of S_i; we reserve the prime ' to denote points on lower edges.

The point $p'_t = q_t$ in the intersection of S_i with S_{i-1} indicates that, at time t, point p' on the lower edge of B_i coincides with point q on the upper edge of B_{i-1}. If the traveller stood in q at time t, he could now change to B_i. Thanks to the L_1-movement, we may w. l. o. g. assume that his walk on B_i starts with a vertical segment that lets him arrive, at time $t + h_i$, at point p on B_i's upper edge. Then he could walk the upper edge horizontally in either direction at innate speed 1. Wedge W_i in Figure 2 (i) indicates when the points on B_i's upper edge can be reached. The slopes of W_i equal $\frac{1}{v_i - 1}$ and $\frac{1}{v_i + 1}$, since the traveller's maximum innate speed is 1. More generally, let

$$M_{i-1} := \left\{ q_t \in S_{i-1} \;\middle|\; \begin{array}{l} q \text{ belongs to upper edge of } B_{i-1} \\ \text{and is reachable at time } t \end{array} \right\}.$$

We show by induction that M_i is a convex set whose boundary edges have at most $3m$ different slopes, and how to construct M_i from M_{i-1} in time $O(\log m)$; see Figure 2 (ii) for an illustration. The case $m = 1$ is settled by Figure 2 (i) for $i = 1$ and $t = 0$.[1] Now we apply the above reasoning to M_{i-1}. First, we intersect M_{i-1} with S_i to find all possible changing points to B_i. This set is shifted by the vector $(v_i h_i, h_i)$ along S_i, to account for the vertical walk in B_i. Let N_i denote the shifted set. Each point on the upper edge of B_i can be reached vertically from below, or horizontally from some other point on the upper edge. Therefore, we form the Minkowski sum of the shifted set, N_i with the wedge W_i, in order to obtain M_i. This can be computed in time logarithmic in the number of edges of N_i. To this end, two binary searches for the slopes of W_i in the set of the slopes of the convex chain formed by the edges of N_i are done. Since for each speed v_i only edges with slopes in $\{\frac{1}{v_i-1}, \frac{1}{v_i}, \frac{1}{v_i+1}\}$ can occur, no more than $3m$ edges can appear on the convex boundary of any set considered.

If M_n is non-empty, the goal is reachable (since the traveller can walk along the far bank), and it is easy to compute his earliest arrival time. All this can be accomplished in total time $O(n \log m)$. □

If we consider the problem with *dist* as the L_2-metric instead of L_1, the curves bounding the sets M_i become curves of high degree. This prevents us from extending our above solution to the Euclidean case. However, the results of the following Sections are valid for both cases, L_1 and L_2. The presentation of the pseudo-polynomial approximation in Section 5.3 is adapted to the Euclidean case.

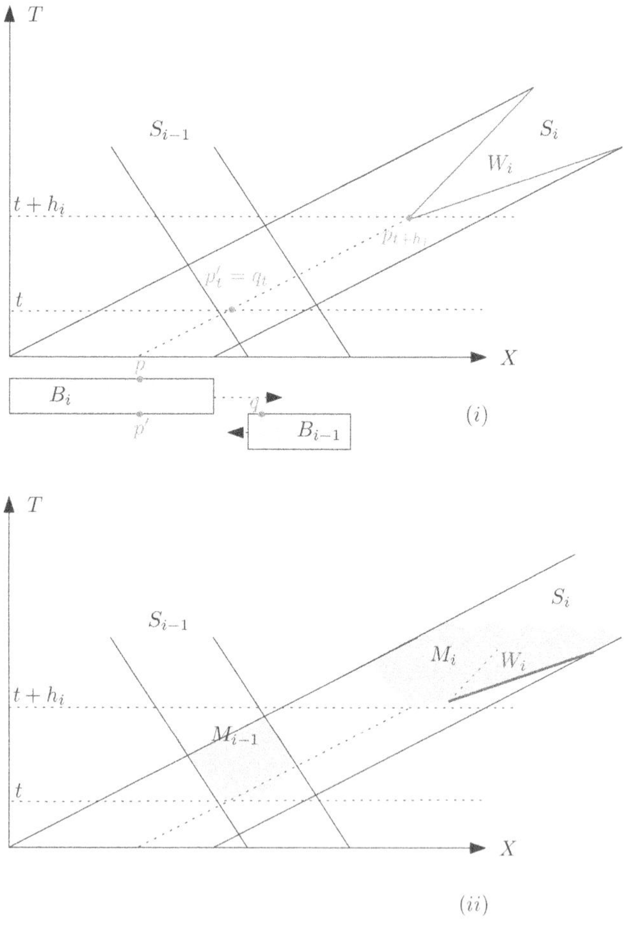

Figure 2: Changing from B_{i-1} to B_i at time t.

4. HIGHER DIMENSIONS

Now we show that Traveller's Problem is undecidable in dimension $d \geq 8$. To this end we employ the following recent result by Bell and Potapov [4]. Let us recall that a two-dimensional affine mapping over $\mathbb{Q}$ acts on (x, y) as follows.

[1] Assuming that $s = p'$ is contained in the bottom edge of B_1 at time $t = 0$. Otherwise, the apex of W_1 is located on the boundary of S_1— an even simpler case.

First, (x, y) is multiplied by a 2×2 matrix with rational coefficients, then a rational vector (v, w) is added to the result.

THEOREM 2. *The following problem is undecidable [4]. Given five affine mappings $f_1, f_2, \ldots f_5$ from $\mathbb{Q}^2$ to $\mathbb{Q}^2$ and two rational vectors $q = (x, y)$ and $q' = (x', y')$. Is there a finite product of mappings from $\{f_1, f_2, \ldots f_5\}$ that maps q to q'?*

Their elegant proof is by reduction from Post's correspondence problem, replacing letters with 2×2 matrices that form a free semigroup. Now we use this result to prove the following.

THEOREM 3. *Traveller's problem with innate speed zero is undecidable in dimension $d \geq 8$.*

PROOF. First, we demonstrate how to simulate the application of a single linear function of one variable. This function is $f(X) = a \cdot X$, where $a > 0$. Our construction uses seven unbounded carriers moving in $XYZV$-space. Only the directions of their speed vectors matter, not their lengths.

Figure 3 depicts the corresponding journey. We start with the traveller at an arbitrary point $e > 0$ on the X-axis. Our first carrier is the XY-plane itself, moving upwards. The traveller can use it to get up to the graph of the mapping $f(X) = aX$. Here he can change to the plane $\{(x, ax, z) | x, z \in \mathbb{R}\}$ that moves into direction $(0, 0, 1)$. At $Z = 1$, he can get off, and change to the third carrier—the plane $\{(x, y, 1) | x, y \in \mathbb{R}\}$ moving leftwards. It gets the traveller to $(0, ae, 1)$. At this point, he can enter dimension 4. To this end, he uses the plane $\{(0, y, 1, v) | y, v \in \mathbb{R}\}$, which moves in positive V-direction. At $(0, ae, 1, 1)$ the traveller can board the next carrier $\{(x, y, 1, 1) | x, y \in \mathbb{R}\}$ whose velocity vector equals $(1, -1, 0, 0)$. It gets him to the point $(ae, 0, 1, 1)$, where he can change to the sixth carrier, which is given by the plane $\{(x, 0, 1, v) | x, v \in \mathbb{R}\}$ moving in negative V-direction. Back to 3-space at the point $(ae, 0, 1)$, he can finally catch the plane $\{(x, 0, z) | x, z \in \mathbb{R}\}$; it moves in negative Z-direction and gets the traveller back to the X-axis, at point $ae = f(e)$.

Two observations are crucial. While the definition of carriers does depend on the coefficient a of mapping f, it works for any argument e.[2] Second, if the traveller leaves the X-axis (at some point e), then his only chance of returning to the X-axis is to ride the seven carriers the way explained above. This gets him to point $f(e)$.

Our construction generalizes to two-dimensional affine mappings $f(X_1, X_2)$. Here, we need to make sure that the traveller, after starting from some point (e, g) in the X_1X_2-plane, can return to this plane only at the point $(r, s) = f(e, g)$. This can be achieved by introducing extra dimensions, so that the computations of r and s take place in disjoint affine subspaces and, consequently, do not interfere. We can deal similarly with five such affine mappings acting independently on the X_1X_2-plane, and thus simulate the problem of Theorem 2. It turns out that dimension 8 provides us with sufficiently many disjoint affine subspaces for this purpose. □

[2]We must add three alternative carriers to deal with arguments $e < 0$.

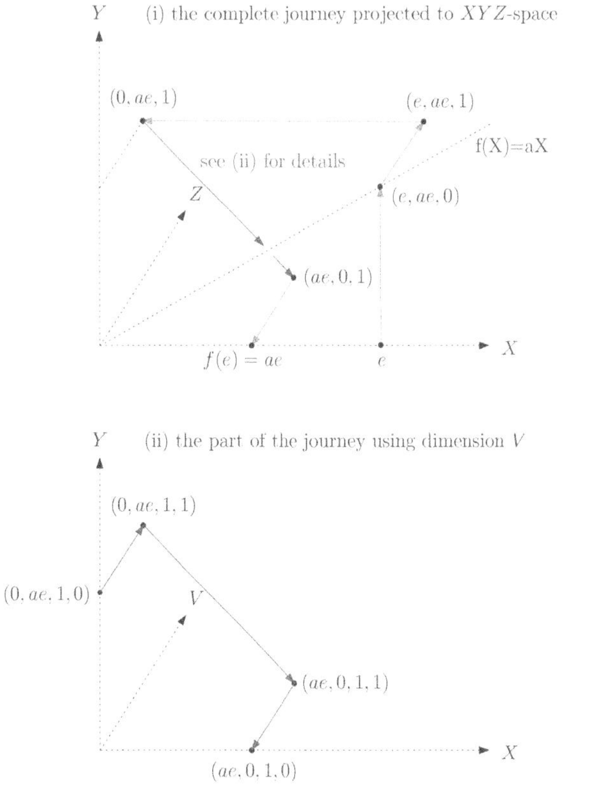

Figure 3: A linear mapping $f(x)$ simulated by carrier movements.

5. DIMENSION TWO

Clearly, Traveller's Problem is most interesting in dimension 2 and 3. In this section we provide some results for the two-dimensional case.

5.1 NP-hardness

The first result shows that the Traveller's Problem in the plane is NP-hard, and does not even admit a constant factor approximation, unless P=NP, even if all carriers are vertical line segments. Our reduction is from the NP-complete problem

PARTITION Given n natural numbers $a_1, a_2, \ldots, a_n$, let $S := \sum_{i=1}^{n} a_i$. Does there exist a subset $I \subset \{1, \ldots, n\}$ such that $\frac{S}{2} = \sum_{i \in I} a_i$?

THEOREM 4. *Traveller's Problem in dimension two is NP-hard for arbitrary innate speed v. There is no constant factor approximation, unless P=NP.*

PROOF. Let us first assume that $v = 0$ holds. Our construction uses vertical segments as carriers. These carriers are C, C' and $A_i, B_i, 1 \leq i \leq n,$. All of them have height S. The carriers C and C' are aligned and do not move. The bottommost point of C equals s, while g is the center point of C; see Figure 4. For each i, carrier A_i moves in such a way that, at some time, it is congruent with C, and has gained a_i in height on reaching C' afterwards. B_i traverses the horizontal strip containing C, C' from right to left. These carriers pass over C, C' in the order $A_1, B_1, A_2, B_2, \ldots, A_n, B_n$, with plenty of time in between so that no interference is possible.

The traveller, located at some point on C, may choose to board a carrier A_i. It will get him to C', at a point by a_i higher than his point of departure from C. Then, he can use B_i, or one of the later carriers B_j, to return to C while maintaining his height. In other words, for each index i, the traveller has the option to move a distance a_i upwards on C. Thus, he is able to reach its middle point, g if, and only if, a partition of the given numbers is possible.

Now assume that a partition is impossible. Then the traveller misses g by a distance at least $\frac{1}{2}$, since all a_i are natural numbers. If $v = 0$ the traveller will never get to g. Now let $v > 0$, and assume that there exists an approximation algorithm with approximation factor $< \alpha$. By speeding up the carriers we can ensure that $T = \frac{1}{2\alpha v}$ holds for the time T where B_n hits C. At this point, the traveller has walked a total distance of at most $Tv = \frac{1}{2\alpha}$, so that he is at least $d := \frac{1}{2} - \frac{1}{2\alpha}$ away from g, if he has reached C at all. To walk distance d takes time at least $\frac{d}{v} = d2\alpha T = (\alpha - 1)T$, so that the whole journey needs time αT at least. Thus, the approximation algorithm would decide PARTITION. □

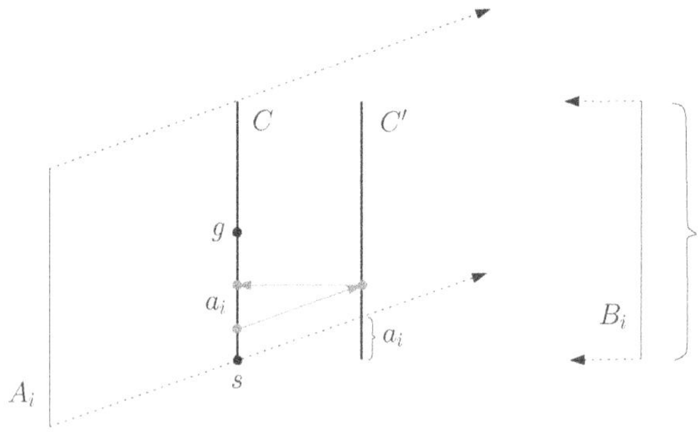

Figure 4: Proving Traveller's Problem NP-hard.

5.2 Decidability

The challenge is to upper bound the complexity of Traveller's Problem in dimension 2. Straightforward attempts meet with firm resistance, caused by the following fact. There are very simple scenes where the goal can be reached in finite time, but only by an infinite number of carrier changes. An example is shown in Figure 5 (i). The three line segments A, B, C are very long, but bounded. Their velocity vectors have large axial and small lateral components. This causes the segments to intersect in point z at some time T. The fast point-shaped carrier D will pass through z at time T, too, and then speed on to meet carrier E that consists just of the goal point, g.

The traveller's innate speed is zero. He sets out from point s on A. In order to reach g, he needs to catch carrier D, because A's upward movement is too slow, and because staying on A would get the traveller too far to the left, anyway. The only occasion when one of A, B, C contains D is at time T in point z. Until then, the traveller must keep cycling through the ever contracting triangle formed by A, B, C. Suppose that point z can be reached at time T after only a finite number of carrier changes. Consider the last change, and suppose it was from carrier C to carrier A. Clearly, it takes place before time T (or it would be unnecessary, because the traveller has already arrived at z). So imagine the traveller standing at the intersection point—let's call it p—of C and A in Figure 5 (i). He can only reach z without further carrier changes if the speed vector of A, that is, the sum of the components parallel and orthogonal to A, points from p to z. But that may never happen, for example, if the triangle is always equilateral, and centered at z, and if all the speed vectors form angles < 30 degrees with their carriers. Hence, the traveller must keep cycling through the ever contracting triangle formed by A, B, C an infinite number of times!

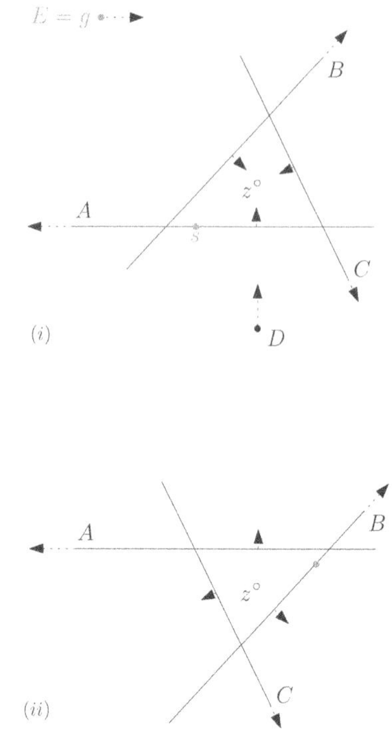

Figure 5: (i) The traveller must pass through the cycle A, B, C infinitely often before he can board carrier D at Zeno point z. (ii) The carriers A, B, C after their meeting at z at time T.

Using a notation from the field of hybrid automata [7], we call z a *Zeno* point, because the situation resembles the paradox of Achilles and the tortoise. In the example above, the cycle A, B, C gives rise to the Zeno point z. In general, Zeno points are defined by the property that there is at least one cycle containing ≥ 3 carriers which can be travelled infinitely often in a finite time interval. This definition ensures that almost all of the infinitely many cycles have arbitrary small travel time which means in the limit that all carriers belonging to such a cycle intersect at one point — namely the Zeno point. It is possible that many different cycles give rise to one Zeno point. In this case, the traveller may run the cycles in arbitrary order which causes a situation looking very complicated compared to the simple triangle example above. Of course, even if an instance of Traveller's Problem contains a Zeno point, this does not imply that the traveller has to run the corresponding cycles an infinite number of times. It might also be the case that a finite number of cycles brings the traveller to a location from where he can successfully reach the goal.

At least three carriers are necessary to give rise to a Zeno point and each triple of carriers causes at most one Zeno point. Hence, the total number of Zeno points is in $O(n^3)$.

Although Zeno points cause complications, they are not strong enough to provide universal computing power in our model. Indeed, we have the following result.

THEOREM 5. *Traveller's Problem is decidable in the plane if all carriers are lines, half-lines, or line segments.*

PROOF. (Sketch) For the sake of simplicity, we assume that there is only one Zeno point. After some time, the combinatorial structure of the carriers' arrangement does not change anymore; in particular, the Zeno point event happens before. This makes it possible to efficiently compute an upper time bound U to the traveller's journey: if he can reach the goal at all, he can get there before U.

In order to decide this question, we would like to maintain, for each time $t \leq U$, on each carrier a list of intervals containing all points the traveller could have reached by time t. Where carriers intersect, intervals must be propagated. A simple example is shown in Figure 6.

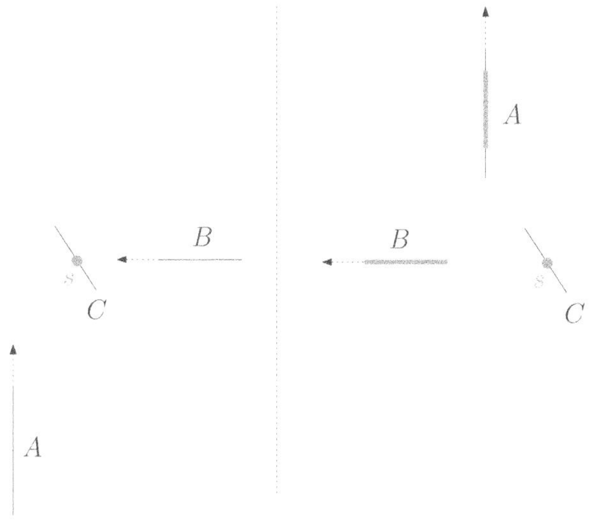

Figure 6: Propagation of reachable intervals. Carrier C is static and contains the traveller at start point s.

On segments involved in a Zeno point, the situation is more complicated. As an example, Figure 7 depicts the points reachable on segment A shown in Figure 5, at some time after T. There is an infinite sequence of points converging to z from the left; they correspond to the traveller's positions while riding carrier A in each of the infinitely many cycles *before* time T. To the right of z, there is an interval of points reachable through z *after* T. It originates in the following way. Just as any point moving through the cycles will eventually reach z at time T, afterwards each point of the expanding triangle formed by carriers A, B, C is reachable from z—by the same argument applied backwards; see Figure 5 (ii).

To avoid dealing with infinitely many points, we interrupt the propagation shortly before time T. This interruption of

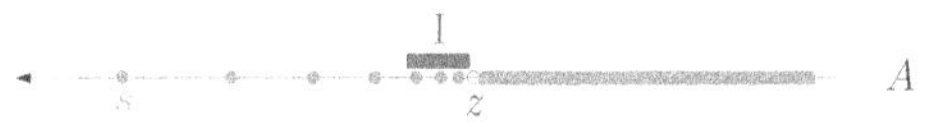

Figure 7: Reachable points on segment A of Figure 5 at some time after T.

propagation is restricted to a very small environment around the Zeno point. At time T, all points on carriers whose reachability information is missing due to the interruption of the propagation, have the common property to be in a small environment around z. This crucial property enables us to create artificial intervals on the carriers containing all such points. These artificial intervals are created at time T. An example is the interval I shown in Figure 7. After time T, artificial intervals are propagated where carriers intersect, just like regular intervals; their offspring is marked artificial, too.

At time U, we stop the propagation process and inspect the goal point g. If it lies in a "real" interval, we report g to be reachable.[3] If g is not contained in any interval, we output that the goal cannot be reached. If g is contained only in artificial intervals, more work is needed.

For all artificial intervals J containing g at time U, we have to check whether the process leading to J can be realized by a traveller path. To this end, we enhance the forward propagation by saving the history leading to the intervals. The history of each interval is encoded by the corresponding sequence of carrier changes.

As in Figure 7, let I denote the artificial interval that was predecessor to J. Starting from g at time U, we do a propagation backwards in time which is restricted to the finitely many carrier changes possible by the history of J. This restriction ensures that the number of steps needed to perform the backwards propagation is finite. At time T, we end up with a closed interval R to the left of z from which g can be reached. The interval R does not include z, since J was not reached through z, but fathered by the artificial interval I. Now, we can continue the forwards propagation from that moment where we interrupted it in the first run. We continue until the neighborhood around z, where reachable points with missing reachability information at time T could be, gets so small that it does not intersect R. Afterwards, we know whether R contains a reachable interval, which is equivalent to the existence of a traveller path to the goal with history matching J.

In case of multiple Zeno points, the above procedure can be extended to "remove" one Zeno point after the other in reverse chronological order. Since there are at most $O(n^3)$ Zeno points, this algorithm terminates. □

We conjecture that the two-dimensional Traveller's Problem is also decidable without the requirement that all carriers are lines, half-lines, or line segments.

5.3 Pseudo-polynomial approximation

Now we present a pseudo-polynomial approximation algorithm for the case of bounded carriers in the plane. Let traveller's maximum innate speed $v = 1$. Let us assume that an s-to-g paths exists in our model, and let P^* be a path of minimum travel time, W. We will establish an algorithm

[3]With some more effort, we can also report the minimum travel time and a quickest path.

that computes an s-to-g path of almost minimum travel time. However, this path may only be feasible in a *relaxed model*, where the traveller can walk at innate speed $1+\varepsilon$, and use a carrier although it is a distance of μ away. Both relaxation parameters, ε and μ, can be chosen arbitrarily small.

Our algorithm works by discretising time and space. The time difference between two consecutive discrete time points is $\Delta := \frac{\mu}{4+8v_{\max}}$, where $v_{\max}$ denotes the maximum speed of all carriers. Space is discretised by a regular grid of width $\kappa := \frac{1}{4}\min(\mu, \varepsilon\Delta)$.

It is easy to show the following lemma.

LEMMA 1. *There exists a function $Q : [0, W] \to \mathbb{R}^2$, such that*

- $\|Q(t)\| \le \frac{\sqrt{2}}{2}\kappa$ *for all* $t \in [0, W]$, *and*
- $P^* + Q$ *is a path visiting grid points at all discrete time points* $j\Delta$, *and*
- $P^* + Q$ *is feasible in the relaxed model.*

Function $Q(t)$ can be obtained as follows. We snap $P^*(t)$ to nearest grid points at all times $j\Delta$, and linearly interpolate the difference of $P^*(t)$ and its snapped version. Thanks to Lemma 1, we need only consider such paths that visit grid points at all times $j\Delta$. This will get us to the goal location at most Δ later than W.

Suppose, the traveller is located at the grid point p at time $j\Delta$. Which grid points can be reached from there at time $(j+1)\Delta$? The crucial idea is to restrict this path planning to a set of *θ-usable* carriers, which contains all carriers having distance at most $\theta := \frac{\sqrt{2}}{2}\kappa + (1+2v_{\max})\Delta$ from p at time $j\Delta$.

If a carrier has distance greater than θ from p at time $j\Delta$, it is redundant by Lemma 1. Namely, the traveller's distance to this carrier exceeds $\frac{\sqrt{2}}{2}\kappa$ not only at time $j\Delta$, but throughout a time interval of length Δ, during which traveller and carrier could get closer by $(1+2v_{\max})\Delta$. On the other hand, if a carrier is at most θ away from p at time $j\Delta$, then the distance cannot exceed $\theta + (1+2v_{\max})\Delta < \frac{3}{4}\mu$ during the time interval from $j\Delta$ to $(j+1)\Delta$. Hence, no matter how the traveller changes between the θ-usable carriers, or walks on them, all extended carrier restrictions are respected. He does not have to care about the borders of the θ-usable carriers and can even imagine them to be unbounded and cover the whole plane.

This freedom allows to linearly combine carrier motions. It turns out that the reachability from p at time $j\Delta$ to q at time $(j+1)\Delta$ can be checked by testing whether the convex hull of the velocity vectors of the θ-usable carriers intersects a certain disc.

The rest of the algorithm is straightforward. Based on the information of reachable grid points at time $j\Delta$, grid points reachable at time $(j+1)\Delta$, and having distance at most $\frac{\sqrt{2}}{2}\kappa$ from their nearest carrier, are computed. The latter property can be tested in $O(\log L)$ after preprocessing time $O(L \log L)$, where L denotes the total number of edges of carriers.

Let $r_{\max}$ denote the maximum carrier diameter. The number of reachable grid points at any discrete time point is at most $O\left(n\left(\frac{r_{\max}+\mu}{\varepsilon\mu}v_{\max}\right)^2\right)$. For each grid point p at time $j\Delta$, reachability to at most $O\left((\frac{v_{\max}}{\varepsilon})^2\right)$ grid points at time $(j+1)\Delta$ has to be tested. The number of discrete time points until time W is in $O(\frac{v_{\max}}{\mu}W)$. Finally, we obtain:

THEOREM 6. *A feasible path in the relaxed model with travel time at most $W+\Delta$ can be computed in running time:*

$$O\left(\frac{nL\log(L)(r_{\max})^2(v_{\max})^5}{\mu^3\varepsilon^4}W\right)$$

6. CONCLUSION

We have introduced a new motion planning problem and shown that its complexity ranges from near linear, in simple cases, to undecidable in higher dimensions. For dimension 2, the problem is decidable, but NP-hard. Its "true" complexity in dimension 2 and 3 remains open. We believe that our pseudo-approximation algorithm can be generalized to higher dimensions. Whether it can be strengthened is another interesting question.

7. ACKNOWLEDGEMENT

The authors are grateful to Frank Dehne, Günter Rote, and Jörg-Rüdiger Sack for very fruitful discussions.

8. REFERENCES

[1] O. Aichholzer, F. Aurenhammer, and B. Palop. Quickest Paths, Straight Skeletons, and the City Voronoi Diagram. Discrete and Computational Geometry 31(7), pp. 17–35, 2004.

[2] E. M. Arkin, J. S. B. Mitchell, and V. Polishchuk. Maximum Thick Paths in Static and Dynamic Environments. Proc. 24th Annual ACM Symposium on Computational Geometry, pp. 20–27, June 2008.

[3] S. W. Bae, J.-H. Kim, and K.-Y. Chwa, Optimal Construction of the City Voronoi Diagram. Int. J. Comput. Geometry Appl., 19(2), pp. 95, 2009.

[4] P. Bell and I. Potapov. On Undecidability Bounds for Matrix Decision Problems. Theor. Comput. Sci. 391(1-2), pp. 3–13, 2008.

[5] R. Görke, Ch.-Su Shin, and A. Wolff. Constructing the City Voronoi Diagram Faster. Int. J. Comput. Geometry Appl, 18(4), pp. 275–294, 2008.

[6] J. Gudmundsson. Dagstuhl, November 2009.

[7] K. H. Johanson, J. Lygeros, S. Sastry, and M. Egerstedt. Simulation of Zeno Hybrid Automata. IEEE Conference on Decision and Control, Phoenix, 1999.

[8] F. Leber. Diploma Thesis, in preparation. Bonn, 2009.

[9] J. S. B. Mitchell. L_1-shortest paths among polygonal obstacles in the plane. Algorithmica 8(1), pp. 55–88, 1992.

A Constant-Factor Approximation Algorithm for TSP with Pairwise-Disjoint Connected Neighborhoods in the Plane

Joseph S. B. Mitchell*
Stony Brook University
Stony Brook, NY 11794-3600
joseph.mitchell@stonybrook.edu

ABSTRACT

In the Euclidean TSP with neighborhoods (TSPN) problem we seek a shortest tour that visits a given set of n *neighborhoods*. The Euclidean TSPN generalizes the standard TSP on points.

We present the first constant-factor approximation algorithm for planar TSPN with pairwise-disjoint connected neighborhoods of any size or shape. Prior approximation bounds were $O(\log n)$, except in special cases.

Categories and Subject Descriptors

F.2.2 [**Analysis of Algorithms and Problem Complexity**]: Nonnumerical Algorithms and Problems—*Geometrical problems and computations*

General Terms

Algorithms

1. INTRODUCTION

The traveling salesperson problem with neighborhoods (or, TSPN) is a generalization of the classic TSP in which the traveler is to visit a of neighborhoods rather than a set of specific points. We focus primarily on the case in which the neighborhoods are *connected* regions in the plane.

The TSPN was introduced by Arkin and Hassin [1], who gave the first algorithmic study of the problem and provided the first approximation algorithms for special cases of the problem. The problem arises naturally in in various optimal covering tour problems, network design problems, relay placement in sensor networks, robotics mission planning, and robot localization.

Our main result is a polynomial-time algorithm that gives the first constant-factor approximation for the TSPN for the general case of disjoint connected neighborhoods in the plane. The regions can be of arbitrary size and shape. In contrast, the best approximation ratio previously known for the problem is $O(\log n)$. Only special cases in which the regions are fat and/or of nearly the same size (diameter) were known previously to have constant-factor approximation algorithms or a polynomial-time approximation scheme (PTAS).

1.1 Related Work

The TSP with neighborhoods has been actively studied since its first formalization and study by Arkin and Hassin [1].

The TSPN is a generalization of the classic geometric TSP on points and is therefore NP-hard. While the TSP on point sets in geometric domains admits a PTAS by the results of Arora [2], Mitchell [15], and Rao and Smith [19], the TSP with neighborhoods seems to be a considerably harder optimization problem to approximate.

Dumitrescu and Mitchell [7] give a PTAS, based on the m-guillotine method, if the regions are all about the same size (the ratio of largest to smallest diameter is bounded), have bounded depth (no point lies in more than a constant number of regions), and are *fat*. Feremans and Grigoriev [11] give a PTAS, based on the method of Arora [2], if the regions are disjoint fat polygons of comparable size in the plane; their algorithm applies also in higher dimensions.

By mapping to the "one-of-a-set" TSP, de Berg et al. [5] gave an $O(1)$-approximation for disjoint fat convex regions. Elbassioni et al. [8, 10] improved the running time and generalized to the case in which the neighborhoods to be visited may be arbitrary sets of points, with each set lying within a (disjoint) fat region that is not necessarily convex. Elbassioni, Fishkin, and Sitters [9, 10] consider the case in which the corresponding regions are intersecting, convex, and fat, of comparable size; they give an $O(1)$-approximation.

Mitchell [18] obtained a PTAS for bounded depth fat regions in the plane, allowing them to be of arbitrary sizes. His definition of "fat" is very weak; he requires only that the area is at least a constant times the square of the diameter. His results apply also to the case in which the regions to be visited may be disconnected sets of points that each lie within one of the (nearly) disjoint fat polygons.

Very recently, Chan and Elbassioni [4] have given a quasi-polynomial-time approximation scheme (QPTAS) for geometric instances of TSPN in any fixed dimension for the case of *fat, weakly disjoint* regions; their results apply also to metric spaces of bounded doubling dimension.

*Partially supported by grants from the National Science Foundation (CCF-0729019), Metron Aviation, and NASA Ames.

If the regions are allowed to overlap, the problem is APX-hard [5, 20], even if the regions are segments all of very nearly the same length [9]. The problem is also APX-hard if the regions are disconnected, with each being a pair of points in the plane [6]. Thus, we do not expect to find a PTAS for the general case. There might be a PTAS in the case of disjoint regions (the case for which we give the first constant-factor approximation); this is a fascinating open problem.

For connected sets in the plane, possibly overlapping, the best known approximation ratio is $O(\log n)$, given in an algorithm discovered more than 15 years ago [14]; the running time has been improved more recently [9, 12].

For further background about the geometric TSP, the TSP with neighborhoods, and related problems, see the surveys [3, 16, 17].

1.2 Our Contribution

All prior constant-factor approximation algorithms (and PTAS's) relied on exploiting special structure that comes from assuming that regions are either all about the same size or all are fat in some sense. Fatness was crucial in order to apply a packing argument to give effective lower bounds on the length of an optimal tour. Even the special case of horizontal line segments has had no constant-factor approximation prior to this work.

Several new ideas are needed in order to address the general case in which the given regions, $\{P_1, P_2, \ldots, P_n\}$, can be of arbitrary sizes and are not fat. We outline our approach:

1. We address the "skinniness" of general regions by surrounding each region by its four "directional hulls", which we prove are fat, for an appropriate choice of one of *two* coordinate systems. This allows us to partition the regions into two sets ("blue" regions and "red" regions); we separately find approximating tours of each set, and then appeal to the Combination Lemma of [1] to combine them into a tour of the entire set. Thus, it suffices to consider only the set of blue regions, which have all four of their directional hulls in our (x, y)-coordinate system fat.

2. Let T be a tour that visits all of the fat blue directional hulls. We convert T into a polygonal subdivision, G, each of whose faces are *histograms*; this increases the total length of T by a constant factor.

3. We argue that if all four of the (fat) directional hulls of the original (possibly skinny) input region P_i is visited by G, then G also visits P_i. This follows from the fact that the faces of G are histograms. (Thus, if G happens to visit all of the directional hulls of all of the (blue) regions, then G already visits all of the regions themselves, and we are done.)

   This allows us to conclude with our first result (Proposition 1), a problem reduction: A c-approximation for the case of computing a tour T for arbitrary *fat* connected regions implies an $O(c)$-approximation for arbitrary connected regions, *even if the input regions are not disjoint.*

4. Since we do not yet know a method to compute an $O(1)$-approximation for arbitrary fat connected regions in the plane, we need some further ideas to obtain our second (and main) result, a constant-factor approximation for the case of *disjoint* connected regions (Theorem 1).

   We assume now that our original regions are disjoint. Their minimum enclosing balls (MEB's) are fat, of course, but they overlap. We select a disjoint subset, $\mathcal{E}_0$, of the MEB's; we do this greedily, in order of increasing size. We use the algorithm of [18] to compute an approximately optimal tour, T, of the disjoint subset $\mathcal{E}_0$ of MEB's. We convert T into a polygonal subdivision, G, each of whose faces are *histograms*; this increases the total length of T by a constant factor.

5. The fact that the regions $\mathcal{E}_0$ were selected greedily by size allows us to argue that any region P_i that is *not* visited already by T must be *close* to the tour T (and therefore close to the boundaries of faces of G), where "close" means within distance that is $O(diam(P_i))$. (I.e., there can be no "missed" regions P_i that are substantially interior to some face of G.) This motivates the definition of a *stratified grid* within a histogram face, H; this grid has small squares near the boundary of H, then progressively larger squares as the distance to the boundary increases. Since regions P_i that are "far" from the boundary of H must be "large", we know that we are able to visit all regions with a slight refinement of the squares of the stratified grid. Also, each square of the stratified grid can be attached to the boundary of H by a connection whose length is proportional to the size of the square.

6. We then focus on a single histogram face, H, and its stratified grid. We first argue a lower bound on the total length of any forest F that visits all regions P_i interior to H and for which the union $F \cup \partial H$ is connected: Such a forest must have length at least a constant fraction of the weight of a minimum-weight cover of the regions P_i by squares of the stratified grid, where "weight" refers to the sum of the sizes of the squares. Thus, our goal is to solve a weighted set cover problem that has special structure. We are able to exploit the disjointness of the regions P_i to obtain a dynamic programming algorithm to compute a minimum-weight cover.

2. PRELIMINARIES

Let $\mathcal{R} = \{P_1, P_2, \ldots, P_n\}$ be the input set of n disjoint, connected regions in the plane.

We say that a tree or a tour T *visits* region P_i if $T \cap P_i \neq \emptyset$. We say that T visits $\mathcal{R}$ if T visits each of the regions P_i, for $i = 1, \ldots, n$. Let L^* denote the length of an optimal tour.

We utilize some basic notation and observations from [18]. Let R_0 be a minimum-diameter (blue) axis-aligned rectangle that intersects or contains all regions P_i, and let D be the diameter of R_0. (Note that R_0 is easily computed in polynomial time by critical placement arguments; for our purposes, a constant-factor approximation suffices, and this is even more readily computed.) Then, bounds on the length, L^*, of an optimal tour can be written in terms of D; specifically, as shown in [18], Lemma 2.2, $2D \leq L^* \leq nD$. Let $\mathcal{G}$ denote the regular grid (lattice) of points $(i\delta, j\delta)$, for integers i and j, where $\delta = D/n$. We let Γ_i denote the subset of grid points $\mathcal{G}$ at distance at most $\delta/\sqrt{2}$ from region P_i. Then, $\Gamma_i \neq \emptyset$.

Note that it may be that $\Gamma_i = \Gamma_j$ for distinct regions P_i and P_j, $i \neq j$. (In particular, many "tiny" regions may all map to the same singleton grid point.) By Lemma 2.3 of [18] (with $\epsilon = 1$), we know that any tour T, of length L, that visits $\mathcal{R} = \{P_1, P_2, \ldots, P_n\}$ can be modified (by adding n detours, each of length at most $2\delta/\sqrt{2} = \sqrt{2}D/n \le L^*/(\sqrt{2}n)$) to be a tour $T_\mathcal{G}$, of length $O(L)$, that visits $\{\Gamma_1, \Gamma_2, \ldots, \Gamma_n\}$. Similarly, any tour $T_\mathcal{G}$, of length $L_\mathcal{G}$, that visits $\{\Gamma_1, \Gamma_2, \ldots, \Gamma_n\}$ can be modified to be a tour T, of length $O(L_\mathcal{G})$, that visits $\mathcal{R} = \{P_1, P_2, \ldots, P_n\}$. Further, by Lemma 2.4 of [18], it suffices to search for optimal tours within the ball, $B(c_0, 2D)$, of radius $2D$ centered at the center point, c_0, of R_0; this *localizes* our problem.

Thus, for our approximation purposes, it suffices to consider polygonal tours whose vertices lie on the grid $\mathcal{G}$ (and within distance $O(D)$ of the point c_0); in fact, giving up at most a factor $\sqrt{2}$, we can assume, for simplicity, that we are searching over the set of rectilinear tours on $\mathcal{G}$, with all edges axis-parallel, on the grid. By rescaling, we can also assume that $\delta = 1$, without loss of generality.

Finally, it suffices to give an approximation algorithm for the *minimum spanning tree with neighborhoods* (MSTN) problem, since associated with a spanning tree T of length $|T|$ is a tour of length $2|T|$ obtained by walking around the tree T. Thus, we desire a tree, T, that visits all of the regions $\mathcal{R} = \{P_1, P_2, \ldots, P_n\}$ and has (Euclidean) length close to $|T^*|$, the length of an optimal spanning tree, T^*. We can assume that the tree is rectilinear, lies on the integer grid, and the goal is to find a short tree T that visits, or comes close (within distance $1/\sqrt{2}$) to, each region P_i.

3. REDUCTION TO CASE OF OVERLAPPING FAT REGIONS

We consider two Cartesian coordinate systems: (1) The "base" (or "blue") system has coordinates (x, y), and (2) the "rotated" (or "red") system is rotated by 45 degrees with respect to the blue system and has coordinates (x', y'). Each region P_i has an axis-aligned bounding box in each of the two coordinate systems; we let $BB(P_i)$ denote the blue bounding box and $BB'(P_i)$ denote the red bounding box.

We let $E^{+x}(P_i) \subseteq BB(P_i)$ denote the set of all points $p \in BB(P_i)$ for which the rightwards ray (in the $+x$ direction) from p intersects P_i. We similarly define $E^{-x}(P_i)$, $E^{+y}(P_i)$, and $E^{-y}(P_i)$, and refer to these as the *blue directional hulls* of P_i. Exactly analogously, we define the four red directional hulls of P_i, with respect to the red coordinates x', y' and the red bounding box, $BB'(P_i)$. Refer to Figure 1.

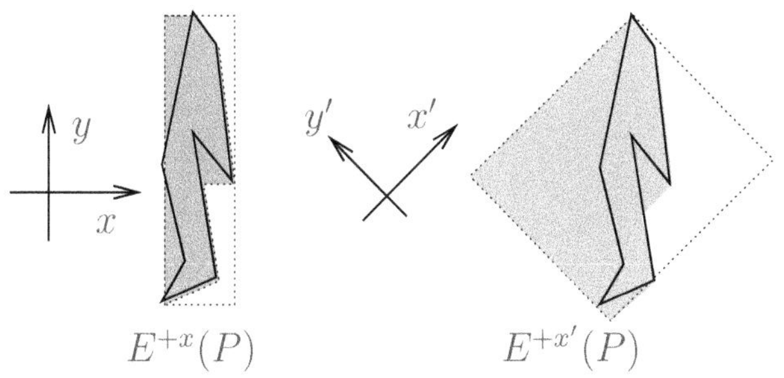

Figure 1: Directional hulls: blue $E^{+x}(P)$ and red $E^{+x'}(P)$ for polygon P.

We use the same definition of fatness as in [18]: a connected planar region X is *α-fat* (or simply *fat*) if X contains a disk of radius at least $diam(X)/\alpha$, where $diam(X)$ denotes the diameter of X. Note that this definition of fat applies to convex as well as non-convex regions.

LEMMA 1. *Let X be a connected subset of the plane. Either the four blue directional hulls of X are fat or the four red directional hulls of X are fat.*

PROOF. If the four blue directional hulls are fat, we are done. Thus, assume that at least one of the blue directional hulls, say $E^{-y}(X)$, is not fat.

We claim that all four red directional hulls are fat.

There are two cases: (1) The aspect ratio of $BB(X)$ is at least 10; and (2) The aspect ratio of $BB(X)$ is less that 10. (The number 10 is not specially significant or optimally chosen, but it suffices for our purposes.)

In case (1) we assume, without loss of generality, that $BB(X)$ has its longer sides horizontal (in the (x, y)-coordinate system), and we partition $BB(X)$ into a chain of 10 subrectangles by partitioning the longer dimension of $BB(X)$ into 10 equal-length pieces. By the fact that $BB(X)$ is a minimal bounding box, we know that there must be a point $a \in X$ within the first subrectangle and a point $b \in X$ within the last (10th) subrectangle of the chain. (In fact, by connectivity, each subrectangle has a connected portion of X within it.) We readily see that the red bounding box $BB'(\{a, b\})$ extends enough outside $BB(X)$ to contain the (x', y')-aligned square, A, of size $diam(X)/10$ in the upper corner of $BB'(\{a, b\})$; similarly, there is a square B of size $diam(X)/10$ in the lower corner of $BB'(\{a, b\})$. Refer to Figure 2. Since X is connected, there is a path, γ, within X (and therefore within $BB(X)$ and $BB'(X)$) connecting a and b. We see that $A \subset BB'(\{a, b\}) \subseteq BB'(X)$, and, by definition of directional hulls, $A \subset E^{-y'}(X)$ and $A \subset E^{-x'}(X)$; similarly, $B \subset BB'(\{a, b\}) \subseteq BB'(X)$, and $B \subset E^{+y'}(X)$ and $B \subset E^{+x'}(X)$. Thus, $BB'(X)$ has all four of its red directional hulls fat (containing A or B, each of which has a constant fraction fraction of the area of $BB'(X)$).

In case (2), we again assume, without loss of generality, that $BB(X)$ has its longer sides horizontal (in the (x, y)-coordinate system). We partition the longer dimension of $BB(X)$ into 10 equal-length pieces, and consider the 10 corresponding squares within $BB(X)$ along the bottom edge of $BB(X)$. Refer to Figure 2. Since $E^{-y}(X)$ is not fat, we know that none of these squares is disjoint from X (otherwise, such a square would lie inside $E^{-y}(X)$, contradicting the assumption that $E^{-y}(X)$ is not fat). Thus, we know that there must be a point $a \in X$ within the leftmost square and a point $b \in X$ within the rightmost square. While the red bounding box $BB'(\{a, b\})$ extends enough below $BB(X)$ to contain the (x', y')-aligned square, B, of size $diam(X)/10$ in the lower corner of $BB'(\{a, b\})$, the similar square, A, in the upper corner of $BB'(\{a, b\})$ may lie partly or entirely within $BB(X)$. We have $B \subset BB'(\{a, b\}) \subseteq BB'(X)$, $B \subset E^{+y'}(X)$ and $B \subset E^{+x'}(X)$; thus, $E^{+y'}(X)$ and $E^{+x'}(X)$ are fat. We need a different argument to show that $E^{-y'}(X)$ and $E^{-x'}(X)$ are fat, since it may be that X enters square A, so it is not immediate that A is contained in $E^{-y'}(X)$ and $E^{-x'}(X)$. Consider a path γ within X from b to a. Such a path must at some point cross the polygonal path (p, q, r) shown in Figure 2. (Here, pq lies on the vertical (y-parallel) line supporting A on its right; qr lies on the y'-parallel line supporting A from below.) If the path γ hits segment pq before segment qr, then γ is a witness to the containment of square C within $E^{-y}(X)$, a contradiction to the fact that $E^{-y}(X)$ is assumed not to be fat. Otherwise, if γ hits segment qr before (or at the same point as) it hits segment pq, then γ is a witness to the containment of A in the red directional hull $E^{-y'}(X)$, showing that $E^{-y'}(X)$ is fat. A similar argument shows that $E^{-x'}(X)$ is fat. □

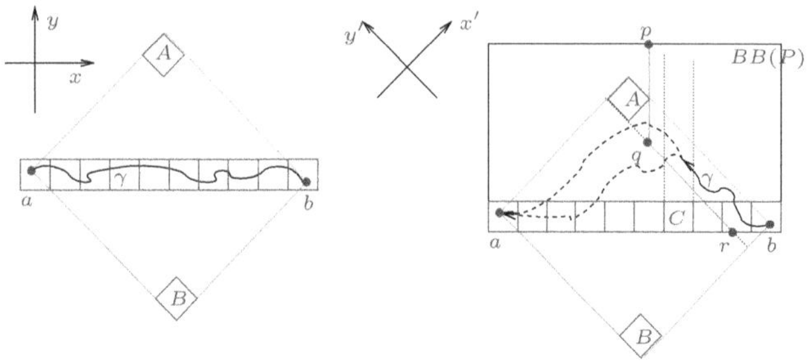

Figure 2: Proof of Lemma 1. Left: Case (1), aspect ratio is high; Right: Case (2), aspect ratio is low.

The next lemma shows that the problem of visiting a set of arbitrary connected regions can be reduced to the problem of visiting a set of fat regions (that may overlap, even if the original regions are disjoint).

LEMMA 2. *Let T be a tree that visits all four of the blue directional hulls of each of the regions, $\mathcal{R} = \{P_1, P_2, \ldots, P_n\}$. Then there exists a connected planar network, $G \supseteq T$, of length $|G| = O(|T|)$ that visits the regions in $\mathcal{R}$.*

PROOF. We can assume that T is rectilinear (with axis-parallel edges). First, we add to T the boundary of the (axis-aligned) bounding box, $BB(T)$, of tree T. The set $BB(T) \setminus T$ consists of a set of simple rectilinear polygonal *pockets*, each with at least one edge (the pocket "lid") on the boundary of $BB(T)$.

For each pocket, Q, we build its *histogram decomposition*, as follows. Let e be one edge of Q; for specificity, we can take e to be a lid of pocket Q, and assume that e is horizontal. We illuminate edge e within Q, using *rectilinear visibility*: the set $VP(e, Q)$ of all points in Q that are rectilinearly visible from e is the set of all points $q \in Q$ for which the axis-parallel segment, $qq_\perp$, joining q to the point $q_\perp$ that is the orthogonal projection of q onto the line through e, satisfies $q_\perp \in e$ and $qq_\perp \subset Q$. The set $VP(e, Q)$ is a (rectilinear) histogram with base e. (A *histogram* is a polygon H having an edge β, the *base* of the histogram, such that the segment $pp_\perp \subset H$ for every $p \in H$, where $p_\perp$ is the perpendicular projection of p onto the line through β.) The boundary of $VP(e, Q)$ consists of segments contained in the tree T and chord segments, known as *windows*, that pass through the interior of Q. Each window segment w is a chord separating $VP(e, Q)$ from a subpolygon ("subpocket") of Q. We then consider each window w, and the corresponding subpocket Q', and determine the histogram, $VP(w, Q')$, consisting of the points within Q' (and therefore within Q) that are rectilinearly visible from w. We continue this process until each subpocket has no windows (only edges contained in T). This process is a rectilinear version of the "window partition tree" used to compute link distances in polygons [21]. It was used also in [14], where it was argued that the total length of the resulting histogram decomposition is $O(|T|)$, where $|T|$ denotes the total length of tree T: The key observation is that any axis-parallel chord of Q crosses at most two windows; thus, the length of each window (the edges that were added to T to make the decomposition) can be charged to the length of T.

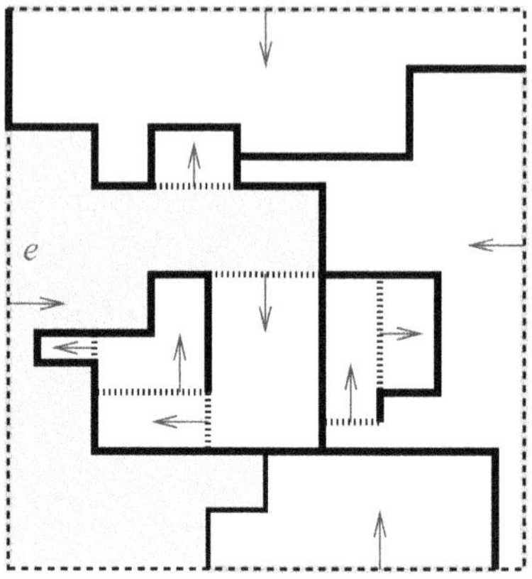

Figure 3: The histogram decomposition of tree T (shown bold black). $VP(e, Q)$ is shaded light gray for the edge e (shown in medium gray) on the boundary of the bounding box. Windows are shown dashed, with a short arrow indicating the direction of illumination into the subpocket.

Next we argue that the connected planar network, G, given by the union of the histogram decompositions of the pockets of T, visits all of the original regions, $\mathcal{R}$. Suppose to the contrary that P_i lies fully interior to a (histogram) face, H, of G. (We assume here that H is a bounded face, not the face at infinity; however, the argument below applies even more readily to the case that H is the face at infinity, i.e., the complement of the rectangle $BB(T)$.) Suppose that H is a *vertical histogram*, meaning its base is horizontal (x-parallel). Since T visits all four of the blue directional hulls of P_i, we know that G (whose edges are a superset of T) visits the hull $E^{+y}(P_i)$ in particular.

If some point $p \in E^{+y}(P_i)$ lies left of the leftmost (vertical) side of H, then, by definition of $E^{+y}(P_i)$, the upwards ray from p intersects P_i at some point $p' \in P_i$; thus, p' lies to the left of the bounding box of H, so p' is a point of P_i outside H, a contradiction. Similarly, we know that no part of $E^{+y}(P_i)$ lies to the right of the rightmost (vertical) side of H.

If the bottom edge (base) of $E^{+y}(P_i)$ lies below the bottom edge (base) of H, then some point of P_i that supports the base of $E^{+y}(P_i)$ lies outside H, a contradiction.

Finally, if some point $p \in E^{+y}(P_i)$ lies above the top (x-monotone) boundary of H, then, by definition of $E^{+y}(P_i)$, the upwards ray from p intersects P_i at some point $p' \in P_i$; thus, p' lies above the top boundary of H, so p' is a point of P_i outside H, a contradiction. Thus, $E^{+y}(P_i)$ lies completely below the top boundary of H. Since $E^{+y}(P_i)$ also lies completely above the base of H and to the right of the left side of H and to the left of the right side of H, we conclude that $E^{+y}(P_i)$ lies interior to H, a contradiction to the fact that G visits $E^{+y}(P_i)$. □

Based on the above lemmas, we suggest an approach to computing a constant-factor approximation for an arbitrary set of connected regions $\mathcal{R}$ in the plane. First, we partition the regions $\mathcal{R}$ into two sets – the "blue" regions that all four blue directional hulls fat, and the remaining "red" regions, which, by Lemma 1, must have all four red directional hulls fat. Then we compute a tree, T_{blue}, visiting all of the (fat) blue directional hulls of the blue regions and separately a tree, T_{red}, visiting all of the (fat) red directional hulls of the red regions. By Lemma 2, we know that T_{blue} visits all of the blue regions and T_{red} visits all of the red regions. We can then add a segment of length $O(D)$ (and recall that $L^* \geq 2D$) connecting T_{blue} and T_{red}, forming a single tree that visits all of the regions. If we have a constant-factor approximation algorithm for computing a short tree spanning a set of (overlapping) fat regions, then this approach yields an overall constant-factor approximation for MSTN (and therefore for TSPN). Note that this approach applies to *arbitrarily overlapping* regions $\mathcal{R}$; we made no assumption about disjointness. We summarize:

PROPOSITION 1. *A c-approximation for TSPN/MSTN for arbitrary connected fat regions in the plane yields an $O(c)$-approximation for TSPN/MSTN for arbitrary connected regions in the plane.*

The difficulty with the above approach is that we do not yet know how to give a constant-factor approximation for TSPN on a set of arbitrarily overlapping fat regions. Thus, we take a different approach. We *do* know how to compute a nearly optimal tree/tour of a set of *disjoint* fat regions (even if the regions are not disjoint, but have bounded depth); in fact, a PTAS is given in [18]. Thus, we will compute such an approximating tree/tour T of an appropriately chosen subset of *disjoint* fat regions, and then augment T so that it visits all of those original regions that T does not already visit. Since we can afford to add to T its histogram decomposition, and still have total length $O(|T|)$, it suffices to solve the augmentation problem for regions that lie within a single face (histogram), H, of the decomposition.

It is important for our approach that we have additional structure associated with the "floating" regions that lie interior to faces of the histogram decomposition. This structure comes from the method we use to select the set of disjoint fat regions. We now describe that method.

Let $\mathcal{E} = \{E_1, E_2, \ldots\}$ be the minimum enclosing balls (MEB's) of the input regions $\mathcal{R}$. We pick a subset $\mathcal{E}_0 \subseteq \mathcal{E}$ of *disjoint* MEB's by an iterative algorithm, examining the E_i's in increasing order of diameter, $diam(E_i)$. As we examine E_i, if it is disjoint from the MEB's already placed in the set $\mathcal{E}_0$, then we add it to $\mathcal{E}_0$; otherwise, we skip it and go to the next larger MEB. (In case of ties, we examine the MEB's of equal diameter in arbitrary order.)

Next, we compute a tree, $T_{\mathcal{E}_0}$, visiting the MEB's $\mathcal{E}_0$. For this, we can use the PTAS of [18]. We know that the length of an optimal tree/tour of $\mathcal{R}$ is at least the length of an optimal tree/tour of $\mathcal{E}_0$. We then extend $T_{\mathcal{E}_0}$ to a histogram decomposition, G, of the bounding box and pockets of $T_{\mathcal{E}_0}$.

Now, the remaining problem is that of augmenting G so that the augmented graph, $\overline{G}$, is connected and visits *all* of the regions $\mathcal{R}$. It suffices to consider one face, H, in the histogram decomposition G, and the set $\mathcal{R}_H$ of (input) regions that lie interior to H. We will exploit special structure of the set of regions $\mathcal{R}_H$ with respect to the boundary of H.

LEMMA 3. *Each $P \in \mathcal{R}_H$ lies within distance $O(diam(P))$ of the boundary, ∂H, of H.*

PROOF. Let $P \in \mathcal{R}_H$. If the MEB of P is in $\mathcal{E}_0$, then we know that $T_{\mathcal{E}_0}$ comes within distance $diam(P)$ of P. If the MEB of P is not in $\mathcal{E}_0$, then there must be another region $E' \in \mathcal{E}_0$ with diameter at most $diam(P) = diam(E)$ and with $E \cap E' \neq \emptyset$. Since $T_{\mathcal{E}_0}$ visits E', $T_{\mathcal{E}_0}$ comes within distance $diam(E') \leq diam(P)$ of E', and therefore within distance at most $2 \cdot diam(P)$ of P. Thus, P lies within distance $O(diam(P))$ of ∂H. □

In the next section, we give an algorithm to solve (approximately) the *histogram problem*, which is the following: For a histogram H and a set $\mathcal{R}_H$ of connected regions interior to H, with each $P \in \mathcal{R}_H$ within distance $O(diam(P))$ of ∂H, construct a minimum-length network, F, such that $F \cup \partial H$ is connected and visits all of the regions $\mathcal{R}_H$.

4. SOLVING THE HISTOGRAM PROBLEM

Let $\mathcal{R}_H$ be a set of disjoint regions interior to a histogram H. As discussed earlier, we can assume that the vertices of H are integral (on the grid $\mathcal{G}$). Also, without loss of generality, H is a vertical histogram (i.e., H has a horizontal base). By Lemma 3, we know that each $P \in \mathcal{R}_H$ lies within distance $O(diam(P))$ of ∂H. Our goal is to construct a minimum-length network of edges, F, such that $F \cup \partial H$ is connected and visits all of the regions $\mathcal{R}_H$. If F is truly of minimum-length, it is a forest (since any cycle can be cut); we let F^* denote an optimal forest, with length $|F^*|$. The network we construct for our approximation will not, in general, be a forest, but it will have length $O(|F^*|)$.

4.1 The Stratified Grid

We now define the *stratified grid* decomposition of H. Informally, the decomposition is formed as follows: We place squares of size 1 (forming the first strata, S_1) inside H, around its boundary; this results in an "eroded" (shrunk by L_∞ distance 1) region. We then place squares of size 2 (forming the second strata, S_2) inside each component of the eroded region, around its boundary; this results in the eroded region getting smaller by L_∞ distance 2. This process continues until all of H has been packed (and covered) by squares of sizes 1, 2, 4, 8, etc., forming the strata $S_1, S_2, S_4, \ldots$. This description is informal since it does not take into account the situation in which the eroded region may contain narrow "necks" of insufficient width to accommodate squares of the appropriate size for the next strata of erosion. Thus, we make the process more formal with the following definitions. (There are multiple ways to establish stratified grids that work equally well to the method we describe here; we will point out below the basic properties that we need the stratification to have.)

The *standard squares* of size 2^i (or *standard 2^i-squares*) are those squares of size 2^i whose defining coordinates are integer multiples of 2^i $(i = 0, 1, 2, \ldots)$.

The stratified grid decomposition of H is a polygonal subdivision of H into standard squares of sizes 1, 2, 4, 8, etc; we let S_i denote the set of squares of size i. We abuse notation slightly by using S_i also to denote the region within H that is the union of the squares of S_i.

Let H_{-1} denote the 1-offset of H, consisting of the set of all points within H that are at L_∞ distance at least 1 from the boundary of H. (Note that H_{-1} may consist of more than one connected component, each of which is a histogram with integral coordinates.) Let $H_{-1}^{(2)}$ denote the union of all standard 2-squares within H_{-1}. (Note that $H_{-1}^{(2)}$ is a union of histograms whose vertex coordinates are multiples of 2; thus, $H_{-1}^{(2)}$ can be exactly tiled by standard 2-squares.) We define the *1-strata*, S_1, to be the set of all (standard) 1-squares that lie within $H \setminus H_{-1}^{(2)}$. Note that each 1-square of S_1 is either in contact with the boundary of H or at L_∞ distance 1 from the boundary of H.

We define H_{-2} to be the 2-offset of $H_{-1}^{(2)}$, and $H_{-2}^{(4)}$ to be the union of all standard 4-squares within H_{-2}. The *2-strata*, S_2, is the set of all standard 2-squares that lie within $H_{-1}^{(2)} \setminus H_{-2}^{(4)}$. We similarly define H_{-2^i} and the regions $H_{-2^i}^{(2^{i+1})}$ for $i = 0, 1, 2, \ldots$; the 2^i-strata, S_{2^i}, is the set of all standard 2^i-squares that lie within $H_{-2^{i-1}}^{(2^i)} \setminus H_{-2^i}^{(2^{i+1})}$. (Note that both $H_{-2^{i-1}}^{(2^i)}$ and $H_{-2^i}^{(2^{i+1})}$ can be exactly tiled by standard 2^i-squares.) An example of a stratified grid of H is shown in Figure 4.

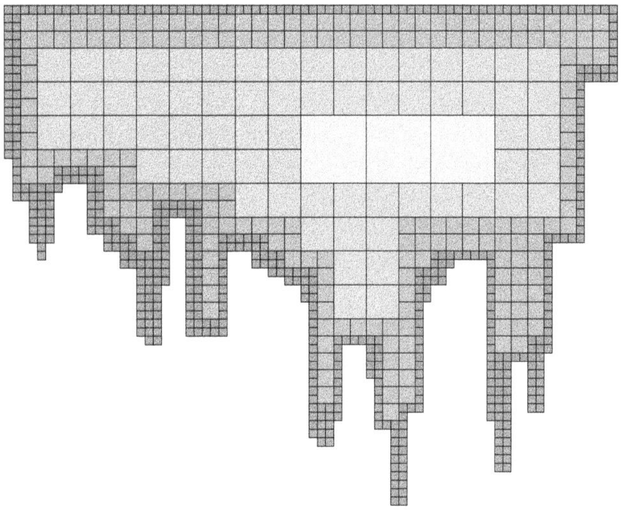

Figure 4: The stratified grid of a histogram H.

By the specification of the stratified grid, each grid square σ of size $|\sigma| = 2^i$ lies at L_∞ distance $\Theta(|\sigma|)$ from ∂H, (More precisely, the L_∞ distance is between $2^i - 1$ and $3 \cdot 2^i - 2$.)

We subdivide each grid square of the stratified grid into a constant number of subsquares. This is done so that no region $P \in \mathcal{R}_H$ can lie substantially inside any square (after subdivision), where "substantially" means at distance more than $1/\sqrt{2}$ (recall that we only need to get within distance $\delta/\sqrt{2}$ of each region, and we rescaled so that $\delta = 1$). There is no need to subdivide the finest squares (the squares of size 1 or 2). For all other squares σ, it suffices to partition σ with a "+" *mullion* into 4 equal-size "panes" (subsquares), each of half the size. We consider these mullions to be associated with each square σ having $|\sigma| > 1$. Then, since σ is at distance at least $|\sigma| - 1$ to ∂H, and we know that any $P \in \mathcal{R}_H$ is at distance $O(diam(P))$ from ∂H, we know that, while P may lie inside a square σ, it cannot avoid being intersected by the mullions of σ, since each subsquare has diameter $|\sigma|/\sqrt{2}$, and we have that $|\sigma|/\sqrt{2} < |\sigma| - 1$ for sizes $|\sigma| \geq 4$.

4.2 A Lower Bound on OPT

We establish a lower bound on the length, $|F^*|$, of a minimum-length forest, F^* whose addition to ∂H spans all of the regions, with $F^* \cup \partial H$ being connected. We argue that we can replace the forest F^* with the network consisting of the boundaries of the set S_{F^*} of all grid squares that F^* intersects, and that this network has length $O(F^*)$. This is a nontrivial statement and utilizes the special structure of the stratified grid, since, in a general tiling by squares of different sizes, a curve of length ℓ can intersect a set of n squares whose total perimeter is $\Omega(|\ell| \log n)$; see the example in [18].

LEMMA 4. *The total perimeter of the stratified grid squares in the set S_γ of squares intersected by a curve $\gamma \subset H$ of length $|\gamma|$ is $O(|\gamma|)$ plus the sizes of the squares containing γ's endpoints.*

PROOF. Suppose γ's starting endpoint, g_0, lies in a grid square of size 2^i (within strata $S^{(0)} = S_{2^i}$). As we traverse γ, starting at g_0, we either get to the ending point of γ without ever leaving the initial strata, $S^{(0)}$, or we enter a second, neighboring strata, $S^{(1)}$ (which is either $S_{2^{i-1}}$ or $S_{2^{i+1}}$). If we stay within a single strata, then our result follows immediately by standard packing arguments (a curve of length ℓ can intersect only $O(|\ell|)$ unit disks). Thus, assume we change strata. Then, γ stays within these two strata for some time, until we either reach the endpoint (in which case we are again done, since we have encountered only two different sizes of squares), or we enter a new strata, $S^{(3)}$. We mark this first entry point, g_3 along γ. Then, γ continues within the two strata $S^{(2)}$ and $S^{(3)}$, possibly zig-zagging back and forth, until it finally reaches a new strata $S^{(4)}$ (adjacent to $S^{(2)}$ or to $S^{(3)}$) for the first time at point g_4, etc. The standard packing argument applies to the portion of γ from g_3 to g_4, since the curve lies within squares of only two different sizes (one being twice the size of the other). Further, we know that γ had to traverse a distance of at least the size of one of the squares in the smaller strata. Thus, the sum of the sizes of the squares traversed by γ between point g_j and g_{j+1} is at most $O(|\gamma_{j,j+1}|)$ (the length of the subcurve), *plus* the sizes of the squares at g_j and at g_{j+1}, which we know is also $O(|\gamma_{j,j+1}|)$, since $\gamma_{j,j+1}$ had to cross one of the two strata. Thus, summing along γ, we get the claimed bound. □

LEMMA 5. *Let F^* be a minimum-length forest whose addition to ∂H spans the regions $\mathcal{R}_H$ inside histogram H, with $F^* \cup \partial H$ being connected. Then $|F^*|$ has length at least a constant times the sum of the sizes of the set S_{F^*} of stratified grid squares intersected by F^*.*

PROOF. The forest F^* can be traversed by a set of paths, one path walking around each tree (connected component of F^*), starting and ending at the point where the tree connects to ∂H. We then apply Lemma 4 to each such path. □

Our histogram problem is now reduced to the following minimum-weight cover problem: Find a minimum-weight set $\mathcal{S}$ of grid squares within the stratified grid of H such that each region of $\mathcal{R}_H$ is intersected by at least one square of $\mathcal{S}$. (The weight of the set of squares is the sum of the sizes of the squares in the set.) For a set $\mathcal{S}$ of squares covering $\mathcal{R}_H$, we can construct a network, F, of length proportional to the weight of $\mathcal{S}$, that visits all of the regions $\mathcal{R}_H$ and is connected to ∂H: The network consists of the boundaries of the squares in $\mathcal{S}$, together with the mullions of these squares, and together with a segment joining each square σ to ∂H (each segment is of length $O(|\sigma|)$).

The next subsection gives a constant-factor approximation algorithm to the minimum-weight cover problem.

4.3 The Minimum-Weight Cover Problem

We begin by defining a notion of "maximal" squares in the stratified grid. Consider the following embedded planar dual graph, $\mathcal{G}'$, of the stratified grid. The nodes of $\mathcal{G}'$ are the centerpoints of the grid squares; two nodes are joined by an edge (straight line segment) if the corresponding squares are edge-adjacent. (By construction, two edge-adjacent squares are either of the same size, or one square is twice the size of the other.) We augment $\mathcal{G}'$ with a node s_0, corresponding to ∂H, and a set of edges, each of length $1/2$, linking s_0 to each of the centerpoints of the 1-squares that are (edge) adjacent to the boundary, ∂H. Now consider the set of *all* shortest paths from s_0 to nodes of $\mathcal{G}'$. Those squares of the grid whose centerpoints are *not* internal to *any* shortest path from s_0 are said to be *maximal squares*; they are, in a sense, "locally furthest" from the boundary, ∂H. (An alternative definition that works for our purposes is to define a maximal square to be a square σ such that it and any of its neighboring grid squares of size $|\sigma|$ are not adjacent to any grid squares of size $2|\sigma|$.) We let $\mathcal{M}_H$ denote the set of maximal squares in H.

Consider the set of all maximal shortest paths from s_0 to the centerpoints of maximal squares. There is a subset, $\mathcal{P}$, of noncrossing maximal shortest paths, with each non-maximal square σ lying internal to at least one path in $\mathcal{P}$. Such a set $\mathcal{P}$ of noncrossing paths can be constructed incrementally, starting with any one path, π_0, and then adding maximal shortest paths one by one, maintaining the non-crossing property; for any non-maximal square σ, there is always a maximal shortest path through it that does not cross the paths already in the set $\mathcal{P}$. The paths of $\mathcal{P}$ have a natural ordering, starting at π_0 and proceeding counter-clockwise around the boundary of H. We say that $\pi \prec \pi'$, for $\pi, \pi' \in \mathcal{P}$, if π attaches to ∂H at a point between the attachment points of π_0 and π' (going counterclockwise around ∂H from π_0 to π') and, if π and π' share the same attachment point on ∂H, then at the point along the paths where the paths first diverge, π turns to the left from π'.

The following lemma justifies that, in solving the minimum-weight cover problem, we can afford to add to F the boundaries (and mullions) of the maximal squares of the stratified grid, since their length is $O(|\partial H|)$, and we know (Lemma 2) that the total length of the histogram decomposition, G, is $\sum_H |\partial H| = O(L^*)$.

LEMMA 6. *The sum of the sizes of all maximal squares within H is $O(|\partial H|)$.*

PROOF. This follows from a charging argument whose details are deferred to the full paper. We assume that H is a vertical histogram with a horizontal base across its top, as in Figure 4. The boundary of each maximal square is charged off to the boundary of H (such that no portion of ∂H is charged more than $O(1)$ times). We argue that each maximal square σ is either "horizontally chargeable", meaning that there is length $\Omega(|\sigma|)$ of ∂H that lies in the horizontal strip of height $2|\sigma|$ and width $O(|\sigma|)$ whose top edge is aligned with the top of σ, or "vertically" chargeable to the boundary of ∂H below σ or to the horizontal chords corresponding to horizontally charged squares. □

In addition to the boundaries of maximal squares (and their mullions), we add to our network F a shortest path (the *spoke* associated with σ) in $\mathcal{G}'$ linking each maximal square σ to ∂H. Since each square σ is within distance $O(|\sigma|)$ of ∂H, the total length of the spokes is also $O(|\partial H|)$, so we can afford it. We can assume that the spokes are noncrossing, since any pair of crossing shortest paths can be uncrossed.

Each grid square, $\sigma \in S_i$, of the stratified grid has an associated shortest path, $\pi_\sigma \in \mathcal{P}$ that passes through its center. We let L_σ denote the subpath of π_σ from s_0 to σ, and refer to L_σ as the *stem* of σ. The stems connect each non-maximal square to the boundary ∂H. We know that $|L_\sigma| = O(|\sigma|)$. Let M_σ denote the maximal square at the end of path π_σ, and let U_σ denote the subpath of π_σ joining σ to M_σ. (Thus, π_σ is the concatenation of L_σ and U_σ.)

The portion of H that is not covered by maximal squares, $H \setminus \mathcal{M}$, is partitioned by the spokes into *zones*. It suffices to solve our minimum-weight cover problem in each zone Z independently. For a given zone Z, our goal is to find a minimum-weight *covering* set of grid squares within Z that is covering in the sense that all regions P interior to Z are intersected by the square (and therefore by its boundary or mullions) or its stem that joins it to ∂H; the weight is the sum of the square sizes, which is proportional to the sum of the perimeters, lengths of mullions, and lengths of stems.

For this optimization problem, we use a dynamic programming algorithm. Our approach is similar to that of Katz et al. [13], who study the following covering problem: Given a set of downward-pointing rays and a set of disjoint line segments in the plane, each of which is stabbed by at least one ray, find a minimum-cardinality set of rays that stab all line segments. (In fact, our results here generalize and extend the results of [13] to the problem of covering a set of disjoint *polygons* with a set of downwards-point rays.) The stemmed squares (squares with their associated stems), serve as the set of "rays" that are "downward" in the sense that the stems point to points that get closer and closer to ∂H.

We need a bit more notation. Let $\mathcal{R}_\sigma$ denote the set of regions intersected by $\sigma \cup L_\sigma$. Let r_σ be the "rightmost" point of $\partial\sigma \cup \mathcal{R}_\sigma$, and let P_σ denote the region (or σ) containing r_σ, where we say that $p \in Z$ is to the *right* of $q \in Z$ if the non-maximal square of Z containing p (resp., q) lies on a path $\pi_p \in \mathcal{P}$ (resp., $\pi_q \in \mathcal{P}$) with $\pi_q \prec \pi_p$ in the counterclockwise ordering of paths $\mathcal{P}$. (Possibly p and q lie within the same non-maximal square, in which case the points are considered to be "equal" in this ordering, since then $\pi_p = \pi_q$.) We let A_σ denote the subpath joining the non-maximal square containing r_σ to its terminus (a maximal square, one of the two that define the zone Z).

We define a partial order on stemmed squares within Z. Consider two distinct squares, σ and σ'. We say that σ *dominates* σ' if $\mathcal{R}_\sigma$ intersects $A_{\sigma'}$ and σ' lies to the left of the path, ν_σ, from ∂H to P_σ (along L_σ), then along the boundary of the region that contains r_σ, to r_σ, then to the boundary of Z along A_σ. (We think of ν_σ as the "vertical line" through σ.) The partial order is well defined. It is easy to verify transitivity. Also, if σ dominates σ', then σ'

does not dominate σ. (This follows from the fact that if $\mathcal{R}_\sigma$ intersects $A_{\sigma'}$, then $\mathcal{R}_{\sigma'}$ does not intersect A_σ: If $P \in \mathcal{R}_\sigma$ intersects $A_{\sigma'}$, then the rightmost point of P must be to the right of the point $r_{\sigma'}$ that defines $A_{\sigma'}$, and we know that $r_{\sigma'}$ is rightmost among regions $\mathcal{R}_{\sigma'}$.)

If σ is undominated among squares in Z, then no region $P \in \mathcal{R}_H$ crosses A_σ, since any such region P has a rightmost point to the right of r_σ, and there is some other grid square σ' for which $P \in \mathcal{R}_{\sigma'}$ (e.g., the square σ' that intersects P works).

The above observation allows us to write a dynamic program as follows. The set of stemmed squares within Z are ordered, $(\sigma_1, \ldots, \sigma_{K-1}, \sigma_K)$, according to ruling given by the noncrossing paths $\mathcal{P}$ within Z. (Since the paths are noncrossing, they are ordered about ∂H.) Additionally, we let σ_0 (resp., σ_{K+1}) denote the spoke that defines the "left" (resp., "right") side of Z.

A *subproblem* within zone Z is specified by giving two stemmed squares, (σ_i, σ_j), with the property that no regions intersect A_{σ_i} or A_{σ_j}. The subproblem asks us to find a minimum-weight set of stemmed squares in the subzone between ν_{σ_i} and ν_{σ_j} that stab all of the regions P that lie *fully* between ν_{σ_i} and ν_{σ_j}.

The important property about the subproblem is that we are able to specify *exactly which regions are the responsibility of the subproblem* – there are no regions that "sneak across" the boundary and would need to be specified, potentially causing the state space to explode. (This is the typical difficulty with recursive methods of trying to solve TSPN; see [18].) This is where we critically use the disjointness of the regions: No regions can cross the left boundary of the subproblem, ν_{σ_i}, along a portion of the curve ν_{σ_i} that lies inside a region. (And we know separately, from undominance, that no region crosses A_{σ_i}, and any region crossing the stem of σ_i is already visited by the stem, so we need not worry further about them in the subproblem.)

Let $f(i,j)$ be the optimal value associated with the subproblem. Then, we get the dynamic programming recursion: $f(i,j) = \min_{k \in K(i,j)}(weight(\sigma_k) + f(i,k) + f(k,j))$, where $K(i,j)$ is the set of all $k \in (i,j)$ such that σ_k is undominated among stemmed squares that lie between ν_{σ_i} and ν_{σ_j}.

Correctness of the dynamic program follows from the observation that there *exists* an undominated stemmed square in any optimal solution, and the principle of optimality. The output is a set of stemmed squares that have a minimum total weight among sets of stemmed squares that cover all regions interior to the zone.

5. THE MAIN THEOREM

THEOREM 1. *There is a polynomial-time $O(1)$-approximation algorithm for the TSP with neighborhoods in the plane for a set $\mathcal{R}$ of disjoint, connected regions.*

PROOF. Our algorithm computes a tree $T_{\mathcal{E}_0}$ visiting a disjoint subset, $\mathcal{E}_0$, of the MEB's of the regions. It does so with a known algorithm ([18]) that yields an approximately optimal tree/tour that visits $\mathcal{E}_0$. We know that an optimal tree/tour T^* must visit all of $\mathcal{R}$ and, therefore, must visit all of the regions $\mathcal{E}_0$ (each of which contains a region of $\mathcal{R}$). Thus, the tree $T_{\mathcal{E}_0}$ that we produce has length $O(L^*)$. Then, using the fact that the histogram decomposition of $T_{\mathcal{E}_0}$ has length within a constant factor of the length of $T_{\mathcal{E}_0}$ (see the

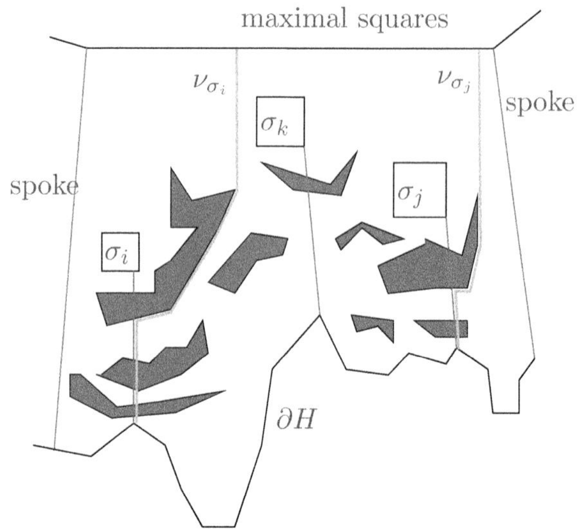

Figure 5: Illustration of the dynamic program. (The diagram is not intended to be an accurate depiction of the histogram, grid squares, etc.)

first part of the proof of Lemma 2 and reference [14]), the network G that we compute from $T_{\mathcal{E}_0}$ is also of length $O(L^*)$.

The output of our algorithm is the network G, augmented by a set of networks F, one per face H of G. We know that T^* restricted to any one face H of G is a forest of trees, each of which is connected to ∂H, spanning the regions that lie interior to H. Since we compute a set of networks, one per face H (spanning the regions within H, and connecting to ∂H), each of which is within a constant factor of optimal for the subproblem H, we know that the total length of all forests we compute is $O(L^*)$.

Since our solution that is output is the union of the edge set of G and the set of computed networks F for each face H of G, we conclude that the network we compute, which spans $\mathcal{R}$, is of length $O(L^*)$. □

6. CONCLUSION

We have given the first constant-factor approximation algorithm for TSPN in the plane for a set of arbitrary disjoint connected regions. We have not yet attempted to optimize (or even to compute exactly) the constant factor in our approximation bounds for our algorithm; however, the factor is not particularly large, and we conjecture that with some care, it can be reduced to $(2+\epsilon)$.

There are two main directions we are pursuing for future work on TSPN in the plane: (1) In the case of disjoint regions, it is not known if a PTAS may exist; (2) In the case of overlapping regions of arbitrary depth, it is not known if a constant-factor approximation may exist. Our results point to a possible approach: It suffices, using our results, to obtain a constant-factor approximation to visit a set of *fat* overlapping regions (the four directional hulls of the blue regions) that have the property that each region lies within a constant factor of its diameter to the boundary of a containing histogram (Proposition 1). (Using a modification of an argument in [10], we can show that the problem of visiting a set of overlapping fat convex regions is APX-hard, so we do not expect to obtain a PTAS.) Our dynamic programming algorithm exploits disjointness (though did not require fatness).

Additionally, we are pursuing approximation algorithms for TSPN in higher dimensions for general regions (not necessarily fat, as required in [4]).

7. REFERENCES

[1] E. M. Arkin and R. Hassin. Approximation algorithms for the geometric covering salesman problem. *Discrete Appl. Math.*, 55:197–218, 1994.

[2] S. Arora. Polynomial time approximation schemes for Euclidean traveling salesman and other geometric problems. *J. ACM*, 45(5):753–782, 1998.

[3] S. Arora. Approximation schemes for NP-hard geometric optimization problems: A survey. *Mathematical Programming*, 97(1-2):43–69, 2003.

[4] T.-H. H. Chan and K. Elbassioni. A QPTAS for TSP with fat weakly disjoint neighborhoods in doubling metrics. In *Proc.21st ACM-SIAM Symposium on Discrete Algorithms*, pages 256–267, 2010.

[5] M. de Berg, J. Gudmundsson, M. J. Katz, C. Levcopoulos, M. H. Overmars, and A. F. van der Stappen. TSP with neighborhoods of varying size. *Journal of Algorithms*, 57:22–36, 2005.

[6] M. Dror and J. B. Orlin. Combinatorial optimization with explicit delineation of the ground set by a collection of subsets. Technical report, MIT, 2004.

[7] A. Dumitrescu and J. S. B. Mitchell. Approximation algorithms for TSP with neighborhoods in the plane. *Journal of Algorithms*, 48:135–159, 2003.

[8] K. Elbassioni, A. V. Fishkin, N. H. Mustafa, and R. Sitters. Approximation algorithms for Euclidean group TSP. In *Proc. 32nd Internat. Colloq. Automata Lang. Prog.*, volume 3580 of *Lecture Notes Comput. Sci.*, pages 1115–1126. Springer-Verlag, 2005.

[9] K. Elbassioni, A. V. Fishkin, and R. Sitters. On approximating the TSP with intersecting neighborhoods. In *Proc. 17th Internat. Sympos. Algorithms Comput.*, volume 4288 of *Lecture Notes Comput. Sci.*, pages 213–222. Springer-Verlag, 2006.

[10] K. M. Elbassioni, A. V. Fishkin, and R. Sitters. Approximation algorithms for the Euclidean traveling salesman problem with discrete and continuous neighborhoods. *Int. J. Comput. Geometry Appl.*, 19(2):173–193, 2009.

[11] C. Feremans and A. Grigoriev. Approximation schemes for the generalized geometric problems with geographic clustering. In *Abstracts 21st European Workshop Comput. Geom.*, pages 101–102, 2005.

[12] J. Gudmundsson and C. Levcopoulos. A fast approximation algorithm for TSP with neighborhoods. *Nordic J. Comput.*, 6:469–488, 1999.

[13] M. Katz, J. S. B. Mitchell, and Y. Nir. Orthogonal segment stabbing. *Comput. Geom. Theory Appl.*, 30(2):197–205, 2005.

[14] C. Mata and J. S. B. Mitchell. Approximation algorithms for geometric tour and network design problems. In *Proc. 11th ACM Sympos. Comput. Geom.*, pages 360–369, 1995.

[15] J. S. B. Mitchell. Guillotine subdivisions approximate polygonal subdivisions: A simple polynomial-time approximation scheme for geometric TSP, k-MST, and related problems. *SIAM J. Comput.*, 28(4):1298–1309, 1999.

[16] J. S. B. Mitchell. Geometric shortest paths and network optimization. In J.-R. Sack and J. Urrutia, editors, *Handbook of Computational Geometry*, pages 633–701. Elsevier Science Publishers B.V. North-Holland, Amsterdam, 2000.

[17] J. S. B. Mitchell. Shortest paths and networks. In J. E. Goodman and J. O'Rourke, editors, *Handbook of Discrete and Computational Geometry (2nd Edition)*, chapter 27, pages 607–641. Chapman & Hall/CRC, Boca Raton, FL, 2004.

[18] J. S. B. Mitchell. A PTAS for TSP with neighborhoods among fat regions in the plane. In *Proc. 18th ACM-SIAM Symposium on Discrete Algorithms*, pages 11–18, 2007.

[19] S. B. Rao and W. D. Smith. Approximating geometrical graphs via "spanners" and "banyans". In *Proc. 30th ACM Sympos. Theory Comput.*, pages 540–550, 1998.

[20] S. Safra and O. Schwartz. On the complexity of approximating TSP with neighborhoods and related problems. In *Proc. 11th Annu. European Sympos. Algorithms*, volume 2832 of *Lecture Notes Comput. Sci.*, pages 446–458. Springer-Verlag, 2003.

[21] S. Suri. A linear time algorithm for minimum link paths inside a simple polygon. *Comput. Vision Graph. Image Process.*, 35:99–110, 1986.

New Constructions of SSPDs and their Applications*

Mohammad Ali Abam[†]
Dept. Computer Science
Technische Universität Dortmund
Germany
mohammad-ali.abam@tu-dortmund.de

Sariel Har-Peled[‡]
Dept. Computer Science;
University of Illinois;
201 N. Goodwin Avenue;
Urbana, IL, 61801, USA;
http://www.uiuc.edu/~sariel/

ABSTRACT

We present a new optimal construction of semi-separated pair decomposition (SSPD) for a set of n points in $\mathbb{R}^d$. In the new construction each point participates in a few pairs, and it extends easily to spaces with low doubling dimension. This is the first optimal construction with these properties.

As an application of the new construction, for a fixed $t > 1$, we present a new construction of a t-spanner with $O(n)$ edges and maximum degree $O(\log^2 n)$ that has a separator of size $O\left(n^{1-1/d}\right)$.

Categories and Subject Descriptors

F.2.2 [**Analysis of Algorithms and problem complexity**]: Nonnumerical Algorithms and Problems—*Geometrical problems and computations*

General Terms

Algorithms, Theory

Keywords

Geometric spanners, Separated pair decomposition, Separators

1. INTRODUCTION

For a point-set P, a pair decomposition of P is a set of pairs of subsets of P, such that for every pair of points of $p, q \in P$ there exists a pair $\{\mathcal{X}, \mathcal{Y}\} \in \mathcal{W}$ such that $p \in \mathcal{X}$ and $q \in \mathcal{Y}$—see Section 2 for the formal definition. A well-separated pair decomposition (WSPD) of P is a pair decomposition of P such that for every pair $\{\mathcal{X}, \mathcal{Y}\}$, the distance between $\mathcal{X}$ and $\mathcal{Y}$ is large when compared to the maximum diameter of the two point sets. The notion of WSPD was developed by Callahan and Kosaraju [7], and it provides a compact representation of the quadratic pairwise distances of the point-set P, since there is a WSPD with a linear number of pairs.

The total weight of a pair decomposition $\mathcal{W}$ is the total size of the sets involved; that is $\omega(\mathcal{W}) = \sum_{\{\mathcal{X},\mathcal{Y}\}\in\mathcal{W}}(|\mathcal{X}| + |\mathcal{Y}|)$. Naturally, a WSPD with near linear weight is easier to manipulate and can be used in applications where the total weight effects the overall performance. Unfortunately, it is easy to see that, in the worst case, the total weight of any WSPD is $\Omega(n^2)$. Callahan and Kosaraju [7] overcame this issue by generating an implicit representation of the WSPD using a tree. Indeed, they build a tree $\mathcal{T}$ (usually a compressed quadtree, or some other variant) that stores the points of the given point set in the leaves. Pairs are reported as $\{u, v\}$ where u and v are nodes in the tree such that their respective pair $\mathcal{S}(u) \otimes \mathcal{S}(v)$ is well separated, where $\mathcal{S}(u)$ denotes the set of points stored at the subtree of u.

SSPD*s*.. To overcome this obesity problem, a weaker notion of semi-separated pair decomposition (SSPD) had been recently suggested by Varadarajan [20]. Here, an SSPD $\mathcal{S}$ of a point set has the property that for each pair $\{\mathcal{X}, \mathcal{Y}\} \in \mathcal{S}$ the distance between $\mathcal{X}$ and $\mathcal{Y}$ is large when compared to the *minimum* diameter of the two point sets (in the WSPD case this was the *maximum* of the diameters). See figure 1 for an example of a semi-separated pair that is not well-separated.

By weakening the separation, one can get an SSPD with near-linear total weight. Specifically, Varadarajan [20] provided an algorithm for computing an SSPD of total weight $O(n \log^4 n)$ for a set of n points in the plane, in $O(n \log^5 n)$ time (for a constant separation factor). He used SSPD for speeding up his algorithm for the min-cost perfect-matching in the plane. Recently, Abam *et al.* [3] presented an algorithm which improves the construction time to $O(\varepsilon^{-2} n \log n)$ and the weight to $O(\varepsilon^{-2} n \log n)$, where $1/\varepsilon$ is the separation

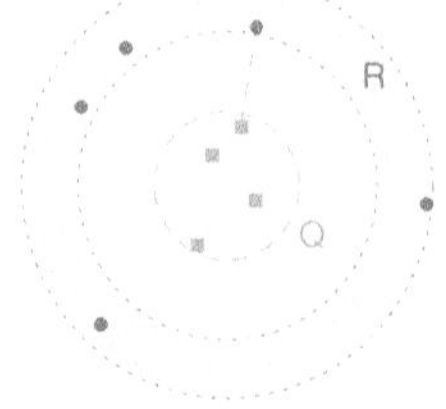

Figure 1: A semi-separated pair.

*The latest version of this paper is available online [4].

[†]MAA was suported by Technische Universität Dortmund, and the MADALGO Center for Massive Data Algorithmics, a Center of the Danish National Research Foundation

[‡]Work on this paper by SH was partially supported by a NSF AF award CCF-0915984.

SCG'10, June 13–16, 2010, Snowbird, Utah, USA.

required between pairs. It is known that any pair decomposition has $\Omega(n \log n)$ size [6], implying that the result of Abam *et al.* [3] is optimal. This construction was generalized to $\mathbb{R}^d$ with the construction time being $O(\varepsilon^{-d} n \log n)$ and the total weight of the SSPD being $O(\varepsilon^{-d} n \log n)$, see [2].

Spanners. More recently SSPDs were used in constructing certain geometric spanners [3, 2, 1]. Let $\mathcal{G} = (\mathsf{P}, \mathsf{E})$ be a geometric graph on a set P of n points in $\mathbb{R}^d$. That is, $\mathcal{G}$ is an edge-weighted graph where the weight of an edge $\mathsf{pq} \in \mathsf{E}$ is the Euclidean distance between p and q. The distance in $\mathcal{G}$ between two points p and q, denoted by $\mathsf{d}_\mathcal{G}(\mathsf{p}, \mathsf{q})$, is the length of the shortest (that is, minimum-weight) path between p and q in $\mathcal{G}$. A graph $\mathcal{G}$ is a (geometric) ***t*-spanner**, for some $t \geq 1$, if for any two points $\mathsf{p}, \mathsf{q} \in \mathsf{P}$ we have $\mathsf{d}_\mathcal{G}(\mathsf{p}, \mathsf{q}) \leq t \cdot \|\mathsf{pq}\|$. Note that the concept of geometric spanners can be easily extended to any metric space. Geometric spanners have received considerable attention in the past few years—see [18] and references therein. Obviously, the complete graph is a t-spanner, but a preferable spanner would provide short paths between its nodes, while having few edges. Other properties considered include (i) low total length of edges, (ii) low diameter, (iii) low maximum degree, and (iv) having small separators.

Separators. A graph $\mathcal{G}$ is said to have a ***k*-separator** if its vertices can be decomposed into three sets $\mathcal{X}$, $\mathcal{Y}$ and $\mathcal{Z}$ such that both $|\mathcal{X}|$ and $|\mathcal{Y}|$ are $\Omega(n)$ and $|\mathcal{Z}| \leq k$ (i.e., the set $\mathcal{Z}$ is the *separator*). Furthermore, there is *no* edge in $\mathcal{G}$ connecting a vertex in $\mathcal{X}$ to a vertex in $\mathcal{Y}$. Graphs with good separators are the best candidates to applying the divide and conquer approach—see [15, 17, 19] and reference therein for more results and applications. Lipton and Tarjan [15] showed that any planar graph has an $O(\sqrt{n})$-separator. The Delaunay triangulation of a planar point-set P is an $O(1)$-spanner [14], it is a planar graph, and is thus a $O(1)$-spanner with an $O(\sqrt{n})$-separator. Fürer and Kasiviswandathan [9] recently presented a t-spanner for a ball graph which is an intersection graph of a set of n ball in $\mathbb{R}^d$ with arbitrary radii which has $O\left(n^{1-1/d}\right)$-separator. Since complete Euclidean graphs are a special case of unit ball graphs, their results yields a new construction of t-spanner for geometric graphs with small separators.

Metric spaces with low doubling dimension. Recently the notation of doubling dimension [5, 11, 12] which is a generalization of the Euclidean dimension, had received considerable attention. The *doubling constant* of a metric space $\mathcal{M}$ is the maximum, over all balls b in the metric space $\mathcal{M}$, of the minimum number of balls needed to cover b, using balls with half the radius of b. The logarithm of the doubling constant is the ***doubling dimension*** of the space—note that $\mathbb{R}^d$ has $\Theta(d)$ doubling dimension. Constructions of WSPD, spanners, and a data-structure for approximate nearest neighbor for metric spaces with fixed doubling dimension were provided by Har-Peled and Mendel [13].

Limitations of known constructions of SSPDs. The optimal construction of SSPDs of [3] uses BAR-trees [8], and as such it is not applicable to metric spaces with constant doubling dimension. Moreover, in all previously known constructions of SSPDs a point might appear in many (i.e., linear number of) pairs. In particular, in all previous constructions of spanners with small separators the degree of a point might be $\Omega(n)$.

Our results. Interestingly, building an SSPD for a point set with polynomially bounded spread is relatively easy, as we point out in Section 2 (see Remark 2.9). However, extending this construction to the unbounded spread is quite challenging. Intuitively, this is because the standard WSPD construction is local and greedy in nature, and does not take the global structure of the point set into account (in particular, it ignore weight issues all together), which is necessary when handling unbounded spread.

Building on the bounded spread construction, we present two new constructions of SSPDs for a point set in $\mathbb{R}^d$. The first construction guarantees that each point appears in $O(\log^2 n)$ pairs and the resulting SSPD is of total weight $O(n \log^2 n)$. This construction seems to be simpler than previous constructions.

The second construction uses a randomized scheme, which is of independent interest, and results in an optimal SSPD where each point appears in $O(\log n)$ pairs, with high probability. This is the first construction to guarantee that no point participates in too many pairs. The two new constructions of SSPDs work also in finite metric spaces with low doubling dimension. This enables us to extend, in a plug and play fashion, several results from Euclidean space to spaces with low doubling dimension—see Section 5.1 for details.

We also present an algorithm for constructing a spanner in Euclidean space from any SSPD. Since this is a simple generalization of the algorithm given in [3], we delegate the description of this algorithm to Appendix A. The new proof showing that the output graph is t-spanner is independent of the SSPD construction, unlike the previous proof of Abam *et al.* [3].

As a result of the new constructions, for a fixed t, we present a new construction of a t-spanner with $O(n)$ edges and maximum degree of $O\left(\log^2 n\right)$. The construction time of this spanner is $O\left(n \log^2 n\right)$ and it provides $O\left(n^{1-1/d}\right)$-separators. Note that, in the worst case, the separator can not be much smaller. The previous construction of Fürer and Kasiviswandathan [9] is slower, and the maximum degree in the resulting spanner is unbounded—see Theorem 5.4 for details.

The paper is organized as follows: In Section 2 we formally define some of the concepts we need and prove some basic lemmas. Section 3 presents a simple but optimal construction of SSPDs. In Section 4 we present the new optimal construction of SSPDs. In Section 5 we present the new construction of a spanner with a small separator. We depart with a few concluding remarks in Section 6.

2. PRELIMINARIES

Definitions and notation. Let $\mathsf{b}(\mathsf{p}, r)$ denote the closed ball centered at a point p of radius r. Let $\mathrm{ring}\left(\mathsf{p}, r, R\right) = \mathsf{b}(\mathsf{p}, R) \setminus \mathsf{b}(\mathsf{p}, r)$ denote the ring centered at p with outer radius R and inner radius r.

For two sets of points P and Q in $\mathbb{R}^d$, we denote the distance between the sets P and Q by $d(P, Q) = \min_{p \in P, q \in Q} \|p - q\|$. We also use to denote all the (unordered) pairs of points formed by the sets P and Q.

Definition 2.1 (Pair decomposition.) *For a point-set* P, *a* **pair decomposition** *of* P *is defined to be a set of pairs* $\mathcal{W} = \left\{ \{\mathcal{X}_1, \mathcal{Y}_1\}, \ldots, \{\mathcal{X}_s, \mathcal{Y}_s\} \right\}$, *such that (i)* $\mathcal{X}_i, \mathcal{Y}_i \subset P$ *for every* i, *(ii)* $\mathcal{X}_i \cap \mathcal{Y}_i = \emptyset$ *for every* i, *and (iii)* $\cup_{i=1}^{s} \mathcal{X}_i \otimes \mathcal{Y}_i = P \otimes P$.

The **weight** *of a pair decomposition* $\mathcal{W}$ *is defined to be* $\omega(\mathcal{W}) = \sum_{i=1}^{s}(|\mathcal{X}_i| + |\mathcal{Y}_i|)$.

As just mentioned, such a pair decomposition is described implicitly by reporting pairs $\{u, v\}$ where u and v are nodes of a tree $\mathcal{T}$ that stores the points of the given point set in the leaves and is used to construct the decomposition. As such, a pair $\{u, v\}$ represents the pairs $\mathcal{S}(u) \otimes \mathcal{S}(v)$, where $\mathcal{S}(u)$ is the set of points stored in the subtree of u.

Definition 2.2 *A pair of sets* R *and* S *is* **$(1/\varepsilon)$-separated** *if* $\max(\mathrm{diam}(R), \mathrm{diam}(S)) \leq \varepsilon \cdot d(R, S)$. *Furthermore, they are* **$(1/\varepsilon)$-semi-separated** *if* $\min(\mathrm{diam}(R), \mathrm{diam}(S)) \leq \varepsilon \cdot d(R, S)$.

Definition 2.3 (WSPD) *For a point-set* P, *a* **well-separated pair decomposition** *of* P *with parameter* $1/\varepsilon$ *is a pair decomposition* $\mathcal{W}$ *of* P, *such that for any pair* $\{\mathcal{X}_i, \mathcal{Y}_i\} \in \mathcal{W}$, *the sets* $\mathcal{X}_i$ *and* $\mathcal{Y}_i$ *are* $(1/\varepsilon)$*-separated.*

Definition 2.4 (SSPD) *For a point-set* P, *a* **semi-separated pair decomposition** *of* P *with parameter* $1/\varepsilon$, *denoted by* $(1/\varepsilon)$*-SSPD, is a pair decomposition of* P *formed by a set of pairs* $\mathcal{S}$, *such that all the pairs of* $\mathcal{S}$ *are* $(1/\varepsilon)$*-semi-separated.*

Note that, by definition, a $(1/\varepsilon)$-WSPD of P is also a $(1/\varepsilon)$-SSPD for P. Interestingly, one can split any pair decomposition such that it covers only pairs that appear in some desired cut.

Lemma 2.5 *Given any pair decomposition* $\mathcal{W}$ *of a point-set* P, *and given a subset* Q, *one can compute a pair decomposition* $\mathcal{W}'$ *for* $Q \otimes \overline{Q}$ *(that covers only these pairs), where* $\overline{Q} = P \setminus Q$. *Furthermore, the following properties hold. (A) If a point appears in* k *pairs of* $\mathcal{W}$ *then it would appear in at most* k *pairs of* $\mathcal{W}'$. *(B) We have* $\omega(\mathcal{W}') \leq \omega(\mathcal{W})$. *(C) The number of pairs in* $\mathcal{W}'$ *is at most twice the number of pairs in* $\mathcal{W}$. *(D) For any pair* $\{\mathcal{X}', \mathcal{Y}'\} \in \mathcal{W}'$ *there exists a pair* $\{\mathcal{X}, \mathcal{Y}\} \in \mathcal{W}$ *such that* $\mathcal{X}' \subseteq \mathcal{X}$ *and* $\mathcal{Y}' \subseteq \mathcal{Y}$.

PROOF. Let

$$\mathcal{W}' = \left\{ \{\mathcal{X} \cap Q, \mathcal{Y} \cap \overline{Q}\}, \{\mathcal{X} \cap \overline{Q}, \mathcal{Y} \cap Q\} \;\middle|\; \{\mathcal{X}, \mathcal{Y}\} \in \mathcal{W} \right\}.$$

Naturally, we can throw away pairs $\{X, Y\} \in \mathcal{W}'$ such that X or Y are empty sets. It is now easy to check that the above properties hold for the pair decomposition $\mathcal{W}'$. □

Lemma 2.6 ([13]) *Given any set* P *of* n *points in* $\mathbb{R}^d$, *an arbitrary constant* $\mu \geq 1$, *and a sufficiently large constant* $c \geq 1$ *(that depends only on* μ *and the dimension* d*), one can compute, in expected linear time, a ball* $b(p, r)$ *that contains* n/c *points of* P, *such that* $b(p, \mu r)$ *contains at most* $n/2$ *points of* P.

PROOF. Pick randomly a point p from P, and compute the ball $b(p, r)$ of smallest radius around p containing at least n/c points. Next, consider the ball of radius $b(p, \mu r)$. If it contains $\leq n/2$ points, we are done. Otherwise, we repeat this procedure until we succeed.

To see why this algorithm succeeds with constant probability in each iteration, consider the smallest ball $Q = P \cap b(q, r_{\mathrm{opt}})$ that contains at least $m = n/c$ points of P, for $q \in P$. Observe that any ball of radius $r_{\mathrm{opt}}/2$ contains less than m points (the ball is not necessarily centered at a point of P). With probability $1/c$ our sample $p \in Q$ and then $r \leq 2r_{\mathrm{opt}}$.

Furthermore, the ball $b(p, \mu r_{\mathrm{opt}})$ can be covered by $O(1)$ balls of radius $r_{\mathrm{opt}}/2$. Indeed, consider the axis parallel box of side length $2\mu r_{\mathrm{opt}}$ centered at p, and partition it into a grid with sidelength $r_{\mathrm{opt}}/\sqrt{d}$. Observe that every grid cell can be covered by a ball of radius $r_{\mathrm{opt}}/2$, and this grid has at most $c' = (2\mu r_{\mathrm{opt}}/(r_{\mathrm{opt}}/\sqrt{d}) + 1)^d = \left(2\mu\sqrt{d} + 1\right)^d$ cells. Hence it holds that $|P \cap b(p, \mu r)| < c'm \leq n/2$, by requiring that $c \geq 2c'$.

Thus, the algorithm succeeds with probability $1/c$ in each iteration, and the expected number of iterations performed is $O(c)$. This imply the result, as each iteration takes $O(n)$ time. □

This lemma helps us to establish the main basic tool in our SSPD construction.

Lemma 2.7 *Let* P *be a set of* n *points in* $\mathbb{R}^d$, $t > 0$ *be a parameter, and let* c *be a sufficiently large constant. Then one can compute in linear time a ball* $b = b(p, r)$, *such that (i)* $|b \cap P| \geq n/c$, *(ii)* $\left|\mathrm{ring}\left(p, r, r(1 + 1/t)\right) \cap P\right| \leq n/2t$, *and (iii)* $|P \setminus b(p, 2r)| \geq n/2$.

PROOF. Let $b = b(p, \alpha)$ be the ball computed, in $O(n)$ time, by Lemma 2.6 such that $|b(p, \alpha) \cap P| = n/c$ and $|b(p, 8\alpha) \cap P| \leq n/2$. We will set $r \in [\alpha, e\alpha]$ in such a way that property (ii) will hold for it. Indeed, set $r_i = \alpha(1 + 1/t)^i$, for $i = 0, \ldots, t$, and consider the rings $\mathcal{R}_i = \mathrm{ring}\left(p, r_{i-1}, r_i\right)$, for $i = 1, \ldots, t$. We have that $r_t = \alpha(1 + 1/t)^t \leq \alpha(\exp(1/t))^t \leq \alpha e$, since $1 + x \leq e^x$ for all $x \geq 0$. As such, all these (interior disjoint) rings are contained inside $b(p, 4\alpha)$. It follows that one of these rings, say the ith ring $\mathcal{R}_i$, contains at most $(n/2)/t$ of the points of P (since $b(p, 8\alpha)$ contains at most half of the points of P). For $r = r_{i-1} \leq 4\alpha$ the ball $b = b(p, r)$ has the required properties, as $b(p, 2r) \subseteq b(p, 8\alpha)$. □

The ***spread*** of a point-set P is defined to be the quantity $\Phi(P) = \left(\max_{p,q \in P} \|pq\|\right) / \left(\min_{p,q \in P, p \neq q} \|pq\|\right)$. We next describe a simple WSPD construction whose weight depends on the spread of the point set. The idea is to use a regular quadtree of height $O(\log \Phi)$ to compute the WSPD, and observe that each node participates in $O(1/\varepsilon^d)$ pairs.

Lemma 2.8 *Let* P *be a set of* n *points in* $\mathbb{R}^d$, *with spread* $\Phi = \Phi(P)$, *and let* $\varepsilon > 0$ *be a parameter. Then, one can* *compute a $(1/\varepsilon)$-WSPD (and thus a $(1/\varepsilon)$-SSPD) for P of total weight $O(n\varepsilon^{-d}\log\Phi)$. Furthermore, any point of P participates in at most $O(\varepsilon^{-d}\log\Phi)$ pairs.*

Proof. Build a regular (i.e., not compressed) quadtree for P and observe that its height is $h = O(\log\Phi)$. To avoid some minor technicalities, if a leaf contains a point of P and its height $< h$ then continue refining it till it is of height h. Now, all the leafs of the quadtree that have a point of P stored in them are of the same height h. Clearly, the time to construct this quadtree is $O(n\log\Phi)$

Now, construct a $(1/\varepsilon)$-WSPD for P using this quadtree, such that a node participates only in pairs with nodes that are of the exact same level in the quadtree. This requires to slightly modify the algorithm of [7], such that if it fails to separate the pair of nodes $\{u, v\}$, then it recursively try to separate all the children of u from all the children of v, thus keeping the invariant that all the pairs considered involves nodes of the same level of the quadtree.

We claim that every node participates in $O(\varepsilon^{-d})$ pairs in the resulting WSPD. Indeed, a WSPD pair $\{u, v\}$ corresponds to two cells $\square_u$ and $\square_v$ that are cubes of the same size, such that $\mathrm{diam}(\square_u)/\varepsilon \le \mathsf{d}(\square_u, \square_v)$. However, for such a pair, we must also have that $\mathsf{d}(\square_u, \square_v) \le 4d\cdot\mathrm{diam}(\square_u)/\varepsilon$. Otherwise, the parents of u and v would be $(1/\varepsilon)$-separated, and the algorithm would use them as a pair instead of $\{u, v\}$.

As such, all the pairs involving a node u in the quadtree must use nodes in the same level of the quadtree, and they are in a ring of radius $\Theta(\mathrm{diam}(\square_u)/\varepsilon)$ around it. Clearly, there are $O(1/\varepsilon^d)$ such nodes. Implying that u participates in at most $O(1/\varepsilon^d)$ pairs.

Now, a point $\mathsf{p} \in \mathsf{P}$ participates in pairs involving nodes v, such that v is on the path of p from its leaf to the root of the quadtree. As such there are $O(\log\Phi)$ such nodes. As such, p will appear in $U = O(\varepsilon^{-d}\log\Phi)$ pairs in the WSPD. This implies that the total weight of this WSPD is $nU = O(n\varepsilon^{-d}\log\Phi)$, as claimed. □

Remark 2.9 Lemma 2.8 implies the desired result (i.e., an SSPD with low weight) if the spread of P is polynomial in $|\mathsf{P}|$.

3. A SIMPLE CONSTRUCTION OF SSPDs

We first describe a simple construction of SSPDs for a point-set P, which is suboptimal.

Theorem 3.1 *Let P be a set of points in $\mathbb{R}^d$, and let $\varepsilon > 0$ be a parameter. Then, one can compute a $(1/\varepsilon)$-SSPD for P of total weight $O(n\varepsilon^{-d}\log^2 n)$.*

Proof. Using Lemma 2.7, with $t = n$, we compute a ball $\mathsf{b}(\mathsf{p}, r)$ that contains at least n/c points of P, and such that $\mathrm{ring}\big(\mathsf{p}, r, (1 + 1/2t)r\big)$ contains no point of P.

Let $\mathsf{P}_{\mathrm{in}} = \mathsf{P} \cap \mathsf{b}(\mathsf{p}, r)$, $\mathsf{P}_{\mathrm{out}} = \mathsf{P} \cap \mathrm{ring}\big(\mathsf{p}, r, 2r/\varepsilon\big)$, and $\mathsf{P}_{\mathrm{outer}} = \mathsf{P} \setminus (\mathsf{P}_{\mathrm{in}} \cup \mathsf{P}_{\mathrm{out}})$—see Fig. 2. Clearly, $(\mathsf{P}_{\mathrm{in}}, \mathsf{P}_{\mathrm{outer}})$ is a $(1/\varepsilon)$-semi-separated pair, which we add to our SSPD. Let $\ell = \mathsf{d}(\mathsf{P}_{\mathrm{in}}, \mathsf{P}_{\mathrm{out}})$ and observe that $\ell \ge r/2n$.

We would like to compute the SSPD for all pairs of points in $X = \mathsf{P}_{\mathrm{in}} \otimes \mathsf{P}_{\mathrm{out}}$. Observe that none of these pairs has length smaller than ℓ, and the diameter of the point-set $\mathsf{Q} = \mathsf{P}_{\mathrm{in}} \cup \mathsf{P}_{\mathrm{out}}$ is $\mathrm{diam}(\mathsf{Q}) \le 4\ell n/\varepsilon$. Thus, we can snap the point-set Q to a grid of sidelength $\varepsilon\ell/2\sqrt{d}$. The resulting

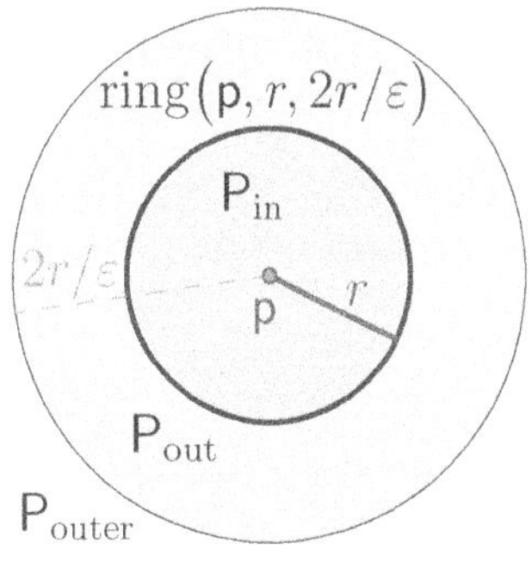

Figure 2: Decomposing the space into rings.

point-set Q' has spread $O(n/\varepsilon^2)$. Next, compute a $(2/\varepsilon)$-SSPD for the snapped point-set Q', using the algorithm of Lemma 2.8. Clearly, the computed SSPD when interpreted on the original point-set Q would cover all the pairs of X, and it would provide an $(1/\varepsilon)$-SSPD for these pairs. By Lemma 2.8, every point of Q would participate in at most $O(\varepsilon^{-d}\log(n/\varepsilon)) = O(\varepsilon^{-d}\log n)$ pairs.

To complete the construction, we need to construct a $(1/\varepsilon)$-SSPD for the pairs $\mathsf{P}_{\mathrm{in}} \otimes \mathsf{P}_{\mathrm{in}}$ and $(\mathsf{P}_{\mathrm{out}} \cup \mathsf{P}_{\mathrm{outer}}) \otimes (\mathsf{P}_{\mathrm{out}} \cup \mathsf{P}_{\mathrm{outer}})$. To this end, we continue the construction recursively on the point-sets P_{in} and $\mathsf{P}_{\mathrm{out}} \cup \mathsf{P}_{\mathrm{outer}}$.

In the resulting SSPD, every point participates in at most $T(n) = 1 + O(\varepsilon^{-d}\log n) + \max(T(n_1), T(n_2))$, where $n_1 = |\mathsf{P}_{\mathrm{in}}|$ and $n_2 = |\mathsf{P}_{\mathrm{out}} \cup \mathsf{P}_{\mathrm{outer}}|$. Since $n_1 + n_2 = n$ and $n_1, n_2 \ge n/c$, where c is some constant. It follows that $T(n) = O(\varepsilon^{-d}\log^2 n)$. Now, a point participates in at most $T(n)$ pairs, and as such the total weight of the SSPD is $O(nT(n))$, as claimed. □

4. OPTIMAL CONSTRUCTION OF SSPDs

4.1 The construction

Let P be a set of n points in $\mathbb{R}^d$. If $n = O(1/\varepsilon^d)$ then we compute a $(1/\varepsilon)$-WSPD of the point set and return it as the SSPD. Otherwise, we compute a ball $\mathsf{b}(\mathsf{p}, r)$ that contains at least n/c points of P and such that $\mathsf{P} \setminus \mathsf{b}(\mathsf{p}, 20r)$ contains at most $n/2$ of the points of P, where c is a sufficiently large constant that depends only on the dimension d.

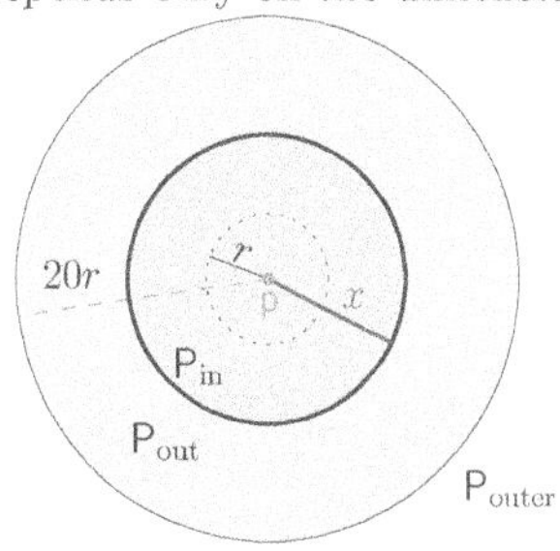

We randomly choose a number x in the range $[5r, 6r]$, and consider the sets:

$$\mathsf{P}_{\mathrm{in}} = \mathsf{P} \cap \mathsf{b}(\mathsf{p}, x), \qquad \mathsf{P}_{\mathrm{out}} = \mathsf{P} \cap \mathrm{ring}\big(\mathsf{p}, x, 20r\big), \qquad \text{and} \qquad \mathsf{P}_{\mathrm{outer}} = \mathsf{P} \setminus \mathsf{b}(\mathsf{p}, 20r).$$

We recursively compute an SSPD for the set P_{in} and an SSPD for the set $\mathsf{P}_{\mathrm{out}} \cup \mathsf{P}_{\mathrm{outer}}$.

It remains to separate all the pairs of points in $\mathsf{P}_{\mathrm{in}} \otimes$

$(\mathsf{P}_{\text{out}} \cup \mathsf{P}_{\text{outer}})$. We do this in two steps, and merge all these pair decompositions together to get the desired SSPD of P.

Separating P_{in} *from* $\mathsf{P}_{\text{outer}}$. Partition the points of P_{in} into $O(1/\varepsilon^d)$ clusters, such that each cluster has diameter $\le \varepsilon r/20$. Clearly, we need $m = O(1/\varepsilon^d)$ such clusters $C_1'', \ldots, C_m''$. Now, since $\mathsf{d}(C_i'', \mathsf{P}_{\text{outer}}) \ge r$, it follows that C_i'' and $\mathsf{P}_{\text{outer}}$ are $(1/\varepsilon)$-semi-separated, for all i. Therefore, we create the pair separating them $C_i \otimes \mathsf{P}_{\text{outer}}$, for all i. Each point of P participates in $O(1/\varepsilon^d)$ such pairs.

We will refer to all the pairs generated in this stage as being ***long*** pairs.

Separating P_{in} *from* P_{out}. This is the more challenging partition to implement as there is no gap between the two sets. We build a quadtree $\mathcal{T}$ for $\mathsf{R} = \mathsf{P}_{\text{in}} \cup \mathsf{P}_{\text{out}} = \mathsf{P} \cap \mathsf{b}(\mathsf{p}, 20r)$ and compute a ρ-WSPD on this quadtree, where $\rho = 4/\varepsilon$. Namely, a pair in this decomposition is a pair of two nodes u and v in the quadtree $\mathcal{T}$, such that $\mathrm{diam}(\Box_u) = \mathrm{diam}(\Box_v) \le (1/\rho)\mathsf{d}(\Box_u, \Box_v)$, where $\Box_u$ and $\Box_v$ denote the cells in $\mathbb{R}^d$ that u and v corresponds to.

We clean up this WSPD by repeatedly throwing away all pairs $\{A, B\}$ such that $(A \otimes B) \cap (\mathsf{P}_{\text{in}} \otimes \mathsf{P}_{\text{out}}) = \emptyset$; namely, a pair $\{A, B\}$ is thrown away if it does not separate any point of P_{in} from any point of P_{out}.

To do this efficiently, we do not compute the quadtree in advance. Rather, we start with a root node containing all the points of R. Whenever the algorithm for computing the pair decomposition try to access a child of a node v, such that v exists in the tree but not its children, we compute the children of v, and split the points currently stored in v (i.e., $\mathcal{S}(v)$) into the children of v. Then, the regular execution of the algorithm for computing a pair decomposition resumes. A similar idea of doing on the fly implicit construction of a quadtree while generating some subset of a pair decomposition was used by Har-Peled [Har01].

Note that since we are using a *regular* quadtree to compute the pair decomposition, we can guarantee that any pair of nodes $\{u, v\}$ realizing a pair (i.e., $\mathcal{S}(u) \otimes \mathcal{S}(v)$) belongs to the same level of the quadtree. Namely, the sidelength of the two cells $\Box_u$ and $\Box_v$ is the same. (It is easy to verify that using a regular quadtree to construct WSPD, instead of compressed quadtrees, increases the number of pairs in the WSPD only by a constant factor.)

We will refer to all the pairs generated in this stage as being ***short*** pairs.

4.2 Analysis

4.2.1 Separating P_{in} from P_{out}

We first concentrate on analyzing the weight of the pairs in the SSPD separating P_{in} from P_{out}. Let $\mathsf{R} = \mathsf{P} \cap \mathsf{b}(\mathsf{p}, 20r)$, and for a point $\mathsf{q} \in \mathsf{R}$, let D_q be the random variable which is the (signed) distance of q from the boundary of the ball $\mathsf{b}(\mathsf{p}, x)$. Formally, we have

$$D_\mathsf{q} = \|\mathsf{p} - \mathsf{q}\| - x.$$

The random variable D_q is uniformly distributed in an interval of length r.

Claim 4.1 *Consider a point* $\mathsf{q} \in \mathsf{R}$*, and a pair of nodes of the quadtree* $\{u, v\}$ *that is in the generated SSPD of* $\mathsf{P}_{\text{in}} \otimes \mathsf{P}_{\text{out}}$ *and such that* $\mathsf{q} \in \mathcal{S}(u)$*. Then* $\mathrm{depth}(u) = \mathrm{depth}(v) \in \left[\lg \frac{1}{\varepsilon},\ \lg \frac{1}{\varepsilon} + \beta + \lg \frac{r}{|D_\mathsf{q}|}\right]$*, where* β *is some constant.*

PROOF. Assume that $\mathsf{q} \in \mathsf{P}_{\text{in}}$ (a symmetric argument would work for the case that $\mathsf{q} \in \mathsf{P}_{\text{out}}$), and observe that q is in distance at least $|D_\mathsf{q}|$ from all the points of P_{out}. Consider any pair of nodes of the quadtree u and v such that: (i) u and v are in the same level in the quadtree, (ii) $\mathsf{q} \in \mathcal{S}(u)$, (iii) the cells of u and v have diameter $\Delta = \mathrm{diam}(\Box_u) = \mathrm{diam}(\Box_v)$, such that $\Delta \le \varepsilon |D_\mathsf{q}| / c$ (for c to be specified shortly), and (iv) $\mathcal{S}(v) \cap \mathsf{P}_{\text{out}} \ne \emptyset$. Now, $\Box_u$ and $\Box_v$ have the same side length, and the distance between the two cells is at least

$$\begin{aligned}
\mathsf{d}(\Box_u, \Box_v) &\ge \mathsf{d}\Big(\mathsf{q}, \mathbb{R}^d \setminus \mathsf{b}(\mathsf{p}, x)\Big) - 2\Delta \\
&\ge |D_\mathsf{q}| - \frac{2\varepsilon |D_\mathsf{q}|}{c} = \left(1 - \frac{2\varepsilon}{c}\right) \frac{c}{\varepsilon} \cdot \frac{\varepsilon}{c} |D_\mathsf{q}| \\
&\ge \frac{c - 2\varepsilon}{\varepsilon} \Delta.
\end{aligned}$$

Namely, u and v are α-separated, for $\alpha = (c - 2\varepsilon)/\varepsilon$. In particular, by picking c to be sufficiently large, we can guarantee that their respective parents $\overline{\mathsf{p}}(u)$ and $\overline{\mathsf{p}}(v)$ are $\alpha/4$-separated, and $\alpha/4 \ge 1/\rho$. This implies that $\overline{\mathsf{p}}(u)$ and $\overline{\mathsf{p}}(v)$ are $1/\rho$-separated, and the algorithm would have included $\{\overline{\mathsf{p}}(u), \overline{\mathsf{p}}(v)\}$ in the SSPD, never generating the pair $\{u, v\}$.

Namely, a node u in the quadtree that contains p and also participates in an SSPD pair, has $\mathrm{diam}(\Box_u) \ge \varepsilon |D_\mathsf{q}| / c$. As such, the node u has depth at most

$$\begin{aligned}
O(1) + \lg \frac{\mathrm{diam}(\mathsf{P}_{\text{in}} \cup \mathsf{P}_{\text{out}})}{\varepsilon |D_\mathsf{q}| / c} &= O(1) + \lg \frac{20r}{\varepsilon |D_\mathsf{q}| / c} \\
&= O(1) + \lg \frac{1}{\varepsilon} + \lg \frac{r}{|D_\mathsf{q}|},
\end{aligned}$$

as claimed.

As for the lower bound, observe that the point-set R has diameter diam(R), as such to get $(1/\rho)$-separation of any two points of R, one needs to use cells with diameter $\le \rho \mathrm{diam}(\mathsf{R})$. The depth of such nodes in the quadtree is $\ge \left\lceil \lg \frac{\mathrm{diam}(\mathsf{R})}{\rho \mathrm{diam}(\mathsf{R})} \right\rceil \ge \lg \frac{1}{\varepsilon}$, as claimed. $\Box$

Claim 4.2 *For a point* $\mathsf{q} \in \mathsf{R}$ *we have that* $\mathbf{E}\left[\lg \frac{r}{|D_\mathsf{q}|}\right] = O(1)$.

PROOF. Let I be the interval of length r, such that D_q distributed uniformly in I. Clearly $i \le \lg \frac{r}{|D_\mathsf{q}|} \le i + 1$ if and only if $r2^{-i-1} \le |D_\mathsf{q}| \le r2^{-i}$. Namely, $D_\mathsf{q} \in J_i$ or $D_\mathsf{q} \in -J_i$, where $J_i = \left[r2^{-i-1}, r2^{-i}\right]$. Therefore,

$$\mathbf{Pr}\left[i \le \lg \frac{r}{|D_\mathsf{q}|} \le i + 1\right] \le \frac{2|J_i|}{r} \le \frac{1}{2^i},$$

and $\mathbf{E}\left[\lg \frac{r}{|D_\mathsf{q}|}\right] \le \sum_{i=0}^{\infty} (i+1) \cdot \frac{1}{2^i} = O(1)$. $\Box$

Lemma 4.3 *The expected total weight of the pairs of the SSPD of* $\mathsf{P}_{\text{in}} \otimes \mathsf{P}_{\text{out}}$ *is* $O(n/\varepsilon^d)$*, and the expected time to compute this SSPD is* $O(n/\varepsilon^d)$.

PROOF. By Claim 4.1 we have that every point $\mathsf{q} \in \mathsf{R}$ (in expectation) participates in nodes that have depth in the range $[\lg \frac{1}{\varepsilon}, X + O(1) + \lg \frac{1}{\varepsilon}]$, where $X = \lg \frac{r}{|D_q|}$. Now, since every node of the regular quadtree participates in at most $O(1/\varepsilon^d)$ WSPD pairs, we conclude that q participates in at most $O((1+X)/\varepsilon^d)$ pairs. By Claim 4.2, we have that $O(\mathbf{E}[((1+X)/\varepsilon^d)]) = O(1/\varepsilon^d)$. The claim now follows by summing this up over all the points of R.

The time required to move every point of R down the quadtree to the leaf where it is being stored is bounded by,the number of pairs it participates in plus the $O(\log \varepsilon^{-1})$ top levels of the quadtree, where no pair is being generated. As such, in expectation, this is bounded by $O(n \log 1/\varepsilon + n/\varepsilon^d)$, by the above. Clearly, the time to compute the pairs themselves is dominated by the total weight of the pairs. Putting these two observations together implies the bound on the expected running time. □

4.2.2 *Bounding the total weight*

Lemma 4.4 *In the SSPD computed, every point participates in $O(\varepsilon^{-d} \log n)$ pairs, both in expectation and with high probability.*

PROOF. Consider a point $q \in P$, and let X_k be the number of short pairs it appears in when considering the subproblem containing it in the kth level of the recursion. By Claim 4.1 and Claim 4.2, the variable X_k is either bounded by $O(1/\varepsilon^d)$, or it is bounded by $O((1+Z_k)/\varepsilon^d)$, where Z_k is a geometric variable with expectation $O(1)$. Therefore, the number of pairs q participates in is bounded by a sum of h geometric variables, each one with expectation $O(1/\varepsilon^d)$, where $h = O(\log n)$ is the depth of the recursion. Now, there are Chernoff type inequalities for such summations that immediately imply the claim—see [16]. □

Lemma 4.5 *Given a point-set P in $\mathbb{R}^d$, and parameter $\varepsilon > 0$, one can compute, in $O(n\varepsilon^{-d} \log n)$ expected time, an SSPD of P of total expected weight $O(n\varepsilon^{-d} \log n)$. Furthermore, every point participates in $O(\varepsilon^{-d} \log n)$ pairs with high probability.*

PROOF. The bound on the total weight of the SSPD generated is implied by Lemma 4.4. As for the running time, Lemma 4.3 implies that in expectation the divide stage takes $O(n/\varepsilon^d)$ time, and since the two subproblems have size which is a constant fraction of n, the result follows. □

Reducing the number of pairs. To reduce the number of pairs generated requires some additional work. The idea is to merge together pairs of the SSPD that are still well separated together.

Lemma 4.6 *Given an SSPD as constructed above with U pairs, one can reduce the number of pairs in the SSPD to $O(n/\varepsilon^d)$, and this can be done in $O(n \log n + n\varepsilon^{-d} + U)$ time.*

PROOF. The number of long pairs created is $O(n/\varepsilon^d)$, as the divide stage generates $O(1/\varepsilon^d)$ long pairs, and we stop the recursive construction bottoms out when the size of the subproblem drops below $O(1/\varepsilon^d)$.

Let $\mathcal{S}$ be the computed $2/\varepsilon$-SSPD (we require a slightly stronger separation to implement this part). Construct a $O(1/\varepsilon)$-WSPD $\mathcal{W}$ of the point-set P. For each *short* pair $A \otimes B \in \mathcal{S}$, pick an arbitrary point $q \in A$ and $r \in B$, and find the pair $X \otimes Y$ in $\mathcal{W}$ such that $q \in X$ and $r \in Y$. Associate the pair $A \otimes B$ with the pair $X \otimes Y$. Repeat this for all the pairs in $\mathcal{S}$.

Given a pair of points q, r finding the pair of the WSPD containing the two points can be done in constant time [10]. As such, we can compute, in $O((n/\varepsilon^d) \log n)$ time, for all the short pairs in the SSPD $\mathcal{S}$ its associated pair in the WSPD. Now, take all the SSPD pairs $\{\mathcal{X}_1, \mathcal{Y}_1\}, \ldots, \{\mathcal{X}_k, \mathcal{Y}_k\}$ that are associated with a single pair $\{X, Y\}$ of the WSPD, such that $\mathcal{X}_i \cap X \neq \emptyset$ and $\mathcal{Y}_i \cap Y \neq \emptyset$ for all i. We replace all these short pairs in the SSPD $\mathcal{S}$ by the single short pair

$$X' \otimes Y' \text{ where } X' = \left(\bigcup_i \mathcal{X}_i\right) \text{ and } Y' = \left(\bigcup_i \mathcal{Y}_i\right).$$

It is easy to verify that X' and Y' are $1/\varepsilon$-separated. As such, in the end of this replacement process, we have a $1/\varepsilon$-SSPD that have $O(n/\varepsilon^d)$ long pairs and $|\mathcal{W}|$ short pairs, where $|\mathcal{W}|$ is the number of pairs in the WSPD $\mathcal{W}$. Overall, this merge process takes time that is proportional to the total weight of the original SSPD.

Thus, we get a SSPD that has $O(n/\varepsilon^d)$ pairs overall, and clearly this merging process did not increase the total weight of the SSPD. □

4.3 The results

Putting the above together we get our main result.

Theorem 4.7 *Given a point-set P in $\mathbb{R}^d$, and parameter $\varepsilon > 0$, then one can compute, in $O(n\varepsilon^{-d} \log n)$ expected time, an SSPD $\mathcal{S}$ of P, such that: (A) The total expected weight of the pairs of $\mathcal{S}$ is $O(n\varepsilon^{-d} \log n)$. (B) Every point of P participates in $O(\varepsilon^{-d} \log n)$ pairs, with high probability. (C) The total number of pairs in $\mathcal{S}$ is $O(n/\varepsilon^d)$.*

One can extend the result also to an n-point metric space with bounded doubling dimension.

Theorem 4.8 *Let P be an n-point metric space with doubling dimension* dim, *and parameter $\varepsilon > 0$, then one can compute, in $O(n\varepsilon^{-O(\mathrm{dim})} \log n)$ expected time, an SSPD $\mathcal{S}$ of P, such that: (A) The total expected weight of the pairs of $\mathcal{S}$ is $O\left(n\varepsilon^{-O(\mathrm{dim})} \log n\right)$. (B) Every point of P participates in $O\left(\varepsilon^{-O(\mathrm{dim})} \log n\right)$ pairs, with high probability. Furthermore, by investing an additional $O\left(n\varepsilon^{-O(\mathrm{dim})} \log^2 n\right)$ time one can reduce the number of pairs in $\mathcal{S}$ to $O(n/\varepsilon^d)$.*

PROOF. This follows by an immediate plug and chug of our algorithm into the machinery of Har-Peled and Mendel [13]. Observe that our algorithm only used distances in the computation. In particular, we replace the use of quadtrees by net-trees, see [13].

The deterioration in the running time to reduce the number of pairs is caused by the longer time it takes to perform a "pair-location" query; that is, locating the pair containing a specific pair of points takes $O(\log n)$ time instead of constant time. □

It seems that by redesigning the algorithm one can remove the extra log factor needed to reduce the number of pairs in the resulting SSPD. However, the resulting algorithm is somewhat more involved and less clear, and we decided to present here the slightly less efficient variant.

5. APPLICATIONS

5.1 Immediate applications

We now have a near-linear weight SSPD for any point set from a finite metric space with low doubling dimension. We can use this SSPD in any application that uses only the SSPD property, and do not use any special properties that exist only in Euclidean space. So, let P be an n-point metric space with constant doubling dimension. By plugging in the above construction we get the following new results:

(A) A $(1+\varepsilon)$-spanner for P with diameter 2 and $O(n \log n)$ edges [1].

(B) A $(3+\varepsilon)$-spanner of a complete bipartite graph [1]. (This can also be done directly by using WSPD.)

(C) An additively $(2+\varepsilon)$-spanner with $O(n \log n)$ edges [2] can be constructed for P. See [2] for exact definitions.

One can also extract a spanner from any SSPD, as the following theorem states. Since the proof of this is quite standard by now, we delegate the proof to Appendix A.

Theorem 5.1 *Given a $8/\varepsilon$-SSPD $\mathcal{S}$ for a point-set P in $\mathbb{R}^d$, one can compute a $(1+\varepsilon)$-spanner of P with $O(|\mathcal{S}|/\varepsilon^{d-1})$ edges. The construction time is proportional to the total weight of $\mathcal{S}$. In particular, a point appears in k pairs of the SSPD is of degree $O(k/\varepsilon^{d-1})$ in the resulting spanner.*

5.2 Spanners with $O(n^{1-1/d})$-separator

Let P be a set of n points in $\mathbb{R}^d$, and let $\varepsilon > 0$ be a parameter. We next describe a modified construction of SSPDs given in Section 3 for the point-set P, such that when converting it into a spanner, it has a small separator.

5.2.1 The SSPD construction

Compute a ball $\mathsf{b}(\mathsf{p}, r)$, using Lemma 2.7, setting $t = (1/2)n^{1/d}$. Let $r' = (1+1/t)r$. We have that $\mathrm{ring}(\mathsf{p}, r, r')$ contains at most $n^{1-1/d}$ points of P. We partition P as follows:

$$\mathsf{P}_{\mathrm{in}} = \mathsf{P} \cap \mathsf{b}(\mathsf{p}, r), \qquad \mathsf{P}_{\mathrm{ring}} = \mathsf{P} \cap \mathrm{ring}(\mathsf{p}, r, r'),$$

$$\mathsf{P}_{\mathrm{out}} = \mathsf{P} \cap \mathrm{ring}(\mathsf{p}, r', 2r), \quad \text{and} \quad \mathsf{P}_{\mathrm{outer}} = \mathsf{P} \setminus \mathsf{b}(\mathsf{p}, 2r).$$

We have that $|\mathsf{P}_{\mathrm{in}}| \geq n/c$, $|\mathsf{P}_{\mathrm{ring}}| \leq n^{1-1/d}$, and $|\mathsf{P}_{\mathrm{outer}}| \geq n/2$ where c is a constant that depends only on d. We add the following pairs to the SSPD $\mathcal{S}$.

(A) $\mathsf{P}_{\mathrm{ring}} \otimes (\mathsf{P} \setminus \mathsf{P}_{\mathrm{ring}})$: We compute a $(1/\varepsilon)$-SSPD for P using Theorem 4.7, and we split it using Lemma 2.5 to get a $(1/\varepsilon)$-SSPD for $\mathsf{P}_{\mathrm{ring}} \oplus (\mathsf{P} \setminus \mathsf{P}_{\mathrm{ring}})$ (with the same parameters as the original SSPD of Theorem 4.7).

(B) $\mathsf{P}_{\mathrm{in}} \otimes \mathsf{P}_{\mathrm{outer}}$: We decompose P_{in} into $O(1/\varepsilon^d)$ clusters each with diameter $\varepsilon r/10$ (for example, by using a grid of the appropriate size). Let $\mathcal{F}$ be the resulting set of subsets of P_{in}. For each $X \in \mathcal{F}$, we add $\{X, \mathsf{P}_{\mathrm{outer}}\}$ as a $(1/\varepsilon)$-semi-separated pair to $\mathcal{S}$.

(C) $\mathsf{P}_{\mathrm{in}} \otimes \mathsf{P}_{\mathrm{out}}$: We have $\mathsf{d}(\mathsf{P}_{\mathrm{in}}, \mathsf{P}_{\mathrm{out}}) \geq r/t$, and we can apply the approach used in the simple SSPD construction of Section 3. We construct a grid covering $\mathsf{b}(\mathsf{p}, 2r)$, each cell with side $\ell = \varepsilon r/(4\sqrt{d}t)$ and snap points to grid points—note that each side of the grid consists of $4r/\ell = O(n^{1/d}/\varepsilon)$ segments. Next, build a $(2/\varepsilon)$-WSPD for this snapped point set, and interpret it as a WSPD for the original point set. We split this WSPD so that it covers $\mathsf{P}_{\mathrm{in}} \otimes \mathsf{P}_{\mathrm{out}}$ using Lemma 2.5. This results in $O(n^{1-1/d}/\varepsilon^d)$ $(1/\varepsilon)$-semi separated pairs of the form $\{\mathcal{X}_i, \mathcal{Y}_i\}$ that covers $\mathsf{P}_{\mathrm{in}} \otimes \mathsf{P}_{\mathrm{out}}$. Observe that any point participates in at most $O(\varepsilon^{-d}\log(n/\varepsilon))$ pairs.

(D) $\mathsf{P}_{\mathrm{in}} \otimes \mathsf{P}_{\mathrm{in}}$ and $(\mathsf{P}_{\mathrm{out}} \cup \mathsf{P}_{\mathrm{outer}}) \otimes (\mathsf{P}_{\mathrm{out}} \cup \mathsf{P}_{\mathrm{outer}})$: We construct the SSPD for these two sets of pairs by recursively calling the algorithm on P_{in} and on $\mathsf{P}_{\mathrm{out}} \bigcup \mathsf{P}_{\mathrm{outer}}$.

Lemma 5.2 *For a point-set P of n points in $\mathbb{R}^d$, and a parameter ε, the $(1/\varepsilon)$-SSPD generated by the above construction has: (i) $O(n/\varepsilon^d)$ pairs, (ii) every point is contained in $O(\varepsilon^{-d}\log^2 n)$ pairs, (iii) the total weight of the SSPD is $O(n\varepsilon^{-d}\log^2 n)$, and (iv) the construction time is $O(n\varepsilon^{-d}\log^2 n)$.*

PROOF. (i) To bound the number of pairs generated for $\mathsf{P}_{\mathrm{in}} \otimes \mathsf{P}_{\mathrm{ring}}$, observe that every point participates in at most $O(\varepsilon^{-d}\log n)$ pairs, and there are $O(n^{1-1/d})$ points in $\mathsf{P}_{\mathrm{ring}}$. As such, the number of pairs generated in this step is at most $O\left(\left(n^{1-1/d}/\varepsilon^d\right)\log n\right)$, as every pair must involve at least one point of $\mathsf{P}_{\mathrm{ring}}$. This also bound the number of pairs generated for $(\mathsf{P}_{\mathrm{out}} \cup \mathsf{P}_{\mathrm{outer}}) \otimes \mathsf{P}_{\mathrm{ring}}$. As such, we have that $T(n) = O\left(\left(n^{1-1/d}/\varepsilon^d\right)\log n\right) + T(|\mathsf{P}_{\mathrm{in}}|) + T(|\mathsf{P}_{\mathrm{out}} \cup \mathsf{P}_{\mathrm{outer}}|)$. And the solution to this recurrence is $O(n/\varepsilon^d)$.

(ii) We have that a point participates in at most $D(n) = O(\varepsilon^{-d}\log n) + O(\varepsilon^{-d}\log(n/\varepsilon)) + D(n/2)$ pairs. The solution to this recurrence is $O(\varepsilon^{-d}\log^2 n)$ since we can assume that $\varepsilon > 1/n$.

(iii) By the above, the total weight of the SSPD generated is $O(n\varepsilon^{-d}\log^2 n)$.

(iv) As for the construction time $T(n) = O(n\varepsilon^{-d}\log n) + T(n_1) + T(n_2)$, where $n_1 + n_2 \leq n$. As such, the construction time is $O(n\varepsilon^{-d}\log^2 n)$. □

5.2.2 Converting into spanner

We plug the above SSPD construction into Theorem 5.1 to get a spanner. We remind the reader that the construction uses a cone decomposition around the smaller part of each pair in the SSPD and connects the apex of the cone to the closest point in the other side of the pair inside the cone, as such every SSPD pair give rise to $O(1/\varepsilon^{d-1})$ edges, which all share a single vertex called the ***hub*** of the pair. Let $\mathcal{G}$ be the resulting spanner.

Lemma 5.3 *The graph $\mathcal{G}$ has a vertex separator of size $O(n^{1-1/d}/\varepsilon^d)$.*

PROOF. If we remove all the points of $\mathsf{P}_{\mathrm{ring}}$, the graph $\mathcal{G}$ is almost disconnected. Indeed, removing all $O(n^{1-1/d})$ points of $\mathsf{P}_{\mathrm{ring}}$ immediately kills all the edges of the spanner that rise out of stage (A). Stage (B) gives rise to $O(1/\varepsilon^d)$ pairs and consequently $O(1/\varepsilon^{2d-1})$ edges. Eliminating $O(1/\varepsilon^d)$ hub vertices eliminates all such edges. Stage (C) gives rise to $O(n^{1-1/d}/\varepsilon^d)$ pairs, which in turn induces $O\left(n^{1-1/d}/\varepsilon^{2d-1}\right)$ edges in the spanner. Again, removing $O(n^{1-1/d}/\varepsilon^d)$ hub vertices eliminates all such edges. Therefore the set $\mathcal{X}$ of all $O(n^{1-1/d}/\varepsilon^d)$ removed vertices is an $O(n^{1-1/d}/\varepsilon^d)$-separator for graph $\mathcal{G}$ which indeed separates P_{in} from $\mathsf{P}_{\mathrm{out}} \cup \mathsf{P}_{\mathrm{outer}}$. □

Theorem 5.4 *For any $\varepsilon > 0$ and any set P of n points in $\mathbb{R}^d$, there is a $(1+\varepsilon)$-spanner $\mathcal{G}$ with (i) $O(n/\varepsilon^{2d-1})$ edges, (ii) maximum degree $O((1/\varepsilon^{2d-1})\log^2 n)$, and (iii) a* *separator of size $O(n^{1-1/d}/\varepsilon^d)$. The $(1+\varepsilon)$-spanner can be constructed in $O\big((n/\varepsilon^d)\log^2 n\big)$ time.*

PROOF. The SSPD computation takes $O\big((n/\varepsilon^d)\log^2 n\big)$ time, and this also bounds the total weight of the SSPD. Theorem 5.1 converts this into the desired spanner in time proportional to the total weight of the SSPD. □

Theorem 5.4 compares favorably with the result of Fürer and Kasiviswandathan [9]. Indeed, the stated running time of their algorithm is $O\Big(n^{2-2/(\lceil k/2\rceil+1)}\Big)$ (ignoring polylog factors and the dependency on ε). It is quite plausible that their algorithm can be made to be faster (most likely $O(n\log^{d-1} n)$) for this special case. However, in the worst case, the maximum degree of a vertex in their spanner is $\Omega(n)$, while in our construction the maximum degree is $O(\log^2 n)$.

6. CONCLUSIONS

We presented several new constructions of SSPDs that have several additional properties that previous constructions did not have. Our construction relied on finding a good ring separator in low dimension, an idea that should have other applications. To get an optimal construction we used a random partition scheme which might be of independent interest.

Many of the applications of SSPDs uses cones and angles. It would be interesting to extend some of these applications to spaces with low doubling dimension. In particular, can one construct a spanner for a point set, with low degree and a small separator, in a low-doubling-dimension space?

7. REFERENCES

[1] M. A. Abam, P. Carmi, M. Farshi, and M. H. M. Smid. On the power of the semi-separated pair decomposition. In *Proc. 11th Workshop Algorithms Data Struct.*, pages 1–12, 2009.

[2] M. A. Abam, M. de Berg, M. Farshi, J. Gudmundsson, and M. H. M. Smid. Geometric spanners for weighted point sets. In *Proc. 17th Annu. European Sympos. Algorithms*, pages 190–202, 2009.

[3] M. A. Abam, M. de Berg, M. Farshi, and J. Gudmundsson. Region-fault tolerant geometric spanners. *Discrete Comput. Geom.*, 41(4):556–582, 2009.

[4] M. A. Abam and S. Har-Peled. New constructions of SSPDs and their applications. `http://cs.uiuc.edu/~sariel/papers/09/sspd/`, 2010.

[5] P. Assouad. Plongements lipschitziens dans $\mathbf{R}^n$. *Bull. Soc. Math. France*, 111(4):429–448, 1983.

[6] B. Bollobás and A. Scott. On separating systems. *Eur. J. Comb.*, 28(4):1068–1071, 2007.

[7] P. B. Callahan and S. R. Kosaraju. A decomposition of multidimensional point sets with applications to k-nearest-neighbors and n-body potential fields. *J. Assoc. Comput. Mach.*, 42:67–90, 1995.

[8] C. A. Duncan, M. T. Goodrich, and S. Kobourov. Balanced aspect ratio trees: combining the advantages of k-d trees and octrees. *J. Algorithms*, 38:303–333, 2001.

[9] M. Fürer and S. P. Kasiviswanathan. Spanners for geometric intersection graphs. In *Proc. 10th Workshop Algorithms Data Struct.*, pages 312–324, 2007.

[10] S. Funke, D. Matijevic, and P. Sanders. Approximating energy efficient paths in wireless multi-hop networks. In *Proc. 11th Annu. European Sympos. Algorithms*, pages 230–241, 2003.

[11] A. Gupta, R. Krauthgamer, and J. R. Lee. Bounded geometries, fractals, and low-distortion embeddings. In *Proc. 44th Annu. IEEE Sympos. Found. Comput. Sci.*, pages 534–543, 2003.

S. Har-Peled. A practical approach for computing the diameter of a point-set. In *Proc. 17th Annu. ACM Sympos. Comput. Geom.*, pages 177–186, 2001.

[12] J. Heinonen. *Lectures on analysis on metric spaces.* Universitext. Springer-Verlag, New York, 2001.

[13] S. Har-Peled and S. Mazumdar. Fast algorithms for computing the smallest k-enclosing disc. *Algorithmica*, 41(3):147–157, 2005.

[14] M. J. Keil and C. A. Gutwin. Classes of graphs which approximate the complete euclidean graph. *Discrete Comput. Geom.*, 7:13–28, 1992.

[15] R. J. Lipton and R. E. Tarjan. Applications of a planar separator theorem. *SIAM J. Comput.*, 9(3):615–627, 1980.

[16] R. Motwani and P. Raghavan. *Randomized Algorithms.* Cambridge University Press, New York, NY, 1995.

[17] G. L. Miller, S. H. Teng, W. P. Thurston, and S. A. Vavasis. Separators for sphere-packings and nearest neighbor graphs. *J. Assoc. Comput. Mach.*, 44(1):1–29, 1997.

[18] G. Narasimhan and M. Smid. *Geometric spanner networks.* Cambridge University Press, 2007.

[19] W. D. Smith and N. C. Wormald. Geometric separator theorems and applications. In *Proc. 39th Annu. IEEE Sympos. Found. Comput. Sci.*, pages 232–243, 1998.

[20] K. R. Varadarajan. A divide-and-conquer algorithm for min-cost perfect matching in the plane. In *Proc. 39th Annu. IEEE Sympos. Found. Comput. Sci.*, pages 320–331, 1998.

APPENDIX

A. FROM SSPD TO SPANNER

Abam *et al.* [3] showed how to construct a $(1+\varepsilon)$-spanner from their SSPD for a set of n points in a plane. The proof of the resulting graph is $(1+\varepsilon)$-spanner depends on the SSPD construction, namely the monotonicity property of the SSPD—see [3] for the definition and details. Our spanner construction from a SSPD $\mathcal{S}$ of a set $\mathsf{P} \subseteq \mathbb{R}^d$ of n points, as describe next, is just a simple generalization of the construction given in [3] but the proof is independent of the construction.

A.1 The construction

For a parameter ψ, we define a ***ψ-cone*** to be the intersection of d non-parallel half-spaces such that the angle of any two rays emanating at the cone's apex and being inside the cone is at most ψ. Let $\mathcal{C}$ be a collection of $O(1/\psi^{d-1})$ interior-disjoint ψ-cones, each with their apex at the origin, that together cover $\mathbb{R}^d$. We can construct this collection of cones by a grid induced by a system of halfspaces, such that given a direction, we can find the cone containing this direction in constant time.

We call the cones in $\mathcal{C}$ ***canonical cones***. For a cone $\sigma \in \mathcal{C}$

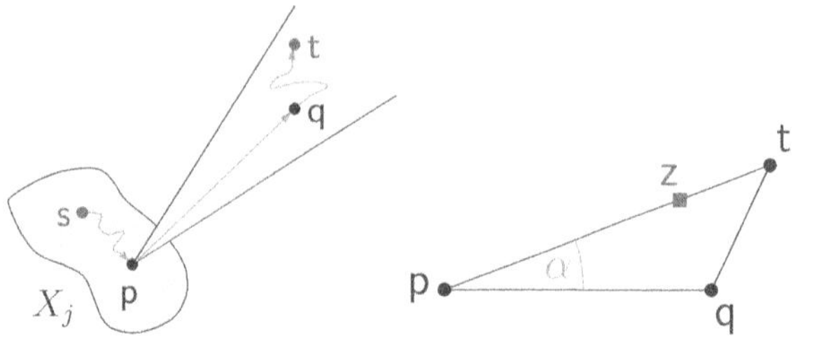

Figure 3: Illustration of the proof of Theorem 5.1.

and a point $p \in \mathbb{R}^d$, let $\sigma(p)$ denote the translated copy of σ whose apex coincides with p.

A.1.1 The spanner construction

We are given a $1/\rho$-SSPD $\mathcal{S}$ of a point-set P in $\mathbb{R}^d$, where $\rho \leq \varepsilon/8$. We next show how to convert this SSPD into a $(1+\varepsilon)$-spanner of P.

Let $\psi = \varepsilon/40$. We build a graph $\mathcal{G}$ having P as its vertices set. Initially the graph has no edges. Next, for each pair $\{\mathcal{X}, \mathcal{Y}\} \in \mathcal{S}$ pick an arbitrary point p from the set with smaller diameter, say $\mathcal{X}$. We will refer to p as the ***hub*** of $\mathcal{X}$, denoted by $\mathrm{hub}(X)$. For each cone $\sigma \in \mathcal{C}$, we connect p to its nearest neighbor in $\mathcal{Y} \cap \sigma(\mathsf{p})$ (denoted by q); that is, we insert the edge pq into $\mathcal{G}$, with $\|\mathsf{pq}\|$ as its weight. Thus, every pair of $\mathcal{S}$ contributes $|\mathcal{C}|$ edges to $\mathcal{G}$.

We claim that $\mathcal{G}$ is the desired spanner.

A.2 Analysis

Restatement of Theorem 5.1 *Given a $8/\varepsilon$-SSPD $\mathcal{S}$ for a point-set P in $\mathbb{R}^d$, one can compute a $(1+\varepsilon)$-spanner of P with $O(|\mathcal{S}|/\varepsilon^{d-1})$ edges. The construction time is proportional to the total weight of $\mathcal{S}$. In particular, a point appears in k pairs of the SSPD is of degree $O(k/\varepsilon^{d-1})$ in the resulting spanner.*

PROOF. The construction is described above (using $\rho = \varepsilon/8$ and $\psi = \varepsilon/40$), and the bound on the number of edges in the spanner follows immediately.

The proof of the spanner property is by induction. Sort the pairs of points in P by their distance and let $p_1q_1, \ldots, p_uq_u$ be these $u = \binom{n}{2}$ pairs sorted by their length, where $n = |\mathsf{P}|$.

It is easy to verify that p_1q_1 must be in the spanner. so, assume it holds that $\mathsf{d}_{\mathcal{G}}(p_i, q_i) \leq (1+\varepsilon)\|p_iq_i\|$, for all $i \leq k$. We now prove the claim holds for st, where $\mathsf{s} = p_{k+1}$ and $\mathsf{t} = q_{k+1}$.

Assume $\mathsf{s} \in \mathcal{X}_j$ and $\mathsf{t} \in \mathcal{Y}_j$ for some pair $\{\mathcal{X}_j, \mathcal{Y}_j\}$ of $\mathcal{S}$. Furthermore, assume that $\mathcal{X}_j$ is the set with the smaller diameter, and let $\mathsf{p} = \mathrm{hub}(\mathcal{X}_j)$. Let q be the closest neighbor to p inside the cone containing t. By construction, the edge pq is in the spanner.

Since $\mathsf{s}, \mathsf{p} \in \mathcal{X}_j$, and $\mathsf{t} \in \mathcal{Y}_j$ it follows that $\|\mathsf{sp}\| < \|\mathsf{st}\|$. As such, by induction, we have that $\mathsf{d}_{\mathcal{G}}(\mathsf{s}, \mathsf{p}) \leq (1+\varepsilon)\|\mathsf{sp}\|$. It is also easy to verify that $\|\mathsf{qt}\| < \|\mathsf{st}\|$ (this also follows from the calculations below), which implies that $\mathsf{d}_{\mathcal{G}}(\mathsf{q}, \mathsf{t}) \leq (1+\varepsilon)\|\mathsf{qt}\|$.

As such, we have that

$$\begin{aligned}\mathcal{E} &= \mathsf{d}_{\mathcal{G}}(\mathsf{s},\mathsf{t}) - \|\mathsf{st}\| \\ &\leq (1+\varepsilon)\|\mathsf{sp}\| + \|\mathsf{pq}\| + (1+\varepsilon)\|\mathsf{qt}\| - \|\mathsf{st}\| \\ &\leq 2\|\mathsf{sp}\| + \|\mathsf{pq}\| + (1+\varepsilon)\|\mathsf{qt}\| - \|\mathsf{pt}\| + \|\mathsf{sp}\| \\ &\leq 3\|\mathsf{sp}\| + \overbrace{\|\mathsf{pq}\| + (1+\varepsilon)\|\mathsf{qt}\| - \|\mathsf{pt}\|}^{\Delta=}.\end{aligned}$$

Let z be the projection of q on the segment pt. It holds $\|\mathsf{pt}\| = \|\mathsf{pz}\| + \|\mathsf{zt}\|$. Let $\alpha = \angle \mathsf{tpq} \leq \psi$. Now, observe that $\tan\alpha = \dfrac{\sin\alpha}{\cos\alpha} \leq 2\psi$, because $\sin\alpha \leq \alpha \leq \psi$, and $\cos\alpha \geq \cos\psi \geq 1/2$, since $\psi \leq \pi/3$. As such $\|\mathsf{zq}\| = \|\mathsf{pz}\|\tan\alpha \leq 2\psi\|\mathsf{pz}\|$. This implies that

$$\begin{aligned}\Delta &= \|\mathsf{pq}\| + (1+\varepsilon)\|\mathsf{qt}\| - \|\mathsf{pt}\| \\ &\leq \|\mathsf{pz}\| + \|\mathsf{zq}\| + (1+\varepsilon)(\|\mathsf{zq}\| + \|\mathsf{zt}\|) - \|\mathsf{pz}\| - \|\mathsf{zt}\| \\ &\leq (2+\varepsilon)\|\mathsf{zq}\| + \varepsilon\|\mathsf{zt}\| \\ &\leq 2\psi(2+\varepsilon)\|\mathsf{pz}\| + \varepsilon\|\mathsf{zt}\| \\ &\leq 6\psi\|\mathsf{pz}\| + \varepsilon\|\mathsf{zt}\| \\ &\leq (6\psi - \varepsilon)\|\mathsf{pz}\| + \varepsilon(\|\mathsf{pz}\| + \|\mathsf{zt}\|) \\ &\leq (6\psi - \varepsilon)\|\mathsf{pz}\| + \varepsilon\|\mathsf{pt}\|.\end{aligned}$$

Now, by the above $\|\mathsf{pz}\| \leq \|\mathsf{pq}\|$ and $\|\mathsf{sp}\| \leq (\varepsilon/8)\|\mathsf{pq}\|$. As such,

$$\begin{aligned}\mathcal{E} &\leq 3\|\mathsf{sp}\| + \Delta \leq 3\|\mathsf{sp}\| + (6\psi - \varepsilon)\|\mathsf{pz}\| + \varepsilon(\|\mathsf{sp}\| + \|\mathsf{st}\|) \\ &\leq 4\|\mathsf{sp}\| + (6\psi - \varepsilon)\|\mathsf{pz}\| + \varepsilon\|\mathsf{st}\| \\ &\leq frac\varepsilon 2\|\mathsf{pq}\| + (6\psi - \varepsilon)\|\mathsf{pq}\| + \varepsilon\|\mathsf{st}\| \\ &= \left(6\psi - \frac{\varepsilon}{2}\right)\|\mathsf{pq}\| + \varepsilon\|\mathsf{st}\| \leq \varepsilon\|\mathsf{st}\|,\end{aligned}$$

since $\psi \leq \varepsilon/12$ implies that $\left(6\psi - \frac{\varepsilon}{2}\right) \leq 0$. This implies that $\mathsf{d}_{\mathcal{G}}(\mathsf{s},\mathsf{t}) \leq (1+\varepsilon)\|\mathsf{st}\|$.

Construction time. To implement this construction scan the pairs of the SSPD one by one. For each such pair $\{\mathcal{X}, \mathcal{Y}\}$, we do the following.

First, we need to determine if $\mathrm{diam}(\mathcal{X}) = O(\mathrm{diam}(\mathcal{Y}))$ or $\mathrm{diam}(\mathcal{Y}) = O(\mathrm{diam}(\mathcal{X}))$ (so we known which set is roughly smaller). This can be done in $O(|\mathcal{X}| + |\mathcal{Y}|)$ by approximating the diameter of both sets in linear time. Next, for each such pair (assume $\mathcal{X}$ has a smaller diameter than $\mathcal{Y}$), we need to find the nearest neighbor to $\mathrm{hub}(\mathcal{X})$ in $\mathcal{Y}$, in each one of the cones. To this end, we have a grid of directions around $\mathrm{hub}(\mathcal{X})$, and we compute for each grid cell all the points of $\mathcal{Y}$ falling into this cell. Next, for all the points in such a grid cell, we find the closest point to $\mathrm{hub}(\mathcal{X})$ in linear time.

This takes $O(|\mathcal{X}| + |\mathcal{Y}|)$ time for the pair $\{X, Y\}$. Overall, this takes time linear in the total weight of the given SSPD. □

The Complexity of the Normal Surface Solution Space*

Benjamin A. Burton†
School of Mathematics and Physics
The University of Queensland
Brisbane QLD 4072, Australia
bab@maths.uq.edu.au

ABSTRACT

Normal surface theory is a central tool in algorithmic three-dimensional topology, and the enumeration of vertex normal surfaces is the computational bottleneck in many important algorithms. However, it is not well understood how the number of such surfaces grows in relation to the size of the underlying triangulation. Here we address this problem in both theory and practice. In theory, we tighten the exponential upper bound substantially; furthermore, we construct pathological triangulations that prove an exponential bound to be unavoidable. In practice, we undertake a comprehensive analysis of millions of triangulations and find that in general the number of vertex normal surfaces is remarkably small, with strong evidence that our pathological triangulations may in fact be the worst case scenarios. This analysis is the first of its kind, and the striking behaviour that we observe has important implications for the feasibility of topological algorithms in three dimensions.

Categories and Subject Descriptors

F.2.2 [**Analysis of Algorithms and Problem Complexity**]: Nonnumerical Algorithms and Problems—*Geometrical problems and computations*; G.2.1 [**Discrete Mathematics**]: Combinatorics

General Terms

Performance, theory, experimentation

Keywords

Computational topology, 3-manifolds, normal surfaces, vertex enumeration, complexity

*A more detailed version of this paper will be available as *Extreme cases in normal surface enumeration* (in preparation).

†Supported by the Australian Research Council under the Discovery Projects funding scheme (project DP1094516).

1. INTRODUCTION

Geometric topology is an inherently algorithmic subject, asking fundamental questions such as the *homeomorphism problem* (find an algorithm to determine whether two given spaces are topologically equivalent) and the *identification problem* (find an algorithm that can determine the topological name and/or structure of a given space). Three-dimensional topology is of particular interest, since in lower dimensions such problems become trivial [27], and in higher dimensions they become unsolvable [25].

Throughout this paper we restrict our attention to *closed 3-manifolds*. In essence, a closed 3-manifold is a compact 3-dimensional topological space that locally looks like $\mathbb{R}^3$ at every point. Much recent progress has been made on algorithms in 3-manifold topology. For example:

- Rubinstein gave an algorithm in 1992 for recognising the simplest of all closed 3-manifolds, namely the 3-sphere [32, 33]; this algorithm has been refined several times since [8, 19, 34].
- In 1995, Jaco and Tollefson presented an algorithm for breaking a 3-manifold down into a connected sum decomposition (essentially a topological "prime decomposition") [21].
- Perelman's proof of the geometrisation conjecture in 2002 finally resolved the general homeomorphism problem for 3-manifolds, completing a programme initiated decades earlier by pioneers such as Haken [15] and Thurston [36]. The full homeomorphism algorithm is a fusion of diverse and complex components, including both the 3-sphere recognition and connected sum decomposition algorithms above.

A recurring theme in these algorithms (and many others) is that they rely upon *normal surface theory*, a tool that allows us to convert difficult topology problems into simpler linear programming problems. In particular, we can search for an interesting surface within a 3-manifold by (i) constructing a high-dimensional polytope, (ii) enumerating the "admissible" vertices of this polytope, and then (iii) testing each admissible vertex to see whether it encodes the interesting surface that we are searching for.[1]

The concept of an "interesting surface" depends on the application at hand. For instance, in the connected sum

[1]Some other algorithms (such as knot genus [16] and Heegaard genus [24]) replace step (ii) with the more difficult enumeration of a Hilbert basis for a polyhedral cone, yielding what are known as *fundamental surfaces*.

decomposition algorithm we search for embedded spheres within our 3-manifold; in other algorithms we might search for non-trivial embedded discs [14] or embedded incompressible surfaces [17]. However, in all of these applications the high-dimensional polytope and its admissible vertices remain the same. That is, the polytope vertex enumeration problem is a *common component* for all of these topological algorithms and many others besides.

Furthermore, this common vertex enumeration problem is in fact the computational bottleneck for many of these algorithms [8, 10]. It is therefore important to improve the efficiency and understand the complexity of this vertex enumeration problem, since any improvements or results will have a widespread impact on computational 3-manifold topology as a whole. This impact also extends beyond three dimensions—for instance, in *4-manifold topology*, to understand whether a given triangulation represents a 4-manifold we require all of the complex machinery of 3-sphere recognition as discussed above.

In general, polytope vertex enumeration is difficult. The general problem is known to be NP-hard [12, 22], and the range of available algorithms is matched by a range of pathological cases that exploit their weaknesses [2]. However, in our context we have two advantages:

- We are not dealing with an arbitrary polytope, but rather one that derives from the machinery of normal surface theory; this polytope is known as the *projective solution space*. Such polytopes have additional constraints on their dimensions and the equalities and inequalities that define them.

- We do not need to enumerate all vertices of the polytope, but only the *admissible vertices*. These are the vertices that satisfy an additional family of non-linear constraints, known as the *quadrilateral constraints*.

These contextual advantages can be exploited in vertex enumeration algorithms with great success; see [7, 8, 9, 37] for details. Nevertheless, the enumeration problem remains a difficult one. In particular, Agol et al. [1] show that determining knot genus—yet another problem that employs normal surface theory—is in fact NP-complete.

In this paper we concern ourselves with the *complexity* of the enumeration problem. More specifically, we focus on the *number of admissible vertices* of the projective solution space, which we denote by σ. This quantity is important for the following reasons:

- The admissible vertex count σ gives a lower bound for the time complexity of vertex enumeration. Moreover, for the quadrilateral-to-standard conversion algorithm (a key component of the current state-of-the-art enumeration algorithm), there is strong evidence to suggest that the running time is in fact a low-degree polynomial in σ [7].

- Each admissible vertex corresponds to a surface in our 3-manifold upon which we must run some subsequent test. For some problems (such as Hakenness testing [10, 17]) this test is extremely expensive, and so the number of admissible vertices becomes a critical factor in the overall time complexity.

The input for a typical normal surface algorithm is a *3-manifold triangulation*, formed from n tetrahedra by joining their $4n$ faces together in pairs. We call n the *size* of the triangulation; not only does n represent the complexity of the input, but both the dimension and the number of facets of the projective solution space are linear in n.

The growth of σ as a function of n is currently not well understood. The only general theoretical bound in the literature is $\sigma \leq 128^n$, proven by Hass et al. [16]; in the special case of a one-vertex triangulation this has been improved to $\sigma \in O(15^n)$ [9]. Very little is known about the growth of σ in practice, though initial observations suggest that σ is in fact far smaller [7]. For example, in the proof that the Weber-Seifert dodecahedral space is non-Haken (one of the first significant computer proofs to employ normal surface theory), a "typical" triangulation of size $n = 23$ is found to generate just $\sigma = 1751$ admissible vertices [10].

In this paper we shed more light on the growth of σ, including new theoretical bounds and comprehensive practical experimentation. Following a brief outline of normal surface theory in Section 2, we present the following results:

- In Section 3 we show that $\sigma \in O(\phi^{7n})$, where ϕ is the golden ratio $(1+\sqrt{5})/2$. This tightens the general theoretical bound on σ from 128^n to just over $O(29^n)$. We prove this by extending McMullen's upper bound theorem [31] to show that any convex polytope with k facets must have $O(\phi^k)$ vertices.

  We push this bound from the other direction in Section 4 by constructing an infinite family of 3-manifold triangulations for which $\sigma = 17^{n/4} + n/4$. This yields the first known family for which σ is exponential in n, and disproves an earlier conjecture of the author that $\sigma \in O(2^n)$. By extending this family to all $n > 5$ we show that any theoretical upper bound must grow at least as fast as $\Omega(17^{n/4}) \simeq \Omega(2.03^n)$.

- In Section 5 we build a comprehensive census of *all* 3-manifold triangulations of size $n \leq 9$, and measure σ for each of the ~ 150 million triangulations that ensue. We find a remarkably slow growth rate—for $n > 5$ the worst cases are precisely the infinite family above, suggesting that the lower limit of $\Omega(17^{n/4}) \simeq \Omega(2.03^n)$ may in fact be tight. In the average case the mean $\overline{\sigma}$ appears to grow even slower, with an apparent growth rate of less than ϕ^n and a final mean of just $\overline{\sigma} \simeq 78.49$ for $n = 9$.

  This analysis is the first of its kind, primarily because the complex algorithms and software required for such a comprehensive study did not exist until very recently [5, 7]. Previous censuses have focused on restricted classes of triangulations (such as minimal triangulations of irreducible or hyperbolic manifolds [5, 11, 26, 30]), and previous measurements of σ have been for isolated or ad-hoc collections of cases [7, 10, 28].

Throughout this paper we work with Haken's original formulation of normal surface theory [14, 15]. Tollefson defines an alternative formulation called *quadrilateral coordinates* [37], which is only applicable for some problems but where the polytope becomes much simpler. In quadrilateral coordinates an upper bound of $\sigma \leq 4^n$ can be obtained through an analysis of *zero sets* [9], but again the growth rate is found to be significantly slower in practice. We address quadrilateral coordinates in detail in the full version of this paper.

2. PRELIMINARIES

Throughout this paper we assume that we are working with a *3-manifold triangulation of size n*. By this we mean a collection of n tetrahedra, some of whose $4n$ faces are affinely identified (or "glued together") in pairs so that the resulting topological space is a 3-manifold (possibly with boundary). If all $4n$ faces are identified in $2n$ pairs then we obtain a closed 3-manifold; otherwise we obtain a *triangulation with boundary*, and the unidentified faces become *boundary faces*. Unless otherwise specified, all triangulations in this paper are of closed 3-manifolds.

There is no need for a 3-manifold triangulation to be rigidly embedded in some larger space—tetrahedra can be "bent" or "stretched". Moreover, we allow multiple vertices of the same tetrahedron to be identified as a result of our face gluings, and likewise with edges. This allows us to build triangulations using very few tetrahedra, which becomes useful for computation.

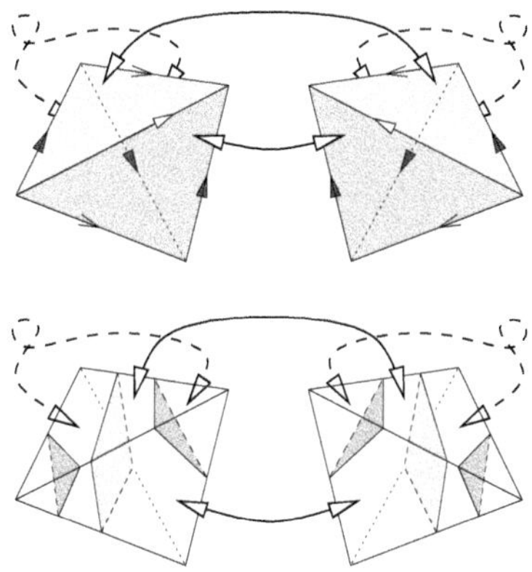

Figure 1: A 3-manifold triangulation and an embedded normal surface

To illustrate, the upper diagram of Figure 1 shows a triangulation of the product space $S^2 \times S^1$ using just $n = 2$ tetrahedra—the back two faces of each tetrahedron are identified with a twist, and the front two faces of the left tetrahedron are identified directly with the front two faces of the right tetrahedron. All eight vertices become identified together, and the 12 edges become identified in three distinct classes (represented in the diagram by three different types of arrowhead). We say that the resulting triangulation has *one vertex* and *three edges*.

Normal surfaces were introduced by Kneser [23], and further developed by Haken [14, 15] for use in algorithms. A *normal surface* is a 2-dimensional surface embedded within a 3-manifold triangulation that meets each tetrahedron in a (possibly empty) collection of *triangles* and/or *quadrilaterals*, as illustrated in Figure 2. For example, a normal surface within our $S^2 \times S^1$ triangulation is shown in the lower diagram of Figure 1; as a consequence of the tetrahedron gluings, the six triangles and quadrilaterals join together to form a 2-dimensional sphere.

There are four distinct *types* of triangle and three distinct *types* of quadrilateral within each tetrahedron (defined by which edges of the tetrahedron they meet). The *vector representation* of a normal surface is a collection of $7n$ integers counting the number of pieces of each type in each tetrahedron; from this vector in $\mathbb{R}^{7n}$ we can completely reconstruct the original surface. We treat surfaces and their vectors interchangeably (so, for instance, "adding" two surfaces means adding their two vectors and reconstructing a new surface from the result).

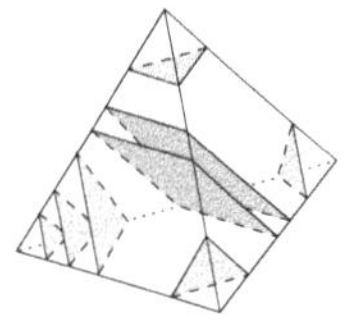

Figure 2: Normal triangles and quadrilaterals within a tetrahedron

An early result of Haken is a set of necessary and sufficient conditions for a vector to represent a normal surface: (i) all coordinates must be non-negative; (ii) the vector must satisfy a set of linear homogeneous equations (the *matching equations*); and (iii) there can be at most one non-zero quadrilateral coordinate corresponding to each tetrahedron (the *quadrilateral constraints*). Vectors that satisfy all of these conditions are called *admissible*.

Jaco and Oertel [17] define the *projective solution space* to be the polytope in $\mathbb{R}^{7n}$ obtained as a cross-section of the cone defined by (i) and (ii) above. A *vertex normal surface* lies on an extremal ray of this cone and is not a multiple of some smaller surface. The vertex normal surfaces are in bijection with the admissible vertices of the projective solution space; we let σ denote the number of vertex normal surfaces, and we call σ the *admissible vertex count*.

The enumeration of vertex normal surfaces is a critical component—and often the computational bottleneck—for many important topological algorithms. This is because one can often prove that, if an interesting surface exists (such as an incompressible surface or an essential sphere), then one must appear as a vertex normal surface. See Hass et al. [16] for a more detailed introduction to normal surface theory and its role in computational topology.

3. THEORETICAL BOUNDS

As noted in the introduction, the best bound known to date for the admissible vertex count is $\sigma \le 128^n$, proven by Hass et al. [16]. We begin by tightening this exponential bound as follows:

THEOREM 1. *Let $\phi = (1+\sqrt{5})/2$. Then the admissible vertex count σ is bounded above by $O(\phi^{7n}) \simeq O(29.03^n)$.*

We prove this through a simple extension of McMullen's upper bound theorem [31]. McMullen gives a tight bound on the number of vertices for a convex polytope with k facets and d dimensions; we extend this here to a loose bound that covers all possible dimensions.

LEMMA 2. *Let $F_0 = 0$, $F_1 = 1$, $F_2 = 1$, ... represent the Fibonacci sequence, where $F_{i+2} = F_{i+1} + F_i$. Then for any $k \ge 3$, a convex polytope with precisely k facets has $\le F_{k+1}$ vertices.*

PROOF. Suppose the polytope P is d-dimensional with precisely k facets. Then McMullen's theorem (taken in dual

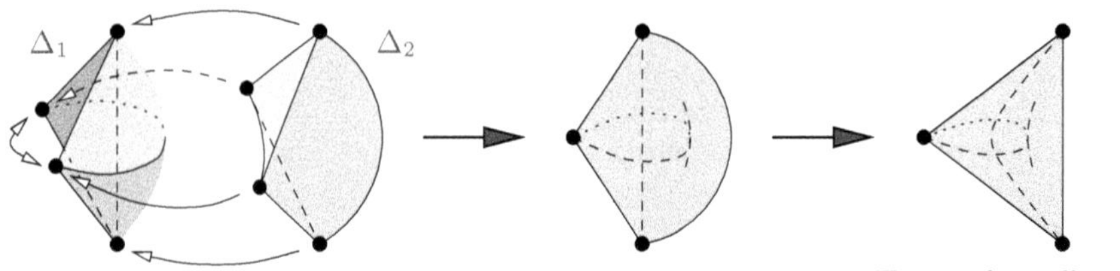

Figure 3: The two-tetrahedron triangular pillow at the centre of a 4-block

form) shows that P has at most

$$\binom{k-\lfloor\frac{d+1}{2}\rfloor}{k-d}+\binom{k-\lfloor\frac{d+2}{2}\rfloor}{k-d}$$
$$=\binom{k-\lfloor\frac{d+1}{2}\rfloor}{d-\lfloor\frac{d+1}{2}\rfloor}+\binom{k-\lfloor\frac{d+2}{2}\rfloor}{d-\lfloor\frac{d+2}{2}\rfloor} \quad (1)$$

vertices.[2] For even d this can be rewritten as $\binom{k-a}{a}+\binom{(k-2)-b}{b}$ for suitable integers a, b, and for odd d it can be rewritten as $2\binom{(k-1)-a}{a}$ for a suitable integer a.

We now claim that $\binom{k-a}{a} \leq F_k$ for any k, a with $k \geq 1$. This is easily established for $k = 1, 2$, and the full claim follows from the inductive step $\binom{k-a}{a} = \binom{k-1-a}{a}+\binom{k-1-a}{a-1} = \binom{(k-1)-a}{a} + \binom{(k-2)-(a-1)}{a-1} \leq F_{k-1} + F_{k-2} = F_k$.

From here our lemma is straightforward. If d is even then the number of vertices of P is at most $\binom{k-a}{a} + \binom{(k-2)-b}{b} \leq F_k + F_{k-2} \leq F_k + F_{k-1} = F_{k+1}$, and if d is odd then the number of vertices is at most $2\binom{(k-1)-a}{a} \leq 2F_{k-1} \leq F_k + F_{k-1} = F_{k+1}$. □

Unlike McMullen's result, Lemma 2 is not tight. Nevertheless, it gives us a very good[3] asymptotic upper bound of $O(\phi^k)$, which is enough to prove our main theorem.

PROOF OF THEOREM 1. The facets of the projective solution space in $\mathbb{R}^{7n}$ are defined by the $7n$ inequalities $x_1 \geq 0$, ..., $x_{7n} \geq 0$, and so there are at most $7n$ facets in total. Lemma 2 then shows that the projective solution space has at most F_{7n+1} vertices, and so $\sigma \leq F_{7n+1}$. Using the standard formula $F_k = \lfloor \phi^k/\sqrt{5} + \frac{1}{2} \rfloor$ it follows that $\sigma \in O(\phi^{7n})$. □

It is interesting to note that Theorem 1 makes no use of admissibility—this suggests that, although the bound of ϕ^{7n} is a strong improvement on 128^n, this bound is still very loose. We confirm this through experimentation in Section 5. Although we only consider closed 3-manifolds in this paper, it should be noted that Theorem 1 and its proof apply equally well to triangulations with boundary, and also to the *ideal triangulations* of Thurston [35].

4. EXTREME CASES

Having tightened the upper bound from above, we now turn our attention to limiting the upper bound from below.

[2]This is the number of facets of the cyclic d-dimensional polytope with k vertices [13].

[3]Experimentation shows that this asymptotic upper bound of $\phi^k \simeq 1.618^k$ is close to optimal. If we maximise equation (1) over all d for each $k = 100, \ldots, 200$, the maximum grows at a rate of approximately 1.613^k.

We do this by building pathological triangulations for which $\sigma \in \Theta(17^{n/4}) \simeq \Theta(2.03^n)$. This growth rate shows that an exponential upper bound on σ is unavoidable, and furthermore disproves an earlier conjecture of the author that $\sigma \in O(2^n)$.

We begin by describing 4-blocks, which are small building blocks that appear repeatedly throughout our triangulations. Using these building blocks, we then construct the family of pathological triangulations $\mathcal{X}_1, \mathcal{X}_2, \ldots$.

Definition (4-block). A *4-block* is a triangulation with boundary, built from the four tetrahedra $\Delta_1, \Delta_2, \Delta_3, \Delta_4$ using the following construction.

We begin by folding together two faces of Δ_1, and then wrapping Δ_2 around the remaining two faces as illustrated in Figure 3. This forms a *triangular pillow* with three vertices, three boundary edges, two internal edges, and two boundary faces.

Next we fold together two faces of Δ_3 and two faces of Δ_4, as illustrated in the leftmost column of Figure 4. To finish, we join the pillow to both Δ_3 and Δ_4 as illustrated in the central column of Figure 4—the upper face $A_1B_1A_2$ of the pillow is glued to the lower face $A_3B_2A_3$ of Δ_3, and the lower face $A_1B_1A_2$ of the pillow is glued to the upper face $A_4B_3A_4$ of Δ_4.

The final result is shown in the rightmost column of Figure 4, with three boundary vertices and one internal vertex. The triangular pillow is buried in the middle of this structure, wrapped around the internal vertex; for simplicity the two edges inside the pillow are not shown.

Definition (Pathological triangulation $\mathcal{X}_k$). For each integer $k \geq 1$, the *pathological triangulation* $\mathcal{X}_k$ is constructed from $n = 4k$ tetrahedra in the following manner.

From these $4k$ tetrahedra we build k distinct 4-blocks, labelled $\mathcal{B}_1, \ldots, \mathcal{B}_k$. Within each 4-block $\mathcal{B}_i$ we label the three boundary vertices P_i, Q_i, R_i, where P_i sits between both boundary triangles as illustrated in Figure 5.

For each $i = 1, \ldots, k$ we join blocks $\mathcal{B}_i$ and $\mathcal{B}_{i+1}$ as follows (where $\mathcal{B}_{k+1}$ is taken to mean $\mathcal{B}_1$). Triangle $P_iP_iR_i$ is joined to triangle $Q_{i+1}P_{i+1}P_{i+1}$; note that this is "twisted", not a direct gluing, since it maps $P_i \leftrightarrow Q_{i+1}$ and $P_{i+1} \leftrightarrow R_i$. There are in fact two ways this gluing can be performed (one a reflection of the other); we resolve this ambiguity by orienting each block consistently, and then choosing the gluing that preserves orientation.

An effect of these gluings is to identify all of the P_i, Q_i and R_i to a single vertex, so that $\mathcal{X}_k$ has $k+1$ vertices in total (counting also the k internal vertices from each original block).

It is not clear that each $\mathcal{X}_k$ is a 3-manifold triangulation (in particular, that $\mathcal{X}_k$ looks like $\mathbb{R}^3$ in the vicinity of each

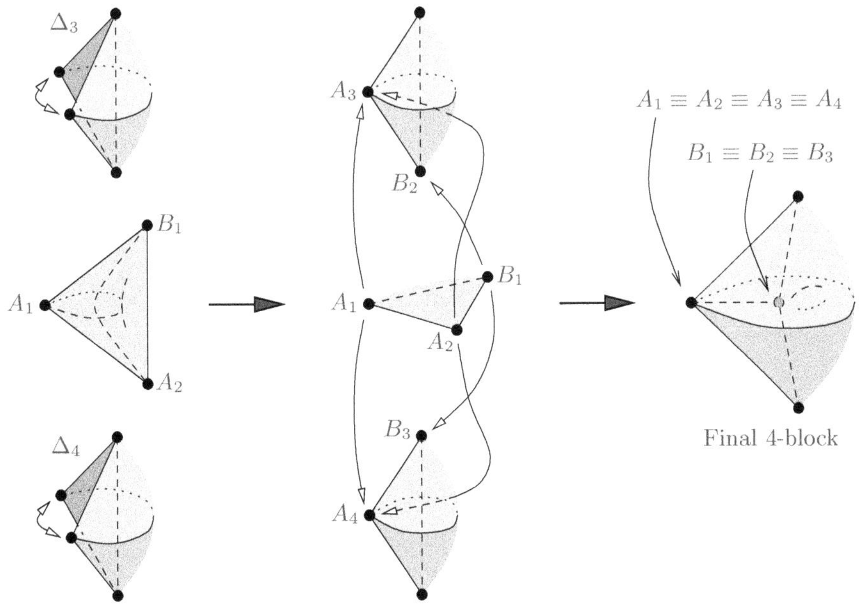

Figure 4: Building a 4-block from two tetrahedra and a triangular pillow

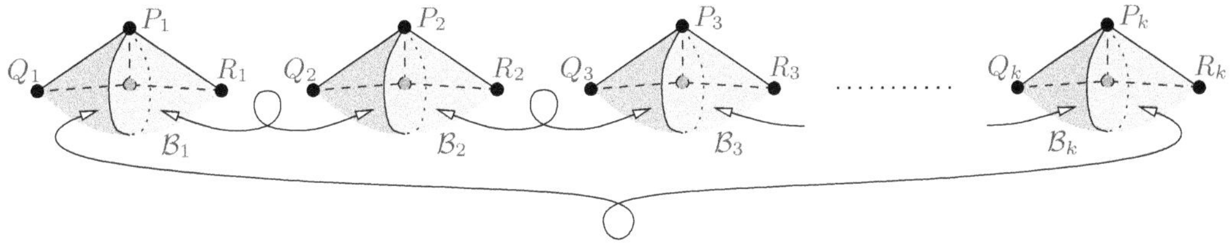

Figure 5: Building the pathological triangulation $\mathcal{X}_k$ from k distinct 4-blocks

vertex). The following sequence of results proves this by showing that every $\mathcal{X}_k$ is in fact a triangulation of the 3-sphere.

LEMMA 3. *A 4-block is a triangulation of the 3-ball (i.e., the solid 3-dimensional ball), with a boundary consisting of two triangles in the formation shown in Figure 6.*

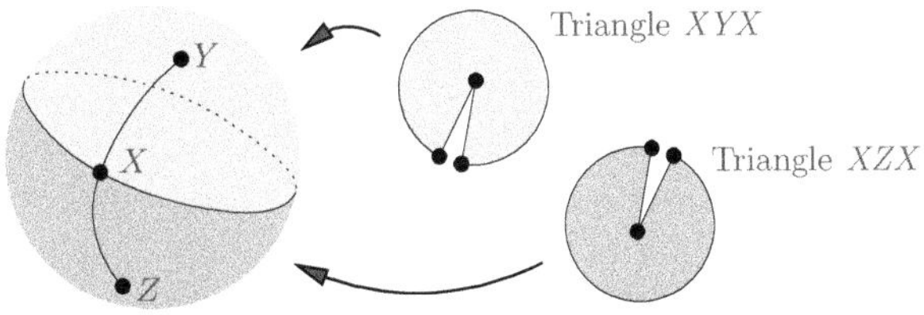

Figure 6: A 3-ball whose boundary consists of two triangles

PROOF. This is evident from the construction in Figure 4. It can also be verified computationally using the software package *Regina* [3], which implements 3-sphere and 3-ball recognition [4]. □

LEMMA 4. *Let $\mathcal{T}_1$ and $\mathcal{T}_2$ each be triangulations of the 3-ball with boundaries in the formation shown in Figure 6. If we identify one boundary triangle of $\mathcal{T}_1$ with one boundary triangle of $\mathcal{T}_2$ under any of the six possible identifications, the result is always another triangulation of the 3-ball with boundary in the formation shown in Figure 6.*

LEMMA 5. *Let $\mathcal{T}$ be a triangulation of the 3-ball with boundary in the formation shown in Figure 6. If we identify the two boundary triangles under any of the three possible orientation-preserving identifications, the result is always a closed 3-manifold triangulation of the 3-sphere.*

PROOF. Both of these results are essentially properties of 3-manifolds, not their underlying triangulations—if they hold for any selection of triangulations $\mathcal{T}_1, \mathcal{T}_2, \mathcal{T}$ then they must hold for all such selections. We verify these results using *Regina* by choosing 4-blocks for our triangulations and testing all six/three possible identifications. □

Since each $\mathcal{X}_k$ is built by joining together 4-blocks along boundary triangles in an orientation-preserving fashion, the following result follows immediately from Lemmata 3–5.

COROLLARY 6. *For each $k \geq 1$, $\mathcal{X}_k$ is a closed 3-manifold triangulation of the 3-sphere.*

We turn our attention now to counting the vertex normal surfaces for each triangulation $\mathcal{X}_k$. Recalling that $k = n/4$, the following result shows that for these pathological triangulations we have $\sigma \in \Theta(17^{n/4}) \simeq \Theta(2.03^n)$.

Lemma 7. *For each $k \geq 1$, $\mathcal{X}_k$ has precisely $\sigma = 17^k + k$ vertex normal surfaces.*

Proof. Consider a single 4-block with boundary vertices labelled P, Q, R as before, and let S denote the internal vertex. Define α, β and γ to be small loops on the 4-block boundary surrounding P, Q and R respectively, as illustrated in Figure 7.

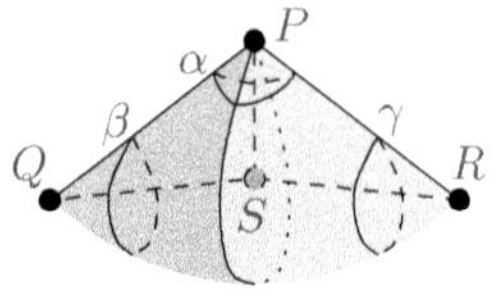

Figure 7: The curves α, β, γ on the boundary of a 4-block

Using the software package *Regina*, we can construct the projective solution space for this 4-block. There are 17 admissible vertices in total, corresponding to 17 vertex normal surfaces: one with empty boundary, and 16 whose boundary consists of some combination of α, β and γ. These surfaces are summarised in Table 1, and we label them $\mathbf{a}, \mathbf{b}, \ldots, \mathbf{q}$ as shown.

It is important to note that $\mathbf{a}, \mathbf{b}, \ldots, \mathbf{q}$ are all *compatible*; that is, no combination of their vectors can ever violate the quadrilateral constraints.[4] This is an unusual but extremely helpful state of affairs, since we can effectively ignore the quadrilateral constraints from here onwards.

Now consider the entire set of 4-blocks $\mathcal{B}_1, \ldots, \mathcal{B}_k$. Let $\mathbf{a}_i, \mathbf{b}_i, \ldots, \mathbf{q}_i$ denote the corresponding surfaces in $\mathcal{B}_i$, and let $\alpha_i, \beta_i, \gamma_i$ denote the corresponding boundary curves. Any normal surface in $\mathcal{X}_k$ is a union of normal surfaces in the individual blocks $\mathcal{B}_1, \ldots, \mathcal{B}_k$, and hence can be expressed as

$$(\lambda_{1,1}\,\mathbf{a}_1 + \ldots + \lambda_{1,17}\,\mathbf{q}_1) + \ldots + (\lambda_{k,1}\,\mathbf{a}_k + \ldots + \lambda_{k,17}\,\mathbf{q}_k)$$

for some family of constants $\lambda_{1,1}, \ldots, \lambda_{k,17} \geq 0$. In this form, it can be shown[5] that the matching equations for $\mathcal{X}_k$ reduce to the following statement:

> There is some non-negative $\mu \in \mathbb{R}$ such that, for every i, the sum $\lambda_{i,1}\,\mathbf{a}_i + \ldots + \lambda_{i,17}\,\mathbf{q}_i$ has boundary $\mu\alpha_i + \mu\beta_i + \mu\gamma_i$.

In other words, the portion of the overall surface within each 4-block $\mathcal{B}_i$ must have boundary $\mu\alpha_i + \mu\beta_i + \mu\gamma_i$, where μ is independent of i.

Return now to a single 4-block with admissible vertices $\mathbf{a}, \ldots, \mathbf{q}$, and let $\lambda_1\,\mathbf{a} + \ldots + \lambda_{17}\,\mathbf{q}$ be some point in the projective solution space for this 4-block. We can ensure that the corresponding surface has boundary of the form $\mu\alpha + \mu\beta + \mu\gamma$ by imposing the linear constraints depicted in Table 2 (where each line of these constraints corresponds to a section of the *Boundary* column in Table 1).

This has the effect of intersecting the original projective solution space for the 4-block with two new hyperplanes. A standard application of the filtered double description method [9] shows that the resulting polytope has 18 admissible vertices, described by the following 18 normal surfaces: the original $\mathbf{a}$ with no boundary, and 17 new surfaces[6] all with boundary $\alpha + \beta + \gamma$. Within each block $\mathcal{B}_i$, we label these 17 new surfaces $\mathbf{v}_{i,1}, \ldots, \mathbf{v}_{i,17}$.

Given the formulation of the matching equations above, it follows that the normal surfaces in $\mathcal{X}_k$ are described completely by the linear combinations

$$\rho_{1,1}\,\mathbf{v}_{1,1} + \ldots + \rho_{k,17}\,\mathbf{v}_{k,17} + \eta_1\mathbf{a}_1 + \ldots + \eta_k\mathbf{a}_k,$$

where each $\rho_{i,j}, \eta_i \geq 0$ and where $\sum_j \rho_{1,j} = \sum_j \rho_{2,j} = \ldots = \sum_j \rho_{k,j}$. The full projective solution space for $\mathcal{X}_k$ therefore has $17^k + k$ admissible vertices, corresponding to the k surfaces $\mathbf{a}_1, \ldots, \mathbf{a}_k$ and the 17^k combinations $\mathbf{v}_{1,j_1} + \mathbf{v}_{2,j_2} + \ldots + \mathbf{v}_{k,j_k}$ for $j_1, j_2, \ldots, j_k \in \{1, \ldots, 17\}$. □

The pathological triangulations $\mathcal{X}_1, \mathcal{X}_2, \ldots$ cover all sizes of the form $n = 4k$. We can generalise this construction to include $n = 4k+1$, $4k+2$ and $4k+3$ by replacing one of our 4-blocks with a single "exceptional" block. The general constructions and analyses are detailed in the full version of this paper, and the results are summarised in the following theorem.

Theorem 8. *For every positive $n \neq 1, 2, 3, 5$, there exists a closed 3-manifold triangulation of size n whose admissible vertex count is as follows:*

$$\begin{array}{llcl} n = 4k & (k \geq 1) & \Longrightarrow & \sigma = 17^k + k \\ n = 4k+1 & (k \geq 2) & \Longrightarrow & \sigma = 581 \cdot 17^{k-2} + k + 1 \\ n = 4k+2 & (k \geq 1) & \Longrightarrow & \sigma = 69 \cdot 17^{k-1} + k \\ n = 4k+3 & (k \geq 1) & \Longrightarrow & \sigma = 141 \cdot 17^{k-1} + k + 2 \end{array} \qquad (2)$$

Lemma 7 proves this result for the first case $n = 4k$. For an extra measure of verification, equation (2) has been confirmed numerically for all $n \leq 14$ by building the relevant triangulations and using *Regina* to enumerate all vertex normal surfaces.

The main result of this section is the following limit on any upper bound for σ, which follows immediately from Theorem 8. Moreover, as we discover in the following section, there is reason to believe that this may in fact give the tightest possible asymptotic bound.

Corollary 9. *Any upper bound for the admissible vertex count σ must grow at a rate of at least $\Omega(17^{n/4}) \simeq \Omega(2.03^n)$.*

5. PRACTICAL GROWTH

We turn now to a comprehensive study of the admissible vertex count σ for real 3-manifold triangulations. The basis of this study is a complete census of *all* closed 3-manifold triangulations of size $n \leq 9$. This is a significant undertaking, and such a census has never been compiled before; the paper [5] details some of the sophisticated algorithms involved.

The result is a collection of 149 676 922 triangulations, each counted once up to *isomorphism* (a relabelling of tetrahedra and their vertices). It is worth noting that within this large collection of triangulations there is a much smaller

[4] This is because, within each tetrahedron, we observe that two of the three quadrilateral types never appear *anywhere* amongst the surfaces $\mathbf{a}, \mathbf{b}, \ldots, \mathbf{q}$.

[5] The argument uses the facts that curves $\alpha_i, \beta_i, \gamma_i$ surround vertices P_i, Q_i, R_i respectively, and that all of these vertices are identified together in the overall triangulation $\mathcal{X}_k$.

[6] These are the six surfaces $(\mathbf{c}+\mathbf{g},\ \mathbf{d}+\mathbf{f},\ \text{or}\ \mathbf{j}) + (\mathbf{b}\ \text{or}\ \mathbf{l})$, the five surfaces $\mathbf{c}+\mathbf{d}+(\mathbf{b},\ \mathbf{e},\ \mathbf{l},\ \mathbf{m},\ \text{or}\ \mathbf{n})$, and the six surfaces $\mathbf{c}+\mathbf{i}$, $\mathbf{c}+\mathbf{p}$, $\mathbf{d}+\mathbf{h}$, $\mathbf{d}+\mathbf{o}$, $\mathbf{k}$ and $\mathbf{q}$.

Label	Boundary	Description
a	—	Small sphere around internal vertex S
b	α	Small disc around boundary vertex P
c	β	Small disc around boundary vertex Q
d	γ	Small disc around boundary vertex R
e	α	Tube from P to S, closed around S
f	β	Tube from Q to S, closed around S
g	γ	Tube from R to S, closed around S
h	$\alpha+\beta$	Tube from P to Q via S, open at both ends
i	$\alpha \quad +\gamma$	Tube from P to R via S, open at both ends
j	$\beta+\gamma$	Tube from Q to R via S, open at both ends
k	$\alpha+\beta+\gamma$	Forked tube joining all of P, Q, R via S, open at all three ends
l	α	Surface **b** with large "balloon" disc attached inside the pillow
m	α	Surface **b** with punctured torus attached inside the pillow
n	α	Surface **e** with punctured torus attached inside the pillow
o	$\alpha+\beta$	Surface **h** with punctured torus attached inside the pillow
p	$\alpha \quad +\gamma$	Surface **i** with punctured torus attached inside the pillow
q	$\alpha+\beta+\gamma$	Surface **k** with punctured torus attached inside the pillow

Table 1: The 17 vertex normal surfaces within a 4-block

$$\begin{aligned} & \lambda_2 + \lambda_5 + \lambda_8 + \lambda_9 + \lambda_{11} + \lambda_{12} + \lambda_{13} + \lambda_{14} + \lambda_{15} + \lambda_{16} + \lambda_{17} \\ = {} & \lambda_3 + \lambda_6 + \lambda_8 + \lambda_{10} + \lambda_{11} + \lambda_{15} + \lambda_{17} \\ = {} & \lambda_4 + \lambda_7 + \lambda_9 + \lambda_{10} + \lambda_{11} + \lambda_{16} + \lambda_{17} \end{aligned}$$

Table 2: Ensuring a boundary of the form $\mu\alpha + \mu\beta + \mu\gamma$ within a single 4-block

number of distinct 3-manifolds, as indicated by the 3-manifold census data of Martelli and Petronio [26] and the author [5].

For each of these ~ 150 million triangulations we enumerate all vertex normal surfaces using the algorithms described in [7, 9]. The resulting admissible vertex counts σ are summarised in Table 3. All computations were performed using the software package *Regina* [3, 4].

Size (n)	Number of triangulations	Admissible vertex count (σ) Mean	Std dev	Min	Max
1	4	2.00	0.71	1	3
2	17	3.94	1.39	2	7
3	81	5.49	1.97	2	11
4	577	8.80	3.38	2	18
5	5 184	13.34	5.49	4	36
6	57 753	20.76	9.21	4	70
7	722 765	32.17	15.29	4	144
8	9 787 509	50.20	25.52	4	291
9	139 103 032	78.49	42.51	4	584

Table 3: Summary of admissible vertex counts for all triangulations ($n \le 9$)

The figures that we see are remarkably small. For $n = 9$ tetrahedra, although Theorem 1 places the theoretical bound at $\simeq O(29^n)$, we have just 584 vertex normal surfaces in the worst case. The mean admissible vertex count for $n = 9$ is much smaller again, evaluated at just 78.49. The full distribution of all admissible vertex counts for $n = 9$ is shown in the upper graph of Figure 8.

Indeed, our pathological triangulations $\mathcal{X}_1, \mathcal{X}_2$ represent the worst cases for $n = 4, 8$ respectively, giving the maximum observed values of $\sigma = 17^1 + 1 = 18$ and $\sigma = 17^2 + 2 = 291$. More generally, the pathological triangulations of Theorem 8 give the maximum cases in our census wherever they are defined (i.e., $n \neq 1, 2, 3, 5$). This leads us to the following general conjecture:

Conjecture 1. *For every positive $n \neq 1, 2, 3, 5$, equation (2) gives a tight upper bound on the admissible vertex count σ. As a consequence, we have $\sigma \in O(17^{n/4})$.*

The growth rate of σ for $n = 1, \ldots, 9$ is illustrated in the lower graph of Figure 8 (note that the vertical axis is plotted on a log scale). The growth rate of the maximum σ is roughly $17^{n/4} \simeq 2.03^n$ as suggested above; the growth rate of the average $\overline{\sigma}$ is in the range 1.5^n to 1.6^n. This is just below the Fibonacci growth rate of $\phi^n \simeq 1.62^n$. Indeed, if we let $\overline{\sigma}_n$ denote the mean admissible vertex count amongst all triangulations of size n, we find that $\overline{\sigma}_n < \overline{\sigma}_{n-1} + \overline{\sigma}_{n-2}$ throughout our census. This leads us to our next general conjecture:

Conjecture 2. *For every $n \geq 3$, the mean admissible vertex count $\overline{\sigma}_n$ satisfies the relation $\overline{\sigma}_n < \overline{\sigma}_{n-1} + \overline{\sigma}_{n-2}$. As a consequence, $\overline{\sigma}_n$ is bounded above by $O(\phi^n)$ where $\phi = (1+\sqrt{5})/2$.*

In particular, our census analysis gives us the following computational result:

Theorem 10. *Conjectures 1 and 2 are true for $n \leq 9$.*

6. CONCLUSIONS

We have pushed the theoretical bounds on the admissible vertex count σ from both directions, and we have shown through an exhaustive study of ~ 150 million triangulations that σ is surprisingly small in practice. We close with a brief discussion of the implications of this study.

Most importantly, it suggests that topological algorithms that employ normal surfaces might not be as infeasible as theory suggests. Hints of this have already been seen with the quadrilateral-to-standard conversion algorithm for normal surfaces [7], which (against theoretical expectations) appears to have a running time polynomial in its output size.

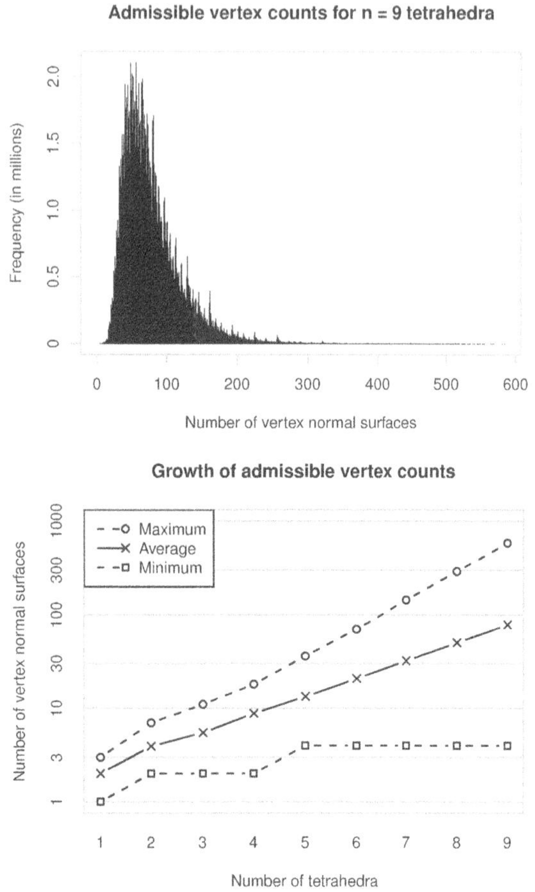

Figure 8: Aggregate results for admissible vertex counts

In many fields, a census for size $n \leq 9$ might not seem large enough for drawing conclusions and conjectures. However, there is evidence elsewhere to suggest that 3-manifold triangulations are flexible enough for important patterns to establish themselves for very low n. For example, the papers [6, 29] discuss several combinatorial patterns for $n \leq 6$; these patterns have later been found to generalise well for larger n [5, 26], and some are now proven in general [18, 20].

Finally, it is clear from this practical study that the theoretical bounds on σ still have much room for improvement. One possible direction is to incorporate the quadrilateral constraints directly into McMullen's theorem. This is difficult because the quadrilateral constraints break convexity, but the outcome may be significantly closer to the $O(17^{n/4})$ that we see in practice.

7. ACKNOWLEDGMENTS

The author is grateful to both the University of Victoria (Canada) and the Victorian Partnership for Advanced Computing (Australia) for the use of their excellent computing resources.

8. REFERENCES

[1] I. Agol, J. Hass, and W. Thurston. 3-manifold knot genus is NP-complete. In *STOC '02: Proceedings of the Thiry-Fourth Annual ACM Symposium on Theory of Computing*, pages 761–766. ACM Press, 2002.

[2] D. Avis, D. Bremner, and R. Seidel. How good are convex hull algorithms? *Comput. Geom.*, 7(5-6):265–301, 1997.

[3] B. A. Burton. Regina: Normal surface and 3-manifold topology software. `http://regina.sourceforge.net/`, 1999–2009.

[4] B. A. Burton. Introducing Regina, the 3-manifold topology software. *Experiment. Math.*, 13(3):267–272, 2004.

[5] B. A. Burton. Enumeration of non-orientable 3-manifolds using face-pairing graphs and union-find. *Discrete Comput. Geom.*, 38(3):527–571, 2007.

[6] B. A. Burton. Structures of small closed non-orientable 3-manifold triangulations. *J. Knot Theory Ramifications*, 16(5):545–574, 2007.

[7] B. A. Burton. Converting between quadrilateral and standard solution sets in normal surface theory. *Algebr. Geom. Topol.*, 9(4):2121–2174, 2009.

[8] B. A. Burton. Quadrilateral-octagon coordinates for almost normal surfaces. To appear in Experiment. Math., `arXiv:0904.3041`, Apr. 2009.

[9] B. A. Burton. Optimizing the double description method for normal surface enumeration. *Math. Comp.*, 79(269):453–484, 2010.

[10] B. A. Burton, J. H. Rubinstein, and S. Tillmann. The Weber-Seifert dodecahedral space is non-Haken. Preprint, `arXiv:0909.4625`, Sept. 2009.

[11] P. J. Callahan, M. V. Hildebrand, and J. R. Weeks. A census of cusped hyperbolic 3-manifolds. *Math. Comp.*, 68(225):321–332, 1999.

[12] M. E. Dyer. The complexity of vertex enumeration methods. *Math. Oper. Res.*, 8(3):381–402, 1983.

[13] B. Grünbaum. *Convex Polytopes*. Number 221 in Graduate Texts in Mathematics. Springer, New York, 2nd edition, 2003.

[14] W. Haken. Theorie der Normalflächen. *Acta Math.*, 105:245–375, 1961.

[15] W. Haken. Über das Homöomorphieproblem der 3-Mannigfaltigkeiten. I. *Math. Z.*, 80:89–120, 1962.

[16] J. Hass, J. C. Lagarias, and N. Pippenger. The computational complexity of knot and link problems. *J. Assoc. Comput. Mach.*, 46(2):185–211, 1999.

[17] W. Jaco and U. Oertel. An algorithm to decide if a 3-manifold is a Haken manifold. *Topology*, 23(2):195–209, 1984.

[18] W. Jaco, H. Rubinstein, and S. Tillmann. Minimal triangulations for an infinite family of lens spaces. *J. Topol.*, 2(1):157–180, 2009.

[19] W. Jaco and J. H. Rubinstein. 0-efficient triangulations of 3-manifolds. *J. Differential Geom.*, 65(1):61–168, 2003.

[20] W. Jaco, J. H. Rubinstein, and S. Tillmann. Coverings and minimal triangulations of 3-manifolds. To appear in Algebr. Geom. Topol., `arXiv:0903.0112`, Feb. 2009.

[21] W. Jaco and J. L. Tollefson. Algorithms for the complete decomposition of a closed 3-manifold. *Illinois J. Math.*, 39(3):358–406, 1995.

[22] L. Khachiyan, E. Boros, K. Borys, K. Elbassioni, and

V. Gurvich. Generating all vertices of a polyhedron is hard. *Discrete Comput. Geom.*, 39(1-3):174–190, 2008.

[23] H. Kneser. Geschlossene Flächen in dreidimensionalen Mannigfaltigkeiten. *Jahresbericht der Deut. Math. Verein.*, 38:248–260, 1929.

[24] T. Li. An algorithm to determine the Heegaard genus of a 3-manifold. Preprint, `arXiv:1002.1958`, Feb. 2010.

[25] A. A. Markov. Insolubility of the problem of homeomorphy. In *Proc. Internat. Congress Math. 1958*, pages 300–306. Cambridge Univ. Press, New York, 1960.

[26] B. Martelli and C. Petronio. Three-manifolds having complexity at most 9. *Experiment. Math.*, 10(2):207–236, 2001.

[27] W. S. Massey. *A Basic Course in Algebraic Topology.* Number 127 in Graduate Texts in Mathematics. Springer-Verlag, New York, 1991.

[28] S. Matsumoto and R. Rannard. The regular projective solution space of the figure-eight knot complement. *Experiment. Math.*, 9(2):221–234, 2000.

[29] S. V. Matveev. Tables of 3-manifolds up to complexity 6. *Max-Planck-Institut für Mathematik Preprint Series*, (67), 1998. Available from `http://www.mpim-bonn.mpg.de/html/preprints/preprints.html`.

[30] S. V. Matveev. Recognition and tabulation of three-dimensional manifolds. *Dokl. Akad. Nauk*, 400(1):26–28, 2005.

[31] P. McMullen. The maximum numbers of faces of a convex polytope. *Mathematika*, 17:179–184, 1970.

[32] J. H. Rubinstein. An algorithm to recognize the 3-sphere. In *Proceedings of the International Congress of Mathematicians (Zürich, 1994)*, volume 1, pages 601–611. Birkhäuser, 1995.

[33] J. H. Rubinstein. Polyhedral minimal surfaces, Heegaard splittings and decision problems for 3-dimensional manifolds. In *Geometric Topology (Athens, GA, 1993)*, volume 2 of *AMS/IP Stud. Adv. Math.*, pages 1–20. Amer. Math. Soc., 1997.

[34] A. Thompson. Thin position and the recognition problem for S^3. *Math. Res. Lett.*, 1(5):613–630, 1994.

[35] W. P. Thurston. The geometry and topology of 3-manifolds. Lecture notes, Princeton University, 1978.

[36] W. P. Thurston. Three-dimensional manifolds, Kleinian groups and hyperbolic geometry. *Bull. Amer. Math. Soc. (N.S.)*, 6(3):357–381, 1982.

[37] J. L. Tollefson. Normal surface Q-theory. *Pacific J. Math.*, 183(2):359–374, 1998.

Distance k-Sectors Exist*

Keiko Imai
Chuo University
imai@ise.chuo-u.ac.jp

Akitoshi Kawamura
University of Toronto
kawamura@cs.toronto.edu

Jiří Matoušek
Charles University
matousek@kam.mff.cuni.cz

Daniel Reem
The Technion
dream@tx.technion.ac.il

Takeshi Tokuyama
Tohoku University
tokuyama@dais.is.tohoku.ac.jp

ABSTRACT

The *bisector* of two nonempty sets P and Q in $\mathbb{R}^d$ is the set of all points with equal distance to P and to Q. A *distance k-sector* of P and Q, where $k \geq 2$ is an integer, is a $(k-1)$-tuple $(C_1, C_2, \ldots, C_{k-1})$ such that C_i is the bisector of C_{i-1} and C_{i+1} for every $i = 1, 2, \ldots, k-1$, where $C_0 = P$ and $C_k = Q$. This notion, for the case where P and Q are points in $\mathbb{R}^2$, was introduced by Asano, Matoušek, and Tokuyama, motivated by a question of Murata in VLSI design. They established the existence and uniqueness of the distance 3-sector in this special case. We prove the existence of a distance k-sector for all k and for every two disjoint, nonempty, closed sets P and Q in Euclidean spaces of any (finite) dimension (uniqueness remains open), or more generally, in proper geodesic spaces. The core of the proof is a new notion of *k-gradation* for P and Q, whose existence (even in an arbitrary metric space) is proved using the Knaster–Tarski fixed point theorem, by a method introduced by Reem and Reich for a slightly different purpose.

Categories and Subject Descriptors

F.2.2 [**Analysis of Algorithms and Problem Complexity**]: Nonnumerical Algorithms and Problems—*Geometrical problems and computations*; G.0 [**Mathematics of Computing**]: General

General Terms

Theory

Keywords

distance k-sectors, Knaster–Tarski fixed point theorem

*A preliminary form of the results was announced in Section 4 of [5]. For the case $k = 3$, some of the methods and results were found essentially independently in [8].

SCG'10, June 13–16, 2010, Snowbird, Utah, USA.

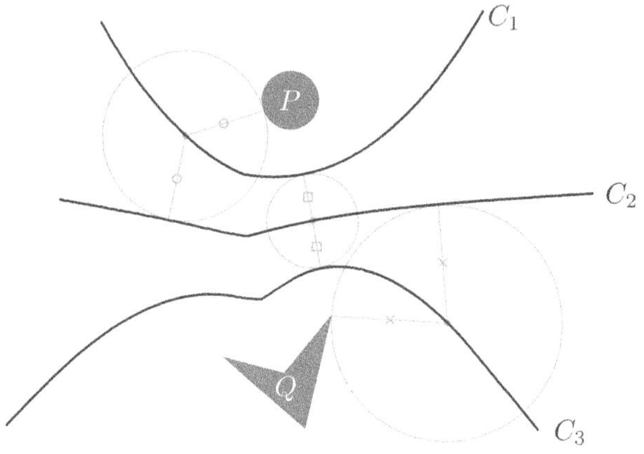

Figure 1: A 4-sector (C_1, C_2, C_3) of sets P and Q in Euclidean plane. Each point on the curve C_i is at the same distance from C_{i-1} and C_{i+1}. Note that C_2 is not the bisector of P and Q.

1. INTRODUCTION

The *bisector* of two nonempty sets X and Y in Euclidean space, or in an arbitrary metric space (M, dist), is defined as

$$\mathrm{bisect}(X, Y) = \{ z \in M : \mathrm{dist}(z, X) = \mathrm{dist}(z, Y) \}, \quad (1)$$

where $\mathrm{dist}(z, X) = \inf_{x \in X} \mathrm{dist}(z, x)$ denotes the distance of z from a set X.

Let $k \geq 2$ be an integer and let P, Q be disjoint nonempty sets in M called the *sites*. A *distance k-sector* (or simply *k-sector*) of P and Q is a $(k-1)$-tuple $(C_1, \ldots, C_{k-1})$ of nonempty subsets of M such that

$$C_i = \mathrm{bisect}(C_{i-1}, C_{i+1}), \qquad i = 1, \ldots, k-1, \quad (2)$$

where $C_0 = P$ and $C_k = Q$ (see Figures 1 and 2).

Distance k-sectors were introduced by Asano et al. [3] for Euclidean plane, motivated by a question of Murata from VLSI design: Suppose that we are given a topology of a circuit layer, and we need to put $k-1$ wires through a corridor between given two sets of obstacles (modules and other wires) on the board. To minimize the chance of failure, we want to keep the wires far apart from each other. In this situation, it seems reasonable to let each wire bisect the adjacent ones, as in the definition of a k-sector.

A similar problem occurs also in designing routes of $k-1$ autonomous robots moving in a narrow polygonal corridor.

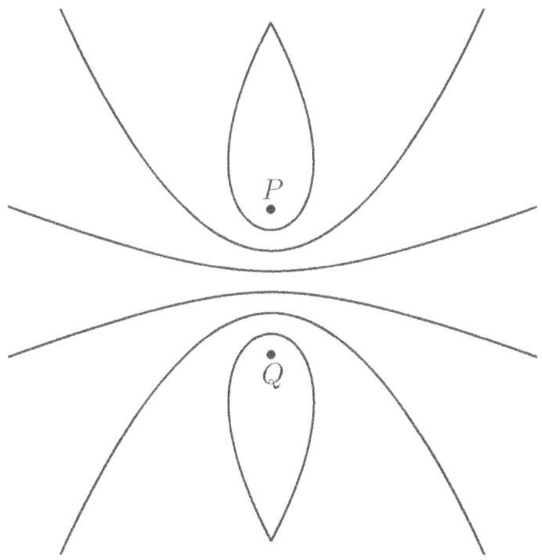

Figure 2: A 7-sector of two singleton sets P and Q in Euclidean plane.

Each robot has its own predetermined route (say, it is drawn on the floor with a coloured tape that the robot can recognize) and tries to follow it. We want to design the routes to be far away from each other so that the robots can easily avoid collision.

Despite its innocent definition, it is nontrivial to find a k-sector even in Euclidean plane. The bisector of two point sites P and Q in $\mathbb{R}^2$ is a line, and it is easy to see that there is a 4-sector of them consisting of a line and two parabolas. However, the problem was not investigated for other values of k until Asano et al. [3] proved the existence and uniqueness of the 3-sector (trisector) of two points in Euclidean plane. Chun et al. [4] extended this to the case where Q is a line segment.

We give the first proof of existence of k-sectors in Euclidean spaces for a general k. This improves on the previous proofs in generality and simplicity even for $k = 3$. Note that a k-sector need not exist in arbitrary metric spaces: there is no 3-sector of sites $P = \{p\}$ and $Q = \{q\}$ in the two-point metric space $\{p, q\}$.

Main Theorem. *Every two disjoint nonempty closed sets P and Q in Euclidean space $\mathbb{R}^d$, or more generally, in a proper geodesic metric space, have at least one k-sector.*

Here, a metric space (M, dist) is called *proper* if all closed balls are compact. It is called *geodesic* if for every two distinct points $x, y \in M$ there is a *metric segment* in M connecting them, i.e., an isometric mapping $\gamma: [a, b] \to M$ of an interval $[a, b] \subset \mathbb{R}$ with $\gamma(a) = x$ and $\gamma(b) = y$. In particular, a convex subset of a normed space is a geodesic metric space. Another example is the surface of a sphere, where the distance between two points is measured by the length of the shortest path on the surface connecting them. Geodesic metric spaces are a reasonably general class of metric spaces in which our arguments go through, although one could probably make up even more general conditions.

We remark that if $\text{dist}(P, Q) > 0$ and $k = 3$, then the properness assumption can be omitted; see [8] for a proof.

From now on, unless otherwise noted, subscripts i and j range over $1, \ldots, k-1$. For example, $(C_i)_i$ stands for the $(k-1)$-tuple $(C_1, \ldots, C_{k-1})$.

Gradations.

One of the main steps in the proof of the main theorem is introducing the notion of a *k-gradation* of P and Q, which is related to a k-sector but easier to work with. First, for nonempty sets X, Y in a metric space (M, dist), we define the *dominance region* of X over Y by

$$\text{dom}(X, Y) = \{\, z \in M : \text{dist}(z, X) \leq \text{dist}(z, Y) \,\}. \qquad (3)$$

A *k-gradation* between nonempty subsets P and Q of M is a $(k-1)$-tuple $(R_i, S_i)_i$ of pairs of subsets of M satisfying

$$R_i = \text{dom}(R_{i-1}, S_{i+1}), \qquad S_i = \text{dom}(S_{i+1}, R_{i-1}), \qquad i = 1, \ldots, k-1, \qquad (4)$$

where $R_0 = P$ and $S_k = Q$.

Using the Knaster–Tarski fixed point theorem [10], we prove in Section 2 that k-gradations always exist:

Proposition 1. *For every nonempty sets P and Q in an arbitrary metric space (M, dist), there exists at least one k-gradation.*

The idea of applying the Knaster–Tarski theorem to a similar setting is from [9], where it is used to prove the existence of *double zone diagrams*. A slight modification of Proposition 1 also holds in the more general setting of *m-spaces* [9].

In Section 3, we establish the following connection between k-gradations and k-sectors. The main theorem is an immediate consequence of Propositions 1 and 2.

Proposition 2. *Let P, Q be nonempty, disjoint, closed sets in a proper geodesic metric space. Then a $(k-1)$-tuple $(C_i)_i$ of sets is a k-sector of P and Q if and only if*

$$C_i = R_i \cap S_i, \qquad i = 1, \ldots, k-1 \qquad (5)$$

for some k-gradation $(R_i, S_i)_i$ between P and Q.

For instance, the k-sectors $(C_i)_i$ in Figures 1, 2 and 3 correspond to the k-gradations $(R_i, S_i)_i$ where each R_i is the union of C_i and the region above it, and each S_i is the union of C_i and the region below it.

3-gradations and zone diagrams.

A *zone diagram* of P, Q is, according to the general definition of Asano et al. [2], a pair of sets (A, B) such that $A = \text{dom}(P, B)$ and $B = \text{dom}(Q, A)$. By comparing the definitions, we can see that if $((R_1, S_1), (R_2, S_2))$ is a 3-gradation for P, Q, then (R_1, S_2) is a zone diagram of P, Q. Conversely, given a zone diagram (A, B), we can set $R_1 := A$, $S_2 := B$, $R_2 := \text{dom}(R_1, Q)$, $S_1 := \text{dom}(S_2, P)$ to obtain a 3-gradation (we note that R_2 and S_1 are uniquely determined by R_1 and S_2).

The existence of zone diagrams of arbitrary two nonempty sets in an arbitrary metric space (and even in the still more general setting of m-spaces) was proved by Reem and Reich [9, Theorem 5.6]. By the above, it immediately implies the existence of 3-gradations, a special case of Proposition 1.

Uniqueness.

Kawamura et al. [6] (also see [5] for a preliminary version) proved the existence and uniqueness of zone diagrams in $\mathbb{R}^d$ (for finitely many closed and pairwise separated sites) under the Euclidean distance, and more generally, under any smooth and uniformly convex norm. By Proposition 2,

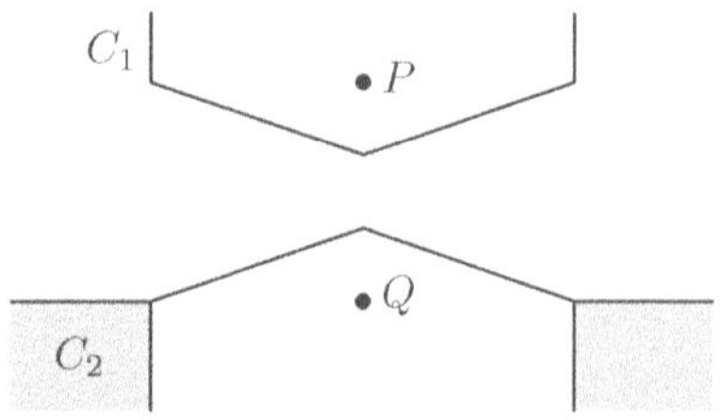

Figure 3: A 3-sector (C_1, C_2) of P and Q under the ℓ_1 norm.

this implies the uniqueness of 3-sectors under the same conditions. This is the most general uniqueness result for k-sectors we are aware of.

For general metrics, k-sectors need not be unique. A simple example, for the ℓ_1 metric in the plane (given by $\operatorname{dist}(x,y) = |x_1 - y_1| + |x_2 - y_2|$), is shown in Figure 3; it was essentially discovered by Asano and Kirkpatrick [1]. The set C_1 is a polygonal curve, while C_2 is "fat", consisting of two straight segments and two quadrants. A different 3-sector is obtained as a mirror reflection of the one shown.

Thus, uniqueness of k-sectors requires some geometric assumptions on the underlying metric space. We will further comment on this issue in Section 4.

Construction of k-sectors.

Our existence proof for k-sectors, based on the Knaster–Tarski theorem, is somewhat nonconstructive. Section 4 discusses a more constructive approach, which re-establishes Proposition 1 under stronger assumptions, but which yields an iterative algorithm (in a similar spirit as in [2]). We have no rigorous results about the speed of its convergence, but in practice it has been used successfully for approximating k-sectors and drawing pictures such as Figure 1. Such computations also support our belief that k-sectors in Euclidean spaces are unique, at least for two point sites in the plane.

2. THE EXISTENCE OF *k*-GRADATIONS

Here we prove Proposition 1. A set $\mathcal{L}$ equipped with a partial order $\leq$ is called a *complete lattice* if every subset $\mathcal{D} \subseteq \mathcal{L}$ has an infimum $\bigwedge \mathcal{D}$ (the greatest $x \in \mathcal{L}$ such that $x \leq y$ for all $y \in \mathcal{D}$) and a supremum $\bigvee \mathcal{D}$ (the least $x \in \mathcal{L}$ such that $x \geq y$ for all $y \in \mathcal{D}$). We say that a function $F\colon \mathcal{L} \to \mathcal{L}$ on a complete lattice $\mathcal{L}$ is *monotone* if $x \leq y$ implies $F(x) \leq F(y)$.

Knaster–Tarski Theorem ([10]). *Every monotone function on a complete lattice has a fixed point.*

The proof of this theorem is simple: It is routine to verify that the least and the greatest fixed points of a monotone function $F\colon \mathcal{L} \to \mathcal{L}$ are given by

$$\bigwedge\{x \in \mathcal{L} : x \geq F(x)\}, \qquad \bigvee\{x \in \mathcal{L} : x \leq F(x)\}, \tag{6}$$

respectively.

Proof of Proposition 1. Let $\mathcal{L}$ be the set of all $(k-1)$-tuples $(R_i, S_i)_i$ of pairs of subsets of the considered metric space M satisfying $R_i \supseteq P$, $S_i \supseteq Q$ and $R_i \cup S_i = M$. We define the order $\leq$ on $\mathcal{L}$ by setting $(R_i, S_i)_i \leq (R'_i, S'_i)_i$ if $R_i \subseteq R'_i$ and $S_i \supseteq S'_i$ for all $i = 1, \ldots, k-1$. It is easy to see that $\mathcal{L}$ with this order $\leq$ is a complete lattice in which the infimum and supremum of $\mathcal{D} \subseteq \mathcal{L}$ are given by

$$\bigwedge \mathcal{D} = \Big(\bigcap_{(R_j,S_j)_j \in \mathcal{D}} R_i, \bigcup_{(R_j,S_j)_j \in \mathcal{D}} S_i \Big)_i, \tag{7}$$

$$\bigvee \mathcal{D} = \Big(\bigcup_{(R_j,S_j)_j \in \mathcal{D}} R_i, \bigcap_{(R_j,S_j)_j \in \mathcal{D}} S_i \Big)_i. \tag{8}$$

We define $F\colon \mathcal{L} \to \mathcal{L}$ by

$$F\big((R_i, S_i)_i\big) = \big(\operatorname{dom}(R_{i-1}, S_{i+1}), \operatorname{dom}(S_{i+1}, R_{i-1})\big)_i, \tag{9}$$

where $R_0 = P$ and $S_k = Q$. It is easy to see that F is well-defined and monotone. By the Knaster–Tarski Theorem, F has a fixed point, which is a k-gradation by definition. $\square$

3. DOMINANCE REGIONS, *k*-GRADATIONS, AND *k*-SECTORS

The goal of this section is to prove Proposition 2. We write ∂Z for the boundary of a closed set Z. We begin with observing that, for arbitrary nonempty sets X, Y in any metric space, the set $\operatorname{bisect}(X,Y) = \operatorname{dom}(X,Y) \cap \operatorname{dom}(Y,X)$ contains $\partial \operatorname{dom}(X,Y)$. Moreover, if the metric space is geodesic (and hence connected), then $\operatorname{bisect}(X,Y)$ is nonempty. For otherwise, $\operatorname{dom}(X,Y)$ and $\operatorname{dom}(Y,X)$ would be two disjoint closed sets covering the whole space.

Lemma 3. *Let X, Y, Z be nonempty closed sets in a proper geodesic metric space. Note that $D = \operatorname{dom}(X,Y)$ and $C = \operatorname{bisect}(X,Y)$ are nonempty. If D and Z are disjoint, then*

(a) $\operatorname{dom}(D,Z) = \operatorname{dom}(C,Z)$, $\operatorname{dom}(Z,D) = \operatorname{dom}(Z,C)$,

(b) $\operatorname{bisect}(D,Z) = \operatorname{bisect}(C,Z)$.

Proof. Part (b) follows from (a) because $\operatorname{bisect}(X,Y) = \operatorname{dom}(X,Y) \cap \operatorname{dom}(Y,X)$.

To show (a), we claim that

$$\operatorname{dist}(a,Z) > \operatorname{dist}(a,C) \qquad \text{for all } a \in D. \tag{10}$$

Indeed, let $z \in Z$ be a point attaining the distance to a; i.e., $\operatorname{dist}(a,z) = \operatorname{dist}(a,Z)$ (the distance is attained since the intersection of Z with the ball of radius $2\operatorname{dist}(a,Z)$ around a is compact). There is a metric segment (see the definition following the Main Theorem; for $\mathbb{R}^d$ this simply means a line segment) connecting a and z. The segment is a connected set containing both $a \in D$ and $z \notin D$, so it meets ∂D, and thus also C, at some point, say c. Hence, $\operatorname{dist}(a,z) = \operatorname{dist}(a,c) + \operatorname{dist}(c,z) > \operatorname{dist}(a,c) \geq \operatorname{dist}(a,C)$. We also have

$$\operatorname{dist}(a,C) = \operatorname{dist}(a,D) \qquad \text{for all } a \notin D. \tag{11}$$

For let $d \in D$ be arbitrary. Again, there is a segment connecting a and d, and it meets ∂D, and thus also C, at some point, say c. Hence, $\operatorname{dist}(a,d) = \operatorname{dist}(a,c) + \operatorname{dist}(c,d) \geq \operatorname{dist}(a,c) \geq \operatorname{dist}(a,C)$. Since $C \subseteq D$, this proves (11).

The first part of (a) comes as follows: Points $a \in D$ belong both to $\operatorname{dom}(D,Z)$ and, by (10), to $\operatorname{dom}(C,Z)$; other points $a \notin D$ belong to $\operatorname{dom}(D,Z)$ and $\operatorname{dom}(C,Z)$ at the same time by (11).

The second part is similar: Points $a \in D$ belong neither to $\operatorname{dom}(Z,D)$ nor to $\operatorname{dom}(Z,C)$ by (10); other points $a \notin D$ belong to $\operatorname{dom}(Z,D)$ and $\operatorname{dom}(Z,C)$ at the same time by (11). $\square$

Now we proceed with k-gradations. We observe that, if $(R_i, S_i)_i$ is a k-gradation for P and Q, then $R_i \cup S_i$ is the whole space and

$$P = R_0 \subseteq R_1 \subseteq \cdots \subseteq R_{k-1}, \tag{12}$$
$$S_1 \supseteq S_2 \supseteq \cdots \supseteq S_k = Q, \tag{13}$$

because $X \subseteq \mathrm{dom}(X, Y)$.

Lemma 4. *Let P, Q be nonempty, disjoint, closed sets in an arbitrary metric space.*

(i) *If $(C_i)_i$ is a k-sector of $C_0 = P$ and $C_k = Q$, then C_{i-1} and C_{i+1} are disjoint for each $i = 1, \ldots, k-1$.*

(ii) *If $(R_i, S_i)_i$ is a k-gradation between $R_0 = P$ and $S_k = Q$, then R_i and S_j are disjoint for each i and j with $0 \leq i < j \leq k$.*

Proof. For (i), suppose that there is a point $a \in C_{i-1} \cap C_{i+1}$. Since $\mathrm{dist}(a, C_{i-1}) = 0 = \mathrm{dist}(a, C_{i+1})$, we have $a \in \mathrm{bisect}(C_{i-1}, C_{i+1}) = C_i$. Since P and Q are disjoint, either $a \notin P$ or $a \notin Q$. By symmetry, we may assume $a \notin P$. Let i^- be the smallest such that $a \in C_j$ for all $j = i^-$, $\ldots$, i. Then $a \in C_{i^-+1} \setminus C_{i^--1}$, contradicting $a \in C_{i^-} = \mathrm{bisect}(C_{i^--1}, C_{i^-+1})$.

For (ii), suppose that there is a point $a \in R_i \cap S_j$ for some $i < j$. Since P and Q are disjoint, either $a \notin P$ or $a \notin Q$. By symmetry, we may assume $a \notin P$. Retake i to be the smallest such that $a \in R_i$. Then $a \notin R_{i-1}$ and $a \in S_j \subseteq S_{i+1}$, contradicting $a \in R_i = \mathrm{dom}(R_{i-1}, S_{i+1})$. □

Proof of Proposition 2. For one direction, let $(R_i, S_i)_i$ be a k-gradation and let $C_i = R_i \cap S_i$ for each $i = 1, \ldots, k-1$. Then $C_i = \mathrm{dom}(R_{i-1}, S_{i+1}) \cap \mathrm{dom}(S_{i+1}, R_{i-1}) = \mathrm{bisect}(R_{i-1}, S_{i+1})$ is nonempty. Furthermore, this equals $\mathrm{bisect}(C_{i-1}, C_{i+1})$ by Lemma 3(b), because R_{i-1} and S_{i+1} are disjoint according to Lemma 4(ii).

For the other direction, we suppose that $(C_i)_i$ is a k-sector. Let $R_i = \mathrm{dom}(C_{i-1}, C_{i+1})$ and $S_i = \mathrm{dom}(C_{i+1}, C_{i-1})$ for each $i = 1, \ldots, k-1$. Then $C_i = R_i \cap S_i$ by the definition of a k-sector. By Lemma 4(i), we have $R_i \cap C_{i+1} = \emptyset$, and similarly $S_{i+1} \cap C_i = \emptyset$. Therefore, $R_i \cap S_{i+1}$ is disjoint from $C_i \cup C_{i+1} \supseteq \partial R_i \cup \partial S_{i+1} \supseteq \partial(R_i \cap S_{i+1})$. This means that $R_i \cap S_{i+1}$ has an empty boundary, and thus is itself empty, because the whole space is geodesic and hence connected. By this and the fact that $R_i \cup S_i$ covers the whole space, we have $P \subseteq R_1 \subseteq \cdots \subseteq R_{k-1}$ and $S_1 \supseteq S_2 \supseteq \cdots \supseteq S_{k-1} \supseteq Q$. Because R_i and S_{i+1} are disjoint, so are R_{i-1} and S_{i+1}. This allows us to apply Lemma 3(a), which yields $\mathrm{dom}(R_{i-1}, S_{i+1}) = \mathrm{dom}(C_{i-1}, C_{i+1}) = R_i$ and similarly $\mathrm{dom}(S_{i+1}, R_{i-1}) = S_i$. □

The following example shows that the assumption of the space being geodesic cannot be dropped. Consider the distance on $\mathbb{R}$ defined by $\mathrm{dist}(x, y) = f(|x - y|)$, where f is given by

$$f(r) = \begin{cases} r & \text{if } r \leq 1, \\ 1 & \text{if } 1 \leq r \leq 2, \\ r/2 & \text{if } r \geq 2. \end{cases} \tag{14}$$

Thus, dist is almost like the usual metric, except that it "thinks of any distance between 1 and 2 as the same." Then there is no 3-sector between $P = (-\infty, 0]$ and $Q = [1, +\infty)$ (whereas there is a gradation by Proposition 1). For suppose that (C_1, C_2) is a 3-sector. By Lemma 4(i), the set C_2 cannot overlap P or Q, so it is a nonempty subset of $(0, 1)$. Hence, the point 2 is equidistant from C_2 and P, and thus belongs to C_1. This contradicts Lemma 4(i).

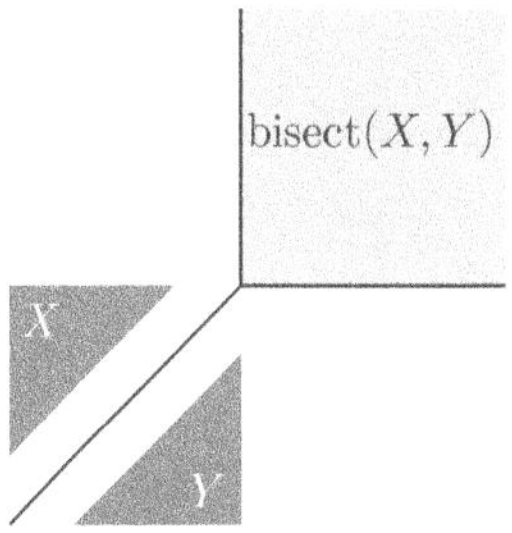

Figure 4: A bisector may be fat in the plane with the ℓ_1 metric. Every point in the shaded region is at the same distance from X and Y. The equation in Lemma 6 does not hold.

4. DRAWING k-SECTORS

Here we provide a more constructive proof of the existence of k-gradations, but only under stronger assumptions than in Proposition 1. Later we discuss how this approach can be used for approximate computation of bisectors. We write $\overline{X}$ for the closure of a set X.

Proposition 5. *Suppose that P and Q are disjoint nonempty closed sets in $\mathbb{R}^d$ with the Euclidean norm (or, more generally, with an arbitrary strictly convex norm). Let the lattice $\mathcal{L}$ and the function $F\colon \mathcal{L} \to \mathcal{L}$ be as in the the proof of Proposition 1 (Section 2). Let $(R_i^0, S_i^0)_i$ be an element of $\mathcal{L}$ with $(R_i^0, S_i^0)_i \leq F((R_i^0, S_i^0)_i)$. Define $(R_i^{n+1}, S_i^{n+1})_i := F((R_i^n, S_i^n)_i)$ for each $n \in \mathbb{N}$ (thus, $(R_i^0, S_i^0)_i \leq (R_i^1, S_i^1)_i \leq (R_i^2, S_i^2)_i \leq \cdots$), and let $(R_i^\infty, S_i^\infty)_i = \bigvee\{(R_i^n, S_i^n)_i : n \in \mathbb{N}\}$. Then $(\overline{R_i^\infty}, S_i^\infty)_i$ is a k-gradation.*

We begin proving this proposition. We write $R_0^n = P$ and $S_k^n = Q$ for each $n \in \mathbb{N} \cup \{\infty\}$.

Lemma 6. *For any disjoint nonempty closed sets X, Y in $\mathbb{R}^d$ with the Euclidean metric (or with a strictly convex norm),* $\mathrm{dom}(Y, X) = \overline{\mathbb{R}^d \setminus \mathrm{dom}(X, Y)}$.

We note that the assumption on the considered metric in this lemma is necessary: As Figure 4 illustrates, the claim is not valid with the ℓ_1 norm.

Proof of Lemma 6. We have $\mathrm{dom}(Y, X) \supseteq \overline{\mathbb{R}^d \setminus \mathrm{dom}(X, Y)}$ because $\mathrm{dom}(Y, X)$ is closed and $\mathrm{dom}(Y, X) \cup \mathrm{dom}(X, Y) = \mathbb{R}^d$. For the other inclusion, let $z \in \mathrm{dom}(Y, X)$ and let y be a closest point in Y to z. Since X does not intersect the open ball with centre z and radius $\mathrm{dist}(y, z)$, any point $z' \neq z$ on the segment zy is strictly closer to y than to X (Figure 5), and thus is not in $\mathrm{dom}(X, Y)$. Since z' can be arbitrarily close to z, we have $z \in \overline{\mathbb{R}^d \setminus \mathrm{dom}(X, Y)}$. □

Lemma 7. *If $(R_i^\infty, S_i^\infty)_i$ is as in Proposition 5, then $\overline{R_i^\infty} \cap S_j^\infty = \emptyset$ whenever $0 \leq i < j \leq k$.*

Proof. For contradiction, suppose that there is some $a \in \overline{R_i^\infty} \cap S_j^\infty$.

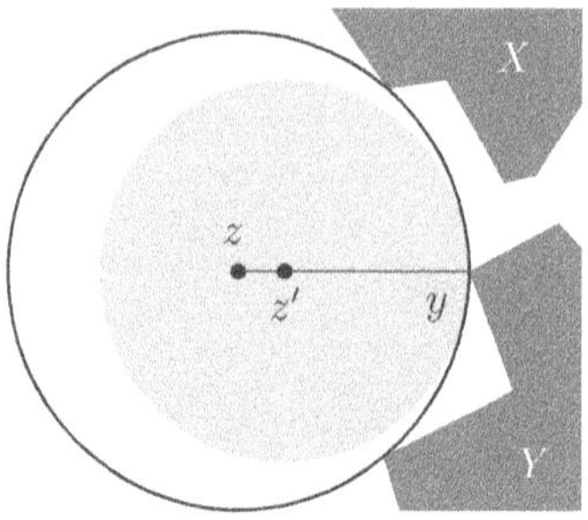

Figure 5: Since X does not intersect the interior of the ball around z, it does not touch the ball around z'.

If $i > 0$, then for each $n \in \mathbb{N}$ we have $a \in S_j^\infty \subseteq S_j^n \subseteq S_{i+1}^n$, so $\mathrm{dom}(R_{i-1}^n, \{a\}) \supseteq \mathrm{dom}(R_{i-1}^n, S_{i+1}^n) = R_i^{n+1}$. This implies $\mathrm{dist}(a, R_{i-1}^n) \leq 2 \cdot \mathrm{dist}(a, R_i^{n+1})$. Since $a \in \overline{R_i^\infty}$, the right-hand side tends to 0 as $n \to \infty$, and hence, so does $\mathrm{dist}(a, R_{i-1}^n)$. Thus, $a \in \overline{R_{i-1}^\infty}$. Repeating the same argument for $i-1$, $i-2$, ..., we arrive at $a \in \overline{R_0^\infty} = P$.

Similarly, if $j < k$, then we have $a \in S_j^\infty \subseteq S_j^{n+1} = \mathrm{dom}(S_{j+1}^n, R_{j-1}^n)$ for all $n \in \mathbb{N}$. Therefore, $\mathrm{dist}(a, S_{j+1}^n) \leq \mathrm{dist}(a, R_{j-1}^n) \leq \mathrm{dist}(a, R_i^n) \to 0$ as $n \to \infty$ because $a \in \overline{R_i^\infty}$. So $a \in S_{j+1}^\infty$. Repeating the argument for $j+1$, $j+2$, ..., we obtain $a \in S_k^\infty = Q$.

Thus we have $a \in P \cap Q$, contradicting the assumption that P and Q are disjoint. □

Proof of Proposition 5. By the definition of a k-gradation, our goal is to prove $F((\overline{R_i^\infty}, S_i^\infty)_i) = (\overline{R_i^\infty}, S_i^\infty)_i$. Since F is monotone, $F((\overline{R_i^\infty}, S_i^\infty)_i) \geq F((R_i^n, S_i^n)_i) \geq (R_i^n, S_i^n)_i$ for each n, and hence $F((\overline{R_i^\infty}, S_i^\infty)_i) \geq (\overline{R_i^\infty}, S_i^\infty)_i$. It remains to show that $F((\overline{R_i^\infty}, S_i^\infty)_i) \leq (\overline{R_i^\infty}, S_i^\infty)_i$, which means, by the definition of F, that

$$\mathrm{dom}(S_{i+1}^\infty, \overline{R_{i-1}^\infty}) \supseteq S_i^\infty, \tag{15}$$

and

$$\mathrm{dom}(\overline{R_{i-1}^\infty}, S_{i+1}^\infty) \subseteq \overline{R_i^\infty}. \tag{16}$$

The inclusion (15) follows just by the continuity of the distance function: $S_i^\infty = \bigcap_{n\in\mathbb{N}} S_i^{n+1} = \bigcap_{n\in\mathbb{N}} \mathrm{dom}(S_{i+1}^n, R_{i-1}^n)$. So for $x \in S_i^\infty$ we have $\mathrm{dist}(x, S_{i+1}^n) \leq \mathrm{dist}(x, R_{i-1}^n)$ for every n, and $\mathrm{dist}(x, S_{i+1}^\infty) = \lim_{n\to\infty} \mathrm{dist}(x, S_{i+1}^n) \leq \lim_{n\to\infty} \mathrm{dist}(x, R_{i-1}^n) = \mathrm{dist}(x, \overline{R_{i-1}^\infty})$. Hence $x \in \mathrm{dom}(S_{i+1}^\infty, \overline{R_{i-1}^\infty})$ and (15) is proved.

For proving (16), we need the previous lemmas. By (15), we have

$$\mathbb{R}^d \setminus \mathrm{dom}(S_{i+1}^\infty, \overline{R_{i-1}^\infty}) \subseteq \mathbb{R}^d \setminus S_i^\infty \subseteq R_i^\infty, \tag{17}$$

where the latter inclusion is because $R_i^n \cup S_i^n = \mathbb{R}^d$ for every n (this was part of the definition of $\mathcal{L}$). We obtain (16) by taking the closure of (17), using Lemma 6 for the left-hand side; for applying this lemma, we need $\overline{R_{i-1}^\infty} \cap S_{i+1}^\infty = \emptyset$, which holds by Lemma 7. □

If the initial element $(R_i^0, S_i^0)_i$ in Proposition 5 is less than or equal to all k-gradations (with respect to the ordering $\leq$), then so is $(R_i^n, S_i^n)_i$ for all n (inductively by the monotonicity of F), and therefore, the resulting $(\overline{R_i^\infty}, S_i^\infty)_i$ is the *least* k-gradation. This is the case when, for example, $(R_i^0, S_i^0)_i$ is the least element $(P, \mathbb{R}^d)_i$ of $\mathcal{L}$.

Note that the 3-sector in Figure 3 corresponds to the least 3-gradation, but this 3-gradation is not obtained by iteration from the least element of $\mathcal{L}$. This witnesses that Proposition 5 may indeed fail for norms that are not strictly convex.

Computational issues.

Proposition 5 gives a method to draw a k-sector in Euclidean spaces: By applying F iteratively, we get an ascending chain $(R_i^0, S_i^0)_i \leq (R_i^1, S_i^1)_i \leq \cdots$ whose supremum $(R_i^\infty, S_i^\infty)_i$ gives a k-gradation $(\overline{R_i^\infty}, S_i^\infty)_i$. If we stop the iteration after sufficiently many steps, we obtain an approximation of $(\overline{R_i^\infty}, S_i^\infty)_i$.

However, implementing the algorithm is not entirely trivial, because even if the sites are simple, applying F repeatedly gives rise to regions that are hard to describe. For example, consider the case where P and Q are points in the plane, and we begin with $(R_i^0, S_i^0)_i = (P, \mathbb{R}^2)_i$. Then ∂R_{k-1}^1 is the line bisecting P and Q, and ∂R_{k-2}^2 is the parabola bisecting P and this line. The next iteration yields the curve ∂R_{k-3}^3 (or ∂R_{k-1}^3) which bisects between a parabola and a point.

Thus, unlike typical basic operations allowed in computational geometry, taking the bisector gives rise to increasingly complicated curves. If we have an analytic description of the boundary curves of the regions R_i^n and S_i^n, each of the curves defining R_i^{n+1} and S_i^{n+1} is described by a system of differential equations associated with the bisecting condition. But solving such equations exactly in each iterative step is computationally expensive. Therefore, we need to find a practical method for approximating the bisectors. In the following, we assume that we only compute the regions in a bounded area.

One method is to approximate each region by a polygon. We start with some polygonal approximations $\tilde{P}$, $\tilde{Q}$ of P, Q, and let $(\tilde{R}_i^0, \tilde{S}_i^0)_i := (\tilde{P}, \mathbb{R}^d)_i$. Then for each n, we compute an approximation $(\tilde{R}_i^{n+1}, \tilde{S}_i^{n+1})_i$ to $F((\tilde{R}_i^n, \tilde{S}_i^n)_i)$, where the bisector of two polygonal regions, which is a piecewise quadratic curve, is approximated by a suitable polygonal region. To ensure that $(\tilde{R}_i^n, \tilde{S}_i^n)_i$ converges to an underestimate (with respect to $\leq$) of the least k-gradation $(\overline{R_i^\infty}, S_i^\infty)_i$, we should have $(\tilde{R}_i^n, \tilde{S}_i^n)_i \leq (\tilde{R}_i^{n+1}, \tilde{S}_i^{n+1})_i \leq F((\tilde{R}_i^n, \tilde{S}_i^n)_i)$. This can be achieved by computing an inner approximation of R_i^{n+1} and an outer approximation of S_i^{n+1}.

Another method is to consider the problem in the pixel geometry, where each of the approximate regions $\tilde{R}_i^n$, $\tilde{S}_i^n$ is a set of pixels. In computing $(\tilde{R}_i^{n+1}, \tilde{S}_i^{n+1})_i$, we again make sure that $(\tilde{R}_i^n, \tilde{S}_i^n)_i \leq (\tilde{R}_i^{n+1}, \tilde{S}_i^{n+1})_i \leq F((\tilde{R}_i^n, \tilde{S}_i^n)_i)$. Then $(\tilde{R}_i^n, \tilde{S}_i^n)_i$ stabilizes eventually, providing a lower estimate of the least k-gradation.

As a third approach, some of the methods of [7, 8] may also be applicable.

The analysis of time complexity (as a function of precision) of these methods is left as a future research problem.

Uniqueness.

The curves in Figure 1 were drawn using the pixel geometry model explained above. As we mentioned there, they are guaranteed to lie on P's side of any true 4-sector curves. By exchanging P and Q, we obtain also an approximate 4-sector that lies on Q's side of any true 4-sector. We tried computing these lower and upper estimates for several different P, Q and k in Euclidean plane, but we did not find them differ by a significant amount. Because of this, we suspect that the k-sector is always unique:

Conjecture. *The k-sector of any two disjoint nonempty closed sets in Euclidean space is unique.*

5. ACKNOWLEDGEMENTS

We gratefully acknowledge valuable discussions with many friends including Tetsuo Asano and Günter Rote; indeed, we owe Tetsuo for precious information of his recent work on convex distance cases. We also thank Yu Muramatsu for his programming work in drawing figures. D. R. would like to express his thanks to Simeon Reich for his helpful discussion. Finally, we remark that the warm comments from the audience of the preliminary announcement at EuroCG 2009 encouraged us to work further on the subject.

A. K. is supported by the Nakajima Foundation and by the Natural Sciences and Engineering Research Council of Canada. The part of this research by T. T. was partially supported by the JSPS Grant-in-Aid for Scientific Research (B) 18300001.

6. REFERENCES

[1] T. Asano and D. Kirkpatrick. Distance trisector curves in regular convex distance metrics. In *Proceedings of the 3rd International Symposium on Voronoi Diagrams in Science and Engineering (ISVD 2006)*, pp. 8–17.

[2] T. Asano, J. Matoušek, and T. Tokuyama. Zone diagrams: Existence, uniqueness, and algorithmic challenge. *SIAM Journal on Computing*, 37(4):1182–1198, 2007.

[3] T. Asano, J. Matoušek, and T. Tokuyama. The distance trisector curve. *Advances in Mathematics*, 212(1):338–360, 2007.

[4] J. Chun, Y. Okada, and T. Tokuyama. Distance trisector of segments and zone diagram of segments in a plane. In *Proceedings of the 4th International Symposium on Voronoi Diagrams in Science and Engineering (ISVD 2007)*, pp. 66–73.

[5] K. Imai, A. Kawamura, J. Matoušek, Y. Muramatsu, and T. Tokuyama. Distance k-sectors and zone diagrams. In *Proceedings of the 25th European Workshop on Computational Geometry (EuroCG 2009)*, pp. 191–194.

[6] A. Kawamura, J. Matoušek, and T. Tokuyama. Zone diagrams in Euclidean spaces and in other normed spaces. In *Proceedings of the 26th Annual Symposium on Computational Geometry (SoCG 2010)*.

[7] D. Reem. An algorithm for computing Voronoi diagrams of general generators in general spaces. In *Proceedings of the 6th International Symposium on Voronoi Diagrams in Science and Engineering (ISVD 2009)*, pp. 144–152.

[8] D. Reem. Voronoi and zone diagrams. PhD Thesis, The Technion, Haifa, 2010.

[9] D. Reem and S. Reich. Zone and double zone diagrams in abstract spaces. *Colloquium Mathematicum*, 115(1):129–145, 2009.

[10] A. Tarski. A lattice-theoretical fixpoint theorem and its applications. *Pacific Journal of Mathematics*, 5:285–309, 1955.

Zone Diagrams in Euclidean Spaces and in Other Normed Spaces

Akitoshi Kawamura
University of Toronto
kawamura@cs.toronto.edu

Jiří Matoušek
Charles University
and ETH Zürich
matousek@kam.mff.cuni.cz

Takeshi Tokuyama
Tohoku University
tokuyama@dais.is.tohoku.ac.jp

ABSTRACT

Zone diagrams are a variation on the classical concept of Voronoi diagrams. Given n sites in a metric space that compete for territory, the zone diagram is an equilibrium state in the competition. Formally it is defined as a fixed point of a certain "dominance" map.

Asano, Matoušek, and Tokuyama proved the existence and uniqueness of a zone diagram for point sites in Euclidean plane, and Reem and Reich showed existence for two arbitrary sites in an arbitrary metric space. We establish existence and uniqueness for n disjoint compact sites in a Euclidean space of arbitrary (finite) dimension, and more generally, in a finite-dimensional normed space with a smooth and rotund norm. The proof is considerably simpler than that of Asano et al. We also provide an example of non-uniqueness for a norm that is rotund but not smooth. Finally, we prove existence and uniqueness for two point sites in the plane with a smooth (but not necessarily rotund) norm.

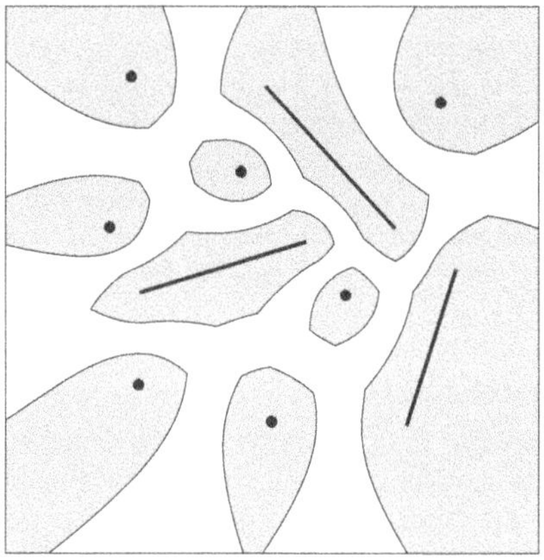

Figure 1: A zone diagram of points and segments.

Categories and Subject Descriptors

F.2.2 [**Analysis of Algorithms and Problem Complexity**]: Nonnumerical Algorithms and Problems—*Geometrical problems and computations*; G.0 [**Mathematics of Computing**]: General

General Terms

Theory

Keywords

Knaster–Tarski fixed point theorem, zone diagrams

1. INTRODUCTION

Zone diagrams are a metric notion somewhat similar to the classical concept of Voronoi diagrams. Let (X, dist) be a metric space and let $\mathbf{P} = (P_1, \ldots, P_n)$ be an n-tuple of nonempty subsets of X called the *sites*. To avoid unpleasant trivialities, we will always assume in this paper that the sites are closed and pairwise disjoint.

A *zone diagram* of $\mathbf{P}$ is an n-tuple $\mathbf{R} = (R_1, \ldots, R_n)$ of subsets of X, called the *regions* of the zone diagram, with the following defining property: Each R_i consists of all points $x \in X$ that are closer (non-strictly) to P_i than to the union $\bigcup_{j \neq i} R_j$ of all the other regions.

Informally, one can imagine that the sites compete for territory, and a site P_i can defend only a territory R_i that is closer to P_i than to all the territories of the other sites. A zone diagram is an equilibrium state in this "war game".

Fig. 1 shows a zone diagram in Euclidean plane whose sites are points and segments. While in the Voronoi diagram the regions partition the whole space, in a zone diagram the union of the regions typically has a nonempty complement, called the *neutral zone*.

The definition of the zone diagram is implicit, since each region is determined in terms of the remaining ones. So neither existence nor uniqueness of the zone diagram is obvious, and so far only partial results in this direction have been known.

Asano et al. [2] introduced the notion of a zone diagram, for the case of n point sites in Euclidean plane, and in this setting they proved existence and uniqueness. The proof involves a case analysis specific to $\mathbb{R}^2$.

Reem and Reich [10] established, by a simple and elegant argument, the existence of a zone diagram for *two* sites in an arbitrary metric space (and even in a still more general setting, which they call *m-spaces*).

On the negative side, they gave an example of a three-point metric space in which the zone diagram of two point sites is not unique; thus, *uniqueness* needs additional assumptions. On the other hand, for all we know, it is possible that a zone diagram always exists, for arbitrary sites in an arbitrary metric space.

Arbitrary sites in Euclidean spaces.

In this paper, we establish the existence and uniqueness of zone diagrams in Euclidean spaces. This generalizes the main result of [2] with a considerably simpler argument. For the case of two point sites in the plane, we also obtain a new and simpler proof of the existence and uniqueness of the *distance trisector curve* considered by Asano et al. [3].

THEOREM 1.1. *Let the considered metric space* (X, dist) *be* $\mathbb{R}^d$ *with the Euclidean distance. Then for every n-tuple* $\mathbf{P} = (P_1, \ldots, P_n)$ *of nonempty closed sites in* $\mathbb{R}^d$ *such that* $\mathrm{dist}(P_i, P_j) > 0$ *for every* $i \neq j$*, there exists exactly one zone diagram* $\mathbf{R}$.

The full proof is contained in Sections 2 (general preliminaries) and 3. The same proof yields existence and uniqueness also for infinitely many sites in $\mathbb{R}^d$, provided that every two of them have distance at least 1 (or some fixed $\varepsilon > 0$). Moreover, with some extra effort it may be possible to extend the proof to compact sites in a Hilbert space, for example, but in this paper we restrict ourselves to the finite-dimensional setting.

Normed spaces.

We also investigate zone diagrams in a more general class of metric spaces, namely, finite-dimensional normed spaces.[1] Normed spaces are among the most important classes of metric spaces. Moreover, as we will see, studying arbitrary norms also sheds some light on the Euclidean case. Earlier Asano and Kirkpatrick [1] investigated distance trisector curves (which are essentially equivalent to two-site zone diagrams) of two point sites under polygonal norms in the plane, obtaining results for the Euclidean case through approximation arguments.

For us, a crucial observation is that the uniqueness of zone diagrams does *not* hold for normed spaces. Let us consider $\mathbb{R}^2$ with the ℓ_1 norm $\|\cdot\|_1$, given by $\|x\|_1 = |x_1| + |x_2|$. It is easy to check that the two point sites $(0,0)$ and $(0,3)$ have at least two different zone diagrams, as drawn in Fig. 2. This example was essentially contained already in Asano and Kirkpatrick [1], although in a different context.

[1]A finite-dimensional (real) normed space can be thought of as the real vector space $\mathbb{R}^d$ with some *norm*, which is a mapping that assigns a nonnegative real number $\|x\|$ to each $x \in \mathbb{R}^d$ so that $\|x\| = 0$ implies $x = 0$, $\|\alpha x\| = |\alpha| \cdot \|x\|$ for all $\alpha \in \mathbb{R}$, and the triangle inequality holds: $\|x+y\| \leq \|x\| + \|y\|$. Each norm $\|\cdot\|$ defines a metric by $\mathrm{dist}(x,y) := \|x - y\|$. For studying a norm $\|\cdot\|$, it is usually good to look at its *unit ball* $\{x \in \mathbb{R}^d : \|x\| \leq 1\}$. The unit ball of any norm is a closed convex body K that is symmetric about 0 and contains 0 in the interior. Conversely, any $K \subset \mathbb{R}^d$ with the listed properties is the unit ball of a (uniquely determined) norm.

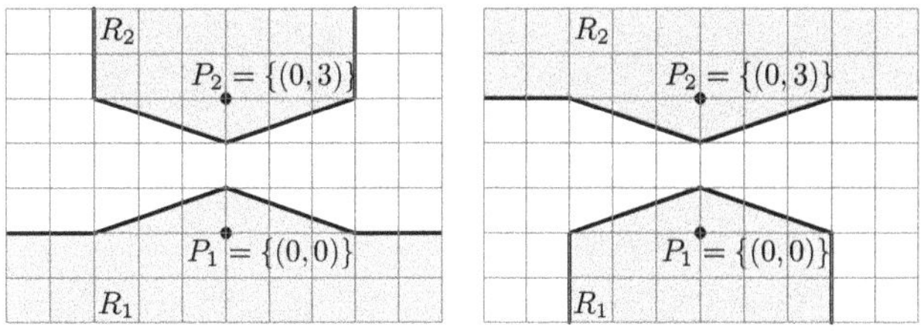

Figure 2: Two different zone diagrams under the ℓ_1 metric (drawn in the grid with unit spacing).

Figure 3: Rotundity and smoothness of norms.

The ℓ_1 norm differs from the Euclidean norm in two basic respects: the unit ball has sharp corners and straight edges; in other words, the ℓ_1 norm is neither smooth nor rotund.

We recall that a norm $\|\cdot\|$ on $\mathbb{R}^d$ is called *smooth* if the function $x \mapsto \|x\|$ is differentiable (geometrically, the unit ball of a smooth norm has no "sharp corners"; see Fig. 3). The property that we are actually going to use in the proof is *uniform smoothness*, which can be formulated as follows: The function $\rho\colon (0,\infty) \to [0,\infty)$ defined by

$$\rho(t) := \sup\left\{ \frac{\|u - tv\| + \|u + tv\|}{2} - 1 : \|u\| = \|v\| = 1 \right\}, \tag{1}$$

the *modulus of smoothness*, satisfies $\rho(t) = o(t)$ as $t \to 0$. A compactness argument shows that every smooth *finite-dimensional* Banach space is also uniformly smooth (we refer, e.g., to [5] or [7] for this and other facts on norms mentioned without proofs).

Notions dual to smoothness and uniform smoothness are rotundity and uniform convexity, respectively. A norm $\|\cdot\|$ on $\mathbb{R}^d$ is called *rotund* (or *strictly convex*) if for all $x, y \in \mathbb{R}^d$ with $\|x\| = \|y\| = 1$ and $x \neq y$ we have $\|\frac{x+y}{2}\| < 1$. Geometrically, the unit sphere of $\|\cdot\|$ contains no segment. A rotund norm on a finite-dimensional space is also *uniformly convex*, which means that for every $\varepsilon > 0$ there is $\mu = \mu(\varepsilon) > 0$ such that if x, y are unit vectors with $\|x - y\| \geq \varepsilon$, then

$$\left\| \frac{x+y}{2} \right\| \leq 1 - \mu.$$

The Euclidean norm $\|\cdot\|_2$, and more generally the ℓ_p norms with $1 < p < \infty$, are both rotund and smooth. We have the following generalization of Theorem 1.1:

THEOREM 1.2. *Let the considered metric space* (X, dist) *be* $\mathbb{R}^d$ *with a norm* $\|\cdot\|$ *that is both smooth and rotund. For every n-tuple* $\mathbf{P} = (P_1, \ldots, P_n)$ *of nonempty closed sites in* $\mathbb{R}^d$ *such that* $\mathrm{dist}(P_i, P_j) > 0$ *for every* $i \neq j$*, there exists exactly one zone diagram* $\mathbf{R}$.

The proof for the Euclidean case (Theorem 1.1) is set up

so that it generalizes to smooth and rotund norms more or less immediately; there is only one lemma where we need to work harder—see Section 4.

Our current proof method apparently depends both on smoothness and on rotundity. We know that smoothness is indeed essential (see the full version [8] for a proof):

PROPOSITION 1.3. *There exist a rotund norm in the plane* $\mathbb{R}^2$ *and two distinct point sites which have (at least) two different zone diagrams.*

On the other hand, we suspect that the assumption of rotundity in Theorem 1.2 can be dropped. Currently we have a proof (see [8]) only in a rather special case:

THEOREM 1.4. *For two point sites* $P_0 = \{p_0\}$ *and* $P_1 = \{p_1\}$ *in the plane* $\mathbb{R}^2$ *with a smooth norm, there exists exactly one zone diagram.*

2. PRELIMINARIES

Here we introduce notation and present some results from the literature, some of them in a more general context than in the original publications.

Let (X, dist) be a general metric space. The closure of a set $A \subseteq X$ is denoted by $\overline{A}$, while ∂A stands for its boundary. The (closed) ball of radius r centered at x is denoted by $\mathrm{B}(x, r)$.

For sets $A, B \subseteq X$, not both empty, we define the *dominance region* of A over B as the set

$$\mathrm{dom}(A, B) := \{ x \in X : \mathrm{dist}(x, A) \le \mathrm{dist}(x, B) \},$$

where

$$\mathrm{dist}(C, D) := \inf_{x \in C,\ y \in D} \mathrm{dist}(x, y) \in [0, +\infty]$$

denotes the distance of sets C and D.

Let us fix an n-tuple $\mathbf{P} = (P_1, \ldots, P_n)$ of sites (which are, as above, pairwise disjoint nonempty closed subsets of X). For an n-tuple $\mathbf{R} = (R_1, \ldots, R_n)$ of arbitrary subsets of X, we define another n-tuple of regions $\mathbf{R}' = (R'_1, \ldots, R'_n)$ denoted by $\mathbf{Dom}\,\mathbf{R}$ and given by

$$R'_i := \mathrm{dom}\Big(P_i, \bigcup_{j \ne i} R_j\Big), \qquad i = 1, \ldots, n$$

(the sites are considered fixed and they are a part of the definition of the operator $\mathbf{Dom}$).

The definition of a zone diagram can now be expressed as follows: An n-tuple $\mathbf{R}$ is called a *zone diagram* for the n-tuple $\mathbf{P}$ of sites if $\mathbf{R} = \mathbf{Dom}\,\mathbf{R}$ (componentwise equality, i.e., $R_i = \mathrm{dom}(P_i, \bigcup_{j \ne i} R_j)$ for all i).

For two n-tuples $\mathbf{R}$ and $\mathbf{S}$ of sets, we write $\mathbf{R} \preceq \mathbf{S}$ if $R_i \subseteq S_i$ for every i. It is easily seen (see, e.g., [2]) that the operator $\mathbf{Dom}$ is antimonotone, i.e., $\mathbf{R} \preceq \mathbf{S}$ implies $\mathbf{Dom}\,\mathbf{R} \succeq \mathbf{Dom}\,\mathbf{S}$. Our starting point in the proof of Theorems 1.1 and 1.2 is the following general result.

THEOREM 2.1. *For every* n*-tuple* $\mathbf{P}$ *of sites (in any metric space), there exist* n*-tuples* $\mathbf{R}$ *and* $\mathbf{S}$ *such that* $\mathbf{R} = \mathbf{Dom}\,\mathbf{S}$ *and* $\mathbf{S} = \mathbf{Dom}\,\mathbf{R}$*, and moreover, for every* n*-tuples* $\mathbf{R}', \mathbf{S}'$ *with* $\mathbf{R}' = \mathbf{Dom}\,\mathbf{S}'$ *and* $\mathbf{S}' = \mathbf{Dom}\,\mathbf{R}'$*, we have* $\mathbf{R} \preceq \mathbf{R}'$ *and* $\mathbf{S}' \preceq \mathbf{S}$ *(and in particular,* $\mathbf{R} \preceq \mathbf{S}$*).*

A special case of this result, for point sites in the Euclidean plane, was first proved by Asano et al. [2, Lemma 5.1], while the general case is due to Reem and Reich [10]. We recall their proof for the reader's convenience.

PROOF. We use the following theorem of Knaster and Tarski (see [11]): *If* $\mathcal{L} = (L, \preceq)$ *is a complete lattice and* $g\colon \mathcal{L} \to \mathcal{L}$ *is a monotone mapping, then* g *has at least one fixed point (i.e.,* $x \in L$ *with* $g(x) = x$*), and moreover, there exists a smallest fixed point* x_0 *and a largest fixed point* x_1*, i.e., such that* $x_0 \preceq x \preceq x_1$ *for every fixed point* x*.*

To prove Theorem 2.1, we let L be the system of all ordered n-tuples $\mathbf{D}$ such that $P_i \subseteq D_i$ for every i. It is easy to check that $\mathcal{L} = (L, \preceq)$ (where $\preceq$ is defined as above) is a complete lattice. Let $g := \mathbf{Dom}^2$; that is, $g(\mathbf{D}) := \mathbf{Dom}(\mathbf{Dom}\,\mathbf{D})$. Then we let $\mathbf{R}$ be the smallest fixed point of g as in the Knaster–Tarski theorem, and $\mathbf{S} := \mathbf{Dom}\,\mathbf{R}$. Clearly $\mathbf{Dom}\,\mathbf{S} = \mathbf{Dom}^2\,\mathbf{R} = g(\mathbf{R}) = \mathbf{R}$. Moreover, if $\mathbf{R}'$ and $\mathbf{S}'$ satisfy $\mathbf{R}' = \mathbf{Dom}\,\mathbf{S}'$ and $\mathbf{S}' = \mathbf{Dom}\,\mathbf{R}'$, then $\mathbf{R}'$ and $\mathbf{S}'$ are both fixed points of $\mathbf{Dom}^2$, and thus $\mathbf{R} \preceq \mathbf{R}'$, $\mathbf{S}' \preceq \mathbf{S}$ as claimed. □

Let us remark that the earlier proof by Asano et al. [2] can easily be extended so that it yields the special case of Theorem 2.1 where the metric space is a finite-dimensional normed space with a rotund norm (and the sites are arbitrary). This is discussed in more detail in an ArXiv version of the present paper [8]. That proof is still of some interest, since it is more "constructive" than the one shown above, in that the alleged n-tuples $\mathbf{R}$ and $\mathbf{S}$ are obtained by an iterative process.

We finish this section with a simple geometric lemma. It was used in a less general setting in [2] (proof of Lemma 4.3).

OBSERVATION 2.2. *Let* $\mathbf{P}$ *be an* n*-tuple of sites (in any metric space), and suppose that* $\varepsilon := \min_{i \ne j} \mathrm{dist}(P_i, P_j) > 0$ *and that* $\mathbf{R}$ *and* $\mathbf{S}$ *satisfy* $\mathbf{R} = \mathbf{Dom}\,\mathbf{S}$ *and* $\mathbf{S} = \mathbf{Dom}\,\mathbf{R}$*. Then we have* $\mathrm{dist}(P_i, \bigcup_{j \ne i} S_j) \ge \frac{\varepsilon}{2}$*, and consequently, the* $\frac{\varepsilon}{4}$*-neighborhood of each* P_i *is contained in* R_i*.*

PROOF. We recall the simple proof from [2]. We first note that $\mathbf{V} = (V_1, \ldots, V_n) := \mathbf{Dom}\,\mathbf{P}$ is the classical Voronoi diagram of $\mathbf{P}$, and the open $\frac{\varepsilon}{2}$-neighborhood of P_i does not intersect $\bigcup_{j \ne i} V_j$. Since $\mathbf{P} \preceq \mathbf{R}$, we have $\mathbf{Dom}\,\mathbf{P} \succeq \mathbf{Dom}\,\mathbf{R} = \mathbf{S}$, and hence the open $\frac{\varepsilon}{2}$-neighborhood of P_i is disjoint from $\bigcup_{j \ne i} S_j$ as well, as claimed. □

3. THE EUCLIDEAN CASE

Here we prove Theorem 1.1; throughout this section, dist denotes the Euclidean distance. In addition to Theorem 2.1 and Observation 2.2, we also need the next lemma.

LEMMA 3.1 (CONE LEMMA, EUCLIDEAN CASE). *Let* $\mathbf{P}$ *be an* n*-tuple of (nonempty closed) sites in* $\mathbb{R}^d$ *with the Euclidean metric with* $\varepsilon := \min_{i \ne j} \mathrm{dist}(P_i, P_j) > 0$*, and let* $\mathbf{R}$ *and* $\mathbf{S}$ *satisfy* $\mathbf{R} = \mathbf{Dom}\,\mathbf{S}$ *and* $\mathbf{S} = \mathbf{Dom}\,\mathbf{R}$*. Let* a *be a point of some* R_i*, and let* $p \in P_i$ *be a point of the corresponding site closest to* a *(such a nearest point exists by compactness). Then the set*

$$K := \mathrm{conv}\big(\{a\} \cup \mathrm{B}(p, \tfrac{\varepsilon}{4})\big)$$

is contained in R_i*; see Fig. 4.*

The following proof is rather specific for the Euclidean metric (the lemma fails for the ℓ_1 metric, for example).

PROOF. The region $\mathrm{dom}(p, \bigcup_{j \ne i} S_j)$ contains both a and $\mathrm{B}(p, \frac{\varepsilon}{4})$ (the latter by Observation 2.2). For the Euclidean metric, the dominance region of a point over any set is convex, since it is the intersection of halfspaces. Hence $K \subseteq \mathrm{dom}(p, \bigcup_{j \ne i} S_j) \subseteq R_i$. □

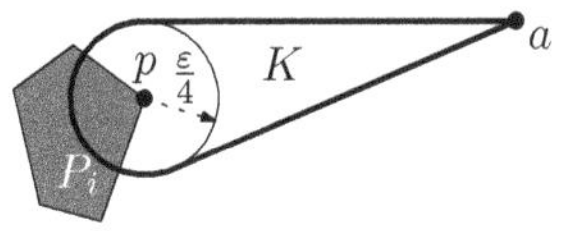

Figure 4: The cone K.

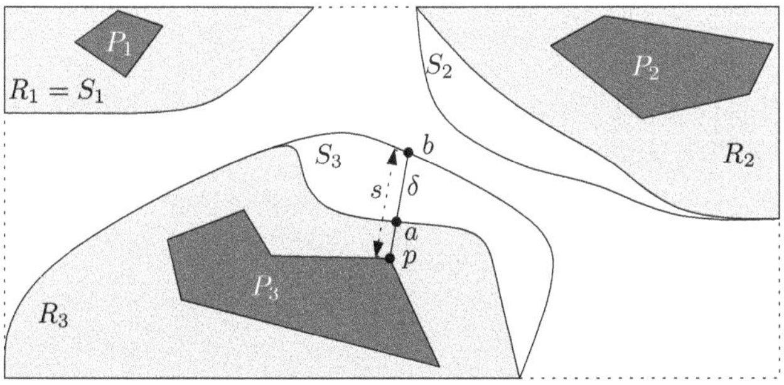

Figure 5: The setting of the proof of Theorem 1.1 (a schematic picture).

Now we describe the general strategy of the proof of Theorem 1.1. With $\mathbf{R}$ and $\mathbf{S}$ as in Theorem 2.1, it suffices to prove $\mathbf{R} = \mathbf{S}$. For contradiction, we assume that it is not the case, i.e., that $R := \bigcup_{i=1}^{n} R_i$ is properly contained in $S := \bigcup_{i=1}^{n} S_i$; see the schematic illustration in Fig. 5.

For a point $b \in S \setminus \bigcup_{i=1}^{n} P_i$, let $s(b) := \mathrm{dist}(b, P_i)$ be the distance from the nearest site P_i, and let $p = p(b) \in P_i$ be a point where this distance is attained. Let $a = a(b)$ be the closest point to b that lies in the intersection of R_i with the segment bp. It is easily seen, using the triangle inequality, that p is also a nearest point of P_i to a. Thus, the set K in Lemma 3.1 is contained in R_i, and in particular, a is the only intersection of the segment bp with ∂R_i. We set $\delta(b) := \mathrm{dist}(b, a)$. The parameters $s(b)$ and $\delta(b)$ will measure, in some sense, how much S differs from R "at b".

Assuming $\mathbf{R} \neq \mathbf{S}$, we choose a point $b_0 \in S \setminus R$. Then, using b_0, we find $b_1 \in S \setminus R$ where S differs from R "more than" at b_0. Iterating the same procedure we obtain an infinite sequence $b_0, b_1, b_2, b_3, \ldots$ of points, and the difference will "grow" beyond bounds, while, on the other hand, it has to stay bounded—and this way we reach a contradiction.

More concretely, for every integer $t \geq 1$ we will construct b_t from b_{t-1} so that, with $s := s(b_{t-1})$, $s' := s(b_t)$, $\delta := \delta(b_{t-1})$, and $\delta' := \delta(b_t)$, we have

(A) $s' \leq s - \alpha$, or

(B) $s' \leq s - \delta$ and $\delta' \geq \delta$,

where $\alpha > 0$ is a constant that depends on $s_0 := s(b_0)$ and ε, but not on t.

Thus, as t increases, $s(b_t)$ keeps decreasing. Since $s(b_t)$ is bounded from below by $\frac{\varepsilon}{4}$ by Observation 2.2, case (A) can happen only finitely many times. Therefore, from some t on, we have case (B) only. But this also causes $s(b_t)$ to decrease towards 0—a contradiction.

It remains to describe the construction of b_t from b_{t-1}, and this is done in the next lemma.

Lemma 3.2. *For every s_0 and $\varepsilon > 0$ there exists $\alpha > 0$ such that if $b \in S \setminus R$ satisfies $s := s(b) \leq s_0$, then there exists another point $b' \in S \setminus R$ such that $s' := s(b')$, $\delta := \delta(b)$ and $\delta' := \delta(b')$ satisfy* (A) *or* (B).

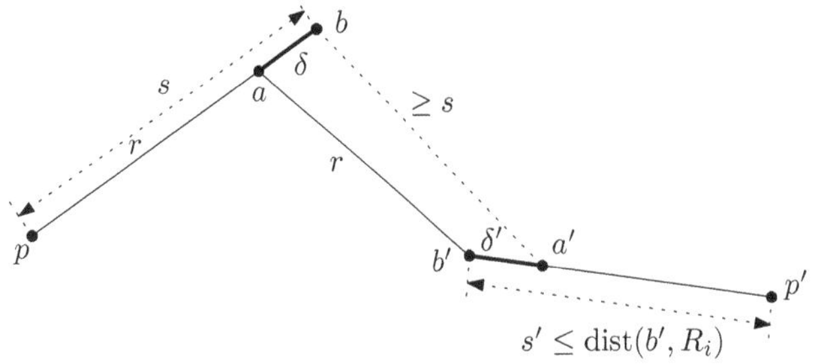

Figure 6: The construction of b'.

Proof. Let $b \in S_i$, let $a := a(b)$, $p := p(b)$, and write $r = \mathrm{dist}(a, p)$; see Fig. 6. Since $a \in \partial R_i$ and $\mathbf{R} = \mathbf{Dom}\,\mathbf{S}$, there exist $j \neq i$ and $b' \in S_j$ with $\mathrm{dist}(a, b') = r$. If there are several possible b', we choose one of them arbitrarily.

First we check that $b' \notin R$, or in other words, that $\delta' > 0$. During this step we also derive a lower bound for δ' that will be useful later. Since $b \in S$, $a' \in R$, and $\mathbf{S} = \mathbf{Dom}\,\mathbf{R}$, we have $\mathrm{dist}(a', b) \geq s$. Then we bound, using the triangle inequality,

$$\delta' \geq \mathrm{dist}(a', b) - \mathrm{dist}(b, b') \geq s - \mathrm{dist}(b, b'). \tag{2}$$

Supposing for contradiction that $\delta' = 0$, we get $\mathrm{dist}(b, b') \geq s$. But the triangle inequality gives $\mathrm{dist}(b, b') \leq \mathrm{dist}(b, a) + \mathrm{dist}(a, b') = r + \delta = s$, and hence the triangle inequality here holds with equality. For the Euclidean metric, this can happen only if a lies on the segment bb', and then b' has to coincide with p, which is impossible. So $\delta' > 0$ indeed.

Since $\mathbf{S} = \mathbf{Dom}\,\mathbf{R}$ and $b' \in S$, we have $s' \leq \mathrm{dist}(b', R_i)$. An obvious upper bound on $\mathrm{dist}(b', R_i)$ is $\mathrm{dist}(b', a) = r = s - \delta$, and thus the first inequality in (B), namely, $s' \leq s - \delta$, always holds.

Moreover, if $\delta \geq \alpha$, then $s' \leq s - \delta \leq s - \alpha$, and we have (A). For the rest of the proof we thus assume that $\delta < \alpha$ (where α hasn't been fixed yet—so far we're free to choose it as a positive function of ε and s_0 in any way we like).

Let us consider the ball $\mathrm{B}(b', r)$; see Fig. 7. If it contains b, as in the left picture, we have $\mathrm{dist}(b', b) \leq r$, and thus by (2) we have $\delta' \geq s - r = \delta$. Then (B) holds. Thus, the last case to deal with is $b \notin \mathrm{B}(b', r)$.

Let us consider the cone $K = \mathrm{conv}(\{a\} \cup \mathrm{B}(p, \frac{\varepsilon}{4}))$ as in Lemma 3.1. Its opening angle γ is bounded away from 0 in terms of ε and s_0 (here and in the further steps we use that r and s are bounded from below by ε and from above by s_0).

Let Π be a 2-dimensional plane containing p, a, b'; it also contains b since p, a, b are collinear. Let k be the ray originating at a and containing b, and let ℓ be the ray in Π originating at a and making the angle $\pi - \frac{\gamma}{2}$ with k (on the side of b'); see Fig. 7 bottom.

Since the angle of the rays k and ℓ is bounded away from the straight angle, the Euclidean ball $\mathrm{B}(b', r)$ cuts a segment of significant length from at least one of these rays. This length can be bounded from below by a positive quantity β depending only on s_0 and ε. Indeed, in the extreme case where k and ℓ make the same angle $\frac{\gamma}{4}$ with the tangent

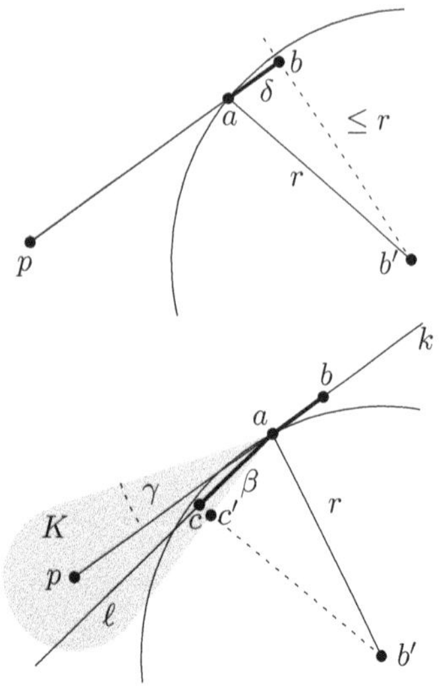

Figure 7: The r-ball around b'.

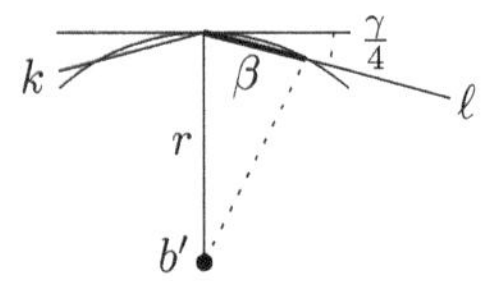

Figure 8: Bounding the quantity β from below in the Euclidean case.

of $\mathrm{B}(b', r)$, shown in Fig. 8, easy trigonometry yields $\beta = 2r \sin \frac{\gamma}{4}$.

So far we have not fixed α, and so now we can make sure that $\alpha < \beta$. Since we assume $b \notin \mathrm{B}(b', r)$, the segment of length β cut out by $\mathrm{B}(b', r)$ can't belong to the ray k. So the situation is as in the Fig. 7 bottom: $\mathrm{B}(b', r)$ contains the initial segment ac of ℓ of length β. Hence $\mathrm{dist}(b', c) \leq r$.

The distance $\mathrm{dist}(c, \mathbb{R}^d \setminus K)$ is bounded away from 0 in terms of β and γ, and so we may fix α so that $\mathrm{dist}(c, \mathbb{R}^d \setminus K) \geq \alpha$.

Let c' be the point where the segment $b'c$ meets the boundary of K. We have

$$\begin{aligned} \mathrm{dist}(b', K) &\leq \mathrm{dist}(b', c') = \mathrm{dist}(b', c) - \mathrm{dist}(c, c') \\ &\leq r - \mathrm{dist}(c, \mathbb{R}^d \setminus K) \leq r - \alpha. \end{aligned}$$

Then, finally, using $K \subseteq R_i$, we have

$$s' \leq \mathrm{dist}(b', R_i) \leq \mathrm{dist}(b', K) \leq r - \alpha < s - \alpha,$$

and so (A) holds. This concludes the proof of Lemma 3.2, as well as that of Theorem 1.1. $\square$

4. THE CASE OF SMOOTH AND ROTUND NORMS

In this section we establish Theorem 1.2. We begin with the part where the proof differs from the Euclidean case: the cone lemma. In the Euclidean case, we used the fact that for points $p \neq q$, $\mathrm{dom}(p, q)$ is a halfspace, and consequently, $\mathrm{dom}(p, X)$ is convex for arbitrary X. For other norms $\mathrm{dom}(p, q)$ need not be convex, though; see Fig. 9.

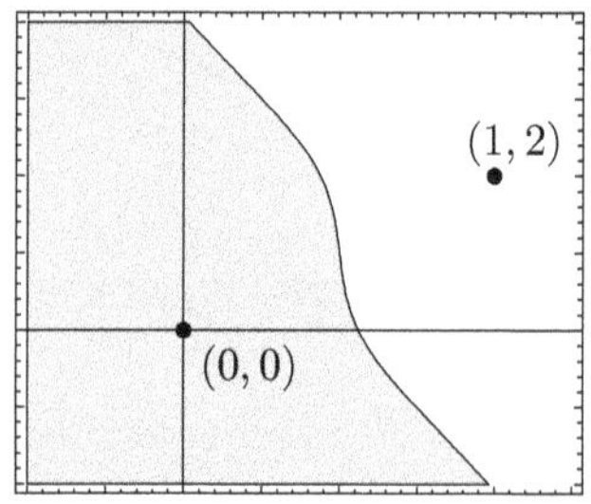

Figure 9: The dominance region of the point $(0, 0)$ against $(2, 1)$ in the ℓ_4 norm.

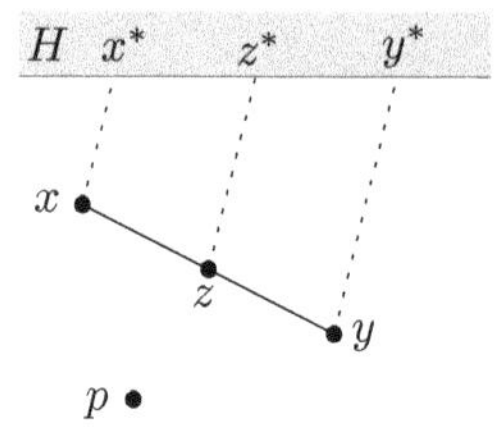

Figure 10: The dominance region of a point against a halfspace.

We have at least the following convexity result.

LEMMA 4.1. *Let us consider $\mathbb{R}^d$ with an arbitrary norm $\|\cdot\|$, let H be a closed halfspace, and let $p \notin H$ be a point. Then $\mathrm{dom}(p, H)$ is convex.*

Consequently, if the complement of a closed set $A \subseteq \mathbb{R}^d$ is convex and $p \notin A$, then $\mathrm{dom}(p, A)$ is convex.

PROOF. Let $x \notin H$ be a point and let $x^* \in \partial H$ be a point where $\mathrm{dist}(x, H)$, the distance of x to H measured by $\|\cdot\|$, is attained. If $y \notin H$ is another point and $y^* \in \partial H$ is the point such that the vectors $x - x^*$ and $y - y^*$ are parallel, then $\|y - y^*\| = \mathrm{dist}(y, H)$; see Fig. 10.

Now let $x, y \in \mathrm{dom}(p, H)$, let x^*, y^* be as above, set $z := (x+y)/2$, and let z^* be defined analogously to y^*. Then we get $\mathrm{dist}(z, H) = \|z - z^*\| = (\|x - x^*\| + \|y - y^*\|)/2 = (\mathrm{dist}(x, H) + \mathrm{dist}(y, H))/2$. From this $z \in \mathrm{dom}(p, H)$ is immediate, since $\|p - z\| \leq (\|p - x\| + \|p - y\|)/2 \leq (\mathrm{dist}(x, H) + \mathrm{dist}(y, H))/2 = \mathrm{dist}(z, H)$. This proves the first part of the lemma.

The second part follows easily: A can be expressed as a union of closed halfspaces H, and $\mathrm{dom}(p, A)$ is the intersection of the convex sets $\mathrm{dom}(p, H)$. $\square$

Now we prove a cone lemma, similar to Lemma 3.1:

LEMMA 4.2 (CONE LEMMA FOR ROTUND NORMS). *Let $\|\cdot\|$ be a rotund norm on $\mathbb{R}^d$. Suppose that an n-tuple $\mathbf{P}$ of sites satisfies $\varepsilon := \min_{i \neq j} \mathrm{dist}(P_i, P_j) > 0$, and $\mathbf{R}$ and $\mathbf{S}$ satisfy $\mathbf{R} = \mathbf{Dom}\,\mathbf{S}$ and $\mathbf{S} = \mathbf{Dom}\,\mathbf{R}$. Then for every $s_0 > 0$ there is $\rho > 0$ (also depending on ε and on $\|\cdot\|$) such that the following holds: If $a \in R_i$ with $r := \mathrm{dist}(a, P_i) \leq s_0$ and $p \in P_i$ is a point attaining the distance $\mathrm{dist}(a, P_i)$, then the set*

$$K := \mathrm{conv}\big(\{a\} \cup \mathrm{B}(p, \rho)\big)$$

is contained in R_i.

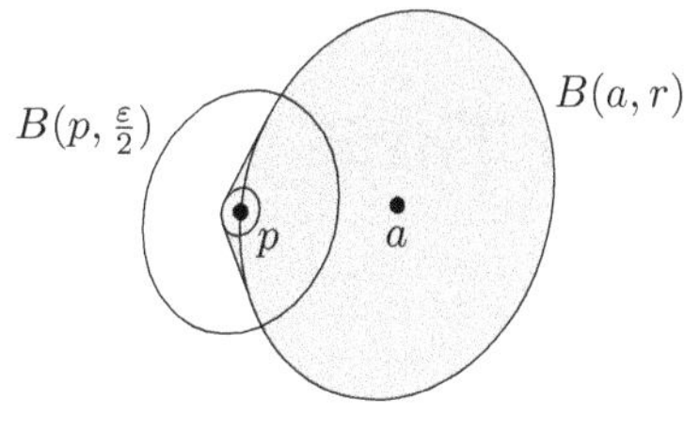

Figure 11: The sets C (shaded) and D.

PROOF. As in the Euclidean case, we begin by noting that $a \in \mathrm{dom}(p, \bigcup_{j \neq i} S_j)$ and also $\mathrm{B}(p, \frac{\varepsilon}{4}) \subseteq \mathrm{dom}(p, \bigcup_{j \neq i} S_j)$ by Observation 2.2. Thus, the set $D := \mathrm{B}(a, r) \cup \mathrm{B}(p, \frac{\varepsilon}{2})$ is contained in the closure of $\mathbb{R}^d \setminus \bigcup_{j \neq i} S_j$. We now want to find a open convex subset $C \subseteq D$ such that a and $B(p, \rho)$ are contained in $\mathrm{dom}(p, \mathbb{R}^d \setminus C)$, since the latter region is convex by Lemma 4.1 and thus it contains K as well.

We let C be the interior of $\mathrm{conv}(B(a, r) \cup B(p, 2\rho))$ with ρ sufficiently small (the restrictions on it will be apparent from the proof below); see Fig. 11. It is clear that $\{a\} \cup B(p, \rho) \subseteq \mathrm{dom}(p, \mathbb{R}^d \setminus C)$, and so it remains to prove $C \subseteq D$.

To this end, it is sufficient to prove the following: If $B := \mathrm{B}(0, 1)$ is the unit ball of $\|\cdot\|$ and $\eta > 0$ is given, then there exists $\delta > 0$ such that for every $x \in \mathbb{R}^d$ with $\|x\| \leq 1+\delta$, the "cap" $\mathrm{conv}(B \cup \{x\}) \setminus B$ has diameter at most η. This is a well-known and easily proved property of uniformly convex norms. (Proof sketch: If x with $\|x\| = 1+\delta$ has a cap of large diameter, then there is z of norm 1 and half of the diameter away from x such that the line xz avoids the interior of B. Let y be the other intersection of this line with $\partial \mathrm{B}(0, 1+\delta)$—then xy is a long segment that cuts in $\mathrm{B}(0, 1+\delta)$ into depth only δ.) □

PROOF OF THEOREM 1.2. The overall strategy is exactly as for Theorem 1.1 (see Section 3). The constant α in (A) may also depend on the considered norm $\|\cdot\|$. This quantification also needs to be added in the appropriate version of Lemma 3.2.

In the proof of that lemma, the first place where we use a property not shared by all norms is below (2); we need that the triangle inequality may hold with equality only for collinear points—this remains true for all *rotund* norms.

Then we proceed as in the Euclidean case, introducing the the cone $K = \mathrm{conv}(\{a\} \cup B(p, \rho))$ as in Lemma 4.2. There is some $\gamma > 0$, depending on ε, s_0, and the norm $\|\cdot\|$, such that the appropriate Euclidean cone with opening angle γ is contained in K. (Here and in the sequel we implicitly use the fact that every norm on $\mathbb{R}^d$ is between two constant multiples of the Euclidean norm, which is well known and immediate by compactness. All angles are measured in the usual Euclidean sense.)

We define the rays k and ℓ, again following the Euclidean proof. For the next step, we need that, since the angle of these rays is bounded away from the straight angle, at least one of k, ℓ cuts a segment of a significant length β from the ball $\mathrm{B}(b', r)$. Instead of an explicit formula as in the Euclidean case, we use the *uniform smoothness* of the norm (formula (1) in Section 1); thus, β also depends on the modulus of smoothness of the norm. The rest of the proof goes through unchanged. □

5. ACKNOWLEDGEMENTS

We are grateful to Tetsuo Asano for valuable discussions including those on non-uniqueness examples for polygonal distances. We also express our gratitude to Daniel Reem for careful reading and useful suggestions on the manuscript. Finally, we remark that the warm comments from the audience of our preliminary announcement of partial results at EuroCG 2009 encouraged us to work further.

Part of this work was done while A.K. was visiting ETH Zürich, whose support and hospitality he gratefully acknowledges. His research is also supported by the Nakajima Foundation and the Natural Sciences and Engineering Research Council of Canada. The part of this research by T.T. was partially supported by the JSPS Grant-in-Aid for Scientific Research (B) 18300001.

6. REFERENCES

[1] T. Asano and D. Kirkpatrick. Distance trisector curves in regular convex distance metrics. In *Proc. 3rd International Symposium on Voronoi Diagrams in Science and Engineering*, IEEE Computer Society, pages 8–17, 2006.

[2] T. Asano, J. Matoušek, and T. Tokuyama. Zone diagrams: Existence, uniqueness, and algorithmic challenge. *SIAM Journal on Computing*, 37(4):1182–1198, 2007.

[3] T. Asano, J. Matoušek, and T. Tokuyama. The distance trisector curve. *Advances in Mathematics*, 212(1):338–360, 2007.

[4] F. Aurenhammer. Voronoi diagrams—a survey of a fundamental geometric data structure. *ACM Computing Surveys*, 23(3):345–405, 1991.

[5] Y. Benyamini and J. Lindenstrauss. *Nonlinear Functional Analysis, Vol. I, Colloquium Publications 48*. American Mathematical Society (AMS), Providence, RI, 1999.

[6] J. Chun, Y. Okada, and T. Tokuyama. Distance trisector of segments and zone diagram of segments in a plane. In *Proc. 4th International Symposium on Voronoi Diagrams in Science and Engineering*, IEEE Computer Society, pages 66–73, 2007.

[7] M. I. Kadets, B. M. Levitan: Banach space, in *Encyclopedia of Mathematics*, M. Hazewinkel ed., Springer 2002, available online at `http://eom.springer.de/b/b015190.htm`.

[8] A. Kawamura, J. Matoušek, and T. Tokuyama. Zone diagrams in Euclidean spaces and in other normed spaces. Preprint, arXiv:0912.3016.

[9] A. Okabe, B. Boots, K. Sugihara, and S. N. Chiu. *Spatial Tessellations: Concepts and Applications of Voronoi Diagrams*. Probability and Statistics. Wiley, second edition, 2000.

[10] D. Reem and S. Reich. Zone and double zone diagrams in abstract spaces. *Colloquium Mathematicum*, 115(1):129–145, 2009.

[11] A. Tarski. A lattice-theoretical fixpoint theorem and its applications. *Pacific Journal of Mathematics*, 5:285–309, 1955.

Klee's Measure Problem on Fat Boxes in Time $\mathcal{O}(n^{(d+2)/3})$

Karl Bringmann
Saarland University
Postfach 151150
66041 Saarbrücken, Germany
s9kabrin@stud.uni-saarland.de

ABSTRACT

The measure problem of Klee asks for the volume of the union of n axis-parallel boxes in a fixed dimension d. We give an $\mathcal{O}(n^{(d+2)/3})$ time algorithm for the special case of all boxes being cubes or, more generally, fat boxes. Previously, the fastest run-time was $n^{d/2}\,2^{\mathcal{O}(\log^* n)}$, achieved by the general case algorithm of Chan [SoCG 2008]. For the general problem our run-time would imply a complexity theoretic breakthrough for the k-clique problem and can thus be considered extremely unlikely.

Categories and Subject Descriptors

F.2.2 [**Theory of Computation**]: Analysis of Algorithm and Problem Complexity, Nonnumerical Algorithms and Problems [Computations on discrete structures, geometrical problems and computations]

General Terms

Algorithms, Theory

Keywords

Geometric data structures, Union of Cubes

1. INTRODUCTION

We consider a natural geometric problem: Computing the volume of the union of n axis-parallel boxes in $\mathbb{R}^d$, where d is considered to be constant. This problem was first stated by Klee [11], who gave an $\mathcal{O}(n \log n)$ algorithm for the case of $d = 1$ and asked if this was optimal, while leaving the question open how to extend this to arbitrary dimension $d > 1$. Bentley [3] gave an algorithm with run-time $\mathcal{O}(n^{d-1} \log n)$ for $d \geq 2$, which is optimal for $d = 2$. As Chan [7] noted, this is better than explicitly constructing the union of the given boxes, which has a worst-case combinatorial complexity of $\Theta(n^d)$. The next breakthrough was a paper by Overmars and Yap [13] giving an algorithm with run-time $\mathcal{O}(n^{d/2} \log n)$ for $d \geq 2$, which was the fastest known until Chan [7] slightly improved their approach to get a run-time of $n^{d/2}\,2^{\mathcal{O}(\log^* n)}$. Interestingly, there is also an $\mathcal{O}(\frac{dn}{\varepsilon^2})$ Monte Carlo $(1+\varepsilon)$-approximation algorithm for Klee's measure problem (KMP) [5].

So far, the only known lower bound is $\Omega(n \log n)$ for any d [9]. Additionally, there are a few known hardness results for KMP: Suzuki and Ibaraki [14] showed that it is #P-hard for $d \to \infty$, i.e., if we do not consider d to be constant. Furthermore, Chan [7] showed W[1]-hardness of KMP, meaning that no algorithm of run-time $f(d)\, n^{\mathcal{O}(1)}$ is likely to exist for any function f depending only on d. His proof relies on a reduction of KMP to the k-clique problem, i.e., checking whether a graph with n vertices contains a clique of size k. Since the best-known algorithm for the latter problem has a run-time of $\mathcal{O}(n^{\omega\lfloor k/3 \rfloor + (k \bmod 3)})$ [12], where $\omega = 2.376..$ is the exponent occuring in fast matrix multiplication, he concludes that any $\mathcal{O}(n^{0.396d})$ algorithm for KMP, and even a combinatorial $\mathcal{O}(n^{(\frac{1}{2}-\varepsilon)d})$ algorithm, would require a breakthrough in the k-clique problem.

This raises the question whether there are easier special cases of KMP. To develop algorithms for such special cases is also one of the open problems posed by Jeff Erickson [8]. The two special cases that got attention so far, are the case of all boxes being cubes (or fat boxes), or unit cubes (fat boxes of roughly equal size), respectively:

Klee's measure problem on cubes (C-KMP) can be solved in time $\mathcal{O}(n^{4/3} \log n)$ for $d = 3$, using an algorithm of Agarwal, Kaplan, and Sharir [2]. This runtime has just been improved to $\mathcal{O}(n \log^4 n)$ [1]. For higher dimensions, Chan's KMP algorithm is the fastest known. One may generalize the case of cubes to the one of α-fat boxes for some constant $\alpha \geq 1$, where we say that a box is α-fat, if its maximal side length is at most a factor of α larger than its minimal side length. A simple reduction shows that both problems can be solved in the same asymptotic run-time: Represent a fat box by a union of possibly overlapping cubes. You need at most $\lceil \alpha \rceil^{d-1}$ cubes for such a representation. Then the volume of the union of the cubes is the same as the volume of the union of the fat boxes, and we increased the number of boxes only by a constant factor. Hence, all algorithms for C-KMP also solve the case of fat boxes.

We speak of Klee's measure problem on unit cubes (UC-KMP) if all cubes have the same side length. As the union of n unit cubes has combinatorial complexity $\Theta(n^{\lfloor d/2 \rfloor})$ [4], this special case can be solved in $\mathcal{O}(n^{\lfloor d/2 \rfloor} \text{polylog}\, n)$ [10], which improves upon general KMP algorithms in odd dimensions. Furthermore, an elaborate algorithm runs in $\mathcal{O}(n^{\lceil d/2 \rceil - 1 + \frac{1}{\lceil d/2 \rceil}} \operatorname{polylog} n)$ [6], which improves in even dimensions. This case can be generalized to fat boxes of roughly equal size, analogously to cubes and fat boxes. Note that all of these algorithms have run-time $\Omega(n^{d/2-1})$ in the worst case.

The Result.

In this paper we are improving upon the algorithms for both of these special cases (in high dimensions) by giving a better algorithm for C-KMP. As customary, we assume d to be constant.

THEOREM 1. *Given a set M of n axis-parallel cubes in $\mathbb{R}^d$, $d \geq 2$, we can compute the volume of the union of these cubes, i.e, solve C-KMP, in time $\mathcal{O}(n^{(d+2)/3})$.*

Note that this is faster than any known algorithm for C-KMP in dimensions $d \geq 4$ (at least by a factor of $2^{\mathcal{O}(\log^*(n))}$) and faster than any known algorithm for UC-KMP in dimensions $d > 8$. More importantly, we reduce the exponent from $\frac{d}{2} + \mathcal{O}(1)$ to $\frac{d}{3} + \mathcal{O}(1)$. As this is notably faster than the bound $n^{0.396d}$, finding such a good algorithm for the general case would imply a breakthrough in more classical areas (k-clique).

The space requirement of our algorithm, as we will present it in this paper, is also $\mathcal{O}(n^{(d+2)/3})$ and cannot be bounded by an asymptotically smaller function. However, one may use the very same trick as Overmars and Yap [13] who show in their Section 5 how to reduce the amount of storage to $\mathcal{O}(n)$.

Our result uses some ideas from Overmars and Yap [13] as well as from Agarwal et al. [2]. However, it is no generalization of the latter, which works only for $d = 3$. Instead, we switch our view to another base case. The contribution of this paper can be seen as the identification of the this simpler base case, and the idea how to solve it. The differences to existing algorithms will be highlighted again in Section 2.

In the following section we give a structural overview of our algorithm for C-KMP. Sections 3 to 5 give the details of the algorithm in 3 steps. In the last part we give concluding remarks.

2. STRUCTURAL OVERVIEW

In this section we give a rough overview of the algorithm. We start by defining some notation and the problem: In dimension $d \in \mathbb{N}$ we define a *box* to be a set $[x_1, y_1] \times \ldots \times [x_d, y_d] \subseteq \mathbb{R}^d$, $x_i \leq y_i$ for all i. A *cube* is a box with $y_i - x_i = y_j - x_j$ for all dimensions i, j, i.e., for $1 \leq i, j \leq d$. We refer to x_i (y_i) as the lower (upper) i-th coordinate of the box or cube. For a set $U \subseteq \mathbb{R}^d$ we define $\mathrm{Vol}(U)$ as the Lebesgue measure of U. If we want to point out the dimension we are working in, we use Vol^d instead of Vol. Moreover, for a box C we define $\mathrm{Vol}_C(U) := \mathrm{Vol}(C \cap U)$, the volume of U inside C. For a set of boxes M, we define $\mathcal{U}(M) := \bigcup_{B \in M} B$. Then $\mathrm{Vol}(\mathcal{U}(M))$ is the volume of the union of the boxes in M.

The problem C-KMP now is to compute $\mathrm{Vol}(\mathcal{U}(M))$ for a given set M of n cubes. Using a bounding box $\mathcal{BB}$ of all the boxes in M, this quantity is the same as $\mathrm{Vol}_{\mathcal{BB}}(\mathcal{U}(M))$.

Representation of sets of boxes.

Similar to a construction of Overmars and Yap [13], we will represent a set of boxes M in the following way: We have sorted lists L_i of reals, $1 \leq i \leq d$, containing the i-th (upper and lower) coordinates of the boxes in M. Thus, every box occurs $2d$ times in the d lists. Furthermore, each occurence of a box will have a pointer to the next occurence, such that all occurrences of a box are in a cyclic structure of $2d$ pointers.

Such a representation allows us to do several things quickly: For example, given a pointer to one occurence of a box, we can delete this box from the set M in time $\mathcal{O}(1)$, as we can iterate through all occurences of the box in constant time. Also, we may iterate through all boxes sorted by lower i-th coordinate or sorted by upper i-th coordinate. More importantly, we will at some points in this paper be in the position that we iterate through some L_i and define a subset M' of M by deciding during the iteration whether the current box belongs to M' or not. Then a representation of M' can be computed in time $\mathcal{O}(|M|)$ by marking elements of M' in all lists L_i and computing L'_i by iterating through L_i and taking marked elements.

This representation will save us a logarithmic factor in run-time. Computing this representation when given any standard representation of sets of boxes can be done in time $\mathcal{O}(n \log n)$. This does not increase the overall run-time for $d \geq 2$.

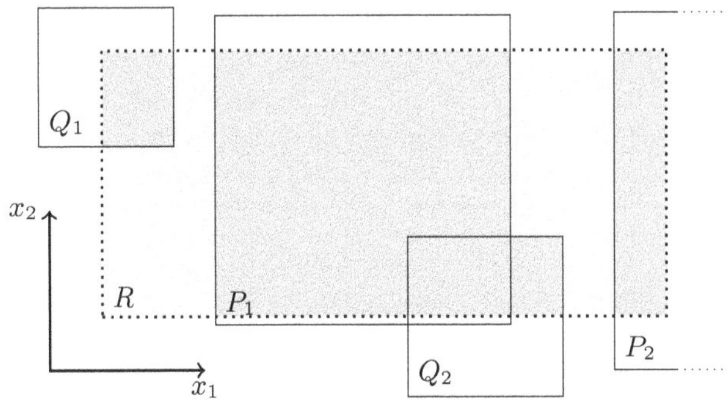

Figure 1: An example of piles and quasi-piles of a region R. P_1 and P_2 are 1-piles, Q_1 and Q_2 are $(1, 2)$-quasi-piles. Note that in 2D all cubes partially covering R are piles or quasi-piles. This does not hold in higher dimensions.

2.1 Space partitioning

We compute the volume $\mathrm{Vol}_{\mathcal{BB}}(\mathcal{U}(M))$ by splitting up the bounding box: We define a *partitioning* of a box B to be a finite set P of boxes with $\bigcup_{R \in P} R = B$ and that for two different boxes $R, R' \in P$ the intersection is a null set, i.e., $\mathrm{Vol}(R \cap R') = 0$. We refer to the boxes in a partitioning as *regions*.

Now, if we have a partitioning P of the bounding box $\mathcal{BB}$, we can compute the quantity of interest as $\mathrm{Vol}(\mathcal{U}(M)) = \mathrm{Vol}_{\mathcal{BB}}(\mathcal{U}(M)) = \sum_{R \in P} \mathrm{Vol}_R(\mathcal{U}(M))$.

We want such a partitioning to have several nice properties and we need some definitions to state them: We say that a box B *partially covers* a region R, if $\mathrm{Vol}(R) > \mathrm{Vol}_R(B) > 0$. A region is said to be *fully covered* by a box B, if $R \subseteq B$. Furthermore, for a box $B = [x_1, y_1] \times \ldots \times [x_d, y_d]$ we call $B_i := [x_i, y_i]$ the *i-interval* and $|B_i| = y_i - x_i$ the *i-th side length* of B. We call a box B an *i-pile* for region R and a dimension i, if we have $R_k \subseteq B_k$ for all dimensions $k \neq i$, and $\emptyset \subsetneq R_k \cap B_k \subsetneq R_k$ for $k = i$. We call B an (i, j)-

quasi-pile, $i \neq j$, if we have $R_k \subseteq B_k$ for all dimensions $k \neq i, k \neq j$, and $\emptyset \subsetneq R_k \cap B_k \subsetneq R_k$ for $k = i$ and $k = j$. We call it a pile, if it is an i-pile for some i, similarly for quasi-pile. Note that any (quasi-)pile of a region R partially covers R. Intuitively, a box is a pile (quasi-pile), if it covers the region R in all but one (two) dimensions, see Figure 1 for an example.

Now, we can state the two properties we want from a partitioning P of the bounding box:

(P1) Every region $R \in P$ is partially covered by $\mathcal{O}(n^{2/3})$ cubes in M, of which $\mathcal{O}(n^{1/3})$ are quasi-piles for R and all other are piles for R.

(P2) The number of regions in P is $\mathcal{O}(n^{d/3})$.

Note that property (P1) does not state anything about the number of fully covering boxes of R, as we explicitly defined piles and quasi-piles not to be fully covering.

In Section 3 we will give a construction for such a partitioning. It returns the set of regions together with their sets of partially covering cubes and a fully covering box, if there exists one, in time $\mathcal{O}(n^{(d+2)/3})$ for $d \geq 2$. As it does not matter whether we have one or all fully covering boxes for computing $\mathrm{Vol}_R(\mathcal{U}(M))$, we can assume that each region has at most one fully covering box in the remainder.

The partitioning we build is very similar to the one of Overmars and Yap [13], just with a different parameter, and the same as a generalized Agarwal et al. [2] would do. The only difference is that we solve a static problem, while the mentioned algorithms do a sweep first and solve a dynamic problem. This is why they need to handle a partition *tree*, where one can insert and delete boxes, while we only need a partitioning, without any tree build on it. The reason for us solving the static problem is that the dynamic problem seems too hard to be solved fast enough to get a better algorithm, i.e., I do not know how to solve it.

2.2 Solving the base case

We are left with the following *base case*: Computing $\mathrm{Vol}_R(\mathcal{U}(M))$ for a region R and a set M of cubes containing at most one fully covering box for R, $\mathcal{O}(n^{1/3})$ quasi-piles, and $\mathcal{O}(n^{2/3})$ piles. If M contains a fully covering box, computing this volume is trivial. Otherwise, we will split up this base case into a few easier problems. For this, we refer to the points $(z_1, \ldots, z_d)$ with $z_i \in \{x_i, y_i\}$ for all dimensions i as the *vertices* of a region $R = [x_1, y_1] \times \ldots \times [x_d, y_d]$. We call a (quasi-)pile of R *vertex-containing*, if it contains a vertex of R.

The motivation of splitting up the base case is that we found a way to solve the following *reduced base case* efficiently: We are given a region R in $\mathbb{R}^{d'}$ and a set M' of m boxes partially covering R, which are all vertex-containing piles or vertex-containing quasi-piles. Compute $\mathrm{Vol}_R^{d'}(\mathcal{U}(M'))$.

First of all, we found a way to solve the base case (on $\mathcal{O}(n^{1/3})$ quasi-piles and $\mathcal{O}(n^{2/3})$ piles) by solving $\mathcal{O}(n^{1/3})$ reduced base cases (on $\mathcal{O}(n^{1/3})$ boxes) using additional time $\mathcal{O}(n^{2/3})$. This can be seen as a Turing reduction from the base case to the reduced base case. This reduction is where we use the fact that we are facing cubes, not general boxes. In Section 4 this step will be described in detail.

Secondly, we found a way to solve the reduced base case in time $\mathcal{O}(m)$. Here, we use the standard technique of a space sweep to get a dynamic problem with dynamic piles and static quasi-piles. Then we solve this dynamic problem by considering a few smaller dynamic problems. The elaborate details of this step can be found in Section 5.

Note that this leaves us with an $\mathcal{O}(n^{(d+2)/3})$ algorithm for C-KMP.

For differentiating between our approach and [13] or [2], one has to point out that our base case is a static problem, while the mentioned algorithms solve a dynamic one. Furthermore, the identification and solution of our *reduced base case* is completely novel.

2.3 Subsumption

Summing up, we see that the algorithm consists of 3 steps:

- We construct a partitioning P of a bounding box $\mathcal{BB}$ with properties (P1) and (P2). Having this, we compute the volume $\mathrm{Vol}_R(M)$ inside every region $R \in P$ and sum up.
- We transform the base case of computing $\mathrm{Vol}_R(M)$ into easier reduced base cases.
- We solve the reduced base case.

These three steps will be described in the following 3 sections.

3. CONSTRUCTION OF THE SPACE PARTITIONING

In this section we describe how to compute a partitioning of the bounding box of M with properties (P1) and (P2) in time $\mathcal{O}(n^{(d+2)/3})$. Our construction will, additionally, compute for each region R the set of partially covering cubes of R in M and a fully covering cube, if there exists one.

The Construction.

Say the bounding box of M is $\mathcal{BB} = [x_1, y_1] \times \ldots \times [x_d, y_d]$. We will proceed in d levels, starting with $\mathcal{BB}$ on level 1: On a level $1 \leq \ell \leq d$ we are given a box $B = [x'_1, y'_1] \times \ldots \times [x'_{\ell-1}, y'_{\ell-1}] \times [x_\ell, y_\ell] \times \ldots \times [x_d, y_d]$ and the set $M_{B,\ell} \subseteq M$ of cubes partially covering B. For a cube C in $M_{B,\ell}$ let v be the number of dimensions k, $1 \leq k < \ell$ such that C has a k-th coordinate in the open interval (x'_k, y'_k). We split $M_{B,\ell}$ into three subsets: $M^i_{B,\ell}$ contains all cubes with $v = i$ for $i \in \{0, 1, 2\}$. We will show in a moment, that no cube has $v > 2$. Now, we split the interval $[x_\ell, y_\ell]$ into $\mathcal{O}(n^{1/3})$ intervals, each of whose interior contains at most $n^{2/3}$ ℓ-th coordinates of cubes in $M^0_{B,\ell}$, at most $n^{1/3}$ ℓ-th coordinates of cubes in $M^1_{B,\ell}$ and no ℓ-th coordinate of a cube in $M^2_{B,\ell}$. This splits the box B into $\mathcal{O}(n^{1/3})$ smaller boxes (children), on which we recurse to level $\ell + 1$ after computing their sets of partially covering cubes $M_{B',\ell+1}$.

All the boxes we end up with on level $d + 1$ will be the regions of our partitioning. For each such region R, we are given $M_{R,d+1}$, the set of partially covering cubes of R in M, and split it into three subsets, $M^i_{R,d+1}$, $i \in \{0, 1, 2\}$, just as we did on lower levels.

Correctness.

We need to prove two facts to show that this construction works: The first is that no cube will ever have $v > 2$ (on any level $1 \leq \ell \leq d + 1$). Any such cube would have $v = 2$

on some lower level $\ell' < \ell$, so it would be in $M^2_{B,\ell'}$ on that level. But then we split so that no coordinate of the cube is in the interior of a new interval, so its v-value cannot grow.

The second fact is that we need at most $\mathcal{O}(n^{1/3})$ splits to assure that each interior of a new interval contains at most $n^{2/3}$ ℓ-th coordinates of cubes in $M^0_{B,\ell}$, at most $n^{1/3}$ ℓ-th coordinates of cubes in $M^1_{B,\ell}$ and no ℓ-th coordinate of a cube in $M^2_{B,\ell}$. To prove this, it suffices to show the upper bounds $|M^1_{B,\ell}| = \mathcal{O}(n^{2/3})$ and $|M^2_{B,\ell}| = \mathcal{O}(n^{1/3})$ for $1 \leq \ell \leq d+1$, as we can assure that each interval includes $|M^i_{B,\ell}|/\mathcal{O}(n^{1/3})$ coordinates of cubes in $M^i_{B,\ell}$ for each i by splitting at $\mathcal{O}(n^{1/3})$ positions. These inequalities are trivially true on the first level, as those sets are empty there. Also, they are maintained during the split at a level ℓ: For each child B' of the box B (corresponding to an interval $[x'_\ell, y'_\ell]$) we have $|M^1_{B',\ell+1}| \leq |M^1_{B,\ell}| + n^{2/3}$, as new such cubes may only come from a box in $M^0_{B,\ell}$, whose ℓ-th coordinate is contained in (x'_ℓ, y'_ℓ), and this number is bounded from above by $n^{2/3}$ by our construction. As the number of levels is d, a constant, the upper bound holds in all levels. We get the inequality for $|M^2_{B,\ell}|$ similarly.

It is now very easy to show the following lemma:

LEMMA 2. *The above construction yields a partitioning with properties (P1) and (P2).*

PROOF. Observe that the set of quasi-piles of R is exactly $M^2_{R,d+1}$ and the set of piles of R is $M^1_{R,d+1}$. Moreover, the way we constructed $M^0_{R,d+1}$ no cube in it can *partially* cover R, since every cube in this set has no k-th coordinate contained in the interior of the interval R_k for any k, so this set is empty. Since we proved $|M^2_{R,d+1}| = \mathcal{O}(n^{1/3})$ and $|M^1_{R,d+1}| = \mathcal{O}(n^{2/3})$, this shows that each region is partially covered by $\mathcal{O}(n^{2/3})$ piles, $\mathcal{O}(n^{1/3})$ quasi-piles, and no other boxes in M, which is property (P1).

For (P2) note that we split the box into $\mathcal{O}(n^{1/3})$ smaller boxes at each of the d levels. Hence, we create $\mathcal{O}(n^{d/3})$ regions. □

Implementation Details.

Now we have a construction of a partitioning with the properties we wanted. However, it is not so clear how to implement this with the aforementioned runtime of $\mathcal{O}(n^{(d+2)/3})$, for the intuitive upper bound being $\mathcal{O}(n^{(d+3)/3}\log n)$. We use here, that we represent sets of cubes by sorted lists of coordinates in every dimension. Having these lists, we can split the set $M_{B,\ell}$ into $M^i_{B,\ell}$ and find the split of the current interval in time $\mathcal{O}(n)$ (this would not be possible without a sorted order). After we split the box into $\mathcal{O}(n^{1/3})$ children, we compute the set of partially covering boxes for each child and build sorted lists of coordinates of these boxes from the sorted lists we got for $M_{B,\ell}$. This can be done in $\mathcal{O}(n)$ per child. For each level $1 \leq \ell < d$, this run-time is admissible, as we get a run-time of $\mathcal{O}(n \cdot n^{(d-1)/3}) = \mathcal{O}(n^{(d+2)/3})$.

On the last level $\ell = d$, finding the positions for splits can be done in $\mathcal{O}(n)$, too, which is admissible, as there are $\mathcal{O}(n^{(d-1)/3})$ problem instances on level d. However, computing the sets of partially covering cubes for the children has to be done in (amortized) time $\mathcal{O}(n^{2/3})$ per child. This is easy for cubes that become i-piles or (i,j)-quasi-piles with $i,j < d$ in the children: Any such (quasi-)pile is partially covering one child if and only if it partially covers all children. Thus, a list of these (quasi-)piles can be constructed in time $\mathcal{O}(n)$, i.e., $\mathcal{O}(n^{2/3})$ per child. For cubes that become d-piles or (i,d)-quasi-piles, $i < d$, we use that any such (quasi-)pile is partially covering at most 2 children, since each of its two d-th coordinates may lie in the interior of another child. If we go through the children and the sorted list of d-th coordinates of these cubes "in parallel", we can also find the children a cube partially covers in (amortized) constant time. Hence, also these (quasi-)piles can be computed in $\mathcal{O}(n^{2/3})$ per child. Since any partially covering cube of a child is a pile or quasi-pile by property (P1), we are done with these two cases. After this, we have to split the set $M_{R,d+1}$ into the sets $M^i_{R,d+1}$. Note that this can be done in $\mathcal{O}(n^{2/3})$ trivially, as we proved above that $|M^0_{R,d+1}| = 0, |M^1_{R,d+1}| = \mathcal{O}(n^{2/3})$ and $|M^2_{R,d+1}| = \mathcal{O}(n^{1/3})$, so that the overall number of cubes in $M_{R,d+1}$ is small enough to allow linear time procedures.

So far we lack the computation of a fully covering box for each fully covered region. We will compute those boxes on level d, too. For this, we go through the sorted list of d-th coordinates of *all* cubes in M. At the same time, we go through the children in the same sorted order. For a cube we can tell in constant time, whether it fully covers the current child. If so, we save it as a fully covering box for this child and go on in the list of children (and check the current cube with the next child). If not, we go on in the list of cubes or of children, respectively. This way, we compute a fully covering box for any child in time linear in the number of cubes in M and the number of children, i.e., in $\mathcal{O}(n)$, which is $\mathcal{O}(n^{2/3})$ per child.

Thus, we have seen a construction of a partitioning with properties (P1) and (P2) that computes for each region its set of partially covering boxes and one fully covering box, if there is one.

4. SIMPLIFYING THE BASE CASE

In this section we show how to simplify the base case to the reduced base case. Recall that the base case is the problem of computing $\mathrm{Vol}^d_R(\mathcal{U}(M))$ for a region R and a set of cubes M containing $\mathcal{O}(n^{1/3})$ quasi-piles and $\mathcal{O}(n^{2/3})$ piles (and no other boxes). The reduced base case is the problem of computing $\mathrm{Vol}^{d'}_R(\mathcal{U}(M'))$ of a set of boxes M' consisting of vertex-containing piles and vertex-containing quasi-piles (in some dimension $1 \leq d' \leq d$). We describe how to solve the base case by solving $\mathcal{O}(n^{1/3})$ reduced base cases on $\mathcal{O}(n^{1/3})$ boxes using additional run-time of $\mathcal{O}(n^{2/3})$. This is the point where we use that we are dealing with cubes rather than general boxes.

Dealing with most piles.

Without loss of generality we may assume that the side lengths of region R are in sorted order $|R_1| \leq |R_2| \leq \ldots \leq |R_d|$. An i-pile B of R is vertex-containing iff the interval B_i contains an endpoint of the interval R_i. Thus, any i-pile B of R with $i < d$ is already vertex-containing, since otherwise we would have $B_i \subsetneq R_i$, thus $|B_i| < |R_i| \leq |R_d|$, so that we cannot have $R_d \subseteq B_d$, as B is a cube, but this contradicts B being a pile.

Dealing with these vertex-containing i-piles, $i < d$, in the computation of $\mathrm{Vol}_R(\mathcal{U}(M))$ is easy: Out of the i-piles B

with B_i containing the lower i-th coordinate of R we take the pile P_1 with largest interval $B_i \cap R_i$. Similarly, out of the i-piles B with B_i containing the upper i-th coordinate of R we take the pile P_2 with the largest interval $B_i \cap R_i$. Then we have for any i-pile B: $B \cap R \subseteq (P_1 \cup P_2) \cap R$. Thus, we can remove all i-piles other than P_1, P_2 from M and still get the same volume $\mathrm{Vol}_R(\mathcal{U}(M))$. We reduced the number of i-piles, $i < d$, to a constant this way.

Sweep along dimension d.

Now we sweep along dimension d. Let $R_d = [y_1, y_2]$ and let $z_1 \leq \ldots \leq z_m$ be the d-th coordinates of boxes in M that lie in R_d. Let $z_0 := y_1, z_{m+1} := y_2$. We sweep a horizontal hyperplane along dimension d from y_1 to y_2 stopping at each z_i, $0 \leq i \leq m+1$. Let $\Pi(t)$ be the hyperplane satisfying $x_d = t$. For each $0 \leq i \leq m$ the cross-section $\Pi(z) \cap R \cap \mathcal{U}(M)$ is the same for all $z \in (z_i, z_{i+1})$. Let v_i denote the $(d-1)$-dimensional volume of this cross-section. Then $\mathrm{Vol}_R(\mathcal{U}(M)) = \sum_{i=0}^{m} v_i(z_{i+1} - z_i)$. In every interval (z_i, z_{i+1}) where a d-pile is active, i.e., where there exists a d-pile B of R with $(z_i, z_{i+1}) \subseteq B_d$, the volume v_i is trivially equal to $\prod_{j \neq d} |R_j|$. Not looking at these trivial v_i, the sequence of v_i's changes only if a box in M, which is no d-pile, is inserted or deleted. The number of those boxes is bounded by $\mathcal{O}(n^{1/3})$, as we reduced the number of i-piles, $i < d$, to a constant. Thus, we have to compute $\mathcal{O}(n^{1/3})$ v_i's, each with $\mathcal{O}(n^{1/3})$ partially covering boxes and no fully covering ones. We spent time $\mathcal{O}(n^{2/3})$ so far, since all this can be implemented in linear time with the coordinates already sorted. Note that we are not trying to compute v_i dynamically by updating v_{i-1}, but consider them as static problems.

Most boxes are vertex-containing.

We are left with $\mathcal{O}(n^{1/3})$ $(d-1)$-dimensional base cases, but not in its full generality. In fact, every (quasi-)pile is vertex-containing in these instances, except the $(d-1)$-piles (that stem from $(d-1, d)$-quasi-piles in the d-dimensional problem). We use the fact that we are facing cubes to prove this: As in the second paragraph of this section we show that every i-pile, $i < d-1$, is already vertex-containing. This holds in general for the base case. A non-vertex-containing (i, j)-quasi-pile B, $i < j < d$, has side length $|B_i| < |R_i| \leq |R_j| \leq |R_d|$. But then B cannot stem from a pile or quasi-pile of the original region R, as B_k does not include R_k for $k = i, j, d$.

Cutting out $(d-1)$-piles.

What do we do with the remaining $(d-1)$-piles that are non-vertex-containing? We simply cut them out of dimension $d-1$: Let $R_{d-1} = [y_1, y_2]$ and let $y_1 = z_0 \leq \ldots \leq z_{2m} = y_2$ be a partitioning of R_{d-1} such that each $R_1 \times \ldots \times R_{d-2} \times (z_i, z_{i+1})$ is fully covered by some $(d-1)$-pile for even i but neither fully nor partially covered by a $(d-1)$-pile for odd i, and $m = \mathcal{O}(n^{1/3})$. In this partitioning we want to cut out the intervals (z_{2i}, z_{2i+1}), as depicted in Figure 2. Formally, one can write this using a compression function κ defined as follows: For an $x \in (y_1, y_2]$ we find the i with $x \in (z_i, z_{i+1}]$. If i is odd, i.e., we do not cut out (z_i, z_{i+1}), we define $\kappa(x) := x - \sum_{j=0}^{(i-1)/2}(z_{2j+1} - z_{2j})$, if i is even we define $\kappa(x) := z_i - \sum_{j=0}^{(i-2)/2}(z_{2j+1} - z_{2j})$. Moreover, we set $\kappa(x) := x$ for $x \leq y_1$, and $\kappa(x) := x - Z$ for $x > y_2$, where $Z := \sum_{j=0}^{m-1}(z_{2j+1} - z_{2j})$ is the total length of cut intervals. For a box $B = [x_1, x_1'] \times \ldots \times [x_{d-1}, x_{d-1}']$ we define $\kappa(B) := [x_1, x_1'] \times \ldots \times [x_{d-2}, x_{d-2}'] \times [\kappa(x_{d-1}), \kappa(x_{d-1}')]$, for a set of boxes M we define $\kappa(M) := \{\kappa(B) \mid B \in M\}$. Computing $\mathrm{Vol}_{\kappa(R)}^{d-1}(\mathcal{U}(\kappa(M)))$ is then the compressed problem on the right hand side in Figure 2. We now have $\mathrm{Vol}_R^{d-1}(\mathcal{U}(M)) = \mathrm{Vol}_{\kappa(R)}^{d-1}(\mathcal{U}(\kappa(M))) + Z \cdot \prod_{j=1}^{d-2} |R_j|$. Observe that we can compute $\kappa(R), \kappa(M)$ and Z in time $\mathcal{O}(n^{1/3})$, as we have sorted lists of coordinates.

In the problem $\mathrm{Vol}_{\kappa(R)}^{d-1}(\mathcal{U}(\kappa(M)))$ all partially covering boxes of $\kappa(R)$ are vertex-containing piles or vertex-containing quasi-piles, as we cut out the $(d-1)$-piles and all other boxes where vertex-containing before. Note that the function κ may destroy the property of being a cube, but we did not require this for the reduced base case. It follows that the problem of computing $\mathrm{Vol}_{\kappa(R)}^{d-1}(\mathcal{U}(\kappa(M)))$ is a reduced base case. This finishes the reduction.

5. SOLVING THE REDUCED BASE CASE

In the last step we are left with solving the reduced base case: Compute $\mathrm{Vol}_R^d(\mathcal{U}(M))$ of a set of boxes M consisting of vertex-containing piles and vertex-containing quasi-piles for some $d \in \mathbb{N}$. It will be shown how to solve this problem in time $\mathcal{O}(m)$ for $m = |M|$, d constant. We may assume without loss of generality that each box in M is contained in R. This simplifies the representation of sets of piles and sets of quasi-piles.

5.1 The static problem

We will call the reduced base case the *static problem*. The reason for this is that we solve it by sweeping along dimension d, which leaves us with a dynamic problem. As described in more detail in the previous section, we sweep a horizontal hyperplane along dimension d from y_1 to y_2 for $R_d = [y_1, y_2]$, stopping at each d-th coordinate z_i of a box in M. Between two such stops the $(d-1)$-dimensional volume v_i stays the same, so that we get $\mathrm{Vol}_R(\mathcal{U}(M))$ as $\sum_i v_i(z_{i+1} - z_i)$. In the dynamic problem of computing those v_i all (j,k)-quasi-piles and j-piles of R, $j, k < d$, are contributing to all v_i, so they are static, and all (j,d)-quasi-piles become dynamic j-piles, that may get inserted or deleted. Observe that each (j,d)-quasi-piles is either already present in the initialization of the dynamic problem and may be deleted, or may be inserted but never deleted, as we are facing vertex-covering (quasi-)piles. A d-pile of R becomes a fully covering box in the $(d-1)$-dimensional problem. As computing v_i is trivial if a d-pile B is active, i.e., if $(z_i, z_{i+1}) \subseteq B_d$, we may assume that there are no fully covering boxes in the dynamic problem.

With this sweep approach we get

$$T_{stat}(m, d) \leq T_{dyn}(m, d-1) + \mathcal{O}(m), \tag{1}$$

where $T_{stat}(m, d)$ denotes the run-time of our algorithm for solving the static problem on m boxes in d dimensions, and $T_{dyn}(m, d)$ denotes the run-time for solving the dynamic problem in d dimensions, where the number of boxes we initialize the problem with plus the number of updates is bounded from above by m.

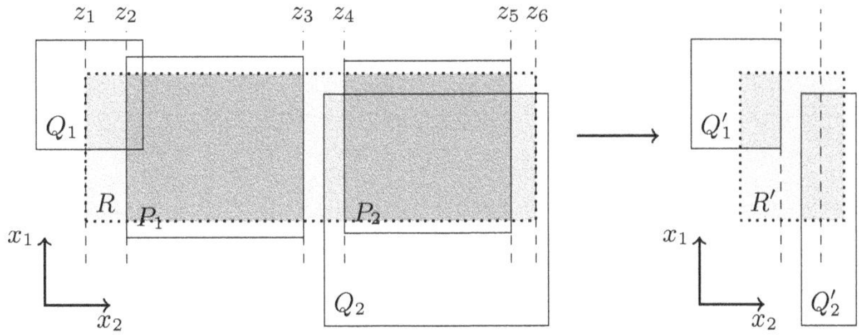

Figure 2: We want to cut out the 2-piles P_1 and P_2. This is done by cutting out the intervals (z_2, z_3) and (z_4, z_5). On the right hand side you see the result, where dashed lines denote that we deleted an interval there.

5.2 The dynamic problem

More precisely, the *dynamic problem* is the following: On initialization we get a region $R \subseteq \mathbb{R}^{d'}$, a set of vertex-containing quasi-piles Q and a set of vertex-containing piles P^0 and return $\mathrm{Vol}_R^{d'}(\mathcal{U}(Q \cup P^0))$. There are two types of updates: Firstly, a vertex-containing pile may be inserted, call the set of these inserted piles P^1. Secondly, a pile from P^0 may be deleted. After each update we have to return the current volume $\mathrm{Vol}_R^{d'}(\mathcal{U}(Q \cup P^0 \cup P^1))$.

In the remainder of this section we will describe how to solve the dynamic problem. We need to define some notions first. Beside the dimensions $1, \ldots, d'$ we will speak of the $2d'$ *directions* $+1, -1, \ldots, +d', -d'$. Intuitively, $\pm i$ points to $\pm\infty$ along dimension i. We define the *opposite direction* $\bar{r}$ as $-i$ if $r = +i$ and $+i$ if $r = -i$. We say that two directions r, r' are *perpendicular*, $r \perp r'$, if $r' \neq r$ and $r' \neq \bar{r}$. We can canonically assign to each vertex-containing pile a direction: An i-pile B gets assigned to direction $+i$, if the interval B_i contains the upper i-th coordinate of R, and it gets assigned to $-i$, if B_i contains the lower i-th coordinate of R. It will be more convenient to speak of *r-piles* in the remainder, for directions r, not i-piles, for dimensions i. We can do the same for quasi-piles: An (i, j)-quasi-piles Q gets assigned the directions $r = \pm i$, $r' = \pm j$, depending on whether Q_i contains the upper or lower i-th coordinate of R (and the same for j), so that we can speak of an *(r, r')-quasi-pile*. As shorthands we write $P = P^1 \cup P^0$ and P_r^0 for the r-piles in P^0, similarly for P_r^1 and P_r. We will store only the sets Q, P_r^0 and P_r^1 explicitly. Iterating through all boxes can then be accomplished by iterating through these $4d' + 1$ sets "in parallel".

For a direction $r = +i$ we define the *rim* to be the hyperplane Π_r defined by the equation $x_i = \min\{y_i \mid (y_1, \ldots, y_{d'}) \in \mathcal{U}(P_r)\}$, or $x_i = u_i$, if the set P_r is empty and u_i is the upper i-th coordinate of R. For a direction $r = -i$ we replace min by max and u_i by ℓ_i, the lower i-th coordinate of R. This is the hyperplane that splits R into the part covered by r-piles and the part not influenced by r-piles. We take any r-pile that has non-empty intersection with Π_r (normally, this pile will be uniquely determined) and call it the *rim-defining* pile of direction r. Figure 3(a) shows an example with the rims indicated. The rim-defining piles of directions -1 and $+2$ are P_1 and P_3, respectively, the other two directions do not have a rim-defining pile.

Initialization.

We are given the sets Q and P^0 and have to return $\mathrm{Vol}_R^{d'}(\mathcal{U}(Q \cup P^0))$, so we simply solve this as a static problem. This costs time $T_{stat}(m, d') + \mathcal{O}(m)$.

Moreover, we initialize dynamic problems D_r for each direction $r = \pm i$ with the $(d'-1)$-dimensional region $\prod_{j \neq i} R_j$ and all boxes in $Q \cup P \setminus (P_r \cup P_{\bar{r}})$ intersecting Π_r, the rim in this direction. During the algorithm the following invariant I_r will hold for all directions r after the initialization and each update: The dynamic problem D_r contains exactly the boxes in $Q \cup P \setminus (P_r \cup P_{\bar{r}})$ that intersect Π_r. We will show that initialization and updates of the instance D_r are of the form we defined above for the dynamic problem, if we re-initialize D_r at the right point.

Insertions and Deletions.

When we have to delete an r-pile B, we delete it from P_r^0 (assuming that we are given a pointer to B in P_r^0 this can be done in $\mathcal{O}(1)$). It may be that it was the rim-defining pile in its direction. Then the volume $\mathrm{Vol}_R^{d'}(Q \cup P)$ changes. Figure 3(b) shows this situation, where the old rim was at p_{old} and the new will be at p_{new}. We may do a differential volume update, as we already have computed $\mathrm{Vol}_R^{d'}(Q \cup P)$ before the deletion. For this we need the volume v overlapped by boxes in $Q \cup P$ in the subregion from p_{old} to p_{new} of R. This volume can be computed by a sweep: We sweep a hyperplane Π parallel to Π_r from p_{old} to p_{new} stopping at all coordinates of boxes in Q. We need to compute the $(d'-1)$-dimensional volume of the cross-section $\Pi \cap R \cap \mathcal{U}(Q \cup P \setminus (P_r \cup P_{\bar{r}}))$. This is exactly what the dynamic problem D_r gives us, so we insert or delete the boxes in Q we stop at into or from problem D_r. This way, we can do the sweep by utilizing the lower dimensional dynamic problem D_r. At the end of this sweep the invariant I_r is fulfilled again.

Additionally, we have to update the dynamic problems in the other directions: We delete the r-pile B from $D_{r'}$ for any direction $r' \perp r$. After this, invariant $I_{r'}$ holds again.

An insertion of a pile works analogously. Here, we need that we only insert a pile B, if it is not already contained in some other pile B' in P^1, i.e., if $B \cap R \not\subseteq B' \cap R$. If we do this, then any newly inserted r-pile is "the largest" in P_r^1, so that we can insert it in time $\mathcal{O}(1)$ into P_r^1.

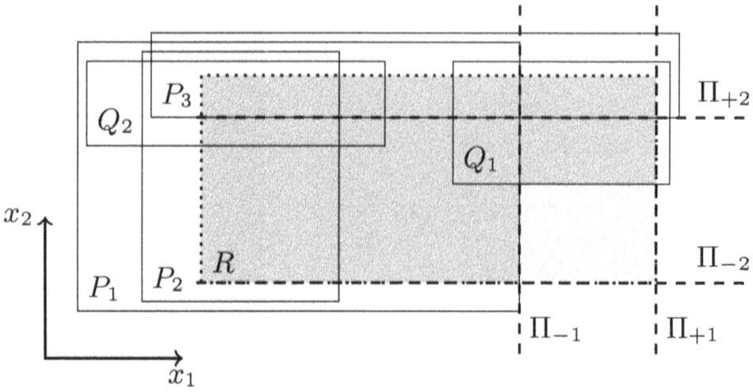

(a) An example with rims indicated

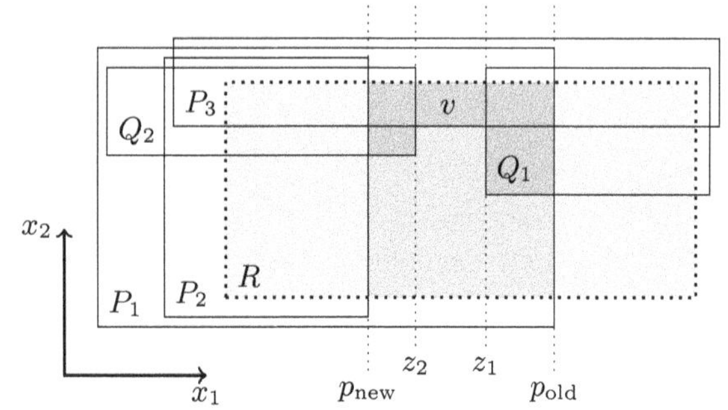

(b) The deletion of P_1 demands a sweep

Figure 3: An example of the dynamic problem with piles P_1, P_2, P_3 and quasi-piles Q_1, Q_2. In part (b) pile P_1 gets deleted, so that we have to compute the volume v for a differential volume update. We do a sweep from p_{old} to p_{new} stopping at z_1 and z_2 to delete Q_1 and insert Q_2 into D_{-1}. We also have to delete P_1 from D_{+2} and D_{-2}.

D_r is really a dynamic problem.

Note that the sequence of insertions and deletions of r-piles that actually change the volume inside R has a very simple form: It may start with some deletions. Eventually, an insertion changes the volume inside R, implying that the rim-defining pile will be one of P_r^1. From this point on no box in P_r^0 can be rim-defining anymore, so that no deletions will change the volume in R. Hence, this sequence of insertions and deletions starts with a sequence of deletions followed by a sequence of insertions. This also shows that the rim is monotonically decreasing up to some point, and is monotonically increasing afterwards. Observe that during each of these two phases the updates to the dynamic problem D_r are of the demanded form: Each pile in $P \setminus (P_r \cup P_{\bar{r}})$ always intersects Π_r, and they are either there at the initialization, so also at the initialization of D_r, and may get deleted, or may get inserted but never deleted. Each (r', r'')-quasi-pile in Q, $r \perp r', r''$, always intersects Π_r, so always is in D_r. An (r', r)-quasi-pile with $r' \perp r$ may get inserted into D_r when sweeping Π_r during the deletion of an r-pile. But then it is never deleted from D_r in a deletion of an r-pile anymore. Similar statements hold for insertions and $(r', \bar{r})$-quasi-piles.

We use a trick now to make all dynamic problems of the demanded form: At the point we switch to the second phase in direction r (which is easy to recognize) we re-initialize problem D_r. Without this re-initialization D_r would not necessarily be of the demanded form, as a quasi-pile might get inserted into D_r during the deletion of a pile and get deleted from D_r again during the insertion of a pile. With this trick, the dynamic problems are of the demanded form and we now have at most $4d'$ of them: For all of the $2d'$ directions we may initialize the problem twice.

A Detail.

So far during a sweep of an insertion or deletion of an r-pile we considered only the boxes in Q and $P \setminus (P_r \cup P_{\bar{r}})$ for computing the differential volume update. However, the piles in $P_{\bar{r}}$ may also influence this volume: If the two rims of r and $\bar{r}$ cross each other we get $\mathcal{U}(P_r \cup P_{\bar{r}}) = R$, but this is not taken into account by our differential volume update so far (and we would probably return a volume greater than $\text{Vol}(R)$). This detail has a simple fix: During each sweep we have another stop at the point where the rim crosses its opposite rim, if this happens at all. If this cross is of the form, that $\mathcal{U}(P_r \cup P_{\bar{r}}) = R$ afterwards, then we note this and return at the end of the update not the volume we computed, but $\text{Vol}(R)$. If the cross is of the form, that $\mathcal{U}(P_{r'} \cup P_{\bar{r}'}) \subsetneq R$ for each direction r' afterwards, then we reset the current volume to $\text{Vol}(R)$ at this point. This simple fix can be seen to work trivially. It ends our description of the solution of the dynamic problem.

Run-time.

To compute the required run-time we note that the number of boxes in each of the $4d'$ dynamic problems is bounded by m and all sweeps (and the rest) can be implemeted in linear time, as we have sorted lists of coordinates. Hence, we get

$$T_{\text{dyn}}(m, d') \leq T_{\text{stat}}(m, d') + 4d' \cdot T_{\text{dyn}}(m, d' - 1) + \mathcal{O}(m).$$

Using the bound (1) we get

$$T_{\text{dyn}}(m, d') \leq (4d' + 1) \cdot T_{\text{dyn}}(m, d' - 1) + \mathcal{O}(m).$$

As d' is constant, this solves to $T_{\text{dyn}}(m, d') = \mathcal{O}(m)$. Here, we used the observation that the dynamic problem can be solved in linear time in dimension 1: After each update we have to know the rim-defining $+1$-pile and the rim-defining -1-pile to compute the current volume inside the region. But this is simple since we are given sorted lists of coordinates.

6. CONCLUSION

In this paper we reduced the exponent β in the run-time of $\mathcal{O}(n^{\beta})$ for Klee's measure problem on cubes from $\beta = \frac{d}{2} + \mathcal{O}(1)$ to $\beta = \frac{d}{3} + \mathcal{O}(1)$.

However, it is not clear so far, whether an algorithm for C-KMP needs a run-time of $n^{\Theta(d)}$. Proving W[1]-hardness of C-KMP would give such a result, conditioned on certain complexity theoretic assumptions, but this remains open. On the other hand, there may also be a "fast" algorithm for this problem, waiting to be found.

References

[1] P. K. Agarwal. An improved algorithm for computing the volume of the union of cubes. In *Proc. 26rd annual Symposium on Computational Geometry (SoCG '10)*, 2010. To appear.

[2] P. K. Agarwal, H. Kaplan, and M. Sharir. Computing the volume of the union of cubes. In *Proc. 23rd annual Symposium on Computational Geometry (SoCG '07)*, pp. 294–301, 2007.

[3] J. L. Bentley. Algorithms for Klee's rectangle problems, 1977. Department of Computer Science, Carnegie Mellon University, Unpublished notes.

[4] J.-D. Boissonnat, M. Sharir, B. Tagansky, and M. Yvinec. Voronoi diagrams in higher dimensions under certain polyhedral distance functions. In *Proceedings of the eleventh annual symposium on Computational geometry (SoCG '95)*, pp. 79–88, 1995.

[5] K. Bringmann and T. Friedrich. Approximating the volume of unions and intersections of high-dimensional geometric objects. In *Proc. 19th International Symposium on Algorithms and Computation (ISAAC '08)*, Vol. 5369 of *LNCS*, pp. 436–447, 2008.

[6] T. M. Chan. Semi-online maintenance of geometric optima and measures. *SIAM J. Comput.*, 32:700–716, 2003.

[7] T. M. Chan. A (slightly) faster algorithm for Klee's measure problem. *Computational Geometry: Theory and Applications*, 2009+. To appear, preliminary version appeared in *Proc. 24th ACM Symposium on Computational Geometry (SoCG '08)*.

[8] J. Erickson. Klee's measure problem, 1998. http://compgeom.cs.uiuc.edu/~jeffe/open/klee.html.

[9] M. L. Fredman and B. W. Weide. On the complexity of computing the measure of $\bigcup[a_i, b_i]$. *Commun. ACM*, 21:540–544, 1978.

[10] H. Kaplan, N. Rubin, M. Sharir, and E. Verbin. Counting colors in boxes. In *Proc. 18th Annual ACM-SIAM Symposium on Discrete Algorithms (SODA '07)*, pp. 785–794, 2007.

[11] V. Klee. Can the measure of $\bigcup[a_i, b_i]$ be computed in less than $O(n \log n)$ steps? *American Mathematical Monthly*, 84:284–285, 1977.

[12] J. Nešetřil and S. Poljak. On the complexity of the subgraph problem. *Commentationes Mathematicae Universitatis Carolinae*, 26:415–419, 1985.

[13] M. H. Overmars and C.-K. Yap. New upper bounds in Klee's measure problem. *SIAM J. Comput.*, 20: 1034–1045, 1991.

[14] S. Suzuki and T. Ibaraki. An average running time analysis of a backtracking algorithm to calculate the measure of the union of hyperrectangles in d dimensions. In *Proc. 16th Canadian Conference on Computational Geometry (CCCG '04)*, pp. 196–199, 2004.

An Improved Algorithm for Computing the Volume of the Union of Cubes*

Pankaj K. Agarwal
Department of Computer Science
Duke University

Abstract

Let $\mathcal{C}$ be a set of n axis-aligned cubes in $\mathbb{R}^3$, and let $\mathcal{U}(\mathcal{C})$ denote the union of $\mathcal{C}$. We present an algorithm that computes the volume of $\mathcal{U}(\mathcal{C})$ in time $O(n\,\mathrm{polylog}(n))$. The previously best known algorithm takes $O(n^{4/3}\log^2 n)$ time.

Categories and Subject Descriptors

F.2.2 [**Analysis of Algorithms and Problem Complexity**]: Nonnumerical Algorithms and Problems—*Computations on discrete structures, geometrical problems and computations*

General Terms

Algorithms, Theory.

Keywords

Geometric data structures, Union of cubes.

1. INTRODUCTION

Let $\mathcal{C}$ be a set of n axis-aligned cubes in $\mathbb{R}^3$, and let $\mathcal{U}(\mathcal{C})$ denote the union of $\mathcal{C}$. Computing the volume of $\mathcal{U}(\mathcal{C})$ efficiently is related to the well-known *Klee's measure problem.* In 1977 Victor Klee [13] had presented an $O(n \log n)$ time algorithm for computing the union of n intervals in $\mathbb{R}^1$ and had asked whether his algorithm was optimal. An $\Omega(n \log n)$ lower bound was proved by Fredmen and Weide [11]. Bentley [4] studied the two-dimensional version of Klee's measure problem. When extended to computing the volume of the union of n d-dimensional axis-aligned boxes, the running time of Bentley's algorithm is $O(n^{d-1} \log n)$. Later, van Leeuwen and Wood [12] improved the running time to $O(n^2)$ for $d = 3$. The problem lay dormant for a while until Overmars and Yap presented an algorithm with $O(n^{d/2} \log n)$ running time [15]. Recently, Chan [7] slightly improved the running time of their algorithm to $n^{d/2} 2^{O(\log^* n)}$; see also [8, 9] for some other related results. The lower bounds proved in [7, 16] suggest that improving the running time to $O(n^{d/2-\varepsilon})$, for any constant $\varepsilon > 0$, might be hard. See [1] for a brief history of the problem. Boissonnat *et al.* [5] proved that the combinatorial complexity of n axis-aligned cubes in $\mathbb{R}^d$ is $\Theta(n^{\lceil d/2 \rceil})$, and it is $\Theta(n^{\lfloor d/2 \rfloor})$ if all the cubes have the same size. Note that this bound is considerably better than the $\Theta(n^d)$ worst-case bound on the union of n axis-aligned boxes in $\mathbb{R}^d$. This suggests that it might be easier to compute the volume of the union of n cubes. Indeed, the volume of the union of n axis-aligned unit cubes in $\mathbb{R}^3$ can be computed in $O(n \log n)$ time, by computing their union explicitly (which has linear complexity), but this will not lead to an efficient algorithm for cubes of different sizes. Agarwal *et al.* [2] presented an $O(n^{4/3} \log^2 n)$ algorithm for computing the volume of the union of n axis-aligned cubes in $\mathbb{R}^3$, by exploiting the special structure of cubes. Recently Bringmann [6] extended the result to higher dimensions and proposed an $O(n^{(d+2)/3})$ algorithm for computing the volume of the union of n hypercubes in $\mathbb{R}^d$. In this paper we significantly improve the result in [2].

THEOREM 1.1. *The volume of the union of a set of n axis-aligned cubes in $\mathbb{R}^3$ can be computed in time $O(n \log^4 n)$.*

Although there are some similarities between the new algorithm and [2], several new ideas and data structures are needed to improve the running time. The algorithm asserted in Theorem 1.1 is presented in the following four sections. Section 2 gives a high-level description of the algorithm, and describes a data structure for maintaining the area of the union of a set of squares in $\mathbb{R}^2$ under certain assumptions on the sequence of updates. Section 3 describes the update procedure for the data structure, Section 4 presents auxiliary procedures needed by our algorithm in Section 3, and Section 5 presents secondary data structures needed in Section 4.

2. THE GLOBAL STRUCTURE

We assume that the cubes of $\mathcal{C}$ are in *general position*. In particular, we assume that no plane support facets of two distinct cubes in $\mathcal{C}$. Let $z_1 < \cdots < z_{2n}$ be the (distinct) z-coordinates of the vertices of cubes in $\mathcal{C}$, sorted in increasing order. We sweep a horizontal plane Π in the $(+z)$-direction from $-\infty$ to $+\infty$, stopping at each z_i. Let $\Pi(t)$ denote the horizontal plane at $z = t$. For each $1 \leq i < 2n$, the cross-section $\mathcal{U}(\mathcal{C}) \cap \Pi(z)$ is the same for all $z \in (z_i, z_{i+1})$. Let α_i denote the area of this cross-section. Then $\mathrm{Vol}\,\mathcal{U}(\mathcal{C}) = \sum_{i=1}^{2n-1} \alpha_i (z_{i+1} - z_i)$. We thus need to maintain α_i as we sweep the horizontal plane. The intersection of $\Pi(z)$ with $\mathcal{U}(\mathcal{C})$ is the union of a set $\mathbb{S}$ of squares that changes dynamically—a square is added to the intersection when Π sweeps through the bottom facet of its corresponding cube, and is removed from the intersection when Π sweeps through the top facet of its cube. Let

*Supported by NSF under grants CNS-05-40347, CCF-06 -35000, IIS-07-13498, and CCF-09-40671, by ARO grants W911NF-07-1-0376 and W911NF-08-1-0452, by an NIH grant 1P50-GM-08183-01, by a DOE grant OEG-P200A070505, and by a grant from the U.S.–Israel Binational Science Foundation.

SCG'10, June 13–16, 2010, Snowbird, Utah, USA.

S_1 and S_2 be two squares that are inserted into $\mathbb{S}$. If S_1 is bigger than S_2 and S_1 is inserted after S_2, then S_1 is deleted after S_2 has been deleted (because S_1 and S_2 are intersections of cubes with the sweep line). We capture this observation by defining the notion of a *size preserving* update sequence:

> *A sequence of insertions and deletions is called size preserving if a square S is deleted only after all squares that were smaller than S and inserted before S have been deleted.*

We describe a dynamic data structure that maintains, in $O(\log^4 n)$ amortized time (see Lemma 3.2), the area of the union of $\mathbb{S}$, denoted by $\mu(\mathbb{S})$, for a size-preserving update sequence. This implies Theorem 1.1.

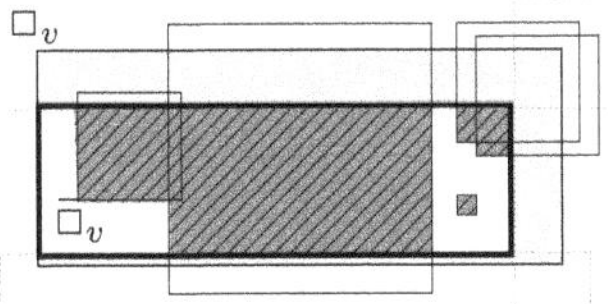

Figure 1. Long (dotted lines) and short (solid lines) squares in $\square_v$, $\bar{\square}_v$ (thick rectangle). Lightly shaded region is $\mathcal{U}(\mathbb{L}_v) \cap \square_v$, and the hatched region is $\mathcal{U}(\mathbb{G}_v) \cap \bar{\square}_v$.

Here is a rough sketch of the overall data structure for maintaining $\mu(\mathbb{S})$. $\mathbb{S}$ is stored in a partition tree $\mathbb{T}$, which is a variant of a kd-tree. Each node v of $\mathbb{T}$ is associated with a rectangle $\square_v$. The squares of $\mathbb{S}$ intersecting $\square_v$ are partitioned into two sets $\mathbb{L}_v$ and $\mathbb{G}_v$, the sets of *long* and *short* squares, respectively. A square is long if at most one of its edges intersects $\square_v$, and short if at least two edges intersects $\square_v$. Let $\bar{\square}_v = \square_v \setminus \mathcal{U}(\mathbb{L}_v)$, which is a rectangle; see Figure 1. The basic idea is to maintain $\mathbb{L}_v$ and $\bar{\square}_v$ at v, to store $\mathbb{G}_v$ recursively at the descendents of v, and to compute $\tilde{\alpha}(v) = \operatorname{Area} \mathcal{U}(\mathbb{G}_v) \cap \bar{\square}_v$ from the information stored at the children of v. There are, however, several challenges in accomplishing this: First, a square may appear short at $\Omega(\sqrt{n})$ nodes in a kd-tree, so how do we ensure that a square appears as a short square only at polylog(n) nodes of $\mathbb{T}$? Exploiting that $\mathbb{S}$ is a set of squares, we describe a variant of kd-tree that guarantees this property. Second, and even more challenging issue, is to maintain $\bar{\square}_v$ and $\tilde{\alpha}(v)$ efficiently. A square can be long at too many nodes of $\mathbb{T}$, so a long square is stored only at the highest nodes at which it is long (analogous to how intervals are stored in a segment tree). But then $\bar{\square}_v$ cannot be not maintained explicitly at v, making the maintenance of $\tilde{\alpha}(v)$ hard. We circumvent this problem by maintaining an approximation $\boxplus_v$ of $\bar{\square}_v$, maintaining $\alpha(v) = \operatorname{Area} \mathcal{U}(\mathbb{G}_v) \cap \boxplus_v$, pushing certain information related to $\mathbb{L}_v$ to the descendents of v in a lazy manner, and maintaining secondary structures to compute $\tilde{\alpha}(v)$ from $\alpha(v)$ quickly whenever needed. A clever charging scheme is used to bound the time spent in maintaining this information. The charging scheme exploits, in a crucial though subtle way, the special (obvious) property that the *life-time* of a square of side length h (regarding the z-direction as "time") is also h time units.

For a horizontal (resp. vertical) edge e lying on the line $y = a$ (resp. $x = a$), we refer to a as the *value* of e and denote it by $\varphi(e)$. For two sets A and B of squares and a rectangle ρ, let $\mathcal{U}(A, B, \rho)$ denote $(\mathcal{U}(A) \cap \rho) \setminus \mathcal{U}(B)$, and $\mu(A, B, \rho)$ denote $\operatorname{Area} \mathcal{U}(A, B, \rho)$. For brevity, we set $\mathcal{U}(A, \rho) := \mathcal{U}(A, \emptyset, \rho)$ and $\mathcal{U}(A, B) := \mathcal{U}(A, B, \mathbb{R}^2)$. We define $\mu(A, \rho)$ and $\mu(A, B)$ analogously. We will repeatedly use the following simple equality

$$\mu(A \cup B, \rho) = \mu(B, \rho) + \mu(A, B, \rho)\,. \tag{1}$$

Primary data structure. In our case, we know in advance the set $\mathcal{S}$ of all squares that will ever be inserted into $\mathbb{S}$. $\mathcal{S}$ is the set of the xy-projections of cubes in $\mathcal{C}$; $|\mathcal{S}| = n$. Let $\square$ be the smallest axis-parallel rectangle containing all squares in $\mathcal{S}$. We build a binary space partition tree $\mathbb{T}$ on $\mathcal{S}$, the so-called *longest-sided kd-tree* [10], that is similar to a kd-tree [3]. The structure of $\mathbb{T}$ will be static but the information stored at each node of $\mathbb{T}$ will change as the set $\mathbb{S}$ changes.

Each node v of $\mathbb{T}$ is associated with a rectangle $\square_v = [x_v^-, x_v^+] \times [y_v^-, y_v^+] \subseteq \square$ and a subset $\mathcal{S}_v \subseteq \mathcal{S}$ of squares. For the root node u of $\mathbb{T}$, $\square_u = \square$ and $\mathcal{S}_u = \mathcal{S}$. If the horizontal edge of $\square_v$ is longer than its vertical edge (i.e., $x_v^+ - x_v^- \geq y_v^+ - y_v^-$), then we call v a $\obar$-type node, otherwise we call v a $\ominus$-type node; see Figure 3. We classify a square $S \in \mathcal{S}$ that intersects $\square_v$ into one of the following mutually disjoint categories (see Figure 2): S is called a *cover* if $\square_v \subseteq S$. S is an *anchor* if S contains exactly one edge of $\square_v$ — exactly one edge e of S intersects the interior of $\square_v$. We set $\varphi(S) := \varphi(e)$. If S contains a long edge of $\square_v$, then S is called a *long* anchor, and a *short* anchor otherwise. S is a *bar* if $\square_v$ does not contain a vertex of S and two parallel edges of S—the ones parallel to a short edge of $\square_v$—intersect the interior of $\square_v$. If v is $\obar$-type (resp. $\ominus$-type), then only the vertical (resp. horizontal) edges of S can intersect the horizontal (resp. vertical) edges of $\square_v$. Finally, S is called a *corner* and a *floater* if $\square_v$ contains one vertex and at least two vertices of S, respectively, in its interior.

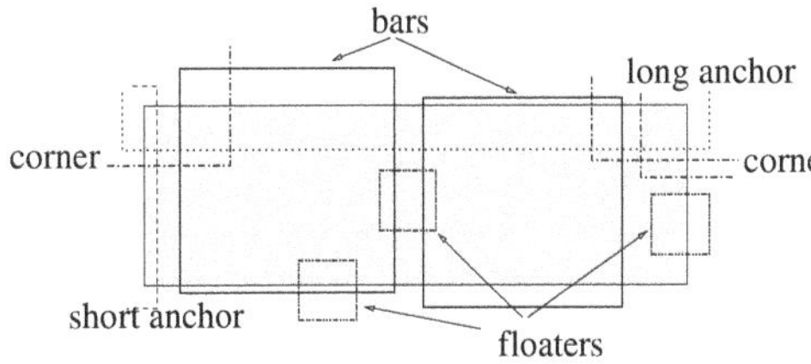

Figure 2. Partition of $\mathcal{S}$ into various categories.

We refer to bars, corners, and floaters as *short* squares (at least two edges of a short square intersect $\square_v$), and to anchors and covers as *long* squares. We call a square S *active* at v if it is not a cover or a long anchor at any proper ancestor of v. All short squares at v are active, and an active anchor at v is allowed to be an active short anchor at $p(v)$, the parent of v. Let $\mathcal{S}_v \subseteq \mathcal{S}$ be the subset of active squares at v. For a square $S \in \mathcal{S}$, let $\Xi(S)$ be the set of lowest nodes of $\mathbb{T}$ at which S is active, and let $\mathcal{N}(S)$ be the set of (proper) ancestors of nodes in $\Xi(S)$. S is active at all nodes in $\mathcal{N}(S) \cup \Xi(S)$, and it is stored at these nodes. Similarly, we call an orthogonal segment e intersecting $\square_v$ *short* at v if $\square_v$ contains an endpoint of e, and *long* otherwise. We call e *active* at v if there is no proper ancestor u of v at which e is long and parallel to a long edge of $\square_w$; this definition is similar to a square being active at a node v. Finally, we define $\Xi(e)$ and $\mathcal{N}(e)$ for an edge e as for a square.

If there are no short squares at v, then v is a leaf. Otherwise, v is an interior node, and we split $\square_v$ into two rectangles by splitting its longer edges, as follows. Suppose v is $\obar$-type. Let $\mathcal{X}_v$ be the set of x-coordinates of the vertices of short squares at v that lie in the interval $[x_v^-, x_v^+]$, i.e., the set of x-coordinates of the vertices of: (i) $\mathcal{S}$ that lie inside $\square_v$, and (ii) of bars at v. Let χ_v be the median of $\mathcal{X}_v$. We split $\square_v$ into two rectangles by drawing the vertical line $\ell_v : x = \chi_v$. The resulting left (resp. right) subrectangle is associated with the left (resp. right) child of v. If v is $\ominus$-type, then we split $\square_v$ by the horizontal line $\ell_v : y = \chi_v$, where χ_v is the median of the y-coordinates of the vertices of short squares at v that lie in the interval $[y_v^-, y_v^+]$; see Figure 3. We associate the bottom (resp. top) subrectangle with the left (resp. right) child of v. We call ℓ_v the *separator line* at v.

We define a subtree $\mathbb{T}(v)$ of $\mathbb{T}$ rooted at v, as follows: we recursively visit the subtree rooted at v. Suppose we are at a node w. If w is a leaf of $\mathbb{T}$ or a node of different type than v, we stop. Otherwise, we recursively visit the children of v. $\mathbb{T}(v)$ is the set of nodes visited by this procedure. Let $\mathbb{D}(v)$ denote the set of leaves of $\mathbb{T}(v)$. All interior nodes of $\mathbb{T}(v)$ are of the same type as v. See Figure 3.

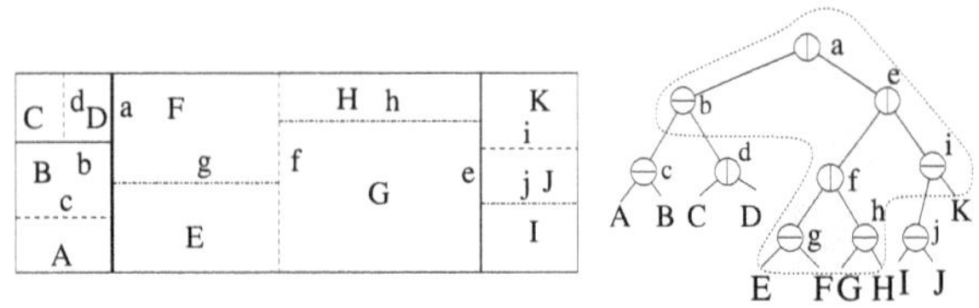

Figure 3. A recursive partition of $\square$ and the corresponding $\mathbb{T}$; lower-case letters denote the separator lines, and upper-case letters denote the cells associated with the leaves of $\mathbb{T}$; shaded region denotes $\mathbb{T}(\text{rt})$.

Each square is a floater at the root of $\mathbb{T}$. Let $S \in \mathbb{S}$ be a square, and let v be a node such that S is active at v and the separating line ℓ_v intersects the interior of S. If $S \subset \text{int}\,\square_v$, S splits into two floaters. Assume that S intersects $\partial\square_v$. If S is a floater at v, then either S splits into two corner squares, or into a bar and a floater. If S is a bar at v, it splits into two (active) anchors. (Note that since ℓ_v splits the long edges of $\square_v$, a bar is never split into two bars.) If S is a corner at v, then it splits into an (active) anchor and a corner. Finally, if S is an active short anchor at v, it splits into a cover and an anchor. See Figure 4. The following lemma will be used to bound the size of the data structure.

LEMMA 2.1. *(i) $\mathbb{T}$ has $O(n \log n)$ leaves, and the depth of $\mathbb{T}$ is $O(\log n)$. (ii) A square appears as a floater, a corner, or an active long anchor at $O(\log n)$ nodes, and as a bar, an active short anchor, or an active cover at $O(\log^2 n)$ nodes.*

Proof: Let Δ be the depth of $\mathbb{T}$, and let S be a square in $\mathbb{S}$. If S is a floater or a corner at a node v, then $\square_v$ contains at least one vertex of S. Since there are at most four nodes v of $\mathbb{T}$ at any given level for which $\square_v$ contains a vertex of S, S appears as a floater or a corner in at most 4Δ nodes. Next, if S appears as a bar at a node v, then S appears at $p(v)$ as a bar or a floater and does not appear as a bar at the sibling of v. Therefore the nodes at which S appears as a bar can be partitioned into a family $\Pi_B(S)$ of paths, each of length at most Δ, such that S appears as a floater at the parent of the root of each path. See Figure 4. Since S appears as a floater in at most 4Δ nodes, S appears as a bar in at most $4\Delta^2$ nodes. If S appears as an active short anchor at v, then there are two cases:

(i) S appears as a bar at $p(v)$, S intersects $\ell_{p(v)}$, and S appears as an anchor at the sibling of v, or

(ii) S appears as a corner or an active short anchor at $p(v)$ and does not appear as a short anchor at the sibling of v.

We can thus partition the nodes at which S appears as an active short anchor into a family Π_A of paths each of length at most Δ so that either the parent w of the root of each path is a leaf of a path in Π_B, or S appears as a corner at w. Hence, the number of paths in Π_A is $O(\Delta)$, and S appears as an active short anchor at $O(\Delta^2)$ nodes. If S appears as an active cover at a node v, then S appears as an active short anchor at $p(v)$, implying that S appears as an active cover at $O(\Delta^2)$ nodes. Finally, if S appears as a long anchor at v, then either $p(v)$ is the leaf of a path in $\Pi_A \cup \Pi_B$ or S appears as a corner at $p(v)$. Since there are $O(\Delta)$ such nodes, S appears an active long anchor at $O(\Delta)$ nodes. Next, we prove that $\Delta = O(\log n)$, which will complete the proof of (ii).

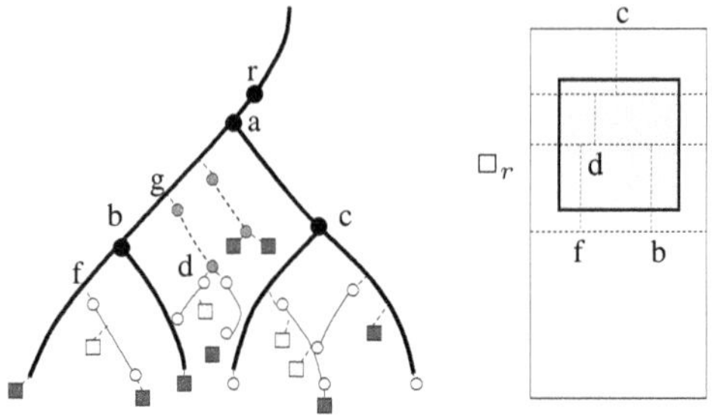

Figure 4. Trace of a square S through $\mathbb{T}$. Left: S appears as a corner or floater along thick paths; paths in $\Pi_B(S)$ (resp. $\Pi_A(S)$) are denoted by dashed (resp. solid) lines; S appears as a cover (resp. long anchor) at light (resp. dark) squares, and as a short anchor (resp. bar) at hollow (resp. filled) circles. Right: Separator lines inside $\square_r$ corresponding to the marked nodes on the left.

Let $L(m, k)$ denote the maximum number of leaves in a subtree rooted at a node v so that $\mathbb{S}_v$ contains m bars and $\square_v$ contains k vertices of $\mathbb{S}$. Let $\Delta(m, k)$ denote the maximum depth of such a subtree. If $m + k \le 1$, then $\Delta(m, k) \le 1$ and $L(m, k) \le 2$. For $m + k \ge 1$, let w_1, w_2 be the two children of v. For $i = 1, 2$, let m_i, k_i denote the number of bars at w_i and the number of vertices that lie in $\square_{w_i}$. Then

$$L(m,k) \le L(m_1,k_1) + L(m_2,k_2),$$

$$\Delta(m,k) \le 1 + \max\{\Delta(m_1,k_1), \Delta(m_2,k_2)\}.$$

A bar at v contributes at most one bar at a child of v, and a floater at v contributes at most one bar at a child of v. At least two of the vertices of a floater at v lie in $\square_v$, so the number of floaters at v is at most $k/2$, thereby implying that $m_1 + m_2 \le m + k/2$ and $k_1 + k_2 \le k$. Since the separator line chooses the median of $2m+k$ values, namely the (x- or y-) coordinates of the vertices of bars and of the vertices that lie in $\square_v$, $2m_i + k_i \le (2m + k)/2$ for $i = 1, 2$. The solution to the above recurrence is

$$\Delta(m,k) \le A_1 \log_2(2m+k),$$

$$L(m,k) \le A_2(m + (k/2)\log_2(2m+k)),$$

where $A_1, A_2 \ge 1$ are constants. Since there are no bars at the root of $\mathbb{T}$ and $\mathbb{S}$ has at most $4n$ vertices, the depth of $\mathbb{T}$ is $O(\log n)$ and it has $O(n \log n)$ leaves, as claimed. □

Information stored at a node v. Let $\mathbb{S} \subseteq \mathbb{S}$ be the current set of squares. Let $\mathbb{S}_v = \mathbb{S}_v \cap \mathbb{S}$ be the subset of current squares that are active at v; $\mathbb{T}$ stores $\mathbb{S}_v$ at v. Let $\mathbb{B}_v$ (resp. $\mathbb{C}_v$, $\mathbb{F}_v$) be the subset of squares in $\mathbb{S}_v$ that are bar (resp. corner, floater) squares at v. Set $\mathbb{G}_v := \mathbb{F}_v \cup \mathbb{B}_v \cup \mathbb{C}_v \subseteq \mathbb{S}_v$ to be the set of short squares of $\mathbb{S}_v$. Let $\mathbb{X}_v$ (resp. $\mathbb{LA}_v$, $\mathbb{SA}_v$) be the subset of active covers (resp. long anchors, short anchors) at v. Set $\mathbb{L}_v := \mathbb{LA}_v \cup \mathbb{SA}_v \cup \mathbb{X}_v \subseteq \mathbb{S}_v$ to be the set of long squares of $\mathbb{S}_v$, and $\mathbb{L}_v^* = \bigcup_u \mathbb{L}_v$ where the union is taken over all ancestors of v including v itself. The following lemma is straightforward:

LEMMA 2.2. *Let w be a descendent of v. Then $\mathbb{F}_w \subseteq \mathbb{F}_v$ and $\mathbb{G}_w \subseteq \mathbb{G}_v$. Moreover, if w is a node of $\mathbb{T}(v)$ of the same type as v, then $\mathbb{B}_w \subseteq \mathbb{B}_v$, otherwise $\mathbb{B}_w \subseteq \mathbb{F}_v$.*

We call $\bar{\square} := \square_v \setminus \mathcal{U}(\mathbb{L}_v{}^*)$ an *anchored window*, which is a (possibly empty) rectangle lying inside $\square_v$. By (1),

$$\begin{aligned}\mu(\mathbb{S}, \square_v) &= \mu(\mathbb{L}_v^*, \square_v) + \mu(\mathbb{G}_v, \mathbb{L}_v^*, \square_v) \\ &= \text{Area}(\square_v) - \text{Area}(\bar{\square}_v) + \mu(\mathbb{G}_v, \bar{\square}_v)\,.\end{aligned}$$

See Figure 5 (left). Ideally, we would like to maintain $\bar{\square}_v$ and $\mu(\mathbb{G}_v, \bar{\square}_v)$ at each node v, from which $\mu(\mathbb{S}, \square_v)$ can be computed. It is, however, too expensive to maintain them explicitly at each node because the insertion or deletion of a square may change $\bar{\square}$ at several nodes. We therefore maintain another window $\boxplus_v$ called *exposed window*, an approximation of $\bar{\square}_v$ defined below, and maintain $\mu(\mathbb{G}_v, \boxplus_v)$.

If v is $\obar$-type (resp. $\ominus$-type), then we define $\text{LB}_v^-, \text{LB}_v^+$ to be the bottom and top (resp. left and right) edges of $\square_v$, and $\text{SB}_v^-, \text{SB}_v^+$ to be the left and right (resp. bottom and top) edges of $\square_v$—the former two are the long edges of $\square_v$ and the latter two are the short edges of $\square_v$. Let $\text{lb}_v^-, \text{lb}_v^+, \text{sb}_v^-$, and sb_v^+ denote the values of LB_v^- (i.e., $\text{lb}_v^- = \varphi(\text{LB}_v^-)$), $\text{LB}_v^+, \text{SB}_v^-$, and SB_v^+, respectively. $\square_v$ is thus $[\text{sb}_v^-, \text{sb}_v^+] \times [\text{lb}_v^-, \text{lb}_v^+]$ if v is $\obar$-type, and $[\text{lb}_v^-, \text{lb}_v^+] \times [\text{sb}_v^-, \text{sb}_v^+]$ otherwise. We divide active long and short anchors at v into two sets each: $\mathbb{LA}_v^-$ (resp. $\mathbb{LA}_v^+$) is the subset of $\mathbb{LA}_v$ that contains the edge LB_v^- (resp. LB_v^+), and $\mathbb{SA}_v^-$ (resp. $\mathbb{SA}_v^+$) is the subset of $\mathbb{SA}_v$ that contains the edge SB_v^- (resp. SB_v^+). To maintain $\boxplus_v$ and to compute $\bar{\square}_v$, we maintain the following information at v:

I. The sets $\mathbb{F}_v, \mathbb{C}_v, \mathbb{B}_v, \mathbb{LA}_v, \mathbb{SA}_v$, and the size $|\mathbb{X}_v|$.

II. The sequence $\mathsf{La}_v^- = \langle \varphi(S) \mid S \in \mathbb{LA}_v^- \rangle$ in decreasing order, and the sequence $\mathsf{La}_v^+ = \langle \varphi(S) \mid S \in \mathbb{LA}_v^+ \rangle$ in increasing order. For technical reasons, we add lb_v^- (resp. lb_v^+) at the end of La_v^- (resp. La_v^+).

III. The sequence $\mathsf{Sa}_v^- = \langle \varphi(S) \mid S \in \mathbb{SA}_v^- \rangle$ in decreasing order, and the sequence $\mathsf{Sa}_v^+ = \langle \varphi(S) \mid S \in \mathbb{SA}_v^+ \rangle$ in increasing order. For technical reasons, we add sb_v^- (resp. sb_v^+) at the end of Sa_v^- (resp. Sa_v^+).

IV. F_v: the edges of squares in $\mathbb{F}_v$ parallel to the long edges of $\square_v$ sorted in increasing order of their values.

Anchored window. $\bar{\square}_v$ is also defined by four edges $\text{LA}_v^-, \text{LA}_v^+, \text{SA}_v^-, \text{SA}_v^+$, and let $\text{la}_v^-, \text{la}_v^+, \text{sa}_v^-, \text{sa}_v^+$ be their values. If $\bar{\square} = \emptyset$, then these values are not well defined. We define them directly so that they are well defined even if $\bar{\square} = \emptyset$, and view $\bar{\square}_v$ as the intersection of four halfplanes defined by the lines supporting these edges. We describe la_v^+: Set $\tilde{\lambda}_v = \min_{\varphi \in \mathsf{La}_v^+} \varphi$, and let $\hat{\lambda}_v = \text{la}_{p(v)}^+$ if $p(v)$ and v are of the same type and $\hat{\lambda}_v = \text{sa}_{p(v)}^+$ otherwise. Then la_v^+ is defined to be the minimum of $\tilde{\lambda}_v$ and $\hat{\lambda}_v$ but its value cannot be less than lb_v^- (to ensure that $\text{la}_v^+ \in [\text{lb}_v^-, \text{lb}_v^+]$), i.e., $\text{la}_v^+ = \max\{\text{lb}_v^-, \min\{\hat{\lambda}_v, \tilde{\lambda}_v\}\}$. Values of the other edges of $\bar{\square}_v$ are described similarly. These values, and thus $\bar{\square}_v$, can be computed by traversing the path in $\mathbb{T}$ from the root to v.

Exposed window. The exposed window at v, $\boxplus_v \subseteq \square_v$, is also composed of four edges, called *virtual walls*, $\text{LE}_v^-, \text{LE}_v^+, \text{SE}_v^-, \text{SE}_v^+$ and whose values are $\text{le}_v^-, \text{le}_v^+, \text{se}_v^-, \text{se}_v^+$, respectively. See Figure 5. For each node, the algorithm maintains these edges and the quantity

$$\alpha(v) := \mu(\mathbb{G}_v, \boxplus_v) = \mu(\mathbb{F}_v \cup \mathbb{B}_v \cup \mathbb{C}_v, \boxplus_v), \qquad (2)$$

i.e., the area of the union of short squares (at v) lying inside $\boxplus_v$. If $\text{se}_v^- \geq \text{se}_v^+$ or $\text{le}_v^- \geq \text{le}_v^+$, then $\boxplus_v = \emptyset$. For the root rt of $\mathbb{T}$, the algorithm ensures that $\boxplus_{\text{rt}} = \square_{\text{rt}}$, implying that $\alpha(\text{rt}) = \mu(\mathbb{S})$. For a leaf v and for a node v with $\boxplus_v = \emptyset$, $\alpha(v) = 0$. If $\boxplus_v = \bar{\square}_v$, then $\boxplus_v$ is called *tight* (see Figure 5 (i)); otherwise it is called *loose*. If $\boxplus_v$ is tight, then $\alpha(v) = \mu(\mathbb{G}_v, \bar{\square}_v)$, as desired. As mentioned above, it is too expensive to ensure that $\boxplus_v$ is tight at all nodes of $\mathbb{T}$. The algorithm lets $\boxplus_v$ be loose at many nodes, and updates them carefully in a lazy manner so that the following two invariants are maintained at every node $v \in \mathbb{T}$; see Figure 5 (ii):

(I1) *If v is $\obar$-type (resp. $\ominus$-type), then the y-coordinate (resp. x-coordinate) of none of the vertices of a square in $\mathbb{F}_v$ lies between le_v^- and la_v^- or between le_v^+ and la_v^+.*

(I2) *If v is $\obar$-type (resp. $\ominus$-type), then the x-coordinate (resp. y-coordinate) of none of the vertices of a square in $\mathbb{F}_v \cup \mathbb{B}_v$ lies between se_v^- and sa_v^- or between se_v^+ and sa_v^+.*

Figure 5 (iii) illustrates an example of an exposed window that violates (I1) and (I2). Intuitively, (I1) and (I2) ensure that no edge of $\mathbb{F}_v \cup \mathbb{B}_v$ that is parallel to LE_v^+ lies between LE_v^+ and LA_v^+, though an edge of $\mathbb{C}_v$ may lie there; the same holds for the other three virtual walls of $\boxplus_v$. These invariants enable us to compute $\mu(\mathbb{F}_v \cup \mathbb{B}_v, \rho)$, for any $\rho \subseteq \boxplus_v \oplus \bar{\square}_v$, by reducing it to a 1D problem. The secondary data structures described below will facilitate the computation of $\mu(\mathbb{G}_v, \rho)$ (provided I1 and I2 are maintained), which in turn is used to update $\alpha(v)$ as $\boxplus_v$ is made tight.

Secondary structures at v. For a square S, with a slight abuse of notation, we use S_v^- (resp. S_v^+) to denote the interval in $\mathbb{R}^1$ formed by the intersection of $S \cap \square_v$ and the line containing the edge LE_v^- (resp. LE_v^+) of $\boxplus_v$. (See Figure 6.) Let $\mathbb{I}_v^- = \{S_v^- \mid S \in \mathbb{B}_v \cup \mathbb{F}_v\}$, and let $\mathbb{I}_v^+ = \{S_v^+ \mid S \in \mathbb{B}_v \cup \mathbb{F}_v\}$. For an interval $I \in \mathbb{I}_v^- \cup \mathbb{I}_v^+$, let I'' be the rectangle $I \times [y_v^-, y_v^+]$ if v is $\obar$-type and $[x_v^-, x_v^+] \times I$ if v is $\ominus$-type. Set $\mathbb{P}_v^- = \{I'' \mid I \in \mathbb{I}_v^-\}$ and $\mathbb{P}_v^+ = \{I'' \mid I \in \mathbb{I}_v^+\}$. The following two secondary data structures are maintained at v.

Wall structure. Store $\mathbb{I}_v^-$ into a dynamic segment tree that supports the following two operations in $O(\log n)$ time [3]: (i) insertion or deletion of an interval to $\mathbb{I}_v^-$, and (ii) for a query interval δ, return $\text{UL}^-(v, \delta) = |\mathcal{U}(\mathbb{I}_v^-) \cap \delta|$. Similarly, store $\mathbb{I}_v^+$ into a segment tree so that $\mathbb{I}_v^+$ can be updated and $\text{UL}^+(v, \delta) = |\mathcal{U}(\mathbb{I}_v^+) \cap \delta|$, for a query interval δ, can be computed in $O(\log n)$ time.

Corner structure. We process $\mathbb{C}_v$ and $\mathbb{I}_v^-$ into a data structure that supports the following operations: (i) insertion or deletion of a square to $\mathbb{C}_v$ and an interval to $\mathbb{I}_v^-$; (ii) for a query rectangle $\rho \subseteq \square_v$, compute $\text{CA}^-(v, \rho) = \mu(\mathbb{C}_v, \mathbb{P}_v^-, \rho)$. Similarly, maintain $\mathbb{C}_v$ and $\mathbb{I}_v^+$ into a data structure to compute $\text{CA}^+(v, \rho) = \mu(\mathbb{C}_v, \mathbb{P}_v^+, \rho)$ for a query rectangle ρ. The corner data structure is described in Section 5 and used in Section 4. By Lemma 5.1, a query is answered in $O(\log n)$ time and an update can be performed in $O(\log^2 n)$ time.

3. UPDATE PROCEDURES

This section describes the procedures for updating $\mathbb{T}$ and the secondary structures stored at its various nodes, as a square is inserted or deleted. The update procedures maintain (I1) and (I2) and use the following auxiliary procedures.

ADJUSTWALL(v, WL, ξ). Shift $\text{WL} \in \{\text{LE}_v^-, \text{LE}_v^+, \text{SE}_v^-, \text{SE}_v^+\}$ of the exposed window $\boxplus_v$ at v from its current position to ξ. The value of ξ is such that the invariants (I1) and (I2) are not violated by the shift. The procedure returns the updated value of $\alpha(v)$.

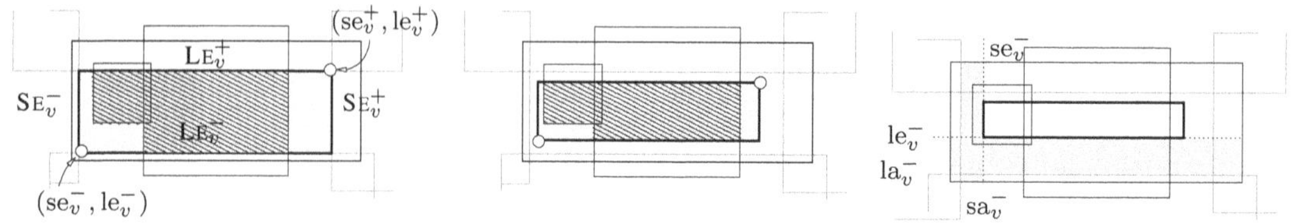

Figure 5. Exposed window $\boxplus_v$ (lightly shaded rectangles) and its virtual walls, hatched region is $\mathcal{U}(\mathbb{G}_v, \boxplus_v)$. Left: $\boxplus_v$ is tight; middle: $\boxplus_v$ satisfies invariants (I1) and (I2); right: $\boxplus_v$ violates both (I1) and (I2) — shaded strips contain vertices of floaters.

TIGHTENWINDOW(v). Tighten the exposed window $\boxplus_v$ so that it becomes the same as $\bar{\square}_v$. The procedure returns the updated value of $\alpha(v)$.

PUSHUP(v). Let w, z be the children of v. Assuming $\boxplus_v, \boxplus_w, \boxplus_z$ are tight, the procedure computes the value of $\alpha(v)$ from $\alpha(w)$ and $\alpha(z)$ and returns it.

These procedures are described in Section 4. ADJUSTWALL and TIGHTENWINDOW procedures take $O(\log^2 n)$ time, and PUSHUP takes $O(1)$ time. Assuming that we have these procedures at our disposal, we describe the procedure for inserting a square; the deletion procedure is symmetric.

Inserting a square. Let S be a square that we wish to insert into $\mathbb{S}$. We update the information stored at various nodes of $\mathbb{T}$, including $\alpha(\cdot)$. The new value of $\alpha(\mathrm{rt})$ is precisely the new value of $\mu(\mathbb{S})$.

We first visit the nodes of $\mathcal{N}(S)$ and their children in a top-down manner, starting from the root, and call the function TIGHTENWINDOW at each node. This ensures that the exposed window is tight at all these nodes before S is actually inserted. Next, for each node $v \in \mathcal{N}(S) \cup \Xi(S)$, we insert S at v, as described below, in a top-down manner. Finally, we visit the nodes $v \in \mathcal{N}(S) \cup \Xi(S)$ in a bottom-up manner to update the value of $\alpha(v)$. For $v \in \Xi(S)$, $\alpha(v)$ is updated directly as described below, and for $v \in \mathcal{N}(S)$, it is updated using the procedure PUSHUP(v); the exposed windows at v and its children will be tight before PUSHUP(v) is invoked at v; it ensures that $\alpha(v)$ is correctly computed.

The processing of S at a node $v \in \mathcal{N}(S) \cup \Xi(S)$ depends on the status of S at v. Recall that if S is a cover or a long anchor at v, then $v \in \Xi(S)$; if S is a floater, corner, or bar, then $v \in \mathcal{N}(S)$; if S is an active short anchor and v is a leaf (resp. an interior node) of $\mathbb{T}$, then $v \in \Xi(S)$ (resp. $v \in \mathcal{N}(S)$). If S is a short square or a short anchor at v, then we simply insert S at v and update the information (I)-(IV) and the secondary structures at v in a straightforward manner in $O(\log^2 n)$ time. Inserting an active long anchor or cover at v is more involved, as it may violate (I1) and (I2) at many of its descendents. Additional processing is needed at these descendents to restore (I1) and (I2). We describe these two cases in detail.

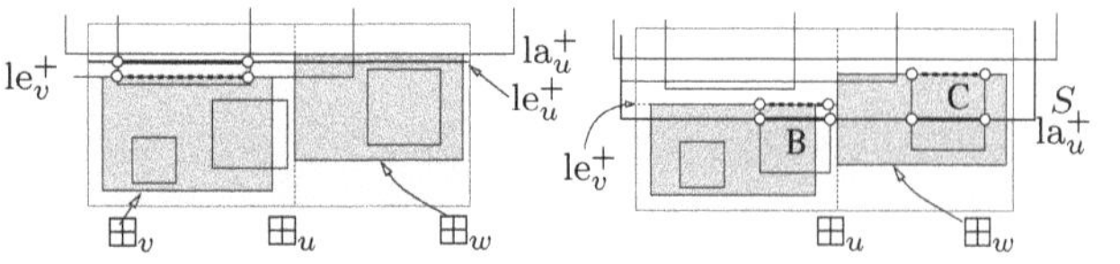

Figure 6. Insertion of a long anchor. Solid (dashed) intervals belong to $\mathbb{I}_u^+$ ($\mathbb{I}_v^+$). Left: before the insertion of S. Right: after the insertion of S; PUSHDOWN procedure lowers LE_u^+ to the bottom edge of S, LE_v^+ to the top edge of B, and LE_w^+ to the top edge of C.

Long anchor. If $S \in \mathbb{LA}_v^+$, we insert $\varphi(S)$ into La_v^+, and into La_v^- otherwise. Next, we update the exposed windows at v and some of the descendents of v to ensure that (I1) and (I2) are not violated after the insertion of S. We refer to this procedure as PUSHDOWN; it also updates the value of $\alpha(\cdot)$. For the sake of concreteness, we assume that $S \in \mathbb{LA}_v^+$ and that v is $\oplus$-type; this implies that $\mathrm{LA}_v^+, \mathrm{LE}_v^+$ are the top edges of $\bar{\square}_v, \boxplus_v$. TIGHTENWINDOW was called at v in the beginning of the insertion procedure, so $\boxplus_v$ was tight before the insertion of S. If $\varphi(S) \geq \mathrm{la}_v^+$, then $\boxplus_v$ remains tight even after the insertion of S and we do nothing. If $\varphi(S) < \mathrm{la}_v^+$ then LA_v^+ lowers to $\varphi(S)$. We *lower* LE_v^+ of $\boxplus_v$ to $\varphi(S)$, by sweeping from its current position to $\varphi(S)$ and stopping at all values in F_v, which we refer to as *events*. An event due to an edge $e \in \mathsf{F}_v$ indicates that (I1) or (I2) is violated at v (and some of its descendents) because of e. For technical reasons, we lower $\mathrm{LA}_v^+, \mathrm{LE}_v^+$ simultaneously through the sweep process. Let ξ denote the value of le_v^+ at the current event and η at the last event. Initially, we set ξ to the original value of le_v^+ (before the insertion of S) and $\eta = +\infty$. If LE_v^+ reaches $\varphi(S)$, set $\alpha(v)$:=ADJUSTWALL($v, \mathrm{LE}_v^+, \varphi(S)$) and $\mathrm{le}_v^+ = \mathrm{la}_v^+ = \varphi(S)$, and stop. If LE_v^+ reaches an edge $e \in \mathsf{F}_v$, where e is an edge of a floater $\sigma \in \mathbb{F}_v$, set η to ξ and ξ to $\varphi(e)$.

Let $\mathcal{Z}(v, e)$ be the subtree consisting of the descendents w of v that lie in $\mathcal{N}(e)$, at which σ is floater or bar, and for which its top virtual wall if above e. $\mathcal{Z}(v, e)$ can be computed in $O(\log^2 n)$ time by traversing $\mathbb{T}$ in a top-down manner, starting from v. Let w be a node in $\mathcal{Z}(v, e)$. The insertion of S causes the top edge of $\bar{\square}_w$ to pass below γ and thus the top virtual wall of $\boxplus_w$, denoted by WL, needs to be aligned with e to maintain (I1) and (I2); WL is SE_w^+ (resp. LE_w^+) if v is $\ominus$-type (resp. $\oplus$-type). We set $\alpha(w)$:=ADJUSTWALL(w, WL, ξ). If w is $\oplus$-type, we also update the secondary data structures at w: we insert the interval σ_v^+ into $\mathbb{I}_w^+$ if e is the top edge of σ (LE_w^+ starts intersecting σ as we lower it beyond e) and delete it from $\mathbb{I}_w^+$ if e is the bottom edge (LE_w^+ no longer intersects σ as we lower it beyond e), and we update the wall and corner data structures at w. See Figure 6.

For each node $w \in \mathcal{Z}(v, e)$, we say that S *encountered* e at node w. The procedure spends $O(\log^2 n)$ time in computing $\mathcal{Z}(v, e)$ and $O(\log^2 n)$ time at each node $w \in \mathcal{Z}(v, e)$; we charge the former to the "encounter" of e at v. For $S \in \mathbb{LA}_v^-$ and for a $\ominus$-type node, the PUSHDOWN procedure is symmetric. The total running time is $O((1 + \sum_w \kappa_w) \log^2 n)$, where κ_w is the number of edges encountered by S at w.

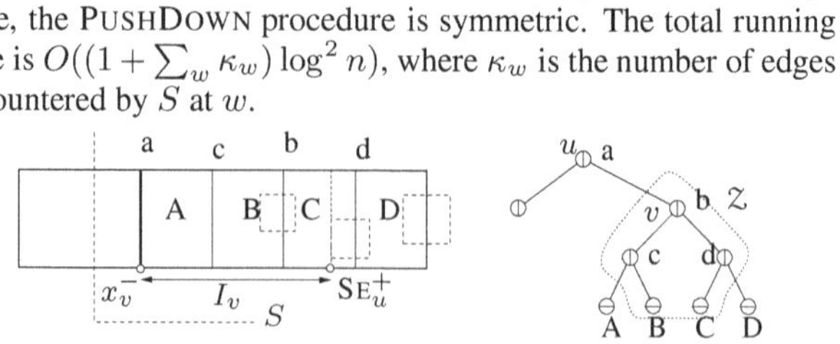

Figure 7. Insertion of a cover square and the subtree $\mathcal{Z}$. Left: shaded region is $\square_v$, dotted line is SE_v^+.

Cover. We increment the value of $|\mathbb{X}_v|$. If $|\mathbb{X}_v| = 1$, we update $\boxplus_v$ and further processing is needed at v and its descendents to ensure (I1) and (I2) and to update the secondary structures. Let $u = p(v)$. Suppose u is $\oplus$-type and v is the right child of u, in which case $S \in \mathbb{SA}_u^+$; see Figure 7. We move the right virtual wall of $\boxplus_v$ (which is LE_v^+ if v is $\ominus$-type and SE_v^+ otherwise) from its current position, say, ξ, to x_v^-, the value of the left boundary of $\square_v$. Let $I_v = [x_v^-, \xi]$, and let $\mathbb{Z} \subseteq \mathbb{T}(u)$ be the set of nodes z such that $[x_z^-, x_z^+] \cap I_v \neq \emptyset$ and $\mathbb{F}_z \cup \mathbb{B}_z \neq \emptyset$. $\mathbb{Z}$ forms a subtree of $\mathbb{T}(u)$ rooted at v; if v is $\ominus$-type, then $\mathbb{Z} = \{v\}$. The total time spent in computing $\mathbb{Z}$ is $O((1+\beta_v)\log n)$ where β_v is the number of edges in $\mathbb{F}_v \cup \mathbb{B}_v$ whose values lie in the interval I_v. To ensure (I1) and (I2), we call the PUSHDOWN procedure at the leaves w of $\mathbb{Z}$ that are of $\oplus$-type to move LE_w^+ to the left edge of $\square_w$. At other nodes w of $\mathbb{Z}$, we set $\alpha(w) = 0$ and SE_w^+ to the left edge of $\square_w$. The insertion procedure for other cases—when v is the left child of u or when u is $\ominus$-type—is similar. The total time spent in inserting a cover at v is $O((1+\sum_w \kappa_w)\log^2 n + \beta_v \log n)$, where w is a descendent of a leaf of $\mathbb{Z}$ and κ_w is the number of edges encountered by the PUSHDOWN procedure at w.

A square can be deleted using a similar procedure. The correctness of the update procedures follows from the following lemma. The proof of the lemma, tedious but not difficult, is omitted from this extended abstract because of lack of space.

LEMMA 3.1. *Invariants (I1)–(I2) are maintained at each node of $\mathbb{T}$ after inserting a square into $\mathbb{S}$ or deleting from it.*

Since (I1) and (I2) hold at all times, the auxiliary procedures compute the value of $\alpha(\cdot)$ correctly, which in turn implies that the algorithm correctly maintains $\alpha(v)$ at each node v of $\mathbb{T}$ at all times. In particular $\alpha(\text{rt}) = \mu(\mathbb{S})$ at all times. The next lemma bounds the amortized update time.

LEMMA 3.2. *We can maintain $\mathbb{S}$ into a data structure so that $\mu(\mathbb{S})$ can be updated in $O(\log^4 n)$ amortized time, as we insert or delete a square, provided that the sequence of updates is size preserving.*

Proof: The argument in the update procedure implies that the insertion/deletion time of a square S is $O(\log^4 n + \sum_v \kappa_v \log^2 n + \sum_w \beta_w \log n)$, where κ_v is the number of edges encountered at v by S during the update procedure, w is a node at which S is a cover, and β_w is as defined above. We charge $O(\log^4 n)$ time to the insertion of S. We prove that the amortized cost of the second term is also $O(\log^4 n)$; a similar argument bounds the amortized cost of the third term by $O(\log^4 n)$. We charge $\log^2 n$ units to each edge encountered by S during its insertion or deletion. We claim that an edge γ of a square $\sigma \in \mathbb{S}$ is charged at most twice at a node w of $\mathbb{T}$ by the insertion and deletion procedures each. Since $w \in \mathcal{N}(\gamma)$ and $\sigma \in \mathbb{F}_v \cup \mathbb{B}_v$, γ is charged a total of $O(\log^2 n)$ times. Hence γ is charged a total of $O(\log^4 n)$ units, which can be charged to the insertion of σ. This implies that the amortized update time of a square is $O(\log^4 n)$.

To prove the above claim, suppose γ is parallel to the long edges of $\square_w$; the other case is symmetric. First consider the insertion procedure. Suppose γ was encountered by S at w while lowering le_w^+ (actually, $\gamma \in \mathsf{F}_w$ in this case). Recall that γ is encountered at w because the PUSHDOWN procedure swept through γ at an ancestor v of w while lowering $\text{LE}_v^+, \text{LA}_v^+$, where $\gamma \in \mathsf{F}_v$ and $S \in \mathbb{LA}_v \cup \mathbb{X}_v$. Since $\sigma \in \mathbb{F}_v$, one of the edges of σ lies inside $\square_v$ while S contains a long edge of $\square_v$, which implies that $|\mathsf{X}(\sigma)| < (\text{le}_v^+ - \text{le}_v^-) \leq |\mathsf{X}(S)|$, i.e., S is bigger than σ. (Note that this claim might not be true if S is a short anchor at $\square_v$ and thus only contains a short edge of $\square_v$.) Moreover, σ is inserted into $\mathbb{S}$ before S. We have assumed the update sequence to be size preserving (see Section 2), therefore σ will be deleted before S is deleted, implying that la_v^+, and thus la_w^+, remain less than $\varphi(\gamma)$ until σ is deleted. Since $\sigma \in \mathbb{F}_w$ and invariants (I1) and (I2) are maintained, $\text{le}_w^+ \leq \varphi(\gamma)$ until γ is deleted. Hence, γ will not be encountered again at w while lowering LE_w^+. Similarly, γ will be encountered at w at most once by the insertion procedure while raising LE_w^-. Similar arguments show that γ is charged at w at most twice by the deletion procedure or when γ is parallel to the short edges of $\square_w$. $\square$

Remark. The proof of the above lemma crucially uses the observations that if the PUSHDOWN procedure at v because of the insertion of a long anchor S sweeps through the edge γ of a floater square σ then S is bigger than σ, and that the size-preserving order ensures that an edge is encountered only $O(1)$ times for a fixed node. These claims are not true if PUSHDOWN is called to move a short virtual edge. That is why short and long anchors (and edges of $\square_v$) are treated differently and auxiliary data structures are stored only with respect to long edges.

4. AUXILIARY PROCEDURES

If $\alpha(v) \neq 0$ and $\boxplus_v, \boxplus_w, \boxplus_z$ are tight, where w and z are the children of v, then

$$\alpha(v) = \alpha(w) + \alpha(z) + \text{Area}(\boxplus_v \setminus (\boxplus_w \cup \boxplus_z)).$$

Using this observation, PUSHUP(v) can be implemented in $O(1)$ time. TIGHTENWINDOW can be implemented by invoking ADJUSTWALL at most four times. We thus describe ADJUSTWALL, which uses the secondary structures (wall and corner structures) stored at the nodes of $\mathbb{T}$ and relies on invariants (I1) and (I2).

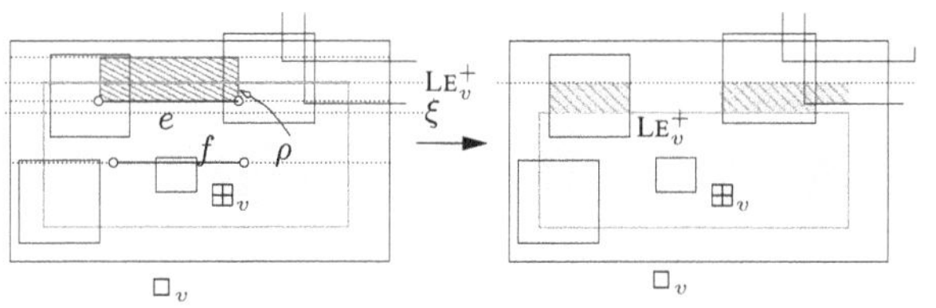

Figure 8. ADJUSTWALL(v, LE_v^+,ξ): current $\boxplus_v$ and after adjusting LE_v^+ (lightly shaded rectangles). Left: Segment e and rectangle ρ are compatible with LE_v^+; segment f is not compatible with LE_v^+. Right: area of the hatched region is the change in $\alpha(v)$.

ADJUSTWALL(v, WL, ξ). This procedure shifts the virtual wall WL of $\boxplus_v$ from its current position to ξ, assuming that the value of ξ is such that the invariants (I1) and (I2) are not violated by the shift. The procedure returns the updated value of $\alpha(v)$. See Figure 8. Let $R \subseteq \square_v$ be the rectangle obtained by sweeping WL from its current position to ξ, then $\alpha(v)$ changes by $\mu(\mathbb{G}_v, R)$.

We call an orthogonal segment $e \subseteq \square_w$ *compatible* with a virtual wall WL of $\boxplus_v$ parallel to e if the strip W_e bounded by the lines supporting e and WL does not contain a vertex of any square in $\mathbb{F}_v \cup \mathbb{B}_v$. That is, no square of $\mathbb{F}_v \cup \mathbb{B}_v$ is contained in W_e and the two boundary lines of W_e intersect the same set of squares in $\mathbb{F}_v \cup \mathbb{B}_v$. We call a rectangle $\rho \subseteq \square_v$ compatible with WL if the two edges of ρ that are parallel to WL are compatible with e. See Figure 8.

For a square $\rho \subseteq \square_v$ that is compatible with one of the virtual walls of $\boxplus_v$, we describe a procedure that computes $\mu(\mathbb{G}_v, \rho)$. By (I1) and (I2), R is compatible with WL, so $\mu(\mathbb{G}_v, R)$ can be computed using this procedure. First, consider the case when ρ is compatible with LE_v^+. In this case, ρ intersects a square $S \in \mathbb{F}_v \cup \mathbb{B}_v$ if the interval $I := S_v^+$ lies in $\mathbb{I}_v^+$. Furthermore, $S \cap \rho = I'' \cap \rho$, S

be regarded as a bar. Let $\rho = \mathsf{x}_\rho \times \mathsf{y}_\rho$. By (1),

$$\begin{aligned}\mu(\mathbb{G}_v, \rho) &= \mu(\mathbb{F}_v \cup \mathbb{B}_v, \rho) + \mu(\mathbb{C}_v, \mathbb{F}_v \cup \mathbb{B}_v, \rho) \\ &= \mu(\mathbb{P}_v^+, \rho) + \mu(\mathbb{C}_v, \mathbb{P}_v^+, \rho) \\ &= \textsc{Ul}^+(v, \mathsf{x}_\rho)|\mathsf{y}_\rho| + \textsc{Ca}^+(v, \rho).\end{aligned}$$

Similarly if ρ is compatible with $\textsc{Le}_v^-$, then

$$\mu(\mathbb{G}_v, \rho) = \textsc{Ul}^-(v, \mathsf{x}_\rho)|\mathsf{y}_\rho| + \textsc{Ca}^-(v, \rho).$$

Using the wall and corner structures stored at v, $\mu(\mathbb{G}_v, \rho)$ can be computed in $O(\log n)$ time.

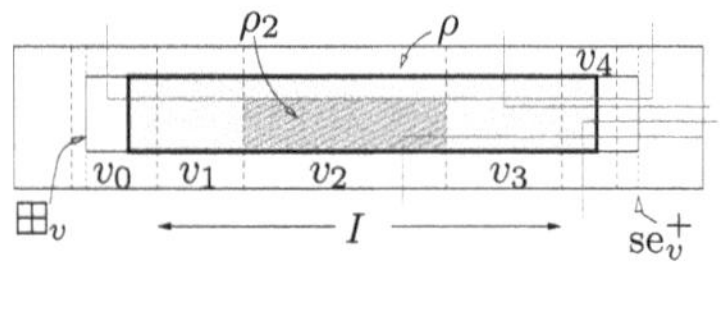

Figure 9. Computing $\mu(\mathbb{G}_v, \rho)$ for a rectangle ρ compatible with $\textsc{Se}_v^+$; thick rectangle is ρ and dashed lines are separator lines.

Next, suppose ρ is compatible with $\textsc{Se}_v^+$ and v is $\oplus$-type. Since we do not store secondary structure for short edges of $\square_v$, answering the query is more involved in this case. By (I2), no vertical edge of a square in $\mathbb{F}_v \cup \mathbb{B}_v$ intersects ρ. Hence, if a square in $\mathbb{B}_v$ intersects ρ, it contains ρ and $\mu(\mathbb{G}_v, \rho) = \text{Area}(\rho)$. We can check this condition in $O(\log n)$ time using the wall data structure. So assume that ρ does not intersect any square in $\mathbb{B}_v$. Let v_0 (resp. v_k) be the node in $\mathbb{D}(v)$ (cf. Section 2) such that $\square_{v_0}$ (resp. $\square_{v_k}$) contains the left (resp. right) edge of ρ. Let I be the x-projection of $\rho \setminus (\square_{v_0} \cup \square_{v_k})$, and let $v_1, \ldots, v_{k-1}$ be the nodes in $\Xi(I)$; each v_i lies in $\mathbb{T}(v)$. See Figure 9. For $1 \le i < k$, let $\mathbb{H}_i = \mathbb{G}_v \setminus \mathbb{G}_{v_i} = \bigcup_w \mathbb{LA}_w \cup \mathbb{SA}_w$, where $w \ne v$ is a node lying on the path from v to v_i. Let

$$\rho_i := (\rho \cap \square_{v_i}) \setminus \mathcal{U}(\mathbb{H}_i), \qquad (3)$$

which is a rectangle obtained by clipping ρ from top and bottom (e.g. hatched rectangle in Figure 9 is ρ_2). By construction, ρ_i is compatible with the right virtual wall of $\square_{v_i}$. Using (1) and (3),

$$\begin{aligned}\mu(\mathbb{G}_v, \rho) &= \sum_{i=0}^{k} \mu(\mathbb{H}_i, \rho \cap \square_{v_i}) + \mu(\mathbb{G}_{v_i}, \mathbb{H}_i, \rho \cap \square_{v_i}) \\ &= \sum_{i=0}^{k} \mu(\mathbb{H}_i, \rho \cap \square_{v_i}) + \mu(\mathbb{G}_{v_i}, \rho_i).\end{aligned}$$

The first term can be computed in $O(\log n)$ time. As for the second term, if v_i is a leaf of $\mathbb{T}$, then $\mathbb{G}_{v_i} = \emptyset$ and $\mu(\mathbb{G}_{v_i}, \rho) = 0$, so assume that v_i is an interior node of $\mathbb{T}$. If $v_i \in \mathbb{D}(v)$, then v_i is $\ominus$-type and ρ_i is compatible with $\textsc{Le}_{v_i}^+$ (e.g. v_1, v_3 in Figure 9). We can therefore compute $\mu(\mathbb{G}_{v_i}, \rho_i)$ in $O(\log n)$ time, as described above. If $v_i \notin \mathbb{D}(v)$, i.e., v_i is $\oplus$-type and $1 \le i < k$ (e.g. v_2 in Figure 9), then it can be proved that $\mathbb{B}_{v_i} \cup \mathbb{F}_{v_i} = \emptyset$ and

$$\mu(\mathbb{G}_{v_i}, \rho_i) = \mu(\mathbb{C}_{v_i}, \rho_i) = \mu(\mathbb{C}_{v_i}, \mathbb{P}_{v_i}^+, \rho_i) = \textsc{Ca}^+(v, \rho_i).$$

By Lemma 5.1, $\mu(\mathbb{G}_{v_i}, \rho_i)$ can be computed in $O(\log n)$ time. Putting everything together, $\mu(\mathbb{G}_v, \rho)$ can be computed in $O(\log^2 n)$ time, and ADJUSTWALL thus takes $O(\log^2 n)$ time.

LEMMA 4.1. ADJUSTWALL *and* TIGHTENWINDOW *procedures take* $O(\log^2 n)$ *time, and* PUSHDOWN *takes* $O(1)$ *time.*

5. CORNER DATA STRUCTURE

Let $\square := [0, 0] \times [a, b]$ be a rectangle with $p_0, \ldots, p_3$ as its vertices. Without loss of generality, assume that $a \ge b$. Let $\mathbb{C}$ be a set of corner squares with respect to $\square$, let $\mathbb{B}$ be a set of rectangles, called *bars*, whose horizontal edges lie on the top and bottom edges of $\square$. Let $\mathbb{I}$ be the set of x-projections of bars in $\mathbb{B}$. We describe a data structure that supports the following operations: insertion or deletion of a corner or a bar; for a query rectangle $\rho \subseteq \square$, compute $\textsc{Ca}(\rho) = \mu(\mathbb{C}, \mathbb{B}, \rho)$. We assume that we have the wall data structure, described in Section 2, so that for any interval I, $\varepsilon(I) = |I \setminus \mathcal{U}(\mathbb{I})|$ can be computed in $O(\log n)$ time.

For a corner square S, let $q(S)$ be the vertex of S that lies inside $\square$. For $0 \le i \le 3$, let $\mathbb{C}_i \subseteq \mathbb{C}$ be the set of corners that contain the vertex p_i of $\square$, and let $\mathcal{Q}_i = \{q(S) \mid S \in \mathbb{C}_i\}$; see Figure 10 (ii). We call a (rectilinear) polygon *staircase* if it consists of a rectilinear chain that is both x- and y-monotone (in each coordinate it can be either increasing or decreasing), and the endpoints of the chain are connected together by a horizontal and a vertical edge; see Figure 10 (i). The common endpoint of the horizontal and the vertical edge is called the *apex* of the polygon. For each i, $\mathcal{U}(\mathbb{C}_i, \square)$ is a staircase polygon whose apex is p_i. We construct the following data structures:

- We preprocess $\mathbb{C}_0$ and $\mathbb{B}$ into a data structure Ψ_0 so that, for a query rectangle $\rho \subseteq \square$, $\mu(\mathbb{C}_0, \mathbb{B}, \rho)$ can be computed in $O(\log n)$ time. We construct a similar data structure Ψ_1 on $\mathbb{C}_1$ and $\mathbb{B}$ for computing $\mu(\mathbb{C}_1, \mathbb{B}, \rho)$.
- We preprocess $\mathbb{C}_0, \mathbb{C}_2, \mathbb{B}$ into a data structure Ψ_2 so that, for a rectangle $\rho \subseteq \square$, $\mu(\mathbb{C}_2, \mathbb{B} \cup \mathbb{C}_0, \rho)$ can be computed in $O(\log n)$ time. We construct a similar data structure Ψ_3 on $\mathbb{C}_1, \mathbb{C}_3, \mathbb{B}$ for computing $\mu(\mathbb{C}_3, \mathbb{B} \cup \mathbb{C}_1, \rho)$.

Before describing $\Psi_0, \ldots, \Psi_3$, we explain how they can be used to compute $\textsc{Ca}(\rho)$ in $O(\log n)$ time. For $0 \le i \le 3$, let Γ_i be the rectilinear chain of $\mathcal{U}(\mathbb{C}_i)$; Figure 10 (i). Γ_i and Γ_{i+1} intersect in at most one point, but Γ_i and Γ_{i+2} may intersect several times. For each i, we define a point r_i, as follows. If Γ_i and Γ_{i+1} (mod 4) do not intersect, then r_i is the endpoint of Γ_i that lies on the edge $p_i p_{i+1}$, otherwise r_i is the (orthogonal) projection of the intersection point of Γ_i and Γ_{i+1} on the edge $p_i p_{i+1}$. Finally, let $\square_i$ be the rectangle formed by r_{i-1} and r_i as two of its diagonally opposite vertices; see Figure 10 (iv) and (v). The interiors of $\square_i$ and $\square_{i+1}$ are disjoint but those of $\square_i$ and $\square_{i+2}$ may intersect. However, if $\square_0$ and $\square_2$ intersect, then $\square_1$ and $\square_3$ are disjoint, and vice-versa; Figure 10 (iv). Note that $\square_0, \ldots, \square_3$ may not cover $\square$; Figure 10 (v). Nevertheless, $\mathcal{U}(\mathbb{C}, \square) \subseteq \bigcup_{i=0}^3 \square_i$ and Γ_i appears on $\partial\mathcal{U}(\mathbb{C}, \square)$ only inside $\square_i$; see Figure 10. The following equality is straightforward: $\mathcal{U}(\mathbb{C}, \square) = \bigcup_{i=0}^3 \mathcal{U}(\mathbb{C}_i, \square_i)$. For a rectangle ρ, we set $\rho_i = \rho \cap \square_i$. Then

$$\mathcal{U}(\mathbb{C}, \mathbb{B}, \rho) = \bigcup_{i=0}^{3} \mathcal{U}(\mathbb{C}_i, \mathbb{B}, \rho_i).$$

Since the interiors of $\square_i$ and $\square_{i+1}$ are disjoint,

$$\begin{aligned}\mu(\mathbb{C}, \mathbb{B}, \rho) &= \mu(\mathbb{C}_0, \mathbb{B}, \rho_0) + \mu(\mathbb{C}_1, \mathbb{B}, \rho_1) + \\ &\quad \mu(\mathbb{C}_2, \mathbb{C}_0 \cup \mathbb{B}, \rho_2) + \mu(\mathbb{C}_3, \mathbb{C}_1 \cup \mathbb{B}, \rho_3).\end{aligned}$$

Let $\mathcal{V}_i \subseteq \mathcal{Q}_i$ be the subset of points that appear as (convex) vertices of $\mathcal{U}(\mathbb{C}_i)$. We maintain $\mathcal{V}_i$ sorted from left to right. By performing a binary search on $\mathcal{V}_i$ and $\mathcal{V}_{i+1}$, r_i can be computed in $O(\log n)$ time. We can then compute $\rho_0, \ldots, \rho_3$ in additional $O(1)$ time. Each of the terms on the right hand side of the above equation can be computed in $O(\log n)$ time using $\Psi_0, \ldots, \Psi_3$, therefore

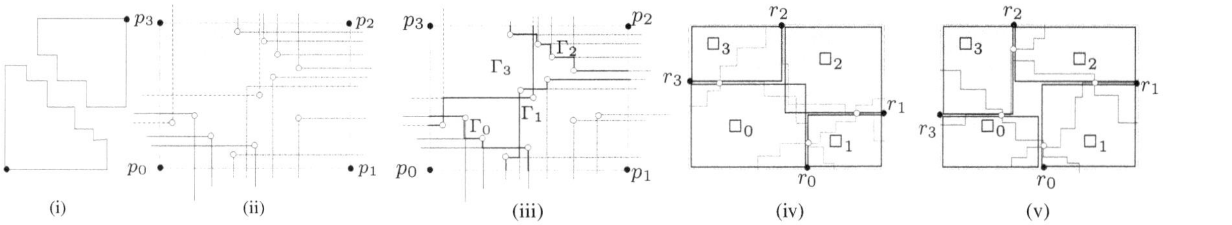

Figure 10. (i) Staircase polygons. (ii) Four different types of corner squares. (iii) rectilinear chains $\Gamma_0, \ldots, \Gamma_3$. (iv) $\square_0, \ldots, \square_3$ cover $\square$; $\square_0$ and $\square_2$ intersect. (v) $\square_0, \ldots, \square_3$ that do not cover $\square$.

$\mu(\mathbb{C}, \mathbb{B}, \rho)$ can also be computed in $O(\log n)$ time. We now describe Ψ_0 and Ψ_2; Ψ_1 and Ψ_3 are symmetric to Ψ_0 and Ψ_2, respectively. Although Ψ_0 is a special case of Ψ_2, we first describe Ψ_0 and then describe how we extend it to construct Ψ_2.

Preprocessing $\mathbb{C}_0$ and $\mathbb{B}$. For simplicity, we replace each square C in $\mathbb{C}_0$ into a quadrant with apex $q(C)$ and containing p_0; Let $\mathbb{Q}$ be the resulting set of quadrants. We describe the data structure to preprocess $\mathbb{Q}$ and $\mathbb{B}$ to compute $\mu(\mathbb{Q}, \mathbb{B}, \rho)$ for a query rectangle $\rho \subseteq \square$. $\mathcal{U}(\mathbb{Q})$ can be maintained using the data structure by Overmars and van Leeuwen [14] but the interaction of $\mathbb{Q}$ and $\mathbb{B}$ makes the maintenance of $\mathcal{U}(\mathbb{Q}, \mathbb{B})$ difficult: a bar in $\mathbb{B}$ may intersect many edges of $\partial\mathcal{U}(\mathbb{Q})$, and many bars in $\mathbb{B}$ may intersect the same edge of $\mathcal{U}(\mathbb{Q})$; see Figure 11. The insertion or deletion of a corner square or a bar may thus cause many changes in the boundary structure of $\mathcal{U}(\mathbb{Q}, \mathbb{B})$, making it expensive to update $\mathcal{U}(\mathbb{Q}, \mathbb{B})$. We circumvent this problem by maintaining the edges of $\mathcal{U}(\mathbb{Q}, \mathbb{B})$ implicitly, as described below.

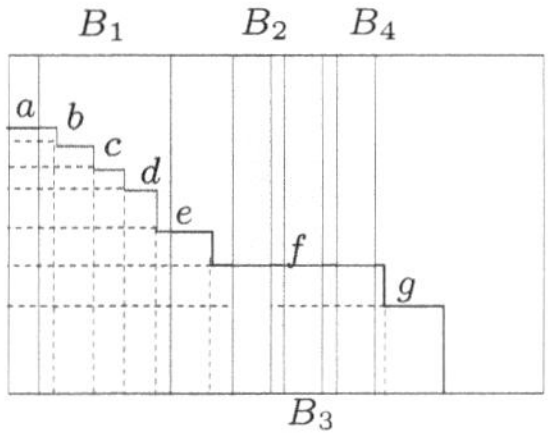

Figure 11. Interaction of $\mathbb{Q}$ and $\mathbb{B}$. $\Gamma = \langle a, \ldots, g \rangle$; b, c, d do not appear on $\Sigma(\Gamma, \mathbb{B})$; $\hat{\Sigma} = \langle \hat{a}, \hat{e}, \hat{f}.\hat{g} \rangle$.

Operations on a monotone chain. For a rectilinear xy-monotone chain $\Gamma \subset \square$, let $\mathcal{P}(\Gamma)$ be the staircase polygon formed by the set of points in $\square$ that lie below Γ. We represent Γ by its sequence of horizontal edges, and we will use Γ to denote both the chain as well as the sequence of its horizontal edges. For a subset $\mathcal{B} \subseteq \mathbb{B}$, let $\Sigma(\Gamma, \mathcal{B})$ be the sequence of horizontal edges of $\Gamma \setminus \mathcal{U}(\mathcal{B})$. An edge of Γ may get split into many edges in $\Sigma(\Gamma, \mathcal{B})$. We represent $\Sigma(\Gamma, \mathcal{B})$ implicitly: For an edge $e \in \Gamma$, define a 4-tuple $\hat{e} = \langle x^-(e), x^+(e), y(e), \varepsilon(e) \rangle$, where $x^-(e), x^+(e)$ are the x-coordinates of the left and right endpoints of e, $y(e)$ is the y-coordinate of e, and $\varepsilon(e) = |e \setminus \mathcal{U}(\mathcal{B})|$ is the *exposed* portion of e on Σ; $\hat{e}$ is the representation of e. We say that e *appears* in Σ if $\varepsilon(e) > 0$. We represent Σ as the sequence $\hat{\Sigma} = \langle \hat{e}_1, \hat{e}_2, \ldots, \rangle$, where $e_1, e_2, \ldots$ is the subsequence of the edges of Γ that appear in Σ. Note that $\text{Area}(\mathcal{P}(\Gamma) \setminus \mathcal{U}(\mathcal{B})) = \sum_{\hat{e} \in \Sigma} \varepsilon(e) \cdot y(e)$. Abusing the notation slightly, we do not distinguish between Σ and its representation. For $A \subset \mathbb{R}^2$, let $\mathsf{X}(A)$ denote the x-projection of A. We perform the following operations on Σ.

(i) SPLIT(Σ, a): Given a rectilinear chain Σ and a value $a \geq 0$, let $\Sigma^+ = \langle e \in \Sigma \mid y(e) > a \rangle$ and $\Sigma^- = \langle e \in \Sigma \mid y(e) < a \rangle$. Split Σ into Σ^-, Σ^+. If Σ contains an edge e with $y(e) = a$, then the procedure returns $\hat{e}$ separately. See Figure 12.

(ii) MERGE(Σ^-, Σ^+, e): Let Σ^-, Σ^+ be two xy-monotone rectilinear and e a horizontal edge so that $\Sigma = \Sigma^- \circ \langle e \rangle \circ \Sigma^+$ is also a xy-monotone rectilinear chain. Given Σ^-, Σ^+, and $\hat{e}$, compute Σ. If the edge e is not specified or $\varepsilon(e) = 0$, the procedure computes $\Sigma_1 \circ \Sigma_2$.

(iii) QUERY(Σ, I): Given a chain Σ and an interval I, compute

$$\alpha(\Sigma, I) = \sum_{e \in \Sigma, \mathsf{X}(e) \subseteq I} \varepsilon(e) \cdot y(e).$$

Suppose $e_i, \ldots, e_j$ are the edges of Σ whose x-projections are contained in I. Then $\alpha(\Sigma, I)$ is the area of $(\mathcal{P}(\Gamma) \setminus \mathcal{U}(\mathbb{B})) \cap R_I$, where $R_I = [x^-(e_i), x^+(e_j)] \times [0, b]$.

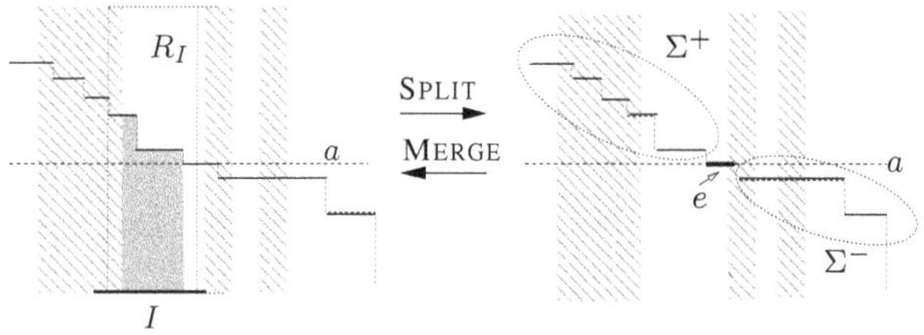

Figure 12. Operations on chains; I is a query interval, darker region is $(\mathcal{P}(\Gamma) \setminus \mathcal{U}(\mathbb{B})) \cap R_I$ (left).

By maintaining Σ in a height-balanced tree, which we denote by $\mathcal{H}(\Sigma)$, each of these operations can be performed in $O(\log n)$ time. Using the wall data structure, for an edge e of Γ, $\varepsilon(e)$ can be computed in $O(\log n)$ time.

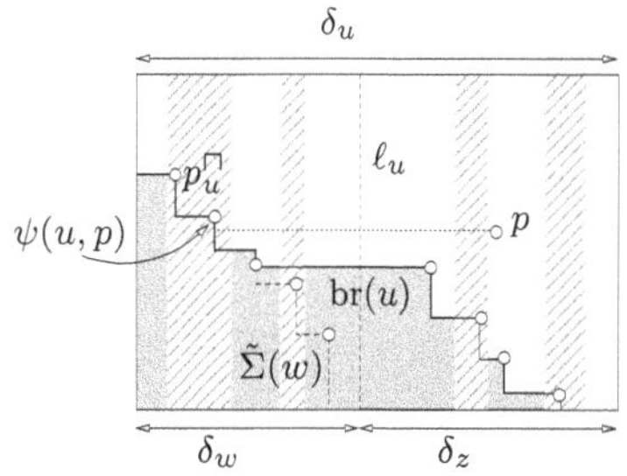

Figure 13. A node u and its children w and z. $\mathbb{B}^*(u)$ is the hatched area and $\mathcal{U}(\mathbb{Q}_u, \mathbb{B}_u^*, \square_u)$ is the darker region.

Structure of Ψ_0. Let $\mathcal{Q} = \{q(S) \mid S \in \mathbb{Q}\}$, and let $\mathcal{X} \subseteq [0, a]$ be the set of points in $\mathbb{R}$ that are x-coordinates of points in $\mathcal{Q}$ and vertices in $\mathbb{B}$. $\mathcal{X}$ partitions the interval $(0, a]$ into a set of atomic intervals; we regard each of these intervals semiclosed — the right endpoint lies in the interval but the left endpoint does not lie in the interval. We build a height-balanced binary tree $\mathcal{T}$ on these atomic intervals. Each node $v \in \mathcal{T}$ is associated with an interval $\delta_v = (x_v^-, x_v^+]$ and a rectangle $\square_v = \delta_v \times [0, b]$. If v is the i-th leaf of $\mathcal{T}$, then δ_v is the i-th (semiclosed) atomic interval. For an interior node v, let $\delta_v = \delta_{\mathrm{L}(v)} \cup \delta_{\mathrm{R}(v)}$, $\square_v = \delta_v \times [0, b]$, and let ξ_v be the common endpoint of $\delta_{\mathrm{L}(v)}$ and $\delta_{\mathrm{R}(v)}$. Let $\ell_v : x = \xi_v$ be the separator line at v. For an interval $I \subseteq [0, a]$, let $\Xi(I)$ be the set of nodes $u \in \mathcal{T}$ for which $\mathrm{cl}\delta_u \subseteq I$ and $\mathrm{cl}\delta_{p(u)} \not\subseteq I$, and let $\mathcal{N}(I)$ be the set of ancestors of nodes in $\Xi(I)$. Similarly, we define $\Xi(B)$ and $\mathcal{N}(B)$ for a bar in $\mathbb{B}$. For a node u, let $\mathcal{Q}_u = \square_u \cap \mathcal{Q}$, $\mathbb{Q}_u = \{S \in \mathbb{Q} \mid q(S) \in \mathcal{Q}_u\}$, $\mathbb{B}_u \subseteq \mathbb{B}$ (resp. $\mathbb{B}_u^* \subseteq \mathbb{B}$) be the set of bars B such that $u \in \Xi(B)$ (resp. $u \in \Xi(B) \cup \mathcal{N}(B)$), and $p_u^{\sqcap}$ be the point of $\mathcal{Q}_u$ with the maximum y-coordinate. Let $\beta(u) = |\mathsf{X}(\mathbb{B}^*(u)) \cap \delta_v|$, which is $|\delta_u|$ if $|\mathbb{B}_u| > 0$, and $\beta(\mathrm{L}(u)) + \beta(\mathrm{R}(u))$ otherwise.

$\mathcal{U}(\mathbb{Q}_u, \square_u)$ is a staircase polygon. Let $\Gamma(u)$ be its rectilinear chain. Set $\Sigma(u) = \Sigma(\Gamma(u), \mathbb{B}_u^*)$, the portion of $\partial\mathcal{U}(\mathbb{Q}_u, \mathbb{B}_u^*, \square_u)$ that lies on $\Gamma(u)$. For an interior node u, let $\mathrm{br}(u)$ be the edge of $\Gamma(u)$ that intersects ℓ_u, and let $\tilde{\Sigma}(u) = \Sigma(u) \setminus \Sigma(p(u))$ (Figure 15 (i)). If $\varepsilon(\mathrm{br}(u)) > 0$, then $\mathrm{br}(u) \in \Sigma(u)$. For the root rt of $\mathcal{T}$, $\tilde{\Sigma}(\mathrm{rt}) = \Sigma(\mathrm{rt})$. At each node u we store: $\tilde{\Sigma}(u)$, $\mathrm{br}(u)$, $\beta(u)$, $|\mathbb{B}_u|$, and $p^{\sqcap}(u)$. For a node u and for a point p, let $\psi(u, p)$ denote the rightmost point in $\mathcal{Q}_u$ whose y-coordinate is greater than that of p; $\psi(u, p)$ can be computed in $O(\log n)$ time.

Updating Ψ_0. Using the following two procedures, each of which takes $O(\log n)$ time, a corner or a bar can be inserted/deleted in $O(\log^2 n)$ time. Let u be a node of $\mathcal{T}$, and let w and z be the left and right child of u, respectively.

ASCEND(u): It computes $\Sigma(u)$, $\tilde{\Sigma}(w)$, $\tilde{\Sigma}(z)$ from $\Sigma(w)$ and $\Sigma(z)$. If $\beta(u) = \delta_u$, then we set $\Sigma(u) = \emptyset$, $\tilde{\Sigma}(w) = \Sigma(w)$, and $\tilde{\Sigma}(z) = \Sigma(z)$, and we stop. So assume that $\beta(u) < \delta_u$. Let $p_R = p^{\sqcap}(z)$. We compute $p_L = \psi(w, p_R)$. If p_L does not exist, then the left endpoint of $\mathrm{br}(u)$ is $(x_u^-, y(p_R))$, otherwise it is $(x(p_L), y(p_R))$. The right endpoint of $\mathrm{br}(u)$ is p_R. Let $I = [x(p_L), x(p_R)]$ be the projection of $\mathrm{br}(u)$. We compute $\varepsilon(\mathrm{br}(u))$, in $O(\log n)$ time. If $\varepsilon(\mathrm{br}(u)) = 0$, we set $\mathrm{br}(u) = \emptyset$. Next, we call SPLIT($\Sigma(w)$, $y(p_R)$). Let Σ^-, Σ^+ be the subchains returned by the procedure. We set $\tilde{\Sigma}(w) = \Sigma^+$. If $\Sigma(z)$ contains the horizontal edge at height $y(p_R)$, we delete it, and we set $\Sigma(u)$ = MERGE(Σ^-, $\Sigma(z)$, $\mathrm{br}(u)$).

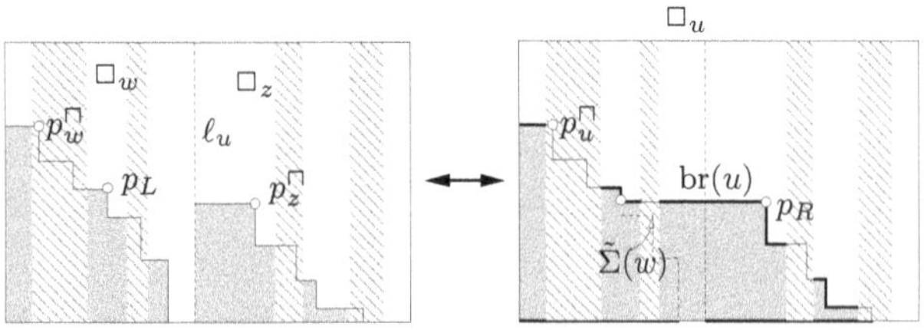

Figure 14. ASCEND(u) and DESCEND(u) procedures.

DESCEND(u): Assuming $\Sigma(u)$ is at our disposal, this procedure computes $\Sigma(w)$ and $\Sigma(z)$. If $\beta(u) = \delta_u$, then we set $\Sigma_w = \tilde{\Sigma}_w$ and $\Sigma(z) = \tilde{\Sigma}(z)$ and stop. Otherwise, let $p_R = p^{\sqcap}(z)$. We call SPLIT($\Sigma(u)$, $y(p_R)$). Let Σ^-, Σ^+ be the two chains returned by this procedure; if $\varepsilon(\mathrm{br}(u)) > 0$, then the procedure also returns $\mathrm{br}(u)$. We set $\Sigma(w)$ = MERGE(Σ^-, $\tilde{\Sigma}(w)$). Let $e = \mathrm{br}(u) \cap \square_z$. We compute $\varepsilon(e)$ and set $\Sigma(z)$ = MERGE($\emptyset$, Σ^+, e).

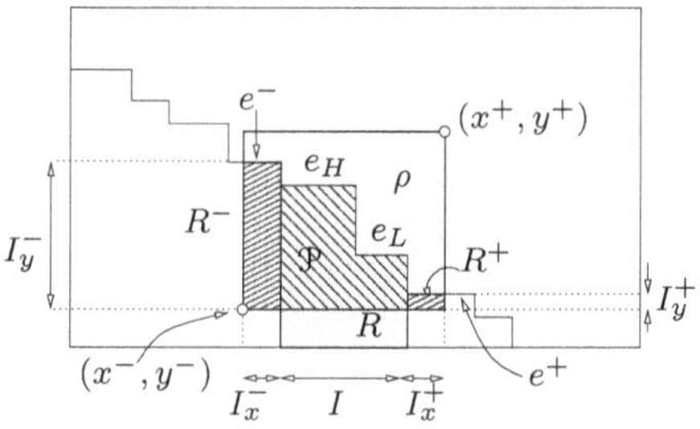

Figure 15. Answering a query on Ψ_0.

Answering a query. Let $\rho = [x^-, x^+] \times [y^-, y^+] \subseteq \square$ be a query rectangle. We wish to compute $\mu(\mathbb{Q}, \mathbb{B}, \rho)$. Let rt be the root of $\mathcal{T}$, and let $\Gamma = \Gamma(\mathrm{rt})$ and $\Sigma = \Sigma(\mathrm{rt})$. By searching with ρ in $\mathcal{H}(\Sigma)$, stored at rt, we find the highest (resp. lowest) edge e_H (resp. e_L) of Γ that appears in Σ and that lies completely inside ρ. Let $\mathcal{P}$ be the staircase polygon formed by the edges $e_H, \ldots, e_L$ of Σ. Let e^- be the predecessor of e_H and e^+ the successor of e_L in Σ. Set $I = [x^-(e_H), x^+(e_L)]$, $R = I \times [0, y^-]$, $I_x^- = \mathsf{X}(e^-) \cap [x^-, x^+]$, $I_x^+ = \mathsf{X}(e^+) \cap [x^-, x^+]$, $I_y^- = [0, y(e^-)] \cap [y^-, y^+]$, and $I_y^+ = [0, y(e^+)] \cap [y^-, y^+]$. Set $R^- = I_x^- \times I_y^-$ and $R^+ = I^+ \times I_y^+$. See Figure 15 (ii). Let A (resp. A^-, A^+) denote the area of R (resp. R^-, R^+) not lyig in $\mathcal{U}(\mathbb{B})$. Then

$$\begin{aligned}\mu(\mathbb{Q}, \mathbb{B}, \rho) &= \alpha(\Sigma, I) - \mathsf{A} + \mathsf{A}^- + \mathsf{A}^+ \\ &= \alpha(\Sigma, I) - \varepsilon(I) y_L + \varepsilon(I_x^-)|I_y^-| + \varepsilon(I^+)|I_y^+|.\end{aligned}$$

Each of these quantities can be computed in $O(\log n)$ time either querying $\mathcal{H}(\Sigma)$ or the wall data structure. Hence, $\mu(\mathbb{Q}, \mathbb{B}, \rho)$ can be computed in $O(\log n)$ time.

Preprocessing $\mathbb{C}_0$, $\mathbb{C}_2$, and $\mathbb{B}$. The overall structure of Ψ_2 is similar to that of Ψ_0, but it is more complex because of the interaction between $\mathbb{C}_0$ and $\mathbb{C}_2$. To keep the presentation analogous to Ψ_0, we describe the data structure for computing $\mu(\mathbb{C}_0, \mathbb{C}_2 \cup \mathbb{B}, \rho)$; $\mu(\mathbb{C}_2, \mathbb{C}_0 \cup \mathbb{B}, \rho)$ can be computed by reversing the directions of $(+x)$- and $(+y)$-axes and constructing the data structure in this new coordinate frame.

Let $\mathbb{Q}^+$ (resp. $\mathbb{Q}^-$) be the set of quadrants corresponding to the squares in $\mathbb{C}_0$ and $\mathbb{C}_2$. For a query rectangle $\rho \subseteq \square$, we wish to compute $\mu(\mathbb{Q}^+, \mathbb{Q}^- \cup \mathbb{B}, \rho)$. We begin by describing the representation of $\mathcal{U}(\mathbb{Q}^+, \mathbb{Q}^- \cup \mathbb{B}, \square)$ and the operations performed on it.

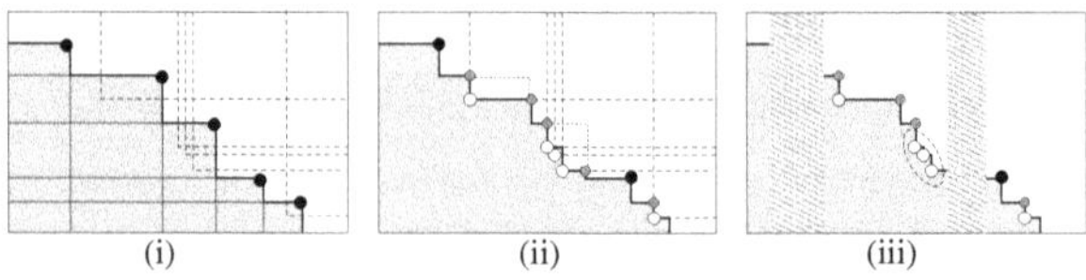

Figure 16. Representation of $\Sigma(\mathbb{Q}^+, \mathbb{Q}^-, \mathbb{B})$. (i) $\mathcal{U}(\mathbb{Q}^+)$. (ii) $\mathcal{U}(\mathbb{Q}^+, \mathbb{Q}^-)$, black (resp. white) points are vertices of squares in $\mathbb{Q}^+$ (resp. $\mathbb{Q}^-$), and gray vertices are mixed vertices. (iii) $\mathcal{U}(\mathbb{Q}^+, \mathbb{Q}^- \cup \mathbb{B})$; edges inside the ellipse form a superedge.

Representation of $\mathcal{U}(\mathbb{Q}^+, \mathbb{Q}^- \cup \mathcal{B}, \square)$. $\mathcal{U}(\mathbb{Q}^+, \mathbb{Q}^-, \square)$ is a staircase polygon, with four types of vertices: vertices of $\mathbb{Q}^+$, vertices of $\mathbb{Q}^-$, intersection points of two edges of $\mathbb{Q}^+$ (or $\mathbb{Q}^-$), and intersection points of an edge of $\partial\mathcal{U}(\mathbb{Q}^+)$ with an edge of $\partial\mathcal{U}(\mathbb{Q}^-)$. The first and the last type are convex vertices, the second type are reflex vertices, and the third type can be both convex and reflex. We refer to the last ones as *mixed* vertices. An edge of $\mathcal{U}(\mathbb{Q}^+, \mathbb{Q}^-)$ is called *purple* if one of its endpoints is a mixed vertex, *blue* if it is an edge of $\mathcal{U}(\mathbb{Q}^+)$, and *red* if it is an edge of $\mathcal{U}(\mathbb{Q}^-)$. Let

$\Gamma(\mathbb{Q}^+, \mathbb{Q}^-)$ be the rectilinear chain of $\mathcal{U}(\mathbb{Q}^+, \mathbb{Q}^-, \square)$. As in the previous case, Γ is represented as the sequence of its horizontal edges. Let $\Sigma := \Sigma(\mathbb{Q}^+, \mathbb{Q}^-, \mathbb{B})$ be the sequence of edges of $\Gamma(\mathbb{Q}^+, \mathbb{Q}^-) \setminus \mathcal{U}(\mathcal{B})$, and let $\Sigma(\mathbb{Q}^-, \mathbb{B})$ be the sequence of edges in $\Gamma(\mathbb{Q}^-) \setminus \mathcal{U}(\mathcal{B})$. Σ is represented implicitly using $\Sigma(\mathbb{Q}^-, \mathbb{B})$: Let $E = \langle e_1, e_2, \ldots, e_k \rangle$ be the sequence of edges of $\Gamma(\mathbb{Q}^+, \mathbb{Q}^-)$ that appear in Σ. Every red edge in E also appears in $\Sigma(\mathbb{Q}^-, \mathbb{B})$. We call a contiguous subsequence $e_i, e_{i+1}, \ldots, e_j$ of red edges in E as a *super-edge* σ_{ij} (see Figure 16 (iii)), and represent it as a five-tuple:

$$\hat{\sigma}_{ij} = \langle x^-(\sigma_{ij}), x^+(\sigma_{ij}), y^-(\sigma_{ij}), y^+(\sigma_{ij}), \varepsilon(\sigma_{ij}) \rangle,$$

where $x^-(\sigma_{ij}) = x^-(e_i)$, $x^+(\sigma_{ij}) = x^+(e_j)$, $y^-(\sigma_{ij}) = y(e_j)$, $y^+(\sigma_{ij}) = y(e_i)$, and $\varepsilon(\sigma_{ij}) = \sum_{l=i}^{j} \varepsilon(e_l) y(e_l)$. We represent $\Sigma = \hat{\Sigma} = \langle \gamma_1, \gamma_2, \ldots, \gamma_s \rangle$ as a sequence of blue edges, purple edges, and super-edges; either $\gamma_i = \hat{e}_j$ for a blue or purple edge in E or $\gamma_i = \hat{\sigma}_{jl}$ for a super-edge σ_{jl}. By definition, a super-edge may consist of a single red edge. We assume that each super-edge in $\hat{\Sigma}$ is maximal in the sense that if γ_i is a super-edge then γ_{i+1} is not a super-edge. By storing both $\Sigma(\mathbb{Q}^+, \mathbb{Q}^-, \mathbb{B})$ and $\Sigma(\mathbb{Q}^-, \mathbb{B})$ in height balanced binary trees, each of the following operations can be performed in $O(\log n)$ time.

(i) SPLIT(Σ, a): Given a rectilinear chain Σ and a value $a \geq 0$, let $\Sigma^+ = \langle e \in \Sigma \mid y(e) > a \rangle$ and $\Sigma^- = \langle e \in \Sigma \mid y(e) < a \rangle$. Split Σ into Σ^-, Σ^+. If Σ contains an edge e with $y(e) = a$, then the procedure returns $\hat{e}$ separately. If there is a super-edge σ_{jl} in $\hat{\Sigma}$ with $a \in [y^-(\sigma_{jl}), y^+(\sigma_{jl})]$, then the procedure splits the super-edge into two: one of which lies above a and appears at the end of Σ^-, and the other lies below a and appears at the beginning of Σ^+.

(ii) MERGE(Σ^-, Σ^+, e): Let Σ^-, Σ^+ be two xy-monotone rectilinear chains and e a horizontal edge so that $\Sigma = \Sigma^- \circ \langle e \rangle \circ \Sigma^+$ is also a xy-monotone rectilinear chain. Given Σ^-, Σ^+, and $\hat{e}$, compute Σ. If the edge e is not specified or $\varepsilon(e) = 0$, the procedure computes $\Sigma^- \circ \Sigma^+$. Finally, if there are two consecutive super-edges in $\hat{\Sigma}$, then we merge them.

(iii) QUERY(Σ, I): Given a chain Σ and an interval I, compute

$$\alpha(\Sigma, I) = \sum_{e \in \Sigma, \mathsf{X}(e) \subseteq I} \varepsilon(e) \cdot y(e).$$

Since some of the edges of Σ are implicitly represented as super-edges, computing $\alpha(\Sigma, I)$ now is more involved than for Ψ_0 but nevertheless can be computed in $O(\log n)$ time.

Structure of Ψ_2. Let $\mathcal{Q}^- = \{q(S) \mid S \in \mathbb{Q}^-\}$ and $\mathcal{Q}^+ = \{q(S) \mid S \in \mathbb{Q}^+\}$. Let $\mathcal{X} \subseteq [0, a]$ be the set of x-coordinates of points in $\mathcal{Q}^+ \cup \mathcal{Q}^-$ and edges in $\mathbb{B}$. We construct a binary tree $\mathcal{T}$ as for Ψ_0. For each node u, we define $\mathbb{Q}_u^+, \mathbb{Q}_u^-, \mathbb{B}_u, \mathbb{B}_u^*$ in a manner similar to Ψ_0. Let $\Gamma^+(u) = \Gamma(\mathbb{Q}_u^+, \mathbb{Q}_u^-)$, $\Gamma^-(u) = \Gamma(\mathbb{Q}_u^-)$, $\Sigma^+(u) = \Sigma(\mathbb{Q}_u^+, \mathbb{Q}_u^-, \mathbb{B}_u^*)$, and $\Sigma^-(u) = \Sigma(\mathbb{Q}_u^-, \mathbb{B}_u^*)$. In addition, let $\tilde{\Sigma}^+(u) = \Sigma^+(u) \setminus \Sigma^+(p(u))$ and $\tilde{\Sigma}^-(u) = \Sigma^-(u) \setminus \Sigma^-(p(u))$. We define $\mathrm{br}^+(u)$ (resp. $\mathrm{br}^-(u)$) be the edge of $\Gamma^+(u)$ (resp. $\Gamma^-(u)$) that intersects ℓ_u. At each node u, we store compact representations of $\tilde{\Sigma}^+(u)$ and $\tilde{\Sigma}^-(u)$, as described above, and we also store $\mathrm{br}^+(u)$ and $\mathrm{br}^-(u)$.

As for Ψ_0, we again describe ASCEND, DESCEND procedures to compute $\Sigma^+(u)$ from $\Sigma^+(w)$ and $\Sigma^+(z)$, and vice-versa, where w and z are the children of v. Each of them takes $O(\log n)$ time, and they are used to insert and delete corners and bars. Putting everything together, we conclude the following:

LEMMA 5.1. *A set $\mathbb{C}$ of corner squares and a set $\mathbb{B}$ of bars can be maintained in a dynamic data structure under insertion/deletion so that for a query rectangle ρ, $\mu(\mathbb{C}, \mathbb{B}, \rho)$ can be computed in $O(\log n)$ time. The insertion and deletion operations take $O(\log^2 n)$ time.*

References

[1] http://en.wikipedia.org/wiki/Klee's_measure_problem

[2] P. K. Agarwal, H. Kaplan, and M. Sharir, Computing the volume of the union of cubes, *Proc. 23rd Annu. Sympos. Comput. Geom.*, 2007, 294–301.

[3] M. de Berg, M. van Kreveld, M. Overmars and O. Schwarzkopf, *Computational Geometry: Algorithms and Applications*, 2nd edition, Springer Verlag, Heidelberg, 2000.

[4] J. L. Bentley, Algorithms for Klee's rectangle problems. Unpublished notes, Computer Science Department, Carnegie Mellon University, 1977.

[5] J.D. Boissonnat, M. Sharir, B. Tagansky and M. Yvinec, Voronoi diagrams in higher dimensions under certain polyhedral distance functions, *Discrete Comput. Geom.* 19 (1998), 485–519.

[6] K. Bringmann, Klee's measure problem on fat boxes, *Proc. 26th Annu. Sympos. Comput. Geom.*, 2010, to appear.

[7] T. M. Chan, A (slightly) faster algorithm for Klee's measure problem, *Comput. Geom.: Theory Appls.* 43 (2010), 243-250.

[8] E. Chen and T. M. Chan, Space-efficient algorithms for Klee's measure problem, *Proc. 17th Canadian Conf. Comput. Geom.*, 2005.

[9] B. S. Chlebus, On the Klee's measure problem in small dimensions, *Proc. 25th Conf. Current Trends in Theory and Practice of Informatics*, 1998, 304-311.

[10] M. Dickerson, C. A. Duncan, and M. T. Goodrich, K-d trees are better when cut on the longest side, *Proc. 8th European Sympos. Algorithms*, 2000, 179190.

[11] M. L. Fredman and B. Weide, The complexity of computing the measure of $\bigcup[a_i, b_i]$, *Commun. ACM* 21 (1978), 540–544.

[12] J. van Leeuwen and D. Wood, The measure problem for rectangular ranges in d-space, *J. Algorithms* 2 (1981), 282–300.

[13] V. Klee, Can the measure of $\bigcup[a_i, b_i]$ be computed in less than $O(n \log n)$ steps? *Amer. Math. Monthly* 84 (1977), 284–285.

[14] M. Overmars and J. Leeuwen, Maintenance of configurations in the plane, *J. Comput. Syst. Sci.* 23 (1981), 166–204.

[15] M. Overmars and C.K. Yap, New upper bounds in Klee's measure problem, *SIAM J. Comput.* 20 (1991), 1034–1045.

[16] S. Suzuki and T. Ibaki, An average running time analysis of a backtracking algorithm to calculate the measure of the union of hyperrectangles in d dimensions, *Proc. 16th Canadian Conf. Comput. Geom.*, 2004, 196–199.

Orthogonal Range Reporting: Query Lower Bounds, Optimal Structures in 3-d, and Higher-dimensional Improvements

Peyman Afshani* Lars Arge* Kasper Dalgaard Larsen*
MADALGO†
Department of Computer Science
Aarhus University, Denmark.
{peyman,large,larsen}@madalgo.au.dk

ABSTRACT

Orthogonal range reporting is the problem of storing a set of n points in d-dimensional space, such that the k points in an axis-orthogonal query box can be reported efficiently. While the 2-d version of the problem was completely characterized in the pointer machine model more than two decades ago, this is not the case in higher dimensions.

In this paper we provide a space optimal pointer machine data structure for 3-d orthogonal range reporting that answers queries in $O(\log n + k)$ time. Thus we settle the complexity of the problem in 3-d. We use this result to obtain improved structures in higher dimensions, namely structures with a $\log n/\log\log n$ factor increase in space and query time per dimension. Thus for $d \geq 3$ we obtain a structure that both uses optimal $O(n(\log n/\log\log n)^{d-1})$ space and answers queries in the best known query bound $O(\log n(\log n/\log\log n)^{d-3} + k)$.

Furthermore, we show that any data structure for the d-dimensional orthogonal range reporting problem in the pointer machine model of computation that uses $S(n)$ space must spend $\Omega((\log n/\log(S(n)/n))^{\lfloor d/2\rfloor-1})$ time to answer queries. Thus, if $S(n)/n$ is poly-logarithmic, then the query time is at least $\Omega((\log n/\log\log n)^{\lfloor d/2\rfloor-1})$. This is the first known non-trivial higher dimensional orthogonal range reporting query lower bound and it has two important implications. First, it shows that the query bound increases with dimension. Second, in combination with our upper bounds it shows that the optimal query bound increases from $\Theta(\log n + k)$ to $\Omega((\log n/\log\log n)^2 + k)$ somewhere between three and six dimensions.

Finally, we show that our techniques also lead to improved structures for point location in rectilinear subdivisions, that is, the problem of storing a set of n disjoint d-dimensional axis-orthogonal rectangles, such that the rectangle containing a query point q can be found efficiently.

*Work was supported in part by the Danish National Research Foundation, the Danish Strategic Research Council, and by US Army Research Office Grant W911NF-08-1-0452.
†Center for Massive Data Algorithmics—a center of the Danish National Research Foundation.

SCG'10, June 13–16, 2010, Snowbird, Utah, USA.

Categories and Subject Descriptors

E.1 [**Data Structures**]: Miscellaneous

General Terms

Algorithms, Theory

Keywords

Data structures, orthogonal range reporting, pointer machine, lower bounds

1. INTRODUCTION

Orthogonal range reporting is the problem of storing a set of n points in d-dimensional space, such that the k points in an axis-orthogonal query box can be reported efficiently. This is a fundamental problem in several fields, including spatial databases and computational geometry, and it has been studied extensively [3, 4]. We study the problem in the pointer machine model of computation [16]. While the two-dimensional version of the problem was completely characterized in this model more than two decades ago, this is not the case in higher dimensions.

1.1 Previous results

In this section we review previous orthogonal range reporting results. For brevity we only review the structures most relevant to our work, that is, static pointer machine structures with poly-logarithmic query bounds. Refer to surveys for further results [3, 4].

In two dimensions the orthogonal range reporting problem can be solved in $O(\log n+k)$ time using $O(n\log n/\log\log n)$ space [8]. This is optimal since Chazelle proved that any d-dimensional structure with an $O(\log^{O(1)} n+k)$ query bound has to use $\Omega(n(\log n/\log\log n)^{d-1})$ space [9].

However, for $d \geq 3$ no optimal $O(\log n + k)$ time and $O(n(\log n/\log\log n)^{d-1})$ space structure is known. Until recently, the known space-optimal $O(n(\log n/\log\log n)^{d-1})$ structure answered queries in $O(\log^{d-1+\varepsilon} n + k)$ time [9]. Using $O(n\log^{d-1} n/\log\log n)$ space another structure could

Space	Query	Ref.
$n(\log n/\log\log n)^3$	$\log n + k$	[2]
$n(\log n/\log\log n)^2$	$\log n(\log n/\log\log n) + k$	[2]
$n(\log n/\log\log n)^2$	$\log n + k$	new

Table 1: Our results compared to the best previous 3-d orthogonal range reporting results.

Space	Query	Ref.
$n\log^d n/(\log\log n)^3$	$\log^{d-2} n + k$	[2]
$n(\log n/\log\log n)^{d-1}$	$\log n(\log n/\log\log n)^{d-2} + k$	[2]
$n(\log n/\log\log n)^{d-1}$	$\log n(\log n/\log\log n)^{d-3} + k$	new

Table 2: Our results compared to the best previous d-dimensional orthogonal range reporting results.

answer queries in $O(\log^{d-1} n + k)$ time [8]. A structure with an $O(\log^{d-2} n + k)$ query bound, that is, an optimal query bound in 3-d, was also known but it uses $O(n\log^d n)$ space [7, 11]. An improved space-optimal structure that could answer queries in $O(\log n(\log n/\log\log n)^{d-2}+k)$ time developed recently, as well as an improved $O(\log^{d-2} n + k)$ query time structure using $O(n\log^d n/(\log\log n)^3)$ space [2]. These two structures are the currently best known structures in d-dimensions.

The lower bound of Chazelle discussed above provides a space lower bound for poly-logarithmic query structures. However, no non-trivial query lower bound is known for super-linear space structures. It is not even known if the query time increases with dimension; the existence of both 2-d and 3-d $O(\log n+k)$ query structures might suggest this is not the case. Furthermore, since the two best known structures answer 3-d queries in $O(\log n + k)$ time using $O(n(\log n/\log\log n)^3)$ space and $O(\log n\cdot(\log n/\log\log n)+k)$ time using $O(n(\log n/\log\log n)^2)$ space, respectively, one might also suspect that a $\log n/\log\log n$ factor improvement in query time (resp. space) is only possible with a corresponding increase in space (resp. query time). In fact, in a previous paper we conjectured that the space-query product of any orthogonal range reporting structure has to be $\Omega(n\log^{2d-2} n/(\log\log n)^{2d-3})$ [2].

1.2 Our results

In Section 2 of this paper we describe the first 3-d orthogonal range reporting data structure that both uses optimal $O(n(\log n/\log\log n)^2)$ space and answers queries in optimal $O(\log n + k)$ time. Not only does this structure settle the complexity of the problem in 3-d, but also disproves our query-space product conjecture. Refer to Table 1. The structure relies on a new $O(n\log n/\log\log n)$ space and $O(\log n + k)$ query time structure for 3-d orthogonal range reporting where the query box is unbounded (in one direction) in *one* of the three dimensions. This is optimal (since the structure can be used to answer 2-d queries) and (maybe surprisingly) the bounds match the bounds of the known optimal structure for the case where the query box is unbounded in *two* of the three dimensions [2].

In Section 2 we show how our 3-d structure can be extended to higher dimensions with a $\log n/\log\log n$ factor increase in both query time and space per dimension. For $d \geq 3$, the resulting d-dimensional data structure uses optimal $O(n(\log n/\log\log n)^{d-1})$ space and answers queries in $O(\log n(\log n/\log\log n)^{d-3} + k)$ time, which improves the two best previous results. See Table 2.

In Section 3 we then show that any d-dimensional orthogonal range reporting data structure in the pointer machine model that uses $S(n)$ space and answers queries in $Q(n) + O(k)$ time must have $Q(n) = \Omega((\log n/\log(S(n)/n))^{\lfloor d/2\rfloor-1})$. Thus, if $S(n)/n$ is poly-logarithmic, then the query time is at least $\Omega((\log n/\log\log n)^{\lfloor d/2\rfloor-1} + k)$. This is the first non-trivial query lower bound and it has two important implications. First, it shows that the query bound increases with dimension. Second, in combination with our upper bounds it shows that the optimal query bound increases from $\Theta(\log n + k)$ to $\Omega((\log n/\log\log n)^2 + k)$ somewhere between three and six dimensions.

Rectilinear subdivision point location..

We also consider point location in rectilinear subdivisions, since the ideas used in our orthogonal range reporting structures can be used to develop improved structures for this problem as well. The point location in rectilinear subdivisions problem is the problem of storing a set of n disjoint d-dimensional axis-orthogonal rectangles, such that the rectangle (if any) containing a query point q can be found efficiently. The previously best known pointer machine structure for this problem uses linear space and answers queries in $O(\log^{d-1} n)$ time [12]. In Section 4, we design an improved structure for $d \geq 3$, that can answer queries in $O(\log n(\log n/\log\log n)^{d-2})$ time using linear space.

2. NEW DATA STRUCTURES

In this section, we describe our new orthogonal range reporting data structures. Our structures rely on improved solutions to various special cases of the problem, where the query box can be unbounded or the points colored.

We use $Q(d,k)$ to refer to the special case in which the query boxes have finite ranges in k of the d dimensions, that is, are unbounded in $d-k$ dimensions. Refer to Fig. 1. The $Q(2,1)$ and $Q(d,0)$ problems are often called *3-sided planar range reporting* and *dominance reporting*, respectively. We then define the (more difficult) *concurrent $Q(d,k)$ problem* as follows: Let S be a set of n points in d-dimensional space, $A : S \to \mathcal{C}$ a function that assigns a color from a color set $\mathcal{C}$ to each point, and $\mathcal{P}$ a set of color sets (that is, $\mathcal{P} \subset 2^{\mathcal{C}}$). The problem is to store S such that for any query tuple (q, L) consisting of a $Q(d,k)$ query q and a set $L \in \mathcal{P}$ of colors, all points $p \in S$ with $p \in q$ and $A(p) \in L$ can found efficiently.

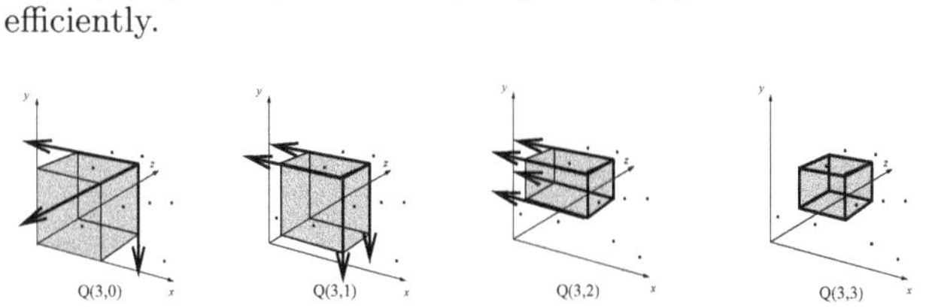

Figure 1: Three-dimensional queries.

In Subsection 2.1 below we first show how to solve the concurrent $Q(3,2)$ problem efficiently. In Subsection 2.2 we then use this solution to obtain efficient solutions for the

$Q(3,3)$ and $Q(d,d)$ problems, that is, for orthogonal range reporting.

2.1 Solving Concurrent $Q(3,2)$

In this section we show how to solve the concurrent $Q(3,2)$ problem efficiently. To do so we first solve the concurrent $Q(3,0)$ problem.

Throughout the section, we use the following notations: Given two points v and w, we say v *dominates* w if and only if all the coordinates of v are greater than those of w. For a set S of points we let $\mathrm{Dom}_S(v)$ denote the subset of S dominated by v. A *shallow cutting for the k-level of S*, or a *k-shallow cutting* for short, is a set R of $O(|S|/k)$ points such that any 3-d point p that dominates at most k points of S is dominated by a point in R, and such that every point of R dominates $O(k)$ points of S. The existence of this kind of shallow cuttings is known [1], and more general shallow cuttings have been used extensively in the computational geometry literature (see e.g. [15]).

The following lemma and its proof play an important role in our concurrent $Q(3,0)$ data structure.

LEMMA 1. *(Makris and Tsakalidis [14]) Let S be a set of n points in 3-d. It is possible to construct a subdivision $\mathcal{A}_S$ of the plane of size $O(n)$ using orthogonal line segments, such that for any query point q in 3-d, one can use the result of a point location query on $\mathcal{A}_S$ to find a point that dominates q or conclude that no such point exists.*

PROOF. Let $p_1,\ldots,p_n$ be the points in S projected onto the xy-plane, sorted decreasingly by their z-coordinates (Figure 2(a)). Now consider the iterative process of shooting two rays from p_i, starting with $i=1$, one vertical towards $y=-\infty$ and another horizontal towards $x=-\infty$, until they intersect any pre-existing ray. Next, remove all the points p_j, $j>i$, that are dominated by p_i and continue with the next point. It is easy to realise that the resulting planar subdivision, $\mathcal{A}_S$, is of size $O(n)$. Refer to Figure 2(b).

Now let q' be the projection of q onto the xy-plane and let $p\in S$ be the point at the top-right corner of the region of $\mathcal{A}_S$ containing q'. Observe that p has the largest z-coordinate among all the points that dominate q' in the xy-plane. Thus if the z-coordinate of p is greater than that of q then p dominates q. Otherwise, no point dominates q. Therefore the domination query q can easily be answered once q' is located in $\mathcal{A}_S$. □

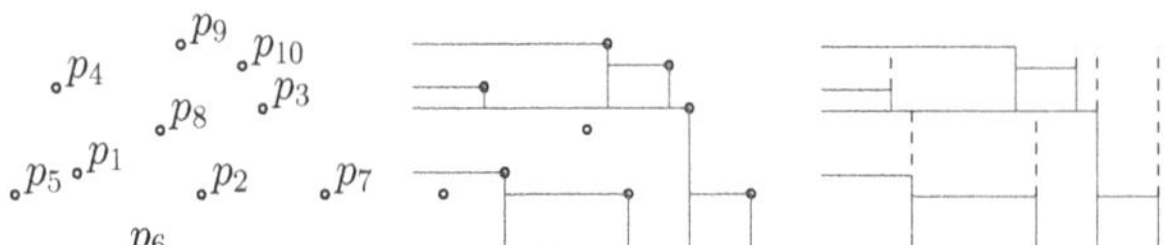

Figure 2: (a) The projection of 3-d point set S onto the xy-plane (numbered by z-coordinate). (b) The subdivision $\mathcal{A}_S$. (c) The trapezoid decomposition of $\mathcal{A}_S$.

LEMMA 2. *There exists an $O(n)$ space structure for the concurrent $Q(3,0)$ problem that answers queries in $O(|\mathcal{C}|\log\log n+\log n+k)$ time.*

PROOF. Our concurrent $Q(3,0)$ structure is constructed as follows. For each color $c\in\mathcal{C}$, we build a $(\log n)$-shallow cutting R_c for the set $S_c := \{p\in S|\mathcal{A}(p)=c\}$. For every point $v\in R_c$, we then store $\mathrm{Dom}_{S_c}(v)$ in a dominance reporting data structure and also store S_c in a linear-space dominance reporting structure [1] (that is, a $Q(3,0)$ structure). Furthermore, using Lemma 1, we build the subdivision $\mathcal{A}_c$ for the set R_c. We apply trapezoid decomposition on $\mathcal{A}_c$ (that is, we shoot vertical rays towards $y=\infty$ from every vertex; refer to Figure 2(c)) and obtain a set of $O(|R_c|)$ boxes. Then we construct a linear-space point enclosure data structure [8] on the union of the boxes obtained from $\mathcal{A}_c$ for all $c\in\mathcal{C}$, that is, a structure that can be used to find all boxes containing a given query point.

That the above structure uses linear space can be seen as follows. Each point in the shallow cutting R_c dominates $O(\log n)$ points, so $|R_c|=O(|S_c|/\log n)$. By the properties of the shallow cutting, we know that $|\mathrm{Dom}_{S_c}(v)|=O(\log n)$ for every $v\in R_c$. Since the dominance data structure of [1] uses linear space, it follows that the combined space usage of all the dominance data structures is $O(n)$. Finally, the total number of boxes in the subdivisions $\mathcal{A}_c$ over all $c\in\mathcal{C}$ is $O(n/\log n)$. Thus, since the point enclosure structure of [8] also uses linear space, the space usage of the point enclosure data structure is $O(n/\log n)$.

Now consider a query tuple (q,L). With a little abuse of notation, we let q denote the point defining the $Q(3,0)$ query q. For a color c, we let $k_c=|\mathrm{Dom}_{S_c}(q)|$. Clearly, $\sum_{c\in L}k_c=k$. For every $c\in L$, we want to perform a point location query with q on $\mathcal{A}_c$. Since the boxes defined from $\mathcal{A}_c$ are disjoint, we can do so in $O(\log n+|\mathcal{C}|)$ time simply by querying the point enclosure data structure with q and this way obtain a box for each of the $|\mathcal{C}|$ colors. By Lemma 1, having the point location result for $\mathcal{A}_c$ enables us to determine if (i) there is a point $v\in R_c$ that dominates q or (ii) no point of R_c dominates q. In case (i), it follows that $\mathrm{Dom}_{S_c}(q)\subseteq\mathrm{Dom}_{S_c}(v)$ and thus $\mathrm{Dom}_{S_c}(q)$ can be reported by querying the dominance reporting data structure on $\mathrm{Dom}_{S_c}(v)$; this takes $O(\log|\mathrm{Dom}_{S_c}(v)|+k_c)=O(\log\log n+k_c)$ time. In case (ii), it follows from the properties of the shallow cutting that $k_c>\log n$. In this case, we query the dominance data structure implemented on S_c using $O(\log|S_c|+k_c)=O(k_c)$ time. Summing the query time over all $c\in L$, we obtain a total query time of $O(\log n+|\mathcal{C}|+|L|\log\log n+k)=O(|\mathcal{C}|\log\log n+\log n+k)$. □

Below we show how Lemma 2 combined with a grid building technique can be used to solve the concurrent $Q(3,2)$ problem. Our strategy is inspired by previous grid building techniques [5, 13], in particular the work of Karpinski and Nekrich [13]. We need the following technical observation.

OBSERVATION 1. *Define $f(n)=\sqrt{nt}$, $f^{(1)}(n)=f(n)$ and $f^{(k)}(n)=f(f^{(k-1)}(n))$. Let $f^*(n)$ be the minimum integer k s.t., $f^{(k)}(n)\le t\log n$. We have $f^*(n)\le\lceil\log\log n-\log\log\log n\rceil$.*

PROOF. It is easy to check that $f^{(i)}(n)=t^{(2^i-1)/2^i}n^{1/2^i}\le tn^{1/2^i}$. Thus, $f^{(\lceil\log\log n-\log\log\log n\rceil)}\le tn^{\log\log n/\log n}=t\log n$. □

We are now ready to describe our concurrent $Q(3,2)$ structure, assuming without loss of generality that the query boxes are unbounded towards $-\infty$ along the z-axis.

Structure: Let $t := |\mathcal{P}||\mathcal{C}|\log^2 n$. Consider the projection of the points in S on the xy-plane and a $(\sqrt{n/t}) \times (\sqrt{n/t})$ grid such that each vertical or horizontal slab contains the projection of $\sqrt{nt}$ points. In each slab we construct a concurrent $Q(3,0)$ queries structure (Lemma 2). We also construct a grid data structure on all the points in S. We will describe this structure below. Finally we recurse on the points in each slab. Note that in the recursions, the grid size and the value of t vary according to the size of the subproblem. We stop the recursion when a subproblem contains less than $(|\mathcal{C}||\mathcal{P}|)^2\sqrt{\log n}$ points.

The grid data structure is defined as follows. First consider altering the x- and y-coordinates of the points in S such that if the projection of a point p lies in a cell c of the grid, then the x- and y-coordinates of p are changed to those of the bottom-left vertex of c. Let S' denote the set of modified points. The modification ensures that the points of S' lie on the grid vertices when projected onto the xy-plane. For every grid vertex p and every color c, we use $S'_{p,c}$ to denote the points of S' that have color c and lie on p when projected onto the xy-plane. The grid data structure now consists of a number of linked lists, combined denoted by D_g, and a number of the query-optimal $Q(3,2)$ structure by Chazelle and Guibas [11] called D. D_g consists of a list on the points in each $S'_{p,c}$, sorted by increasing z-coordinate. D consists of a $Q(3,2)$ structure for each colorset $L \in \mathcal{P}$, constructed on a set S'_L consisting of the points with the smallest z-coordinate for every set $S'_{p,c}$ with $c \in L$. Note that $|S'_L| = O(n|L|/t) = O(n|\mathcal{C}|/t)$.

Space use: The combined size of the $Q(3,0)$ data structures is $O(n)$ by Lemma 2. We claim that the grid data structures take $O(n)$ space as well. Clearly this is true for D_g, as each point is stored only once. This is also true for D since the $Q(3,2)$ data structure for S'_L takes $O(|S'_L|\log^2|S'_L|) = O(n/|\mathcal{P}|)$ space [11] and there are $|\mathcal{P}|$ such sets. Thus, the space use, $S(n)$, of the data structure is given by the recurrance

$$S(n) = 2\sqrt{\frac{n}{t}}\,S(\sqrt{nt}) + O(n), \quad t = |\mathcal{C}||\mathcal{P}|\log^2 n.$$

This solves to $S(n) = 2^r O(n)$ where r is the number of recursion steps. By Observation 1, after $f^*(n)$ steps of recursion the size of the subproblems are reduced to $O(t\log n) = O(|\mathcal{C}||\mathcal{P}|\log^3 n)$. Note that in these subproblems the value of t is $O(|\mathcal{C}||\mathcal{P}|\log^2(|\mathcal{C}||\mathcal{P}|\log^3 n))$. It is easily verified that three more recursion steps reduce the size of the subproblem to $O(|\mathcal{C}||\mathcal{P}|\log^{3/8} n \log^{O(1)}(|\mathcal{C}||\mathcal{P}|\log n)) < (|\mathcal{C}||\mathcal{P}|)^2\sqrt{\log n}$. Thus, the number of recursions is bounded by $r = \log\log n - \log\log\log n + O(1)$ and we get $S(n) = O(n\log n/\log\log n)$.

Queries: Consider a query tuple (q, L) and the projection of q on the xy-plane (Figure 3(a)). If the projection is completely contained in a horizontal or vertical slab, then we answer the query recursively in that slab; at the bottom of the recursions where the number of points is less than $(|\mathcal{C}||\mathcal{P}|)^2\sqrt{\log n}$ we simply answer the query brute-force. Otherwise, q can be decomposed into two "vertical" $Q(3,1)$ queries (Figure 3(b)), two "horizontal" $Q(3,1)$ queries (Figure 3(c)), and one "grid" query, q_g, (Figure 3(d)).

We use D_g to answer the grid query. Note that as the grid query completely spans all the grid cells it intersects, answering the grid query on S' yields the same result as answering it on S. We first query D_L with q_g. This takes $O(\log n + k)$ time since all the reported points have colors from L and are contained in q_g. For every output point, we go to the corresponding list in D_g, and traverse the list until the z-coordinate of the points exceed that of q_g. It is easy to see that this procedure answers q_g correctly in $O(\log n + k)$ time.

Now, consider a vertical $Q(3,1)$ query q_1 (the horizontal queries can be answered similarly). We answer q_1 recursively on the corresponding slab. One step down in the recursion, q_1 will be decomposed into one vertical $Q(3,1)$ query, two horizontal $Q(3,0)$ queries, and one grid query. The grid query is answered as above, the $Q(3,0)$ queries are answered using the $Q(3,0)$ data structures built in each slab, and the $Q(3,1)$ query is answered recursively. Thus, the query time for a $Q(3,1)$ query is given by the recurrance

$$Q(n) = Q(\sqrt{nt}) + O(|\mathcal{C}|\log\log n + \log n)$$

which solves to $Q(n) = O(|\mathcal{C}|(\log\log n)^2 + \log n)$. Overall, the query time is $O(|\mathcal{C}|(\log\log n)^2 + (|\mathcal{C}||\mathcal{P}|)^2\sqrt{\log n} + \log n + k) = O((|\mathcal{C}||\mathcal{P}|)^2\sqrt{\log n} + \log n + k)$. Thus, we obtain the following:

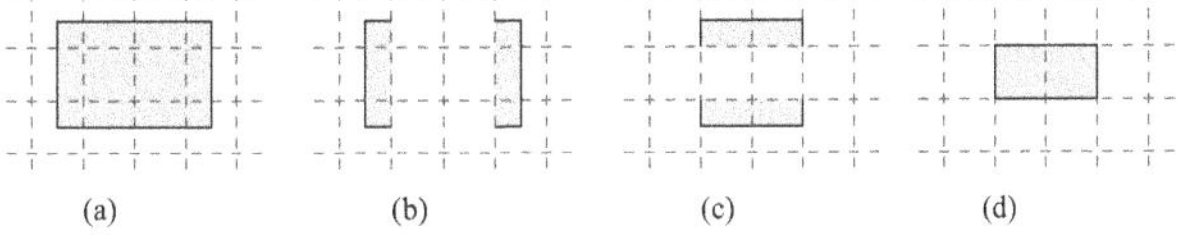

Figure 3: (a) The projection of the $Q(3,2)$ query on the xy-plane. (b) The two vertical queries. (c) The two horizontal queries. (d) The grid query.

THEOREM 1. *There exists an $O(n\log n/\log\log n)$ space structure for the concurrent $Q(3,2)$ problem that answers queries in $O((|\mathcal{C}||\mathcal{P}|)^2\sqrt{\log n} + \log n + k)$ time.*

COROLLARY 1. *There exists an $O(n\log n/\log\log n)$ space structure for the $Q(3,2)$ problem that can answer queries in $O(\log n + k)$ time. This is optimal.*

PROOF. A $Q(3,2)$ problem is a concurrent $Q(3,2)$ problem with $|\mathcal{C}| = |\mathcal{P}| = 1$ and thus the bounds follow from Theorem 1. Since a data structure for $Q(3,2)$ problem solves $Q(2,2)$, the optimality of the space bound follows from [9]. □

2.2 Solving $Q(3,3)$ and $Q(d,d)$

Having solved the concurrent $Q(3,2)$ problem efficiently, we can now obtain our efficient structures for the $Q(3,3)$ and $Q(d,d)$ problems in a simple way using the following lemma, where $Q_{\mathcal{A},\mathcal{C},\mathcal{P}}(d,k)$ denotes a concurrent $Q(d,k)$ problem.

LEMMA 3. *(Afshani et al. [2]) Assume for any $S, \mathcal{C}, \mathcal{A}$, and $\mathcal{P}$ in which S is a set of n points in d-dimensional space, $\mathcal{C}$ is a set of colors, $\mathcal{A} : S \to \mathcal{C}$ and $\mathcal{P} \subset 2^{\mathcal{C}}$, that there exists a data structure that solves the $Q_{\mathcal{A},\mathcal{C},\mathcal{P}}(d,k)$ problem using $S(n, |\mathcal{C}|, |\mathcal{P}|)$ space and with $Q(n, |\mathcal{C}|, |\mathcal{P}|) + O(k)$ query time. Then a $Q_{\mathcal{A}',\mathcal{C}',\mathcal{P}'}(d+1, k+1)$ problem (respectively a $Q_{\mathcal{A}',\mathcal{C}',\mathcal{P}'}(d, k+1)$ problem) can be solved using $O(\sum_{i=1}^{\log_\alpha n} \alpha^i S(n/\alpha^i, |\mathcal{C}'|\alpha, |\mathcal{P}'|\alpha))$ space and with the query time of $O(\log_\alpha n \cdot Q(n, |\mathcal{C}'|\alpha, |\mathcal{P}'|\alpha) + k)$ (respectively $O(Q(n, |\mathcal{C}'|\alpha, |\mathcal{P}'|\alpha) + k)$) for any parameter α.*

THEOREM 2. *There exists an $O(n(\log n/\log\log n)^2)$ space data structure for the concurrent $Q(3,3)$ problem that can answer queries in $O((|\mathcal{C}||\mathcal{P}|)^2 \log^{3/4} n + \log n + k)$ time.*

PROOF. Apply Lemma 3 with $\alpha = \log^{1/16} n$ to Theorem 1. □

COROLLARY 2. *In three-dimensions, there exists an optimal orthogonal range reporting data structure that answers queries in $O(\log n + k)$ time and uses $O(n(\log n/\log\log n)^2)$ space.*

COROLLARY 3. *In d-dimensions, there exists an orthogonal range reporting data structure that can answer queries in $O(\log n(\log n/\log\log n)^{d-3} + k)$ time and uses optimal $O(n(\log n/\log\log n)^{d-1})$ space.*

PROOF. We apply Lemma 3 $d-3$ times to Theorem 2 with $\alpha = \log^{\varepsilon} n$, for a sufficiently small constant $\varepsilon > 0$. □

3. LOWER BOUND

In this section, we prove a query lower bound for the orthogonal range reporting problem in d dimensions. To do so, we utilize the general pointer machine lower bound technique of Chazelle [9]. However, to obtain a query lower bound rather than a space lower bound, we apply the technique to the seemingly "dual" problem of point enclosure, and then reduce point enclosure to orthogonal range reporting.

In the point enclosure problem we are to preprocess a set of axis-aligned boxes in d-dimensional space such that we can report the boxes that contain a query point. Our lower bound proof is inspired by the lower bound of Arge et al. [6] for the 2-d point enclosure problem in the I/O-model. The following theorem is the main result of this section.

THEOREM 3. *Any pointer machine structure for the d-dimensional point enclosure problem that uses $S(n)$ space and answers queries in $Q(n)+O(k)$ time must have $Q(n) = \Omega((\log n/\log(S(n)/n))^{d-1})$.*

To prove Theorem 3, we will use the following result.

THEOREM 4. *(Chazelle [9]) Consider a reporting problem on a set S of n input elements and assume a data structure of size $S(n)$ achieves the query time of $Q(n)+O(k)$. If there exists a set $\mathcal{Q} \subset 2^S$ such that*

(i) for every $q \in \mathcal{Q}$ there exists a query that outputs q

(ii) for every $q \in \mathcal{Q}$, $|q| = \Omega(Q(n))$

(iii) for every two $q_1, q_2 \in \mathcal{Q}$, $|q_1 \cap q_2| = O(1)$

then $S(n) = \Omega(|\mathcal{Q}|Q(n))$.

In our proof of Theorem 3, the input set S will be a set of boxes in d-dimensional space and each of the sets $q \in \mathcal{Q}$ will be a set of boxes corresponding to the output of a point enclosure query on S for some query point p. With a little abuse of notation, we will refer to the elements of $\mathcal{Q}$ as queries.

We thus prove our lower bound by constructing two sets S and $\mathcal{Q}$ (of boxes and points, respectively) that satisfy the conditions of Theorem 4.

The input set S. Let M, α and t be parameters to be fixed later. Consider a d-dimensional box B with side lengths M. All the input boxes will have a fixed volume of αM^{d-1} and will be contained in B. For every combination of indices $i_1, \dots, i_{d-1} \in \{1, \dots, \lfloor (1/d)\log_t M \rfloor\}$, we construct a box of dimensions $M/t^{i_1} \times M/t^{i_2} \times \cdots \times M/t^{i_{d-1}} \times \alpha t^{i_1+\cdots+i_{d-1}}$ and add it to a set of boxes R. We refer to the set R as the set of box types, and say that a box has type $(i_1, \dots, i_{d-1})$ if its dimensions equal those of the box in R constructed from those indices. It is easy to see that $|R| = \Theta(\log_t^{d-1} M)$. Our input set S is now obtained as follows: for each $r \in R$, place $\Theta(M/\alpha)$ boxes of type r inside B. The boxes are placed by tiling them from the lower corner of B, so that the boxes of the same type are disjoint. However, note that, two boxes of different type can intersect. For simplicity, we assume the boxes of each type completely cover B.

The query set $\mathcal{Q}$. Essentially, what we need is a point set of size $\Theta(M)$ with the property that any orthogonal box that contains $k \geq 2$ points has volume $\Omega(kM^{d-1})$. Intuitively, a point set placed uniformly at random inside B has this property "on average" [9]. However, such a set can also be constructed deterministically [10].
The number of boxes in the input set is $\Theta((M/\alpha)\log_t^{d-1} M)$. We thus have:

$$n = \Theta((M/\alpha)\log_t^{d-1} M). \qquad \text{(C-1)}$$

We are now ready assign values to M, α and t that satisfy conditions (i) and (ii) of Theorem 4. Because of the tiling, any given query point is contained in precisely $\Theta(\log_t^{d-1} M)$ boxes, one for each type. To satisfy condition (i) of Theorem 4, we therefore require that

$$\log_t^{d-1} M \geq Q(n). \qquad \text{(C-2)}$$

Now consider two query points p_1 and p_2. To ensure condition (ii) of Theorem 4, we need to select M, α and t such that only a constant number of input boxes can contain both p_1 and p_2. By the property of the point set, the box b spanned by p_1 and p_2 has volume $\Omega(M^{d-1})$. Letting $w_1 \times w_2 \times \cdots \times w_d$ be the dimensions of b, this translates to $\Pi_{i=1}^d w_i = \Omega(M^{d-1})$. Clearly any input box that contains both p_1 and p_2 must also contain b. Since only one box of each type can contain b, we simply need to bound the maximum number of different types that can potentially contain b. A box of type $(i_1, \dots, i_{d-1})$ can contain b only if

$$M/t^{i_j} \geq w_j \quad \text{for } 1 \leq j \leq d-1 \quad \text{and} \qquad (1)$$
$$\alpha t^{i_1+\cdots+i_{d-1}} \geq w_d \qquad (2)$$

By multiplying all the inequalities of (1) we obtain that $M^{d-1}/t^{i_1+\cdots+i_{d-1}} \geq w_1 \dots w_{d-1} = \Omega(M^{d-1}/w_d)$, which results in the requirement $w_d = \Omega(t^{i_1+\cdots+i_{d-1}})$. Combined with (2) we get that a box of type $(i_1, \dots, i_{d-1})$ can contain b only if $c_1 \cdot w_d \geq t^{i_1+\cdots+i_{d-1}} \geq w_d/\alpha$ for some constant c_1. Thus there are only $O(\log_t \alpha)$ different values of $s = i_1 + \cdots + i_{d-1}$ that satisfy (1) and (2), and these values are consecutive integers. By (1) we get that the lowest value of s satisfying the requirements is obtained by letting $i_j = \lceil \log_t(M/w_j) \rceil$ for all j. It follows that i_j must satisfy $\log_t(M/w_j) \leq i_j \leq \log_t(M/w_j) + O(\log_t \alpha)$, which means the total number of different choices of indices, and thus types possibly containing b, is bounded by $O(\log_t^{d-1} \alpha)$. To satisfy condition (ii) of Theorem 4 we therefore must have

$$\log_t^{d-1} \alpha = O(1). \qquad \text{(C-3)}$$

Any choice of parameters M, α and t that satisfy conditions (C-1),(C-2), and (C-3) will give us a space lower bound of $\Omega(|\mathcal{Q}|Q(n))$. To satisfy (C-3), we set $t = \alpha$, to satisfy (C-2) we pick α such that $\log_\alpha^{d-1} M = Q(n)$, and by rearranging (C-1) we get a value for M. It can be easily verified that with this choice of parameters $\log M = \Theta(\log n)$. These values give the space lower bound of $\Omega(|\mathcal{Q}|Q(n)) = \Omega(MQ(n)) = \Omega(M \log_\alpha^{d-1} M) = \Omega(n\alpha)$. Combined with (C-2) this gives $\log_\alpha^{d-1} n = \Theta(Q(n))$. We solve this for α and obtain that $\log \alpha = \Theta(\log n / Q(n))^{1/(d-1)})$. Substituting this value in the space lower bound we obtain that

$$Q(n) = \Omega\left(\left(\frac{\log n}{\log \frac{S(n)}{n}}\right)^{d-1}\right).$$

This concludes the proof of Theorem 3.

COROLLARY 4. *Any pointer machine structure for the d-dimensional orthogonal range reporting problem that uses $S(n)$ space and answers queries in $Q(n) + O(k)$ time must have $Q(n) = \Omega((\log n / \log(S(n)/n))^{\lfloor d/2 \rfloor - 1})$.*

PROOF. It is easy to see that d-dimensional point enclosure reduces to $(2 \cdot d)$-dimensional orthogonal range reporting: an input box $[a_1, b_1] \times \cdots \times [a_d, b_d]$ is mapped to an input point $(a_1, b_1, \ldots, a_d, b_d)$ and a query point $(q_1, \ldots, q_d)$ is mapped to a query box $[-\infty, q_1] \times [q_1, \infty] \times \ldots [-\infty, q_d] \times [q_d, \infty]$. □

4. RECTILINEAR POINT LOCATION

In this section we consider point location in d-dimensional rectilinear subdivisions. We improve the bounds for this problem using an approach similar to the one employed in Section 2.

The input to the concurrent version of the problem is a set S of n boxes in d dimensions and a color assignment $\mathcal{A} : S \to \mathcal{C}$. The color assignment has the property that all the boxes mapped to the same color are disjoint. A query consists of a point q and a set of colors $L \subseteq \mathcal{C}$. The task is to preprocess the input, such that given a query (q, L), we can report the boxes r in S for which $q \in r$ and $\mathcal{A}(r) \in L$. We use $P_{\mathcal{A},\mathcal{C}}(d)$ to denote this problem.

First we solve the concurrent 2-d point location in rectilinear subdivisions problem, $P_{\mathcal{A},\mathcal{C}}(2)$.

LEMMA 4. *There exists an $O(n)$ space structure for $P_{\mathcal{A},\mathcal{C}}(2)$ that answers queries in $O(|\mathcal{C}|^2 + \log n)$ time.*

PROOF. We construct a linear-space 2-d point enclosure data structure on all the input boxes [8]. To answer a query (q, L), we query the point enclosure data structure with q. This returns a set R of all boxes in S that contain q and takes $O(\log n + |R|)$ time. We output each $r \in R$ if $\mathcal{A}(r) \in L$. The total time is then bounded by $O(|R||\mathcal{C}| + \log n)$. Since the boxes with the same color are disjoint, at most one box of each color can contain q, thus $|R| \leq |\mathcal{C}|$ and the result follows. □

Structure. To obtain our high dimensional point location data structure we need an analogous of Lemma 3. Let X_{d+1} be a sorted set containing the $2n$ values of the coordinates of the last dimension of boxes in S. Build a balanced tree T of fanout t on X_{d+1} and associate each box $r \in S$ with the least common ancestor of the two leaf nodes containing the coordinates of r in the last dimension. Thus, every node v in T is associated with a set $S_v \subseteq S$ of input boxes. We project S_v into the first d dimensions and implement a data structure for $P_{\mathcal{A}_v,\mathcal{C}_v}(d)$ on the projected points in which $\mathcal{A}_v$ and $\mathcal{C}_v$ are defined as follows: Let $c_1, \ldots, c_t$ be the children of v. Define $\mathcal{C}_v = \mathcal{C} \times \{1, \ldots, t\} \times \{1, \ldots, t\}$, and for a box $r \in S_v$, we define $\mathcal{A}_v(r) = (\mathcal{A}(r), i, j)$, in which where i is the index of the child whose subtree contains the smallest of r's coordinates in the last dimension, and j is the index of the child containing the largest.

Answering Queries. Let (q, L) be a $P_{\mathcal{A},\mathcal{C}}(d+1)$ query. We start out at the root node v in T, and compute the index i of the child c_i of v containing the last coordinate of q. We then query the $P_{\mathcal{A}_v,\mathcal{C}_v}(d)$ data structure stored in v with (q', L') as the query, in which $L' = L \times \{1, \ldots, i\} \times \{i, \ldots, t\}$ and q' is the projection of q onto the first d dimensions. This returns a set $R \subseteq S_v$ of boxes. For each box $r \in R$, we check whether q is inside r in the last dimension, and if so we report r. Finally, we recurse on child c_i.

Analysis. First we argue that our color assignments satisfy the disjointness requirement: Consider two d-dimensional boxes r_1 and r_2 in S_v such that $\mathcal{A}_v(r_1) = \mathcal{A}_v(r_2) = (c, i, j)$. Let r_1' and r_2' be the $(d+1)$-dimensional boxes whose projection onto the first d dimensions is r_1 and r_2, respectively. Since $\mathcal{A}(r_1') = \mathcal{A}(r_1') = c$, we know r_1' and r_2' are disjoint. Furthermore, in the last dimension, both r_1' and r_2' contain the coordinate separating c_i and c_{i+1}. This implies r_1 and r_2 are disjoint. That the query algorithm returns the correct boxes when querying for (q, L) follows from the definition of (q', L'). Thus, we get the following lemma.

LEMMA 5. *Assume for any $S, \mathcal{C}$, and $\mathcal{A}$ there exists a data structure that solves $P_{\mathcal{A},\mathcal{C}}(d+1)$ using $S(n, |\mathcal{C}|)$ space and with $Q(n, |\mathcal{C}|)$ query time. Then, $P_{\mathcal{A}',\mathcal{C}'}(d+1)$ can be solved using $S(n, |\mathcal{C}'|\alpha)$ space and with the query time of $O(\log_\alpha n \cdot Q(n, |\mathcal{C}'|\alpha))$ for any parameter α.*

Combining Lemma 5 and Lemma 4 gives us the following result.

THEOREM 5. *There exists an $O(n)$ space data structure for point location in d-dimensional rectilinear subdivisions that answers queries in $O(\log n (\log n / \log\log n)^{d-2})$ time.*

PROOF. We get a data structure with the claimed bounds after $d - 2$ applications of Lemma 5 to Lemma 4 with $\alpha = \log^\varepsilon n$ for a sufficiently small constant $\varepsilon > 0$. □

5. CONCLUSION

In this paper we described a space optimal pointer machine data structure for 3-d orthogonal range reporting that answers queries in optimal $O(\log n + k)$ time. We also described improved higher-dimensional structure and gave the first non-trivial query lower bound for the problem.

One important implication of our results is that the optimal query bound has to increase from $O(\log n + k)$ to $\Omega((\log n / \log\log n)^2 + k)$ somewhere between three and six dimensions. One intriguing open problem is of course to pinpoint the dimension where the optimal query bound jumps. We conjecture that it happens in four dimensions.

Our query upper bound increases by a $\log n / \log\log n$ factor every dimension while the increase in the lower bound happens every other dimension. Another interesting question is therefore which of the two is closer to the behavior of the optimal query bound. In this context, it is worth noting that many other bounds in computational geometry (such as the worst case convex hull complexity, and halfspace range reporting query bounds) increase every other dimension.

6. REFERENCES

[1] P. Afshani. On dominance reporting in 3D. In *Proc. European Symposium on Algorithms*, pages 41–51, 2008.

[2] P. Afshani, L. Arge, and K. D. Larsen. Orthogonal range reporting in three and higher dimensions. In *Proc. IEEE Symposium on Foundations of Computer Science*, pages 149–158, 2009.

[3] P. K. Agarwal. Range searching. In J. E. Goodman and J. O'Rourke, editors, *CRC Handbook of Discrete and Computational Geometry*. CRC Press, Inc., 2004.

[4] P. K. Agarwal and J. Erickson. Geometric range searching and its relatives. In B. Chazelle, E. Goodman, and R. Pollack, editors, *Discrete and Computational Geometry: Ten Years Later*. Mathematical Society Press, 1997.

[5] S. Alstrup, G. S. Brodal, and T. Rauhe. New data structures for orthogonal range searching. In *Proc. 41st Annual Symposium on Foundations of Computer Science*, pages 198–207, 2000.

[6] L. Arge, V. Samoladas, and K. Yi. Optimal external memory planar point enclosure. In *Proc. European Symposium on Algorithms, LNCS 3221*, pages 40–52, 2004.

[7] P. Bozanis, N. Kitsios, C. Makris, and A. Tsakalidis. New results on intersection query problems. *The Computer Journal*, 40:22–29, 1997.

[8] B. Chazelle. Filtering search: a new approach to query-answering. *SIAM J. Comput.*, 15(3):703–724, 1986.

[9] B. Chazelle. Lower bounds for orthogonal range searching: I. the reporting case. *Journal of the ACM*, 37(2):200–212, Apr. 1990.

[10] B. Chazelle. Lower bounds for off-line range searching. In *STOC '95: Proceedings of the twenty-seventh annual ACM symposium on Theory of computing*, pages 733–740, New York, NY, USA, 1995. ACM.

[11] B. Chazelle and L. J. Guibas. Fractional cascading: II.Applications. *Algorithmica*, 1:163–191, 1986.

[12] H. Edelsbrunner, G. Haring, and D. Hilbert. Rectangular point location in d dimensions with applications. *The Computer journal*, 29:76–82, 1986.

[13] M. Karpinski and Y. Nekrich. Space efficient multi-dimensional range reporting. In *COCOON '09: Proceedings of the 15th Annual International Conference on Computing and Combinatorics*, pages 215–224, 2009.

[14] C. Makris and A. Tsakalidis. Algorithms for three-dimensional dominance searching in linear space. *Information Processing Letters*, 66(6):277 – 283, 1998.

[15] J. Matoušek. Reporting points in halfspaces. *Computational Geometry: Theory and Applications*, 2(3):169–186, 1992.

[16] R. E. Tarjan. A class of algorithms that require nonlinear time to maintain disjoint sets. *Journal of Computer and System Sciences*, 18:110–127, 1979.

A Dynamic Data Structure for Approximate Range Searching*

David M. Mount
Department of Computer Science
University of Maryland
College Park, Maryland
mount@cs.umd.edu

Eunhui Park
Department of Computer Science
University of Maryland
College Park, Maryland
ehpark@cs.umd.edu

ABSTRACT

In this paper, we introduce a simple, randomized dynamic data structure for storing multidimensional point sets, called a *quadtreap*. This data structure is a randomized, balanced variant of a quadtree data structure. In particular, it defines a hierarchical decomposition of space into cells, which are based on hyperrectangles of bounded aspect ratio, each of constant combinatorial complexity. It can be viewed as a multidimensional generalization of the treap data structure of Seidel and Aragon. When inserted, points are assigned random priorities, and the tree is restructured through rotations as if the points had been inserted in priority order.

In any fixed dimension d, we show it is possible to store a set of n points in a quadtreap of space $O(n)$. The height h of the tree is $O(\log n)$ with high probability. It supports point insertion in time $O(h)$. It supports point deletion in worst-case time $O(h^2)$ and expected-case time $O(h)$, averaged over the points of the tree. It can answer ε-approximate spherical range counting queries over groups and approximate nearest neighbor queries in time $O\big(h + (\frac{1}{\varepsilon})^{d-1}\big)$.

Categories and Subject Descriptors

F.2.2 [**Analysis of Algorithms and Problem Complexity**]: Nonnumerical Algorithms and Problems—*Geometrical problems and computations*

General Terms

Algorithms

Keywords

Geometric data structures, dynamic data structures, quadtrees, range searching, approximation algorithms

*This work has been supported by the National Science Foundation under grant CCR-0635099 and the Office of Naval Research under grant N00014-08-1-1015.

SCG'10, June 13–16, 2010, Snowbird, Utah, USA.

1. INTRODUCTION

Recent decades have witnessed the development of many data structures for efficient geometric search and retrieval. A fundamental issue in the design of these data structures is the balance between efficiency, generality, and simplicity. One of the most successful domains in terms of simple, practical approaches has been the development of linear-sized data structures for approximate geometric retrieval problems involving points sets in low dimensional spaces. In this paper, our particular interest is in dynamic data structures, which allow the insertion and deletion of points for use in approximate retrieval problems, such as range searching and nearest neighbor searching. A number of data structures have been proposed for approximate retrieval problems for points sets. The simplicity and general utility of these data structures is evident by the wide variety of problems to which they have been applied. We will focus on methods based on partition trees, and in particular, on those based on quadtrees and their multidimensional extensions (see, e.g., [18]). One nice feature of the quadtree, which makes it appropriate for approximate retrieval problems, is that it decomposes space into disjoint hypercubes, which are of constant combinatorial complexity and bounded aspect ratio, two important properties in geometric approximation.

Because the size and depth of a quadtree generally depends on the ratio of the maximum and minimum point distances, it is common to consider the compressed quadtree [5, 9,16], which can store n points in space $O(n)$, irrespective of their distribution. A compressed quadtree may have height $\Theta(n)$, and so it is often combined with an auxiliary search structure for efficient access. This can be done by applying some form of centroid decomposition to the tree [10]or by imposing a general-purpose data structure, like a link-cut tree [6, 20]. These approaches are rather inelegant, however, due to their reliance on relatively heavyweight auxiliary structures.

A much simpler and more elegant solution, called the *skip quadtree*, was proposed by Eppstein *et al.* [14]. It consists of a series of compressed quadtrees, each for a successively sparser random sample of the point set, together with links between corresponding nodes of consecutive trees. The result is a multidimensional analog of the well known skip list data structure [17]. The skip quadtree can be used to answer approximate nearest neighbor queries and approximate range-reporting queries. Another creative solution, due to Chan [7,8], involves a simple in-place data structure based on the bit-interleaved ordering of point coordinates. He shows that this trivial "data structure," which is really just a sorted array of points, supports efficient nearest neighbor searching without explicitly storing any tree. The general approach of linearizing point sets through bit interleaving is well known, and is the basis of a structure called the linear quadtree [15]. Another approach for achieving balance is to modify the definition of the decomposition process. Examples of this include the BBD-tree [2–4], which uses an operation called centroid-shrinking to produce a balanced tree, and the BAR tree [13], which uses splitting planes that are not axis-aligned.

As mentioned above, our interest is in approximate range counting. Consider a set P of n points in $\mathbb{R}^d$, for some constant d. It is common to assume that each point $p \in P$ is associated with a numeric weight, $\mathrm{wgt}(p)$. After preprocessing, we are given a query range Q, and the problem is to compute the sum of weights of the points lying within Q. It is generally assumed that the weights are drawn from a commutative semigroup. In some cases the semigroup is actually a group, and if so, subtraction of weights is also allowed. In *approximate range searching*, the range Q is assumed to be approximated by two convex shapes, an inner range Q^- and an outer range Q^+, where $Q^- \subset Q^+$. Points lying within the inner range must be counted and points lying outside the outer range must not. It is assumed that the boundaries of these two shapes are separated by a distance of at least $\varepsilon \cdot \mathrm{diam}(Q)$. Space and query times are expressed as a function of both ε and n. The only other assumption imposed on the query shapes is the *unit-cost assumption*, which states that it is possible to determine whether a quadtree box lies entirely inside Q^+ or entirely outside Q^- in constant time. Arya and Mount [3] showed that, under the unit-cost assumption, approximate range queries could be answered with space $O(n)$ and query time $O\big(\log n + (\frac{1}{\varepsilon})^{d-1}\big)$. They showed that this is essentially optimal for methods based on partition trees. Although data structures exist with asymptotically better performance, these methods require ε to be fixed at construction time. The BBD-tree has the nice feature that preprocessing is independent of ε, and hence a single structure can be used to answer queries of all degrees of accuracy.

One significant shortcoming of the aforementioned data structures, is that none of them admits an efficient solution to the important problem of approximate range counting together with efficient insertion and deletion. The BBD-tree and BAR tree do not support efficient insertion and deletion (except in the amortized sense, through the process of completely rebuilding unbalanced subtrees [1, 12]). Chan's implicit data structure and the skip quadtree both support efficient insertion and deletion, but neither supports range-counting queries. Intuitively, to support range-counting queries, each internal node of a partition tree maintains the total weight of all the points residing in the subtree rooted at this node. With each insertion or deletion, these counts are updated from the point of insertion to the tree's root. In Chan's structure there is no tree, and hence no internal nodes. The skip quadtree is based on the compressed quadtree, which may have height $\Theta(n)$. (The skip quadtree does support efficient range-reporting queries, however, because even an unbalanced subtree of size k can be traversed in $O(k)$ time.)

In this paper, we introduce a simple dynamic data structure, which supports efficient approximate range counting and approximate nearest neighbor searching. This tree structure is similar in spirit to the BBD-tree, but whereas the BBD-tree is static, our data structure employs a dynamic rebalancing method based on rotations. Similar to the skip quadtree, which is based on combining quadtrees and the 1-dimensional skip list, our data structure can be viewed as a combination of the quadtree and the treap data structure of Seidel and Aragon [19].

A *treap* is a randomized data structure for storing 1-dimensional keys, which is based on a combination of a binary search tree and a heap. A treap assigns random priorities to the keys, and the tree behaves at all times as if the points had been inserted in order of increasing priority. It relies on the fact that, if nodes are inserted in random order into a binary tree, then the tree's height is $O(\log n)$ with high probability. Our structure also assigns priorities to points, and maintains the tree as if the points had been inserted in this order. Our tree structure maintains something akin to the heap property of the treap (but each node of our structure is associated with two priority values, not one). Because of its similarity to the treap, we call our data structure the *quadtreap*. Our main result is stated below.

THEOREM 1.1. *Given a set of n points in $\mathbb{R}^d$, a quadtreap storing these points has space $O(n)$. The tree structure is randomized and, with high probability, it has height $O(\log n)$. Letting h denote the height of the tree:*

(*i*) *It supports point insertion in time $O(h)$.*
(*ii*) *It supports point deletion in worst-case time $O(h^2)$, and in expected-case time $O(h)$ (averaged over all the points of the tree).*
(*iii*) *Approximate range-counting queries can be answered in time:*
  - $O\big(h + (\frac{1}{\varepsilon})^{d-1}\big)$, *when the point weights are drawn from a commutative group,*
  - $O\big(h \cdot (\frac{1}{\varepsilon})^{d-1}\big)$, *when the point weights are drawn from a commutative semigroup.*

(*iv*) *Approximate range-reporting queries can be answered in time $O\big(h + (\frac{1}{\varepsilon})^{d-1} + k\big)$, where k is the output size.*
(*v*) *Approximate nearest neighbor queries can be answered in time $O\big(h + (\frac{1}{\varepsilon})^{d-1}\big)$.*

For approximate range-counting, it is assumed that the inner and outer ranges are convex, and satisfy the unit-cost assumption. (See the definition given above).

The rest of the paper is organized as follows. In Section 2 we introduce the BD-tree data structure and present a simple incremental algorithm for its construction. In Section 3 we present our dynamic data structure and show how insertions and deletions are performed. In Section 4 we present the range query algorithm. In Section 5 we discuss processing of approximate nearest neighbor queries.

2. INCREMENTAL CONSTRUCTION OF A BD-TREE

To motivate our data structure, we begin by recalling some of the basic elements of quadtrees and BD-trees. A *quadtree* is a hierarchical decomposition of space into d-dimensional hypercubes, called *cells*. The root of the quadtree is associated with a unit hypercube $[0, 1]^d$, and we assume that (through an appropriate scaling) all the points fit within this hypercube. Each internal node has 2^d children corresponding to a subdivision of its cell into 2^d disjoint hypercubes, each having half the side length. Given a set P of points, this decomposition process is applied until each cell contains at most one point, and these terminal cells form the leaves of the trees. A *compressed quadtree*, is obtained by replacing all maximal chains of nodes that have a single non-empty child by a single node associated with the coordinates of the smallest quadtree box containing the data points. The size of a compressed quadtree is $O(n)$, and it can be constructed in time $O(n \log n)$ time (see, e.g., [9]).

If the dimension of the space is much larger than a small constant, it is impractical to split each internal node into 2^d cells, many of which may contain no points. For this reason, we consider a binary variant of the quadtree. Each decomposition step splits a cell by an axis-orthogonal hyperplane that bisects the cell's longest side. If there are ties, the side with the smallest coordinate index is selected. Each cell has constant aspect ratio, and so the essential packing properties of cells still hold. Henceforth, we use the terms *compressed quadtree* and *quadtree box* in this binary context. As with standard quadtree boxes, it is easy to prove that two quadtree boxes in this binary context are either spatially disjoint or one is nested within the other. Assuming a model of computation that supports exclusive bitwise-or and base-2 logarithms on point coordinates, the smallest quadtree box enclosing a pair of points (or more generally a pair of quadtree boxes) can be computed in constant time.

If the point distribution is highly skewed, a compressed quadtree may have height $\Theta(n)$. One way to deal with this is to introduce a partitioning mechanism that allows the algorithm to "zoom" into regions of dense concentration. In [3,4] a subdivision operation, called *shrinking*, was proposed to achieve this. The resulting data structure is called a *box-decomposition tree* (*BD-tree*). This is a binary tree in which the cell associated with each node is either a quadtree box or the set theoretic difference of two such boxes, one enclosed within the other. Thus, each cell is defined by an *outer box* and an optional *inner box*. The *size* of a cell is defined to be the maximum side length of its outer box. Although cells are not convex, they have bounded aspect ratio and are of constant combinatorial complexity.

We say that a cell of a BD-tree is *crowded* if it contains two or more points or if it contains an inner box and at least one point. Each crowded cell is partitioned into two smaller cells by one of two partitioning operations (see Fig. 1). The first operation, called a *split*, partitions a cell by an axis-orthogonal hyperplane in the same manner described above for the binary quadtree. The associated node has two children, one associated with each of these cells, called the *left child* and *right child*. In contrast to traditional partition-tree definitions, we do not assume that the coordinates of points in the left node are smaller than those of the the right node. Instead (for reasons to be discussed later), it will be convenient to assume that, if the original cell contains an inner box, this inner box lies within the left cell. We call this the *inner-left convention*. Otherwise, the nodes may be labeled left and right arbitrarily.

The second operation, called a *shrink*, partitions a cell by a quadtree box (called the *shrinking box*), which lies within the cell. It partitions the cell into two parts, one lying within the shrinking box (called the *inner cell*), and the other being the set-theoretic difference of the original cell and the shrinking

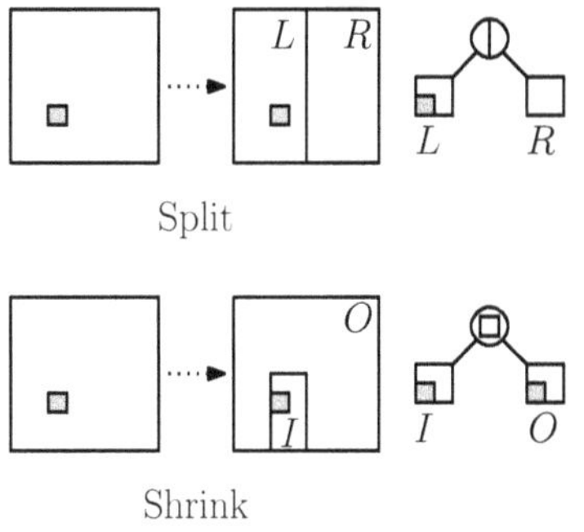

Figure 1: Splitting (above) and shrinking (below). In each case the initial cell contains an inner box, which is indicated by a small gray square.

box (called the *outer cell*). The associated child nodes are called the *inner child* and *outer child*, respectively. (In our figures, the inner child will always be on the left side.)

We will maintain the invariant that, whenever a shrink operation is applied to a cell that contains an inner box, the shrinking box (properly) contains the inner box. This implies that a cell never has more than one inner box. We allow a degenerate shrink to occur, where the shrinking box is equal to the cell's outer box. In this case, the outer box is said to be a *vacuous leaf* since it has no area, and hence no points can be inserted into it. In summary, there are two types of internal nodes in a BD-tree, *split nodes* and *shrink nodes*, depending on the choice of the partitioning operation.

The decomposition process terminates when the cell associated with the current node contains either a single point or a single inner box. The resulting node is a *leaf*.

2.1 Incremental Construction Algorithm

In [3,4], a bottom-up method for constructing a BD-tree of height $O(\log n)$ was proposed. The starting point for our discussion is a simple (top down) incremental algorithm for constructing a BD-tree through repeated insertion. This construction does not guarantee logarithmic height, but in Section 2.3 we will show that, if the points are inserted in random order, the height will be $O(\log n)$ with high probability. Ignoring the trivial case, where the tree is empty, we will maintain the invariant that the cell associated with each leaf node contains either a single point or a single inner box, which we call its *contents*.

Given a point set $P = \{p_1, \ldots, p_n\}$, the incremental construction algorithm begins with an empty tree, whose only cell is the unit hypercube, and it proceeds by repeatedly inserting each point $p \in P$ into the tree as follows. First, through a top-down descent, we find the leaf node u that contains p (see Fig. 2). Let b denote u's contents (either a point or an inner box), and let C denote u's outer box. We compute the minimum quadtree box enclosing both p and b, denoted E. By the minimality of E and basic properties of quadtree boxes, applying a split to E will produce two cells, one containing b and the other containing p.

We replace u with a pair of internal nodes v and w. The node v shrinks from u's outer box down to E. The outer child of v is a leaf node with outer box C and inner box E. (Note that E might be equal to u's outer box C), in which case the outer child is a vacuous leaf.) The inner child of

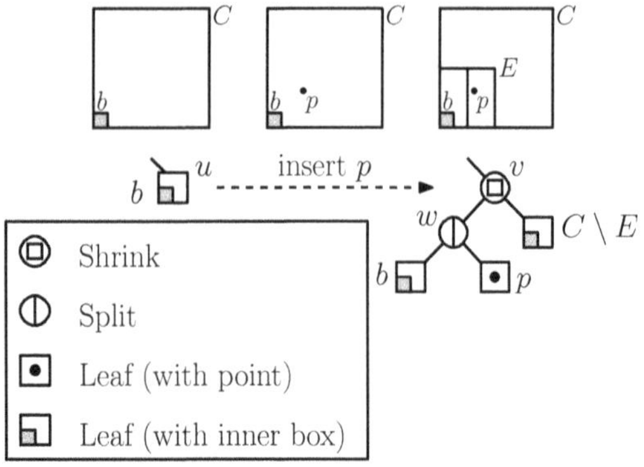

Figure 2: Insertion algorithm

v is a split node w that separates b from p. The children of w are two leaves. By the inner-left convention, the left child has b as its contents, and the right child contains p. (Recall that the left child does not necessarily correspond to points with smaller coordinates.) Observe that this insertion process generates nodes in pairs, a shrink node whose inner child is a split node. Irrespective of the insertion order, the following invariants are preserved after creation:

- Each cell contains at most one inner box.
- Each leaf cell contains either a single point or a single inner box (unless the tree is empty, in which case it contains nothing).
- The inner child of each shrink node is a split node.

An example showing two different insertion orders is given in Fig. 3. Although the tree structure depends on the insertion order, the following lemma shows that the subdivision induced by the tree does not. The proof is based on an inductive argument. The key is that, irrespective of the insertion order, the highest level decomposition step (which need not be at the root node) is a function of the smallest quadtree box containing all the points.

LEMMA 2.1. *Let T be a BD-tree resulting from applying the incremental algorithm to a set P of points. The subdivision induced by the leaf cells of T is independent of the insertion order.*

Due to space limitations, many proofs have been omitted.

2.2 Node Labels and the Heap Property

In this section we show that, if points are labeled with their insertion times, then it is possible to assign labels to the internal nodes of the tree based on the labels of its descendant leaves, so that these labels satisfy a heap ordering. This observation is analogous to the heap condition in the treap data structure of Seidel and Aragon [19].

To motivate this labeling, observe that each newly created internal node is added by the incremental algorithm in order to separate two entities, the newly inserted point and the existing contents of the leaf node in which the new point resides. If we were to label every point with its insertion time (and also provide an appropriate label value to each inner box), it follows that the creation time of any internal node is the *second smallest* label over all the points in the subtree rooted at this node. This suggests a labeling approach based

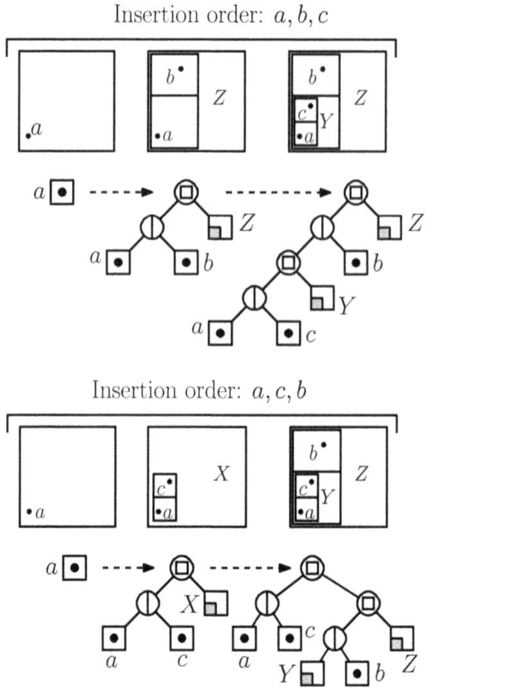

Figure 3: The tree on the left has been created with the sequence $\langle a, b, c\rangle$ and the one on the right with $\langle a, c, b\rangle$. Uppercase letters identify the outer cells of shrink nodes.

on maintaining the smallest and second smallest labels of the descendant points.

To make this more formal, we define the following *node-labeling rule*. First, we define two symbols, $\downarrow$ and $\uparrow$ denote, respectively, numeric values smaller and larger than any insertion times. We create a labeled pair for each node of the BD-tree. First, each leaf that contains a point is labeled with the pair $(t, \uparrow)$, where t is the insertion time of the associated point. Each leaf that contains only an inner box is given the label $(\downarrow, \uparrow)$. For each internal node u, let v and w be its two children, and let $(v^{[1]}, v^{[2]})$ and $(w^{[1]}, w^{[2]})$ denote the labels of its children. If u is a split node it has the label

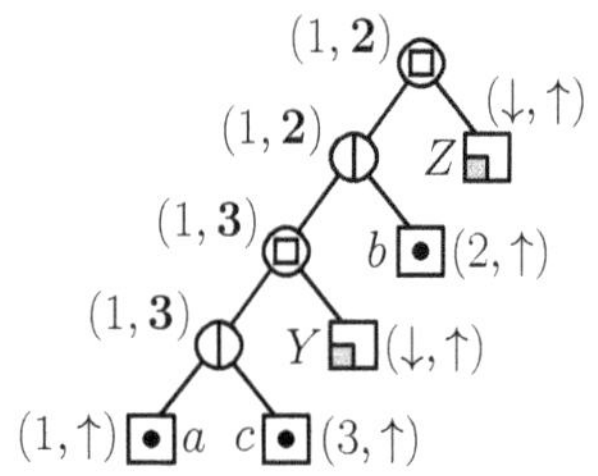

Figure 4: Node labeling for the insertion order $\langle a, b, c\rangle$.

$$(u^{[1]}, u^{[2]}) \leftarrow \left(\min\left(v^{[1]}, w^{[1]}\right), \max\left(v^{[1]}, w^{[1]}\right)\right).$$

If u is a shrink node, it is given the label of its inner child (the split node). An example of such a labeling is shown in Fig. 4. The following lemma establishes some useful observations regarding the relationships between the labels of nodes in the tree and the insertion times of the points in their associated subtrees.

LEMMA 2.2. *Consider the labeled BD-tree resulting from the incremental insertion algorithm. For any node u in this tree:*

(i) If u's cell has an inner box, then $u^{[1]} = \downarrow$, and in particular, this holds for the outer child of any shrink node. Otherwise $u^{[1]}$ is equal to the earliest insertion time of any point in u's subtree.
(ii) If u is an internal node, then $u^{[2]}$ is equal to the node's creation time, and in particular, $u^{[2]} \notin \{\downarrow, \uparrow\}$.
(iii) If u is a shrink node, then for every node v in its outer subtree $v^{[2]} > u^{[2]}$.

With the aid of this observation, the node labels satisfy the following properties. The second property is called the *heap property.*

LEMMA 2.3. *The labeled BD-tree resulting from the incremental insertion algorithm satisfies the following properties:*

(i) If v and w are left and right children of a split node, respectively, then $v^{[1]} < w^{[1]}$.
(ii) Given any pair consisting of a parent u and child v, we have $u^{[2]} \leq v^{[2]}$. If u is a split node, the inequality is proper.

2.3 Randomized Incremental Construction

In this section we show that, if points are inserted in random order into the BD-tree by the above incremental algorithm, with high probability, the resulting tree has $O(\log n)$ height. We begin by showing that the search depth of any query point is $O(\log n)$ in expectation (over all possible insertion orders). The proof is a standard application of backwards analysis [11]. It is based on the observations that (1) the subdivision induced by the tree is independent of the insertion order (as shown in Lemma 2.1), and (2) the existence of each cell of the subdivision depends only on a constant number of points. Thus, the probability that any one insertion affects the leaf cell containing the query point is inversely proportional to the number of points inserted thus far.

LEMMA 2.4. *Consider the BD-tree resulting from incrementally inserting an n-element point set P in random order. Given an arbitrary point q, the expected depth in the tree (averaged over all insertion orders) of the leaf containing q is $O(\log n)$.*

The following theorem strengthens the above result by showing that the height bound holds with high probability. A bound on the construction time and space follow immediately. Again, this is a straightforward generalization of analyses of other randomized incremental algorithms (see, e.g., [11]).

THEOREM 2.1. *Consider the BD-tree resulting from incrementally inserting an n-element point set in random order. The tree has space $O(n)$ (unconditionally). With high probability, the height of the tree is $O(\log n)$, and the time needed to construct the tree is $O(n \log n)$.*

3. THE QUADTREAP

In this section we define our dynamic data structure, which we call the *quadtreap.* Before presenting the algorithm, we discuss the basic rebalancing operation upon which the data structure is based.

3.1 Pseudo-nodes and Rotation

The BD-tree depends on the insertion order, but we will show in this section that it can be rebalanced through a simple local operation, which we refer to variously as *rotation* or *promotion.* This operation is much like the familiar rotation operation defined on binary search trees, but some modifications will be needed in the context of BD-trees. This operation will be a central primitive in maintaining balance in our data structure as points are inserted and deleted.

Throughout this section we assume that the BD-tree satisfies the property that the internal nodes of the BD-tree can be partitioned into pairs, such that each pair consists of a shrink node as a parent and a split node as its inner child. We call this the *shrink-split property.* As mentioned in Section 2, the BD-tree resulting from our incremental construction algorithm satisfies this property.

This assumption allows us to view each shrink-split combination as single decomposition operation, which subdivides a cell into three subcells. Thus, we can conceptually merge each shrink-split pair into a single node, called a *pseudo-node* (see Fig. 5), which has three children. The first two children, called the *left* and *right child,* correspond to the children of the split node, and the third child, called the *outer child,* corresponds to the outer child of the shrink node. Note that this is a conceptual device and does not involve any structural changes to the tree.

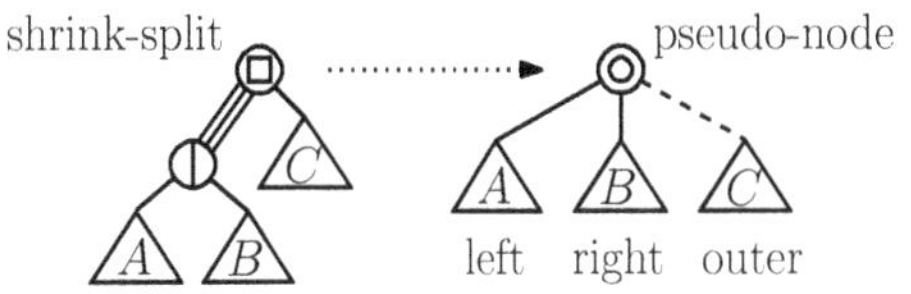

Figure 5: The pseudo-node corresponding to a shrink-split pair.

Let us now define rotation on pseudo-nodes. We call the operation a *promotion* and it is specified by giving a node y of the tree that is either a left child or an outer child. Let x denote y's parent. If y is a left child, the operation promote(y) makes x the outer child of y, and y's old outer child becomes the new left child of x. Observe that the inner-left convention is preserved, since y's left child is unchanged, and x's left child (labeled w in the figure) contains the inner box (consisting of the union of A and B's cells in the figure).

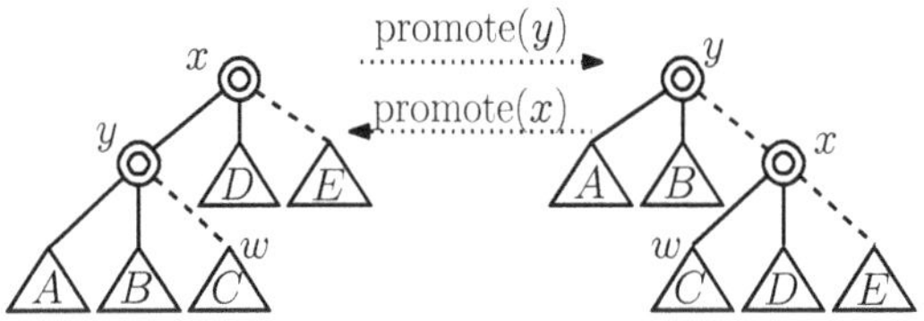

Figure 6: Rotation operation on pseudo-nodes.

Next, let us consider the promotion of an outer child x. Let y denote its parent. The operation promote(x) is the inverse of the previously described left-child promotion. It makes y the left child of x, and x's old left child becomes the new outer child of y. Again, the inner-left convention is preserved, since prior to the promotion, if y's cell had an inner box it must lie in its left child A, and so after promotion it lies in x's left child y. (The reason for the inner-left convention is to allow us to define one promotion rule. Otherwise, there would need to be a third promotion rule involving the right-child edge.)

Based on the above descriptions, it is easy to see that the essential properties of the BD-tree are preserved after applying either promotion operation. Note that promotion does not alter the underlying spatial decomposition, just the tree structure. Since it is a purely local operation, promotion can be performed in $O(1)$ time.

3.2 Point Insertion

We have seen that, if the points are inserted in random order, the height of the BD-tree is $O(\log n)$ with high probability, but a particularly bad insertion order could result in a tree of height $\Omega(n)$. In order to make the tree's height independent of the insertion order, we assign each point a random numeric *priority* at the time it is inserted, and we maintain the tree *as if* the points had been inserted in increasing priority order. This is essentially the same insight underlying the treap data structure [19]. Intuitively, since the priorities are not revealed to the user of the data structure, the tree effectively behaves as if the insertion order had been random.

The tree's structure is determined by the node-labeling rule described in Section 2.2 and the properties of Lemmas 2.2 and 2.3. Recall that the labeling procedure of that section gives both nodes of each shrink-split pair the same label. We define the label of each pseudo-node to be this value. Whenever a new point is inserted into or deleted from the tree, we need to restructure the tree so that its structure is consistent with the heap property. Thus, the tree behaves *as if* the nodes of the tree had been inserted in priority order. We begin with the insertion algorithm.

A newly inserted point is assigned a random priority $0 < t < 1$. It is then inserted into the tree, by the incremental algorithm. The newly created nodes (three leaves, one split node, and one shrink node) generated by the incremental algorithm are labeled as if the insertion took place at time t. The resulting tree may violate the heap properties, however, and the tree needs to be restructured to restore this property. The restructuring algorithm is presented in Algorithm 1. Recall that the label of a node u is denoted by $(u^{[1]}, u^{[2]})$. The restructuring procedure makes use of the following simple utility functions:

- adjust-left-right(u): Let v and w be the left and right children of u, respectively. If $w^{[1]} < v^{[1]}$, swap these children. (This enforces property (i) of Lemma 2.3.)
- update-label(u): Let w_1 and w_2 denote u's left and right children, respectively, Set

$$(u^{[1]}, u^{[2]}) \leftarrow ({w_1}^{[1]}, {w_2}^{[1]}).$$

Finally, the operation update(u) invokes both of these functions on u.

An example of the insertion and subsequent restructuring is shown in Fig. 7. (For ease of illustration, we assume that priorities are positive integers.) Consider the insertion of a point with priority 2, which lies within the leaf node indicated in Fig. 7(a). This insertion creates a pseudo-node v with label $(\downarrow, 2)$, which violates Lemma 2.3(ii) with respect to its parent u (see (b)), thus causing a promotion. After

Algorithm 1: Tree restructuring after inserting a point in a new leaf node v.

while $v \neq root(T)$ **do**
  $u \leftarrow$ parent(v);
  if *v is a left or right child* **then**
    update(u);
    if $v^{[2]} < u^{[2]}$ **then**
      promote(v); update(u);
    else $v \leftarrow u$;
  else if $v^{[2]} < u^{[2]}$ **then**
    promote(v); update(v);
  else break

the promotion, there is a violation of Lemma 2.3(ii) between v and its new parent, whose label is $(\downarrow, 6)$ (see (c)), resulting in another promotion. There is now violation of the heap property with the root node (see (d)), causing a final promotion. At this point v is the root, and we obtain the final tree (see (e)).

The following lemmas establish the correctness and running time of this procedure. The proof involves a straightforward induction involving a case analysis of the relationships between the labels of nodes before and after each promotion. Together, they establish Theorem 1.1(i).

LEMMA 3.1. *After inserting a point and applying Algorithm 1, the quadtreap satisfies Lemma 2.3.*

LEMMA 3.2. *The time to insert a point in a quadtreap of size n and height h is $O(h)$. Thus, the insertion time is $O(\log n)$ with high probability.*

PROOF. The promotion and updating of priority values can be performed in $O(1)$ time per node. The time needed to locate the point to be inserted is $O(h)$. The time to insert the point is $O(1)$. Since the algorithm traces the path from the insertion point to the root, the time to perform the restoration of the heap properties by Algorithm 1 is $O(h)$. Thus, the entire insertion time is $O(h)$. By Theorem 2.1, $h = O(\log n)$ time with high probability. □

3.3 Point Deletion

Next, we consider the deletion of a point, p. We first determine the leaf node v containing this point. We handle deletion by reversing the insertion process. In particular, we effectively set the deleted point's priority to $\uparrow$ by assigning v a label of $(\uparrow, \uparrow)$. We then restructure the tree, described below, so that the properties of Lemmas 2.3 are satisfied. Because of p's high priority, the tree's structure would be the same as if p had been the last point to be inserted. When viewed from the perspective of pseudo-nodes, when a point is inserted into the tree, it is placed within a leaf cell that is the right child of its parent, and its two siblings are both leaves. To establish this claim, observe first that v cannot be an outer child because the cell associated with an outer child has an inner box. Since v contains a point, it cannot also contain an inner box. Also, v cannot be a left child since this would violate Lemma 2.3(i). Therefore, v is the right child of its parent. To show that v's siblings are leaves, note that by the node-labeling rule, v's parent's second label component is $\uparrow$. If its siblings were not leaves, their second label components would be strictly smaller than this,

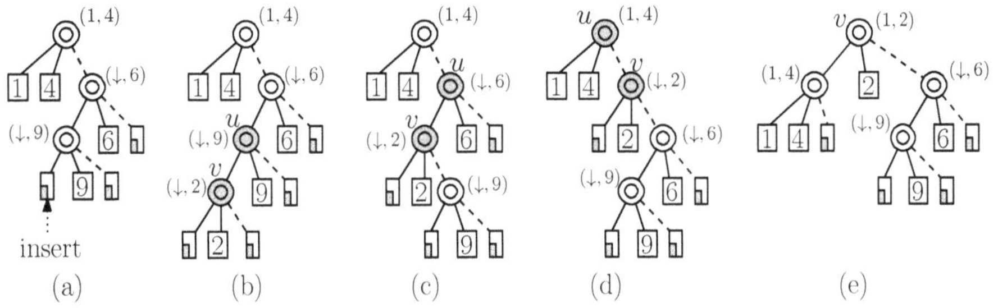

Figure 7: Example of quadtreap restructuring after insertion.

thus violating property (ii) of Lemma 2.3. Therefore, after restructuring, we can delete p by simply "undoing" the insertion procedure by replacing the subtree rooted at v's parent with a single leaf node. All that remains is to describe the above restructuring process. This is given in Algorithm 2.

Algorithm 2: Restructuring the tree as part of the deletion of a point in a leaf node v.

```
1  label(v) ← (↑, ↑);
2  r ← parent(v);
3  while r ≠ null do
4      u ← r;  r ← parent(r);
5      update(u);
6      w ← left(u);  x ← outer(u);
7      while w^[2] < u^[2] or x^[2] < u^[2] do
8          if w^[2] < x^[2] then
9              promote(w);  update(u);
10             w ← left(u);
11         else
12             promote(x)  update(x);
13             x ← outer(u);
```

An example of the restructuring for the deletion process is shown in Fig. 8. (For ease of illustration, let us assume that priorities are positive integers.) The point to be deleted lies in node v (see (a)). We set its label to $(\uparrow, \uparrow)$, set u to v's parent and then invoke the update procedure on line 5 of Algorithm 2. As a result, u's left and right children are swapped, and u's label is updated (see (b)). A sequence of promotions (actually "demotions") is then applied to restore the heap properties (see (c)–(e)). Finally, the subtree rooted at v's parent is replaced by a single leaf node (see (f)).

The following lemmas establish the correctness of this procedure. As with insertion, the proof involves a straightforward induction involving a case analysis of the relationships between the labels of nodes before and after each promotion.

THEOREM 3.1. *After deleting a point and applying the restructuring procedure of Algorithm 2, the quadtreap satisfies Lemma 2.3.*

Deletion requires $O(\log^2 n)$ time. Intuitively, the reason that deletion is more complicated than insertion is because the deleted node's priority may exist among the label components along the entire search path to the root. (Consider, for example, the deletion of the point with the lowest priority in the tree.) Deleting the point involves updating the label of each such node. Each update may result in $O(\log n)$ promotions.

LEMMA 3.3. *The time to delete a point from a quadtreap of size n and height h is $O(h^2)$. Thus, the deletion time is $O(\log^2 n)$ with high probability.*

PROOF. The promotion and updating of each label can be performed in time $O(1)$. Each iteration of the inner loop of Algorithm 2 takes time proportional to the height of node u. This inner loop may be repeated for each ancestor of the leaf v containing the deleted point. Therefore, the total deletion time is at most $O(h^2)$. Since the depth of the tree by Theorem 2.1 is $O(\log n)$ with high probability, the deletion time is $O(\log^2 n)$, also with high probability. □

The worst case scenario for point deletion is rather pessimistic. The following lemma shows that the expected time to delete a random point of the tree is linear in the tree's height. The expectation is over the choices of which point to delete, whereas the high-probability bound is over the assignment of priorities. This establishes Theorem 1.1(ii).

LEMMA 3.4. *The expected time to delete a random point from a quadtreap T of size n and height h is $O(h)$. Thus, the expected deletion time is $O(\log n)$ with high probability*

PROOF. Before giving the proof, we begin with a useful observation. Consider a node u visited in an arbitrary iteration of the outer while loop of Algorithm 2 during the deletion of some point p. We claim that the inner loop will be entered only if p's priority is among the two smallest in the subtree rooted at u. First, observe u is an ancestor of the leaf containing p. The second component of u's label is equal to the second smallest priority in u's subtree, which implies that this component's value can be changed only if p has one of the two smallest priorities in u's subtree. If this observation holds for p and u, p applies a charge to u.

Define an indicator variable, $\chi(u, p)$ as follows.

$$\chi(u,p) = \begin{cases} 1 & \text{if } p \text{ charges } u, \\ 0 & \text{otherwise.} \end{cases}$$

Thus, the expected deletion time t is

$$E(t) \le \frac{1}{n} \sum_{p \in P} \sum_{u \in T} \mathit{height}(u) \cdot \chi(u,p).$$

Each node is charged by at most two points, and thus,

$$\begin{aligned} E(t) &\le \frac{1}{n} \sum_{u \in T} 2 \cdot \mathit{height}(u) \le \frac{1}{n} \cdot n \cdot 2h \\ &= O(h) = O(\log n), \end{aligned}$$

as desired. □

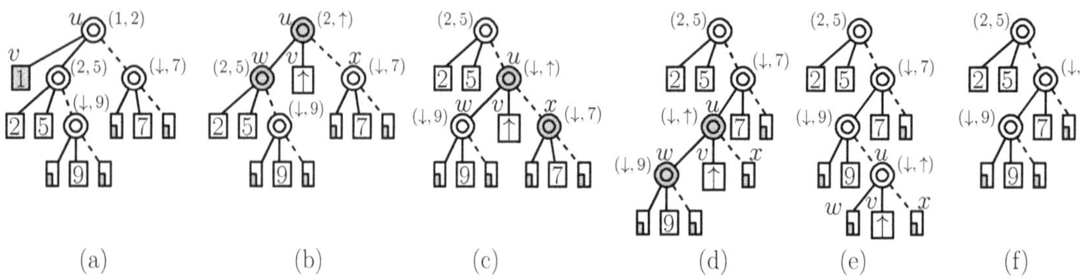

Figure 8: Example of deletion from a quadtreap.

4. APPROXIMATE RANGE QUERIES

In this section we present an algorithm for answering approximate range-counting queries using the quadtreap. Recall the problem description from Section 1. Because promotions will not be needed here, most of the description here will be based on the simpler representation of the tree as a BD-tree with split and shrink nodes.

In order to provide efficient response to queries, we will need to add a couple of enhancements to the basic data structure. Before discussing these enhancements, let us recall that we are given a set P of n points $\mathbb{R}^d$, for fixed d. Let $\mathrm{wgt}(p)$ denote the weight of point p. Recall that a query is presented in the form of two convex shapes, an inner range and outer range, Q^- and Q^+, respectively, whose boundaries are separated by a distance of at least $\varepsilon \cdot \mathrm{diam}(Q)$. Let T be a BD-tree storing these points, and let h denote its height. For the sake of generality, we will express running times (deterministically) in terms of n, h, and ε, but as shown in the previous sections, if the BD-tree is a quadtreap, then h will be $O(\log n)$ with high probability. Our best results are for range counting where the weights are drawn from a commutative group, but we will also consider the case of commutative semigroups and range reporting.

The first enhancement to the tree is to maintain at each node v the total weight of the points in the associated subtree. Given a node v, let P_v denote the points of P lying within v's subtree, and let $\mathrm{wgt}(v)$ denote their total weight. Observe that this sum can be updated as points are inserted or deleted, without altering the construction time or space bounds.

The second enhancement is a structural addition to the tree. To motivate the addition, it is useful to recall how approximate range queries are answered in partition trees. We apply a standard top-down recursive algorithm (see for example [3]). Starting at the root, let v denote the current node being visited. We compare v's cell C to the range. If the cell lies outside the inner range or inside the outer range or is a leaf, we can process it in $O(1)$ time. Otherwise, we recurse on its children. (See the code block.)

The key issue in analyzing the algorithm is determining the number of internal nodes that are *expanded*, which means that a recursive call is made to the node's two children. Recall that the *size* of a cell in the tree is the maximum side length of its outer box. The analysis classifies expanded nodes as being of two types: *large nodes* are those whose cell size is at least $2 \cdot \mathrm{diam}(Q)$, and remainder are called *small nodes*. To understand the issue, recall the analysis of the small expanded nodes given in [3]. It relies on an crucial property of the BBD-tree, namely that whenever the search

Procedure range(v, Q)

```
C ← cell(v);
if C ∩ Q⁻ = ∅ then return 0;
else if C ⊆ Q⁺ then return wgt(v);
else if v is a leaf then
  | if v contains a point in Q then return wgt(p);
  | else return 0;
else if v is a split node then
  | return range(left(v), Q) + range(right(v), Q);
else // v is a shrink node
  └ return range(inner(v), Q) + range(outer(v), Q);
```

descends a constant number of levels, the size of the associated cells decreases by a constant factor. This property holds for the binary quadtree, since with each d levels of descent in the tree, every side is bisected and so the cell size is halved. However, this generally does not hold for BD-tree. The problem arises from the fact that a the outer child of a shrink node has the same outer box as its parent. Thus, there may arbitrarily long chains of shrink nodes, for which the cell size does not decrease. We define a *shrink chain* to be a maximal sequence of shrink nodes, where each node is the outer child of its predecessor.

We fix this problem by adding a special pointer, called a *link*, which points from the first node of each shrink chain to its last node (see Fig. 9). We also assume that each node of the tree stores a pointer to its parent. A BD-tree with all the above enhancements (internal weights, parent pointers, and links) is called an *augmented BD-tree.* A quadtreap based on such a tree is called an *augmented quadtreap.*

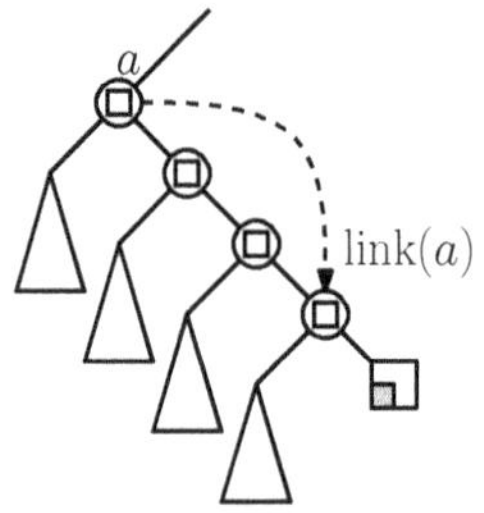

Figure 9: A link.

In Section 3.1 we discussed promotions. It is easy to modify the promotion process to maintain node weights and links. To see this, let us briefly return to the pseudo-node view of the tree. Consider the operation promote(y), where y is the left child of some node x (recall Fig. 6). Let w be y's outer child. The associated weights $\mathrm{wgt}(x)$ and $\mathrm{wgt}(y)$ can be updated by assigning each the sum of the weights of their new children. The links are updated as follows. Prior to the promotion, x and y may each have been the head of some shrink chain. Therefore, each may have a link. If y was the first node of a shrink chain prior to the promotion, w is now the head of this chain, and so w is assigned y's old link. If x was the first node of a shrink chain prior to the promotion, y now becomes the first node of the chain after the promotion, and so y is assigned x's old link. The modifications for the promotion of an outer child are symmetrical. (In particular, x is assigned y's old link, and y is assigned w's old link.)

Let us see how the link is used in answering range searching. Given an augmented tree, when the search arrives at the start of a shrink chain and the node is small, rather than descending the chain from top to bottom, as the above search algorithm would, it will traverse the chain from bottom to top. Why does this work? Recall from Section 2 our invariant that, if the cell of a shrink node has an inner box, the shrinking box properly contains this inner box. This implies that, when considered from bottom to top, the sizes of the inner boxes decrease monotonically. This is exactly the property we desire when visiting small nodes.

There is a simple and elegant way in which to implement the modified search algorithm. The algorithm is exactly as described above, but whenever we visit a small shrink node, we "redefine" the meanings of the various tree primitives for each node: left, right, cell, and weight. To motivate this modification, observe that it is possible to transform each shrink chain, into one in which each node in the transformed sequence is the inner child of its parent (see Fig. 10). Let T^* denote the resulting transformed tree.[1] Note that this transformed tree exists merely for conceptual purposes (we do not actually modify the tree).

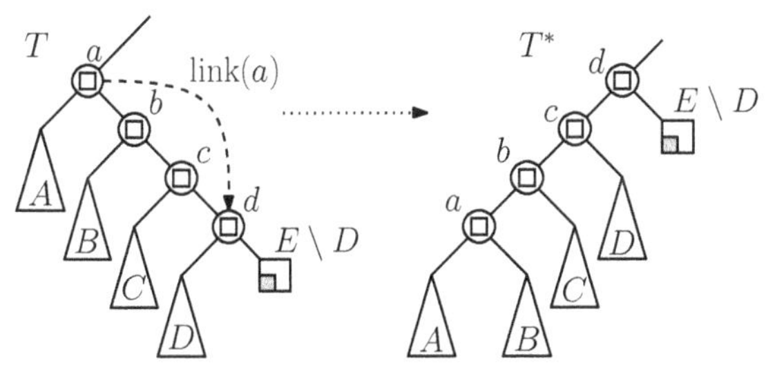

Figure 10: A shrink chain and the transformed tree.

As mentioned above, this transformation can be achieved "on the fly" by appropriately redefining the primitive tree operations as the range search algorithm is running. The algorithm proceeds as before, but whenever a shrink node is first encountered, we save this node, which is called the *head* of the chain (labeled "a" in Fig. 10). We then immediately follow its link to obtain the next node to be visited by the search. As long as we continue to visit shrink nodes, we apply the alternate definitions of the various tree primitives given in Fig. 11. On returning to a leaf or split node, we return to the standard definitions. Note that the modified weight function requires the use of a subtraction operator.

For example, in Fig. 10, in the tree T^* the outer child of

[1]The conversion of each shrink chain can be viewed as arising from a series of promotions to the nodes of the shrink chain, but, since we are not considering nodes at the level of pseudo-nodes here, the resulting transformed tree does not satisfy the shrink-split property. Nonetheless, it is equivalent to the original tree from the perspective of the subdivision of space that it defines, and thus it is a valid BD-tree. This is the only property that the range-search procedure requires.

$$\begin{aligned}
\text{inner}^*(v) &\equiv (v = \textit{head})\ ?\ \text{inner}(v) : \text{parent}(v)\\
\text{outer}^*(v) &\equiv (\text{outer}(v) \text{ is a leaf})\ ?\\
&\quad\ \text{outer}(v) : \text{inner}(\text{outer}(v))\\
\text{cell}^*(v) &\equiv (\text{outer}(v) \text{ is a leaf})\ ?\\
&\quad\ \text{cell}(\textit{head}) : \text{cell}(\textit{head}) \setminus \text{cell}(\text{outer}(\text{outer}(v)))\\
\text{wgt}^*(v) &\equiv (\text{outer}(v) \text{ is a leaf})\ ?\\
&\quad\ \text{wgt}(\textit{head}) : \text{wgt}(\textit{head}) - \text{wgt}(\text{outer}(\text{outer}(v)))
\end{aligned}$$

Figure 11: Redefined tree primitives.

b is C, which is equivalent to inner(outer(b)) in the original tree T, and this matches the definition of outer$^*(b)$.

Because the search algorithm does not rely on the shrink-split property, establishing correctness of the modified range-search algorithm involves showing that the modified primitives achieve the desired transformation.

LEMMA 4.1. *Given a set of points with weights drawn from a commutative group and an augmented BD-tree storing these points (which need not satisfy the shrink-split property), the modified query algorithm correctly returns a count that includes all the points lying inside the inner range and excludes all the points lying outside the outer range.*

The transformed tree T^* satisfies the property that the cell sizes decrease by a constant factor with every constant number of levels of descent. The original tree T is of height h. It follows from a straightforward generalization of the analysis of [3] (using T for the large expanded nodes and T^* for the small expanded nodes) that the query time is $O(h + (1/\varepsilon)^{d-1})$. Because the use of wgt* requires subtraction, this query time applies only if the weights are drawn from a group. In the case of semigroup weights, we perform the entire query in T. In the absence of the size-decreasing property, the query time that results is the product (not the sum) of h and $(1/\varepsilon)^{d-1}$. (Answering an approximate range query can be reduced to $O((1/\varepsilon)^{d-1})$ cell queries in T [14], each of which takes $O(h)$ time.)

The above query algorithm (for the group case) can be adapted to answer range reporting queries. Whenever we encounter a node whose cell lies entirely inside Q^+, rather than returning the sum of the weights of the points in this node, the algorithm traverses the associated subtree and enumerates all its points.

Summarizing all of these observations, we have the following result, which establishes Theorem 1.1(iii) and (iv).

THEOREM 4.1. *Consider a set of n points in $\mathbb{R}^d$ that have been stored in an augmented BD-tree of height h. Then, for any $\varepsilon > 0$ and any convex range Q satisfying the unit-cost assumption:*

(i) If the point weights are drawn from a commutative group, it is possible to answer ε-approximate range counting queries in time $O(h + (1/\varepsilon)^{d-1})$.

(ii) If the point weights are drawn from a commutative semigroup, it is possible to answer ε-approximate counting queries in time $O(h \cdot (1/\varepsilon)^{d-1})$.

(iii) It is possible to answer ε-approximate range reporting queries in time $O(h + (1/\varepsilon)^{d-1} + k)$, where k is the number of points reported.

5. NEAREST NEIGHBOR QUERIES

In this section we briefly outline how to answer approximate nearest neighbor queries in BD-trees. To do so, we assume that the tree is augmented with the link pointers of the previous section. We also assume that each internal node u of the tree stores an arbitrary one of its descendant points, called its *representative*. (A convenient choice is the point that provides the value of $u^{[2]}$.) This point can be maintained throughout our update procedures.

Let T denote the BD-tree, and let h denote its height. Let q denote the query point, and let ε denote the desired approximation factor. Observe that approximate nearest neighbor searching can be reduced to approximate spherical range emptiness queries. By invoking the algorithm of [4] on the BD-tree, it is possible to compute a factor-2 approximation $\widehat{r}$ to the nearest neighbor distance in $O(h)$ time. (There is no need to deal with the transformed tree T^*, since only large nodes are visited.) From this, it is possible to compute an ε-approximate nearest neighbor by employing a bisecting search over the interval $[\widehat{r}/2, \widehat{r}]$. The resulting query time is $O((h + (1/\varepsilon)^{d-1}) \log(1/\varepsilon))$.

We can eliminate the additional factor of $O(\log(1/\varepsilon))$ by employing a more careful search. The idea is to run a type of breadth-first search based on the sizes of the cells involved. Given the value of $\widehat{r}$, it is possible in $O(\log n)$ time to determine a constant number of maximal nodes (depending on dimension) of size at most $2\widehat{r}$ whose cells form a disjoint cover of the ball of radius $\widehat{r}$ centered at q. These form an initial set of *active nodes*. We maintain a variable r, which holds the distance from q to the closest representative so far. Initially, $r = \widehat{r}$. We keep the active nodes in a priority queue, sorted by decreasing cell sizes. We process each active node as follows. First, if its representative is closer to q than r, we update the value of r. If the distance from q to the node's cell is greater than $r/(1+\varepsilon)$, we discard it. Otherwise, we expand the node by placing its two children in the priority queue of active cells. As in the previous section, all shrink node expansions are performed in the transformed tree T^* (thus, all nodes are treated as if they are small nodes). We apply this until no active nodes remain.

As shown in [4], the search is guaranteed to stop when the sizes of the cells being processed is smaller than $\varepsilon r/\sqrt{d}$, which is as least $\varepsilon\widehat{r}/2\sqrt{d}$. There are $O(\log(1/\varepsilon))$ different quadtree cell size possible in the range from $\widehat{r}$ down to $\varepsilon\widehat{r}/2\sqrt{d}$. We implement the priority queue as an array of lists, which allows us to perform each priority queue operation in $O(1)$ time (with a one-time additive cost of $O(\log(1/\varepsilon))$. Although space does not permit, it can be shown that (even with the dynamically varying radius r) the total number of nodes expanded is $O(1/\varepsilon^{d-1})$. We obtain the following result, which establishes Theorem 1.1(v).

THEOREM 5.1. *Consider a set of n points in $\mathbb{R}^d$ that have been stored in an augmented BD-tree of height h. Then, for any $\varepsilon > 0$, it is possible to answer ε-approximate nearest neighbor queries in time $O(h + (1/\varepsilon)^{d-1})$.*

Acknowledgments

We would like to thank Guilherme da Fonseca for suggesting the original motivating application for this work and the reviewers for their many helpful suggestions.

6. REFERENCES

[1] A. Andersson. General balanced trees. *J. Algorithms*, 30:1–18, 1999.
[2] S. Arya and D. M. Mount. Algorithms for fast vector quantization. In *Data Compression Conference*, pages 381–390. IEEE Press, 1993.
[3] S. Arya and D. M. Mount. Approximate range searching. *Comput. Geom. Theory Appl.*, 17:135–163, 2001.
[4] S. Arya, D. M. Mount, N. S. Netanyahu, R. Silverman, and A. Wu. An optimal algorithm for approximate nearest neighbor searching. *J. Assoc. Comput. Mach.*, 45:891–923, 1998.
[5] M. Bern. Approximate closest-point queries in high dimensions. *Inform. Process. Lett.*, 45:95–99, 1993.
[6] S. N. Bespamyatnikh. Dynamic algorithms for approximate neighbor searching. In *Proc. Eighth Canad. Conf. Comput. Geom.*, pages 252–257, 1996.
[7] T. Chan. A minimalist's implementation of an approximate nearest neighbor algorithm in fixed dimensions. (See `http://www.cs.uwaterloo.ca/-~tmchan/pub.html`), 2006.
[8] T. M. Chan. Closest-point problems simplified on the RAM. In *Proc. 13th Annu. ACM-SIAM Sympos. Discrete Algorithms*, pages 472–473, 2002.
[9] K. L. Clarkson. Fast algorithms for the all nearest neighbors problem. In *Proc. 24th Annu. IEEE Sympos. Found. Comput. Sci.*, pages 226–232, 1983.
[10] R. Cole and U. Vishkin. The accelerated centroid decomposition technique for optimal parallel tree evaluation in logarithmic time. *Algorithmica*, 3:329–346, 2005.
[11] M. de Berg, M. van Kreveld, M. Overmars, and O. Schwarzkopf. *Computational Geometry: Algorithms and Applications*. Springer-Verlag, Berlin, Germany, 3rd edition, 2008.
[12] C. A. Duncan. *Balanced Aspect Ratio Trees*. PhD dissertation, Johns Hopkins University, Department of Computer Science, 1999.
[13] C. A. Duncan, M. T. Goodrich, and S. Kobourov. Balanced aspect ratio trees: Combining the advantages of k-d trees and octrees. *J. Algorithms*, 38:303–333, 2001.
[14] D. Eppstein, M. T. Goodrich, and J. Z. Sun. The skip quadtree: A simple dynamic data structure for multidimensional data. *Intl. J. Comp. Geom. Appl.*, 18:131–160, 2008.
[15] I. Gargantini. An effective way to represent quadtrees. *Commun. ACM*, 25:905–910, 1982.
[16] S. Har-Peled. Notes on geometric approximation algorithms. (`http://valis.cs.uiuc.edu/~sariel/-teach/notes/aprx/`), 2009.
[17] W. Pugh. Skip lists: A probabilistic alternative to balanced trees. *Commun. ACM*, 33:668–676, 1990.
[18] H. Samet. *Foundations of Multidimensional and Metric Data Structures*. Morgan-Kaufmann, San Francisco, 2006.
[19] R. Seidel and C. Aragon. Randomized search trees. *Algorithmica*, 16:464–497, 1996.
[20] D. D. Sleator and R. E. Tarjan. A data structure for dynamic trees. *J. Comput. Sys. Sci.*, 26:362–391, 1983.

The Tidy Set: A Minimal Simplicial Set for Computing Homology of Clique Complexes*

[Extended Abstract]

Afra Zomorodian
Department of Computer Science
Dartmouth College
Hanover, New Hampshire
afra@cs.dartmouth.edu

ABSTRACT

We introduce the tidy set, a minimal simplicial set that captures the topology of a simplicial complex. The tidy set is particularly effective for computing the homology of clique complexes. This family of complexes include the Vietoris-Rips complex and the weak witness complex, methods that are popular in topological data analysis. The key feature of our approach is that it skips constructing the clique complex. We give algorithms for constructing tidy sets, implement them, and present experiments. Our preliminary results show that tidy sets are orders of magnitude smaller than clique complexes, giving us a homology engine with small memory requirements.

Categories and Subject Descriptors

I.3.5 [**Computer Graphics**]: Computational Geometry and Object Modeling—*Curve, surface, solid, and object representations*; F.2.2 [**Analysis of Algorithms and Problem Complexity**]: Nonnumerical Algorithms and Problems—*Computations on discrete structures*

General Terms

Algorithms, Theory

Keywords

computational topology, Vietoris-Rips complex, witness complex, simplicial set

*Research by the author was partially supported by DARPA HR 0011-06-1-0038, ONR N 00014-08-1-0908, and NSF CAREER CCF-0845716.

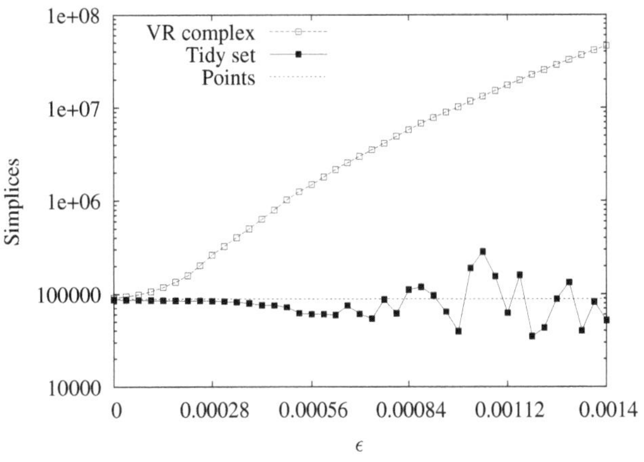

Figure 1: Size of the Vietoris-Rips complex versus the tidy set at scale ϵ for dataset D in Section 5.1, a set of 88,571 points in $\mathbb{R}^3$. Note: y-axis is log scale.

1. INTRODUCTION

In this paper, we introduce the tidy set, a minimal simplicial set that captures the topology of a simplicial complex. We give algorithms for computing the tidy set, implement the algorithms, and present preliminary experimental results. Our method is particularly effective computing the homology of clique complexes without first constructing them. To inspire the reader, Figure 1 compares computing homology of a point set with a clique complex, the Vietoris-Rips complex, versus the tidy set. At the highest scale ϵ, the standard method constructs a simplicial complex with 46M simplices. Our method produces a simplicial set that has the same homology but is nearly three orders of magnitude smaller. With only 51K simplices, this tidy set is even smaller than the input point set. Our method is also five times faster than the standard method.

1.1 Motivation

We are motivated by *topological data analysis*, where the goal is recovering the lost topology of sampled data [31]. The standard recovery process has two steps: First, we approximate the underlying space of data using a combinatorial structure; Second, we compute topological invariants of this structure, such as homology. There are a number of methods for completing the first step, such as the Čech complex [15], the alpha complex [10], and the flow complex [12], to name a few. These methods, especially when geometric in nature, do not scale to large datasets or extend to high dimensions. For example, we currently do not have efficient software for computing the alpha complex in dimensions higher than three. There are currently two methods used in practice. The Vietoris-Rips complex [14] is popular due to its algorithmic simplicity, but yields massive non-embedded complexes even for small point sets. The (weak) witness complex [9] mitigates the problem of size by only approximating the topology over a subset of the data. Both of these complexes are clique complexes of certain graphs. Therefore, our goal is to find methods for computing homology of clique complexes of large datasets. We do so by computing a minimal simplicial set directly from the graph itself without first constructing the clique complex. We call this simplicial set the tidy set.

1.2 Prior Work

A common assumption in topological analysis is that step one – constructing a complex – is easy, while step two – computing homology – is hard. This assumption is somewhat justified since the classic *reduction algorithm* for computing homology over integers has supercubical complexity in the size of the complex [28]. Over field coefficients, reduction simplifies to Gaussian elimination, still having quadratic space and cubic time complexity. It is a reasonable strategy to search for heuristics that reduce the size of the complex while preserving its topology. There have been a number of reduction techniques proposed for different categories of structures. For simplicial complexes, the earliest and perhaps simplest method is *elementary contraction*, proposed by Whitehead in defining the simple homotopy type [29]. A stronger technique is the recent *LC-reduction* [5] that produces not only a homotopic, but isomorphic complex [19, 1]. Both these techniques produce simplicial complexes with fewer simplices. Due to the popularity of simplicial complexes in computational topology, the techniques have been widely used.

For *cubical complexes*, the CHomP project [4] has examined a large number of heuristics over the years, resulting in an array of homology engines [16]. Our methods in this paper are analogous to those by Mrozek et al. [22]. Our work was done independently from this group and applies to arbitrary-dimensional simplicial complexes, not three-dimensional cubical complexes. The primary characteristic that unifies both works is using cell collapses. This reduction moves us from the familiar simplicial complex category to the unfamiliar simplicial set category. The only instance of simplicial sets in computational topology that we know of is Perry [24] who describes an implementation of simplicial sets and an algorithm for computing their homology.

1.3 Our Approach

Our approach is based on our experience in applying topological techniques to problems in a number of areas, such as shape description [6], biophysics [17], and computer vision [2]. We find that the opposite of the traditional assumption is true: Constructing a complex is hard as non-embedded complexes, such as clique complexes, can get very large, very fast, requiring large construction time and storage. Also, computing homology over fields is easy using the *persistence algorithm* [33] as it represents matrices sparsely, resulting in linear time behavior. A significant repercussion of these two observations is that standard reduction techniques are not competitive for us. We spend most of time building a massive complex, not computing its homology.

Our approach, then, is to avoid constructing the full complex by reducing it *during* its construction. We make reduction techniques effective by applying them to high-dimensional simplices only as simplices have exponential complexity. We maintain a compact representation of the structure throughout computation and postpone enumerating the structure and computing its homology as long as possible.

The contributions of this paper are as follows. In Section 3, we define the tidy set, a minimal simplicial set that has the same homology as an input simplicial complex. In Section 4, we give algorithms for computing the tidy set as well as for computing homology of clique complexes directly. In Section 5, we give preliminary results of our implementation of the algorithms, including computing homology of point sets using the Vietoris-Rips complex. Our implementation can process large datasets in arbitrary dimensions, datasets that are currently not handled by any existing software. It is also fast, takes less memory, and produces tidy sets that are orders of magnitude smaller, often sublinear in input size.

2. BACKGROUND

We begin with a review of simplicial complexes and their generalization, simplicial sets. We are interested in simplicial sets that may be derived from simplicial complexes via collapses, which we describe next. We then describe homology for both categories. We end this section with clique complexes, the family of complexes whose homology we wish to compute. For an accessible introduction to computational topology, see [31].

2.1 Simplicial Complex

A *simplicial complex* is a set K of finite sets, closed under the subset relation: If $\sigma \in K$ and $\tau \subseteq \sigma$, then $\tau \in K$. We then say that τ is a *face* of σ, its *coface*. A simplex is *maximal* if it has no proper coface in K. If $\sigma \in K$ has cardinality $|\sigma| = k+1$, we call σ a *k-simplex* of *dimension* k, denoted $\dim \sigma = k$. K is d-dimensional if $d = \dim K = \max_{\sigma \in K} \dim \sigma$. Given a subset $L \subseteq K$, L is a *subcomplex* if it is a simplicial complex. Otherwise, the smallest subcomplex containing L is its *closure* under subset: $\mathrm{Cl}\, L = \{\tau \in K \mid \tau \subseteq \sigma \in L\}$. A key subcomplex is the *k-skeleton* consisting of simplices in K of dimension less than or equal to k.

2.2 Simplicial Set

A *simplicial set*, initially called the *complete semi-simplicial complex* or *c.s.s. complex*, generalizes a simplicial complex to model a well-behaved topological space [8, 11, 20]. Informally, a simplicial set is like a simplicial complex where simplices may be collapsed to a point, and vertices may be identified. Formally, a *simplicial set* X is a collection of sets $\{X_n\}_n$ together with maps

$$d_i \colon X_n \to X_{n-1},$$
$$s_i \colon X_n \to X_{n+1},$$

for $0 \leq i \leq n$, that satisfy the following identities:

$$
\begin{aligned}
d_i \circ d_j &= d_{j-1} \circ d_i, \quad \text{if } i < j. \\
s_i \circ s_j &= s_{j+1} \circ s_i, \quad \text{if } i \leq j. \\
d_i \circ s_j &= \begin{cases} s_{j-1} \circ d_i, & \text{if } i < j, \\ 1_{X_n}, & \text{if } i = j \text{ or } i = j+1, \\ s_j \circ d_{i-1}, & \text{if } i > j+1, \end{cases}
\end{aligned}
$$

where 1_{X_n} is the identity on X_n. An element of X_n is an *n-simplex*, the map d_i is the *ith face operator*, and s_i is the *ith degeneracy operator* [8, 20]. Simplicial sets may be elegantly reinterpreted in the language of category theory [13].

In this paper, we are interested simplicial sets that are derived from simplicial complexes, such as the seven 2-simplices in Figure 2. Let K be a simplicial complex and denote its n-simplices by K_n. We assume that the vertices in each simplex are ordered. For instance, a total order on the vertices in the complex implies an order for each simplex. We define the simplicial set X that corresponds to simplicial complex K inductively:

$$
\begin{aligned}
X_0 &= K_0, \\
X_n &= K_n \cup \cup_i^n s_i(X_{n-1}), \quad n > 0.
\end{aligned}
$$

The ith face operator d_i deletes the ith vertex, and the ith degeneracy operator s_i repeats it:

$$
\begin{aligned}
d_i([v_0, \ldots, v_n]) &= [v_0, \ldots, \hat{v}_i, \ldots, v_n], \\
s_i([v_0, \ldots, v_n]) &= [v_0, \ldots, v_i, v_i, \ldots, v_n].
\end{aligned}
$$

It is easy to verify that these operators satisfy the simplicial identities. A simplex that may be written as $s_i(\sigma)$ for some σ is *degenerate* and is not in the simplicial complex. Otherwise, the simplex is *non-degenerate*.

Example 1 (triangle) Consider the triangle abc in Figure 2. As a simplicial complex K, abc has

$$
\begin{aligned}
K_0 &= \{a, b, c\}, \\
K_1 &= \{ab, bc, ac\}, \\
K_2 &= \{abc\},
\end{aligned}
$$

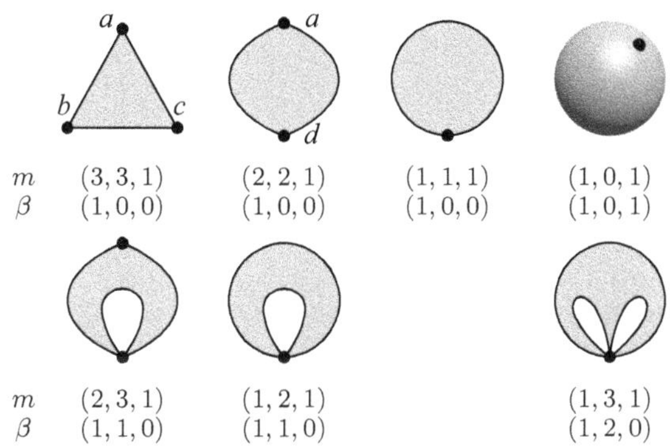

Figure 2: The 7 possible 2-simplices in a simplicial set. The triangle is the only one allowed in a complex. The rest have collapsed edges (top row), identified vertices (bottom row), or both. The vector m counts the non-degenerate simplices and the vector β holds the Betti numbers.

where we denote simplices as strings for brevity. As a simplicial set X, abc has

$$
\begin{aligned}
X_0 &= \{a, b, c\}, \\
X_1 &= \{ab, bc, ac, aa, bb, cc\}, \\
X_2 &= \{abc, aab, abb, bbc, bcc, aac, acc, aaa, bbb, ccc\}.
\end{aligned}
$$

Note the addition of degenerate simplices. For example, abb may be viewed as a collapsed triangle.

2.3 Simplicial Collapse

Simplicial sets may be constructed directly, but we are interested in sets that is derived from complexes by collapses only. Given a simplicial set X and an n-simplex $\sigma \in X$, the *collapse* of σ identifies it to a single point, giving us a new simplicial set $X' = X/\sigma$. To construct X', we introduce a new vertex v and replace σ, its faces, and its degeneracies, with the degeneracies of v. We first gather its non-degenerate k-faces inductively for $k \geq 0$:

$$
\bar{F}_k(\sigma) = \begin{cases} \emptyset, & \text{if } k > n, \\ \{\sigma\}, & \text{if } k = n, \\ \cup_{i=0}^{k+1} d_i(\bar{F}_{k+1}(\sigma)), & \text{if } k < n. \end{cases}
$$

By adding the degenerate faces, we get all the faces.

$$
F_k(\sigma) = \begin{cases} \bar{F}_0(\sigma), & \text{if } k = 0, \\ \bar{F}_k(\sigma) \cup \bigcup_{i=0}^{k-1} s_i(F_{k-1}(\sigma)), & \text{if } k > 0. \end{cases}
$$

We may now define the k-simplices for X' as

$$
X'_k = (X_k - F_k(\sigma)) \cup \{s_0^k(v)\},
$$

where s_0^k denotes applying the degeneracy operator k times. We next define the operators for the new set:

$$
\begin{aligned}
d'_i(\tau) &= \begin{cases} d_i(\tau), & \text{if } d_i(\tau) \notin F_{i-1}(\sigma), \\ s_0^{i-1}(v), & \text{otherwise.} \end{cases} \\
s'_i(\tau) &= \begin{cases} s_i(\tau), & \text{if } s_i(\tau) \notin F_{i+1}(\sigma), \\ s_0^{i+1}(v), & \text{otherwise.} \end{cases}
\end{aligned}
$$

Example 2 (2-gon) In Example 1, we listed the n-simplices of the triangle abc in Figure 2 as a simplicial set X. We now collapse edge bc to a new vertex d to get the 2-gon $X' = ad$ in the figure. We have

$$
\begin{aligned}
\bar{F}_2(bc) &= \emptyset, \\
\bar{F}_1(bc) &= \{bc\}, \\
\bar{F}_0(bc) &= F_0(bc) = \{b, c\}, \\
F_1(bc) &= \{bc, bb, cc\}, \\
F_2(bc) &= \{bbc, bcc, bbb, ccc\}, \\
X'_0 &= \{a, d\}, \\
X'_1 &= \{ab, ac, aa, dd\}, \\
X'_2 &= \{abc, aab, abb, aac, acc, aaa, ddd\}.
\end{aligned}
$$

The operators follow easily, e.g. $d'_0(abc) = dd$.

Generally, we may also identify vertices in constructing simplicial sets. While we do not use vertex identifications in this paper, vertices may be identified by collapsed neighbors.

2.4 Simplicial Homology

Simplicial homology extends naturally to simplicial sets. Let X be a simplicial set. The *nth chain group* $C_n(X)$ of X is the free Abelian group on K's set of oriented, non-degenerate, n-simplices. The *boundary homomorphism* $\partial_n : C_n(X) \to C_{n-1}(X)$ is the linear extension of

$$\partial_n = \sum_{i=0}^{n} (-1)^i d_i,$$

where d_i are the face operators and a degenerate face is treated as 0. The fundamental property of the boundary homomorphism is that $\partial_n \partial_{n+1} = 0$ for all n.

Example 3 (collapsed ∂) The face operators for our collapsed set in Example 2 give us the correct boundary. For instance, we have $d_0(abc) = dd$, $d_1(abc) = ac$, and $d_2(abc) = ab$, giving us $\partial_2(abc) = -ac + ab$, as dd is degenerate. Taking another boundary, we have

$$\partial_1 \partial_2(abc) = \partial_1(-ac) + \partial_1(ab) = -(d-a) + (d-a) = 0.$$

The boundary homomorphism connects the chain groups into a *chain complex* C_*:

$$\cdots \to C_{n+1}(X) \xrightarrow{\partial_{n+1}} C_n(X) \xrightarrow{\partial_n} C_{n-1}(X) \to \cdots.$$

Given any chain complex, the *nth homology group* is

$$H_n(X) = \ker \partial_n / \operatorname{im} \partial_{n+1}.$$

Homology is a functor that we may apply to C_* to get another sequence H_*:

$$\cdots \to H_{n+1}(X) \xrightarrow{H(\partial_{n+1})} H_n(X) \xrightarrow{H(\partial_n)} H_{n-1}(X) \to \cdots.$$

Given a subset $A \subseteq X$ that is a simplicial set, we may also define the *relative homology groups* $H_n(X, A)$, where we view the subset A as collapsed onto a single point. A *contractible* space has the homotopy type of a point, and it is often convenient for it to have trivial homology in all dimensions, including zero. For this, we define *reduced homology groups* $\tilde{H}_n(X)$, so that $H_0(X) \cong \tilde{H}_0(X) \oplus \mathbb{Z}$ and $H_n(X) \cong \tilde{H}_n(X)$ for $n > 0$. We say that a space X is *acyclic* if it has trivial reduced homology, i.e. $\tilde{H}_n(X) = 0$ for all n. Contractible spaces, such as simplices in a simplicial complex, are acyclic.

We end this section with an integer topological invariant that is coarser than homology, but may be computed by simple counting. Given a simplicial set X, the *Euler characteristic* $\chi(X)$ is

$$\chi(X) = \sum_n (-1)^n c_n = \sum_n (-1)^n \beta_n,$$

where c_n is the number of non-degenerate simplices in X and $\beta_n = \operatorname{rank} H_n(X)$ [15]. The second equality is the *Euler-Poincaré formula* that allows us to conclude that an acyclic space X has $\chi(X) = 1$, such as the three spaces on the left in Figure 2. The figure also lists m_n and β_n for each space and we may confirm the Euler-Poincaré formula readily.

2.5 Clique Complex

Suppose we are given a graph $G = (V, E)$, such as the graph in Figure 3(a). A *clique* is a set of vertices $Q \subseteq V$ that induces a complete subgraph in G. A clique is *maximal* if it cannot be made any larger. Figure 3(a) highlights the 9 maximal cliques of the graph with shaded ovals. The *clique complex* $\mathcal{C}(G)$ has the maximal cliques of G as its maximal simplices [18]. Since subsets of cliques are also cliques, the clique complex is a simplicial complex, as shown in Figure 3(b) for our example. Different graphs give rise to different families of clique complexes.

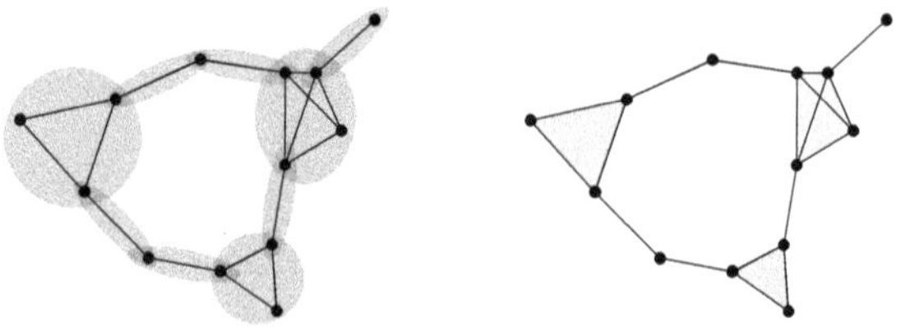

(a) $G = (V, E)$ (b) $\mathcal{C}(G)$

Figure 3: A graph G (a) with shaded ovals highlighting its nine maximal cliques that become maximal simplices in its clique complex $\mathcal{C}(G)$ (b).

Example 4 (Vietoris-Rips) given a finite point set $S \subseteq \mathbb{R}^d$, the *Vietoris-Rips graph (VR graph)* at scale $\epsilon \in \mathbb{R}$ is the geometric graph $G_\epsilon(S) = (S, E_\epsilon(S))$, where $E_\epsilon(S) = \{\{u, v\} \mid \mathrm{d}(u, v) \leq \epsilon, u \neq v \in S\}$. That is, vertices within distance ϵ are connected. The graph in Figure 3(a) is a VR graph. The clique complex of the VR graph is the *Vietoris-Rips complex (VR complex)* [14].

Example 5 (witness) Given a finite point set $S \subseteq \mathbb{R}^d$, choose a subset Alternatively, we may also choose a subset $L \subseteq S$ of *landmarks* and let $W = S - L$. The *witness graph* at scale $\epsilon \in \mathbb{R}$ is the graph $G = (L, E_{\epsilon,L})$, where $\{l_1, l_2\} \in E_{\epsilon,L}$ if there exists a *witness* $w \in W$ that is closer to l_i than any other landmark, and $\mathrm{d}(w, l_i) \leq \epsilon$ for $i = 1, 2$. The clique complex of this graph is the *(weak) witness complex* [9].

Each method defines a one-parameter filtered family of complexes that describe the shape of the point set at different scales. Both methods are currently popular in topological data analysis and motivate our work on clique complexes.

3. TIDY SET

In this section, we define the tidy set, a minimal simplicial complex. We begin by describing two reductions that we use in deriving the tidy set, as previewed in Figure 3. We then describe a minimal representation for simplicial sets. Our representation both simplifies and increases the efficacy of the reductions. We end by showing that the tidy set is minimal with respect to both reductions.

3.1 Reductions

Our first reduction technique is trimming leaves. Intuitively, a leaf in a simplicial complex has an acyclic intersection with the rest of the complex, the intersection being its "stem". We generalize this notion for simplicial sets.

Definition 1 (leaf) *Let X be a simplicial set. A simplex $\sigma \in X$ is a* leaf *if for all n,*

$$H_n(Cl\sigma, Cl\sigma \cap Cl(X - Cl\sigma)) = 0.$$

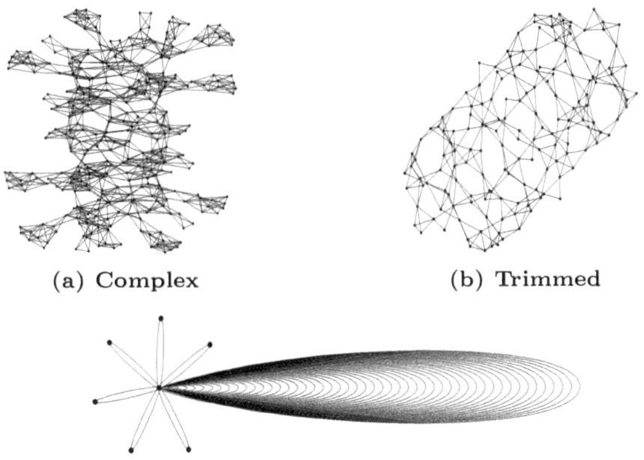

(c) Tidy Set

Figure 4: 1-skeletons of homologous complexes: Complex (a), trimmed complex (b), and tidy set (c) for dataset G in Section 5.1.

Here, $\mathrm{Cl}\,\sigma$ is σ as a simplicial complex, and $\mathrm{Cl}\,(X - \mathrm{Cl}\,\sigma)$ is the rest of the complex. In a simplicial complex, the definition simplifies to our earlier intuition.

Theorem 1 (complex leaf) *Let K be a simplicial complex and $\sigma \in K$ be a leaf. Then for all n,*

$$\tilde{H}_n(Cl\sigma \cap Cl(X - Cl\sigma)) = 0.$$

PROOF. From the definition of a leaf and an application of the Mayer-Vietoris sequence [15], we have

$$H_n(\mathrm{Cl}\,\sigma) \cong H_n(\mathrm{Cl}\,\sigma \cap \mathrm{Cl}\,(X - \mathrm{Cl}\,\sigma))$$

Simplices in simplicial complexes are contractible and therefore acyclic, so $\tilde{H}_n(\mathrm{Cl}\,(\sigma)) = 0$ for all n. □

Leaves may be deleted without any change in homology.

Theorem 2 *Let X be a simplicial set and $\sigma \in X$ be a leaf. Then for all n, $H_n(X) \cong H_n(Cl(X - Cl\sigma))$.*

PROOF. Let $A = \mathrm{Cl}\,(X - \mathrm{Cl}\,\sigma)$ and $B = \mathrm{Cl}\,\sigma$ and note that $X = A \cup B$. By the definition of a leaf, we have $H_n(B, A \cap B) = 0$ for all n. By excision [15, Corollary 2.24], we have $H_n(B, A \cap B) \cong H_n(X, A)$ for all n. Combining, we get $H_n(X, A) = 0$ giving us $H_n(X) \cong H_n(A)$ for all n through Mayer-Vietoris. □

The idea of removing leaves is not new. For instance, it is called *shaving* for full-dimensional cubes within cubical complexes [25]. Deleting is a favored technique as it reduces the size of a complex without changing its category.

Our second reduction technique is collapsing as defined in Section 2.2. Collapsing changes the category of the structure, from a simplicial complex to a simplicial set, but sometimes, does not change its homology:

Theorem 3 (collapse) *Let X be a simplicial set and $\sigma \in X$. If $Cl\sigma$ is acyclic, then for all n, $H_n(X) \cong H_n(X/\sigma)$.*

PROOF. The proof follows [15, Theorem 2.13]. □

3.2 Definition

A key feature of our approach is that we use a minimal description for representing simplicial sets. We narrow our focus to sets that are complexes with collapsed maximal simplices.

Definition 2 ($\mathcal{X}$) *Let Q and C be disjoint sets of maximal sets. Then $\mathcal{X}(Q, C)$ is the simplicial set having the sets in Q as maximal simplices and the sets in C as collapsed maximal simplices. We use the tuple (Q, C) to denote $\mathcal{X}(Q, C)$.*

Our representation is a natural extension of a minimum representation for simplicial complexes, with $\mathcal{X}$ extending closure as the face enumeration operator.

Definition 3 ($\mathcal{Q}$) *Let K be a simplicial complex. We define $\mathcal{Q}(K)$ to be the set of maximal simplices.*

Theorem 4 (representation) *$\mathcal{Q}(K)$ is a unique representation of minimum size for simplicial complex K.*

PROOF. $\mathcal{Q}(K)$ is a set of maximal sets, where maximality is with respect to subset. Now, $\mathrm{Cl}\,\mathcal{Q}(K) = K$, so $\mathcal{Q}(K)$ generates K. Uniqueness follows from the definition of maximal sets and axioms of specification and extension. For minimality, observe that a maximal set σ must be in any description of K as σ is not a subset of any other set. We may prove this formally using order theory. □

We may denote K with $(\mathcal{Q}(K), \emptyset)$ as a simplicial set. For general simplicial sets, the representation is not unique as we may build the same set through different operations. It also does not have minimum size necessarily, as we may collapse any acyclic set to a single point. It does, however, make reduction operations very easy.

Definition 4 (trim & thin) *Let (Q, C) denote a simplicial set. For $\sigma \in Q$, we have two homology-preserving reductions:*

$$\begin{array}{lll} \text{trim:} & (Q, C) \mapsto (Q - \{\sigma\}, C) & \sigma,\ \textit{a leaf} \\ \text{thin:} & (Q, C) \mapsto (Q - \{\sigma\}, C \cup \{\sigma\}) & \sigma,\ \textit{acyclic} \end{array}$$

Note that both reductions maintain the invariant that Q and C are disjoint. Our representation also enables us to postpone enumeration of simplicial sets until we require it for computing homology. We are now ready to define the tidy set.

Definition 5 (tidy set) *A* tidy set *is a trimmed, then thinned, simplicial complex.*

That is, we first delete all maximal leaves in the input simplicial complex. We then collapse all maximal acyclic simplices to get a simplicial set, as shown in Figure 3.

3.3 Minimality

The order in which we do reduction is important. Indeed, it may seem reasonable to try trimming a tidy set again, as we currently trim complex leaves only. The following theorem states, however, that collapses do not grow leaves.

Theorem 5 (minimal) *A tidy set has no leaves. That is, it is minimal with respect to trimming and thinning.*

PROOF. Recall Definition 1. For any $\sigma \in Q$, let $c \in H_n(\mathrm{Cl}\,\sigma)$ be a nontrivial homology class for some n. We know that this class exists as otherwise, σ would be acyclic and collapsed, $\sigma \in C$, but we know $Q \cap C = \emptyset$. Initially, however, σ was acyclic as a simplex within the input simplicial complex. So, c developed within $\mathrm{Cl}\,\sigma$ due to the collapse of a neighboring simplex. But this development was through σ's intersection with the neighbor and this intersection was also collapsed, so $c \notin H_n(\mathrm{Cl}\,\sigma \cap \mathrm{Cl}\,(X - \mathrm{Cl}\,\sigma))$. Therefore, σ is not a leaf. □

Because of the theorem above, a tidy set is a minimal model for representing a simplicial complex. It is not unique as it depends on the ordering of the sequence of deletions and collapses.

4. ALGORITHMS

In this section, we describe algorithms for computing homology by first constructing a tidy set. We begin with a quick look at data structures as well as algorithms for computing homology. We then describe algorithms for acquiring the minimal representations for simplicial complexes. For reduction, we give a recursive algorithm for trimming, and a two-phase algorithm for thinning.

4.1 Basic Blocks

We begin with a brief discussion on data structures for computing homology with simplicial sets. A crucial aspect of our approach is having two representations: For most of the computation, we represent a simplicial set $\mathcal{X}(Q, C)$ using the tuple (Q, C). But when required, we enumerate the simplices as a set. We represent each simplex or clique as a set of vertices, with the boundary operator being implicit. This implicit representation means that we need to maintain vertex identifications that may result from simplicial collapses. The vertices form *disjoint sets*, so we utilize a *union-find* data structure [7]. To determine whether a simplex σ is degenerate, we check to see if σ is a subset of any set in C, and we only keep non-degenerate faces during enumeration. Consequently, a simplicial set, unlike a simplicial complex, is not closed in our representation. However, this design decision allows our sets to remain small, a principle goal of our paper.

An important structure is the dual graph, which captures the intersection pattern of the maximal simplices.

Definition 6 (dual graph) *Let Q be a set of maximal sets. The* dual graph *is $G = (Q, E)$, where $E = \{\{\sigma, \tau\} \mid \sigma \cap \tau \neq \emptyset, \sigma \neq \tau \in Q\}$.*

For sparse complexes, such as clique complexes of sparse graphs, we represent the dual complex explicitly for quick access to neighbors of simplices. For denser complexes, however, explicit construction is computationally infeasible and we must construct the graph locally as needed. For the rest of the section, we assume the procedure DUAL-GRAPH(Q) returns the dual graph for a set of maximal sets Q.

For reduction, we need to compute homology, and we may do so by using the reduction algorithm [23]. However, placing any arbitrary filtration on a simplicial set turns it into a *based persistence complex* [34], allowing us to use the persistence algorithm over fields. Below, we assume that the procedure BETTI(X) returns the reduced Betti numbers of a given simplicial set X in a vector by first computing homology over $\mathbb{Z}_2$ coefficients using the generalized persistence algorithm [34]. We use the same implementation of the algorithm for computing homology of simplicial complexes.

While a clique complex may have high dimension, a space does not have non-trivial homology in dimensions higher than its embedding dimension [15]. So, for geometric simplicial sets embedded in $\mathbb{R}^d$, we only require the d-skeleton in computing homology. Similarly, in many applications, we only need the ith homology, which requires the $(i+1)$th skeleton. Therefore, in practice, we parameterize our algorithms with the maximum dimension of the skeleton we are interested in. In the discussion below, we hide this parameter to simplify presentation.

4.2 Maximal Simplices

Given a simplicial complex K, we need to compute its minimum representation $\mathcal{Q}(K)$, its maximal simplices, which is equivalent to maximal sets in K. Yellin [30] gives an output-sensitive iterative algorithm for this problem with complexity $O(mn)$, where m is the number of maximal sets and $n = \sum_{\sigma \in K} |\sigma|$ is the complexity of K. As described, the algorithm requires a prohibitive $\Theta(|K|^2)$ additional space for storing an array of counters. We observe, however, that these counters are used locally in each iteration of the algorithm. This observation allows us to reduce the space complexity to $\Theta(\dim K)$, making the algorithm feasible for large complexes. We define MAXIMAL-SETS(K) to be the function that returns the set of maximal simplices in K.

For clique complexes, we may compute our representation directly from the input graph G as maximal simplices are maximal cliques. This correspondence reduces our problem to enumerating maximal cliques of a graph. An n-vertex graph may have up to $3^{n/2}$ maximal cliques in the worst case [21], so this problem is hard in general. There have been a number of algorithms based on greedy or output sensitive approaches. We define MAXIMAL-CLIQUES(G) to be the function that computes the set of maximal cliques in G using the IK-GX algorithm [3]. We emphasize that we do not have to construct the complex $\mathcal{C}(G)$ to find its minimal representation $\mathcal{Q}(\mathcal{C}(G))$.

4.3 Greedy Reduction

We employ an iterative scheme for both trimming and thinning the complex. Our approach is greedy as a simplex has exponential number of faces, so eliminating large simplices has enormous payoff. Therefore, we always maintain sets of simplices in decreasing order of size. We define GREEDY(Q, C, *Is-Reducible*, *Reduce*) to be the procedure that reduces the simplicial set denoted (Q, C) by the reduction technique specified by predicate *Is-Reducible* and action *Reduce*.

```
GREEDY(Q, C, Is-Reducible, Reduce)
P ← Q
while P ≠ ∅                                  ▷ Potential
      do R ← ∅                               ▷ Reduced
         foreach σ ∈ P
               do if Is-Reducible(σ, Q, C)
                     then (Q, C) ← Reduce(σ, Q, C)
                          R ← R ∪ {σ}
         P ← NEIGHBORS(R, Q)
return (Q, C)
```

The algorithm maintains a set P of potentially reducible simplices, initializing it to Q. In each round, the algorithm collects reduced simplices in set and uses their neighbors in Q as candidates for the next round. We use this scheme, along with another greedy thinning algorithm, DFS-THIN, to define the procedure TIDY-SET(Q), which reduces a simplicial complex with maximal simplices Q and returns the tidy set as a tuple (Q, C).

TIDY-SET(Q)

$(Q, C) \leftarrow$ GREEDY($Q, \emptyset$, IS-LEAF, TRIM)
$(Q, C) \leftarrow$ DFS-THIN(Q, C)
$(Q, C) \leftarrow$ GREEDY(Q, C, IS-ACYCLIC, THIN)
return (Q, C)

4.4 Recursive Trimming

To trim using the greedy scheme, we define the action TRIM and the predicate IS-LEAF. By Theorem 5, we only need to trim leaves in the simplicial complex, so we use the definition of complex leaves in Theorem 1. For this reason, TRIM follows Definition 4, and $C = \emptyset$ is not used below.

TRIM(σ, Q, C)

return $(Q - \{\sigma\}, C)$

IS-LEAF(σ, Q, C)

$I \leftarrow \bigcup_{\tau \in Q - \{\sigma\}} (\sigma \cap \tau)$ ▷ Stem
$M \leftarrow$ MAXIMAL-SETS(I)
if $|M| = 1$ ▷ Single set
  then return TRUE
elseif $(\max_{\tau \in M} \dim \tau) >$ MAX-DIM
  then $(Q_M, C_M) \leftarrow$ TIDY-SET(M) ▷ Recurse
    $X_M \leftarrow \mathcal{X}(Q_M, C_M)$
    if $\chi(X_M) = 1$
      then return BETTI$(X_M) = 0$
      else return FALSE
  else $K_M \leftarrow \mathrm{Cl}\, M$ ▷ Direct
    if $\chi(K_M) = 1$
      then return BETTI$(K_M) = 0$
      else return FALSE

To determine if σ is a leaf in the simplicial complex, the predicate IS-LEAF needs to determine if the intersection I of σ and the rest of the complex is acyclic. The procedure computes I and represents it with maximal simplices M by using MAXIMAL-SETS from Section 4.2. If the intersection has only one maximal set, it immediately returns true as a maximal set corresponds to a simplex which is acyclic in a complex. If the intersection has high dimension, it recurses by using the procedure TIDY-SET as it now has a smaller instance of the original problem. It then enumerates the resulting simplicial set and checks if its reduced Betti numbers are all zero. Since both TIDY-SET and IS-LEAF call each other, the two procedures become mutually recursive. Otherwise, when the intersection has low dimension, it directly computes homology by enumerating the simplicial complex. In both cases, it uses the Euler characteristic to skip homology computation whenever possible. Based on our experiments, we currently set MAX-DIM to 5. It is important to emphasize that the minimal representation is key to the efficiency of our trimming procedure: It allows both simple acyclicity testing as well as recursive evaluation, using direct homology testing of small complexes as a base case.

4.5 Two-Phase Thinning

We thin the trimmed complex in two phases, corresponding to complex and set thinning, respectively. Within a complex, all simplices are acyclic, but collapsing any simplex may cause a neighboring simplex to have non-trivial homology. For this reason, we attempt to find a large set of non-neighboring simplices that we may collapse at once. This idea may remind the reader of an *independent set*, a set of vertices in a graph that are pairwise non-adjacent. Indeed, vertices in an independent set of the dual graph correspond to non-intersecting maximal simplices. We may collect a larger set, however.

Theorem 6 *A simplex with one collapsed neighbor remains acyclic.*

PROOF. Two simplices intersect along a shared face. If we collapse one of the simplices, the shared face is also collapsed, and this does not cause the other simplex to develop non-trivial homology. □

Given this observation, we search the dual graph using *depth-first-search (DFS)* [7] to collect a set of acyclic simplices. DFS-THIN reduces a simplicial set denoted by (Q, C) by searching the dual graph and collecting acyclic simplices using THIN-DFS-VISITOR upon node discovery. We use the *algorithm visitor* paradigm [27] along with a generic version of DFS and define action THIN exactly as in Definition 4. Note that this is a fast and simple procedure as it does not require either face enumeration or homology computation.

THIN(σ, Q, C)

return $(Q - \{\sigma\}, C \cup \{\sigma\})$

DFS-THIN(Q, C)

return DFS(DUAL-GRAPH(Q), THIN-DFS-VISITOR)

THIN-DFS-VISITOR(σ, Q, C)

$N \leftarrow$ NEIGHBORS(σ, C) ▷ Collapsed neighbors
if $|N| \leq 1$
  then return THIN(σ, Q, C)

Having thinned the complex, we move into the category of simplicial sets. To thin using the greedy scheme, we define the predicate IS-ACYCLIC, having defined action THIN already. The procedure now needs to enumerate the full simplicial set. As with trimming, we attempt to avoid computing homology by using the Euler characteristic.

IS-ACYCLIC(σ, Q, C)

$X_\sigma \leftarrow \mathcal{X}(\{\sigma\}, C)$
if $\chi(X_\sigma) = 1$
  then return BETTI$(X_\sigma) = 0$
  else return FALSE

5. EXPERIMENTS

In this section, we describe an implementation of our algorithms, examine its performance on real and synthetic data, and compare it with existing software. Our implementation is in generic C++ and part of a library we are currently developing for computational topology. All our timings are done on a 64-bit GNU/Linux machine with two dual-core 3

S	$\dim S$	$\|S\|$	ϵ	$G_\epsilon = (S, E)$ time	$\|E\|$	$\mathcal{C}(G_\epsilon)$ time	size	β time	total time
G	3	318	5.00	0.00	3,960	0.11	71,032	0.12	0.23
M	8	10,000	0.13	0.22	36,263	48.74	13,234,966	126.01	174.97
B	3	34,837	0.05	0.38	489,876	19.29	9,714,912	26.35	46.02
S	8	50,000	0.18	2.17	546,388	49.25	19,134,612	76.66	128.08
D	3	88,571	0.0014	1.08	543,996	168.40	45,995,489	297.71	467.19

Table 1: Data sets and statistics on computing the VR graph G_ϵ at scale ϵ, the complex $\mathcal{C}(G_\epsilon)$, and computing its homology. All times are in seconds.

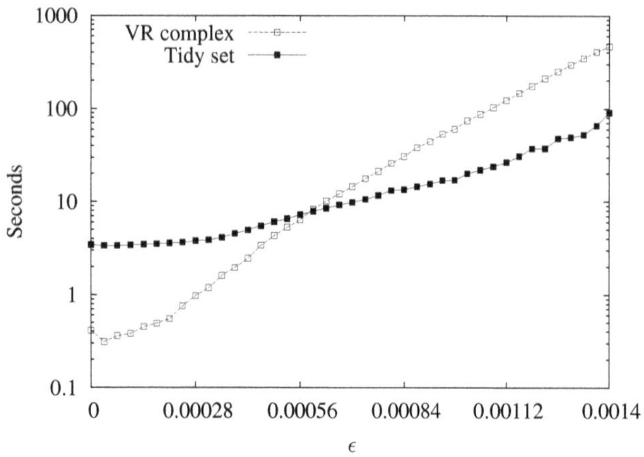

Figure 5: Homology time using the VR complex versus the tidy set at scale ϵ for dataset D.

GHz Xeon processors, although our software is not threaded and uses only one core. We measured all timings with `clock` from the Standard C library, and zero means that measured time was below the granularity of this function.

5.1 Data

Our datasets are listed in in Table 1. G is Gramicidin A, a small protein. M is a portion of the *van Hateren-Mumford dataset* with parameters $k = 30$ and cut $= 20\%$ [2]. B and D are points sampled from the surface of the *Stanford bunny* and *dragon*, respectively. S is sampled from a unit 3-sphere, diagonally embedded in $\mathbb{R}^8$. The standard method for computing homology involves constructing the VR complex for which we give timing and statistics in Table 1. We use the ANN library to build the VR graph G_ϵ, and modify algorithm INCREMENTAL-VR [32] to build a non-filtered VR complex $\mathcal{C}(G_\epsilon)$ in the ambient dimension, e.g. an 8-dimensional complex for S. Finally, we compute Betti numbers β using the persistence algorithm [34].

5.2 Timing

We build the tidy set directly from the graph G_ϵ. Figure 5 shows the performance of our algorithm for dataset D across scale. We showed the size of the resulting tidy set in Figure 1. Figure 6 compares our method for the 8-dimensional dataset M. Note that the complex is just beginning to connect and develop topological attributes at the scales we are examining. Table 2 lists the times for all phases of our method at the maximum scale for each dataset. We observe that our algorithm is generally much faster than computing with the VR complex, and competitive for smaller sets.

S	$\mathcal{Q}$	dual	trim	dfs	thin	$\mathcal{X}$	β	total
G	0.03	0.01	0.13	0.00	0.00	0.00	0.00	0.17
M	0.34	0.60	3.81	0.00	1.75	0.14	0.20	7.06
B	8.45	3.95	25.22	0.01	0.01	0.00	0.00	38.02
S	8.03	3.45	32.43	0.08	17.39	3.19	4.16	70.09
D	37.63	15.36	33.12	0.04	3.53	0.11	0.11	90.98

Table 2: Time, in seconds, for computing cliques $\mathcal{Q}$ of the VR graph G_ϵ, the dual graph, trimming, thinning using DFS and greedy scheme, enumerating the tidy set, and computing homology. The total includes time for computing G_ϵ from Table 1.

Moreover, our method requires much less memory. For example, computing the VR complex and homology for D requires 5 GB and 10 GB of memory, respectively, while our method only needs 500 MB, a factor of 20 times less.

5.3 Statistics

Table 3 gives statistics on the number and size of cliques in the VR graph, the efficacy of our trimming and two thinning procedures, and the size of the resulting tidy set. We generally have a great number of cliques, including large ones, such as a 73-clique for D that generates $\binom{73}{4}$ or roughly 1M tetrahedra in the VR complex. Our methods are highly effective in reducing cliques. For G, we are left with a single 9-clique that generates 264 simplices, as compared to 71K simplices in the VR complex. For B, we have a tidy set that has a factor of 9,000 fewer simplices. The tidy set for S has nearly 21K cliques, although its topological complexity ($\sum_i |\beta_i|$) is 2,223. We hope to examine such hard cases to look for further reduction.

In general, the effectiveness of reduction techniques vary across scale, as illustrated by Figure 7 for G. The techniques, however, are complementary, removing nearly 90% of maximal cliques at all scales. Initially, the graph is just a set of points, which DFS "contracts" trivially. With increasing scale, as the graph becomes denser, the complex gains thickness, allowing us to trim from the boundary inward. What is intriguing is that the efficacy of the methods as displayed in in the figure reflects the underlying topology of the point set: The first local minimum for trimming is near 2 Angstroms, slightly larger than radii of atoms, when atoms connect and form a large number of 1-cycles.

We end by comparing our methods with *JPlex* [26] the only publicly available software that implements VR complexes and computes homology using the persistence algorithm. Figure 8 compares total computation time for B, our largest dataset that JPlex is able to process. At the highest scale, our methods run about 13 times faster and requires 5

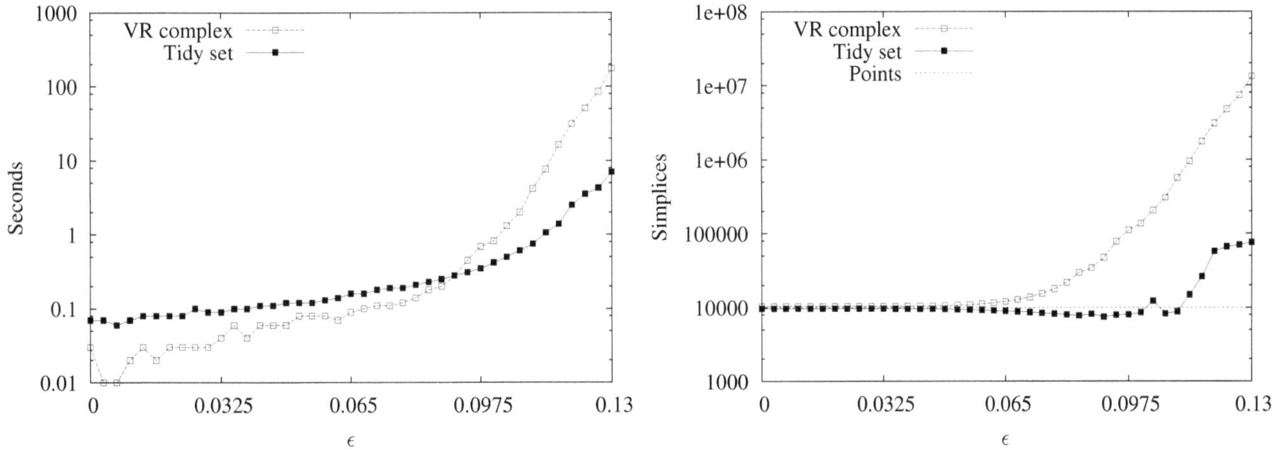

(a) Time

(b) Size

Figure 6: Homology times and sizes of the VR complex and tidy sets for dataset M.

S	cliques $\mathcal{Q}$ ave	max	num	− trim	− dfs	− thin	= tidy	$\vert\mathcal{X}\vert$
G	8.97	13	870	853	8	8	1	246
M	5.31	22	16,114	10,626	3,702	644	1,142	76,008
B	9.40	16	140,052	139,679	358	9	6	1,104
S	6.56	18	167,742	129,835	7,986	8,938	20,983	1,477,416
D	6.91	73	123,091	87,336	25,773	3,079	6,903	51,448

Table 3: Average and maximum clique size, and number of cliques, number removed by trimming using DFS and greedy scheme, remaining cliques in the tidy set, and its enumerated size.

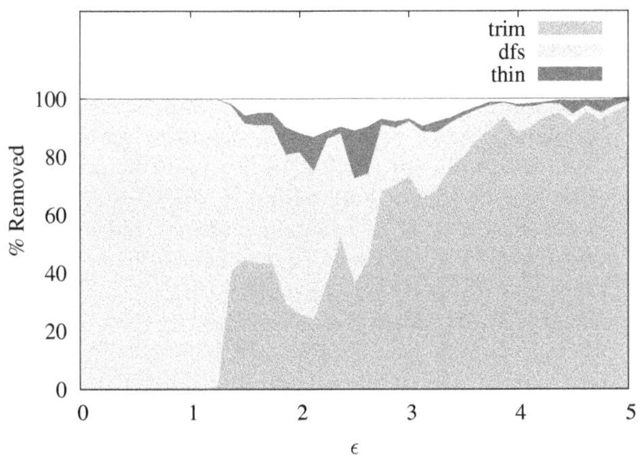

Figure 7: Cumulative graphs showing percentage of cliques removed by our three reduction techniques: trimming, DFS thinning, and greedy thinning for dataset G.

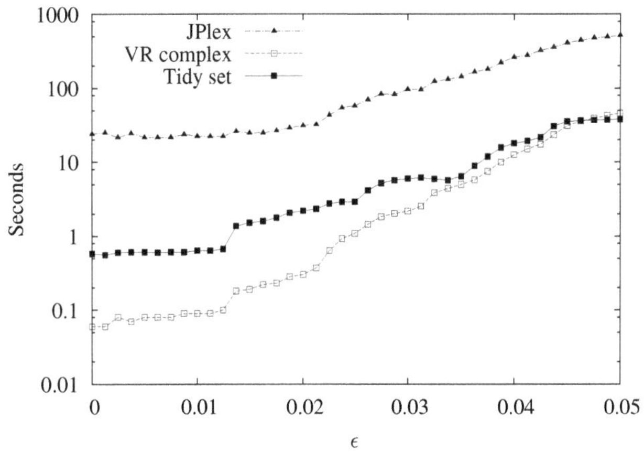

Figure 8: Comparison of our methods with JPlex for dataset B.

times less memory (4.7 GB vs. 958 MB) even though JPlex is optimized for simplicial complexes in low dimensions.

6. CONCLUSION

In this paper, we define the tidy set, a minimal simplicial set, for computing homology of clique complexes. We give recursive algorithms for computing the tidy set, implement them, and experimentally verify their effectiveness by computing homology of large datasets. Our software enables a number of interesting applications. For instance, we may compute geometric descriptions of homological cycles of tidy sets and expand them back onto the original point set to identify regions with nontrivial homology.

There are a number of rich avenues for research. While we focus on clique complexes in this paper, our work applies to arbitrary simplicial complexes, provided we compute maximal simplices efficiently. We also have not applied our methods toward computing witness complexes: We may now use large sets of landmarks for massive datasets. Dense graphs behave very differently from sparse graphs, and we are working on algorithms for computing their clique homology. We plan to extend our methods to filtered complexes to enable computation of persistence barcodes. Finally, almost every step of our method is parallelizable by design.

Acknowledgments

The author would like to thank Gunnar Carlsson for initial discussions and support.

7. REFERENCES

[1] Barmak, J., and Minian, E. Strong homotopy types, nerves and collapses, 2009. arXiv:0907.2954v1 [math.GT].

[2] Carlsson, G., Ishkhanov, T., de Silva, V., and Zomorodian, A. On the local behavior of spaces of natural images. *International Journal of Computer Vision 76*, 1 (2008), 1–12.

[3] Cazals, F., and Karande, C. Reporting maximal cliques: new insights into an old problem. Research Report 5642, INRIA, 2005.

[4] CHomP: Computational Homology Project. `http://chomp.rutgers.edu`.

[5] Civan, Y., and Yalçin, E. Linear colorings of simplicial complexes and collapsing. *Journal of Combinatorial Theory Series A 114*, 7 (2007), 1315–1331.

[6] Collins, A., Zomorodian, A., Carlsson, G., and Guibas, L. A barcode shape descriptor for curve point cloud data. *Computers and Graphics 28*, 6 (2004), 881–894.

[7] Cormen, T. H., Leiserson, C. E., Rivest, R. L., and Stein, C. *Introduction to Algorithms*, third ed. The MIT Press, Cambridge, MA, 2009.

[8] Curtis, E. B. Simplicial homotopy theory. *Advances in Mathematics 6* (1971), 107–209.

[9] de Silva, V., and Carlsson, G. Topological estimation using witness complexes. In *Proc. IEEE/Eurographics Symposium on Point-Based Graphics* (2004), pp. 157–166.

[10] Edelsbrunner, H., and Mücke, E. P. Three-dimensional alpha shapes. *ACM Transactions on Graphics 13* (1994), 43–72.

[11] Eilenberg, S., and Zilber, J. A. Semi-simplicial complexes and singular homology. *Annals of Mathematics 51*, 3 (1950), 499–513.

[12] Giesen, J., and John, M. The flow complex: A data structure for geometric modeling. In *Proc. Symposium on Discrete Algorithms* (2003), pp. 285–294.

[13] Goerss, P. G., and Jardine, J. F. *Simplicial homotopy theory*, vol. 174 of *Progress in Mathematics*. Birkhäuser-Verlag, Basel, Switzerland, 1999.

[14] Gromov, M. Hyperbolic groups. In *Essays in Group Theory*, S. Gersten, Ed. Springer-Verlag, New York, NY, 1987, pp. 75–263.

[15] Hatcher, A. *Algebraic Topology*. Cambridge University Press, New York, NY, 2002. `http://www.math.cornell.edu/~hatcher/AT/ATpage.html`.

[16] Kaczynski, T., Mischaikow, K., and Mrozek, M. *Computational Homology*. Springer-Verlag, New York, NY, 2004.

[17] Kasson, P. M., Zomorodian, A., Park, S., Singhal, N., Guibas, L. J., and Pande, V. S. Persistent voids: a new structural metric for membrane fusion. *Bioinformatics 23*, 14 (2007), 1753–1759.

[18] Kozlov, D. *Combinatorial Algebraic Topology*. Springer-Verlag, New York, NY, 2008.

[19] Matoušek, J. LC reductions yield isomorphic simplicial complexes. *Contributions to Discrete Mathematics 3*, 2 (2008), 37–39.

[20] May, J. P. *Simplicial Objects in Algebraic Topology*. D. Van Nostrand Co., Inc., Princeton, NJ, 1967.

[21] Moon, J. W., and Moser, L. On cliques in graphs. *Israel Journal of Mathematics 3*, 1 (1965), 23–28.

[22] Mrozek, M., Pilarczyk, P., and Żelazna, N. Homology algorithm based on acyclic subspace. *Computers and Mathematics with Applications 55*, 11 (2008), 2395–2412.

[23] Munkres, J. R. *Elements of Algebraic Topology*. Addison-Wesley, Reading, MA, 1984.

[24] Perry, P. Application of simplicial sets to computational topology. Senior thesis, Stanford University, 2003.

[25] Pilarczyk, P. Computer assisted method for proving existence of periodic orbits. *Topological Methods in Nonlinear Analysis 13* (1999), 365–377.

[26] Sexton, H., and Johansson, M. V. JPlex, 2009. `http://comptop.stanford.edu/programs/jplex/`.

[27] Siek, J., Lee, L.-Q., and Lumsdaine, A. *The Boost Graph Library: user guide and reference manual*. Pearson Education, Inc., Upper Saddle River, NJ, 2002.

[28] Storjohann, A. Near optimal algorithms for computing Smith normal forms of integer matrices. In *Proc. International Conference on Symbolic and Algebraic Computation* (1996), pp. 267–274.

[29] Whitehead, J. H. C. Simplicial spaces, nuclei, and m-groups. *Proceedings of the London Mathematical Society s2-45*, 1 (1939), 243–327.

[30] Yellin, D. M. Algorithms for subset testing and finding maximal sets. In *Proc. ACM-SIAM Symposium on Discrete Algorithms* (1992), pp. 386–392.

[31] Zomorodian, A. Computational topology. In *Algorithms and Theory of Computation Handbook*, M. Atallah and M. Blanton, Eds., second ed., vol. 2. Chapman & Hall/CRC Press, Boca Raton, FL, 2010, ch. 3.

[32] Zomorodian, A. Fast construction of the Vietoris-Rips complex. *Computers & Graphics* (2010). (To appear).

[33] Zomorodian, A., and Carlsson, G. Computing persistent homology. *Discrete & Computational Geometry 33*, 2 (2005), 249–274.

[34] Zomorodian, A., and Carlsson, G. Localized homology. *Computational Geometry: Theory & Applications 41*, 3 (2008), 126–148.

A Randomized $O(m \log m)$ Time Algorithm for Computing Reeb Graphs of Arbitrary Simplicial Complexes

William Harvey
Department of Computer Science and Engineering
The Ohio State University
Columbus, OH 43210, USA
harvey@cse.ohio-state.edu

Yusu Wang
Computer Science and Engineering Department
The Ohio State University
Columbus, OH 43210, USA
yusu@cse.ohio-state.edu

Rephael Wenger
Computer Science and Engineering Department
The Ohio State University
Columbus, OH 43210,USA
wenger@cse.ohio-state.edu

ABSTRACT

Given a continuous scalar field $f : X \to \mathbb{R}$ where X is a topological space, a *level set* of f is a set $\{x \in X : f(x) = \alpha\}$ for some value $\alpha \in \mathbb{R}$. The level sets of f can be subdivided into connected components. As α changes continuously, the connected components in the level sets appear, disappear, split and merge. The Reeb graph of f encodes these changes in connected components of level sets. It provides a simple yet meaningful abstraction of the input domain. As such, it has been used in a range of applications in fields such as graphics and scientific visualization.

In this paper, we present the first sub-quadratic algorithm to compute the Reeb graph for a function on an arbitrary simplicial complex K. Our algorithm is randomized with an expected running time $O(m \log n)$, where m is the size of the 2-skeleton of K (i.e, total number of vertices, edges and triangles), and n is the number of vertices. This presents a significant improvement over the previous $\Theta(mn)$ time complexity for arbitrary complex, matches (although in expectation only) the best known result for the special case of 2-manifolds, and is faster than current algorithms for any other special cases (e.g, 3-manifolds). Our algorithm is also very simple to implement. Preliminary experimental results show that it performs well in practice.

Categories and Subject Descriptors

F.2.2 [**Analysis of Algorithms and Problem Complexity**]: Nonnumerical Algorithms and Problems—*Geometrical problems and computations*

General Terms

Algorithms, Theory

Keywords

Randomized algorithms, Reeb graph, topology.

1. INTRODUCTION

Let $f : X \to \mathbb{R}$ be a continuous function defined on a topological space X. For each scalar value $\alpha \in \mathbb{R}$, the set $\{x \in X : f(x) = \alpha\}$ is called a *level set* of f. A level set of f can be partitioned into connected components. The *Reeb graph* of f is obtained by continuously collapsing every component of each level set into a single point. As α increases, connected components appear, disappear, split and merge, and the Reeb graph of f tracks such changes.

The mathematical concept of the Reeb graph was first defined by George Reeb [22] for smooth manifolds. It was introduced in graphics applications by Shinagawa et al. [25]. Since then, it has been used in a range of shape analysis applications, including shape understanding [3, 4, 25], segmentation and matching [17, 23, 28, 30], shape repairing and animation [18, 32], surface quadrangulations and parametrization [16, 21, 33]. See [5] for a survey on the Reeb graph and its applications. The loop-free version of the Reeb graph, commonly known as the contour tree, is also a popular tool for analyzing scalar fields [6], and has a long history in fields such as geographic information systems and scientific visualization. In all these applications, it is important to be able to construct the Reeb graph in an efficient manner.

We consider the problem of computing Reeb graphs of $f : X \to \mathbb{R}$, where f is a piecewise linear function defined on a simplicial complex X. A straightforward approach to do so is to track the connected components of the level sets and update the Reeb graph as the components change. While this approach is conceptually simple, it can be tricky to implement. Moreover, on a 2-complex with n vertices and m triangles, this approach can take $\Theta(mn)$ time.

Our contribution. As discussed in Section 2, a number of papers present efficient algorithms for computing Reeb graphs in special cases, such as when X is a two or three manifold. This paper describes an efficient randomized algorithm for arbitrary simplicial complexes. The algorithm runs in $O(m \log n)$ expected time, where m is the number of 0, 1, and 2-simplices (i.e, vertices, edges and triangle) in the complex, and n is the number of vertices.

Specifically, for a point $q \in X$, let L_q be the level set $\{x \in X : f(x) = f(q)\}$ and let C_q be the connected component of L_q which contains q. Our algorithm picks a random vertex q in the complex and "collapses" all the triangles intersecting C_q onto q and its adjacent edges. The algorithm then picks another random vertex and repeats this collapse

References	Underlying Domain	Time Complexity
[9]	2-manifolds	$O(n \log n) = O(m \log m)$
[12]	3-manifolds	$O(m \log m + m \log g(\log \log g)^3)$
	3-manifolds	$O(mg \log^2 m)$ (implemented algorithm)
	d-manifolds	$O(m \log m(\log \log m)^3)$
[11]	3-manifolds	$O(m \log m + L) = \Theta(mn)$
	arbitrary simplicial complex	$O(mn)$
[29]	3-manifolds embedded in $\mathbb{R}^3$	$O(m \log m + hm) = \Theta(mn)$
[20]	arbitrary simplicial complex	$O(mn)$

Table 1: Current best algorithms to compute Reeb graph for a simplicial complex X. m is the size of the 2-skeleton of X (i.e, total number of vertices, edges and triangles), and n is the number of vertices.

procedure. New triangles will be created and collapsed during the process, and the expected total number of these intermediate triangles is $O(m \log n)$. As a result, the expected running time of our algorithm is also $O(m \log n)$. Our contributions are as follows:

- We give the first sub-quadratic time algorithm for an arbitrary simplicial complex. Our expected running time matches the running time of the best current algorithm for 2-manifolds (although only in expectation) and is faster than any other current algorithm.
- Our algorithm and its implementation are very simple. The implementation uses a repetition of just one "collapse" operation, and involves only array and linked-list data structures.
- We show preliminary experimental results to demonstrate the practical potential of our algorithm.

The software for computing the Reeb graph using our algorithm is publicly available at the authors' web pages.

2. RELATED WORK

In [7], Carr et al. presented an elegant and efficient algorithm to compute the contour tree of an arbitrary simply-connected, simplicial complex domain X in $O(n \log n + N\alpha(N))$ time, where n is the number of vertices in the input simplicial complex and N is the total number of vertices and edges. The algorithm improved ideas from several previous contour-tree algorithms [27, 31].

Shinagawa and Kunii presented the first provably correct algorithm to compute Reeb Graphs for a triangulation of a 2-manifold [24]. Their algorithm runs in $\Theta(n^2)$ time. It sweeps vertices of the mesh in increasing order of function values, and maintains the level-sets explicitly during the sweeping. This sweeping idea can be used to compute the Reeb graph for arbitrary simplicial complex in $\Theta(nm)$ time, where n is still the number of vertices, and m is the total number of vertices, edges, and triangles in the complex. Since then, there have been several more efficient algorithms, mainly focusing on 2 or 3-manifolds. We summarize the results in Table 1 and briefly review them below.

For the case of 2-manifold, Cole-McLaughlin et al. [9] improved the running time from $O(n^2)$ to $O(n \log n)$ based on their insights in the structure of the level sets and Reeb graph for 2-manifolds. Doraiswamy and Natarajan [12] further extended the sweeping idea to handle 3-manifolds, and presented an $O(m \log m + m \log g(\log \log g)^3)$ time algorithm, where g is the maximum genus of any iso-surface. Their algorithm uses dynamic spanning tree / co-trees to maintain connectivity of level sets during the sweeping. It can be extended to d-manifolds in time $O(m \log m(\log \log m)^3)$, by using a fully-dynamic graph connectivity algorithm. They also provided a simpler but slower implementation that runs in $O(mg \log^2 m)$ time to compute the Reeb graph for functions on 3-manifolds. An interesting and simple semi-output sensitive algorithm is proposed in [11] to compute the Reeb graph of 3-manifolds in time $O(m \log m + L)$, where L is the total complexity of all level-sets passing through critical points and can be $\Theta(nm)$ in worst case. The same algorithm can handle arbitrary simplicial complexes, but the bound of $O(m \log m + L)$ will then not hold.

Very recently in [29], Tierny et al. proposed an algorithm that computes the Reeb graph for a 3-manifold with boundary embedded in $\mathbb{R}^3$ in time $O(m \log m + hm)$, where h is number of independent loops in the Reeb graph. Their approach leverages the efficient contour tree algorithm in [6] by using a novel surgery idea to first cut the input simplicial complex so that its Reeb graph is loop-free. The worst case time complexity can be $\Theta(nm)$, but it runs much faster in practice as h is usually small for 3D volumetric data. Finally, a streaming algorithm was presented in [20] to compute the Reeb graph for an arbitrary simplicial complex in $\Theta(nm)$ time. Reeb graphs for time-varying functions defined on 3-dimensional domains was studied in [14] exploiting Jacobi sets. In the field of graphics, there are also several practical implementations to *approximate* the Reeb graphs for triangular meshes (see references in [5]).

3. PROBLEM DEFINITION AND PRELIMINARIES

Reeb graphs. Let X be a topological space, and $f : X \to \mathbb{R}$ a continuous function defined on X. The level-set of f with respect to a value $\alpha \in \mathbb{R}$ is denoted by $f^{-1}(\alpha) = \{x \in X \mid f(x) = \alpha\}$. Two points $x, y \in X$ are *equivalent*, denoted by $x \sim y$, if and only if x and y belong to the same connected component of some $f^{-1}(\alpha)$; that is, $\alpha = f(x) = f(y)$ and x is connected to y in $f^{-1}(\alpha)$. Now consider the quotient space $X_\sim$, which is the set of equivalent classes equipped with the quotient topology induced by this equivalent relation; $X_\sim$ is also called the *Reeb graph* of X with respect to f, denoted by $\mathcal{R}_X(f)$ from now on, where X may be omitted when its choice is clear.

Note that $\mathcal{R}_X(f)$ can also be thought of as the image of the continuous surjection map $\Phi_f : X \to X_\sim$ where $\Phi_f(x) = \Phi_f(y)$ *if and only if* x and y come from the same connected component of a level set of f. In this sense,

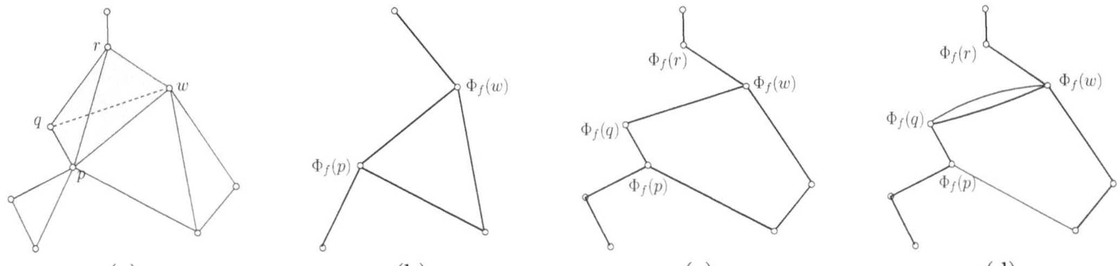

Figure 1: (a) A simplicial complex K and (b) Reeb graph of the height function on K. Shaded triangles are 2-simplices in K, and the two front faces of the tetrahedron $pqrw$ as well as one back face $\triangle qrw$ are present in K. (c) shows the corresponding augmented Reeb graph. One can obtain (b) by removing monotonic degree-2 nodes from (c). If the back face $\triangle qrw$ is missing, then the corresponding augmented Reeb graph is (d).

$\mathcal{R}_X(f)$ is obtained by continuously identifying each connected component C. The map Φ_f induces a scalar function $\tilde{f} : \mathcal{R}_X(f) \to \mathbb{R}$ on $\mathcal{R}_X(f)$ where $\tilde{f}(p) = f(x)$ if $p = \Phi_f(x)$. Since $f(x) = f(y)$ whenever $\Phi_f(x) = \Phi_f(y)$, the function $\tilde{f}$ is well-defined. Since f is continuous, so is $\tilde{f}$.

Reeb graph nodes and arcs. As the name suggests, the Reeb graph $\mathcal{R}_X(f)$ can be represented as a graph. See Figure 1 (b) for an example, where the height of a point $q \in \mathcal{R}_X(f)$ is simply $\tilde{f}(q)$. Now for every point $q \in \mathcal{R}_X(f)$, there is a sufficiently small neighborhood $\mathcal{R}' \subseteq \mathcal{R}_X(f)$ containing q such that $\mathcal{R}'$ is connected, has no loops, and $\tilde{f}(p) \neq \tilde{f}(q)$ for any point $p \in \mathcal{R}' - \{q\}$. Let γ be a connected component of $\mathcal{R}' - \{q\}$. Since $\tilde{f}(p) \neq \tilde{f}(q)$ for any point $p \in \gamma$ and $\tilde{f}$ is continuous, either $\tilde{f}(p) > \tilde{f}(q)$ for all $p \in \gamma$ or $\tilde{f}(p) < \tilde{f}(q)$ for all $p \in \gamma$. The *up degree* of a point $q \in \mathcal{R}_X(f)$ is the number of connected components γ in $\mathcal{R}' - \{q\}$ where $\tilde{f}(p) > \tilde{f}(q)$ for $p \in \gamma$. The *down degree* of $q \in \mathcal{R}_X(f)$ is the number of connected components γ in $\mathcal{R}' - \{q\}$ where $\tilde{f}(p) < \tilde{f}(q)$ for $p \in \gamma$. A *node* of $\mathcal{R}_X(f)$ is a point $q \in \mathcal{R}_X(f)$ whose up degree is not one or whose down degree is not one. Deleting the nodes of $\mathcal{R}_X(f)$ from $\mathcal{R}_X(f)$ leaves a set of curves which are the *arcs* of the Reeb graph.

The Reeb graph $\mathcal{R}_X(f)$ encodes partial information about the 0-th and 1-st homology group information of the topological space X. Specifically, it can be shown [13] that $\beta_0(\mathcal{R}(f)) = \beta_0(X)$ and $\beta_1(\mathcal{R}(f)) \leq \beta_1(X)$. If X is an orientable 2-manifold, then one can in fact obtain the full 1-st homology group information (including its rank and generators) about X from $\mathcal{R}(f)$ [9].

Piecewise-linear (PL) settings. Consider a simplicial complex K and a piecewise-linear (PL) function $f : K \to \mathbb{R}$ on K. Specifically, f is defined at vertices of K, and linearly interpolated in the interior of every simplex of dimension higher than 0. Since $\mathcal{R}(f)$ depends only on the connectivity of each level set, for a generic function f (where no two vertices have the same function value), the Reeb graph of f depends only on the 2-skeleton of K. Hence from now on, we assume that f is generic and $K = (V, E, T)$ is a simplicial 2-complex with vertices V, edges E and triangles T.

Augmented Reeb graph. An *augmented Reeb graph* of $f : X \to \mathbb{R}$ is a Reeb graph of f with some additional degree-2 vertices inserted in the original Reeb graph arcs. In particular, if f is a piecewise-linear function on a simplicial complex K, then the *augmented Reeb graph generated by* K is a Reeb graph of f whose nodes are $\{\Phi_f(v) : v \in V(K)\}$. Note that all nodes of the original Reeb graph are in $\{\Phi_f(v) : v \in V(K)\}$. See Figure 1 (c) and (d). One can obtain the original Reeb graph from the augmented one by removing *monotonic* degree-2 nodes, which are nodes with up-degree 1 and down-degree 1. (The augmented Reeb graph generated by K is similar to the augmented contour tree in [6].)

Some notations. Let f be a function on triangle $t = \triangle pqr$ such that $f(p)$, $f(q)$ and $f(r)$ are all distinct. The *middle vertex* of t, denoted by mid(t), is the vertex q where $f(p) < f(q) < f(r)$. The edge of t opposite to mid(t), pr in this example, spans the range of function values for all points in t, and is called *the spanning edge of* t.

Our initial input K is a simplicial complex. However, as our algorithm proceeds, we will obtain intermediate complexes that may no longer be simplicial. Specifically, there may be multiple edges between the same pair of vertices. Similarly, two triangles may have the same set of vertices but not the same set of edges. Hence we usually denote a triangle t by its boundary edges $t(e_1, e_2, e_3)$. However, for simplicity, we sometimes still denote a triangle by its vertices $\triangle pqr$ when its choice of edges is clear.

4. ALGORITHM

Input to Algorithm RANDREEB is a simplicial 2-complex $K = (V, E, T)$ and a piecewise linear function $f : K \to \mathbb{R}$. We assume that $f(v)$ are distinct for all $v \in V(K)$. We can enforce this condition by symbolically perturbing the scalar value at all vertices. The algorithm computes the augmented Reeb graph of f in expected time $O(m \log n)$ where $n = |V|$ and $m = |V| + |E| + |T|$ is the size of K. Below we introduce the main components of our algorithm. From now on, in all figures, we use the height function as the input piecewise-linear function f.

Data structure. The set of vertices is stored in an array. The set of edges and triangles are each stored in a doubly-linked list. Each edge e maintains a list of (pointers to) triangles incident on e, denoted by $IncT(e)$. Each triangle maintains three pointers to its three boundary edges, e_1, e_2 and e_3, and three pointers to its position in these incident lists, $IncT(e_1)$, $IncT(e_2)$ and $IncT(e_3)$. Similarly, a vertex v maintains a list of triangles having v as middle-vertex, and each triangle stores a pointer to its position in the corresponding list. Adding or removing a triangle takes $O(1)$ time. The total size of the data structure is $O(|V| + |E| + |T|)$.

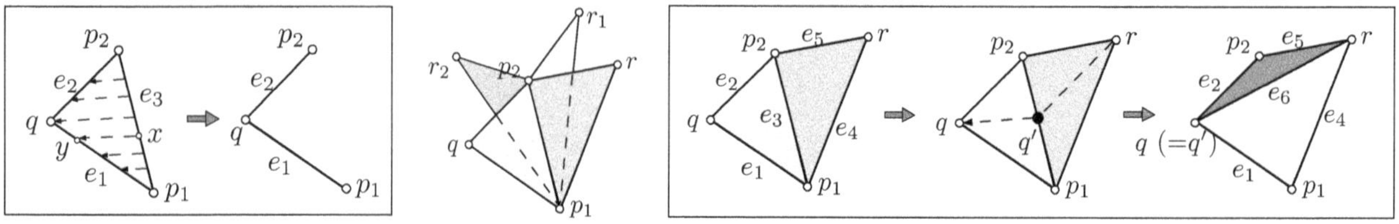

(a) (b) (c)

Figure 2: (a) *Collapse*(t) with $t = (e_1, e_2, e_3)$. All points from t on the same contour (e.g, segment xy) collapse onto its corresponding point on edges e_1 or e_2 (e.g, point y). (b) Edge e_3 has three incident triangles other than t. (c) Each incident triangle of e_3, say $\triangle rp_1p_2$, will be split into two ($\triangle rp_1q', \triangle rp_2q'$ with $f(q) = f(q')$).

4.1 The Collapse Operation

A fundamental operation of our algorithm is the *Collapse*(t) procedure defined for a triangle t. Let e_1 and e_2 be the edges of t incident on $q = \text{mid}(t)$, and let e_3 be the edge of t opposite q. Since e_3 is the spanning edge of t, no two points in $e_1 \cup e_2$ share the same function value. Procedure *Collapse*(t) collapses t by mapping $\{x \in t : f(x) = f(y)\}$ to the point $y \in e_1 \cup e_2$. See Figure 2 (a) for an illustration.

Collapsing t splits all the other triangles incident on the spanning edge e_3. Let $\sigma = (e_3, e_4, e_5)$ be a triangle incident on e_3, where e_4 shares a vertex with edge $e_1 \in t$ and e_5 shares a vertex with edge $e_2 \in t$. Triangle σ has a vertex r opposite e_3. We add the edge e_6 with endpoints q, r and replace σ with triangles (e_1, e_4, e_6) and (e_2, e_5, e_6). See Figure 2 (c). We refer to σ as a *splitting triangle.* Every incident triangle to edge e_3 other than t itself is a splitting triangle. We remark that one should consider simplicial complexes in this paper as abstract simplicial complexes. After the collapse operation, it is possible that the geometric realization of the new complex in the embedding Euclidean space may have self-intersections.

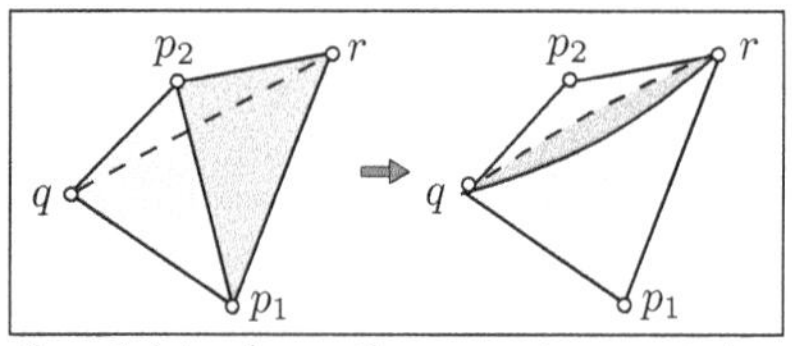

Procedure *Collapse* described above may create double or even multiple edges between the same two points. For example, see the figure on the right where the complex contains four faces of a tetrahedron. Collapsing $\triangle qp_1p_2$ splits $\triangle p_1p_2r$ and creates a double edge between q and r. (Also, recall Figure 1 (b) where such a pair of double edge creates a loop in the final Reeb graph.) Hence the resulting complex may not be a simplicial complex any more, but rather, is a cell complex with the property that each face is a simplex.

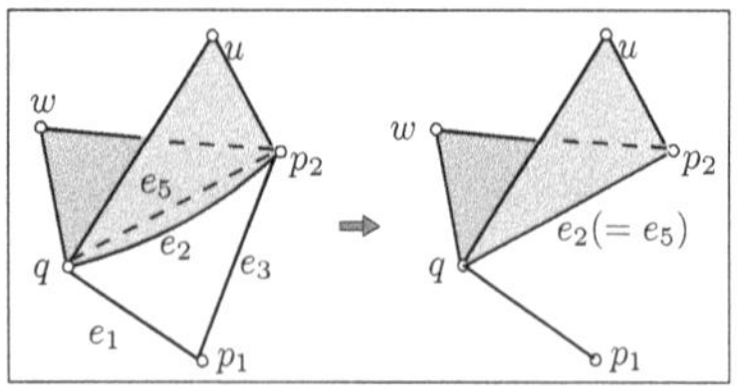

Because the complexes created by Procedure *Collapse* are not necessarily simplicial, a triangle σ incident to the spanning edge e_3 of t may have the same vertices as the collapsing triangle t (i.e, $r = q$ in Figure 2 (c)). In this case, edges e_1 and e_4 may be the same edges or they may be "double" edges, sharing the same endpoints but nevertheless distinct. Similarly, edges e_2 and e_5 may be the same edges or they may be distinct double edges. For example, in the figure on the right, there are two edges e_2 and e_5 between q and p_2 and two triangles with the same set of vertices q, p_1, p_2. One triangle has edges e_1, e_3 and e_2 while the other one has edges e_1, e_3 and e_5.

In the case where σ and t share the same vertices, collapsing t and splitting σ would create two degenerate triangles, spanned by edges e_1 and e_4, and by edge e_2 and e_5, respectively. Instead of creating such degenerate triangles, if edges e_1 and e_4 are the same edge, then no new triangle is created and nothing is done. If they are distinct double edges, then we simply identify these two edges. Similarly, if edges e_2 and e_5 are distinct, then we identify e_2 and e_5. In each case the algorithm calls a procedure to merge the two edges and their data structures into a single edge. In the previous example on the right, triangle $t_1(e_2, qu, up_2)$ is incident to edge e_2 while triangle $t_2(e_5, qw, wp_2)$ is incident to edge e_5. Collapsing triangle $t(e_1, e_2, e_3)$ causes the deletion of triangle $\sigma(e_1, e_5, e_3)$ and the identification of edge e_5 with e_2. After the identification of e_2 and e_5, both t_1 and t_2 are incident to edge e_2 and edge e_5 is removed. The pseudo-code of Procedure *Collapse* is described in Figure 3.

Finally, let K_1 and K_2 denote the complex before and after Procedure *Collapse*(t). Note that K_1 and K_2 share the same set of vertices V, and each cell in K_2 is still a simplex. Let e_1 and e_2 be the edges of t incident on mid(t). Procedure *Collapse*(t) induces a continuous surjection $\phi_t : |K_1| \to |K_2|$ where $\phi_t(y) = y$ if $y \notin t$, and $\phi_t(y) = \phi_t(x)$ if $y \in t$ and $x \in e_1 \cup e_2$ with $f(x) = f(y)$. Since each cell in K_2 is still a simplex, it can be shown that the function $f_t : |K_2| \to \mathbb{R}$ defined as $f_t := f \circ \phi_t$ is exactly the piecewise-linear function on K_2 induced by the function values $f(v)$ at $v \in V$. We thus abuse the notation slightly and still refer to f_t as f.

Lemma 4.1 *Let K_1 and K_2 denote the complex before and after a collapse operation. The augmented Reeb graphs remains the same; that is, $\mathcal{R}_{K_1}(f) = \mathcal{R}_{K_2}(f)$.*

PROOF. Let $\Phi_2 : |K_2| \to \mathcal{R}_{K_2}(f)$ be the surjection mapping K_2 to its Reeb graph. Set $\Phi = \Phi_2 \circ \phi_t$. Function Φ maps each connected component of a level set to a distinct point. Thus $\mathcal{R}_{K_2}(f)$ equals $\mathcal{R}_{K_1}(f)$. □

Vertex-collapse with respect to q. A *vertex-collapse w.r.t a vertex q*, denoted by *SeqCollapse*(q), refers to a sequence of collapse operations for all triangles with q being the middle vertex. These triangles may include new triangles created from earlier collapse operations involving q. In fact, it is necessary that one of the two new triangles created by every splitting triangle during *Collapse*(t) will have q as the middle vertex, and thus may be later destroyed while executing *SeqCollapse*(q). For example, in Figure 2 (c), the triangle $\triangle qp_1r$ may be later also collapsed in *SeqCollapse*(q).

```
     Procedure COLLAPSE(t)
(1)      remove triangle t
(2)      let q = mid(t), and e3 = (p1, p2) the spanning edge of t
(3)      let e1 = (q, p1) and e2 = (q, p2) be the edges of t incident on q
(4)      merge all edges identified with e3
(5)      For (every σ incident to e3 and σ ≠ t)
(6)          set r be the vertex of σ opposite to e3
(7)          let e4 = (r, p1) and e5 = (r, p2) be the edges of σ incident on r
(8)          If (r == q)             // then t and σ have the same vertices
(9)              If (e1 ≠ e4)        Then   identifyEdges(e1, e4);
(10)             If (e2 ≠ e5)        Then   identifyEdges(e2, e5);
(11)         Else
(12)             create new edge e6 with endpoints q, r
(13)             create triangle (e1, e4, e6) and triangle (e2, e5, e6)
(14)         Endif
(15)         remove triangle σ;
(16)     Endfor
(17)     remove edge e3;
```

Figure 3: Pseudo-code for the collapse operation.

SeqCollapse(q) systematically collapses the entire contour passing through q onto q. At the end of *SeqCollapse*(q) operation, there is no triangle left with q being the middle-vertex. See Figure 4 for an example.

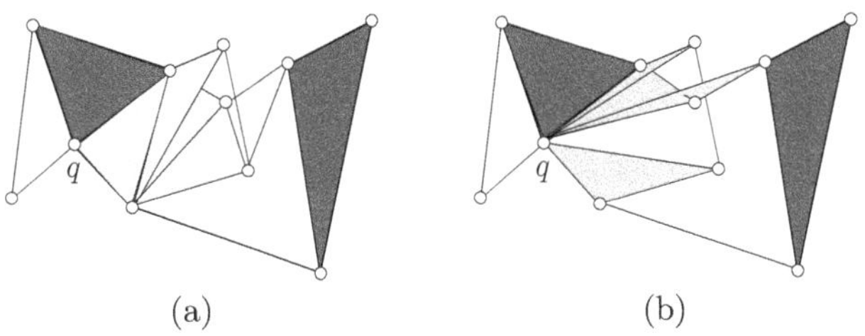

Figure 4: (a) Before and (b) after vertex-collapse operation *SeqCollapse*(q). Shaded triangles are 2-simplices. Two dark-shaded triangles are not affected by this operation.

Claim 4.2 *After performing SeqCollapse(q), no subsequent vertex-collapse operations can ever create a triangle with q being the middle vertex.*

PROOF. Each splitting triangle σ will create two new triangles σ_1 and σ_2. The key observation is that the two extreme vertices of σ (i.e, the vertex with largest and smallest function values) remain extreme in the new triangles. Hence after Procedure *SeqCollapse*(q) (at which point q is not the middle-vertex of any triangle), no subsequent collapse operation can change q from being an extreme vertex of some triangle to being the middle vertex of another triangle. The claim then follows. □

4.2 Identifying Edges

The last components to be described are *identifyEdges*(e, e') in Steps (9) and (10) of Procedure *Collapse* and the merging of these edges in Step (4) in Figure 3. The simplest way to implement *identifyEdges* is to traverse the lists of triangles, $IncT(e)$ and $IncT(e')$, merging the two lists into one and updating the incident triangles. However, this merging and updating associated data-structures of incident triangles takes time proportional to the length of one of the two lists. If the simplicial complex is a 2-manifold, then each list $IncT(e)$ never has more than two elements (see Appendix A). However, for a general simplicial complex, each such list may grow very long, say $O(|T|)$, and it is not clear how to merge two lists in amortized $O(1)$ time, which is required to obtain our desired time complexity [1]. Hence to ensure that Steps (9) and (10) do not take too much time, we use a "lazy" identification procedure.

Specifically, instead of merging e, e' and their associated data structures, *identifyEdges*(e, e') simply records the identity relation between e and e'. Each edge has a list of edges with which it has such a relation. Calling *identifyEdges*(e, e') adds e' to the list of e and adds e' to the list of e.

The actual merging of edges only occurs in Step (4) of Procedure *Collapse*. All the edges identified *transitively* with the spanning edge e_3 and their associated incident triangle lists are merged with e_3. Note that e_3 is removed at the end of the call to *Collapse*(t). All the edges identified with e_3 and all the triangles incident on those edges are also removed in this call. Thus, each edge is only involved in one merge operation.

4.3 The Randomized Algorithm

Algorithm RANDREEB(K, f) randomly permutes vertices of K and performs *SeqCollapse*(v) for each vertex v in the permuted order. Because of lazy edge identification, some edges may be identified but not yet merged. As a final step, RANDREEB merges these edges using a linear scan.

Termination. Algorithm RANDREEB calls, for every vertex v of K, Procedure *SeqCollapse*(v), which subsequently calls procedure *Collapse*(t) for each triangle t whose middle vertex is v. Procedure *Collapse*(t) can create new trian-

[1]As will be seen later in our time analysis, the number of duplicate edges that created can be proportional to the total number of triangles every created, which is $O(m \log n)$ in expectation. Hence to obtain the $O(m \log n)$ final time complexity, it is necessary that each *identifyEdges* operation is handled in $O(1)$ amortized time.

gles whose middle vertex is v. However, as we will show later, each triangle split during $SeqCollapse(v)$ can create at most one new triangle that survives after $SeqCollapse(v)$. Hence the number of such triangles is bounded by the number of triangles intersected by the level set $f^{-}(v)$. Therefore, $SeqCollapse(v)$ creates only a finite number of new triangles and Algorithm RANDREEB terminates.

Correctness. Let $(v_1, v_2, \ldots, v_n)$ be the vertices of K listed in their permuted order. At the i'th iteration of the algorithm, any triangle with middle vertex v_i will be destroyed. By Claim 4.2, no new triangle can be created with middle vertex v_i after the i'th iteration. Hence no triangle with middle vertex v_i can remain at the end of the algorithm, for any $i \in [1, n]$. Thus, Algorithm RANDREEB constructs a graph $G = (V, E_r)$, possibly with multiple edges having the same endpoints. Finally, note that our algorithm consists of simply a sequence of *Collapse* procedures. By Lemma 4.1, Procedure *Collapse* does not change the Reeb graph. Thus, the final outcome, which is itself a graph, is exactly the augmented Reeb graph $\mathcal{R}_K(f)$.

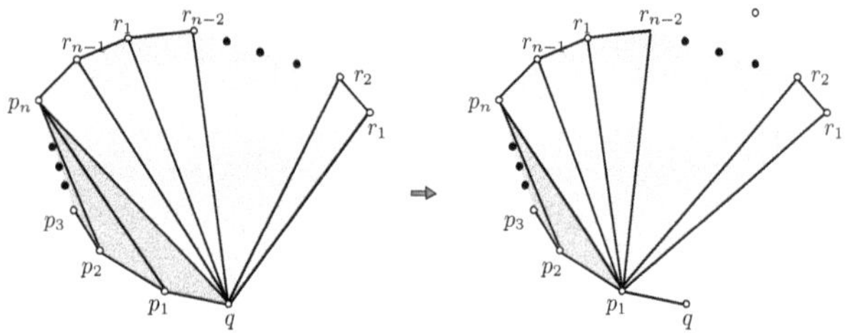

Figure 5: A lower-bound example for the worst-case time complexity of RANDREEB(K, f) performed on a manifold with boundary.

4.4 Time Complexity

The worst case time complexity of the above randomized algorithm RANDREEB(K, f) is $\Omega(|V||T|)$ even when K is a 2-manifold without boundary. A lower-bound example is shown in Figure 5. In this example, we process the vertices $\{p_1, p_2, \ldots, p_n\}$ in order. Each $SeqCollapse(p_i)$ will destroy all $\Theta(n)$ triangles of the form $\triangle p_{i-1} r_j r_{j+1}$ and create $\Theta(n)$ triangles of the form $\triangle p_i r_j r_{j+1}$. Simple modifications of this example give a worst case $\Omega(|V||T|)$ bound for a 2-manifold without boundary.

We now claim that for an arbitrary simplicial 2-complex K, the expected running time of RANDREEB is $O(m \log n)$, where m is the size of K and n is the number of vertices. Below we first argue that each *Collapse* procedure takes time proportional to the number of triangles it collapses and splits. We then bound the (expected) total number of triangles that will ever be collapsed or split.

One collapse operation. Given a triangle $t = (e_1, e_2, e_3)$ with spanning edge e_3, $Collapse(t)$ destroys all $k = |IncT(e_3)|$ triangles incident to edge e_3, and creates at most $2(k-1)$ new triangles. Destroying the triangle t itself takes $O(1)$ time. Consider a splitting triangle σ incident to e_3. If σ and t do not share the same vertices, then splitting σ creates two new triangles, which can be done in $O(1)$ time. If they share the same vertices, then edges e_1 and e_4 (or e_2 and e_5) may need to be identified. Using lazy edge identification, the identity relation between e_1 and e_4 is recorded in $O(1)$ time. Thus Steps (5)–(17) run in time $O(k)$.

Step (4) merges all the edges identified with e_3, as well as their lists of incident triangles. Since each incident triangle merged becomes an entry in $IncT(e_3)$, merging all incident triangles takes $O(|IncT(e_3)|) = O(k)$ time. The cost of finding and merging all edges identified with e_3 in a transitive way is proportional to the total number of identify-relations recorded in all these edges. We charge the cost of processing each entry to the cost of creating this identity relation in Steps (9) and (10). Since each identity relation, once processed, will be destroyed, each Step (9) or (10) is charged at most once. Thus bounding the total time of Steps (5)–(17) over all calls to Procedure *Collapse* bounds also the total time for Step (4).

Overall analysis. The above analysis says that the total time for all executions of Step (4) is bounded by the total time for all executions of Steps (5)–(17). Hence the total number of triangles ever destroyed provides an upper bound for Algorithm RANDREEB. We now focus on bounding total number of triangles ever destroyed.

Note that a triangle σ can be destroyed either by performing *Collapse* procedure on this triangle itself, or by splitting it while collapsing some other triangle. We call σ a collapsing triangle in the former case, and a splitting triangle as usual in the latter case.

If σ is a collapsing triangle, then it will not create any new triangle. Now suppose σ is split while performing Procedure $Collapse(t)$. If σ shares the same vertices with t, then we call it a *degenerate splitting triangle*. In this case, it will not create any further triangle either, only potentially identity-relations between edges. Otherwise, σ is a *non-degenerate splitting triangle*, and creates two new triangles σ_1 and σ_2.

Exactly one of these two new triangles, say σ_2, shares the middle-vertex $q = \mathrm{mid}(t)$ with t (e.g, $\triangle q p_1 r$ in Figure 2 (c)). Hence σ_2 will be destroyed within the same $SeqCollapse(q)$ operation as t, either being collapsed or split. In fact, if σ_2 is destroyed by splitting, then it must be that σ_2 is destroyed when the algorithm collapses another triangle t' that shares the same vertices as σ_2 (which is q and the vertices of the common edge between σ and t'). In this case σ_2 has to be a degenerate splitting triangle. This means, whether σ_2 is a collapsing or a splitting triangle, it will be destroyed within Procedure $SeqCollapse(q)$, and will not create any new triangle. The other new triangle σ_1 will remain untouched throughout the $SeqCollapse(q)$ operation.

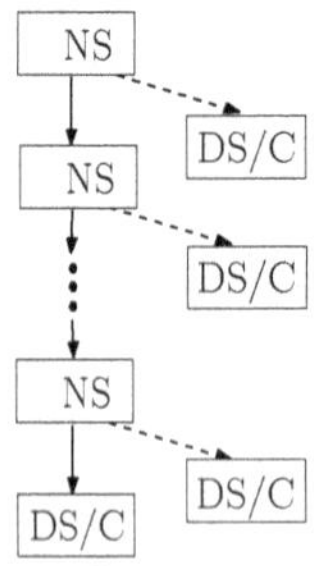

We now charge the existence of the short-lived triangle σ_2 to σ. We say that σ_1, the triangle survived the $SeqCollapse(q)$ operation, is the *child* of the splitting triangle σ, and σ is the *parent* of σ_1. If σ_1 turns out to be also a collapsing triangle, we charge it to σ as well. In summary, each splitting triangle has at most one child, and can be charged at most twice. These relations are illustrated in the right figure, where 'NS', 'DS' and 'C' stand for non-degenerate splitting, degenerate splitting, and collapsing triangles, respectively. Solid segments indicate parent-child relations, and dotted segments indicate charging relations.

Note that the parent-child relations induce a collection of directed paths (the solid path in the right figure is one example). Each such path starts with a triangle $t \in T$ from the original complex K, consists of a sequence of non-degenerate splitting triangles descended from t, and ends with either a collapsing triangle or a degenerate splitting triangle. We call such a path the *descendant-path with head t*. There are exactly $|T|$ number of descendant-paths, each headed by an original triangle from K. If an original triangle is a collapsing triangle, then its descendant-path has length 1 (containing only itself). Every non-degenerate splitting triangle belongs to exactly one descendant-path. The total size of these paths upper-bounds the total number of splitting and collapsing triangles ever existed. We now bound the expected length of each descendant-path.

Expected length of a descendant-path. Let the *index* of a vertex $v \in V$, denoted by $\mathcal{I}(v)$, be its position in the sorted list of vertices based on their function values; that is, $f(v_i) > f(v_j)$ if and only if $\mathcal{I}(v_i) > \mathcal{I}(v_j)$. Given a triangle $\sigma = \triangle abc$, its *span*, denoted by $Span(\sigma)$, is the interval spanned by maximum and minimum indices of vertices of t; i.e, $Span(\sigma) = [\min\{\mathcal{I}(a), \mathcal{I}(b), \mathcal{I}(c)\}, \max\{\mathcal{I}(a), \mathcal{I}(b), \mathcal{I}(c)\}]$. Let V_σ be the set of vertices v of K such that the level set connected component containing v intersects the triangle σ. The *range of the triangle σ*, denoted by $rg(\sigma)$, is the set of indices of vertices in V_σ in increasing order. Obviously, all indices in $rg(\sigma)$ fall in $Span(\sigma)$.

If we perform $SeqCollapse(v)$ for any vertex $v \in V_\sigma$, then, the triangle σ will either be collapsed (thus terminating the descending-path it lies in), or be split. In the latter case, the span of its child σ_1 is either $[I_1, \mathcal{I}(v)]$ or $[\mathcal{I}(v), I_2]$. In either case, $Span(\sigma_1)$ is strictly contained in the span $Span(\sigma)$ of its parent σ, and the range of σ_1 is the subsequence of $rg(\sigma)$ contained in $Span(\sigma_1)$. Furthermore, if we choose v randomly from V_σ, then with constant probability, the size of $rg(\sigma_1)$ (thus also of V_{σ_1}) is at most half of that of $rg(\sigma)$. Thus intuitively, it can be further split $O(\log |V_\sigma|) = O(\log |V|)$ expected number of times.

This can be made more precise by a standard probabilistic analysis using indicator functions for the size of the range that may appear in a dependent-path with a fixed head. Alternatively, this can be seen by thinking of this splitting process as building a randomized binary search tree, where splitting σ against a vertex $q \in V_\sigma$ corresponds to insert a random key $\mathcal{I}(q)$. At each node of the tree, we record the range of keys in its subtree. The sequence of ranges of triangles on the descendant-path with head σ corresponds to ranges of nodes along some tree path in a randomly built binary tree over keys $rg(\sigma)$. Since the expected height of such a tree is $O(\log |rg(\sigma)|) = O(\log |V|)$ [10], the dependent path has expected length of $O(\log |V|)$. Since there are $|T|$ number of descendant-paths, putting everything together, we conclude with our main result:

Theorem 4.3 *Given an arbitrary simplicial complex K with 2-skeleton (V, E, T) and a piecewise-linear function $f : K \to \mathbb{R}$, Algorithm* RANDREEB*(K, f) computes the augmented Reeb graph $\mathcal{R}(f)$ in expected time $O(m \log n)$ where $m = |V| + |T| + |E|$ and $n = |V|$.*

4.5 Variations

2-manifolds. When K is the triangulation of a 2-manifold, there is no need to use lazy edge identification. Thus Algorithm RANDREEB can be simplified while retaining its $O(|V| \log |V|)$ expected running time. The details can be found in Appendix A.

Using potential critical points. As we sweep K in increasing function values, the 0-th homology of the level sets does not change till some "critical" moments (corresponding to nodes in the Reeb graph). For example, if $|K|$ is a manifold and f is a Morse function, then these critical moments correspond to a certain subset of critical points of f. Instead of applying the $SeqCollapse(v)$ to all the vertices of K, we need only apply it to the "critical" vertices of K.

Specifically, we identify a subset of vertices $V_c \subseteq V$ which we call *potential critical points*, randomly permute them, and then apply Procedure *SeqCollapse* to only these vertices in their permuted order. The resulting complex is not a graph, but it turns out that the Reeb graph can be easily extracted from this complex in linear time. The time complexity of running RANDREEB using only the potential critical vertices is $O(m \log |V_c|) = O(m \log n)$. In the worst case, this running time is the same as the running time when all vertices are processed, but the revised algorithm is faster when $|V_c|$ is substantially smaller than m. The details are in Appendix B.

5. EXPERIMENTS

We implemented Algorithm RANDREEB() using the version where we only collapse w.r.t potential critical points as discussed in Section 4.5. In our experiments, this usually improves the running time of the version that processes all points by 10%–50%. Experiments are conducted on a standard desktop with a 64-bit 3.16 GHz Intel Core 2 Duo CPU and 8 GB of RAM.

Data sets. The tetrahedral meshes are downloaded from AIM@SHAPE database [1], and were used in previous papers [11, 29]. For non-manifold data set, the *Simulation* data is obtained by constructing the Rips complex from a set of high-dimensional points, where each point corresponds to a protein conformation produced by a molecular simulation process [19]. The function value at a point is the energy of the corresponding protein conformation. The *Camel* data is the Rips complex constructed from an incomplete point clouds of a camel model. The function value is the heat-signature defined in [26]. The *Hand* data is obtained from AIM@SHAPE database.

Performance comparison. We compare the performance of our algorithm with that of two state-of-the-art algorithms: the output-sensitive algorithm proposed in [11], denoted by OS, and the loop-surgery algorithm proposed in [29], denoted by LS. Algorithm OS can handle arbitrary simplicial complexes. We use the original implementation of OS, denoted by OS-v1, as well as a very recent improved implementation that we just obtained [2], denoted by OS-v2, both kindly provided by the authors of [11]. Algorithm LS processes only tetrahedral meshes modeling 3-manifolds with boundary embedded in $\mathbb{R}^3$. We use published running times reported in [29], which were obtained on a computer of similar configuration as ours. Time for our algorithm is averaged over 5 runs.

[2]The new version incorporate heuristics to prune certain unnecessary critical points.

Dataset Statistics					Running Time (sec)			
Classification	Dataset	#Triangles	$\|V_c\|$	# Loops	Our	OS-v1 [11]	OS-v2	LS [29]
Tetra-mesh	Fighter	143881	3618	0	5.36	629.40	96.19	0.35
	Plasma	2646016	2852	0	114.76	3772.42	339.89	2.20
	Earthquake	4198057	11896	0	150.28	5866.71	534.20	4.07
	Buckyball	2524284	4378	0	56.75	1602.01	178.61	2.51
	Post	1243200	132	1	13.91	18.05	13.38	0.69
Non-manifold	Hand	1676884	209	0	6.60	14.10	10.05	*
	Camel	144971	176	24	0.26	0.86	0.89	*
	Simulation	104127	11804	214	1.31	193.966	10.15	*

Table 2: Entries marked with * are unavailable. V_c is the set of potential critical points used by our algorithm.

Table 2 compares the running times of the three algorithms on a set of tetrahedral meshes (i.e, 3-manifolds with boundary embedded in $\mathbb{R}^3$) used in previous papers [11, 29], and on a set of non-manifold simplicial complexes.

Our algorithm outperforms both implementations of algorithm OS in almost all cases. Algorithm LS is specifically designed for 3-manifolds with boundary embedded in $\mathbb{R}^3$ and gives superior performance on all tetrahedral meshes.

Both our algorithm and algorithm LS identify and use a few potential critical points. Based on a nice observation about 3-manifolds embedded in $\mathbb{R}^3$, Algorithm LS processes only critical points which form a loop in the Reeb graph of the boundary of the 3-manifold. Thus its running time depends on the number of loops in this Reeb graph. While [29] reported timing results for some tetrahedral meshes whose boundary Reeb graphs contained 30-80 such loops, these data sets are not in the public domain. The tetrahedral mesh data sets listed in Table 2 all have 0 or 1 loops. Since the observation used in [29] does not hold for arbitrary simplicial complexes, Algorithm RandReeb needs to consider a much larger set of potentially critical points, not just the ones contributing to loops in the Reeb graph of domain boundary. The number of such points are on the order of several thousands in the data sets we tested. (See column 4 in Table 2).

Dataset	# Triangles	$\|V_c\|$	*AvgSeq*	*AvgRand*
Fighter	143881	3618	1138.40	21.16
Plasma	2646016	2852	*	15.57
Earthquake	4198057	11896	*	13.95
Buckyball	2524284	4378	104.3	11.1
Post	1243200	132	9.97	5.62
Hand	1676884	209	2.34	2.3
Camel	144971	176	3.44	3.16
Simulation	104127	11804	40.92	7.64

Table 3: The average number of times an input triangle is split, using sequential vertex-collapsing (*AvgSeq*) and random vertex-collapsing (*AvgRand*). Only input triangles that are destroyed are counted when computing this average. V_c is the set of potential critical points that our algorithm processes. Entries marked with (*) indicate the algorithm runs out of memory during the execution.

Effect of random collapsing. To measure the effect of collapsing in random order, we removed randomization from RandReeb and called *SeqCollapse* on potential critical points in order of increasing function values. We counted the average number of times an input triangle was split by the original randomized version of RandReeb (*AvgRand*) and by the sequential, non-random version (*AvgSeq*). See Table 3 for some results. For example, the *Fighter* data has 3618 potential critical points, RandReeb splits each triangle 21.16 times on average, while the sequential version splits each triangle 1138 times on average. Note that 21 is on the order of $\log_2(1138)$ which is what we expect by using a random order of collapsing.

Let C_q denote the connected component of $f^{-1}(q)$ that contains vertex q. *AvgSeq* is a lower bound on the number of times that a triangle intersects C_q for all potential critical points q. Thus each triangle in the *Fighter* data set intersects an average of (at least) 1138 such connected components. This may in some sense explain the performance difference between our algorithm and algorithm OS from [11], as it may process a triangle every time it is intersected by such a connected component.

6. CONCLUSION

In this paper, we proposed the first algorithm to compute the Reeb graph for an arbitrary simplicial complex in near linear time (although in expectation). The algorithm is simple to implement and performs reasonably well in practice.

It will be interesting to see whether one can further improve the practical performance of the current algorithm, while still maintaining its simplicity. Another open question is how to simplify the Reeb graph efficiently in $O(n \log n)$ time as well, where n is the number of edges in the final Reeb graph. This boils down to computing the topological features and their importance for the Reeb graph. There is a natural way to pair up nodes of Reeb graph [2] governed by the extended persistence [8]. However, the best algorithm to compute this pairing takes $O(n \log^2 n)$ by the data-structure proposed in [15]. It will be interesting to see whether there is a simple procedure to compute it in $O(n \log n)$ time.

Acknowledgments. The authors would like to thank Vijay Natarajan and Harish Doraiswamy for kindly providing their software, as well as help with it. This work is in part supported by the National Science Foundation (NSF) under grants CCF-0747082, CCF-0635008, and DBI-0750891.

7. REFERENCES

[1] Aim@shape shape repository, 2006. `http://shapes.aimatshape.net/`.

[2] P. K. Agarwal, H. Edelsbrunner, J. Harer, and Y. Wang. Extreme elevation on a 2-manifold. *Discrete Comput. Geom.*, 36(4):553–572, 2006.

[3] M. Attene, S. Biasotti, and M. Spagnuolo. Shape understanding by contour driven retiling. *The Visual Computer*, 19(2-3):127–138, 2003.

[4] S. Biasotti, B. Falcidieno, and M. Spagnuolo. Extended Reeb graphs for surface understanding and description. In *Proc. 9th Internat. Conf. Discrete Geom. for Computer Imagery*, pages 185–197, 2000.

[5] S. Biasotti, D. Giorgi, M. Spagnuolo, and B. Falcidieno. Reeb graphs for shape analysis and applications. *Theor. Comput. Sci.*, 392(1-3):5–22, 2008.

[6] H. Carr. *Topological manipulation of isosurfaces.* PhD thesis, The University of British Columbia (Canada), 2004. Adviser-Panne, Michiel Van.

[7] H. Carr, J. Snoeyink, and U. Axen. Computing contour trees in all dimensions. *Comput. Geom*, 24(2):75–94, 2003.

[8] D. Cohen-Steiner, H. Edelsbrunner, and J. Harer. Extending persistence using poincaré and lefschetz duality. *Found. of Comput. Math.*, 9(1):79–103, 2009.

[9] K. Cole-McLaughlin, H. Edelsbrunner, J. Harer, V. Natarajan, and V. Pascucci. Loops in Reeb graphs of 2-manifolds. *Discrete Comput. Geom.*, 32(2):231–244, 2004.

[10] T. H. Cormen, C. E. Leiserson, R. L. Rivest, and C. Stein. *Introduction to Algorithms.* MIT Press, Cambridge, MA, second edition, 2001.

[11] H. Doraiswamy and V. Natarajan. Efficient output-sensitive construction of Reeb graphs. In *Proc. 19th Internat. Sym. Alg. and Comput.*, pages 556–567, 2008.

[12] H. Doraiswamy and V. Natarajan. Efficient algorithms for computing Reeb graphs. *Computational Geometry: Theory and Applications*, 42:606–616, 2009.

[13] H. Edelsbrunner and J. Harer. *Computational Topology. An Introduction.* Amer. Math. Soc., Providence, Rhode Island, 2009.

[14] H. Edelsbrunner, J. Harer, A. Mascarenhas, V. Pascucci, and J. Snoeyink. Time-varying Reeb graphs for continuous space-time data. *Comput. Geom.*, 41(3):149–166, 2008.

[15] L. Georgiadis, R. E. Tarjan, and R. F. F. Werneck. Design of data structures for mergeable trees. In *Proc. 17th ACM-SIAM Sympos. Discrete Alg.*, pages 394–403, 2006.

[16] F. Hétroy and D. Attali. Topological quadrangulations of closed triangulated surfaces using the Reeb graph. *Graph. Models*, 65(1-3):131–148, 2003.

[17] M. Hilaga, Y. Shinagawa, T. Kohmura, and T. L. Kunii. Topology matching for fully automatic similarity estimation of 3d shapes. In *Proc. SIGGRAPH '01*, pages 203–212, 2001.

[18] P. Kanongchaiyos and Y. Shinagawa. Articulated Reeb graphs for interactive skeleton animation. In S. Hashimoto, editor, *Multimedia Modeling: Modeling Multimedia Information and System*, pages 451–467. World Scientific, 2000.

[19] I.-H. Park and C. Li. Novel dynamic ligand-induced-fit simulation via enhanced conformational samplings and ensemble dockings: a survivin example, 2009. Submitted to The Journal of Physical Chemistry, B.

[20] V. Pascucci, G. Scorzelli, P.-T. Bremer, and A. Mascarenhas. Robust on-line computation of Reeb graphs: simplicity and speed. *ACM Trans. Graph.*, 26(3):58, 2007.

[21] G. Patanè, M. Spagnuolo, and B. Falcidieno. Para-graph: Graph-based parameterization of triangle meshes with arbitrary genus. *Comput. Graph. Forum*, 23(4):783–797, 2004.

[22] G. Reeb. Sur les points singuliers d'une forme de Pfaff complètement intégrable ou d'une fonction numérique. *Comptes Rendus Hebdomadaires des Séances de l'Académie des Sciences*, 222:847–849, 1946.

[23] Y. Shi, R. Lai, S. Krishna, N. Sicotte, I. Dinov, and A. W. Toga. Anisotropic Laplace-Beltrami eigenmaps: Bridging Reeb graphs and skeletons. *Computer Vision and Pattern Recognition Workshop*, 0:1–7, 2008.

[24] Y. Shinagawa and T. L. Kunii. Constructing a Reeb graph automatically from cross sections. *IEEE Comput. Graph. Appl.*, 11(6):44–51, 1991.

[25] Y. Shinagawa, T. L. Kunii, and Y. L. Kergosien. Surface coding based on morse theory. *IEEE Comput. Graph. Appl.*, 11(5):66–78, 1991.

[26] J. Sun, M. Ovsjanikov, and L. J. Guibas. A concise and provably informative multi-scale signature based on heat diffusion. *Comput. Graph. Forum*, 28(5):1383–1392, 2009.

[27] S. P. Tarasov and M. N. Vyalyi. Construction of contour trees in 3D in $o(nlogn)$ steps. In *Proc. 14th Annu. ACM Sympos. Comput. Geom.*, pages 68–75, 1998.

[28] J. Tierny. *Reeb graph based 3D shape modeling and applications.* PhD thesis, Universite des Sciences et Technologies de Lille, 2008.

[29] J. Tierny, A. Gyulassy, E. Simon, and V. Pascucci. Loop surgery for volumetric meshes: Reeb graphs reduced to contour trees. *IEEE Trans. Vis. Comput. Graph.*, 15(6):1177–1184, 2009.

[30] T. Tung and F. Schmitt. The augmented multiresolution Reeb graph approach for content-based retrieval of 3d shapes. *Internat. J. Shape Modeling*, 11(1):91–120, 2005.

[31] M. van Kreveld, R. van Oostrum, C. Bajaj, V. Pascucci, and D. Schikore. Contour trees and small seed sets for isosurface traversal. In *Proc. 13th Annu. ACM Sympos. Comput. Geom.*, pages 212–220, 1997.

[32] Z. Wood, H. Hoppe, M. Desbrun, and P. Schröder. Removing excess topology from isosurfaces. *ACM Trans. Graph.*, 23(2):190–208, 2004.

[33] E. Zhang, K. Mischaikow, and G. Turk. Feature-based surface parameterization and texture mapping. *ACM Trans. Graph.*, 24(1):1–27, 2005.

APPENDIX

A. 2-MANIFOLDS

When K is the triangulation of a 2-manifold, it turns out that there is no need to use lazy edge identification. Thus Algorithm RandReeb can be simplified while retaining its $O(|V| \log |V|)$ expected running time. The simplification is based on the following so that performing merging directly in Steps (9) and (10) takes constant time.

Claim A.1 *If K is the triangulation of a 2-manifold (with or without boundary,) then $|IncT(e)| \leq 2$ for any edge e in any intermediate complex produced by* RANDREEB*(K, f).*

PROOF. The claim holds at the beginning for K, since its underlying space is a 2-manifold. Let $IncT_{K'}(e)$ denote the incident list of an edge e in an intermediate complex K'. Let K_1 and K_2 be the complex before and after a $Collapse(t)$ operation with $t = \triangle(qp_1p_2)$ and $q = \mathrm{mid}(t)$. Recall Figure 2. Procedure $Collapse(t)$ will collapse t and split all the other $k-1$ triangles incident to the edge p_1p_2, where $k = |IncT_{K_1}(p_1p_2)| \leq 2$. In other words, there is at most one triangle we split, say, it is $\sigma = \triangle p_1p_2r$.

If $r \neq q$, then after the collapse operation, edge qp_1 will lose one incident triangle (which is t), but gain one incident triangle as well. Hence $|IncT_{K_2}(qp_1)| = |IncT_{K_1}(qp_1)| - 1 + (k-1) \leq 2$ as both $|IncT_{K_1}(qp_1)|$ and k are bounded by 2. The same argument holds for edge qp_2. The edge p_1r (resp. p_2r) of the splitting triangle σ will lose one triangle (i.e, σ) in its incident list, but gain one triangle $\triangle qp_1r$ (resp. $\triangle qp_2r$). Hence the size of its incident list remains the same.

In the case that $r = q$ and a pair of double edges e_1 and e_2 are identified, we have that $|IncT_{K_2}(e_1)| = |IncT_{K_1}(e_1)| - 1 + |IncT_{K_1}(e_2)| - 1 \leq 2$. The claim thus holds at any time during the algorithm. □

B. USING POTENTIAL CRITICAL POINTS

Algorithm RANDREEB is conceptually simple and easy to implement. However, it ignores any property that input data may have. Specifically, observe that as we sweep K in increasing function values, the H_0 homology of the level sets does not change till some "critical" moments (corresponding to nodes in the Reeb graph). For example, if the $|K|$ is a 2-manifold (resp. d-manifold) and f is a Morse function, then these critical moments correspond to the set of critical points (resp. a certain subset of critical points) of f. Thus it seems wasteful that we perform Procedure $SeqCollapse$ for all vertices in K, even though many of them do not carry key information.

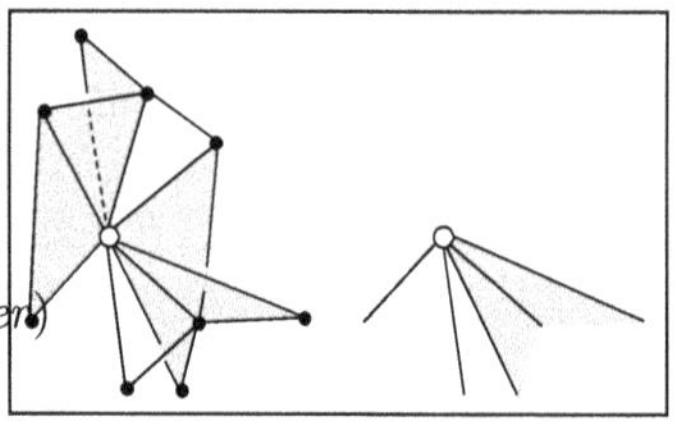

We thus present a revised algorithm RANDREEB() to potentially reduce the number of $Collapse$ operations. First, we say that a simplex α_1 is *lower* (resp. *higher*) than another simplex α_2, if for any two points x and y in the interior of α_1 and α_2 respectively, we have that $f(x) < f(y)$ (resp. $f(x) > f(y)$). Given a vertex $v \in K$, its *lower star* (resp. *upper star*) is the union of the interior of simplices incident to v which are lower (resp. higher) than v. See the right figure for an example: The left illustration shows the closure of all simplices incident to the empty dot, and the right one shows its lower star, which contains three components. We say that a vertex $v \in K$ is a *potential critical point* if its lower star or upper star has more than one component. It is easy to verify that the pre-image of any node in the Reeb graph $\mathcal{R}_K(f)$ necessarily contains a potential critical point. The inverse is not true – the image of a potential critical point v may be a monotonic degree-2 point in the interior of an arc of $\mathcal{R}_K(f)$.

We now modify Algorithm RANDREEB(K, f) as follows. First, we compute the set of potential critical vertices $V_c \subseteq V$. In the second step, we randomly permute vertices in V_c and perform Procedure $SeqCollapse$ for only these vertices. Let K' denote the resulting complex after these $SeqCollapse$ operations. By Lemma 4.1, K' shares the same Reeb graph as K; that is, $\mathcal{R}_{K'}(f) = \mathcal{R}_K(f)$. Furthermore, the following result suggests that K' almost has the structure of its Reeb graph, even though it is not yet a graph.

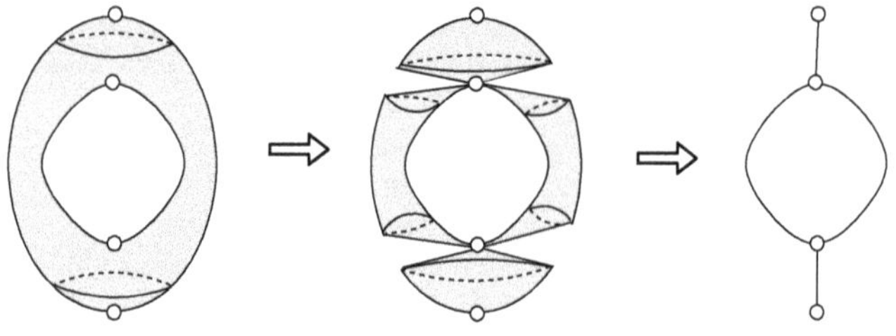

Figure 6: Performing Procedure $Collapse$ only to the four potential critical points (empty dots).

Lemma B.1 *Let $\Phi_f : |K'| \to \mathcal{R}_{K'}(f)$ be the continuous surjection from $|K'|$ to its Reeb graph. For every point $v \in V$, there is a one-to-one correspondence between components in the upper-star of v in K' and the up-branches of $\Phi_f(v)$ in $\mathcal{R}(f)$. Similarly, there is a one-to-one correspondence between components in the lower-star of v in K' and the lower-branches of $\Phi_f(v)$ in $\mathcal{R}(f)$.*

See Figure 6 for an example where the underlying domain of input simplicial complex is a torus. There are four potential critical points in V_c in this case (empty dots). Consider the lower saddle point p. Note that its lower star in the input manifold has two components. After performing $SeqCollapse$ for all points in V_c in K' (middle figure), the lower star of p has only one component, just like in the final Reeb graph (right figure).

Lemma B.1 states that the local neighborhood of every vertex in K' has the same connected component information as its image in the final Reeb graph $\mathcal{R}(f)$. Hence in the third step of the algorithm, we use K' to connect vertices in V_c to obtain the Reeb graph of f[3]. In particular, for every $v \in V_c$ and for each component of its upper star, we start an upward path by connecting v to an arbitrary vertex v' of K in the closure of that component. We then connect v' to an arbitrary vertex v'' connected to v' by an edge and with a higher function value. We continue this tracing until we reach another potential critical vertex from V_c. Note that any intermediate vertex we reach along this upward path can have only one component in its upper star (as otherwise, this vertex should be in V_c and the tracing is terminated). It follows from Lemma B.1 that the resulting graph consisting of the upward tracing paths is the Reeb graph of f.

It is easy to see that the expected time complexity of the revised algorithm RANDREEBis $O(m \log |V_c|) = O(m \log n)$. In worst case this is the same as as the running time when processing all vertices, but is faster when V_c is substantially smaller than n.

[3]Note that this is not the augmented Reeb graph generated by K any more, as not all vertices will appear as a node in the final Reeb graph. It is a Reeb graph of f augmented by some vertices from K.

Topological Inference via Meshing * †

Benoît Hudson
Autodesk, Inc.

Gary L. Miller
Computer Science Dept.
Carnegie Mellon University
5000 Forbes Avenue
Pittsburgh, PA 15217
glmiller@cs.cmu.edu

Steve Y. Oudot
INRIA Saclay
Geometrica Group
4 rue Jacques Monod
91893 ORSAY, France
steve.oudot@inria.fr

Donald R. Sheehy
Computer Science Dept.
Carnegie Mellon University
5000 Forbes Avenue
Pittsburgh, PA 15217
dsheehy@cs.cmu.edu

ABSTRACT

We apply ideas from mesh generation to improve the time and space complexities of computing the full persistent homological information associated with a point cloud P in Euclidean space $\mathbb{R}^d$. Classical approaches rely on the Čech, Rips, α-complex, or witness complex filtrations of P, whose complexities scale up very badly with d. For instance, the α-complex filtration incurs the $n^{\Omega(d)}$ size of the Delaunay triangulation, where n is the size of P. The common alternative is to truncate the filtrations when the sizes of the complexes become prohibitive, possibly before discovering the most relevant topological features. In this paper we propose a new collection of filtrations, based on the Delaunay triangulation of a carefully-chosen superset of P, whose sizes are reduced to $2^{O(d^2)}n$. Our filtrations interleave multiplicatively with the family of offsets of P, so that the persistence diagram of P can be approximated in $2^{O(d^2)}n^3$ time in theory, with a near-linear observed running time in practice. Thus, our approach remains tractable in medium dimensions, say 4 to 10.

Categories and Subject Descriptors

F.2.2 [**Analysis of Algorithms and Problem Complexity**]: Nonnumerical Algorithms and Problems—*Computations on discrete structures, Geometrical problems and computations*

*This work was partially supported by the National Science Foundation under grant number CCF-0635257.

†The full version of the paper is available as INRIA research report number RR-7125. It can be downloaded at `http://hal.inria.fr/inria-00436891/en/`.

SCG'10, June 13–16, 2010, Snowbird, Utah, USA.

General Terms

Algorithms, Theory

Keywords

topological inference, persistent homology, mesh generation, sparse Voronoi refinement

1. INTRODUCTION

The goal of topological inference is to infer topological invariants of a space given only a sample of the space. In the setting of geometric points, it is natural to consider the point set at different scales by blowing the points up to balls. Persistent homology is a powerful tool for understanding the topological structure of a point cloud across these different scales. Given a point cloud P in Euclidean space $\mathbb{R}^d$, one can build a simplicial complex over P, then associate a time of appearance $t(\sigma)$ to each simplex σ (full-dimensional or lower-dimensional) in the complex. This defines a nested family of simplicial complexes indexed by time, known as a *filtration*. As simplices are added to the complex, the set of topological features (connected components, holes, tunnels, voids, etc.) changes: new ones are created, and old ones destroyed. The persistence algorithm [13, 26] takes the filtration and produces a *persistence diagram* that encodes the lifespans of these topological features. Given an appropriate choice of filtration, one can prove that short-lived features correspond to sampling noise, while long-lived features correspond to relevant topological structures underlying the input set.

Several filtrations have been used with success in the past, including the α-complex [12] and witness complex [10, 11] filtrations, which are based on the Delaunay triangulation of P or an approximation of it, and the Čech [14] and Vietoris-Rips [25] filtrations, which are derived from the nerves of collections of congruent balls centered at the data points. The ability of these filtrations to capture the homological information associated with a point cloud is certified by a well-founded theory [3], which largely explains their success from a theoretical point of view. In practice however, the cost to build them makes their use prohibitive, even in medium dimensions, say 4 to 10. When α becomes large, the size of the α-complex approaches that of the Delaunay triangulation: $n^{\Omega(d)}$ for n data points in d dimensions, even for some relatively "nice" inputs [15, 16]. The sizes of the Čech, Rips and (relaxed) witness complexes grow even more quickly, as $2^{\Omega(n)}$.

To avoid this issue, researchers usually resort to truncating the filtrations at a prescribed size limit. This truncation is equivalent to looking at the data at small scales only, and can make the algorithm miss relevant structures at larger scales. A typical scenario, inspired from [17], is described in Figure 1 (left): it consists of a point cloud sampled evenly from a helicoidal curve drawn on the Clifford torus in $\mathbb{R}^4$. In this case, the point cloud admits at least three candidate underlying spaces: at a small scale, the curve; at a larger scale, the torus; and at an even larger scale, the 3-sphere of radius $\sqrt{2}$ on which the Clifford torus is naturally embedded. One might also add the point cloud itself and $\mathbb{R}^4$ at either ends of the spectrum.

In order to analyze such data sets at different scales using only truncated filtrations, Chazal and Oudot [6] proposed a *landmarking* strategy in the spirit of [17], which maintains a growing subset of the data points, on which the simplicial complexes are built. However, their approach produces a weaker form of data representation than persistence diagrams, which does not explicitly correlate the features visible at different scales. As a result, they can get false positives when retrieving the set of persistent topological features. See e.g. [17, Fig. 7] for an example.

A simple algorithm. In this paper, we use techniques from finite element mesh generation to build a complex on the input set with some extra vertices that is guaranteed to have small size. We then order the simplices in a natural and easy to compute way in order to generate a filtration. This complex can then be input directly to standard algorithms to discover the persistent topological features. In its simplest form our algorithm can be implemented using both the mesh generator and the persistence computation as black boxes. Thus, the only new code to implement is the filtering of the mesh.

Consequently, the work in this paper is primarily in the analysis of the theoretical guarantees. We show how varying the mesh generation techniques, one can get different guarantees with respect to the size of the complex and the tightness of the approximation.

Enter Sparse Voronoi Refinement. We preprocess the point cloud P using techniques inspired by Delaunay refinement, iteratively inserting new points of $\mathbb{R}^d$ called *Steiner points* into P until some quality criterion is met. Here, quality will be measured by the aspect ratios of the Voronoi cells, so as to guarantee that the size of the Delaunay triangulation of the augmented set $P \cup S$ drops down to $2^{O(d^2)}(n + |S|)$ when the criterion is met. Furthermore, the number of Steiner points needed to meet the criterion is $2^{O(d \log d)}n$, which makes the size of the final triangulation only $2^{O(d^2)}n$. In order to realize the benefits of the refined mesh, we compute it without first constructing the Delaunay triangulation, as is possible using the Sparse Voronoi Refinement (SVR) algorithm [19]. In addition, we partition the input into *well-paced* sets which guarantees that the size of the filtration stays linear in n, modulo a constant factor that depends exponentially on d [21].

Once the augmented point cloud $P \cup S$ has been computed, we order the simplices of its Delaunay triangulation according to a filter $t : \mathrm{Del}(P \cup S) \to \mathbb{R}$. Several different filters are analyzed in the paper, yielding filtrations with different properties: some are easier to build, others come with better approximation guarantees. The choice of a particular filter depends on the application considered and is therefore left to the user. Note that all our filters are based on distances to the input point cloud P, as illustrated in Figure 2. This enables us to show that the corresponding filtrations are interleaved on a logarithmic scale with the filtration of the offsets of P, in the sense of [4], from which we can deduce that they produce accurate (approximate) persistence diagrams. Computing the persistence diagram takes time cubic in the number of simplices and thus dominates our worst-case $2^{O(d^2)}n^3$ overall runtime. This bound, though large, is still a significant improvement over $n^{\Omega(d)}$. Moreover, in practice, the persistence diagram computation takes near-linear time (on an input with $2^{O(d^2)}n$ simplices), which makes our approach tractable in small to medium dimensions (4-10) for moderate input sizes (thousands to tens of thousands of points). A preliminary implementation bears out these predictions (see Section 6).

Layout of the paper. In Section 2 we recall the necessary background on Sparse Voronoi Refinement and on persistent homology. The rest of the paper is devoted to the description of our approach. We first present a simplified version in Section 3 that produces a filtration that is $\log(\rho)$-interleaved with the offsets filtration of P, for some constant $\rho \geq 2$. The size of this filtration is $2^{O(d^2)}n\log(\Delta(P))$, where $\Delta(P)$ denotes the *spread* of P. We then show in Section 4 how the interleaving between our filtration and the offsets filtration can be tightened, so that we can produce persistence diagrams that are accurate within any arbitrarily small error. Finally, in Section 5 we concentrate on the size of the filtration and show how to eliminate its dependence on the spread by a recursive decomposition of the input.

2. PRELIMINARIES

Throughout the paper, the ambient space is $\mathbb{R}^d$, endowed with the standard Euclidean norm, noted $|\cdot|$. We use singular homology with coefficients in a field, omitted in our notations for simplicity. We refer the reader to [18] for a thorough introduction to homology theory.

2.1 Clipped Voronoi Diagrams and Sparse Voronoi Refinement

Let P be a finite set of distinct points lying in general position in $\mathbb{R}^d$. We denote by $\mathrm{Vor}(P)$ the *Voronoi diagram* of P, defined as a collection of closed cells $\{\mathrm{Vor}(p) : p \in P\}$, where each cell $\mathrm{Vor}(p)$ is the locus of the points of $\mathbb{R}^d$ that are at least as close to p as to any other point of P. Its dual complex is known as the *Delaunay triangulation* $\mathrm{Del}(P)$. Since P lies in general position, $\mathrm{Del}(P)$ is an embedded simplicial complex in $\mathbb{R}^d$, whose underlying space coincides with the convex hull of P.

Given an axis-aligned box BB containing P, we consider the restrictions of the Voronoi diagram and Delaunay triangulation to BB. Specifically, given a point $p \in P$, we

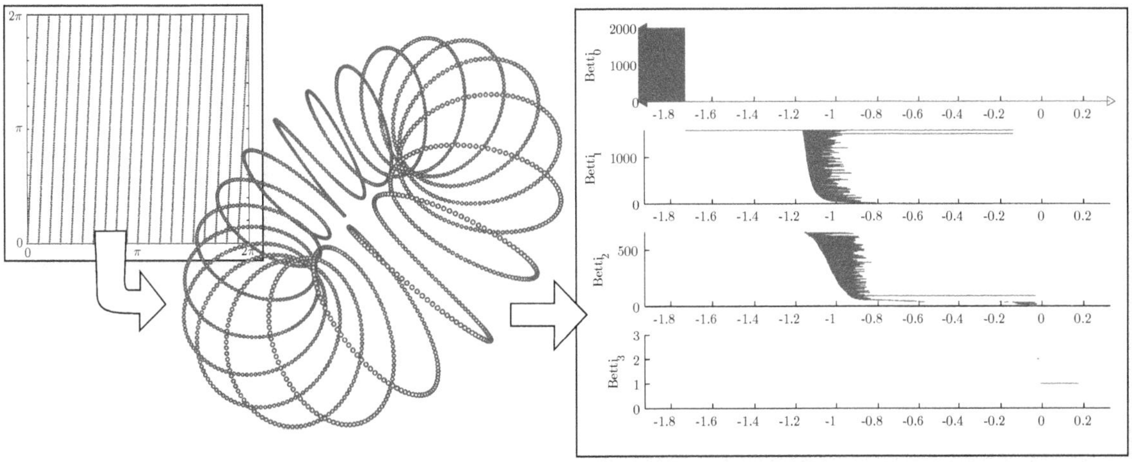

Figure 1: The Clifford data set. Left: point cloud sampled uniformly along a periodic curve in $[0, 2\pi]^2$, then mapped onto a helicoidal curve drawn on the Clifford torus in $\mathbb{R}^4$ via the canonical embedding $(u, v) \mapsto (\cos u, \sin u, \cos v, \sin v)$. Right: log-scale barcode obtained on this data set using the filtration of Section 3.2.

call $\mathrm{Vor}_\square(p)$ its Voronoi cell clipped to BB: $\mathrm{Vor}_\square(p) = \mathrm{Vor}(p) \cap BB$. We call $\mathrm{Vor}_\square(P)$ the Voronoi diagram clipped to BB, and $\mathrm{Del}_\square(P)$ its dual complex, which is a subcomplex of $\mathrm{Del}(P)$. For a clipped Voronoi cell $\mathrm{Vor}_\square(p)$, we let R_p be the radius of the smallest Euclidean ball centered at p that contains all of $\mathrm{Vor}_\square(p)$, and we let r_p be the radius of the largest Euclidean ball centered at p that is entirely contained in $\mathrm{Vor}_\square(v)$. We define the *aspect ratio* of the clipped Voronoi cell to be R_p/r_p.

*Sparse Voronoi Refinement (*Svr*).* The Svr algorithm takes a finite point cloud P as input and returns a finite superset M of P that satisfies the following properties:

(i) M is a point sampling of some axis-aligned bounding box BB of side length $O(\mathrm{diam}(P))$ around P,

(ii) $\mathrm{Del}_\square(M) = \mathrm{Del}(M)$, where $\mathrm{Del}_\square(M)$ denotes the Delaunay triangulation clipped to BB,

(iii) the clipped Voronoi cells have aspect ratios bounded from above by an absolute constant $\rho \geq 2$,

(iv) The size of $\mathrm{Del}(M)$ is $2^{O(d^2)}|M|$,

(v) The size of M is $2^{O(d)} n \log(\Delta(P))$, where $\Delta(P)$ denotes the *spread* of P, i.e. the ratio of the largest to smallest interpoint distances among the points of P.

As shown in [20], the extra work needed to fill in the entire bounding box BB with point samples is negligible. The points of $S = M \setminus P$ added by the algorithm are called *Steiner points.* We will refer to the point set M along with its Delaunay triangulation as the *mesh.* The Svr algorithm can produce M in near-optimal $2^{O(d)} n \log(\Delta(P)) + O(|M|)$ time [19]. As shown in [21], it is possible to reduce the output-sensitive term $|M|$ to $2^{O(d \log d)} n$ by applying Svr to well-chosen subsets of the input called *well-paced sets.* This technique will be used in Section 5 to improve the complexity of our method, which uses Svr as a black box.

2.2 Filtrations, persistence diagrams and stability

A *filtration* is a one-parameter family $\mathcal{F} = \{F_\alpha\}_{\alpha \geq 0}$ of topological spaces that is nested with respect to inclusion, that is: $F_\alpha \subseteq F_\beta$ for all $\beta \geq \alpha \geq 0$. Persistence theory describes the evolution of the homology of the sets F_α as α ranges from 0 to $+\infty$. This is done through a special type of planar representation called a *persistence diagram.* When the parameter of $\mathcal{F}$ is clear and varies over all of $[0, +\infty]$, we write simply $\{F_\alpha\}$ rather than $\{F_\alpha\}_{\alpha \geq 0}$. Given a discrete subset $A = \{\cdots, \alpha_i, \alpha_j, \alpha_k, \cdots\}$ of $[0, +\infty)$ that has no accumulation point, the canonical inclusions $\cdots \hookrightarrow F_{\alpha_i} \hookrightarrow F_{\alpha_j} \hookrightarrow F_{\alpha_k} \hookrightarrow \cdots$ induce a directed system of vector spaces involving the r-dimensional homology groups:

$$\cdots \longrightarrow H_r(F_{\alpha_i}) \longrightarrow H_r(F_{\alpha_j}) \longrightarrow H_r(F_{\alpha_k}) \longrightarrow \cdots$$

If all the vector spaces are finite-dimensional, then the filtration, $\mathcal{F}$, is said to be *tame*, and the algebraic structure of this system can be encoded as a multi-set of points in $[0, +\infty]^2$. The *r-th persistence diagram* of $\mathcal{F}$ is then obtained by considering a growing family $\{A_i\}_{i \in \mathbb{N}}$ of discrete sets, whose union is dense in $[0, +\infty)$, and by taking the well-defined limit of their corresponding multi-sets, which does not depend on the choice of the family $\{A_i\}_{i \in \mathbb{N}}$. The union of all such diagrams for r ranging over $\mathbb{N}$ is called the *persistence diagram* of $\mathcal{F}$, noted $\mathrm{D}\mathcal{F}$. Intuitively, each point $p \in \mathrm{D}f$ encodes the lifespan of some homological feature (connected component, hole, void, etc.) appearing at time p_x and dying at time p_y in the filtration. For formal developments on this topic, please refer to [4], whose framework is adopted here.

An important property of persistence diagrams is to be stable under small perturbations of the filtrations. Proximity between filtrations is defined in terms of mutual nesting: specifically, two tame filtrations $\mathcal{F}, \mathcal{G}$ are said to be ε-*interleaved* if we have $F_\alpha \subseteq G_{\alpha+\varepsilon}$ and $G_\alpha \subseteq F_{\alpha+\varepsilon}$ for all $\alpha \geq 0$. Under this condition, it is known that the persistence diagrams $\mathrm{D}\mathcal{F}$ and $\mathrm{D}\mathcal{G}$ are ε-close in the bottleneck distance [4, 8]. Recall that the bottleneck distance $\mathrm{d}_B^\infty(A, B)$ between two multi-sets $A, B \subset [0, +\infty]^2$ is defined as the quantity $\min_\gamma \max_{p \in A} \|p - \gamma(p)\|_\infty$, where $\|\cdot\|_\infty$ denotes the l_∞-norm and γ ranges over all bijections from A to B. To make sure that such bijections always exist, all persistence diagrams are enriched with the diagonal $\{(x, x) : x \in [0, +\infty]\}$, whose multiplicity is set to infinity. The formal statement goes as follows:

THEOREM 2.1. (STABILITY [4, 8]). *If two tame filtrations $\mathcal{F}, \mathcal{G}$ are ε-interleaved, then $\mathrm{d}_B^\infty(\mathrm{D}\mathcal{F}, \mathrm{D}\mathcal{G}) \leq \varepsilon$.*

Multiplicative interleaving. In this paper we consider filtrations $\mathcal{F}, \mathcal{G}$ that are ε-interleaved *multiplicatively*, that is: $F_\alpha \subseteq G_{\alpha\varepsilon}$ and $G_\alpha \subseteq F_{\alpha\varepsilon}$ for all $\alpha \geq 0$. Consider $\log \mathcal{F}$ and $\log \mathcal{G}$, the reparametrizations of the filtrations $\mathcal{F}$ and $\mathcal{G}$ on the natural logarithmic scale[1]: $\forall \alpha \in \mathbb{R}$, $\log F_\alpha = F_{\exp(\alpha)}$ and $\log G_\alpha = G_{\exp(\alpha)}$. Multiplicative ε-interleaving of $\mathcal{F}$ and $\mathcal{G}$ implies additive $\log(\varepsilon)$-interleaving of their reparametrizations, $\log \mathcal{F}$ and $\log \mathcal{G}$, that is: $\forall \alpha \in \mathbb{R}$, $\log F_\alpha \subseteq \log G_{\alpha + \log \varepsilon}$ and $\log G_\alpha \subseteq \log F_{\alpha + \log \varepsilon}$.

As a result, multiplicative interleaving of filtrations implies the following weaker form of proximity between their persistence diagrams, where the notation $\mathrm{d}_{\mathrm{D}}^{\log}(\mathcal{F}, \mathcal{G})$ stands for the quantity $\mathrm{d}_B^\infty(\mathrm{D}\log\mathcal{F}, \mathrm{D}\log\mathcal{G})$:

COROLLARY 2.2. *If two filtrations $\mathcal{F}, \mathcal{G}$ are ε-interleaved multiplicatively, then $\mathrm{d}_{\mathrm{D}}^{\log}(\mathcal{F}, \mathcal{G}) \leq \log \varepsilon$.*

The persistence diagram of a simplicial filtration (i.e. a finite family of nested finite abstract simplicial complexes) can be computed using the persistence algorithm [13, 26]. Its runtime is determined by the total number of simplices m in the filtration; in the worst case, it can take $O(m^3)$ time, although in practice near-linear times are common. Constructing the filtration itself will take us near-linear time as well: reducing the size of the filtration represents a large win for computing persistent homology.

2.3 Filters and projections

In addition to filtering simplicial complexes, a filtration can also be defined by considering a topological space X and a non-negative function $t : X \to [0, +\infty)$, called a *filter*, which encodes the time at which each point of X appears in the filtration. The spaces forming the filtration are the sublevel-sets of t, i.e. the sets of the form $F_\alpha = t^{-1}([0, \alpha])$. In this setting, a filtered simplicial complex is a piecewise constant function that maps the interior of a simplex σ to $t(\sigma)$.

Distance functions are an important class of filters considered in the paper. Given a compact set P in Euclidean space $\mathbb{R}^d$, let $\mathrm{d}_P(x)$ denote the distance from $x \in \mathbb{R}^d$ to the nearest point in P:

$$\mathrm{d}_P(x) = \min_{p \in P} |x - p|.$$

For any $\alpha \geq 0$, the sublevel-set $P^\alpha = \mathrm{d}_P^{-1}([0, \alpha])$ is the union of the closed Euclidean balls of same radius α about the points of P, called the *α-offset* of P. The family of sublevel-sets of d_P is thus known as the *offsets filtration* of P in the literature. This filtration has played an important role in topological inference from point cloud data, where it has been used as a central theoretical tool for proving the correctness of existing methods [5, 6, 8, 22].

We will also be using a related distance function induced by $P \subset \mathbb{R}^d$. The Ruppert local feature size, $f_P(x)$, is the distance from x to its second nearest neighbor in P [23]:

$$f_P(x) = \min_{p_1 \neq p_2 \in P} \max\{|x - p_1|, |x - p_2|\}.$$

[1]Throughout the paper, log denotes the natural logarithm.

The triangle inequality implies that f_P is 1-Lipschitz. The function f_P is a standard tool in mesh generation as it bounds the size of Voronoi cells locally in an optimal, bounded aspect ratio mesh.

To conclude this preliminary section, let us mention another important function derived from a compact set P: the metric projection $\pi_P : \mathbb{R}^d \to \mathbb{R}^d$, defined by $\pi_P(x) = \mathrm{argmin}_{y \in P}|x - y|$ for all $x \in \mathbb{R}^d$. This function will be instrumental in showing topological equivalence between various families of spaces. In particular, we will rely on the following classical result of convex geometry, whose proof is recalled for completeness in the full version of the paper:

LEMMA 2.3. *If $P \subset \mathbb{R}^d$ is compact and convex, then the projection π_P is well-defined and 1-Lipschitz over $\mathbb{R}^d$.*

3. THE α-MESH FILTRATION

Our strategy is to build a superset M of the input point set P, and then to filter the Delaunay triangulation of M in order to obtain a filtration that can be related to the offsets filtration of P. In Section 3.1 we present a simplified version of our filter that yields a partial approximation (Theorem 3.5). This version may not always be useful in practice, however it is more intuitive and will enable us to emphasize the key ingredients of our approach. In Section 3.2 we will reuse these ingredients and expand upon them to improve our filter and obtain a full approximation guarantee (Theorem 3.7).

3.1 Basic filter

Our input is a finite set P of points in general position in $\mathbb{R}^d$. We first apply the SVR algorithm to construct a superset $M \supseteq P$ that satisfies conditions (i) through (v) of Section 2.1. We then define the filter $t : \mathrm{Del}(M) \to \mathbb{R}$ as follows, identifying each k-simplex $\sigma \in \mathrm{Del}(M)$ with its vertex set $\{v_0, \ldots, v_k\} \subseteq M$:

$$t(\sigma) = \max_{v \in \sigma} d_P(v).$$

We define the *α-mesh filtration* $\{D_M^\alpha\}$ as the sublevel-sets filtration of t: for every $\alpha \geq 0$, let D_M^α be the subcomplex of $\mathrm{Del}(M)$ made of all simplices σ with $t(\sigma) \leq \alpha$. Note that if τ is a face of σ then $t(\tau) \leq t(\sigma)$, so the spaces forming the filtration are proper simplicial complexes. Furthermore, $D_M^\alpha \subseteq D_M^\beta$ for all $\beta \geq \alpha \geq 0$.

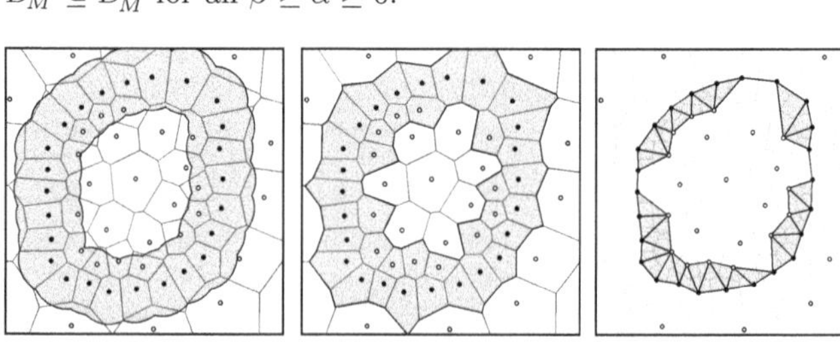

Figure 2: From left to right: the offset P^α, the α-Voronoi V_M^α and its dual α-mesh D_M^α.

Intuitively, our basic filter sorts the simplices of $\mathrm{Del}(M)$ according to their distances to P, in order to simulate within $\mathrm{Del}(M)$ the growth of the offsets of P — see Figure 2 for an illustration. Our analysis shows that this simulation process works thanks to the fact that Voronoi cells have bounded aspect ratios.

Theoretical analysis. Our goal is to relate $\{D_M^\alpha\}$ to the offsets filtration $\{P^\alpha\}$. We do the analysis in terms of a dual filtration, $\{V_M^\alpha\}$, based on the clipped Voronoi diagram $\mathrm{Vor}_\square(M)$ — see Figure 2 (center) for an example. To each point $v \in M$ we assign a closed convex set $U_\alpha(v)$ as follows:

$$U_\alpha(v) = \begin{cases} \emptyset & \text{if } \alpha < t(v), \\ \mathrm{Vor}_\square(v) & \text{otherwise.} \end{cases}$$

The filtration $\{V_M^\alpha\}$ is defined by $V_M^\alpha = \bigcup_{v\in M} U_\alpha(v)$ for all $\alpha \geq 0$, and the collection $\mathcal{U}_\alpha = \{U_\alpha(v)\}_{v\in M}$ forms a closed cover of V_M^α. Let $\mathcal{N}\mathcal{U}_\alpha$ denote its nerve, i.e. the simplicial complex containing one k-simplex for each non-empty intersection of $k+1$ elements in $\mathcal{U}_\alpha$. Both D_M^α and $\mathcal{N}\mathcal{U}_\alpha$ are embedded as subcomplexes of the full simplex 2^M over the vertex set M, and the following lemma stresses their relationship:

LEMMA 3.1. *For all $\alpha \geq 0$, the subcomplexes D_M^α and $\mathcal{N}\mathcal{U}_\alpha$ of the full simplex 2^M are equal.*

PROOF. Consider first the case of a zero-dimensional simplex $\sigma = \{v\}$. The definition of D_M^α states that $\{v\} \in D_M^\alpha$ if and only if $\mathrm{d}_P(v) \leq \alpha$, which is also the criterion for which $U_\alpha(v)$ is not empty and hence belongs to the collection $\mathcal{U}_\alpha$. Thus, $\{v\} \in D_M^\alpha \Leftrightarrow \{v\} \in \mathcal{N}\mathcal{U}_\alpha$.

Consider now the case of a higher-dimensional simplex $\sigma = \{v_0, \cdots, v_k\}$. The definition of D_M^α states that $\sigma \in D_M^\alpha$ if and only if $\sigma \in \mathrm{Del}(M)$ and $\max_i t(v_i) \leq \alpha$, which is equivalent to $\bigcap_{i=0}^k \mathrm{Vor}(v_i) \neq \emptyset$ and $\max_i t(v_i) \leq \alpha$. By assertion (ii) of Section 2.1, we have $\bigcap_{i=0}^k \mathrm{Vor}(v_i) \neq \emptyset \Leftrightarrow \bigcap_{i=0}^k \mathrm{Vor}(v_i) \cap BB \neq \emptyset \Leftrightarrow \bigcap_{i=0}^k \mathrm{Vor}_\square(v_i) \neq \emptyset$. Hence, $\sigma \in D_M^\alpha$ if and only if $\sigma \in \mathcal{N}\mathcal{U}_\alpha$. □

Since the sets $U_\alpha(v)$ in the cover of V_M^α are convex, the Nerve Theorem [18, §4G] implies that V_M^α and its nerve $\mathcal{N}\mathcal{U}_\alpha$ are homotopy equivalent. Furthermore, since the sets $U_\alpha(v)$ are monotonically increasing with α, it follows from the Persistent Nerve Theorem [6] that the filtration $\{V_M^\alpha\}$ and the family of nerves $\{\mathcal{N}\mathcal{U}_\alpha\}$ have identical persistence diagrams (see the full version of the paper for the details of the argument). Combined with Lemma 3.1, this fact draws a connection between the persistence diagrams of $\{V_M^\alpha\}$ and $\{D_M^\alpha\}$:

LEMMA 3.2. *The persistence diagrams of the filtrations $\{V_M^\alpha\}$ and $\{D_M^\alpha\}$ are identical.*

Let the clipped offsets be defined as follows, in analogy with the clipped Voronoi cells: $P_\square^\alpha = P^\alpha \cap BB = \{x \in BB \mid \mathrm{d}_P(x) \leq \alpha\}$. Let also $r_P = \frac{1}{2}\max_{p\in P} \mathrm{d}_{M\setminus\{p\}}(p)$. Using the fact that the clipped Voronoi cells have bounded aspect ratios, we can show that the clipped offsets filtration is multiplicatively interleaved with $\{V_M^\alpha\}$, starting at time $\alpha = r_P$:

LEMMA 3.3. *For all $\alpha \geq r_P$, we have $V_M^{\alpha/\rho} \subseteq P_\square^\alpha \subseteq V_M^{\rho\alpha}$.*

PROOF. Let $x \in V_M^{\alpha/\rho} \subseteq BB$, and let $v \in M$ be such that $x \in U_{\alpha/\rho}(v)$. Let also $p \in P$ be closest to v. If $v \in P$, then assertion (iii) of Section 2.1 implies that $\mathrm{d}_P(x) \leq |x - v| \leq \frac{\rho}{2}\mathrm{d}_{M\setminus\{v\}}(v) \leq r_P \leq \alpha$. If $v \in M \setminus P$, then the fact that $U_{\alpha/\rho}(v) \neq \emptyset$ implies that $|v - p| \leq \alpha/\rho$ and $U_{\alpha/\rho}(v) = \mathrm{Vor}_\square(v)$. This implies that $|x - p| \leq |x - v| + |v - p| \leq |x - v| + \alpha/\rho$. Now, assertion (iii) of Section 2.1 guarantees that the aspect ratio of $\mathrm{Vor}_\square(v)$ is at most ρ, implying that $|x - v| \leq \frac{\rho}{2}\mathrm{d}_{M\setminus\{v\}}(v) \leq \frac{\rho}{2}|v - p| \leq \frac{\alpha}{2}$. Thus, $\mathrm{d}_P(x) \leq |x - p| \leq \alpha(\frac{1}{2} + \frac{1}{\rho})$. Since $\rho \geq 2$, we conclude that $\mathrm{d}_P(x) \leq \alpha$. Hence, in all cases we have $\mathrm{d}_P(x) \leq \alpha$, which means that $x \in P_\square^\alpha$.

Let now $x \in P_\square^\alpha$, and let $v \in M$ and $p \in P$ be closest to x. Then, x belongs both to $\mathrm{Vor}_\square(v)$ and to the Euclidean ball of center p and radius α. It follows that $\mathrm{d}_P(v) \leq |v - p| \leq |v - x| + |x - p| \leq 2|x - p| \leq 2\alpha \leq \rho\alpha$. This means that $U_{\rho\alpha}(v) = \mathrm{Vor}_\square(v)$, which contains x. As a consequence, we have $x \in V_M^{\rho\alpha}$. □

Finally, we relate the clipped offsets filtration to the real offsets filtration:

LEMMA 3.4. *For all $\alpha \geq 0$, the canonical inclusion $P_\square^\alpha \hookrightarrow P^\alpha$ is a homotopy equivalence.*

PROOF. Let π_{BB} denote the metric projection onto BB, that is: $\pi_{BB}(x) = \mathrm{argmin}_{y\in BB}|x - y|$. Since BB is compact and convex, Lemma 2.3 ensures that π_{BB} is well-defined and 1-Lipschitz over the entire space $\mathbb{R}^d$. Let x be a point of P^α, and let $x' = \pi_{BB}(x)$. We will show that the line segment $[x, x']$ is included in P^α. Let $p \in P$ be such that $|x - p| \leq \alpha$. Since BB contains P, we have $\pi_{BB}(p) = p$, and therefore $|p - x'| \leq |p - x|$ since π_{BB} is 1-Lipschitz. It follows that both x and x' belong to the ball of center p and radius α. Since this ball is convex, it contains in fact the whole line segment $[x, x']$.

Let now $F : [0, 1] \times P^\alpha \to \mathbb{R}^d$ be defined by $F(t, x) = (1-t)x + t\pi_{BB}(x)$. Since π_{BB} is 1-Lipschitz, F is continuous. In addition, the above discussion shows that $F(t, P^\alpha) \subseteq P^\alpha$ for all $t \in [0, 1]$. Also, since $P_\square^\alpha \subseteq BB$, the restriction of π_{BB} to $P_\square^\alpha$ is the identity, therefore so is the restriction of F. Finally, for all $x \in P^\alpha$ we have $F(1, x) = \pi_{BB}(x) \in P^\alpha \cap BB = P_\square^\alpha$. Hence, F is a deformation retraction of P^α onto $P_\square^\alpha$, which implies that the canonical inclusion $P_\square^\alpha \hookrightarrow P^\alpha$ is a homotopy equivalence. □

With the above results we can compare the diagrams of the *truncated*[2] filtrations $\{P^\alpha\}_{\alpha\geq r_P}$ and $\{D_M^\alpha\}_{\alpha\geq r_P}$:

THEOREM 3.5. *On the natural logarithmic scale, the persistence diagrams of the truncated filtrations $\{P^\alpha\}_{\alpha\geq r_P}$ and $\{D_M^\alpha\}_{\alpha\geq r_P}$ are $\log\rho$-close in the bottleneck-distance, i.e. $\mathrm{d}_\mathrm{D}^{\log}(\{P^\alpha\}_{\alpha\geq r_P}, \{D_M^\alpha\}_{\alpha\geq r_P}) \leq \log\rho$.*

PROOF. By Lemma 3.4, the canonical inclusions $P_\square^\alpha \hookrightarrow P^\alpha$ and $P_\square^\beta \hookrightarrow P^\beta$ are homotopy equivalences that commute with the inclusions $P_\square^\alpha \hookrightarrow P_\square^\beta$ and $P^\alpha \hookrightarrow P^\beta$ for all $\beta \geq \alpha \geq 0$, so the filtrations $\{P^\alpha\}$ and $\{P_\square^\alpha\}$ have identical persistence diagrams. In addition, Lemma 3.2 implies that $\{D_M^\alpha\}_{\alpha\geq 0}$ and $\{V_M^\alpha\}$ have identical diagrams. The result follows then from the interleaving of the truncated filtrations $\{P_\square^\alpha\}_{\alpha\geq r_P}$ and $\{V_M^\alpha\}_{\alpha\geq r_P}$ (Lemma 3.3) and its consequences on the proximity of their diagrams (Corollary 2.2). □

Intuitively, Theorem 3.5 means that homological features appearing in the offsets filtration after time $\alpha = r_P$ are captured by the α-mesh filtration, with approximately the same birth and death times on the natural logarithmic scale; features appearing before r_P and dying after r_P are also captured, but starting at times potentially as late as r_P,

[2]Although these filtrations are only indexed over a subinterval of $[0, +\infty)$, their persistence diagrams can be defined using the same process as in Section 2.2, and the proofs of Theorem 2.1 and Corollary 2.2 carry over.

the death times remaining approximately the same; finally, features appearing and dying before r_P may not be captured at all by the α-mesh filtration.

3.2 Full filter

The basic filter only enables us to approximate the persistence diagram of the offsets filtration after a certain time $\alpha = r_P$ (Theorem 3.5). The reason for this appears clearly in the proof of Lemma 3.3: even though we have $P^\alpha_\square \subseteq V^{\rho\alpha}_M$ for all $\alpha \geq 0$, the symmetric inclusion $V^\alpha_M \subseteq P^{\rho\alpha}_\square$ only holds when $\alpha \geq r_P$, since the clipped Voronoi cells of the input points appear in V^α_M at time $\alpha = 0$ and are not covered by P^α before $\alpha = \rho r_P$. In the dual α-mesh, this phenomenon translates into the appearance of edges between the points of P at time $\alpha = 0$, whereas such edges should normally appear when α-balls around these points touch one another.

In this section we propose a solution to this issue, which consists in modifying the filter of $\mathrm{Del}(M)$ so as to somewhat delay the appearances of the simplices incident to the points of P in the α-mesh filtration. The rest of the approach remains unchanged: we apply SVR on the input point cloud P, to get a vertex set $M \supseteq P$, then we define a modified filter $\tilde{t} : \mathrm{Del}(M) \to \mathbb{R}$ and build its sublevel-sets filtration $\{\tilde{D}^\alpha_M\}$.

Filter modification. We follow the above recommendations and modify our filter to be a little more careful in the region close to the input points. Let $s(v) = \frac{1}{2} f_M(v)$ if $v \in P$ and $s(v) = \mathrm{d}_P(v)$ otherwise, where f_M denotes the Ruppert local feature size of M. Then, we modify our filter as follows:

$$\tilde{t}(\sigma) = \begin{cases} d_P(v) & \text{if } \sigma \text{ is a vertex } v \in M, \\ \max_{v\in\sigma} s(v) & \text{otherwise.} \end{cases}$$

In other words, we delay the time at which Delaunay simplices incident to the points of P appear, although the points themselves still appear as vertices at time $\alpha = 0$. The amount of the delay is based on the Ruppert local feature size of the augmented point set M.

Theoretical analysis. We resort again to a dual filtration $\{\tilde{V}^\alpha_M\}$ with $\tilde{V}^\alpha_M = \bigcup_{v\in M} \tilde{U}_\alpha(v)$, where the sets $\tilde{U}_\alpha(v)$ are slightly modified versions of the sets $U_\alpha(v)$ from Section 3.1:

$$\tilde{U}_\alpha(v) = \begin{cases} \emptyset & \text{if } \alpha < \tilde{t}(v), \\ \mathrm{ball}(v,\alpha) & \text{if } v \in P \text{ and } \tilde{t}(v) \leq \alpha < s(v), \\ \mathrm{Vor}_\square(v) & \text{otherwise.} \end{cases}$$

Making $\tilde{U}_\alpha(v)$ equal to $\mathrm{ball}(v, \alpha)$ instead of the empty set when $v \in P$ and $\alpha < s(v)$ enables us to obtain an interleaving between the entire filtrations $\{\tilde{V}^\alpha_M\}$ and $\{P^\alpha_\square\}$:

LEMMA 3.6 (ANALOG OF LEMMA 3.3). *For all $\alpha \geq 0$, we have $\tilde{V}^{\alpha/\rho}_M \subseteq P^\alpha_\square \subseteq \tilde{V}^{\rho\alpha}_M$.*

PROOF. Let x be a point of $\tilde{V}^{\alpha/\rho}_M \subseteq BB$, and let $v \in M$ be such that $x \in \tilde{U}_{\alpha/\rho}(v)$. If $v \in P$ with $\mathrm{d}_{M\setminus\{v\}}(v) > 2\alpha/\rho$, then $x \in \mathrm{ball}(v, \alpha/\rho)$ and thus $x \in P^{\alpha/\rho}_\square \subseteq P^\alpha_\square$. If $v \in P$ with $\mathrm{d}_{M\setminus\{v\}}(v) \leq 2\alpha/\rho$, then condition (iii) of Section 2.1 guarantees that $|x - v| \leq \alpha$ and thus $x \in P^\alpha_\square$. If $v \in S$, then the analysis is exactly the same as in the proof of Lemma 3.3. So, we have $\tilde{V}^{\alpha/\rho}_M \subseteq P^\alpha_\square$.

For the second inclusion, let x be a point of $P^\alpha_\square$. We want to show that $x \in \tilde{V}^{\rho\alpha}_M$. Let $v \in M$ be closest to x. If $v \in P$, then $x \in \mathrm{ball}(v, \alpha) \cap \mathrm{Vor}_\square(v)$, which is included in $\tilde{U}_\alpha(v)$ by definition (recall that we have $\tilde{t}(v) = 0$). As a result, $x \in \tilde{V}^{\rho\alpha}_M$. If $v \in S$, then the analysis is the same as in the proof of Lemma 3.3. So, we have $P^\alpha_\square \subseteq \tilde{V}^{\rho\alpha}_M$. □

The rest of the analysis is roughly the same as in Section 3.1, and we refer the reader to the full version of the paper for the details:

THEOREM 3.7 (ANALOGUE OF THEOREM 3.5). *On the natural logarithmic scale, the persistence diagrams of $\{P^\alpha\}$ and $\{\tilde{D}^\alpha_M\}$ are $\log\rho$-close in the bottleneck-distance, that is, $\mathrm{d}^{\log}_{\mathrm{D}}\left(\{P^\alpha\},\ \{\tilde{D}^\alpha_M\}\right) \leq \log\rho$.*

4. TIGHTER INTERLEAVING VIA OVERMESHING

It follows from Theorem 3.7 that the approximation error induced by our approach diminishes as parameter ρ shrinks. However, recall from assertion (iii) of Section 2.1 that the mesher requires $\rho \geq 2$ in order to terminate. In this section we show how we can reduce the approximation error to any arbitrarily small $\varepsilon > 0$ by inserting a controlled number of extra Steiner points and by using a more elaborate filter, which rids our analysis of its dependence on parameter ρ. Let $f : \mathbb{R}^d \to \mathbb{R}$ be a sizing function. As long as f is bounded from above by the Ruppert local feature size f_P, SVR can return a mesh M such that the radius R_v of every Voronoi cell $\mathrm{Vor}(v)$ is at most $f(v)$. Given a parameter $\varepsilon > 0$, let $f(x) = \frac{1}{3(1+1/\varepsilon)} f_P(x)$. This means that for any $v \in M$ and any $x \in \mathrm{Vor}_\square(v)$, $f_P(v) \geq 3(1 + \frac{1}{\varepsilon})|x - v|$. The standard mesh size analysis implies that the size m of our output mesh M will be bounded as follows:

$$m = O\left(\int_{BB} \frac{1}{f(z)^d} dz\right) = O\left(\left(3(1+\frac{1}{\varepsilon})\right)^d \int_{BB} \frac{1}{f_P(z)^d} dz\right).$$

In other words, our new sizing function f will only increase the mesh size by a factor of $\left(3(1 + \frac{1}{\varepsilon})\right)^d$.

Modified α-mesh filtration. As before, we run SVR on the input point set P, but this time using the sizing function f described above. Letting M denote the output superset of P, we modify the filter on $\mathrm{Del}(M)$ in such a way that the Voronoi cells of mesh vertices that are significantly closer to a given point $p \in P$ than to the others appear only once p lies within $\alpha/2$ of its nearest neighbor in $P \setminus \{p\}$.

More precisely, for every point $x \in \mathbb{R}^d$ let n_x denote the point of P closest to x — if there are two or more such points, then choose either of them as n_x. We define the following function on the mesh vertices:

$$\forall v \in M,\ s'(v) = \max\left\{\mathrm{d}_P(v),\ \frac{1}{2} f_P(n_v)\right\}. \qquad (1)$$

Note that when v belongs to P, we have $n_v = v$ and $s'(v) = \frac{1}{2} f_P(v)$. Also, if v is equidistant to two vertices $p, q \in P$, then $\mathrm{d}_P(v) \geq \frac{1}{2} f_P(p)$ and $\mathrm{d}_P(v) \geq \frac{1}{2} f_P(q)$, so the choice of which serves as n_v is irrelevant. Our new filter $t' : \mathrm{Del}(M) \to \mathbb{R}$ is defined as follows:

- for every vertex $v \in M$, let $t'(v) = 0$ if $v \in P$ and $t'(v) = s'(v)$ if $v \in M \setminus P$,
- for every higher-dimensional simplex $\sigma = \{v_0, \cdots, v_k\} \in \mathrm{Del}(M)$, let $t'(\sigma) = \max_{i\in\{0,\cdots,k\}} s'(v_i)$.

The modified α-mesh filtration $\{D'^{\alpha}_M\}_{\alpha\geq}$ is defined as the sublevel-sets filtration of t', so once again each space D'^{α}_M is a subcomplex of Del(M).

Approximation guarantee. Here again the analysis is done in terms of a dual filtration $\{V'^{\alpha}_M\}$, defined by $V'^{\alpha}_M = \bigcup_{v\in M} U'_\alpha(v)$, where

$$U'_\alpha(v) = \begin{cases} \emptyset & \text{if } v \in M \setminus P \text{ and } \alpha < s'(v), \\ \text{ball}(v, \frac{\alpha}{1+\varepsilon}) & \text{if } v \in P \text{ and } \alpha < s'(v), \\ \text{Vor}_\Box(v) & \text{otherwise.} \end{cases}$$

Let $\mathcal{U}'_\alpha$ denote the collection of sets $\{U'_\alpha(v)\}_{v\in M}$. In contrast with Section 3, the sets $U'_\alpha(v) \in \mathcal{U}'_\alpha$ are not monotonically increasing with α, the problem being that $U'_\alpha(v) \not\subseteq U'_\beta(v)$ when $v \in P$ and $\alpha < s'(v) \leq \beta$. Nevertheless, for our choice of sizing field f the family $\{V'^{\alpha}_M\}$ is still a valid filtration and D'^{α}_M is the nerve of its cover. These two facts are proved respectively in Lemmas A.3 and A.4 of Appendix A.

As in the previous section, the filtration $\{V'^{\alpha}_M\}$ is interleaved multiplicatively with $\{P^{\alpha}_\Box\}$, however this time with an arbitrarily small interleaving factor:

LEMMA 4.1. *Given $\varepsilon \leq \frac{1}{2}$, for all $\alpha \geq 0$, $V'^{\alpha/(1+\varepsilon)}_M \subseteq P^{\alpha}_\Box \subseteq V'^{\alpha(1+\varepsilon)}_M$.*

PROOF. First we prove $V'^{\alpha/(1+\varepsilon)}_M \subseteq P^{\alpha}_\Box$. Let x be a point in $V'^{\alpha/(1+\varepsilon)}_M$, and let $v \in M$ be such that $x \in U'_{\alpha/(1+\varepsilon)}(v)$. There are two cases to consider, depending on the value of α and on the location of v. In each case, the goal is to show that $\text{d}_P(x) \leq \alpha$.

Case $\alpha/(1+\varepsilon) < s'(v)$:
In this case we have $v \in P$ and $U'_{\alpha/(1+\varepsilon)}(v) = \text{ball}(v, \alpha/(1+\varepsilon)^2)$, which gives $\text{d}_P(x) \leq |x-v| \leq \frac{\alpha}{(1+\varepsilon)^2} \leq \alpha$.

Case $\alpha/(1+\varepsilon) \geq s'(v)$:
Since f_P is 1-Lipschitz, we have $f_P(v) \leq f_P(n_v) + \text{d}_P(v)$, which by (1) is at most $3s'(v)$. Hence,

$$\text{d}_P(x) \leq \text{d}_P(v) + |x-v| \leq s'(v) + f(v)$$

$$\leq s'(v) + \frac{\varepsilon}{3(1+\varepsilon)} f_P(v) \leq s'(v)(1+\varepsilon) \leq \alpha.$$

Now we prove the other inclusion, namely $P^{\alpha}_\Box \subseteq V'^{\alpha(1+\varepsilon)}_M$. Let x be a point in $P^{\alpha}_\Box$, and let $v \in M$ be closest to x. Then, $x \in \text{Vor}_\Box(v)$, and we will show that either $x \in U'_{\alpha(1+\varepsilon)}(v)$ or $x \in U'_{\alpha(1+\varepsilon)}(n_v)$. If $\alpha(1+\varepsilon) \geq s'(v)$ then $U'_{\alpha(1+\varepsilon)}(v) = \text{Vor}_\Box(v)$, which contains x, so we may assume $\alpha(1+\varepsilon) < s'(v)$. Once again we distinguish between several cases:

Case $v \in P$:
In this case we have $U'_{\alpha(1+\varepsilon)}(v) = \text{ball}(v, \alpha)$, which contains x by hypothesis.

Case $v \in M \setminus P$ and $s'(v) = \frac{1}{2} f_P(n_v)$:
Our assumption that $\alpha < \frac{s'(v)}{1+\varepsilon}$ implies $|x - n_x| \leq \alpha < \frac{f_P(n_v)}{2(1+\varepsilon)}$. It turns out that points x and v have a common nearest neighbor in P. Indeed, otherwise we can derive the following contradiction:

$$f_P(n_v) \leq |n_v - n_x| \leq |n_v - v| + |v - x| + |x - n_x|$$

$$\leq \text{d}_P(v) + \frac{\varepsilon}{3(1+\varepsilon)} f_P(v) + \alpha$$

$$< \left(\frac{1}{2} + \frac{\varepsilon}{2(1+\varepsilon)} + \frac{1}{2(1+\varepsilon)}\right) f_P(n_v) = f_P(n_v).$$

So, $n_x = n_v$. Since in addition $\alpha(1+\varepsilon) < s'(v) = \frac{1}{2} f_P(n_v) \leq s'(n_v)$, we deduce that $U'_{\alpha(1+\varepsilon)}(n_v) = \text{ball}(n_v, \alpha) = \text{ball}(n_x, \alpha)$, which contains x.

Case $v \in M \setminus P$ and $s'(v) = \text{d}_P(v)$:
In fact, this case cannot occur. Indeed, our assumption that $\alpha < \frac{s'(v)}{1+\varepsilon}$ implies $|x - n_x| < \frac{s'(v)}{1+\varepsilon}$, which enables us to derive the following contradiction:

$$s'(v) = \text{d}_P(v) \leq |v - x| + |x - n_x|$$

$$< \frac{\varepsilon}{3(1+\varepsilon)} f_P(v) + \frac{1}{1+\varepsilon} s'(v)$$

$$\leq \frac{\varepsilon}{3(1+\varepsilon)} f_P(n_v) + \frac{\varepsilon}{3(1+\varepsilon)} \text{d}_P(v) + \frac{1}{1+\varepsilon} s'(v)$$

$$< \frac{2\varepsilon}{3(1+\varepsilon)} s'(v) + \frac{\varepsilon}{3(1+\varepsilon)} s'(v) + \frac{1}{1+\varepsilon} s'(v) = s'(v).$$

□

The usual approach to relating the persistence diagrams of $\{D'^{\alpha}_M\}$ and $\{V'^{\alpha}_M\}$ cannot be used directly here because, although D'^{α}_M is the nerve of a good closed cover of V'^{α}_M, the sets $U'_\alpha(v)$ in that cover do not grow monotonically with α.

Consequently, we use an intermediate filtration, $\{\mathcal{NU}''_\alpha\}$, where each space $\mathcal{NU}''_\alpha$ is defined as the nerve of the collection of sets $\mathcal{U}''_\alpha = \{U''_\alpha(v)\}_{v\in M}$ where $U''_\alpha(v) = U'_\alpha(v) \cap \text{Vor}_\Box(v)$. It turns out that $\mathcal{NU}''_\alpha$ and D'^{α}_M are isomorphic cell complexes. The proof of this fact is a simple exercise, recalled in Lemma A.5 of Appendix A for completeness.

Let now $V''^{\alpha}_M = \bigcup_{v\in M} U''_\alpha(v)$. Obviously, we have $V''^{\alpha}_M \subseteq V'^{\alpha}_M$ since $U''_\alpha(v) \subseteq U'_\alpha(v)$ for all $v \in M$. It turns out that the canonical inclusion $V''^{\alpha}_M \hookrightarrow V'^{\alpha}_M$ is a homotopy equivalence, as proved in Lemma A.6 of Appendix A.

Equipped with these definitions and properties, we can prove the main result of the section:

THEOREM 4.2. *Given a user-defined parameter $\varepsilon \in (0, \frac{1}{2}]$ controlling the sizing function for M, the persistence diagrams of $\{P^\alpha\}$ and $\{D'^{\alpha}_M\}$ on the natural logarithmic scale are ε-close in the bottleneck-distance, i.e. $\text{d}^{\log}_{\text{D}}(\{P^\alpha\}, \{D'^{\alpha}_M\}) \leq \varepsilon$.*

PROOF. The persistence diagrams of $\{D'^{\alpha}_M\}$ and $\{\mathcal{NU}''_\alpha\}$ are identical because $\mathcal{NU}''_\alpha$ and D'^{α}_M are isomorphic cell complexes. In addition, since the sets $U''_\alpha(v)$ are convex and monotonically increasing with α, the same standard arguments of algebraic topology as the ones used in Section 3.1 show that the persistence diagrams of $\{\mathcal{NU}''_\alpha\}$ and $\{V''^{\alpha}_M\}$ are identical. Finally, the persistence diagrams of $\{V''^{\alpha}_M\}$ and $\{V'^{\alpha}_M\}$ are the same because the canonical inclusion $V''^{\alpha}_M \hookrightarrow V'^{\alpha}_M$ is a homotopy equivalence for all $\alpha \geq 0$. Combining these equivalences, we obtain that $\{D'^{\alpha}_M\}$ and $\{V'^{\alpha}_M\}$ have identical persistence diagrams. Now, it follows from Lemma 4.1 and Corollary 2.2 that $\text{d}^{\log}_{\text{D}}(\{V'^{\alpha}_M\}, \{P^{\alpha}_\Box\}_{\alpha\geq 0}) \leq \log(1+\varepsilon) \leq \varepsilon$. And to complete the proof, recall from Lemma 3.4 that $\{P^{\alpha}_\Box\}$ and $\{P^\alpha\}$ have identical persistence diagrams. □

5. RECURSIVELY WELL-PACED SUBSETS

Under some restrictions on P, we can guarantee that $|M| = 2^{O(d)}|P|$ [20]; however, in general, the mesh can have size up to $2^{O(d)}|P|\log(\Delta(P))$, and the bound is tight. We now define a filtration over the point cloud that recursively partitions the points so that each mesh has linear size, and the same interleavings as before still hold. Let BB be a bounding box around the input point set P. Given an ordering $(p_1, \ldots, p_n)$ of P, let $P^{(0)} = P \cap BB$ and $P^{(i)} = \{p_1, \ldots, p_i\} \cap BB$ for all $i = 1, \cdots, n$. For any $\theta \in (0, 1)$, we say that P is *θ-well-paced* with respect to BB if there is an ordering of P such that $\mathrm{d}_{P^{(i)}}(p_{i+1}) \geq \theta f_{P^{(i)}}(p_{i+1})$ for all $i = 0, \cdots, n-1$, where $f_{P^{(i)}}$ is the Ruppert feature size with respect to $P^{(i)}$ as defined in Section 2.3. The output of SVR has linear size when the input is a well-paced set [21].

A simple greedy algorithm can be used to find a maximal θ-well-paced subset P_1 of the input P. The remaining points of $P \setminus P_1$ are assigned to clusters around the points in P_1 based on their nearest neighbor in P_1. The greedy algorithm is repeated recursively on the clusters, each given a reasonably-sized bounding box, producing a collection of θ-well-paced point sets $P_1, \ldots, P_k$. As in Section 4, we construct a mesh M_i for each P_i as well as the corresponding filtration $D'^{\alpha}_{M_i}$. We can then define a new (abstract) filtration $D^{\alpha}_{M_*} = \bigcup_{i=1}^{k} D'^{\alpha}_{M_i}$, and by applying the proof methods of Section 4 to the individual meshes M_i, we obtain the following theorem, the detailed proof of which can be found in the full version of the paper:

THEOREM 5.1. *The persistence diagrams of $\{D^{\alpha}_{M_*}\}$ and $\{P^{\alpha}\}$ on the natural logarithmic scale are $(3\theta + \varepsilon)$-close in the bottleneck distance, i.e.* $\mathrm{d}_{\mathrm{D}}^{\log}(\{D^{\alpha}_{M_*}\}, \{P^{\alpha}\}) \leq 3\theta + \varepsilon$.

The advantage of this slightly more complicated construction is that it only runs SVR on well-paced points and thus, the size of the filtration does not depend on the spread of the input. There is a tradeoff however, since the size can increase by a factor of $1/\theta^{O(d)}$.

6. EXPERIMENTS

As a proof of concept, we experimented on 2,000 points chosen on the 4-dimensional Clifford torus (see Figure 1). We modified a pre-existing SVR implementation [1] to run in 4D and compute the filtration of Section 3.2. We used the Plex library [27] to compute the persistence diagram. To the 2,000 input points, SVR added approximately 71,000 Steiner points to achieve an aspect ratio $\rho = 3.08$ (a value chosen for technical reasons). The mesh contained 2 million pentahedra, or 12 million simplices. It took approximately 1 hour to compute the mesh and filtration, and another 7 hours to compute the persistence diagram.

Figure 1 (right) displays the persistence diagram thus obtained as a *persistence barcode* [2] on the natural logarithmic scale, where homological features are sorted first by their dimension, then by their birth time, and drawn as intervals. Intervals with arrow heads extend to infinity. The qualitative interpretation of the barcode is straightforward: scanning through the scales from smallest to largest, we see the disconnected point cloud, the helicoidal curve, the Clifford torus, the 3-sphere of radius $\sqrt{2}$, and finally the ambient space $\mathbb{R}^4$, represented simply as a space with trivial reduced homology groups. Note that the topological noise appearing in the 2-dimensional barcode between -0.2 and 0 is made of many short intervals of length less than 0.05. The 3-sphere structure is of particular interest because it had never been observed before, being too far from the beginning of the filtration for Rips or Čech filtrations to capture it.

Quantitatively, the curve appears at time $\log \alpha = -1.73$, which corresponds roughly to half the distance between consecutive points along the curve. The second 1-cycle of the torus appears around $\log \alpha = -1.2$, which is only slightly sooner than the time ($\log \alpha = -1.16$) at which consecutive periods of the curve start being connected in the offsets filtration. The 2-cycle of the torus appears soon afterwards, since the square $[0, 2\pi]^2$ gets filled in rapidly once consecutive periods of the curve start to connect. The isolines $u = \mathrm{C^t}$ and $v = \mathrm{C^t}$ are mapped to unit circles in $\mathbb{R}^4$, so both 1-cycles as well as the 2-cycle should disappear at $\log \alpha = \log 1 = 0$ in the barcode, which is close to being the case. Now, the Euclidean distance to the Clifford torus over the 3-sphere reaches its maximum at point $(\sqrt{2}, 0, 0, 0)$, where its value is $\sqrt{4 - 2\sqrt{2}} \approx 1.08$, so the 3-sphere should appear around $\log \alpha = \log 1.08 \approx 0.08$ in the barcode, which is indeed the case in our result. Finally, at the end of the barcode the approximation quality worsens slightly: since the 3-sphere has radius $\sqrt{2}$, the 3-cycle should disappear at $\log \sqrt{2} \approx 0.35$, but in reality it does so sooner, around $\log \alpha = 0.18$. Nevertheless, the absolute error is still within $\log 1.18$, meaning that our result is as good as if a multiplicative 1.18-interleaving had been obtained, whereas the aspect ratio bound ρ used by the SVR algorithm was 3.08. These observations suggest that our approach can perform better in practice than expected from the theory.

Comparison. The 4-skeleton of the Rips filtration of P reaches an equivalent size (2 million pentahedra) as early as $\log \alpha = -0.75$, which makes it difficult with this budget to detect the torus, and impossible to detect the 3-sphere. Increasing the limit to a mere $\log \alpha = -0.5$ already raises the size of the 4-skeleton to more than 10 million pentahedra. The Clifford torus is not a worst case for the α-complex filtration. However, as mentioned previously, the α-complex is susceptible to pathological behaviour on some other very reasonable inputs.

Engineering issues. Our implementation is very preliminary and would benefit from substantial engineering. In particular, the SVR implementation we adapted creates a bounding box to avoid dealing with boundary issues. The box includes a number of vertices that grows proportionally to $1/(\rho-1)^{d-1}$; with $\rho = 3.08$ in 4D, this is 2,800 points. No research is needed to solve this issue. In addition, since we did not have access to efficient staged predicates and constructions in 4D, we used exact rational arithmetic, which in 3D slows SVR down by a factor of worse than 20. Despite this, meshing was not the bottleneck.

7. DISCUSSION

Steiner point choice. Since all our filtrations are derived from the mesh $\mathrm{Del}(M)$, their sizes (and therefore the complexity of the whole approach) depend heavily on the size of M. Some work has been done in two and three dimensions to optimize point placement (e.g. [24]), reducing the mesh size for any requested quality. Furthermore, there is a huge industry in mesh smoothing, which in practice improves the quality of a mesh as a post-processing step. Reductions in the number of Steiner points are particularly important as the dimension increases; meanwhile, improving the mesh quality reduces the approximation error.

Higher dimensions. A major limitation of our approach lies in the fact that it is tied to the ambient space $\mathbb{R}^d$, which is fine only in small to moderate dimensions. One possibility for improvement would be to refine the approach and its analysis, so as to make its complexity depend on the dimensionality of the topological features the user is interested in. For instance, in scenarios where the data are high-dimensional but the user is only interested in low-dimensional structures, it would be interesting to devise a mechanism that captures low-dimensional topological features at all scales, at a cost that does not depend exponentially on the ambient dimension. Some work has been done in this direction [6], but many problems remain open. It would be interesting to see if meshing techniques could help in this context.

Approximating other filtrations. Our family of filtrations enables us to approximate the persistence diagrams of other filtrations besides the offsets filtration. An interesting example is the *Ruppert filtration*, i.e. the sublevel-sets filtration of the Ruppert local feature size f_P. Using the same machinery as in Section 3, we can devise a filtration of the mesh $\mathrm{Del}(M)$ that is interleaved with the Ruppert filtration of P, thus making it possible to approximate the persistence diagram of f_P through meshing. The details are provided in the full version of the paper. We believe the Ruppert local feature size has a role to play in topological inference, due to its close connections to distance functions (f_P is the distance to the second nearest neighbor in P) and to meshing algorithms.

Superlevel-sets filtrations. Given a point cloud $P \subset \mathbb{R}^d$, our approach can also yield filtrations that are interleaved with the family of superlevel-sets of d_P. However, in $\mathbb{R}^d$ the persistence diagram of the superlevel-sets filtration of d_P provides in fact the same information as the diagram of the sublevel-sets filtration [9][3]. It would be interesting to see if our approach can be extended to other ambient spaces where approximating the superlevel-sets of distance functions would make sense.

8. REFERENCES

[1] U. A. Acar, B. Hudson, G. L. Miller, and T. Phillips. SVR: Practical engineering of a fast 3D meshing algorithm. In *Proc. 16th International Meshing Roundtable*, pages 45–62, 2007.

[2] G. Carlsson, A. Zomorodian, A. Collins, and L. Guibas. Persistence barcodes for shapes. *Internat. Journal of Shape Modeling*, 11:149–187, 2005.

[3] F. Chazal and D. Cohen-Steiner. *Geometric Inference.* to appear as a book chapter, Springer, 2007.

[4] F. Chazal, D. Cohen-Steiner, M. Glisse, L. J. Guibas, and S. Y. Oudot. Proximity of persistence modules and their diagrams. In *Proceedings of the 25th ACM Symposium on Computational Geometry*, 2009.

[5] F. Chazal and A. Lieutier. Stability and computation of topological invariants of solids in R^n. *GEOMETRY: Discrete & Computational Geometry*, 37(4):601–617, 2007.

[6] F. Chazal and S. Y. Oudot. Towards persistence-based reconstruction in euclidean spaces. In *Proceedings of the 24th ACM Symposium on Computational Geometry*, 2008.

[7] D. Cohen-Steiner. Private communication.

[8] D. Cohen-Steiner, H. Edelsbrunner, and J. Harer. Stability of persistence diagrams. In *Proceedings of the 21st ACM Symposium on Computational Geometry*, 2005.

[9] D. Cohen-Steiner, H. Edelsbrunner, and J. Harer. Extending persistence using Poincaré and Lefschetz duality. *Found. Comput. Math.*, 2008. To appear.

[10] V. de Silva. A weak characterisation of the Delaunay triangulation. *Geometriae Dedicata*, 2008. to appear.

[11] V. de Silva and G. Carlsson. Topological estimation using witness complexes. In *Proc. Sympos. Point-Based Graphics*, pages 157–166, 2004.

[12] H. Edelsbrunner. The union of balls and its dual shape. In *SCG '93: Proceedings of the ninth annual symposium on Computational geometry*, pages 218–231, New York, NY, USA, 1993. ACM.

[13] H. Edelsbrunner, D. Letscher, and A. Zomorodian. Topological persistence and simplification. *Discrete Compututational Geometry*, 28:511–533, 2002.

[14] S. Eilenberg and N. Steenrod. *Foundations of Algebraic Topology.* Princeton University Press, 1952.

[15] J. Erickson. Nice point sets can have nasty delaunay triangulations. In *Symposium on Computational Geometry*, pages 96–105, 2001.

[16] J. Erickson and S. Kim. Arbitrarily large neighborly families of congruent symmetric convex 3-polytopes. *Discrete Geometry* (A. Bezdek, editor), pages 267–278, 2003.

[17] L. J. Guibas and S. Y. Oudot. Reconstruction using witness complexes. *Discrete and Computational Geometry*, 40:325–356, 2008.

[18] A. Hatcher. *Algebraic Topology.* Cambridge University Press, 2001.

[19] B. Hudson, G. Miller, and T. Phillips. Sparse Voronoi Refinement. In *Proceedings of the 15th International Meshing Roundtable*, pages 339–356, Birmingham, Alabama, 2006. Long version available as Carnegie Mellon University Technical Report CMU-CS-06-132.

[20] B. Hudson, G. L. Miller, T. Phillips, and D. R. Sheehy. Size complexity of volume meshes vs. surface meshes. In *SODA: ACM-SIAM Symposium on Discrete Algorithms*, 2009.

[21] G. L. Miller, T. Phillips, and D. R. Sheehy. Linear-size meshes. In *CCCG: Canadian Conference in Computational Geometry*, 2008.

[22] P. Niyogi, S. Smale, and S. Weinberger. Finding the homology of submanifolds with high confidence from random samples. *Discrete Comput. Geom.*, 39(1-3):419–441, March 2008.

[23] J. Ruppert. A Delaunay refinement algorithm for quality 2-dimensional mesh generation. *J. Algorithms*, 18(3):548–585, 1995. Fourth Annual ACM-SIAM Symposium on Discrete Algorithms (SODA) (Austin, TX, 1993).

[3] The result of [9] is stated for continuous real-valued functions over compact manifolds without boundary. In our setting, even though $\mathbb{R}^d$ is not compact, the result of [9] carries over by an easy reduction [7].

[24] A. Üngör. Off-centers: A new type of steiner points for computing size-optimal quality-guaranteed delaunay triangulations. *Comput. Geom.*, 42(2):109–118, 2009.
[25] L. Vietoris. Über den höheren Zusammenhang kompakter Räume und eine Klasse von zusammenhangstreuen Abbildungen. *Mathematische Annalen*, 97(1):454–472, 1927.
[26] A. Zomorodian and G. Carlsson. Computing persistent homology. *GEOMETRY: Discrete & Computational Geometry*, 33(2):249–274, 2005.
[27] PLEX 2.5. See `http://comptop.stanford.edu/programs/plex.html`.

A. APPENDIX: MISSING PROOFS FROM SECTION 4

The proofs of Lemmas A.3 through A.6 rely on the following technical results:

LEMMA A.1. *For all $v \in P$,*

$$\text{ball}\left(v, \frac{s'(v)}{1+\varepsilon}\right) \subseteq \bigcup_{\substack{u \in M:\\ |u-v| \le s'(v)}} \text{Vor}_\square(u),$$

where $\varepsilon \le \frac{1}{2}$ is a user defined parameter that controls the sizing function for M.

PROOF. Assume for a contradiction that $\text{ball}(v, \frac{s'(v)}{1+\varepsilon})$ intersects $\text{Vor}_\square(u)$ for some $u \in M$ such that $|u-v| > s'(v) = \frac{1}{2} f_P(v)$, and let x be a point in the intersection. Using the triangle inequality, the sizing function $f = \frac{\varepsilon}{3(1+\varepsilon)} f_P$, and the 1-Lipschitz property of f_P, we obtain:

$$\begin{aligned}|u-v| &\le |v-x| + |x-u| \\ &\le \frac{s'(v)}{1+\varepsilon} + \frac{\varepsilon}{3(1+\varepsilon)} f_P(u) \\ &\le \frac{1}{2(1+\varepsilon)} f_P(v) + \frac{\varepsilon}{3(1+\varepsilon)} f_P(u) \\ &\le f_P(v)\left(\frac{1}{2(1+\varepsilon)} + \frac{\varepsilon}{3(1+\varepsilon)}\right) + \frac{\varepsilon}{3(1+\varepsilon)}|u-v|,\end{aligned}$$

which implies that $|u-v| \le f_P(v)\left(\frac{\frac{1}{2(1+\varepsilon)} + \frac{\varepsilon}{3(1+\varepsilon)}}{1 - \frac{\varepsilon}{3(1+\varepsilon)}}\right) = \frac{1}{2} f_P(v)$, which contradicts our hypothesis. □

LEMMA A.2. *For all $\alpha \ge 0$ and all $v \in P$, if $s'(v) > \alpha$ then $U'_\alpha(v) \cap U'_\alpha(u) = \emptyset$ for all other $u \in M$.*

PROOF. Suppose for a contradiction that there exists some $u \in M$ such that $U'_\alpha(v) \cap U'_\alpha(u) \ne \emptyset$. If $U'_\alpha(u) = \text{ball}(u, \frac{\alpha}{1+\varepsilon})$ then $u \in P$ and we get the following contradiction:

$$f_P(v) \le |u-v| \le \frac{2\alpha}{1+\varepsilon} < 2\alpha < 2s'(v) = f_P(v).$$

If $U'_\alpha(u) = \text{Vor}_\square(u)$ then $s'(u) \le \alpha < s'(v)$. By Lemma A.1, if the Voronoi cell $\text{Vor}_\square(u)$ intersects $U'_\alpha(v) = \text{ball}(v, \frac{\alpha}{1+\varepsilon})$ then $|u-v| \le s'(v)$. In this case, we get the following contradiction:

$$\begin{aligned}s'(v) &= \frac{1}{2} f_P(v) \le \frac{1}{2}|v-n_u| \le \frac{1}{2}(|v-u| + |u-n_u|) \\ &\le \frac{1}{2}(s'(v) + d_P(u)) \le \frac{1}{2}(s'(v) + s'(u)) < s'(v).\end{aligned}$$

□

With these technical results at hand, we can prove Lemmas A.3 through A.6:

LEMMA A.3. *Given $\varepsilon \le \frac{1}{2}$, the family $\{V'^\alpha_M\}_{\alpha \ge 0}$ is a valid filtration.*

PROOF. Let $v \in M$ and $\beta \ge \alpha \ge 0$. By definition, we have $U'_\alpha(v) \subseteq U'_\beta(v)$ unless $v \in P$ and $\alpha < s'(v) \le \beta$, which is the case we will now address. In this case, we have $U'_\alpha(v) = \text{ball}(v, \frac{\alpha}{1+\varepsilon})$ and $U'_\beta(v) = \text{Vor}_\square(v)$. Let S denote the set $M \cap \text{ball}(v, s'(v))$. For every $u \in S$ we must have $v = n_u$, for otherwise the triangle inequality would imply that $f_P(v) \le |v - n_u| < 2s'(v) = f_P(v)$, a contradiction. As a result, $s'(u) = s'(v) \le \beta$, and thus $U'_\beta(u) = \text{Vor}_\square(u)$. Then, Lemma A.1 implies that $U'_\alpha(v) \subseteq \bigcup_{u \in S} \text{Vor}_\square(u) = \bigcup_{u \in S} U'_\beta(u) \subseteq V'^\beta_M$. □

LEMMA A.4. *Given $\varepsilon < \frac{3}{2}$, the complex D'^α_M coincides with the nerve of the cover $\mathcal{U}'_\alpha$ of V'^α_M.*

PROOF. For an input vertex $p \in P$, we have $\{p\} \in D'^\alpha_M$ and $U'_\alpha(p) \ne \emptyset$ for any $\alpha \ge 0$. For a Steiner vertex $v \in M \setminus P$, we have $\{v\} \in D'^\alpha_M \Leftrightarrow s'(v) \le \alpha \Leftrightarrow U'_\alpha(v) \ne \emptyset$. So, for all $\alpha \ge 0$ the vertices of D'^α_M and of the nerve of $\mathcal{U}'_\alpha$ coincide.

Before moving on to higher-dimensional simplices, let us make the following claim. Let $v \in P$ be such that $s'(v) > \alpha$, and thus $U'_\alpha(v) = \text{ball}(v, \frac{\alpha}{1+\varepsilon})$. By Lemma A.2, $\{v\}$ is the only simplex of the nerve of $\mathcal{U}'_\alpha$ that contains v. We claim that $\{v\}$ is also the only simplex of D'^α_M that contains v. Indeed, let $u \in M$ be any neighbor of v in $\text{Del}(M)$. First, we have $u \in M \setminus P$. Indeed, $|v-u| \le f(v) + f(u) \le \frac{\varepsilon}{3(1+\varepsilon)}(f_P(v) + f_P(u))$, which is at most $\frac{2\varepsilon}{3(1+\varepsilon)} f_P(v) + \frac{\varepsilon}{3(1+\varepsilon)}|u-v|$ since f_P is 1-Lipschitz. It follows that $|u-v| \le \frac{2\varepsilon}{3+2\varepsilon} f_P(v) < f_P(v)$, which means that $u \notin P$. Second, we have $n_u = v$. Indeed, $|v - n_u| \le |v-u| + |u-n_u| \le 2|v-u| \le \frac{4\varepsilon}{3+2\varepsilon} f_P(v)$, which is less than $f_P(v)$ since $\varepsilon < \frac{3}{2}$. This means that $n_u = v$. It follows that $s'(u) \ge \frac{1}{2} f_P(n_u) = \frac{1}{2} f_P(v) = s'(v) > \alpha$, which proves our claim.

Our claim implies that any simplex $\sigma = \{v_0, \ldots, v_k\}$ with $k \ge 1$ that appears in D'^α_M or in the nerve of $\mathcal{U}'_\alpha$ satisfies $U'_\alpha(v_i) = \text{Vor}_\square(v_i)$ for all $i = 0 \ldots k$. Hence, $\sigma \in D'^\alpha_M$ if and only if σ belongs to the nerve of $\mathcal{U}'_\alpha$. □

LEMMA A.5. *For all $\alpha \ge 0$, $\mathcal{N}\mathcal{U}''_\alpha = D'^\alpha_M$.*

PROOF. Observe that $U''_\alpha(v) \subseteq U'_\alpha(v)$ for all points $v \in M$, so $\mathcal{N}\mathcal{U}''_\alpha$ is naturally included in the nerve of $\mathcal{U}'_\alpha$, which by Lemma A.4 coincides with D'^α_M. For the other inclusion, we observe that $U'_\alpha(v) \subseteq U''_\alpha(v)$ unless $v \in P$ and $\alpha < s'(v)$. However, by Lemma A.2, such vertices v only appear in 0-simplices of D'^α_M. These 0-simplices also appear in $\mathcal{N}\mathcal{U}''_\alpha$ since $\text{Vor}_\square(v) \cap \text{ball}(v, \frac{\alpha}{1+\varepsilon}) \ne \emptyset$, so indeed, $D'^\alpha_M \subseteq \mathcal{N}\mathcal{U}''_\alpha$. □

LEMMA A.6. *For all $\alpha \ge 0$, the canonical inclusion $V''^\alpha_M \hookrightarrow V'^\alpha_M$ is a homotopy equivalence.*

PROOF. We will exhibit a deformation retraction of V'^α_M onto V''^α_M on each connected component of V'^α_M separately. By Lemma A.2, every vertex $v \in P$ with $s'(v) > \alpha$ has the property that $U'_\alpha(v)$ is disjoint from all other sets $U'_\alpha(u)$ and thus forms a separate connected component. On this component the deformation retraction is easily defined using the metric projection onto the convex set $U''_\alpha(v)$, as in Lemma 3.4. All other connected components of V'^α_M can be expressed as unions of $U'_\alpha(u)$'s, each of which is equal to $\text{Vor}_\square(u)$. For these components the identity map is a trivial deformation retraction. □

Geometric Tomography With Topological Guarantees

Omid Amini
CNRS – DMA,
École Normale Supérieure,
Paris, France
omid.amini@ens.fr

Jean-Daniel Boissonnat
INRIA Sophia Antipolis - Méditerranée, France
jean-daniel.boissonnat@sophia.inria.fr

Pooran Memari
INRIA Sophia Antipolis - Méditerranée, France
pooran.memari@sophia.inria.fr

ABSTRACT

We consider the problem of reconstructing a compact 3-manifold (with boundary) embedded in $\mathbb{R}^3$ from its cross-sections with a given set of cutting planes having arbitrary orientations. Under appropriate sampling conditions that are satisfied when the set of cutting planes is dense enough, we prove that the algorithm presented by Liu et al. in [LBD$^+$08] preserves the homotopy type of the original object. Using the homotopy equivalence, we also show that the reconstructed object is homeomorphic (and isotopic) to the original object. This is the first time that shape reconstruction from cross-sections comes with such theoretical guarantees.

Categories and Subject Descriptors

F.2.2 [**Nonnumerical Algorithms and Problems**]: Geometrical problems and computations; I.3.5 [**Computational Geometry and Object Modeling**]: Curve, surface, solid, and object representations

General Terms

Algorithms, Reliability, Theory.

1. INTRODUCTION

Overview.

This paper deals with the reconstruction of 3-dimensional geometric shapes from unorganized planar cross-sections. The need for such reconstructions is a result of the advances in medical imaging technology, specially in ultrasound tomography. In this context, the purpose is to construct a 3D model of an organ from a collection of ultrasonic images. When the images are provided by free-hand ultrasound devices, the cross-sections of the organ belong to planes that are not necessarily parallel. However, it is only very recently that reconstruction from unorganized cross-sections has been considered: A very first work [PT94] by Payne and Toga was restricted to easy cases of reconstruction that do not require branching between sections. In [BG93], Boissonnat and Geiger proposed a Delaunay-based algorithm for the case of serial planes, that has been generalized to arbitrarily oriented planes in [DP97] and [BM07]. Some more recent work ([JWC$^+$05] and [LBD$^+$08]) can handle the case of multilabel sections (multiple materials). Barequet and Vaxman's work [BV09] extends the work of [LBD$^+$08] and can handle the case where the sections are only partially known.

Most of previous work has been restricted to the case of parallel cross-sections and is mostly based on the simple idea of connecting two sections if their orthogonal projections overlap. This paper, analyzes a natural generalization of this idea for the case of non parallel sections, that has been proposed in [LBD$^+$08]. We prove that under appropriate sampling conditions, the connection between the sections provided by this generalization is coherent with the connectivity structure of the object and the proposed reconstructed object is homeomorphic to the object. To the best of our knowledge, this work is the first to provide such a topological study in shape modeling from planar cross-sectional data. The only existing results studying the topology of the reconstructed object are restricted to the 2D variant of the problem ([SBG06] and [MB08]).

Reconstruction Problem.

Let $\mathcal{O} \subset \mathbb{R}^3$ be a compact 3-manifold with boundary (denoted by $\partial\mathcal{O}$) of class $C^{1,1}$. The manifold $\mathcal{O}$ is cut by a set $\mathcal{P}$ of so-called cutting planes that are supposed to be in general position in the sense that none of these cutting planes are tangent to $\partial\mathcal{O}$. For any cutting plane $P \in \mathcal{P}$, we are given the intersection $\mathcal{O} \cap P$. There is no assumption on the geometry or the topology of these intersections. The goal is to reconstruct $\mathcal{O}$ from the given intersections.

Arrangement of the Cutting Planes.

We can decompose the problem into several subproblems as follows. Consider the arrangement of the cutting planes, i.e., the subdivision of $\mathbb{R}^3$ into convex polyhedral cells induced by the cutting planes. Without loss of generality, we can restrict our attention to a cell of this arrangement and reduce the reconstruction of $\mathcal{O}$ to the reconstruction of $\mathcal{O}_\mathcal{C} := \mathcal{O} \cap \mathcal{C}$ for all cells $\mathcal{C}$ of the arrangement. Since the various reconstructed pieces will conform to the given sections, it will be easy to glue them together in the end to get the overall reconstructed object $\mathcal{R}$.

SCG'10, June 13–16, 2010, Snowbird, Utah, USA.

Sections: Input of the Reconstruction Algorithm.

We now focus on a cell $\mathcal{C}$ of the arrangement and describe how the reconstructed object $\mathcal{R}_\mathcal{C}$ is defined in $\mathcal{C}$. On each face f of $\mathcal{C}$, the intersection of the object $\mathcal{O}$ with f is given and consists of a set of connected regions called *sections*. By definition, the sections of a face of $\mathcal{C}$ are disjoint. However, two sections (on two neighbor faces of $\mathcal{C}$) may intersect along the intersection between their two corresponding faces. The boundary of a section A is denoted by ∂A and is a set of closed curves, called *section-contours*, that may be nested.

Let us write $\partial\mathcal{C}$ for the boundary of $\mathcal{C}$, and $\mathcal{F}_\mathcal{C}$ for the set of faces of $\mathcal{C}$. In the sequel, $\mathcal{S}_\mathcal{C}$ denotes the union of sections of all the faces of $\mathcal{C}$ and a point of $\mathcal{S}_\mathcal{C}$ is called a *section-point.*

Methodology.

We know that a point on the boundary of $\mathcal{C}$ is in $\mathcal{O}$ if it lies in $\mathcal{S}_\mathcal{C}$. The goal is now to determine whether a point x inside $\mathcal{C}$ belongs to $\mathcal{O}$ or not. The reconstruction method that we will present here is based on the notion of *distance from* $\partial\mathcal{C}$:

> A point $x \in \mathcal{C}$ is in the reconstructed object if one of its **nearest points** in $\partial\mathcal{C}$ is in $\mathcal{S}_\mathcal{C}$.

Different distance function (from the boundary of $\mathcal{C}$) may be used in order to satisfy properties of interest for different applications (for example, to promote the connection between sections in the case of sparse data, or to impose a favorite direction to connect the sections, etc). A natural idea is to use the Euclidean distance as the distance function from $\partial\mathcal{C}$. In this case, the reconstructed object coincides with the method introduced by Liu et al in [LBD+08]. In this paper, we analyze this method and present appropriate sampling conditions providing topological guarantees for the resulting reconstructed object.

Organization of the paper.

After this brief introduction, in Section 2 we provide the definition of the reconstructed object $\mathcal{R}$. The rest of the paper will be then devoted to prove that in the general case, under two appropriate sampling conditions, $\mathcal{R}$ and $\mathcal{O}$ are homotopy equivalent, and are more strongly homeomorphic. Indeed, the first sampling condition, called the *Separation Condition*, discussed in Section 2.1, ensures good connectivity between the sections, but does not necessarily imply the homotopy equivalence.

As we will see, in order to ensure the homotopy equivalence between $\mathcal{R}$ and $\mathcal{O}$, a second so-called *Intersection Condition* is required, c.f., Section 3.4. To make the connection between the upcoming sections more clear, we shortly outline the general strategy employed in proving the homotopy equivalence between $\mathcal{R}$ and $\mathcal{O}$. In Section 3.5, we provide a set of properties on the sampling of cutting planes to ensure the Separation and the Intersection Conditions. Finally, in Section 3.6 we show that the two shapes $\mathcal{O}$ and $\mathcal{R}$ are indeed homeomorphic (and even isotopic). Some preliminary notions of homotopy theory we use here are recalled in the full version of the paper [ABM09].

2. RECONSTRUCTED OBJECT DEFINITION

Let us first give a definition of the reconstructed object in a cell $\mathcal{C}$ of the arrangement of the cutting planes, which is related to the Voronoi diagram of $\mathcal{C}$ defined as follows.

Voronoi Diagram of a Cell.

For a face f of $\mathcal{C}$, the Voronoi cell of f, denoted by $\mathrm{Vor}_\mathcal{C}(f)$, is defined as the set of all points in $\mathcal{C}$ that have f as the nearest face of $\mathcal{C}$, i.e.,

$$\mathrm{Vor}_\mathcal{C}(f) = \{\, x \in \mathcal{C} \mid d(x,f) \leq d(x,f'),\ \forall \text{ face } f' \text{ of } \mathcal{C} \,\}.$$

Where $d(.,.)$ denotes the Euclidean distance. The collection of all $\mathrm{Vor}_\mathcal{C}(f)$ of the faces of $\mathcal{C}$ forms a tiling of $\mathcal{C}$, called the *Voronoi diagram of* $\mathcal{C}$.

We write $\partial\mathrm{Vor}_\mathcal{C}(f)$ for the boundary of $\mathrm{Vor}_\mathcal{C}(f)$. The union of $\partial\mathrm{Vor}_\mathcal{C}(f)$ for all the faces f of $\mathcal{C}$ is called the *Voronoi Skeleton of* $\mathcal{C}$, and is denoted by VorSkel($\mathcal{C}$). VorSkel($\mathcal{C}$) is also called *the medial axis of the cell,* and is the locus of points in $\mathcal{C}$ that are at the same distance from at least two faces of $\mathcal{C}$. To simplify notation, when the cell $\mathcal{C}$ is understood from the context, we simply remove the index $\mathcal{C}$ and write $\mathrm{Vor}(f)$, $\partial\mathrm{Vor}(f)$, etc.

Definition 1 (Nearest Point) *For any point x in $\mathcal{C}$, the* nearest point *in $\partial\mathcal{C}$ to x is the orthogonal projection of x onto the nearest face f of $\mathcal{C}$. This projection is denoted by* $\mathrm{np}_f(x)$*. The set of all nearest points to x in $\partial\mathcal{C}$ is denoted by* $\mathrm{Np}_\mathcal{C}(x)$*. Note that for any $x \notin$* VorSkel($\mathcal{C}$)*,* $\mathrm{Np}_\mathcal{C}(x)$ *is reduced to a single point. Based on this, and to simplify the presentation, sometimes we drop the index f, and by* $\mathrm{np}(x)$ *we denote a point of* $\mathrm{Np}_\mathcal{C}(x)$*.*

We can now define the reconstructed object in a given cell $\mathcal{C}$. We first give the formal definition, and then present a more detailed geometric characterization of the reconstructed object using the lifting procedure described below.

Definition 2 (Reconstructed Object $\mathcal{R}_\mathcal{C}$ in $\mathcal{C}$) *The* reconstructed object $\mathcal{R}_\mathcal{C}$ *is the set of all points x in $\mathcal{C}$ such that a nearest point* $\mathrm{np}(x)$ *lies in $\mathcal{S}_\mathcal{C}$, i.e.,* $\mathrm{Np}_\mathcal{C}(x) \cap \mathcal{S}_\mathcal{C} \neq \emptyset$*. Note that in the case where $\mathcal{S}_\mathcal{C}$ is empty, $\mathcal{R}_\mathcal{C}$ will be the empty set as well.*

Definition 3 (Lift Function) *Let $x \in \mathcal{C}$ be a point in the Voronoi cell of a face f of $\mathcal{C}$. The lift of x in $\mathcal{C}$, denoted by* $\mathrm{lift}_\mathcal{C}(x)$ *(or simply* $\mathrm{lift}(x)$ *if $\mathcal{C}$ is trivially implied), is defined to be the unique point of* $\partial\mathrm{Vor}_\mathcal{C}(f)$ *such that the line defined by the segment* $[x, \mathrm{lift}(x)]$ *is orthogonal to f. In other words,* $\mathrm{lift}(x)$ *is the unique point in* $\partial\mathrm{Vor}_\mathcal{C}(f)$ *whose the orthogonal projection onto f is* $\mathrm{np}(x)$*.*

The lift of a set of points $X \subseteq \mathcal{C}$, denoted by $\mathrm{lift}(X)$*, is the set of all the points* $\mathrm{lift}(x)$ *for $x \in X$, i.e.,* $\mathrm{lift}(X) := \{\, \mathrm{lift}(x) \mid x \in X \,\}$*.*

The function $\mathcal{L} : \mathcal{C} \to$ VorSkel($\mathcal{C}$) *that maps each point $x \in \mathcal{C}$ to its lift in* VorSkel($\mathcal{C}$) *will be called the* lift function *in the sequel. For any $Y \subset$* VorSkel($\mathcal{C}$)*, $\mathcal{L}^{-1}(Y)$ denotes the set of points $x \in \mathcal{C}$ such that* $\mathrm{lift}(x) = y$ *for some $y \in Y$.*

Characterization of the Reconstructed Object $\mathcal{R}_\mathcal{C}$.

If $\mathcal{S}_\mathcal{C} = \emptyset$, then, as we said before, for any point $x \in \mathcal{C}$, $\mathrm{np}(x) \notin \mathcal{S}_\mathcal{C}$, and so $\mathcal{R}_\mathcal{C}$ is empty. Otherwise, let $A \in \mathcal{S}_\mathcal{C}$ be a section lying on a face of $\mathcal{C}$. For each point $a \in A$, the locus of all the points $x \in \mathcal{C}$ that have a as their nearest point in $\partial\mathcal{C}$ is the line segment $[a, \mathrm{lift}(a)]$ joining a to its

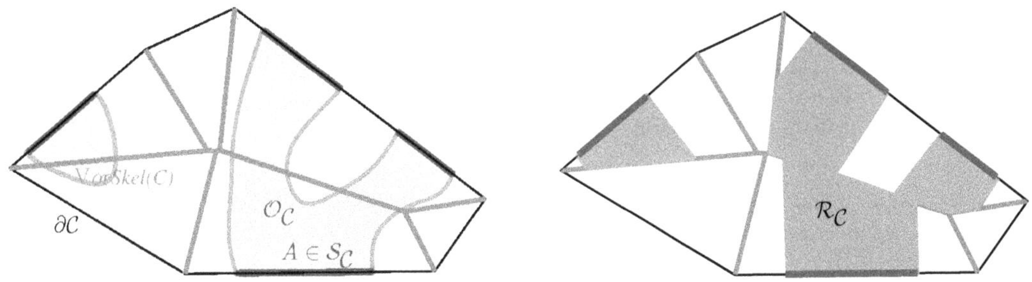

Figure 1: A 2D illustration of the partition of a cell $\mathcal{C}$ by the Voronoi Skeleton VorSkel($\mathcal{C}$). **Left) The original shape $\mathcal{O}_\mathcal{C}$. Right) The reconstructed object $\mathcal{R}_\mathcal{C}$.**

lift. Therefore, the reconstructed object $\mathcal{R}_\mathcal{C}$ is the union of all the line-segments $[a, \text{lift}(a)]$ for a point a in a section $A \in \mathcal{S}_\mathcal{C}$, i.e.,

$$\mathcal{R}_\mathcal{C} = \bigcup_{A \in \mathcal{S}_\mathcal{C}} \bigcup_{a \in A} [a, \text{lift}(a)] = \mathcal{L}^{-1}(\text{lift}(\mathcal{S}_\mathcal{C})).$$

Note that according to this characterization, if the lifts of two sections intersect in VorSkel($\mathcal{C}$), then these two sections are connected in $\mathcal{R}_\mathcal{C}$. This generalizes the classical overlapping criterion for the case of parallel cutting planes. The union of all the pieces $\mathcal{R}_\mathcal{C}$ over all cells $\mathcal{C}$ will be the overall reconstructed object $\mathcal{R}$.

The rest of the paper is devoted to prove that under two appropriate sampling conditions, $\mathcal{R}$ and $\mathcal{O}$ are homotopy equivalent, and are indeed homeomorphic (and isotopic).

2.1 First Sampling Condition: Separation Condition

In this section, we provide the first sampling condition, under which the connection between the sections in the reconstructed object $\mathcal{R}$ are the same as in the original object $\mathcal{O}$. Our discussion will be essentially based on the study of the *medial axis*, that we define now.

Definition 4 (Medial Axis of $\partial\mathcal{O}$) *Consider $\partial\mathcal{O}$ as a 2-manifold without boundary embedded in $\mathbb{R}^3$. The medial axis of $\partial\mathcal{O}$, denoted by $MA(\partial\mathcal{O})$, contains two different parts: the so-called* internal *part, denoted by $MA_i(\partial\mathcal{O})$, which lies in $\mathcal{O}$ and the so-called* external *part, denoted by $MA_e(\partial\mathcal{O})$, which lies in $\mathbb{R}^3 \setminus \mathcal{O}$.*

The *internal retract* $m_i : \partial\mathcal{O} \to \text{MA}_i(\partial\mathcal{O})$ is defined as follows: for a point $x \in \partial\mathcal{O}$, $m_i(x)$ is the center of the maximum ball entirely included in $\mathcal{O}$ which passes through x. For any $x \in \partial\mathcal{O}$, $m_i(x)$ is unique. Symmetrically, we define *the external retract* $m_e : \partial\mathcal{O} \to \text{MA}_e(\partial\mathcal{O})$: for a point $x \in \partial\mathcal{O}$, $m_e(x)$ is the center of the maximum ball entirely included in $\mathbb{R}^3 \setminus \mathcal{O}$ which passes through x. For any $x \in \partial\mathcal{O}$, $m_e(x)$ is unique but may be at infinity. In the sequel, we may write $m(a)$ for a point in $\{m_i(a), m_e(a)\}$.

The interesting point is that as discussed below if the sample of cutting planes is sufficiently dense, then the internal part of $\text{MA}(\partial\mathcal{O})$ lies inside the defined reconstructed object and the external part of this medial axis lies outside the reconstructed object.

Definition 5 (Separation Condition) *We say that the set of cutting planes verifies the Separation Condition if*

$$MA_i(\partial\mathcal{O}) \subset \mathcal{R} \text{ and } MA_e(\partial\mathcal{O}) \subset \mathbb{R}^3 \setminus \mathcal{R}.$$

In other words, $\partial\mathcal{R}$ separates the internal and the external parts of the medial axis of $\partial\mathcal{O}$. (That is where the name comes from.)

We will show that in each cell $\mathcal{C}$, the Separation Condition implies that $\partial\mathcal{R}_\mathcal{C}$ separates the internal and the external parts of the medial axis of $\partial\mathcal{O}_\mathcal{C}$.

Definition 6 (Medial Axis of $\partial\mathcal{O}_\mathcal{C}$) *In order to study the Separation Condition in a cell $\mathcal{C}$, we will need to consider the medial axis of $\mathcal{O}_\mathcal{C}$, denoted by $MA(\partial\mathcal{O}_\mathcal{C})$, defined as the set of points in $\mathcal{C}$ with at least two closest points in $\partial\mathcal{O}_\mathcal{C}$. By $MA_i(\partial\mathcal{O}_\mathcal{C})$ (resp. $MA_e(\partial\mathcal{O}_\mathcal{C})$) we denote the part of $MA(\partial\mathcal{O}_\mathcal{C})$ that lies inside (resp. outside) $\mathcal{O}_\mathcal{C}$. Note that the two sets $MA(\partial\mathcal{O}_\mathcal{C})$ and $MA(\partial\mathcal{O}) \cap \mathcal{C}$ may be different.*

We also consider the *internal retract* $m_{i,\mathcal{C}} : \partial\mathcal{O}_\mathcal{C} \to \text{MA}_i(\partial\mathcal{O}_\mathcal{C})$ defined as follows: for a point $x \in \partial\mathcal{O}_\mathcal{C}$, $m_{i,\mathcal{C}}(x)$ is the center of the maximum ball entirely included in $\mathcal{O}_\mathcal{C}$ which passes through x. Symmetrically, we can define *the external retract* $m_{e,\mathcal{C}} : \partial\mathcal{O}_\mathcal{C} \to \text{MA}_e(\partial\mathcal{O}_\mathcal{C})$: for a point $x \in \partial\mathcal{O}_\mathcal{C}$, $m_{e,\mathcal{C}}(x)$ is the center of the maximum ball entirely included in $\mathcal{C} \setminus \mathcal{O}_\mathcal{C}$ which passes through x. It is easy to see that for any $x \in \partial\mathcal{O} \cap \mathcal{C}$, the segments $[x, m_{i,\mathcal{C}}(x)]$ and $[x, m_{e,\mathcal{C}}(x)]$ are subsegments of $[x, m_i(x)]$ and $[x, m_e(x)]$ respectively, and lie on the line defined by the normal to $\partial\mathcal{O}$ at x.

Lemma 1 (Separation Condition Restricted to $\mathcal{C}$) *If the Separation Condition is verified then $MA_i(\partial\mathcal{O}_\mathcal{C}) \subset \mathcal{R}_\mathcal{C}$ and $MA_e(\partial\mathcal{O}_\mathcal{C}) \subseteq \mathcal{C} \setminus \mathcal{R}_\mathcal{C}$.*

PROOF. We prove the first part, $\text{MA}_i(\partial\mathcal{O}_\mathcal{C}) \subset \mathcal{R}_\mathcal{C}$. A similar proof gives the second part.
Let m be a point in $\text{MA}_i(\partial\mathcal{O}_\mathcal{C})$, and $B(m)$ be the open medial ball centered at m. Two cases can happen:

- Either, the closest points to m in $\partial\mathcal{O}_\mathcal{C}$ are in $\partial\mathcal{O}$, in which case m is a point in $\text{MA}_i(\partial\mathcal{O})$. The Separation Condition states that $\text{MA}_i(\partial\mathcal{O}) \subset \mathcal{R}$, and so $m \in \mathcal{R}_\mathcal{C} = \mathcal{R} \cap \mathcal{C}$.

- Otherwise, one of the closest points to m in $\partial\mathcal{O}_\mathcal{C}$ is a point a in some section $A \in \mathcal{S}_\mathcal{C}$. If a is on the boundary of A, then since along the section-contours $\partial\mathcal{O}_\mathcal{C}$ is non-smooth, a lies in $\text{MA}_i(\partial\mathcal{O}_\mathcal{C})$ and coincides with m, and $m = a$ is trivially in $\mathcal{R}_\mathcal{C}$. Hence, we may assume that a lies in the interior of A. Therefore, the ball $B(m)$ is tangent to A at a, and the line segment $[a, m]$ is orthogonal to A. Since $B(m) \cap \partial\mathcal{C} = \emptyset$, m and a are in the same Voronoi cell of the Voronoi diagram of $\mathcal{C}$. Thus, $a \in \mathcal{S}_\mathcal{C}$ is the nearest point in $\partial\mathcal{C}$ to m. By the definition of $\mathcal{R}_\mathcal{C}$, we deduce that $m \in \mathcal{R}_\mathcal{C}$. □

Assume that the Separation Condition is verified. The first idea which comes to mind is to retract points of $\partial\mathcal{O}$ to $\partial\mathcal{R}$ by following the normal-directions. A point $x \in \partial\mathcal{O}$ which lies outside $\mathcal{R}$ can move towards $m_i(x) \in \mathcal{R}$ and stop when $\partial\mathcal{R}$ is reached. A point $x \in \partial\mathcal{O}$ which lies inside $\mathcal{R}$, can move toward $m_e(x)$ and stop when $\partial\mathcal{R}$ is reached. Since $\partial\mathcal{O}$ is assumed to be of class $C^{1,1}$, the normals form a continuous vector field. Hence, this deformation will be a continuous retraction if each normal intersects $\partial\mathcal{R}$ at a single point. In such a case, $\partial\mathcal{O}$ can be deformed to $\partial\mathcal{R}$ homeomorphically. But a major problem is that $\mathcal{R}$ may have a complex shape (with cavities), so that a normal to $\partial\mathcal{O}$ intersects $\partial\mathcal{R}$ in several points. In such a case, such a retraction is not continuous and does not provide a deformation retract of $\mathcal{O}$ onto $\mathcal{R}$. However, we will be essentially following this intuitive idea by looking for a similar deformation retract of $\mathcal{O}$ onto a subshape of $\mathcal{R}$ (the so-called medial shape).

2.2 Guarantees on the Connections Between the Sections

We now show that if the sample of cutting planes verifies the Separation Condition, then in each cell $\mathcal{C}$ of the arrangement, the connection between the sections is the same in $\mathcal{O}_\mathcal{C}$ and $\mathcal{R}_\mathcal{C}$.

Theorem 1 *If the sample of cutting planes verifies the Separation Condition, $\mathcal{R}_\mathcal{C}$ and $\mathcal{O}_\mathcal{C}$ induce the same connectivity components on the sections of $\mathcal{C}$.*

PROOF. The proof is given in two parts:

(I) **If two sections are connected in $\mathcal{R}_\mathcal{C}$, then they are connected in $\mathcal{O}_\mathcal{C}$.** Let A and A' be two sections connected in $\mathcal{R}_\mathcal{C}$. Let γ be a path in $\mathcal{R}_\mathcal{C}$ that connects a point $a \in A$ to a point $a' \in A'$. For the sake of a contradiction, suppose that a and a' are not in the same connected component of $\mathcal{O}_\mathcal{C}$. In this case, as γ joins two points in two different connected components of $\mathcal{O}_\mathcal{C}$, it intersects $\mathrm{MA}_e(\partial\mathcal{O}_\mathcal{C})$. This is a contradiction with the fact that $\gamma \subset \mathcal{R}_\mathcal{C}$, since according to Lemma 1 we have $\mathrm{MA}_e(\partial\mathcal{O}_\mathcal{C}) \cap \mathcal{R}_\mathcal{C} = \emptyset$.

(II) **If two sections are connected in $\mathcal{O}_\mathcal{C}$, then they are connected in $\mathcal{R}_\mathcal{C}$.** Let A and A' be two sections in a same connected component K of $\mathcal{O}_\mathcal{C}$. According to the non-smoothness of $\partial\mathcal{O}_\mathcal{C}$ at the boundary of the sections, ∂A and $\partial A'$ are contained in $\mathrm{MA}_i(\partial\mathcal{O}_\mathcal{C})$. Thus, there is a path γ in $\mathrm{MA}_i(\partial\mathcal{O}_\mathcal{C}) \cap K$ that connects a point $a \in \partial A$ to a point $a' \in \partial A'$. According to Lemma 1, $\mathrm{MA}_i(\partial\mathcal{O}_\mathcal{C}) \subset \mathcal{R}_\mathcal{C}$. Thus, γ is a path in $\mathcal{R}_\mathcal{C}$ that connects A to A'.

□

2.3 How to Ensure the Separation Condition?

In this section we provide a sufficient condition for ensuring the Separation Condition. For this, we need first some definitions.

Definition 7 (Reach) *Let $\mathcal{O}$ be a connected compact 3-manifold with smooth boundary $\partial\mathcal{O}$ in $\mathbb{R}^3$. For $a \in \partial\mathcal{O}$, we define reach$(a) = \min(d(a, m_i(a)), d(a, m_e(a)))$. The quantity reach$(\mathcal{O})$ is defined as the minimum distance of $\partial\mathcal{O}$ from the medial axis of $\partial\mathcal{O}$:*

$$reach(\mathcal{O}) := \min_{m \in MA(\partial\mathcal{O})} d(m, \partial\mathcal{O}) = \min_{a \in \partial\mathcal{O}} reach(a).$$

Note that as $\mathcal{O}$ is compact and $\partial\mathcal{O}$ is of class $C^{1,1}$, reach$(\mathcal{O})$ is strictly positive.

Definition 8 (Reach restricted to a cell) *Given a cell $\mathcal{C}$ of the arrangement, we define reach$_\mathcal{C}(\mathcal{O}) = \min d(a, m(a))$, where either $a \in \partial\mathcal{O} \cap \mathcal{C}$ or $m(a) \in MA(\partial\mathcal{O}) \cap \mathcal{C}$. By definition, we have reach$(\mathcal{O}) = \min_\mathcal{C}$ (reach$_\mathcal{C}(\mathcal{O})$).*

Definition 9 (Height of a Cell) *Let $\mathcal{C}$ be a cell of the arrangement of the cutting planes. The* height *of $\mathcal{C}$, denoted by $h_\mathcal{C}$, is defined as the maximum distance of a point $x \in \mathcal{C}$ to its nearest point in the boundary of $\mathcal{C}$. In other words, $h_\mathcal{C} := \max_{x \in \mathcal{C}} d(x, \mathrm{np}(x))$.*

We now show that by upper-bounding the height of the cells by a factor related to the reach of the object, we can ensure the Separation Condition.

Lemma 2 (Sufficient Condition) *If $h_\mathcal{C} <$ reach$_\mathcal{C}(\mathcal{O})$, for any cell $\mathcal{C}$ of the arrangement, then the Separation Condition is verified.*

PROOF. The proof is straightforward. Let m be a point in $\mathrm{MA}(\partial\mathcal{O})$ in a cell $\mathcal{C}$ of the arrangement. We have

$$d(m, \mathrm{np}(m)) \leq h_\mathcal{C} < \mathrm{reach}_\mathcal{C}(\mathcal{O}) \leq d(m, \partial\mathcal{O}).$$

Therefore the Separation Condition is verified. □

We proved that under the Separation condition, the connectivity between the sections of $\mathcal{C}$ induced by the reconstructed object $\mathcal{R}_\mathcal{C}$ is coherent with the original shape $\mathcal{O}_\mathcal{C}$. This implies the homotopy equivalence between $\mathcal{R}_\mathcal{C}$ and $\mathcal{O}_\mathcal{C}$ for the 2-dimensional variant of the reconstruction problem.

2.4 Guarantees for 2D Shape Reconstruction from Line Cross-Sections

Consider the 2-dimensional variant of the reconstruction problem, that consists of constructing a 2D-shape from its intersections with arbitrarily oriented *cutting lines*. In this case the sections are line-segments.
We can focus on a cell $\mathcal{C}$ of the arrangement of the plane by the cutting lines. Similar definitions for the Voronoi diagram and the Voronoi skeleton of $\mathcal{C}$, the lift function and the reconstructed object $\mathcal{R}_\mathcal{C}$ can be considered. If for any cell $\mathcal{C}$ of the arrangement, $h_\mathcal{C} < \mathrm{reach}_\mathcal{C}(\mathcal{O})$ then the Separation Condition is ensured. Under the Separation Condition, there is a bijection between the connected components of $\mathcal{R}_\mathcal{C}$ and $\mathcal{O}_\mathcal{C}$. By the definition of the reconstructed object, it is easy to see that any connected component of $\mathcal{R}_\mathcal{C}$ is a topological disk. On the other hand, under the Separation Condition, any connected component of $\partial\mathcal{O}$ is cut by at least one cutting line. We easily deduce that any connected component of $\mathcal{O}_\mathcal{C}$ is a topological disk.

Using the sufficient condition presented in the last section that implies the separation condition, we deduce the following theorem.

Theorem 2 (Provably Good 2D Reconstruction) *If for any cell $\mathcal{C}$ of the arrangement of the cutting lines, $h_{\mathcal{C}} < reach_{\mathcal{C}}(\mathcal{O})$ then $\mathcal{R}$ is homeomorphic to $\mathcal{O}$.*

PROOF. We proved that under the separation condition, there is a bijection between the connected components of $\mathcal{R}_{\mathcal{C}}$ and $\mathcal{O}_{\mathcal{C}}$. On the other hand, according to the previous lemma, all the connected components of $\mathcal{O}_{\mathcal{C}}$ or $\mathcal{R}_{\mathcal{C}}$ are 2-dimensional disks. Therefore, there is a homotopy equivalence between each pair of corresponding connected components of $\mathcal{O}_{\mathcal{C}}$ or $\mathcal{R}_{\mathcal{C}}$. This provides a homotopy equivalence between $\mathcal{R}_{\mathcal{C}}$ and $\mathcal{O}_{\mathcal{C}}$. As we will explain in detail in Section 3.4.1, the homotopy equivalences in the different cells of the arrangement can be extended to a homotopy equivalence between $\mathcal{R}$ and $\mathcal{O}$. Finally, since $\mathcal{R}$ and $\mathcal{O}$ are two homotopy equivalent 2-dimensional topological manifolds, we deduce that there is a homeomorphism between $\mathcal{R}$ and $\mathcal{O}$. □

3. TOPOLOGICAL GUARANTEES

To clarify the connection between the upcoming sections, let us shortly outline the general strategy employed in proving the homotopy equivalence between $\mathcal{R}$ and $\mathcal{O}$.

3.1 Proof Outline of the Homotopy Equivalence Between $\mathcal{R}$ and $\mathcal{O}$

We will provide a homotopy equivalence between $\mathcal{R}_{\mathcal{C}}$ and $\mathcal{O}_{\mathcal{C}}$ in each cell of the arrangement. (And then glue these homotopy equivalences together to form a global homotopy equivalence between $\mathcal{R}$ and $\mathcal{O}$.) In Section 2.2 we showed that under the first sampling condition called Separation Condition the connection between the sections in the reconstructed object $\mathcal{R}_{\mathcal{C}}$ is the same as in $\mathcal{O}_{\mathcal{C}}$, in the sense that there is a bijection between the connected components of $\mathcal{R}_{\mathcal{C}}$ and the connected components of $\mathcal{O}_{\mathcal{C}}$. This implies that for proving the homotopy equivalence between $\mathcal{R}_{\mathcal{C}}$ and $\mathcal{O}_{\mathcal{C}}$, it will be enough to show that the corresponding connected components have the same homotopy type. In order to extend these homotopy equivalences to a homotopy equivalence between $\mathcal{R}$ and $\mathcal{O}$, we will have to glue together the homotopy equivalences we obtain in the cells of the arrangement. This needs some care since the restriction to a section S of the two homotopy equivalences defined in the two adjacent cells of S may be different. To overcome this problem, we need to define an intermediate shape $\mathcal{M}_{\mathcal{C}}$ in each cell $\mathcal{C}$, called the *medial shape*. The medial shape has the following three properties:

(i) The medial shape contains the sections of $\mathcal{C}$, i.e., $\mathcal{S}_{\mathcal{C}} \subseteq \mathcal{M}_{\mathcal{C}}$.

(ii) There is a (strong) deformation retract r from $\mathcal{O}_{\mathcal{C}}$ to $\mathcal{M}_{\mathcal{C}}$. In particular, this map is a homotopy equivalence between $\mathcal{O}_{\mathcal{C}}$ and $\mathcal{M}_{\mathcal{C}}$. And its restriction to $\mathcal{S}_{\mathcal{C}}$ is the identity map.

(iii) Under the first sampling condition (Separation Condition), $\mathcal{M}_{\mathcal{C}} \subseteq \mathcal{R}_{\mathcal{C}}$.

The first two properties will be crucial to guarantee that the homotopy equivalences conform on each section under the Separation Condition. Indeed, the map $\mathcal{O}_{\mathcal{C}} \to \mathcal{M}_{\mathcal{C}} \hookrightarrow \mathcal{R}_{\mathcal{C}}$, obtained by composing the deformation retract and the inclusion, restricts to the identity map on each section of $\mathcal{S}_{\mathcal{C}}$. Thus, we can glue all these maps to obtain a global map from $\mathcal{O}$ to $\mathcal{R}$.

Using a generalized version of the nerve theorem (see Section 3.4.1) and property (ii) above, we can then reduce the problem to proving that the inclusion $i : \mathcal{M}_{\mathcal{C}} \hookrightarrow \mathcal{R}_{\mathcal{C}}$ forms a homotopy equivalence in each cell. Using Whitehead's theorem, it will be enough to show that the inclusion i induces isomorphisms between the corresponding homotopy groups. Under the Separation Condition, we prove that i induces an injective map on the first homotopy groups, and that all higher homotopy groups of $\mathcal{M}_{\mathcal{C}}$ and $\mathcal{R}_{\mathcal{C}}$ are trivial. Unfortunately, the Separation Condition does not ensure in general the surjectivity of i on the first homotopy groups. To overcome this problem, we need to impose a second condition called *Intersection Condition*. Under the Intersection Condition, the map i will be surjective on the first homotopy groups, leading to a homotopy equivalence between $\mathcal{O}$ and $\mathcal{R}$.

According to the guarantees on the connectivity between the sections (Theorem 1), to prove the homotopy equivalence between $\mathcal{R}_{\mathcal{C}}$ and $\mathcal{O}_{\mathcal{C}}$ under the Separation Condition, we may restrict to each of the corresponding connected components.

> *In the sequel, to simplify the notations and the presentation, we suppose that $\mathcal{O}_{\mathcal{C}}$ and thus $\mathcal{R}_{\mathcal{C}}$ are connected, and we show that $\mathcal{O}_{\mathcal{C}}$ and $\mathcal{R}_{\mathcal{C}}$ have the same homotopy type. It is clear that the same proofs can be applied to each corresponding connected components of $\mathcal{O}_{\mathcal{C}}$ and $\mathcal{R}_{\mathcal{C}}$ to imply the homotopy equivalence in the general case of multiple connected components.*

3.2 Medial Shape

We now define an intermediate shape in each cell $\mathcal{C}$ of the arrangement called the *medial shape*. The medial shape enjoys a certain number of important properties, discussed in this section, which makes it playing an important role in obtaining the homotopy equivalence between $\mathcal{O}_{\mathcal{C}}$ and $\mathcal{R}_{\mathcal{C}}$.

Definition 10 (Medial Shape $\mathcal{M}_{\mathcal{C}}$) *Let x be a point in $\mathcal{S}_{\mathcal{C}} \subset \partial\mathcal{O}_{\mathcal{C}}$. Let $w(x) = [x, m_{i,\mathcal{C}}(x)]$ be the segment in the direction of the normal to $\partial\mathcal{O}_{\mathcal{C}}$ at x which connects x to the point $m_{i,\mathcal{C}}(x) \in MA_i(\partial\mathcal{O}_{\mathcal{C}})$. We add to $MA_i(\partial\mathcal{O}_{\mathcal{C}})$ all the segment $w(x)$ for all the points $x \in \mathcal{S}_{\mathcal{C}}$. We call the resulting shape $\mathcal{M}_{\mathcal{C}}$, see Figure 2. More precisely,*

$$\mathcal{M}_{\mathcal{C}} := MA_i(\partial\mathcal{O}_{\mathcal{C}}) \cup (\bigcup_{x \in \mathcal{S}_{\mathcal{C}}} w(x)).$$

Proposition 1 *The medial shape verifies the following set of properties:*

(i) *The medial shape contains the sections of $\mathcal{C}$, i.e., $\mathcal{S}_{\mathcal{C}} \subseteq \mathcal{M}_{\mathcal{C}}$.*

(ii) *There is a (strong) deformation retract r from $\mathcal{O}_{\mathcal{C}}$ to $\mathcal{M}_{\mathcal{C}}$. In particular, this map is a homotopy equivalence between $\mathcal{O}_{\mathcal{C}}$ and $\mathcal{M}_{\mathcal{C}}$. And its restriction to $\mathcal{S}_{\mathcal{C}}$ is the identity map.*

(iii) *Under the Separation Condition, $\mathcal{M}_{\mathcal{C}} \subseteq \mathcal{R}_{\mathcal{C}}$.*

PROOF. (i) This property is true by the definition of the medial shape.

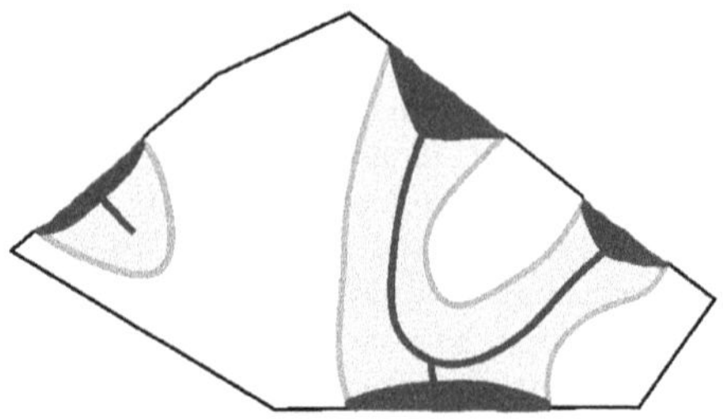

Figure 2: A 2D illustration of the medial shape.

(*ii*) This is obtained by deforming $\mathcal{O}_\mathcal{C}$ to $\mathcal{M}_\mathcal{C}$ in the direction of the normals to the boundary $\partial\mathcal{O}_\mathcal{C}$. Note that the boundary $\partial\mathcal{O}_\mathcal{C}$ is smooth except on the boundaries of sections in $\mathcal{S}_\mathcal{C}$, and the boundaries of the sections in $\mathcal{S}_\mathcal{C}$ are already in $\mathcal{M}_\mathcal{C}$, thus the deformation retract is well defined and easily seen to be continuous. (We refer the interested reader to Lieutier's paper [Lie04], for a more general result on the homotopy equivalence between any open bounded set in $\mathbb{R}^n$ and its medial axis.)

(*iii*) Since $\mathcal{M}_\mathcal{C} = \text{MA}_i(\partial\mathcal{O}_\mathcal{C}) \cup \left(\bigcup_{x\in\mathcal{S}_\mathcal{C}} w(x)\right)$ and in addition $\text{MA}_i(\partial\mathcal{O}_\mathcal{C}) \subset \mathcal{R}_\mathcal{C}$, it will be sufficient to show that for any x in a section $A \in \mathcal{S}_\mathcal{C}$, $w(x) \subset \mathcal{R}_\mathcal{C}$. (Recall that $w(x)$ is the orthogonal segment to $\partial\mathcal{O}_\mathcal{C}$ at x that joins x to the corresponding medial point $m_{i,\mathcal{C}}(x)$ in $\text{MA}_i(\partial\mathcal{O}_\mathcal{C})$.) We will show that $w(x)$ is contained in the segment $[x, \text{lift}(x)]$. The point x is the closest point in $\partial\mathcal{O}_\mathcal{C}$ to $m_{i,\mathcal{C}}(x)$. Thus, the ball centered at $m_{i,\mathcal{C}}(a)$ and passing through x is entirely contained in $\mathcal{O}$ and its interior is empty of points of $\partial\mathcal{C}$. Thus, in the Voronoi diagram of $\mathcal{C}$, $m_{i,\mathcal{C}}(a)$ is in the same Voronoi cell as x. On the other hand, x is the closest point in $\mathcal{S}_\mathcal{C} \subset \partial\mathcal{O}_\mathcal{C}$ to $\text{lift}(x)$. It easily follows that $d(x, \text{lift}(x)) \geq d(x, m_{i,\mathcal{C}}(x))$. It follows that the segment $[x, m_{i,\mathcal{C}}(x)] = w(x)$ is a subsegment of $[x, \text{lift}(x)]$. Therefore, by the definition of $\mathcal{R}_\mathcal{C}$, $w(x) \subset \mathcal{R}_\mathcal{C}$.

□

We end this section with the following important remark and proposition which will be used in the next section. By replacing the shape $\mathcal{O}_\mathcal{C}$ with its complementary set we may define an *exterior medial shape* $\widetilde{\mathcal{M}}_\mathcal{C}$. This is more precisely defined as follows. Let $\widetilde{\mathcal{O}}$ be the closure of the complementary set of $\mathcal{O}$ in $\mathbb{R}^3$. And let $\widetilde{\mathcal{O}}_\mathcal{C}$ be the intersection of $\widetilde{\mathcal{O}}$ with the cell $\mathcal{C}$. The medial shape of $\widetilde{\mathcal{O}}_\mathcal{C}$, denoted by $\widetilde{\mathcal{M}}_\mathcal{C}$, is the union of the medial shapes of the connected components of $\widetilde{\mathcal{O}}_\mathcal{C}$. Similarly, under the Separation Condition, the following proposition holds.

Proposition 2 *Let $\widetilde{\mathcal{O}}_\mathcal{C}$ be the closure of the complementary set of $\mathcal{O}_\mathcal{C}$ in $\mathcal{C}$ and $\widetilde{\mathcal{M}}_\mathcal{C}$ be the medial shape of $\widetilde{\mathcal{O}}_\mathcal{C}$. Under the Separation Condition: (i) There is a strong deformation retract from $\mathcal{C} \setminus \widetilde{\mathcal{M}}_\mathcal{C}$ to $\mathcal{O}_\mathcal{C}$, and (ii) We have $\mathcal{R}_\mathcal{C} \subset \mathcal{C} \setminus \widetilde{\mathcal{M}}_\mathcal{C}$.*

PROOF. The proof of Property (*i*) is similar to the proof of Proposition 1 by deforming along the normal vectors to the boundary of $\widetilde{\mathcal{O}}_\mathcal{C}$. The second property (*ii*) is equivalent to $\widetilde{\mathcal{M}}_\mathcal{C} \subset \mathcal{C} \setminus \mathcal{R}_\mathcal{C}$. □

3.3 Topological Guarantees Implied by the Separation Condition

Throughout this section, we suppose that the Separation Condition holds. By the discussion at the end of Section 3.1, and without loss of generality, we may suppose that $\mathcal{O}_\mathcal{C}$ and hence $\mathcal{R}_\mathcal{C}$ are connected. Thus, $\mathcal{O}_\mathcal{C}$ and $\mathcal{R}_\mathcal{C}$ are connected compact topological 3-manifolds embedded in $\mathbb{R}^3$.

In Section 3.2, we defined the medial shape $\mathcal{M}_\mathcal{C}$ and showed that $\mathcal{M}_\mathcal{C}$ is homotopy equivalent to $\mathcal{O}_\mathcal{C}$, by giving a (strong) deformation retract from $\mathcal{O}_\mathcal{C}$ onto $\mathcal{M}_\mathcal{C}$. We have also shown that under the Separation Condition, $\mathcal{M}_\mathcal{C} \subset \mathcal{R}_\mathcal{C}$. Using these properties, the goal will be to prove that the inclusion $i : \mathcal{M}_\mathcal{C} \hookrightarrow \mathcal{R}_\mathcal{C}$ is a homotopy equivalence. As the objects we are manipulating are all CW-complexes, homotopy equivalence is equivalent to weak homotopy equivalence according to Whitehead's theorem.

Hence, it will be enough to show that $i : \mathcal{M}_\mathcal{C} \hookrightarrow \mathcal{R}_\mathcal{C}$ induces isomorphism between the corresponding homotopy groups.

3.3.1 *Injectivity on the Level of Homotopy Groups*

We will make use of the lift function in $\mathcal{C}$, c.f. Section 2. We consider the restriction of the lift function to the reconstructed object $\mathcal{R}_\mathcal{C}$. According to the definition of $\mathcal{R}_\mathcal{C}$, $\mathcal{R}_\mathcal{C}$ is the union of all the segments $[a, \text{lift}(a)]$, for $a \in \mathcal{S}_\mathcal{C}$. On the other hand, the lift function retracts each segment $[a, \text{lift}(a)]$ to $\text{lift}(a)$ continuously. We infer the following simple observation.

Proposition 3 *The lift function $\mathcal{L} : \mathcal{R}_\mathcal{C} \to \text{lift}(\mathcal{S}_\mathcal{C})$ is a homotopy equivalence.*

According to the above proposition and the following diagram, to show that $i : \mathcal{M}_\mathcal{C} \hookrightarrow \mathcal{R}_\mathcal{C}$ is a homotopy equivalence, using Whitehead's theorem it will be sufficient to show that the restriction of the lift function to $\mathcal{M}_\mathcal{C}$ is a weak homotopy equivalence.

$$\begin{array}{ccc} \mathcal{M}_\mathcal{C} & \overset{i}{\hookrightarrow} & \mathcal{R}_\mathcal{C} \\ & {\scriptstyle\mathcal{L}}\searrow & \downarrow{\scriptstyle\mathcal{L}} \\ & & \text{lift}(\mathcal{S}_\mathcal{C}) \end{array}$$

More precisely, if $\mathcal{L} : \mathcal{M}_\mathcal{C} \to \text{lift}(\mathcal{S}_\mathcal{C})$ is a weak homotopy equivalence (what we will prove below), since $\mathcal{L} : \mathcal{R}_\mathcal{C} \to \text{lift}(\mathcal{S}_\mathcal{C})$ is also a homotopy equivalence and because of the commutativity of the above diagram, the inclusion $i : \mathcal{M}_\mathcal{C} \hookrightarrow \mathcal{R}_\mathcal{C}$ induces isomorphisms between the homotopy groups of $\mathcal{M}_\mathcal{C}$ and $\mathcal{R}_\mathcal{C}$. Thus, Whitehead's theorem implies that i is a homotopy equivalence. We first show that under the Separation Condition, the restricted lift function $\mathcal{L}_{|\mathcal{M}_\mathcal{C}}$ induces injections on the level of homotopy groups.

Theorem 3 (Injectivity) *Under the Separation Condition, the homomorphisms between the homotopy groups of $\mathcal{M}_\mathcal{C}$ and $\text{lift}(\mathcal{S}_\mathcal{C})$, induced by the lift function $\mathcal{L}$, are injective.*

PROOF. Under the Separation Condition, we have $\mathcal{M}_\mathcal{C} \subset \mathcal{R}_\mathcal{C}$. Let $\widetilde{\mathcal{M}}_\mathcal{C}$ be the medial shape of the closure of the complementary set of $\mathcal{O}_\mathcal{C}$ in $\mathcal{C}$. We refer to the discussion at the end of the previous section for more details. Recall that by Proposition 2, we have $\mathcal{R_C} \subset \mathcal{C} \setminus \widetilde{\mathcal{M}}_\mathcal{C}$, and there exists a deformation retract from $\mathcal{C} \setminus \widetilde{\mathcal{M}}_\mathcal{C}$ to $\mathcal{O_C}$ (in particular $\mathcal{O_C}$ and $\mathcal{C} \setminus \widetilde{\mathcal{M}}_\mathcal{C}$ are homotopy equivalent). We have now the following commutative diagram in which every map (except the lift function $\mathcal{L}$) is an injection (or an isomorphism) on the level of homotopy groups.

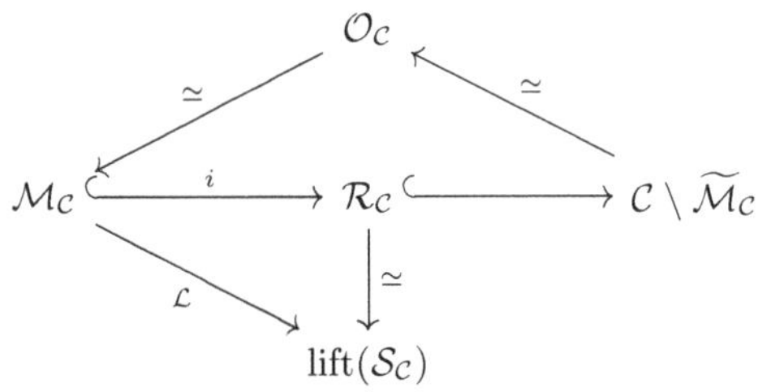

Using this diagram, the injectivity on the level of homotopy groups is clear: For any integer $j \geq 1$, consider the induced homomorphism $\mathcal{L}_* : \pi_j(\mathcal{M_C}) \to \pi_j(\text{lift}(\mathcal{S_C}))$. Let $x \in \pi_j(\mathcal{M_C})$ be so that $\mathcal{L}_*(x)$ is the zero element of $\pi_j(\text{lift}(\mathcal{S_C}))$. It is sufficient to show that x is the zero element of $\pi_j(\mathcal{M_C})$. Following the maps of the diagram, and using the homotopy equivalence between lift$(\mathcal{S_C})$ and $\mathcal{R_C}$, we have that $i_*(x)$ is mapped to the zero element of $\pi_j(\mathcal{R_C})$. Then, by the inclusion $\mathcal{R_C} \hookrightarrow \mathcal{C} \setminus \widetilde{\mathcal{M}}_\mathcal{C}$, it goes to the zero element of $\mathcal{C} \setminus \widetilde{\mathcal{M}}_\mathcal{C}$, and by the two retractions, it will be mapped to the zero element of $\mathcal{M_C}$. As this diagram is commutative, we infer that x is the zero element of $\mathcal{M_C}$. Thus, $\mathcal{L}_* : \pi_j(\mathcal{M_C}) \to \pi_j(\text{lift}(\mathcal{S_C}))$ is injective for all $j \geq 1$. The injectivity for $j = 0$ is already proved in Theorem 1. ☐

We have shown that under the Separation Condition, the lift function $\mathcal{L} : \mathcal{M_C} \to \text{lift}(\mathcal{S_C})$ induces injective morphisms between the homotopy groups of $\mathcal{M_C}$ and lift$(\mathcal{S_C})$. If these induced morphisms were surjective, then $\mathcal{L}$ would be a homotopy equivalence (by Whitehead's theorem). We will show in Section 3.3.2 that the Separation Condition implies the surjectivity for all the homotopy groups except for dimension one (fundamental groups). Indeed, we will show that under the Separation Condition, all the i-dimensional homotopy groups of $\mathcal{M_C}$ and lift$(\mathcal{S_C})$ for $i \geq 2$ are trivial. Once this is proved, it will be sufficient to study the surjectivity of $\mathcal{L}_* : \pi_1(\mathcal{M_C}) \to \pi_1(\text{lift}(\mathcal{S_C}))$.

Remark 1 *Note that the injectivity in the general form above remains valid for the corresponding reconstruction problems in dimensions greater than three. However, the vanishing results on higher homotopy groups of $\mathcal{O_C}$ and $\mathcal{R_C}$ are only valid in dimensions two and three.*

3.3.2 *The topological structures of $\mathcal{R_C}$ and $\mathcal{O_C}$ are determined by their fundamental groups*

In this section, we show that if the Separation Condition is verified, then the topological structure of the portion of $\mathcal{O}$ in a cell $\mathcal{C}$ (i.e., $\mathcal{O_C}$) is simple enough, in the sense that for all $i \geq 2$, the i-dimensional homotopy group of $\mathcal{O_C}$ is trivial. We can easily show that $\mathcal{R_C}$ has the same property.[1] As a consequence, the topological structures of $\mathcal{O_C}$ and $\mathcal{R_C}$ are determined by their fundamental group, $\pi_1(\mathcal{O_C})$ and $\pi_1(\mathcal{R_C})$.

We first state the following general theorem for an arbitrary embedded 3-manifold with connected boundary.

Theorem 4 *Let K be a connected 3-manifold in $\mathbb{R}^3$ with a (non-empty) connected boundary. Then for all $i \geq 2$, $\pi_i(K) = \{0\}$.*

This theorem can be obtained from Corollary 3.9 of [Hat02]. We also provide a proof of this theorem in the long version of the paper [ABM09]. From this theorem, we infer the two following theorems.

Theorem 5 *Under the Separation Condition, $\pi_i(\mathcal{O_C}) = \{0\}$, for all $i \geq 2$.*

PROOF. We only make use of the fact that under the Separation Condition, any connected component of $\partial\mathcal{O}$ is cut by at least one cutting plane. In this case, every connected component of $\mathcal{O_C}$ is a 3-manifold with connected boundary. The theorem follows as a corollary of Theorem 4. ☐

Theorem 6 *$\pi_i(\mathcal{R_C}) = \{0\}$, for all $i \geq 2$.*

PROOF. Using Theorem 4, it will be sufficient to show that the boundary of any connected component K of $\mathcal{R_C}$ is connected. Let x and y be two points on the boundary of K, and let S and S' be two sections so that $x \in [a, \text{lift}(a)]$ for some $a \in S$ and $y \in [b, \text{lift}(b)]$ for some $b \in S'$. By the definition of $\mathcal{R_C}$, x is connected to S in $\partial\mathcal{R_C}$, and y is connected to S' in $\partial\mathcal{R_C}$. On the other hand, since S and S' are two sections in the connected component K of $\mathcal{R_C}$, they lie on ∂K and are connected to each other in ∂K (and so in $\partial\mathcal{R_C}$). Thus, x is connected to y in $\partial\mathcal{R_C}$. ☐

3.4 Second Condition: Intersection Condition

In the previous section, we saw that under the Separation Condition, the topological structures of $\mathcal{O_C}$ and $\mathcal{R_C}$ are determined by their fundamental group $\pi_1(\mathcal{O_C})$ and $\pi_1(\mathcal{R_C})$, respectively. The goal of this section is to find a way to ensure an isomorphism between the fundamental groups of $\mathcal{R_C}$ and $\mathcal{O_C}$. We recall that as $\mathcal{O_C}$ and $\mathcal{M_C}$ are homotopy equivalent, $\pi_1(\mathcal{O_C})$ is isomorphic to $\pi_1(\mathcal{M_C})$. On the other hand, $\mathcal{R_C}$ and lift$(\mathcal{S_C})$ are homotopy equivalent, and $\pi_1(\mathcal{R_C})$ is isomorphic to $\pi_1(\text{lift}(\mathcal{S_C}))$ (c.f. last diagram). Thus, it will be sufficient to compare $\pi_1(\mathcal{M_C})$ and $\pi_1(\text{lift}(\mathcal{S_C}))$.

We consider $\mathcal{L}_* : \pi_1(\mathcal{M_C}) \to \pi_1(\text{lift}(\mathcal{S_C}))$, the map induced by the lift function from $\mathcal{M_C}$ to lift$(\mathcal{S_C})$ on fundamental groups . We showed that $\mathcal{L}_*$ is injective. A natural condition to ensure that $\mathcal{L}_*$ is an isomorphism is to imply that *any connected component of* lift$(\mathcal{S_C})$ *is contractible.* This is very common in practice, where the sections are contractible and sufficiently close to each other. In this case, since $\pi_1(\text{lift}(\mathcal{S_C}))$ is trivial and $\mathcal{L}_*$ is surjective. Hence, the homotopy equivalence between $\mathcal{R_C}$ and $\mathcal{O_C}$ can be deduced.

However, the map $\mathcal{L}_* : \pi_1(\mathcal{M_C}) \to \pi_1(\text{lift}(\mathcal{S_C}))$ fails to be surjective in general (where the connected components of lift$(\mathcal{S_C})$ are not necessarily contractible). Figure 3 shows two shapes with different topologies, a torus and a (*twisted*) cylinder, that have the same (inter)sections with a set of (two) cutting planes.
Hence, whatever is the reconstructed object from these sections, it would not be topologically consistent for at least one

[1] Recall that for simplifying the presentation, we assume that $\mathcal{O_C}$ and so $\mathcal{R_C}$ are connected. The same proof shows that in the general case, the same property holds for each connected component of $\mathcal{O_C}$ or $\mathcal{R_C}$.

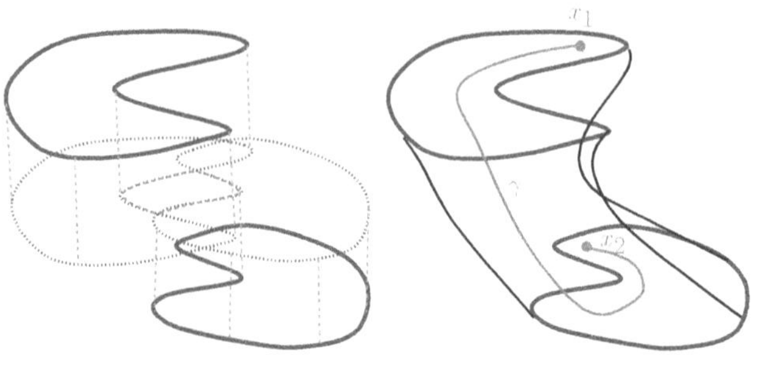

Figure 3: An example of the case where the lift function from $\mathcal{M}_C$ to lift($\mathcal{S}_C$) fails to be surjective: x_1 and x_2 are two points with the same lift in lift($\mathcal{S}_C$). The lift of any curve γ connecting x_1 and x_2 in $\mathcal{M}_C$ provides a non-zero element of $\pi_1(\text{lift}(\mathcal{S}_C), x)$. The reconstructed object (at left) is a torus and is not homotopy equivalent to the original shape (at right) which is a twisted cylinder.

of these objects. In particular, the proposed reconstructed object ($\mathcal{R}$) is a torus which is not homotopy equivalent to the (*twisted*) cylinder ($\mathcal{O}$). In addition, we note that the Separation Condition may be verified for such a situation. Indeed, such a situation is exactly the case when the injective morphism between the fundamental groups of $\mathcal{O}$ and $\mathcal{R}$ is not surjective. This situation can be explained as follows: let x_1 and x_2 be two points in the sections S_1 and S_2 with the same lift x in lift($\mathcal{S}_C$). The lift of any curve γ connecting x_1 and x_2 in $\mathcal{M}_C$ provides a non-zero element of $\pi_1(\text{lift}(\mathcal{S}_C), x)$ which is not in the image of $\mathcal{L}_*$. We may avoid this situation with the following condition.

Definition 11 (Intersection Condition) *We say that the set of cutting planes verifies the Intersection Condition if for any pair of sections S_i and S_j in $\mathcal{S}_C$, and for any connected component X of* lift$(S_i) \cap$ lift(S_j)*, the following holds: there is a path $\gamma \subset \mathcal{M}_C$ from a point $a \in S_i$ to a point $b \in S_j$ with* lift$(a) =$ lift$(b) = x \in X$ *so that $\mathcal{L}_*(\gamma)$ is the zero element of $\pi_1(\text{lift}(\mathcal{S}_C), x)$, i.e., is contractible in* lift($\mathcal{S}_C$) *with a homotopy respecting the base point x.*

In Section 3.5, we will show how to verify the Intersection Condition. Let us first prove the surjectivity of the map $\mathcal{L}_*$ which is deduced directly from the Intersection Condition.

Theorem 7 *Under the Intersection Condition, the induced map $\mathcal{L}_* : \pi_1(\mathcal{M}_C) \to \pi_1(\text{lift}(\mathcal{S}_C))$ is surjective.*

PROOF. Let y_0 be a fixed point for $\mathcal{M}_C$ and $x_0 = \mathcal{L}(y_0)$. We show that $\mathcal{L}_* : \pi_1(\mathcal{M}_C, y_0) \to \pi_1(\text{lift}(\mathcal{S}_C), x_0)$ is surjective. Let α be a closed curve in lift($\mathcal{S}_C$) which represents an element of $\pi_1(\text{lift}(\mathcal{S}_C), x_0)$. We show the existence of an element $\beta \in \pi_1(\mathcal{M}_C, y_0)$ such that $\mathcal{L}_*(\beta) = [\alpha]$, where $[\alpha]$ denotes the homotopy class of α in $\pi_1(\text{lift}(\mathcal{S}_C), x_0)$.
We can divide α into subcurves $\alpha_1, \ldots, \alpha_m$ such that α_j joins two points x_{j-1} and x_j, and is entirely in the lift of one of the sections S_j, for $j = 1, \ldots, m$. We may assume $y_0 \in S_1 = S_m$. For each $j = 1, \ldots, m$, let β_j be the curve in S_j, joining two points z_j to w_j, which is mapped to α_j under $\mathcal{L}$. Note that w_j and z_{j+1} (possibly) live in two different sections, but have the same image (x_j) under the lift map $\mathcal{L}$. Let X_j be the connected component of lift$(S_j) \cap$ lift(S_{j+1}) which contains x_j, see Figure 4. According to the Intersection Condition, there is a path $\gamma_j \subset \mathcal{M}_C$ connecting a point $a_j \in S_j$ to a point $b_{j+1} \in S_{j+1}$ such that lift$(a_j) =$ lift$(b_{j+1}) = x'_j \in X_j$ and the image of γ_j under $\mathcal{L}$ is the zero element of $\pi_1(\text{lift}(\mathcal{S}_C), x'_j)$ (i.e., is contractible with a homotopy respecting the base point x'_j). Since X_j is connected, there is a path from x_j to x'_j in X_j, so lifting back this path to two paths from w_j to a_j in S_j and from b_{j+1} to z_{j+1} and taking the union of these two paths with γ_j, we infer the existence of a path $\gamma'_j \subset \mathcal{M}_C$ connecting w_j to z_{j+1}, such that the image of γ'_j under $\mathcal{L}$ is contractible in lift($\mathcal{S}_C$) with a homotopy respecting the base point x_j.

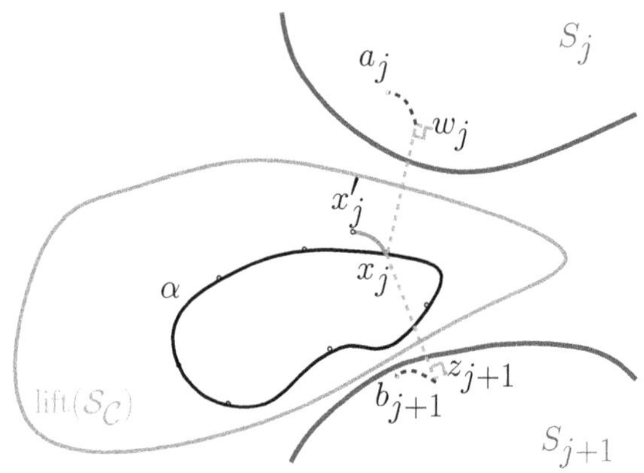

Figure 4: For the proof of Theorem 7.

Let β be the path from x_0 to x_0 obtained by concatenating β_j and γ'_j alternatively, i.e., $\beta = \beta_1\gamma'_1\beta_2\gamma'_2 \ldots \beta_{m-1}\gamma'_m\beta_m\gamma'_m$. We claim that $\mathcal{L}_*([\beta]) = [\alpha]$. This is now easy to show: we have $\mathcal{L}_*(\beta) = \alpha_1\mathcal{L}_*(\gamma'_1)\alpha_2 \ldots \mathcal{L}_*(\gamma'_m)\alpha_m$, and all the paths $\mathcal{L}_*(\gamma'_j)$ are contractible to the constant path $[x_j]$ by a homotopy fixing x_j all the time. We deduce that under a homotopy fixing x_0, $\alpha_1\mathcal{L}_*(\gamma'_1) \ldots \mathcal{L}_*(\gamma'_m)\alpha_m$ is homotopic to $\alpha_1\alpha_2 \ldots \alpha_m = \alpha$, and this is exactly saying that $\mathcal{L}_*([\beta]) = [\alpha]$. And the surjectivity follows. □

Putting together all the materials we have obtained, we infer the main theorem of this section.

Theorem 8 (Main Theorem-Part 0) *Under the Separation and the Intersection Conditions, $\mathcal{R}_C$ is homotopy equivalent to $\mathcal{O}_C$, for any cell C of the arrangement.*

3.4.1 Generalized Nerve Theorem and Homotopy Equivalence of $\mathcal{R}$ and $\mathcal{O}$

In this section, we extend the homotopy equivalence between $\mathcal{R}_C$ and $\mathcal{O}_C$, in each cell $\mathcal{C}$, to a global homotopy equivalence between $\mathcal{R}$ and $\mathcal{O}$. To this end, we make use of a generalization of the nerve theorem. This is a folklore theorem and has been observed and used by different authors. For a modern proof of a still more general result, we refer to Segal's paper [Seg68]. (See also [May03], for a survey of similar results.)

Theorem 9 (Generalized Nerve Theorem) *Let $H : X \to Y$ be a continuous map. Suppose that Y has an open cover $\mathcal{K}$ with the following two properties:*

- *Finite intersections of sets in $\mathcal{K}$ are in $\mathcal{K}$.*
- *For each $U \in \mathcal{K}$, the restriction $H : H^{-1}(U) \to U$ is a weak homotopy equivalence.*

Then H is a weak homotopy equivalence.

Let $H_\mathcal{C} : \mathcal{O}_\mathcal{C} \to \mathcal{R}_\mathcal{C}$ be the homotopy equivalence obtained in the previous sections between $\mathcal{O}_\mathcal{C}$ and $\mathcal{R}_\mathcal{C}$. (So $H_\mathcal{C}$ is the composition of the retraction $\mathcal{O}_\mathcal{C} \to \mathcal{M}_\mathcal{C}$ and the inclusion $\mathcal{M}_\mathcal{C} \hookrightarrow \mathcal{R}_\mathcal{C}$.) Let $H : \mathcal{O} \to \mathcal{R}$ be the map defined by $H(x) = H_\mathcal{C}(x)$ if $x \in \mathcal{O}_\mathcal{C}$ for a cell $\mathcal{C}$ of the arrangement of the cutting planes. Note that H is well-defined since $H_\mathcal{C}|_{\mathcal{S}_\mathcal{C}} = id_{\mathcal{S}_\mathcal{C}}$, for all $\mathcal{C}$. In addition, since for all cell $\mathcal{C}$, $H_\mathcal{C}$ is continuous, H is continuous as well.
We can now apply the generalized nerve theorem by the following simple trick. Let ϵ be an infinitesimal positive value. For any cell $\mathcal{C}$ of the arrangement of the cutting planes, we define $\mathcal{O}_\mathcal{C}^\epsilon = \{x \in \mathbb{R}^3,\ d(x, \mathcal{O}_\mathcal{C}) < \epsilon\ \}$. Let us now consider the open covering $\mathcal{K}$ of $\mathcal{O}$ by these open sets and all their finite intersections. It is straightforward to check that for ϵ small enough, the restriction of H to each element of $\mathcal{K}$ is a weak homotopy equivalence. Therefore, according to the generalized nerve theorem, H is a weak homotopy equivalence between $\mathcal{R}$ and $\mathcal{O}$. And by Whitehead's theorem, H is a homotopy equivalence between $\mathcal{R}$ and $\mathcal{O}$. Thus, we have:

Theorem 10 (Main Theorem-Part I) *Under the Separation and Intersection Conditions, the reconstructed object $\mathcal{R}$ is homotopy equivalent to the unknown original shape $\mathcal{O}$.*

3.5 How to Ensure the Intersection Condition?

In Section 2.2, we showed that the Separation Condition can be ensured with a sufficiently dense sample of cutting planes. In this section we provide a sufficient condition that implies the Intersection Condition.

We showed that by upper-bounding the height of the cells by the reach of the object, we can ensure the Separation Condition. In order to ensure the Intersection Condition, we need a stronger condition on the height of the cells. As we will see, this condition is a *transversality* condition on the cutting planes that can be measured by the angle between the cutting planes and the normal to $\partial\mathcal{O}$ at contour-points.

Definition 12 (Angle α_a) *Let a be a point on the boundary of a section $A \in \mathcal{S}_\mathcal{C}$ on the plane P_A. We consider $m_i(a)$, that may be outside the cell $\mathcal{C}$. We define α_a as the angle between P_A and the normal to $\partial\mathcal{O}$ at a, see Figure 5:* $\alpha_a := \text{angle}(P_A, [a, m_i(a)])$.

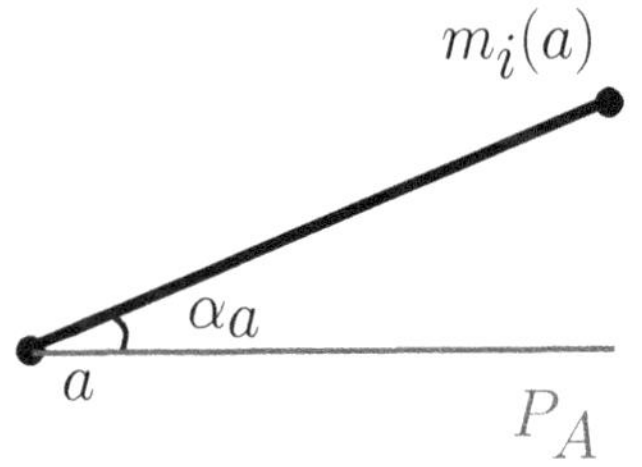

Figure 5: Definition of α_a

Sufficient Conditions.

We now define the sampling conditions on the cutting planes. (See 2.3 for the definitions of $h_\mathcal{C}$ and $\text{reach}_\mathcal{C}(\mathcal{O})$.)

(C1) Density Condition For any cell $\mathcal{C}$ of the arrangement, $h_\mathcal{C} < \text{reach}_\mathcal{C}(\mathcal{O})$.

(C2) Transversality Condition For any cell $\mathcal{C}$,

$$h_\mathcal{C} < \frac{1}{2}\left(1 - \sin(\alpha_a)\right) \text{reach}(a), \forall a \in \partial\mathcal{S}_\mathcal{C}.$$

The Density Condition is based on the density of the sections. The Transversality Condition is defined in a way that the transversality of the cutting planes to $\partial\mathcal{O}$ and the distance between the sections are controlled simultaneously. (Indeed, $\sin(\alpha_a)$ is to control the transversality, and upper-bounding $h_\mathcal{C}$ allows us to control the distance between the sections.)

Remark on the Transversality Condition.

The transversality of the cutting planes to $\partial\mathcal{O}$ seems to be a reasonable condition in practice, specially for applications in 3D ultrasound. Indeed, according to [Rou03] Section 1.2.1, from a technical point of view if a cut is not sufficiently transversal to the organ, the quality of the resulting 2D ultrasonic image is not acceptable for diagnosis.

According to Lemma 2 in Section 2.2, the Density Condition implies the Separation Condition. Also we can show that under the Transversality Condition, the Intersection Condition is verified (the proof is provided in the full version [ABM09]). Therefore, by increasing the density of the sections of $\mathcal{O}$, with preferably transversal cutting planes, we can ensure the required sampling conditions, and consequently, provide a topologically consistent reconstruction of $\mathcal{O}$.

Theorem 11 (Main Theorem-Part II) *If the set of cutting planes verifies the* Density *and the* Transversality Conditions, *then the* Separation *and the* Intersection Conditions *are verified. Therefore, the proposed reconstructed object $\mathcal{R}$ is homotopy equivalent to the unknown original shape $\mathcal{O}$.*

3.6 Deforming the Homotopy Equivalence to a Homeomorphism

Using the homotopy equivalence between $\mathcal{R}$ and $\mathcal{O}$, we can show that they are indeed isotopic.

Theorem 12 (Main Theorem-Part III) *Under the Separation and the Intersection Conditions, the two topological manifolds $\mathcal{R}$ and $\mathcal{O}$ are homeomorphic (in addition, they are isotopic).*

Although, this result is stronger than the homotopy equivalence, the way our proof works makes essentially use of the topological study of the previous sections.

Proof.

Again, we first argue in each cell of the arrangement and show the existence of a homeomorphism between $\mathcal{O}_\mathcal{C}$ and $\mathcal{R}_\mathcal{C}$ whose restriction to $\mathcal{S}_\mathcal{C}$ is the identity map. Gluing these homeomorphisms together, one obtains a global homeomorphism between $\mathcal{R}$ and $\mathcal{O}$. Let $\mathcal{C}$ be a cell of the arrangement of the cutting planes. A similar method used to prove the homotopy equivalence between $\mathcal{R}_\mathcal{C}$ and $\mathcal{O}_\mathcal{C}$ shows that $\partial\mathcal{R}\cap\mathcal{C}$ and $\partial\mathcal{O}\cap\mathcal{C}$ are homotopy equivalent 2-manifolds and are therefore homeomorphic, and in addition there exists a homeomorphism $\beta_\mathcal{C} : \partial\mathcal{O} \cap \mathcal{C} \to \partial\mathcal{R} \cap \mathcal{C}$ which induces identity on the boundary of sections in $\mathcal{S}_\mathcal{C}$. We showed that the topology of $\mathcal{R}_\mathcal{C}$ and $\mathcal{O}_\mathcal{C}$ is completely determined by their fundamental groups, i.e., all the higher homotopy groups of $\mathcal{R}_\mathcal{C}$ and $\mathcal{O}_\mathcal{C}$ are trivial. Moreover, there is an isomorphism between $\pi_1(\mathcal{O}_\mathcal{C})$ and $\pi_1(\mathcal{R}_\mathcal{C})$, and the induced map $(\beta_\mathcal{C})_* : \pi_1(\partial\mathcal{O}\cap\mathcal{C}) \to \pi_1(\partial\mathcal{R}\cap\mathcal{C})$ on first homotopy groups is consistent with this isomorphism (in the sense that there exists a commutative diagram of first homotopy groups). This shows that there is no obstruction in extending $\beta_\mathcal{C}$ to a map $\alpha_\mathcal{C} : \mathcal{O}_\mathcal{C} \to \mathcal{R}_\mathcal{C}$, inducing the corresponding isomorphism between $\pi_1(\mathcal{O}_\mathcal{C})$ and $\pi_1(\mathcal{R}_\mathcal{C})$, and such that the restriction of $\alpha_\mathcal{C}$ to $\mathcal{S}_\mathcal{C}$ remains identity. Since all the higher homotopy groups of $\mathcal{O}_\mathcal{C}$ and $\mathcal{R}_\mathcal{C}$ are trivial, it follows that $\alpha_\mathcal{C}$ is a homotopy equivalence. We can now apply the following theorem due to Waldhausen, which shows that α can be deformed to homeomorphism between $\mathcal{O}_\mathcal{C}$ and $\mathcal{R}_\mathcal{C}$, by a deformation which does not change the homeomorphism $\alpha_\mathcal{C}$ between the boundaries. A compact 3-manifold M is called *irreducible* if $\pi_2(M)$ is trivial. We note that $\mathcal{O}_\mathcal{C}$ and $\mathcal{R}_\mathcal{C}$ are irreducible.

Theorem 13 (Waldhausen) *Let $f : M \to M'$ be a homotopy equivalence between orientable irreducible 3-manifolds with boundaries such that f takes the boundary of M onto the boundary of M' homeomorphically. Then f can be deformed to a homeomorphism $M \to M'$ by a homotopy which is fixed all the time on the boundary of M. (See [Mat03], page 220, for a proof.)*

Applying Waldhausen's theorem, one obtains a homeomorphism $\tilde{\alpha}_\mathcal{C}$ from $\mathcal{O}_\mathcal{C}$ to $\mathcal{R}_\mathcal{C}$ which is identity on the sections in $\mathcal{S}_\mathcal{C}$. Gluing $\tilde{\alpha}_\mathcal{C}$, one obtain a global homeomorphism form $\mathcal{O}$ to $\mathcal{R}$. Moreover, according to Chazal and Cohen-Steiner's work [CCS05] (Corollary 3.1), since $\mathcal{R}$ and $\mathcal{O}$ are homeomorphic and $\mathcal{R}$ contains the medial axis of $\mathcal{O}$, $\mathcal{R}$ is isotopic to $\mathcal{O}$. □

Conclusion

In this paper, we presented the first topological studies in shape reconstruction from cross-sectional data. We showed that the generalization of the classical overlapping criterion to solve the correspondence problem between unorganized cross-sections, proposed by Liu et al. in [LBD+08], preserves the homotopy type of the shape under some appropriate sampling conditions. In addition, we proved that in this case, the homotopy equivalence between the reconstructed object and the original shape can be deformed to a homeomorphism. Even, more strongly, the two objects are isotopic.

Acknowledgments

This work has been partially supported by the High Council for Scientific and Technological Cooperation between Israel and France (research networks program in medical and biological imaging).

4. REFERENCES

[ABM09] O. Amini, J-D. Boissonnat, and P. Memari. Geometric Tomography with Topological Guarantees. *INRIA Report 7147*, 2009.

[BG93] J.D. Boissonnat and B. Geiger. Three dimensional reconstruction of complex shapes based on the delaunay triangulation. *Biomedical Image Processing and Visualization*, page 964, 1993.

[BM07] J.D. Boissonnat and P. Memari. Shape reconstruction from unorganized cross sections. *Symposium on Geometry Processing*, pages 89–98, 2007.

[BV09] G. Barequet and A. Vaxman. Reconstruction of multi-label domains from partial planar cross-sections. *Symposium on Geometry Processing*, 2009.

[CCS05] F. Chazal and D. Cohen-Steiner. A condition for isotopic approximation. *Graphical Models*, 67(5):390–404, 2005.

[DP97] C.R. Dance and R.W. Prager. Delaunay Reconstruction from Multiaxial Planar Cross-Sections. *Research Report*, 1997.

[Hat02] A. Hatcher. *Algebraic topology*. Cambridge University Press, 2002.

[JWC+05] T. Ju, J. Warren, J. Carson, G. Eichele, C. Thaller, W. Chiu, M. Bello, and I. Kakadiaris. Building 3D surface networks from 2D curve networks with application to anatomical modeling. *The Visual Computer*, 21(8):764–773, 2005.

[LBD+08] L. Liu, C.L. Bajaj, J.O. Deasy, D.A. Low, and T. Ju. Surface reconstruction from non-parallel curve networks. *Computer Graphics Forum*, 27:155–163, 2008.

[Lie04] A. Lieutier. Any open bounded subset of $\mathbb{R}^n$ has the same homotopy type as its medial axis. *Computer-Aided Design*, 36(11):1029–1046, 2004.

[Mat03] S.V. Matveev. *Algorithmic topology and classification of 3-manifolds*. Springer, 2003.

[May03] J.P. May. Finite spaces and simplicial complexes. *Notes for REU*, 2003.

[MB08] P. Memari and J.D. Boissonnat. Provably good 2d shape reconstruction from unorganized cross sections. *Computer Graphics Forum*, 27(5):1403–1410, 2008.

[PT94] B.A. Payne and A.W. Toga. Surface reconstruction by multiaxial triangulation. *IEEE Computer Graphics and Applications*, 14(6):28–35, 1994.

[Rou03] F. Rousseau. *Méthodes d'analyse d'images et de calibration pour l'échographie 3D en mode main-libre*. PhD thesis, 2003.

[SBG06] A. Sidlesky, G. Barequet, and C. Gotsman. Polygon reconstruction from line cross-sections. *Canadian Conference on Computational Geometry*, 2006.

[Seg68] G. Segal. Classifying spaces and spectral sequences. *Publications Mathématiques de l'IHÉS*, 34(1):105–112, 1968.

On Degrees in Random Triangulations of Point Sets*

Micha Sharir
School of Computer Science
Tel Aviv University
Tel Aviv 69978, Israel
Courant Inst. of Math. Sci.
New York University
New York, NY 10012, USA
michas@tau.ac.il

Adam Sheffer
School of Computer Science
Tel Aviv University
Tel Aviv 69978, Israel
sheffera@tau.ac.il

Emo Welzl
Institut für Theoretische
Informatik, ETH Zürich
CH-8092 Zürich, Switzerland
emo@inf.ethz.ch

ABSTRACT

We study the expected number of interior vertices of degree i in a triangulation of a point set S, drawn uniformly at random from the set of all triangulations of S, and derive various bounds and inequalities for these expected values. One of our main results is: For any set S of N points in general position, and for any fixed i, the expected number of vertices of degree i in a random triangulation is at least $\gamma_i N$, for some fixed positive constant γ_i (assuming that $N > i$ and that at least some fixed fraction of the points are interior).

We also present a new application for these expected values, using upper bounds on the expected number of interior vertices of degree 3 to get a new lower bound, $\Omega(2.4317^N)$, for the minimal number of triangulations any N-element planar point set in general position must have. This improves the previously best known lower bound of $\Omega(2.33^N)$.

Categories and Subject Descriptors

G.2.1 [**Discrete Mathematics**]: Combinatorics—*Counting Problems*

General Terms

Theory

Keywords

random triangulation, counting, degree sequences, number of triangulations, plane graphs, crossing-free geometric graphs, charging

*Work on this paper was partially supported by Grants 155/05 and 338/09 from the Israel Science Fund. Work by Micha Sharir was also supported by NSF Grants CCF-05-14079 and CCF-08-30272, by Grant 2006/194 from the U.S.-Israel Binational Science Foundation, and by the Hermann Minkowski–MINERVA Center for Geometry at Tel Aviv University. Research by Emo Welzl was supported by the Swiss National Science Foundation, SNF Project 200020-125027.

1. INTRODUCTION

A *planar graph* is a graph that can be drawn in the plane in such a way that its edges intersect only at their endpoints. A *plane straight-line graph* is an embedding of a planar graph in the plane such that its edges are mapped to non-crossing straight line segments. In this paper, we consider only plane *straight-line* graphs, but refer to them as plane graphs or non-crossing graphs, for simplicity.

A *triangulation* of a finite point set S in the plane is a maximal plane graph on S. Let $\mathcal{T}(S)$ denote the set of all triangulations of S and let $\mathcal{P}(S)$ denote the set of all plane graphs of S. Moreover, $\mathsf{tr}(S) := |\mathcal{T}(S)|$ and $\mathsf{pg}(S) := |\mathcal{P}(S)|$.

Improved bounds on the number of plane graphs of several special kinds on a set S of N points have been obtained by studying the properties of a graph chosen uniformly at random from the set of all such graphs on a fixed set S.

- $\mathsf{pg}(S) \leq \mathsf{tr}(S) \cdot 8^N$ holds for any planar point set S of N points, because each triangulation has at most $3N$ edges and each plane graph is contained in some triangulation. Razen et al. [9] proved that this relation is not tight with an exponentially better bound of $\mathsf{pg}(S) = O\left(\mathsf{tr}(S) \cdot 7.98^N\right)$. The new bound is established by showing that the expected number of edges in a plane graph, uniformly chosen from $\mathcal{P}(S)$, is at least $\frac{M}{2} + \frac{N-4}{16}$, where $M \leq 3N-6$ is the number of edges in a triangulation of S.
- Upper bounds for the maximal value of $\mathsf{tr}(S)$, for sets S of N points in the plane, have been studied during the past three decades ([1, 3, 10, 11, 14, 13]). The best known bound is $\mathsf{tr}(S) < 30^N$ from [12]. It is obtained by showing that the expected number of vertices of degree 3 in a triangulation, drawn uniformly at random from $\mathcal{T}(S)$, exceeds $N/30$.

(Abstract random planar graphs of a given size have been considered, for example, in [4, 6, 8].) Here we continue the study of random triangulations of planar point sets, initiated in [13], investigating the number of vertices of degree i in a random triangulation. For $T \in \mathcal{T}(S)$, let $v_i(T)$ denote the number of interior vertices (i.e., points which are not vertices of the convex hull of S) of degree i in T. Furthermore, let

$$\hat{v}_i = \hat{v}_i(S) := \mathbb{E}(v_i(T)) = \frac{\sum_{T \in \mathcal{T}(S)} v_i(T)}{\mathsf{tr}(S)},$$

i.e., the expected number of interior vertices of degree i in a random triangulation of S. Due to linearity of expectation, any linear identity or inequality in the $v_i(T)$'s will also be satisfied by the $\hat{v}_i$'s. However, as noted in [13], the $\hat{v}_i$'s are more constrained than the v_i's. Charging schemes seem to provide an efficient way to bound the $\hat{v}_i$'s; they are the main tool used throughout this paper. In [12, 13] considerations were restricted to point sets with triangular convex hull. Here we abandon this restriction. For this purpose, we define S^o as the set of interior points of S, and write $N = n + h$, with h the number of hull vertices and $n := |S^o|$.

Section 2 establishes the upper bounds $\hat{v}_3 \leq \frac{2n+h/2}{5}$ and $\hat{v}_3 \leq n/2$ (for $N \geq 7$), and it is shown how these bounds imply a lower bound of $\Omega\left(2.4317^N\right)$ on the minimal number of triangulations any set of N points in general position must have. This improves the previous bound of $\Omega\left(2.33^N\right)$ in Aichholzer et al. [2]. A construction with $O(3.455^N)$ triangulations is presented by Hurtado and Noy [5], the currently best known upper bound on the minimum number of triangulations. McCabe and Seidel [7] proved that when h is constant, there are $\Omega\left(2.63^N\right)$ triangulations (full proof not yet published). This is sharper than our bound. More specifically, our bound depends on the ratio between n and N, and attains the minimum when $n \approx 0.89901N$. When $N-n = O(1)$, as in [7], our bound is $\Omega\left(2.5^N\right)$, short of their bound.

In Section 3, we derive inequalities relating the $\hat{v}_i$'s and we show that the inequalities imply the bound

$$\hat{v}_4 \geq \max\left\{\tfrac{1}{340}\left(n + 15 - \tfrac{8h}{3}\right), \tfrac{1}{1360}\left(n + 18 - 2h\right)\right\};$$

(this will prove useful in the later sections).

Following the lower bounds on $\hat{v}_3$ in [12, 13] and on $\hat{v}_4$ (just stated), we complete the picture in Section 4, where we derive linear lower bounds on $\hat{v}_i$ for any $i \geq 5$. Specifically, we show that for each $i \geq 5$, $\varepsilon > 0$, and $3 \leq h \leq \left(\frac{1}{2} - \varepsilon\right) n$, there exists a positive constant $\delta_{i,h}$ such that, for any N-element point set S with h hull vertices, we have $\hat{v}_i \geq \delta_{i,h} n$. That is, a random triangulation of S is expected to contain many interior vertices (at least a constant fraction of the points) of degree i, for *every* $3 \leq i < N$.

We end Section 4 with observations on improved lower bounds on the expected number of low-degree vertices in a random triangulation, which are sharper than the bounds that we can get for individual degrees: $\max\{\hat{v}_3, \hat{v}_4, \hat{v}_5, \hat{v}_6\} \geq \frac{n-h+9}{10}$ and $\max\{\hat{v}_4, \hat{v}_5, \ldots, \hat{v}_{11}\} \geq \frac{12n-9.5h+45}{180}$.

1.1 Notations

Vints and bints. As in [12, 13], we consider $S^o \times \mathcal{T}(S)$ and call each of its elements a *vint* (*v*ertex *in* triangulation), i.e. a vint is an instance of a vertex in a specific triangulation. The degree of a vint (p, T) is the degree (number of neighbors) of p in T; a vint of degree i is called an *i-vint*. Note that hull vertices do not participate in this definition.

The *link* of a vint (p, T) is the face obtained by removing p with incident edges from T, a star-shaped polygon with respect to p; its number of edges equals the degree of p.

Let B denote the set of edges of the convex hull of S. Similarly to the set of vints, we consider $B \times \mathcal{T}(S)$ and call each of its elements a *bint* (*b*oundary edge *in* triangulation).

Catalan numbers. $C_m := \frac{1}{m+1}\binom{2m}{m} = \Theta(m^{-3/2}4^m) = \Theta^*(4^m)$, $m \in \mathbb{N}_0$, denotes the mth *Catalan number*. (In $O^*()$, $\Theta^*()$, and $\Omega^*()$, we neglect polynomial factors.) The number of triangulations of h points in convex position is C_{h-2} and the number of subtrees of the complete binary tree, that contain exactly k nodes, is C_k (see [15, section 5.3]), properties useful later in the paper.

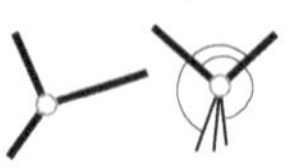

Figure 1: Separable edges.

Separable edges. Let $w = (p, T)$ be a vint. We call an edge e incident to p in T *separable at* w if it can be separated from the other edges incident to p by a line through p. Equivalently, the two angles between e and its clockwise and counterclockwise neighboring edges (around p) have to sum up to more than π. We observe the easy following properties.

(S0) No edge is separable at both vints induced by its endpoints.

(S1) If w has degree 3, every edge incident to its point is separable at w (recall that points of vints are interior).

(S2) If w has degree at least 4, at most two incident edges can be separable at w; if two edges are separable at w, they must be consecutive.

External chords. Let o be a link of a vint. An edge, which is openly disjoint from o but its endpoints are vertices of o, is called an *external chord* of o (see Figure 2). Observe that a link with i edges can have at most $i - 3$ external chords.

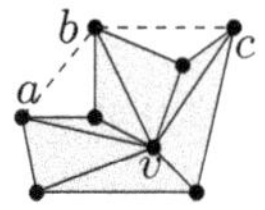

Figure 2: External chords ab and bc.

"Flips-down-to" relation. For vints $u = (p_u, T_u)$ and $v = (p_v, T_v)$, we define $u \to v$ if $p_v = p_u$ and T_v is obtained by flipping one edge incident to p_u in T_u. We see that u and v are associated with the same point but in different triangulations; u is an $(i+1)$-vint and v an i-vint, for some $i \geq 3$. We let $\to^*$ denote the transitive reflexive closure of $\to$. If $u \to^* v$, we say that *u can be flipped down to v*.

2. UPPER BOUNDS FOR $\hat{v}_3$

We derive upper bounds on $\hat{v}_3$. Upper bounds of this kind translate into lower bounds on the number of triangulations every N-element point set in general position must have.

The following lemma with proof is taken from [13] (with "3" there replaced by "h" here). The main raison d'être of this first lemma is to introduce its proof technique, which we will adapt in two lemmas to obtain the improvements relevant for our lower bounds on the number of triangulations.

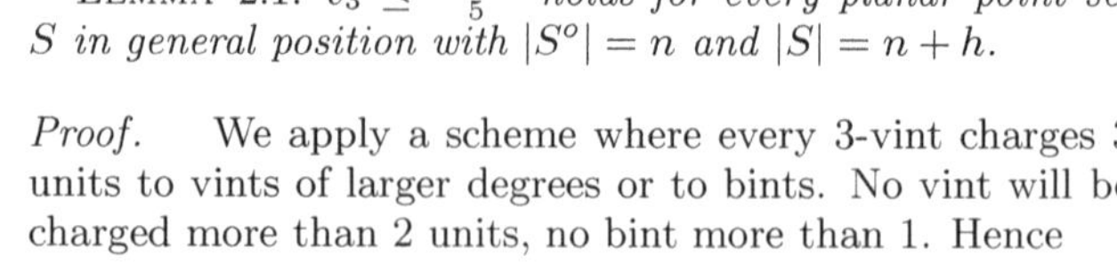

Figure 3: The various types of charges of a 3-vint in the proof of Lemma 2.1.

LEMMA 2.1. *$\hat{v}_3 \leq \frac{2n+h}{5}$ holds for every planar point set S in general position with $|S^o| = n$ and $|S| = n + h$.*

Proof. We apply a scheme where every 3-vint charges 3 units to vints of larger degrees or to bints. No vint will be charged more than 2 units, no bint more than 1. Hence

$$3\hat{v}_3 \leq h + 2\textstyle\sum_{j \geq 4} \hat{v}_j = h + 2(n - \hat{v}_3), \qquad (1)$$

which yields the asserted inequality.

Let $v = (p, T)$ be a 3-vint, and let o_v denote its link, which is a triangle. For each edge e of o_v we do the following, depending on the nature of e; see Figure 3.

(1) *e is an edge of the hull.* Then we let v charge 1 to bint (e, T); we call this a *boundary-charge*.

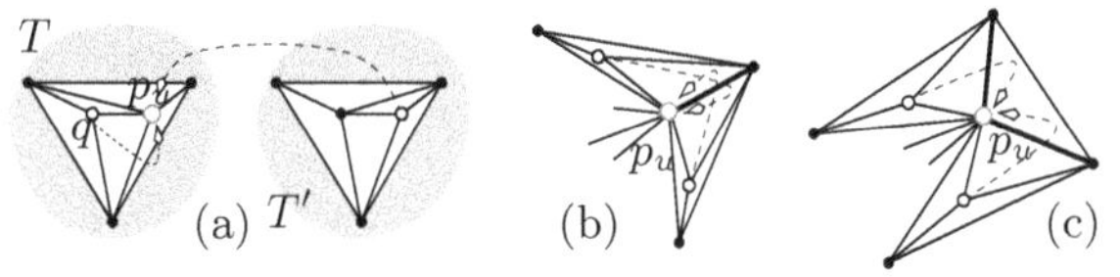

Figure 5: (a) 4-vint (p_u, T) with non-convex link is charged once by a flip-charge (right) and once by a neighbor-charge (left). (b) Two neighbor-charges to vint u with one separable edge. (c) Neighbor-charges to vint u with two separable edges.

(2) *There is a triangle t incident to e on its other side:*

(2.1) *t forms with p a convex quadrilateral.* We flip e to get a 4-vint (in a different triangulation!) to which v charges 1; we call this a *flip-charge*.

(2.2) *t forms with p a non-convex quadrilateral.* Let a be the endpoint of e that is reflex; a cannot be a hull vertex and it has to be of degree at least 4, since interior vertices of degree 3 are never adjacent. Here v charges 1 to vint (a, T); we call this a *neighbor-charge*. (e must be separable at (a, T).)

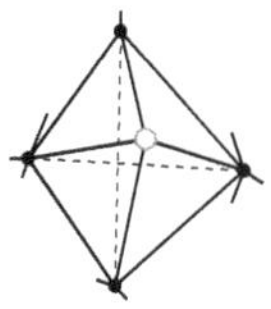

Figure 4: A 4-vint with two flippable incident edges.

The fact that no bint is charged more than once is obvious, so we turn to show that no vint u can be charged more than twice. Consider first the case of a 4-vint $u = (p_u, T_u)$. Let o_u denote the quadrangular link of p_u. We note that at most two edges incident to p_u are flippable: One out of each pair of opposite edges is separable at u (regardless of whether the link of v is convex or not), and thus unflippable; see Figure 4. We distinguish between the following two cases:

(a) *o_u is a convex quadrilateral*, as depicted in Figure 4. In this case, u receives exactly two flip-charges. Moreover, u cannot be charged as a neighbor, since no vertex of o_u can be interior and of degree 3.

(b) *o_u has a reflex vertex*, as depicted in Figure 5(a). Here u receives exactly one flip-charge. This obvious fact is a special case of a more general analysis, given in Lemma 3.2. Moreover, u can be charged at most once as a neighbor. Indeed, if q is a vertex of o_u of degree 3, then it must be a reflex vertex of o_u and there can be at most one such vertex. (q, T_u) cannot charge u twice through two edges of the link of (q, T_u), for then these two edges have to be separable at p, but they are not consecutive around p; cf. (S2).

Consider next the case where $u = (p_u, T_u)$ is a vint of degree at least 5. Each flip-charge is to a 4-vint and therefore u receives neighbor-charges only. Neighbor-charges are made within the *same* triangulation and in this case p_u can be a neighbor of at most two points of degree 3 that charge it as a neighbor (as just noted, no point can charge u twice in this manner). Recall the ingredients necessary for such a neighbor-charge to be made to u: (i) an edge e that is separable at u, and (ii) a neighbor a of p_u that has degree 3 so that the edges e and $p_u a$ are consecutive around p_u. Clearly, if there is only one edge separable at u then there are at most two such constellations; see Figure 5(b). If there are two separable edges at u, then they have to be consecutive around p_u, cf. (S2). This rules out the possibility that any of these two edges is involved in more than one neighbor-charge, since an edge cannot be both separable at p_u and connect to an interior point of degree 3 (Figure 5(c)). ☐

With slight changes to the charging scheme, the two following lemmas improve the result of Lemma 2.1.

LEMMA 2.2. *$\hat{v}_3 \leq \frac{n}{2}$ holds for every point set S in general position with $|S^\circ| = n$ and $|S| \geq 7$.*

Proof. A refined version of Inequality (1) in the proof of Lemma 2.1 is $3\hat{v}_3 \leq h_c + 2(n - \hat{v}_3)$, where h_c is the expected number of charged bints in a uniformly chosen triangulation. We now change the charging scheme so that we can show $h_c \leq \hat{v}_3$; combining this bound with the inequality implies the assertion of the lemma.

We change the charging scheme as follows. For each 3-vint that charges two bints, we move the charge from one of these bints to a vint of degree at least 5, such that the overall number of charges made to a vint is at most two.

First, consider a point p such that any triangle (spanned by S) that contains only p in its interior, is incident to at most one boundary edge. Such a case is depicted in Figure 6(a), where p has to be above the dotted edges. Equivalently, the condition says that, for each triangle t, two of whose edges are consecutive edges of the hull, either p lies outside this triangle t or it lies in t with at least one additional interior point. In this case, each 3-vint with p as a vertex charges at most one bint; thus we leave the charges made by p as in the preceding scheme.

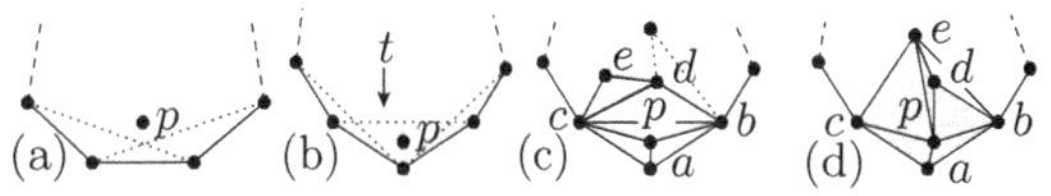

Figure 6: (a) No triangle incident to two boundary edges contains p in its interior. (b) Only the shaded triangle t is incident to two boundary edges and contains p in its interior. (c) bc and cd are flippable. (d) The link of the 5-vint of p is not convex.

Next, assume that there is a single triangle t that is incident to two boundary edges and contains only p in its interior, as depicted in Figure 6(b). We notice that the 3-vints of p which charge two bints are exactly those for which the link of p is t. Consider such a 3-vint $v = (p, T)$, and denote the vertices of the link of v as a, b, and c, such that ab and ac are boundary edges (as depicted in Figure 6(c)). It is easily checked that the edge bc must be flippable; let us denote the third vertex of the other triangle incident to bc as d. Moreover, we notice that, after flipping bc, at least one of the edges bd and cd is flippable. Without loss of generality, we assume that cd is flippable (after flipping bc), and denote the third vertex of the other triangle incident to cd as e (as depicted in Figure 6(c)).

Consider the pentagon $abdec$, which is the link of a 5-vint of p (in a different triangulation). First, assume that this is a convex pentagon, as depicted in Figure 6(c). In triangulations where the pentagon is the link of a 5-vint of p, it cannot contain any 3-vints on its boundary (recall that a vint can use only interior vertices, so we are claiming that neither d nor e can be a 3-vint in such a triangulation), and thus the 5-vint is not charged at all in the charging scheme of Lemma 2.1. We move the charge from one of the bints of v to this 5-vint. There are two 3-vints which can charge the 5-vint in this new manner—v and the symmetric 3-vint of p, with the same link and with the edge be replacing cd. Therefore, the 5-vint gets charged exactly twice overall.

Assume next that the pentagon is not convex, which implies that e cannot "see" b from within the pentagon, and perhaps also a (notice that e cannot "hide" from a behind c, since c is a hull vertex). In such a case, v is the only 3-vint that will charge the 5-vint in the new manner (since the quadrilateral $bced$—the complement of the link of v inside the pentagon—has a single triangulation). Moreover, there may be a 3-vint of d adjacent to the 5-vint, which may charge the 5-vint (only once) by a neighbor-charge, as depicted in Figure 6(d), where the link of the 5-vint is shaded. No other 3-vint can charge the 5-vint by a neighbor-charge, which implies that the 5-vint is charged, in the modified scheme, at most twice.

Finally, assume that there are two distinct triangles, each incident to two boundary edges and containing only p, as depicted in Figure 7(a) (notice that there cannot exist more than two such triangles). Let us denote the vertices of these triangles as a, b, c, and d, appearing in this order along the convex hull, so the two triangles are Δabc and Δbcd, and the non-boundary edges are ac and bd (as depicted in Figure 7(a)). Consider a 3-vint $v = (p, T)$ with Δabc as its link (the case where the link is Δbcd is handled symmetrically). v can be analyzed as before, flipping edges to turn it into a 5-vint and charging this 5-vint, except for the case where the resulting pentagon contains the quadrilateral $abcd$ (as depicted in Figure 7(b)). In such a case, the pentagon must be convex, and four 3-vints of p that charge two bints have their links contained in the pentagon—two with Δabc as the link of p and two with Δbcd as the link, and they all charge the 5-vint.

We thus need to find additional "victims" to distribute charges to. To this end, we denote the fifth vertex of this convex pentagon as e, as depicted in Figure 7(b), and note that, after flipping ac and ad, at least one of the edges ae and de is flippable (since $|S| \geq 7$). Without loss of generality, we assume that ae is flippable (after flipping ac and ad), and denote the third vertex of the other triangle incident to ae as f.

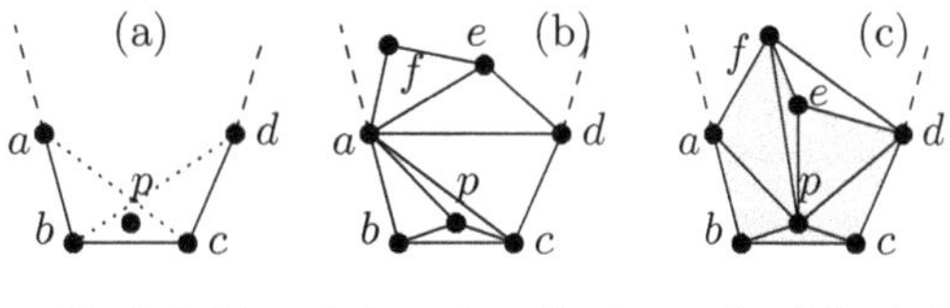

Figure 7: (a) Two triangles that are incident to two boundary edges and contain p only in their interiors. (b) ad and ae are flippable; the resulting hexagon is convex. (c) 6-vint with non-convex link.

Consider the hexagon $abcdef$, which is the link of a 6-vint of p (in an appropriate triangulation). First, assume that this is a convex hexagon, as depicted in Figure 7(b). Such a hexagon contains the links of ten 3-vints of p that charge two bints (five with Δabc as their link and five with Δbcd as their link; the number 5 is C_3, the number of triangulations of the pentagon completing the link of the 3-vint into the hexagon). Moreover, in triangulations where such a hexagon is the link of a 6-vint of p, it cannot contain any 3-vints on its boundary, and thus the 6-vint is not charged at all in the charging scheme of Lemma 2.1. This also applies to the four convex 5-vints obtained by removing either a, d, e, or f from the hexagon. (Note that the link of each of the "truncated" 5-vints contains at least one of the triangles Δabc, Δbcd, and that p lies in both of these triangles, so the link of each of these 5-vints does indeed contain p in its interior, as it should.) Therefore, we have five vints which are not charged at all. We can therefore shift ten boundary charges from the above ten 3-vints to those five vints, so each of those latter vints is charged exactly twice.

Assume next that the hexagon is not convex, which implies that f cannot "see" d within the hexagon and perhaps also c, as depicted in Figure 7(c), where the link of the 6-vint is shaded. In such a case, the link of the hexagon contains the links of at most six 3-vints of p that charge two bints (three with Δabc as their link and three with Δbcd as their link; here 3 is the maximum number of triangulations of the non-convex pentagon completing the link of the 3-vint into the hexagon). There may be a 3-vint of e adjacent to the 6-vint, as depicted in Figure 7(c). However, since both fp and dp are flippable, the 6-vint is not charged at all by the old scheme. A similar analysis also applies to the 5-vints obtained by removing either a or d from the 6-vint. (Again, the links of these 5-vints do indeed contain p.) The 5-vint obtained by removing f also does not get charged, since its link is a convex pentagon. Therefore, we can shift one boundary charge from each of the (at most) six 3-vints to one of the four larger vints, with enough room to conclude that each of these latter vints gets charged at most twice.

We have thus established the bound $h_c \leq \hat{v}_3$, and this completes the proof of the lemma. $\square$

LEMMA 2.3. *$\hat{v}_3 \leq \frac{2n+h/2}{5}$ holds for every point set S in general position with $|S^o| = n$ and $|S| = n + h \geq 6$.*

Proof. We use the same inequality $3\hat{v}_3 \leq h_c + 2(n - \hat{v}_3)$ as in the preceding proof, where h_c is the expected number of charged bints in a uniformly chosen triangulation. Again we modify the charging scheme, now in order to ensure $h_c \leq h/2$; combining this bound with the above inequality implies the assertion of the lemma. This bound is achieved by decomposing the collection of all bints into sets of at most nine bints each, such that the total charge in each set is at most half its size. The sets are not necessarily disjoint, but only charged bints can appear in more than one set, which is only to our advantage in establishing the bound $h_c \leq h/2$.

A bint β gets charged if and only if the third vertex of the triangle incident to β is a 3-vint. Consider such a bint $\beta = (b, T)$ that is charged by a 3-vint $v = (p, T)$, as depicted in Figure 8(a) (where b is the edge ac). Following the notations in the figure, we notice that at least one of the edges ad and cd must be flippable, and assume, without loss of generality, that cd is flippable (as depicted in the figure). Let T' denote the triangulation obtained by flipping cd in T. Notice that the bint $\beta' = (b, T')$ is not charged, since it is adjacent to the 4-vint $v' = (p, T')$ (depicted in Figure 8(b)). If v' cannot flip-down to another 3-vint with a link that contains b, we create the set $\{\beta, \beta'\}$, which has two elements, only one of which is charged.

Suppose that v' can flip down to another 3-vint with a link containing b, as in Figure 8(c) (note here that the link of v', the quadrilateral $aced$, has to be convex and p has to lie below its diagonals). Since the link of v' is convex and contains a boundary edge, one of its edges must be flippable. Let us denote one of the 5-vints obtained by flipping such an

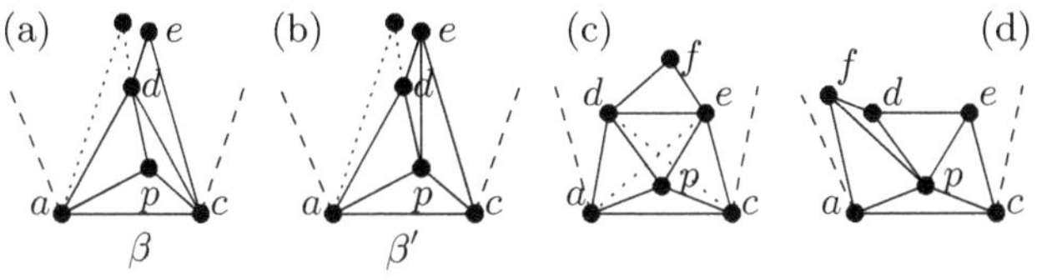

Figure 8: (a) The link of the 3-vint has at least one flippable edge. (b) A 4-vint that flips down to v. (c) A link of a 4-vint that flips down to two 3-vints that charge β. (d) A 5-vint with a non-convex link.

edge as $v'' = (p, T'')$ and let f be the vertex that is in the link of v'' but not in the link of v'. First, assume that the link of v'' is a convex pentagon, as depicted in Figure 8(c), where we flip de in T' to get v''. The link of v'' contains the links of five 3-vints (there are five ways to triangulate a convex pentagon and to insert p as a 3-vint into it) and three 4-vints of p (by removing either d, e, or f from the pentagon—note that any of these removals keeps p inside the resulting quadrilateral) that are adjacent to the edge b. Since the link of v'' is convex, it is not charged at all in the original scheme, and thus we can charge it twice. Notice that ad and bc might be boundary edges, so they could induce bints that also get charged by some 3-vints of p. Nevertheless, the assumption on the location of p (depicted in Figure 8(c)) implies that, even if there is a 3-vint of p which charges bints of ad or ce, the respective 4-vints cannot flip down to another 3-vint of p that charges the same edge, which implies that such bints belong to the previous case. Therefore, there is a unique case where v'' gets charged. In conclusion, we have a set of nine bints, all involving edge b (five adjacent to 3-vints, three to 4-vints, and one to a 5-vint), with a total modified charge of $5 - 2 = 3 < 9/2$ (only 3-vints charge b in the original scheme).

Finally, assume that the link of v'' is not convex. This implies that, in the link of v'', f cannot see either one or two of the other vertices. Figure 8(d) depicts such a case, where f is adjacent to ad and only e is invisible from f (the following analysis does not refer specifically to this example, though). Let x denote the number of 3-vints of p that are adjacent to b and have their link contained in the link of v''. Notice that $x \le 3$, since there are at most three ways to triangulate the non-convex 5-gon and then insert p as the 3-vint. We can always obtain a 4-vint of p that is adjacent to b by removing f from the 5-vint, and an additional 4-vint by removing either d or e (or both, depending on the position of f). Therefore, we have a set of at least $x + 3$ bints, all involving the edge b (x bints adjacent to 3-vints, one adjacent to a 5-vint, and at least two adjacent to 4-vints), with $x \le \frac{x+3}{2}$ of them charged.

We have shown $\hat{h}_c \le h/2$ as claimed ◻

Let $\mathsf{tr}^-(n, h)$ denote the minimal number of triangulations for point sets with n interior points and h boundary points and set $\mathsf{tr}^-(N) := \min_{n+h=N} \mathsf{tr}^-(n, h)$. We now employ the upper bounds for $\hat{v}_3$ for a lower bound for $\mathsf{tr}^-(N)$. The following is a generalization of [13, Lemma 2.1(ii)].

LEMMA 2.4. *For $n \ge 1$, let $\delta_{n,h} > 0$ be a real number, such that $\hat{v}_3 \le \delta_{n,h} n$ holds for any set of n interior points and h boundary points in general position. Then,*

$$\mathsf{tr}^-(n, h) \ge \tfrac{1}{\delta_{n,h}} \mathsf{tr}^-(n-1, h)\ .$$

Proof. Let S be a set that minimizes $\mathsf{tr}(S)$ among all sets with n interior points and h boundary points in general position. As easily seen and argued for [13, Lemma 2.1(ii)], we have

$$\hat{v}_3 \cdot \mathsf{tr}(S) = \textstyle\sum_{T \in \mathcal{T}(S)} v_3(T) = \sum_{q \in S^o} \mathcal{T}(S \setminus \{q\}).$$

The leftmost expression equals $\hat{v}_3 \cdot \mathsf{tr}^-(n, h)$, the rightmost one is at least $n \cdot \mathsf{tr}^-(n-1, h)$. Hence, with $\hat{v}_3 \le \delta_{n,h}\, n$, $\mathsf{tr}^-(n, h) \ge \frac{n}{\hat{v}_3} \cdot \mathsf{tr}^-((n-1, h) \ge \frac{1}{\delta_{n,h}} \cdot \mathsf{tr}^-(n-1, h)$. ◻

THEOREM 2.5. $\mathsf{tr}^-(N) = \Omega\left(2.4317^N\right)$.

Proof. We know $\mathsf{tr}^-(0, h) = C_{h-2} = \Theta^*(4^h)$. Moreover, combining the results of Lemmas 2.2, 2.3, and 2.4 yields

$$\mathsf{tr}^-(n, h) \ge 2 \cdot \mathsf{tr}^-(n-1, h) \quad \text{and} \tag{2}$$
$$\mathsf{tr}^-(n, h) \ge \tfrac{5n}{2n+h/2} \cdot \mathsf{tr}^-(n-1, h) = \tfrac{10n}{3n+N} \cdot \mathsf{tr}^-(n-1, h) \tag{3}$$

for $n \ge 1$ and $N \ge 7$. (3) is stronger iff $n > N/2$, and therefore, for any point set S with $n \le N/2$ and $N \ge 7$,

$$\mathsf{tr}(S) \ge 2^n \cdot \mathsf{tr}^-(0, N-n) = \Omega^*\left(2^{2N-n}\right) = \Omega^*\left(2^{3N/2}\right) \tag{4}$$

with $2^{3/2} = 2.828\ldots$. Next, assume that $n > N/2$, so (3) is the stronger inequality. Let x be the maximal number of interior points we can remove before (2) becomes the stronger; x is the maximal with $\frac{10(n-x)}{(N-x)+3(n-x)} \ge 2$, that is, $x = 2n - N$. Using the above, we derive the bound (assuming that $N + 3n$ is divisible by 4, which, if true initially, remains true as we remove interior points)

$$\begin{aligned}\mathsf{tr}^-(N) &\ge \tfrac{10n}{N+3n} \cdot \tfrac{10(n-1)}{N+3n-4} \cdots \tfrac{10(n-x+1)}{N+3n-4(x+1)} \cdot 2^{n-x} \cdot \Theta^*(4^{N-n}) \\ &= \tfrac{10^x \cdot n!}{(n-x)!} \cdot \tfrac{((N+3n)/4-x)!}{4^x \cdot ((N+3n)/4)!} \cdot 2^{n-x} \cdot \Theta^*(4^{N-n})\,.\end{aligned}$$

In order to simplify this bound, we use Stirling's approximation. Since we are only interested in the exponential part of the bound, we can simply replace $m!$ by $(m/e)^m$. Therefore, $\mathsf{tr}^-(N)$ is lower bounded by

$$\Omega^*\Bigl(2^{2N-n-2x} \cdot 5^x \cdot \tfrac{n^n}{e^n} \cdot \tfrac{e^{n-x}}{(n-x)^{n-x}} \cdot \tfrac{((N+3n)/4-x)^{(N+3n)/4-x}}{e^{(N+3n)/4-x}} \cdot \tfrac{e^{(N+3n)/4}}{((N+3n)/4)^{(N+3n)/4}}\Bigr),$$

and after some cleanup, we get a lower bound of

$$\Omega^*\left(2^{2N-n} \cdot 5^x \cdot \frac{n^n}{(n-x)^{n-x}} \cdot \frac{(N+3n-4x)^{(N+3n)/4-x}}{(N+3n)^{(N+3n)/4}}\right).$$

After replacing x with $2n - N$, substituting $n = tN$, $0.5 < t < 1$, and performing some additional cleanup, we get

$$\mathsf{tr}^-(N) = \Omega^*\left(2^{2N-n} \cdot 5^{(3n+N)/4} \cdot n^n \cdot \frac{(N-n)^{(N-n)/4}}{(N+3n)^{(N+3n)/4}}\right)$$

$$= \Omega^*\left(\left(2^{2-t} \cdot 5^{(3t+1)/4} \cdot t^t \cdot \frac{(1-t)^{(1-t)/4}}{(1+3t)^{(1+3t)/4}}\right)^N\right). \tag{5}$$

Finding the t minimizing this expression (for given N) can be done either numerically or through differentiation. The latter approach produces the quartic equation $t^4 - 288t^2 - 128t - 16 = 0$, whose solution is $t \approx 0.89901$, which implies a minimum of $\Omega\left(2.4317^N\right)$. We have thus shown that for every $n + h = N$, we have $\mathsf{tr}^-(N) = \Omega\left(2.4317^N\right)$. ◻

Remark. The analysis provides lower bounds on $\mathsf{tr}^-(n,h)$, for any n and h. Collecting the bounds in (4) and (5), with $t = N/n$, $0 \le t < 1$, we have lower bounds on $\mathsf{tr}^-(n,h)$ of

$$\Omega^*\left(\left(2^{2-t}\right)^N\right) \qquad 0 \le t \le 0.5$$

$$\Omega^*\left(\left(2^{2-t}\cdot 5^{(3t+1)/4}\cdot t^t \cdot \frac{(1-t)^{(1-t)/4}}{(1+3t)^{(1+3t)/4}}\right)^N\right) \qquad 0.5 < t < 1.$$

The base in the bound starts at 4 for $t = 0$ and ends at the limit 2.5 for $n = N - 3$ (where t is almost 1). This latter value is still not as large as the base of 2.63 in [7].

3. RELATING THE $\hat{v}_i$'S

We derive inequalities among the $\hat{v}_i$'s which we then manipulate for a lower bound on $\hat{v}_4$. These facts are required for the proof of Theorem 4.1 in Section 4, which yields linear lower bounds for all $\hat{v}_i$'s, $i \ge 4$. We first recall the notion of a flip-tree studied in [12, 13] (and implicitly in [10]).

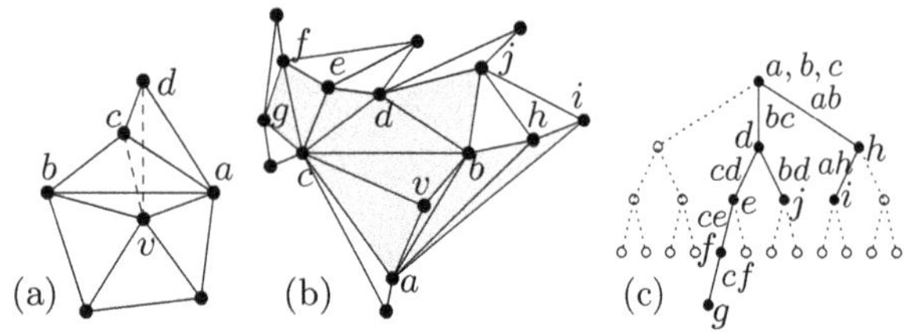

Figure 9: (a) A 5- and a 6-vint that can be flipped down to the same 4-vint. (b) The shaded area is dual to the flip tree of the 3-vint v. (c) The flip-tree itself (solid edges only).

The flip-tree of a vint. How do we find the vints that flip down to a given i-vint $v = (p_v, T_v)$? Clearly, there is v itself. Consider a flippable edge e (in T_v) that is not incident to p_v but is part of the boundary of its link. Flipping e yields an $(i+1)$-vint $u = (p_v, T_u)$ that can be flipped down to v (by reversing the preceding flip). Similarly, if in the triangulation T_u there is a flippable edge that is not incident to p_v but is part of its link, then we can flip this edge to get an $(i+2)$-vint that can be flipped down to v, and so on. Figure 9(a) depicts a 4-vint v, that, by flipping ab to cv, turns into a 5-vint that can be flipped down to v (and which, by flipping ac to dv, turns into a 6-vint that can also be flipped down to v).

In order to represent this structure, we associate with an i-vint $v = (p_v, T_v)$ a *flip-tree* $\tau(v)$, defined as follows. The root of the tree is labeled by the pair (o_v, N_v), where o_v is the link of v (an i-gon) and N_v is the set of vertices of o_v (the neighbors of p_v in T_v). Any other node of the tree is associated with a pair (t, q), where t is a face of T_v and q is a vertex of that face, which does not belong to the union of the faces labeling the ancestors of the present node (note, though, that o_v from the root is not a face of T_v—it is the union of the i faces incident to p_v). The associated faces represent a duality between the flip-tree and part of the triangulation T_v (which will be explained momentarily). While defining the structure of the flip-tree in the following paragraphs, we refer to an example depicted in Figures 9(b) and 9(c). These figures depict a 3-vint v and its flip-tree, and the nodes of this flip-tree are labeled only by their vertex (and not by their triangle).

(i) Every edge e of o_v gives rise to a child if it can be flipped in T_v. If so, this child is labeled by the triangle incident to e that is not incident to p_v, and by the vertex of this triangle which is not incident to e. Therefore, the root has at most i children. In our example, the root has two children—$(\Delta bcd, d)$ (since bc is flippable) and $(\Delta abh, h)$ (since ab is flippable). In what follows, as in Figure 9, we will often suppress the triangle t in the label (t, q) of a node of the flip-tree, and just use the vertex q. The triangle t is the unique triangle of T_v into which the segment qp_v enters as we trace it from q.

(ii) Consider now a non-root node of the tree labeled by (t, q) and an edge e of t incident to q. If e is a boundary edge, no child will be obtained via e. Otherwise, let t' be the other triangle incident to e. If t' together with the triangle formed by e and p_v is a convex quadrilateral (in which e can be flipped), then this gives rise to a child of (t, q) labeled by (t', q'), where q' is the vertex of t' that is not incident to e. Therefore, a non-root node has at most two children. In our example, the node corresponding to h has the single child i, since the quadrilateral $vhia$ is convex, but the other potential quadrilateral $vbjh$ is not.

Note that the union of all triangles of the nodes of any subtree of $\tau(v)$ (containing the root) form a polygon which is star-shaped with respect to p_v; this follows easily by the inductive definition of $\tau(v)$. The triangles of the original T_v form a triangulation of the polygon, and the subtree is actually the dual tree of this triangulation. The shaded area in Figure 9(b) is the portion of the triangulation dual to the entire flip-tree of v. Also, an edge in the flip-tree incident to two nodes that are dual to (i.e., labeled by) the triangles Δ_1, Δ_2 in T_v, can be regarded as dual to the edge in T_v incident to both Δ_1 and Δ_2. If we retriangulate this polygon in T_v by connecting p_v to all vertices of the polygon, we get a vint that flips down to v. Moreover, every vint u that flips down to v can be obtained in this way (by taking the subtree dual to the link of u). That is:

LEMMA 3.1. *The subtrees of $\tau(v)$ containing its root are in bijective correspondence to the vints that flip down to v.*

We recall a basic fact about flippable edges.

LEMMA 3.2. *Each i-vint, $i \ge 4$, is incident to a flippable edge.*

Proof. The link of a vint (p, T) has at least three vertices with a convex angle (less than π) and at most two edges are separable at p. Hence, there is an edge incident to p that is separable at none of its endpoints – thus flippable. □

The next lemma is from [13, Lemma 4.1] with its proof based on [10, Lemma 4]. (Note that h does not play a role.)

LEMMA 3.3. *For all integers $3 \le i < j$ there is a positive integer $\delta_{i,j}$ such that $\hat{v}_i \ge \frac{\hat{v}_j}{\delta_{i,j}}$. In particular, $\hat{v}_i \ge \frac{\hat{v}_{i+1}}{i}$, $\hat{v}_3 \ge \frac{\hat{v}_j}{C_{j-1}-C_{j-2}}$ for $j \ge 4$, and $\hat{v}_4 \ge \frac{\hat{v}_j}{C_{j-1}-2C_{j-2}}$ for $j \ge 5$.*

Proof. For a proof of $\hat{v}_i \ge \frac{\hat{v}_{i+1}}{i}$, we let every $(i+1)$-vint charge some i-vint it can be flipped down to, by Lemma 3.2 this is possible, since $i + 1 \ge 4$. In this way an i-vint can be charged at most i times, so the first inequality holds.

For the general inequality we let every j-vint charge some i-vint it can be flipped down to. By Lemma 3.1, every j-vint that flips down to an i-vint v corresponds to a subtree of the flip-tree of v. More precisely, since the root of the flip-tree of

v corresponds to an i-gon in the triangulation of v, every j-vint corresponds to a subtree with $j-i+1$ nodes. Therefore, an i-vint can be charged at most $t_{i,j-i+1}$ times, where $t_{i,k}$ denotes the number of (ordered) binary trees with k nodes and with an exceptional root of degree i; that is, the root has i potential children pointers, but not all of them need to be used (just like binary nodes distinguish between a left and a right child, the root discriminates its children via an index in $\{1, 2, \dots, i\}$). For example, $t_{i,1} = 1$ and $t_{i,2} = i$. Hence, as in the case of $j = i + 1$, we can take $\delta_{i,j} = t_{i,j-i+1}$. The number of ordered binary trees is known to be $t_{2,k} = C_k$ (see Subsection 1.1), which also implies that $t_{1,k} = C_{k-1}$. Furthermore, a recurrence of $t_{i,k} = t_{i-1,k+1} - t_{i-2,k+1}$ can be derived, cf. [10]. This allows us to choose

$$\begin{aligned} \delta_{3,j} &\le t_{3,j-2} = t_{2,j-1} - t_{1,j-1} = C_{j-1} - C_{j-2}, \text{ and} \\ \delta_{4,j} &\le t_{4,j-3} = t_{3,j-2} - t_{2,j-2} = C_{j-1} - 2C_{j-2}. \end{aligned}$$ ◻

We will now improve the bound for $\delta_{4,j}$, which we will use to derive a reasonably large lower bound on $\hat{v}_4$.

Lemma 3.4. *$\hat{v}_4 \ge \frac{3\hat{v}_j}{C_{j-1}-C_{j-2}}$ holds for all integers $j \ge 5$.*

Proof. In the previous proof we made a j-vint charge a single 4-vint, a scheme now modified. For u a vint, let $supp_4(u) := |\{v \mid v \text{ 4-vint with } u \to^* v\}|$, called *4-support of u*. We let every j-vint split a charge of 1 evenly among the 4-vints it can be flipped down to, i.e., $\frac{1}{supp_4(u)}$ each.

Given a 4-vint v, let w be a 3-vint such that $v \to w$, and let τ be the flip-tree of w. The subtree of τ which corresponds to v consists of a single level-1 edge e (i.e., an edge emanating from the root). Therefore, there is a bijective correspondence between the vints that flip down to v and subtrees of τ that contain e. Counting the number of such subtrees of size $j-2$ (i.e., the number of j-vints that flip down to v) implies our previous result of $t_{3,j-2} - t_{2,j-2} = C_{j-1} - 2C_{j-2}$.

τ might have two additional level-1 edges e_2 and e_3. Let v_2 (v_3) denote the 4-vint corresponding to the subtree of τ which consists of edge e_2 (e_3, resp.) only. A subtree containing e_2 can flip down to v_2, a subtree containing e_3 can flip down to v_3. Hence, a vint with a subtree that contains two level-1 edges has a 4-support of at least 2, and a vint with a subtree that contains all three level-1 edges has a support of at least 3. For example, out of the four possible 5-vints that can flip down to a certain 4-vint, if they all exist, two contain two level-1 edges, and thus have a support of at least 2. Figure 10(a) depicts a subtree of a 5-vint that might have a support of 1, and Figure 10(b) depicts a subtree of a 5-vint that has a support of at least 2.

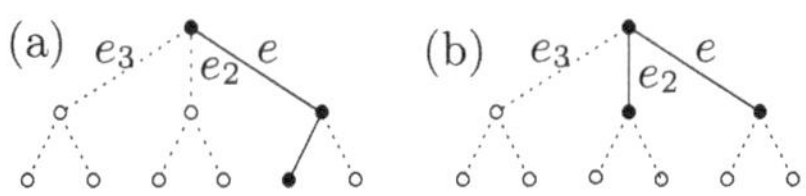

Figure 10: (a) One of two subtrees that correspond to a 5-vint with a support of at least 1. (b) One of two subtrees of a 5-vint with a support of at least 2.

Therefore, the number of j-vints that flip down to v and have a support of 1, is at most $t_{1,j-2}$. The number of j-vints that flip down to v with a subtree having exactly two level-1 edges, is at most $2(t_{2,j-2} - 2t_{1,j-2})$ (choose one of e_2, e_3 and count subtrees containing both e and the chosen edge but not the third). The number of j-vints that flip down to v with their corresponding subtrees having three level-1 edges, is at most $t_{3,j-2} - 3t_{2,j-2} + 3t_{1,j-2}$ (inclusion-exclusion principle). Therefore, v receives a charge of at most

$$t_{1,j-2} + \tfrac{1}{2}2(t_{2,j-2} - 2t_{1,j-2}) + \tfrac{1}{3}(t_{3,j-2} - 3t_{2,j-2} + 3t_{1,j-2})$$

which equals $\frac{1}{3}t_{3,j-2} = \frac{1}{3}(C_{j-1} - C_{j-2})$. ◻

Lemma 3.5. *If $|S^o| \ge 3$, we have $\sum_i i\hat{v}_i \le 6n + h - 9$.*

Proof. The number of edges in a triangulation of S is $3n + 2h - 3$, therefore $\sum_i iv_i = 2(3n + 2h - 3) - D$, where D is the sum of the degrees of the hull vertices. One can show $D \ge 3h + 3$ – details omitted –, provided there are at least 3 interior points. This yields the bound for the v_i's which carries over to the $\hat{v}_i$'s via linearity of expectation. ◻

Lemma 3.6. *For $n \ge 3$, we have $\hat{v}_4 \ge \frac{1}{340}\left(n + 15 - \frac{8h}{3}\right)$. In particular, when S has a triangular convex hull, $\hat{v}_4 > \frac{n}{340}$.*

Proof. $\sum_i (9-i)\hat{v}_i \ge 9n - (6n + h - 9) = 3n - h + 9$ (by Lemma 3.5), $\hat{v}_3 \le \frac{2n+h/2}{5}$ (Lemma 2.3), and by Lemma 3.4

$$\begin{aligned} \hat{v}_5 &\le \tfrac{C_4-C_3}{3}\hat{v}_4 = 3\hat{v}_4 & \hat{v}_7 &\le \tfrac{C_6-C_5}{3}\hat{v}_4 = 30\hat{v}_4 \\ \hat{v}_6 &\le \tfrac{C_5-C_4}{3}\hat{v}_4 = \tfrac{28}{3}\hat{v}_4 & \hat{v}_8 &\le \tfrac{C_7-C_6}{3}\hat{v}_4 = 99\hat{v}_4. \end{aligned} \quad (6)$$

Hence,

$$\begin{aligned} 3n + 9 - h &\le 6\hat{v}_3 + 5\hat{v}_4 + 4\hat{v}_5 + 3\hat{v}_6 + 2\hat{v}_7 + \hat{v}_8 \\ &\le \tfrac{6(2n+h/2)}{5} + \hat{v}_4\left(5 + 4\cdot 3 + 3\cdot\tfrac{28}{3} + 2\cdot 30 + 99\right) \\ &= \tfrac{12n+3h}{5} + 204\hat{v}_4\ , \end{aligned}$$

implying that $\hat{v}_4 \ge \frac{1}{340}\left(n + 15 - \frac{8h}{3}\right)$, as asserted. ◻

Here is an alternative lower bound whose dependence on h is better, while the dependence on n is worse.

Lemma 3.7. *For $n \ge 4$, we have $\hat{v}_4 \ge \frac{1}{1360}(n + 18 - 2h)$.*

Proof. Lemma 3.5, again, delivers $\sum_i (10-i)\hat{v}_i \ge 4n - h + 9$. From Lemma 2.2, we employ $\hat{v}_3 \le \frac{n}{2}$ and from Lemma 3.4, we use (6) and $\hat{v}_9 \le \frac{C_8-C_7}{3}\hat{v}_4 = \frac{1001}{3}\hat{v}_4$. Hence, we get

$$\begin{aligned} 4n - h + 9 &\le 7\hat{v}_3 + 6\hat{v}_4 + 5\hat{v}_5 + 4\hat{v}_6 + 3\hat{v}_7 + 2\hat{v}_8 + \hat{v}_9 \\ &\le \tfrac{7n}{2} + \hat{v}_4\cdot\left(6 + 5\cdot 3 + 4\cdot\tfrac{28}{3} + 3\cdot 30 + 2\cdot 99 + \tfrac{1001}{3}\right) \\ &= \tfrac{7n}{2} + 680\hat{v}_4\ . \end{aligned}$$ ◻

4. LOWER BOUNDS FOR ALL $\hat{v}_i$'S

In this section, we establish lower bounds for each of the quantities $\hat{v}_i$. The bound $\hat{v}_3 > \frac{n}{30}$ was proved in [12] (for a triangular convex hull), and in Section 3 we derived the bound $\hat{v}_4 \ge \frac{1}{1360}(n + 18 - 2h)$. We now present a generalized bound which holds for each $i \ge 4$.

Theorem 4.1. *For each $N > i \ge 4$, $\varepsilon > 0$, and $3 \le h \le \left(\frac{1}{2} - \varepsilon\right)n$, there exists a constant $\gamma_{i,h} = \gamma_{i,h}(\varepsilon)$, which depends on i, h, and ε, such that, for any set S with h hull vertices and n interior vertices, we have $\hat{v}_i \ge \gamma_{i,h}n$.*

Proof. The proof is by induction on i, where the base case $i = 4$ has already been established. More precisely, Lemma 3.7 implies that, when $h \le \left(\frac{1}{2} - \varepsilon\right)n$, there is a constant $c_\varepsilon > 0$ such that $\hat{v}_4 \ge c_\varepsilon n$, and we use this inequality as our induction basis, with $\gamma_{4,h} = c_\varepsilon$.

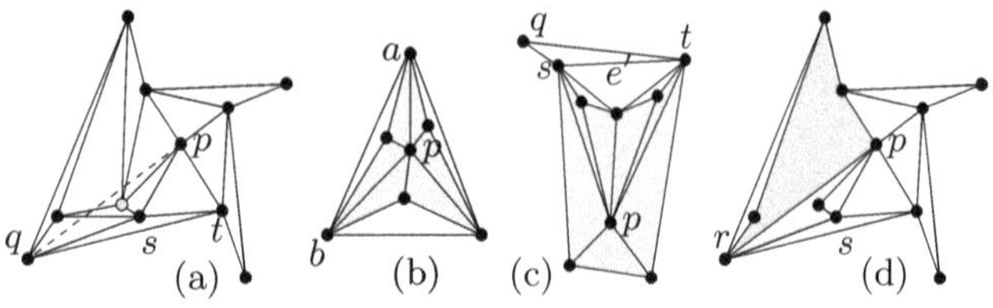

Figure 13: (a) The grey vertex is a vertex of the link that is contained in Δpsq. (b) No edge of the link is incident to a triangle with a third vertex not contained in o. (c) There is a path from the link of p to the triangle containing q. (d) The link is split into two corridors.

For the general induction step, we assume $\hat{v}_{i-1} \geq \gamma_{i-1,h}n$ and proceed to establish a similar inequality on $\hat{v}_i$. This will be done by charging each $(i-1)$-vint v to various vints of degree at least i. This will yield an inequality involving the quantities $\hat{v}_k$, for $k \geq i-1$, which we will then combine with the inequalities of Lemma 3.3, to replace all $\hat{v}_k$, for $k > i$, by $\hat{v}_i$, and thereby obtain the desired lower bound on $\hat{v}_i$.

Let $v = (p, T)$ be a fixed $(i-1)$-vint, and let o denote its link. The charging that v makes depends on the structure of o and of the triangles of T in its vicinity. The charging is performed depending on the following cases:

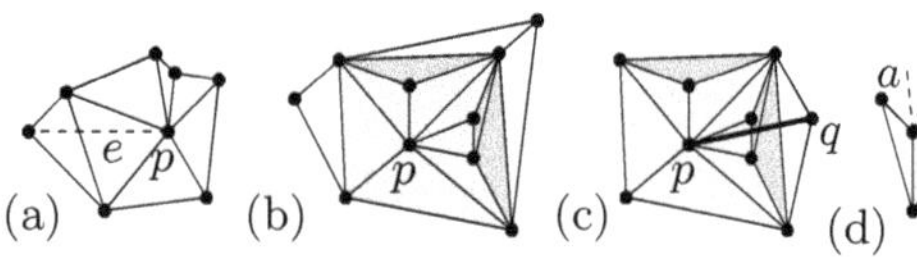

Figure 11: (a) A link with a flippable edge. (b) The lightly shaded portion is the link, and the union of the shaded portions is the extended link. (c) The edge pq crosses only edges of the extended link. (d) Two vertices "hiding" from p.

(a) *o has a flippable bounding edge e,* as depicted in Figure 11(a). In this case we flip e to turn v into an i-vint, and charge that i-vint. Clearly, any i-vint can be charged in this way at most i times.

(b) *No edge of o is flippable, and all the vertices of o that are interior to the hull have degree at most $i-1$.* We argue that the following property holds in such a case.

LEMMA 4.2. *In case (b), we can connect p to some point $r \in S$ outside o, such that pr crosses at most $(i-2)(i-4)+1$ edges of T.*

Proof. Recall $N > i$, so there is at least one point not connected to p. First, assume that there exists an edge e of the link, such that e is incident to a triangle with a third vertex that is not a vertex of o (see below for an illustration and analysis of the complementary situation). Let s and t be the endpoints of e, and let q be the third vertex of the triangle. Without loss of generality, assume that the edge sq is shorter than the edge tq (i.e., that q is "hiding" from p behind s). Such a case is depicted in Figure 12 (for now, ignore the non-solid lines and the shading).

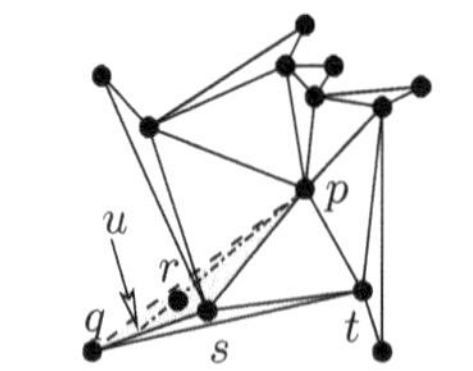

Figure 12: Case (b).

We consider the triangle Δpsq, and notice that it may contain additional vertices of o, as well as other points of S. Such a case is depicted in Figure 13(a), where the grey vertex is a vertex of o that is contained in Δpsq. Let $S_{\Delta psq}$ be the set of points of S contained in Δpsq, but not in o (including q, but not p). Let r be the vertex in $S_{\Delta psq}$ that minimizes the angle $\angle spr$ (r is well defined, because $S_{\Delta psq}$ is nonempty—it contains q). Let ℓ denote the line containing the edge pr, and let u denote the point where ℓ crosses sq (by definition, ℓ must indeed cross sq; the crossing could be at q if $r = q$). Our choice of r implies that the interior of the triangle Δspu does not contain any point of $S_{\Delta psq}$, so the only points of S it can contain are vertices of o. We again refer the reader to Figure 12, where Δpsq is shaded.

We now show that pr can cross at most $(i-2)(i-4)+1$ edges of T. For an edge of T to cross pr, exactly one of its vertices must lie in the triangle Δspu (this is only a necessary condition). However, we have just argued that this triangle can only contain vertices of o. Since t lies outside Δspu, there are at most $i-2$ vertices in this triangle (including s). Each of these vertices is of degree at most $i-1$, one of its incident edges is connected to p, and two other edges are part of the boundary of o. Therefore, excluding the single crossing between pr and o, each of the $i-2$ vertices can participate in at most $i-4$ edges that cross pr.

Next, assume that there is no edge e with an incident triangle on the other side which has a vertex not in o (such a case is depicted in Figure 13(b)). Every edge of o interior to the hull must be incident to a triangle that has an external chord as an edge.

We walk through T, starting at some edge e of o and walking away from o, crossing from each visited triangle to an adjacent one through a common external chord, until we get to a triangle incident to an external chord e' and to a vertex q which is not contained in o. It is easily seen that the rules for the walk are well-defined: we can either find an external chord to cross into the next triangle, or get stuck with a terminal triangle as above. Moreover, since $N > i$, the walk will always end in such a terminal triangle. Such a walk is depicted in Figure 13(c), where the link is shaded, and there is a path that leads to q. Now, denoting the endpoints of e' as s and t, we can apply the same analysis as above. That is, assume first that q hides behind s, as above, and denote by r the vertex in $S_{\Delta psq}$ that minimizes the angle $\angle spr$. In this case one can argue, as above, that pr can cross at most $(i-2)(i-4)+1$ edges. However, here (unlike in the preceding analysis) it is also possible for q not to hide at all, that is, pq can cross e'. In this case, we can choose q as the point r, and notice that pq can only cross external chords and a single edge of o, which implies that there are at most $(i-3)+1 = i-2$ crossings ($< (i-2)(i-4)+1$ for $i \geq 5$). ◻

We now explain how to deal with an $(i-1)$-vint v that falls under case (b) of the present analysis. We charge v to a vint $v' = (p, T')$ obtained as follows. Let r be the point provided in Lemma 4.2. Delete from T all the $\mu \leq i^2 - 6i + 9$ edges that cross pr, and add pr to the new graph. This leaves two links, referred to as "corridors", with pr as a common edge. We triangulate each of the corridors in an arbitrary manner, leaving the rest of T untouched, to obtain a triangulation T', and then charge v to $v' = (p, T')$. In Figure 13(d), the shaded areas are the two untriangulated corridors obtained from the vint depicted in Figure 13(a).

Note that the degree of v' is at least i (because we have added pr as an edge). It can be larger than i, if the triangulations of the corridors use additional edges incident to p.

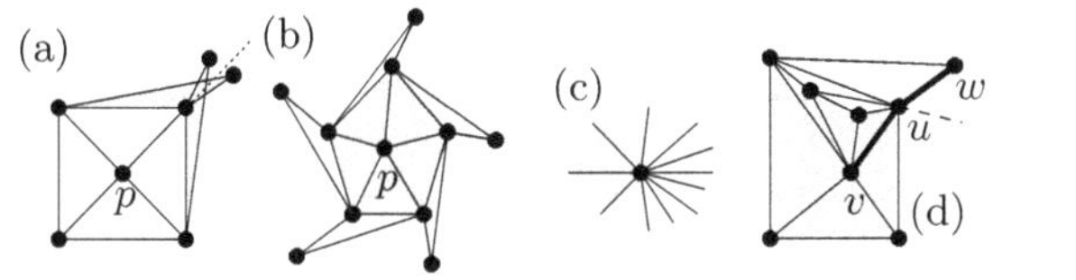

Figure 14: (a) Two vertices cannot hide behind the same vertex of o'. (b) All the vertices of S' hide in a clockwise manner. (c) The shaded area is a dominating sequence of size 4. (d) There is a dominating sequence of u from pu clockwise to uw.

Since we have removed μ edges from T, and then inserted the edge pr, the re-triangulation of the corridors requires $\mu - 1$ additional edges. The maximal degree of v' is obtained when all of these additional edges are incident to p. Hence, the degree of p is at most $i+(\mu-1) \le i+(i^2-6i+9-1) = i^2-5i+8$.

We next show that the number of $(i-1)$-vints, that fall under case (b) and charge the fixed vint v', is at most some (large) quantity M_i that depends only on i. By the preceding discussion, we can assume that the degree d of v' is at most i^2-5i+8. Given v', we can reconstruct v as follows. We first choose the vertex r from the d neighbors of p in T'. Next, we choose the two corridors bounded by pr. To do so, we recall that, together, these corridors consisted of at most $i^2-6i+10$ triangles (in the original triangulation T), so T' uses the same number of triangles to fill them up. Thus, starting from the two triangles of T' that are adjacent to pr, we append to them up to i^2-6i+8 additional triangles, in a breadth-first manner. Specifically, we maintain a queue of triangles to be appended to the corridors. When appending a triangle, we have already used one of its edges to reach it from its predecessor (the same holds for the two initial triangles, which cannot reach other triangles through their common edge pr). We therefore have up to two other edges that we can cross to reach other triangles. Hence, when appending a triangle, we have up to four choices: append its two neighboring triangles, append only the first of them, append only the second, or not append any of them. (Some of these neighbor triangles may have already been appended; this only limits our choices.) We continue this process until we collect the desired number of triangles. Hence, a crude upper bound for the number of such choices is $4^{i^2-6i+10}$.

Finally, having guessed these triangles, we remove from T' all the inner edges of their union (i.e., edges adjacent to two of these triangles), and re-triangulate the resulting link in an arbitrary manner (using only edges that cross pr). Notice that the number of ways to triangulate this polygon is maximized when it is convex (since every triangulation of a non-convex polygon is combinatorially equivalent to a triangulation of a convex polygon with the same number of edges). The polygon has at most $i^2-6i+12$ vertices, and thus it has $M_i' = O^*\left(4^{i^2-6i+10}\right)$ triangulations.

In conclusion, the number of $(i-1)$-vints, that fall under case (b) and charge the fixed vint v', is at most

$$M_i = (i^2-5i+8)\cdot 4^{i^2-6i+10}\cdot M_i'.$$

In the remaining cases (c) and (d) to come, we assume that no edge of o is flippable and that o contains a vint u of degree at least i. Define the *extended link* o' of o by iteratively repeating the following process — find in T a triangle Δ incident to two (consecutive) edges of the current link o^* and lying in the exterior of o^*, and append Δ to o^*. When we can no longer find such a triangle, we have obtained the extended link $o' = o^*$; see Figure 11(b). Note that all the edges of the triangles Δ encountered in this process are either edges of o or extended chords of o.

(c) *There exists a vertex q which is not a vertex of o, and the line segment pq crosses only edges contained in o'.* Such a case is depicted in Figure 11(c). Notice that pq crosses a single edge of o, and possibly some external chords. Therefore, pq cannot cross more than $(i-4)+1 = i-3$ edges of T. Similarly to case (b), we can remove the edges that cross pq, insert pq, retriangulate the two resulting "corridors", and charge the resulting j-vint of p (where $j \ge i$). As in the previous case, such a j-vint cannot get charged more than L_i times in this manner, for some L_i depending only on i.

(d) *For every $q \in S$, either q is a vertex of o or the line segment pq crosses at least one edge not contained in o'.* By definition, every triangle of T not contained in o' is incident to at most one edge of o'. Let S' be the set of third vertices (not contained in o) of triangles incident to edges of o'.

For each $s \in S'$, its corresponding vint in T must "hide" from p, either in a *clockwise* manner (such as a in Figure 11(d)), or in a *counterclockwise* manner (such as b in Figure 11(d)). Notice that two such vints cannot hide behind the same vertex of o, one in a clockwise manner and the other in a counterclockwise manner, since this would imply that their corresponding triangles overlap (see Figure 14(a)). Therefore, either all of the vertices of S' hide in a clockwise manner, or they all hide in a counterclockwise manner; see Figure 14(b). This also implies that o' cannot contain an edge of the convex hull.

Consider a j-vint w. Its link o_w consists of j triangles, all incident to w, such that the sum of the angles at w over all j triangles is 2π. We say that a set D of consecutive triangles is a *dominating sequence* if the sum of the angles in those triangles is larger than π. Figure 14(c) depicts an 11-vint, and the four shaded triangles form a dominating sequence. Note that a separable edge defines a dominating sequence of size 2 (see Figure 1).

LEMMA 4.3. *For every $i \in \mathbb{N}$, every vint has fewer than $3i^2$ dominating sequences of size at most i.*

Proof. Consider a j-vint w with at least one dominating sequence D of size at most i. A subset of the complementary set D' cannot be dominating. Thus every dominating sequence of w must include at least one triangle of D. There are less than i^2 contiguous subsequences of D. For sequences of size at most i not completely contained in D, we note that there are at most $2i$ such sequences with one element from D, at most $2i$ such sequences with two elements from D, ..., for a total of at most $2i^2$ sequences. □

Recall that we assume that there exists a vint $u = (p_u, T)$ in o of degree at least i. From the above, there is another vint $w = (p_w, T)$ hiding from v behind u (Figure 14(d)). Note that, because of the 'hiding', there is a dominating sequence of v starting from uv and going clockwise up to uw. The edges between the triangles of this sequence are external chords and a single edge of o. Thus the size of the set is at most $i-2$. In this case, we let v charge u. Since uv is on the boundary of a dominating sequence of u of size at most $i-2$, u is charged fewer than $6i^2$ times in this manner.

Recurrence with solution. Summing up the charges in

all three cases and averaging over all $(i-1)$-vints, we obtain

$$\begin{aligned}\hat{v}_{i-1} &\le i\hat{v}_i + L_i \sum_{k\ge i}\hat{v}_k + 6i^2\sum_{k\ge i}\hat{v}_k + M_i\sum_{k\ge i}\hat{v}_k\\ &= (i+M_i+L_i+6i^2)\hat{v}_i + (M_i+L_i+6i^2)\sum_{k\ge i+1}\hat{v}_k\\ &= A_i\hat{v}_i + B_i\sum_{k=i+1}^{t}\hat{v}_k + B_i\sum_{k>t}\hat{v}_k,\end{aligned}$$

where $A_i = i + M_i + L_i + 6i^2$, $B_i = M_i + L_i + 6i^2$, and where t is chosen so that $t > 14B_i/\gamma_{i-1,h}$. Note that t too depends only on i (and on h). By Lemma 3.5, $\sum_{k\ge 3} k\hat{v}_k \le 6n + h - 9 < 7n$, and thus

$$B_i\sum_{k>t}\hat{v}_k \le \frac{B_i}{t}\sum_{k>t}k\hat{v}_k < \frac{B_i\cdot 7n}{t} < \tfrac{1}{2}\gamma_{i-1,h}n.$$

By the induction hypothesis, $\gamma_{i-1,h}n \le \hat{v}_{i-1} \le A_i\hat{v}_i + B_i\sum_{k=i+1}^{t}\hat{v}_k + \frac{1}{2}\gamma_{i-1,h}n$. By Lemma 3.3, for each $k \ge i+1$ there is a constant $\delta_{i,k}$ such that $\hat{v}_k \le \delta_{i,k}\hat{v}_i$. Putting $D_i = \sum_{k=i+1}^{t}\delta_{i,k}$, we get

$$\tfrac{1}{2}\gamma_{i-1,h}n \le (A_i + B_iD_i)\hat{v}_i \text{ , and } \hat{v}_i \ge \frac{\gamma_{i-1,h}}{2(A_i+B_iD_i)}n.$$

This establishes $\gamma_{i,h} = \frac{\gamma_{i-1,h}}{2(A_i+B_iD_i)}$ for induction on i and so completes the proof of Theorem 4.1. □

4.1 Large $\hat{v}_i$'s must always exist

The lower bounds for the v_i's, presented above come with small constants. We complement the analysis by showing, using a simple counting argument, that, for every point set with sufficiently many interior points, there are $\hat{v}_i$'s with much larger values, for small values of the index i. The "catch" is that we use an averaging argument, so we do not know which specific $\hat{v}_i$ has to be large.

LEMMA 4.4. *For every planar set of N points in general position, where n of them are interior and h are hull vertices, we have* $\max\{\hat{v}_3,\hat{v}_4,\hat{v}_5,\hat{v}_6\} \ge \frac{(n-h+9)}{10}$. *In particular, when the convex hull is triangular,* $\max\{\hat{v}_3,\hat{v}_4,\hat{v}_5,\hat{v}_6\} > \frac{N}{10}$ *holds.*

Proof. Consider a charging scheme for a triangulation T, where each i-vint of T is charged $7-i$. By Lemma 3.5, we get the following lower bound on the total charge in T:

$$\begin{aligned}\textstyle\sum_i(7-i)v_i(T) &= \textstyle\sum_i 7v_i(T) - \sum_i iv_i(T)\\ &\ge 7n - (6n+h-9) = n-h+9.\end{aligned}$$

Charges of i-vints with $i \ge 7$ are non-positive, thus ignoring them can only increase the total charge. Hence

$$4v_3(T)+3v_4(T)+2v_5(T)+v_6(T) \ge \textstyle\sum_i(7-i)v_i(T) \ge n-h+9.$$

By linearity of expectation, $4\hat{v}_3 + 3\hat{v}_4 + 2\hat{v}_5 + \hat{v}_6 \ge n-h+9$. Letting $\hat{m} = \max\{\hat{v}_3,\hat{v}_4,\hat{v}_5,\hat{v}_6\}$, we have

$$10\hat{m} \ge 4\hat{v}_3 + 3\hat{v}_4 + 2\hat{v}_5 + \hat{v}_6 \ge n-h+9,$$

so $\hat{m} \ge \frac{n-h+9}{10}$, as asserted. □

Looking at the preceding lemma, one might suspect that the larger lower bound that it yields is due to $\hat{v}_3$ being large (as also suggested by the lower bound of [12], even though this latter bound is only $N/30$), and that the other $\hat{v}_i$'s are probably much smaller. As the following lemma shows, this is not the case, and some other large $\hat{v}_i$'s must also exist.

LEMMA 4.5. *For every point set in general position, with parameters N, n, and h, as above,* $\max\{\hat{v}_4,\hat{v}_5,\ldots,\hat{v}_{11}\} \ge \frac{12n-9.5h+45}{180}$. *In particular, when the convex hull is triangular, we have* $\max\{\hat{v}_4,\hat{v}_5,\ldots,\hat{v}_{11}\} \ge \frac{N-39/24}{15}$.

Proof. Similarly to Lemma 4.4, we consider a charging scheme for a triangulation T, where each i-vint of T is charged $12-i$. Once again, Lemma 3.5 provides the following lower bound on the total charge in T (with $v_i = v_i(T)$):

$$\textstyle\sum_i(12-i)v_i \ge 12n - (6n+h-9) = 6n-h+9.$$

Ignoring the charge of i-vints with $i \ge 12$ can only increase the total charge. Let $m := \max\{v_4, v_5, \ldots, v_{11}\}$ and obtain

$$9v_3+36m \ge 9v_3+8v_4+\cdots+v_{11} \ge \textstyle\sum_i(12-i)v_i \ge 6n-h+9.$$

Using linearity of expectation and arguing as in the previous proof, we have $\hat{m} \ge \frac{6n-h+9-9\hat{v}_3}{36}$, where we set $\hat{m} := \max\{\hat{v}_4,\hat{v}_5,\ldots,\hat{v}_{11}\}$. With the inequality $\hat{v}_3 \le \frac{2n+h/2}{5}$ from Lemma 2.3 this yields the asserted bound. □

5. REFERENCES

[1] M. Ajtai, V. Chvátal, M. M. Newborn, and E. Szemerédi, Crossing-free subgraphs, *Annals Discrete Math.* **12** (1982), 9–12.

[2] O. Aichholzer, F. Hurtado, and M. Noy, A lower bound on the number of triangulations of planar point sets, *Comput. Geom. Theory Appl.* **29**(2) (2004), 135–145.

[3] M.O. Denny and C.A. Sohler, Encoding a triangulation as a permutation of its point set, *Proc. 9th Canadian Conf. on Computational Geometry* (1997), 39–43.

[4] O. Giménez and M. Noy, The number of planar graphs and properties of random planar graphs, Proc. International Conf. on Analysis of Algorithms, *Discrete Math. & Theoretical Computer Sci.* **AD** (2005), 147–156.

[5] F. Hurtado, M. Noy, Counting triangulations of almost-convex polygons, *Ars Combin.* **45** (1997), 169–179.

[6] V. A. Liskovets, A pattern of asymptotic vertex valency distributions in planar maps, *J. Combinat. Theory*, Ser. B **75** (1999), 116–133.

[7] P. McCabe and R. Seidel, New lower bounds for the number of straight-edge triangulations of a planar point set, *Proc. 20th European Workshop Comput. Geom.* (2004).

[8] C. McDiarmid, A. Steger, and D.J.A. Welsh, Random planar graphs, *J. Combinat. Theory*, Ser. B **93** (2005), 187–205.

[9] A. Razen, J. Snoeyink, E. Welzl, Number of crossing-free geometric graphs vs. triangulations, *Electronic Notes in Discrete Math.* **31** (2008), 195–200.

[10] F. Santos and R. Seidel, A better upper bound on the number of triangulations of a planar point set, *J. Combinat. Theory*, Ser. A **102**(1) (2003), 186–193.

[11] R. Seidel, On the number of triangulations of planar point sets, *Combinatorica* **18**(2) (1998), 297–299.

[12] M. Sharir and A. Sheffer, Counting triangulations of planar point sets, 0911.3352v2 (improves [13]).

[13] M. Sharir and E. Welzl, Random triangulations of planar point sets, *Proc. 22nd ACM Symp. on Computational Geometry* (2006), 273–281.

[14] W. S. Smith, *Studies in Computational Geometry Motivated by Mesh Generation*, Ph. D. Thesis, Princeton University, 1989.

[15] R. P. Stanley, *Enumerative Combinatorics*, vol. **2**, Cambridge University Press, Cambridge, 1999.

Acute Triangulations of Polyhedra and the Euclidean Space

[Extended Abstract] *

Eryk Kopczyński
Institute of Informatics,
Warsaw University
Banacha 2, 02-097
Warsaw, Poland
erykk@mimuw.edu.pl

Igor Pak
Department of Mathematics,
UCLA
Los Angeles, CA 90095, USA
pak@math.ucla.edu

Piotr Przytycki
Institute of Mathematics,
Polish Academy of Sciences
Śniadeckich 8, 00-956
Warsaw, Poland
pprzytyc@mimuw.edu.pl

ABSTRACT

We study the problem of *acute triangulations* of convex polyhedra and the space $\mathbb{R}^n$. Here an acute triangulation is a triangulation into simplices whose dihedral angles are acute. We prove that acute triangulations of the n–cube do not exist for $n \geq 4$. Further, we prove that acute triangulations of the space $\mathbb{R}^n$ do not exist for $n \geq 5$. In the opposite direction, in $\mathbb{R}^3$ we construct nontrivial acute triangulations of all Platonic solids. We also prove nonexistence of an acute triangulation of $\mathbb{R}^4$ if all dihedral angles are bounded away from $\pi/2$.

Categories and Subject Descriptors

G.2.1 [**Mathematics of Computing**]: Discrete mathematics—*Combinatorics*

General Terms

Design

1. INTRODUCTION

The problem of finding acute triangulations has a long history going back to the early days of Discrete and Computational Geometry. It has a number of connections to other areas and some real world applications, most notably the finite element method. Until recently, most results dealt with the 2–dimensional case, where the problem has been largely resolved; it is now known that every n–gon in the plane has an acute triangulation into $O(n)$ triangles (a combination of results in [BGR] and [Mae]).

*A full version of this article [KPP] is available at arXiv:0909.3706.

SCG'10, June 13–16, 2010, Snowbird, Utah, USA.

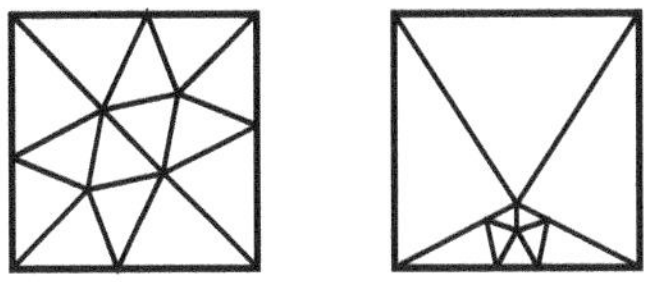

Figure 1: A subdivision which forms a simplicial complex and one which does not.

In the last few years, several papers [ESÜ, Kří, VHZG] broke the dimension barrier in both positive and negative direction (see below). In this paper we continue this exploration, nearly completely (negatively) resolving the problem in dimension 4 and higher, and making further advancement in dimension 3. This extended abstract is based on [KPP].

We must address one important limitation of our paper, essentially highlighting the current poor state of art. The real problem (both in theory and in application) is to find acute triangulations *efficiently* (say, in polynomial time). Instead, we prove that such algorithm is theoretically impossible in dimension $n \geq 5$, and in practice for $n \geq 4$. In a positive direction, we make the first real effort to prove that the general goal can conceivably be accomplished in 3 dimensions.

1.1 Definitions and main results

For a polytope $P \subset \mathbb{R}^n$, an *acute triangulation* is a subdivision of P into finitely many *acute simplices* (i.e. with acute dihedral angles[1]) which form a simplicial complex, so e.g. in the plane, a vertex of one simplex cannot lie in the interior of an edge of another. (See Figure 1, where on the left we have a subdivision of the square which forms a simplicial complex, and on the right we have a subdivision which does not.) A triangulation is *non-trivial* if it has at least one interior vertex. An *acute triangulation* of $\mathbb{R}^n$ is a subdivision of $\mathbb{R}^n$ into acute (infinitely many) simplices which form a simplicial complex.

THEOREM A. *Every Platonic solid in* $\mathbb{R}^3$ *has a non-trivial acute triangulation.*

For an important example of the cube, we roughly do the following. We first triangulate the cube into a regular 3–

[1]A dihedral angle of a polytope in $\mathbb{R}^n$ is called *acute* if the scalar product of outward normal vectors is negative.

simplex and four standard 3–simplices. We then subdivide each of these 3–simplices into 543 pieces, to obtain combinatorially what we call the *special subdivision* (based on the 600–cell, see Section 2).

THEOREM B. *There are no non-trivial acute triangulations of polytopes in* $\mathbb{R}^n$, *for all* $n \geq 5$. *In particular there are no acute triangulations of* $\mathbb{R}^n$, *for* $n \geq 5$.

THEOREM C. *The 4–cube does not have an acute triangulation. Neither do the* isosceles 4–orthoscheme[2] *and the* Schläfli simplex $\widetilde{D}_4$.[3]

Together, Theorems A,B and C imply the following result which remained open for nearly 50 years:

COROLLARY D. *The* n*–cube has an acute triangulation if and only if* $n \leq 3$.

The next two theorems are successive far-reaching extensions of Theorem C.

THEOREM E. *The space* $\mathbb{R}^4$ *has no periodic acute triangulation.*

THEOREM F. *The space* $\mathbb{R}^4$ *has no acute triangulation into simplices whose dihedral angles are less than* $\pi/2 - \varepsilon$, *for any given* $\varepsilon > 0$.

Theorem F is a *bounded geometry* version of Křížek's conjecture stating that $\mathbb{R}^4$ has no acute triangulation [Kří]. Theorems B, C and E are proved by a topological argument using a (known) advanced extension of Dehn–Sommerville equations. The proof of the strongest result (Theorem F) uses the concept of p–parabilicity of graphs, its recent properties, and our new advanced isoperimetric type inequality.

1.2 Previous work

The problem of finding acute triangulations has a long history in classical geometry, and is elegantly surveyed in [BKKS], which argues that it goes back to Aristotle. In recent decades, it was further motivated by the *finite element method* which requires "good" meshes (triangulations of surfaces) for the numerical algorithms to run. Although the requirements for meshes largely depend on the algorithm, the sharp angle conditions seem to be a common feature, and especially important in this context. We refer to [SF] for the introduction to the subject, and to [She] for the state of art.[4]

It is important to emphasize that for a given convex polygon $P \subset \mathbb{R}^2$, the real difficulty in the acute triangulation problem is finding the positions of Steiner points in the interior and on the boundary of P. Once such set of points is fixed, the unique triangulation on these vertices that can possibly be acute is the corresponding *Delaunay triangulation* (see [Ede]), and the latter can be constructed efficiently (see [Aur, For]). This makes this problem different from most problems in [DRS], where typically an optimal triangulation is sought on a fixed set of vertices.

Let us mention also a motivation coming from the recreational literature, where the subject of dissections has been popular in general (see [Lin]), and of acute triangulations in particular [CL, Man]. In this context, the problem of acute triangulations of a square, cube, and hypercubes seem to be of special interest [Epp]. It is crucial in this context that the simplices must be acute rather than non-obtuse (when the angle $\pi/2$ is allowed), since in the latter case every n–cube can be triangulated into $n!$ non-obtuse (path-) simplices.

In one of the first papers on the subject, Burago and Zalgaller proved in [BZ] that any non-convex polygon (possibly, with holes) has an acute triangulation. Unfortunately, their argument was largely forgotten as it was inexplicit and did not give a bound on the number of triangles required. In a long series of papers [BE, BGR, BMR, Mae, Sar, Yuan] first polynomial, and then linear bounds were obtained for non-obtuse, and, eventually, for acute triangulations. We refer to [Zam] for the historical outline, a short survey, and further references.

In higher dimensions, several results have been recently obtained. First, Eppstein, Sullivan and Üngör [ESÜ] showed that the space $\mathbb{R}^3$ has a periodic acute triangulation. Then, Křížek [Kří] showed that no vertex in $\mathbb{R}^n$ for $n \geq 5$ can be surrounded by a finite number of acute simplices (as in Theorem B),[5] and conjectured that the space $\mathbb{R}^4$ also cannot be triangulated into acute tetrahedra. Finally, most recently (and independently from our [KPP]), VanderZee, Hirani, Zharnitsky and Guoy [VHZG] used an advanced numerical simulation technique to find an acute triangulation for the (usual) cube in $\mathbb{R}^3$ (as in Theorem A). Their construction is ad hoc, but better suitable for applications (it uses 1370 tetrahedra as opposed to 2715 tetrahedra in our construction).

The main approach in our paper is topological, both in motivation of the positive results, and in the tools for negative results. A variation on the use of 600–cell to obtain a topological version of Theorem A was used previously by Świątkowski and the third named author in [PŚ], to construct the so called *flag-no-square* subdivisions in dimension 3, used originally to construct Gromov hyperbolic groups with prescribed boundaries. A variation on Theorem B was previously obtained by Kalai in [Kal] (in fact, both results are extension of the same special case).

Finally, the idea behind both the statement and the proof of Theorem F is based on large body of work on tessellations of the space by convex polyhedra with bounded geometry. Perhaps the earliest, is the result of Alexandrov that in every triangulation of the plane into bounded triangles the average degree of vertices (when defined) must be at least 6 [Ale]. Another is a classical result by Niven that convex n–gons of bounded geometry cannot tile the plane for $n \geq 7$ [Niv] (see also [Ful]). The idea is always to use the isoperimetric inequalities compared with direct counting estimates, an approach which works in higher dimensions as well (see e.g. [KS, LM]). Our proof of Theorem F is a variation on the same line of argument. We refer to [GS] for historical background and further references.

[2]This is a path-simplex in $\mathbb{R}^4$ with intervals of unit lengths, which can be defined by the inequalities $0 \leq x_1 \leq x_2 \leq x_3 \leq x_4 \leq 1$.

[3]This 4–simplex is sometimes called *cube corner* and can be defined by $x_1 + x_2 + x_3 + x_4 \leq 1$, and $x_1, x_2, x_3, x_4 \geq 0$.

[4]Proceedings of recent *International Meshing Roundtable* conferences, specifically their *tetrahedral meshes* sections, provide further up-to-date results on both theoretical and practical aspects of this important problem.

[5]There is a crucial error in this proof, see Křížek's correction in *Disc. Comp. Geom.* (to appear).

1.3 Implications of our work for the finite element method

This paper has both good and bad news for the finite element method practitioners. We start with the good. Until now, a typical (far from optimal) practical approach to getting an acute triangulation of a given (non-convex) polyhedron, would be to start with the triangulation of the interior along the fundamental tetrahedron in the BCC lattice, and then improve and refine the triangulation near the boundary.[6] This tetrahedron, one of the Sommerville's tetrahedra, tiles the space, but although not acute, it is non-obtuse and highly symmetric. The acute triangulation in [ESÜ] suggests that at a cost of creating less symmetric triangles, one can ensure that the same approach can make all but "boundary" tetrahedra to be acute. Our work (Theorem A) suggests that perhaps one can abandon this periodicity approach altogether and create an acute triangulation of the whole polyhedron.

MAIN CONJECTURE G. *Every (possibly, non-convex) polyhedron $P \subset \mathbb{R}^3$ has an acute triangulation. Moreover, such triangulation will have a polynomial number of tetrahedra (in the number of vertices of P), and can be computed in polynomial time.*

Given how little is known (basically, nearly nothing until recently) this might sound too speculative. We refer to [KPP] for a reasoning behind (based on this work).

Now for the bad news. In many practical applications, mostly when time is a dimension, the finite element method is applied in $\mathbb{R}^4$. Our Theorem E shows that the periodicity approach (as in [ESÜ]) cannot be implemented. Moreover, Theorem F proves that the very large dihedral angles are unavoidable in any large simplicial acute triangulation in $\mathbb{R}^4$, which suggests that some numerical methods might be slow in four dimensions.

Convention. In the entire article we adopt a convention that simplicial complexes and triangulations of (homology) manifolds are not allowed to have edges connecting a vertex to itself, and they are also not allowed to have multiple simplices spanned on the same set of vertices.

2. ACUTE TRIANGULATIONS IN THE 3–DIMENSIONAL EUCLIDEAN SPACE

In this section we describe acute triangulations of the 3–cube and the regular octahedron. The starting point is the following observation:

OBSERVATION 2.1. *The link of an interior edge of an acute triangulation of a polyhedron in $\mathbb{R}^3$ is a simplicial loop of length at least 5.*

In view of this observation, let us make the following definition.

DEFINITION 2.2. *A triangulation of an n-dimensional homology manifold is* rich *if the links of all interior $(n-2)$-simplices are loops of length at least 5.*

[6]This makes such triangulations useful for some but not all applications.

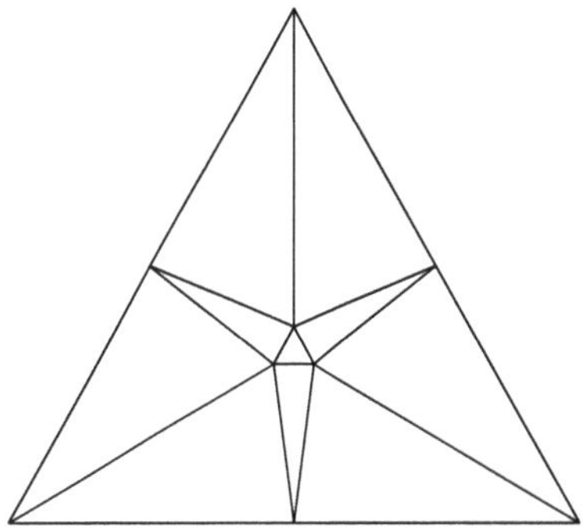

Figure 2: Special subdivision of a 2–simplex.

Note that being rich is a purely combinatorial (i.e. non-metric) property. Observation 2.1 states that an acute triangulation of the 3–cube (or a regular octahedron) must be rich.

Consider the 600–cell, the convex regular 4–polytope with Schläfli symbol $\{3;3;5\}$ (see, e.g., [Cox]). Denote by X_{600} the boundary of the 600–cell, a 3–dimensional simplicial polyhedron homeomorphic to the 3–dimensional sphere. It consists of 600 3–simplices[7] and has 120 vertices. Its vertex links are icosahedra and its edge links are pentagons. We first focus on the combinatorial simplicial structure of X_{600}. Denote by X_{543} the subcomplex of X_{600} which we obtain by removing from X_{600} the interiors of all simplices intersecting a fixed 3–simplex. (The number 543 in the subscript refers to the number of 3–simplices in X_{543}.)

LEMMA 2.3 ([PŚ, LEMMAS 2.5 AND 2.7]).

(1) X_{543} is topologically a 3-ball. It is rich.

(2) Its boundary is a 2–sphere simplicially isomorphic to the simplicial complex which we obtain from the boundary of a 3–simplex by subdividing each face as in Figure 2.

We recall from [PŚ, Definitions 2.2 and 2.8] the following definition:

DEFINITION 2.4. *Given a simplicial complex of dimension at most 3, its* special subdivision *is the simplicial complex obtained by:*

(i) subdividing each edge into two (by adding an extra vertex in the interior of the edge),

(ii) subdividing each 2–simplex as in Figure 2,

(iii) subdividing each 3–simplex so that it becomes isomorphic to X_{543}.

We are ready to describe the combinatorial structure of our triangulation of the 3–cube and the regular octahedron. Assume that the cube lies in $\mathbb{R}^3$ with the vertices at points $(\pm1, \pm1, \pm1)$. Consider the triangulation W of the cube into five 3–simplices so that one of them (denote it by T_0) has vertices $(1, 1, 1), (-1, -1, 1), (-1, 1, -1)$ and $(1, -1, -1)$, while the remaining four 3–simplices (denote them $T_1, \ldots, T_4$) are the components of the complement of T_0 in the cube. Note that $T_1, \ldots, T_4$ are congruent (equal up to a rigid motion);

[7]To streamline and simplify the presentation, we refer to triangles as 2–simplices, to tetrahedra as 3–simplices, etc.

we call such 3–simplices *standard* (see e.g. [Pak]).[8] Let W^* be the special subdivision of W defined as above.

Similarly, let Y be the triangulation of the regular octahedron into eight standard 3–simplices obtained as cones from the center over the faces. Let Y^* be the special subdivision of Y.

By [PŚ, Proposition 2.13], subdivisions W^* and Y^* are both rich and hence have a potential of having acute realizations. This is true indeed, and proves Theorem A for the cube and the regular octahedron: In fact, we provide acute triangulations of all 3–simplices of W and Y, combinatorially equivalent to X_{543}, and matching on common part of the boundary. In other words, we prove the following intermediate result:

THEOREM 2.5. *There is a (non-trivial) acute triangulation, combinatorially equivalent to X_{543}, of*

(i) the regular 3-simplex, and

(ii) the standard 3-simplex.

Below we describe the construction for the 3–cube. At some points we use a computer program. We provide the exact position of all vertices of both triangulations from Theorem 2.5 in Appendix A of [KPP]. There are three steps of the construction. First, we construct an acute triangulation of T_0. Then we "flatten" it to obtain an acute triangulation of T_1. Then we construct another acute triangulation of T_0 so that it matches the one of T_1 on the common part of the boundary.

Step 1. Note that the vertices of the 600–cell, whose boundary we called X_{600}, lie on a sphere in $\mathbb{R}^4$. Moreover all 3–simplices in this realization of X_{600} are regular, hence acute. Let now $\widetilde{X}_{543}$ be the realization of X_{543} in $\mathbb{R}^3$, whose vertices are obtained by stereographic projection of the $\mathbb{R}^4$ realization. We choose the center of the projection to be the center of the (spherical) 3–simplex in X_{600} disjoint from X_{543}. It turns out that this mapping does not disturb the angles significantly.

We move the vertices of $\partial\widetilde{X}_{543}$ radially so that they arrange on the boundary of a regular 3–simplex which we identify with T_0. If we scale the size of ∂T_0 correctly, this triangulation of T_0 is already acute, i.e. it satisfies Theorem 2.5(i). However, we will modify it later in Step 3.

Step 2. The subdivision of the standard 3–simplex, say T_1, is more difficult. Our computer program uses the following algorithm to find the position of the vertices. We "flatten" the acute triangulation of T_0 obtained in Step 1 in order to obtain an acute triangulation of T_1. We gradually move one of the boundary vertices (marked A on Figure 3) towards the center, keeping the three vertices marked C in the points where the circles inscribed into triangles AB_iB_j meet the edges AB_i. We also keep the nine points marked D on their faces, and scale and translate together all the interior vertices.

Whenever some angle stops being acute during this operation, we suspend the flattening process to correct the angles. This is done by slightly moving the responsible vertices so that the angle becomes smaller. More precisely, suppose that the dihedral angle between faces PQR and PQS is not acute. Let T and U be the middle points of the edges

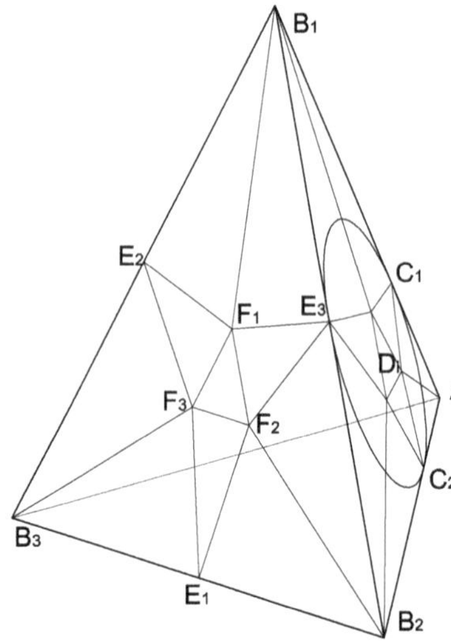

Figure 3: The flattening process.

PQ and RS, respectively. Let v be a small vector colinear with the projection of TU to the plane orthogonal to PQ. Then we translate the points R and S by the vector v, and the points P and Q by $-v$. However, this movement is restricted so that the combinatorial structure is not disturbed, i.e. A, B_i, C_i, E_i are not moved at all; movement of D_i and F_i is restricted to their faces.[9]

When all the angles are corrected, we resume the flattening, until we obtain the standard 3–simplex T_1. This completes the description of the triangulation in Theorem 2.5, part (ii).

Step 3. The position of the vertices F_i on the equilateral face of T_1 is now different from their position on the face of T_0, because we had to move F_i during the correcting process in Step 2. So in the triangulation of T_0 constructed in Step 1 we move all 12 vertices corresponding to F_i to the position matching with the standard T_i. It turns out that it is then enough to scale the interior structure to obtain an acute triangulation.

Now we attach acute triangulations of all T_i, constructed in Steps 2 and 3, to obtain an acute triangulation of the cube (see Remark 2.6 below). Similarly, by attaching eight copies of the standard 3–simplex triangulated as in Step 2, we obtain an acute triangulation of the regular octahedron.

For the last two Platonic solids, note that the regular icosahedron has a straightforward acute triangulation as a union of cones from the center over the faces. Finally, for the regular dodecahedron, first subdivide it into a union of 120 path tetrahedra. Then take their special subdivision and realize it metrically in a similar manner as with the standard 3–simplex. We omit the details.

REMARK 2.6. *The animation of our triangulation of the 3-cube is available at* `http://www.mimuw.edu.pl/~erykk/papers/acute.html`. *For the details and the exact values of all the parameters which have been guessed, see Appendix A of [KPP] and the*

[8]This tetrahedron is also called the *cube-corner*.

[9]We can also require that all the interior vertices except the two outermost layers (of 12 and 16 vertices, respectively) are not moved in the correcting process.

implementation of above algorithm, available with the animation.

3. DEHN–SOMMERVILLE EQUATIONS IN DIMENSION 4

In this short section we present some known results in geometric combinatorics.

Denote by $f_i(M)$, $f_i(\partial M)$ (we later abbreviate this to f_i, f_i^∂), the number of i–dimensional simplices of a triangulation of a compact m–dimensional homology manifold M and its boundary ∂M. Recall the following Dehn–Sommerville type equations.

THEOREM 3.1 ([KLA, THEOREM 1.1] AND [NS]). *Let M be a compact m–dimensional triangulated homology manifold with boundary. For $k = 0, \dots, m$ we have*

$$f_k(M) - f_k(\partial M) = \sum_{i=k}^{m} (-1)^{i+m} \binom{i+1}{k+1} f_i(M).$$

If $m = 4$, then for $k = 1, 2$ we obtain the following.

COROLLARY 3.2. *If M is 4-dimensional, and $f_i = f_i(M), f_i^\partial = f_i(\partial M)$, then:*

(i) $2f_1 - f_1^\partial = 3f_2 - 6f_3 + 10f_4$,

(ii) $-f_2^\partial = -4f_3 + 10f_4$.

These equalities will be used repeatedly in the next two sections.

4. RICH TRIANGULATIONS OF 4–MANIFOLDS

In this section we prove the following combinatorial result on rich triangulations (see Definition 2.2) of 4–dimensional homology manifolds. We keep the notation f_i, f_i^∂ from Section 3.

THEOREM 4.1. *Every rich triangulation of a compact 4–dimensional homology manifold M with Euler characteristic χ satisfies*

$$2f_0 \leq 2\chi + f_1^\partial.$$

In particular, if M is closed, then $f_0 \leq \chi$.

Before we present the proof of the theorem, let us give the following corollaries in the case when the homology manifold M is closed.

PROOF OF THEOREMS C AND E. A periodic triangulation τ of $\mathbb{R}^4$ descends to a triangulation τ' of a 4–torus. Since the Euler characteristic of a 4–torus equals 0, by Theorem 4.1, triangulation τ' is not rich. Hence, by Observation 2.1, τ is not acute. This proves Theorem E. For Theorem C, observe that an acute triangulation of the 4–cube could be promoted, by reflecting, to a periodic acute triangulation of $\mathbb{R}^4$. For the isosceles orthoscheme, observe that it tiles the cube and thus (periodically) the whole space $\mathbb{R}^4$ by reflections. Similarly, albeit less obviously, the cube corner 4–simplex tiles the space $\mathbb{R}^4$ according to reflections of the affine Lie group $\widetilde{D}_4$. □

PROOF OF THEOREM B. Let v be an interior vertex and let ρ be a codimension 5 simplex (a vertex for $\mathbb{R}^5$, an edge for $\mathbb{R}^6$ etc) containing v. The link L of ρ is a 4–dimensional homology sphere, hence its Euler characteristic equals 2. Since L is 4–dimensional, it must have at least 6 vertices. Hence, by Theorem 4.1, L is not rich. Thus the link of one of the codimension 2 simplices containing ρ is a cycle of length shorter than 5. Hence one of the dihedral angles adjacent to v is not acute. □

PROOF OF THEOREM 4.1. Let τ be a rich triangulation of M. We compute the number N of flags ($\rho_2 \subset \rho_4$) of a 2–simplex ρ_2 contained in a 4–simplex ρ_4. On one hand, it is equal to $10f_4$, since each 4–simplex has ten 2–dimensional faces. On the other hand, by richness, each interior 2–simplex (there are $f_2 - f_2^\partial$ of those) is contained in at least five 4–simplices. Thus, we have:

$$10f_4 = N \geq 5(f_2 - f_2^\partial). \tag{1}$$

By the definition of the Euler characteristic, we have:

$$\chi - f_0 = -f_1 + f_2 - f_3 + f_4. \tag{2}$$

Applying consecutively formula (2), then Corollary 3.2 parts (i) and (ii), and formula (1), we obtain:

$$\begin{aligned}
&2(\chi - f_0) + f_1^\partial \\
&= -2f_1 + 2(f_2 - f_3 + f_4) + f_1^\partial = \\
&= -(f_1^\partial + 3f_2 - 6f_3 + 10f_4) + 2(f_2 - f_3 + f_4) + f_1^\partial = \\
&= -f_2 + 4f_3 - 8f_4 = -f_2 + (f_2^\partial + 10f_4) - 8f_4 = \\
&= 2f_4 - (f_2 - f_2^\partial) \geq 0,
\end{aligned}$$

as desired. □

5. ACUTE TRIANGULATIONS OF THE 4–DIMENSIONAL EUCLIDEAN SPACE

In this section we address the problem whether there is an acute triangulation of $\mathbb{R}^4$. We know already that every such acute triangulation of $\mathbb{R}^4$ cannot be periodic (Theorem E).

We say that a triangulation of $\mathbb{R}^p$ has *bounded geometry* if there is a global upper bound on the ratio of edge lengths in every p–simplex.

THEOREM 5.1. *There is no acute triangulation of $\mathbb{R}^4$ with bounded geometry.*

This result easily implies Theorem F, as the following argument shows.

PROOF OF THEOREM F MODULO THEOREM 5.1. If the dihedral angles are bounded away from $\frac{\pi}{2}$, then the angles of 2–simplices are bounded away from $\frac{\pi}{2}$ (see e.g. [Kří]). Hence the angles of 2–simplices are also bounded away from 0. By the sine law, this gives a bound on the ratio of lengths of edges in each 2–simplex, which results in a bound of the ratio of lengths of edges in each 4–simplex. □

Now Theorem 5.1 follows from the following intermediate results which are proved in the expanded version of our article [KPP].

DEFINITION 5.2. *Let $G = (V, E)$ be a connected locally finite infinite graph, and let $\Omega \subset V$ be a finite subset of vertices. Denote by $\partial\Omega$ the* vertex-boundary *of Ω, defined as the subset of $V \setminus \Omega$ consisting of vertices adjacent to vertices in Ω.*

We say that $I: \mathbb{Z}_{\geq 0} \to \mathbb{Z}_{\geq 0}$ is an isoperimetric function *for G, if the inequality $I(|\Omega|) \leq |\partial\Omega|$ holds for every finite $\Omega \subset V$.*

PROPOSITION 5.3 ([KPP, PROPOSITION 5.7]). *The 1–skeleton of any acute triangulation of $\mathbb{R}^4$ with bounded geometry has linear isoperimetric function.*

Following Benjamini–Curien [BC, Section 2.2], we recall the following definition:

DEFINITION 5.4. *Let $G = (V, E)$ be a locally finite connected graph and let $\Gamma(v)$ be the set of all semi-infinite self avoiding simplicial paths in G starting from $v \in V$. For any $m: V \to \mathbb{R}_+$ (so called* metric*), the* length *of a path γ in G is defined by*

$$Length_m(\gamma) = \sum_{v\in\gamma} m(v).$$

If $m \in L^p(V)$, we denote by $||m||_p$ the usual L^p norm. The graph G is p–parabolic *if the* p–extremal length *of $\Gamma(v)$,*

$$\sup_{m\in L^p(V)} \inf_{\gamma\in\Gamma(v)} \frac{Length_m(\gamma)^p}{||m||_p^p}$$

is infinite. This definition does not depend on the choice of $v \in V$.

LEMMA 5.5. *Let G be the 1–skeleton of a triangulation of $\mathbb{R}^p$ with bounded geometry, where $p \geq 2$. Then G is p–parabolic.*

This lemma can be obtained from the Bonk and Kleiner result [BK, Corollary 8.8]. To make the proof complete and self-contained, we include a concise proof in [KPP].

To finish the proof, we need the following recent result by Benjamini and Curien:

PROPOSITION 5.6 ([BC, PROPOSITION 4.1(1)]). *Let $G = (V, E)$ be an infinite locally finite connected graph. If G is p–parabolic and I is an isoperimetric function, then we have*

$$\sum_{k=1}^{\infty} \frac{1}{I(k)^{\frac{p}{p-1}}} = \infty.$$

PROOF OF THEOREM 5.1. Assume that there is is an acute triangulation τ of $\mathbb{R}^4$ with bounded geometry. Let G be the 1–skeleton of τ. By Lemma 5.5 we have that the graph G is 4–parabolic. By Proposition 5.6, we have that $k \to Ck$ is not an isoperimetric function for G. This contradicts Proposition 5.3. □

6. CONCLUSION

We presented both positive and negative results on acute triangulations of polytopes and acute triangulations of the space $\mathbb{R}^n$. The results suggest that it is often possible to obtain acute triangulations in $\mathbb{R}^3$. We do this explicitly for all Platonic solids. Independently with [VHZG], this is is the first ever construction of a non-trivial acute triangulation of the 3–cube. Our construction is based on geometry of the 600–cell, a regular polytope in $\mathbb{R}^4$, and topological considerations. In addition, we resolved an old folklore conjecture of Gardner, et al. finding that the n–cube has an acute triangulation if and only if $n \leq 3$.

In the negative direction, we show that the standard finite element idea cannot possibly work in dimensions higher than 4, since there are no periodic acute triangulations in $\mathbb{R}^4$ and any non-trivial acute triangulations in $\mathbb{R}^n$, $n \geq 5$. We proved that several examples of convex polytopes in $\mathbb{R}^4$ (the 4–cube, the 4–dimensional cube corner, and the 4–dimensional isosceles orthoscheme) do not have an acute triangulation. These are the first (correct) negative results in higher dimension. Finally, we give a partial solution of Křížek's conjecture (Theorem F).[10]

7. ACKNOWLEDGMENTS

This work was initiated at Université Paul Sabatier in Toulouse, where the second and the third author were visiting. We thank the university and Jean-Marc Schlenker for their hospitality.

We thank Marc Bourdon, who suggested the final argument of Section 5. We are grateful to Anil Hirani for telling us about [VHZG] and explaining the ideas behind this work, and to Evan VanderZee for giving us his numerical estimates. We are thankful to Michal Křížek for confirming the crucial error in his paper [Kří] and telling us about a forthcoming correction. We are grateful to Jon McCammond for pointing out a technical error in our earlier version of the proof of Proposition 5.3. We also thank Itai Benjamini, Jesús De Loera, Gil Kalai, Isabella Novik, Vic Reiner, Egon Schulte and Alex Vladimirsky for help with the references.

The second author was partially supported by UCLA, University of Minnesota, Université Paul Sabatier and the NSA. The third author was partially supported by MNiSW grant N201 012 32/0718, the Foundation for Polish Science, and ANR grant ZR58.

8. REFERENCES

[Ale] A. D. Alexandrov, On partitions and tessellations of the plane (in Russian), *Mat. Sbornik* **2** (1937), 307–318.

[Aur] F. Aurenhammer, Voronoi diagrams—a survey of a fundamental geometric data structure, *ACM Comput. Surv.* **23** (1991), 345–405.

[BGR] B. S. Baker, E. Grosse, and C. S. Rafferty, Nonobtuse triangulations of polygons, *Discrete Comput. Geom.* **3** (1988), 147–168.

[BC] I. Benjamini and N. Curien, Local limit of packable graphs, `arXiv:0907.2609`.

[BE] M. Bern and D. Eppstein, Polynomial-size nonobtuse triangulation of polygons. *Int. J. Comp. Geometry and Applications* **2** (1992), 241–255.

[BMR] M. Bern, S. Mitchell and J. Ruppert, Linear-size nonobtuse triangulations of polygons, *Discrete Comput. Geom.* **14** (1995), 411–428.

[10] In fact, we do not believe in the conjecture in full generality (see [KPP] for the reasoning).

[BK] M. Bonk and B. Kleiner, Quasisymmetric parametrizations of two-dimensional metric spheres, *Invent. Math.* **150** (2002), 127–183.

[BKKS] J. Brandts, S. Korotov, M. Křížek and J. Šolc, On Nonobtuse Simplicial Partitions, *SIAM Rev.* **51** (2009), 317–335.

[BZ] Ju. D. Burago and V. A. Zalgaller, Polyhedral embedding of a net (in Russian), *Vestnik Leningrad. Univ.* **15** (1960), no. 7, 66–80.

[CL] C. Cassidy and G. Lord, A square acutely triangulated, *J. Rec. Math.* **13** (1980), 263–268.

[Cox] H. S. M. Coxeter, *Regular polytopes* (Third edition), Dover, New York, 1973.

[DRS] J. A. De Loera, J. Rambau and F. Santos, *Triangulations: Structures and Algorithms*, Springer, 2008.

[Ede] H. Edelsbrunner, *Geometry and topology for mesh generation*, Cambridge University Press, Cambridge, 2001.

[Epp] D. Eppstein, Acute square triangulation, 1997; available at `http://www.ics.uci.edu/~eppstein/junkyard/acute-square/`

[ESÜ] D. Eppstein, J. M. Sullivan and A. Üngör, Tiling space and slabs with acute tetrahedra, *Comput. Geom.* **27** (2004), 237–255; `arXiv:cs.CG/0302027`.

[For] S. Fortune, Voronoi diagrams and Delaunay triangulations, in *Computing in Euclidean geometry* (F. Hwang and D. Z. Du, eds.), World Scientific, Singapore, 1995, 225–265.

[Ful] C. Fulton, Tessellations, *Amer. Math. Monthly* **99** (1992), 442–445.

[GS] B. Grünbaum and G. C. Shephard, *Tilings and patterns*, Freeman, New York, 1987.

[Kal] G. Kalai, On low-dimensional faces that high-dimensional polytopes must have, *Combinatorica* 10 (1990), no. 3, 271–280.

[Kla] D. A. Klain, Dehn–Sommerville relations for triangulated manifolds, unpublished note; available at `http://faculty.uml.edu/dklain/ds.pdf`.

[KPP] E. Kopczyński, I. Pak and P. Przytycki, Acute triangulations of polyhedra and $\mathbb{R}^n$, `arXiv:0909.3706`, submitted.

[Kří] M. Křížek, There is no face-to-face partition of $\mathbf{R}^5$ into acute simplices, *Discrete Comput. Geom.* **36** (2006), 381–390; errata will appear in *Proc. ENUMATH 2009 Conf.*, Uppsala, Springer, Berlin, 2010, and *Discrete Comput. Geom.* (2010+).

[KS] G. Kuperberg and O. Schramm, Average kissing numbers for noncongruent sphere packings, *Math. Res. Lett.* **1** (1994), 339–344.

[LM] J. C. Lagarias and D. Moews, Polytopes that fill $\mathbb{R}^n$ and scissors congruence, *Discrete Comput. Geom.* **13** (1995), 573–583.

[Lin] H. Lindgren, *Geometric dissections*, Van Nostrand, Princeton, N.J., 1964.

[Mae] H. Maehara, Acute triangulations of polygons, *Europ. J. Combin.* **23** (2002), 45–55.

[Man] W. Manheimer, Solution to problem E1406: Dissecting an obtuse triangle into acute triangles, *Amer. Math. Monthly* **67** (1960).

[Niv] I. Niven, Convex polygons that cannot tile the plane, *Amer. Math. Monthly* **85** (1978), 785–792.

[NS] I. Novik and E. Swartz, Applications of Klee's Dehn-Sommerville relations, *Discrete Comput. Geom.* **42** (2009), 261–276.

[Pak] I. Pak, *Lectures on Discrete and Polyhedral Geometry*, monograph to appear, available at `http://www.math.umn.edu/~pak/book.htm`.

[PŚ] P. Przytycki and J. Świątkowski, Flag-no-square triangulations and Gromov boundaries in dimension 3, *Groups, Geometry & Dynamics* **3** (2009), 453–468.

[Sar] S. Saraf, Acute and nonobtuse triangulations of polyhedral surfaces, *Europ. J. Combin.* **30** (2009), 833–840.

[She] J. R. Shewchuk, What Is a Good Linear Finite Element? Interpolation, Conditioning, Anisotropy, and Quality Measures, preprint, 2002; available at `http://www.cs.cmu.edu/~jrs/jrspapers.html`

[SF] G. Strang and G. J. Fix, *An analysis of the finite element method*, Prentice-Hall, Englewood Cliffs, N.J., 1973.

[VHZG] E. VanderZee, A. N. Hirani, V. Zharnitsky and D. Guoy, A dihedral acute triangulation of the cube, to appear in *Comput. Geom.*, `arXiv:0905.3715`.

[Yuan] L. Yuan, Acute triangulations of polygons, *Discrete Comput. Geom.* **34** (2005), 697–706.

[Zam] T. Zamfirescu, Acute triangulations: a short survey, in *Proc. Sixth Conf. of R.S.M.S.*, Bucharest, Romania, 2003, 10–18.

Dynamic Well-Spaced Point Sets

Umut A. Acar[*]
Max-Planck Institute for Software Systems
umut@mpi-sws.org

Andrew Cotter Benoît Hudson
Toyota Technological Institute at Chicago
{cotter,bhudson}@tti-c.org

Duru Türkoğlu[†]
Dept. of Computer Science
University of Chicago
duru@cs.uchicago.edu

ABSTRACT

In a *well-spaced point set* the Voronoi cells all have bounded aspect ratio, i.e., the distance from the Voronoi site to the farthest point in the Voronoi cell divided by the distance to the nearest neighbor in the set is bounded by a small constant. Well-spaced point sets satisfy some important geometric properties and yield quality Voronoi or simplicial meshes that can be important in scientific computations. In this paper, we consider the dynamic well-spaced point sets problem, which requires computing the well-spaced superset of a dynamically changing input set, e.g., as input points are inserted or deleted. We present a dynamic algorithm that allows inserting/deleting points into/from the input in worst-case $O(\log \Delta)$ time, where Δ is the geometric spread, a natural measure that yields an $O(\log n)$ bound when input points are represented by log-size words. We show that the runtime of the dynamic update algorithm is optimal in the worst case. Our algorithm generates size-optimal outputs: the resulting output sets are never more than a constant factor larger than the minimum size necessary. A preliminary implementation indicates that the algorithm is indeed fast in practice. To the best of our knowledge, this is the first time- and size-optimal dynamic algorithm for well-spaced point sets.

Categories and Subject Descriptors

F.2.2 [**Analysis of Algorithms and Problem Complexity**]: Nonnumerical Algorithms and Problems—*Geometrical problems and computations*

General Terms

Algorithms, Theory

Keywords

Well-spaced point sets, Voronoi diagrams, mesh generation, dynamization, self-adjusting computation, dynamic stability

[*]Acar is partially supported by gifts from Intel and Microsoft Research.

[†]Türkoğlu is partially supported by a gift from Intel.

SCG'10, June 13–16, 2010, Snowbird, Utah, USA.

1. INTRODUCTION

Given a hypercube B in $\mathbb{R}^d$, we call a set of points $\mathsf{M} \subset B$ *well-spaced* if for each point $p \in \mathsf{M}$ the ratio of the distance to the farthest point of B in the Voronoi cell of p divided by the distance to the nearest neighbor of p in M is small [Tal97]. Well-spaced point sets are strongly related to meshing and triangulation for scientific computing, which require meshes to have certain qualities. In two dimensions, a well-spaced point set induces a Delaunay triangulation with no small angles, which is known to be a good mesh for the finite element method. In higher dimensions, well-spaced point sets can be post-processed to generate good simplicial meshes [LT01, CDE$^+$00]. The Voronoi diagram of a well-spaced point set is also immediately useful for the control volume method [MTT$^+$96].

Given a d-dimensional hypercube $B \subset \mathbb{R}^d$, we define the well-spaced point set problem as constructing a well-spaced output $\mathsf{M} \subset B$ that is a superset of a given set of input points $\mathsf{N} \subset B$. We can construct the output by extending the input set with so called *Steiner* points, taking care to insert as few Steiner points as possible. We call the output and the algorithm *size-optimal* if the size of the output, $|\mathsf{M}|$, is within a constant factor of the size of the smallest possible well-spaced superset of the input. This problem has been studied since the late 1980s (e.g., [Che89, BEG94, Rup95]), with several recent results obtaining fast runtimes [HPÜ05, HMP06, STÜ07, HT08]. We are interested in the dynamic version of the problem, which requires maintaining a well-spaced output (M) while the input (N) changes dynamically due to insertion and deletion of points. Upon a modification to the input, the dynamic algorithm should efficiently update the output preserving size-optimality with respect to the new input. There has been relatively little progress on solving the dynamic problem. Existing solutions either do not produce size-optimal outputs (e.g., [NvdS04, CAR$^+$09]) or they are asymptotically no faster than running a static algorithm from scratch [LTÜ99, MBF04, CGS06].

In this paper, we present a dynamic algorithm for the well-spaced point set problem. Our algorithm always returns size-optimal outputs and requires worst-case $O(\log \Delta)$ time for an input modification (an insertion or a deletion). Here Δ is the *geometric spread*, a common measure, defined as the ratio of the diameter of the input space to the distance between the closest pair of points in the input. If the geometric spread is polynomially bounded in the size of the input, n, then $\log \Delta = O(\log n)$ (e.g., when the input is specified using $\log n$-bit number). Our algorithm consumes linear space in the size of the output and our update runtime is optimal in the worst-case.

To solve the dynamic problem, we first present an efficient algorithm for constructing size-optimal, well-spaced supersets (Sections 3, 4, and 5). To enable dynamization, in addition to the output, the algorithm constructs a *computation graph* that represents the operations performed during the execution and the dependencies between them. A key property of this algorithm is that it is *stable* in the sense that it produces similar computation graphs and outputs with similar inputs, e.g., that differ by one point. We make this property precise by describing a *distance* measure between the computation graphs and bounding this distance by $O(\log \Delta)$ when inputs differ by a single point (Lemma 6.5). Taking advantage of this bound, we design a change-propagation algorithm that performs dynamic updates in $O(\log \Delta)$ time by identifying the operations that are affected by the modification to the input and deleting/re-executing them as necessary (Section 7). For the lower bound, we show that there exist inputs and modifications that require $\Omega(\log \Delta)$ Steiner points to be inserted to the output (Section 8).

The approach of designing a stable algorithm and then providing a dynamic update algorithm based on change propagation is inspired by recent advances on *self-adjusting computation* (e.g., [ABBT06, LWAF09]). In self-adjusting computation, programs can respond automatically to modifications to their data by invoking a change propagation algorithm [Aca05]. The data structures required by change propagation are constructed automatically. Our computation graphs are abstract representations of these data structures. Similarly our dynamic update algorithm is an adaptation of the change propagation algorithm for the problem of well-spaced point sets. Self-adjusting computation is found to be effective in kinetic motion simulation of three-dimensional convex hulls [ABTT08]. Although these initial findings are empiricial, they have motivated the approach that we present in this paper. Since our approach takes advantage of the structure of a static algorithm to perform dynamic updates, it can be viewed as a dynamization technique, which has been used effectively for a relatively broad range of algorithms (e.g., [Mul91, Sch91, BDS+92, CMS93]).

The efficiency of our dynamic update algorithm directly depends on stability. We design a stable algorithm that maintains several invariants. First, we structure the computation into $\Theta(\log \Delta)$ levels—ranks and colors—such that the operations in each level depend only on the previous levels [STÜ07]. Second, we pick Steiner points by making local decisions only, using clipped Voronoi cells [HT08]. These techniques enable us to process each point only once and help isolate and limit the effects of a modification. Furthermore, our dynamic update algorithm returns an output and a computation graph that are isomorphic to those that would be obtained by executing from scratch the static algorithm with the modified input (Lemma 7.2). Consequently, the output remains both well-spaced and size-optimal with respect to the modified input (Theorem 7.3).

To assess the effectiveness of the proposed dynamic algorithm, we present a prototype implementation and report the results of a preliminary experimental evaluation (Section 9). Our experimental results confirm our theoretical bounds, showing linear speedups over re-computing from scratch. These results suggest that a well-optimized implementation can perform very well in practice.

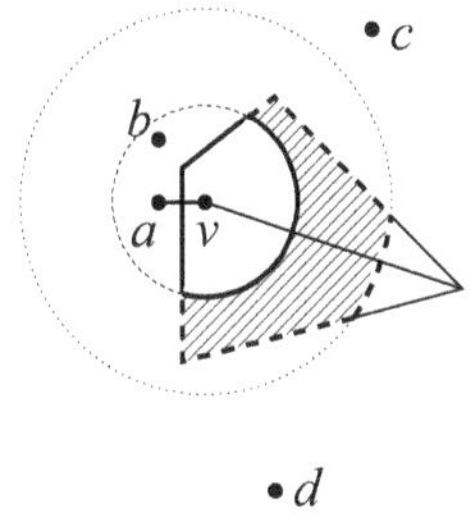

Figure 1: $\mathcal{M} = \{a, b, c, d, v\}$. $\mathrm{NN}_{\mathcal{M}}(v) = |va|$. Thick solid and dashed boundaries show $\mathrm{Vor}^{\rho}_{\mathcal{M}}(v)$ and $\mathrm{Vor}^{\beta}_{\mathcal{M}}(v)$, where $\rho = 2$ and $\beta = 4$. The ρ-clipped Voronoi neighbors of v are a and b. Shaded region is the (ρ, β) picking region of v.

2. PRELIMINARIES

Given a set of points N, we define the *geometric spread* (Δ) to be the ratio of the diameter of N to the distance between the closest pair in N. We say that a d-dimensional hypercube B is a *bounding box* if $\mathsf{N} \subset B$ and each edge of B has length within a constant factor of the diameter of N. Without loss of generality, we scale and shift the point set N such that $B = [0, 1]^d$ becomes a bounding box.

Given N as input, our algorithm constructs a well-spaced output $\mathsf{M} \subset B$ that is a superset of N. We use the term *point* to refer to any point in B and the term *vertex* to refer to the input and output points. Consider a vertex set $\mathcal{M} \subset B$. The *nearest-neighbor distance of v in $\mathcal{M}$*, written $\mathrm{NN}_{\mathcal{M}}(v)$, is the distance from v to the nearest other vertex in $\mathcal{M}$. The *Voronoi cell* of v in $\mathcal{M}$, written $\mathrm{Vor}_{\mathcal{M}}(v)$, consists of points $x \in B$ such that for all $u \in \mathcal{M}, |vx| \leq |ux|$. Following Talmor [Tal97], a vertex is *ρ-well-spaced* if the intersection of its Voronoi cell with B is contained in the ball of radius $\rho\,\mathrm{NN}_{\mathcal{M}}(v)$ centered at v; $\mathcal{M}$ is ρ-well-spaced if every vertex in $\mathcal{M}$ is ρ-well-spaced. The *β-clipped Voronoi cell* of v, written $\mathrm{Vor}^{\beta}_{\mathcal{M}}(v)$, is the intersection of $\mathrm{Vor}_{\mathcal{M}}(v)$ with the ball of radius $\beta\,\mathrm{NN}_{\mathcal{M}}(v)$ centered at v [HT08]. For any $\beta > \rho$, we define the *(ρ, β) picking region* of v, written $\mathrm{Vor}^{(\rho,\beta)}_{\mathcal{M}}(v)$, as $\mathrm{Vor}^{\beta}_{\mathcal{M}}(v) \setminus \mathrm{Vor}^{\rho}_{\mathcal{M}}(v)$, the region of the Voronoi cell bounded by concentric balls of radius $\rho\,\mathrm{NN}_{\mathcal{M}}(v)$ and $\beta\,\mathrm{NN}_{\mathcal{M}}(v)$. A vertex u is a *(β-clipped) Voronoi neighbor* of v if the (β-clipped) Voronoi cell of v contains a point equidistant from v and u. Note that v is ρ-well-spaced if and only if $\mathrm{Vor}^{\rho}_{\mathcal{M}}(v) = \mathrm{Vor}_{\mathcal{M}}(v)$. Figure 1 illustrates some of these definitions.

Given an input set N, the *local feature size* of a point $x \in B$, written $\mathrm{lfs}(x)$, is the distance from x to the second-nearest vertex in N. The output M is *size-conforming* if there exists a constant c independent of N such that for all $v \in \mathsf{M}$, $\mathrm{NN}_{\mathsf{M}}(v) < c \cdot \mathrm{lfs}(v)$. Our algorithm guarantees that the output is size-conforming; this implies size-optimality [Rup95].

Our algorithm uses a point location structure based on the balanced quadtree of Bern, Eppstein, and Gilbert [BEG94]. It is relatively easy to dynamize the balanced quadtree and to extend it to d dimensions. We explain the details of this structure in a technical report [ACHT10]. We use "quadtree" to mean 2^d-tree and "quadtree node" to mean d-hypercube. We treat the quadtree almost as a black box; we only use the leaves of the quadtree, which we refer to as *squares*. The quadtree squares store neighbor pointers and a list of the vertices they contain to support fast searches. Vertices store the square that contains them, avoiding the need to search through the tree structure. The quadtree supports the functions `QTBuild`, `QTAdd`, `QTRemove`, `QTApxNN`, and `QTClippedVoronoi`. The function `QTBuild(N)` constructs a quadtree for a set of n vertices N in $O(n \log \Delta)$ time. The functions `QTAdd(Π, v)` and `QTRemove(Π, v)` respectively add or remove an input vertex v into or from N and update the quadtree Π to match the new input in $O(\log \Delta)$ time. They return the updated quadtree and the set of squares that are deleted or that become internal quadtree nodes. For any square $s \in \Pi$ that is returned by QTAdd(Π, v) or QTRemove(Π, v) we have $|vs| \in O(|s|)$, where $|s|$ is the size (length of an edge) of s [ACHT10]. The function QTApxNN(v) returns the size of the quadtree square that contains v. The quadtree guarantees that this value is in $\Omega(\mathrm{NN}_{\mathsf{N}}(v))$ and less than $\mathrm{NN}_{\mathsf{N}}(v)$. The function QTClippedVoronoi(v, β) returns the β-clipped Voronoi cell of v in $O(1)$ time under certain assumptions that our algorithm meets [HT08]. It also returns the nearest neighbor distance of v.

3. A STABLE ALGORITHM

We can construct a well-spaced superset of an input set by repeatedly "filling" each vertex of the superset by applying a *fill* operation to it. When applied to some vertex v, which we say that it *acts on*, a fill operation makes the vertex ρ-well-spaced by inserting Steiner vertices into its Voronoi cell. Although correct, this basic algorithm is not efficient because the Voronoi cells can be arbitrarily complex (thus requiring super-constant time to compute), and because filling a vertex may adversely affect the well-spacedness of already processed vertices requiring them to be filled multiple times. This algorithm is also unstable, because inserting/deleting a single vertex into/from the input can result in very different outputs because the presence/absence of a vertex can affect the choice of many subsequent Steiner vertices.

To address these problems, we refine the basic algorithm to schedule carefully the fill operations such that 1) each fill operation requires constant time, 2) each vertex is filled at most once, 3) the algorithm is stable. To achieve these three properties, which we make precise and prove in the rest of the paper, we start by refining the fill operation so that instead of inserting points inside the Voronoi cell, it inserts points within the (ρ, β) picking region of the vertex that it acts on (Figure 1). We then carefully order the fill operations so that no vertex is filled more than once and fill operations can be performed in constant time. These refinements yield an efficient algorithm. To ensure stability, we further refine the algorithm to identify certain fill operations as independent, which makes it possible to re-execute one operation without affecting another independent operation. In the rest of this section, we briefly describe these refinements and present the pseudo-code for the algorithm, which is sufficiently precise for an implementation (Figure 3).

Given a vertex set $\mathcal{M}$, consider applying a fill operation to a vertex $v \in \mathcal{M}$ that is not ρ-well-spaced. Let w be a Steiner vertex this operation inserts.

FACT 1. *The Steiner vertex w is in $\mathrm{Vor}_{\mathcal{M}}^{(\rho,\beta)}(v)$. That is, $\forall u \in \mathcal{M}, |wv| \leq |wu|$ and $\rho\,\mathrm{NN}_{\mathcal{M}}(v) \leq |wv| < \beta\,\mathrm{NN}_{\mathcal{M}}(v)$.*

Since v is the nearest neighbor of w, this fact implies that $\mathrm{NN}_{\mathcal{M}}(w) \geq \rho\,\mathrm{NN}_{\mathcal{M}}(v)$. Generalizing this simple observation, we infer the following.

FACT 2. *For any given $\alpha > 0$ if every vertex $u \in \mathcal{M}$ with $\mathrm{NN}_{\mathcal{M}}(u) < \alpha$ is ρ-well-spaced then $\mathrm{NN}_{\mathcal{M}}(w) \geq \rho\alpha$.*

Suppose that vertices whose nearest neighbors are at distance less than α are all ρ-well-spaced. The second fact implies that inserting a Steiner vertex does not change the nearest neighbors and hence the well-spacedness of the vertices whose nearest neighbors are at distance less than $\rho\alpha$.

Taking advantage of this property, we partially order the vertices by assigning *ranks* to them. More precisely, we define the rank of a vertex v in a vertex set $\mathcal{M}$ as the the logarithm in base ρ of its nearest neighbor distance, i.e., $\lfloor \log_\rho \mathrm{NN}_{\mathcal{M}}(v) \rfloor$. We then fill the vertices in the order of their ranks. With this partial ordering, for example, the fill operations acting on vertices with nearest neighbor distances in $[\rho^r, \rho^{r+1})$ would be at rank r. Note that for any $\rho > 1$, this partial order has only a logarithmic number of levels, $O(\log \Delta)$ in particular. As we prove in Lemma 5.3, this ordering ensures that fill operations run in $O(1)$ time.

We ensure stability by identifying independent fill operations. We say that two fill operations at rank r are *independent* if, when executed (in either order), no operation inserts a Steiner vertex that becomes a β-clipped Voronoi neighbor of the vertex acted on by the other. We identify independent fill operations by using a *coloring scheme* that partitions the space based on a *coloring parameter* κ, and a real valued function $\ell(r)$ defined on ranks. At each rank r, we partition the space into d-dimensional hypercubes or r-*tiles* with side length $\ell(r)$. We color r-tiles such that they are colored periodically in each dimension with period κ, using κ^d *colors* in total. A fill operation at rank r that acts on a vertex v has color $c \in \{1, 2, \ldots, \kappa^d\}$ if v lies in a c colored r-tile. Figure 2 illustrates a coloring scheme in 2D. By choosing $\ell(r)$ small enough and κ large enough, we prove that two fill operations at the same rank are independent if they have the same color (Lemma 6.1).

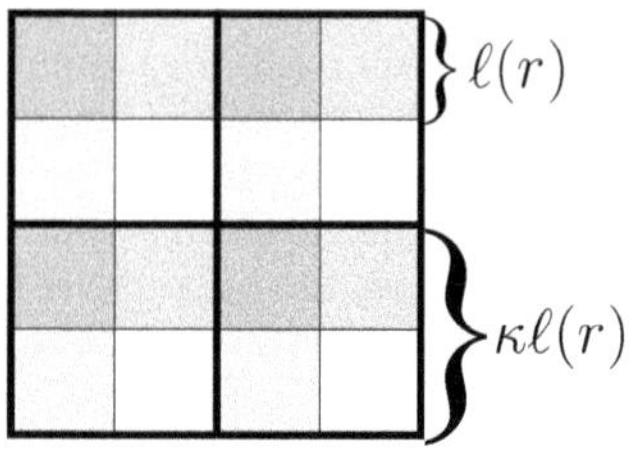

Figure 2: Illustration of a coloring scheme ($\kappa = 2$).

Figure 3 shows the pseudo-code of the algorithm. The pseudo-code follows the description quite closely except for the computation of ranks. Our algorithm critically relies on ordering the computation by assigning ranks to vertices and filling them in that order. Since the rank of a vertex depends on its nearest neighbor and since that can change as Steiner vertices are inserted, we need to update ranks dynamically. To achieve this, we assign ranks to fill operations and use another type of operation, called *dispatch*, to compute and update ranks. The unique dispatch operation acting on a vertex v also has a rank and runs before the fill operations acting on v. The rank of a dispatch operation acting on an input vertex v is an $O(1)$-approximation (from below) of the rank of v, and those that act on Steiner vertices are assigned exact ranks. When executed, a dispatch operation computes the rank of v, creates a fill operation for v at that rank, and creates fill operations for its β-clipped Voronoi neighbors in order to update their ranks. This approach guarantees that after the execution of the dispatch operations at rank r, every vertex either has a fill operation at its up-to-date rank, or a dispatch operation at rank greater than r. When executed, a fill operation makes well-spaced the vertex it acts on, subsequent fill operations terminate immediately without inserting Steiner vertices. We prefer this approach because it simplifies the analysis by making explicit the dependencies between operations.[1] As we prove

[1]In an implementation we would create one fill operation for each vertex and update its rank. In fact this is how our implementation (Section 9) operates.

```
Dimension:  d, Parameters:  ρ, β, κ, ℓ(r)
StableWS (N) =
  Ω ← ∅ ; Π ← QTBuild(N)
  for each v ∈ N do
    Ω ← Ω ∪ {NewOp(v, ⌊log_ρ QTApxNN(v)⌋ , 0, nil)}
  for r = min rank in Ω to ⌊log_ρ √d⌋ do
    for each op ∈ Ω|_{r,0} do Dispatch (op, Ω)
    for c = 1 to κ^d do
      for each op ∈ Ω|_{r,c} do Fill (op, Ω)
  return (N, Π)

Dispatch (op, Ω) =
  (v, nnv, CV) ← QTClippedVoronoi(op, β)
  r ← ⌊log_ρ nnv⌋
  if r ≥ op.rank then Ω ← Ω ∪ {NewOp(v, r, Color(v, r), op)}
  for each β-clipped Voronoi neighbor w of v (via CV) do
    r ← ⌊log_ρ |wv|⌋
    if r ≥ op.rank then Ω ← Ω ∪ {NewOp(w, r, Color(w, r), op)}

Fill (op, Ω) =
  (v, nnv, CV) ← QTClippedVoronoi(op, β)
  while v is not ρ-well-spaced (via CV) do
    choose w ∈ CV such that |vw| ≥ ρ · nnv
    op.steiners ← op.steiners ∪ {w}
    Ω ← Ω ∪ {NewOp(w, ⌊log_ρ |wv|⌋ , 0, op)}
    update CV with w

Color (v, r) =
  for i = 1 to d do c_i ← ⌊v_i/ℓ(r)⌋  mod κ
  return (c_1, c_2, ..., c_d) as a d digit number

NewOp (v, r, c, parent) =
  op ← CreateOp(v) ; op.rank ← r ; op.color ← c
  parent.children ← parent.children ∪ {op}
  op.children, op.steiners ← ∅ ; return op
```

Figure 3: Pseudo-code for our stable algorithm.

in Theorem 4.4 this algorithm computes correctly and efficiently a ρ-well-spaced superset of its input.

The algorithm `StableWS` starts by constructing a quadtree Π and stores it for use in dynamic updates. It then computes the output M by creating (via `NewOp`) and performing dispatch and fill operations which it stores in Ω. The algorithm assigns a rank and a color, the pair of which we refer to as *time*, to each operation and executes them in time order. The dispatch operations are assigned the color zero. In the pseudo-code, we use $\Omega|_{r,c}$ to refer to the operations with time (r, c). In the analysis, we refer to time as a single entity rather than its components (rank and color). For brevity, we define time $t = 0$ to be the beginning of time, when the dispatch operations for the input are created but before any operations are performed, and define time $t = \infty$ to be the end of the algorithm. We write M_t to refer to the output at time t, e.g., M_0 is the input, N, and M_∞ is the output, M. For readability, we use t instead of M_t in the subscript, e.g., NN_t instead of $\mathrm{NN}_{\mathsf{M}_t}$.

To support efficient dynamic updates, while executing, the algorithm constructs a computation graph of all executed operations and dependencies between them. The *computation graph* $G = (V, E)$ consists of nodes, $V = \Sigma \cup \Omega$, comprised of the set of squares (Σ) and the set of all operations (Ω), and directed edges representing various dependencies between operations and squares. Consider executing an operation *op*. If *op* creates an operation *op'* then $(op, op') \in E$ becomes an edge (recorded by storing *op'* in the `children` field of *op*). If *op* reads a square s via `QTClippedVoronoi` then (s, op) becomes an edge (recorded in the square s). Finally, if *op* writes into a square s by inserting a Steiner vertex w into it then (op, s) becomes an edge (recorded by storing w in the `steiners` field of *op*).

4. OUTPUT QUALITY AND SIZE

We prove that the output of our algorithm, M, is ρ-well-spaced and size-optimal. We prove size-optimality by showing that M is size-conforming. The first two lemmas prove that our algorithm incrementally progresses towards a ρ-well-spaced output. In these two lemmas, let $\mathcal{M}$ be the set of vertices in the output at the beginning of rank r.

LEMMA 4.1. *At the beginning of rank r, assume that every vertex $u \in \mathcal{M}$ with $\mathrm{NN}_\mathcal{M}(u) < \rho^r$ is ρ-well-spaced. Then, for every vertex $w \in \mathcal{M}$ with $\mathrm{NN}_\mathcal{M}(w) \in [\rho^r, \rho^{r+1})$, there exists a fill operation that acts on w at rank r.*

PROOF. Pick a vertex $w \in \mathcal{M}$, let u be its nearest neighbor in $\mathcal{M}$, and assume that $\rho^r \leq |wu| < \rho^{r+1}$. Let op_w and op_u be the dispatch operations that act on w and u respectively. If op_w runs at rank $\leq r$ and u is in the output when op_w is executed then op_w schedules a fill operation that acts on w at rank r. Alternatively, op_u schedules such a fill operation if op_u runs at rank $\leq r$ and w is a β-clipped Voronoi neighbor of u when op_u is executed.

Analyzing the vertices w and u, in two cases, we prove that the first condition holds. If both w and u are input vertices then op_w runs at rank $\leq r$. In the case that w is a Steiner vertex consider the vertex v that creates w. If u is in the output when w is being created, by Fact 1 we know that $|wv| \leq |wu|$, which implies that op_w runs at rank $\leq r$.

We prove that the second condition holds in the remaining case, that u is a Steiner vertex and that w is already in the output when u is being created. Similar to the previous case, we deduct that op_u runs at rank $\leq r$. Since u is the nearest neighbor of w in $\mathcal{M}$, w is a Voronoi neighbor of u in $\mathcal{M}'$, where $\mathcal{M}' \subset \mathcal{M}$ is the set of vertices in the output when op_u is executed. If u is ρ-well-spaced in $\mathcal{M}$ then $|wu| \leq 2\rho\,\mathrm{NN}_\mathcal{M}(u) < 2\beta\,\mathrm{NN}_{\mathcal{M}'}(u)$. Otherwise, the assumption of the lemma implies $\rho^r \leq \mathrm{NN}_\mathcal{M}(u)$. Since $|wu| < \rho^{r+1}$, we get $|wu| < \rho\,\mathrm{NN}_\mathcal{M}(u) < 2\beta\,\mathrm{NN}_{\mathcal{M}'}(u)$. Either way, w is a β-clipped Voronoi neighbor of u in $\mathcal{M}'$. □

LEMMA 4.2 (PROGRESS). *At the beginning of rank r, every vertex $u \in \mathcal{M}$ with $\mathrm{NN}_\mathcal{M}(u) < \rho^r$ is ρ-well-spaced.*

PROOF. We use induction. At the minimum rank, there are no vertices with smaller nearest neighbor distance, so the claim is trivially true. Assume that the lemma holds up to rank r, that is, every vertex $u \in \mathcal{M}$ with $\mathrm{NN}_\mathcal{M}(u) < \rho^r$ is ρ-well-spaced. For rank $r+1$, let $\mathcal{M}' \supset \mathcal{M}$ be the set of vertices in the output at the beginning of rank $r+1$ and consider a vertex $w \in \mathcal{M}'$ with $\mathrm{NN}_{\mathcal{M}'}(w) < \rho^{r+1}$. If $w \in \mathcal{M}' \setminus \mathcal{M}$ then w is a Steiner vertex inserted at rank r. Repeatedly applying Fact 2 for each (Steiner) vertex in $\mathcal{M}' \setminus \mathcal{M}$, we see that the nearest neighbors of these Steiner vertices are at distance $\geq \rho^{r+1}$; in particular, $\mathrm{NN}_{\mathcal{M}'}(w) \geq \rho^{r+1}$. This is a contradiction, thus, $w \in \mathcal{M}$. Furthermore, $\mathrm{NN}_\mathcal{M}(w) < \rho^{r+1}$ for similar reasons. If $\mathrm{NN}_\mathcal{M}(w) < \rho^r$ then by our induction hypothesis w is ρ-well-spaced. Otherwise, by Lemma 4.1, there exists a fill operation that acts on w at rank r. After executing that operation, w becomes ρ-well-spaced. Finally, once again, Fact 2 implies that w remains ρ-well-spaced. Therefore, our claim holds. □

LEMMA 4.3. *The output* M *is size-conforming and size-optimal with respect to* N.

PROOF. We use induction over the order in which the algorithm inserts Steiner vertices and show that there exists a constant c such that for every $v \in \mathsf{M}$, we have $c\,\mathrm{NN}_{\mathsf{M}}(v) \geq \mathrm{lfs}(v)$, thereby proving that M is size-conforming. In the base case, every vertex is an input vertex and the nearest neighbor of an input vertex is exactly the local feature size. For the inductive case, assume that there exists a constant c such that, for every $v \in \mathcal{M}$, we have $c\,\mathrm{NN}_{\mathcal{M}}(v) \geq \mathrm{lfs}(v)$. Furthermore, assume that v inserts a Steiner vertex w and the new output is $\mathcal{M}' = \mathcal{M} \cup \{w\}$. We analyze the inductive claim for w and for any vertex $u \in \mathcal{M}$ separately. For w, Fact 1 states that $|wv| \geq \rho\,\mathrm{NN}_{\mathcal{M}}(v)$ and implies that $\mathrm{NN}_{\mathcal{M}'}(w) = |wv|$. By the triangle inequality, lfs satisfies the Lipschitz condition: $\mathrm{lfs}(v) + |wv| \geq \mathrm{lfs}(w)$. By the inductive hypothesis, $c\,\mathrm{NN}_{\mathcal{M}}(v) \geq \mathrm{lfs}(v)$. Therefore, we have $(\frac{c}{\rho}+1)|wv| = (\frac{c}{\rho}+1)\,\mathrm{NN}_{\mathcal{M}'}(w) \geq \mathrm{lfs}(w)$. For any vertex $u \in \mathcal{M}$, if $\mathrm{NN}_{\mathcal{M}}(u) = \mathrm{NN}_{\mathcal{M}'}(u)$ then the claim holds trivially. Otherwise, assume $\mathrm{NN}_{\mathcal{M}}(u) > \mathrm{NN}_{\mathcal{M}'}(u) = |wu|$. By the Lipschitz condition, $|wu| + \mathrm{lfs}(w) \geq \mathrm{lfs}(u)$. Fact 1 implies $|wu| \geq |wv|$. Combining these facts by the bound we obtained for $\mathrm{lfs}(w)$, we get $(\frac{c}{\rho}+2)|wu| = (\frac{c}{\rho}+2)\,\mathrm{NN}_{\mathcal{M}'}(u) \geq \mathrm{lfs}(u)$. Solving for $c \geq \frac{c}{\rho}+2$, we conclude that any $c \geq \frac{2\rho}{\rho-1}$ suffices to prove the inductive step. Therefore, M is size-conforming and hence size-optimal [Rup95]. □

THEOREM 4.4. ***StableWS*** *constructs a size-optimal ρ-well-spaced superset* M *of its input* N.

PROOF. The quality property that M is ρ-well-spaced follows from the Progress Lemma and the fact that `StableWS` iterates over all ranks. Lemma 4.3 proves the size bound. □

5. RUNTIME

We analyze the running time of our static algorithm and emphasize two lemmas that are useful in the analysis of our dynamic algorithm. The first lemma (Lemma 5.1) proves that throughout the algorithm, the nearest neighbor distance of a vertex v changes only by a constant factor. The second (Lemma 5.2) proves that all operations acting on v have rank $\lfloor \log_\rho \mathrm{NN}_\infty(v) \rfloor \pm O(1)$; none are scheduled too early or too late.

LEMMA 5.1. *Let t be the time at which v is created ($t = 0$ for input vertices). Then,* $\mathrm{NN}_t(v) \in \Theta(\mathrm{NN}_\infty(v))$.

PROOF. As time progresses, more vertices are added, so the nearest neighbor distance can only shrink: $\mathrm{NN}_t(v) \geq \mathrm{NN}_\infty(v)$. For the upper bound, we analyze input vertices and Steiner vertices separately. By definition, an input vertex v has $\mathrm{lfs}(v) = \mathrm{NN}_0(v)$. The algorithm is size-conforming (Lemma 4.3), so $\mathrm{NN}_0(v) = \mathrm{lfs}(v) \in O(\mathrm{NN}_\infty(v))$. For a Steiner vertex w that is created at time $t = (r, c)$, Fact 1 implies that $\rho^{r+1} \leq \mathrm{NN}_t(w) \leq \beta\rho^{r+1}$. For any other Steiner vertex u that is created later, the same fact implies that $\rho^{r+1} \leq |uw|$ which means $\rho^{r+1} \leq \mathrm{NN}_\infty(w)$. Therefore, $\mathrm{NN}_t(w) \leq \beta\rho^{r+1} \leq \beta\,\mathrm{NN}_\infty(w)$. □

LEMMA 5.2. *If an operation at rank r acts on v then* $\mathrm{NN}_\infty(v) \in \Theta(\rho^r)$.

PROOF. Consider an operation op that acts on a vertex v at time $t = (r, c)$. If op is a dispatch operation and v is an input vertex then the call `QTApxNN`(v) returns a value in $\Theta(\mathrm{NN}_0(v))$ which implies $\mathrm{NN}_0(v) \in \Theta(\rho^r)$. By Lemma 5.1, we know that $\mathrm{NN}_0(v) \in \Theta(\mathrm{NN}_\infty(v))$; the result follows.

Otherwise, let op' be the operation that creates op, and assume that op' acts on u at time $t' = (r', c')$; hence, $r = \lfloor \log_\rho |uv| \rfloor$. Since $\mathrm{NN}_t(v) \leq |uv|$, we get $\mathrm{NN}_t(v) < \rho^{r+1}$. Thus, the upper bound holds: $\mathrm{NN}_\infty(v) \leq \mathrm{NN}_t(v) \in O(\rho^r)$. For the lower bound, from Lemma 4.3, we have $\mathrm{NN}_\infty(v) \in \Omega(\mathrm{lfs}(v))$. By definition, $\mathrm{lfs}(v) \geq \mathrm{NN}_{t'}(v)$, and since $r = \lfloor \log_\rho |uv| \rfloor$, we have $|uv| \geq \rho^r$. Thus, it suffices to show that $\mathrm{NN}_{t'}(v) \in \Omega(|uv|)$. Since op' creates op, we know that v is a β-clipped Voronoi neighbor of u at time t', which means that u is a Voronoi neighbor of v at time t'. If $\mathrm{NN}_{t'}(v) < \rho^{r'}$ then by Progress Lemma, v is ρ-well-spaced at time t'. Therefore, $2\rho\,\mathrm{NN}_{t'}(v) \geq |uv|$ and we are done. If $\mathrm{NN}_{t'}(v) \geq \rho^{r'}$, since v is a β-clipped Voronoi neighbor of u, i.e., $|uv| \leq 2\beta\,\mathrm{NN}_{t'}(u)$. Applying the upper bound result from above for op', we get $\mathrm{NN}_{t'}(u) \in O(\rho^{r'})$, thus, $|uv| \in O(\rho^{r'})$. Since $\mathrm{NN}_{t'}(v) \geq \rho^{r'}$, this implies $\mathrm{NN}_{t'}(v) \in \Omega(|uv|)$. □

LEMMA 5.3. *Every operation runs in $O(1)$ time.*

PROOF. Pick an operation acting on v at time $t = (r, c)$. The main costs are the `QTClippedVoronoi` calls and the loops. The Progress Lemma shows that every vertex $u \in \mathsf{M}_t$ with $\mathrm{NN}_t(u) < \rho^r$ is ρ-well-spaced and Lemmas 5.2 and 5.1 together show that $\mathrm{NN}_t(v) \in \Theta(\rho^r)$. Hudson and Türkoğlu show that these are sufficient conditions to guarantee that `QTClippedVoronoi` runs in constant time [HT08].

The dispatch operation loops as many times as there are β-clipped Voronoi neighbors. Since `QTClippedVoronoi` runs in constant time, there is only $O(1)$ neighbors. The fill operation has a loop that inserts Steiner vertices until v is ρ-well-spaced. For each inserted Steiner vertex w, Fact 1 implies $\mathrm{NN}_t(w) \geq \rho\,\mathrm{NN}_t(v)$. Thus, we can associate non-overlapping empty balls of radius $\rho\,\mathrm{NN}_t(v)/2$ around every Steiner vertex. Since the Steiner vertices are in a ball of radius $\beta\,\mathrm{NN}_t(v)$ around v, a packing argument shows that each fill operation inserts $O(1)$ Steiner vertices. □

LEMMA 5.4. *For every vertex $v \in \mathsf{M}$, there are $O(1)$ operations that act on v.*

PROOF. By Lemma 5.2, we know that any operation that acts on v has rank $\lfloor \log_\rho \mathrm{NN}_\infty(v) \rfloor \pm O(1)$. Therefore, if we can show that the number of the operations that acts on v at each rank is constant, our claim will hold. There is only one dispatch operation for each vertex, so we only need to count fill operations scheduled by other dispatch operations. Fix r and consider a dispatch operation at time $t' = (r', 0)$ that acts on u and schedules a fill operation that acts on v at rank r. Then, v is β-clipped Voronoi neighbor of u, in other words, $|uv| \leq 2\beta\,\mathrm{NN}_{t'}(u)$. The fact that the fill operation is scheduled for rank r implies $\rho^r \leq |uv| < \rho^{r+1}$. Considering the dispatch operation, Lemmas 5.1 and 5.2 show that $\mathrm{NN}_{t'}(u) = O(\rho^{r'})$. These facts altogether imply $\rho^r = O(\rho^{r'})$. Again by Lemma 5.2, we know that there exists an empty ball around u with radius $\Omega(\rho^{r'})$ which is $\Omega(\rho^r)$ by the previous assertion. We already know that $|uv| < \rho^{r+1}$, therefore, a packing argument proves our claim. □

THEOREM 5.5. *StableWS runs in* $O(n \log \Delta)$ *time.*

PROOF. Building the quadtree takes $O(n \log \Delta)$ time. By Lemmas 5.3 and 5.4, the rest of the algorithm takes $O(m)$ time, where $m = |\mathsf{M}|$. The total runtime is $O(n \log \Delta + m)$. That $m \in O(n \log \Delta)$ follows from our dynamic bounds. □

6. DYNAMIC STABILITY

We call two inputs N and N' *related* if they differ by one vertex, i.e., N' can be obtained from N by inserting or deleting a vertex. To analyze the stability of the algorithm `StableWS`, we define a notion of distance between two executions with related inputs. We prove that this distance is bounded by $O(\log \Delta)$ in the worst-case, where Δ is the larger geometric spread of the inputs N and N' (Lemma 6.5).

As described in Section 3, `StableWS(N)` creates a computation graph $G = (V, E)$ by building quadtree squares Σ and a set of operations Ω. The set of nodes V is $\Sigma \cup \Omega$; the edges E represent the dependencies in the computation. For another input set N' which is related to N, consider running `StableWS(N')` and creating $G' = (V', E')$, Σ', and Ω' similarly. We define two squares $s \in \Sigma$ and $s' \in \Sigma'$ to be *identical*, written $s \equiv s'$, if s and s' have the same corner points. Also, two operations $op \in \Omega$ and $op' \in \Omega'$ are *identical*, written $op \equiv op'$, if op and op' have the same time and act on the same vertex. There exists a unique function $\mu : V' \to V$, $\mu = \mu_o \cup \mu_s$, where μ_o is the largest set satisfying $\mu_o = \{(op', op) \mid op' \in \Omega' \wedge op \in \Omega \wedge (op' \equiv op) \wedge (\text{parent}(op'), \text{parent}(op)) \in \mu_o\}$ and $\mu_s = \{(s', s) \mid s' \in \Sigma' \wedge s \in \Sigma \wedge s' \equiv s\}$. We call μ the *matching* between G' and G. Informally, μ pairs squares of G' with identical squares of G and pairs operations of G' with identical operations of G as long as their parents (the operations that create them, if any) are also paired. We say that nodes $u' \in V'$ and $u \in V$ *match* if $\mu(u') = u$. We denote the domain and the range of μ by $\mathsf{dom}(\mu)$ and $\mathsf{range}(\mu)$.

Given $G = (V, E)$ and $G' = (V', E')$ and their matching μ, let $\mu' = \mu \cup \{(u, u) \mid u \in V' \setminus \mathsf{dom}(\mu)\}$ be a total function defined on the nodes V' of G'. We combine the computation graphs in a *union graph* $G^{\cup} = (V \cup \mu'(V'), E \cup \mu'(E'))$, where $\mu'(E') = \{(\mu'(u), \mu'(v)) \mid (u, v) \in E'\}$. The union graph injects G' into G under the guidance of μ by extending G with the unmatched nodes of G', unifying the matched nodes, and adding the edges of G' while redirecting them to the matched nodes appropriately. In order to capture the dependencies between two operations, we define a path in the union graph to be a dependency path if the times of the edges on the path do not decrease. Lemma 6.1 allows us to refine this definition: a path $(u_0, u_1, \ldots, u_h)$ is a *dependency path* if the times of the edges $(u_0, u_1), (u_1, u_2), \ldots, (u_{h-1}, u_h)$ increase monotonically.

LEMMA 6.1. *Set coloring parameters* $\ell(r)$ *and* κ *such that* $\ell(r) < \rho^r/\sqrt{d}$ *and* $\kappa > 1 + 3\beta\rho^{r+1}/\ell(r)$. *Then, any two fill operations at the same rank are independent if they have the same color.*

PROOF. Consider two fill operations, op_v and op_u, at the same rank and color acting on vertices v and u respectively. Let r be the rank of these operations and $\mathcal{M}$ be the set of vertices in the output at the beginning of rank r. If both v and u are ρ-well-spaced in $\mathcal{M}$ then op_v and op_u do not insert any Steiner vertices. Thus, op_v and op_u are independent. Otherwise, if v is not ρ-well-spaced the Progress Lemma implies that $\text{NN}_{\mathcal{M}}(v) \geq \rho^r$. Since $\ell(r) < \rho^r/\sqrt{d}$, the diameter of an r-tile is less than ρ^r, and thus v and u cannot be in the same r-tile. Since op_v and op_u have the same color, v and u are far apart, more precisely, $|vu| \geq (\kappa - 1)\ell(r) > 3\beta\rho^{r+1}$. By Fact 1, we know that any Steiner vertex w that op_v inserts satisfies $|vw| \leq \beta\,\text{NN}_{\mathcal{M}}(v)$. By the existence of op_v and op_u, we already know $\text{NN}_{\mathcal{M}}(v), \text{NN}_{\mathcal{M}}(u) < \rho^{r+1}$. Using the triangle inequality, we get $|uw| \geq |vu| - |vw| > 2\beta\rho^{r+1} > 2\beta\,\text{NN}_{\mathcal{M}}(u)$. The last inequality asserts that w cannot be a β-clipped Voronoi neighbor of u. Similar arguments can be made for u as well; therefore, the operations op_v and op_u are independent. □

We partition the nodes of the union graph $G^{\cup} = (V^{\cup}, E^{\cup})$ into several categories. The nodes $V^- = V \setminus \mathsf{range}(\mu)$ are called *obsolete* (squares Σ^-, operations Ω^-); these are the nodes of G that have no matching pairs in G'. The nodes $V^+ = V' \setminus \mathsf{dom}(\mu)$ are called *fresh* (squares Σ^+, operations Ω^+); these are the nodes of G' that have no matching pairs in G. Furthermore, we call a square $s \in V^{\cup}$ *inconsistent* if it is fresh or obsolete, or if it contains the vertex v^* of the symmetric difference of N and N'. We define an operation $op \in \mathsf{range}(\mu)$ to be *inconsistent* if it is reachable from an inconsistent square via a dependency path. We represent inconsistent nodes with $V^{\times}$ (squares $\Sigma^{\times}$, operations $\Omega^{\times}$). We define the *distance* between the executions with related inputs N and N' to be the number of obsolete, fresh, or inconsistent operations of the union graph, i.e., $|\Omega^- \cup \Omega^+ \cup \Omega^{\times}|$.

LEMMA 6.2. *For every operation in* $\Omega^- \cup \Omega^+ \cup \Omega^{\times}$, *there exists a dependency path from a square in* $\Sigma^{\times}$.

PROOF. By definition of inconsistent operations, an operation $op \in \Omega^{\times}$ can be reachable via a dependency path from $\Sigma^{\times}$. For unmatched operations, assume towards a contradiction that there exist an operation in $\Omega^- \cup \Omega^+$ that is not reachable from $\Sigma^{\times}$. Let op be the earliest of such operations. Let us assume that op is a dispatch operation acting on an input vertex v. Since op does not depend on an inconsistent square, it does not read an inconsistent square. Therefore, v is in $\mathsf{N} \cap \mathsf{N}'$ and lies in identical squares in both executions, which implies that `QTApxNN(v)` returns the same value for v in both executions and that their ranks are the same. Then, the definition of μ_o matches op with op' because op and op' are identical. Therefore, op is not a dispatch operation acting on an input vertex. Then, consider the operation op'' that creates op. By minimality of op, op'' can be reached via a dependency path from a square in $\Sigma^{\times}$. Extending that path to op proves the contradiction. □

As proven by Hudson and Türkoğlu [HT08], the function `QTClippedVoronoi` satisfies the following locality property: for a given input N, a size-conforming set of vertices $\mathcal{M} \supset \mathsf{N}$, and a square s read by `QTClippedVoronoi`, for all $x \in s$, $|vx| \in O(\text{NN}_{\mathcal{M}}(v))$. This property allows us to relate the operations on a dependency path geometrically.

LEMMA 6.3. *Consider two operations* op *and* op' *in* $G^{\cup}$ *acting on vertices* v *and* w. *If there exists a dependency path from* op' *to* op *and* op *is at rank* r, *then* $|vw| \in O(\rho^r)$.

PROOF. First, we show that for any edge in $G^{\cup}$, the distance between its nodes is short. We define the distance between a square and an operation to be the distance from the vertex of the operation to the farthest point in the square, and the distance between two operations to be the distance between the vertices on which they act. Consider an edge $e \in E$ with time $t_e = (r_e, c_e)$. The edge e consists of an operation $op_1 \in \Omega$ acting on v at time t_e and either a square s that it accesses (reads/writes) or another operation op_2 that it schedules. Using the locality result stated above, we bound the distance between op_1 and s by $O(\mathrm{NN}_{t_e}(v))$. Also, op_2 is within the same distance. Lemmas 5.1 and 5.2 bound $\mathrm{NN}_{t_e}(v)$ by $O(\rho^{r_e})$; thus, the distance between the nodes of e is at most $\alpha\rho^{r_e}$, where α is a constant. The same analysis applies for any edge $e' \in E^{\cup}$.

By definition of dependency paths, the times of the edges on a dependency path from op' to op monotonically increase. Assuming that the rank of op' is r', there can be at most κ^d edges for each rank between r' and r. Therefore, in the worst case, the distance between v and w is bounded by $\sum_{i=r'}^{r} \kappa^d \alpha \rho^i = \alpha\kappa^d \frac{\rho^{r+1}-\rho^{r'}}{\rho-1} < \alpha\kappa^d \frac{\rho^{r+1}}{\rho-1}$. Consequently, $|vw| \in O(\rho^r)$. □

In order to bound the distance between the executions with inputs N and N' which generate outputs M and M', we focus on the vertices rather than the operations. We define a vertex to be *affected* if there exists an obsolete, a fresh, or an inconsistent operation that acts on it. Since there is a constant number of operations acting on a given vertex (Lemma 5.4), the number of affected vertices measures the distance asymptotically. We define the sets of affected vertices in both executions: $\widehat{\mathsf{M}} = \{v \mid op \in \Omega^- \cup \Omega^\times \text{ acts on } v\}$ and $\widehat{\mathsf{M}}' = \{v \mid op \in \Omega^+ \cup \Omega^\times \text{ acts on } v\}$. The next two lemmas bound the number of affected vertices.

LEMMA 6.4. *For any vertex $v \in \widehat{\mathsf{M}}$, $|vv^*| \in O(\mathrm{NN}_{\mathsf{M}}(v))$ and for any $v \in \widehat{\mathsf{M}}'$, $|vv^*| \in O(\mathrm{NN}_{\mathsf{M}'}(v))$.*

PROOF. We prove the lemma for $v \in \widehat{\mathsf{M}}$; symmetric arguments apply for $\widehat{\mathsf{M}}'$. By definition of $\widehat{\mathsf{M}}$, there exists an operation $op_v \in \Omega^- \cup \Omega^\times$ acting on v at rank r. Lemma 6.2 suggests that there exists a dependency path from a square $s \in \Sigma^\times$ to op_v. Let op_u be the operation on this path that reads s; op_u acts on a vertex u at rank r_u. By Lemma 6.3, we know that $|vu| \in O(\rho^r)$. By that fact that op_u reads s, we know $|us|$ is in $O(\rho^{r_u})$ and the quadtree functions `QTAdd` and `QTRemove` guarantee that $|sv^*| \in O(|s|)$ which is in $O(\rho^{r_u})$ as well. Using the triangle inequality and the fact that $r_u \le r$, we bound $|vv^*|$ by $O(\rho^r)$. It only remains to prove that there is a ball around v of radius $\Omega(\rho^r)$ empty of vertices of M. Lemma 5.2 proves precisely this. □

LEMMA 6.5 (DISTANCE). *The distance between two executions with related inputs is bounded by $O(\log \Delta)$.*

PROOF. The distance is asymptotically bounded by $|\widehat{\mathsf{M}}| + |\widehat{\mathsf{M}}'|$. Consider the vertices $v \in \widehat{\mathsf{M}}$ with $|vv^*| \in [2^i, 2^{i+1})$. By Lemma 6.4, we can assign non-overlapping empty balls of radius $\Omega(2^i)$ to them. Therefore, there is a constant number of such vertices for any i. At most $O(\log \Delta)$ values of i cover $\widehat{\mathsf{M}}$, so $|\widehat{\mathsf{M}}| \in O(\log \Delta)$. Similar arguments apply to $\widehat{\mathsf{M}}'$. □

7. DYNAMIC UPDATE ALGORITHM

We describe an algorithm for dynamically updating the output of `StableWS` when the input is modified by insertion/deletion of a vertex, prove it correct (Lemma 7.2) and efficient (Theorem 7.3).

```
Global queues:  Ω⊖, Ω⊕, Ω⊗
Add (N, Π, v*) =
  (Π′, Σ⁻) ← QTAdd(Π, v*)
  Ω⊕ ← {NewOp(v*, ⌊log_ρ QTApxNN(v*)⌋, 0, nil)};  Ω⊖, Ω⊗ ← ∅
  PropagateWS(N, Σ⁻ ∪ {square of v*}) ; return (N ∪ {v*}, Π′)

Remove (N, Π, v*) =
  (Π′, Σ⁻) ← QTRemove(Π, v*)
  Ω⊖ ← {Dispatch of v*};  Ω⊕, Ω⊗ ← ∅
  PropagateWS(N, Σ⁻ ∪ {square of v*}) ; return (N \ {v*}, Π′)

PropagateWS (N, Σ⊗) =
  MarkReaders (Σ⊗, 0)
  for each s ∈ Σ⊗ and each v ∈ N ∩ vertices of s do
    Ω⊖ ← Ω⊖ ∪ {Dispatch of v}
    Ω⊕ ← Ω⊕ ∪ {NewOp(v, ⌊log_ρ QTApxNN(v)⌋, 0, nil)}
  for r = min rank in Ω⊖ ∪ Ω⊕ ∪ Ω⊗ to ⌊log_ρ √d⌋ do
    UndoOps (r, 0)
    for each op ∈ (Ω⊕ ∪ Ω⊗)|_{r,0} do Dispatch (op, Ω⊕)
    for c = 1 to κ^d do
      UndoOps (r, c)
      for each op ∈ (Ω⊕ ∪ Ω⊗)|_{r,c} do
        Fill (op, Ω⊕)
        MarkReaders (squares containing op.steiners, (r, c))

UndoOps (r, c) =
  for each op ∈ (Ω⊖ ∪ Ω⊗)|_{r,c} do
    Ω⊖ ← Ω⊖ ∪ op.children
    MarkReaders (squares containing op.steiners, (r, c))
    remove all vertices in op.steiners
  Ω⊗ ← Ω⊗ \ Ω⊖|_{r,c}
  ResetEdges(Ω⊗|_{r,c})

MarkReaders (Σ̂, t) =
  for each s ∈ Σ̂ and each op that reads s do
    if (op.rank, op.color) > t then Ω⊗ ← Ω⊗ ∪ {op}
```

Figure 4: Pseudo-code for the dynamic algorithm.

Our dynamic update algorithm is a change-propagation algorithm. Given the input modification, the update algorithm re-executes the actions of the stable algorithm for the part of the computation affected by the modification and undoes the part of the computation that becomes obsolete. More precisely, the algorithm maintains distinct set of operations for removal $\Omega^\ominus$ (obsolete operations), for execution $\Omega^\oplus$ (fresh operations), and for re-execution $\Omega^\otimes$ (inconsistent operations), which contain the operations that become obsolete, that need to be executed, and that become inconsistent respectively; inconsistent operations are updated by deleting their old versions and executing them again, which may now perform actions different than before. The algorithm removes and executes operations in the same order as the stable algorithm and uses the `Dispatch` and `Fill` operations of the stable algorithm for executing fresh operations.

Figure 4 shows the pseudo-code for the `Add` and `Remove` functions for inserting and deleting a vertex v^* into and from the input, and the `PropagateWS` function for dynamic updates. Given v^*, `Add`/`Remove` updates the quadtree, determines the set of inconsistent squares $\Sigma^\otimes$, and initializes the fresh/obsolete set by creating a dispatch operation or by marking the old dispatch operation acting on v^*. Both functions then call `PropagateWS`.

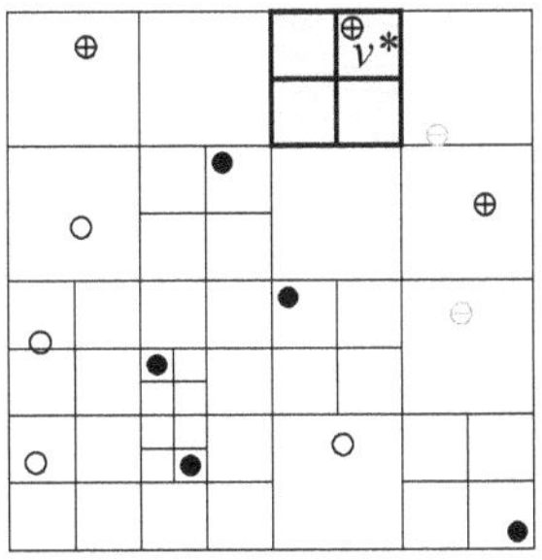

Figure 5: Dynamic update after insertion of v^*. Solid vertices are input (N), vertices marked + are inserted, vertices marked − are deleted. Gray squares are inconsistent. The four smaller gray squares are fresh; they replace the bigger obsolete square.

The PropagateWS function starts by updating the operation sets by finding the input vertices that are contained in the inconsistent squares, deleting their dispatch operations, and creating new dispatch operations for them. It also initializes the inconsistent operation set, as MarkReaders marks inconsistent all operations that read a square in $\Sigma^{\otimes}$. The algorithm then proceeds in time order, first undoing the obsolete and inconsistent operations and then performing the fresh and inconsistent operations by calling Dispatch and Fill (Figure 3). The UndoOps function undoes the work of obsolete and fresh operations by marking all of their children for removal and by deleting quadtree dependencies (edges) from the computation graph. It also prepares the live inconsistent operations for re-execution by resetting their dependencies. The MarkReaders function expands the set of inconsistent operations as the set of vertices in a square changes due to removed or freshly executed fill operations.

As their notation suggests, the obsolete, fresh, and inconsistent operations used by the algorithm correspond to those defined in the stability analysis; Lemma 7.1 makes this correspondence precise.

LEMMA 7.1. *The set of operations processed in the dynamic update algorithm, $\Omega^{\ominus} \cup \Omega^{\oplus} \cup \Omega^{\otimes}$, is equal to the set of obsolete, fresh, and inconsistent operations, $\Omega^{-} \cup \Omega^{+} \cup \Omega^{\times}$.*

PROOF. Let $A = \Omega^{\ominus} \cup \Omega^{\oplus} \cup \Omega^{\otimes}$ and $B = \Omega^{-} \cup \Omega^{+} \cup \Omega^{\times}$. We prove the equality by showing containment in both directions; for space restrictions, we only show one direction. The other direction is similarly shown in [ACHT10]. Towards a contradiction, assume that $B \not\subset A$ and let *op* be the earliest operation in $B \setminus A$. If $op \in \Omega^{-}$ then either *op* is a dispatch operation acting on an input vertex or there is another operation $op' \in \Omega^{-} \cup \Omega^{\times}$ that creates *op*. In the first case, *op* depends on a square in $\Sigma^{\times}$, which implies $op \in A$. In the second case, by the minimality of *op*, $op' \in A$. Since the update algorithm processes all children of op', $op \in A$. Similar arguments show that $op \in \Omega^{+}$ implies $op \in A$. Therefore *op* must be in $\Omega^{\times}$, i.e., there exists a dependency path from a square $s \in \Sigma^{\times}$ to *op*. Pick the longest dependency path that reaches *op* and let $op' \neq op$ be the latest operation on that path. If no such op' exists then *op* is a dispatch operation acting on an input vertex that reads a square from $\Sigma^{\times}$. The initialization in PropagateWS puts *op* in A. In the other case that op' exists, by minimality of *op*, op' is in A and the dependency path from op' to *op* ensures that our update algorithm schedules *op* to one of the sets $\Omega^{\ominus}$, $\Omega^{\oplus}$, or $\Omega^{\otimes}$, depending on the type of dependency between *op* and op'. Contradiction. □

When completed, PropagateWS updates the output to $\tilde{\mathsf{M}}$ and the computation graph to $\tilde{G}$ as if StableWS is run from-scratch with N' as input, computing M' and G'.

LEMMA 7.2 (ISOMORPHISM). *The output sets $\tilde{\mathsf{M}}$ and M' are equal and there exists an isomorphism $\phi : \tilde{G} \rightarrow G'$ that preserves the vertex and time of each operation.*

PROOF. Due to space restrictions we skip some parts of the proof. We prove equality of the output and build ϕ inductively. Define the sets of operations according to their creation times: $\Omega_t^{\ominus} = \{op \in \Omega^{\ominus} \mid op \text{ is created at time} < t\}$ ($\Omega_0^{\ominus}$ is the set of dispatch operations acting on input vertices). Define a similar assemblage for the $^{\oplus}$, $^{\otimes}$, and $'$ sets. Let $\tilde{G}_t$ be the subgraph of $\tilde{G}$ induced by the nodes $\tilde{\Omega}_t \cup \tilde{\Sigma}$ excluding the edges with time $\geq t$; the excluded edges are related to the execution of operations at time $\geq t$. Define G'_t similarly and let $\tilde{\mathsf{M}}_t$ be the updated set of vertices obtained by removing and inserting vertices until time t, just before the executing operations at time t.

Initially, $\tilde{\mathsf{M}}_0 = \mathsf{M}'_0 = \mathsf{N}'$ and $\tilde{\Sigma} = \Sigma'$. Therefore, there exists an isomorphism $\phi_0 : \tilde{G}_0 \rightarrow G'_0$. Assume the inductive hypothesis at time t, that $\tilde{\mathsf{M}}_t = \mathsf{M}'_t$ and that we have an isomorphism $\phi_t : \tilde{G}_t \rightarrow G'_t$. Pick $op \in \tilde{\Omega}_t$ with time t and let $op' = \phi_t(op)$. There are three cases: *op* is either in $\Omega_t^{\oplus}$, or in $\Omega_t^{\otimes}$, or otherwise *op* is an operation that has not been modified. In all the cases, one can show that the operations *op* and op' read the same data. Because our functions are all deterministic, *op* and op' execute similarly.

Then, we have a natural correspondence between the operations that *op* and op' create and the Steiner vertices they insert (in any). Therefore, $\tilde{\mathsf{M}}_{t+1} = \mathsf{M}'_{t+1}$. Furthermore, because *op* and op' read and write the same squares the edges incident to these operations have natural correspondences as well. Extending ϕ_t to ϕ_{t+1} by adding these correspondences completes proof of the inductive step. □

THEOREM 7.3. *The **Add** and **Remove** functions modify the output in $O(\log \Delta)$ time and maintain a ρ-well-spaced output of optimal-size with respect to the updated input.*

PROOF. By Lemma 7.2, we know that the output is the same as what would have been generated by executing from scratch StableWS with the new input, therefore, Theorem 4.4 applies. The quadtree can be updated in $O(\log \Delta)$ time. Furthermore, Lemma 7.1 relates the runtime of the update algorithm to the distance between the executions with the old and the new inputs. Finally, Lemma 6.5 bounds the runtime of PropagateWS as desired. □

8. LOWER BOUND

We present a lower bound proving that any algorithm which explicitly maintains a well-spaced superset requires $\Omega(\log \Delta)$ time per dynamic update. Consider dynamically inserting a new point very close to an existing input vertex. Even the optimal dynamic algorithm is forced to insert geometrically growing rings of new Steiner vertices around the dynamically inserted vertex. We prove that we can iterate this process using a gadget. This shows that our algorithm is worst-case optimal compared to all other explicit algorithms, even in an amortized setting.

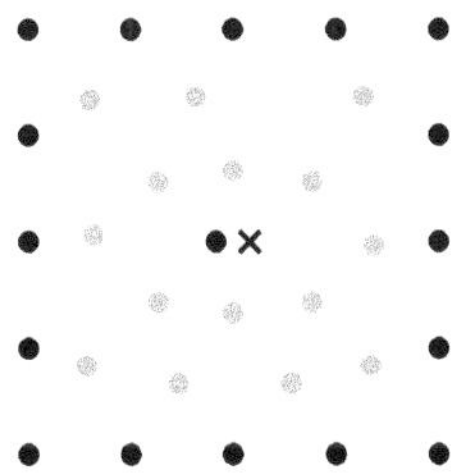

Figure 6: Inserting x creates $\Omega(\log \Delta)$ fresh Steiner vertices.

We define a gadget (see Figure 6) consisting of points in the hypercube $[0, k^{-1/d}]^d$. Consider two vertices at distance

$1/\Delta$ from each other in the middle of the box; let one of them be the *dynamic vertex* x which will be inserted later. Also, consider a grid of $O(1)$ vertices on each of the faces of the hypercube, chosen according to the scheme of Hudson [Hud07, p.79]. The input N consists of tiling $[0,1]^d$ with the gadgets, $k^{1/d}$ for each dimension, without any dynamic vertex. The dynamic modification sequence consists of inserting k dynamic vertices, one for each gadget.

LEMMA 8.1. *Inserting the dynamic vertex to a single gadget requires inserting $\Omega(\log \Delta)$ Steiner vertices.*

PROOF. Let N be the input before adding the dynamic vertex x. Any size-optimal output M of N has $O(1)$ Steiner vertices inside the gadget box. Consider inserting x and let $\mathsf{N}' = \mathsf{N} \cup \{x\}$ and $\delta = \mathrm{NN}_{\mathsf{N}'}(x)$. Draw the segment from x to the farthest point in $\mathrm{Vor}_{\mathsf{N}'}(x)$. This segment has length at least $\ell = \frac{1}{4} - \frac{\delta}{2}$. Consider the Voronoi diagram of a ρ-well-spaced superset M' of N' and consider the Voronoi cells that this segment cuts. Let $v_1, v_2, \ldots$ be the vertices of those Voronoi cells, in order. We know that the vertices in M' are ρ-well-spaced, therefore, $|v_1x| \leq 2\rho\,\mathrm{NN}_{\mathsf{N}'}(x) = 2\rho\delta$. Also, the nearest neighbour distance of v_1 is at most $|v_1x|$. We can use the same argument to get $|v_1v_2| \leq 2\rho|v_1x|$ and repeat. In other words, distance from x grows only geometrically as we walk down the segment: covering the distance ℓ requires $\Omega(\log 1/\delta) = \Omega(\log \Delta)$ many Steiner vertices. This implies that M differs from M' in at least $O(\log \Delta)$ vertices. □

THEOREM 8.2 (LOWER BOUND). *There exists an initial input and a set of n dynamic insertions that forces any algorithm to insert $\Omega(n \log \Delta)$ new Steiner vertices.*

PROOF. In the above scheme, let $k = n$. Then, we would like to prove that inserting n dynamic vertices requires inserting $\Omega(n \log \Delta)$ Steiner vertices. We refer to a technique of inserting vertices to the hypercube faces [Hud07]. It was developed precisely to make sure that certain algorithms need not add vertices outside the hypercube when making the interior ρ-well-spaced. Contrapositively, adding vertices outside a gadget does not help make the gadget, with its dynamic vertex, be ρ-well-spaced. Thus the prior lemma applies to each gadget individually, showing that the final ρ-well-spaced superset must contain at least $\Omega(n \log \Delta)$ Steiner vertices, for a carefully selected ρ. Since there exists a constant $\rho > 1$ such that the original input of n gadgets is ρ-well-spaced, the initial output must be of size $O(n)$. This completes our proof. □

9. IMPLEMENTATION & EXPERIMENTS

We implemented[2] the `StableWS` and `PropagateWS` algorithms in C++. Given a set of vertices N, `StableWS` computes a well-spaced superset M of N and `PropagateWS` updates the output dynamically as the input is modified by insertions and deletions. Our implementation is a preliminary prototype: it follows closely the algorithmic description with minor optimizations. As with other meshing software (e.g., [She97]), ours is highly susceptible to numerical error. We therefore used an exact arithmetic package based on floating-point filters. We have verified the correctness of our implementation by considering numerous randomly generated inputs and some real models.

Figure 8: A model of Lake Superior meshed by `StableWS`.

[2]Source code is available for download at http://nagoya.uchicago.edu/~cotter/projects/wsp

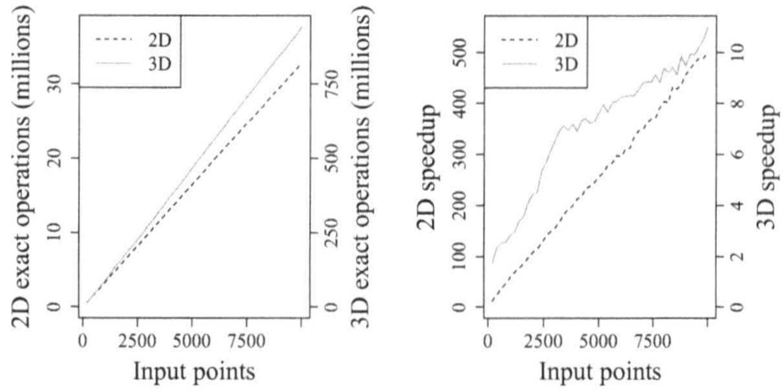

Figure 7: Left: cost of `StableWS` on random inputs. Right: speedup of `PropagateWS` one unit changes relative to `StableWS` from scratch.

In experiments, we generate point sets of double-precision floating-point numbers drawn uniformly at random from the unit box in 2D and 3D. For a given input, we measure the cost of running `StableWS` on the entire input, and the average cost of performing an update after a *unit dynamic change* that removes a random input vertex, updates the output using `PropagateWS`, adds a new vertex, and updates again. To focus on algorithmic concerns we use exact arithmetic operation counts to measure run-time cost. These dominate runtime even in highly optimized implementations. In all experiments, we chose $\rho = \sqrt{2}$, and $\beta = 2$ in 2D or $\beta = 2\sqrt{2}/\sqrt{3}$ in 3D, with the color parameters $\ell(r) = \rho^{r-1/2}/\sqrt{d}$ and $\kappa = \lceil 1 + 3\sqrt{d}\beta\rho^{3/2} \rceil$. For both two and three dimensions κ is 16; the number of colors in 2D is $16^2 = 256$ and in 3D it is $16^3 = 4096$.

Figure 7 shows the speedup of dynamic updates calculated as the ratio of the cost of running `StableWS` to the average cost of one dynamic update with `PropagateWS`. Each plotted point is the average over 100 different unit dynamic changes on each of 10 random inputs. We include 2D and 3D measurements on the same plot; note that the y-axis scales are different (the constant factors are larger in 3D). Consistent with our analysis, the measurements indicate that in both 2D and 3D the cost of `StableWS` grows close to linearly with the input sizes, while dynamic updates yield linear speedups.

10. CONCLUSION

We present a dynamic algorithm for computing a well-spaced point set of a dynamically changing set of input points. Our algorithm is efficient, finds an optimal-size output, consumes linear space, and responds to dynamic modifications in worst-case optimal time. The underlying technique to these results is a stable algorithm for computing well-spaced point sets whose executions can be represented with computation graphs that remain similar when the input sets themselves are similar. Our dynamic update algorithm takes advantage of stability to update the output efficiently by propagating the input modification through the computation graph. To assess the practicality of our approach we present a prototype implementation. Our experiments show that the algorithm can be implemented efficiently such that it delivers performance consistent with our theoretical bounds. We expect a well-polished implementation will provide static performance comparable to the state of the art, and dynamic performance orders of magnitude faster.

11. REFERENCES

[ABBT06] Umut A. Acar, Guy E. Blelloch, Matthias Blume, and Kanat Tangwongsan. An experimental analysis of self-adjusting computation. In *Proceedings of the ACM SIGPLAN Conference on PLDI*, 2006.

[ABTT08] Umut A. Acar, Guy E. Blelloch, Kanat Tangwongsan, and Duru Türkoğlu. Robust Kinetic Convex Hulls in 3D. In *16th Annual European Symposium on Algorithms*, 2008.

[Aca05] Umut A. Acar. *Self-Adjusting Computation.* PhD thesis, Department of Computer Science, Carnegie Mellon University, May 2005.

[ACHT10] Umut A. Acar, Andrew Cotter, Benoît Hudson, and Duru Türkoğlu. Dynamic well-spaced point sets. Technical Report TTIC-TR-2010-1, Toyota Technological Institute at Chicago, 2010.

[BDS+92] J.-D. Boissonnat, O. Devillers, R. Schott, M. Teillaud, and M. Yvinec. Applications of random sampling to on-line algorithms in computational geometry. *Discrete Computional Geometry*, 8:51–71, 1992.

[BEG94] Marshall Bern, David Eppstein, and John R. Gilbert. Provably Good Mesh Generation. *Journal of Computer and System Sciences*, 48(3):384–409, 1994.

[CAR+09] Nuttapong Chentanez, Ron Alterovitz, Daniel Ritchie, Lita Cho, Kris K. Hauser, Ken Goldberg, Jonathan R. Shewchuk, and James F. O'Brien. Interactive simulation of surgical needle insertion and steering. In *Proceedings of ACM SIGGRAPH*, Aug 2009.

[CDE+00] Siu-Wing Cheng, Tamal Krishna Dey, Herbert Edelsbrunner, Michael A. Facello, and Shang-Hua Teng. Sliver Exudation. *Journal of the ACM*, 47(5):883–904, 2000.

[CGS06] Narcis Coll, Marité Guerrieri, and J. Antoni Sellarès. Mesh modification under local domain changes. In *15th Intl. Meshing Roundtable*, pages 39–56, 2006.

[Che89] L. Paul Chew. Guaranteed-quality triangular meshes. Technical Report TR-89-983, Department of Computer Science, Cornell University, 1989.

[CMS93] Kenneth L. Clarkson, Kurt Mehlhorn, and Raimund Seidel. Four results on randomized incremental constructions. *Computational Geometry Theory and Application*, 3:185–212, 1993.

[HMP06] Benoît Hudson, Gary L. Miller, and Todd Phillips. Sparse Voronoi Refinement. In *15th Intl. Meshing Roundtable*, pages 339–356, 2006. Long version in Carnegie Mellon University Tech. Report CMU-CS-06-132.

[HPÜ05] Sariel Har-Peled and Alper Üngör. A time-optimal Delaunay refinement algorithm in two dimensions. In *21st Symposium on Computational Geometry*, pages 228–236, 2005.

[HT08] Benoît Hudson and Duru Türkoğlu. An efficient query structure for mesh refinement. In *Canadian Conf. on Comp. Geometry*, 2008.

[Hud07] Benoît Hudson. *Dynamic Mesh Refinement.* PhD thesis, School of Computer Science, Carnegie Mellon University, December 2007. Available as Technical Report CMU-CS-07-162.

[LT01] Xiang-Yang Li and Shang-Hua Teng. Generating well-shaped Delaunay meshes in 3D. In *Proceedings of the 12th Annual ACM-SIAM Symposium on Discrete Algorithms*, pages 28–37, 2001.

[LTÜ99] Xiang-Yang Li, Shang-Hua Teng, and Alper Üngör. Simultaneous refinement and coarsening for adaptive meshing. *Engineering with Computers*, 15(3):280–291, 1999.

[LWAF09] Ruy Ley-Wild, Umut A. Acar, and Matthew Fluet. A cost semantics for self-adjusting computation. In *Proceedings of the 26th Annual ACM Symposium on Principles of Programming Languages*, 2009.

[MBF04] Neil Molino, Zhaosheng Bao, and Ron Fedkiw. A virtual node algorithm for changing mesh topology during simulation. In *SIGGRAPH*, 2004.

[MTT+96] Gary L. Miller, Dafna Talmor, Shang-Hua Teng, Noel Walkington, and Han Wang. Control Volume Meshes Using Sphere Packing: Generation, Refinement and Coarsening. In *5th Intl. Meshing Roundtable*, pages 47–61, 1996.

[Mul91] Ketan Mulmuley. Randomized multidimensional search trees (extended abstract): dynamic sampling. In *Proceedings of the 7th Annual Symposium on Computational Geometry*, pages 121–131, 1991.

[NvdS04] Han-Wen Nienhuys and A. Frank van der Stappen. A Delaunay approach to interactive cutting in triangulated surfaces. In *fifth Intl. Workshop on Algorithmic Foundations of Robotics*, 2004.

[Rup95] Jim Ruppert. A Delaunay refinement algorithm for quality 2-dimensional mesh generation. *J. Algorithms*, 18(3):548–585, 1995.

[Sch91] Otfried Schwarzkopf. Dynamic maintenance of geometric structures made easy. In *Proceedings of the 32nd Annual Symposium on Foundations of Computer Science*, pages 197–206, 1991.

[She97] Jonathan Richard Shewchuk. Adaptive Precision Floating-Point Arithmetic and Fast Robust Geometric Predicates. *Discrete & Computational Geometry*, 18(3):305–363, 1997.

[STÜ07] Daniel Spielman, Shang-Hua Teng, and Alper Üngör. Parallel Delaunay refinement: Algorithms and analyses. *IJCGA*, 17:1–30, 2007.

[Tal97] Dafna Talmor. *Well-Spaced Points for Numerical Methods.* PhD thesis, Carnegie Mellon University, August 1997. Available as Technical Report CMU-CS-97-164.

Manifold Reconstruction using Tangential Delaunay Complexes *

Jean-Daniel Boissonnat
Jean-Daniel.Boissonnat@sophia.inria.fr

Arijit Ghosh
Arijit.Ghosh@sophia.inria.fr

INRIA, Team Geometrica
2004 route des Lucioles
06902 Sophia-Antipolis, France

ABSTRACT

We give a provably correct algorithm to reconstruct a k-dimensional manifold embedded in d-dimensional Euclidean space. Input to our algorithm is a point sample coming from an unknown manifold. Our approach is based on two main ideas : the notion of tangential Delaunay complex defined in [6, 19, 20], and the technique of sliver removal by weighting the sample points [13]. Differently from previous methods, we do not construct any subdivision of the embedding d-dimensional space. As a result, the running time of our algorithm depends only linearly on the extrinsic dimension d while it depends quadratically on the size of the input sample, and exponentially on the intrinsic dimension k. To the best of our knowledge, this is the first certified algorithm for manifold reconstruction whose complexity depends linearly on the ambient dimension. We also prove that for a dense enough sample the output of our algorithm is isotopic to the manifold and a close geometric approximation of the manifold.

Categories and Subject Descriptors

F.2.2 [**Nonnumerical Algorithms and problems**]: Geometrical problems and computations; I.3.5 [**Computational Geometry and Object Modeling**]: Curve, surface, solid, and object representations.

General Terms

Algorithms, Theory.

Keywords

Tangential Delaunay complex, Weighted Delaunay triangulation, manifold reconstruction, manifold learning, sampling conditions, sliver exudation.

*This work was partially supported by the ANR project GAIA. For the full version of the paper refer to [7].

1. INTRODUCTION

Manifold reconstruction consists in computing a PL approximation of an unknown manifold $\mathbb{M} \subset \mathbb{R}^d$ from a finite sample of unorganized points $\mathcal{P}$ lying on $\mathbb{M}$ or close to $\mathbb{M}$. When the manifold is a two-dimensional surface embedded in $\mathbb{R}^3$, the problem is known as the surface reconstruction problem. Surface reconstruction is a problem of major practical interest which has been extensively studied in the fields of Computational Geometry, Computer Graphics and Computer Vision. In the last decade, solid foundations have been established and the problem is now pretty well understood. Refer to Dey's book [17], and the survey by Cazals and Giesen in [10] for recent results. The output of those methods is a triangulated surface that approximates $\mathbb{M}$. This triangulated surface is usually extracted from a 3-dimensional subdivision of the ambient space (typically a grid or a triangulation). Although rather inoffensive in 3-dimensional space, such data structures depend exponentially on the dimension of the ambient space, and all attempts to extend those geometric approaches to more general manifolds has led to algorithms whose complexities depend exponentially on d [26, 11, 14].

The problem in higher dimensions is also of great practical interest in data analysis and machine learning. In those fields, the general assumption is that, even if the data are represented as points in a very high dimensional space $\mathbb{R}^d$, they in fact live on a manifold of much smaller intrinsic dimension [28]. If the manifold is linear, well-known global techniques like principal component analysis (PCA) or multi-dimensional scaling (MDS) can be efficiently applied. When the manifold is highly nonlinear, several more local techniques have attracted much attention in visual perception and many other areas of science. Among the prominent algorithms are Isomap [30], LLE [27], Laplacian eigenmaps [4], Hessian eigenmaps [18], diffusion maps [24, 25], principal manifolds [31]. Most of those methods reduces to computing an eigendecomposition of some connection matrix. In all cases, the output is a mapping of the original data points into $\mathbb{R}^k$ where k is the estimated intrinsic dimension of $\mathbb{M}$. Those methods come with no or very limited guarantees. For example, Isomap provides a correct embedding only if $\mathbb{M}$ is isometric to a convex open set of $\mathbb{R}^k$. To be able to better approximate the sampled manifold, another route is to extend the work on surface reconstruction and to construct a PL approximation of $\mathbb{M}$ from the sample in such a way that, under appropriate sampling conditions, the quality of the approximation can be guaranteed. First investigations along this line can be found in the work of

Cheng, Dey and Ramos [14], and Boissonnat, Guibas and Oudot [8]. In both cases, however, the complexity of the algorithms is exponential in the ambient dimension d, which highly reduces their practical relevance.

In this paper, we extend the geometric techniques developped in small dimensions and propose a way to avoid computing data structures in the ambient space. We assume that $\mathbb{M}$ is a smooth manifold of known dimension k and that we can compute the tangent space to $\mathbb{M}$ at any sample point. Under those conditions, we propose a provably correct algorithm that allows to construct a simplicial complex of dimension k that approximates $\mathbb{M}$. The complexity of the algorithm is linear in d, quadratic in the size n of the sample, and exponential in k. Our work builds on [14] and [8] but dramatically reduces the dependance on d. To the best of our knowledge, this is the first certified algorithm for manifold reconstruction whose complexity depends only linearly on the ambient dimension. In the same spirit, Chazal and Oudot [12] have devised an algorithm of intrinsic complexity to solve the easier problem of computing the homology of a manifold from a sample.

Our approach is based on two main ideas : the notion of *tangential Delaunay complex* defined in [20, 6, 19], and the technique of sliver removal by weighting the sample points [13]. The tangential complex is obtained by gluing local (Delaunay) triangulations around each sample point. The tangential complex is a subcomplex of the d-dimensional Delaunay triangulation of the sample points but it can be computed using mostly operations in the k-dimensional tangent spaces at the sample points. Hence the dependence on k rather than d in the complexity. However, due to the presence of so-called inconsistencies, the local triangulations may not form a triangulated manifold. Although this problem has already been reported [20], no solution was known except for the case of curves ($k = 1$) [19]. We show that we can remove inconsistencies by weighting the sample points under appropriate sample conditions. We can then prove that the approximation returned by our algorithm is isotopic to $\mathbb{M}$, and a close geometric approximation of $\mathbb{M}$.

Our algorithm can be seen as a *local* version of the cocone algorithm of Cheng et al. [14]. By local, we mean that we do not compute any d-dimensional data structure like a grid or a triangulation of the ambient space. Still, the tangential complex is a subcomplex of the d-dimensional Delaunay triangulation of the data points and therefore implicitly relies on a global partition of the ambient space. This is key to our analysis and makes our method depart from other local algorithms that have been proposed in the surface reconstruction literature [16, 23].

Notations

In the rest of the paper, we assume that $\mathbb{M}$ is a smooth manifold of dimension k embedded in $\mathbb{R}^d$. We call $\mathcal{P} = \{p_1, \ldots, p_n\}$ a finite sample of points from $\mathbb{M}$. We denote by T_p the k-dimensional tangent space at point $p \in \mathbb{M}$. We write $B(c, r)$ for the d-dimensional ball centered at c of radius r. We define the angle between two vector spaces U and V as

$$UV = \max_{u \in U} \min_{v \in V} \angle uv. \tag{1}$$

If τ is a j-simplex, the $(d-j)$-dimensional normal space of $\text{aff}(\tau)$ is denoted by N_τ.

2. DEFINITIONS AND PRELIMINARIES

2.1 Weighted Delaunay triangulation

2.1.1 Weighted points

A weighted point is a pair consisting of a point p of $\mathbb{R}^d$, called the *center* of the weighted point, and a non-negative real number $\omega(p)$, called the *weight* of the weighted point. It might be convenient to visualize the weighted point $(p, \omega(p))$ as the hypersphere (we will simply say sphere in the sequel) centered at p of radius $\omega(p)$.

Two weighted points (or spheres) $(p, \omega(p))$ and $(q, \omega(q))$ are called *orthogonal* when $\|p-q\|^2 = \omega(p)^2 + \omega(q)^2$, *further than orthogonal* when $\|p-q\|^2 > \omega(p)^2 + \omega(q)^2$, and *closer than orthogonal* when $\|p-q\|^2 < \omega(p)^2 + \omega(q)^2$.

Given a point set $\mathcal{P} = \{p_1, \ldots, p_n\} \subseteq \mathbb{R}^d$, a *weight function* on $\mathcal{P}$ is a non-negative real-valued function $\omega : \mathcal{P} \to [0, \infty)$. Write $p_i^\omega = (p_i, \omega(p_i))$ and $\mathcal{P}^\omega = \{p_1^\omega, \ldots, p_n^\omega\}$.

We define the *relative amplitude* of ω, denoted as $\tilde{\omega}$, as $\max_{p \in \mathcal{P}, q \in \mathcal{P}\setminus\{p\}} \frac{\omega(p)}{\|p-q\|}$. In the paper, we assume that $\tilde{\omega} \leq \omega_0 < 1/2$, for some constant ω_0 to be fixed later.

Given a subset τ of $d+1$ weighted points whose centers are affinely independent, there exists a unique sphere orthogonal to the weighted points of τ. The sphere is called the *orthosphere* of τ and its center and radius are called the *orthocenter* and the *orthoradius* of τ. If τ is a j-simplex, $j < d$, the orthosphere of τ is the smallest sphere that is orthogonal to the (weighted) vertices of τ. Plainly, its center o_τ lies in $\text{aff}(\tau)$. The radius of the orthosphere of τ is denoted by R'_τ.

A finite set of weighted points $\mathcal{P}^\omega$ is said to be in *general position* if there exists no sphere orthogonal to $d+2$ weighted points of $\mathcal{P}^\omega$.

2.1.2 Weighted Voronoi diagram and Delaunay triangulation

Let ω be a weight function defined over $\mathcal{P}$. We define the weighted Voronoi cell of $p \in \mathcal{P}$ as

$$\begin{aligned} \text{Vor}^\omega(p) = \{x \in \mathbb{R}^d \quad &: \quad \|p-x\|^2 - \omega^2(p) \\ &\leq \quad \|q-x\|^2 - \omega^2(q), \forall q \in \mathcal{P}\}. \end{aligned}$$

The weighted Voronoi cells and their k-dimensional faces, $0 \leq k \leq d$, form a cell complex, called the weighted Voronoi diagram of $\mathcal{P}$, that decomposes $\mathbb{R}^d$ into convex polyhedral cells. See [2].

Let τ be a subset of points of $\mathcal{P}$ and write $\text{Vor}^\omega(\tau) = \cap_{x \in \tau} \text{Vor}^\omega(x)$. If the points of $\mathcal{P}$ are in general position, $\text{Vor}^\omega(\tau) = \emptyset$ when $|\tau| > d+1$. The collection of all simplices $\text{conv}(\tau)$ such that $\text{Vor}^\omega(\tau) \neq \emptyset$ constitutes the weighted Delaunay triangulation $\text{Del}^\omega(\mathcal{P})$. The mapping that associates to the face $\text{Vor}^\omega(\tau)$ of $\text{Vor}^\omega(\mathcal{P})$ the face $\text{conv}(\tau)$ of $\text{Del}^\omega(\mathcal{P})$ is a *duality*, i.e. a bijection that reverses the inclusion relation.

Alternatively, a d-simplex τ is in $\text{Del}^\omega(\mathcal{P})$ if the orthosphere of τ is further than orthogonal from all weighted points in $\mathcal{P}^\omega \setminus \{\tau^\omega\}$.

The weighted Delaunay triangulation of a set of weighted points can be computed efficiently in small dimensions and has found many applications, see e.g. [3, 10]. In this paper, we use weighted Delaunay triangulations for two main reasons. The first one is that the restriction of a d-dimensional weighted Voronoi diagram to an affine space of dimension

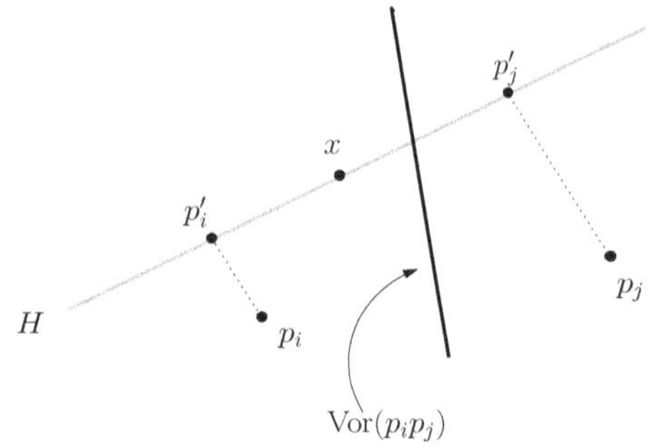

Figure 1: Refer to Lemma 1. The red line denotes the k-dimensional plane H and the black line denotes $\mathrm{Vor}^\omega(p_ip_j)$.

k is a k-dimensional weighted Voronoi diagram that can be computed without computing the d-dimensional diagram (see Lemma 1). The other main reason is that some flat simplices named slivers can be removed from a Delaunay triangulation by weighting the vertices (see [14, 8, 13] and Section 4).

LEMMA 1. *Let H be a k-dimensional affine space of $\mathbb{R}^d$. The restriction of the weighted Voronoi diagram of $\mathcal{P}$ to H is the k-dimensional weighted Voronoi diagram of $\mathcal{P}'$ where $\mathcal{P}'$ is the orthogonal projection of $\mathcal{P}$ onto H and the squared weight of p'_i is $\omega^2(p_i) - \|p_i - p'_i\|^2$.*

PROOF. By Pythagoras theorem, we have $\forall x \in H \cap \mathrm{Vor}^\omega(p_i)$, $\|x-p_i\|^2 - \omega^2(p_i) \le \|x-p_j\|^2 - \omega^2(p_j) \Leftrightarrow \|x - p'_i\|^2 + \|p_i - p'_i\|^2 - \omega^2(p_i) \le \|x - p'_j\|^2 + \|p_j - p'_j\|^2 - \omega^2(p_j)$, where p'_i denotes the orthogonal projection of $p_i \in \mathcal{P}$ onto H. Hence the restriction of $\mathrm{Vor}^\omega(\mathcal{P})$ to H is the weighted Voronoi diagram of the weighted points $(p'_i, \omega_i) \in H$ where $\omega_i^2 = -\|p_i - p'_i\|^2 + \omega^2(p_i)$. □

LEMMA 2 ([13]). *If τ is a simplex of $\mathrm{Del}^\omega(\mathcal{P})$, then*

1. *$\forall z \in \mathrm{aff}(\mathrm{Vor}^\omega(\tau))$ and $\forall p, q \in \tau$ we have $\|q - z\| \le \frac{\|p-z\|}{\sqrt{1-4\omega_0^2}}$.*
2. *$R_\tau \le \frac{R'_\tau}{\sqrt{1-4\omega_0^2}}$.*
3. *$\forall z \in \mathrm{aff}(\mathrm{Vor}^\omega(\tau))$ and $\forall p \in \tau$, $r_z = \sqrt{\|p - z\|^2 - \omega^2(p)} \ge R'_\tau$.*

2.2 Sampling conditions

2.2.1 Local feature size

The *medial axis* of $\mathbb{M}$ is the closure of the sets of points of $\mathbb{R}^d$ that have more than one nearest neighbor on $\mathbb{M}$. The *local feature size* of $x \in \mathbb{M}$, $\mathrm{lfs}(x)$, is the distance of x to the medial axis of $\mathbb{M}$. As is well known and can be easily proved, lfs is *Lipschitz continuous* i.e, $\mathrm{lfs}(x) \le \mathrm{lfs}(y) + \|x - y\|$.

2.2.2 (ε, δ)-sample

The point sample $\mathcal{P}$ is said to be an (ε, δ)-sample (where $0 < \delta < \varepsilon < 1$) if (1) for any point $x \in \mathbb{M}$ there exists a point $p \in \mathcal{P}$ such that $\|x - p\| \le \varepsilon\ \mathrm{lfs}(x)$, and (2) for any two distinct points $p, q \in \mathcal{P}$, $\|p - q\| \ge \delta\ \mathrm{lfs}(p)$.[1] The ratio ε/δ is called the *relative density* of $\mathcal{P}$.

[1] Observe that the sparsity condition (2) is mandatory if one wants to infer the dimension of $\mathbb{M}$ from a sample [22].

We will use the following results from [22]. We write l_p for the distance between $p \in \mathcal{P}$ and its nearest neighbor in $\mathcal{P} \setminus \{p\}$.

LEMMA 3. *Given an (ε, δ)-sample $\mathcal{P}$ of $\mathbb{M}$, we have*

1. *$\delta\,\mathrm{lfs}(p) \le l_p \le \frac{2\varepsilon}{1-\varepsilon}\mathrm{lfs}(p)$.*
2. *For any two points $p, q \in \mathbb{M}$ such that $\|p-q\| = t\,\mathrm{lfs}(p)$, $0 < t < 1$, $\sin\angle(pq, T_p) \le t/2$.*
3. *Let p be a point in $\mathbb{M}$. Let x be a point in T_p such that $\|p - x\| \le t\,\mathrm{lfs}(p)$ for some $0 < t \le 1/4$. Let x' be the point on $\mathbb{M}$ closest to x. Then $\|x - x'\| \le 2t^2\,\mathrm{lfs}(p)$.*

2.3 Slivers and good simplices

Consider a j-simplex τ, where $1 \le j \le k+1$. We denote by R_τ, L_τ, V_τ and $\rho(\tau) = R_\tau/L_\tau$ the circumradius, the shortest edge length, the volume, and the radius-edge ratio of τ respectively. We further define $\sigma(\tau) = \left(V_\tau/L_\tau^j\right)^{1/j}$, as the *sliverity measure* of τ. The orthocenter of τ is denoted by o_τ and its orthoradius by R'_τ.

If $p \in \tau$, we define $\tau_p = \tau \setminus \{p\}$ to be the $(j-1)$-face of τ opposite to p. We also write $D_\tau(p)$ for the distance from p to the affine hull of τ_p, and $H_\tau(p)$ for the *signed distance*[2] from o_τ to $\mathrm{aff}(\tau_p)$. We state without proof the following easy lemma.

LEMMA 4. *Let τ be a simplex of $\mathrm{Del}^\omega(\mathcal{P})$ and $p \in \tau$ s.t.*

1. *There exists $z \in \mathrm{aff}(\mathrm{Vor}^\omega(\tau))$ s.t. $\|z - p\| \le L_1$.*
2. *$\|p - q\| \le L_2$ for all vertices q of τ.*
3. *$R'_\tau \le \gamma_0 L_\tau$.*

Then $|H_\tau(x)| = \mathrm{dist}(o_\tau, \mathrm{aff}(\tau_x)) \le L_1 + (1 + \gamma_0 + \omega_0)L_2$ for all vertices x of τ.

LEMMA 5 ([13]). *Let τ be a simplex of $\mathrm{Del}^\omega(\mathcal{P})$. Let p be any vertex of τ and write $H_\tau(\omega(p))$ (instead of $H_\tau(p)$) for the signed distance of o_τ to $\mathrm{aff}(\tau_p)$ parametrized by the weight of p. We have $H_\tau(\omega(p)) = H_\tau(0) - \frac{\omega^2(p)}{2D_\tau(p)}$.*

Slivers are a special type of flat simplices. The property of being a sliver is measured in terms of a parameter σ_0, called the *sliverity bound*, to be fixed later in Section 4.

DEFINITION 1 (SLIVER). *Given a positive parameter σ_0, slivers are defined by induction on the dimension : (1) a simplex of dimension less than 3 is not a σ_0-sliver, and (2) for $j \ge 3$, a j-simplex τ is a σ_0-sliver if $\sigma(\tau) < \sigma_0$ and, $\forall \tau' \subset \tau$, $\sigma(\tau') \ge \sigma_0$.*

LEMMA 6. *If a j-simplex τ is a σ_0-sliver, then $D_\tau(p) < j\sigma_0 L_\tau$ for all vertices $p \in \tau$.*

PROOF. The volume of τ is

$$V_\tau = \frac{V_{\tau_p} \,.\, D_\tau(p)}{j} = \frac{\sigma^{j-1}(\tau_p) L_{\tau_p}^{j-1} \,.\, D_\tau(p)}{j}$$

and it is also equal to $\sigma^j(\tau)L_\tau^j$. Since τ is a σ_0-sliver, we have $\sigma(\tau) < \sigma_0$ and $\sigma(\tau_p) \ge \sigma_0$. Therefore we get

$$D_\tau(p) = j\,\frac{\sigma^j(\tau)}{\sigma^{j-1}(\tau_p)} \times \frac{L_\tau^j}{L_{\tau_p}^{j-1}} < j\sigma_0 L_\tau.$$

□

[2] $H(p)$ is positive if $o_\tau \in \mathrm{aff}(\tau)$ and p lie on the same side of $\mathrm{aff}(\tau_p)$, and it is negative if they lie on different sides of $\mathrm{aff}(\tau_p)$.

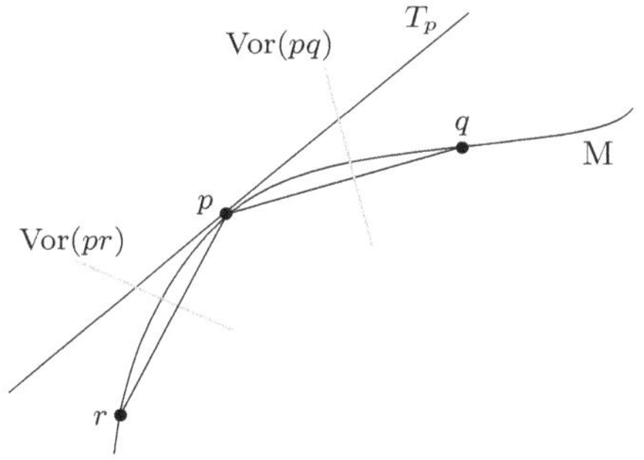

Figure 2: $[pq]$ and $[pr]$ are edges of the star of p in $\mathrm{Del}^{\omega}_{T\mathbb{M}}(\mathcal{P})$ since their dual Voronoi edges intersect the tangent space T_p at p.

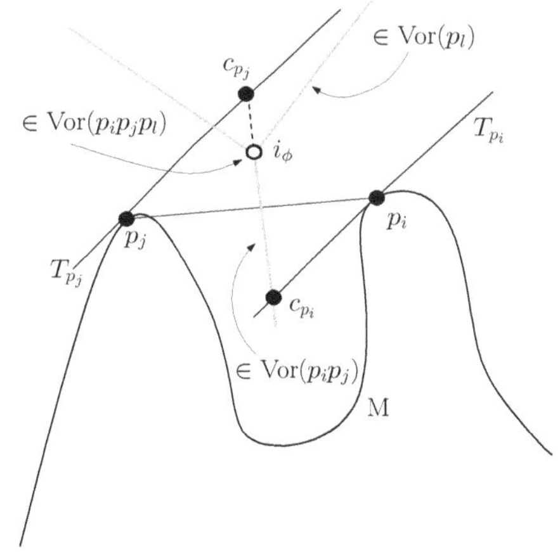

Figure 3: An inconsistent configuration in the unweighted case. Edge $[p_ip_j]$ is in $\mathrm{Del}_{p_i}(\mathcal{P})$ but not in $\mathrm{Del}_{p_j}(\mathcal{P})$ since $\mathrm{Vor}(p_ip_j)$ intersects T_{p_i} but not T_{p_j}. This happens because $[c_{p_i}c_{p_j}]$ penetrates (at i_ϕ) the Voronoi cell of a point $p_l \neq p_i, p_j$, therefore creating an inconsistent configuration $\phi = [p_i, p_j, p_l]$.

DEFINITION 2 (GOOD SIMPLEX). *Given two positive constants ρ_0 and σ_0, a simplex τ is called a (ρ_0, σ_0)-good simplex if $\rho(\tau) \leq \rho_0$ and τ nor its subsimplices are σ_0-slivers.*

The following important lemma is known (see e.g. [14]).

LEMMA 7 (NORMAL APPROXIMATION). *Let τ be a (ρ_0, σ_0)-good j-simplex for $j \leq k$ with vertices on a k-dimensional smooth manifold $\mathbb{M}$, and $p \in \tau$ s.t. the lengths of the edges of τ that are incident to p are less than $c_3\varepsilon\mathrm{lfs}(p)$ for $c_3\varepsilon < 1$. Then, for any normal vector n_p of $\mathbb{M}$ at p, τ has a normal n_τ such that $\angle n_p n_\tau \leq \alpha_j(\sigma_0)\varepsilon$ where $\alpha_j(\sigma_0)$ depends on j, σ_0, ρ_0 and c_3, and $1/\alpha_j(\sigma_0)$ vanishes with σ_0.*

In the sequel, we will simply write $\alpha(\sigma_0)$ for $\alpha_k(\sigma_0)$.

2.4 Tangential Delaunay complex and inconsistent configurations

Let $\mathrm{Del}^{\omega}_{p_i}(\mathcal{P})$ be the weighted Delaunay triangulation of $\mathcal{P}$ restricted to the tangent space T_{p_i}. Equivalently, the simplices of $\mathrm{Del}^{\omega}_{p_i}(\mathcal{P})$ are the simplices of $\mathrm{Del}^{\omega}(\mathcal{P})$ whose Voronoi dual faces intersect T_{p_i}, i.e. $\tau \in \mathrm{Del}^{\omega}_{p_i}(\mathcal{P})$ iff $\mathrm{Vor}^{\omega}(\tau) \cap T_{p_i} \neq \emptyset$. Observe that $\mathrm{Del}^{\omega}_{p_i}(\mathcal{P})$ is in general a k-dimensional triangulation. Since this situation can always be ensured by applying some infinitesimal perturbation on $\mathcal{P}$, we will assume, in the rest of the paper, that all $\mathrm{Del}^{\omega}_{p_i}(\mathcal{P})$ are k-dimensional triangulations. Finally, write $\mathrm{star}(p_i)$ for the star of p_i in $\mathrm{Del}^{\omega}_{p_i}(\mathcal{P})$, i.e. the set of simplices that are incident to p_i in $\mathrm{Del}^{\omega}_{p_i}(\mathcal{P})$.

We call *tangential Delaunay complex* or tangential complex for short, the simplicial complex $\{\tau, \tau \in \mathrm{star}(p), p \in \mathcal{P}\}$. We denote it by $\mathrm{Del}^{\omega}_{T\mathbb{M}}(\mathcal{P})$. By our assumption above, $\mathrm{Del}^{\omega}_{T\mathbb{M}}(\mathcal{P})$ is a k-dimensional complex contained in $\mathrm{Del}^{\omega}(\mathcal{P})$.

By duality, computing $\mathrm{star}(p_i)$ is equivalent to computing the restriction of the (weighted) Voronoi cell of p_i to T_{p_i}, which, by Lemma 1, reduces to computing a cell in a k-dimensional weighted Voronoi diagram embedded in T_{p_i}. It follows that the tangential complex can be computed without constructing any data structure of dimension higher than k, the intrinsic dimension of $\mathbb{M}$.

The tangential Delaunay complex is *not* in general a triangulated manifold and therefore not a good approximation of $\mathbb{M}$. This is due to the presence of so-called inconsistencies. Consider a k-simplex τ of $\mathrm{Del}^{\omega}_{T\mathbb{M}}(\mathcal{P})$ with two vertices p_i and p_j such that τ is in $\mathrm{star}(p_i)$ but not in $\mathrm{star}(p_j)$ (refer to Fig. 3). We write $B_i(\tau)$ for the open ball centered on T_{p_i} that is orthogonal to the (weighted) vertices of τ^{ω}, and denote by c_{p_i} and r_{p_i} its center and its radius. According to our definition, τ is inconsistent iff $B_i(\tau)$ is further than orthogonal from all weighted points in $\mathcal{P}^{\omega} \setminus \tau^{\omega}$ while there exists a weighted point of $\mathcal{P}^{\omega} \setminus \tau^{\omega}$, say p_l^{ω}, that is closer than orthogonal from $B_j(\tau)$. We deduce from the above discussion that the line segment $[c_{p_i}c_{p_j}]$ has to penetrate the interior of $\mathrm{Vor}^{\omega}(p_l)$.

We formally define an inconsistent configuration as follows.

DEFINITION 3 (INCONSISTENT CONFIGURATION). $\phi = [p_1, \ldots, p_{k+2}]$ *is called an inconsistent configuration of* $\mathrm{Del}^{\omega}_{T\mathbb{M}}(\mathcal{P})$ *witnessed by the triplet* (p_i, p_j, p_l) *if*

- *The k-simplex $\tau = \phi \setminus \{p_l\}$ is in* $\mathrm{star}(p_i)$ *but not in* $\mathrm{star}(p_j)$.
- *τ is a (ρ_0, σ_0)-good simplex.*
- $\mathrm{Vor}^{\omega}(p_l)$ *is the first cell of* $\mathrm{Vor}^{\omega}(\mathcal{P})$ *whose interior is intersected (at a point denoted by i_ϕ) by the line segment $[c_{p_i}c_{p_j}]$ oriented from c_{p_i} to c_{p_j}. Here $c_{p_i} = T_{p_i} \cap \mathrm{Vor}^{\omega}(\tau)$ and $c_{p_j} = T_{p_j} \cap \mathrm{aff}(\mathrm{Vor}^{\omega}(\tau))$.*

Note that i_ϕ is the center of a sphere that is orthogonal to the weighted vertices of τ and also to p_l^{ω}, and further than orthogonal from all the other weighted points of $\mathcal{P}^{\omega}$. Equivalenty, i_ϕ is the point on $[c_{p_i}c_{p_j}]$ that belongs to $\mathrm{Vor}^{\omega}(\phi)$.

An inconsistent configuration is thus a $(k+1)$-simplex of $\mathrm{Del}^{\omega}(\mathcal{P})$. Such a configuration or its subfaces do not necessarily belong to $\mathrm{Del}^{\omega}_{T\mathbb{M}}(\mathcal{P})$[3] We write $\mathrm{In}^{\omega}(\mathcal{P})$ for the subcomplex of $\mathrm{Del}(\mathcal{P})$ consisting of all the inconsistent configurations of $\mathrm{Del}^{\omega}_{T\mathbb{M}}(\mathcal{P})$ and their subfaces.

3. STRUCTURAL RESULTS

In the rest of the paper, we will need several constants : ω_0, ρ_0 and σ_0 (to define slivers, good simplices and inconsistent configurations), and c_3 (to be able to use lemma 7).

[3]In fact, as already noted, no $(k+1)$-simplex belongs to $\mathrm{Del}^{\omega}_{T\mathbb{M}}(\mathcal{P})$ when the points are in general position.

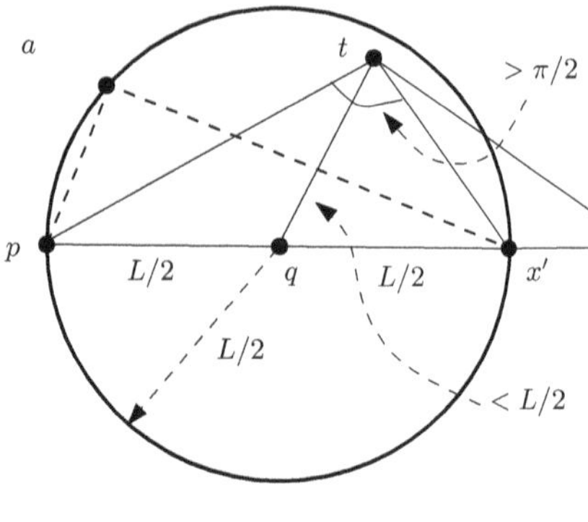

Figure 4: Refer to Lemma 8. x' is a point on the line segment such that $||p - x'|| = c_1\varepsilon\,\text{lfs}(p)$, $L = c_1\varepsilon\,\text{lfs}(p)$, $\angle pax' = \pi/2$ and $\angle ptx \geq \angle ptx' > \pi/2$.

These constants will be fixed in Section 3 and in Section 4. For simplicity, we will write sliver for σ_0-sliver and inconsistent configuration for (ρ_0, σ_0)-inconsistent configuration.

We give now an hypothesis which is assumed to be satisfied in the following results.

HYPOTHESIS 1. *$\mathcal{P}$ is an (ε, δ)-sample of $\mathbb{M}$ of bounded relative density, i.e. $\varepsilon/\delta \leq \eta_0$ for some positive constant η_0. We assume further that ε is small enough and that $2\alpha(\sigma_0)\varepsilon < 1$. Finally, we assume that $\tilde{\omega} \leq \omega_0$ where $\tilde{\omega}$ is the relative amplitude of the weight assignement ω and ω_0 is a positive constant less than $1/2$.*

3.1 Properties of the tangential Delaunay complex

We now give the following two lemmas which are slight variants of results of [14].

LEMMA 8. *For all $x \in T_p \cap \text{Vor}^\omega(p)$, there exists a positive constant c_1 such that $||p - x|| \leq c_1\varepsilon\text{lfs}(p)$.*

PROOF. Assume for a contradiction that there exists a point $x \in \text{Vor}^\omega(p) \cap T_p$ s.t. $||p - x|| > c_1\varepsilon\text{lfs}(p)$ with $c_1(1 - c_1\varepsilon) > 2 + c_1\varepsilon(1 + c_1\varepsilon)$ (*). Let q be a point on the line segment $[px]$ such that $||p - q|| = c_1\varepsilon\text{lfs}(p)/2$. Let q' be the point nearest to q on $\mathbb{M}$. From Lemma 3, we have $||q - q'|| \leq c_1^2\varepsilon^2\text{lfs}(p)/2$.

Hence, $||p - q'|| \leq ||p - q|| + ||q - q'|| < \frac{c_1}{2}\varepsilon(1 + c_1\varepsilon)\text{lfs}(p)$. From the 1-Lipschitz property, $\text{lfs}(q') \leq \text{lfs}(p) + ||p - q'|| < (1 + \frac{c_1}{2}\varepsilon(1 + c_1\varepsilon))\,\text{lfs}(p) < \frac{c_1}{2}(1 - c_1\varepsilon)\,\text{lfs}(p)$, which yields

$$||p - q'|| \geq ||p - q|| - ||q - q'|| > \frac{c_1}{2}\varepsilon(1 - c_1\varepsilon)\,\text{lfs}(p)$$

Since $\mathcal{P}$ is an ε-sample, there exists a point $t \in \mathcal{P}$, s.t. $||q' - t|| \leq \varepsilon\text{lfs}(q') < \frac{c_1}{2}\varepsilon(1 - c_1\varepsilon)\,\text{lfs}(p)$. We thus have

$$||q - t|| \leq ||q - q'|| + ||q' - t|| < \frac{c_1}{2}\,\varepsilon\text{lfs}(p).$$

From Fig. 4, we can see that $\angle ptx > \pi/2$. This implies that $||x - p||^2 - ||x - t||^2 - ||p - t||^2 > 0$. Hence,

$$\begin{aligned} ||x - p||^2 \;\; - & \;\; ||x - t||^2 - \omega^2(p) + \omega^2(t) \\ \geq & \;\; ||p - t||^2 - \omega^2(p) \\ \geq & \;\; ||p - t||^2 - \omega_0^2.||p - t||^2 \\ > & \;\; 0 \;\; (\text{as } \omega_0 < \tfrac{1}{2}) \end{aligned}$$

This implies $x \notin \text{Vor}^\omega(p)$, which contradicts our initial assumption. We conclude that $\text{Vor}^\omega(p) \cap T_p \subseteq B(p, c_1\varepsilon\text{lfs}(p))$ if Inequality (*) is satisfied, which is true for all $c_1 = 3 + \sqrt{2} \approx 4.41$ and $\varepsilon < 0.09$. □

LEMMA 9. *There exists positive constants c_2 and ρ_0' s.t.*

1. *If pq is an edge of $\text{Del}^\omega_{T\mathbb{M}}(\mathcal{P})$, then $||p - q|| \leq c_2\varepsilon\text{lfs}(p)$.*
2. *If τ is a simplex of $\text{Del}^\omega_{T\mathbb{M}}(\mathcal{P})$, then $R'_\tau \leq \rho_0' L_\tau$ and $\rho(\tau) = R_\tau/L_\tau \leq \rho_0'$.*

PROOF. 1a. Consider first the case where pq is an edge of $\text{Del}^\omega_p(\mathcal{P})$. Then $T_p \cap \text{Vor}^\omega(pq) \neq \emptyset$. Let $x \in T_p \cap \text{Vor}^\omega(pq)$. From Lemma 8, we have $||p - x|| \leq c_1\varepsilon\text{lfs}(p)$. By Lemma 2, $||q - x|| \leq \frac{||p-x||}{\sqrt{1-4\omega_0^2}} \leq \frac{c_1\varepsilon\text{lfs}(p)}{\sqrt{1-4\omega_0^2}}$. Hence, $||p - q|| \leq c_2'\varepsilon\text{lfs}(p)$ where $c_2' = c_1(1 + 1/\sqrt{1 - 4\omega_0^2}) > 2c_1$.

1b. From the definition of $\text{Del}^\omega_{T\mathbb{M}}(\mathcal{P})$, there exists a vertex r of τ such that $[pq] \in \text{star}(r)$. From 1a, $||r - p||$ and $||r - q||$ are at most $c_2'\varepsilon\text{lfs}(r)$. From the 1-Lipschitz property of lfs and assuming that $2c_2'\varepsilon < 1$, we have $\text{lfs}(r) \leq \text{lfs}(p) + ||p - r|| \leq \frac{\text{lfs}(p)}{1-c_2'\varepsilon} \leq 2\,\text{lfs}(p)$. It follows that $||p - q|| \leq ||p - r|| + ||r - q|| \leq 4c_2'\varepsilon\text{lfs}(p)$. The first part of the lemma is proved by taking $c_2 = 4c_2' > 8c_1$.

2. Assume that $\tau \in \text{star}(p)$. Let $z \in \text{Vor}^\omega(\tau) \cap T_p$, and $r_z = \sqrt{||z - p||^2 - \omega^2(p)}$. By definition, the ball centered at z with radius r_z is orthogonal to the weighted vertices of τ. From Lemma 2, we have $r_z \geq R'_\tau$. Hence it suffices to prove $r_z \leq \rho_0' L_\tau$. Since $z \in \text{Vor}^\omega(\tau) \cap T_p$, we deduce from Lemma 8 that $||z - p|| \leq c_1\varepsilon\text{lfs}(p)$. Therefore

$$r_z = \sqrt{||z - p||^2 - \omega^2(p)} \leq ||z - p|| \leq c_1\varepsilon\text{lfs}(p).$$

For any vertex q of τ, we have $||p - q|| \leq c_2\varepsilon\text{lfs}(p)$ (By 1.). Assuming $2c_2\varepsilon \leq 1$ and using the fact that lfs is 1-Lipschitz, $\text{lfs}(p) \leq 2\text{lfs}(q)$. Therefore, taking for q a vertex of the shortest edge of τ, we have, using Lemma 3,

$$\begin{aligned} r_z \;\; \leq & \;\; c_1\left(\frac{\varepsilon}{\delta}\right)\delta\,\text{lfs}(p) \leq c_1\left(\frac{\varepsilon}{\delta}\right)\delta \,\times\, 2\text{lfs}(q) \\ \leq & \;\; 2c_1\eta_0\,L_\tau = \rho_0''L_\tau. \end{aligned}$$

From Lemma 2, we have $R_\tau \leq \frac{R'_\tau}{\sqrt{1-4\omega_0^2}}$. Therefore $\rho(\tau) \leq \rho_0' = \frac{\rho_0''}{\sqrt{1-4\omega_0^2}}$. □

3.2 Properties of inconsistent configurations

We now give the lemmas on inconsistent configurations which are central to the proof of correctness of the reconstruction algorithm given later in the paper.

LEMMA 10. *Let $\phi \in \text{In}^\omega(\mathcal{P})$ be an inconsistent configuration witnessed by (p_i, p_j, p_l). Then, there exists positive constants $c_3 > c_2$ and $\rho_0 > \rho_0'$ s.t.*

1. *$||p - \text{i}_\phi|| \leq \frac{c_3}{2}\,\varepsilon\text{lfs}(p)$ for all vertices p of ϕ.*
2. *If pq is an edge of ϕ then $||p - q|| \leq c_3\varepsilon\,\text{lfs}(p)$.*
3. *If τ is a j-dimensional face of ϕ ($j \leq k + 1$) and R'_τ is the orthosphere of τ, then $R'_\tau \leq \rho_0 L_\tau$ and $R_\tau/L_\tau \leq \rho_0$.*

PROOF. From the definition, $\tau = \phi \setminus \{p_l\}$ belongs to $\text{Del}^\omega_{p_i}(\mathcal{P})$. We first bound $\text{dist}(\text{i}_\phi, \text{aff}(\tau)) = ||\text{o}_\tau - \text{i}_\phi||$ where

o_τ is the orthocenter of τ. By Lemma 8, $\|p_i - c_{p_i}\| \leq c_1\varepsilon \mathrm{lfs}(p_i)$ and, by Lemma 2, we have

$$\|p_j - c_{p_i}\| \leq \frac{\|p_i - c_{p_i}\|}{\sqrt{1-4\omega_0^2}} \leq \frac{c_1\varepsilon \,\mathrm{lfs}(p_i)}{\sqrt{1-4\omega_0^2}}$$

Let $c_3 = c_2/\sqrt{1-4\omega_0^2} > c_2$. By Lemma 7, $\angle(\mathrm{aff}(\tau), T_{p_i}) \leq \alpha(\sigma_0)\,\varepsilon$, which implies that $\sin\angle(\mathrm{aff}(\tau), T_{p_i}) \leq \alpha(\sigma_0)\varepsilon$ and

$$\tan^2\angle(\mathrm{aff}(\tau), T_{p_i}) \leq \frac{\alpha^2(\sigma_0)\,\varepsilon^2}{1-\alpha^2(\sigma_0)\,\varepsilon^2} < 4\,\alpha^2(\sigma_0)\,\varepsilon^2,$$

since $2\alpha(\sigma_0)\varepsilon < 1$ (Hypothesis 1). Observing that $\|p_i - o_\tau\| \leq \|p_i - c_{p_i}\|$, since o_τ belongs to $\mathrm{aff}(\mathrm{Vor}^\omega(\tau))$ and therefore is the closest point to p_i in $\mathrm{aff}(\mathrm{Vor}^\omega(\tau))$, we deduce

$$\|c_{p_i} - o_\tau\| \leq \|c_{p_i} - p_i\| \sin\angle(\mathrm{aff}(\tau), T_{p_i}) \leq \alpha(\sigma_0)c_1\varepsilon^2 \mathrm{lfs}(p_i).$$

Moreover, $\|p_j - o_\tau\| \leq \|p_j - c_{p_i}\|$ as o_τ is the closest point to p_j in $\mathrm{aff}(\mathrm{Vor}^\omega(\tau))$. Hence we have,

$$\begin{aligned}\|c_{p_j} - o_\tau\| &\leq \|p_j - o_\tau\| \tan\angle(\mathrm{aff}(\tau), T_{p_j}) \\ &< \frac{2\,\alpha(\sigma_0)\,c_1\,\varepsilon^2}{\sqrt{1-4\omega_0^2}}\,\mathrm{lfs}(p_i)\end{aligned}$$

As $i_\phi \in [c_{p_i}c_{p_j}]$, we conclude that

$$\|o_\tau - i_\phi\| \leq \frac{2\,\alpha(\sigma_0)\,c_1\,\varepsilon^2}{\sqrt{1-4\omega_0^2}}\,\mathrm{lfs}(p_i).$$

1. Assuming that $2\alpha(\sigma_0)\,\varepsilon < 1$ and using the facts that $\|p_i - o_\tau\| \leq \|p_i - i_\phi\|$, we get

$$\begin{aligned}\|p_i - i_\phi\| &\leq \|p_i - o_\tau\| + \|o_\tau - i_\phi\| \\ &\leq \|p_i - c_{p_i}\| + \|o_\tau - i_\phi\| \\ &\leq \left(c_1\varepsilon + \frac{2\alpha(\sigma_0)c_1\varepsilon^2}{\sqrt{1-4\omega_0^2}}\right)\mathrm{lfs}(p_i) \\ &\leq \frac{c_2}{4}\,\varepsilon \mathrm{lfs}(p_i)\end{aligned}$$

From Lemma 2, we have $\|p - i_\phi\| \leq \frac{\|p_i - i_\phi\|}{\sqrt{1-4\omega_0^2}} = \frac{c_3}{4}\,\varepsilon \mathrm{lfs}(p_i)$ for all vertices p of ϕ.

2. Using part 1 of this lemma, we have

$$\|p - q\| \leq \|p - i_\phi\| + \|q - i_\phi\| \leq \frac{c_3}{2}\,\varepsilon \mathrm{lfs}(p_i)$$

Moreover, $\mathrm{lfs}(p_i) \leq 2\mathrm{lfs}(p)$ since lfs is a 1-Lipschitz function and by taking $c_3\varepsilon < 1$. Hence $\|p - i_\phi\| \leq \frac{c_3}{2}\varepsilon \mathrm{lfs}(p)$ and $\|p - q\| \leq c_3\varepsilon\,\mathrm{lfs}(p)$.

3. Let $r_\phi = \sqrt{\|i_\phi - p_i\|^2 - \omega^2(p_i)}$. Since $i_\phi \in \mathrm{Vor}^\omega(\tau)$, the ball centered at i_ϕ with radius r_ϕ is orthogonal to the weighted vertices of τ. From Lemma 2, we have $r_\phi \geq R'_\tau$. Hence it suffices to show that $r_\phi \leq \rho_0 L_\tau$. Using $\|p_i - i_\phi\| \leq \frac{c_3}{4}\,\varepsilon \mathrm{lfs}(p_i)$ we get

$$r_\phi = \sqrt{\|i_\phi - p_i\| - \omega^2(p_i)} \leq \|i_\phi - p_i\| \leq \frac{c_3}{4}\,\varepsilon \mathrm{lfs}(p_i).$$

Let q be a vertex of a shortest edge of τ. We have, from part 2 of this lemma, $\|p_i - q\| \leq c_3\,\varepsilon \mathrm{lfs}(q)$. Therefore

$$R'_\tau \leq r_\phi \leq c_3\,\varepsilon \mathrm{lfs}(q) \leq c_3\left(\frac{\varepsilon}{\delta}\right)\delta \times \mathrm{lfs}(q) \leq c_3\,\eta_0\,L_\tau$$

From Lemma 2, we have $R_\tau \leq R'_\tau/\sqrt{1-4\omega_0^2}$. Therefore , $R_\tau/L_\tau \leq \rho_0 = c_3\eta_0/\sqrt{1-4\omega_0^2}$. □

LEMMA 11. *Let τ be a j-simplex of $\mathrm{Del}^\omega_{TM}(\mathcal{P}) \cup \mathrm{In}^\omega(\mathcal{P})$, $j \leq k+1$. For any vertex p of τ, there exists a constant c_4 s.t. the distance between the orthocenter $o(\tau)$ of τ and $\mathrm{aff}(\tau_p)$ is at most $c_4\varepsilon \mathrm{lfs}(p)$.*

PROOF. 1. We first consider the case where $\tau \in \mathrm{In}^\omega(\mathcal{P})$. Then there exists an inconsistent configuration ϕ witnessed by points (p_i, p_j, p_l) s.t. τ is a j-dimensional subsimplex of ϕ. From Lemma 10, we have $\|i_\phi - p\| \leq \frac{c_3}{2}\,\varepsilon \mathrm{lfs}(p)$, $\|q - p\| \leq c_3 \mathrm{lfs}(p)$ for all $q \in \phi$ and, since $\tau \in \mathrm{In}^\omega(\mathcal{P})$, $\rho(\tau) \leq \rho_0$. Using the above facts and Lemma 4, we get

$$\begin{aligned}\mathrm{dist}(o_\tau, \mathrm{aff}(\tau_p)) &\leq \mathrm{dist}(i_\phi, \mathrm{aff}(\tau_p)) \\ &\leq \frac{c_3}{2}\,\varepsilon \mathrm{lfs}(p) + (1+\rho_0+\omega_0)c_3 \mathrm{lfs}(p) \\ &\leq (\frac{3}{2} + \rho_0 + \omega_0)c_3\varepsilon \mathrm{lfs}(p) = c_4\varepsilon \mathrm{lfs}(p),\end{aligned}$$

2. Consider now the case where $\tau \in \mathrm{Del}^\omega_{TM}(\mathcal{P})$. By definition, $\tau \in \mathrm{Del}^\omega_q(\mathcal{P})$ for some vertex q of τ. From Lemma 8, we have $\|q - c_q\| \leq c_1\varepsilon \mathrm{lfs}(q) \leq 2c_1\varepsilon \mathrm{lfs}(p)$ where $c_q = \mathrm{Vor}^\omega(\tau) \cap T_q$ and p is any vertex of τ. The last inequality follows from the facts that lfs is 1-Lipschitz, $\|p - q\| \leq c_2\varepsilon \mathrm{lfs}(p)$ (Lemma 9) and by taking $c_2\varepsilon \leq 1$. Therefore, using Lemma 4, we get

$$\mathrm{dist}(o_\tau, \mathrm{aff}(\tau_p)) \leq \frac{2c_1\varepsilon \mathrm{lfs}(p)}{\sqrt{1-4\omega_0^2}} + (1+\rho'_0+\omega_0)c_2\,\varepsilon \mathrm{lfs}(p).$$

□

The next lemma shows that inconsistent configurations are slivers provided that σ_0 is sufficiently large wrt ε.

LEMMA 12. *Let ϕ be an inconsistent configuration and*

$$\varepsilon < \mathrm{f}(\sigma_0) = \frac{(k+1)\,\sigma_0}{\rho_0\,(c_3 + 2\,\alpha(\sigma_0))}.$$

If the subfaces of ϕ are not slivers, then ϕ is a sliver.

PROOF. Let pq be the smallest edge of ϕ and let r be a vertex in $\phi \setminus \{p, q\}$. Since $\phi_r = \phi \setminus \{r\}$ is not a sliver (as all subfaces of ϕ are not slivers) and $\|r - x\| \leq c_3 \mathrm{lfs}(x)$ (Lemma 10), we have $\sin\angle(\mathrm{aff}(\phi_r), T_x) \leq \alpha(\sigma_0)\,\varepsilon$ for all vertices x of ϕ_r by Lemma 7. From Lemma 3, $\sin\angle(pr, T_p) \leq \frac{c_3}{2}\,\varepsilon$. Therefore

$$\begin{aligned}D_\phi(r) &= \sin\angle(pr, \mathrm{aff}(\phi_r)) \times \|p - r\| \\ &\leq (\sin\angle(pr, T_p) + \sin\angle(\mathrm{aff}(\phi_r), T_p)) \times \|p - r\| \\ &\leq (\frac{c_3}{2} + \alpha(\sigma_0))\,\varepsilon\|p - r\|.\end{aligned}$$

Using the facts that $\mathrm{vol}(\phi_r) = \sigma^k(\phi_r)\,L^k_{\phi_r}$, $\sigma(\phi_r) \geq \sigma_0$, $\|p - r\| \leq 2R_\phi$, $\rho(\phi_r) \leq \rho_0$ and $\varepsilon < \mathrm{f}(\sigma_0)$, we get

$$\begin{aligned}\mathrm{vol}(\phi) &= D_\phi(r) \times \frac{\mathrm{vol}(\phi_r)}{k+1} \\ &\leq \left(\frac{c_3}{2} + \alpha(\sigma_0)\right)\varepsilon\|p - r\| \times \frac{\sigma^k(\phi_r)L^k_\phi}{k+1} \\ &\leq (c_3 + 2\alpha(\sigma_0))\,\varepsilon R_\phi \times \frac{\sigma_0^k L^k_\phi}{k+1} \\ &\leq \frac{\rho_0(c_3 + 2\alpha(\sigma_0))\varepsilon}{k+1} \times \sigma_0^k\,L^{k+1}_\phi \\ &< \sigma_0^{k+1}\,L^{k+1}_\phi\end{aligned}$$

□

3.3 Number of local neighbors

Lemmas 9 and 10 show that, in order to construct star(p) and search for inconsistencies involving p, it is enough to consider the points of $\mathcal{P}$ that lie in ball $B_p = B(p, c_3\varepsilon\text{lfs}(p))$. Since ε and lfs(p) are not known in practice, we will consider instead the ball $B'_p = B(p, c_3\eta_0\, l_p)$ where

$$l_x = \min_{q\in\mathcal{P}, q\neq x} \|x - q\|.$$

It is easily seen that $l_x : \mathbb{M} \to \mathbb{R}$ is 1-Lipschitz and, by Lemma 3, we have $\delta\text{lfs}(p) \leq l_p \leq \frac{2\varepsilon}{1-\varepsilon}\text{lfs}(p)$. It follows that B'_p contains B_p if $\varepsilon/\delta \leq \eta_0$. We call $LN_p = B'_p \cap \mathcal{P}$ the *local neighborhood* of p.

LEMMA 13. *The number of points of LN_p is less than $N < 2^{O(k)}$.*

PROOF. For convenience, write $\nu = 4c_3\eta_0\varepsilon$ and assume that $\nu \leq 1/2$. We observe that $LN_p \subset B''_p = B(p, \nu\text{lfs}(p))$ since, by Lemma 3, $l_p \leq \frac{2\varepsilon}{1-\varepsilon}\text{lfs}(p) \leq 4\varepsilon\text{lfs}(p)$. We will count the number of points in $B''_p \cap \mathcal{P}$. Let x and y be two points of $B''_p \cap \mathcal{P}$. We have $\text{lfs}(x), \text{lfs}(y) \geq \text{lfs}(p)(1-\nu) \geq \text{lfs}(p)/2$, since lfs is 1-Lipschitz. The balls $B(x, l_x/2)$ and $B(y, l_y/2)$ are disjoint, and, since $l_x \geq \delta\,\text{lfs}(x) \geq \frac{\delta}{2}\text{lfs}(p)$ (and similarly for l_y), the balls $B_x = B(x, \frac{\delta}{4}\text{lfs}(p))$ and $B_y = B(y, \frac{\delta}{4}\text{lfs}(p))$ are also disjoint. Observe that both balls B_x and B_y are contained in $B^+_p = B(p, \mu\,\varepsilon\text{lfs}(p))$ where $\mu = \frac{\nu}{\varepsilon} + \frac{\delta}{4\varepsilon} \leq 4c_3\eta_0 + \frac{1}{4}$.

A packing argument now allows to conclude. Specifically, by Lemma 15, we have that $\text{vol}(B_x \cap \mathbb{M}) > \phi_k\left(\frac{\delta\,\text{lfs}(p)}{8}\right)^k$ and $\text{vol}(B^+_p \cap \mathbb{M}) < \phi_k\,(\mu\varepsilon\text{lfs}(p))^k$, where ϕ_k is the volume of the k-dimensional unit ball. We conclude that the number of points of $\mathcal{P} \cap B''_p$ is less than $\left(\frac{8\mu\varepsilon}{\delta}\right)^k \leq (32c_3\eta_0 + 2)^k\,\eta_0^k = 2^{O(k)}$. □

4. MANIFOLD RECONSTRUCTION

In this section, we will show how to find a weight assignment for the point set $\mathcal{P}$ so that we can remove all inconsistent configurations. Once this is done, all the stars become coherent and the resulting weighted tangential Delaunay complex is a simplicial k-manifold.

4.1 Algorithm

The input to the algorithm is a point sample $\mathcal{P} = \{p_1, \ldots, p_n\}$ together with a bound on the relative density η_0 of $\mathcal{P}$. We assume in addition that the dimension k of $\mathbb{M}$ is given and that we know the tangent space T_p at each point $p \in \mathcal{P}$.

The algorithm fixes ω_0 in $(0, 1/2)$ and then computes a weight assignment $\omega \in [0, \omega_0]$ such that no inconsistent configuration remains in the weighted tangential Delaunay complex. More precisely, we will assign a weight to each point $p \in \mathcal{P}$ in turn so as to remove all j-dimensional slivers incident to p in $\text{Del}^{\omega}_{T\mathbb{M}}(\mathcal{P}) \cup \text{In}^{\omega}(\mathcal{P})$ for $j \in \{3, \ldots, k+1\}$. By Lemma 12, we know that, if σ_0 is large enough, removing inconsistent configurations from the tangential Delaunay complex reduces to removing slivers.

For a given j-simplex $\tau = [p_0, \ldots, p_j] \in \text{Del}^{\omega}_{T\mathbb{M}}(\mathcal{P}) \cup \text{In}^{\omega}(\mathcal{P})$ we have

$$\sigma^j(\tau) = \frac{|\det(p_1 - p_0, \ldots, p_j - p_0)|}{j!\, L^j_\tau} \leq \frac{\Pi^j_{i=1}\|p_i - p_0\|}{j!\, L^j_\tau} \leq \frac{2^j\rho^j_0}{j!} \leq 2\rho^j_0,$$

the last inequalities follow from the facts that $L_\tau \leq 2R_\tau$, and the radius-edge ratio of the simplices in $\text{Del}^{\omega}_{T\mathbb{M}}(\mathcal{P}) \cup \text{In}^{\omega}(\mathcal{P})$ is $\leq \rho_0$ (Lemmas 9 and 10). This implies that $\sigma(\tau) \in (0, 2\rho_0]$. In the first step of our reconstruction algorithm, we pick a random value of σ_0 from $(0, 2\rho_0]$, and once σ_0 is selected, we try to remove all slivers from $\text{Del}^{\omega}_{T\mathbb{M}}(\mathcal{P}) \cup \text{In}^{\omega}(\mathcal{P})$. If we fail to remove slivers or if we still have inconsistencies, then we go back and select a new value of σ_0.

Manifold-Reconstruction($\mathcal{P} = \{p_1, \ldots, p_n\}$)

S0 Calculate $LN_{p_i}\ \forall p_i \in \mathcal{P}$ and ρ_1

S1 Select σ_0 at random from $(0, 2\rho_1]$

S2 **for** $i = 1$ **to** n **do**
  if weight(p_i, σ_0) = "FAIL" **then go-to** S1
  else update($\text{Del}^{\omega}_{T\mathbb{M}}(\mathcal{P}), p_i$)

S3 **if** $\text{In}^{\omega}(\mathcal{P}) \neq \emptyset$ **then go-to** S1
  else output $\text{Del}^{\omega}_{T\mathbb{M}}(\mathcal{P})$

Before we give the details of the function **weight**() we first define the subroutine **skyline**(p, S, σ_0) that will be used in the function. Let S be a set of simplices incident on p.

Let τ be a simplex in S whose subfaces are not σ_0-slivers. Such a simplex is called a *candidate simplex*. We associate to τ interval $W(\tau)$ that consists of all squared weights $\omega^2(p)$ for which τ appears as a simplex in $\text{Del}^{\omega}_{T\mathbb{M}}(\mathcal{P}) \cup \text{In}^{\omega}(\mathcal{P})$. We define the skyline of p as the lower boundary of the union of all rectangles $R(\tau) = W(\tau) \times [\sigma(\tau), +\infty)$ for all candidate simplices over $W(p) = [0, \omega_0^2\, l_p^2]$, see Figure 5. For any $\omega^2(p)$, the minimum sliverity ratio of any *candidate simplex* incident to p is the height of **skyline**(p, S_p, σ_0) over $\omega^2(p) \in W(p)$. The best choice for $\omega(p)$ is the weight of p corresponding to the highest point on the **skyline**(p, S_p, σ_0), i.e **skyline**(p, S_p, σ_0) has the maximum height over $\omega^2(p)$.

Function **weight**(p, σ_0)

S1 $S_p \leftarrow$ **detect_simplices**(p, σ_0)

S2 **skyline**(p, S_p, σ_0) **begin**
  for $i = 1$ **to** n **do**
    if none of the subfaces of τ are σ_0-slivers **then**
      include $R(\tau) = W(\tau) \times [\sigma(\tau), +\infty)$
  end

S3 $\Theta \leftarrow$ highest point on **skyline**(p, S_p, σ_0)

S4 **if** $\Theta < \sigma_0$ **then return** "FAIL"
  else $\omega(p) \leftarrow$ weight of p corresponding to a highest point on **skyline**(p, S_p, σ_0)

Function **update**($\text{Del}^{\omega}_{T\mathbb{M}}(\mathcal{P}), p$)

- Update the stars of p and of all points $x \in LN_p$ by modifying $\text{Del}^{\omega}_x(LN_x)$.

Function **detect_simplices**(p, σ_0)

1. We first detect all possible j-simplices for all $3 \leq j \leq k+1$ of $\text{Del}^{\omega}_{T\mathbb{M}}(\mathcal{P})$ incident on p for all possible $\omega(p)$. This is done in the following way: (1) we vary the weight of p from 0 to to $\omega_0 l_p$, keeping the weights of the other points constant; (2) for each new weight assignment to p, we modify the stars of the points in LN_p and detect from the stars the new j-simplices incident

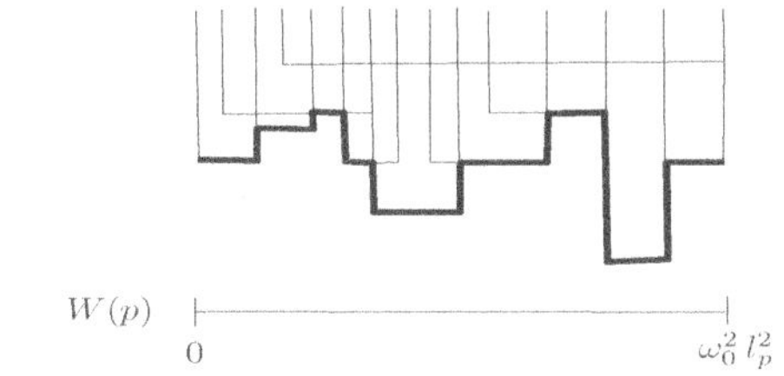

Figure 5: The above figure shows a skyline(p, S_p, σ_0) over $W(p) = [0, \omega^2 l_p^2]$ for point p.

to p that have not been detected thus far. The weight of point p changes only in a finite number of instances $0 = P_0 < P_1 < \cdots < P_{n-1} < P_n = \omega_0 l_p$.

We determine the next weight assignment of p in the following way. For each new simplex τ currently incident to p, we keep it in a priority queue ordered by the weight of p at which τ will disappear for the first time. Hence the minimum weight in the priority queue gives the next weight assignment for p. Since the number of points in LN_p is bounded, the number of simplices incident to p is also bounded, as well as the number of times we have to change the weight of p.

2. Once we have detected all possible j-simplices, for all $j \in \{1, \ldots, k+1\}$, that can be incident on p in the weighted tangential Delaunay complex, we then detect all possible inconsistent configurations incident on p, by calling the function **detect_inconsistent-configuration**(p, σ_0).

Function **detect_inconsistent-configurations**(p, σ_0)

1. We vary the weight of p from 0 to $\omega_0 l_p$, keeping the weight of the rest of the points constant. Once we have assigned a new weight to p we modify the stars of the points in LN_p.

2. Detecting the inconsistent configurations incident to p is more complicated than detecting the simplices incident to p. We consider all points p_i in LN_p. Let τ be a k-simplex in the star of p_i, and let p_j be a vertex of τ such that τ is not in the star of p_j. We calculate the Voronoi diagram of the points in LN_p restricted to the line segment $[c_{p_i} c_{p_j}]$, where $c_{p_i} = T_{p_i} \cap \mathrm{Vor}^{\omega}(\tau)$ and $c_{p_j} = T_{p_j} \cap \mathrm{aff}(\mathrm{Vor}^{\omega}(\tau))$. From the restricted Voronoi diagram, we find a point p whose Voronoi cell intersects for the first time the line segment $[c_{p_i} c_{p_j}]$ oriented from c_{p_i} to c_{p_j}. If $p \in \phi = \tau \cup \{l\}$, then we report ϕ.

3. As in the **detect_simplices** function the weight of p is changed only a finite number of times. For each current inconsistent configuration ϕ incident to p, we keep in a priority queue the weight of p for which ϕ will disappear for the first time. The minimum weight in the priority queue gives the next weight assignment of p.

4.2 Analysis of the algorithm

DEFINITION 4 (SLIVERITY RANGE). *Let ω be a weight assignment of relative amplitude at most ω_0 we keep fixed except for $\omega(p)$. The sliverity range of a point $p \in \mathcal{P}$ is the measure of the set of all squared weights $\omega^2(p)$ for which p is incident to a sliver in $\mathrm{Del}^{\omega}_{T\mathbb{M}}(\mathcal{P}) \cup \mathrm{In}^{\omega}(\mathcal{P})$.*

LEMMA 14. *Under Hypothesis 1, the sliverity range of p is at most $\Sigma(p) = N^{k+2}(k+1) c_5\, \sigma_0\, l_p^2$ for some constant c_5.*

PROOF. Let τ be a simplex incident on p. We call the sliverity range of τ the measure of the set of squared weights for which τ is a sliver in $\mathrm{Del}^{\omega}_{T\mathbb{M}}(\mathcal{P}) \cup \mathrm{In}^{\omega}(\mathcal{P})$. If $\omega(p)$ is the weight of p, we write $H(\omega(p))$ for the signed distance of the orthocenter of τ to $\mathrm{aff}(\tau_p)$. From Lemma 11, we have $|H(\omega(p))| \leq c_4 \varepsilon \mathrm{lfs}(p)$, for all $\tau \in \mathrm{Del}^{\omega}_{T\mathbb{M}}(\mathcal{P}) \cup \mathrm{In}^{\omega}(\mathcal{P})$. Moreover, using Lemma 5 and the fact that τ is a sliver, $H(\omega(p)) = H(0) - \frac{\omega^2(p)}{2D_p} \leq H(0) - \frac{\omega^2(p)}{2j\sigma_0 L_\tau}$. It follows that the sliverity range of τ is at most $4j\sigma_0 L_\tau c_4 \varepsilon \mathrm{lfs}(p)$. Using the facts that $L_\tau \leq c_3 \varepsilon \mathrm{lfs}(p)$ (from Lemmas 9 and 10), $\mathrm{lfs}(p) \leq l_p/\delta$ and $\varepsilon/\delta \leq \eta_0$, the sliverity range of τ is less than $4jc_3c_4\sigma_0\eta_0^2 l_p^2 = j\, c_5 \sigma_0\, l_p^2$. By Lemma 13, the number of j-simplices that are incident to p is at most N^j. Hence, the sliverity range of p is less that

$$\Sigma(p) = \sum_{3}^{k+1} N^j\, j c_5\, \sigma_0\, l_p^2 \leq N^{k+2}(k+1) c_5\, \sigma_0\, l_p^2.$$

□

THEOREM 1. *Under Hypothesis 1 and if*

$$\sigma_{\max} = \frac{\omega_0^2}{(k+1)\, c_5\, N^{k+2}} > \sigma_{\min} = \inf\{\sigma | \varepsilon < \mathrm{f}(\sigma)\},$$

then, for any $\sigma_0 \in [\sigma_{\min}, \sigma_{\max}]$, the above algorithm outputs $\mathrm{Del}^{\omega}_{T\mathbb{M}}(\mathcal{P})$ without any slivers nor inconsistent configuration.

PROOF. As in subroutine **skyline**(), let S_p denotes the set of all possible simplices that can be incident on p in the complex $\mathrm{Del}^{\omega}_{T\mathbb{M}}(\mathcal{P}) \cup \mathrm{In}^{\omega}(\mathcal{P})$ for all possible weight assignments ω of relative amplitude $\tilde{\omega} \leq \omega_0$. By Lemma 14, the sliverity range of p is less than $N^{k+2}(k+1)c_5\, \sigma_0\, l_p^2$. If the sliverity range of p is less than $\omega_0^2 l_p^2$, the total range of all possible squared weights, or, equivalently, if

$$\sigma_0 < \sigma_{\max} = \frac{\omega_0^2}{(k+1)\, c_5\, N^{k+2}},$$

then we will be able to remove all slivers incident on p by selecting the highest point on the skyline.

If we select a value of σ_0 in the interval $(\sigma_{\min}, \sigma_{\max}]$, Lemma 14 ensures that removing all j-dimensional slivers for all $j \in \{3, \ldots, k+1\}$ in $\mathrm{Del}^{\omega}_{T\mathbb{M}}(\mathcal{P}) \cup \mathrm{In}^{\omega}(\mathcal{P})$ will also result in removing inconsistent configurations from $\mathrm{Del}^{\omega}_{T\mathbb{M}}(\mathcal{P})$, i.e. $\mathrm{In}^{\omega}(\mathcal{P}) = \emptyset$. □

4.3 Time and space complexity

THEOREM 2. *The time complexity of the algorithm is*

$$O(d)\, |\mathcal{P}|^2 + \frac{1}{\lambda} \times 2^{O(k^2)+\log d}\, |\mathcal{P}|,$$

where $\lambda = (\sigma_{\max} - \sigma_{\min})/(2\rho_0)$, and its space complexity is

$$2^{O(k^2)+\log d}\, |\mathcal{P}|.$$

PROOF. We only sketch the complexity analysis. See [7] for a detailed discussion. Step S0 of **Manifold-Reconstruction** can easily be performed in $O(d)\, |\mathcal{P}|^2$ time.

We show now that the expected number of times Step **S1** of **ManifoldReconstruction** is repeated is $\frac{1}{\lambda}$. Indeed, for any simplex $\tau \in \mathrm{Del}^{\omega}_{T\mathbb{M}}(\mathcal{P}) \cup \mathrm{In}^{\omega}(\mathcal{P})$, we have $\sigma(\tau) \in (0, 2\rho_0]$. Hence, the probability that, for the selected value of σ_0, the algorithm removes all slivers and inconsistencies is at least $\lambda = (\sigma_{\max} - \sigma_{\min})/(2\rho_0)$. It follows that the expected number of times **S1** is performed is less than

$$\sum_{i=1}^{\infty} i(1-\lambda)^{i-1}\lambda = \frac{1}{\lambda}.$$

The time complexities of functions **update**$(\mathrm{Del}^{\omega}_{T\mathbb{M}}(\mathcal{P}), p)$, **detect_simplices** (p, σ_0), and **detect_inconsistent-configurations**(p, σ_0) are $2^{O(k(k+\log d))}$. Indeed, we need to project $|LN_p| < N < 2^{O(k)}$ points onto T_p, which costs $O(kd) \times |LN_p| = O(d)\, 2^{O(k)}$ time. The Delaunay simplices that are computed have their vertices in LN_p and are of dimension at most $k+1$. Hence their number is $2^{O(k^2)}$. The basic operations (mainly in-sphere predicates) amount to evaluating signs of determinants of $k \times k$ matrices. The cost of such a basic operation is $O(k^3)$. The total cost of both functions is thus $O(d)\, 2^{O(k)} + O(k^3)\, 2^{O(k^2)} = 2^{O(k^2)+\log d}$.

We deduce that the expected time complexity of **ManifoldReconstruction** is

$$O(d)\, |\mathcal{P}|^2 + \frac{1}{\lambda} \times 2^{O(k^2)+\log d}\, |\mathcal{P}|.$$

We easily deduce from the above discussion that the total space complexity of the algorithm is

$$2^{O(k^2)+\log d}\, |\mathcal{P}|. \tag{2}$$

□

4.4 Topological and Geometric guarantees

We assume that the conditions of Theorem 1 are satisfied and denote by $\mathrm{Del}^{\omega}_{T\mathbb{M}}(\mathcal{P})$ the tangential complex output by our algorithm. Let π be the mapping that maps any point of $\mathrm{Del}^{\omega}_{T\mathbb{M}}(\mathcal{P})$ to its closest point on $\mathbb{M}$. The proof of topological correctness (see [7]) uses ideas from [1, 8, 11, 14].

THEOREM 3. *Under the conditions of Theorem 1, our algorithm outputs $\mathrm{Del}^{\omega}_{T\mathbb{M}}(\mathcal{P})$ without any slivers and inconsistent configurations, and $\mathrm{Del}^{\omega}_{T\mathbb{M}}(\mathcal{P})$ has the following properties*

- **Bijection :** *The restriction of π to $\mathrm{Del}^{\omega}_{T\mathbb{M}}(\mathcal{P})$ is a bijection;*
- **Pointwise approximation :** $\forall x \in \mathbb{M}$, $\mathrm{dist}(x, \pi^{-1}(x)) = O(\varepsilon^2 \mathrm{lfs}(x))$;
- **Normal approximation :** $\forall x \in \mathbb{M}$, $\angle N_x N_\tau = O(\varepsilon)$, *where τ is a k-simplex of $\mathrm{Del}^{\omega}_{T\mathbb{M}}(\mathcal{P})$ containing the point $\pi^{-1}(x)$,*
- **Topological correctness :** *π defines an isotopy between $\mathrm{Del}^{\omega}_{T\mathbb{M}}(\mathcal{P})$ and $\mathbb{M}$.*

PROOF SKETCH. By Lemma 7, one can show that the maximum distance from a point of a simplex $\tau \in \mathrm{Del}^{\omega}_{T\mathbb{M}}(\mathcal{P})$ to the closest point on $\mathbb{M}$ is $O(\varepsilon^2 \mathrm{lfs}(x))$. It follows that the projection π that maps every point of τ to its closest point on $\mathbb{M}$ is injective: if we extend an open segment of length $\mathrm{lfs}(y)$ from every manifold point y in all normal directions to $\mathbb{M}$, these segments do not intersect, and they can be used as the fibers of a tubular neighborhood $\hat{\mathbb{M}}$ of $\mathbb{M}$. Each point of such a segment has y as its unique closest neighbor on $\mathbb{M}$. For small enough ε, the simplex τ is contained in $\hat{\mathbb{M}}$. Thus, the mapping π defines an isotopy between τ and a corresponding manifold patch.

One can show that two k-simplices of $\mathrm{Del}^{\omega}_{T\mathbb{M}}(\mathcal{P})$ that share a subface have normal spaces that differ by at most $O(\varepsilon)$, and that the mapping π extends continuously across the subfaces. It follows that the projection π restricted to the two adjacent k-simplices is a homeomorphism that is invertible locally. (In topological terms, $\pi\colon \mathrm{Del}^{\omega}_{T\mathbb{M}}(\mathcal{P}) \to \mathbb{M}$ is a covering map, if we can establish that it is surjective.) By assumption, on every component, there is at least one vertex of a simplex of $\mathrm{Del}^{\omega}_{T\mathbb{M}}(\mathcal{P})$. This ensures that $\pi(\mathrm{Del}^{\omega}_{T\mathbb{M}}(\mathcal{P}))$ contains that vertex, and since the mapping can be continued locally, it follows that every component of S is covered at least once. It is now still possible that some component is covered more than once by π. This would imply that some sample point $p \in P$ is covered more than once. However, one can show quite easily that no point p of $\mathrm{Del}^{\omega}_{T\mathbb{M}}(\mathcal{P})$ except p itself has p as its closest neighbor on $\mathbb{M}$.

It follows that the mapping π defines an ambient isotopy between $\mathrm{Del}^{\omega}_{T\mathbb{M}}(\mathcal{P})$ and $\mathbb{M}$. □

5. CONCLUSION

We have given the first algorithm that is able to reconstruct a smooth manifold in a time that depends only linearly on the dimension of the ambient space. We believe that our algorithm is of practical interest when the dimension of the manifold is small, even if it is embedded in a space of very high dimension. This situation is quite common in practical applications in machine learning.

The algorithm is rather simple. The basic ingredients we need are data structures for constructing weighted Delaunay triangulations in k-flats. We will report experimental results in a forthcoming paper.

We have assumed that dimension of $\mathbb{M}$ is known. If not, we can use algorithms given in [22, 15] to estimate the dimension of $\mathbb{M}$ and the tangent space at each sample point. One interesting feature of our approach is that it is pretty robust and still works if we only have approximate tangent spaces at the sample points.

We have also assumed that we know an upper bound on the relative density η_0 of the input sample $\mathcal{P}$. Ideas from [21, 8] may be useful to convert a sample to a subsample with a bounded relative density.

We forsee other applications of the tangential complex and of our construction each time computations in the tangent space of a manifold are required, e.g. for dimensionality reduction and approximating the Laplace Beltrami operator [5].

Finally, let us mention that removing inconsistencies among stars that have been computed independently is a useful paradigm that has already been used for maintaining dynamic meshes [29] and generating anisotropic meshes [9]. We hope that this paper will motivate further applications.

6. ACKNOWLEDGEMENTS

The authors thank the anonymous referees for their insightful comments, and Mariette Yvinec for helpful discussions.

7. REFERENCES

[1] N. Amenta, S. Choi, T. K. Dey, , and N. Leekha. A simple algorithm for homeomorphic surface reconstruction. *Intl. Journal of Computational Geometry and Application*, 12:125–141, 2002.

[2] F. Aurenhammer. Power diagrams: properties, algorithms and applications. *SIAM J. Comput.*, 16(1), 1987.

[3] F. Aurenhammer and H. Edelsbrunner. An optimal algorithm for constructing the weighted voronoi diagram in the plane. *Pattern Recognition*, 17(2):251–257, 1984.

[4] M. Belkin and P. Niyogi. Laplacian eigenmaps and spectral techniques for embedding and clustering. *Advances in Neural Information Processing Systems*, 2001.

[5] M. Belkin, J. Sun, and Y. Wang. Discrete laplace operator on meshed surfaces. In *Proc. ACM Symp. on Computational Geometry*, 2008.

[6] J.-D. Boissonnat and J. Flötotto. A coordinate system associated with points scattered on a surface. *Computer-Aided Design*, 36:161–174, 2004.

[7] J.-D. Boissonnat and A. Ghosh. Manifold Reconstruction using Tangential Delaunay Complexes. *INRIA Research Report 7142*, 2009.

[8] J. D. Boissonnat, L. Guibas, and S. Y. Oudot. Manifold reconstruction in arbitary dimensions using witness complexes. In *Proc. ACM Symp. on Computational Geometry*, pages 193–204, 2007.

[9] J.-D. Boissonnat, C. Wormser, and M. Yvinec. Locally uniform anisotropic meshing. In *Proc. ACM Symp. on Computational Geometry*, pages 270–277, 2008.

[10] F. Cazals and J. Giesen. Delaunay triangulation based surface reconstruction. In J. Boissonnat and M. Teillaud, editors, *Effective Computational Geometry for Curve and Surfaces*. Springer, 2006.

[11] F. Chazal and A. Lieutier. Smooth Manifold Reconstruction from Noisy and Non uniform Approximation with Guarantees. *Comp. Geom: Theory and Applications*, 40:156–170, 2008.

[12] F. Chazal and S. Y. Oudot. Towards Persistence-Based Reconstruction in Euclidean Spaces. In *Proc. ACM Symp. on Computational Geometry*, pages 232–241, 2008.

[13] S.-W. Cheng, T. K. Dey, H. Edelsbrunner, M. A. Facello, and S.-H. Teng. Sliver Exudation. *Journal of ACM*, 47:883–904, 2000.

[14] S.-W. Cheng, T. K. Dey, and E. A. Ramos. Manifold Reconstruction from Point Samples. In *Proc. ACM-SIAM Symp. Discrete Algorithms*, pages 1018–1027, 2005.

[15] S.-W. Cheng, Y. Wang, and Z. Wu. Provable Dimension Detection using Principle Component Analysis. *Intl. Journal of Computational Geometry and Application*, 18(5):415–440, 2008.

[16] D. Cohen-Steiner and T. K. F. Da. A greedy Delaunay Based Surface Reconstruction Algorithm. *The Visual Computer*, 20:4–16, 2004.

[17] T. K. Dey. *Curve and Surface Reconstruction: Algorithms with Mathematical Analysis*. Cambridge University Press, 2006.

[18] D. L. Donohu and C. Grimes. Hessian eigenmaps: new locally linear embedding techniques for high dimensional data. *Proceedings of the Natural Academy of Sciences*, 100:5591–5596, 2003.

[19] J. Flötotto. *A coordinate system associated to a point cloud issued from a manifold: definition, properties and applications*. PhD thesis, Université of Nice Sophia-Antipolis, 2003.

[20] D. Freedman. Efficient simplicial reconstructions of manifolds from their samples. *IEEE Trans. on Pattern Analysis and Machine Intelligence*, 24(10), 2002.

[21] S. Funke and E. Ramos. Smooth-surface reconstruction in near-linear time. In *Proc. ACM-SIAM Symp. Discrete Algorithms*, pages 781–780, 2002.

[22] J. Giesen and U. Wagner. Shape dimension and intrinsic metric from samples of manifolds. In *Proc. ACM Symp. on Computational Geometry*, pages 329–337, 2003.

[23] M. Gopi, S. Khrisnan, and C. T. Silva. Surface Reconstruction based on Lower Dimensional Localized Delaunay Triangulation. *Eurographics*, 19 (3), 2000.

[24] S. Lafon and A. B. Lee. Diffusion Maps and Coarse-Graining: A Unified Framework for Dimensionality Reduction, Graph Partitioning, and Data Set Parameterization. *IEEE Transactions on Pattern Analysis and Machine Intelligence*, 28:1393–1403, 2006.

[25] B. Nadler, S. Lafon, R. R. Coifman, and I. G. Kevrekidis. Diffusion maps, spectral clustering and eigenfunctions of fokker-planck operators. *Neural Information Processing Systems*, 18, 2005.

[26] P. Niyogi, S. Smale, and S. Weinberger. Finding the Homology of Submanifolds with High Confidence from Random Samples. *Discrete and Computational Geometry*, 39(1-3), March 2008.

[27] S. T. Roweis and L. K. Saul. Nonlinear dimensionality reduction by locally linear embedding. *Science*, 290:2323–2326, 2000.

[28] H. S. Seung and D. D. lee. The manifold ways of perception. *Science*, 290:2268–2269, 2000.

[29] J. Shewchuk. Star splaying: An algorithm for repairing delaunay triangulations and convex hulls. In *Proc. ACM Symp. on Computational Geometry*, pages 237–246, 2005.

[30] J. B. Tenenbaum, V. deSilva, and J. C. Langford. A global geometric framework for nonlinear dimensionality reduction. *Science*, 290:2319–2323, 2000.

[31] Z. Zhang and H. Zha. Principal manifolds and nonlinear dimension reduction via local tangent space alignment. *SIAM Journal of Scientific Computing*, 26(1):313–338, 2004.

APPENDIX

LEMMA 15 ([26]). *Let $A = B(p, r) \cap \mathbb{M}$ where $r \leq \varepsilon \mathrm{lfs}(\mathbb{M})$. Then, $\phi_k r^k \geq \mathrm{vol}(A) \phi_k r^k / 2^k$, where ϕ_k is volume of the k-dimensional unit ball.*

Optimal Reconstruction Might be Hard*

[Extended Abstract]

Dominique Attali
Gipsa-lab, Grenoble, France
Dominique.Attali@grenoble-inp.fr

André Lieutier
Aix-en-Provence, France
Andre.Lieutier@wanadoo.dr

ABSTRACT

Sampling conditions for recovering the homology of a set using topological persistence are much weaker than sampling conditions required by any known polynomial time algorithm for producing a topologically correct reconstruction. Under the former sampling conditions which we call *weak sampling conditions*, we give an algorithm that outputs a topologically correct reconstruction. Unfortunately, even though the algorithm terminates, its time complexity is unbounded. Motivated by the question of knowing if a polynomial time algorithm for reconstruction exists under the weak sampling conditions, we identify at the heart of our algorithm a test which requires answering the following question: given two 2-dimensional simplicial complexes $L \subset K$, does there exist a simplicial complex containing L and contained in K which realizes the persistent homology of L into K? We call this problem the *homological simplification* of the pair (K, L) and prove that this problem is NP-complete, using a reduction from 3SAT.

Categories and Subject Descriptors

F.2.2 [**Analysis of Algorithms and Problem Complexity**]: Nonnumerical Algorithms and Problems—*Geometrical problems and computations, Computations on discrete structures*; I.3.5 [**Computer Graphics**]: Computational Geometry and Object Modeling

General Terms

Algorithms, Theory

Keywords

Shape reconstruction, topological persistence, sampling conditions, homological simplification, NP-completeness, 3SAT

*This work is partially supported by ANR Project *GIGA* ANR-09-BLAN-0331-01.

1. INTRODUCTION

Previous works.

In the last decade, several authors have proposed algorithms for reconstructing shapes with topological guarantees. First results considered compact smooth surfaces embedded in the Euclidean three-dimensional space and assumed surfaces to be known through noise-free samples [5, 1, 3, 9, 22, 4]. Since then, an effort has been made to generalize such results to wider classes of shapes and sampling conditions [24, 21, 32, 15, 10, 25].

An important extension allows samples to be noisy: each point of the sample is required to lie within some distance of the sampled shape (the sample is *accurate*) and each point of the sampled shape must lie within some distance of a sample point (the sample is *dense*). When both distances are bounded by the same value ε, the sampling condition can be expressed by saying that the *Hausdorff distance* between the shape and the sample is upper bounded by ε.

In 2006, several algorithms for reconstructing non-smooth objects with topological guarantees have been designed. In [33, 11], Boissonnat and Oudot considered Lipschitz manifolds while Chazal, Cohen-Steiner and Lieutier in [12] considered a large class of non-smooth compact sets called *sets with positive μ-reach.* In particular, the latter gave a polynomial time algorithm that is able to output what we will call in the paper a *faithful reconstruction* (see Definition 1).

In 2002, a fruitful point of view in computational topology, called *topological persistence*, has been introduced [26]. Within this context, the theorem on the stability of persistence diagrams [18] allows to infer the homology of shapes known through a sample. The sampling condition is significantly milder than the one required by the previously mentioned algorithm for computing a faithful reconstruction. We refer to this mild sampling condition sufficient for recovering homology as the *weak sampling condition.* This condition is tight.

Optimal reconstruction.

We call any algorithm that would be able to produce a faithful reconstruction under the weak sampling condition an *optimal reconstruction algorithm.* We explain in Section 2.3 that, even though no realistic version of an optimal reconstruction algorithm is known today, the weak sampling condition ensures that the sample contains in principle enough information on the sampled shape to produce without ambiguity a faithful reconstruction of it. Starting from this observation, we give in Section 2.4 a "naive" algorithm which, at the expense of not being efficient, produces a faithful reconstruction under the weak sampling condition.

The main question we pursue is: can we do better? More precisely, does there exist a polynomial time optimal reconstruction algorithm? Such an algorithm would have applications in several fields such as shape reconstruction or machine learning. While [6] gives a partially positive answer for subsets of $\mathbb{R}^2$, the question remains open for higher dimensions. Indeed, this problem is closely related to the persistence-sensitive simplification of real-valued functions, whose goal is to filter out topological noise in sub-level sets. Indeed, reconstruction can be thought of as the simplification of distance functions to the samples. For functions defined on triangulated 2-manifolds, polynomial algorithms have been devised [27, 6, 30]. Still, persistence-sensitive simplification of functions in higher dimension remains elusive.

Homological simplification.

In Section 3, we focus on the test at the heart of our naive algorithm. This test requires to answer the following question: given two 2-dimensional simplicial complexes $L \subset K$, does there exist a simplicial complex X containing L and contained in K such that the maps induced by the inclusions $L \hookrightarrow X$ and $X \hookrightarrow K$ on all modulo 2 homology groups are respectively surjective and injective. We call this problem the *homological simplification* of the pair (K, L) and prove that it is NP-complete.

Although this result is negative, we believe that it casts new light on the problem of finding a faithful reconstruction under weak sampling conditions and opens further research tracks as mentioned in Section 4. In particular, it suggests that, in order to design efficient reconstruction algorithms under weak sampling conditions, one has to make additional hypotheses. For instance, one can assume shapes are embedded in $\mathbb{R}^3$ and/or require some specific properties on embedded simplicial complexes.

2. THE QUEST FOR AN OPTIMAL RECONSTRUCTION ALGORITHM

Section 2.1 presents the necessary background. Section 2.2 contains our definition of a (homological) faithful reconstruction. We then define weak sampling condition and optimal reconstruction algorithms in Section 2.3. Finally, Section 2.4 presents a naive algorithm that outputs a homological faithful reconstruction under a condition approaching the weak sampling condition.

2.1 Background

The goal of this section is to recall three closely related concepts useful for the expression of sampling conditions in shape reconstruction. Given a shape $\mathcal{A}$, we define the reach $r_1(\mathcal{A})$, the μ-reach $r_\mu(\mathcal{A})$ for any $\mu \in (0,1]$ and the weak feature size $\text{wfs}(\mathcal{A})$. As we shall see, these quantities are related by the following inequality: $r_1(\mathcal{A}) \leq r_\mu(\mathcal{A}) \leq \text{wfs}(\mathcal{A})$. All three concepts can be derived from the critical function of the shape. This leads us to introduce the critical function, which requires first to define the norm of the gradient to the distance function.

The distance function to a compact set plays a central role in several recent works related to topologically guaranteed reconstruction [29, 23, 12]. For a compact set $\mathcal{A} \subset \mathbb{R}^N$, the distance function $d_\mathcal{A} : \mathbb{R}^N \to \mathbb{R}^+$ maps every point $q \in \mathbb{R}^N$ to

$$d_\mathcal{A}(q) = \min_{a \in \mathcal{A}} \|a - q\|.$$

Although not differentiable, $d_\mathcal{A}$ admits several extended notions of gradient [16, 29]. For our purpose, we will introduce a real valued function $\Psi_\mathcal{A} : \mathbb{R}^N \setminus \mathcal{A} \to [0,1]$ which corresponds to the norm of the gradient defined in [29]. Let $\frac{\mathrm{d}}{\mathrm{d}t^+}(\cdot)_{|t=0}$ denote the right derivative with respect to the variable t at $t=0$. For $q \in \mathbb{R}^N \setminus \mathcal{A}$ and $v \in \mathbb{S}^{N-1}$, one can check [29] that the quantity $\frac{\mathrm{d}}{\mathrm{d}t^+} d_\mathcal{A}(q+tv)_{|t=0}$ is well-defined and belongs to $[-1,1]$. We define $\Psi_\mathcal{A}$ as:

$$\Psi_\mathcal{A}(q) = \max\left\{0, \sup_{v \in \mathbb{S}^{N-1}} \frac{\mathrm{d}}{\mathrm{d}t^+} d_\mathcal{A}(q+tv)_{|t=0}\right\}.$$

Roughly speaking, $\Psi_\mathcal{A}(q)$ quantifies at which maximal speed the distance function to $\mathcal{A}$ can increase in a neighborhood of q. We are now ready to recall the definition of the critical function $\chi_\mathcal{A}$ introduced in [12]. The critical function maps every positive real number $\rho > 0$ to the infimum of $\Psi_\mathcal{A}$ over the set of points at distance ρ from $\mathcal{A}$:

$$\chi_\mathcal{A}(\rho) = \inf_{d_\mathcal{A}(q)=\rho} \Psi_\mathcal{A}(q).$$

The critical function is lower semi-continuous [12] and allows to define two quantities, the *μ-reach* and the *weak feature size* of $\mathcal{A}$ denoted respectively $r_\mu(\mathcal{A})$ and $\text{wfs}(\mathcal{A})$:

$$r_\mu(\mathcal{A}) = \inf\{\rho > 0,\ \chi_\mathcal{A}(\rho) < \mu\},$$
$$\text{wfs}(\mathcal{A}) = \inf\{\rho > 0,\ \chi_\mathcal{A}(\rho) = 0\}.$$

The reach of $\mathcal{A}$ is equal to $r_1(\mathcal{A})$. From the definition, it is clear that $r_1(\mathcal{A}) \leq r_\mu(\mathcal{A}) \leq \text{wfs}(\mathcal{A})$ for any $\mu \in (0,1]$. Figure 1 shows the critical function $\chi_\mathcal{A}$ for a simple shape $\mathcal{A}$ in the Euclidean plane, which consists of the points at distance R from a full rectangle of width ℓ and length L.

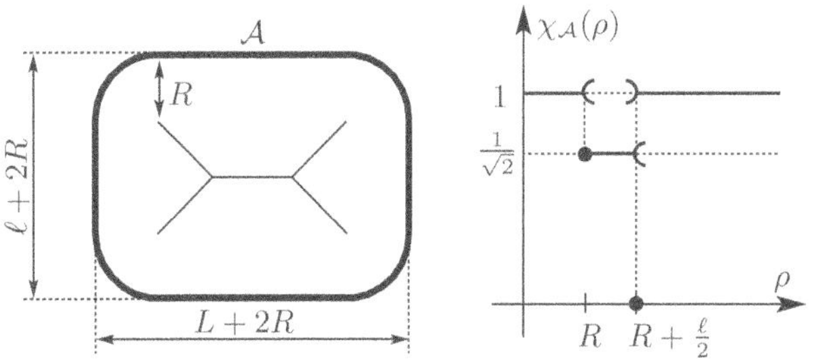

Figure 1: Left: the shape $\mathcal{A}$ is the outer closed thick curve and its medial axis consists of the five thin inner segments. Right: critical function $\chi_\mathcal{A}$. We have $r_\mu(\mathcal{A}) = R$ for $\mu > \frac{1}{\sqrt{2}}$ and $r_\mu(\mathcal{A}) = R + \frac{l}{2} = \text{wfs}(A)$ for $\mu \leq \frac{1}{\sqrt{2}}$.

To shed light on these notions, it is useful to make some connections with the medial axis. The *medial axis* of $\mathcal{A}$ is the set of points $q \notin \mathcal{A}$ which have at least two closest points in $\mathcal{A}$. Alternatively, it is the locus of points q for which $\Psi_\mathcal{A}(q) < 1$. Any point q for which $\Psi_\mathcal{A}(q) = 0$ is called a *critical point* of the distance function and lies on the medial axis. The reach is the minimum of distances between points in $\mathcal{A}$ and in its medial axis. The weak feature size is the minimum of distances between points in $\mathcal{A}$ and critical points.

For instance, the function $\Psi_\mathcal{A}$ of the shape $\mathcal{A}$ depicted in Figure 1 evaluates to 0 on the horizontal line of the medial axis which constitutes the only critical points in this case, evaluates to $\frac{1}{\sqrt{2}}$ on the other points of the medial axis and evaluates to 0 on all points of the plane that neither belong to $\mathcal{A}$ nor to its medial axis.

For completeness, we also recall the related notion of local feature size, introduced by Amenta [2] for reconstructing smooth shapes. The *local feature size* is a real-valued function which maps every point of $\mathcal{A}$ to its distance to the medial axis. Notice that the local feature size and its infimum, the reach, vanish on non-smooth objects as soon as they contain a sharp concave corner or edge. For this reason, we will focus in Section 2.3 on sampling conditions based on the weak feature size and μ-reaches which apply to a large class of non-smooth shapes.

Given $\eta > 0$, the η-offset of $\mathcal{A}$ is the set of points at distance η or less from $\mathcal{A}$, $\mathcal{A}^\eta = d_\mathcal{A}^{-1}([0,\eta])$. As in Morse theory, topological changes in offsets occur only at critical values. More precisely, as stated in [28, 14]:

Lemma 1 (Topological Stability of Offsets). *If $0 < x < y < \mathrm{wfs}(\mathcal{A})$, then the inclusion map $\mathcal{A}^x \hookrightarrow \mathcal{A}^y$ is a homotopy equivalence.*

2.2 Faithful reconstructions

Let us now give our definitions of a faithful reconstruction and a faithful homological reconstruction. For the second definition, we will consider a fixed field F and take coefficients in F for homology [31, Chapter 1]. Hence, the property of being a faithful homological reconstruction will depend on the choice of F.

Definition 1. *We say that a subset $\mathcal{R} \subset \mathbb{R}^N$ is a* faithful reconstruction *of the compact set $\mathcal{A} \subset \mathbb{R}^N$ if there exist real numbers x, y such that $0 < x < y < \mathrm{wfs}(\mathcal{A})$ and the following two properties hold:*

- $\mathcal{A}^x \subset \mathcal{R} \subset \mathcal{A}^y$
- *the inclusion maps $\mathcal{A}^x \hookrightarrow \mathcal{R}$ and $\mathcal{R} \hookrightarrow \mathcal{A}^y$ are homotopy equivalences.*

We say that $\mathcal{R}$ is a faithful homological reconstruction *when the last condition is relaxed by:*

- *the inclusion maps $\mathcal{A}^x \hookrightarrow \mathcal{R}$ and $\mathcal{R} \hookrightarrow \mathcal{A}^y$ induces isomorphisms on all homology groups.*

A faithful reconstruction is always a faithful homological reconstruction. As expected, the converse is not true: a punctured Poincaré sphere nested between a point and a ball is an example where inclusions are not homotopy equivalences but yet induce isomorphisms on homology groups [17]. Interestingly, this example does not embed in $\mathbb{R}^3$.

Note that in the above definition, if one of the two inclusion maps $\mathcal{A}^x \hookrightarrow \mathcal{R}$ or $\mathcal{R} \hookrightarrow \mathcal{A}^y$ is a homotopy equivalence, so is the other one. Indeed, by Lemma 1, $\mathcal{A}^x \hookrightarrow \mathcal{A}^y$ is a homotopy equivalence and we can conclude by applying Lemma 2 below. A similar statement can be made for the second part of the definition.

Lemma 2. *Consider three nested spaces $\mathcal{A} \subset \mathcal{B} \subset \mathcal{C}$. If two of the three inclusions $i : \mathcal{A} \hookrightarrow \mathcal{B}$, $j : \mathcal{B} \hookrightarrow \mathcal{C}$ and $k = j \circ i : \mathcal{A} \hookrightarrow \mathcal{C}$ are homotopy equivalences, then the third one is also a homotopy equivalence.*

Proof. If i and j are homotopy equivalences with homotopy inverses i' and j' respectively, then $i' \circ j'$ is clearly a homotopy inverse of $k = j \circ i$.

If j and k are homotopy equivalences with homotopy inverses j' and k' respectively, then using $k = j \circ i$ we get that $j' \circ k = j' \circ j \circ i \simeq i$ and $k' \circ j$ is a homotopy inverse of $i \simeq j' \circ k$.

Similarly, if i and k are homotopy equivalences with homotopy inverses i' and k' respectively, then using $k = j \circ i$ we get that $k \circ i' = j \circ i \circ i' \simeq j$ and $i \circ k'$ is a homotopic inverse of $j \simeq k \circ i'$. □

2.3 Sampling conditions

In this section, we compare inputs, preconditions and outputs of two algorithms that infer information on a shape $\mathcal{A}$ known through a finite sample $\mathcal{S}$. Specifically, the first algorithm recovers Betti numbers of $\mathcal{A}$ and the second one constructs a faithful approximation of $\mathcal{A}$. Each algorithm relies on a key theorem that states sampling conditions ensuring correctness. Both algorithms are polynomial in the size of the sample. We then define an *optimal reconstruction algorithm* as one that would produce the output of the second algorithm with the input and precondition of the first algorithm.

We recall that the *Hausdorff distance* between two compact sets $\mathcal{A}$ and $\mathcal{A}'$ of $\mathbb{R}^N$ is defined by:

$$d_H(\mathcal{A}, \mathcal{A}') = \|d_{\mathcal{A}'} - d_\mathcal{A}\|_\infty = \sup_{q \in \mathbb{R}^N} |d_{\mathcal{A}'}(q) - d_\mathcal{A}(q)|.$$

Computing Betti numbers.

A powerful tool for inferring Betti numbers from geometric approximations is topological persistence [26]. Theorem 3 below is a corollary of the Persistence Stability Theorem [18] and can also be derived by flow based arguments [14]. Before stating it, we need the following definition.

Definition 2. *Let $\mathcal{A} \subset \mathbb{R}^N$ be a compact set and let $0 \leq x \leq y$. The* p-th (x, y)-persistent Betti number *of $\mathcal{A}$ is the rank of the homomorphism induced by inclusion $\mathcal{A}^x \hookrightarrow \mathcal{A}^y$:*

$$\beta_p^{x,y}(\mathcal{A}) = \mathrm{rank}\left(\mathbf{H}_p(\mathcal{A}^x) \hookrightarrow \mathbf{H}_p(\mathcal{A}^y)\right)$$

It is worth noting that the (x, y)-persistent Betti numbers are finite whenever $x < y$ [20].

Theorem 3 (Homology Inference [18, 14]). *Let $\mathcal{A}$ and $\mathcal{S}$ be two compact subsets of $\mathbb{R}^N$ and suppose there exists a real number $\alpha > 0$ such that*

$$d_H(\mathcal{S}, \mathcal{A}) < \alpha < \frac{1}{4}\,\mathrm{wfs}(\mathcal{A})$$

Then, $\beta_p(\mathcal{A}) = \beta_p^{\alpha,3\alpha}(\mathcal{S})$.

The above theorem leads immediately to a polynomial time algorithm for inferring Betti numbers of a shape $\mathcal{A}$ when the sample $\mathcal{S}$ of $\mathcal{A}$ is finite. Indeed, writing $K_\alpha(\mathcal{S})$ for the α-complex of $\mathcal{S}$, the persistent Betti numbers can be expressed as

$$\beta_p^{\alpha,3\alpha}(\mathcal{S}) = \mathrm{rank}\left(\mathbf{H}_p(K_\alpha(\mathcal{S})) \hookrightarrow \mathbf{H}_p(K_{3\alpha}(\mathcal{S}))\right).$$

In particular, they can be computed in time cubic the size of $K_{3\alpha}(\mathcal{S})$. Since for a fixed dimension, the size of α-complexes is polynomial in the number of vertices, it follows that $\beta_p(\mathcal{A})$ can also be computed in polynomial time the size of the sample.

Table 1: Input, precondition and output of two polynomial time algorithms derived from Theorem 3 and Theorem 4. The notation "$\exists\mathcal{A}$" stands for "there exists a compact set $\mathcal{A} \subset \mathbb{R}^N$". $\mathcal{S}$ designates a finite set of $\mathbb{R}^N$. α and μ designate two real numbers with $\alpha > 0$ and $\mu \in (0,1]$.

Input	Precondition	Output
$\mathcal{S}$, α	$\exists\mathcal{A}, d_H(\mathcal{S},\mathcal{A}) < \alpha < \frac{1}{4}\,\mathrm{wfs}(\mathcal{A})$	Betti numbers of $\mathcal{A}$
$\mathcal{S}$, α, μ	$\exists\mathcal{A}, d_H(\mathcal{S},\mathcal{A}) < \alpha < \frac{\mu^2}{5\mu^2+12} r_\mu(\mathcal{A})$	a faithful reconstruction of $\mathcal{A}$

Computing a faithful reconstruction.
For a shape $\mathcal{A}$ with a positive μ-reach, authors in [12] describe a simple procedure for computing a faithful reconstruction of $\mathcal{A}$, given as input a sample $\mathcal{S}$ of $\mathcal{A}$. The procedure consists merely of outputting an r-offset of the sample, for a suitable value of the offset parameter r (see Theorem 4 below for the precise value of r). In practice, this computation can be replaced by the computation of $K_r(\mathcal{S})$, which shares the same homotopy type. Both computations can be done in polynomial time if the sample is finite. The sampling condition required by the procedure is that the Hausdorff distance between the sample $\mathcal{S}$ and the sampled shape $\mathcal{A}$ is less than a fraction the μ-reach of $\mathcal{A}$. More precisely:

THEOREM 4 (RECONSTRUCTION THEOREM [12]). *Let $\mathcal{A}$ and $\mathcal{S}$ be two compact subsets of $\mathbb{R}^N$ and suppose there exists two real numbers $\alpha > 0$ and $\mu \in (0,1]$ such that*

$$d_H(\mathcal{S},\mathcal{A}) < \alpha < \frac{\mu^2}{5\mu^2+12} r_\mu(\mathcal{A})$$

Then, $\mathcal{S}^{\frac{4\alpha}{\mu^2}}$ is a faithful reconstruction of $\mathcal{A}$.

Comparing sampling conditions.
Table 1 summarizes inputs, preconditions and outputs of the two polynomial time algorithms described above and inspired by Theorems 3 and 4. Note that the precondition required by the first algorithm which we call the *weak precondition* is equivalent to saying that the following set is non-empty:

$$W(\mathcal{S},\alpha) = \left\{\mathcal{X} \mid d_H(\mathcal{S},\mathcal{X}) < \alpha < \frac{1}{4}\,\mathrm{wfs}(\mathcal{X})\right\} \neq \emptyset, \quad (1)$$

where $\mathcal{X}$ ranges over all compact sets of $\mathbb{R}^N$. By Theorem 3, all shapes in $W(\mathcal{S},\alpha)$ share the same Betti numbers and the first algorithm returns the Betti numbers of any $\mathcal{A} \in W(\mathcal{S},\alpha)$. Since $r_\mu(\mathcal{A})$ is by definition upper bounded by $\mathrm{wfs}(\mathcal{A})$, the first precondition is significantly weaker than the second precondition, especially when μ is small. We now claim that, in some sense, the input of the first algorithm together with its weak precondition determines completely the output of the second. Indeed, let us recall from [14] the following theorem:

THEOREM 5 ([14]). *Let $\mathcal{A}$ and $\mathcal{X}$ be two compact subsets of $\mathbb{R}^N$ and $\alpha > 0$ a real number such that*

$$d_H(\mathcal{A},\mathcal{X}) < 2\alpha < \frac{1}{2}\min\{\mathrm{wfs}(\mathcal{A}), \mathrm{wfs}(\mathcal{X})\}$$

Then, $\mathcal{X}^{2\alpha}$ is a faithful reconstruction of $\mathcal{A}$.

Suppose $\mathcal{A}$ and $\mathcal{X}$ both belong to $W(\mathcal{S},\alpha)$. Applying a triangular inequality, we get that $\mathcal{A}$, $\mathcal{X}$ and α fulfill conditions of Theorem 5 and therefore, $\mathcal{X}^{2\alpha}$ is a faithful reconstruction of $\mathcal{A}$. Hence, any 2α-offset of a shape $\mathcal{X} \in W(\mathcal{S},\alpha)$ is a faithful reconstruction of any shape $\mathcal{A} \in W(\mathcal{S},\alpha)$. In other words, all shapes in $W(\mathcal{S},\alpha)$ share a common set of faithful reconstructions which contains 2α-offsets of $W(\mathcal{S},\alpha)$. For this reason, we say that, under the weak precondition, inputs $\mathcal{S}$ and α carry in principle enough information about the unknown shape $\mathcal{A}$ to determine without ambiguity a faithful reconstruction of it.

Optimal reconstruction algorithms.
The weak precondition is tight, by which we mean that for any $\eta > 0$, the set $W_\eta(\mathcal{S},\alpha) = \{\mathcal{X} \text{ compact set of } \mathbb{R}^N \mid d_H(\mathcal{S},\mathcal{X}) < \alpha < \frac{1}{4}\,\mathrm{wfs}(\mathcal{X}) + \eta\}$ may contain objects that do not have the same homology. To construct such an example, consider the two shapes $\mathcal{O}$ and $\mathcal{U}$ described in [14] and the sample $\mathcal{S}$ pictured on Figure 2. By construction, we have $\mathrm{wfs}(\mathcal{O}) = 2$, $\mathrm{wfs}(\mathcal{U}) = +\infty$ and $d_H(S,\mathcal{O}) = d_H(S,\mathcal{U}) = \frac{1+\eta}{2}$. Hence, both $\mathcal{O}$ and $\mathcal{U}$ belong to $W_\eta(\mathcal{S}, \frac{1}{2} + \frac{3\eta}{4})$ but $\beta_1(\mathcal{O}) \neq \beta_1(\mathcal{U})$. Therefore, the weak precondition is the weakest amongst the preconditions expressed in terms of Hausdorff distance and critical functions that allows to retrieve a faithful reconstruction without ambiguity.

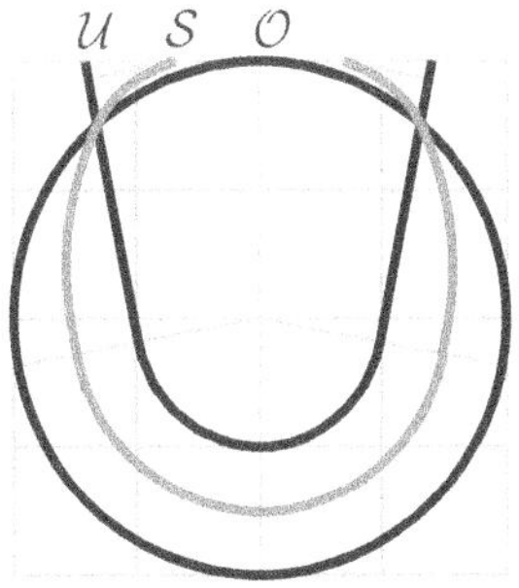

Figure 2: The angle between the two bars in shape $\mathcal{U}$ is adjusted such that $d_H(\mathcal{S},\mathcal{O}) = d_H(\mathcal{S},\mathcal{U}) = \frac{1+\eta}{2}$.

Because of that, we call any algorithm that would be able to output a faithful reconstruction under the weak precondition and associated inputs an *optimal reconstruction algorithm*. In Section 2.4, we describe a naive algorithm that outputs a faithful homological reconstruction under the weak precondition. We call it "naive" since it has an unbounded time complexity. The main question motivating our work is whether there exists a polynomial time optimal reconstruction algorithm. Section 3 suggests a negative answer if no additional condition is assumed.

2.4 Naive algorithms for reconstruction

Given as input a pair $(\mathcal{S}, \alpha)$ satisfying the weak precondition, the previous section suggests the following strategy for computing a faithful reconstruction: enumerate all compact sets in $\mathbb{R}^N$ and return the 2α-offset of the first compact set $\mathcal{X}$ that belongs to $W(\mathcal{S}, \alpha)$. Of course, this procedure is unrealistic and the goal of this section is to present an effective version of it. Specifically, given as input a sample $\mathcal{S}$ and two real numbers α and η satisfying the precondition:

$$\exists \mathcal{A},\ d_H(\mathcal{S}, \mathcal{A}) < \alpha < \frac{1}{4}(\mathrm{wfs}(\mathcal{A}) - \eta), \qquad (2)$$

we describe an algorithm that computes a faithful homological reconstruction of $\mathcal{A}$ and whose pseudocode is given in Table 2. The idea is to replace the enumeration on compact sets by an enumeration on cubical sets and refine the size of the cubes until we find a solution. We also simplify the problem, replacing the search for a faithful reconstruction by the search of a faithful homological simplification. We proceed in two steps. First, we give an algorithm for shapes with a positive μ-reach (`NAIVE_1`) and then, derive an algorithm for shapes with a lower bounded weak feature size (`NAIVE_2`).

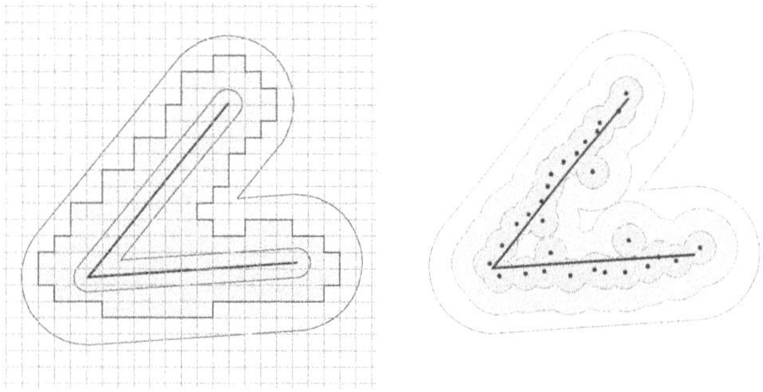

Figure 3: Left: the cubical set (in pink) is nested between two offsets (in light purple) of the V-shaped black curve and is a faithful reconstruction of it. Right: offsets $\mathcal{S}^l$ and $\mathcal{S}^k$ of the sample.

We start with some definitions. An *ε-voxel* is a closed cube with edge length ε and whose vertices belong to the lattice $\varepsilon\mathbb{Z}^N$. We call any finite union of ε-voxels an *ε-cubical set*. Assuming a shape $\mathcal{A}$ has a positive μ-reach, next lemma states the existence of a cubical set which is a faithful reconstruction of $\mathcal{A}$. This is a key ingredient in establishing the correctness of the naive algorithms.

LEMMA 6. *There exists a positive constant c_N depending only upon the ambient dimension N such that the following property holds: for all real numbers x, y and $\mu \in (0,1]$ and all compact sets $\mathcal{A} \subset \mathbb{R}^N$ satisfying $r_\mu(\mathcal{A}) > y > x > 0$, there exists a $(c_N\mu(y-x))$-cubical set $\mathcal{X}$ such that $\mathcal{A}^x \subset \mathcal{X} \subset \mathcal{A}^y$ and the inclusion maps $\mathcal{A}^x \hookrightarrow \mathcal{X}$ and $\mathcal{X} \hookrightarrow \mathcal{A}^y$ are homotopy equivalences. In particular, the cubical set $\mathcal{X}$ is a faithful reconstruction of $\mathcal{A}$ (see Figure 3, left).*

The proof is in the appendix and relies on a result in [8].

First naive reconstruction algorithm.

Under precondition (2), the algorithm `NAIVE_1` outputs either the empty set or a faithful homological reconstruction

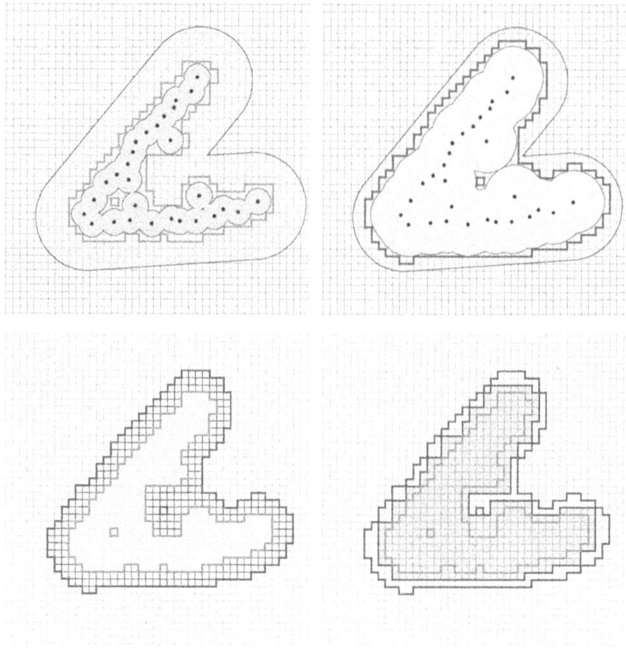

Figure 4: Illustration of algorithm `NAIVE_1`. Top: boundaries of $\mathcal{L} = V_\varepsilon(\mathcal{S}^l)$ and $\mathcal{K} = V_\varepsilon(\mathcal{S}^k)$ are depicted in red and dark green. Bottom: the cubical set $\mathcal{X}$ in blue is nested between $\mathcal{L}$ and $\mathcal{K}$ and is a faithful homological reconstruction of $\mathcal{A}$.

of $\mathcal{A}$. Its pseudocode is given in Table 2, left. The algorithm proceeds as follows. It chooses a voxel size ε, two offset parameters l and k and derives from the sample $\mathcal{S}$ two ε-cubical sets $\mathcal{L} = V_\varepsilon(\mathcal{S}^l)$ and $\mathcal{K} = V_\varepsilon(\mathcal{S}^k)$, obtained by collecting all ε-voxels intersecting respectively $\mathcal{S}^l$ and $\mathcal{S}^k$ (see Figures 3 and 4). For all cubical sets $\mathcal{X}$ containing $\mathcal{L}$ and contained in $\mathcal{K}$, the algorithm then considers three nested simplicial complexes $L \subset X \subset K$ triangulating the three cubical sets $\mathcal{L} \subset \mathcal{X} \subset \mathcal{K}$ in a way that is consistent with the grid. It then returns $\mathcal{X}$ if the simplicial complex X is a homological simplification of the pair (K, L) (see definition below). If no homological simplification X is found between L and K, the algorithm returns the empty set.

DEFINITION 3 (HOMOLOGICAL SIMPLIFICATION). *Let $L \subset K$ be two simplicial complexes. The simplicial complex X is said to be a* homological simplification *of the pair (K, L) if $L \subset X \subset K$ and the maps $j_* : \mathbf{H}_p(L) \to \mathbf{H}_p(X)$ and $i_* : \mathbf{H}_p(X) \to \mathbf{H}_p(K)$ induced by inclusions are respectively surjective and injective for all integers $p \geq 0$ (see Figure 5).*

$$\mathbf{H}_p(L) \xrightarrow{\ j_*\ } \mathbf{H}_p(X) \xrightarrow{\ i_*\ } \mathbf{H}_p(K)$$

Figure 5: Notations for Definition 3 and the proof of Lemma 7.

The correctness of the algorithm relies on several lemmas stated in the appendix. Under precondition (2), if X is a homological simplification of the pair (K, L), then Lemma 12 implies that $\mathcal{X} = |X|$ is a faithful homological reconstruction

Table 2: Naive reconstruction algorithms. $|X|$ denotes the underlying space of the simplicial complex X. $sc(\mathcal{X})$ denotes a triangulation of the cubical set $\mathcal{X}$ compatible with inclusion.

```
NAIVE_1( S, α, η, μ )
PRECONDITION: ∃A, d_H(S,A) < α < 1/4(wfs(A) − η)
OUTPUT: either ∅ or a faithful homological reconstruction
of A.

ε ← η / (4√N + 2/(c_N μ))
l ← η/2 + α;            k ← η + 3α − ε√N
L ← sc(V_ε(S^l));        K ← sc(V_ε(S^k))

for all ( X such that L ⊂ X ⊂ K )
    if ( X is a homological simplification of (K, L) )
    return |X|
end for
return ∅
```

```
NAIVE_2( S, α, η )
PRECONDITION: ∃A, d_H(S,A) < α < 1/4(wfs(A) − η)
OUTPUT: a faithful homological reconstruction of A

μ ← 1
α' ← α + η/8
η' ← η/4

while ( TRUE )
    X ← NAIVE_1(S, α', η', μ)
    if ( X != ∅ ) return X
    μ ← μ/2
end while
```

of $\mathcal{A}$. Furthermore, under the stronger precondition (3):

$$\exists \mathcal{A},\ d_H(\mathcal{S},\mathcal{A}) < \alpha < \frac{1}{4}\left(r_\mu(\mathcal{A}) - \eta\right), \tag{3}$$

Lemma 11 guarantees that the algorithm always returns a faithful homological simplification (and not $\emptyset$). Let us bound the time complexity of a more efficient version of the algorithm in which voxels are not decomposed into simplices. Let D be the diameter of $\mathcal{S}$ and set $D' = D + 2(\nu + 3\alpha)$. It is not difficult to check that this simpler algorithm has time complexity $O\left(2^{|K|}|K|^3\right) = O\left(2^{\left(\frac{D'}{\varepsilon}\right)^N}\left(\frac{D'}{\varepsilon}\right)^{3N}\right)$. Indeed, the size of K is $O((D'/\varepsilon)^N)$. Checking if X is a homological simplification of (K, L) takes cubic time the size of K and the number of cubical sets $\mathcal{X}$ between $\mathcal{L}$ and $\mathcal{K}$ is $O(2^{|\mathcal{K}|})$.

Second naive reconstruction algorithm.

Under precondition (2), the algorithm `NAIVE_2` outputs a faithful homological reconstruction of $\mathcal{A}$ after a finite number of iterations. Its pseudocode is given in Table 2, right. Starting with $\mu = 1$, it calls `NAIVE_1` with decreasing values of μ until `NAIVE_1` returns a faithful homological reconstruction. The algorithm terminates thanks to the lower semi-continuity of the critical function $\chi_\mathcal{A}$. Indeed, $\chi_\mathcal{A}$ attains its minimum $\mu' > 0$ over the interval $[\frac{\eta}{8}, 4\alpha + \frac{7\eta}{8}]$. Setting $\mathcal{A}' = \mathcal{A}^{\frac{\eta}{8}}$, $\alpha' = \alpha + \frac{\eta}{8}$ and $\eta' = \frac{\eta}{4}$, we have $r_{\mu'}(\mathcal{A}') > 4\alpha + \frac{3\eta}{4} = 4\alpha' + \eta'$ (see Figure 6 for an explanation) and therefore precondition (3) is satisfied for $\mathcal{A} = \mathcal{A}'$, $\alpha = \alpha'$, $\mu = \mu'$ and $\eta = \eta'$. Note that even though the algorithm terminates, its time complexity is unbounded.

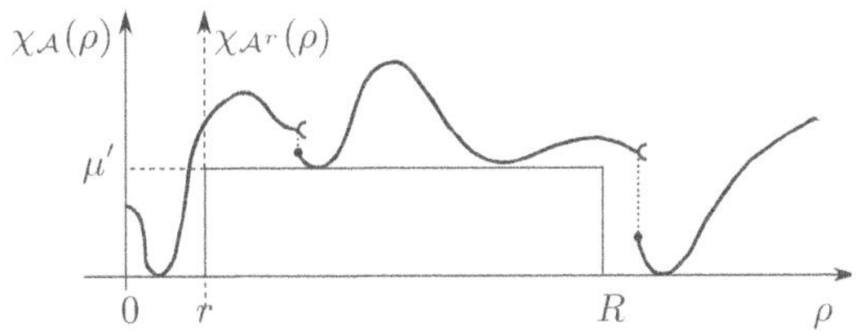

Figure 6: Performing an r-offset translates into translating the critical function to the left by r [12]. Thus, $\chi_\mathcal{A}(\rho) \geq \mu'$ on $[r, R]$ implies $r_{\mu'}(\mathcal{A}^r) > R - r$.

3. HOMOLOGICAL SIMPLIFICATION IS NP-COMPLETE

In this section, we focus on the problem of computing a homological simplification and prove that this problem is NP-complete. We denote the *p-th homology group* of K by $\mathbf{H}_p(K)$ and work with coefficients in the field $\mathbb{Z}_2$ of integers modulo 2. A *simplicial pair* (K, L) consists of a (finite) simplicial complex K and a subcomplex $L \subset K$. When clear from the context, we will simply speak of the pair (K, L) and omit "simplicial". We say that the pair (K, L) is *p-dimensional* if the simplicial complex K has dimension p.

DEFINITION 4. *The homological simplification problem takes as input a simplicial pair (K, L) and asks whether there exists a simplicial complex X which is a homological simplification of the pair (K, L).*

The size of the problem is the number of simplices in K. A useful observation is that since we are working with coefficients in $\mathbb{Z}_2$ and homology groups are finite-dimensional vector spaces, X is a homological simplification of the pair (K, L) if and only if X realizes the persistent homology of L into K. Formally, we have:

LEMMA 7. *Consider a sequence of simplicial complexes $L \subset X \subset K$. The simplicial complex X is a homological simplification of the pair (K, L) if and only if $\mathbf{H}_p(X)$ is isomorphic to the image of the homomorphism $\mathbf{H}_p(L) \to \mathbf{H}_p(K)$ induced by the inclusion $L \subset K$, for all integers $p \geq 0$.*

PROOF. See Figure 5. If X is a homological simplification of the pair (K, L), then the injectivity of the map $i_* : \mathbf{H}_p(X) \to \mathbf{H}_p(K)$ induced by the inclusion $X \subset K$ implies that $\mathbf{H}_p(X)$ is isomorphic to $i_*(\mathbf{H}_p(X))$ and the surjectivity of the map $j_* : \mathbf{H}_p(L) \to \mathbf{H}_p(X)$ induced by inclusion $L \subset X$ implies that $\mathbf{H}_p(X) = j_*(\mathbf{H}_p(L))$. It follows that $\mathbf{H}_p(X)$ is isomorphic to $i_* \circ j_*(\mathbf{H}_p(L))$ for all p.

Conversely, suppose $\mathbf{H}_p(X)$ is isomorphic to $i_* \circ j_*(\mathbf{H}_p(L))$. Then, j_* is surjective because $\dim j_*(\mathbf{H}_p(L)) \geq \dim i_* \circ j_*(\mathbf{H}_p(L)) = \dim \mathbf{H}_p(X)$. Furthermore, i_* is injective because the surjectivity of j_* implies $i_*(\mathbf{H}_p(X)) = i_* \circ j_*(\mathbf{H}_p(L))$ which is isomorphic to $\mathbf{H}_p(X)$. □

We are now ready to state our main theorem:

THEOREM 8. *The homological simplification problem of 2-dimensional simplicial pairs is NP-complete.*

PROOF. To check that a candidate X is a homological simplification of the p-dimensional pair (K, L), it is enough to compute the dimension of the p-th homology group of X and compare it to the rank of the persistent p-th homology group of K into L, for all p. Since all computations can be done in time cubic in the number of simplices in K, we deduce that the homological simplification problem of p-dimensional simplicial pairs is in NP. In Section 3.1, we prove that this problem is NP-hard for $p = 2$ by reducing 3SAT to it in polynomial time. Figure 7 summarizes the reduction. □

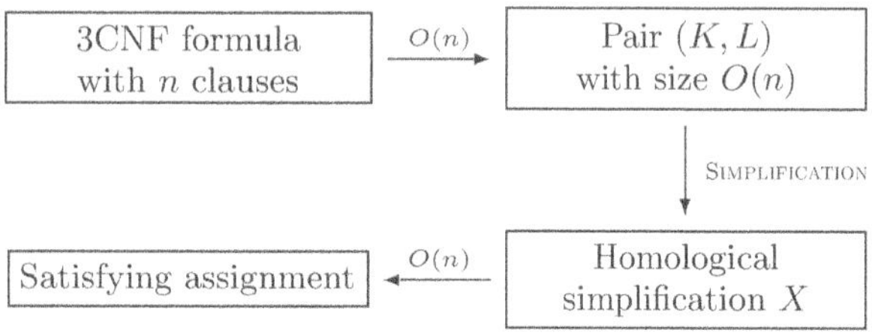

Figure 7: Diagram of the reduction.

3.1 Reduction from 3SAT

A Boolean formula E is in *3-conjunctive normal form*, or 3CNF, if it is a conjunction (AND) of n clauses $c_1, c_2, \ldots, c_n$, each of which is a disjunction (OR) of three literals, each literal being a Boolean variable or its negation [19]. Specifically, $E = \bigwedge_{1 \le i \le n} c_i$ and each clause c_i has the form

$$c_i = \left(e_i^1 v_{j_i^1}\right) \vee \left(e_i^2 v_{j_i^2}\right) \vee \left(e_i^3 v_{j_i^3}\right),$$

where $j_i^k \in \{1, \ldots, m\}$, $v_{j_i^k}$ is a Boolean variable and $e_i^k \in \{\mathbf{1}, \neg\}$ is either the identity symbol $\mathbf{1}$ or the negation symbol $\neg$, for $1 \le k \le 3$. The 3SAT problem takes as input a 3CNF formula E and determines whether one can assign a value TRUE or FALSE to each variable of E such that E evaluates to TRUE. An assignment of variables which makes E evaluates to TRUE is called a *satisfying assignment.* Since the number m of variables used in formula E is at most three times the number n of clauses, *i.e.* $m \le 3n$, we let n be the size of the 3SAT problem. 3SAT is known to be NP-complete.

Reduction algorithm.

We describe a reduction algorithm that transforms in linear time any instance E of the 3SAT problem into an instance (K, L) of the homological simplification problem in such a way that (K, L) has a homological simplification if and only if E has a satisfying assignment. Given a 3CNF formula E of n clauses $c_1, \ldots, c_n$ and m variables $v_1, \ldots, v_m$, we construct a 2-dimensional simplicial pair (K, L) as follows; see Figure 8. The simplicial complex L consists of

- a vertex A;
- two vertices B_i and C_i and three edges AB_i, B_iC_i and C_iA for each clause c_i;
- two vertices V_j and W_j and the edge V_jW_j for each variable v_j.

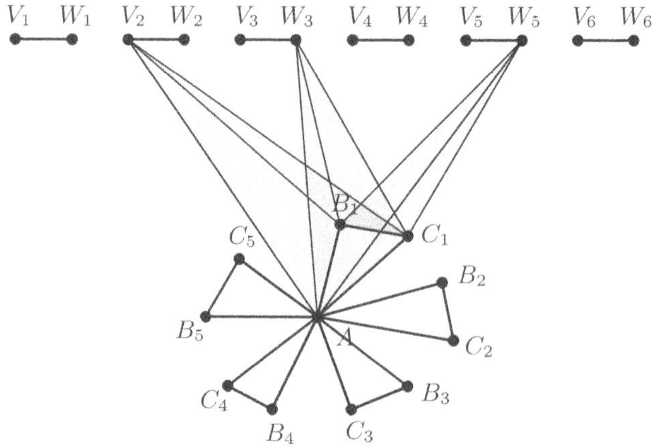

Figure 8: Simplicial complex L output by the reduction of a formula with five clauses and six variables and triangles in K created by clause $c_1 = v_2 \vee \neg v_3 \vee \neg v_5$.

Besides simplices in L, the simplicial complex K contains three triangles per literal and two edges per variable. Specifically, if $e_i^k = \mathbf{1}$, we add the three triangles $AB_iV_{j_i^k}$, $B_iC_iV_{j_i^k}$ and $C_iAV_{j_i^k}$ and their edges. If $e_i^k = \neg$, we add the three triangles $AB_iW_{j_i^k}$, $B_iC_iW_{j_i^k}$ and $C_iAW_{j_i^k}$ and their edges. Moreover, we add edges AV_j and AW_j for all $j \in \{1, \ldots, m\}$. Observe that the size of K is only a constant factor larger than the size of E and its construction requires linear time in n.

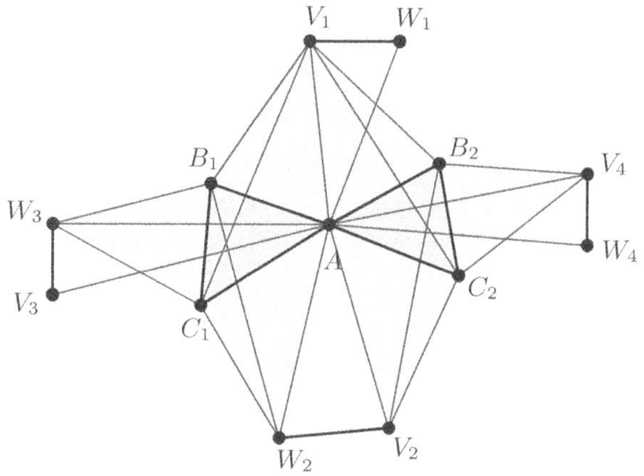

Figure 9: Pair (K, L) produced by the reduction of formula $(v_1 \vee \neg v_2 \vee \neg v_3) \wedge (v_1 \vee v_2 \vee v_4)$. L consists of the vertices and bold edges.

Let $f_* : \mathbf{H}_p(L) \to \mathbf{H}_p(K)$ be the homomorphism induced by the inclusion $L \subset K$. Since K is connected, we have $f_*(\mathbf{H}_0(L)) = \mathbb{Z}_2$. Furthermore, $f_*(\mathbf{H}_1(L)) = 0$ since a base of the 1-cycles in L is given by the n cycles $\sigma_i = AB_i + B_iC_i + C_iA$ and σ_i is homologous to 0 in K for each $i \in \{1, \ldots, n\}$. Last, $f_*(\mathbf{H}_2(L)) = 0$ since L contains no 2-simplices. By Lemma 7, we obtain that X is a homological simplification of the pair (K, L) if and only if $\mathbf{H}_0(X) = \mathbb{Z}_2$, $\mathbf{H}_1(X) = 0$ and $\mathbf{H}_2(X) = 0$. Keeping this in mind, we establish the following lemma, in which (K, L) designates the pair output by our reduction algorithm when applied to formula E.

LEMMA 9. *The pair (K, L) has a homological simplification if and only if the formula E has a satisfying assignment. Furthermore, given a homological simplification of the pair (K, L), computing a satisfying assignment for E takes linear time.*

PROOF. Suppose the pair (K, L) has a homological simplification X and let us prove that E has a satisfying assignment. First, we claim that X cannot contain both edges AV_j and AW_j, for $1 \leq j \leq m$. Indeed, if both edges AV_j and AW_j were in X, we could consider the cycle $\tau = AV_j + V_jW_j + W_jA$. Since the edge V_jW_j bounds no triangle in K, the cycle τ cannot be homologous to 0 in X, contradicting $\mathbf{H}_1(X) = 0$.

The claim allows us to assign to each variable v_j either the value `TRUE` if the edge AV_j belongs to X or the value `FALSE` if the edge AW_j belongs to X. If none of the edges AV_j and AW_j belong to X, then we assign to v_j an arbitrary value in $\{\texttt{TRUE}, \texttt{FALSE}\}$; see Figure 10. Note that the computation of this assignment can be done in linear time. We now check that this assignment of boolean values to the variables v_j is a satisfying assignment, in other words we show that all clauses c_i are satisfied for $1 \leq i \leq n$.

Since $\mathbf{H}_1(X) = 0$, the 1-cycle $AB_i + B_iC_i + C_iA$ is a boundary in X. This implies that at least one triangle of X contains AB_i on its boundary. By construction, AB_i belongs to exactly three triangles in K, namely the triangles $AB_iY_i^k$ for $1 \leq k \leq 3$ where Y_i^k designates $V_{j_i^k}$ if $e_i^k = \mathbf{1}$ and $W_{j_i^k}$ if $e_i^k = \neg$. It follows that one of the three triangles $AB_iY_i^k$ must belong to X and, in turn, at least one of the three edges AY_i^k for $1 \leq k \leq 3$ is in X. This implies that one of the three literals $e_i^k v_{j_i^k}$ in clause c_i evaluates to `TRUE` and hence c_i is satisfied.

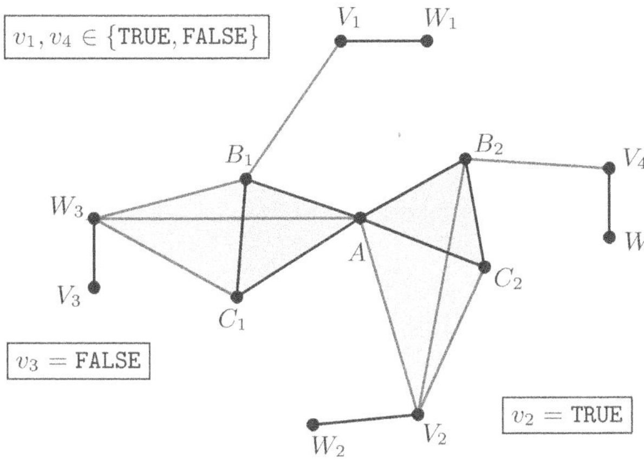

Figure 10: A homological simplification of the pair (K, L) drawn in Figure 9 and output by the reduction of formula $E = (v_1 \vee \neg v_2 \vee \neg v_3) \wedge (v_1 \vee v_2 \vee v_4)$. Corresponding satisfying assignments for E.

Conversely, suppose variables $v_1, \ldots, v_m$ have been assigned values that cause E to evaluate to `TRUE` and let us prove that the pair (K, L) has a homological simplification X. We construct X starting from L and adding some simplices of K as follows; see Figure 11. We begin by adding the edge AV_j if $v_j = \texttt{TRUE}$ and the edge AW_j if $v_j = \texttt{FALSE}$, for all $j \in \{1, \ldots, m\}$. Since values of $v_1, \ldots, v_m$ are a satisfying assignment, we can choose one literal $e_i v_{j_i}$ in each clause c_i that is true. Let $Y_i = V_{j_i}$ if $e_i = \mathbf{1}$ and $Y_i = W_{j_i}$ if $e_i = \neg$. Note that by construction, the edge AY_i is already in X. We then add the three triangles AB_iY_i, $B_iC_iY_i$ and C_iAY_i to X, for all $i \in \{1, \ldots, n\}$.

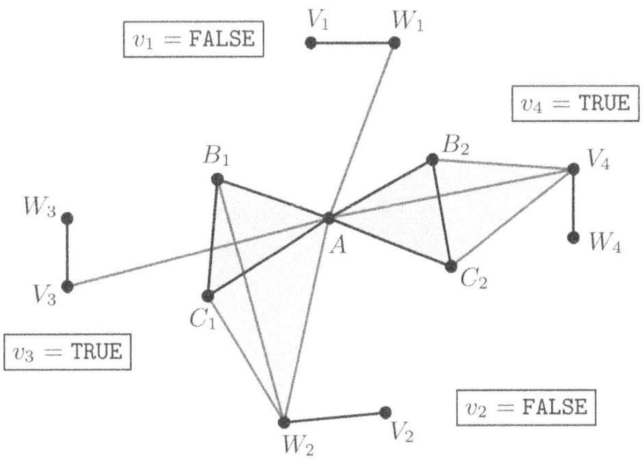

Figure 11: Satisfying assignment for formula $E = (v_1 \vee \neg v_2 \vee \neg v_3) \wedge (v_1 \vee v_2 \vee v_4)$ and corresponding homological simplification of (K, L).

Let us check that X is indeed a solution to the homological simplification problem, *i.e.* $\mathbf{H}_0(X) = \mathbb{Z}_2$, $\mathbf{H}_1(X) = 0$ and $\mathbf{H}_2(X) = 0$. For this, we check that X is contractible by collapsing X to A, using a sequence of elementary collapses. First, observe that exactly one of the two vertices V_j or W_j belongs to no other simplices than the edge V_jW_j. For instance, if $v_j = \texttt{TRUE}$, then by construction $AV_j \in X$ and $AW_j \notin X$. Thus, W_j belongs to no other simplices than V_jW_j and we can collapse the edge V_jW_j to the vertex V_j by removing the pair of simplices (W_j, V_jW_j). Similarly, if $v_j = \texttt{FALSE}$, we collapse the edge V_jW_j to the vertex W_j. For all $i \in \{1, \ldots, n\}$, we apply five elementary collapses, first removing the three triangles AB_iY_i, $B_iC_iY_i$ and C_iAY_i and their edges AB_i, B_iC_i and C_iA, then removing the edges B_iY_i and C_iY_i and their vertices B_i and C_i. In a last step, we collapse every edge AY_i for $1 \leq i \leq n$ to the vertex A. $\square$

4. DISCUSSION

Our work raises several questions and research tracks.

Open questions.

Is there a version of Lemma 6 in which the voxel size does not depend on μ? Is the homological simplification problem in the same class of complexity if we constraint K to be a subcomplex of a triangulation of the sphere $\mathbb{S}^3$?

Optimistic research track.

If a polynomial time optimal reconstruction algorithm exists, it should take advantage of the embedding in Euclidean space or at least lead to a class of simplification problems sufficiently constrained to avoid constructions similar to ours.

Pessimistic research track.

Is it possible to encode 3-SAT as the homological simplification of a pair $(K_{3\alpha}(\mathcal{S}), K_\alpha(\mathcal{S}))$, where $(\mathcal{S}, \alpha)$ satisfies the weak sampling condition? Or, as the homological simplification of a pair of cubical complexes defined by offsets of the sample? If yes, in which minimal dimension?

5. REFERENCES

[1] N. Amenta and M. Bern. Surface reconstruction by Voronoi filtering. *Discrete and Computational Geometry*, 22(4):481–504, 1999.

[2] N. Amenta, M. Bern, and D. Eppstein. The crust and the β-skeleton: Combinatorial curve reconstruction. *Graphical Models and Image Processing*, 60(2):125–135, 1998.

[3] N. Amenta, S. Choi, T. Dey, and N. Leekha. A simple algorithm for homeomorphic surface reconstruction. In *Proceedings of the sixteenth annual symposium on Computational geometry*, pages 213–222. ACM New York, NY, USA, 2000.

[4] N. Amenta, S. Choi, and R. Kolluri. The power crust, unions of balls, and the medial axis transform. *Computational Geometry: Theory and Applications*, 19(2-3):127–153, 2001.

[5] D. Attali. r-regular shape reconstruction from unorganized points. *Computational Geometry: Theory and Applications*, 10:239–247, 1998.

[6] D. Attali, M. Glisse, S. Hornus, F. Lazarus, and D. Morozov. Persistence-sensitive simplification of functions on surfaces in linear time. *Manuscript, INRIA*, 2008.

[7] D. Attali and A. Lieutier. Reconstructing shapes with guarantees by unions of convex sets. http://hal.archives-ouvertes.fr/hal-00427035/en/.

[8] D. Attali and A. Lieutier. Reconstructing shapes with guarantees by unions of convex sets. In *Proc. ACM Symposium on Computational Geometry*, 2010. Submitted.

[9] J. Boissonnat and F. Cazals. Smooth surface reconstruction via natural neighbour interpolation of distance functions. *Computational Geometry: Theory and Applications*, 22(1-3):185–203, 2002.

[10] J. Boissonnat, L. Guibas, and S. Oudot. Manifold reconstruction in arbitrary dimensions using witness complexes. *Discrete and Computational Geometry*, 42(1):37–70, 2009.

[11] J. Boissonnat and S. Oudot. Provably good sampling and meshing of Lipschitz surfaces. In *Proceedings of the twenty-second annual symposium on Computational geometry*, page 346. ACM, 2006.

[12] F. Chazal, D. Cohen-Steiner, and A. Lieutier. A sampling theory for compact sets in Euclidean space. *Discrete and Computational Geometry*, 41(3):461–479, 2009.

[13] F. Chazal, D. Cohen-Steiner, A. Lieutier, and B. Thibert. Shape smoothing using double offsets. In *Proc. of the ACM symposium on Solid and physical modeling*, pages 183–192. ACM New York, NY, USA, 2007.

[14] F. Chazal and A. Lieutier. Stability and computation of topological invariants of solids in $\mathbb{R}^n$. *Discrete and Computational Geometry*, 37(4):601–617, 2007.

[15] F. Chazal and S. Oudot. Towards persistence-based reconstruction in Euclidean spaces. In *Proceedings of the twenty-fourth annual symposium on Computational geometry*, pages 232–241. ACM, 2008.

[16] F. Clarke. *Optimization and nonsmooth analysis.* Society for Industrial Mathematics, 1990.

[17] D. Cohen-Steiner. Personal communication. 2008.

[18] D. Cohen-Steiner, H. Edelsbrunner, and J. Harer. Stability of persistence diagrams. *Discrete and Computational Geometry*, 37(1):103–120, 2007.

[19] T. Cormen, C. Leiserson, R. Rivest, and C. Stein. Introduction to algorithms, 2001.

[20] V. de Silva. Personal communication. 2009.

[21] V. de Silva and G. Carlsson. Topological estimation using witness complexes. *Proc. Sympos. Point-Based Graphics*, pages 157–166, 2004.

[22] T. Dey, S. Funke, and E. Ramos. Surface reconstruction in almost linear time under locally uniform sampling. In *Abstracts 17th European Workshop Comput. Geom*, pages 129–132. Citeseer, 2001.

[23] T. Dey, J. Giesen, E. Ramos, and B. Sadri. Critical points of the distance to an epsilon-sampling of a surface and flow-complex-based surface reconstruction. In *Proc. of the twenty-first annual symposium on Computational geometry*, page 227. ACM, 2005.

[24] T. Dey and S. Goswami. Provable surface reconstruction from noisy samples. *Computational Geometry: Theory and Applications*, 35(1-2):124–141, 2006.

[25] T. Dey and K. Li. Cut locus and topology from surface point data. In *Proceedings of the 25th annual symposium on Computational geometry*, pages 125–134. ACM New York, NY, USA, 2009.

[26] H. Edelsbrunner, D. Letscher, and A. Zomorodian. Topological persistence and simplification. *Discrete and Computational Geometry*, 28(4):511–533, 2002.

[27] H. Edelsbrunner, D. Morozov, and V. Pascucci. Persistence-sensitive simplification functions on 2-manifolds. In *Proceedings of the twenty-second annual symposium on Computational geometry*, page 134. ACM, 2006.

[28] K. Grove. Critical point theory for distance functions. In *Proc. of Symposia in Pure Mathematics*, volume 54, pages 357–386, 1993.

[29] A. Lieutier. Any open bounded subset of R n has the same homotopy type as its medial axis. *Computer-Aided Design*, 36(11):1029–1046, 2004.

[30] D. Morozov. Homological Illusions of Persistence and Stability. *Ph.D. Dissertation, Duke University*, 2008.

[31] J. Munkres. *Elements of algebraic topology.* Perseus Books, 1993.

[32] P. Niyogi, S. Smale, and S. Weinberger. Finding the Homology of Submanifolds with High Confidence from Random Samples. *Discrete Computational Geometry*, 39(1-3):419–441, 2008.

[33] S. Oudot. Échantillonnage et maillage de surfaces avec garanties. *Ph.D. Dissertation, Ecole Polytechnique*, 2005.

APPENDIX

This appendix establishes the correctness of our first naive reconstruction algorithm. First, we establish the existence of cubical sets that are faithful reconstruction of shapes with positive μ-reach, using Corollary 3 in [7]:

LEMMA 10 (COROLLARY 3 IN [7]). *For $d_N = \frac{1}{40N^3\lceil\sqrt{N}\rceil}$ and for all compact sets $\mathcal{A} \subset \mathbb{R}^N$ with reach greater than $\rho > 0$, there exists a $(d_N\rho)$-cubical set $\mathcal{X}$ such that $\mathcal{A} \subset \mathcal{X} \subset \mathcal{A}^\rho$ and the inclusion maps $\mathcal{A} \hookrightarrow \mathcal{X}$ and $\mathcal{X} \hookrightarrow \mathcal{A}^\rho$ are homotopy equivalences.*

PROOF OF LEMMA 6. The proof of Lemma 6 consists in extending the above lemma to the situation where compact sets have a positive μ-reach with the constant $c_N = \frac{d_N}{2}$. Given a set $\mathcal{Y} \subset \mathbb{R}^N$, we denote respectively by $\overline{\mathcal{Y}}$ and $\mathcal{Y}^c$ the closure and the complement of $\mathcal{Y}$. For any compact set $\mathcal{X} \subset \mathbb{R}^N$ and any real number $\rho > 0$, let $\mathcal{X}^{-\rho} = \overline{((\mathcal{X}^c)^\rho)^c}$ and consider the set $\mathcal{B} = (\mathcal{A}^y)^{-\mu(y-x)}$. We know from [13] that the reach of $\mathcal{B}$ is greater than or equal to $\mu(y-x)$ and the inclusion maps corresponding to the sequence

$$\mathcal{A}^x \subset \mathcal{B} \subset \mathcal{A}^y$$

are homotopy equivalences. We can now apply Corollary 3 in [7] to the set $\mathcal{B}$ whose reach is greater than $\rho = \frac{\mu(y-x)}{2}$. This gives the existence of a $(c_N\mu(y-x))$-cubical set $\mathcal{X}$ such that:

$$\mathcal{B} \subset \mathcal{X} \subset \mathcal{B}^\rho$$

and the maps corresponding to inclusions are homotopy equivalences. Using $\mathcal{B}^\rho = ((\mathcal{A}^y)^{-2\rho})^\rho \subset \mathcal{A}^y$, we get the sequence of inclusions

$$\mathcal{A}^x \subset \mathcal{X} \subset \mathcal{A}^y.$$

in which the inclusion map $\mathcal{A}^x \hookrightarrow \mathcal{X}$ is a homotopy equivalence. By Lemma 2, $\mathcal{X}$ is a faithful reconstruction of $\mathcal{A}$. □

Under precondition 3, next lemma states the existence of a cubical set which is a faithful reconstruction nested between two cubical sets that can be deduced from the sample (see Figure 4). Given a compact subset $\mathcal{Y} \subset \mathbb{R}^N$, we recall that $V_\varepsilon(\mathcal{Y})$ designates the union of ε-voxels that intersect $\mathcal{Y}$. The underlying space of the simplicial complex X is denoted $|X|$.

LEMMA 11. *Let $\alpha, \eta > 0$ and $\mu \in (0,1]$ be real numbers and let $\mathcal{A}$ and $\mathcal{S}$ be compact subsets of $\mathbb{R}^N$ such that $d_H(\mathcal{S},\mathcal{A}) < \alpha < \frac{1}{4}(r_\mu(\mathcal{A}) - \eta)$. Then, for:*

$$\varepsilon = \frac{\eta}{4\sqrt{N} + \frac{2}{c_N\mu}}, \quad l = \frac{\eta}{2} + \alpha, \quad k = \eta + 3\alpha - \varepsilon\sqrt{N},$$

there exists an ε-cubical set $\mathcal{X}$ such that:

$$\mathcal{A}^{\frac{\eta}{2}} \subset V_\varepsilon(\mathcal{S}^l) \subset \mathcal{X} \subset V_\varepsilon(\mathcal{S}^k) \subset \mathcal{A}^{\eta+4\alpha}$$

and the inclusion maps $\mathcal{A}^{\frac{\eta}{2}} \hookrightarrow \mathcal{X}$ and $\mathcal{X} \hookrightarrow \mathcal{A}^{4\alpha+\eta}$ are homotopy equivalences. In particular, $\mathcal{X}$ is a faithful reconstruction of $\mathcal{A}$. Furthermore, if we have three nested simplicial complexes $L \subset X \subset K$ such that $V_\varepsilon(\mathcal{S}^l) = |L|$, $\mathcal{X} = |X|$ and $V_\varepsilon(\mathcal{S}^k) = |K|$, then X is a homological simplification of the pair (K, L).

PROOF. Note that for all compact set $\mathcal{Y} \subset \mathbb{R}^N$, we have $\mathcal{Y} \subset V_\varepsilon(\mathcal{Y}) \subset \mathcal{Y}^{\varepsilon\sqrt{N}}$. It follows that for all $t \geq 0$, we have the following sequence of inclusions:

$$\mathcal{A}^t \subset \mathcal{S}^{t+\alpha} \subset V_\varepsilon(\mathcal{S}^{t+\alpha}) \subset \mathcal{S}^{t+\alpha+\varepsilon\sqrt{N}} \subset \mathcal{A}^{t+2\alpha+\varepsilon\sqrt{N}}.$$

Applying this sequence twice, once for $t = \frac{\eta}{2}$ and once for $t = \eta + 2\alpha - \varepsilon\sqrt{N}$, we get that

$$\mathcal{A}^{\frac{\eta}{2}} \subset V_\varepsilon(\mathcal{S}^{\frac{\eta}{2}+\alpha}) \subset \mathcal{A}^{\frac{\eta}{2}+2\alpha+\varepsilon\sqrt{N}}$$
$$\subset \mathcal{A}^{\eta+2\alpha-\varepsilon\sqrt{N}} \subset V_\varepsilon(\mathcal{S}^{\eta+3\alpha-\varepsilon\sqrt{N}}) \subset \mathcal{A}^{\eta+4\alpha}.$$

The value ε has been chosen precisely such that the parameters of the two offsets of $\mathcal{A}$ in the middle differ by $\frac{\varepsilon}{c_N\mu}$. Specifically, writing $x = \frac{\eta}{2}+2\alpha+\varepsilon\sqrt{N}$ and $y = \eta+2\alpha-\varepsilon\sqrt{N}$, we have $y - x = \frac{\varepsilon}{c_N\mu}$. Hence, applying Lemma 6 to $\mathcal{A}$, we get the existence of an ε-cubical set $\mathcal{X}$ such that $\mathcal{A}^x \subset \mathcal{X} \subset \mathcal{A}^y$ and the maps corresponding to the inclusions are homotopy equivalences. The first part of the lemma follows. For the second part, notice that we have the following sequence of homomorphisms induced by inclusion maps:

$$\mathbf{H}_p(\mathcal{A}^{\frac{\eta}{2}}) \to \mathbf{H}_p(|L|) \to \mathbf{H}_p(|X|) \to \mathbf{H}_p(|K|) \to \mathbf{H}_p(\mathcal{A}^{\eta+4\alpha}).$$

We will use the following observation. Consider two functions $i: E \to F$ and $j: F \to G$ such that the composition $j \circ i$ is bijective. Then, i is injective and j is surjective. Since the map $\mathbf{H}_p(\mathcal{A}^{\frac{\eta}{2}}) \to \mathbf{H}_p(|X|)$ induced on homology groups by inclusion is bijective, the map $\mathbf{H}_p(|L|) \to \mathbf{H}_p(|X|)$ is surjective using the observation. Similarly, the map $\mathbf{H}_p(|X|) \to \mathbf{H}_p(|K|)$ is injective and therefore X is a homological simplification of the pair (K, L). □

LEMMA 12. *Let x_1, x_2, x_3 be real numbers and $\mathcal{A}$ a compact subset of $\mathbb{R}^N$ such that $0 < x_1 < x_2 < x_3 < \mathrm{wfs}(\mathcal{A})$. Let $L \subset K$ be two simplicial complexes such that:*

$$\mathcal{A}^{x_1} \subset |L| \subset \mathcal{A}^{x_2} \subset |K| \subset \mathcal{A}^{x_3}$$

If X is a homological simplification of the pair (K, L), then $|X|$ is a faithful homological reconstruction of $\mathcal{A}$.

PROOF. Inclusion maps induce the following commutative diagram between homology groups:

$$\begin{array}{ccccccc}
 & & & \mathbf{H}_p(\mathcal{A}^{x_2}) & & & \\
 & & \nearrow & & \searrow & & \\
\mathbf{H}_p(\mathcal{A}^{x_1}) & \longrightarrow & \mathbf{H}_p(|L|) & & \mathbf{H}_p(|K|) & \longrightarrow & \mathbf{H}_p(\mathcal{A}^{x_3}) \\
 & & \searrow & & \nearrow & & \\
 & & & \mathbf{H}_p(|X|) & & &
\end{array}$$

From Lemma 1, the maps $\mathbf{H}_p(\mathcal{A}^{x_1}) \to \mathbf{H}_p(\mathcal{A}^{x_2}) \to \mathbf{H}_p(\mathcal{A}^{x_3})$ are isomorphisms. Since we take coefficients in a field, homology groups are vector spaces. Since the map $\mathbf{H}_p(\mathcal{A}^{x_1}) \to \mathbf{H}_p(\mathcal{A}^{x_2})$ induced by inclusion is bijective, the map $\mathbf{H}_p(|L|) \to \mathbf{H}_p(\mathcal{A}^{x_2})$ is surjective. Since $\mathbf{H}_p(\mathcal{A}^{x_2}) \to \mathbf{H}_p(\mathcal{A}^{x_3})$ is bijective, $\mathbf{H}_p(\mathcal{A}^{x_2}) \to \mathbf{H}_p(|K|)$ is injective. By an argument similar to the one used in the proof of Lemma 7, we deduce that the dimensions of $\mathbf{H}_p(\mathcal{A}^{x_2})$ and $\mathbf{H}_p(|X|)$ are equal to the rank of $\mathbf{H}_p(|L|) \to \mathbf{H}_p(|K|)$ and therefore $\dim \mathbf{H}_p(|X|) = \dim \mathbf{H}_p(\mathcal{A}^{x_i})$ for all $1 \leq i \leq 3$. Since $\mathbf{H}_p(\mathcal{A}^{x_1}) \to \mathbf{H}_p(\mathcal{A}^{x_3})$ is bijective, $\mathbf{H}_p(\mathcal{A}^{x_1}) \to \mathbf{H}_p(|X|)$ is injective. Because its domain and image have same dimension, it follows that $\mathbf{H}_p(\mathcal{A}^{x_1}) \to \mathbf{H}_p(|X|)$ is an isomorphism. Similarly $\mathbf{H}_p(|X|) \to \mathbf{H}_p(\mathcal{A}^{x_3})$ is an isomorphism and $|X|$ is a faithful homological reconstruction of $\mathcal{A}$. □

Reconstructing Shapes with Guarantees by Unions of Convex Sets*

[Extended Abstract] †

Dominique Attali
Gipsa-lab, Grenoble, France
Dominique.Attali@grenoble-inp.fr

André Lieutier
Aix-en-Provence, France
Andre.Lieutier@wanadoo.fr

ABSTRACT

A simple way to reconstruct a shape $A \subset \mathbb{R}^N$ from a sample P is to output an r-offset $P + rB$, where $B = \{x \in \mathbb{R}^N \mid \|x\| \leq 1\}$ designates the unit Euclidean ball centered at the origin. Recently, it has been proved that the output $P + rB$ is homotopy equivalent to the shape A, for a dense enough sample P of A and for a suitable value of the parameter r [12, 22]. In this paper, we extend this result and find convex sets $C \subset \mathbb{R}^N$, besides the unit Euclidean ball B, for which $P + rC$ reconstructs the topology of A. This class of convex sets includes in particular N-dimensional cubes in $\mathbb{R}^N$. We proceed in two steps. First, we establish the result when P is an ε-offset of A. Building on this first result, we then consider the case when P is a finite noisy sample of A.

Categories and Subject Descriptors

F.2.2 [**Analysis of Algorithms and Problem Complexity**]: Nonnumerical Algorithms and Problems—*Geometrical problems and computations, Computations on discrete structures*; I.3.5 [**Computer Graphics**]: Computational Geometry and Object Modeling

General Terms

Theory, Algorithms

Keywords

Shape reconstruction, offsets, Minkowski sum, union of convex sets, sampling, homotopy equivalence

*This work is partially supported by ANR Project *GIGA* ANR-09-BLAN-0331-01.

†A full version of this paper is available at `http://hal.archives-ouvertes.fr/hal-00427035`

SCG'10, June 13–16, 2010, Snowbird, Utah, USA.

1. INTRODUCTION

In this paper, we study the Minkowski sum between a convex set and a point set that samples a shape, generalizing previous results that establish the Minkowski sum retrieves the topology of the shape when the convex set is a Euclidean ball.

Prior work and problem.

Motivated by surface reconstruction from 3D scan data and manifold learning from point clouds, several authors have formulated precise conditions under which a reconstruction algorithm outputs a topologically correct approximation of a shape, given as input a possibly noisy sample of it [4, 14, 10, 22, 12]. Maybe one of the simplest algorithm consists in outputting a Euclidean r-offset of the sample, that is the union of Euclidean balls with radius r centered on the sample points. Assuming the reach of the shape is positive and data points form a sufficiently dense and accurate sample of the shape, authors in [22, 12] have established that r-offsets of the data points are homotopy equivalent to the shape for suitable values of the offset parameter r (see Figure 1, left). The aim of this work is to understand how this result generalizes when, instead of unions of Euclidean balls, we consider for the reconstruction unions of translated and scaled copies of a convex set C centered on the data points. In other words, writing B for the unit Euclidean ball centered at the origin and letting P be a sample of the shape A, we would like to understand what happens if we replace the Euclidean r-offset $P + rB$ by the Minkowski sum $P + rC$. Do we keep the topology of the shape A as in Figure 1, middle or do we lose it as in Figure 1, right? We are particularly interested in the case where C is a polytope.

Motivation.

Our motivation to study this question is two-fold. First, in many practical applications such as stereo vision or image analysis, the accuracy of measures varies in magnitude according to the direction of measurements. In this context, it seems reasonable to recover the topology of the shape, using a convex set which takes into account the anisotropy of the measurement device. Second, we believe that unions of cubes could present some advantages over unions of Euclidean balls for topological computations in high dimension. In practice, the reconstruction represented by an α-offset is replaced by the more convenient corresponding α-shape which shares the same homotopy type [15]. Indeed, the α-shape has a simpler geometry and, being a simplicial complex, can benefit from existing theorems and algorithms ded-

Figure 1: The union of disks and squares retrieve the topology of the sampled curve unlike the union of triangles.

icated to topological computations. However, if the ambient dimension is large, the α-shape may have a high complexity [1] and its computation may be rather expensive and requires sophisticated data structures [8]. Our idea to circumvent this problem is the following. Given $\varepsilon > 0$, we define the cubical grid $G_\varepsilon = (\varepsilon\mathbb{Z})^N \subset \mathbb{R}^N$ and replace the sample $P \subset \mathbb{R}^N$ by a nearby sample $P_\varepsilon \subset G_\varepsilon$. Applying our result to the unit N-dimensional cube $C = [-1, 1]^N \in \mathbb{R}^N$, we shall see that the set $P_\varepsilon + k\varepsilon C$ retrieves the homotopy type of the shape, for some well-chosen integer k. Hence, our result allows us to reconstruct with the right homotopy type a shape by a union of voxels with vertices the cubical grid (see [5] for a precise statement of this corollary and [6] for an application). Such a "cubical set" has a simpler structure than the α-shape and may be more convenient for topological computations in high dimension. Following this idea, our work might contribute to build a bridge between the point of view of distance functions in computational topology and the world of voxels in digital image processing.

Chosen approach and contributions.

A first idea to tackle the problem mentioned above is to use the framework of semi-concave functions. Specifically, one can associate to any symmetric convex set C with a non-empty interior a norm $\|.\|_C$ defined by $x \mapsto \|x\|_C = \inf\{\alpha > 0 \mid x \in \alpha C\}$. The balls of the associated distance d_C are translated and scaled copies of C. The metric d_C is invariant by translation but is not isotropic unless C is the Euclidean ball. Suppose the boundary of C is smooth with a bounded curvature. Given a subset $Y \subset \mathbb{R}^N$, the squared distance-to-Y function $x \mapsto \min_{y\in Y} \|x - y\|_C^2$ is semi-concave [9] and has therefore a generalized gradient which induces a continuous flow. Hence, a theory similar to what has been done in the Euclidean case [10, 11, 12] can be developed. However, we are interested in convex sets, such as polytopes, whose boundary are not necessarily smooth nor has a bounded curvature. It follows that the semi-concavity property is lost and no generalized gradient of the squared distance-to-Y function can induce a flow. The proof technique used in this paper should be of independent interest since it overcomes the limitation of flow-based methods and applies to convex sets with non-smooth boundary. Taking inspiration in [22] where a deformation retract of a Euclidean offset of the sample onto the shape is constructed explicitly, we move away from this approach and introduce a new proof scheme based a sandwich lemma (Lemma 1). Results in this paper are positive as well as negative. We carefully identify a class of convex sets to which the above result can be extended. We also give examples of convex sets outside this class which won't provide a correct reconstruction. We proceed in two steps. First, we state a reconstruction theorem, when the sample P is an arbitrarily small Euclidean offset of the shape and secondly when P is a finite sample.

Outline.

Section 2 presents definitions and the formal statements of our two reconstruction theorems. Section 3 proves the first reconstruction theorem and Section 4 proves the second. Section 5 concludes the paper.

2. STATEMENT OF RESULTS

Before we state our results in Section 2.3, we first introduce the necessary background in topology in Section 2.1 and identify in Section 2.2 classes of convex sets to which our results will apply.

2.1 Homotopy equivalences

First, we review some classical definitions in topology that can be found for instance in [18, 21]. Two continuous maps $h, k : X \to Y$ are *homotopic* and we write $h \simeq k$ if there is a continuous map $F : X \times [0, 1] \to Y$ such that $F(x, 0) = h(x)$ and $F(x, 1) = k(x)$ for all $x \in X$. Let $f : X \to Y$ and $g : Y \to X$ be two continuous maps. Suppose that $f \circ g : Y \to Y$ is homotopic to the identity map of Y and $g \circ f : X \to X$ is homotopic to the identity map of X, *i.e.* suppose we have $f \circ g \simeq 1_Y$ and $g \circ f \simeq 1_X$. Then, the maps f and g are called *homotopy equivalences*, and each is said to be a *homotopy inverse* of the other. Furthermore, the spaces X and Y are said to have the same *homotopy type*, which we denote by $X \simeq Y$. We say that a subspace A of X is a *deformation retract* of X if there exists a continuous map $H : X \times [0, 1] \to X$ such that $H(x, 0) = x$, $H(x, 1) \in A$ for all $x \in X$ and $H(a, t) = a$ for all $a \in A$ and all $t \in [0, 1]$. Such a function H is called a *deformation retraction* of X onto A. Let $r : X \to A$ be the retraction defined by $r(x) = H(x, 1)$ and let $i : A \to X$ the inclusion map. We have $i \circ r \simeq 1_X$ and $r \circ i = 1_A$. Thus, if A is a deformation retract of X, the inclusion $i : A \to X$ is a homotopy equivalence. Note that assuming X deformation retracts to A is stronger than assuming the inclusion map $A \hookrightarrow X$ is a homotopy equivalence, which in turn is stronger than assuming $A \simeq X$, as illustrated in Figure 2. We now state a technical lemma that will provide us key tools in establishing that two shapes have the same topology.

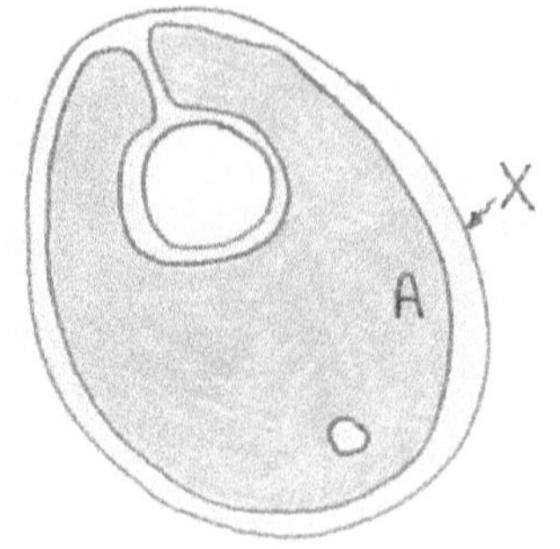

Figure 2: Two nested shapes $A \subset X$ which are close in Hausdorff distance and have the same homotopy type but for which the inclusion $A \hookrightarrow X$ is not a homotopy equivalence.

LEMMA 1 (SANDWICH LEMMA). *Consider four nested spaces $A_0 \subset X_0 \subset A_1 \subset X_1$. If A_1 deformation retracts to A_0 and X_1 deformation retracts to X_0, then X_0 deformation retracts to A_0. If the inclusions $A_0 \hookrightarrow A_1$ and $X_0 \hookrightarrow X_1$ are homotopy equivalences, then the inclusion $A_0 \hookrightarrow X_1$ is a homotopy equivalence.*

PROOF. To prove the first part of the lemma, suppose F is a deformation retraction of A_1 onto A_0 and G is a deformation retraction of X_1 onto X_0. Then, one can check that the map $H : X_0 \times [0,1] \to X_0$ defined by $H(x,t) = G(F(x,t),1)$ is a deformation retraction of X_0 onto A_0.

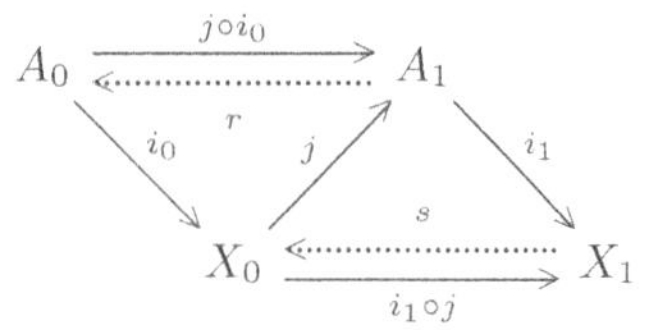

Figure 3: Diagram for the proof of Lemma 1. All arrows but the dotted ones are inclusions.

To prove the second part of the lemma, let $i_0 : A_0 \to X_0$, $j : X_0 \to A_1$ and $i_1 : A_1 \to X_1$ denote inclusions (see Figure 3). Suppose r is a homotopy inverse of $j \circ i_0$ and s is a homotopy inverse of $i_1 \circ j$. We prove that the inclusion $k = i_1 \circ j \circ i_0$ from A_0 to X_1 is a homotopy equivalence with homotopy inverse $r \circ j \circ s$. Indeed, using the fact that composition preserves the relation $\simeq$, we have $k \circ (r \circ j \circ s) = i_1 \circ (j \circ i_0 \circ r) \circ j \circ s \simeq i_1 \circ 1_{A_1} \circ j \circ s \simeq 1_{X_1}$ and similarly $(r \circ j \circ s) \circ k = r \circ j \circ (s \circ i_1 \circ j) \circ i_0 \simeq r \circ j \circ 1_{X_0} \circ i_0 \simeq 1_{A_0}$. □

2.2 Properties on convex sets

In this section, we define two properties that will help us identify classes of convex sets.

2.2.1 θ-roundness

We associate to every compact convex set a non-negative real number called the *θ-roundness* which can be interpreted as a certain kind of curvature. Given a convex set C in $\mathbb{R}^N$, the *normal cone* $\mathcal{N}(x)$ to C at x is the set of unit vectors n such that $(x-y) \cdot n \geq 0$, for all points $y \in C$.

DEFINITION 1. *Let $\theta \in [0,\pi]$ and $\varkappa \geq 0$. We say that the compact convex set C is $(\theta,\varkappa)$-*round *if for all points $c_1, c_2 \in C$ and all vectors $n_1 \in \mathcal{N}(c_1)$ and $n_2 \in \mathcal{N}(c_2)$, the following implication holds:*

$$\angle(n_1,n_2) \geq \theta \implies (c_1 - c_2) \cdot (n_1 - n_2) \geq \varkappa \|c_1 - c_2\|^2.$$

*The θ-*roundness *of C is the supremum of $\varkappa \geq 0$ such that C is $(\theta,\varkappa)$-round.*

Note that if the compact convex set C has θ-roundness $\varkappa$, then C is $(\theta,\varkappa)$-round. If C is $(\theta,\varkappa)$-round, then C is $(\theta',\varkappa')$-round whenever $\theta \leq \theta'$ and $\varkappa' \leq \varkappa$. It is not difficult to see that C is $(\pi,\varkappa)$-round if and only if the diameter of C is upper bounded by $\frac{2}{\varkappa}$. Suppose the boundary of C is a C^2-smooth hypersurface in $\mathbb{R}^N$ and orient ∂C such that normals point outside the convex set. Then, for all points $x \in \partial C$, the normal cone at x is reduced to a single vector which is the normal to ∂C at x. The absolute values of the principal curvatures at point $x \in \partial C$ are non-negative real numbers $|\kappa_1(x)| \geq |\kappa_2(x)| \ldots \geq |\kappa_{N-1}(x)|$ and we let $\kappa_{\min}(C)$ be the minimum of $|\kappa_{N-1}(x)|$ over all points $x \in \partial C$.

LEMMA 2. *A compact convex set C whose boundary is C^2-smooth has 0-roundness $\kappa_{\min}(C)$.*

See Appendix B for a proof. For our reconstruction theorems, we shall consider compact convex sets which have the property to be $(\theta,\varkappa)$-round for a positive $\varkappa$ and a small enough θ. Specifically, we will require $\theta \leq \theta_N = \arccos(-\frac{1}{N})$. Not all convex sets satisfy this property. To construct a counterexample, consider a compact convex set C which is contained in an affine space of dimension i with $0 < i < N$. Let n be a unit vector orthogonal to the smallest affine space containing C. For every point $c \in C$, both n and its opposite vector $-n$ belong to $\mathcal{N}(c)$. Consider two distinct points $c_1, c_2 \in C$ and let $n_1 = n$ and $n_2 = -n$. We have $\angle(n_1,n_2) = \pi$, $(c_1 - c_2) \cdot (n_1 - n_2) = 0$ and $\|c_1 - c_2\| \neq 0$, showing that there are no $\varkappa > 0$ such that C is $(\pi,\varkappa)$-round. Equivalently, the π-roundness of C is zero. As a counterexample with a non-empty interior, take a triangular prism in $\mathbb{R}^3$. Its θ_3-roundness is zero. In the technical report [5], we compute the θ_2-roundness of regular polygons in the plane and establish that the θ_N-roundness of the N-dimensional cube $B_\infty = [-1,1]^N \subset \mathbb{R}^N$ is:

$$\varkappa(B_\infty) = \begin{cases} \frac{1}{2\sqrt{2}}\left(\cos\frac{\pi}{4} + \cos\frac{\pi}{12}\right) & \text{if } N = 2, \\ \frac{1}{\sqrt{6}} & \text{if } N = 3, \\ \frac{1}{(N-2)\sqrt{N}} & \text{if } N \geq 4, \end{cases}$$

2.2.2 Eccentricity

In this section, we associate to every subset $C \subseteq \mathbb{R}^N$ a parameter called *eccentricity*. Intuitively, eccentricity can be thought of as a measure of how much intersections of translated copies of C centered at points in Q deviate from the convex hull of Q. We recall that the *Minkowski sum* of two subsets $X \subset \mathbb{R}^N$ and $Y \subset \mathbb{R}^N$ is the subset defined by $X + Y = \{x + y \mid x \in X, y \in Y\}$. To simplify notations, we shall write $x + Y$ instead of $\{x\} + Y$. Let $B = \{x \in \mathbb{R}^N \mid \|x\| \leq 1\}$ be the unit Euclidean ball centered at the origin. Given a non-negative real number r, we call the Minkowski sum $X + rB$ the Euclidean r-*offset* of X and denote it by X^r. We write $\mathrm{Conv}(Q)$ for the convex hull of $Q \subset \mathbb{R}^N$.

DEFINITION 2. *Given $\xi \geq 0$, we say that C is ξ-eccentric if for all compact $Q \subset \mathbb{R}^N$, the following implication holds (see Figure 4):*

$$\bigcap_{q \in Q} (q + C) \neq \emptyset \implies \left(\bigcap_{q \in Q} (q + C) \right) \cap (\mathrm{Conv}(Q) + \xi C) \neq \emptyset.$$

The eccentricity of C is the infimum of $\xi \geq 0$ such that C is ξ-eccentric.

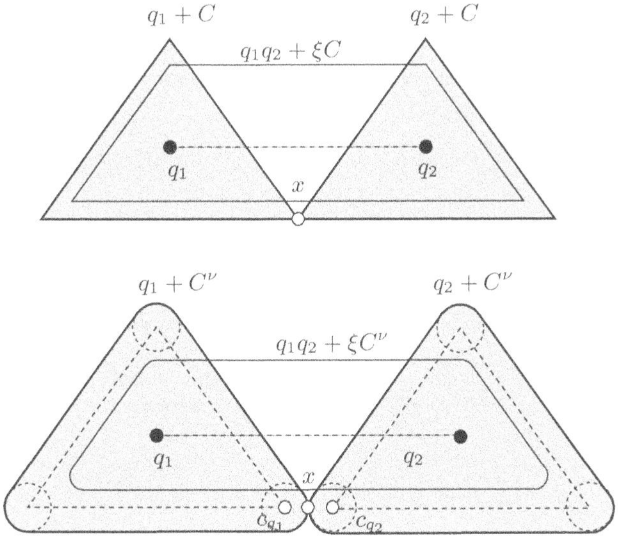

Figure 4: Top: two translated copies of a triangle C. The intersection point x does not belong to any set $\mathrm{Conv}(\{q_1, q_2\}) + \xi C$ for $\xi < 1$, thus showing that the eccentricity is 1. Bottom: bulging the triangle makes its eccentricity drops to a value smaller than 1.

Note that the eccentricity is a real number between 0 and 1. If the eccentricity of a compact set C is ξ, then C is ξ-eccentric. The property to be ξ-eccentric is invariant under bijective linear transformations. We now give eccentricities for simple objects and adopt the convention that all objects we consider in this paragraph have their centroids at the origin. Computations can be found in the technical report [5]. The eccentricity of the unit N-dimensional Euclidean ball B is zero. More generally, i-dimensional Euclidean balls for $0 \leq i \leq N$ have eccentricity 0. Ellipsoids which can be obtained from Euclidean balls by applying a linear transformation also have eccentricity 0. Symmetric compact convex sets in the plane have eccentricity 0 as well. At the opposite end of the spectrum, triangles have eccentricity 1 (see Figure 4). In [5], we show that N-dimensional cubes have eccentricity $1 - \frac{2}{N}$, for $N \geq 2$.

2.3 Reconstruction Theorems

First, we formulate a sampling condition inspired by the work in [2, 3, 10]:

DEFINITION 3. *Given a non-negative real number ε and a subset $C \subset \mathbb{R}^N$, we say that $P \subset \mathbb{R}^N$ is an (ε, C)-sample of $A \subset \mathbb{R}^N$ if $A \subset P + \varepsilon C$ and $P \subset A + \varepsilon B$.*

Notice that P is an (ε, B)-sample of A if and only if the Hausdorff distance between P and A does not exceed ε. If $B \subset C$, then an (ε, B)-sample is also an (ε, C)-sample. The reason why our definition is not symmetric with respect to A and P is to enhance conditions that are used in the proofs of our reconstruction theorems. Given a compact subset A of $\mathbb{R}^N$, we recall that the *medial axis* M of A is the set of points in $\mathbb{R}^N$ which have at least two closest points in A. The *reach* of A is the infimum of distances between points in A and points in M:

$$\mathrm{reach}(A) = \inf_{a \in A, x \in M} \|a - x\|.$$

Shapes with a positive reach include, but are not limited to, compact smooth surfaces with bounded curvatures. Intuitively, a shape with a positive reach cannot have sharp concave edges. Suppose A has a positive reach. Given a convex set C and an (ε, C)-sample P of A, we would like to know whether the Minkowski sum $P + rC$ retrieves the topology of A. Theorem 1 answers the question when $P = A^\varepsilon$ is a Euclidean ε-offset of A and Theorem 2 provides an answer when P is a finite sample of A. Before stating our results, we start with an example which illustrates that not all convex sets C can be used to reconstruct the topology of shapes with a positive reach.

Figure 5: Cycle in the Minkowski sum of the moment curve with a segment.

Specifically, we take A to be the moment curve $A = \{(x_1, x_2, x_3) \in \mathbb{R}^3 \mid x_2 = x_1^2, x_3 = x_1^3\}$ and prove that for r arbitrarily small, we can always find a convex set C such that the Minkowski sum $A + rC$ is not homotopy equivalent to A. For this, let C be a segment of length 2 centered at the origin and contained in the straight-line $L_t = \{(x_1, x_2, x_3) \in \mathbb{R}^3 \mid x_2 = 0, x_3 = t^2 x_1\}$ for some positive real number t. Observe that translated copies of L_t intersect the moment curve A in at most one point, except when the translated copy meets A in the two points $a_t = (t, t^2, t^3)$ and $b_t = (-t, t^2, -t^3)$. Hence, as r increases, the Minkowski sum $A + rC$ undergoes a topology change when the two segments $a_t + rC$ and $b_t + rC$ meet (see Figure 5). This happens for $r = \|a_t - b_t\|/2$ which can be made arbitrarily small by choosing t small enough. We now list conditions we shall need on the compact convex set C, the last condition being only for the second theorem:

(i) $B \subset C \subset \delta B$ for some $\delta \geq 1$;

(ii) C is $(\theta, \varkappa)$-round for $\theta \leq \theta_N = \arccos(-\frac{1}{N})$ and $\varkappa > 0$;

(iii) C is ξ-eccentric for $\xi < 1$.

The two conditions (ii) and (iii) do not imply each other. Indeed, any equilateral triangle in $\mathbb{R}^2$ with centroid the origin has eccentricity 1 and a positive θ-roundness for all $0 < \theta \leq \theta_2$. Hence, it satisfies (ii) for some $\theta \leq \theta_2$ and some $\varkappa > 0$ but not (iii) for any $\xi < 1$. Conversely, a segment in $\mathbb{R}^2$ has θ_2-roundness 0 and eccentricity 0. Hence, it satisfies (iii) for $\xi = 0$ but not (ii) for any $\theta \leq \theta_2$ and $\varkappa > 0$. Table 1 gathers for different compact convex sets C values of δ, θ, $\varkappa$ and ξ for which conditions (i), (ii) and (iii) hold. To state our theorems, let us introduce:

$$R_r = R - \frac{r}{4} - \sqrt{\frac{r}{4}\left(2R + \frac{r}{4}\right)},$$

and note that R_r tends to R as $\frac{r}{R} \to 0$.

THEOREM 1. *Let A be a compact subset of $\mathbb{R}^N$ with positive reach R. Let C be a compact convex set of $\mathbb{R}^N$ satisfying conditions (i) and (ii). Then, $A^\varepsilon + rC$ deformation retracts to A for all real numbers $\varepsilon > 0$ and $r > 0$ such that $\varepsilon + (\delta - 1)r < \min\{R - r, R_{r/\varkappa}\}$.*

The proof of Theorem 1 is given in Section 3. Theorem 1 will be useful in establishing our second theorem:

THEOREM 2. *Let A be a compact subset of $\mathbb{R}^N$ with positive reach R. Let C be a compact convex set of $\mathbb{R}^N$ satisfying conditions (i), (ii) and (iii). Let P be a finite (ε, C)-sample of A. Then, the inclusion $A \hookrightarrow P + rC$ is a homotopy equivalence for all real numbers $\varepsilon > 0$ and $r > 0$ such that (1) $(\delta - 1)r < \min\{R - r, R_{r/\varkappa}\}$, (2) $\delta r < R - \varepsilon$, (3) $\delta(r + \alpha_0) < R$ and (4):*

$$2R - \sqrt{(R-\varepsilon)^2 - (\delta r)^2} - \sqrt{R^2 - \delta^2(r + \alpha_0)^2} < (1 - \xi)r - \varepsilon,$$

where $\alpha_0 = \xi r + R - \sqrt{(R - \varepsilon)^2 - (\delta r)^2}$.

The proof of Theorem 2 is given in Section 4. Notice that Theorem 2 requires that $\theta \leq \theta_N$, $\varkappa > 0$ and $\xi < 1$. If these three conditions are fulfilled, then by choosing $r = \frac{4\varepsilon}{1-\xi}$ and $\frac{\varepsilon}{R}$ small enough, all the assumptions of Theorem 2 are satisfied, implying that the inclusion $A \hookrightarrow P + rC$ is a homotopy equivalence. Given a fixed convex set C, Table 1 gives numerical approximations of the largest value of $\frac{\varepsilon}{R}$ for which assumptions of Theorem 2 hold.

To conclude this section, we prove that condition (iii) in Theorem 2 is necessary. In other words, if we take a compact convex set C which satisfies conditions (i) and (ii) but whose eccentricity is 1, it may happen that for some sample P, the Minkowski sum $P + rC$ does not recover the topology of A, no matter what value r takes in the interval $[\varepsilon, R - \varepsilon]$. To construct such an example, consider a parabola A in the plane with equation $y = x^2$ and a finite sample $P \subset A$ symmetric with respect to the y-coordinate axis. Furthermore, we let C be the equilateral triangle with centroid the origin and vertices $(0, -2)$, $(\sqrt{3}, 1)$ and $(-\sqrt{3}, 1)$. We note that with increasing value of r, holes appear in the Minkowski sum $P + rC$ each time two triangles scaled by r meet at a common vertex on the y-axis (see Figure 6). We then adjust the height of the sample points in such a way that $P + \varepsilon C$ does not have the correct topology and as r increases, a hole appears in $P + rC$ each time a hole gets destroyed, as illustrated in Figure 6.

3. PROOF OF THEOREM 1

In this section, we prove Theorem 1. In other words, we prove that for r and ε small enough with respect to the reach of A, the Minkowski sum $A^\varepsilon + rC$ deformation retracts to A. Our strategy is as follows. We consider two positive real numbers ε' and ε'' such that there is chain of inclusions:

$$A \subset A^\varepsilon + rC \subset A^{\varepsilon'} \subset A^{\varepsilon''} + rC \qquad (1)$$

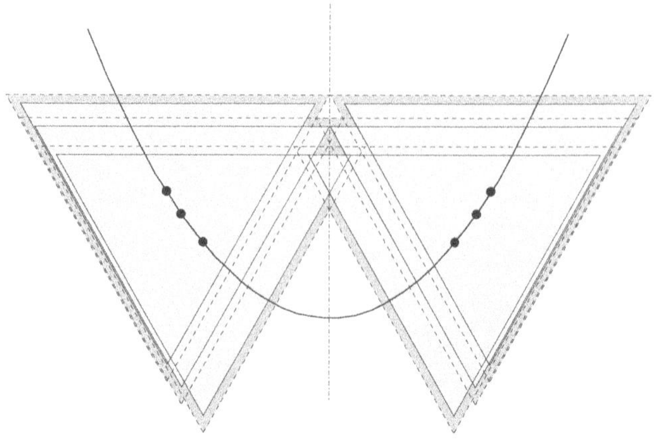

Figure 6: As the size of triangles increases, the hole created by the 4 upper points appears exactly when the hole created by the 4 lower points fills up.

and find conditions under which the third set deformation retracts to the first set and the fourth set deformation retracts to the second set. Applying the Sandwich Lemma allows us to conclude. All the difficulty comes from the second part of the proof which involves comparing the topology of two Euclidean offsets of $A + rC$, namely $A^\varepsilon + rC$ and $A^{\varepsilon''} + rC$. This leads us to study in details Euclidean offsets of Minkowski sums in Section 3.2. A powerful tool for detecting changes in the topology of Euclidean offsets consists in studying the critical points of distance functions. Key results concerning distance functions are recalled in Section 3.1.

3.1 Background on distance functions

The distance function $d(\cdot, Y)$ to the compact subset Y of $\mathbb{R}^N$ associates to each point $x \in \mathbb{R}^N$ its Euclidean distance to Y, $d(x, Y) = \min_{y \in Y} \|x - y\|$. The distance function $d(\cdot, Y)$ is 1-Lipschitz, but is not differentiable in general. Nonetheless, it is possible to define a notion of critical points analogue to the classical one for differentiable functions. Specifically, Grove defines in [17, page 360] critical points for the distance function to a closed subset of a Riemannian manifold. Using Equation (1.1)' in [17, page 360], we recast this definition in our context as follows. Let $\Gamma_Y(x) = \{y \in Y \mid d(x, Y) = \|x - y\|\}$ be the set of points in Y closest to x:

DEFINITION 4. *A point $x \in \mathbb{R}^N$ is a* critical point *of the distance function $d(\cdot, Y)$ if $x \in \mathrm{Conv}(\Gamma_Y(x))$. The* critical values *of $d(\cdot, Y)$ are the images by $d(\cdot, Y)$ of its critical points.*

Slightly recasting Proposition 1.8 in [17, page 362], we have:

LEMMA 3 (ISOTOPY LEMMA [17]). *Let $0 < \varepsilon \leq \varepsilon'$. If the distance function $d(\cdot, Y)$ has no critical value in the interval $[\varepsilon, \varepsilon']$, then Y^ε is a deformation retract of $Y^{\varepsilon'}$.*

If furthermore Y has a positive reach R, then the projection map π_Y which associates to each point $x \in Y^\varepsilon$ its closest point $\pi_Y(x)$ on Y is well defined and continuous [16, page 435]. Thus, the map $H : [0, 1] \times Y^\varepsilon \to Y^\varepsilon$ defined by $H(t, x) = (1 - t)x + t\pi_Y(x)$ is a deformation retraction of Y^ε onto Y. It follows that:

Table 1: Columns 2 to 5: values of δ, θ, $\varkappa$ and ξ for which $B \subset C \subset \delta B$ and the convex set C is $(\theta, \varkappa)$-round and ξ-eccentric. Columns 6 and 7: values of R/ε and r/ε for which Theorem 2 holds. Numerical values are obtained by brute force, enumerating all pairs (ε, r) in a grid, checking if they satisfy conditions of Theorem 2 and keeping the one with largest ε.

convex set C	δ	θ	$\varkappa$	ξ	R/ε	r/ε
Euclidean ball $B \subset \mathbb{R}^N$	1	0	1	0	12.9781	3.95723
cube B_∞ in $\mathbb{R}^N$	$\sqrt{N}$	$\arccos(-\frac{1}{N})$	$\varkappa(B_\infty)$	$1 - \frac{2}{N}$		
cube B_∞ in $\mathbb{R}^2$	$\sqrt{2}$	$\frac{2\pi}{3}$	0.65974	0	24.9973	4.04227
cube B_∞ in $\mathbb{R}^3$	$\sqrt{3}$	$0.608\,\pi$	$\frac{1}{\sqrt{6}}$	1/3	96.4687	6.14485
cube B_∞ in $\mathbb{R}^4$	$\sqrt{4}$	$0.5804\,\pi$	1/4	1/2	247.528	8.1826
cube B_∞ in $\mathbb{R}^5$	$\sqrt{5}$	$0.5641\,\pi$	0.149071	3/5	508.183	10.2006
cube B_∞ in $\mathbb{R}^{10}$	$\sqrt{10}$	$0.5319\,\pi$	0.03953	4/5	4505.44	20.2264
cube B_∞ in $\mathbb{R}^{100}$	10	$0.503183\,\pi$	0.0010204	49/50	4948245	200.232
p-gon $\mathcal{P}_p$ in $\mathbb{R}^2$ (p even)	$\frac{1}{\cos\frac{\pi}{p}}$	$\frac{2\pi}{3}$	$\varkappa(\mathcal{P}_p)$	0		
square in $\mathbb{R}^2$	$\sqrt{2}$	$\frac{2\pi}{3}$	0.65974	0	24.9973	4.04227
hexagon in $\mathbb{R}^2$	1.1547	$\frac{2\pi}{3}$	0.69936	0	16.9858	3.99837
octagon in $\mathbb{R}^2$	1.08239	$\frac{2\pi}{3}$	0.793353	0	15.04119	3.98101
dodecagon in $\mathbb{R}^2$	1.03528	$\frac{2\pi}{3}$	0.8660254	0	13.84148	3.968
36-gon in $\mathbb{R}^2$	1.00382	$\frac{2\pi}{3}$	0.951917	0	13.07011	3.95844
360-gon in $\mathbb{R}^2$	1.00004	$\frac{2\pi}{3}$	0.9949868	0	12.97897	3.95724

LEMMA 4. *If Y has a positive reach R, then Y^ε deformation retracts to Y, for all $0 \le \varepsilon < R$.*

3.2 Distance functions to Minkowski sums

In what follows, A designates a compact subset of $\mathbb{R}^N$ with positive reach R and C designates a compact convex set of $\mathbb{R}^N$. We begin with a technical lemma which will help us to situate critical points of the distance function to $A + C$, assuming C is round enough.

LEMMA 5. *Consider a point $x \in \mathbb{R}^N$ such that $d(x, A + C) < R$. Let $y_1, y_2 \in \Gamma_{A+C}(x)$ be two points on $A + C$ with minimum distance to x. Suppose C is $(\theta, \varkappa)$-round for $\varkappa > 0$ and $\angle y_1 x y_2 \ge \theta$. Then, $d(x, A + C) \ge R_{1/\varkappa}$.*

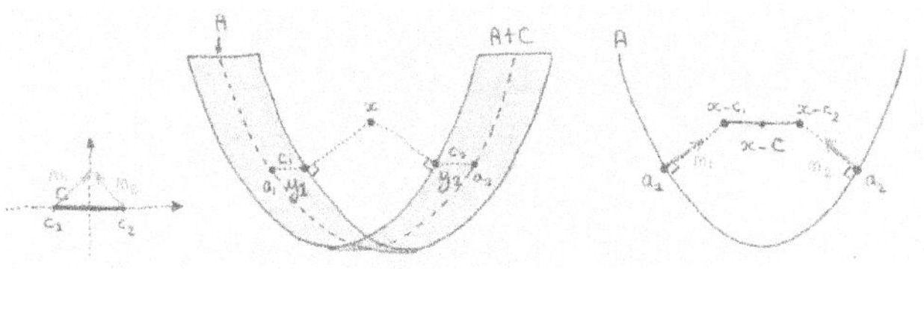

Figure 7: Notations for the proof of Lemma 5.

PROOF. Let $\rho = d(x, A+C)$. For $i \in \{1, 2\}$, let $y_i = a_i + c_i$ with $a_i \in A$ and $c_i \in C$. Since $\rho = \|(x - c_i) - a_i\| < R$, it follows that $x - c_i$ has a unique projection $a_i = \pi_A(x - c_i)$ onto A (see Figure 7). On the other hand, we know from [16, page 435] that the projection map π_A onto A is $\left(\frac{R}{R-\rho}\right)$-Lipschitz for points at distance less than ρ from A. Thus,

$$\|a_1 - a_2\| \le \frac{R}{R - \rho} \|c_1 - c_2\|.$$

Let $n_i = \frac{x - a_i - c_i}{\|x - a_i - c_i\|}$. Squaring both sides of the above inequality and plugging $a_2 - a_1 = c_1 - c_2 + \rho(n_1 - n_2)$ into the left side, we obtain

$$2(c_1 - c_2) \cdot (n_1 - n_2) + \rho \|n_1 - n_2\|^2 \le \frac{2R - \rho}{(R - \rho)^2} \|c_1 - c_2\|^2.$$

For $i \in \{1, 2\}$, the unit vector n_i belongs to $\mathcal{N}(c_i)$. Since C is $(\theta, \varkappa)$-round and $\angle(n_1, n_2) \ge \theta$, it follows that $(c_1 - c_2) \cdot (n_1 - n_2) \ge \varkappa \|c_1 - c_2\|^2$ and

$$\rho \|n_1 - n_2\|^2 \le \left(\frac{2R - \rho}{(R - \rho)^2} - 2\varkappa \right) \|c_1 - c_2\|^2.$$

In particular, this implies that $2\varkappa \le \frac{2R-\rho}{(R-\rho)^2}$ or equivalently $\rho^2 - 2\left(R - \frac{1}{4\varkappa}\right)\rho + R^2 - \frac{R}{\varkappa} \le 0$. Solving this quadratic inequality yields to the result. □

As a consequence of the lemma above, if x is sufficiently close to $A + C$, then the angle between any two vectors connecting x to points in $\Gamma_{A+C}(x)$ is small which implies, in turn, that x is not a critical point of $d(\cdot, A + C)$. The following lemma makes this idea precise.

LEMMA 6. *If C is $(\theta, \varkappa)$-round with $\theta \le \arccos(-\frac{1}{N})$ and $\varkappa > 0$, then the distance function $d(\cdot, A + C)$ has no critical value in the interval $(0, R_{1/\varkappa})$.*

In order to prove Lemma 6, we need the following result also known as *Jung's Theorem*. Given a compact subset $K \subset \mathbb{R}^N$, we denote by $\operatorname{diam}(K) = \max_{p,q \in K} d(p, q)$ the *diameter* of K.

LEMMA 7 (JUNG'S THEOREM). *The smallest ball enclosing a compact subset K of $\mathbb{R}^N$ has radius*

$$r \le \operatorname{diam}(K) \sqrt{\frac{N}{2(N+1)}}.$$

Equality is attained for the regular N-simplex.

For a short proof of Jung's theorem, see [13].

PROOF OF LEMMA 6. Let $x \in \mathbb{R}^N$ and $\rho = d(x, A + C)$. Suppose $0 < \rho < R_{1/\varkappa}$ and let us prove that x is non-critical. By Lemma 5, for all points $y_1, y_2 \in \Gamma_{A+C}(x)$, we have $\angle y_1 x y_2 < \theta$. It follows that $\operatorname{diam}(\Gamma_{A+C}(x)) < 2\rho \sin \frac{\theta}{2}$. Using

$$\sin \frac{\theta}{2} = \sqrt{\frac{1 - \cos\theta}{2}} \leq \sqrt{\frac{N+1}{2N}},$$

and applying Jung's Theorem, we get that the smallest ball B enclosing $\Gamma_{A+C}(x)$ has radius $r < \rho$. Let S denote the sphere centered at x with radius ρ. Observe that $\Gamma_{A+C}(x) \subset S \cap B$. Since the radius of B is smaller than ρ, the radical hyperplane Π of the two spheres S and ∂B separates x from $\Gamma_{A+C}(x)$. Thus $x \notin \operatorname{Conv}(\Gamma_{A+C}(x))$ and x is non-critical. □

Combining Lemma 3 and Lemma 6 and using the fact that if C is $(\theta, \varkappa)$-round, then rC is $(\theta, \frac{\varkappa}{r})$-round, we get immediately conditions under which a Euclidean offset of $A + rC$ deformation retracts to another Euclidean offset:

LEMMA 8. *If C is $(\theta, \varkappa)$-round with $\theta \leq \arccos(-\frac{1}{N})$ and $\varkappa > 0$, then $A^{\varepsilon} + rC$ is a deformation retract of $A^{\varepsilon''} + rC$ for all positive real numbers r, ε and ε'' such that $\varepsilon \leq \varepsilon'' < R_{r/\varkappa}$.*

We are now ready to establish the proof of our first reconstruction theorem.

PROOF OF THEOREM 1. Equation (1) holds whenever $\varepsilon' = \varepsilon + \delta r$ and $\varepsilon'' = \varepsilon + (\delta - 1)r$. Since by hypothesis $\varepsilon \leq \varepsilon'' < R_{r/\varkappa}$, Lemma 8 implies that $A^{\varepsilon''} + rC$ deformation retracts to $A^{\varepsilon} + rC$. By hypothesis, we have $\varepsilon' < R$ and therefore, $A^{\varepsilon'}$ deformation retracts to A from Lemma 4. Applying the Sandwich Lemma allows us to conclude. □

4. PROOF OF THEOREM 2

In this section, we present our proof of Theorem 2. A designates a compact subset of $\mathbb{R}^N$ whose reach R is positive, C is a compact convex set of $\mathbb{R}^N$ satisfying conditions (i), (ii) and (iii) and P is a finite (ε, C)-sample of A. First, we introduce a set which will play a key role. Given three positive real numbers α, β and r, we set $\mathcal{A}_p(\alpha) = (p + rC) \cap (A^{\beta} + \alpha C)$ and define

$$\mathcal{H}(\alpha) = \bigcup_{p \in P} \operatorname{Conv} \mathcal{A}_p(\alpha).$$

Our proof uses two carefully chosen positive constants α_0 and α_1 such that for all sufficiently small β, we have the sequence of inclusions (see Figure 8):

$$A \subset \mathcal{H}(\alpha_0) \subset A^{\beta} + \alpha_1 C \subset P + rC \qquad (2)$$

Having established this sequence of inclusions in Section 4.1, we find in Section 4.2 conditions under which $\mathcal{H}(\alpha_0) \hookrightarrow P + rC$ is a homotopy equivalence. Combined with the conditions we found in Section 3 which ensure that $A \hookrightarrow A^{\beta} + \alpha_1 C$ is a homotopy equivalence, we deduce immediately using Lemma 1 (Sandwich Lemma) conditions under which $A \hookrightarrow P + rC$ is a homotopy equivalence.

4.1 Establishing a key sequence of inclusions

In this section, we find conditions under which inclusions in (2) hold. To establish the middle inclusion, we need the following key inclusion, illustrated in Figure 8:

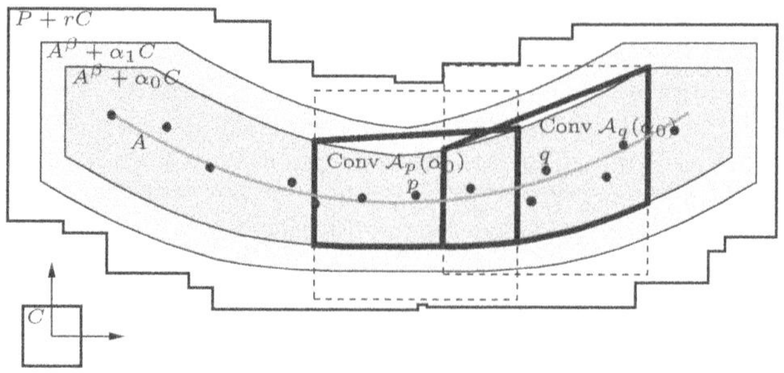

Figure 8: Nested sequence of objects considered for the proof of Theorem 2. Constants α_0 and α_1 are chosen such that $\operatorname{Conv} \mathcal{A}_p(\alpha_0)$ is contained in $A + \alpha_1 C$ for all $p \in P$.

LEMMA 9. *Suppose $\delta(r + \alpha_0) < R - \beta$ and $\alpha_1 - \alpha_0 \geq R - \sqrt{(R-\beta)^2 - \delta^2(r + \alpha_0)^2}$. Then,*

$$\operatorname{Conv} \mathcal{A}_p(\alpha_0) \subset A + \alpha_1 C.$$

PROOF. Let $A' = A^{\beta} \cap (p + rC + \alpha_0(-C))$. Note that $\mathcal{A}_p(\alpha_0) \subset A' + \alpha_0 C$ for if x belongs to $\mathcal{A}_p(\alpha_0) = (p + rC) \cap (A^{\beta} + \alpha_0 C)$, we can find $c_0, c_1 \in C$ and $a' \in A^{\beta}$ such that $x = a' + \alpha_0 c_0 = p + r c_1$, showing that $a' \in A'$ and $x \in A' + \alpha_0 C$. Thus and using lemma 15,

$$\operatorname{Conv} \mathcal{A}_p(\alpha_0) \subset \operatorname{Conv}(A' + \alpha_0 C) = \operatorname{Conv}(A') + \alpha_0 C.$$

By construction, A' is contained in a ball of radius $\delta(r + \alpha_0)$. Applying Lemma 14 with $Q = A'$, $\varepsilon = \beta$ and $\rho = \delta(2r - \varepsilon)$, we get

$$\operatorname{Conv}(A') \subset A + (R - \sqrt{(R-\beta)^2 - \rho^2})B$$

if $\rho < R - \beta$. Thus, for all $p \in P$ we have $\operatorname{Conv} \mathcal{A}_p(\alpha_0) \subset A + \alpha_1 C$ whenever $\delta(r + \alpha_0) < R - \beta$ and $\alpha_1 - \alpha_0 \geq R - \sqrt{(R-\beta)^2 - \delta^2(r + \alpha_0)^2}$. □

Taking the union over all points $p \in P$ on both sides of the inclusion in Lemma 9 we get immediately the middle inclusion in (2), *i.e.* $\mathcal{H}(\alpha_0) \subset A^{\beta} + \alpha_1 C$. The left-most and right-most inclusions in (2) are easy to establish, using $A \subset P + \varepsilon C$ and $B \subset C$.

LEMMA 10. *The sequence of inclusions in (2) holds whenever $\alpha_1 \leq r - \varepsilon - \beta$, $\delta(r + \alpha_0) < R - \beta$ and $\alpha_1 - \alpha_0 \geq R - \sqrt{(R-\beta)^2 - \delta^2(r + \alpha_0)^2}$.*

4.2 A homotopy equivalence for nested collections of convex sets

It is not difficult to see that the inclusion $\mathcal{H}(\alpha) \subset P + rC$ holds for all positive real numbers α and β. The goal of this section is to find conditions under which the inclusion map $\mathcal{H}(\alpha) \hookrightarrow P + rC$ is a homotopy equivalence. For this, we use covers of $\mathcal{H}(\alpha)$ and $P + rC$ by finite collections of convex sets. Specifically, we have $\mathcal{H}(\alpha) = \bigcup_{p \in P} \operatorname{Conv} \mathcal{A}_p(\alpha)$ and $P + rC = \bigcup_{p \in P} (p + rC)$. Since sets in the two collections $\{\operatorname{Conv} \mathcal{A}_p(\alpha)\}_{p \in P}$ and $\{p + rC\}_{p \in P}$ are convex, we can apply Leray's theorem [20] to each, and obtain that the union of sets in each collection has the same homotopy type as its associated nerve:

$$\mathcal{H}(\alpha) \simeq \operatorname{Nerve}\{\operatorname{Conv} \mathcal{A}_p(\alpha)\}_{p \in P}$$
$$P + rC \simeq \operatorname{Nerve}\{p + rC\}_{p \in P}$$

A key step consists in proving that, for suitable values of α, the nerves of the two collections are actually the same. As a consequence, $\mathcal{H}(\alpha)$ and $P + rC$ have the same homotopy type. We strengthen this result thanks to Lemma 11: and state conditions under which the inclusion $\mathcal{H}(\alpha) \hookrightarrow P + rC$ is a homotopy equivalence in Lemma 12.

LEMMA 11. *Consider two finite collections of compact convex sets of $\mathbb{R}^N$, $\mathcal{C} = \{C_i\}_{i\in I}$ and $\mathcal{D} = \{D_i\}_{i\in I}$ such that $C_i \subset D_i$ for all $i \in I$ and suppose the two collections have the same nerve. Then, the inclusion $\bigcup_i C_i \hookrightarrow \bigcup_i D_i$ is a homotopy equivalence.*

From Corollary 4G.3 in [18] also known as Leray's theorem [20] or the Nerve Lemma, it is clear that $\bigcup_i C_i$ and $\bigcup_i D_i$ which share the same nerve have the same homotopy type. But, we need here a stronger result, namely that the inclusion $\bigcup_i C_i \hookrightarrow \bigcup_i D_i$ is a homotopy equivalence. Even though this fact can be deduced from a result in [7], we provide below a short proof to make the paper self-contained.

PROOF. Let $K(\mathcal{C})$ be the abstract simplicial complex whose simplices are the (non-empty) subsets of indices $\sigma \subset I$ such that $\bigcap_{i\in\sigma} C_i \neq \emptyset$. Since the two collections $\mathcal{C}$ and $\mathcal{D}$ have the same nerves, $K(\mathcal{C}) = K(\mathcal{D})$ and we let $K = K(\mathcal{C})$.

For every subset of indices $\sigma \notin K$, a standard compactness argument yields a real number $\rho_\sigma > 0$ such that $\bigcap_{i\in\sigma} D_i^{\rho_\sigma} = \emptyset$. Let $\rho = \min_{\sigma\notin K} \rho_\sigma$ and define the open set $O_i = \{x \in \mathbb{R}^N, d(x, D_i) < \rho\}$ for every $i \in I$. By construction, the nerve of the collection $\mathcal{O} = \{O_i\}_{i\in I}$ is the same as the nerve of $\mathcal{D}$ and $K(\mathcal{O}) = K$. For each $\sigma \in K$, we introduce the possibly empty open set:

$$U_\sigma = \bigcap_{i\in\sigma} O_i \setminus \bigcup_{i\notin\sigma} D_i.$$

It is obvious from the definition that $\bigcup_{\sigma\in K} U_\sigma \subset \bigcup_{i\in I} O_i$. Let us associate to each point $x \in \bigcup_{i\in I} O_i$ the subset of indices $\tau(x) = \{i \in I, x \in O_i\}$. Since $x \in U_{\tau(x)}$, it follows that:

$$\bigcup_{\sigma\in K} U_\sigma = \bigcup_{i\in I} O_i.$$

Let us consider a partition of unity $\{\phi_\sigma\}_{\sigma\in K}$ subordinate to the open cover $\{U_\sigma\}_{\sigma\in K}$ [23, page 22]. Note that the map ϕ_σ is identically zero for the simplices σ for which $U_\sigma = \emptyset$. For each simplex $\sigma \in K$, we choose an arbitrary point $c_\sigma \in \bigcap_{i\in\sigma} C_i$ and introduce the map $h : \bigcup_{i\in I} D_i \to \mathbb{R}^N$ defined by:

$$h(x) = \sum_{\sigma\in K} \phi_\sigma(x) c_\sigma.$$

By construction, h is continuous. We claim that $x \in D_i \implies h(x) \in C_i$. Indeed, if $x \in D_i$ and $\phi_\sigma(x) \neq 0$, one has $i \in \sigma$ and therefore $c_\sigma \in C_i$. Hence, the non-zero terms in the above sum is a convex combination of points in C_i and the claim follows from the convexity of C_i. Let us prove that h is a homotopy inverse of the inclusion map $g : \bigcup_i C_i \to \bigcup_i D_i$. In other words, we have to check that $g \circ h$ is homotopic to the identity of $\bigcup_i D_i$ and $h \circ g$ is homotopic to the identity of $\bigcup_i C_i$. This can be done using twice the homotopy $H(x,t) = (1-t)\cdot x + t\cdot h(x)$, first considered as a map from $\bigcup_i D_i \times [0,1]$ into $\bigcup_i D_i$, second considered as a map from $\bigcup_i C_i \times [0,1]$ into $\bigcup_i C_i$. □

LEMMA 12. *Consider positive real numbers r, ε, α and β such that $\delta r < R - \varepsilon$, $\delta(r+\alpha) < R - \beta$ and $\alpha \geq \xi r + R - \sqrt{(R-\varepsilon)^2 - (\delta r)^2}$. Then, the inclusion $\mathcal{H}(\alpha) \hookrightarrow P + rC$ is a homotopy equivalence.*

PROOF. We prove the lemma in three stages:
(a) First, we prove that for $\delta r < R - \varepsilon$ and $\alpha \geq \xi r + R - \sqrt{(R-\varepsilon)^2 - (\delta r)^2}$, we have

$$\text{Nerve}\{p + rC\}_{p\in P} = \text{Nerve}\{\mathcal{A}_p(\alpha)\}_{p\in P}. \quad (3)$$

Note that this is equivalent to proving that for all subsets $Q \subset P$,

$$\bigcap_{q\in Q} (q + rC) \neq \emptyset \iff \bigcap_{q\in Q} [(q + rC) \cap (A^\beta + \alpha C)] \neq \emptyset.$$

One direction is trivial: if a point belongs to the intersection on the right, then it belongs to the intersection on the left. Suppose now that $\bigcap_{q\in Q}(q + rC) \neq \emptyset$. In particular, using $C \subset \delta B$ this means that Q can be enclosed in a ball of radius $\rho = \delta r$. Since C is ξ-eccentric, there exists $z \in \bigcap_{q\in Q}(q+rC)$ such that $z \in \text{Conv}(Q) + \xi rC$. Since P is an (ε, C)-sample of A, we have $Q \subset P \subset A^\varepsilon$. Applying Lemma 14, we get that $\text{Conv}(Q) \subset A^{\alpha-\xi r}$. Hence and using $B \subset C$, we get $z \in A + (\alpha - \xi r)B + \xi rC \subset A^\beta + \alpha C$.
(b) Second, we prove that

$$\text{Nerve}\{p + rC\}_{p\in P} \;=\; \text{Nerve}\{\text{Conv}\,\mathcal{A}_p(\alpha)\}_{p\in P}. \quad (4)$$

From Lemma 9, we obtain the sequence of inclusions

$$\mathcal{A}_p(\alpha) \;\subset\; \text{Conv}\,\mathcal{A}_p(\alpha) \;\subset\; \mathcal{A}_p(\alpha'),$$

for $\delta(r+\alpha) < R-\beta$ and $\alpha' = \alpha + R - \sqrt{(R-\beta)^2 - \delta^2(r+\alpha)^2}$. Taking the intersection over all points $q \in Q$, we get

$$\bigcap_{q\in Q} \mathcal{A}_q(\alpha) \;\subset\; \bigcap_{q\in Q} \text{Conv}\,\mathcal{A}_q(\alpha) \;\subset\; \bigcap_{q\in Q} \mathcal{A}_q(\alpha'),$$

and consequently

$$\text{Nerve}\{\mathcal{A}_p(\alpha)\} \;\subset\; \text{Nerve}\{\text{Conv}\,\mathcal{A}_p(\alpha)\} \;\subset\; \text{Nerve}\{\mathcal{A}_p(\alpha')\},$$

where p ranges over P. By Equation (3), the two nerves on the left and on the right are equal to $\text{Nerve}\{p + rC\}_{p\in P}$, showing that $\text{Nerve}\{\text{Conv}\,\mathcal{A}_p(\alpha)\}_{p\in P} = \text{Nerve}\{p + rC\}_{p\in P}$.
(c) Third, noticing that $\text{Conv}\,\mathcal{A}_p(\alpha) \subset p + rC$ for all p, we apply Lemma 11 to the two collections of convex sets $\mathcal{C} = \{\text{Conv}\,\mathcal{A}_p(\alpha)\}_{p\in P}$ and $\mathcal{D} = \{p + rC\}_{p\in P}$. □

We conclude this section by the proof of our second reconstruction theorem.

PROOF OF THEOREM 2. For β small enough, we have $\beta + (\delta - 1)r < \min\{R - r, R_{r/\varkappa}\}$, $\delta(r + \alpha_0) < R - \beta$ and

$$2R - \sqrt{(R-\varepsilon)^2 - (\delta r)^2} - \sqrt{(R-\beta)^2 - \delta^2(r+\alpha_0)^2} \leq (1-\xi)r - \varepsilon - \beta.$$

Setting $\alpha_1 = \alpha_0 + R - \sqrt{(R-\beta)^2 - \delta^2(r+\alpha_0)^2}$, the above inequality can be rewritten as $\alpha_1 \leq r - \varepsilon - \beta$. Thus, the sequence of inclusions in (2) holds by Lemma 10. Furthermore, the inclusion $\mathcal{H}(\alpha) \hookrightarrow P + rC$ is a homotopy equivalence by Lemma 12. Since $\alpha_1 \leq r$ and $\beta + (\delta-1)r < \min\{R-r, R_{r/\varkappa}\}$ imply $\beta + (\delta-1)\alpha_1 < \min\{R - \alpha_1, R_{\alpha_1/\varkappa}\}$, the inclusion $A \hookrightarrow A^\beta + \alpha_1 C$ is a homotopy equivalence by Theorem 1. Applying the Sandwich Lemma allows us to conclude. □

5. DISCUSSION

In this paper, we have exhibited a class of compact convex sets whose Minkowski sum with a sufficiently dense sample retrieves the topology of the sampled shape. Compact convex sets in this class possess three properties: a non-empty interior, a positive θ_N-roundness and an eccentricity smaller than 1. In particular, this class contains Euclidean balls but, more interestingly, also includes N-dimensional cubes, with potential algorithmic applications in high dimensions.

Results in this paper raise a number of questions. For instance, it would be interesting to know what is the lowest density of sample points Theorem 2 authorizes and if this number is tight, especially for N-dimensional balls. Also, Theorem 2 requires the sample P to be finite and the shape A to have a positive reach. Can we relax these two conditions?

6. REFERENCES

[1] N. Amenta, D. Attali, and O. Devillers. A tight bound for the Delaunay triangulation of points on a pol yhedron. Research Report 6522, INRIA, May 2008.

[2] N. Amenta and M. Bern. Surface reconstruction by Voronoi filtering. *Discrete and Computational Geometry*, 22(4):481–504, 1999.

[3] N. Amenta, S. Choi, T. Dey, and N. Leekha. A simple algorithm for homeomorphic Surface Reconstruction. *International Journal of Computational Geometry and Applications*, 12:125–141, 2002.

[4] N. Amenta, S. Choi, and R. Kolluri. The power crust, unions of balls, and the medial axis transform. *Computational Geometry: Theory and Applications*, 19(2-3):127–153, 2001.

[5] D. Attali and A. Lieutier. Reconstructing shapes with guarantees by unions of convex sets. *Archive Hal, hal-00427035*, 2009.

[6] D. Attali and A. Lieutier. Optimal reconstruction might be hard. In *26th Ann. Sympos. Comput. Geom.*, Snowbird, Utah, 2010.

[7] P. Bendich, D. Cohen-Steiner, H. Edelsbrunner, J. Harer, and D. Morozov. Inferring local homology from sampled stratified spaces. In *Proc. 48th Ann. Sympos. Found. Comput. Sci.*, pages 536–546, 2007.

[8] J.-D. Boissonnat, O. Devillers, and S. Hornus. Incremental construction of the Delaunay triangulation and the Delaunay graph in medium dimension. In *Proc. ACM Symposium on Computational Geometry*, June 2009.

[9] P. Cannarsa and C. Sinestrari. *Semiconcave functions, Hamilton-Jacobi equations, and optimal control.* Birkhauser, 2004.

[10] F. Chazal, D. Cohen-Steiner, and A. Lieutier. A sampling theory for compact sets in Euclidean space. *Discrete and Computational Geometry*, 41(3):461–479, 2009.

[11] F. Chazal and A. Lieutier. The λ-medial axis. *Graphical Models*, 67(4):304–331, 2005.

[12] F. Chazal and A. Lieutier. Smooth Manifold Reconstruction from Noisy and Non Uniform Approximation with Guarantees. *Computational Geometry: Theory and Applications*, 40:156–170, 2008.

[13] V. de Silva and R. Ghrist. Coverage in sensor networks via persistent homology. *Algebraic & Geometric Topology*, 7:339–358, 2007.

[14] T. Dey, J. Giesen, E. Ramos, and B. Sadri. Critical points of the distance to an epsilon-sampling of a surface and flow-complex-based surface reconstruction. In *Proc. of the twenty-first annual symposium on Computational geometry*, page 227. ACM, 2005.

[15] H. Edelsbrunner. The union of balls and its dual shape. *Discrete Computational Geometry*, 13(1):415–440, 1995.

[16] H. Federer. Curvature measures. *Trans. Amer. Math. Soc*, 93:418–491, 1959.

[17] K. Grove. Critical point theory for distance functions. In *Proc. of Symposia in Pure Mathematics*, volume 54, pages 357–386, 1993.

[18] A. Hatcher. *Algebraic topology.* Cambridge University Press, 2002.

[19] D. Koutroufiotis. On Blaschke's rolling theorems. *Archiv des Mathematik*, 23(1):655–660, 1972.

[20] J. Leray. Sur la forme des espaces topologiques et sur les points fixes des représentations. *J. Math. Pures Appl.*, 24:95–167, 1945.

[21] J. R. Munkres. *Topology.* Prentice Hall, 2000.

[22] P. Niyogi, S. Smale, and S. Weinberger. Finding the Homology of Submanifolds with High Confidence from Random Samples. *Discrete Computational Geometry*, 39(1-3):419–441, 2008.

[23] L. Schwartz. *Théorie des distributions.* Hermann, Paris, 1966.

APPENDIX

A. BASIC PROPERTIES

In this appendix, we present basic properties relating the smallest ball enclosing $Q \subset \mathbb{R}^N$ and the convex hull of Q.

LEMMA 13. *Consider a subset $Q \subset \mathbb{R}^N$ whose smallest enclosing ball has radius r. Then,* $\mathrm{Conv}(Q) \subset \bigcup_{q \in Q} B(q, r)$.

PROOF. For all $q \in \mathrm{Conv}(Q)$, there are points $q_1, \ldots, q_n$ in Q and non-negative real numbers $\alpha_1, \ldots, \alpha_n$ summing up to 1, such that $q = \sum_{i=1}^n \alpha_i q_i$. Let $\pi_i(x) = \|x - q_i\|^2 - r^2$ be the power distance of $x \in \mathbb{R}^N$ from $B_i = B(q_i, r)$ and note that $B_i = \pi_i^{-1}(-\infty, 0]$. Let $\pi(x) = \sum_{i=1}^n \alpha_i \pi_i(x)$ and set $B = \pi^{-1}(-\infty, 0]$. We prove that $\bigcap_{i=1}^n B_i \subset B \subset \bigcup_{i=1}^n B_i$. Indeed, if a point x belongs to all balls B_i, then $\pi_i(x) \leq 0$ for all $1 \leq i \leq n$, which implies $\pi(x) \leq 0$. On the other hand, if $\pi(x) \leq 0$ then $\pi_i(x) \leq 0$ for at least one index i, which implies that x belongs to at least one ball B_i. Now, our choice of r as the radius of the smallest ball enclosing Q implies that $\bigcap_{i=1}^n B_i \neq \emptyset$, showing that B is non-empty. Thus, B is a ball and it is not difficult to see that its center is point q. It follows that $q \in B \subset \bigcup_{i=1}^n B_i$, which concludes the proof. □

The next lemma states that the convex hull of a set of points cannot be too far away from a shape with positive reach, assuming the set of points is close to the shape and are enclosed in a ball of small radius. Formally:

LEMMA 14. *Consider a subset $Q \subset A^\varepsilon$ in $\mathbb{R}^N$ and suppose Q can be enclosed in a ball of radius $\rho < R - \varepsilon$. Then,* $\mathrm{Conv}(Q) \subset A^\alpha$ *for* $\alpha \geq R - \sqrt{(R-\varepsilon)^2 - \rho^2}$.

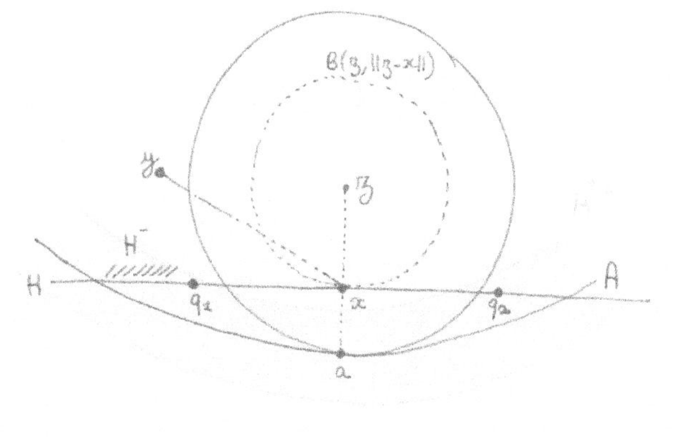

Figure 9: Notations for the proof of Lemma 14.

PROOF. Suppose $R < +\infty$ for otherwise, A is convex and $\mathrm{Conv}(Q) \subset A^{\varepsilon}$. Let x be a point on $\mathrm{Conv}(Q)$ furthest away from A. By Lemma 13, there exists a point $q \in Q$ such that $\|x - q\| \leq \rho$. Thus, $d(x, A) \leq \|x - q\| + d(q, A) \leq \rho + \varepsilon < R$, showing that x has a unique projection a onto A. We claim that the plane H passing through x and orthogonal to the segment xa is a supporting plane of the convex hull of Q. To prove this, consider the two open half-spaces that H bounds and let H^- be the one half-space that does not contain a. Furthermore, consider the half-line with origin a that passes through x and let z be the point on this half-line at distance R from a (see Figure 9). By construction, $B(z, R)$ is tangent to A at a and its interior does not intersect A. We prove that $\mathrm{Conv}(Q) \cap H^- = \emptyset$. Suppose for a contradiction that there exists a point $y \in \mathrm{Conv}(Q) \cap H^-$. Then, the whole segment xy belongs to $\mathrm{Conv}(Q)$ and in particular intersects $B(z, \|z - x\|)$. But points in the interior of $B(z, \|z - x\|)$ are furthest away from A than x, contradicting the definition of x as the point of $\mathrm{Conv}(Q)$ furthest away from A. It follows that H is a supporting plane of the convex hull of Q as claimed. Thus, $Q \cap H$ is non-empty and can be enclosed in a ball of radius smaller or equal to ρ. The convex hull of $Q \cap H$ contains x and by Lemma 13, there exists a point $q' \in Q \cap H$ such that $\|x - q'\| \leq \rho$. On the other hand, $\|z - q'\| \geq R - \varepsilon$. It follows that $\|x - a\| = R - \sqrt{\|z - q'\|^2 - \|x - q'\|^2} \leq \alpha$. $\square$

LEMMA 15. *For any subset $Q \subset \mathbb{R}^N$ and any convex set $C \subset \mathbb{R}^N$, $\mathrm{Conv}(Q + C) = \mathrm{Conv}(Q) + C$.*

The proof is straightforward and hence omitted.

B. PROOF OF LEMMA 2

We start with a preliminary lemma.

LEMMA 16. *For all points $c_1, c_2 \in C$, $c_1 \neq c_2$ and all vectors $n_1 \in \mathcal{N}(c_1)$ and $n_2 \in \mathcal{N}(c_2)$, we have*

$$\frac{(c_1 - c_2) \cdot (n_1 - n_2)}{\|c_1 - c_2\|^2} = \frac{1}{2}(\kappa_{c_1,n_1}(c_2) + \kappa_{c_2,n_2}(c_1)),$$

where $\kappa_{x,n}(y)$ is the curvature of the sphere passing through points x and y and with outer normal n at point x.

PROOF. See Figure 10, left. Let S_i be the sphere passing through points c_1 and c_2 with outer normal n_i at c_i, for $i \in \{1, 2\}$. Let n_2' be the outer unit normal to S_1 at c_2 and n_1' be the outer unit normal to S_2 at c_1. We have

$$\begin{aligned}
(c_1 - c_2) \cdot (n_1 - n_2') &= \kappa_{c_1,n_1}(c_2)\|c_1 - c_2\|^2 \\
(c_1 - c_2) \cdot (n_1' - n_2) &= \kappa_{c_2,n_2}(c_1)\|c_1 - c_2\|^2 \\
(c_1 - c_2) \cdot (n_2' + n_1) &= 0 \\
(c_2 - c_1) \cdot (n_1' + n_2) &= 0
\end{aligned}$$

Summing up these four equations gives the result. $\square$

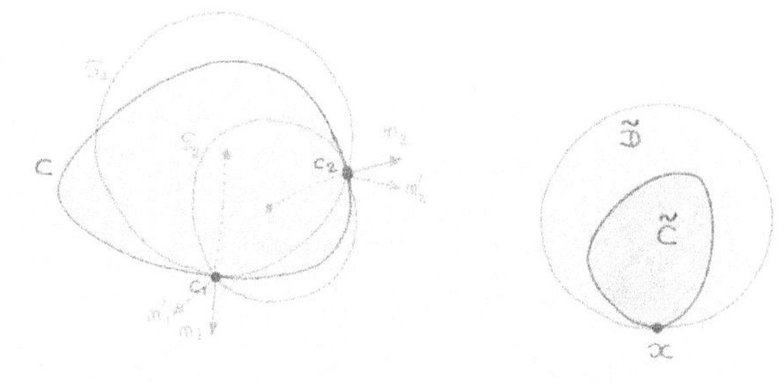

Figure 10: Notations for the proof of Lemma 16 and Lemma 2.

PROOF OF LEMMA 2. We first prove that for all points $c_1, c_2 \in \partial C$ with normals n_1 and n_2 respectively:

$$(c_1 - c_2) \cdot (n_1 - n_2) \geq \kappa_{\min}(C)\|c_1 - c_2\|^2.$$

Consider a sphere S tangent to ∂C at point x and meeting ∂C in another point $y \neq x$. Let D be the ball that S bounds. We begin by proving that $\kappa_{\min}(D) \geq \kappa_{\min}(C)$. Consider a 2-dimensional plane P passing through x and y and containing the common normal to ∂D and ∂C at point x. In particular, P passes through the center of D. We think of $\tilde{D} = D \cap P$ and $\tilde{C} = C \cap P$ as two compact convex sets in $\mathbb{R}^2$. By construction, $\partial\tilde{D}$ and $\partial\tilde{C}$ are C^2-smooth curves tangent at point x and meeting at point $y \neq x$. Thus, we reduced the geometric situation in $\mathbb{R}^N$ to the same situation in $\mathbb{R}^2$. Let us prove that $\kappa_{\min}(\tilde{D}) \geq \kappa_{\min}(\tilde{C})$. Suppose for a contradiction that $\kappa_{\min}(\tilde{D}) < \kappa_{\min}(\tilde{C})$. In other words, the curvature of circle $\tilde{D}$ is smaller than the curvature at any point on the curve $\tilde{C}$. Theorem 1 in [19] tells us that $\tilde{C}$, except for x, lies in the interior of $\tilde{D}$, as illustrated in Figure 10 right. But, this contradicts the fact that $\tilde{C}$ intersects the boundary of $\tilde{D}$ in $y \neq x$. Thus, $\kappa_{\min}(\tilde{D}) \geq \kappa_{\min}(\tilde{C})$ and it follows that $\kappa_{\min}(D) = \kappa_{\min}(D \cap P) \geq \kappa_{\min}(C \cap P) \geq \kappa_{\min}(C)$, as claimed. In other words, given two points $x \neq y$ on the boundary of C and a unit vector $n \in \mathcal{N}(x)$, we have just proved that the curvature $\kappa_{x,n}(y)$ of the sphere passing through x and y with outer normal n at point x satisfies $\kappa_{x,n}(y) \geq \kappa_{\min}(C)$. Applying Lemma 16 gives the claimed inequality.

To prove that the inequality is tight, note that if c_2 tends to c_1 along a curve γ in ∂C, then the ratio

$$\frac{(c_1 - c_2) \cdot (n_1 - n_2)}{\|c_1 - c_2\|^2}$$

tends to the absolute value of the normal curvature of γ at c_1. In particular, if $|\kappa_{N-1}(x)|$ reaches its minimum at $x = c_1$ and the tangent line to γ at c_1 is the associated principal direction, then the ratio tends to $\kappa_{\min}(C)$. $\square$

Improving the First Selection Lemma in $\mathbb{R}^3$

Abdul Basit
Dept. of Computer Science
LUMS, Pakistan
abdulbasit@lums.edu.pk

Nabil H. Mustafa
Dept. of Computer Science
LUMS, Pakistan
nabil@lums.edu.pk

Saurabh Ray
Mathematics department
EPFL, Switzerland
saurabh.ray@epfl.ch

Sarfraz Raza
Dept. of Computer Science
LUMS, Pakistan
sarfrazr@lums.edu.pk

ABSTRACT

We present new bounds on the first selection lemma in $\mathbb{R}^3$. This makes progress on the open problems of Bukh, Matoušek and Nivash [6] and Boros-Füredi [4] for the three-dimensional case, improving the previously best result of Wagner [8]. While our results narrow the gap between the current best lower and upper bounds, they do not settle this question. However, they indicate that it is the current lower-bounds that are not tight, and we conjecture that the lower-bounds can be further improved to match the current upper bound.

Categories and Subject Descriptors

G.2 [**Combinatorics**]: Counting Problems

General Terms

Theory

Keywords

Centerpoints, First Selection Lemma, Hitting Simplices, Location Depth

1. INTRODUCTION

The so-called First Selection Lemma [7] states the following: given any set P of n points in $\mathbb{R}^d$, there exists a point in $\mathbb{R}^d$ contained in at least $c_d n^{d+1} - O(n^d)$ simplices spanned by P. It is a fundamental result that has had several applications in discrete geometry [7]. In particular, it was used to construct weak ϵ-nets [1], which were crucially used in the solution of the famous Hadwiger-Debrunner conjecture [2].

The first selection lemma is closely linked to the following useful property of point sets: given any set P of n points in $\mathbb{R}^d$, there always exists a point q such that any closed halfspace containing q contains at least $n/(d+1)$ points of P. Such a point is called a *centerpoint*. In general, a point p has *depth* t w.r.t. P if any closed halfspace containing p contains at least t points of P. The centerpoint theorem guarantees a point of depth $n/(d+1)$. The depth of P is defined as the maximum depth of any point $p \in \mathbb{R}^d$ w.r.t. P. Currently the best known bounds for c_d for $d \geq 3$ are achieved by using *any* centerpoint.

In the past several decades, the value of the constant c_d has been investigated in a series of papers. Unfortunately, there still remains a large gap between the current upper and lower bounds. Bárány [3] proved that $c_d \geq \frac{1}{d!(d+1)^{d+1}}$. For $d = 2$, this proves the existence of a point in $n^3/54$ of the triangles defined by any point set of size n in the plane. This was improved to $n^3/27$ in [4, 6] and was also shown to be optimal (see Bukh [5] for another proof which is simple and elegant).

Bárány's bound was improved to $\frac{d^2+1}{(d+1)!(d+1)^{d+1}}$ by Wagner [8], who in fact showed that any point of depth τn is contained in at least the following number of simplices:

$$\frac{(d+1)\tau^d - 2d\tau^{d+1}}{(d+1)!} \cdot n^{d+1} - O(n^d) \qquad (1)$$

The recent work of Bukh, Matoušek and Nivash [6] is devoted to the investigation of upper bounds on the value of c_d. In particular, they showed that in $\mathbb{R}^d$, the centerpoint cannot give a better bound than the one above (set $\tau = 1/(d+1)$). Their main result is an elegant construction of a point set P so that no point in $\mathbb{R}^d$ is contained in more than $(n/(d+1))^{d+1}$ simplices defined by P. Furthermore, they conjecture that this is the right bound, and leave improving the lower bound as their main open problem.

Our Result

We make progress on the above problem, which was left as the main open problem in [6], by improving the bounds for the first selection lemma in $\mathbb{R}^3$ by a factor of 1.4, presented in Section 2. In particular, we prove the following:

THEOREM 1. *Let P be a set of n points in $\mathbb{R}^3$. Then there exists a point contained in at least $0.00227 \cdot n^4$ simplices spanned by P.*

The previous best result, which follows from (1), proves that given any P, there exists a point contained in at least $(5/12) \cdot (n/4)^4$ simplices (this is the centerpoint). While our result does not settle the question, it shows that it is the current lower-bounds which are not tight, and gives more strength to their conjecture.

2. IMPROVING FIRST SELECTION LEMMA IN $\mathbb{R}^3$

The bound of Wagner [8] improves with the depth of the point set P. Our simple idea is to show that when the depth of P is low, one can also get a better bound. For example, when $depth(P) = n/(d+1)$, then the conjecture of [6] is in fact proven below. By combining the two, one gets an overall improvement. In particular, let $depth(P) = \tau n$. If $\tau \geq 0.3$, we will apply Wagner's result. We therefore concentrate on the case where $\tau < 0.3$, for which we present an improved bound below. We will use the following lemma, proven in [4].

LEMMA 1 (BOROS-FÜREDI [4]). *Given a set P of n points in $\mathbb{R}^d$, where $depth(P) = \tau n$, there exists a point p with depth τn, and a set $\mathcal{H}$ of $d+1$ halfspaces $\{h_1, \ldots, h_{d+1}\}$, such that i) $|h_i \cap P| = \tau n$, ii) p lies on the boundary plane of each h_i, and iii) $h_1 \cup \ldots \cup h_{d+1}$ cover the entire $\mathbb{R}^d$.*

We first need a technical lemma which can be seen as a generalization of Caratheodory's theorem:

LEMMA 2. *Let $P' = \{p_1, \ldots, p_{d+2}\}$ be a set of $d+2$ points in $\mathbb{R}^d$. Then any point $x \in conv(P')$ lies in at least two d-simplices spanned by P'.*

PROOF. Take any point of P', say p_1, and consider the ray emanating from p_1 and passing through x. This ray, after passing through x, intersects $conv(P')$ in a $(d-1)$-simplex defined by d points, say P''. Then $P'' \cup p_1$ contains x, and has size $d+1$. Let p_i be the remaining point in $P \setminus (P'' \cup \{p_1\})$. Repeating the same procedure of shooting a ray from p_i through x results in another d-simplex, with p_i as one of its points, that contains x. □

Given a set P of n points in $\mathbb{R}^3$, with $depth(P) = \tau n$, use Lemma 1 to get the point p and a set of four halfspaces $\mathcal{H} = \{h_1, h_2, h_3, h_4\}$ satisfying the stated conditions. Define the following subsets of P:

$$\begin{aligned} A_i &= P \cap (\bigcap_{l \neq i} \overline{h}_l) \cap h_i, \\ B_{i,j} &= P \cap (\bigcap_{l \neq i,j} \overline{h}_l) \cap h_i \cap h_j, \\ C_i &= P \cap (\bigcap_{l \neq i} h_l) \cap \overline{h}_i \end{aligned} \quad (2)$$

Set $\alpha_i = |A_i|/n$, $\beta_{i,j} = |B_{i,j}|/n$, and $\gamma_i = |C_i|/n$. Our main lemma is the following.

LEMMA 3. *Let P be a set of n points in $\mathbb{R}^3$, with $depth(P) = \tau n$. Then, there exists a point contained in at least $g(P) \cdot n^4$ simplices spanned by P, where*

$$\begin{aligned} g(P) &= \left(\prod_i \alpha_i\right) + \left(\sum_{i,j} \beta_{i,j} \cdot \frac{\prod_l \alpha_l}{\max(\alpha_i, \alpha_j)}\right) \\ &+ \left(\sum_i \gamma_i \cdot \frac{\prod_l \alpha_l}{\max_{l \neq i} \alpha_l}\right) \end{aligned} \quad (3)$$

PROOF. Let p be the point from Lemma 1, together with the four halfspaces $h_1, \ldots, h_4$. We first show that the simplex spanned by any four points, one from each of A_i, will always contain p.

Claim 1. Let $p_1, p_2, p_3, p_4 \in P$ be four points of P, such that $p_i \in A_i$. Then $p \in conv(\{p_1, p_2, p_3, p_4\})$.

PROOF. For $i \in \{1, 2, 3, 4\}$, let r_i be the ray emanating from p and passing through p_i. Assume, for contradiction, that $conv(\{p_1, p_2, p_3, p_4\})$ does not contain p. Then there exists a hyperplane h that separates p from $conv(\{p_1, p_2, p_3, p_4\})$. For $i \in \{1, 2, 3, 4\}$, define q_i to be the point $r_i \cap h$. By Radon's theorem, there exists disjoint sets Q_1, Q_2 and a point s so that $Q_1 \cup Q_2 = \{q_1, q_2, q_3, q_4\}$ and $s \in conv(Q_1) \cap conv(Q_2)$. For any $i \in \{1, 2, 3, 4\}$, consider the halfspace h_i. By definition h_i passes through p, contains p_i and does not contain any other point p_j with $j \neq i$. Clearly then h_i contains q_i and does not contain any other point q_j with $j \neq i$. Suppose, without loss of generality, that $q_i \in Q_1$. Then, h_i does not contain any of the points in Q_2. Since, $s \in conv(Q_2)$, h_i does not contain s. This implies that none of the h_i's contain s, contradicting the assumption that union of the h_i's covers $\mathbb{R}^3$. □

The total number of such simplices is $n^4 \cdot \prod_i \alpha_i$, which is the first term in Equation (3). Call any such simplex a *basic simplex*, i.e., a simplex on $p_1, p_2, p_3, p_4 \in P$ is basic iff $p_i \in A_i$ for all i. All other simplices are called non-basic.
Now we use basic simplices, which always contain p, to prove the existence of several other simplices which must also contain p.

Claim 2. Let $P' = \{p_1, p_2, p_3, p_4, p_5\} \subset P$ be five points of P, such that $p_k \in A_k$, $k = 1 \ldots 4$, and $p_5 \in B_{i,j}$, for any $1 \leq i < j \leq 4$. Then either the simplex defined by $P' \setminus p_i$ or by $P' \setminus p_j$ contains p.

PROOF. By Claim 1, the basic simplex defined by p_1, p_2, p_3, p_4 contains p. Therefore, by Lemma 2, at least one other simplex spanned by P' must contain p. Note that this simplex must have p_5 as one of its points. Also, it must contain p_k, where $k \neq i, j$, since the plane h_k separates $P' \setminus p_k$ from p, as it follows from the definitions (2) that $p_l \in \overline{h}_k$ for all $l \neq k$, and $p_5 \in \overline{h}_k$ since $p_5 \in B_{i,j}$. So for this second simplex, the only possible choice is for the fourth vertex, which can be either p_i or p_j. □

For any fixed i, j, there are $n^5(\beta_{i,j} \cdot \prod_l \alpha_l)$ 5-tuples as in Claim 2, and each produces one d-simplex containing p. Each such d-simplex may be overcounted at most $n \cdot \max(\alpha_i, \alpha_j)$ times, so the total number of distinct d-simplices of the type in Claim 2 containing p are at least $n^4 \frac{\beta_{i,j} \cdot \prod_i \alpha_i}{\max(\alpha_i, \alpha_j)}$, which when summed over all i, j, forms the second term in (3).

Claim 3. Let $P' = \{p_1, p_2, p_3, p_4, p_5\} \subset P$ be five points of P, such that $p_k \in A_k$, $k = 1 \ldots 4$, and $p_5 \in C_i$, for any $1 \leq i \leq 4$. Then at least one of the three simplices defined by $\{p_5, p_i\} \cup P''$, $|P''| = 2$, contains p, where $P'' \subset P \setminus \{p_5, p_i\}$.

PROOF. As in Claim 2, at least one non-basic simplex spanned by P' must contain p, with p_5 as one of its points. Also, it must contain p_i: the plane h_i separates $P' \setminus p_i$ from p, as $P' \setminus p_i \subseteq \overline{h}_i$. The other two vertices of this second simplex must therefore be a subset of the remaining three vertices in P'. □

By similarly eliminating the overcounting, the d-simplices from Claim 3 form the third term of $g(P)$. Finally, note that no two simplices are counted twice in $g(P)$, since each contains exactly one point from a distinct region (one of $B_{i,j}$ or C_i). This concludes the proof of the lemma. □

It remains to show that regardless of the distribution of the points in A_i, $B_{i,j}$ and C_j, the quantity $g(P)$ is always bounded suitably from below.

LEMMA 4. *Let P be a set of n points in $\mathbb{R}^3$, with $depth(P) = \tau n$, and $g(P)$ as in Lemma 3. Then, if $\tau < 0.3$, $g(P) \geq \tau^2 \cdot (1 - 3\tau)^2 \cdot \frac{5\tau-1}{\tau}$.*

PROOF. Note the following for each $i = 1, \ldots, 4$:

$$\tau = |h_i \cap P| = \alpha_i + \sum_{j \neq i} \beta_{i,j} + \sum_{j \neq i} \gamma_j \qquad (4)$$

Using the fact that $\alpha_i \leq \tau$, we get

$$\begin{aligned} g(P) &= \left(\prod_i \alpha_i\right) + \left(\sum_{i,j} \beta_{i,j} \cdot \frac{\prod_l \alpha_l}{\max(\alpha_i, \alpha_j)}\right) & (5)\\ &+ \left(\sum_i \gamma_i \cdot \frac{\prod_l \alpha_l}{\max_{l \neq i} \alpha_l}\right) \\ &\geq \left(\prod_i \alpha_i\right) + \left(\sum_{i,j} \beta_{i,j} \cdot \frac{\prod_l \alpha_l}{\tau}\right) & (6)\\ &+ \left(\sum_i \gamma_i \cdot \frac{\prod_l \alpha_l}{\tau}\right) \\ &= \left(\prod_i \alpha_i\right)\left(1 + \frac{\sum_{i,j} \beta_{i,j} + \sum_i \gamma_i}{\tau}\right). & (7) \end{aligned}$$

Since $\mathcal{H}$ covers the entire $\mathbb{R}^3$, we have $\cup_i(h_i \cap P) = P$, and so $\sum_i \alpha_i + \sum_{i,j} \beta_{i,j} + \sum_i \gamma_i = 1$. Summing up (4) for all four halfspaces, and subtracting the above from it, we get

$$\sum_{i,j} \beta_{i,j} + 2 \cdot \sum_i \gamma_i = 4 \cdot \tau - 1 \qquad (8)$$

Therefore, $\sum_{i,j} \beta_{i,j} + \sum_i \gamma_i \leq 4\tau - 1$. This, together with Equation (4), implies that $(1 - 3\tau) \leq \alpha_i \leq \tau$ for $i = 1 \ldots 4$. Assuming $\tau < 0.3$, we can show the following:

Claim 4. The bound in equation (7) is minimized when $\sum_{i,j} \beta_{i,j} + \sum_i \gamma_i = 4\tau - 1$ or equivalently, when $\sum_i \gamma_i = 0$ (since $\sum_{i,j} \beta_{i,j} + 2\sum_i \gamma_i = 4\tau - 1$).

PROOF. Suppose that $\sum_i \gamma_i = \epsilon + \epsilon_1$, where $\gamma_1 = \epsilon_1 > 0$. We show that the variables $\alpha_i, \beta_{i,j}, \gamma_1$ can be re-adjusted to new values $\alpha'_i, \beta'_{i,j}, \gamma'_1$ to give a smaller value in Equation (7), while still satisfying all the constraints in Equation (4), and where $\gamma'_1 = 0$. As long as $\sum_i \gamma_i > 0$, we can iteratively apply this procedure for all $\gamma_j > 0$ to make $\sum_i \gamma_i = 0$ without increasing the lower bound. Set $\gamma'_1 = 0$, $\beta'_{i,j} = \beta_{i,j} + \frac{2\epsilon_1}{3}$ for all $i, j \neq 1$, and $\alpha'_i = \alpha_i - \epsilon_1/3$ for all $i \neq 1$. One can verify that Equation (4) still holds for each halfspace, and $\sum \alpha_i + \sum \beta_{i,j} + \sum \gamma_i = 1$. This further implies, as before, that $(1-3\tau) \leq \alpha'_i \leq \tau$; in particular, $\alpha'_i \geq 0.1$ as $\tau \leq 0.3$. We now have to show that the function can only decrease:

$$\left(\prod_i \alpha'_i\right)\left(1 + \frac{\sum \gamma'_i + \sum \beta'_{i,j}}{\tau}\right) \leq \left(\prod_i \alpha_i\right)\left(1 + \frac{\sum \gamma_i + \sum \beta_{i,j}}{\tau}\right)$$

Note that $\sum_{i,j} \beta_{i,j} + \sum_i \gamma_i = 4\tau - 1 - \epsilon - \epsilon_1$, and $\sum_{i,j} \beta'_{i,j} + \sum_i \gamma'_i = 4\tau - 1 - \epsilon$. So

$$\begin{aligned} \left(\prod_{i \neq 1} \alpha_i - \frac{\epsilon_1}{3}\right)\left(\frac{5\tau - 1 - \epsilon}{\tau}\right) &\leq \left(\prod_{i \neq 1} \alpha_i\right)\left(\frac{5\tau - 1 - \epsilon - \epsilon_1}{\tau}\right) \\ \prod_{i \neq 1}\left(1 - \frac{\epsilon_1}{3\alpha_i}\right) &\leq 1 - \frac{\epsilon_1}{5\tau - 1 - \epsilon} \end{aligned}$$

Since each α_i, $i \neq 1$, can be at most $\tau - \epsilon_1$ (from (4)), we have to prove

$$\left(1 - \frac{\epsilon_1}{3(\tau - \epsilon_1)}\right)^3 \leq 1 - \frac{\epsilon_1}{5\tau - 1 - \epsilon}$$

By expanding, dropping the negative cubic term and simplifying, it remains to show that

$$4\tau \geq 1 + \epsilon - \epsilon_1 + \frac{\epsilon_1(5\tau - 1 - \epsilon)}{3(\tau - \epsilon_1)}$$

Since $\sum_{i,j} \beta_{i,j} + 2\sum_i \gamma_i = 4\tau - 1$, we have $\sum \gamma_i = \epsilon + \epsilon_1 \leq (4\tau - 1)/2$. So $4\tau \geq 2\epsilon + 1$, and it remains to show that

$$\frac{\epsilon_1(5\tau - 1 - \epsilon)}{3(\tau - \epsilon_1)} \leq \epsilon_1 \quad \text{or equivalently,} \quad 2\tau \leq 1 + \epsilon - 3\epsilon_1$$

Now one can verify that $2\tau \leq 1 - 3\epsilon_1$, since $\epsilon_1 \leq (4\tau - 1)/2$, and $\tau \leq 0.3$. □

It now follows from Claim 4 that

$$g(P) \geq \left(\prod_i \alpha_i\right)\left(1 + \frac{4\tau - 1}{\tau}\right) = \left(\prod_i \alpha_i\right)\left(\frac{5\tau - 1}{\tau}\right),$$

where $\sum \alpha_i = 2 - 4\tau$. The product $\prod \alpha_i$ is minimized, under the constraint that $\sum \alpha_i = 2 - 4\tau$, when three α_i's are minimum, and one is maximum. However, that is not allowed by Equation (4), as $(1 - 3\tau) \leq \alpha_i \leq \tau$. It turns out that under those constraints, the product is minimized when two of them are maximum, say $\alpha_1 = \alpha_2 = \tau$, and the other two are equally small, $\alpha_3 = \alpha_4 = 1 - 3\tau$, and then $\beta_{3,4} = 4\tau - 1$.

Claim 5. $\prod \alpha_i$ is minimized when $\alpha_1 = \alpha_2 = \tau$, and $\alpha_3 = \alpha_4 = (1 - 3\tau)$.

PROOF. Recall that $(1 - 3\tau) \leq \alpha_i \leq \tau$. If each $\alpha_i > (1 - 3\tau)$, pick the smallest of them, say α_4, and set $\alpha'_4 = \alpha_4 - \epsilon$, for a small enough $\epsilon > 0$, and add this excess to any other variable that is less than τ, say α_3 (there always exists another variable less than τ, else $\sum \alpha_i > (1 - 3\tau) + 3\tau = 1 \geq 2 - 4\tau$ for $\tau \geq 1/4$, a contradiction). Then $(\alpha_3 + \epsilon)(\alpha_4 - \epsilon) < \alpha_3\alpha_4$ since $\alpha_4 \leq \alpha_3$, minimizing the product further. Similarly, α_3 is also $(1 - 3\tau)$ in the configuration minimizing $\prod \alpha_i$. So we get that $\alpha_1 + \alpha_2 = (2 - 4\tau) - 2(1 - 3\tau) = 2\tau$. And as each α is at most τ, this forces $\alpha_1 = \alpha_2 = \tau$. □

It can be verified that all the constraints are satisfied, and so we get the required lower bound for $g(P)$:

$$g(P) \geq \left(\prod_i \alpha_i\right)\left(\frac{5\tau - 1}{\tau}\right) \geq \tau^2 \cdot (1 - 3\tau)^2 \cdot \frac{5\tau - 1}{\tau}$$

This concludes the proof of Lemma 4. □

PROOF OF THEOREM 1. Wagner [8] proved that any point of depth $\tau \cdot n$ in $\mathbb{R}^3$ is contained in at least $(4\tau^3 - 6\tau^4) \cdot \frac{n^4}{4!}$ simplices spanned by P. Setting this equal to the bound from Lemma 4, one gets the value $\tau' = 0.2889$. If $depth(P)$ is less than $\tau' n$, $g(P) \geq 0.00227$. Similarly, for $depth(P) \geq \tau' n$, Wagner's bound gives a point contained in at least $0.00227 \cdot n^4$ simplices. □

3. CONCLUSION

The conjecture of [6], that there always exists a point contained in at least $(n/(d+1))^{d+1}$ simplices spanned by any n points in $\mathbb{R}^d$, is an elegant one. So far, it has only been proven in $\mathbb{R}^2$ [4], and in this paper, we have made a step towards the optimal bound for $\mathbb{R}^3$. This indicates that the current lower-bounds are not tight, and gives more strength to their conjecture. The full conjecture, however, is still open.

Acknowledgements

The second author would like to thank J. Matoušek for his great kindness in answering questions by email. Thanks are also extended to anonymous reviewers whose insightful comments greatly improved the content and presentation of this paper.

4. REFERENCES

[1] N. Alon, I. Bárány, Z. Füredi, and D. J. Kleitman. Point selections and weak e-nets for convex hulls. *Combinatorics, Probability & Computing*, 1:189–200, 1992.

[2] N. Alon and D. Kleitman. Piercing convex sets and the hadwiger debrunner (p, q)-problem. *Adv. Math.*, 96(1):103–112, 1992.

[3] I. Barany. A generalization of caratheodory's theorem. *Discrete Math.*, 40:189–200, 1982.

[4] E. Boros and Z. Furedi. The number of triangles covering the center of an n-set. *Geometriae Dedicata*, 17(1):69–77, 1984.

[5] B. Bukh. A point in many triangles. *Electronic Journal of Combinatorics*, 13(10), 2006.

[6] B. Bukh, M. Matoušek, and G. Nivasch. Stabbing simplices by points and flats. http://arxiv.org/abs/0804.4464, 2008.

[7] J. Matoušek. *Lectures in Discrete Geometry*. Springer-Verlag, New York, NY, 2002.

[8] U. Wagner. *On k-Sets and Applications*. PhD thesis, ETH Zurich, 2003.

Points with Large Quadrant-Depth *

[Extended Abstract] †

Roel Apfelbaum
Mathematics Dept.,
Tel-Aviv University,
Tel-Aviv 69978, Israel.
roel6@hotmail.com.

Itay Ben-Dan
Mathematics Dept.,
Technion—Israel Institute of Technology,
Haifa 32000, Israel.
itaybd@gmail.com.

Stefan Felsner
Inst. f. Mathematik
TU Berlin,
10623 Berlin, Germany.
felsner@math.tu-berlin.de.

Tillmann Miltzow
Inst. f. Mathematik
TU Berlin,
10623 Berlin, Germany.
t.miltzow@googlemail.com.

Rom Pinchasi
Math. Dept.,
Technion—Israel Inst. of Technology,
Haifa 32000, Israel.
room@math.technion.ac.il.

Torsten Ueckerdt
Inst. f. Mathematik
TU Berlin,
10623 Berlin, Germany.
ueckerdt@math.tu-berlin.de.

Ran Ziv
Computer Science Dept.,
Tel-Hai Academic College,
upper Galilee 12210, Israel.
ranziv@telhai.ac.il

ABSTRACT

Given a set P of points in the plane we are interested in points that are 'deep' in the set in the sense that they have two opposite quadrants both containing many points of P. We deal with the extremal version of this problem. A pair (a, b) of numbers is *admissible* if every point set P contains a point $p \in P$ that determines a pair (Q, Q^{op}) of opposite quadrants, such that Q contains at least an a-fraction and Q^{op} contains at least a b-fraction of the points of P. We provide a complete description of the set $\mathcal{F}$ of all admissible pairs (a, b). This amounts to identifying three line segments and a point on the boundary of $\mathcal{F}$.

In higher dimensions we study the maximal a, such that (a, a) is opposite orthant admissible. We show that $1/(2\gamma) \leq a \leq 1/\gamma$ for $\gamma = 2^{2^{d-1}} 2^{d-1}$.

Finally we deal with a variant of the problem where the opposite pairs of orthants need not be determined by a point in P. Again we are interested in values a, such that all subsets P in $\mathbb{R}^d$ admit a pair (O, O^{op}) of opposite orthants both containing at least an a-fraction of the points. The maximal such value is $a = 1/2^d$. Generalizations of the problem are also discussed.

*This research was supported by a Grant from the G.I.F., the German-Israeli Foundation for Scientific Research and Development and also by THE ISRAELI SCIENCE FOUNDATION (grant No. 938/06) and Deutsche Forschungsgemeinschaft (grant DFG Fe340/7-1).

†A full version of this paper is available at `www.math.tu-berlin.de/~felsner/Paper/pwlqd.pdf`

SCG'10, June 13–16, 2010, Snowbird, Utah, USA.

Categories and Subject Descriptors

G.2.1 [**Discrete Mathematics**]: Combinatorics

General Terms

Theory

1. INTRODUCTION

A point $p = (p_1, p_2)$ in the plane defines four quadrants $Q_1(p), Q_2(p), Q_3(p)$ and $Q_4(p)$ centered at p. They are the connected regions left after removing the horizontal and the vertical lines through p from the plane. As usual the quadrants are numbered in counterclockwise order starting from $Q_1 = \{(x_1, x_2) \in \mathbb{R}^2 : x_1 > p_1 \text{ and } x_2 > p_2\}$. There are two pairs of opposite quadrants (Q_1, Q_3) and (Q_2, Q_4). We write Q^{op} to denote the quadrant opposite to Q, e.g., $Q_3^{\text{op}} = Q_1$. Throughout the paper we only consider sets of points in general position; in our context this means that the intersection of any horizontal or vertical line with P consists of at most one point. Actually this assumption is necessary for our results: if the points are not in general position and quadrants are open, then all quadrants of all points in P may have empty intersection with P.

For a given set P of points we ask for points $p \in P$ that are 'deep' in the set in the sense that p has two opposite quadrants both containing many points of P. We deal with the extremal version of this problem. That is, we ask for pairs (a, b), such that for every set P of n points in the plane there is a point $p \in P$ and a pair (Q, Q^{op}) of opposite quadrants centered at p, such that $|Q \cap P| \geq an - c$ and $|Q^{op} \cap P| \geq bn - c$, where c is a small constant. In this case we call the pair (a, b) *admissible* and the pair (Q, Q^{op}) of quadrants (a, b)*-admissible.*

Brönnimann, Lenchner, and Pach [BLP] define the notion of *opposite-quadrant depth* for point sets in the plane as the maximum a, such that (a, a) is admissible. They prove that every set of points in the plane has opposite-quadrant depth at least $\frac{1}{8}$. We give a new and simpler proof of this result below, Theorem 1.1.

In Section 2 we provide a complete description of the set $\mathcal{F}$ of all admissible pairs. The shape of $\mathcal{F}$ turns out to be surprisingly complicated (see Figure 3).

In Section 3 we ask for the maximum a, such that (a, a) is admissible in higher dimensions. In dimension d we obtain upper and lower bounds that differ by a factor of 2. In Section 4 we discuss further generalizations.

The notion of opposite quadrant-depth, resp. opposite orthant-depth is related to *centerpoints* and some measures of statistical depth, like *hyperplane depth.* We refer to [Ede] for information on centerpoints and to [LPS] for statistical depth. Brönnimann et al. [BLP] also mention a connection with conflict-free colorings. Related notions of *depth* have been studied e.g. in [BPZ1] and [BPZ2].

As a warm up and for the purpose of introducing some convenient notations we now reprove the main result from [BLP].

THEOREM 1.1 ([BLP]).

1. *Any set P of n points in general position in the plane has opposite-quadrant depth $\geq \frac{1}{8}$.*

2. *If P is in convex position, then it has opposite-quadrant depth $\geq \frac{1}{4}$.*

Before starting with the proof let us introduce the following convenient notation. The *weight* of a subset A of P with $|P| = n$ is $\omega(A) = \frac{|A|}{n-1}$. For a point $p \in P$ and a quadrant Q centered at p we define the weight of Q as

$$\pi(Q) = \omega(Q \cap P) = \frac{|Q \cap P|}{n-1}.$$

Note that by the general position assumption the quadrants of any point p fulfill $\pi(Q_1(p)) + \pi(Q_2(p)) + \pi(Q_3(p)) + \pi(Q_4(p)) = 1$. In many cases we will need a subset A of P of some specified weight. E.g. when we choose a set A of weight τ from P we mean that $\tau - \frac{1}{n-1} < \omega(A) \leq \tau$. We extend the loose interpretation to general inequalities: let $\omega(A) \leq \tau$ and $\omega(A) \geq \tau$ be abbreviations for $\omega(A) \leq \tau + \frac{c}{n-1}$ and $\omega(A) \geq \tau - \frac{c}{n-1}$ respectively, here c is some constant. The reason for allowing such small errors in inequalities is that our results talk about fractions of the point set, about asymptotic and not about single points. Because the sets considered in our proofs are obtained by at most four iterations of a directive of the form "choose A of weight w from A'" we can assure that the constants c for all inequalities in this paper can be chosen to be ≤ 4.

The theorem is an immediate consequence of the following lemma.

LEMMA 1.2. *Every set P in the plane contains a point p, such that*

$$\min\left(\pi(Q_1(p)), \pi(Q_3(p))\right) + \min\left(\pi(Q_2(p)), \pi(Q_4(p))\right) \geq \frac{1}{4}.$$

Proof. Consider the sets P_L, P_R, P_T and P_B of weight $\frac{1}{4}$ each consisting of the first points in P from the left, right, top and bottom, see Figure 1. From the definition of weights it follows that $P' = P \setminus (P_L \cup P_R \cup P_T \cup P_B) \neq \emptyset$. We claim that every point in P' has the desired property. Let p be such a point and assume that $\min\left(\pi(Q_1(p)), \pi(Q_3(p))\right) = s = \pi(Q_1(p))$. Since P_T is contained in $Q_1(p) \cup Q_2(p)$ it follows that $\pi(Q_2(p)) \geq \frac{1}{4} - s$. Considering P_R we obtain $\pi(Q_4(p)) \geq \frac{1}{4} - s$. Consequently $\min\left(\pi(Q_1(p)), \pi(Q_3(p))\right) = s$ and $\min\left(\pi(Q_2(p)), \pi(Q_4(p))\right) \geq \frac{1}{4} - s$, this proves the lemma. □

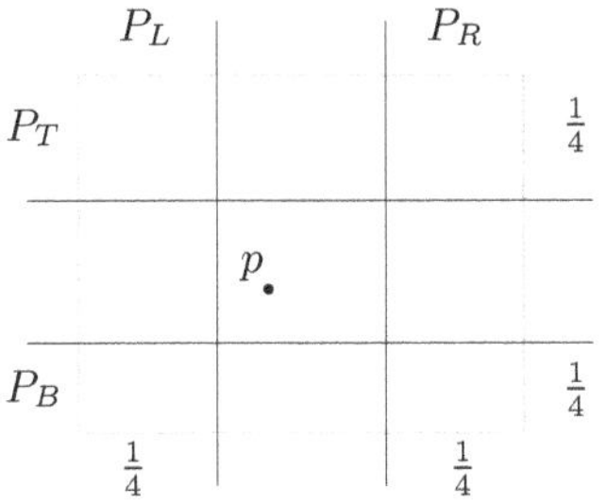

Figure 1: An illustration of the proof of Lemma 1.2.

Proof. (*of Theorem 1.1*) For part one of the theorem it is enough to observe that either s or $\frac{1}{4} - s$ is at least $\frac{1}{8}$. For the second part note that if P is in convex position one of the four quadrants of p is empty. Therefore, one of the two minima in the lemma is zero and the other minimum is at least $\frac{1}{4}$. □

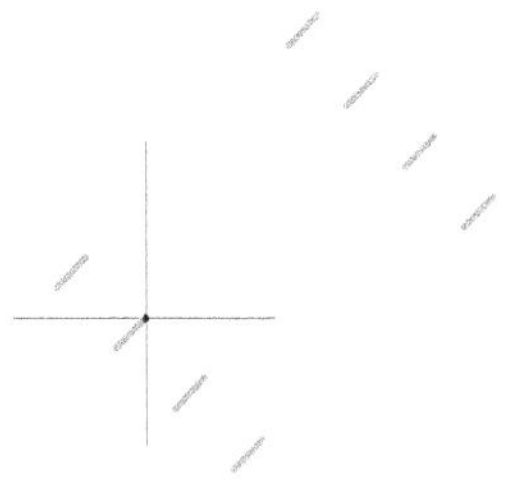

Figure 2: Opposite-quadrant depth $\leq \frac{1}{8}$.

It is easy to see that the second part of Theorem 1.1 is best possible by taking P to be the set of vertices of a regular n-gon. In [BLP] it is shown that the first part of Theorem 1.1 is best possible for arbitrarily large values of n of the form $n = 4 \cdot 3^k$. The example in Figure 2 shows a simple construction that proves that the first part of Theorem 1.1 cannot be improved. To describe the example we identify a point set with the induced dominance order, i.e., we say $p \leq q$ if $p_x \leq q_x$ and $p_y \leq q_y$. Based on this order we can talk about chains and antichains of a point set. The example of Figure 2 consists of eight chains each of weight $\leq \frac{1}{8}$. In the figure the chains are represented by gray segments.

The chains come in two groups of four chains each. One group of weight $\frac{1}{2}$ consists of the first points in P from the top (and the right) and the other group of weight $\frac{1}{2}$ consists of the first points in P from the bottom (and the left).

Since the example is symmetric it is enough to consider points in the first group to prove that there is no point in P with a pair of opposite quadrants each of weight strictly more than $\frac{1}{8}$. We consider two cases: First for $p \in P$ look at the pair $(Q_2(p), Q_4(p))$. The chains in each group are arranged in such a way that $Q_2(p)$ and $Q_4(p)$ both contain an integral number of chains. Therefore in order to have $\pi(Q_2(p)) > \frac{1}{8}$ and $\pi(Q_4(p)) > \frac{1}{8}$ the second and fourth quadrant of p both have to contain at least two chains. But there is no point p with this property.

To complete the argument, we observe that $\pi(Q_1(p)) \leq \frac{1}{8}$ holds for all p in the first group. Hence every point in P has two adjacent quadrants with weight $\leq \frac{1}{8}$.

2. THE SET OF ADMISSIBLE PAIRS

Recall that a pair $(a, b) \in [0, 1]^2$ is called *admissible* if every set P of n points in the plane contains a point $p \in P$, such that there is a quadrant Q centered at p with $\pi(Q) \geq a$ and $\pi(Q^{\text{op}}) \geq b$. For pairs $(a, b) \neq (a', b')$ in $[0, 1]^2$ we write $(a', b') \prec (a, b)$ if $a' \leq a$ and $b' \leq b$.

In this section we provide a full characterization of the set $\mathcal{F}$ of all admissible pairs. We begin with some easy observations.

- $\mathcal{F}$ is symmetric in the sense that if $(a, b) \in \mathcal{F}$, then also $(b, a) \in \mathcal{F}$.
- $\mathcal{F}$ is also monotone decreasing, that is, if $(a, b) \in \mathcal{F}$ and $(0, 0) \prec (a', b') \prec (a, b)$ then $(a', b') \in \mathcal{F}$.

Figure 3 includes the half of the set $\mathcal{F}$, where $a \geq b$, the other half is obtained by reflection about the diagonal line $a = b$. In our analysis, we will determine the part of the boundary of $\mathcal{F}$ shown in the figure. That is, we will always assume that $a \geq b$.

Theorem 1.1 shows that $(\frac{1}{8}, \frac{1}{8}) \in \mathcal{F}$ and the example from Figure 2 implies that if both a and b are greater than $\frac{1}{8}$, then $(a, b) \notin \mathcal{F}$.

To see that no pair (a, b) beyond $(\frac{1}{3}, 0)$ is in $\mathcal{F}$ it is enough to consider three independent chains each of weight $\leq \frac{1}{3}$. In this example $\pi(Q(p)) > \frac{1}{3}$ implies $\pi(Q^{\text{op}}(p)) \leq 0$. Therefore:

OBSERVATION 2.1. *Pairs (a, b) with $a > \frac{1}{3}$ and $b > 0$ are not admissible, i.e., they are not in $\mathcal{F}$.*

Though the next proposition does not really contribute to the boundary of $\mathcal{F}$ it provides a good first approximation to the set.

PROPOSITION 2.2. *Every pair (a, b) with $3a + 5b \leq 1$ is in $\mathcal{F}$.*

Proof. First note that we only have to prove that every pair (a, b), with $3a+5b = 1$, is in $\mathcal{F}$. The proposition then follows for all pairs $(a', b') \prec (a, b)$.

So given a set P of points and a pair (a, b) with $3a+5b = 1$. Choose a vertical line, such that the set A of points left of the line has weight $2a$. Choose another vertical line, such that the set Z of points right of this line has weight $a+b$. Consider the horizontal median point p in the strip S between the vertical lines. From the assumption it follows that $\omega(S) \geq 4b$ (see Figure 4).

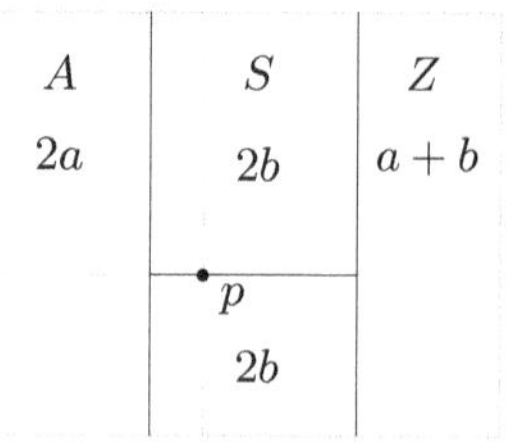

Figure 4: An illustration of the proof of Proposition 2.2.

From $\omega(A) = 2a$ it follows that one of the left quadrants of p has weight $\geq a$ (w.l.o.g. the upper one $Q_2(p)$). If $\pi(Q_4(p)) \geq b$ we are done. Hence, we may assume that $\pi(Q_4(p)) < b$. From the weight of Z it then follows that $\pi(Q_1(p)) \geq a$. The weight of points below p in S is $\geq 2b$, therefore, $\pi(Q_4(p)) < b$ implies that $\pi(Q_3(p)) \geq b$. We have thus found an appropriate pair of opposite quadrants. □

The next observation implies that $(\frac{1}{2}, 0)$ belongs to the boundary of $\mathcal{F}$.

OBSERVATION 2.3. *The pair $(\frac{1}{2}, 0)$ belongs to $\mathcal{F}$. Moreover, for every $a > \frac{1}{2}$ the pair $(a, 0)$ does not belong to $\mathcal{F}$.*

Proof. Let P be a set of n points in the plane and let $p \in P$ be the point of P with the largest x-coordinate. All points of $P \setminus \{p\}$ are contained in the second and third quadrant of p. Hence, one of these two quadrants has weight $\geq \frac{1}{2}$. This shows that $(\frac{1}{2}, 0)$ belongs to $\mathcal{F}$.

To see that $(a, 0)$ does not belong to $\mathcal{F}$ for any $a > \frac{1}{2}$, consider a set P of n points evenly distributed on a circle, or equivalently the vertices of regular n-gon. It is left to the reader to verify that no point in P has a quadrant of weight $> \frac{1}{2}$. □

We now get to the concavity at $(\frac{1}{5}, \frac{1}{10})$ on the boundary of $\mathcal{F}$ and the two segments bounding $\mathcal{F}$ that meet in this point.

THEOREM 2.4. *Every pair (a, b) with $4a + 2b = 1$ and $\frac{3}{16} \leq a \leq \frac{1}{5}$ is on the boundary of $\mathcal{F}$.*

Proof. In the proof we will need that $2a \geq 3b$, this is where the restriction $\frac{3}{16} \leq a$ comes from.

Given a set P of points and a pair (a, b). Choose two vertical lines, such that the set A of points left of both lines has weight $2a-b$, the weight of the set S in the strip between the lines has weight $4b$ and the set Z of points on the right of the two lines has the remaining weight $2a - b$. Consider the horizontal median point p of the middle set S (see Figure 5).

One of the quadrants of p has weight at least $\frac{1}{4}$. Without loss of generality we assume that this is true for $Q_1(p)$, i.e., $\pi(Q_1(p)) \geq \frac{1}{4} \geq a$. If $\pi(Q_3(p)) \geq b$ we are done. Hence, we may assume that $\pi(Q_3(p)) < b$. From the weight of points below p it then follows that $\pi(Q_4) \geq b$. Since the weight of A is $2a - b \geq 2b$ it follows that $\pi(Q_2(p)) \geq b$. If one of the quadrants $Q_2(p)$ and $Q_4(p)$ has weight at least a we are done. But if $\pi(Q_2(p)) < a$ and $\pi(Q_4(p)) < a$ the points in the union of the second, third and fourth quadrant of p

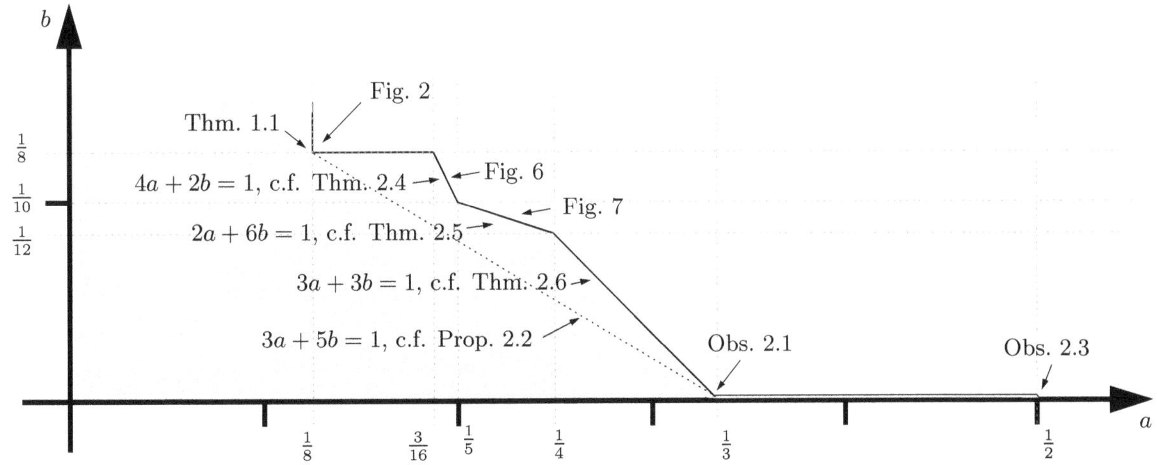

Figure 3: The shape of the set $\mathcal{F}$ of admissible pairs. References show where to find the proofs and constructions.

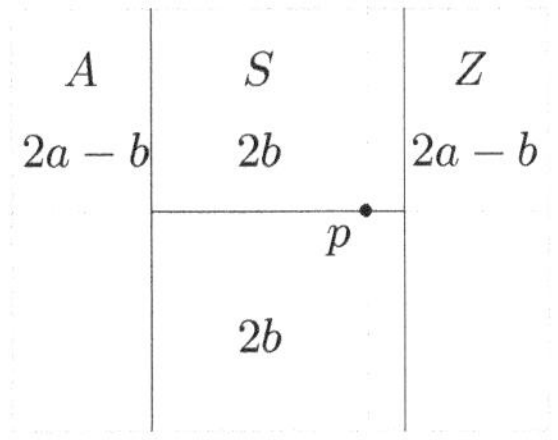

Figure 5: An illustration of the proof of Theorem 2.4.

would have total weight less than $2a+b$ which contradicts the choice of p.

The proof that there are no admissible pairs with $\frac{3}{16} \leq a \leq \frac{1}{5}$ beyond the segment $3a+3b=1$ consists in analysing the example given in Figure 6. $\square$

THEOREM 2.5. *Every pair (a,b) with $2a+6b=1$ and $\frac{1}{5} \leq a \leq \frac{1}{4}$ is on the boundary of $\mathcal{F}$.*

The proof of this theorem is given in the full paper.

THEOREM 2.6. *Every pair (a,b) with $3a+3b=1$ and $\frac{1}{4} \leq a \leq \frac{1}{3}$ is on the boundary of $\mathcal{F}$.*

Proof. Given a set P of points and a pair (a,b). Choose a vertical line, such that the set A of points left of the line has weight $a+b$. Choose another vertical line, such that the set Z of points right of this line has weight $a+b$. The weight of the set S in the strip between the lines also has weight $a+b$. This set S is divided vertically into a top part T, a middle part M and a bottom part B, such that each of T and B has weight $2b$ (see Figure 8). The vertical lines are chosen, such that the weight of M is $(a+b)-4b = a-3b \geq 0$, this is where the restriction $a \geq \frac{1}{4}$ comes from.

Suppose one of the quadrants of p or q has weight at least a. In this case we can simply disregard the middle part M and follow the very same argumentation as in Theorem 2.5 to find an appropriate pair of opposite quadrants.

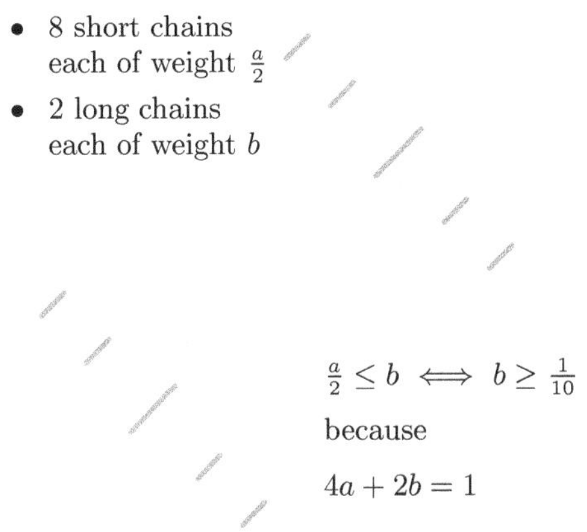

Figure 6: An example showing that the pairs (a,b) from Theorem 2.4 are on the boundary of $\mathcal{F}$.

To see that at least one of the quadrants of p or q has weight at least a we sum up the weights of the first and second quadrant of p and the third and fourth quadrant of q: $\pi(Q_1(p)) + \pi(Q_2(p)) + \pi(Q_3(q)) + \pi(Q_4(q)) = 4a$.

The proof that there are no admissible pairs with $\frac{1}{4} \leq a \leq \frac{1}{3}$ beyond the segment $3a+3b=1$ consists in analysing the example given in Figure 9. $\square$

3. HIGHER DIMENSIONS

A point p in $\mathbb{R}^d$ defines 2^d orthants centered at p. Again there is an obvious notion of an opposite orthant O^{op} of a given orthant O. The weight $\pi(O)$ of an orthant O with respect to a point set P is the fraction of points of P contained in O. For a more formal definition of the weight we refer to the introduction.

Define the *opposite-orthant depth* α_d for point sets in $\mathbb{R}^d$ as the maximum a, such that every point set $P \subset \mathbb{R}^d$ contains a point p that determines a pair (O, O^{op}) of opposite orthants with $\pi(O) \geq a$ and $\pi(O^{\text{op}}) \geq a$. Brönnimann et al. [BLP] have asked for α_3. They also claim that $\alpha_3 \geq n/2016$, this however is based on the false assumption that every set of 9

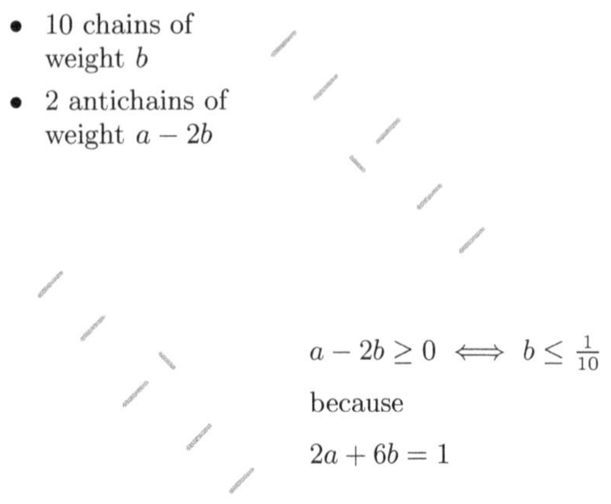

Figure 7: An example showing that the pairs (a, b) from Theorem 2.5 are on the boundary of $\mathcal{F}$.

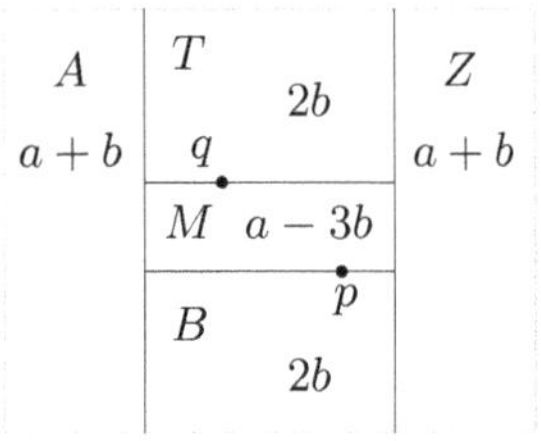

Figure 8: An illustration of the proof of Theorem 2.6.

points in $\mathbb{R}^3$ has a point with two opposite nonempty orthants. Indeed, the least n such that this holds is $n = 17$. With this correction their proof only yields $\alpha_3 \geq n/16320$. The case $d = 3$ of the theorem below gives $\alpha_3 \geq n/32$.

For a point $x \in \mathbb{R}^d$ and $i = 1, \ldots, d$ define the open halfspaces $H_i^+(x) = \{y : y_i > x_i\}$ and $H_i^-(x) = \{y : y_i < x_i\}$. A *sign pattern* is a vector $\sigma = (\sigma_1, \ldots, \sigma_d)$ with $\sigma_i \in \{+, -\}$. For every point x and sign pattern σ we define the orthant $O^\sigma(x) = \bigcap_i H_i^{\sigma_i}(x)$.

THEOREM 3.1 (LOWER BOUND). *The opposite-orthant depth α_d of point sets in $\mathbb{R}^d$ satisfies $\alpha_d \geq 2^{-(2^{d-1}+d)}$.*

Proof. A set of points is *t-good* if it contains no point determining a pair of opposite orthants such that both contain $t+1$ or more points from P.

We will prove that $|P| > 2^{2^{d-1}}(t\,2^d)$ implies that P is not t-good. Hence $\alpha_d(t2^{2^{d-1}+d} + 1) \geq t + 1$ which yields the bound stated in the theorem.

Let P be a t-good set. One of the orthants from each pair of opposite orthants determined by $p \in P$ is *small* in the sense that it contains at most t points from P.

The *pattern* assigned to p is a collection $\phi(p)$ of 2^{d-1} sign vectors, such that

- $O^\sigma(p)$ is small for each $\sigma \in \phi(p)$ and for each pair $(O^\sigma, O^{\bar{\sigma}})$ of opposite orthants determined by p either σ or $\bar{\sigma}$ is in $\phi(p)$.

For a given pattern ϕ we collect all points $p \in P$ with $\phi(p) = \phi$ in a set P_ϕ. Figure 10 shows an example.

Figure 9: An example used to prove that there are no admissible pairs with $\frac{3}{16} \leq a \leq \frac{1}{5}$ beyond the segment $3a + 3b = 1$. The points are distributed to 12 chains/antichains of weight b, 4 chains/antichains of weight $\frac{1}{2}(a - 3b)$ and a circle with equidistributed points of weight $a - 3b$.

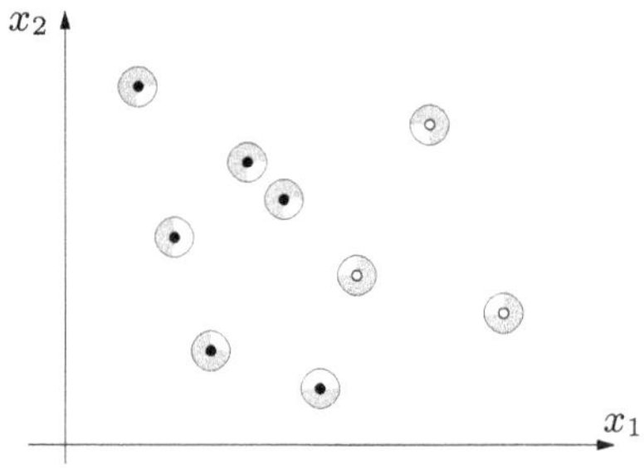

Figure 10: A 2-good set of 9 points in the plane. Small quadrants of points are indicated by gray angles. The white points may get the pattern $\phi = \{(+,+), (+,-)\}$ assigned.

We have partitioned the points of P according to their pattern. The upper bound on the size of any t-good set P follows from counting the possible patterns and bounding the number of points in each class P_ϕ.

There are 2^d sign vectors paired up in 2^{d-1} pairs $\sigma, \bar{\sigma}$ belonging to pairs of opposite orthants. A pattern is a selection of one sign vector from each such pair, therefore:

- There are at most $2^{2^{d-1}}$ different patterns.

For any p and σ let $v_\sigma(p) = |O^\sigma(p) \cap P|$. Define the *score* of p as $s(p) = \sum_{\sigma \in \phi(p)} v_\sigma(p)$. From the definition of $\phi(p)$ it follows that $v_\sigma(p) \leq t$ for all $\sigma \in \phi(p)$, hence, $s(p) \leq t\,2^{d-1}$. Note that the score of p is the number of points in the small orthants $O^\sigma(p)$ with $\sigma \in \phi(p)$.

Consider two points p, q and note that $q \in O^\sigma(p)$ if and only if $p \in O^{\bar{\sigma}}(q)$. Suppose p and q both belong to P_ϕ, since one of σ and $\bar{\sigma}$ is in ϕ we note that either p is counted in the score of q or q is counted in the score of p. From this we obtain:

$$\begin{aligned}\frac{|P_\phi|(|P_\phi| - 1)}{2} &= \binom{|P_\phi|}{2} \leq \sum_{p \in P_\phi} s(p) \\ &\leq \sum_{p \in P_\phi} t\,2^{d-1} = |P_\phi|\,t\,2^{d-1}.\end{aligned}$$

To reduce the upper bound on $\sum s(p)$ by one observe that for each $\sigma \in \phi$ there are points in P_ϕ with $v_\sigma(p) < t$. This yields the following bound on $|P_\phi|$:

- For each class P_ϕ we have $|P_\phi| \leq 2\,t\,2^{d-1}$.

Combining the bounds for the number of patterns and the size of the classes we find that a t-good set P has at most $2^{2^{d-1}}(t\,2^d)$ points. □

The upper bound on the opposite-orthant depth α_d shown with the following theorem is only a factor of two apart from the lower bound of Theorem 3.1. It is evident that the lower bound is not tight. In dimension 2 the upper and lower bounds yield $\frac{1}{16} \leq \alpha_2 \leq \frac{1}{8}$. From Theorem 1.1 and the example of Figure 2 we know that $\alpha_2 = \frac{1}{8}$. Indeed we suspect that in all dimensions the upper bound gives the true value of α_d.

THEOREM 3.2 (UPPER BOUND). *The opposite-orthant depth α_d of point sets in $\mathbb{R}^d$ satisfies $\alpha_d \leq 2^{-(2^{d-1}+d-1)}$.*

Proof. We have to construct large point sets with small opposite-orthant depth. The construction is in two steps. In the first step we build a set P_0 of $2^{2^{d-1}}$ points with opposite-orthant depth zero. In the second step we replace each point of P_0 with a carefully chosen set of $t\,2^{d-1}$ points, such that the depth remains bounded by t. Hence $t+1 \geq \alpha_d(2^{2^{d-1}}\,t\,2^{d-1})$ which yields the bound stated in the theorem.

Let σ be a sign vector and $\bar{\sigma}$ be the sign vector of the orthant opposite to O^σ. Based on σ we define a binary relation on P, let $p \sim_\sigma q$ if $p \in O^\sigma(q)$ or $p \in O^{\bar{\sigma}}(q)$, i.e., $q \in O^\sigma(p)$.

A set M of points in $\mathbb{R}^d$ is *monotone* if there is a sign vector σ, such that $p \sim_\sigma q$ for all $p, q \in M$. Equivalently M is monotone if there is an ordering of the points so that each coordinate is increasing or decreasing in this order. Repeated application of the Lemma of Erdős-Szekeres implies that any n points in $\mathbb{R}^d$ contain a monotone subset of size at least $n^{\frac{1}{2^{d-1}}}$. It is a widely known fact that this bound is best possible. A detailed construction of tight examples can be found e.g. in [Lit]. Due to this result there is a set P_0 of $2^{2^{d-1}}$ points that does not contain a monotone subset of size three. Hence, for every $p \in P_0$ and every pair of opposite orthants (O, O^{op}) determined by p at least one of the orthants contains no point of P_0.

An orthant $O^\sigma(p)$ defined by $p \in P_0$ is *small* if $O^\sigma(p) \cap P_0 = \emptyset$. As in the proof of the previous theorem we collect sign vectors of small orthants of $p \in P_0$ in a pattern $\phi(p)$. Recall that $\phi(p)$ contains the sign vector of one of each pair of opposite orthants. We construct the set P by replacing each point $p \in P_0$ by a set $Q(p)$ of $t\,2^{d-1}$ points, such that $q \in Q(p)$ and $\sigma \in \phi(p)$ implies $|O^\sigma(q) \cap P| = |O^\sigma(q) \cap Q(p)| \leq t$, i.e., the orthant $O^\sigma(q)$ is t-small for all $\sigma \in \phi(p)$.

For each $p \in P_0$ fix a 'small' box $B(p)$ containing p, such that every choice of one point from each of these boxes yields a set of opposite orthant depth zero. Formally, for $p, q \in P_0$ with $p \sim_\sigma q$ we require that $p' \sim_\sigma q'$ for all $p' \in B(p)$ and $q' \in B(q)$. For the construction of $Q(p)$ in the box $B(p)$ it is convenient to think of $B(p)$ as an open set. To begin with let $\sigma_0, \sigma_1, \sigma_2, \ldots$ be an ordering of the 2^{d-1} sign vectors in $\phi(p)$. Starting with $S_0 = \emptyset$ we inductively define subboxes S_i for $i = 1, \ldots, 2^{d-1}-1$ of $B_0 = B(p)$ as follows: If S_{i-1} and B_{i-1} are defined choose a point s_i in B_{i-1} and let $S_i = O^{\sigma_i}(s_i) \cap B_{i-1}$ and $B_i = O^{\bar{\sigma}_i}(s_i) \cap B_{i-1}$. Finally let $S_{2^{d-1}} = B_{2^{d-1}-1}$. An example is given in Figure 11.

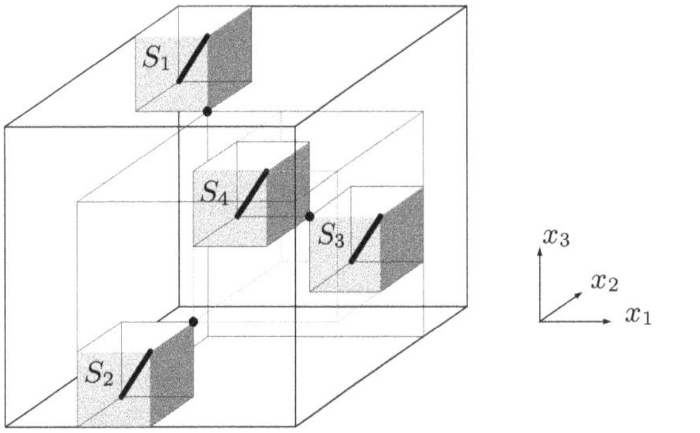

Figure 11: A point set $Q(p)$. The points of $Q(p)$ are aligned along diagonals of the subboxes S_i as indicated by the black bars. The pattern $\phi(p)$ of the point replaced by $Q(p)$ is $\sigma_0 = (-,+,-)$, $\sigma_1 = (-,+,+)$, $\sigma_2 = (-,-,-)$ and $\sigma_3 = (+,+,-)$.

From the construction rules it follows that for $i < j$ and any points $p_i \in S_i$ and $p_j \in S_j$ we have $p_j \in O^{\bar{\sigma}_i}(p_i)$ and consequently $p_i \in O^{\sigma_i}(p_j)$. This shows that inserting t points into each S_i, such that any two of these points are in relation σ_0 yields a set $Q(p)$ with the desired properties.

- $|Q(p)| = t\,2^{d-1}$
- $|O^\sigma(q) \cap P| = |O^\sigma(q) \cap Q(p)| \leq t$ for all $q \in Q(p)$ and $\sigma \in \phi(p)$.

This completes the construction of a t-good set P and the proof of the upper bound on α_d. □

4. FURTHER GENERALIZATIONS

The set $\mathcal{F}$ of all admissible pairs was defined as the set of all pairs (a, b), such that every set P in the plane contains a point $p \in P$ that determines two opposite quadrants with weights at least a and b. What if we do not require the point p to belong to the set P, and only seek for a point z in the plane with the same property of two opposite quadrants determined by it. It is not hard to see that (a, b) is admissible in this model whenever, $a + b \leq 1/2$. In addition we have the admissible pairs $(a, 0)$ for all $a \leq 1$. A set of points uniformly distributed on a circle shows that this is the complete description of the set of admissible pairs.

One way to generalize the setting is by considering two opposite quadrants determined by a vertical and a horizontal line as a *diagonal* in the 2-by-2 array of cells determined by these two lines. Then it is natural to consider $n-1$ vertical lines and $n-1$ horizontal lines and to find a *generalized diagonal* of cells in the n-by-n arrangement of cells, determined by these lines, such that each of the cells contains 'many' points of P. By a generalized diagonal we mean a set of n cells, such that no two are in the same row or in the same column (see Figure 12).

Since we do not require the vertical and horizontal lines to intersect in points of the set in question, it is equivalent to consider a continuous probability measure in the plane and to seek for $n-1$ vertical lines and $n-1$ horizontal lines and a generalized diagonal in the arrangement of the n-by-n cells, determined by these lines, such that each of the cells has

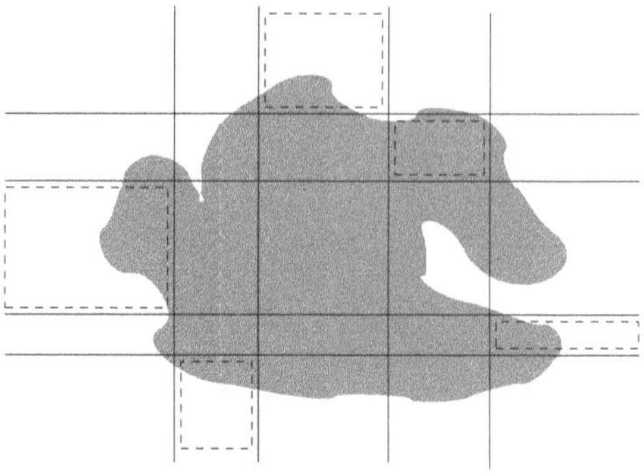

Figure 12: A continuous measure splitted to cells by 4 vertical and 4 horizontal lines. A generalized diagonal is illustrated in the dotted squares.

'large' measure (see Figure 12). This naturally generalizes to higher dimensions as well. The following theorem gives a partial answer to this problem in any dimension d:

THEOREM 4.1. *Let μ be a continuous probability measure in $[0,1]^d$. Let n be a positive integer and let $\alpha_1,\ldots,\alpha_n$ be a sequence of positive real numbers such that $\sum_{i=1}^n \alpha_i = \frac{1}{n^{d-1}}$. Then there exist numbers $x_{i,j}$, where $1 \le i \le d$ and $0 \le j \le n$, and d permutations $\pi_1,\ldots,\pi_d$ on $\{1,\ldots,n\}$ with the following properties:*

1. *For every $1 \le i \le d$ $x_{i,0} = 0 < x_{i,1} < \ldots < x_{i,n-1} < x_{i,n} = 1$.*

2. *For every $1 \le j \le n$ we have $\mu([x_{1,\pi_1(j)-1}, x_{1,\pi_1(j)}] \times \ldots \times [x_{d,\pi_d(j)-1}, x_{d,\pi_d(j)}]) \ge \alpha_j$.*

Remark. Intuitively speaking, the numbers $x_{i,j}$ in Theorem 4.1 define the d dimensional array of n^d cells generated by the hyper-planes $H_{i,j} = \{(x_1,\ldots,x_d) \in \mathbb{R}^d \mid x_i = x_{i,j}\}$, for all $1 \le i \le n$ and $1 \le j \le d$. The theorem then says that there exists such an array (while the measure μ is given) that contains a generalized diagonal of n boxes with measures of at least $\alpha_1,\ldots,\alpha_n$, respectively.

Proof. The proof is a rather straightforward induction on d. Details omitted. □

Recall that when $d = 2$ and $n = 2$, the example where the measure μ is evenly distributed on a circle C shows that the result in Theorem 4.1 is best possible apart from the case where $\alpha_i = 0$ for some i. In the full paper we show the result is not best possible in dimension $d > 2$. However, when the values α_i in Theorem 4.1 are all equal, then the result is indeed best possible in any dimension. This is a consequence of the following simple proposition.

PROPOSITION 4.2. *Let λ be the standard Lebesgue measure on $[0,1]^d$ and let n be a positive integer. Then one cannot find numbers $x_{i,j}$, where $1 \le i \le d$ and $0 \le j \le n$, such that the arrangement of n^d bounded cells determined by the hyperplanes $H_{i,j} = \{z : z_i = x_{i,j}\}$ has a generalized diagonal, such that each cell of the generalized diagonal has measure strictly larger than $1/n^d$.*

Proof. Assume to the contrary that there are numbers $x_{i,j}$ and permutations π_i, such that for each j with $0 \le j \le n$:

$$\lambda([x_{1,\pi_1(j)-1}, x_{1,\pi_1(j)}] \times \ldots \times [x_{d,\pi_d(j)-1}, x_{d,\pi_d(j)}]) > \frac{1}{n^d}.$$

We will use the means inequality, by which, for every d positive numbers $a_1,\ldots,a_d$ we have $d^{-1}(a_1 + \cdots + a_d) \ge (a_1 a_2 \cdots a_d)^{\frac{1}{d}}$.

For every $1 \le i \le d$ and $1 \le j \le n$ put $a_{i,j} = x_{i,\pi_i(j)} - x_{i,\pi_i(j)-1}$. For every $1 \le i \le d$ we may assume that $x_{i,0} = 0$ and $x_{i,n} = 1$, hence, $\sum_{j=1}^n a_{i,j} = 1$. On the other hand, our assumption on the measure and the cells of the generalized diagonal imply $\prod_{i=1}^d a_{i,j} > \frac{1}{n^d}$ for every $1 \le j \le n$. Therefore, by the means inequality, for every $1 \le j \le n$ we have:

$$\sum_{i=1}^{d} a_{i,j} \ge d(\prod_{i=1}^{d} a_{i,j})^{\frac{1}{d}} > \frac{d}{n} \qquad \Longrightarrow$$

$$d = \sum_{i=1}^{d}\sum_{j=1}^{n} a_{i,j} = \sum_{j=1}^{n}\sum_{i=1}^{d} a_{i,j} > \sum_{j=1}^{n} \frac{d}{n} = d.$$

This contradiction completes the proof. □

5. CONCLUSION

We gave a complete description of the set $\mathcal{F}$ of all admissible pairs (a,b) in the plane. This was done by identifying three line segments and the points $(\frac{1}{8},\frac{1}{8})$ and $(0,\frac{1}{2})$ from the boundary of $\mathcal{F}$.

In higher dimensions we were interested in the maximal number α_d, such that (α_d,α_d) is admissible. We think that our upper bound on α_d is tight, the lower bound leaves room for improvements. It would be interesting to get more information about the set $\mathcal{F}_d$ of all admissible pairs (a,b) for $\mathbb{R}^d$.

In the relaxed setting, where the point determining a pair of opposite orthants need not belong to the point set we could determine the diagonal entry precisely, it is $(\frac{1}{2^d},\frac{1}{2^d})$. This follows from more general bounds on generalized diagonals. In this case we have some additional results concerning admissible pairs (a,b). There remain many questions to be asked and anwered.

6. REFERENCES

[BPZ1] I. Ben-Dan, R. Pinchasi and R. Ziv *On a problem of Felsner about quadrant depth.* submitted

[BPZ2] I. Ben-Dan, R. Pinchasi and R. Ziv *Points with large α-depth.* Journal of Combinatorial Theory A, 116 (2009) 747âĂŞ-755.

[BLP] H. Brönnimann, J. Lenchner, and J. Pach, *Opposite-quadrant depth in the plane.* Graphs and Combinatorics 23, (2007), 145–152.

[Ede] H. Edelsbrunner. Algorithms in Combinatorial Geometry. *Springer*, 1987.

[Lit] L. Heinrich-Litan. *Monotone Subsequences in $\mathbb{R}^d$.* Tech. Rep. B 00-19, FU Berlin, FB Math. u. Inf., 2000. `http://heinrich-litan.de/PUB/MonSeq.pdf`

[LPS] R. Liu, J. Parelius, and K. Singh. *Multivariate analysis by data depth: Descriptive statistics, graphics and inference.* Ann. Stat. 27 (1999) 783–858,

Approximating the Fréchet Distance for Realistic Curves in Near Linear Time*

Anne Driemel†
Dept. Inform. Comput. Sci.
Utrecht University
The Netherlands
anne@cs.uu.nl

Sariel Har-Peled‡
Dept. Computer Science
University of Illinois,
Urbana-Champaign
201 N. Goodwin Avenue
Urbana, IL, 61801, USA
sariel@uiuc.edu

Carola Wenk§
Dept. Computer Science
University of Texas
at San Antonio
One UTSA Circle
San Antonio, TX 78249, USA
carola@cs.utsa.edu

ABSTRACT

We present a simple and practical $(1+\varepsilon)$-approximation algorithm for the Fréchet distance between polygonal curves. To analyze this algorithm we introduce a new realistic family of curves, c-packed curves, that is closed under simplification. We believe the notion of c-packed curves to be of independent interest. We show that our algorithm has near linear running time for c-packed polygonal curves, and show similar results for other input models, such as low density.

Categories and Subject Descriptors

F.2.2 [**Analysis of Algorithms and problem complexity**]: Nonnumerical Algorithms and Problems—*Geometrical problems and computations*

General Terms

Algorithms, Theory

Keywords

Fréchet distance, Approximation algorithms, Realistic input models

1. INTRODUCTION

Comparing geometric shapes is a task that arises in a wide arena of applications. The Fréchet distance and its variants have been used, to this end, to compare curves in applications such as dynamic time-warping [22], speech recognition [24], signature and handwriting recognition [25, 26], matching of time series in databases [23], as well as geographic applications, such as map-matching of vehicle tracking data [10, 27], and moving objects analysis [11, 12].

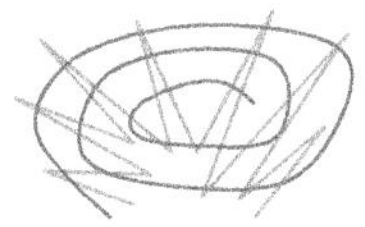

Unlike the Hausdorff distance, which is solely based on nearest neighbor distances between points on the curves, the Fréchet distance requires continuous and order-preserving assignments of points and hence is better suited for comparing curves with respect to their intrinsic structure. See the figure to the right for an example of two dissimilar curves that have a small Hausdorff distance.

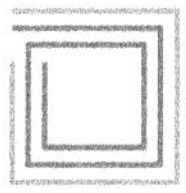

The Fréchet distance between two curves might be arbitrarily larger than their Hausdorff distance, as demonstrated by the figure on the left, and as this example shows, it seems to be a more natural measure of similarity between curves.

Previous results. For two polygonal curves of total complexity n in the plane, their Fréchet distance can be computed in $O(n^2 \log n)$ time [5], and their Hausdorff distance can be computed in $O(n \log n)$ time [2]. It has been an open problem to find a subquadratic algorithm for computing the Fréchet distance for two curves. For the problem of deciding whether the Fréchet distance between two curves is smaller or equal a given value a lower bound of $\Omega(n \log n)$ was given by [13]. Recently, Alt [2] conjectured that the decision problem may be 3SUM-hard. The only subquadratic algorithms known are for quite restricted classes of curves such as for closed convex curves and for κ-bounded curves [6]. For a curve to be κ-bounded means, roughly, that for any two points on the curve the portion of the curve in between them cannot be further away from either point than $\kappa/2$ times the distance between the two points. For closed convex curves the Fréchet distance equals the Hausdorff distance and for κ-bounded curves the Fréchet distance is at most $(1+\kappa)$ times the Hausdorff distance, and hence the $O(n \log n)$ algorithm for the Hausdorff distance applies.

Aronov *et al.* [8] provided a near linear time $(1+\varepsilon)$approximation algorithm for the *discrete* Fréchet distance, which only considers distances between vertices of the curves. This algorithm works for *backbone curves*, which are used for modeling protein backbones in molecular biology. Backbone

*The latest full version of this paper is available online [18].

†Work by AD has been supported by the Netherlands Organisation for Scientific Research (NWO) under RIMGA (Realistic Input Models for Geographic Applications).

‡Work by SH has been supported by a NSF AF award CCF-0915984.

§Work by CW has been supported by the National Science Foundation grant NSF CAREER CCF-0643597.

SCG'10, June 13–16, 2010, Snowbird, Utah, USA.

curves are required to have, roughly, unit edge length and a minimal distance between any pair of vertices. Aronov *et al.* [8] use curve simplification to speed up their algorithm. Agarwal *et al.* [1] studied fast simplification that preserves the Fréchet distance.

The input model. Realistic input models, such as *fatness* and *low density*, were introduced for the analysis of problems where the worst case complexity is dominated by degenerate or contrived configurations which are highly unlikely to occur in practice [17]. We introduce a new class of curves, called c-packed curves, for which we can approximate the Fréchet distance quickly, given that the constant c is small. Intuitively, the constant c measures how "*unrealistic*" the input is.

A curve π is ***c*-packed** if the total length of π inside any ball is bounded by c times the radius of the ball. A κ-bounded curve might have arbitrary length while maintaining a finite diameter, and as such may not be c-packed, see Section 4.2. But unlike κ-bounded curves, the Fréchet distance between two c-packed curves might be arbitrarily larger than their Hausdorff distance. Indeed, c-packed curves are considerably more general and a more natural family of curves. For example, a c-packed curve might self cross and revisit the same location several times, and the class of c-packed curves is closed under concatenation, none of which is true for κ-bounded curves. Intuitively, c-packed curves behave reasonably in any resolution.

See the figure on the right for a few examples of c-packed curves. The boundary of convex polygons, algebraic curves of bounded maximum degree, the boundary of (α, β)-covered shapes [19], and the boundary of γ-fat shapes [16] are all c-packed. Indeed, the boundaries of (α, β)-covered shapes and γ-fat shapes are assumed to be formed by a constant number of algebraic curves of bounded maximum degree. If one removes the requirement that a γ-fat curve be of bounded description complexity, then also fractal curves, like the Koch's snowflake, which can have infinite length within a bounded area, can be fat [9]. Naturally, these curves cannot be c-packed.

Interestingly, one can show that (α, β)-covered polygons are c-packed even if they have unbounded complexity, see [18] and also the result of Bose *et al.* [9]. It is easy to verify that c-packed curves are also low density [17], but a low density curve might not be c-packed, for any bounded c, see Section 4.3. However, the class of c-packed curves is closed under simplification, see Lemma 4.3, and this is not true for low density curves.

Our results. We present a new algorithm for computing a $(1+\varepsilon)$-approximation of the Fréchet distance for polygonal curves in $\mathbb{R}^d$. Underlying the algorithm are several new insights. First, we use the idea of curve simplification to reduce the complexity of the free space diagram, as the simplification of the input curves results in a contraction of the corresponding rows or columns in the free space diagram. We introduce the notion of relative free space complexity to capture the complexity of the free space diagram of two curves, which are simplified to the resolution corresponding to the free space parameter (within a factor of $(1+\varepsilon)$).

Curves type	Running time
Any	$O(\mathsf{N}(\varepsilon, \pi, \sigma) + \mathsf{N}(1, \pi, \sigma) \log n)$ Theorem 3.15
c-packed	$O(cn/\varepsilon + cn \log n)$ Theorem 4.5
κ-straight	Same as 2κ-packed Lemma 4.7
κ-bounded	$O\Big((\kappa/\varepsilon)^d n + \kappa^d n \log n\Big)$ Theorem 4.10
$O(1)$-low density	$O\left(\frac{n^{2(d-1)/d}}{\varepsilon^2} + n^{2(d-1)/d} \log n\right)$ Theorem 4.14
c-packed & closed	$O(c^2 n/\varepsilon^2 + c^2 n \log n)$ Theorem 5.1

Table 1: Summary of new results for computing a $(1+\varepsilon)$-approximation to the Fréchet distance between two curves π and σ with n vertices in $\mathbb{R}^d$. Here $\mathsf{N}(\varepsilon, \pi, \sigma)$ is the relative free space complexity of the two curves, see Definition 3.3.

Surprisingly, without simplification, almost any natural family of curves can have a free space diagram (for the value realizing the Fréchet distance) that has quadratic complexity (even in the plane). Secondly, we present an efficient construction algorithm for this reduced size free space diagram that enables us to solve the decision problem in linear time in the relative free space complexity of the curves. Thirdly, we prove that monotonicity events are sufficiently close to vertex-edge events or an approximate distance between two vertices of the curves. As such, the search for the Fréchet distance can be done efficiently without using parametric search or random sampling, by using approximate distance selection. Carefully combining these insights yields the new algorithm, which has running time near linear in the relative free space complexity of the input curves.

In the second part of the paper, we analyze the relative free space complexity for various families of curves. We prove that c-packed curves have linear relative free space complexity for fixed c and ε. We next prove a subquadratic bound on the relative complexity of the free space of low density curves. This relies on a new packing lemma showing that, if the simplification of a low density curve is long inside a relatively small area, then the original curve must contain many vertices in the vicinity of this region. We also prove that the relative free space complexity of κ-bounded curves is linear for a fixed κ.

Plugging these bounds into our approximation algorithm yields new fast approximation algorithms for the Fréchet distance for all these curves. We also show how to adapt our algorithm to handle closed curves. The new results are summarized in Table 1.

Organization. In Section 2 we provide some background on the Fréchet distance and the notion of the free space diagram. In Section 3, we describe the approximation algorithm that uses simplification. To this end, we show in Section 3.1 that it suffices to only compute the reachable parts of the free space diagram and in Section 3.2 we present a fuzzy decider procedure and show how it can be used to make exact decisions during a binary search for the Fréchet distance. In Section 3.3 we deal with the different subroutines used in the search for the Fréchet distance and in Section 3.4 we give the resulting general algorithm and analyze its correctness and running time, which is near linear in the relative free space complexity. In Section 4 we bound the relative free space complexity of various families of curves. In particular, in Section 4.1, we introduce the notion of c-packed curves, and study their behavior under simplification. In Section 4.2, we bound the relative free space complexity of κ-bounded curves, and in Section 4.3 we handle low density curves. In Section 5 we extend the algorithm to closed curves. We conclude with discussion and some open problems in Section 6.

2. PRELIMINARIES

2.1 Notations and Definitions

Let $\pi \subseteq \mathbb{R}^d$ be a curve; that is, a continuous mapping from $[0,1]$ to $\mathbb{R}^d$. In the following, we will identify π with its range $\pi([0,1]) \subseteq \mathbb{R}^d$ if it is clear from the context. The curve π is ***closed*** only if $\pi(0) = \pi(1)$. We use $\|\cdot\|$ to denote the Euclidean distance as well as the length of a curve. For a polygonal curve π, let $V(\pi)$ denote the set of vertices of π. For two points p and q on a curve π, let $\pi[\mathsf{p},\mathsf{q}]$ denote the portion of the curve between the two points.

We denote with $\mathbf{b}(\mathsf{p}, r)$ the ball of radius r centered at p, and $\mathbb{S}(\mathsf{p}, r)$ denotes the corresponding sphere. For a cube C and a constant s, we denote by sC the cube resulting from scaling C by a factor of s around its center.

Given a set of numbers $U \subseteq \mathbb{R}$, an ***atomic interval*** of U is a (possibly infinite) maximal interval on the real line that does not contain any point of U in its interior.

2.2 Curve simplification

We suggest a straight-forward greedy algorithm for curve simplification, which is sufficient for our purposes. Note that Agarwal *et al.* [1] suggested a more aggressive (but slightly slower and more complicated) simplification algorithm that can be used instead.

Algorithm 2.1 Given a polygonal curve $\pi = \mathsf{p}_1\mathsf{p}_2\mathsf{p}_3\ldots\mathsf{p}_k$ and a parameter $\mu > 0$, consider the following simplification algorithm: First mark the initial vertex p_1 and set it as the current vertex. Now scan the polygonal curve from the current vertex until it reaches the first vertex p_i that is in distance at least μ from the current vertex. Mark p_i and set it as the current vertex. Repeat this until reaching the final vertex of the curve, and also mark this final vertex. Consider the curve that connects only the marked vertices, in their order along π. We refer to the resulting curve $\pi' = \mathrm{simpl}(\pi, \mu)$ as being the ***μ-simplification*** of π. Note, that this simplification can be computed in linear time.

Remark 2.2 The simplified curve has the useful property that all its segments are of length at least μ, except for the last edge that might be shorter. For the sake of simplicity of exposition, we assume that the last segment in the simplified curve also has length at least μ. Our arguments can be easily modified to handle this more general case.

Lemma 2.3 *For any curve π in $\mathbb{R}^d$, and $\mu \geq 0$, we have that $\mathsf{d}_{\mathcal{F}}\Big(\pi, \mathrm{simpl}(\pi,\mu)\Big) \leq \mu$.*

PROOF. Consider a segment u of $\mathrm{simpl}(\pi, \mu)$ and the portion $\widehat{\pi}$ of π that corresponds to it. Clearly, all the vertices of $\widehat{\pi}$ are contained inside a ball of radius μ centered at the first endpoint of u visited by π, except the last vertex of $\widehat{\pi}$. As such, one can parameterize u and $\widehat{\pi}$, such that initially the point stays on the vertex of u while visiting all vertices of $\widehat{\pi}$ (except the last one), and then simultaneously move in sync on u and the last segment of $\widehat{\pi}$, in such a way that the distance is always at most μ. □

2.3 Fréchet Distance and the Free Space Diagram

A ***reparameterization*** is a one-to-one and continuous function $f : [0,1] \to [0,1]$. It is ***orientation-preserving*** if it maps $f(0) = 0$ and $f(1) = 1$. Given two reparameterizations f and g for two curves π and σ, respectively, define their ***width*** as

$$\mathrm{width}_{f,g}(\pi,\sigma) = \max_{s\in[0,1]} \|\pi(f(s)) - \sigma(g(s))\|.$$

This can be interpreted as the maximum length of a leash one needs to walk a dog, where the dog walks monotonically along π according to f, while the handler walks monotonically along σ according to g. In this analogy, the Fréchet distance is the shortest possible leash admitting such a walk.

Formally, given two curves π and σ in $\mathbb{R}^d$, the ***Fréchet distance*** between them is

$$\mathsf{d}_{\mathcal{F}}(\pi,\sigma) = \min_{\substack{f:[0,1]\to[0,1]\\ g:[0,1]\to[0,1]}} \mathrm{width}_{f,g}(\pi,\sigma),$$

where f and g are orientation-preserving reparameterizations of the curves π and σ, respectively. The Fréchet distance complies with the triangle inequality; that is, for any three curves π, σ and τ we have that $\mathsf{d}_{\mathcal{F}}(\pi,\tau) \leq \mathsf{d}_{\mathcal{F}}(\pi,\sigma) + \mathsf{d}_{\mathcal{F}}(\sigma,\tau)$.

Let π, σ be curves and $\delta > 0$ a parameter, the ***free space*** of π and σ of radius δ is defined as

$$\mathcal{D}_{\leq\delta}(\pi,\sigma) = \Big\{(s,t) \in [0,1]^2 \;\Big|\; \|\pi(s) - \sigma(t)\| \leq \delta\Big\}.$$

We are interested only in polygonal curves, which we assume to have natural uniform parameterizations. Then the square $[0,1]^2$ can be broken into a (not necessarily uniform) grid called the ***free space diagram***, where a vertical line corresponds to a vertex of π and a horizontal line corresponds to a vertex of σ. Every two segments of π and σ define a ***free space cell*** in this grid. In particular, let $C_{i,j} = C_{i,j}(\pi,\sigma)$ denote the free space cell that corresponds to the ith edge of π and the jth edge of σ. The cell $C_{i,j}$ is located in the ith column and jth row of this grid.

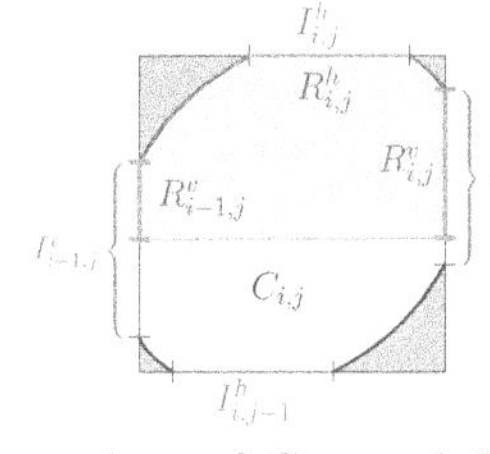

It is known that the free space, for a fixed δ, inside such a cell $C_{i,j}$ (i.e., $\mathcal{D}_{\leq\delta}(\pi,\sigma) \cap C_{i,j}$) is the clipping of an affine transformation of a disk to the cell [5], see the figure to the right; as such, it is convex and of constant complexity. Let $I^h_{i,j}$ denote the horizontal ***free space interval*** at the top boundary of $C_{i,j}$, and $I^v_{i,j}$ denote the vertical free space interval at the right boundary.

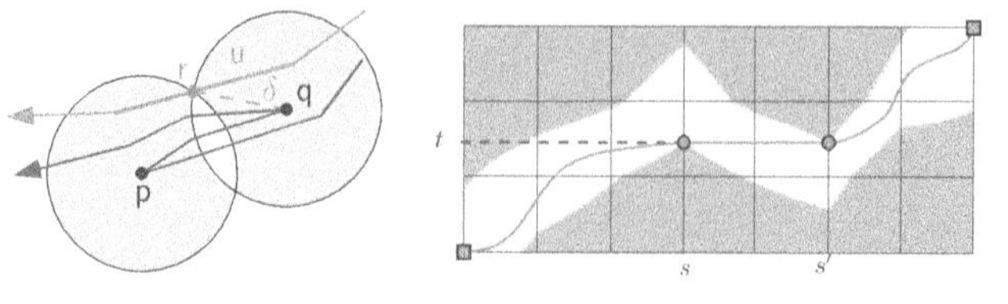

Figure 1: Two curves π and σ and their free space diagram $\mathcal{D}_{\leq\delta}(\pi, \sigma)$, where $\mathsf{p} = \pi(s), \mathsf{q} = \pi(s')$ and $\mathsf{r} = \sigma(t)$. Here, δ is the minimal free space parameter, such that a monotone path exists, i.e., in this example $\mathsf{d}_{\mathcal{F}}(\pi, \sigma)$ coincides with a monotonicity event.

The Fréchet distance between π and σ is at most δ if and only if there is an (x, y)-monotone path in the free space diagram between $(0, 0)$ and $(1, 1)$ that is fully contained in $\mathcal{D}_{\leq\delta}(\pi, \sigma)$. Let the ***reachability intervals*** $R^h_{i,j} \subseteq I^h_{i,j}$ and $R^v_{i,j} \subseteq I^v_{i,j}$ consist of only those points (x, y) on the boundary that are reachable by an (x, y)-monotone path from $(0, 0)$ to (x, y).

Such a path to $(1, 1)$ can be computed, if it exists, in $O(n^2)$ time by dynamic programming, where n is the total complexity of the two polygonal curves π and σ, see [5].

2.3.1 Free Space Events

To compute the Fréchet distance consider increasing δ from 0 to ∞. As δ increases structural changes to the free space happen. We are interested in the radii (i.e., the value of δ) of these events.

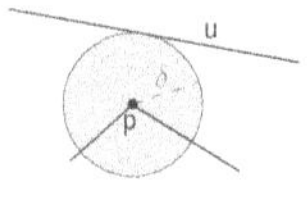

Consider a segment $\mathsf{u} \in \pi$ and a vertex $\mathsf{p} \in \sigma$, a ***vertex-edge event*** corresponds to the minimum value δ such that u is tangent to $\mathbf{b}(\mathsf{p}, \delta)$. In the free space diagram, this corresponds to the event that a free space interval consists of one point only. The line supporting this boundary edge corresponds to the vertex, and the other dimension corresponds to the edge. Naturally, the event could happen at a vertex of u.

The second type of event, a ***monotonicity event***, corresponds to a value δ for which a monotone subpath inside $\mathcal{D}$ becomes feasible, see Figure 1. Geometrically, this corresponds to two vertices p and q on one curve and a directed segment u on the other curve such that: (1) u passes through the intersection of $\mathbb{S}(\mathsf{p}, \delta) \cap \mathbb{S}(\mathsf{q}, \delta)$, and (2) u intersects $\mathbf{b}(\mathsf{q}, \delta)$ first and $\mathbf{b}(\mathsf{p}, \delta)$ second, where p comes before q in the order along the curve π.

Remark 2.4 It might happen that two long edges intersect in their middle (or in higher dimension pass close to each other), and thus contribute an isolated connected component to $\mathcal{D}_{\leq\delta}(\pi', \sigma')$. Such a connected component is a convex set lying completely in the interior of the grid cell of the two segments. Since it is not reachable by a monotone path in the diagram from $(0, 0)$, we can just ignore such ***edge-edge*** events. Such a connected component would grow as δ increases until it hits the boundary of the grid cell. At this point, a vertex-edge event would happen. Other values of δ that would be relevant to our algorithm are the distances between any pair of points of $V(\pi) \cup V(\sigma)$. Technically, apart from the two single events that the endpoints of the curves are being matched to each other, these ***vertex-vertex*** events are vertex-edge events when they are relevant, but they will be handled naturally by our algorithm.

3. THE APPROXIMATION ALGORITHM

3.1 Computing the Reachable Free Space

For two curves π and σ, their ***reachable free space***, denoted by $\mathcal{R} = \mathcal{R}_{\leq\delta}(\pi, \sigma)$, is the set of all the points of $\mathcal{D}_{\leq\delta}(\pi, \sigma)$ that are reachable from $(0, 0)$ by a path that is (x, y)-***monotone***.

The set $\mathcal{R}$ has finite description complexity inside each grid cell, and we need to describe it only for the grid cells that have nonempty intersection with $\mathcal{R}$. Clearly, generating only those grid cells is sufficient to decide if there is a monotone path between $(0, 0)$ and $(1, 1)$, which is equivalent to deciding if the Fréchet distance between π and σ is $\leq \delta$.

In particular, to fully describe $\mathcal{R}$, we will specify the reachability intervals $R^h_{i,j} \subseteq I^h_{i,j}$ and $R^v_{i,j} \subseteq I^v_{i,j}$ for each cell $C_{i,j}$, which describe the intersection of $\mathcal{R}$ with the top and right boundary of $C_{i,j}$. These intervals contain all the needed information, since $\mathcal{R} \cap C_{i,j}$ is convex.

The ***complexity*** of the reachable free space, for distance δ, denoted by $\mathcal{N}_{\leq\delta}(\pi, \sigma)$, is the total number of grid cells with non-empty intersection with $\mathcal{R}$. One can compute this set of cells and extract an existing monotone path in $O(\mathcal{N}_{\leq\delta}(\pi, \sigma))$ time, by performing a BFS of the grid cells that visits only the reachable cells.

This yields the following relatively easy result.

Lemma 3.1 *Given two polygonal curves π and σ in $\mathbb{R}^d$, of total complexity n, and a parameter $\delta \geq 0$, one can compute a representation of $\mathcal{R}_{\leq\delta}(\pi, \sigma)$ in $O(\mathcal{N}_{\leq\delta}(\pi, \sigma))$ time. Furthermore, one can decide if $\mathsf{d}_{\mathcal{F}}(\pi, \sigma) \leq \delta$, and if this is the case also extract the corresponding monotone path in $O(\mathcal{N}_{\leq\delta}(\pi, \sigma))$ time.*

PROOF. Omitted. Available from [18]. □

Observation 3.2 One can compute all relevant vertex-edge events with radius $\leq \delta$ in $O(\mathcal{N}_{\leq\delta}(\pi, \sigma))$ time as follows. We compute the graph representation of $\mathcal{R}_{\leq\delta}(\pi, \sigma)$ using Lemma 3.1. Next, for each reachable cell consider the vertex-edge events at its top and right boundaries and compute their event radii. Recall that a cell boundary corresponds to an edge from the one curve and a vertex from the other curve. Clearly, a cell boundary can be used by the reparameterization of width $\leq \delta$, if and only if the corresponding event radius is smaller or equal δ.

3.2 The Approximate Decision Procedure

In the following, we are interested in the maximum complexity of the reachable free space when considering any radius δ and simplifying the curves with radius $\varepsilon\delta$. The reasons will become apparent only shortly after, in Lemma 3.4 and Lemma 3.5, where we show that the simplification radius chosen this way enables us to either (i) compute a $(1 + \varepsilon)$-approximation of the Fréchet distance, or (ii) solve the decision problem exactly using the simplified curves (see Section 3.3.5).

Definition 3.3 For two curves π and σ, let

$$\mathsf{N}(\varepsilon, \pi, \sigma) = \max_{\delta \geq 0} \mathcal{N}_{\leq\delta}\Big(\mathrm{simpl}(\pi, \varepsilon\delta), \mathrm{simpl}(\sigma, \varepsilon\delta)\Big)$$

be the maximum complexity of the reachable free space for the simplified curves. We refer to $\mathsf{N}(\varepsilon, \pi, \sigma)$ as the ***ε-relative free space complexity*** of π and σ.

We assume that for any $0 < \varepsilon < 1$ the following properties hold for $\mathsf{N}(\cdot, \cdot, \cdot)$.

(P1) For any constant $c' \geq 1$, it holds $\mathsf{N}(\varepsilon/c', \pi, \sigma) = O(\mathsf{N}(\varepsilon, \pi, \sigma))$.

(P2) $\mathsf{N}(\varepsilon, \pi, \sigma) \leq \mathsf{N}(\varepsilon/2, \pi, \sigma)/2$.

The above properties will hold for all the families of curves we consider. In Section 4.1 we show that $\mathsf{N}(\varepsilon, \pi, \sigma)$ is a linear function in the number of vertices of the two curves for a fixed $\varepsilon > 0$ if the curves are sufficiently "nice" (see for example Lemma 4.4).

Lemma 3.4 *Let π and σ be polygonal curves in $\mathbb{R}^d$ with total complexity n, and let $\varepsilon > 0$ and $\delta > 0$ be two parameters. Then, one can output, in $O(\mathsf{N}(\varepsilon, \pi, \sigma))$ time, one of the following:*
(A) "$\mathsf{d}_{\mathcal{F}}(\pi, \sigma) \leq (1+\varepsilon)\delta$", and reparameterizations of width $\leq (1+\varepsilon)\delta$, and this happens if $\mathsf{d}_{\mathcal{F}}(\pi, \sigma) \leq \delta$.
(B) "$\mathsf{d}_{\mathcal{F}}(\pi, \sigma) > \delta$" if $\mathsf{d}_{\mathcal{F}}(\pi, \sigma) > (1+\varepsilon)\delta$.
(C) If $\mathsf{d}_{\mathcal{F}}(\pi, \sigma) \in (\delta, (1+\varepsilon)\delta]$ then the algorithm outputs either of the above outcomes.
In either case, the statement returned is correct.[1]

PROOF. Set $\mu = (\varepsilon/4)\delta$. Compute in linear time the curves $\pi' = \mathrm{simpl}(\pi, \mu)$ and $\sigma' = \mathrm{simpl}(\sigma, \mu)$. Let $\delta' = \delta + 2\mu$. We can decide whether $\mathsf{d}_{\mathcal{F}}(\pi', \sigma') \leq \delta'$ using Lemma 3.1 in

$$O(\mathcal{N}_{\leq \delta'}(\pi', \sigma')) = O(\mathsf{N}(\mu/\delta', \pi, \sigma)) = O(\mathsf{N}(4/\varepsilon + 2, \pi, \sigma)) = O(\mathsf{N}(\varepsilon, \pi, \sigma))$$

time, by assumption (P1). If so, we output the reparameterizations as a proof that

$$\mathsf{d}_{\mathcal{F}}(\pi, \sigma) \leq \mathsf{d}_{\mathcal{F}}(\pi, \pi') + \mathsf{d}_{\mathcal{F}}(\pi', \sigma') + \mathsf{d}_{\mathcal{F}}(\sigma', \sigma) \leq \delta' + 2\mu = \delta + 4(\varepsilon/4)\delta = (1+\varepsilon)\delta.$$

If on the other hand $\mathsf{d}_{\mathcal{F}}(\pi', \sigma') > \delta'$ then this implies, by the triangle inequality, that

$$\mathsf{d}_{\mathcal{F}}(\pi, \sigma) \geq \mathsf{d}_{\mathcal{F}}(\pi', \sigma') - \mathsf{d}_{\mathcal{F}}(\pi, \pi') - \mathsf{d}_{\mathcal{F}}(\sigma', \sigma) > \delta' - 2\mu = \delta.$$

Now, the algorithm outputs "$\mathsf{d}_{\mathcal{F}}(\pi, \sigma) > \delta$" in this case. □

3.2.1 *Using the Approximate Decider in a Binary Search*

In order to use Lemma 3.4 to perform a binary search for the Fréchet distance, we can turn the "fuzzy" decision procedure into a precise one as follows.

Lemma 3.5 *Let π and σ be two polygonal curves in $\mathbb{R}^d$ with total complexity n, and let $1 \geq \varepsilon > 0$ and $\delta > 0$ be two parameters. Then, there is an algorithm $\mathrm{decider}(\pi, \sigma, \delta, \varepsilon)$ that, in $O(\mathsf{N}(\varepsilon, \pi, \sigma))$ time, returns one of the following outputs: (i) a $(1+\varepsilon)$-approximation to $\mathsf{d}_{\mathcal{F}}(\pi, \sigma)$, (ii) $\mathsf{d}_{\mathcal{F}}(\pi, \sigma) < \delta$, or (iii) $\mathsf{d}_{\mathcal{F}}(\pi, \sigma) > \delta$.*

PROOF. Let $\delta' = \delta/(1+\varepsilon')$, for $\varepsilon' = \mathsf{c}\varepsilon$, $\mathsf{c} = 1/3$. We run the algorithm of Lemma 3.4 with parameters δ and ε'. If the call returns "$\mathsf{d}_{\mathcal{F}}(\pi, \sigma) > \delta$", then we know in which direction to continue the search, and we return this result.

Otherwise, we call Lemma 3.4 with parameters δ' and ε'. If it returns that "$\mathsf{d}_{\mathcal{F}}(\pi, \sigma) \leq (1+\varepsilon')\delta'$" then we know in which direction to continue the search since this implies that $\mathsf{d}_{\mathcal{F}}(\pi, \sigma) \leq \delta$, and we return this result.

The only remaining possibility is that the two calls returned "$\mathsf{d}_{\mathcal{F}}(\pi, \sigma) \leq (1+\varepsilon')\delta$" and "$\mathsf{d}_{\mathcal{F}}(\pi, \sigma) > \delta'$". But then we have found the required approximation. As such, the resulting approximation factor of the reparameterizations returned by the call with δ is $\leq \frac{(1+\varepsilon')\delta}{\delta'} = (1+\mathsf{c}\varepsilon)^2 < (1+\varepsilon)$ as can be easily verified, since $0 < \varepsilon \leq 1$. □

[1]To see why this last statement is not redundant, consider a "lesser" decision procedure that inside an interval of uncertainty randomly returns one of the two possible answers. Such a decision procedure will sometimes return the wrong answer inside the uncertainty region.

3.3 Searching for the Fréchet Distance

3.3.1 *Searching in a Fixed Interval*

It is now straightforward to perform a binary search on an interval $[\alpha, \beta]$ to approximate the value of the Fréchet distance, if it falls inside this interval. Indeed, partition this interval into subintervals of length $\varepsilon\alpha$ and perform a binary search to find the interval that contains the Fréchet distance. There are $O(\beta/\varepsilon\alpha)$ intervals, and as such this would require $O(\log(\beta/\varepsilon\alpha))$ calls to decider. By using exponential subintervals, one can do slightly better, as testified by the following lemma.

Lemma 3.6 *Given two curves π and σ in $\mathbb{R}^d$ of total complexity n, a parameter $1 \geq \varepsilon > 0$, and an interval $[\alpha, \beta]$, one can compute a $(1+\varepsilon)$-approximation to $\mathsf{d}_{\mathcal{F}}(\pi, \sigma)$ if $\mathsf{d}_{\mathcal{F}}(\pi, \sigma) \in [\alpha, \beta]$, or report that $\mathsf{d}_{\mathcal{F}}(\pi, \sigma) \notin [\alpha, \beta]$. The algorithm, denoted by $\mathrm{srchInterval}(\pi, \sigma, [\alpha, \beta], \varepsilon)$. Its running time is $O\left(\mathsf{N}(\varepsilon, \pi, \sigma) \log \frac{\log(\beta/\alpha)}{\varepsilon}\right)$.*

PROOF. Omitted. Available from [18]. □

3.3.2 *Searching over Events*

Clearly, the procedure $\mathrm{srchInterval}(\pi, \sigma, [\alpha, \beta], \varepsilon)$ by itself does not suffice to solve our main problem, since the interval of distances we are searching over might have arbitrarily large "spread" (i.e., $\log \beta/\alpha$ might be arbitrarily large). However, the Fréchet distance must be sufficiently close to a free space event in one of the "approximate" diagrams, i.e., a free space diagram of the two simplified curves. Thus, we can identify two kinds of critical values to search over, which are candidate values for the approximate Fréchet distance. These are the events where (i) the simplification of an input curve changes, or (ii) the reachability within the appropriate free space diagram changes (a free space event; see Section 2.3.1).

The traditional solution to overcome this problem is to use parametric search. However, in our case, since we are only interested in approximation, we can use a simpler, "approximate", search. It is sufficient to search over a set of values which approximate the event values by a constant factor, since we will use Lemma 3.6 to refine the resulting search interval in the main algorithm. Note, for instance, that we can easily use this lemma to turn a constant factor approximation of the Fréchet distance into a $(1+\varepsilon)$-approximation of the same.

Algorithm 3.7 Let srchEvents(π, σ, Z) denote the algorithm that performs a binary search over the values of Z, to compute the atomic interval of Z that contains the Fréchet distance between π and σ. This procedure uses decider (Lemma 3.5) to perform the decisions during the search.

3.3.3 Searching over Simplifications

Consider the events when the simplified curves change. Let $\mathcal{W}$ denote the set of all pairwise distances between vertices of π and σ. Observe that it breaks the real line into $\binom{n}{2}+1$ atomic intervals, such that in each such interval the simplification does not change. Thus $\text{simpl}(\pi, \mu)$ might result in $O(n^2)$ different curves depending on the value of μ, where n is the total number of vertices of π and σ. As such, as a first step we would like to use Algorithm 3.7 to perform a binary search over those distances to find the atomic interval that contains the required Fréchet distance. Naively, this would require us to perform distance selection. However, it is believed that exact distance selection requires $\Omega\left(n^{4/3}\right)$ time in the worst case [20]. To overcome this we will perform an approximate distance selection, as suggested by Aronov *et al.* [8]. This is implemented using the well-separated pairs decomposition of Callahan and Kosaraju [14].

Lemma 3.8 *Given a set* P *of* n *points in* $\mathbb{R}^d$, *let* $\binom{\mathsf{P}}{2}$ *be the set of all pairwise distances of points in* P. *Then, one can compute in* $O(n \log n)$ *time a set* Z *of* $O(n)$ *numbers, such that for any* $y \in \binom{\mathsf{P}}{2}$, *there exist numbers* $x, x' \in Z$ *such that* $x \leq y \leq x' \leq 2x$. *Let* approxDists(P) *denote this algorithm.*

Proof. Compute an 8-well-separated pairs decomposition of P. Using the algorithm of Callahan and Kosaraju [14] this can be done in $O(n \log n)$ time, and results in a set of pairs $\{X_1 \otimes Y_1, \ldots, X_m \otimes Y_m\}$, where $m = O(n)$, such that for any two points $\mathsf{p}, \mathsf{q} \in \mathsf{P}$ there exists a pair $X_i \otimes Y_i$ in the above decomposition, such that: (i) $\mathsf{p} \in X_i$ and $\mathsf{q} \in Y_i$ (or vice versa), and (ii) $\max(\text{diam}(X_i), \text{diam}(Y_i)) \leq \|\mathsf{p} - \mathsf{q}\|/8$.

This implies that the distance of any pair of points in X_i and Y_i, respectively, are the same up to a small constant. As such, for every pair $X_i \otimes Y_i$, for $i = 1, \ldots, m$, we pick representative points $\mathsf{p}_i \in X_i$ and $\mathsf{q}_i \in Y_i$, and set $\ell_i = (3/4)\|\mathsf{p}_i - \mathsf{q}_i\|$. Let $Z = \{\ell_1, \ldots, \ell_m, 2\ell_1, \ldots, 2\ell_m\}$ be the computed set of values.

Consider any pair of points $\mathsf{p}, \mathsf{q} \in \mathsf{P}$. For the specific pair $X_i \otimes Y_i$ that contains the pair of points p and q that we are interested in, we have that $\ell_i = (3/4)\|\mathsf{p}_i - \mathsf{q}_i\| \leq \|\mathsf{p}_i - \mathsf{q}_i\| - \text{diam}(X_i) - \text{diam}(Y_i) \leq \|\mathsf{p} - \mathsf{q}\| \leq \|\mathsf{p}_i - \mathsf{q}_i\| + \text{diam}(X_i) + \text{diam}(Y_i) \leq (5/4)\|\mathsf{p}_i - \mathsf{q}_i\| \leq 2\ell_i$, thus establishing the claim. □

3.3.4 Monotonicity Events

The following lemma testifies that the radius of a monotonicity event must be "close" to either a vertex-edge event or to the distance between two vertices. Since we will approximate and perform a binary search over the vertex-vertex distances, this implies that we further only need to consider vertex-edge events. Furthermore, in the remaining search range, by Observation 3.2, the number of those vertex-edge events can be bounded by the total complexity of the free space.

Lemma 3.9 *Let* x *be the radius of a monotonicity event involving vertices* p, q *and a segment* u. *Then there exists a number* y *such that* $y/2 \leq x \leq 3y$, *and* y *is either in* $\mathcal{W} = \binom{V(\pi) \cup V(\sigma)}{2}$ *or* y *is the radius of a vertex-edge event.*

Proof. Let s be the intersection point of $\mathbb{S}(\mathsf{p}, x) \cap \mathbb{S}(\mathsf{q}, x)$ which lies on u. Let p' (resp. q') be the closest point on u to p (resp. q).

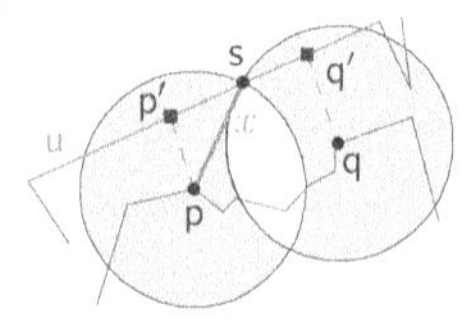

Clearly $\|\mathsf{p}' - \mathsf{q}'\| \leq \|\mathsf{p} - \mathsf{q}\|$ (since the projection onto the nearest neighbor of a convex set is a contraction), and since $\mathsf{p}' \in \mathbf{b}(\mathsf{p}, x)$ and $\mathsf{q}' \in \mathbf{b}(\mathsf{q}, x)$, the point s lies on the segment $\mathsf{p}'\mathsf{q}'$.

This implies that $x = \|\mathsf{p} - \mathsf{s}\| \leq \|\mathsf{p} - \mathsf{p}'\| + \|\mathsf{p}' - \mathsf{s}\| \leq \|\mathsf{p} - \mathsf{p}'\| + \|\mathsf{p}' - \mathsf{q}'\| \leq \|\mathsf{p} - \mathsf{p}'\| + \|\mathsf{p} - \mathsf{q}\|$, by the triangle inequality.

A similar argument implies that

$$x = \|\mathsf{p} - \mathsf{s}\| \geq \|\mathsf{p} - \mathsf{p}'\| - \|\mathsf{p}' - \mathsf{s}\| \geq \|\mathsf{p} - \mathsf{p}'\| - \|\mathsf{p}' - \mathsf{q}'\| \geq \|\mathsf{p} - \mathsf{p}'\| - \|\mathsf{p} - \mathsf{q}\|.$$

If $\|\mathsf{p} - \mathsf{p}'\| \geq 2\|\mathsf{p} - \mathsf{q}\|$ then the above implies that $x \in [1/2, 3/2]\|\mathsf{p} - \mathsf{p}'\|$. If p' is an endpoint of u then $\|\mathsf{p} - \mathsf{p}'\|$ is in $\mathcal{W}$. Otherwise, $\|\mathsf{p} - \mathsf{p}'\|$ is the radius of the vertex-edge event between p and u. In either case, this implies the claim.

If $\|\mathsf{p} - \mathsf{p}'\| \leq 2\|\mathsf{p} - \mathsf{q}\|$ then $x = \|\mathsf{p} - \mathsf{s}\| \leq \|\mathsf{p} - \mathsf{p}'\| + \|\mathsf{p} - \mathsf{q}\| \leq 2\|\mathsf{p} - \mathsf{q}\| + \|\mathsf{p} - \mathsf{q}\| = 3\|\mathsf{p} - \mathsf{q}\|$, and of course $\|\mathsf{p} - \mathsf{q}\| \in \mathcal{W}$. Now, the two balls of radius x centered at p and q, respectively, cover the segment pq, and we have that $\|\mathsf{p} - \mathsf{q}\|/2 \leq x$, which implies the claim. □

3.3.5 Searching with a Fixed Simplification

Assume that we have found simplifications τ and η, such that the Fréchet distance of those curves yields the desired $(1+\varepsilon)$-approximation. Clearly, an approximation of $\mathsf{d}_{\mathcal{F}}(\tau, \eta)$ suffices for our result. To this end, let srchIntrvlNoSimp $(\pi, \sigma, [\alpha, \beta], \varepsilon)$ be the variant of srchInterval (Lemma 3.6) that uses Lemma 3.1 directly instead of calling decider. This version searches for the Fréchet distance in the given interval, but does not perform simplification before calling the decision procedure. It returns a $(1+\varepsilon)$-approximation of the Fréchet distance, given that it is contained in this interval. Note that correctness and running time of Lemma 3.6 are not affected by this modification.

For two real numbers $x, y > 0$, their ***ratio*** is $[x/y] = \max(x, y)/\min(x, y)$.

Lemma 3.10 *Let* τ *and* η *be two given curves in* $\mathbb{R}^d$, *with total complexity* n, *and let* $[h^-, h^+]$ *be an interval, such that (i)* $\mathsf{d}_{\mathcal{F}}(\tau, \eta) \in [h^-, h^+]$, *and (ii) there is no value of* $\mathcal{W} = \binom{V(\tau) \cup V(\eta)}{2}$ *in the interval* $[h^-, h^+]$. *Then, for* $\varepsilon > 0$, *one can* $(1+\varepsilon)$*-approximate* $\mathsf{d}_{\mathcal{F}}(\tau, \eta)$ *in* $O((n+N)\log(N/\varepsilon))$ *time, where* $N = \mathcal{N}_{\leq h^+}(\tau, \eta)$.

Le aprxFrNoSimp$(\tau, \eta, [h^-, h^+], \varepsilon)$ *be this algorithm.*

Proof. Compute $\mathcal{R}_{\leq h^+}(\tau, \eta)$, using Lemma 3.1. Next, using Observation 3.2, compute from $\mathcal{R}_{\leq h^+}(\tau, \eta)$ the set Z of all the radii of the vertex-edge events of τ and η with radius at most h^+. Next, we sort Z, and perform a binary search over Z, using Lemma 3.1, for the atomic interval $\mathcal{I} = [\alpha, \beta]$ of Z that contains the Fréchet distance $\mathsf{d}_{\mathcal{F}}(\tau, \eta)$. Next, call srchIntrvlNoSimp$(\tau, \eta, [\alpha, 8\alpha], \varepsilon)$ and srchIntrvlNoSimp$(\tau, \eta, [\beta/8, \beta], \varepsilon)$. We claim that one of these two searches performed on the respective intervals will discover two consecutive values x and $(1+\varepsilon)x$, such that the two corresponding calls to the algorithm of Lemma 3.6 imply that $\mathsf{d}_{\mathcal{F}}(\tau, \eta) \in [x, (1+\varepsilon)x]$.

Indeed, the interior of $\mathcal{I}$ does not contain any value in $\mathcal{W}$ or a radius of a vertex-edge event of τ and η. As such, $\mathcal{I}$ might contain only monotonicity events of τ and η. By Lemma 3.9, for a monotonicity event with radius r there exists a $y \in Z \cup \mathcal{W}$, such that $\lceil \mathsf{r}/y \rceil \leq 3$. On the other hand, there is no value of $Z \cup \mathcal{W}$ in the interior of $[\alpha, \beta]$, and as such, for any $\mathsf{r}'' \in [8\alpha, \beta/8]$ and $y'' \in Z \cup \mathcal{W}$, we have that $\lceil \mathsf{r}''/y'' \rceil \geq 8$.

We conclude that no monotonicity or vertex-edge events, or a value of $\mathcal{W}$ lies in the interval $[8\alpha, \beta/8]$. Since the Fréchet distance must be equal to one such value, it follows that $\mathsf{d}_{\mathcal{F}}(\tau, \eta) \notin (8\alpha, \beta/8)$, but this implies that either $\mathsf{d}_{\mathcal{F}}(\tau, \eta) \in [\alpha, 8\alpha]$ or $\mathsf{d}_{\mathcal{F}}(\tau, \eta) \in [\beta/8, \beta]$. In either case, the above algorithm would have found the approximate distance.

Computing and sorting the set of vertex-edge events takes $O(N \log N)$ time by Observation 3.2. The binary search requires $O(\log|Z|)$ calls to the algorithm of Lemma 3.1. The two calls to srchIntrvlNoSimp require $O(\log(1/\varepsilon))$ calls to Lemma 3.1. Now, observe that all these calls to the algorithm of Lemma 3.1 are done with values of $\mathsf{r} \leq h^{+}$. As such, the complexity of the reachable free space is bounded (up to a constant factor) by the number of vertex-edge events of values $\leq h^{+}$, and this number is bounded by $|Z|$. As such, a call to Lemma 3.1 takes $O(|Z|)$ time. Thus, the overall running time is $O((n + |Z|) \log(|Z|/\varepsilon))$, and by definition $|Z| = O(\mathcal{N}_{\leq h^{+}}(\tau, \eta))$. □

3.4 The Approximation Algorithm

The resulting approximation algorithm is depicted in Figure 2. It would be used by the final approximation algorithm as a subroutine. We first analyze this basic algorithm. We will then show how to use it, in Lemma 3.14 below, to get a faster approximation algorithm. The algorithm depicted in Figure 2 performs numerous calls to decider, with approximation parameter $\varepsilon > 0$. If any of these calls discover the approximate distance, then the algorithm immediately stops and returns the approximation. As such, at any point in the execution of the algorithm, the assumption is that all previous calls to decider returned a direction where the optimal distance must lie. In particular, a call to srchInterval$(\pi, \sigma, \mathcal{I}, \varepsilon)$, would either find the approximate distance in the interval $\mathcal{I}$ and return immediately, or the desired value is outside this interval.

3.4.1 Correctness

Lemma 3.11 *The algorithm* aprxFréchetI *provides a* $(1+\varepsilon)$*-approximation to* $\mathsf{d}_{\mathcal{F}}(\pi, \sigma)$.

Proof. If the algorithm found the approximation before step (F), then clearly it is the desired approximation, and we are done. (In particular, this must be the case if $4\alpha' > \beta'/4$.)

Otherwise, because of (C), we know that $\mathsf{d}_{\mathcal{F}}(\pi, \sigma) \in [\alpha, \beta]$. By steps (D) and (E) it must be that $\mathsf{d}_{\mathcal{F}}(\pi, \sigma) \in [4\alpha', \beta'/4]$. Since $\mu = 3\alpha \leq \beta'/4$, it follows, by the triangle inequality, that

$$\begin{aligned}\mathsf{d}_{\mathcal{F}}(\pi', \sigma') &\leq \mathsf{d}_{\mathcal{F}}(\pi', \pi) + \mathsf{d}_{\mathcal{F}}(\pi, \sigma) + \mathsf{d}_{\mathcal{F}}(\sigma, \sigma') \\ &\leq 2\mu + \beta'/4 < \beta'.\end{aligned}$$

aprxFréchetI$(\pi, \sigma, \varepsilon)$
- (A) $\mathsf{P} = V(\pi) \cup V(\sigma)$
- (B) $Z \leftarrow$ approxDists(P) (Lemma 3.8)
- (C) $[\alpha, \beta] \leftarrow$ srchEvents$(\pi, \sigma, Z, \varepsilon)$ (Algorithm 3.7)
- (D) Call srchInterval$(\pi, \sigma, [\alpha, 4\alpha'], \varepsilon)$, where $\alpha' = (30/\varepsilon)\alpha$ (Lemma 3.6)
- (E) Call srchInterval$(\pi, \sigma, [\beta'/4, \beta], \varepsilon)$, where $\beta' = \beta/3$
- (F) Let $\pi' = \mathrm{simpl}(\pi, \mu)$ and $\sigma' = \mathrm{simpl}(\sigma, \mu)$, for $\mu = 3\alpha$ (Algorithm 2.1)
- (G) $\delta \leftarrow$ aprxFrNoSimp$(\pi', \sigma', [\alpha', \beta'], \varepsilon/4)$ (Lemma 3.10)
- (H) Return the reparameterizations of π and σ resulting from chaining the reparameterizations of $\pi \Leftrightarrow \pi'$ and $\sigma' \Leftrightarrow \sigma$ and their width as the approximation.

Figure 2: The basic approximation algorithm.

A similar argument shows that $\mathsf{d}_{\mathcal{F}}(\pi', \sigma') > \alpha'$. As such, the algorithm of Lemma 2.3 can be applied to π' and σ' for the range $[\alpha', \beta']$, as $\mathsf{d}_{\mathcal{F}}(\pi', \sigma') \in [\alpha', \beta']$.

Now, by Lemma 2.3, we have that $\delta \in [\mathsf{d}_{\mathcal{F}}(\pi', \sigma'), (1 + \varepsilon/4)\mathsf{d}_{\mathcal{F}}(\pi', \sigma')]$. By the triangle inequality we conclude that the returned Fréchet distance is

$$\begin{aligned}\Delta &\leq \mathsf{d}_{\mathcal{F}}(\pi, \pi') + \delta + \mathsf{d}_{\mathcal{F}}(\sigma, \sigma') \\ &\leq \mathsf{d}_{\mathcal{F}}(\pi, \pi') + (1+\varepsilon/4)\mathsf{d}_{\mathcal{F}}(\pi', \sigma') + \mathsf{d}_{\mathcal{F}}(\sigma', \sigma) \\ &\leq (1+\varepsilon/4)(2\mu + \mathsf{d}_{\mathcal{F}}(\pi, \sigma) + 2\mu) \\ &\leq 5\mu + (1+\varepsilon/4)\mathsf{d}_{\mathcal{F}}(\pi, \sigma) \leq (1+\varepsilon)\mathsf{d}_{\mathcal{F}}(\pi, \sigma),\end{aligned}$$

since $5\mu = 15\alpha = (\varepsilon/2)(30/\varepsilon)\alpha = (\varepsilon/2)\alpha' \leq (\varepsilon/2)\mathsf{d}_{\mathcal{F}}(\pi, \sigma)$.

Note that $\Delta \geq \mathsf{d}_{\mathcal{F}}(\pi, \sigma)$ since it is the width of a specific reparameterization between the two curves. □

3.4.2 Running Time

Lemma 3.12 *For any* $x, y \in (2\alpha, \beta/2)$, *it holds* $\mathrm{simpl}(\pi, x) = \mathrm{simpl}(\pi, y)$ *and* $\mathrm{simpl}(\sigma, x) = \mathrm{simpl}(\sigma, y)$.

Proof. Indeed, the interval (α, β) does not contain any value of Z. As such, by Lemma 3.8, $(2\alpha, \beta/2)$ does not contain any value of $\binom{\mathsf{P}}{2}$ which implies that the simplification is the same for any value inside this interval. □

Lemma 3.13 *Given two polygonal curves* π *and* σ *with a total of* n *vertices in* $\mathbb{R}^d$, *and a parameter* $1 > \varepsilon > 0$, *the running time of* aprxFréchetI$(\pi, \sigma, \varepsilon)$ *is* $O(\mathsf{N}(\varepsilon, \pi, \sigma) \log n)$.

Proof. Computing Z (and sorting it) takes $O(n \log n)$ time. Steps (C), (D) and (E) perform $O(\log n + \log(1/\varepsilon)) = O(\log n)$ calls to decider, by Lemma 3.6. (Here, we assume that $\varepsilon = \Omega(1/n)$. If $1/\varepsilon > n$ then we can just use the exact algorithm since its running time is faster than our approximation algorithm.) Each call to decider takes $O(\mathsf{N}(\varepsilon, \pi, \sigma))$ time, so overall this takes $O(\mathsf{N}(\varepsilon, \pi, \sigma) \log n)$ time. Computing the simplifications in step (F) with Algorithm 2.1 takes $O(n)$ time.

By Lemma 3.10, a call to aprxFrNoSimp$(\pi', \sigma', [\alpha', \beta'], \varepsilon/4)$ takes $T = O((n+N)\log(N/\varepsilon))$ time, where $N = \mathcal{N}_{\leq \beta'}(\pi', \sigma')$. Now, $\mu = 3\alpha$ and β' are both inside the interval $(2\alpha, \beta/2)$, and as such, by Lemma 3.12, we have that $\pi' = \mathrm{simpl}(\pi, \mu) = \mathrm{simpl}(\pi, \beta')$ and $\sigma' = \mathrm{simpl}(\sigma, \mu) =$

simpl(σ, β'). As such, by Lemma 4.4, we have that $N = \mathcal{N}_{\leq \beta'}(\pi', \sigma') = \mathcal{N}_{\leq \beta'}(\text{simpl}(\pi, \beta'), \text{simpl}(\sigma, \beta'))$. Now, this is bounded by $O(\mathsf{N}(1, \pi, \sigma))$.

Thus, step (G) takes $T = O(\mathsf{N}(1, \pi, \sigma) \log(\mathsf{N}(1, \pi, \sigma)\, n/\varepsilon)) = O(\mathsf{N}(1, \pi, \sigma) \log n)$, time since $\mathsf{N}(1, \pi, \sigma) \leq n^2$ and $\varepsilon = \Omega(1/n)$. And clearly, computing the reparameterizations and their width in step (H) also takes $O(n)$ time. Finally, observe that $\mathsf{N}(1, \pi, \sigma) = O(\mathsf{N}(\varepsilon, \pi, \sigma))$. □

The running time of Lemma 3.13 can be slightly improved, see [18] for details.

Lemma 3.14 *The algorithm* aprxFréchetI, *see Figure 2, can be modified to run in time*

$$O(\mathsf{N}(\varepsilon, \pi, \sigma) + \mathsf{N}(1, \pi, \sigma) \log n)$$

(see Definition 3.3).

The Result. Putting the above together, we get the following result.

Theorem 3.15 *Given two polygonal curves π and σ with a total of n vertices in $\mathbb{R}^d$, and a parameter $1 > \varepsilon > 0$, one can $(1+\varepsilon)$-approximate the Fréchet distance between π and σ in $O(\mathsf{N}(\varepsilon, \pi, \sigma) + \mathsf{N}(1, \pi, \sigma) \log n)$ time (see Definition 3.3).*

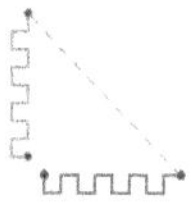

Interestingly, simplification is critical for the efficiency of the above algorithm. Indeed, consider the two nicely behaved curves depicted on the right. The reachable portion of the free space diagram of these two curves, for the distance realizing the Fréchet distance, covers a quadratic number of cells. The algorithm will simplify both curves and thereby contract rows and columns in the relevant diagram to reduce its complexity such that an efficient search for the parametrizations becomes possible.

4. ON THE RELATIVE FREE SPACE COMPLEXITY OF FAMILIES OF CURVES

In this section we are going to bound the relative free space complexity of various families of curves. This will imply various bounds on the running time of the approximation algorithm presented above.

4.1 On c-packed Curves

We introduce a new family of curves, c-packed curves, and prove that their relative free space complexity $\mathsf{N}(\varepsilon, \pi, \sigma)$ is linear, for any two curves π and σ in this family. This implies that Theorem 3.15 works in near linear time for c-packed curves, which is one of our main results.

4.1.1 Definition and basic properties

Definition 4.1 A curve π in $\mathbb{R}^d$ is ***c-packed*** if for any point p in $\mathbb{R}^d$ and any radius $r > 0$, the total length of π inside the ball $\mathbf{b}(\mathsf{p}, r)$ is at most cr.

Lemma 4.2 *Let π be a curve in $\mathbb{R}^d$, $\mu > 0$ be a parameter, and let $\pi' = \text{simpl}(\pi, \mu)$ be the simplified curve. Then $\|\pi \cap \mathbf{b}(\mathsf{p}, \mathsf{r} + \mu)\| \geq \|\pi' \cap \mathbf{b}(\mathsf{p}, \mathsf{r})\|$ for any ball $\mathbf{b}(\mathsf{p}, \mathsf{r})$.*

PROOF. Let u be a segment of π' that intersects $\mathbf{b}(\mathsf{p}, \mathsf{r})$ and let $\mathsf{v} = \mathsf{u} \cap \mathbf{b}(\mathsf{p}, \mathsf{r})$ be this intersection. Let π_u be the portion of π that got simplified into u. Observe that π_u is a polygonal curve that lies inside a hippodrome of radius μ around u; that is, $\pi_\mathsf{u} \subseteq \mathcal{H}_\mathsf{u} = \mathsf{u} \oplus \mathbf{b}(0, \mu)$, where $\oplus$ denotes the Minkowski sum of the two sets, see the figure on the right.

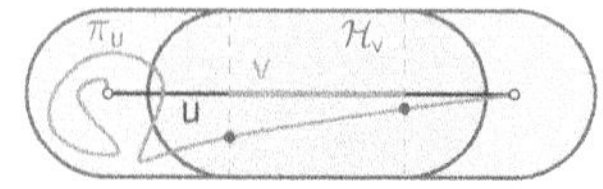

In particular, erect two hyperplanes passing through the endpoints of v that are orthogonal to v, and observe that π_u must intersect both hyperplanes. As such, we conclude that the portions of π_u in the hippodrome $\mathcal{H}_\mathsf{v} = \mathsf{v} \oplus \mathbf{b}(0, \mu)$ are of length at least $\|\mathsf{v}\|$. Clearly, $\mathsf{v} \subseteq \mathbf{b}(\mathsf{p}, \mathsf{r})$ implies that $\mathcal{H}_\mathsf{v} \subseteq \mathbf{b}(\mathsf{p}, \mathsf{r} + \mu)$, which in turn implies that $\pi_\mathsf{u} \cap \mathcal{H}_\mathsf{v} \subseteq \mathbf{b}(\mathsf{p}, \mathsf{r} + \mu)$ and as such $\|\pi_\mathsf{u} \cap \mathbf{b}(\mathsf{p}, \mathsf{r} + \mu)\| \geq \|\mathsf{v}\|$.

Summing over all segments v in $\pi' \cap \mathbf{b}(\mathsf{p}, \mathsf{r})$ implies the claim. □

Lemma 4.3 *Let π be a c-packed curve in $\mathbb{R}^d$, $\mu > 0$ be a parameter, and let $\pi' = \text{simpl}(\pi, \mu)$ be the simplified curve. Then, π' is a $6c$-packed curve.*

PROOF. Assume, for the sake of contradiction, that we have $\|\pi' \cap \mathbf{b}(\mathsf{p}, \mathsf{r})\| > 6c\mathsf{r}$ for some $\mathbf{b}(\mathsf{p}, \mathsf{r})$ in $\mathbb{R}^d$. If $\mathsf{r} \geq \mu$, then set $\mathsf{r}' = 2\mathsf{r}$ and Lemma 4.2 implies that $\|\pi \cap \mathbf{b}(\mathsf{p}, \mathsf{r}')\| \geq \|\pi \cap \mathbf{b}(\mathsf{p}, \mathsf{r} + \mu)\| \geq \|\pi' \cap \mathbf{b}(\mathsf{p}, \mathsf{r})\| > 6c\mathsf{r} = 3c\mathsf{r}'$, which contradicts that π is c-packed.

If $\mathsf{r} < \mu$ then let U denote the segments of π' intersecting $\mathbf{b}(\mathsf{p}, \mathsf{r})$ and let $k = |U|$. Observe that $k > 6c\mathsf{r}/2\mathsf{r} = 3c$, as any segment can contribute at most $2\mathsf{r}$ to the length of π' inside $\mathbf{b}(\mathsf{p}, \mathsf{r})$. As such, we have that $\|\pi' \cap \mathbf{b}(\mathsf{p}, 2\mu)\| \geq \|\pi' \cap \mathbf{b}(\mathsf{p}, \mathsf{r} + \mu)\| \geq \|U \cap \mathbf{b}(\mathsf{p}, \mathsf{r} + \mu)\| \geq k\mu$, since every segment of the simplified curve π' has a minimal length of μ. By Lemma 4.2, this implies that $\|\pi \cap \mathbf{b}(\mathsf{p}, 3\mu)\| \geq \|\pi' \cap \mathbf{b}(\mathsf{p}, 2\mu)\| \geq k\mu > 3c\mu$, which is a contradiction to the c-packedness of π. □

4.1.2 Bounding the relative free space complexity

Lemma 4.4 *For any two c-packed curves π and σ in $\mathbb{R}^d$ of total complexity n, and $0 < \varepsilon < 1$, we have that $\mathsf{N}(\varepsilon, \pi, \sigma) = O(cn/\varepsilon)$.*

PROOF. Let $\delta \geq 0$ be an arbitrary number, $\mu = \varepsilon\delta$, $\pi' = \text{simpl}(\pi, \mu)$ and $\sigma' = \text{simpl}(\sigma, \mu)$

We need to show that the complexity of $\mathcal{D}_{\leq \delta}(\pi', \sigma')$ is $O(cn/\varepsilon)$. A free space cell of $\mathcal{D}_{\leq \delta}(\pi', \sigma')$ corresponds to two segments $\mathsf{u} \in \pi'$ and $\mathsf{v} \in \sigma'$. The free space in this cell is non-empty if and only if there are two points $\mathsf{p} \in \mathsf{u}$ and $\mathsf{q} \in \mathsf{v}$ such that $\|\mathsf{p} - \mathsf{q}\| \leq \delta$. We charge this pair of points to the shorter of the two segments. We claim that a segment cannot be charged too many times.

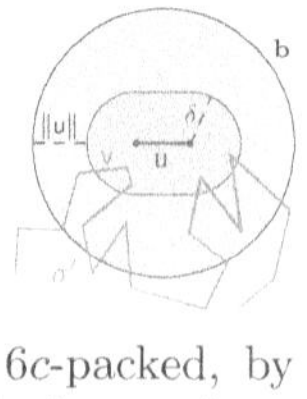

Indeed, consider a segment $\mathsf{u} \in \pi'$, and consider the ball $\mathbf{b}$ of radius $r = (3/2)\|\mathsf{u}\| + \delta$ centered at the midpoint of u, see the figure on the right. Every segment $\mathsf{v} \in \sigma'$ that participates in a close pair as above and charges u for it, is of length at least $\|\mathsf{u}\|$, and the length of $\mathsf{v} \cap \mathbf{b}$ is at least $\|\mathsf{u}\|$. Since σ' is $6c$-packed, by Lemma 4.3, we have that the number of such charges is at most

$$c' = \frac{\|\sigma' \cap \mathbf{b}\|}{\|\mathsf{u}\|} \leq \frac{6cr}{\|\mathsf{u}\|} \leq 9c + \frac{6c\delta}{\mu} = O\Big(\frac{c}{\varepsilon}\Big),$$

since $\|u\| \geq \mu$.

We conclude that there are at most $c'n$ free space cells that contain a point of $\mathcal{D}_{\leq \delta}$. The complexity of the free space inside a cell is a constant, thus implying the claim. □

By plugging the above into Theorem 3.15, we get the following result.

Theorem 4.5 *Given two polygonal c-packed curves π and σ with a total of n vertices in $\mathbb{R}^d$, and a parameter $1 > \varepsilon > 0$, one can $(1+\varepsilon)$-approximate the Fréchet distance between π and σ in $O(cn/\varepsilon + cn \log n)$ time (see Definition 3.3).*

4.2 On the Relative Free Space Complexity of κ-Bounded Curves

Due to space limitations, we only state the results in this section, see [18] for details.

We revisit the definitions of Alt *et al.* [6].

Definition 4.6 Let $\kappa \geq 1$ be a given parameter. A curve π is ***κ-straight*** if for any two points p and q on the curve, it holds that $\|\pi[\mathsf{p},\mathsf{q}]\| \leq \kappa \|\mathsf{p}-\mathsf{q}\|$.

A curve π is a ***κ-bounded*** if for all $\mathsf{p},\mathsf{q} \in \pi$ it holds that the curve $\pi[\mathsf{p},\mathsf{q}]$ is contained inside $\mathbf{b}(\mathsf{p},r) \cup \mathbf{b}(\mathsf{q},r)$, where $r = (\kappa/2)\|\mathsf{p}-\mathsf{q}\|$.

Lemma 4.7 *A κ-straight curve is 2κ-packed.*

Lemma 4.8 *Let π be a κ-bounded polygonal curve in $\mathbb{R}^d$, and let $\mu \leq \delta$ be parameters. Let $\pi' = \mathrm{simpl}(\pi,\mu)$. Then the number of segments of π' intersecting $\mathbf{b}(\mathsf{s},\delta)$ is bounded by $O\big(\kappa^d(1+\delta/\mu)^d\big)$, for any $\mathsf{s} \in \mathbb{R}^d$.*

Lemma 4.9 *For any two κ-bounded polygonal curves in $\mathbb{R}^d$ π and σ of total complexity n, $0 < \varepsilon < 1$, we have $\mathsf{N}(\varepsilon,\pi,\sigma) = O\big((\kappa/\varepsilon)^d n\big)$.*

Theorem 4.10 *Given two κ-bounded polygonal curves π and σ with a total of n vertices in $\mathbb{R}^d$, and a parameter $1 > \varepsilon > 0$, one can $(1+\varepsilon)$-approximate the Fréchet distance between π and σ in $O\Big((\kappa/\varepsilon)^d n + \kappa^d n \log n\Big)$ time.*

4.3 On the Relative Free Space Complexity of Low Density Curves

Due to space limitations, we only state the results in this section, see [18] for details.

Definition 4.11 A polygonal curve π is ***ϕ-low-density*** (in $\mathbb{R}^d$) if any ball $\mathbf{b}(\mathsf{p},r)$ intersects at most ϕ segments of π that are longer than r.

It can be easily seen by a simple packing argument that a polygonal c-packed curve is ϕ-low-density, for $\phi = 2c$. For any ball $\mathbf{b} = \mathbf{b}(\mathsf{p},r)$, consider the ball with the same center that has radius $r' = 2r$. Any edge intersecting $\mathbf{b}$ that is longer than r must contribute at least r to the length of the intersection of the curve with the larger ball, which is bounded by cr'. There can be at most $cr'/r = 2c$ edges of this type. We have been using this property of c-packed curves throughout section Section 4.1 to bound their relative free space complexity.

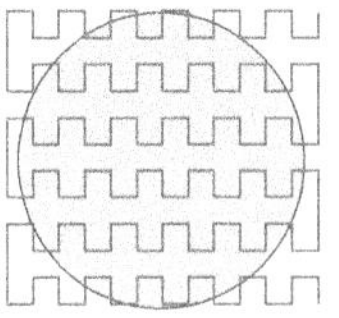

A curve that is low density, however, is not necessarily c-packed for a small value of c. Indeed, a low density curve π might have an arbitrarily long intersection with a ball by having sufficiently small segments, see the figure on the right. However, in this case π must have many vertices in the areas where its length cannot be bounded, as we will show in the following section.

Lemma 4.12 *Let π be a ϕ-low density curve in $\mathbb{R}^d$, and let C be a cube in $\mathbb{R}^d$ with side length r. Let $\alpha = \|\pi \cap C\|$. There must be at least $\Omega((\alpha/r)^{1+1/(d-1)})$ vertices of π contained in 3C, where 3C is the scaling of C by a factor of 3 around its center.*

Lemma 4.13 *For any two low density curves π and σ in $\mathbb{R}^d$ with total complexity n, and $0 < \varepsilon < 1$, we have that $\mathsf{N}(\varepsilon,\pi,\sigma) = O\Big(\frac{n^{2(d-1)/d}}{\varepsilon^2}\Big)$.*

Theorem 4.14 *Given two low-density curves π and σ with a total of n vertices in $\mathbb{R}^d$, and a parameter $\varepsilon > 0$, one can $(1+\varepsilon)$-approximate the Fréchet distance between π and σ in $O\left(\frac{n^{2(d-1)/d}}{\varepsilon^2} + n^{2(d-1)/d}\log n\right)$ time.*

5. EXTENSION TO CLOSED CURVES

Due to space limitations we only state the result. The details are available from the full version [18].

Theorem 5.1 *Given two closed polygonal c-packed curves π and σ with a total of n vertices in $\mathbb{R}^d$, and a parameter $1 > \varepsilon > 0$, one can $(1+\varepsilon)$-approximate the Fréchet distance between π and σ in $O\big(c^2 n(\varepsilon^{-2} + \log n)\big)$ time.*

6. CONCLUSIONS

We presented a new approximation algorithm for Fréchet distance of polygonal curves in any fixed dimension. The new algorithm is surprisingly simple and should be practical, and it works for any kind of polygonal curves. Since the algorithm simplifies the curves to the "right" resolution during the execution, we expect the algorithm to be fast in practice. The algorithm's analysis relies on the concept of the relative free space complexity of curves, which tries to capture the complexity of the free space diagram when simplification is being used.

Next, we introduced the c-packed family of curves. While not all curves are c-packed, it seems that most real life curves are c-packed. The family of c-packed curves is closed under simplification, and the property of a curve being c-packed is independent of the ambient dimension of the space containing the curve. We expect this concept to be used to analyze other algorithms in the future.

Specifically, the relative free space complexity of c-packed curves is linear. We gave bounds for the relative free space complexity for a set of other families of curves, from low density curves to κ-bounded curves. Finally, we also showed that the algorithm can be modified to handle closed curves efficiently.

Open problems. There are many interesting questions for further research – from extending this work to maps [4] to whether or not one can come up with a similar definition for matching realistic surfaces. As of now, not much is known on the efficient computability of the Fréchet distance between surfaces [21, 3]. Finally, it is clear that a variant of our algorithm also works for non-polygonal curves, and in some cases even if they do not have finite complexity. It would be interesting to further pursue this direction.

Acknowledgments. The authors thank Mark de Berg and Marc van Kreveld for insightful discussions on the problems studied in this paper and related problems. The authors would also like to thank the anonymous referees for their insightful comments.

This research was initiated during a workshop supported by the Netherlands Organization for Scientific Research (NWO) under BRICKS/FOCUS grant number 642.065.503.

7. REFERENCES

[1] P. K. Agarwal, S. Har-Peled, N. Mustafa, and Y. Wang. Near-linear time approximation algorithms for curve simplification in two and three dimensions. *Algorithmica*, 42:203–219, 2005.

[2] H. Alt. The computational geometry of comparing shapes. In *Efficient Algorithms: Essays Dedicated to Kurt Mehlhorn on the Occasion of His 60th Birthday*, pages 235–248. Springer-Verlag, 2009.

[3] H. Alt and M. Buchin. Can we compute the similarity between surfaces? *Discrete Comput. Geom.*, 43(1):78–99, 2010.

[4] H. Alt, A. Efrat, G. Rote, and C. Wenk. Matching planar maps. *J. Algorithms*, 49:262–283, 2003.

[5] H. Alt and M. Godau. Computing the Fréchet distance between two polygonal curves. *Internat. J. Comput. Geom. Appl.*, 5:75–91, 1995.

[6] H. Alt, C. Knauer, and C. Wenk. Comparison of distance measures for planar curves. *Algorithmica*, 38(1):45–58, 2004.

[7] B. Aronov and S. Har-Peled. On approximating the depth and related problems. *SIAM J. Comput.*, 38(3):899–921, 2008.

[8] B. Aronov, S. Har-Peled, C. Knauer, Y. Wang, and C. Wenk. Fréchet distance for curves, Revisited. In *Proc. 14th Annu. European Sympos. Algorithms*, pages 52–63, 2006.

[9] P. Bose, O. Cheong, and V. Dujmović. A note on the perimeter of fat objects. *Comput. Geom. Theory Appl.*, 2010. To appear.

[10] S. Brakatsoulas, D. Pfoser, R. Salas, and C. Wenk. On map-matching vehicle tracking data. In *Proc. 31st VLDB Conference*, pages 853–864, 2005.

[11] K. Buchin, M. Buchin, and J. Gudmundsson. Detecting single file movement. In *Proc. 16th ACM SIGSPATIAL Int. Conf. Adv. GIS*, pages 288–297, 2008.

[12] K. Buchin, M. Buchin, J. Gudmundsson, Maarten L., and J. Luo. Detecting commuting patterns by clustering subtrajectories. In *Proc. 19th Annu. Internat. Sympos. Algorithms Comput.*, pages 644–655, 2008.

[13] K. Buchin, M. Buchin, C. Knauer, G. Rote, and C. Wenk. How difficult is it to walk the dog? In *Proc. 23rd Euro. Workshop on Comput. Geom.*, pages 170–173, 2007.

[14] P. B. Callahan and S. R. Kosaraju. A decomposition of multidimensional point sets with applications to k-nearest-neighbors and n-body potential fields. *J. Assoc. Comput. Mach.*, 42:67–90, 1995.

[15] M. de Berg. Linear size binary space partitions for uncluttered scenes. *Algorithmica*, 28:353–366, 2000.

[16] M. de Berg. Improved bounds on the union complexity of fat objects. *Discrete Comput. Geom.*, 40(1):127–140, 2008.

[17] M. de Berg, M. J. Katz, A. F. van der Stappen, and J. Vleugels. Realistic input models for geometric algorithms. *Algorithmica*, 34:81–97, 2002.

[18] A. Driemel, S. Har-Peled, and C. Wenk. Approximating the Fréchet distance for realistic curves in near linear time. `http://arxiv.org/abs/1003.0460`, 2010.

[19] A. Efrat. The complexity of the union of (α, β)-covered objects. *SIAM J. Comput.*, 34(4):775–787, 2005.

[20] J. Erickson. On the relative complexities of some geometric problems. In *Proc. 7th Canad. Conf. Comput. Geom.*, pages 85–90, 1995.

[21] M. Godau. *On the complexity of measuring the similarity between geometric objects in higher dimensions.* PhD thesis, Free University of Berlin, 1999.

[22] E. J. Keogh and M. J. Pazzani. Scaling up dynamic time warping to massive dataset. In *Proc. of the Third Euro. Conf. Princip. Data Mining and Know. Disc.*, pages 1–11, 1999.

[23] M.S. Kim, S.W. Kim, and M. Shin. Optimization of subsequence matching under time warping in time-series databases. In *Proc. ACM symp. Applied comput.*, pages 581–586, New York, NY, USA, 2005.

[24] S. Kwong, Q. H. He, K. F. Man, K. S. Tang, and C. W. Chau. Parallel genetic-based hybrid pattern matching algorithm for isolated word recognition. *Int. J. Pattern Recog. Art. Intel.*, 12(5):573–594, August 1998.

[25] M. E. Munich and P. Perona. Continuous dynamic time warping for translation-invariant curve alignment with applications to signature verification. In *Proc. 7th Int. Conf. Comp. Vision*, pages 108–115, 1999.

[26] E. Sriraghavendra, K. Karthik, and C. Bhattacharyya. Fréchet distance based approach for searching online handwritten documents. In *Proc. 9th Int. Conf. Doc. Analy. Recog.*, pages 461–465, 2007.

[27] C. Wenk, R. Salas, and D. Pfoser. Addressing the need for map-matching speed: Localizing global curve-matching algorithms. In *Proc. 18th Int. Conf. Sci. Statis. Database Manag.*, pages 879–888, 2006.

Computing Similarity between Piecewise-Linear Functions*

Pankaj K. Agarwal
Dept. of Computer Science,
Duke University

Boris Aronov
Dept. of Computer Science
and Engineering
Polytechnic Institute of NYU

Marc van Kreveld
Dept. of Information and
Computing Sciences
Utrecht University

Maarten Löffler
Computer Science Dept.
University of California, Irvine

Rodrigo I. Silveira
Dept. Matemàtica Aplicada II
Universitat Politècnica de
Catalunya

ABSTRACT

We study the problem of computing the similarity between two piecewise-linear bivariate functions defined over a common domain, where the surfaces they define in 3D—polyhedral terrains—can be transformed vertically by a linear transformation of the third coordinate (scaling and translation). We present a randomized algorithm that minimizes the maximum vertical distance between the graphs of the two functions, over all linear transformations of one of the terrains, in $O(n^{4/3} \operatorname{polylog} n)$ expected time, where n is the total number of vertices in the graphs of the two functions. We also study the computation of similarity between two univariate or bivariate functions by minimizing the area or volume between their graphs. For univariate functions we give a $(1+\varepsilon)$-approximation algorithm for minimizing the area that runs in $O(n/\sqrt{\varepsilon})$ time, for any fixed $\varepsilon > 0$. The $(1+\varepsilon)$-approximation algorithm for the bivariate version, where volume is minimized, runs in $O(n/\varepsilon^2)$ time, for any fixed $\varepsilon > 0$, provided the two functions are defined over the same triangulation of their domain.

*Work by P.A. is supported by NSF under grants CNS-05-40347, CCF-06 -35000, IIS-07-13498, and CCF-09-40671, by ARO grants W911NF-07-1-0376 and W911NF-08-1-0452, by an NIH grant 1P50-GM-08183-01, by a DOE grant OEG-P200A070505, and by a grant from the U.S.–Israel Binational Science Foundation. Work by B.A. is supported by a grant from the U.S.-Israel Binational Science Foundation, by NSA MSP Grant H98230-06-1-0016, and NSF Grant CCF-08-30691. Work by M.v.K., M.L., and R.S. is supported by the Netherlands Organisation for Scientific Research (NWO), and M.L. is further supported by the Office of Naval Research under grant N00014-08-1-1015.

Categories and Subject Descriptors

F.2.2 [**Analysis of Algorithms and Problem Complexity**]: Nonnumerical Algorithms and Problems—*computations on discrete structures, geometrical problems and computations*

General Terms

Algorithms, Theory

Keywords

piecewise-linear function, polyhedral terrain, similarity, approximation algorithm, randomized algorithm

1. INTRODUCTION

Many types of spatial data can be modeled mathematically as a bivariate function $f: \mathbb{D} \to \mathbb{R}$, where $\mathbb{D}$ is a (planar) region of interest. Examples include annual precipitation, depth to ground water, soil salinity at the surface, elevation above sea level, and (steepness of) slope of the terrain. Data is usually collected by sampling at a number of points in $\mathbb{D}$, and the function is extended to the entire $\mathbb{D}$ using spatial interpolation schemes [3, 11, 15]. There is much work in many disciplines, including environmental sciences, geology, and statistics on analyzing such data, computing correlations among them, and testing hypotheses and models.

The simplest type of model that may capture the correlation between two types of spatial data is a linear model. If the two types of data are collected at exactly the same set of locations, i.e., data is *isotopic*, then one can apply standard regression analysis on the pairs of values to determine whether a linear dependence of one data set on the other exists [13, 14]. Notwithstanding its popularity because of its simplicity, this approach has two serious shortcomings. First, the two types of data may have been collected at different locations, i.e., data is *heterotopic* [15], due to a difference in resolution of data acquisition techniques or cost factors, or due to inaccessibility of regions for certain types of measurement. Second, it does not account for a possible difference in sampling density in subregions of the region of interest. This will bias the result toward the linear relation that exists in the more densely sampled subregion. The first problem can be handled by using spatial interpolation on one data set to obtain pairs of values at the locations of the other data set.

The second problem can be handled by assigning a weight to each sample location, where the weight is lower in densely sampled subregions. Alternatively, we compute piecewise-linear representations of f and g using spatial interpolation and match them to determine a linear dependence between f and g. This is likely to provide better results than using weights at the sampled locations, which in a sense form a piecewise-constant representation of each function. See [9] for a Morse-theory based method for computing the similarity of two functions.

Contribution. We assume the following representation of a function. Let $\mathbb{M}$ be a triangulation of the domain $\mathbb{D}$. A function value $f(v)$ is assigned to every vertex of $\mathbb{M}$. By linearly interpolating the function value within each triangle of $\mathbb{M}$, we can extend f to the entire $\mathbb{D}$. Thus $\mathbb{M}$ defines a piecewise-linear function $f : \mathbb{D} \to \mathbb{R}$. The graph of f is a polyhedral *terrain*, which can be represented as an xy-monotone triangulated surface whose triangulation is induced by $\mathbb{M}$. Given such representations of two functions f and g, we can *match* them directly, over all possible linear transformations on these functions, to determine a linear correlation of f and g. Note that we apply a linear transformation to only *one* of the functions. Since the functions f and g are scalar-valued, a linear function is determined by two parameters: a *scaling* and a *translation*. Figure 1 shows an example of two terrains representing the functions f and g, and how one can be transformed to match the other one better.

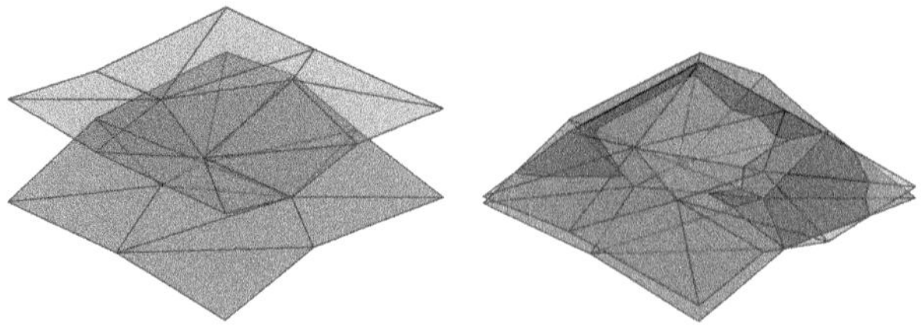
(a) (b)

Figure 1. (a) Two triangulated terrains. (b) The top (red) terrain has been translated and scaled vertically to match the bottom (blue) terrain.

This paper discusses the problem of computing the scaling and translation parameters that provide an optimal matching of two bivariate functions modeled as polyhedral terrains. In particular, let $\mathbb{D}$ be a planar polygonal domain, let $\mathbb{M}_f$ and $\mathbb{M}_g$ be two triangulations of $\mathbb{D}$, and let $f, g : \mathbb{D} \to \mathbb{R}$ be two piecewise-linear functions whose linear pieces correspond to $\mathbb{M}_f$ and $\mathbb{M}_g$, respectively. We assume that $\mathbb{M}_f$ and $\mathbb{M}_g$ together have n vertices. We consider three different measures to determine the matching (similarity, or correlation) between f and g: (i) minimizing the maximum vertical distance (L_∞-norm) between their graphs, (ii) minimizing the volume between their graphs (L_1-norm), and (iii) minimizing the square measure (L_2-norm). More precisely, if s is the scaling parameter and t the translation parameter, we define functions $\mu_p : \mathbb{R}^2 \to \mathbb{R}$, $p = 1, 2, \infty$, to measure how well f and g match for a pair s and t in (1)–(3).

$$\mu_\infty(s,t) = \max_{(x,y)\in\mathbb{D}} |sf(x,y) + t - g(x,y)| \tag{1}$$

$$\mu_1(s,t) = \int_{(x,y)\in\mathbb{D}} |sf(x,y) + t - g(x,y)| \; dxdy \tag{2}$$

$$\mu_2(s,t) = \int_{(x,y)\in\mathbb{D}} (sf(x,y) + t - g(x,y))^2 \; dxdy \tag{3}$$

For $p = 1, 2, \infty$, we can now define the matching between f and g as $\sigma_p(f,g) = \min_{s,t} \mu_p(s,t)$. For each p, our goal is to compute the pair (s^*, t^*) that minimizes the function μ_p and to compute this minimum value $\sigma_p(f,g) = \mu_p(s^*, t^*)$. We note that μ_2 is a linear regression model, μ_1 is similar but uses the L_1-norm, and μ_∞ is similar to the Hausdorff distance, a commonly used measure for shape matching [2].

If the triangulations $\mathbb{M}_f$ and $\mathbb{M}_g$ are identical, then we say that f and g are *aligned*, otherwise they are *unaligned*. We study both aligned and unaligned versions of the problem. We can convert unaligned functions to aligned ones by computing a new triangulation $\mathbb{M}$ that is a common refinement of $\mathbb{M}_f$ and $\mathbb{M}_g$. The number of vertices in $\mathbb{M}$ can vary between $\Theta(n)$ and $\Theta(n^2)$, depending on the complexity of the overlay of $\mathbb{M}_f$ and $\mathbb{M}_g$. If the number of edge-edge intersections between the two triangulations is k, then the overlay has complexity $O(n + k)$ and can be computed in $O(n + k)$ time [10]. A triangulation of the overlay also has complexity $O(n + k)$. For triangulations that satisfy *realistic input assumptions*, one can often show that $k = O(n)$. Several models where this is the case are defined, for example, in [7]. In this case one can align a pair of unaligned functions without loss of asymptotic efficiency.

In Section 2 we develop algorithms for computing $\sigma_\infty(f,g)$. We can compute the optimal linear transformation in linear time for aligned functions, using linear programming. For unaligned terrains, we can avoid the potential quadratic running time by combining various techniques leading to an $O^*(n^{4/3})$ time algorithm (the O^*-notation omits polylogarithmic factors). In Section 4 we discuss the computation of $\sigma_1(f,g)$, but since it is rather technical, we first study the problem for univariate functions in Section 3. This simplified problem is also interesting and has been studied because of its applications in analyzing multivariate time-series data [12, 16]. Computing σ_1 even for univariate functions requires minimizing a linear-size sum of rational functions, which we cannot hope to do exactly. We show that a $(1+\varepsilon)$-approximation algorithm exists that takes $O(n/\sqrt{\varepsilon})$ time for univariate functions (aligned or unaligned), and $O(n/\varepsilon^2)$ time for bivariate functions in the aligned case. The latter extends immediately to $O(n^2/\varepsilon^4)$ time for the non-aligned case, or $O(n/\varepsilon^2)$ time with certain realistic input assumptions. Since the σ_2 measure can easily be computed in linear time for aligned terrains, we do not discuss it further in this paper. To simplify notation, since each section discusses a specific type of measure, we drop the subscript (1 or ∞) from μ and σ in the subsequent sections.

The main novelty and interest of this paper lie in the approach taken to determine correlation of two bivariate functions on the same domain. It gives rise to new geometric problems that can be solved using a suitable combination of advanced algorithmic and approximation techniques. The efficient algorithms that we present are based on geometric properties of the matching functions, which we provide. The convexity of $\mu_1(s,t)$ is especially surprising, as this function is a degree-3 rational function.

2. MINIMIZING THE MAX DISTANCE OF TWO BIVARIATE FUNCTIONS

Let $f, g : \mathbb{D} \to \mathbb{R}$ be two piecewise-linear bivariate functions as defined above. In this section the goal is to find s^*, t^* that minimizes $\mu(s,t)$ according to (1), the maximum vertical distance between the graphs of g and $sf+t$. Let $\mathbb{X}$ be the set of vertices in the overlay of $\mathbb{M}_f$ and $\mathbb{M}_g$. If $\mathbb{M}_f$ and $\mathbb{M}_g$ are identical (f and g are aligned), then $\mathbb{X}$ is the set of its vertices, otherwise $\mathbb{X}$ is the set of vertices in $\mathbb{M}_f$, in $\mathbb{M}_g$, and intersections of their edges. As remarked, $\mathbb{X}$ can be as large as $\Theta(n^2)$ for unaligned functions.

We first observe that the maximum of μ is always realized at a point of $\mathbb{X}$, implying that the problem of computing $\sigma(f,g)$ is inherently discrete. For a point $v \in \mathbb{X}$, we define the function

$$\begin{aligned} d_v(s,t) &= |sf(v) + t - g(v)| \\ &= \max\{sf(v) + t - g(v),\ g(v) - sf(v) - t\}, \end{aligned} \tag{4}$$

which is the vertical height between the two terrains (for a given s and t) at v. Then the above observation implies that $\mu(s,t) = \max_{v \in \mathbb{X}} d_v(s,t)$. Hence, the problem reduces to computing the minimum value on the upper envelope of $\mathcal{D} = \{d_v(s,t) \mid v \in \mathbb{X}\}$. For each v, we define two halfspaces (in the (s,t,z)-space): $\gamma_v^+ : z \geq sf(v) + t - g(v)$ and $\gamma_v^- : z \geq g(v) - sf(v) - t$. Then, by (4), the upper envelope of $\mathcal{D}$ is the same as the boundary of the convex polyhedron $\bigcap_{v \in \mathbb{X}} \gamma_v^+ \cap \gamma_v^-$. The lowest vertex (in z-direction) of this convex polytope can be computed in $O(|\mathbb{X}|)$ expected time, using a linear-time randomized algorithm for linear programming (LP) in fixed dimensions [6].

As mentioned above, if f and g are aligned or they satisfy realistic-input assumptions, then $|\mathbb{X}| = O(n)$, but otherwise it can be $\Theta(n^2)$. In what follows we show how to reduce the potentially quadratic running time for the general case by not computing $\mathbb{X}$ explicitly, but considering only a linear number of intersection points. Roughly speaking, we avoid computing the set $\mathbb{X}$ (and the set of constraints induced by $\mathbb{X}$) explicitly, by using a random-sampling approach; this idea was first presented in [8]. Our method is similar to the LP algorithm in [6], and is sketched in Algorithm MinMaxDistance (Figure 2). For a subset $Y \subseteq \mathbb{X}$, let Optimal(Y) denote the optimal solution for Y, i.e., the lowest vertex in the convex polyhedron $\bigcap_{v \in Y} \gamma_v^+ \cap \gamma_v^-$. As mentioned above, this can be computed in $O(|Y|)$ expected time.

Since $\mathbb{X}$ is not explicitly computed, it is not straightforward to choose R and compute V, the set of *violated* vertices. We describe these two steps in detail. Let $\xi_0 = (s_0, t_0, z_0)$ and $f_0(x,y) = s_0 f(x,y) + t_0$.

Computing the violated vertices. By definition, a point $v \in \mathbb{X}$ is violated if $d_v(s_0, t_0) > z_0$, i.e., the vertical distance between (the graphs of) f_0 and g at v is larger than z_0. The vertical distances between f_0 and g at the vertices of $\mathbb{M}_f$ and $\mathbb{M}_g$ can be computed in a total of $O(n \log n)$ time. More challenging is therefore finding the intersection points of pairs of edges at which the vertical distance is larger than z_0— we want to report them only if there are at most $2n$ of them, without spending more time otherwise.

To report this type of violated points of $\mathbb{X}$, we proceed in two steps. First we use the so-called hereditary segment tree data structure to reduce the vertical-distance problem between line segments to a problem of reporting lines in 3D that are vertically more than z_0 apart. Then we solve that

Algorithm 1: MinMaxDistance

1. $R \leftarrow$ random subset of $\mathbb{X}$ of $\min\{|\mathbb{X}|, 9n\}$ points
2. **repeat**
3. $\quad \xi_0 \leftarrow$ Optimal(R)
4. $\quad V \leftarrow \{v \in \mathbb{X} \mid \xi_0 \notin \gamma_v^+ \cap \gamma_v^-\}$
5. $\quad$ **if** $|V| > 2n$ **then**
6. $\quad\quad R \leftarrow$ random subset of $\mathbb{X}$ of $\min\{|\mathbb{X}|, 9n\}$ points
7. $\quad$ **else** $R \leftarrow R \cup V$
8. **until** $V = \emptyset$
9. **return** ξ_0

Figure 2. The algorithm for computing $\mu_\infty(s,t)$.

problem by mapping the lines in $\mathbb{R}^3$ to Plücker points and Plücker hyperplanes, and solving a halfspace range reporting problem in $\mathbb{R}^5$. By using the trade-off techniques for halfspace range reporting we find all the violated constraints in $O^*(n^{4/3} + |V|)$ time, with the option to stop reporting if $|V| > 2n$. A more detailed description follows.

For the first part, we use a two-level hereditary segment tree T [5]. Let R and B be the sets of edges in $\mathbb{M}_f$ and $\mathbb{M}_g$, respectively. As in [5], T can be augmented to produce a bipartite clique decomposition of the intersecting pairs of segments in $R \times B$. That is, we compute a family $\mathcal{F} = \{(R_1, B_1), \ldots, (R_u, B_u)\}$, where $R_i \subseteq R, B_i \subseteq B$, such that

- (i) every segment in R_i intersects every segment in B_i;
- (ii) the left endpoints of all segments of R_i lie below the lines supporting every segment of B_i, or all of them lie above these lines;
- (iii) for every intersecting pair $(r,b) \in R \times B$ there is an i such that $r \in R_i, b \in B_i$;
- (iv) $\sum_i (|R_i| + |B_i|) = O(n \log^2 n)$.

$\mathcal{F}$ can be computed in $O(n \log^2 n)$ time. For each $(R_i, B_i) \in \mathcal{F}$, we "lift" every line segment $r \in R_i$ (resp. $b \in B_i$) to a line in $\mathbb{R}^3$, namely, the line containing the segment $f_0(r)$ (resp. $g(b)$). Let $\hat{R}_i$ and $\hat{B}_i$ be the sets of resulting lines in $\mathbb{R}^3$. We wish to report the pairs of lines in $\hat{R}_i \times \hat{B}_i$ that are vertically more than z_0 apart.

This second problem is transformed into a halfspace range reporting problem in $\mathbb{R}^5$, as follows. Testing whether two lines ℓ_1, ℓ_2 in $\mathbb{R}^3$ lie at a vertical distance of more than z_0 from each other can be formulated (after translating one of the lines by z_0) as testing whether the Plücker point of ℓ_1 lies in one of the halfspaces bounded by the Plücker hyperplane of ℓ_2. We map the lines from, say, $\hat{B}_i$, to Plücker points and perform a halfspace reporting query with each of the halfspaces bounded by the Plücker hyperplanes of the lines of $\hat{R}_i$. To solve the halfspace reporting problem we apply standard trade-off techniques for geometric range searching (see for example [1]). We build a data structure of size $O^*(n_i^{4/3})$, where $n_i = |R_i| + |B_i|$, that answers halfspace reporting queries in $O(n_i^{1/3} + p)$ time, where p is the output size of the query. In our context, each reported point corresponds to an intersecting pair of segments $(r,b) \in R \times B$ such that $d_v(s_0, t_0) > z_0$. We repeat this procedure for all bipartite cliques in $\mathcal{F}$. Note that in line 4 of the algorithm, we do not need to report all violated vertices of $\mathbb{X}$, but we can stop as soon as the number of reported pairs exceeds $2n$. Thus the total time spent in line 4 is $O^*(n^{4/3})$.

Choosing a random sample. We can use the bipartite clique decomposition $\mathcal{F}$ to choose a random point of $\mathbb{X}$, as follows. We first choose a random bipartite clique $(R_i, B_i) \in \mathcal{F}$; the probability of (R_i, B_i) being chosen is $|R_i| \cdot |B_i|/k$, where $k = \sum_j |R_j| \cdot |B_j|$ is the total number of intersecting pairs in $R \times B$. Next, we choose a random pair $(r, b) \in R_i \times B_i$, each pair is chosen with equal probability, and the desired point is $r \cap b$. After having computed $\mathcal{F}$, it takes $O(\log n)$ time to choose a random point. Hence, we can compute R in $O(n \log n)$ time.

Number of iterations. As argued in [6], it can be shown that line 7 of Algorithm MinMaxDistance (i.e., $|V| \leq 2n$) will be executed at most four times. This is because every time $\xi_0 \neq \text{Optimal}(\mathbb{X})$, i.e., $V \neq \emptyset$, the point of $\mathbb{X}$ corresponding to one of the three constraints that define $\text{Optimal}(\mathbb{X})$ is added to V (and thus to R in line 7), and from then on it remains in R. Therefore after executing line 7 at most three times, R will contain the three vertices that define the optimum, hence the optimum will be found in the next (fourth) iteration. Following the same argument as in [6], based on random sampling, we can prove that the expected number of iterations of the loop is $O(1)$. Hence, we can conclude:

Theorem 1. *Given two bivariate piecewise-linear functions over a common domain, a linear transformation minimizing the maximum distance between them can be found in $O^*(n^{4/3})$ expected time, where n is the total number of vertices in the graphs of these functions. If the functions are aligned, the transformation can be found in linear time.*

3. MINIMIZING THE AREA BETWEEN TWO UNIVARIATE FUNCTIONS

In this section, we assume $\mathbb{D} \subseteq \mathbb{R}$ to be a bounded interval and $f, g : \mathbb{D} \to \mathbb{R}$ to be two univariate piecewise-linear functions. Since the overlay of two one-dimensional subdivisions has linear complexity, we can assume that f and g are aligned and they are defined by a common subdivision $\mathbb{M}$ of $\mathbb{D}$. For any value of s and t, let $\mu(s,t)$ denote the area between $sf+t$ and g over $\mathbb{D}$. The goal is to compute $\arg\min_{s,t} \mu(s,t)$. We begin by analyzing the function μ.

Analytic form of μ. The analytic form of the bivariate function $\mu(s,t)$ depends on the set of pairs of intersecting edges of $sf+t$ and g. Let $x_1 < \cdots < x_n$ be the vertices of $\mathbb{M}$, and let $a_i = f(x_i)$, $b_i = g(x_i)$. Consider the vertical slab $[x_i, x_{i+1}] \times \mathbb{R}$, see Figure 3. Let f_i and g_i be the functions f and g, restricted to the interval $[x_i, x_{i+1}]$, and let μ_i be the area between the graphs of these functions, over the same domain. Unless f_i is constant (we deal with this degenerate situation in the full version of this paper), there is exactly one pair s, t that makes $sf_i + t = g_i$, and $\mu_i(s,t) = 0$. This happens when $sa_i + t = b_i$ and $sa_{i+1} + t = b_{i+1}$ simultaneously.

Lemma 1. *The region in the (s,t)-plane where $sf_i + t$ and g_i intersect is a double wedge whose bounding lines are $\ell_i : t = -a_i s + b_i$ and $\ell_{i+1} : t = -a_{i+1}s + b_{i+1}$. These lines intersect in the apex $(\bar{s}_i, \bar{t}_i)$, where $\bar{s}_i f_i + \bar{t}_i = g_i$ and $\mu_i(\bar{s}_i, \bar{t}_i) = 0$. Above ℓ_i and ℓ_{i+1} (in the direction of t), μ_i is linear in s and t, and the same is true below ℓ_i and ℓ_{i+1}. Below ℓ_i and*

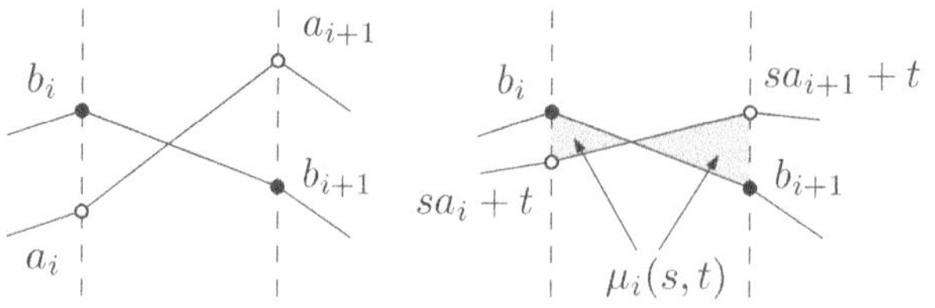

Figure 3. Edges of f and g, and the function $\mu_i(s,t)$.

above ℓ_{i+1} in the (s,t)-plane, we have

$$\mu_i(s,t) = (x_{i+1} - x_i) \cdot \frac{(b_i - sa_i - t)^2 + (sa_{i+1} - b_{i+1} + t)^2}{2(sa_{i+1} - sa_i - b_{i+1} + b_i)}.$$

A similar expression exists for the function that is valid in the wedge above ℓ_i and below ℓ_{i+1}.

Figure 4(a) shows the function $\mu_i(s,t)$ graphically. We observe that inside the double wedge defined by ℓ_i and ℓ_{i+1}, μ_i is a fraction (i.e., rational function) that has the unknown s in the denominator. To minimize μ, we must solve $\min_{s,t} \sum_{i=1}^{n-1} \mu_i(s,t)$, which is a sum of linear and rational functions and involves solving a polynomial of linear degree, if the minimum occurs where many pairs of edges of f and g intersect. We cannot hope to find an exact combinatorial solution in this case.

It will be useful to analyze the function μ_i closer. For a fixed scaling factor $\hat{s}$, consider $\mu_i(\hat{s}, t)$ as a function of t. By Lemma 1, $\mu_i(\hat{s}, t)$ is linear in t below ℓ_i and ℓ_{i+1}, or above both of them, and a quadratic function in t between ℓ_i and ℓ_{i+1}, i.e., $\mu_i(\hat{s}, t)$ consists of three pieces. Moreover, $\mu_i(\hat{s}, t)$ is symmetric and differentiable everywhere; see Figure 4(c). Despite its complicated form, we can prove the following for μ_i:

Lemma 2. *For every i, μ_i is a convex function, and the restriction of μ_i to a ray starting at $(\bar{s}_i, \bar{t}_i)$ is a linear function.*

Proof. For simplicity, we assume that $x_{i+1} - x_i = 1$. The lines ℓ_i and ℓ_{i+1} partition the st-plane into four wedges. The function μ_i is linear in the wedge lying above (or below) both ℓ_i and ℓ_{i+1}, so μ_i is obviously convex within each of these two wedges and linear along any ray emanating from $(\bar{s}_i, \bar{t}_i)$ within them. Next, we prove the convexity within each of the two other wedges. Consider the wedge W^+ lying below ℓ_i and above ℓ_{i+1}; the other case is symmetric. Let $\ell_i(s) = b_i - a_i s$ and $\ell_{i+1}(s) = b_{i+1} - a_{i+1}s$ be the linear functions defined by the lines ℓ_i and ℓ_{i+1}. We can then write $\mu_i(s,t)$ for W^+ (cf. Lemma 1) as

$$\mu_i(s,t) = \frac{(t - (\ell_i(s) + \ell_{i+1}(s))/2)^2}{\ell_i(s) - \ell_{i+1}(s)} + \frac{\ell_i(s) - \ell_{i+1}(s)}{4}.$$

Since a convex (resp. linear) function remains convex (resp. linear) under an affine transformation of its domain, we apply the affine transform $t' = t - (\ell_i(s) + \ell_{i+1}(s))/2$ and $s' = \ell_i(s) - \ell_{i+1}(s)$ and rewrite μ_i as

$$\mu_i(s', t') = \frac{t'^2}{s'} + \frac{s'}{4}.$$

Along a ray from $(s', t') = (0, 0)$ emanating into W^+, $t' = \alpha s'$, $\mu_i(s', \alpha s') = (\alpha^2 + 1/4)s'$ is linear. A similar argument holds in the diametrally opposite wedge W^-. Hence the graph

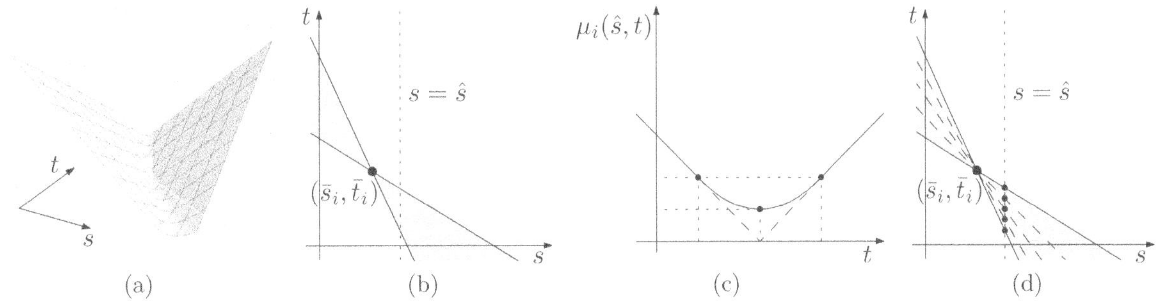

Figure 4. (a) Graph of $\mu_i(s,t)$. (b) Double wedge arising from f_i and g_i in the (s,t)-plane. (c) Cross-section in the plane $s = \hat{s}$ showing $\mu_i(\hat{s},t)$. (d) Subdivision into double wedges in the (s,t)-plane.

of $\mu(s',t')$ is a cone with origin at $(0,0)$ and to check its convexity it is sufficient to consider the univariate function $\mu(\hat{s}',t')$ along the line ℓ: $s' = \hat{s}' > 0$ (a symmetric analysis handles $\hat{s}' < 0$). In W^+, this function has the form $\mu_i(\hat{s}',t') = \frac{t'^2}{\hat{s}'} + \frac{\hat{s}'}{4}$ which is a convex quadratic function. Outside of W^+, $\mu_i(\hat{s}',t') = |t'|$ as is easily checked. Hence, at the point $(\hat{s}', \pm\hat{s}'/2)$ where line ℓ leaves W^+, the slopes of the two expressions for $\mu_i(\hat{s}',t')$ agree, so it is convex as a function of t'. From the above discussion, it follows that $\mu(s',t')$ and therefore $\mu(s,t)$ are convex over their entire range, completing the proof of the lemma. □

COROLLARY 1. *μ is a convex function.*

Approximating μ. Since it is hard to compute the minimum value of $\mu(s,t)$, we define a convex piecewise-linear function $\tilde{\mu}(s,t)$, for a given $\varepsilon > 0$, such that $\mu(s,t) \leq \tilde{\mu}(s,t) \leq (1+\varepsilon)\mu(s,t)$ for all $s,t \in \mathbb{R}$, and we compute $(\tilde{s},\tilde{t}) = \arg\min_{s,t} \tilde{\mu}(s,t)$.

For each i, we define an approximation $\tilde{\mu}_i$ of μ_i: μ_i is already linear outside the double wedge, so we set $\tilde{\mu}_i$ to μ_i outside the double wedges and focus on approximating the quadratic part of $\mu_i(s,t)$ inside the double wedge. We first fix a value $\hat{s}$ and approximate the univariate function $\mu(\hat{s},t)$. We choose $\lceil 2/\sqrt{\varepsilon} \rceil$ points on the graph of $\mu_i(\hat{s},t)$, equally spaced along the line $s = \hat{s}$, such that the maximum distance between the polygonal line through the chosen points and $\mu_i(\hat{s},t)$ itself is at most $\varepsilon\mu_i(\hat{s},t)$, see Figure 4(d). We extend this approximation to all values of s by choosing lines through the new points and $(\bar{s}_i,\bar{t}_i)$, giving a partition of the plane into $\Theta(1/\sqrt{\varepsilon})$ wedges. Lemma 2 ensures that $\tilde{\mu}_i(s,t) \leq (1+\varepsilon)\mu_i(s,t)$ everywhere. We set $\tilde{\mu}(s,t) := \sum_i \tilde{\mu}_i(s,t)$. By construction and the convexity of μ, we can prove the following

LEMMA 3. *$\tilde{\mu}$ is convex and $\mu(s,t) \leq \tilde{\mu}(s,t) \leq (1+\varepsilon)\mu(s,t)$.*

Approximation algorithm. We now describe the algorithm for computing the pair $(\tilde{s},\tilde{t})$ that minimizes $\tilde{\mu}$. Let L be the set of lines in the (s,t)-plane, used to define the functions $\tilde{\mu}_i$. Set $n' := |L| = O(n/\sqrt{\varepsilon})$. The function $\tilde{\mu}$ is linear within each cell of the arrangement $\mathcal{A}(L)$. The minimum is achieved at a vertex of $\mathcal{A}(L)$. By traversing $\mathcal{A}(L)$ and computing the minimum value of $\tilde{\mu}$ at each vertex, $(\tilde{s},\tilde{t})$ can be computed in $O(n^2/\varepsilon)$ time.

A more efficient solution can be obtained by exploiting the convexity of $\tilde{\mu}$ and using a prune-and-search approach. We compute a $(1/2)$-cutting Ξ of L of size $O(1)$ in $O(n')$ time [4]. Ξ is a tiling of the plane by a constant number of triangles with the property that at most half of the lines of L cross each triangle of Ξ and each vertex of Ξ is a vertex of $\mathcal{A}(L)$. Along each of the $O(1)$ edges e of Ξ, we compute $\tilde{\mu}$ over e and find its minimum and gradient at the minimum in $O(n')$ time, which will reveal the triangle $\Delta \in \Xi$ containing $(\tilde{s},\tilde{t})$. We recurse on the lines of L that cross Δ; their number is at most $n'/2$ by the definition of $(1/2)$-cuttings. The contributions from the remaining $\tilde{\mu}_i$ sum up to a single linear function over Δ and can be easily kept track of in constant additional time. After $O(\log n')$ phases of divide-and-conquer, which together take $O(n')$ time, we find a triangle that lies in a single cell of $\mathcal{A}(L)$ and $(\tilde{s},\tilde{t})$ is a vertex of the triangle, from which we can easily compute $(\tilde{s},\tilde{t})$.

THEOREM 2. *Let f and g be two univariate piecewise-linear functions with a total of n pieces. For any fixed $\varepsilon > 0$, a pair $(\tilde{s},\tilde{t})$ can be computed in $O(n/\sqrt{\varepsilon})$ time such that $\sigma(f,g) \leq \mu(\tilde{s},\tilde{t}) \leq (1+\varepsilon)\sigma(f,g)$.*

4. MINIMIZING THE VOLUME BETWEEN TWO BIVARIATE FUNCTIONS

We extend the approach of the previous section to the case where f and g are two aligned bivariate functions, defined by a common triangulation $\mathbb{M}$ of $\mathbb{D}$. The main difficulty in generalizing the above approach is that the analogue of function μ_i, though convex, is much less well behaved. In the previous case, the bivariate function $\mu_i(s,t)$ behaves essentially as a univariate function, in the sense that its graph is a surface of a convex cone. As we require a different method to approximate the volume over a single triangle of $\mathbb{M}$, we obtain an $O(n/\varepsilon^2)$ time algorithm to compute a pair $\tilde{s},\tilde{t}$ such that $\sigma(f,g) \leq \mu(\tilde{s},\tilde{t}) \leq (1+\varepsilon)\sigma(f,g)$.

Analysis of μ over a triangle. Let $\Delta = \Delta v_i v_j v_k$ be a triangle of $\mathbb{M}$, and let Δ_f and Δ_g be the triangles in the graph of f and g, respectively, defined by Δ (i.e., Δ is their xy-projection). Let a_i, a_j, and a_k be the vertices of Δ_f, and let b_i, b_j, and b_k be the corresponding vertices of Δ_g. With slight abuse of notation, we use a_i, a_j, and a_k, and b_i, b_j, and b_k to denote the function values of these vertices as well (i.e., $a_i = f(v_i)$, $b_i = g(v_i)$, etc.). Without loss of generality, we assume that Δ is an equilateral triangle with side length 1. Depending on the scaling s and translation t, triangle $s \cdot \Delta_f + t$ may intersect, be above, or be below Δ_g. The volume between the triangles is therefore composed of one or two parts.

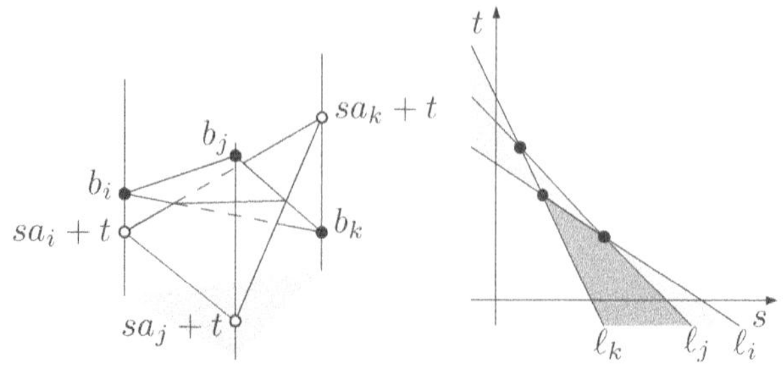

(a) (b)

Figure 5. (a) A pair of intersecting triangles with common (x, y)-projection. (b) The situation of (a) corresponds to values of (s, t) in the dark cell of the parameter space.

In the (s,t)-plane, let $\ell_i : t = b_i - sa_i$ represent the set of points (s, t) at which vertex v_i of Δ_g and $s\Delta_f + t$ coincide; ℓ_j and ℓ_k are defined analogously. We will also view ℓ_i as a univariate function $\ell_i(s) = b_i - sa_i$ and use a similar convention for ℓ_j and ℓ_k. Generally, these three lines partition the (s, t)-plane into seven cells, see Figure 5(b). Let $\mathcal{A}_3$ denote this planar decomposition. Inside a cell of $\mathcal{A}_3$, for every choice of s and t, the same subset of vertices of $s \cdot \Delta_f + t$ lies above Δ_g, and the volume between these triangles can be expressed by a single analytic function. For example, for two triangles in the configuration shown in Figure 5(a), the expression for the volume between the triangles (assuming their projection is equilateral with unit side length) is

$$\begin{aligned}\mu_{ijk}(s,t) = {} & \frac{\sqrt{3}}{12}(\ell_i(s) + \ell_j(s) + \ell_k(s) - 3t) \\ & + \frac{\sqrt{3}}{6} \cdot \frac{(t - \ell_k(s))^3}{(\ell_i(s) - \ell_k(s)) \cdot (\ell_j(s) - \ell_k(s))}.\end{aligned} \tag{5}$$

More precisely, the formula is valid whenever $sa_i + t$ lies below b_i, $sa_j + t$ lies below b_j, and $sa_k + t$ is above b_k. Let us examine a value $\hat{s}$ of s at which the line $s = \hat{s}$ intersects the lines ℓ_k, ℓ_i, ℓ_j, in this order, bottom to top. The form of the function μ_{ijk} in the cells of $\mathcal{A}_3$ met by this line are, in bottom to top order: $\frac{\sqrt{3}}{12}(\ell_i(s) + \ell_j(s) + \ell_k(s) - 3t)$, the form given by (5),

$$\begin{aligned}& \frac{\sqrt{3}}{12}(3t - (\ell_i(s) + \ell_j(s) + \ell_k(s))) \\ & \qquad + \frac{\sqrt{3}}{6} \frac{(\ell_j(s) - t)^3}{(\ell_j(s) - \ell_i(s)) \cdot (\ell_j(s) - \ell_k(s))},\end{aligned} \tag{6}$$

and finally $\frac{\sqrt{3}}{12}(3t - \ell_i(s) - \ell_j(s) - \ell_k(s))$. The equations correspond, respectively, to $s \cdot \Delta_f + t$ lying below all vertices of Δ_g, above only b_k, above b_k and b_i, and above all of them. In the remaining three faces of this arrangement, the form of the function is given by similar formulas, obtained from (5) or (6) by a permutation of indices.

LEMMA 4. *$\mu_{ijk}(s, t)$ is a convex function.*

PROOF. Since μ_{ijk} measures the volume lying vertically between two surfaces in xyz-space, its convexity is not affected by an affine transformation of the (x, y)-plane. In particular, we have already taken the liberty of assuming that Δ is an equilateral triangle with side length 1 in the above expressions for μ_{ijk}.

Our proof consists of two steps: We first verify that μ_{ijk} is convex over every face of $\mathcal{A}_3$ and then check that the convexity is not locally violated along the "seams," i.e., along the three lines separating the cells of $\mathcal{A}_3$, which form the locus of points where the analytic expression defining μ_{ijk} changes.

For the first step, there is nothing to prove in the top and bottom cells of $\mathcal{A}_3$, as the function is linear there. In the other faces, up to a permutation of i, j, k, it has a form given in (5) or (6).

Without loss of generality, suppose the function has the form of (5). For the purpose of determining convexity, since the first term is linear, the function is convex if and only if the second term is convex. By applying an appropriate transform to simplify the second term and computing its Hessian directly (and recalling that, by construction, in the relevant face of $\mathcal{A}_3$, we have $t > \ell_k(s)$, $\ell_i(s) > \ell_k(s)$, and $\ell_j(s) > \ell_k(s)$), we can verify that the Hessian is non-negative in the desired region. We omit the tedious details from this abstract.

For the second step of the proof, let $M = \{(s, t, \mu_{ijk}(s, t)) : (s, t) \in \mathbb{R}^2\}$ be the graph of μ_{ijk}. We will argue that M has a well-defined tangent plane at every point (projecting to a point) on the bounding lines ℓ_i, ℓ_j, ℓ_k, by determining the tangent plane at an interior point (s, t) of a cell of $\mathcal{A}_3$ and computing its limit as (s, t) approaches a bounding line. Since the analytical expressions for the function valid on opposite sides of an arrangement edge agree along the edge (the function is continuous), the "slopes" of the two expressions along the edge agree, so it is sufficient to check that their slopes in some other direction, not parallel to the line, agree as well, to conclude that the tangent planes given by the expressions on both sides of the edge coincide and therefore M has a well-defined tangent plane at the point.

We pick the direction of a line $s = \hat{s}$, for some fixed $\hat{s}$. Our plan is to check that the function $\mu_{ijk}(\hat{s}, t)$ of t has a well-defined tangent at the three points where this line crosses the bounding lines ℓ_i, ℓ_j, ℓ_k; this is done by computing the one-sided derivatives of this univariate function on both sides of each line and verifying that they agree.

For the situation described in Figure 5, $\mu_{ijk}(s, t)$ is given by (5). The following calculation assumes that the line $\gamma : s = \hat{s}$ crosses the lines ℓ_k, ℓ_i, ℓ_j, in this order, bottom to top. (5) applies to the second face from the bottom in $\mathcal{A}_3$ crossed by γ. The one-sided derivative at $\gamma \cap \ell_i$ is given by

$$\begin{aligned}\left.\frac{\partial}{\partial t}\mu_{ijk}(\hat{s}, t)\right|_{t\uparrow\ell_i(\hat{s})} &= \frac{\partial}{\partial t}\left[\frac{\sqrt{3}}{12}(\ell_i(\hat{s}) + \ell_j(\hat{s}) + \ell_k(\hat{s}) - 3t) \right. \\ &\qquad \left. + \frac{\sqrt{3}}{6} \frac{(t - \ell_k(\hat{s}))^3}{(\ell_i(\hat{s}) - \ell_k(\hat{s})) \cdot (\ell_j(\hat{s}) - \ell_k(\hat{s}))}\right]_{t\uparrow\ell_i(\hat{s})} \\ &= \left[-\frac{\sqrt{3}}{4} + \frac{\sqrt{3}}{6} \frac{3(t - \ell_k(\hat{s}))^2}{(\ell_i(\hat{s}) - \ell_k(\hat{s})) \cdot (\ell_j(\hat{s}) - \ell_k(\hat{s}))}\right]_{t\uparrow\ell_i(\hat{s})} \\ &= -\frac{\sqrt{3}}{4} + \frac{\sqrt{3}}{2} \cdot \frac{(\ell_i(\hat{s}) - \ell_k(\hat{s}))^2}{(\ell_i(\hat{s}) - \ell_k(\hat{s})) \cdot (\ell_j(\hat{s}) - \ell_k(\hat{s}))} \\ &= -\frac{\sqrt{3}}{4} + \frac{\sqrt{3}}{2} \cdot \frac{\ell_i(\hat{s}) - \ell_k(\hat{s})}{\ell_j(\hat{s}) - \ell_k(\hat{s})} \\ &= \frac{\sqrt{3}}{4} \cdot \frac{(\ell_i(\hat{s}) - \ell_k(\hat{s})) + (\ell_i(\hat{s}) - \ell_j(\hat{s}))}{\ell_j(\hat{s}) - \ell_k(\hat{s})}.\end{aligned}$$

We now repeat the calculation for $\mu_{ijk}(s, t)$ above the line

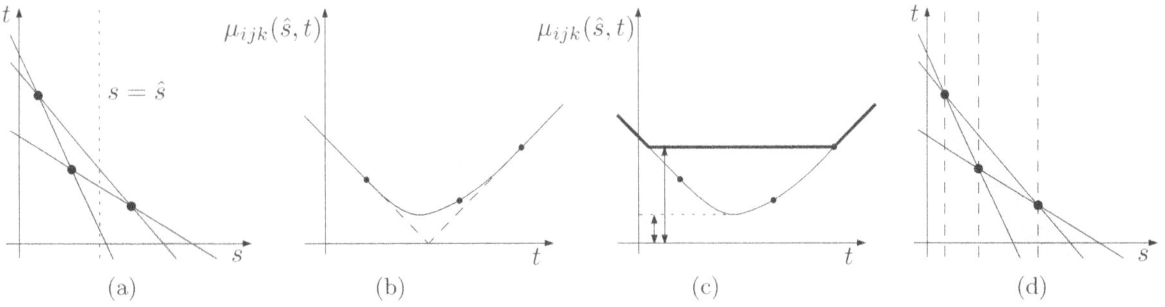

Figure 6. (a) Three lines in the (s,t)-plane corresponding to the three vertices of a triangle of $\mathbb{M}$. (b) The vertical cross-section of the surface $\mu_{ijk}(s,t)$ for a fixed value $s=\hat{s}$ consists of four pieces (two linear and two cubic), separated by three breakpoints that correspond to the three vertices of the triangle. (c) The highest breakpoint is not more than a constant times higher than the lowest point in the cross-section, therefore it can be approximated by a function consisting of three linear pieces. (d) At a value of s where two of the lines in the (s,t)-plane meet, the form of the function in the cross-section changes.

ℓ_i, as given by (6), obtaining

$$\frac{\partial}{\partial t}\mu_{ijk}(\hat{s},t)|_{t\downarrow\ell_i(\hat{s})} = \frac{\sqrt{3}}{4}\cdot\frac{(\ell_i(\hat{s})-\ell_k(\hat{s}))+(\ell_i(\hat{s})-\ell_j(\hat{s}))}{\ell_j(\hat{s})-\ell_k(\hat{s})},$$

showing that indeed $\mu_{ijk}(\hat{s},t)$, as a function of t, is smooth at $t=\ell_i(\hat{s})$. (We have considered the hard case, where two non-linear expressions for μ_{ijk} meet across a line, here ℓ_i. A similar argument can be made where the linear and non-linear portions of μ_{ijk} meet; here at the intersections of γ with ℓ_k and ℓ_j. The details are omitted in this version.) Therefore along the line $s=\hat{s}$, the function $\mu_{ijk}(\hat{s},t)$ is smooth everywhere. By the above argument, $\mu_{ijk}(s,t)$ must have a well-defined tangent plane at every point of its domain. This, together with the fact that it is convex over every cell of $\mathcal{A}_3$, implies that $\mu_{ijk}(s,t)$ is convex everywhere. □

Considering the situation along a line $s=\hat{s}$ again, we see that when $\hat{s}\cdot\Delta_f+t$ and Δ_g do not intersect, $\mu_{ijk}(\hat{s},t)$ is a linear function in t. When they do intersect, the function is piecewise-cubic. More precisely, as can be seen from (5) and (6) by setting $s=\hat{s}$, $\mu_{ijk}(\hat{s},t)$ has (at most) three break points, it is a cubic function between consecutive break points and linear outside the break points, see Figure 6(b). The proof implies that it is differentiable everywhere including at the break points.

A constant-factor approximation for μ_{ijk}. We continue by showing that $\mu_{ijk}(s,t)$ can be approximated within a factor 16 by a constant-complexity piecewise-linear function.

LEMMA 5. *For any fixed $\hat{s}$, the value of $\mu_{ijk}(\hat{s},t)$ at its break points is at most 16 times the value of $\mu_{ijk}(\hat{s},t)$ at its minimum.*

PROOF. By rescaling the triangle, we will assume for the duration of this proof that the xy-projections of Δ_f and Δ_g have unit area. If, for $s=\hat{s}$ and some t, the triangles do not intersect, then the volume between $\hat{s}\cdot\Delta_f+t$ and Δ_g is simply the average distance between the triangles at the three vertices. At the break points, one distance is zero: $a_i\hat{s}+t=b_i$, $a_j\hat{s}+t=b_j$, or $a_k\hat{s}+t=b_k$. Assume without loss of generality that $\hat{s}\cdot\Delta_f+t$ and Δ_g do not properly intersect when $a_j\hat{s}+t=b_j$, nor when $a_k\hat{s}+t=b_k$; they define the extreme break points in Figure 6(b).

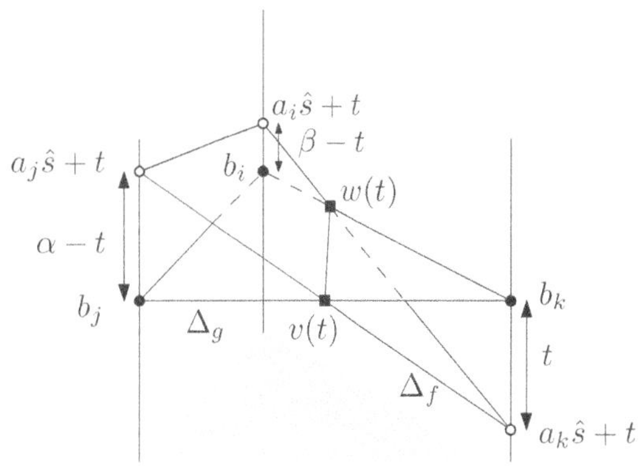

Figure 7. Illustration of the proof of Lemma 5.

Let $\alpha=(a_j\hat{s}+t)-b_j+b_k-(a_k\hat{s}+t)=a_j\hat{s}-b_j+b_k-a_k\hat{s}$ be the maximum vertical distance between any two points on Δ_f and Δ_g if they intersect. Let $\beta=(a_i\hat{s}+t)-b_i+b_k-(a_ks+t)=a_is-b_i+b_k-a_k\hat{s}$, and assume $\beta\geq\alpha/2$ (otherwise, exchange the roles of j and k and we are in the desired situation). Now β is the maximum height difference at the vertices with index i when $\hat{s}\cdot\Delta_f+t$ and Δ_g intersect. See Figure 7.

The maximum volume at a break point then is $(\alpha+\beta+0)/3\leq 2\alpha/3$, which occurs when t is such that $a_k\hat{s}+t=b_k$. Reparameterize t such that $t=0$ in this case, and t is positive when $\hat{s}\cdot\Delta_f+t$ and Δ_g intersect. The minimum volume in between occurs for some $0\leq t\leq\alpha$. We will distinguish two cases depending on the value of t, and show that a relatively big tetrahedron exists between $\hat{s}\cdot\Delta_f+t$ and Δ_g whose volume is at least $\alpha/24$.

Let $e(t)$ be the intersection edge of $\hat{s}\cdot\Delta_f+t$ and Δ_g. Let $v(t)$ be the endpoint of $e(t)$ that lies on the side b_jb_k of Δ_g, and let $w(t)$ be the other endpoint, on b_ib_k or b_ib_j.

First, assume that $t\geq\alpha/2$. If $w(t)\in b_ib_k$, then the projected area of $\triangle b_kv(t)w(t)$ is at least $1/4$, and hence the volume of the tetrahedron $b_kv(t)w(t)(a_k\hat{s}+t)$ is at least $\alpha/24$ because $b_k-(a_k\hat{s}+t)=t\geq\alpha/2$. And if $w(t)\in b_ib_j$, then the projected area of $\triangle b_kv(t)b_i$ is at least $1/2$, and hence the volume of the tetrahedron $b_kv(t)b_i(a_k\hat{s}+t)$ is at least $\alpha/12$.

Second, assume that $t<\alpha/2$. Then $w(t)\in b_ib_k$ by the assumption $\beta\geq\alpha/2$. The projected area of $\triangle b_jb_iv(t)$ is at least 1/2, and the volume of the tetrahedron $b_j b_i v(t)(a_j \hat{s} + t)$ is at least $\alpha/12$ because $(a_j \hat{s} + t) - b_j = t > \alpha/2$.

Hence, the volume at a break point is at most 16 times the volume at the minimum in all cases. □

It follows that we can create a piecewise-linear 16-approximation of $\mu_{ijk}(\hat{s}, t)$ by taking the highest break point, choosing the unique other point on $\mu_{ijk}(\hat{s}, t)$ that has the same height, using a constant function between them, and the linear functions of $\mu_{ijk}(\hat{s}, t)$ outside, see Figure 6(c).

Let $[\tau_1, \tau_2]$ be the interval of t-values for which $\hat{s} \cdot \Delta_f + t$ and Δ_g intersect. We call $[\tau_1, \tau_2]$ the *intersection range* for Δ_f, Δ_g, and $\hat{s}$, and let $r = \tau_2 - \tau_1$.

LEMMA 6. *For a fixed $s = \hat{s}$, the piecewise-linear 16-approximation is exact for all $t \leq \tau_1 - r$ and also for all $t \geq \tau_2 + r$.*

PROOF. First, observe that the extensions of the linear parts of $\mu_{ijk}(\hat{s}, t)$ intersect the s-axis of the (s, t)-plane in the same point, see also Figure 6(b). Since the slopes of the linear parts of $\mu_{ijk}(\hat{s}, t)$ are also the same, the constant part of the 16-approximation has a range for t that cannot be more than twice the intersection range of Δ_f, Δ_g, and $\hat{s}$. The lemma follows. □

Now we go back to the whole (s, t)-plane to extend the 16-approximation to a piecewise-linear bivariate function. If we consider $\mu_{ijk}(\hat{s}, t)$ for changing values of $\hat{s}$, the outer break points translate linearly in $\hat{s}$, because $\mu_{ijk}(s, t)$ is linear in the bottom and top cells of $\mathcal{A}_3$. Hence, extending the 16-approximation of $\mu_{ijk}(\hat{s}, t)$ to a piecewise-linear function over the (s, t)-plane is natural, as long as the same line among ℓ_i, ℓ_j, and ℓ_k defines the highest break point. If we draw vertical (i.e., parallel to the t-axis) lines through the three intersections of ℓ_i, ℓ_j, and ℓ_k, the (s, t)-plane is partitioned into four strips, and inside each strip, we have the same outer two lines, see Figure 6(d). Which one gives the highest $\mu_{ijk}(\hat{s}, .)$ value, for increasing values of $\hat{s}$, can change only once in each strip. We take another vertical line at such a location, giving at most eight strips. Inside each strip, we use three linear functions, and hence the graph of the function consists of no more than 24 patches. Finally, it is not hard to prove that the resulting function is convex, by analysing its behaviour along the breakpoints. Hence, we obtain:

LEMMA 7. *A piecewise-linear convex factor-16 approximation $\tilde{\mu}_{ijk}(s, t)$ of $\mu_{ijk}(s, t)$ exists with $O(1)$ complexity. Moreover, for any $\hat{s}$, $\tilde{\mu}_{ijk}(\hat{s}, t) = \mu_{ijk}(\hat{s}, t)$ for all t at which $\mu_{ijk}(\hat{s}, t) \geq \mu_{ijk}(\hat{s}, \hat{t})$, where $(\hat{s}, \hat{t})$ is the highest break point of the function $\mu_{ijk}(\hat{s}, t)$.*

A $(1 + \varepsilon)$-approximation for μ_{ijk}. To obtain a $(1 + \varepsilon)$-approximation for μ_{ijk}, we will use a different approach than the one in the previous section. Let $\varepsilon > 0$ be given, and assume $\varepsilon \leq \frac{1}{2}$. We will partition Δ into a family Ξ of $\Theta(1/\varepsilon^2)$ equal triangles by partitioning the three edges of Δ using m equally-spaced points on each edge, and choosing edges parallel to the sides of Δ. The parameter m is chosen to be $\lceil c/\varepsilon \rceil$ for a suitable constant c. For each triangle $\rho \in \Xi$, we define the functions μ_ρ and $\tilde{\mu}_\rho$ analogous to μ_{ijk} and $\tilde{\mu}_{ijk}$. By construction, $\sum_{\rho \in \Xi} \mu_\rho(s, t) = \mu_{ijk}(s, t)$.

We now apply Lemma 6 to the subtriangles. Assume that $s \cdot \Delta_f + t$ and Δ_g intersect along an edge e. If we fix s but

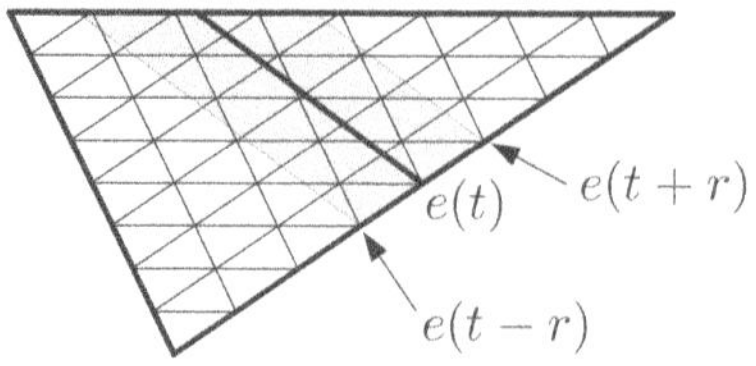

Figure 8. The subtriangles that do not intersect the gray strip Ψ give the exact volume in the 16-approximation.

vary t, the edge $e(t)$ moves parallel to itself in, say, Δ_g. For any subtriangle ρ, the intersection range $[\tau_1, \tau_2]$ is exactly the interval of t where $e(t)$ intersects ρ. By Lemma 6, the 16-approximation of the volume at ρ is exact when $t \leq \tau_1 - r$ or $t \geq \tau_2 + r$. This is true when the supporting line of $e(t)$ misses ρ by a sufficient distance, namely, exactly the same distance as the extent of ρ in the direction normal to $e(t)$. In Figure 8, this is the case for subtriangles that do not intersect the gray strip, which we denote Ψ. Note that if we increase m, the subtriangles shrink, and so does Ψ. Also note that Ψ depends on s, t, m, and the particular triangles Δ_f and Δ_g.

We define the approximation $\tilde{\mu}_{ijk}(s, t) = \sum_{\rho \in \Xi} \tilde{\mu}_\rho(s, t)$. We now prove that $\tilde{\mu}_{ijk}$ is a piecewise-linear convex function and that $\tilde{\mu}_{ijk}(s, t) \leq (1 + \varepsilon)\mu_{ijk}(s, t)$. The convexity of $\tilde{\mu}_{ijk}$ follows directly from Lemma 7. It remains to prove the approximation factor.

The intuition behind the approximation factor is the following. Regardless of the value of s and t, $s \cdot \Delta_f + t$ and Δ_g intersect in at most one segment. The subtriangles that intersect the strip Ψ will give (at worst) a 16-approximation of the volume. All subtriangles that miss Ψ give the exact value of the volume. Since there are many more (by a factor of $\Omega(1/\varepsilon)$) subtriangles that give the exact volume, and the other ones stay within a constant factor, we can argue that our approximation $\tilde{\mu}_{ijk}(s, t)$ stays within a factor $1 + \varepsilon$ of the real $\mu_{ijk}(s, t)$, for the right choice of c.

LEMMA 8. *For any s, t, any subtriangle ρ that intersects $(s \cdot \Delta_f + t) \cap \Delta_g$ defines a volume that is at most twice as large as the volume of a subtriangle that misses $(s \cdot \Delta_f + t) \cap \Delta_g$.*

PROOF. Let h be the vertical difference between $(s \cdot \Delta_f + t)$ and Δ_g along $e(t - r)$ and $e(t + r)$. Along $e(t)$, the difference is 0. So, a subtriangle that intersects $e(t)$ can have, in the best case, two vertices with a height of h and one with 0, leading to an area of at most $\frac{2}{3}hA$ if A is the area of the projection of ρ. On the other hand, a subtriangle that misses $e(t)$ will in the worst case have two vertices with height (almost) 0 and one with height at least h, leading to an area of at least $\frac{1}{3}hA$. □

LEMMA 9. *At most $6m + 3$ subtriangles intersect the strip Ψ, and at least $m^2 - 4m - 3$ subtriangles miss it.*

PROOF. A triangle is partitioned into $m^2 + 2m$ subtriangles. Any line intersects at most $2m + 1$ of them. All subtriangles meeting Ψ meet three lines parallel to $e(t)$. □

Consider the optimal s and t, and consider two triangles $s \cdot \Delta_f + t$ and Δ_g that intersect. Let V be the largest volume that two intersecting subtriangles of $s \cdot \Delta_f + t$ and Δ_g can give. Then all subtriangles that miss Ψ give a total volume in between of at least $(m^2 - 4m - 3)V/2$ by Lemmas 8 and 9, and for them the "approximation" is the exact volume by Lemma 7. The total volume of the triangles intersecting

Ψ that our approximation returns is at most $16(6m+3)V$ by Lemmas 7 and 9. Hence the relative error is at most $16(6m+3) \cdot V/((m^2-4m-3) \cdot V/2) = \Theta(1/m)$. Since $m = \lceil c/\varepsilon \rceil$ and $\varepsilon < \frac{1}{2}$, we can choose c large enough but still constant to obtain a relative error of at most ε.

A $(1+\varepsilon)$-approximation algorithm. We have all ingredients to give a $(1+\varepsilon)$-approximation algorithm for computing $\sigma(f,g)$. For each triangle $\Delta = \triangle v_i v_j v_k$ in $\mathbb{M}$, we compute the piecewise-linear factor-$(1+\varepsilon)$ approximation $\tilde{\mu}_{ijk}$ of μ_{ijk}. We set $\tilde{\mu} = \sum_{\triangle v_i v_j v_k \in \mathbb{M}} \tilde{\mu}_{ijk}$ and observe that $\tilde{\mu}$ is convex as well. We compute the minimum value of $\tilde{\mu}$, using the same prune-and-search procedure as in the previous section. Since each $\tilde{\mu}_{ijk}$ is defined as the sum of $O(1/\varepsilon^2)$ piecewise-linear convex functions, it follows that the total time spent is $O(n/\varepsilon^2)$. Omitting the details, we conclude with the following result.

THEOREM 3. *Let f and g be two aligned piecewise-linear bivariate functions, defined by a triangulation composed of n triangles, and let $\varepsilon > 0$ be a parameter. We can compute in $O(n/\varepsilon^2)$ time a pair $\tilde{s}, \tilde{t}$ and the value $\mu(\tilde{s}, \tilde{t})$ such that $\sigma(f,g) \leq \mu(\tilde{s},\tilde{t}) \leq (1+\varepsilon)\sigma(f,g)$.*

Remark. For unaligned functions, the n in the time bound is replaced by k, the overlay complexity, as described in the introduction. In the worst case, $k = \Theta(n^2)$, but in practice, one can expect it to be close to linear.

5. CONCLUSIONS

We studied the algorithmic aspects of determining the best linear model for two bivariate functions, modeled as polyhedral terrains. A number of open problems remain. It is possible that for the minimum area and volume measures, a strong LTAS exists, where the running time dependence on n and ε is in separate terms. It may also be possible to improve on the worst-case quadratic running time results for the volume and squared measures, in case the two terrains are not aligned. Finally, optimizing over more complex transformations than linear, or finding a linear model for more than two bivariate functions, leads to problems where there are more than two unknowns. These extensions are worth studying further.

6. REFERENCES

[1] P. K. Agarwal and J. Erickson. Geometric range searching and its relatives. In B. Chazelle, J. E. Goodman, and R. Pollack, editors, *Advances in Discrete and Computational Geometry*, volume 223 of *Contemporary Mathematics*, pages 1–56. American Mathematical Society, Providence, RI, 1999.

[2] H. Alt and L. J. Guibas. Discrete geometric shapes: Matching, interpolation, and approximation. In J.-R. Sack and J. Urrutia, editors, *Handbook of Computational Geometry*, pages 121–153. Elsevier, 2000.

[3] P. Burrough and R. McDonnell. *Principles of Geographical Information Systems*. Oxford University Press, 1998.

[4] B. Chazelle. Cutting hyperplanes for divide-and-conquer. *Discrete & Computational Geometry*, 9:145–158, 1993.

[5] B. Chazelle, H. Edelsbrunner, L. J. Guibas, and M. Sharir. Algorithms for bichromatic line segment problems and polyhedral terrains. *Algorithmica*, 11:116–132, 1994.

[6] K. L. Clarkson. Las Vegas algorithms for linear and integer programming when the dimension is small. *Journal of the ACM*, 42:488–499, 1995.

[7] M. de Berg, H. J. Haverkort, S. Thite, and L. Toma. I/O-efficient map overlay and point location in low-density subdivisions. In *Proc. 18th Annu. Int. Symp. on Algorithms and Computation*, volume 4835 of *Lecture Notes in Computer Science*, pages 500–511, 2007.

[8] H. Edelsbrunner, L. J. Guibas, J. Hershberger, R. Seidel, M. Sharir, J. Snoeyink, and E. Welzl. Implicitly representing arrangements of lines or segments. *Discrete & Computational Geometry*, 4:433–466, 1989.

[9] H. Edelsbrunner, J. Harer, V. Natarajan, and V. Pascucci. Local and global comparison of continuous functions. In *IEEE Visualization*, pages 275–280, 2004.

[10] U. Finke and K. Hinrichs. Overlaying simply connected planar subdivisions in linear time. In *Proc. 11th Annu. Symp. on Computational Geometry*, pages 119–126, 1995.

[11] E. Isaaks and R. Srivastava. *Applied Geostatistics*. Oxford University Press, 1989.

[12] H. Li and R. Tasay. A unified approach to identifying multivariate time series models. *Journal of the American Statistical Association*, 93:770–782, 1998.

[13] L. O'Brian. *Introducing Quantitative Geography*. Routledge, 1992.

[14] D. O'Sullivan and D. Unwin. *Geographic Information Analysis*. Wiley, 2003.

[15] H. Wackernagel. *Multivariate Geostatistics: An Introduction with Applications*. Springer, 3rd edition, 2003.

[16] W. Wei. *Time Series Analysis: Univariate and Multivariate Methods*. Addison-Wesley, 1990.

Applications of Geometry and Topology for Quadrilateral Mesh Processing and Verifiable Visualization

Cláudio T. Silva
University of Utah
72 S. Central Campus Dr. WEB 3750
Salt Lake City, UT 84112
csilva@cs.utah.edu

ABSTRACT

Computational geometry, computer graphics, and visualization are closely related ares that have had great synergy over the years. Point-based graphics [8], for example, grew out of contributions from all of these different areas. In this talk, we present results that show non-trivial applications of geometric and topological techniques to graphics and visualization. We also discuss how some of our recent work on graphics and visualization can foster further developments in computational geometry. In particular, we advocate the need for work in quad mesh processing, and a greater emphasis on the verification of geometric algorithms and implementations.

Categories and Subject Descriptors

I.3 [**Computer Graphics**]: Miscellaneous; I.3.5 [**Computational Geometry and Object Modeling**]: Geometric algorithms, languages, and systems

General Terms

Algorithms, Experimentation, Theory, Verification

Keywords

Quadrilateral Mesh Processing, Verifiable Visualization

1. Quadrilateral Mesh Processing

Although in the past geometry processing methods have been dominated by techniques that operate on triangular meshes, there is a growing interest in developing algorithms that operate natively on quad meshes (i.e., meshes composed of only quadrilateral elements). The motivation for the use of this type of mesh has been well articulated in pioneering work on quad re-meshing (see e.g., [1, 5, 10]).

We will present recent work in the general area of quadrilateral mesh processing. We start with the simplification algorithm for meshes composed of quadrilateral elements from Daniels et al [4]. This algorithm is reminiscent of edge-collapse based methods for triangle meshes, but it takes a novel approach to the challenging problem of maintaining the quadrilateral connectivity during level-of-detail creation. The method consists of a set of unit operations applied to the dual of the mesh, each designed to improve mesh structure and maintain topological genus. Geometric shape is maintained by an extension of a quadric error metric to quad meshes. The technique is straightforward to implement and efficient enough to be applied to real-world models. Our technique can handle models with sharp features, and can be used to re-mesh general polygonal, i.e., tri- and quad-dominant, meshes into quad-only meshes. Then, we show how to design a localized *polychord* collapse operator to better control and preserve important surface components [2].

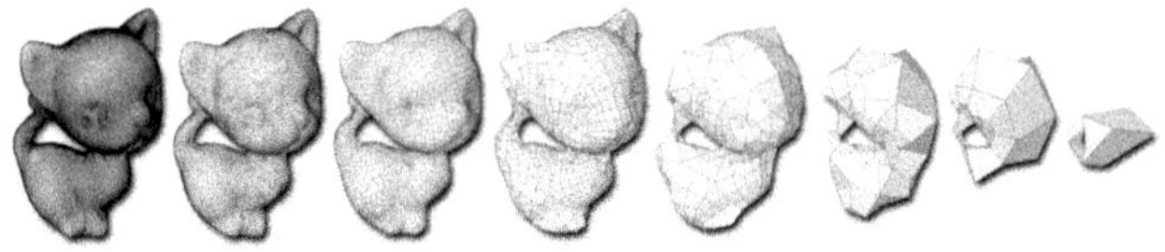

Figure 1: A pure quad level-of-detail hierarchy generated by the algorithm of Daniels et al. [2]. The algorithm preserves topology during simplification, and attempts to optimize geometric fidelity and quad structure (vertex valences near 4) throughout the process.

Semi-regular meshes describe surface models that exhibit a structural regularity that facilitates many geometric processing algorithms. We will review a technique to construct semi-regular, quad-only meshes from input surface meshes of arbitrary polygonal type and genus [3]. The algorithm generates a quad-only model through subdivision of the input polygons, then simplifies to a base domain that is homeomorphic to the original mesh. During the simplification, a novel hierarchical mapping method, *keyframe mapping*, stores specific levels-of-detail to guide the mapping of the original vertices to the base domain. The algorithm implements a scheme for refinement with adaptive resampling of the base domain and backward projects to the original surface. As a byproduct of the remeshing scheme, a surface parameterization is associated with the remesh vertices to facilitate subsequent geometric processing, i.e., texture mapping, subdivision surfaces and spline-based modeling.

The techniques described above are completely automatic. We will briefly touch on a new approach that we have been developing for giving the user more control of the remeshing process. By combining scalar field topology and combinatorial connectivity techniques, our new user-driven framework follows a coarse to fine design philosophy, which allows for explicit control of the output quad mesh at interactive rates. This work is described in Tierny et al. [11].

SCG'10, June 13–16, 2010, Snowbird, Utah, USA.
ACM 978-1-4503-0016-2/10/06.

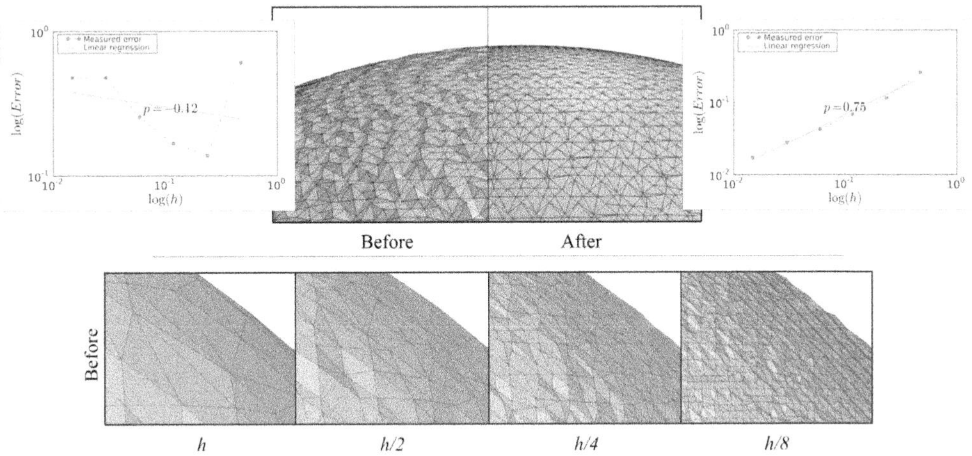

Figure 2: Through the verification methodology presented on Etiene et al. [7], we were able to uncover a convergence problem within a publicly available marching-based isosurfacing code (top left) and fix it (top right). The problem causes the mesh normals to *disagree* with the known gradient field when refining the voxel size h (bottom row). The two graphs show the convergence of the normals before and after fixing the code.

2. Verifiable Visualization

Visualization has become a standard component in many scientific software tools, and it is particularly important for large-scale data analysis. In Kirby and Silva [9], we argue that there is a need for creating a new focus area of visualization research that we tentatively call "verifiable visualizations". We came to this conclusion on the basis of our realization that although strict error analysis and verification has been the norm in simulation science, visualization has lagged behind other computational techniques in this regard. We argue that it is important to consider both the errors of the individual visualization component within the scientific pipeline and the interaction between and interpretation of the accumulated errors generated in the end-to-end computational pipeline.

We will present concrete examples of this idea in the context of verifying the correctness of isosurfacing techniques. In Etiene et al. [7], we derive formulas for the expected *order of accuracy* (or convergence rate) of several isosurface features, and compare them to experimentally observed results in a number of selected isosurfacing codes. We show that this technique exposed actual problems in implementations, and helped to produce improved codes. In ongoing work (see Etiene et al [6]), we extend the approach to use topological properties for verification. Specifically, we use machinery from Stratified Morse Theory and Digital Topology to compute topological invariants that are examined during code verification. This methodology revealed unexpected behavior and coding error in publicly available isosurface codes.

Acknowledgments.

This is joint work with E. Cohen, J. Daniels, T. Etiene, R. M. Kirby, L. G. Nonato, V. Pascucci, T. Peters, C. Scheidegger, and J. Tierny. This work was supported in part by grants from the National Science Foundation (IIS-0905385, CNS-0855167, IIS-0844546, ATM-0835821, CNS-0751152, OCE-0424602, CNS-0514485, IIS-0513692, CNS-0524096, CCF-0401498, OISE-0405402, CCF-0528201, CNS-0551724), the Department of Energy, ExxonMobil, and IBM Faculty Award.

1. REFERENCES

[1] P. Alliez, D. Cohen-Steiner, O. Devillers, B. Lévy, and M. Desbrun. Anisotropic polygonal remeshing. In *ACM SIGGRAPH*, pages 485–493, 2003.

[2] J. Daniels, C. Silva, and E. Cohen. Localized quadrilateral coarsening. *Comp. Graph. Forum.*, 28(5):1436–1444, 2009.

[3] J. Daniels, C. Silva, and E. Cohen. Semi-regular quadrilateral-only mesh generation from simplified base domains. *Comp. Graph. Forum.*, 28(5):1427–1435, 2009.

[4] J. Daniels, C. T. Silva, J. Shepherd, and E. Cohen. Quadrilateral mesh simplification. *ACM Trans. Graph. (Proc of SIGGRAPH Asia)*, 27(5):1–9, 2008.

[5] S. Dong, P.-T. Bremer, M. Garland, V. Pascucci, and J. C. Hart. Spectral surface quadrangulation. In *ACM SIGGRAPH*, pages 1057–1066, 2006.

[6] T. Etiene, L. G. Nonato, C. Scheidegger, J. Tierny, T. J. Peters, V. Pascucci, R. M. Kirby, and C. Silva. Topology verification for isosurface extraction. Unpublished manuscript, 2010.

[7] T. Etiene, C. Scheidegger, L. G. Nonato, R. M. Kirby, and C. Silva. Verifiable visualization for isosurface extraction. *IEEE Transactions on Visualization and Computer Graphics*, 15(6):1227–1234, 2009.

[8] M. Gross and H. Pfister, editors. *Point-Based Graphics*. Morgan Kaufmann, 2007.

[9] R. Kirby and C. Silva. The need for verifiable visualization. *IEEE Computer Graphics and Applications*, 28(5):78–83, 2008.

[10] M. Marinov and L. Kobbelt. A robust two-step procedure for quad-dominant remeshing. *Computer Graphics Forum*, 25(3):537–546, 2006.

[11] J. Tierny, J. Daniels, L. G. Nonato, V. Pascucci, and C. Silva. Interactive quadrangulation with reeb atlases and connectivity textures. Unpublished manuscript, 2010.

Computing Planar Voronoi Diagrams in Double Precision: A Further Example of Degree-driven Algorithm Design

David L. Millman
University of North Carolina
Chapel Hill, North Carolina, USA
dave@cs.unc.edu

Jack Snoeyink
University of North Carolina
Chapel Hill, North Carolina, USA
snoeyink@cs.unc.edu

ABSTRACT

Geometric algorithms use numerical computations to perform geometric tests, so correct algorithms may produce erroneous results if insufficient arithmetic precision is available. Liotta, Preparata, and Tamassia, in 1999, suggested that algorithm design, which traditionally considers running time and memory space, could also consider precision as a resource. They demonstrated that the Voronoi diagram of n sites on a $U \times U$ grid could be rounded to answer nearest neighbor queries on the same grid using only double precision. They still had to compute the Voronoi diagram before rounding, which requires the quadruple-precision InCircle test. We develop a "degree-2 Voronoi diagram" that can be computed using only double precision by a randomized incremental construction in $O(n \log n \log U)$ expected time and $O(n)$ expected space. Our diagram also answers nearest neighbor queries, even though it doesn't even use sufficient precision to determine a Delaunay triangulation.

Categories and Subject Descriptors

F.2.2 [**Analysis of Algorithms and Problem Complexity**]: Nonnumerical Algorithms and Problems—*Geometrical problems and computations*

General Terms

Algorithms, Theory

Keywords

Robust computation, Low-degree primitives, Reduced precision, Voronoi diagrams, Post-office problems

1. INTRODUCTION

Geometric algorithms usually evaluate geometric primitives (e.g., predicates like point/line comparison, left/right turn tests, or constructions like computing the line through two points or the intersection of two lines) by doing numerical computation on coordinate values. Building geometric algorithms on a tower of abstractions—including Euclidean geometry, Cartesian coordinates, and exact arithmetic on RealRAM—has greatly reduced the errors in published papers on geometric algorithms in the last 20 years. Researchers have developed many sophisticated ways to ensure that each layer of abstraction is implemented correctly and efficiently, including the exact geometric computing paradigm [5, 23], arithmetic filters [4, 11], and others [20, 21, 24]. Unfortunately, implementers often rely on the floating point arithmetic supplied by current programming environments. The numerical errors this introduces can undermine the entire tower.

Liotta, Preparata, and Tamassia [16] suggested another approach, which is to consider arithmetic precision to be a resource that should be optimized by the design and analysis of algorithms, much like the traditional resources of running time and memory space. Liotta *et al.* [16] also suggested a measure: the *arithmetic degree* of the predicates used. Most geometric predicates evaluate the sign of a polynomial whose variables are input values. Suppose that input variables can be scaled to b bit integers. Then a degree k term can be evaluated in bk bits, and a polynomial can sum a such terms in $bk + \log_2 a$ bits. Thus, the degree k can be considered the leading term that determines the precision required; we ignore the carry bits, just as we ignore constants in the asymptotic measures used for time and space. (In fact, since most evaluations need only the sign of the polynomial, the $\log_2 a$ can be avoided by Kahan summation [14].) This measure has been used to develop algorithms for intersecting line segments [1, 2, 17].

Liotta *et al.* [16] developed an *implicit Voronoi diagram* to answer Post Office queries for n sites on a $U \times U$ grid – finding the closest site to a query in $O(\log n)$ time and $O(n)$ space, and using predicates whose polynomials have maximum degree 2. (We call degree 2 predicates "double precision.") Unfortunately, their algorithm must first compute the entire Voronoi diagram before rounding it to their structure; Voronoi computation requires the InCircle test, which is an irreducible polynomial of degree 4. (They also sort Voronoi vertices by y coordinate, making their algorithm degree 5.) In subsection 2.1 we look at the degrees of several predicates and algorithms; the degree of an algorithm is the highest degree of its predicates.

We develop a new implicit Voronoi diagram structure that we are able to compute by randomized incremental construc-

SCG'10, June 13–16, 2010, Snowbird, Utah, USA.

tion in $O(n \log n \log U)$ expected time and $O(n)$ expected space, again using only double precision.

To appreciate the challenge in doing so, note that most algorithms compute Voronoi diagrams by computing the Delaunay triangulation, which uses the degree 4 InCircle test to verify that three points define an empty circle [12]. Our algorithms will compute the closest sites only at grid points, which is not enough information to obtain the dual Delaunay triangulation.

Fortune's sweep algorithm [10], computes the Voronoi directly, but uses a degree 6 predicate that orders two circumcircles by their extreme points. The notion of abstract Voronoi diagrams [15] reduces Voronoi computation to ordering bisectors around Voronoi vertices, which again uses InCircle. Sugihara and Iri's incremental construction [22], which tries to avoid geometric tests in favor of topological inference, still relies on InCircle. In their algorithm, the basic step is to carve out the Voronoi cell of a newly inserted site by walking through the current diagram. This doesn't seem to work without a notion of adjacency of cells, which seems difficult to achieve with predicates of degree two.

In earlier work, we were able to implement an $O(n \log(n+U))$-time randomized incremental construction to compute a reduced precision Voronoi diagram [19] using a degree 3 predicate for ordering bisectors along a line. In this paper, we define a trapezoidation of approximate Voronoi cells that is suitable for randomized incremental construction and use a history DAG (directed acyclic graph) rather than a walk to find which trapezoids need to be updated when a new site is inserted.

The nearest-neighbor transform, known as the discrete or digital Voronoi and related to the distance transform, computes nearest sites for for every point in the grid, spending at least $\Omega(U^2)$ time. Breu *et al.* [3] showed that $O(U^2)$ was achievable by computing a Voronoi diagram on the grid by divide and conquer. Chan [7] and Maurer [18] independently developed simpler algorithms that generalized to higher dimensions, and Cao *et al.* [6] gave a fast implementation on GPU processors. These algorithms were described as degree 5, although Chan observed that his was actually degree 3, and could be improved to degree 2 with a little more work; we previously defined the proxy trapezoidation [8] to more compactly store the output of this degree 2 algorithm. This paper extends the definition and shows how to construct the structure directly in linear expected space.

2. DEFINITIONS AND NOTATION

In this section, we first establish some notation for familiar concepts, such as Voronoi diagrams and trapezoid graphs, then define some of the key concepts for our structure.

2.1 The Voronoi Diagram and Grids

Given a set of n sites $S = \{s_1, \ldots s_n\}$ in the plane, the *Voronoi diagram* of S partitions the plane into maximally connected regions with the same set of nearest neighbor sites. Regions with one closest site are called *Voronoi cells*, regions with two closest sites are called *Voronoi edges*, and regions with three or more closest sites are called *Voronoi vertices*. Building a point location structure on top of the Voronoi diagram gives the classical solution to the *Post office problem*; after preprocessing the sites, you can determine the closest site to a query point, q, in $O(\log n)$ time.

We restrict our sites and query points to a $U \times U$ integer grid, denoted $\mathbb{U}$. The *discrete Voronoi diagram* labels only the grid points with their closest sites. Note that a line bisecting two grid points might not hit any points of the grid $\mathbb{U}$. In building our structures, it will be convenient to use the half-integer grid $\mathbb{U}_2 = \frac{1}{2}[2U+1]^2$ and the square $\mathcal{U} = [1/2, U+1/2]^2 \subset \mathbb{R}^2$. That way, at least the midpoint between two sites $(s_i + s_j)/2$ is on the half-integer grid. We sometimes say that a point is *single precision* to mean that it is on the grid $\mathbb{U}_2$.

Consider the degree of one basic construction and four predicates for Voronoi diagrams. We use a model of computation that includes constant-time arithmetic operations, and consider computations both with and without floor or integer division functions. For these basic predicates, floor makes no difference.

`VorVertex`(a, b, c)**:** A Voronoi vertex constructed from grid point sites $a, b, c \in \mathbb{U}$ has coordinates that can be expressed as rational numbers of degree 3 over degree 2.

`Point Comparison` $a \prec b$**:** Compare points by lexicographic order, so that $a \prec b$ if and only if $a_x < b_x$ or ($a_x = b_x$ and $a_y < b_y$). Comparing grid points $a, b \in \mathbb{U}_2$ is degree 1, comparing a grid point with a Voronoi vertex is degree 3, and comparing two Voronoi vertices is degree 5.

q.`Nearer`(s_i, s_j) **or** b_{ij}.`side`(q)**:** A *bisector* $b_{ij} = \{p \in \mathbb{R}^2 : \|p - s_i\| = \|p - s_j\|\}$ is the line equidistant to two sites. Determining if a point q is on a bisector, or determining the closer of the two sites, is degree two—simply compare squared distances.

`InCircle`(a, b, c, q)**:** The basic predicate for Voronoi computation [9], InCircle determines whether q is inside the circumcircle of $a, b, c \in \mathbb{U}$. This could be done by comparing the squared distances from VorVertex(a, b, c) to a and to q, which gives a degree 6 polynomial when you clear fractions, but that polynomial can factor to give the usual InCircle determinant, which is degree 4.

`Orient`(a, b, c)**:** The orientation test, which reports if the path a, b, c makes a right turn, left turn, or goes straight, is a determinant on the homogeneous coordinates of the inputs. It is a degree 2 test on grid points, which is the only way we will use it. Degree goes up by 2 for each Voronoi vertex: it takes degree 8 to determine orientation for three arbitrary Voronoi vertices, and degree-6 to determine the orientation of a grid point relative to an edge of a triangulation of a Voronoi diagram. (Thus, one should avoid point location structures that first triangulate.)

2.2 Trapezoidation and Point Location

Any planar subdivision with line segments can be decomposed into trapezoids by making vertical cuts at the endpoints of each segment that extend until reaching another segment. We define three different, but related, trapezoidations in the next three subsections. Each trapezoid τ will have *top* and *bottom* lines, and a *left* and *right* point, with τ.*left* $\prec$ τ.*right* and both points on or between the *top* and *bottom* lines. Each trapezoid may have up to four neighbors, reached by crossing the vertical lines above or below τ.*left* and τ.*right*, although if the subdivision is into monotone regions, as in Figure 1, then each trapezoid has at most two neighbors. When τ.*left* and τ.*right* have the same x coordinate, we can still think of τ as a trapezoid since the lexicographic order on points used by $\prec$ is consistent with

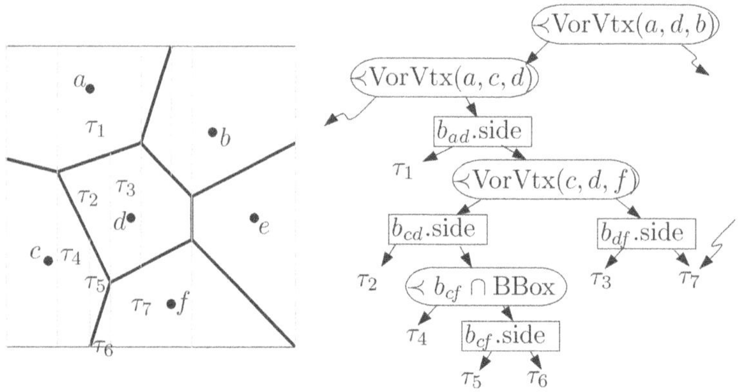

Figure 1: Trapezoidation of a small Voronoi diagram, and a piece of the trapezoid graph for the strip with labeled faces, $\tau_1, \ldots, \tau_7$.

skewing the points slightly, or rotating the vertical direction counter-clockwise. For example, the bisector of d and e in Figure 1 is the bottom edge for an infinitesimally thin trapezoid in the Voronoi cell of d and the top edge for an infinitesimally thin trapezoid in the Voronoi cell of e.

Trapezoid graphs [9, ch. 6] support point location queries, which identify the trapezoid containing a query point q. The *trapezoid graph* is a directed acyclic graph (DAG) with three types of nodes:

x-node: Stores a point v; compares a query $q \prec v$. If both q and v are grid points on $\mathbb{U}_2$, this test is degree 1; if v is a Voronoi vertex, this test is degree 3.

y-node: Given a query point q and a line ℓ, determine if q is above, below, or on ℓ. If ℓ is a bisector of two sites, or if ℓ is defined by two grid points on $\mathbb{U}_2$, then this test is degree 2. On the other hand, if ℓ is defined by two arbitrary Voronoi vertices, this test is degree 6.

leaf node: Leaf nodes represent trapezoids, for which the containing region is known.

Figure 1 shows a portion of the trapezoid graph for seven of the trapezoids in a small Voronoi diagram.

Liotta, Preparata, and Tamassia [16] achieved a degree-two post-office query by building a trapezoid graph for the Voronoi diagram. The straightforward way, depicted in Figure 1, would be to use Voronoi vertices (and intersections of bisectors with the bounding box) at x-nodes and bisectors at y nodes. Liotta *et al.* improve this by a simple observation: since the queries are grid points, rounding non-integer x nodes to half-integers reduces the degree of that test from 3 to 1 without changing any test results. They still used a degree 5 algorithm to compute the Voronoi diagram. Our previous work [19] showed how to build their structure directly with degree three in $O(n \log(n + U))$ expected time.

2.3 Voronoi Polygons on the Grid and Proxy Trapezoidation

Define the *Voronoi polygon* $C_S(s_i)$ to be the convex hull of the grid points of $\mathbb{U}_2$ in the closure of the Voronoi cell of site $s_i \in S$. We omit the subscript S when the set of sites is understood. Voronoi polygon $C(s_i)$ is contained in the Voronoi cell of s_i, and the containment may be proper. As illustrated in Figure 2, the set of all Voronoi polygons may leave *gaps* in $\mathcal{U}$, even though they cover all the grid points.

Define the *cell proxy* of s_i, denoted $P_S(s_i)$, to be the line segment from the minimum to the maximum point of $C_S(s_i)$, as illustrated in the middle of Figure 2. Because the n Voronoi polygons can actually have a total of $\Theta(n \log U)$ sides, we will often prefer to work with the n proxy segments instead. Define the *proxy trapezoidation* to be the vertical visibility map of all cell proxies, as shown in the same figure. Note that the proxy trapezoidation for a set of n sites S has at most $3n+1$ trapezoids, and is canonical—it is completely determined by the sites.

In [8], we observed that if we can compute a proxy trapezoidation, then we can use it to answer post office queries using degree 2, because only the sites contributing the top and bottom proxies are candidates for the closest sites to the grid points inside a proxy trapezoid. (Note that the only grid point actually on a vertical side is the endpoint of a proxy segment that defines the side, and we already know the neighbor of a proxy – the lexicographic ordering used by $\prec$ implicitly perturbs grid points directly above a defining endpoint into the trapezoid to the right, and directly below a defining endpoint into the trapezoid on the left.)

LEMMA 1. *If $q \in \mathbb{U}$ is a query point in a trapezoid τ with $\tau.top = P(s_i)$ and $\tau.bottom = P(s_j)$ then q is in $C(s_i)$ or $C(s_j)$.*

PROOF. Suppose that some grid point $q \in \tau$ belongs in a different Voronoi polygon $C(s_k)$. Since the Voronoi polygons are convex and non-overlapping, the cell proxy $P(s_k)$ must pass through trapezoid τ, which is a contradiction. □

COROLLARY 2. *Given cell proxies $P_S(s_i)$ for all $s_i \in S$, one can build a point location structure that answers post office queries in $O(\log n)$ expected time and linear expected space.*

PROOF. We simply use randomized incremental construction of the trapezoid graph of the proxy trapezoidation, as in [9, ch. 6]. A query determines the trapezoid τ that contains the query point q using degree 1 tests at x-nodes and degree 2 orientation tests at y-nodes. We can then use the degree 2 q.`Nearer`() test to decide which of the two candidate sites is closer. □

2.4 Voronoi Trapezoidation and Conflicts

A few additional concepts will help us describe a randomized incremental construction of the proxy trapezoidation.

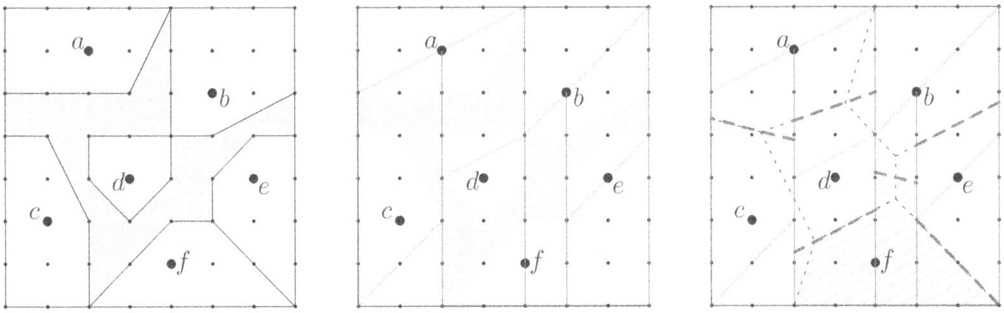

Figure 2: *Left:* **Voronoi polygons of sites on a grid may leave gaps.** *Middle:* **Proxy trapezoidation of proxy segments, which connect the maximal and minimal points in a Voronoi polygon. The lexicographic order for points implies that grid points that appear on the vertical segments are actually in trapezoids to the left or right, unless they are proxy segment endpoints. Thus, f is in the trapezoid that contains d, a is in the trapezoid above the proxy for d, and there is an infinitesimally thin trapezoid between the endpoints of the proxies for c and d.** *Right:* **Splitting trapezoids of the proxy trapezoidation by bisectors gives the Voronoi trapezoidation.**

First, if we split each trapezoid of the proxy trapezoidation with the bisector of sites donating the proxies at top and bottom, then we obtain the Voronoi trapezoidation depicted at the right of Figure 2. This trapezoidation is also canonical, since it is derived from the proxy trapezoidation.

It is important to note that we don't actually compute y-coordinates of bisectors; the *top* and *bottom* pointers just point to line equations for proxies, bounding box sides, or bisectors, each of which can be represented as a degree 2 polynomial. All *left* and *right* points are proxy endpoints or bounding box corners, and all are from $\mathbb{U}_2$. Thus, we observe:

LEMMA 3. *One can test if a grid point q is inside a given trapezoid τ of a Voronoi trapezoidation in constant time using degree 2.*

In the *Voronoi trapezoidation* every trapezoid τ intersects some proxy $P(s_i)$ and either a bisector b_{ij} or a bounding box side; we set $\texttt{site}(\tau) = s_i$ and $\texttt{bisector}(\tau) = b_{ij}$ (or the bounding box side in the latter case).

The trapezoids with $\texttt{site}(\tau) = s_i$ cover the Voronoi polygon $C(s_i)$ and therefore contain all grid points in the Voronoi cell of s_i. We can't really say how the covering trapezoids relate to the true Voronoi cell of s_i; clearly they may miss portions of the cell on the left and right ends, because they all use the proxy $P(s_i)$ as top or bottom. As the striped trapezoids in Figure 2 show, they don't necessarily form a convex region and may contain more or less than the true Voronoi cell – all we guarantee is that they contain the grid points of $C(s_i)$. This means that it would be difficult to bound the work necessary to insert a new site s by walking through the Voronoi trapezoidation of existing sites.

Consider a subset of sites $R \subseteq S$. We say a site $s_k \notin R$ is *in conflict* with trapezoid τ of the Voronoi trapezoidation of R if and only if there exists a $g \in \tau \cap \mathbb{U}_2$ such that $\|g - s_k\| < \|g - \texttt{site}(\tau)\|$, i.e. if some grid point in τ is closer to s_k than to $\texttt{site}(\tau)$. We extend the conflict to the proxy trapezoid whose split produced τ, as well. We call g a *witness* to the conflict.

In the next section we will give a detailed description of how to maintain the proxy/Voronoi trapezoidations as sites are inserted. As in many randomized incremental constructions, we will find it useful to keep the history DAG of the proxy trapezoidation: as a new site is added, some old trapezoids will be deleted and their area filled with new trapezoids – the parents of a new trapezoid will be the minimal set of old trapezoids that cover all the grid points that it contains. This implies that we can trace conflicts through history:

LEMMA 4. *If site $s \in S$ is in conflict with a trapezoid τ of the history DAG, then it is in conflict with at least one parent of τ.*

We will actually be able to use a trapezoid graph to store the history of updates, so parents and children will not be explicit in the data structure, but they will serve a role in the analysis. For sites S, let D2-Voronoi(S) denote the proxy trapezoidation with its history represented in a trapezoid graph, along with the Voronoi trapezoidation implied by introducing bisectors in each trapezoid.

3. CONSTRUCTION

In this section we give the details of our degree 2 randomized incremental construction (RIC). We assume that the sites have been shuffled randomly; let $S_i = \{s_1, s_2, \ldots, s_i\}$. We further assume that we have built the proxy trapezoidation and its history that constitute D2-Voronoi(S_{i-1}) and want to obtain D2-Voronoi(S_i) by inserting s_i.

After observing how incremental construction affects the Voronoi polygons and proxy segments, as defined in Section 2.3, we introduce a few more predicates and constructions for grid points in trapezoids. Finally, we describe the updates to the trapezoidation, and analyze the expected time and space.

LEMMA 5. *In an incremental construction, a Voronoi polygon on the grid can only shrink:*

$$\forall s \in S_{i-1}, \quad C_{S_i}(s) \subseteq C_{S_{i-1}}(s),$$

and a proxy segment changes if and only if the new site s_i is in conflict with at least one of its endpoints:

$$\forall s \in S_{i-1}, \quad P_{S_i}(s) \neq P_{S_{i-1}}(s) \iff$$
$$s_i \text{ conflicts with an endpoint of } P_{S_{i-1}}(s).$$

3.1 Predicates and Constructions

We will continue to use a model of computation in which arithmetic operations are constant-time. Computations do not use floor or integer division unless otherwise stated.

LEMMA 6. *(i) Determining if bisector b_{ij} intersects the vertical segment $\overline{rt}$ with $r, t \in \mathbb{U}_2$ takes degree 2 and constant time. (ii) Determining the shortest subsegment $\overline{ab} \subset \overline{rt}$ with $a, b \in \mathbb{U}_2$ that intersects b_{ij} takes degree 2 and $\log \|r - t\|$ time, or constant time if floor is allowed.*

PROOF. For (i), compare the result of b_{ij}.`side()` on the two endpoints of $\overline{rt}$. (ii) can use floor, or can binary search with b_{ij}.`side()`. □

LEMMA 7. *There is a degree 2 procedure* `HullVertices()`*, taking $O(\log U)$ time, that computes the convex hull of the grid points, if any, that lie in a region bounded by a constant number of bisectors or lines defined by two grid points.*

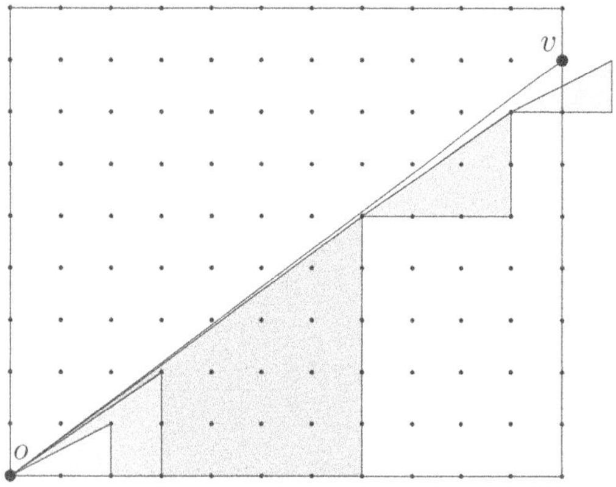

Figure 3: Each darker triangle's hypotenuse at left is an increasingly accurate rational representation of the slope of segment $\overline{ov}$; the `GCD walk` reuses these at right to compute the convex hull of the grid points below $\overline{ov}$.

PROOF. Euclid's GCD algorithm, when interpreted geometrically, gives the sequence of best rational approximations to an arbitrary slope, ordered by increasing denominator. Kahan and Snoeyink [13][Lemma 4.6] turned this into a procedure `HullVertices`(o, v) that takes the origin, an arbitrary point v, and computes the convex hull of the grid points in the bounding box of $\overline{ov}$ that are on or below $\overline{ov}$. Their procedure runs in $\Theta(\log(\|o - v\|)$ time and is degree 2; the highest degree predicate is the orientation test on grid points. The lower bound applies because the convex hull of grid points in the intersection of $O(1)$ halfplanes may have this many vertices.

With a small modification, their procedure can start from a unit segment between grid points, from Lemma 6(ii), and follow a bisector within a region. We call this operation the `GCD walk`. In each step we evaluate the degree 2 predicates, bisector `side`, and `orientation` for grid points. The walk takes time proportional to the log of the maximum side of the bounding box of the region in which it runs. This remains bounded by $O(\log U)$. □

This has two useful corollaries.

COROLLARY 8. *Predicate s_i.*`inConflict`(τ) *determines if s_i is in conflict with trapezoid τ of the Voronoi trapezoidation in $O(\log U)$ time and degree two.*

PROOF. Suppose that s_u = `site`(τ), as in Figure 4. We can use the `GCD walk` to determine the convex hull of grid points that are in τ between τ.*left* and τ.*right* and bounded by `bisector`(τ) and b_{ui}, taking $O(\log U)$ time and degree 2. □

For the next corollary, and as shown with a dash-dotted line in Figure 4, the proxy of any convex hull of grid points is the line segment from the minimum to the maximum under lexicographic order ($\prec$).

COROLLARY 9. *Given a site s_i in conflict with a trapezoid τ of the Voronoi trapezoidation,* `findProxies`(s_i, τ) *constructs, in $O(\log U)$ time and degree 2, the proxies for two convex hulls of the grid points in trapezoid τ of the Voronoi trapezoidation—those that are closer to* `site`(τ)*, and those that are closer to s_i.*

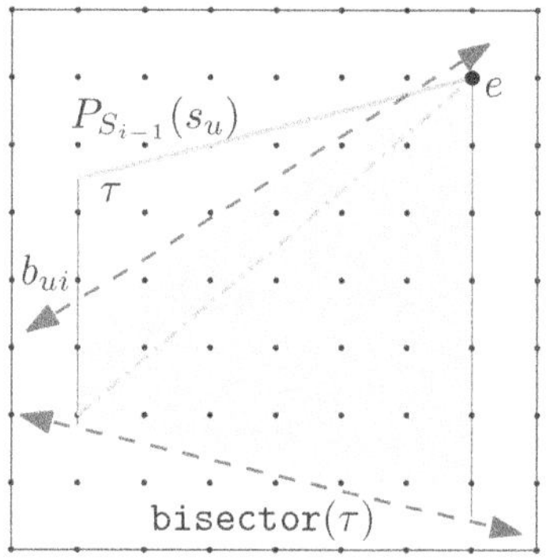

Figure 4: Suppose that new site s_i is in conflict with a Voronoi trapezoid τ, with s_u = `site`(τ). As drawn, τ.*top* is proxy $P_{S_{i-1}}(s_u)$ and τ.*bottom* = `bisector`(τ). The new bisector b_{ui} cuts the shaded area from τ, which is the convex hull of the grid points that witness the conflict by being closer to s_i than s_u. The dash-dotted line depicts the proxy of s_i in τ.

3.2 Incremental construction

Now, suppose that we have constructed D2-Voronoi(S_{i-1}). We update the proxy trapezoidation and its history as we insert the new site s_i using three step. The first step, *Find Conflict*, identifies the set of trapezoids of D2-Voronoi(S_{i-1}) that are in conflict with s_i. The second step, *Proxy Update*, finds the new proxy $P_{S_i}(s_i)$ and updates all other proxies that changed on the insertion of s_i. The third step, *Trapezoidation Update* splits and merges proxy trapezoids to reflect these proxy changes, and updates the trapezoid graph to capture the history, producing D2-Voronoi(S_i).

Find Conflict:.

We collect the trapezoids of the D2-Voronoi(S_{i-1}) that are in conflict with s_i by traversing the history DAG. Starting at the root, we visit only those trapezoids that are in conflict with s_i, or whose parent was in conflict with s_i. At each trapezoid, we test for conflict by Corollary 8, spending $O(\log U)$ time and degree two. By Lemma 4, if there is a conflict, it persists all the way to the root, so we will find it.

Proxy Update:.

Adding s_i to S_{i-1} creates a new proxy $P_{S_i}(s_i)$ for s_i, and usually forces some old proxies to be updated, for example, proxy $P_{S_{i-1}}(s_u)$ in Figure 4. Thanks to Lemma 5, we can identify which proxies must be updated by testing their endpoints: In Figure 4, trapezoid τ is defined in part by endpoint e of proxy $P_{S_{i-1}}(s_u)$. Testing e.`Nearer`(s_i, s_u) identifies, in constant time and degree 2, whether this proxy must be updated. Moreover, we can find all proxies to update by testing only those that define trapezoids in conflict with s_i, since an endpoint that witnesses the need to update the proxy is also a gridpoint that witnesses a conflict with s_i.

For each Voronoi trapezoid τ in conflict with s_i, we can apply Corollary 9 to find the min and max grid points in the regions that we obtain if we split τ by the bisector of `site`(τ) and s_i. The min and max grid points identified from regions on the s_i side of the bisector become the endpoints of the new proxy $P_{S_i}(s_i)$. Similarly, for any proxy that is updated, we take the min and/or max points identified from the regions closer to the corresponding site. Thus, we spend $O(\log U)$ time and degree 2 on each trapezoid in conflict with s_i.

Trapezoidation Update:.

Having identified the updates to proxies, we must now update the trapezoidation and the trapezoid graph. We do this in four substeps.

First, we add all new proxy endpoints, splitting the trapezoids that contain them. In the trapezoid graph, the corresponding leaves (trapezoids to split) become x-nodes that point to two new leaf nodes (the results of the splits).

Second, we add the segment for the new proxy $P_{S_i}(s_i)$ by walking through the trapezoidation, splitting and merging trapezoids as needed. This operation is the same as in any trapezoidation of line segments, and the corresponding updates to the trapezoid graph can be found in textbooks [9, ch. 6]. Briefly, if k trapezoids are crossed by the proxy, then the corresponding k leaves are replaced by copies of a y-node for the segment, which point to $k+1$ new leaves for the resulting trapezoids. (Note that some of the trapezoids crossed may not have been found in the history since they may not have witnesses to conflicts. They did, however, have witnessed conflicts on both ends. This is important, because we could not afford to go walking through trapezoids looking for possible grid points to include in the Voronoi polygon $C_{S_i}(s_i)$.)

Third, we shorten the old proxies that need to be updated. Notice that trapezoids that simply replace $P_{S_{i-1}}(s)$ with a shorter $P_{S_i}(s)$ as the *top* or *bottom* change geometrically, but do not need to change their representations. Thus, this operation is like the inverse of adding a proxy in step two: we erase $P_{S_{i-1}}(s)$ from those trapezoids that do not intersect $P_{S_i}(s)$, merging and splitting as needed.

Fourth, we merge any adjacent trapezoids whose left and right boundaries are defined by grid points that used to be proxy endpoints but are no longer. In the trapezoid graph this just redirects pointers to corresponding leaves.

LEMMA 10. *The leaves of the trapezoid graph corresponding to new trapezoids in the proxy trapezoidation of S_i are $O(1)$ deeper than the leaves for their parent trapezoids in the proxy trapezoidation of S_{i-1}.*

PROOF. Each update in substeps 1–3 adds a single level to the trapezoid graph, and each trapezoid of the proxy trapezoidation can be involved in at most 4 updates (to *top*, *bottom*, *left*, and *right*). □

3.3 Analysis

We can use Mulmuley's general framework of stoppers and triggers (or definers and killers, as described in [9, ch. 9.3]) to analyze the expected time and space for this D2-Voronoi.

LEMMA 11. *The expected size of the D2-Voronoi on n sites is linear in n.*

PROOF. The fact that the proxy trapezoidation is canonical and has linear size implies that the expected amount of work to update while inserting one segment is constant. Thus, the expected size over n insertions is linear. □

LEMMA 12. *The expected time to build the D2-Voronoi on n sites is $O(n \log n \log U)$.*

PROOF. The general analysis framework says that the total number of conflicts that have to be chased through history is $O(n \log n)$. Each conflict is handled by predicate `inConflict` and construction `findProxies`, which give a multiplicative factor of $\log U$. Each update to the trapezoid graph adds at most a constant number of nodes to the search path, so the total time to do the updates is $O(n \log n \log U)$. □

4. CONCLUSION AND OPEN PROBLEMS

Ten years ago Liotta *et al.* [16] described a structure for solving post office queries in double precision. We are happy to report that their structure can also be built efficiently in double precision. To our knowledge, this is the first construction of a planar Voronoi diagram with double precision in sub-quadratic time. We plan to implement the current algorithm to compare with exact arithmetic implementations for building Voronoi diagrams.

It is interesting to note that a randomized incremental construction using the degree 4 InCircle test can be implemented to run in $O(n \log n)$ time, that our earlier degree 3 algorithm is in $O(n \log n + n \log U)$, while this degree 2 algorithm is in $O(n \log n \log U)$. Is there inherent loss of efficiency with restricted predicates? Any lower bound above $\Omega(n \log n)$ would be interesting.

Actually, we believe that by maintaining dynamic convex hulls of grid points in trapezoids and using binary search to test if a witness to a conflict exists before applying our lemmas to extract proxies, we can improve the current algorithm's running time to $O(n \log n \log \log U + n \log U)$. We omit this from the abstract because we prefer the relative simplicity of the current algorithm, and because we would like to reduce the complexity to $O(n \log n + n \log U)$ in the degree 2 case as well.

What other problems are amenable to solution with limitations on the precision? In particular, since degree 2 suffices to compute squared Euclidean distance in any dimensions, what can be said about higher dimensional Voronoi diagrams using restricted predicates?

5. REFERENCES

[1] J.-D. Boissonnat and F. P. Preparata. Robust plane sweep for intersecting segments. *SIAM J. Comput.*, 29(5):1401–1421, 2000.

[2] J.-D. Boissonnat and J. Snoeyink. Efficient algorithms for line and curve segment intersection using restricted predicates. *Comput. Geom. Theory Appl.*, 16(1):35–52, 2000.

[3] H. Breu, J. Gil, D. Kirkpatrick, and M. Werman. Linear time Euclidean distance transform algorithms. *IEEE PAMI*, 17:529–533, 1995.

[4] H. Brönnimann, C. Burnikel, and S. Pion. Interval arithmetic yields efficient dynamic filters for computational geometry. *Discrete Applied Math.*, 1–2:25–47, 2001.

[5] C. Burnikel, J. Könemann, K. Mehlhorn, S. Näher, S. Schirra, and C. Uhrig. Exact geometric computation in LEDA. In *SCG '95: Proceedings of the Eleventh Annual Symposium on Computational Geometry*, pages 418–419, 1995.

[6] T.-T. Cao, K. Tang, A. Mohamed, and T.-S. Tan. Parallel banding algorithm to compute exact distance transform with the GPU. In *I3D '10: Proc. 2010 Symp. on Interactive 3D Graphics and Games*, New York, NY, USA, 2010. ACM.

[7] T. M. Chan. Faster core-set constructions and data-stream algorithms in fixed dimensions. *Comput. Geom. Theory Appl.*, 35(1):20–35, 2006.

[8] T. M. Chan, D. L. Millman, and J. Snoeyink. Discrete Voronoi diagrams and post office query structures without the incircle predicate. In *Proceedings of the Nineteenth Annual Fall Workshop on Computational Geometry*, 2009. `http://cs.unc.edu/~dave/mySite/media/papers/CMS09_FWCG.pdf`.

[9] M. de Berg, O. Cheong, M. van Kreveld, and M. Overmars. *Computational Geometry: Algorithms and Applications*. Springer-Verlag New York, Inc., 3rd edition, 2008.

[10] S. Fortune. A sweepline algorithm for Voronoi diagrams. *Algorithmica*, 2:153–174, 1987.

[11] S. Fortune and C. J. Van Wyk. Static analysis yields efficient exact integer arithmetic for computational geometry. *ACM Trans. Graph.*, 15(3):223–248, July 1996.

[12] L. Guibas and J. Stolfi. Primitives for the manipulation of general subdivisions and the computation of Voronoi. *ACM Trans. Graph.*, 4(2):74–123, 1985.

[13] S. Kahan and J. Snoeyink. On the bit complexity of minimum link paths: Superquadratic algorithms for problems solvable in linear time. *Comput. Geom. Theory Appl.*, 12(1-2):33–44, 1999.

[14] W. Kahan. Pracniques: Further remarks on reducing truncation errors. *Commun. ACM*, 8(1):40, 1965.

[15] R. Klein. *Concrete and Abstract Voronoi Diagrams*, volume 400 of *Lecture Notes Comput. Sci.* Springer-Verlag, 1989.

[16] G. Liotta, F. P. Preparata, and R. Tamassia. Robust proximity queries: An illustration of degree-driven algorithm design. *SIAM J. Comput.*, 28(3):864–889, 1999.

[17] A. Mantler and J. Snoeyink. Intersecting red and blue line segments in optimal time and precision. In *Discrete and Computational Geometry*, number 2098 in LNCS, pages 244–251. Springer Verlag, 2001.

[18] C. R. Maurer, Jr., R. Qi, and V. Raghavan. A linear time algorithm for computing exact Euclidean distance transforms of binary images in arbitrary dimensions. *IEEE Trans. Pattern Anal. Mach. Intell.*, 25(2):265–270, 2003.

[19] D. L. Millman and J. Snoeyink. Computing the implicit Voronoi diagram in triple precision. In *WADS*, volume 5664 of *LNCS*, pages 495–506. Springer Verlag, 2009.

[20] D. Priest. *On properties of floating point arithmetics: numerical stability and the cost of accurate computations*. Ph.D. thesis, Dept. of Mathematics, Univ. of California at Berkeley, 1992.

[21] J. R. Shewchuk. Adaptive precision floating-point arithmetic and fast robust geometric predicates. *Discrete & Computational Geometry*, 18(3):305–363, 1997.

[22] K. Sugihara and M. Iri. Construction of the Voronoi diagram for 'one million' generators in single-precision arithmetic. *Proc. IEEE*, 80(9):1471–1484, Sept. 1992.

[23] C.-K. Yap. Towards exact geometric computation. *Comput. Geom. Theory Appl.*, 7(1-2):3–23, 1997.

[24] C. K. Yap. Robust geometric computation. In *Handbook of Discrete and Computational Geometry*, pages 927–952. CRC Press, Inc., Boca Raton, FL, USA, 2nd edition, 2004.

3D Euler Spirals for 3D Curve Completion

Gur Harary
Dept. of Electrical Engineering
Technion
gur@tx.technion.ac.il

Ayellet Tal
Dept. of Electrical Engineering
Technion
ayellet@ee.technion.ac.il

ABSTRACT

Shape completion is an intriguing problem in geometry processing with applications in CAD and graphics. This paper defines a new type of 3D curves, which can be utilized for curve completion. It can be considered as the extension to three dimensions of the 2D Euler spiral. We prove several properties of these curves – properties that have been shown to be important for the appeal of curves. We illustrate their utility in two applications. The first is "fixing" curves detected by algorithms for edge detection on surfaces. The second is shape illustration in archaeology, where the user would like to draw curves that are missing due to the incompleteness of the input model.

Categories and Subject Descriptors

I.3 [**Computer Graphics**]: Computational Geometry and Object Modeling—*Curve, surface, solid, and object representations*

General Terms

Algorithms, Design

Keywords

Euler spirals, 3D curves

1. INTRODUCTION

Shape completion has been an important task in computational geometry with applications to CAD and computer graphics [2, 3, 28]. While most of the work has focused on completing or repairing polyhedra and CAD models, this paper focuses on completing curves in three dimensions. It presents a practical solution to the problem, which is demonstrated by real-life data.

Given two point-tangent pairs, one way to complete them is to use any of the variety of known splines [7, 10]. Such curves possess many attractive properties, however, Figure 1(b) illustrates that they (in this case Hermite splines) might not always produce the preferable results. This is also supported by psychological studies that indicate that splines may be unsatisfactory for curve completion [30].

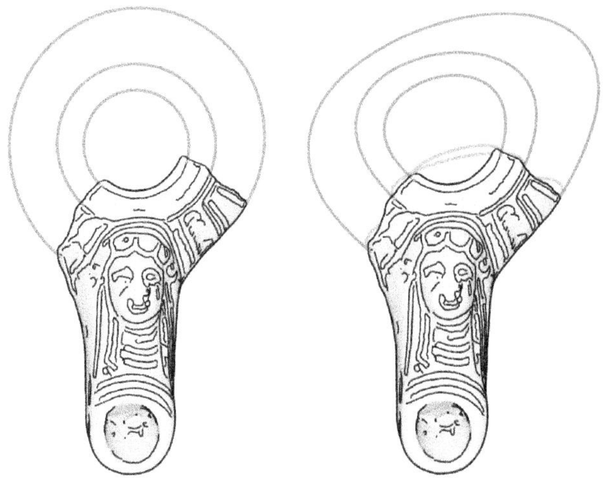

(a) Our completion (b) Hermite completion

Figure 1: 3D Euler spirals (red) complete the curves on a broken Hellenistic oil lamp – curves that would most likely be drawn if the model were complete. The scale of the Hermite splines is determined manually (magenta), since the automatically-scaled splines (green) are inferior due to the large ratio between the length of the curve and the size of the model. Note the perfect circular arcs of our curves.

This paper defines a new type of 3D curves that can be used for this purpose (Figure 1(a)). We show that our curves are not only appealing, but also qualitatively outperform some splines. In a nutshell, our curves can be considered as an extension to 3D of the planar Euler spirals. An important consideration in aesthetic curve design is the curve's fairness [25], which has been shown to be closely related to how little and how smoothly a curve bends. An Euler spiral, also referred to as a *clothoid* or a *Cornu spiral*, is an example of such an aesthetic curve. Its curvature varies linearly with arc-length [16, 20, 21]. Our proposed curve has both its curvature and torsion change linearly with length.

The contribution of this paper is threefold. First, the paper defines the 3D Euler spiral (Section 4) and proves that it satisfies some desirable properties – properties that have been claimed to produce eye-pleasing curves [17] (Section 5).

SCG'10, June 13–16, 2010, Snowbird, Utah, USA.

Figure 2: Archaeological drawing of a broken lamp found in the archaeological site of Dor. This is a manual drawing from [31].

In particular, we prove that our curves are invariant to similarity transformations and that they are symmetric, extensible (i.e., refinable), smooth, and round (i.e., if the boundary conditions lie on a circle, then the curve is a circle, as illustrated in Figure 1(a)). Second, we present a parameter-less algorithm for computing these curves (Section 6). Last but not least, we demonstrate the use of these curves in two curve completion applications (Section 7).

In the first application, our spirals complete curves missing due to "weak" surfaces patches. The second application is curve completion of broken shapes, such as archaeological artifacts. Currently, this task is performed by drawing the missing curves manually in 2D (Figure 2). This is an expensive and time-consuming process, which is prone to biases. Our curves can replace this manual task while performing it in 3D, directly on the scanned artifact. With the growing popularity of digital documentation in archaeology, the ability to draw curves in 3D is becoming ever more important.

2. RELATED WORK

Curve completion: Given two point-tangent pairs, the most common way to perform completion is to use splines, such as a cubic Hermite spline [7, 10]. Splines are fast and easy to compute, but they are not always the curves preferred by the human visual system.

Ullman [32] suggests properties that 2D curves should satisfy: invariance to rigid transformations, smoothness, minimization of the total curvature, and extensibility. These properties led to a Biarc solution – a curve consisting of two circular arcs. Biarcs are smooth and invariant to rigid transformations, but they do not guarantee that the total curvature is minimized and they are not extensible [5]. Biarcs are generalized to 3D in [6, 29].

Knuth [17] proposes different properties of eye-pleasing 2D curves: invariance to similarity transformations and cyclic permutations (for closed curves), extensibility, smoothness, roundness, and being locally constructed. Knuth also shows that the latter four properties cannot take place together. These properties are the base of the METAFONT system of LATEX. [5, 17, 27] propose to use 2D cubic splines, giving up extensibility and roundness.

Another way to construct curves is Elastica [14, 19, 24, 26], which refers to the curves that minimize the total square curvature of the curve: $\mathrm{E}[\kappa(\mathrm{s})] = \int_0^L \kappa^2(s)ds$, where $s \in [0, L]$ is the arc-length parameter and $\kappa(s)$ is the curvature. Horn [14] argues that Elastica is the "smoothest" 2D curve to complete the gap between two point-tangent pairs. It is extensible, but neither scale-variant nor round. Already in 1906 [4] discussed Elastica for 3D curves. A Curve that approximates the solution to Elastica in 3D is explicitly defined in [24]. In 2D this curve is the 2D Euler spiral (discussed next), which has a linear curvature. In 3D, the curvature of this curve is expressed as a hyperbola.

2D Euler spirals: Euler spirals are curves whose curvature evolves linearly along the curve. They were discovered independently by three researchers [20]. In 1694 Bernoulli wrote the equations for the Euler spiral for the first time, but did not draw the spirals or compute them numerically. In 1744 Euler rediscovered the curve's equations, described their properties, and derived a series expansion to the curve's integrals. Later, in 1781, he also computed the spiral's end points. The curves were re-discovered in 1890 for the third time by Talbot, who used them to design railway tracks. Euler spirals are also known as "Cornu spirals" (after Cornu who plotted them) and "Clothoid" (after Clotho, the youngest of the three Fates of Greek mythology). They are defined as the curves that penalize the curvature variation, hence minimizing the following (κ_s is the derivative of κ):

$$\mathrm{E}[\kappa(\mathrm{s})] = \int_0^L \kappa_s^2(s)ds.$$

In [30] psychological experiments show that in 2D an interpolation between two point-tangent pairs using Euler spiral outperforms parabolic curves and circular arcs. This is attributed to its monotonous change in curvature, which has a good fit to the way the human eye interpolates curves.

2D Euler spirals were used in computer aided design. In [14, 23] they are used as an approximation to the solution of Elastica. In [22] the conditions under which the spirals can form a transition curve are investigated. Two spirals are used in [33] to form a parabola-like segment between consecutive points of a control polygon. In [21] a formulation for fitting spiral primitives to a dense polyline data is developed.

In [16] an algorithm is described for 2D curve completion using an Euler spiral. The algorithm is an iterative gradient-descent, initialized by a 2D Biarc. Since there are infinite possible Biarcs, the Biarc that minimizes the total curvature variation is chosen. Some properties that characterize eye-pleasing curves are also proved. In [34] a faster and more accurate algorithm is proposed. It is proved that given two point-tangent pairs, there always exists an Euler spiral that interpolates them.

3D Euler spirals: An attempt to generalize Euler spirals to 3D, maintaining the linearity of the curvature, is presented in [13]. A given polygon is refined, such that the polygon satisfies both arc-length parameterization and linear distribution of the *discrete curvature binormal* vector. The algorithm ignores the torsion, despite being an important characteristic of 3D curves.

We propose a novel algorithm, which produces continuous, rather than discrete, curves and takes both curvature and torsion into account. The algorithm, which is inspired by [16], is general and does not require an initial polygon. We prove that our curve satisfies properties that characterize fair and appealing curves and reduces to the 2D Euler spiral in the planar case.

3. BACKGROUND

A spatial curve $\mathcal{C}(s)$ is determined by its curvature $\kappa(s)$ and its torsion $\tau(s)$. Intuitively, a curve can be obtained from a straight line by bending (curvature) and twisting (torsion).

This section reviews the Frenet-Serret Equations and the Euler-Lagrange Equations, which will be necessary in the derivation of our 3D Euler spirals. In the following, $\vec{T}(s) = \frac{d\mathcal{C}}{ds}(s)$ is the unit tangent vector, $\vec{N}(s)$ is the unit normal vector, and $\vec{B}(s) = \vec{T}(s) \times \vec{N}(s)$ is the binormal vector. We assume an arc-length parameterization.

Frenet-Serret Equations: Given a curvature $\kappa(s) > 0$ and a torsion $\tau(s)$, according to the fundamental theorem of the local theory of curves [9], there exists a unique (up to rigid motion) spatial curve, parameterized by the arc-length s, defined by its Frenet-Serret equations, as follows:

$$\begin{aligned} \frac{d\vec{T}(s)}{ds} &= \kappa(s)\vec{N}(s), \\ \frac{d\vec{N}(s)}{ds} &= -\kappa(s)\vec{T}(s) + \tau(s)\vec{B}(s), \\ \frac{d\vec{B}(s)}{ds} &= -\tau(s)\vec{N}(s). \end{aligned} \tag{1}$$

The curve $\mathcal{C}$ is defined by:

$$\begin{aligned} \mathcal{C}(s) &= \int_0^s \vec{T}(v)\, dv + \mathbf{x}_0 \\ &= \int_0^s \left[\int_0^t \frac{d\vec{T}(u)}{du}\, du + \vec{T}_0 \right] dt + \mathbf{x}_0. \end{aligned} \tag{2}$$

Euler-Lagrange Equation: The Euler-Lagrange Equation is fundamental in *calculus of variations* [11]. It is a differential equation, useful for solving optimization problems in which, given some functional, one seeks the function that optimizes it. It is satisfied by a function q of a real argument s, which is a stationary point of the functional

$$\mathcal{S}(q) = \int_{s_1}^{s_2} \mathcal{L}(s, q(s), q'(s)) ds, \tag{3}$$

where $q = (q_1, \ldots, q_n)$ is the function to be found, $q' = (q'_1, \ldots, q'_n)$, $q'_i = \frac{dq_i}{ds}$, $i = (1, \ldots, n)$, and the positions $q(s_1)$ and $q(s_2)$ are defined.

The function q that optimizes Equation (3) satisfies the Euler-Lagrange Equations:

$$\frac{d}{dt}\left(\frac{\partial \mathcal{L}}{\partial q'_i}\right) - \frac{\partial \mathcal{L}}{\partial q_i} = 0 \quad (i = 1, \ldots, n). \tag{4}$$

4. 3D EULER SPIRALS

This section defines the 3D Euler spiral – the curve having both its curvature and torsion evolve linearly along the curve (Figure 3). Furthermore, we require that our curve conforms with the definition of a 2D Euler spiral. We start with some

Figure 3: A 3D Euler spiral

intuition, then define the 3D Euler spiral, and finally prove its existence and uniqueness up to a rigid transformation.

We seek a functional that will penalize the change in curvature and torsion along the curve. Thus, the curve should minimize the sum of the square variation of the curvature and the torsion. Formally, we require that the following integral be minimized:

$$\mathcal{S}((\kappa, \tau)) = \int_0^L [\kappa_s^2(s) + \tau_s^2(s)]\, ds, \tag{5}$$

where L is the curve's length, $\kappa_s = \frac{\partial \kappa}{\partial s}$, and $\tau_s = \frac{\partial \tau}{\partial s}$. Note that in the planar case $\tau = 0$, therefore our definition indeed conforms with the definition of the 2D Euler spiral.

Minimizing Equation (5) can be performed using the Euler-Lagrange Equation. In our case, Equation (5) corresponds to Equation (3) as follows:

$$\begin{aligned} & q_1(s) \mapsto \kappa(s), \\ & q'_1(s) \mapsto \kappa_s(s), \\ & q_2(s) \mapsto \tau(s), \\ & q'_2(s) \mapsto \tau_s(s), \\ & \mathcal{L}\left(s, q(s), q'(s)\right) \mapsto \left[\kappa_s^2(s) + \tau_s^2(s)\right]. \end{aligned}$$

Hence, the corresponding Euler-Lagrange Equations are (by Equation (4)):

$$\kappa: \quad \frac{d}{ds}\left(\frac{\partial(\kappa_s^2 + \tau_s^2)}{\partial \kappa_s}\right) = 0 \Rightarrow \frac{d}{ds}(2\kappa_s) = 0 \Rightarrow \kappa_{ss} = 0,$$

$$\tau: \quad \frac{d}{ds}\left(\frac{\partial(\kappa_s^2 + \tau_s^2)}{\partial \tau_s}\right) = 0 \Rightarrow \frac{d}{ds}(2\tau_s) = 0 \Rightarrow \tau_{ss} = 0.$$

By integrating κ_{ss} and τ_{ss} twice, these equations lead to a curve whose curvature and torsion evolve linearly. Thus, for some constants $\kappa_0, \tau_0, \gamma, \delta \in \mathbb{R}$, and for $0 \leq s \leq L$:

$$\kappa(s) = \kappa_0 + \gamma s, \quad \tau(s) = \tau_0 + \delta s. \tag{6}$$

In summary, we have shown that the curve that minimizes our functional (Equation (5)) is a curve whose curvature and torsion change linearly along the curve. Note that since our curve has a linear relation between the curvature and torsion, it is a special case of Bertrand curves [12]. This, however, neither helps in deriving the properties proved in Section 5 (which do not hold for general Bertrand curves) nor provides a method for constructing them (Section 6).

Next, we define the curve that satisfies Equation (6). This definition is in the form of a set of differential equations. We assume that we are given the following initial conditions: a point $\mathbf{x}_0$ on the curve, a tangent $\vec{T}_0$ at $\mathbf{x}_0$, and a normal $\vec{N}_0$.

DEFINITION 4.1. **3D Euler spiral:** *The 3D curve that satisfies Equation* (6) *and the initial conditions is the curve* $\mathcal{C}$, *for which the following conditions hold:*

1. $\dfrac{d\mathcal{C}(s)}{ds} = \vec{T}(s)$,

2. $\dfrac{d\vec{T}(s)}{ds} = (\kappa_0 + \gamma s)\vec{N}(s)$,

3. $\dfrac{d\vec{N}(s)}{ds} = -(\kappa_0 + \gamma s)\vec{T}(s) + (\tau_0 + \delta s)\vec{B}(s)$,

4. $\dfrac{d\vec{B}(s)}{ds} = -(\tau_0 + \delta s)\vec{N}(s)$,

5. $\mathcal{C}(0) = \mathbf{x}_0$, $\vec{T}(0) = \vec{T_0}$, $\vec{N}(0) = \vec{N_0}$, $\vec{B}(0) = \vec{T_0} \times \vec{N_0}$.

To understand this definition, observe that 1 is the definition of the tangent, 2–4 are the Frenet-Serret Equations with our curvature and torsion, and 5 represents the initial conditions.

Finally, the following proposition proves the existence of this curve and its uniqueness up to a rigid transformation.

PROPOSITION 4.1. *Given constants* $\kappa_0, \tau_0, \gamma, \delta, \in \mathbb{R}$, *there exists a 3D Euler spiral having a linear curvature* $\kappa(s) = \kappa_0 + \gamma s$ *and a linear torsion* $\tau(s) = \tau_0 + \delta s$. *Moreover, this curve is unique up to a rigid transformation.*

PROOF. By definition of the curvature of curves in $\mathbb{R}^3$, $\kappa(s) = \left|\frac{d^2\vec{C}}{ds^2}(s)\right| \geq 0$. According to the fundamental theorem of local theory of curves, for every differential function with $\kappa(s) > 0$ and $\tau(s)$, there exists a regular parameterized curve, where $\kappa(s)$ is the curvature, $\tau(s)$ is the torsion, and s is the arc-length parameterization [9]. Moreover, any other curve satisfying the same conditions, differs by a rigid motion.

If $\kappa(s) = 0\ \forall s$, the curve is a straight line, which is unique up to a rigid transformation. It is also possible that $\kappa(s) = 0$ for a single point. In this case, the tangent and hence the curve are well-defined at this point, which is the inflection point at which the normal switches directions. (Note that by our definition $\kappa(s)$ may be negative. In this case, we consider $|\kappa(s)|$ and regard the switch of the sign as a change of the normal direction.) □

5. PROPERTIES OF 3D EULER SPIRALS

The aesthetics of curves has been studied in a variety of papers [16, 17, 32]. In addition to having its curvature and torsion change linearly – a property acknowledged to characterize eye-pleasing curves – this section proves that our 3D Euler curves also hold the following properties.

1. Invariance to similarity transformations (translation, rotation, and scaling).

2. Symmetry: The curve leaving the point $\mathbf{x}_0$ with tangent $\vec{T_0}$ and reaching the point $\mathbf{x}_f$ with tangent $\vec{T_f}$, coincides with the curve leaving the point $\mathbf{x}_f$ with tangent $-\vec{T_f}$ and reaching the point $\mathbf{x}_0$ with tangent $-\vec{T_0}$.

3. Extensibility: For every point $\mathbf{x}_m \in \mathcal{C}$ between points $\mathbf{x}_0$ and $\mathbf{x}_f$, the curves $\mathcal{C}_1$ between $\mathbf{x}_0$ and $\mathbf{x}_m$ and $\mathcal{C}_2$ between $\mathbf{x}_m$ and $\mathbf{x}_f$ coincide with $\mathcal{C}$, each in its own section.

4. Smoothness: The tangent is defined at every point, i.e., $\frac{\partial \mathcal{C}}{\partial s}$ is finite. (In fact, our curves are C^∞-smooth.)

5. Roundness: If $\mathcal{C}$ interpolates two point-tangent pairs lying on a circle, then $\mathcal{C}$ is a circle. The importance of this property is demonstrated in Figures 1,6–7, where our spirals are both appealing and correct, since the boundary conditions indicate completion by a circular arc.

PROPOSITION 5.1. *A 3D Euler spiral is invariant to similarity transformations.*

PROOF. Invariance to rotation and translation results from Proposition 4.1. Below we prove invariance to scale. We are given an Euler spiral $\mathcal{C}$ of length L, which interpolates $\mathbf{x}_0 = \mathcal{C}(0)$ and $\mathbf{x}_f = \mathcal{C}(L)$, and whose parameters are $\kappa_0, \tau_0, \gamma, \delta$. We should show that the spiral $\mathcal{C}_\lambda$, which interpolates $\lambda\mathbf{x}_0$ and $\lambda\mathbf{x}_f$ for $\lambda > 0$, is equal to $\mathcal{C}$ multiplied by λ, i.e., $\forall s, 0 \leq s \leq L$:

$$\mathcal{C}_\lambda(s) = \lambda\mathcal{C}(s). \tag{7}$$

Hence, we need to find the constants $\widetilde{\kappa_0}, \widetilde{\tau_0}, \widetilde{\gamma}, \widetilde{\delta}, \widetilde{L}$ that define an Euler spiral $\mathcal{C}_\lambda$ that passes through $\lambda\mathbf{x}_0$ and $\lambda\mathbf{x}_f$ (i.e., $\mathcal{C}_\lambda(0) = \lambda\mathbf{x}_0$ and $\mathcal{C}_\lambda(\lambda L) = \lambda\mathbf{x}_f$) with tangents $\vec{T_0}$ and $\vec{T_f}$ respectively. Moreover, for every point on the curve, it should coincide with $\lambda\mathcal{C}$.

We examine the 3D Euler spiral that satisfies Definition 4.1, having parameters $\widetilde{\kappa_0} = \frac{\kappa_0}{\lambda}, \widetilde{\tau_0} = \frac{\tau_0}{\lambda}, \widetilde{\gamma} = \frac{\gamma}{\lambda^2}, \widetilde{\delta} = \frac{\delta}{\lambda^2}, \widetilde{L} = \lambda L$. According to 2–4 in Definition 4.1, we get:

$$\begin{aligned}
\frac{d\vec{T}(u)}{du} &= \left(\frac{\kappa_0}{\lambda} + \frac{\gamma}{\lambda^2}u\right)\vec{N}(u), \\
\frac{d\vec{N}(u)}{du} &= -\left(\frac{\kappa_0}{\lambda} + \frac{\gamma}{\lambda^2}u\right)\vec{T}(u) + \left(\frac{\tau_0}{\lambda} + \frac{\delta}{\lambda}u\right)\vec{B}(u), \\
\frac{d\vec{B}(u)}{du} &= -\left(\frac{\tau_0}{\lambda} + \frac{\delta}{\lambda^2}u\right)\vec{N}(u).
\end{aligned} \tag{8}$$

By defining a new parameter $v = u/\lambda$ ($\Rightarrow dv = du/\lambda$), we get that $\frac{d\vec{T}}{du} = \frac{d\vec{T}}{dv}\frac{dv}{du} = \frac{1}{\lambda}\frac{d\vec{T}}{dv}$. Similarly, $\frac{d\vec{N}}{du} = \frac{1}{\lambda}\frac{d\vec{N}}{dv}$ and $\frac{d\vec{B}}{du} = \frac{1}{\lambda}\frac{d\vec{B}}{dv}$. Equation (8) now becomes:

$$\begin{aligned}
\frac{d\vec{T}(v)}{dv} &= (\kappa_0 + \gamma v)\vec{N}(v), \\
\frac{d\vec{N}(v)}{dv} &= -(\kappa_0 + \gamma v)\vec{T}(v) + (\tau_0 + \delta v)\vec{B}(v), \\
\frac{d\vec{B}(v)}{dv} &= -(\tau_0 + \delta v)\vec{N}(v).
\end{aligned}$$

Note that this could be done since all the properties of the Frenet-Serret Equations hold for every parameterization, not necessarily the arc-length parameterization [9] .

We can now proceed to calculating the 3D Euler spiral and its tangent:

$$\vec{T_\lambda}(s) = \int_0^{\lambda s} \frac{d\vec{T}}{du}du + \vec{T_0},$$

$$\mathcal{C}_\lambda(s) = \int_0^{\lambda s}\left[\int_0^t \frac{d\vec{T}}{du}du + \vec{T_0}\right]dt + \lambda\mathbf{x}_0.$$

By defining new parameters $v = u/\lambda (\Rightarrow dv = du/\lambda)$ and $\hat{t} = t/\lambda (\Rightarrow d\hat{t} = dt/\lambda)$, we get:

$$\vec{T_\lambda}(s) \overset{v=u/\lambda}{=} \int_0^s \frac{1}{\lambda}\frac{d\vec{T}}{dv}\lambda dv + \vec{T_0} = \vec{T}(s),$$

$$\begin{aligned}\mathcal{C}_\lambda(s) &\overset{v=u/\lambda}{=} \int_0^{\lambda s}\left[\int_0^{t/\lambda}\frac{1}{\lambda}\frac{d\vec{T}}{dv}\lambda dv + \vec{T_0}\right]dt + \lambda\mathbf{x}_0 \\ &\overset{\hat{t}=t/\lambda}{=} \int_0^{s}\left[\int_0^{\hat{t}}\frac{d\vec{T}}{dv}dv + \vec{T_0}\right]\lambda d\hat{t} + \lambda\mathbf{x}_0 \\ &= \lambda\mathcal{C}(s).\end{aligned}$$

Since this holds for every $0 \leq s \leq L$, Equation (7) holds. We also specifically get the boundary conditions $\mathcal{C}_\lambda(0) = \lambda\mathcal{C}(0) = \lambda\mathbf{x}_0, \vec{T}_\lambda(0) = \vec{T}(0) = \vec{T_0}$ and $\mathcal{C}_\lambda(\lambda L) = \lambda\mathcal{C}(L) = \lambda\mathbf{x}_f, \vec{T}_\lambda(\lambda L) = \vec{T}(L) = \vec{T}_f$. □

PROPOSITION 5.2. *A 3D Euler spiral is symmetric. (Proof in Appendix A)*

PROPOSITION 5.3. *A 3D Euler spiral is extensible. (Proof in Appendix B)*

PROPOSITION 5.4. *A 3D Euler spiral is smooth.*

PROOF. According to Proposition 4.1, there exists a solution for the Frenet-Serret equations. Therefore, $\frac{\partial\mathcal{C}}{\partial s} = \vec{T}(s)$ is defined for every $0 \leq s \leq L$. □

PROPOSITION 5.5. *A 3D Euler spiral is round.*

PROOF. For given two point-tangent pairs lying on a circle, the circle defined by $\kappa_0 \neq 0, \tau_0 = 0, \gamma = 0, \delta = 0$ is a solution for the Frenet-Serret Equation. □

6. CURVE CONSTRUCTION ALGORITHM

In Section 4 we have shown that given curve parameters $\kappa_0, \tau_0, \gamma, \delta, L \in \mathbb{R}$ and initial conditions $\mathbf{x}_0$, $\vec{T_0}$ and $\vec{N_0}$, there exists a 3D Euler spiral determined by these parameters and satisfying the initial conditions.

In practice, however, we are given two points and their associated tangents $\left(\mathbf{x}_0, \vec{T_0}\right)$ and $\left(\mathbf{x}_f, \vec{T_f}\right)$. Our goal is to find the parameters $\kappa_0, \tau_0, \gamma, \delta, L \in \mathbb{R}$ that define the 3D Euler spiral that starts at $\mathbf{x}_0$ and $\vec{T_0}$ and minimizes both the difference between the curve's position at $s = L$ and $\mathbf{x}_f$, and the difference between the curve's tangent at $s = L$ and $\vec{T_f}$. In other words, we attempt to minimize the following error:

$$\epsilon = (\epsilon_x + \epsilon_T), \tag{9}$$

$$\epsilon_x = \left[(x(L) - x_f)^2 + (y(L) - y_f)^2 + (z(L) - z_f)^2\right],$$

$$\epsilon_T = \left[(T_x(L) - T_{f,x})^2 + (T_y(L) - T_{f,y})^2 + (T_z(L) - T_{f,z})^2\right].$$

We experimented with other weights of ϵ_x and ϵ_T as well, but they were not proven beneficial.

We propose the Gradient-descent approach to find the parameters of the 3D Euler spiral that minimizes the error in Eq. (9). This approach, which guarantees convergence to a local minimum, is described below and explained thereafter.

Parameter initialization (Step 1): The 3D Euler spiral is initialized using a planar Euler spiral [34]. The question is which plane to choose. We define the plane for which three out of the four boundary conditions hold: $\mathbf{x}_0$, $\mathbf{x}_f$, and $\vec{T_0}$. Therefore, the plane (whose normal is denoted by $\vec{N_0}$) is defined by two vectors: $\vec{T_0}$ and the vector between $\mathbf{x}_0$ and $\mathbf{x}_f$. Note that the resulting planar Euler spiral interpolates $\vec{T_0}$ at $\mathbf{x}_0$ and the projection of $\vec{T_f}$ onto the plane at $\mathbf{x}_f$. The parameters of this 2D spiral κ_0, γ, L are used to initialize our curves. Since it lies on a plane, the torsion's parameters are initialized to zero ($\tau_0 = 0$, $\delta = 0$).

Algorithm 1 Gradient-descent 3D Euler spiral construction

1: Parameter initialization $< \kappa_0, \tau_0, \gamma, \delta, L >$
2: While the current error ϵ and the current step size Δ are large:
3: Calculate the gradient direction
4: Define the step size Δ
5: Update the curve parameters $< \kappa_0, \tau_0, \gamma, \delta, L >$

Our experiments indicate that this initialization gives a good approximation to κ_0 and γ, which hardly change afterwards. We also tested other initialization methods (e.g., Hermite spline, 3D Biarc, and 2D Euler spiral on the binormal plane). We found that our initialization is the fastest and the most accurate.

Iterative step (Steps 3-5): First, the gradient direction, which is the direction of the steepest descent, is calculated. Since the curve is described as a set of differential equations that do not have an explicit solution, we cannot explicitly find the best gradient direction. Instead, at each iteration, we first find the parameters among $\kappa_0, \tau_0, \gamma, \delta, L$, that when modified by $\pm\Delta$, yield a decrease of the error ϵ. We then compare the Euler spirals that result by modifying only one of these parameters to the spiral that results by modifying them all, and choose the spiral that obtains the minimum error ϵ.

Each of these candidate curves is computed by numerically solving the Frenet-Serret Equations (Definition 4.1). This is done by sampling the arc-length parameter s uniformly and solving the equations at these sampled points, using the Euler method [1]. This method only needs the solution at the immediately preceding point to compute the function at the next point. The first point is the input $\mathbf{x}_0$, $\vec{T_0}$ and the normal to the initial plane $\vec{N_0}$ (from Step 1).

Next, the step size is modified. If the error ϵ of the chosen direction is smaller than the error obtained in the previous iteration, Δ is unchanged. Otherwise, it is decreased to $\frac{3\Delta}{4}$.

Finally, the parameters are updated. If Δ is unchanged, the parameters that determined the gradient direction are updated according to the chosen direction.

Termination (Step 2): In our experiments, Δ is initialized to 0.1. The algorithm runs until $\Delta <$ *1e-5* or the error $\epsilon <$ *1e-6*. Smaller values yield negligible changes to the curves.

Optional bound on L (Step 5): Since our curve is a spiral, the obtained solution can have multiple revolutions. For the type of input we expect, it is often desirable to limit the solution to have at most one revolution. This is done by bounding the parameter L, as follows. We first approximate the maximal possible length as the length of the planar Euler spiral with parameters κ_0, γ. Since the tangent angle of such a curve is $\theta(s) = \frac{1}{2}\gamma s^2 + \kappa_0 s + \theta_0$ [16], we require that

$$\theta(L) - \theta_0 = \frac{1}{2}\gamma L^2 + \kappa_0 L \leq 2\pi.$$

Implementation issues: Calculating the numerical solution to the Frenet-Serret Equations at each iteration of the Gradient-descent algorithm might be expensive. In addition,

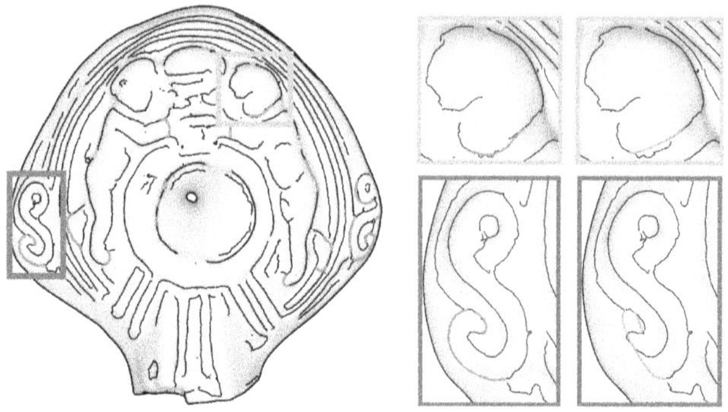

Figure 4: Fixing the curves detected by [18]. Our curves (red) manage to capture the "S" shape, in contrast to the automatically-scaled Hermite splines (green).

Figure 5: Completing the curves produced by [8] on the Buddha – 3D Euler spirals (red) and Hermite splines (green). Note how the spirals nicely capture the "S" shapes.

(a) Our completion (b) Hermite completion

Figure 6: Completing the curves produced by [15] on the Column model: Our Euler-spiral completion (red) is circular and resembles the real column.

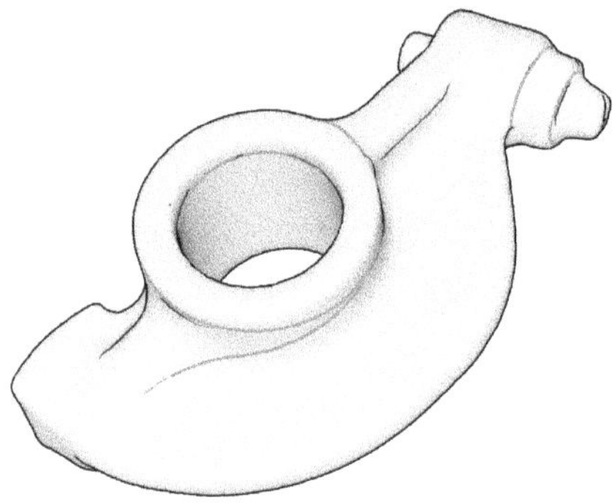

Figure 7: Completing the curves produced by [8] on the Rocker-arm model. The roundness property is visible.

the number of samples along the curve should be carefully determined. Using too many samples will result in a long computation time, while too few samples will cause accuracy problems and result in a large error ϵ. To accelerate the computation while using a fixed and rather small number of samples, we scale the region of interest to the box $(-1,-1,-1)$,$(1,1,1)$, prior to applying Algorithm 1, and then scale it back. Recall that Proposition 5.1 allows us to scale the problem back and forth.

In practice, the problem is first translated by $-x_0$. Then, it is scaled by $D = \max(\Delta x = |x_f - x_0|, \Delta y = |y_f - y_0|, \Delta z = |z_f - z_0|)$, while leaving the tangents at the endpoints unaltered. Then, the curve's parameters are found by Algorithm 1 using 100 samples along the curve for performing the numerical calculations. Once a solution is obtained, it is scaled back to the original range.

7. RESULTS AND APPLICATIONS

This section demonstrates the use of our spirals in two curve completion applications. In the first, the entire model is given, but the algorithm for edge detection on surfaces generates incomplete curves. This is a common problem with most edge-detection algorithms, which may be vital for the shape analysis algorithms that use these curves. In the second application, the given models are broken – a situation prevalent in archaeology. The user is interested in drawing the curves that would be drawn should the entire model be given. In both cases, the user needs only mark the endpoints of the curves and the system creates an Euler spiral between the given endpoints. No parameter tuning is necessary.

Curve completion on polyhedral surfaces: Figures 4–7 demonstrate the use of our spirals for completing the curves detected by various edge detection algorithms: suggestive contours [8], apparent ridges [15], valleys and ridges [35], and demarcating curves [18]. In this application the user needs only choose the endpoints of existing curves that should be connected, since the system can automatically compute the tangents at these endpoints.

Our curves are also compared to the results obtained using Hermite splines. Since Hermite splines depend on the magnitude of the tangent, we used automatic scaling. The

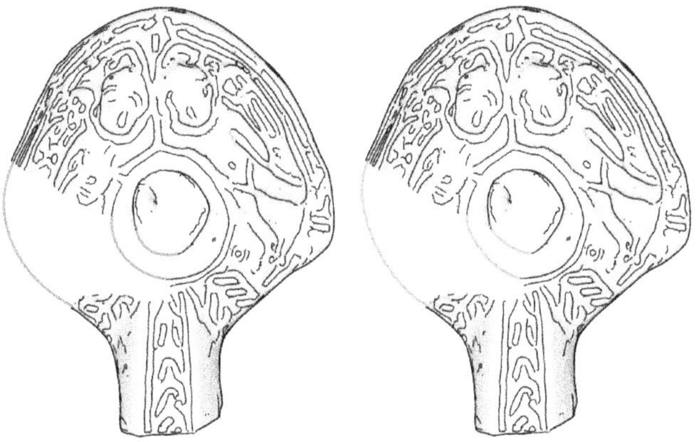

(a) Our completion (b) Hermite completion

Figure 8: Completing a (manually) broken lamp. The 3D Euler spirals (red) are more appealing than the Hermite splines (green) due to the nice circles produced. This is guaranteed by the roundness property of our curves.

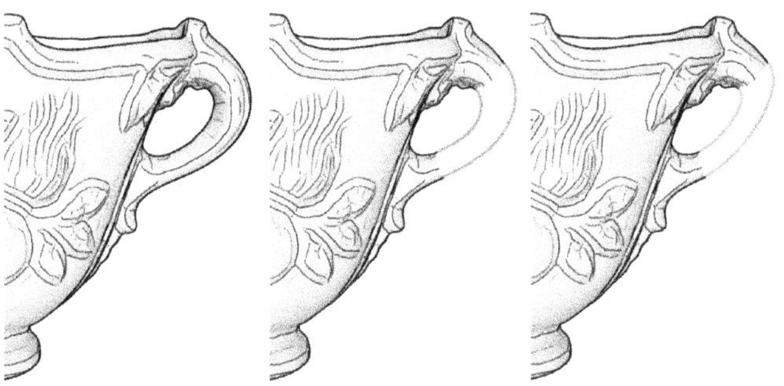

(a) Unbroken model (b) Our completion (c) Hermite

Figure 9: The completion of a (manually) broken pot. Our curves better resemble the original unbroken model.

tangents provided for the computation of the Hermite splines are multiplied by D (described in Section 6), so as to relate their length to the distance between the endpoints.

It can be seen that our curves manage to satisfactorily complete the curves, regardless of how they were created. The two features that are most visible in our spirals, are the ability to create perfect circular arcs (Figures 6–7) and the "natural" S-shapes (Figure 5).

In this application, the generated curves should lie on the surface. Since our curves are not constrained to lie on any surface, the produced 3D Euler curves are projected to the surface. This is done by projecting each point on the curve to its closest point onto the mesh. Though this method is straightforward, it yields good results.

Shape illustration in archaeology: Archaeology sets many challenges to geometry processing. Many of the artifacts found by the archaeologists are scanned and need to be processed and analyzed. These artifacts are often broken and eroded and thus are difficult to handle. One specific problem is the drawing of the artifact, which is traditionally performed manually by archaeological artists in 2D, as shown in Figure 2. This is an expensive and time-consuming procedure, which is prone to biases and inaccuracies. Our curves propose a 3D alternative, as illustrated in Figure 8.

Figures 9–11 show several additional models, which show that our completed curves are not only more appealing, but also better resemble the shape of the original unbroken models. For example, the curl completion in Figure 10 demonstrates the S-shape property of our spirals, while the ear completion illustrates a more "circular" shape. Figure 11 demonstrates that since our curves have more "volume", they avoid intersecting the mesh, which might occur when using the Hermite completion.

Running times: The algorithm was implemented in Matlab and C and ran on a 2Ghz Intel Core 2 Duo-processor laptop with 2Gb of memory. The running time, which depends on the complexity of the required interpolation curve, is 0.01–0.5 second for the curves demonstrated in this paper. The further the curve is from being planar, the longer the time required. This is probably due to initializing the torsion to zero. The size of the model has little affect on the time; it is relevant only when projection is performed. The projection itself is straightforward and quick to compute.

8. CONCLUSION

This paper presented a novel definition of curves, which extends the 2D Euler spiral to 3D. We proved that for given parameters, a unique curve always exists. Moreover, we showed that our curves satisfy several desired aesthetic properties, including invariance to similarity transformation, symmetry, extensibility, smoothness, and roundness. Given boundary conditions – endpoints and tangents – this paper proposed a novel technique for generating these curves, based on the gradient-descent approach.

The utility of our curves is demonstrated for edge completion on polyhedral surfaces and for artifact illustration in archaeology – a task that is traditionally performed manually in 2D. In archaeology, when automatic 3D curve drawing replaces the traditional manual 2D drawing, automatic or interactive curve completion, would be the only alternative. We believe that the proposed curves may be found a feasible alternative for additional applications involving shape design, artistic design, and shape analysis.

In the future, we wish to prove existence of the curves given point–tangent boundary conditions. In 2D, an algorithm was first established [16] before existence was proved several years later [34]. We hope that the same will happen in 3D. In practice a solution exists for all the inputs we tried.

Acknowledgements: This research was supported in part by the Israel Science Foundation (ISF) 628/08, the Goldbers Fund for Electronics Research, and the Ollendorff foundation. We thank Dr. A. Gilboa and the Zinman Institute of Archaeology at the University of Haifa for providing the archaeological models.

9. REFERENCES

[1] U. Ascher and L. Petzold. *Computer methods for ordinary differential equations and differential-algebraic equations.* Society for Industrial Mathematics, 1998.

[2] G. Barequet and S. Kumar. Repairing CAD models. In *IEEE Visualization*, 1997.

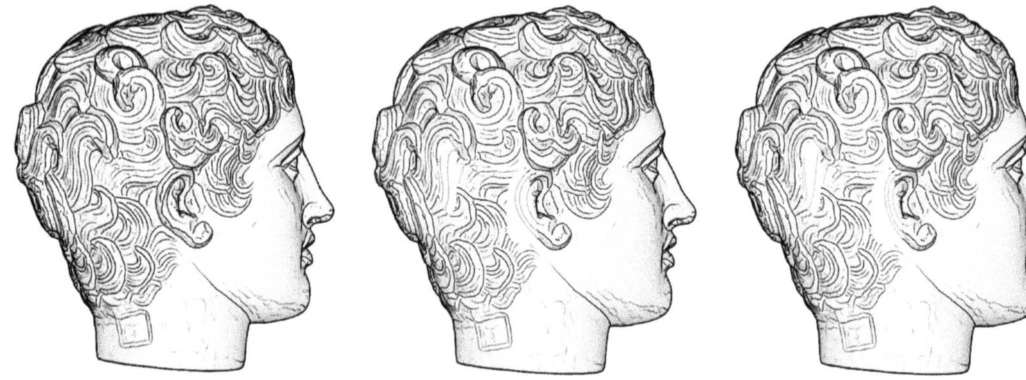

(a) Unbroken model (b) Our completion (c) Hermite completion

Figure 10: Completing a (manually) broken head sculpture. The 3D Euler spirals (red) nicely compute the S-shaped curl. The Euler completion of both the curl and the ear are more similar to the original model than the Hermite completion (green).

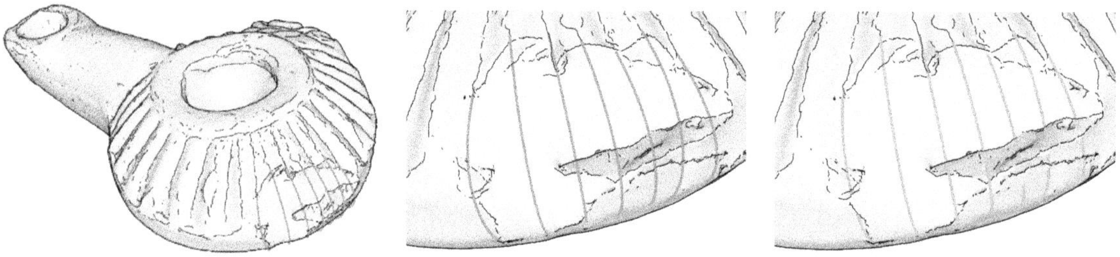

(a) Our completion (b) Zoom in - our completion (c) Hermite completion

Figure 11: Completion of a broken Hellenistic lamp. The curves produced by [35] are used to determine initial conditions. Our curves (red) manage to capture the true volume of the shape, while the Hermite splines (green) intersect the broken model.

[3] G. Barequet and M. Sharir. Filling gaps in the boundary of a polyhedron. *Computer Aided Geometric Design*, 12(2):207–229, 1995.

[4] M. Born. *Untersuchungen über die Stabilität der elastischen Linie in Ebene und Raum: Unter verschiedenen Grenzbedingungen.* Dieterich, 1906.

[5] M. Brady, W. Grimson, and D. Langridge. Shape encoding and subjective contours. In *First Annual National Conference on Artificial Intelligence*, pages 15–17, 1980.

[6] K. Chui, W. Chiu, and K. Yu. Direct 5-axis tool-path generation from point cloud input using 3D biarc fitting. *Robotics and Comp. Integrated Manufacturing*, 24(2):270–286, 2008.

[7] C. De Boor. *A practical guide to splines*. Springer, 2001.

[8] D. DeCarlo, A. Finkelstein, S. Rusinkiewicz, and A. Santella. Suggestive contours for conveying shape. *ACM Trans. Graph.*, 22(3):848–855, 2003.

[9] M. do Carmo. *Differential geometry of curves and surfaces*. Prentice Hall, 1976.

[10] G. Farin. *Curves and surfaces for computer aided geometric design*. Academic Press Professional Inc., 1993.

[11] A. Forsyth. *Calculus of variations*. Dover, NY, 1960.

[12] W. Graustein. *Differential Geometry*. Dover, 2006.

[13] L. Guiqing, L. Xianmin, and L. Hua. 3D discrete clothoid splines. In *CGI '01*, pages 321–324, 2001.

[14] B. Horn. The curve of least energy. *ACM Transactions on Mathematical Software*, 9(4):441–460, 1983.

[15] T. Judd, F. Durand, and E. Adelson. Apparent ridges for line drawing. *ACM Trans. Graph.*, 26(3):19:1–7, 2007.

[16] B. Kimia, I. Frankel, and A. Popescu. Euler spiral for shape completion. *Int. J. Comp. Vision*, 54(1):159–182, 2003.

[17] D. Knuth. Mathematical typography. *American Mathematical Society*, 1(2):337–372, 1979.

[18] M. Kolomenkin, I. Shimshoni, and A. Tal. Demarcating curves for shape illustration. *ACM Trans. Graph.*, 27(5):157:1–9, 2008.

[19] R. Levien. The Elastica: a mathematical history. Technical Report UCB/EECS-2008-103, EECS Department, University of California, Berkeley, 2008.

[20] R. Levien. The Euler spiral: a mathematical history. Technical Report UCB/EECS-2008-111, EECS Department, University of California, Berkeley, 2008.

[21] J. McCrae and K. Singh. Sketching piecewise clothoid curves. In *Sketch-Based Interfaces and Modeling*, 2008.

[22] D. Meek and D. Walton. Clothoid spline transition spirals. *Mathematics of Computation*, 59(199):117–133, 1992.

[23] E. Mehlum. Nonlinear splines. *Computer aided geometric design*, pages 173–207, 1974.
[24] E. Mehlum. Appell and the apple (nonlinear splines in space). In *Mathematical Methods for Curves and Surfaces*, pages 365–384, 1995.
[25] H. Moreton and C. Séquin. Functional optimization for fair surface design. *SIGGRAPH*, 26(2):167–176, 1992.
[26] D. Mumford. Elastica and computer vision. *Algebraic Geometry and Its Applications*, pages 491–506, 1994.
[27] W. Rutkowski. Shape completion. *Computer Graphics and Image Processing*, 9:89–101, 1979.
[28] A. Sharf, M. Alexa, and D. Cohen-Or. Context-based surface completion. *ACM Trans. Graph.*, 23(3):878–887, 2004.
[29] T. Sharrock and R. Martin. Biarc in three dimensions. In *The mathematics of surfaces II*, pages 395–411, 1996.
[30] M. Singh and J. Fulvio. Visual extrapolation of contour geometry. *Natl. Academy of Sciences*, 102(3):939–944, 2005.
[31] E. Stern. *Excavations at Dor.* Jerusalem: Institute of Archaeology of the Hebrew University, 1995.
[32] S. Ullman. Filling-in the gaps: The shape of subjective contours and a model for their generation. *Biological Cybernetics*, 25(1):1–6, 1976.
[33] D. Walton and D. Meek. A controlled clothoid spline. *Computers & Graphics*, 29(3):353–363, 2005.
[34] D. Walton and D. Meek. G1 interpolation with a single cornu spiral segment. *Journal of Computational and Applied Mathematics*, 223(1):86–96, 2007.
[35] S. Yoshizawa, A. Belyaev, and H. P. Seidel. Fast and robust detection of crest lines on meshes. In *ACM Symposium on Solid and Physical Modeling*, pages 227-232, 2005.

APPENDIX

A. SYMMETRY (PROPOSITION 5.3)

Proof: We are given a 3D Euler spiral $\mathcal{C}$ that interpolates the point-tangent pairs $(\mathbf{x}_0, \vec{T}_0)$ and $(\mathbf{x}_f, \vec{T}_f)$ and has parameters $\kappa_0, \tau_0, \gamma, \delta, L$. We need to show that the 3D Euler spiral $\mathcal{C}_{sym}$ that interpolates the point-tangent pairs $(\mathbf{x}_f, -\vec{T}_f)$ and $(\mathbf{x}_0, -\vec{T}_0)$ coincides with $\mathcal{C}$.

Thus, we need to find the constants $\widetilde{\kappa_0}, \widetilde{\tau_0}, \widetilde{\gamma}, \widetilde{\delta}, \widetilde{L}$ that define the Euler spiral $\mathcal{C}_{sym}$ and show that at every point the curves coincide and their tangents are opposite:

$$\vec{T}_{\mathcal{C}_{sym}}(L-s) = -\vec{T}_{\mathcal{C}}(s) \ \ \forall s, 0 \le s \le L,$$

$$\mathcal{C}_{sym}(L-s) = \mathcal{C}(s) \ \ \forall s, 0 \le s \le L.$$

We examine the 3D Euler spiral $\mathcal{C}_{sym}$ that satisfies Definition 4.1 and has parameters $\widetilde{\kappa_0} = \kappa_0 + \gamma L$, $\widetilde{\tau_0} = \tau_0 + \delta s$, $\widetilde{\gamma} = -\gamma$, $\widetilde{\delta} = -\delta$, $\widetilde{L} = L$.

According to 2–4 in Definition 4.1, we get:

$$\begin{aligned}
\frac{d\vec{T}_{\mathcal{C}_{sym}}(u)}{du} &= (\kappa_0 + \gamma L - \gamma u)\, \vec{N}_{\mathcal{C}_{sym}}(u), \\
\frac{d\vec{N}_{\mathcal{C}_{sym}}(u)}{du} &= -(\kappa_0 + \gamma L - \gamma u)\, \vec{T}_{\mathcal{C}_{sym}}(u) \\
&\quad + (\tau_0 + \delta L - \delta u)\, \vec{B}_{\mathcal{C}_{sym}}(u), \\
\frac{d\vec{B}_{\mathcal{C}_{sym}}(u)}{du} &= -(\tau_0 + \delta L - \delta u)\, \vec{N}_{\mathcal{C}_{sym}}(u).
\end{aligned} \tag{10}$$

By defining a new parameter $v = L - u$ ($\Rightarrow dv = -du$), we get that $\frac{d\vec{T}_{\mathcal{C}_{sym}}}{du} = \frac{d\vec{T}_{\mathcal{C}_{sym}}}{dv}\frac{dv}{du} = -\frac{d\vec{T}_{\mathcal{C}_{sym}}}{dv} = \frac{d\vec{T}_{\mathcal{C}}}{dv}$. Similarly, $\frac{d\vec{N}_{\mathcal{C}_{sym}}}{du} = -\frac{d\vec{N}_{\mathcal{C}_{sym}}}{dv}$ and $\frac{d\vec{B}_{\mathcal{C}_{sym}}}{du} = -\frac{d\vec{B}_{\mathcal{C}_{sym}}}{dv}$. This could be done since all the properties of the Frenet-Serret Equations hold for every parameterization, not necessarily the arc-length parameterization [9] . By tangent definition we get:

$$\begin{aligned}
\vec{T}_{\mathcal{C}_{sym}}(L-s) &= \int_0^{L-s} \frac{d\vec{T}_{\mathcal{C}_{sym}}}{du} du - \vec{T}_f \\
&\overset{v=L-u}{=} \int_L^{s} \frac{d\vec{T}_{\mathcal{C}_{sym}}}{dv} dv - \vec{T}_f = -\int_s^{L} \frac{d\vec{T}_{\mathcal{C}_{sym}}}{dv} dv - \vec{T}_f \\
&= \int_s^{L} \frac{d\vec{T}_{\mathcal{C}}}{dv} dv - \vec{T}_f = \int_s^{L} \frac{d\vec{T}_{\mathcal{C}}}{dv} dv - \left(\int_0^{L} \frac{d\vec{T}_{\mathcal{C}}}{dv} dv + \vec{T}_0\right) \\
&= -\int_0^{s} \frac{d\vec{T}_{\mathcal{C}}}{dv} dv - \vec{T}_0 = -\vec{T}_{\mathcal{C}}(s).
\end{aligned}$$

We now show that the curve $\mathcal{C}_{sym}$ coincides with the curve $\mathcal{C}$:

$$\begin{aligned}
\mathcal{C}_{sym}(L-s) &= \mathbf{x}_f + \int_0^{L-s} \left[\int_0^{t} \frac{d\vec{T}_{\mathcal{C}_{sym}}}{du} du - \vec{T}_f\right] dt \\
&\overset{v=L-u}{=} \mathbf{x}_f + \int_0^{L-s} \left[\int_L^{L-t} \frac{d\vec{T}_{\mathcal{C}_{sym}}}{dv} dv - \vec{T}_f\right] dt \\
&= \mathbf{x}_f + \int_0^{L-s} \left[\int_{L-t}^{L} \frac{d\vec{T}_{\mathcal{C}}}{dv} dv - \vec{T}_f\right] dt \\
&\overset{\hat{t}=L-t}{=} \mathbf{x}_f - \int_L^{s} \left[\int_{\hat{t}}^{L} \frac{d\vec{T}_{\mathcal{C}}}{dv} dv - \vec{T}_f\right] d\hat{t} \\
&= \mathbf{x}_f - \int_L^{s} \left[\int_{\hat{t}}^{L} \frac{d\vec{T}_{\mathcal{C}}}{dv} dv - \int_0^{L} \frac{d\vec{T}_{\mathcal{C}}}{dv} dv - \vec{T}_0\right] d\hat{t} \\
&= \mathbf{x}_0 + \int_0^{s} \left[\int_0^{\hat{t}} \frac{d\vec{T}_{\mathcal{C}}}{dv} dv + \vec{T}_0\right] d\hat{t} \overset{Eq.\ (2)}{=} \mathcal{C}(s). \ \square
\end{aligned}$$

B. EXTENSIBILITY (PROPOSITION 5.4)

Proof: Given a 3D Euler spiral $\mathcal{C}$ interpolating the point-tangent pairs $(\mathbf{x}_0, \vec{T}_0)$, $(\mathbf{x}_f, \vec{T}_f)$, we will show that for every $(\mathbf{x}_m, \vec{T}_m)$ on $\mathcal{C}$, the curves $\mathcal{C}_1$ between $\mathbf{x}_0$ and $\mathbf{x}_m$ and $\mathcal{C}_2$ between $\mathbf{x}_m$ and $\mathbf{x}_f$ coincide with $\mathcal{C}$, each in its own section.

Assume that $\mathcal{C}$ has parameters $\kappa_0, \tau_0, \gamma, \delta, L$. Let L_1 be the length of the sub-curve of $\mathcal{C}$ from $\mathbf{x}_0$ to $\mathbf{x}_m$. By the tangent definition and by Equation (2):

$$\vec{T}_m = \int_0^{L_1} \frac{d\vec{T}}{du} du + \vec{T}_0, \tag{11}$$

$$\mathbf{x}_m = \int_0^{L_1} \left[\int_0^{t} \frac{d\vec{T}}{du} du + \vec{T}_0\right] dt + \mathbf{x}_0. \tag{12}$$

Below we first show that $\mathcal{C}_1$ with the parameters $\hat{\kappa_0} = \kappa_0, \hat{\tau_0} = \tau_0, \hat{\gamma} = \gamma, \hat{\delta} = \delta, \hat{L} = L_1$, coincides with $\mathcal{C}$ for $0 \leq s \leq L_1$. Then we show that $\mathcal{C}_2$ with the parameters $\widetilde{\kappa_0} = \kappa_0 + \gamma L_1, \widetilde{\tau_0} = \tau_0 + \delta L_1, \widetilde{\gamma} = \gamma, \widetilde{\delta} = \delta, \widetilde{L} = L - L_1$, coincides with $\mathcal{C}$ for $L_1 \leq s \leq L$. The latter is done in two steps: First we use Equation (11) to prove that the tangents are equal and then we use both Equations (11) and (12) to prove that the coordinates are the same.

The proof that $\mathcal{C}_1$ coincides with $\mathcal{C}$ for $0 \leq s \leq L_1$ is trivial and derived from Proposition 4.1. Since both curves have the same parameters, they must be the same curve, by the uniqueness of the curve.

Let us denote the tangent of the curve $\mathcal{C}$ at $\mathcal{C}(s)$ by $\vec{T_\mathcal{C}}(s)$ and the tangent of the curve $\mathcal{C}_2$ at $\mathcal{C}_2(s)$ by $\vec{T}_{\mathcal{C}_2}(s)$. In order to show that $\mathcal{C}_2$ coincides with $\mathcal{C}$, we need to show that a 3D Euler spiral $\mathcal{C}_2$ that starts at $(\mathbf{x}_m, \vec{T}_m)$ and has parameters $\widetilde{\kappa_0}, \widetilde{\tau_0}, \widetilde{\gamma}, \widetilde{\delta}, \widetilde{L}$, reaches $\mathcal{C}(s)$ with tangent $\vec{T_\mathcal{C}}(s)$, $\forall s, L_1 \leq s \leq L$.

We first show that $\forall s, L_1 \leq s \leq L$, the tangent at $\mathcal{C}_2(s - L_1)$ is $\vec{T_\mathcal{C}}(s)$. According to Definition 4.1, 2–4, we get:

$$\begin{aligned}
\frac{d\vec{T}_{\mathcal{C}_2}(u)}{du} &= (\kappa_0 + \gamma L_1 + \gamma u)\,\vec{N}_{\mathcal{C}_2}(u)\\
\frac{d\vec{N}_{\mathcal{C}_2}(u)}{du} &= -(\kappa_0 + \gamma L_1 + \gamma u)\,\vec{T}_{\mathcal{C}_2}(u) + (\tau_0 + \delta L_1 + \delta u)\,\vec{B}_{\mathcal{C}_2}(u)\\
\frac{d\vec{B}_{\mathcal{C}_2}(u)}{du} &= -(\tau_0 + \delta L_1 + \delta u)\,\vec{N}_{\mathcal{C}_2}(u),
\end{aligned}$$

and by the tangent definition:

$$\vec{T}_{\mathcal{C}_2}(s - L_1) = \int_0^{s-L_1} \frac{d\vec{T}_{\mathcal{C}_2}}{du}du + \vec{T}_m.$$

In a similar manner to the proof of Proposition 5.3, by defining a new integration parameter $v = u + L_1$ and substituting Equation (11), we get:

$$\begin{aligned}
&\vec{T}_{\mathcal{C}_2}(s - L_1) = \int_{L_1}^{s} \frac{d\vec{T_\mathcal{C}}}{dv}dv + \vec{T}_m\\
&= \int_{L_1}^{s} \frac{d\vec{T_\mathcal{C}}}{dv}dv + \int_0^{L_1} \frac{d\vec{T_\mathcal{C}}}{dv}dv + \vec{T_0} = \int_0^{s} \frac{d\vec{T_\mathcal{C}}}{dv}dv + \vec{T_0} = \vec{T_\mathcal{C}}(s).
\end{aligned}$$

Next, we show that $\forall s, L_1 \leq s \leq L, \mathcal{C}_2(s - L_1) = \mathcal{C}(s)$. By Equation (2), we can define the endpoint of $\mathcal{C}_2$ as follows:

$$\begin{aligned}
\mathcal{C}_2(s - L_1) &= \mathbf{x}_m + \int_0^{s-L_1}\left[\int_0^t \frac{d\vec{T}_{\mathcal{C}_2}}{du}du + \vec{T}_m\right]dt\\
&\overset{v=u+L_1}{=} \mathbf{x}_m + \int_0^{s-L_1}\left[\int_{L_1}^{t+L_1} \frac{d\vec{T_\mathcal{C}}}{dv}dv + \vec{T}_m\right]dt \qquad (13)\\
&\overset{\hat{t}=t+L_1}{=} \mathbf{x}_m + \int_{L_1}^{s}\left[\int_{L_1}^{\hat{t}} \frac{d\vec{T_\mathcal{C}}}{dv}dv + \vec{T}_m\right]d\hat{t}.
\end{aligned}$$

Substituting Equation (12) into Equation (13) and then substituting Equation (11) will give us:

$$\begin{aligned}
&\mathcal{C}_2(s - L_1) =\\
&= \mathbf{x}_0 + \int_0^{L_1}\left[\int_0^{\hat{t}} \frac{d\vec{T_\mathcal{C}}}{dv}dv + \vec{T_0}\right]d\hat{t} + \int_{L_1}^{s}\left[\int_{L_1}^{\hat{t}} \frac{d\vec{T_\mathcal{C}}}{dv}dv + \vec{T}_m\right]d\hat{t}\\
&= \mathbf{x}_0 + \int_0^{L_1}\left[\int_0^{\hat{t}} \frac{d\vec{T_\mathcal{C}}}{dv}dv + \vec{T_0}\right]d\hat{t} + \int_{L_1}^{s}\left[\int_0^{\hat{t}} \frac{d\vec{T_\mathcal{C}}}{dv}dv + \vec{T_0}\right]d\hat{t}\\
&= \mathbf{x}_0 + \int_0^{s}\left[\int_0^{\hat{t}} \frac{d\vec{T_\mathcal{C}}}{dv}dv + \vec{T_0}\right]d\hat{t} = \mathcal{C}(s),
\end{aligned}$$

where the last equality holds by Equation (2). □

I/O-Efficient Computation of Water Flow Across a Terrain

Lars Arge*
MADALGO
University of Aarhus
Aarhus, Denmark
large@madalgo.au.dk

Morten Revsbæk*
MADALGO
University of Aarhus
Aarhus, Denmark
mrevs@madalgo.au.dk

Norbert Zeh†
Faculty of Computer Science
Dalhousie University
Halifax, Canada
nzeh@cs.dal.ca

ABSTRACT

Consider rain falling at a uniform rate onto a terrain $\mathcal{T}$ represented as a triangular irregular network. Over time, water collects in the basins of $\mathcal{T}$, forming lakes that spill into adjacent basins. Our goal is to compute, for each terrain vertex, the time this vertex is flooded (covered by water). We present an I/O-efficient algorithm that solves this problem using $O(\mathrm{sort}(X)\log(X/M) + \mathrm{sort}(N))$ I/Os, where N is the number of terrain vertices, X is the number of pits of the terrain, $\mathrm{sort}(N)$ is the cost of sorting N data items, and M is the size of the computer's main memory. Our algorithm assumes that the volumes and watersheds of the basins of $\mathcal{T}$ have been precomputed using existing methods.

Categories and Subject Descriptors

F.2.2 [**Analysis of Algorithms and Problem Complexity**]: Nonnumerical Algorithms and Problems—*Geometrical problems and computations*

General Terms

Algorithms, Theory

Keywords

Terrains, geographical information systems, I/O-efficient algorithms

*Supported in part by the Danish National Research Foundation, the Danish Strategic Research Council, and by the US Army Research office. MADALGO is the Center for Massive Data Algorithmics, a center of the Danish National Research Foundation.

†Supported in part by the Natural Sciences and Engineering Research Council of Canada and the Canada Research Chairs programme. Part of this work was done while on sabbatical at MADALGO.

1. INTRODUCTION

An important problem in terrain analysis is the prediction of water flow across a terrain. Traditional approaches focus on computing the river network of the terrain under the assumption that water does not collect in the basins of the terrain. In reality, water *does* collect in the terrain's basins, particularly during heavy rainfall. This may cause basins to spill into adjacent basins, changing the river network of the terrain as a result. Thus, to model the flow of water across a terrain over time, it is necessary to compute the times at which the basins of the terrain spill. In this paper, we solve the more general problem of computing, for every vertex v of a terrain $\mathcal{T}$, the time t_v at which it is flooded. We assume the terrain $\mathcal{T}$ is represented as a triangular irregular network (TIN) and the amount of rain is uniform across the terrain.

The accuracy of predictions of natural phenomena, such as flooding, depends on the precision of the data used in these predictions. High-resolution elevation models even of fairly small geographic regions often exceed the size of a computer's main memory. Current GIS tools cannot handle data sets of this size efficiently and therefore need to work with models of lower resolutions. This sacrifices accuracy because lower-resolution models do not capture all terrain features. For example, in experiments we conducted to predict the flooding of coastal regions of Denmark due to rising sea levels, an elevation model with one data point every 10m failed to capture a dike around an island, and the island was predicted to be flooded if the sea rises by 2m, while the dike can in fact withstand 2m higher sea levels. Using a higher-resolution model with one data point every 2m, we obtained the correct prediction, but storing elevation data for Denmark alone requires 500GB of space at this resolution, an input size well beyond the size of main memory and beyond the reach of current GIS tools.

To process data sets beyond the size of main memory efficiently, it is necessary to develop I/O-efficient algorithms, that is, algorithms that focus on minimizing the number of disk accesses they perform to swap data between disk and internal memory, as a disk access is orders of magnitude slower than an internal-memory computation step. In this paper, we propose an I/O-efficient algorithm for computing the flooding times of all vertices of a terrain $\mathcal{T}$.

The core of the problem is computing the spill times of all basins of $\mathcal{T}$. A simple method to compute these spill times is to simulate the entire sequence of spill events of the basins of $\mathcal{T}$ and maintain the watersheds of all basins that yet have to spill, as well as predicted spill times for these basins based on their current watersheds. An internal-memory solution based on this idea has been presented in [14]. In Section 3.2, we discuss an $O(N \log N)$ time implementation of this approach using a priority queue and a union-find structure. This simulation approach does not translate into an I/O-efficient algorithm, as the only known I/O-efficient union-find structure [1] requires the sequence of UNION operations to be known in advance. In simulating the sequence of spill events, the *set* of UNION operations is known, but their order depends on the spill times of the basins. Using an internal-memory union-find structure and an I/O-efficient priority queue (e.g., [3,12]), a cost of $O(X\alpha(X) + \text{sort}(N))$ disk accesses can be achieved, where $\alpha(\cdot)$ is the inverse of Ackermann's function, $\text{sort}(N) \ll N$ is the I/O complexity of sorting N data items (see next section), and X is the number of pits of the terrain. In contrast, the algorithm presented in this paper achieves an I/O complexity of $O(\text{sort}(X)\log(X/M) + \text{sort}(N))$ disk accesses.

In the remainder of this section, we formally define the computational model we use, discuss previous work, and give an overview of our algorithm. Section 2 introduces the terminology and notation we use throughout the paper. Section 3 discusses our algorithm for computing the spill times of the terrain's basins and the flooding times of all terrain vertices. This algorithm makes use of an I/O-efficient meldable priority queue, which we discuss in Section 4.

1.1 I/O Model

We use the *I/O model* with one (logical) disk [2] to design and analyze our algorithm. In this model, the computer is equipped with a two-level memory hierarchy consisting of an *internal memory* and a (disk-based) *external memory*. The internal memory is capable of holding M data items (vertices, edges, etc.), while the external memory is of conceptually unlimited size. All computation has to happen on data in internal memory. Data is transferred between internal and external memory in blocks of B consecutive data items. Such a transfer is referred to as an *I/O operation* or *I/O*. The cost of an algorithm is the number of I/Os it performs. The number of I/Os required to read N contiguous items from disk is $\lceil N/B \rceil$. The number of I/Os required to sort N items is $\text{sort}(N) = \Theta((N/B)\log_{M/B}(N/B))$ [2]. For all realistic values of N, M, and B, we have $N/B < \text{sort}(N) \ll N$.

1.2 Related Work

Due to its importance, the problem of computing water flow across a terrain (usually in the form of a river network) has been studied extensively. Most existing methods for computing river networks assume that once water flows into a small basin of the terrain, it never flows out—in other words, basins do not spill. Therefore, to avoid water getting caught in small local basins, most flow modelling approaches first remove all basins by *flooding* the terrain, that is, conceptually pouring water onto the terrain until all basins are filled [4,13,15]. However, this often leads to unrealistic flow patterns, since many important geographical features are removed. Recent papers [1,5] suggested *partial flooding* algorithms that flood only "small" basins, where the size of a basin can be defined using different measures, such as height, volume or area. Agarwal, Arge and Yi [1] described an $O(\text{sort}(N))$ I/O partial flooding algorithm that removes all basins of small height. This is done by computing the *topological persistence* [10,11] of each basin and removing the ones with persistence below a small threshold. The key to obtaining an $O(\text{sort}(N))$ I/O solution to this problem is an algorithm that can process a sequence of N UNION and FIND operations using $O(\text{sort}(N))$ I/Os, assuming the entire sequence of operations is provided in advance. Arge and Revsbæk [5] extended the result of [1] to removing basins based on different geometric measures, including volume and area.

Partial flooding methods provide a basis only for approximate solutions to flow modelling, as the underlying assumption is that all "small" basins are flooded at a certain time, while all "big" basins are not. This assumption may not be true, as the spill time of a basin depends on its volume and its watershed, and the watershed of a basin may grow over time as a result of other basins spilling into it; in particular, the watershed of a big basin may grow to a size far exceeding the size of the watershed of a small basin and, thus, the big basin may spill *before* the small basin. To model the flow network at time t accurately, it is necessary to compute the times the basins of $\mathcal{T}$ fill and remove the basins that are full at time t. This is much harder than the partial flooding approaches discussed above, as the above methods are based on local measures associated with each basin, while the computation of the actual spill time of each basin β depends on the spill times of other basins that spill into β. As mentioned in the introduction, Liu and Snoeyink [14] presented an internal-memory algorithm for computing actual spill times and used it for flow prediction. While the paper does not present the algorithm in detail, we discuss an efficient implementation using a union-find structure and a priority queue in Section 3.2; this implementation is needed as part of our I/O-efficient algorithm.

We also require a tree structure that represents the nesting of the basins of $\mathcal{T}$. This tree has been termed the *merge tree* of $\mathcal{T}$ in [7,8] (also see Section 2) and can be computed using $O(\text{sort}(N))$ I/Os using the topological persistence algorithm of [1]. This algorithm is easily augmented to compute the lowest saddle on the boundary of each basin and, as shown in [5], the volume of each basin.

Computing the watershed sizes of all basins of $\mathcal{T}$ is harder. The watershed sizes of all basins of $\mathcal{T}$ are easily computed from the watershed sizes of all pits by summing watershed sizes bottom up in the merge tree. However, the only I/O-efficient algorithm for computing the watersheds of all pits of a terrain exactly is the one of [9]. This algorithm performs $O(\text{sort}(N + S))$ I/Os for fat terrains, where S is the size of the terrain's strip map. The size of the strip map of a fat terrain is $\Theta(N^2)$ in the worst case [9], in which case the exact computation of watersheds becomes infeasible. An approach often taken in practice [16–18] is to assume that water flows only along terrain edges, allowing the computation of watersheds using $O(\text{sort}(N))$ I/Os. While this may lead to poor approximations of the watersheds for irregular terrains [9], TIN's derived from LIDAR data, for example, are rather regular, and the computed watersheds match the real watersheds rather closely.

1.3 New Result

We present an algorithm that computes the flooding times of all terrain vertices using $O(\text{sort}(X)\log(X/M) + \text{sort}(N))$ I/Os, where N is the size of the terrain and X is the number of pits. This assumes that the watershed sizes and volumes of all basins are given and that every vertex is labelled with the pit whose watershed contains it. The cost of computing this information has been discussed in the previous section. Our algorithm operates on the merge tree $\mathcal{M}$ of the given terrain $\mathcal{T}$. Given a node β of $\mathcal{M}$, we employ a recursive strategy to compute the spill times of all basins represented by descendants of β. If there are at most M such descendants, we use an augmented version of the internal-memory algorithm mentioned in the introduction to compute the spill times of their corresponding basins using O(sort(Y)) I/Os, where Y is the number of descendants of β plus the number of basins that spill into β. Otherwise we consider an appropriate path P from β to a descendant leaf and prove that we can compute the spill times of all basins whose parents belong to P using O(sort(Y)) I/Os, where Y is defined as above. The path P is chosen so that every subtree attached to P contains at most half of β's descendants, and we invoke our algorithm recursively on the root of each such subtree. This ensures that $\log(X/M)$ levels of recursion suffice to break $\mathcal{M}$ into subtrees of size at most M, to which the above internal-memory algorithm can be applied. The cost per level of recursion is O(sort(X)) I/Os. Hence, the total cost of the algorithm is O(sort(X) $\log(X/M)$) I/Os. This gives only the spill times of the basins. To compute the flooding times of *all* terrain vertices, we use a post-processing step that can be seen as a simpler version of the recursive step of our algorithm and performs O(sort(N)) I/Os.

The intuition behind the computation in each recursive step is the following. In general, there are two directions water can flow across any saddle of the terrain $\mathcal{T}$. Given the flow direction for each saddle, spill times could be computed rather easily, but the direction for each saddle is determined by the spill times of the two basins that merge at this saddle. For the saddles between the basins corresponding to the path P in each recursive steps, we can characterize each flow direction as either "confluent" (toward the basin represented by the leaf of P) or "diffluent" (away from the leaf), and we can show that confluent spill events that influence other spill events—we call these *watershed events*—can themselves depend only on confluent watershed events. This allows us to perform a sweep in the confluent direction first to compute the times of all confluent watershed events. In a second phase, we sweep in the diffluent direction and use the times computed in the first phase to compute the correct times for *all* spill events.

2. PRELIMINARIES

In this section, we introduce the basic terminology used throughout this paper. In the following, we make some assumptions about the structure of the terrain that simplify the exposition in the rest of the paper. All these assumptions can be removed using standard perturbation techniques.

Terrains, pits, and basins. We consider the terrain $\mathcal{T}$ to be represented as a triangular irregular network, which is a planar triangulation each of whose vertices v has an associated elevation $\mathcal{T}(v)$. The elevation of a point interior to a triangle is a linear interpolation of the elevations of the triangle vertices. In this manner, the terrain is represented as a continuous piecewise linear surface, and we use $\mathcal{T}(p)$ to refer to the elevation of the point $p \in \mathbb{R}^2$. We assume that no two adjacent vertices have the same elevation. A *pit* of $\mathcal{T}$ is a local minimum, that is, a terrain vertex all of whose neighbours have higher elevations. A *saddle point* of $\mathcal{T}$ is a vertex v with four vertices w_1, w_2, w_3, w_4 among its neighbours that satisfy $\max(\mathcal{T}(w_1), \mathcal{T}(w_3)) < \mathcal{T}(v) < \min(\mathcal{T}(w_2), \mathcal{T}(w_4))$ and appear in the order w_1, w_2, w_3, w_4 clockwise around v.

A *basin* is a maximal connected set of points $\beta \subseteq \mathbb{R}^3$ such that $\mathcal{T}((x,y)) \leq z \leq h_\beta$, for all $(x,y,z) \in \beta$, where h_β is a fixed elevation chosen as the upper boundary of β. A basin β is *maximal* if there exists a saddle point p_β on the boundary of β such that $\mathcal{T}(p_\beta) = h_\beta$. The point p_β is called the *spill point* of basin β, since water poured into β spills over p_β into an adjacent basin once β becomes full. We assume p_β is unique, that is, there are no two saddles with elevation h_β on the boundary of β. We also assume exactly two basins meet in each spill point. Throughout this paper, we are interested almost exclusively in maximal basins and refer to them simply as basins. Every basin contains at least one pit, and for every pit there exists a unique (maximal) basin that contains only this pit. We call such a basin *elementary*.

Trickle paths, watersheds, and tributaries. The *trickle path* of a point $q \in \mathcal{T}$ is the path that starts at q, continues in the direction of steepest descent for every point it visits, and ends either in a pit p or at the boundary of $\mathcal{T}$. In the former case, water falling onto q collects in the elementary basin corresponding to p; in the latter, it flows off the edge of the terrain. The *watershed* of a pit p is the set of points whose trickle paths end in p. The watershed W^0_β of a basin β is the union of the watersheds of all pits contained in β. More generally, we use W^t_β to denote the watershed of basin β at time t, which is the area such that water falling onto W^t_β at time t collects in basin β. A *tributary* of β is a basin τ such that $\tau \cap \beta = \emptyset$, τ spills before β, and water falling onto $W^{t_\tau}_\tau$ at the time t_τ when τ spills collects in β; that is, τ spills into β and the watershed of τ at this time becomes part of the watershed of β. Note that τ is usually a tributary of more than one basin. In particular, if β is the smallest basin that has τ as a tributary, then τ is a tributary of every basin that contains β but not τ.

Merge tree and flow tree. The basins of $\mathcal{T}$ form a hierarchy that is easily represented using a rooted tree, the *merge tree* $\mathcal{M}$ of $\mathcal{T}$. The leaves of $\mathcal{M}$ are the elementary basins of $\mathcal{T}$. A basin β_1 is the parent of a basin β_2 if and only if $\beta_2 \subset \beta_1$ and there exists no basin β_3 such that $\beta_2 \subset \beta_3 \subset \beta_1$. Under the assumptions we made about $\mathcal{T}$, $\mathcal{M}$ is a binary tree. For a subset S of nodes of $\mathcal{M}$, let $\mathcal{M}(S)$ be the subgraph of $\mathcal{M}$ induced by S. For a node α of $\mathcal{M}$, $\mathcal{M}_\alpha$ denotes the subtree of $\mathcal{M}$ induced by α and its descendants. We do not distinguish between merge tree nodes and their corresponding basins. For a basin β, we use V_β to denote β's volume, W^t_β to denote β's watershed at time t or its size (which will be clear from the context), E_β to denote the event that β spills into an adjacent basin, and t_β to denote the time of event E_β. We call E_β the *spill event* associated with β. See Figure 1 for an illustration of these definitions.

Now consider a subset S of nodes of $\mathcal{M}$ such that $\mathcal{M}(S)$ is a tree. The flow paths between the basins in S form a *flow tree* $\mathcal{F}(S)$ defined as follows. Let S' be the set of leaves of $\mathcal{M}(S)$. The elements of S' are the vertices of $\mathcal{F}(S)$. There is an edge between two such vertices α_1 and α_2 if their watersheds touch in the common spill point of two basins $\beta_1, \beta_2 \in S$. See Figure 2.

3. COMPUTING FLOODING TIMES

Our algorithm for computing the flooding times of all terrain vertices has two phases. The first phase (Sections 3.1–3.3) computes the spill times t_β of all basins of $\mathcal{T}$ using

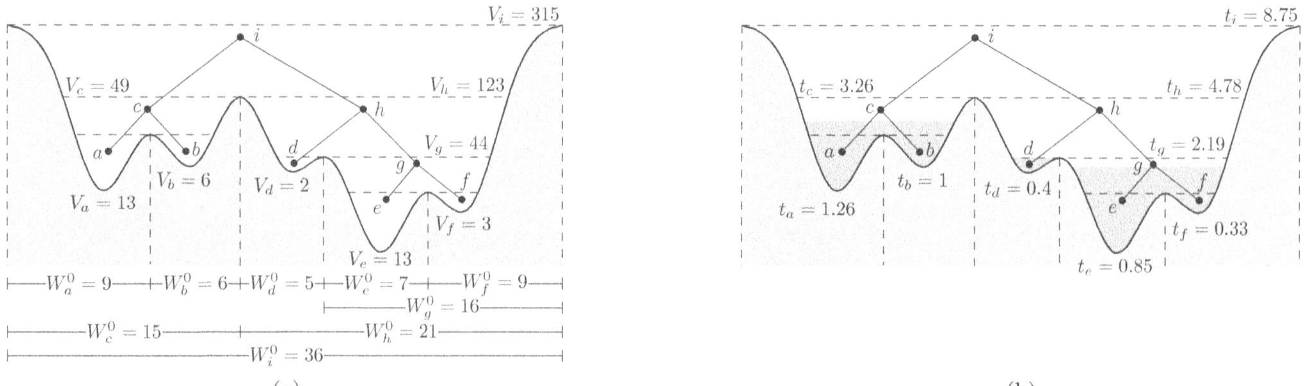

Figure 1: (a) A 1-d terrain with its corresponding merge tree and volumes and initial watersheds of its basins. (b) The spill times of the basins and the water levels in the basins at time $t = 2$.

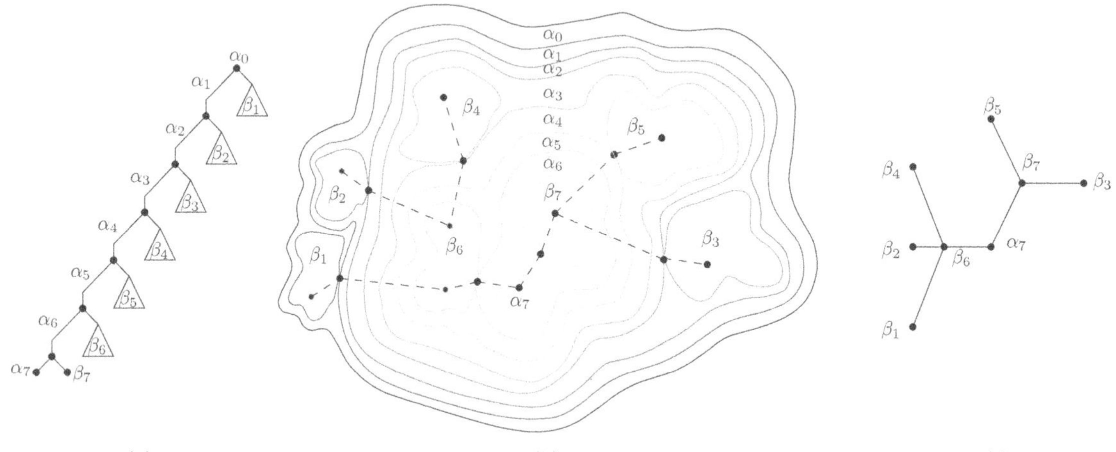

Figure 2: Figure (a) shows the merge tree $\mathcal{M}(S)$ of a set $S = \{\alpha_0, \alpha_1, \beta_1, \ldots, \alpha_7, \beta_7\}$ of basins. Figure (b) illustrates the nesting of these basins using contour lines through their spill points. Figure (c) shows the flow tree of basins $\alpha_7, \beta_1, \beta_2, \ldots, \beta_7$. Every edge corresponds to a spill point and joins the two basins containing the endpoints of the trickle paths starting at this spill point (shown as dashed lines in Figure (b)). Note that the trickle paths corresponding to different edges incident to a flow tree node β_i may end in different pits inside the basin β_i. This is the case for basin β_6 in Figure (b).

O(sort(X) log(X/M)) I/Os. The second phase (Section 3.4) then computes the flooding times of all vertices of $\mathcal{T}$ using O(sort(N)) I/Os.

3.1 Computing Spill Times

We assume the merge tree $\mathcal{M}$ is given and every node $\beta \in \mathcal{M}$ stores V_β, W_β^0, as well as identifiers of the two elementary basins $\lambda_f(\beta)$ and $\lambda_r(\beta)$ such that $\lambda_f(\beta) \in \mathcal{M}_\beta$ and $W^0_{\lambda_f(\beta)}$ and $W^0_{\lambda_r(\beta)}$ touch in p_β; $\lambda_f(\beta)$ is needed for some data structure queries in our algorithm, while $\lambda_r(\beta)$ is the basin where water spilling from β would collect if we poured water only into β. We further assume the elementary basins of $\mathcal{T}$ have been numbered using a preorder traversal of the flow tree $\mathcal{F}$ of $\mathcal{T}$ starting at an arbitrary root, and every elementary basin stores the preorder interval of its descendants. This information can be computed from the input of our algorithm using O(sort(X)) I/Os using standard techniques. Details appear in the full paper.

Our algorithm for computing the spill times of all basins is recursive. Every recursive call takes a node $\beta \in \mathcal{M}$ and a list $\mathcal{R}_\beta$ of all tributaries of β as input. Each tributary $\tau \in \mathcal{R}_\beta$ stores its spill time t_τ, its watershed $W_\tau := W_\tau^{t_\tau}$ at time t_τ, and the preorder number of an elementary basin it contains. The task of the recursive call on a node β is to compute the spill times of all proper descendants of β in $\mathcal{M}$. The top-level invocation takes the root ρ of $\mathcal{M}$ and an empty list of tributaries as input (since ρ has no tributaries). We distinguish two cases for each recursive call.

If $|\mathcal{M}_\beta| \le M$, we use the algorithm in Section 3.2 below to solve the problem using O(sort(X)) I/Os, where X is the total input size of the invocation, that is, $X := |\mathcal{M}_\beta| + |\mathcal{R}_\beta|$.

If $|\mathcal{M}_\beta| > M$, we compute a *heaviest path* P in $\mathcal{M}_\beta$. This path consists of a sequence of nodes $\alpha_0, \alpha_1, \ldots, \alpha_k$, where $\alpha_0 = \beta$, α_k is a leaf, and, for $1 \le i \le k$, α_i is the child of α_{i-1} with the bigger subtree $\mathcal{M}_{\alpha_i}$ among the two children of α_{i-1}. We use β_i to denote the other child of α_{i-1}. See

Figure 2(a). The first step of the algorithm is to compute the spill times t_{α_i} and t_{β_i} and the set $\mathcal{R}_{\beta_i}$ of tributaries of β_i, for all $1 \le i \le k$. To finish the computation of spill times, we recursively invoke the algorithm on each node β_i, $1 \le i \le k$. As we show in Section 3.3, the computation of the spill times t_{α_i} and t_{β_i}, for $1 \le i \le k$, and of the lists of tributaries of the basins $\beta_1, \beta_2, \ldots, \beta_k$ takes $O(\text{sort}(k + |\mathcal{R}_\beta|)) = O(\text{sort}(X))$ I/Os, where $X := |\mathcal{M}_\beta| + |\mathcal{R}_\beta|$. The path P can be computed using $O(\text{sort}(X))$ I/Os using the Euler tour technique and list ranking [6]. This gives the following result.

THEOREM 1. *The spill times of all basins of a terrain $\mathcal{T}$ can be computed using $O(\text{sort}(X) \log(X/M))$ I/Os, where X is the number of elementary basins of $\mathcal{T}$.*

PROOF. We prove in Section 3.2 that, given the tributaries of β, we compute the correct spill times for all basins in $\mathcal{M}_\beta$ in the case $|\mathcal{M}_\beta| \le M$. In Section 3.3, we prove that, in the case $|\mathcal{M}_\beta| > M$, we compute the spill times of basins α_i and β_i and the tributary lists $\mathcal{R}_{\beta_i}$, for $1 \le i \le k$, correctly. The correctness of the algorithm then follows by induction. The I/O complexity of an invocation of the algorithm with total input size $X := |\mathcal{M}_\beta| + |\mathcal{R}_\beta|$ and merge tree size $Y := |\mathcal{M}_\beta|$ is given by the recurrence

$$T(X,Y) = \begin{cases} O(\text{sort}(X)) & Y \le M \\ O(\text{sort}(X)) + \sum_{i=1}^{k} T(X_i, Y_i) & Y > M \end{cases},$$

where $Y_i := |\mathcal{M}_{\beta_i}|$ and $X_i := Y_i + |\mathcal{R}_{\beta_i}|$. By the definition of a tributary, every basin τ with $\tau \in \mathcal{M}_\beta$ or $\tau \in \mathcal{R}_\beta$ can be the tributary of at most one basin β_i. Hence, we have $\sum_{i=1}^{k} X_i \le X$. Furthermore, the choice of the path P as a heaviest path ensures that $Y_i \le Y/2$, for all $1 \le i \le k$. Together, these two facts imply that the recurrence solves to $T(X,Y) = O(\text{sort}(X) \log(Y/M))$. For the root of $\mathcal{M}$, we have $X = Y$, that is, the overall complexity of the algorithm is $O(\text{sort}(X) \log(X/M))$, as claimed. □

3.2 Small Basins

To solve the case $|\mathcal{M}_\beta| \le M$, we provide an implementation of the algorithm of [14] using a union-find structure and a priority queue and extend it to take the tributaries of the basin β into account when computing the spill times of all sub-basins of β. Before running the actual algorithm, we compute, for each tributary τ of β, the elementary sub-basin $\lambda_r(\tau)$ of β that τ spills into; that is, τ spills into β across a saddle on the boundary of $W^0_{\lambda_r(\tau)}$. These basins can be computed from the preorder numbers stored with the tributaries of β and the preorder intervals of the elementary sub-basins of β using $O(\text{sort}(X))$ I/Os. Details appear in the full paper.

The algorithm maintains a set of *active* basins in $\mathcal{M}_\beta$, which are the basins that have not spilled yet but whose children have already spilled. A basin that has spilled is *finished*, and a basin with at least one unfinished child is *inactive*. The set of active basins always contains the next basin in $\mathcal{M}_\beta$ to spill. We maintain the set of active basins using two data structures: a priority queue Q and a union-find structure U. The priority queue stores the active basins with priorities equal to their predicted spill times—these times decrease over time as we discover more tributaries of active basins. The union-find structure stores the elementary basins (leaves) in $\mathcal{M}_\beta$ and allows us to find, for each such basin α, the active basin α' such that W^0_α is currently part of $W_{\alpha'}$. More precisely, a FIND(α) operation returns a representative elementary sub-basin of α', and it is easy to ensure that at all times, the representative of α' stores the ID of α'. Initially, all elementary basins are active and all other basins are inactive; the predicted spill time of an elementary basin α is $t'_\alpha := V_\alpha / W^0_\alpha$. To allow the updating of predicted spill times, each active basin α also stores the time u_α when its watershed changed last—that is, the spill time of its most recent tributary—as well as its residual volume V^r_α at time u_α, which is the portion of V_α left to be filled at this time. Initially, $V^r_\alpha = V_\alpha$ and $u_\alpha = 0$, for every elementary basin α of $\mathcal{T}$.

After initializing the algorithm's data structures as just described, we process the events in Q and $\mathcal{R}_\beta$ by increasing time until Q contains only the basin β. The details of each iteration are as follows. Let τ be the next tributary in $\mathcal{R}_\beta$ to be processed, and let α be the active basin with minimum priority in Q. If $t_\tau < t'_\alpha$, we remove τ from $\mathcal{R}_\beta$ and process E_τ as a *watershed event* with time t_τ, as described below. If $t'_\alpha < t_\tau$, we remove α from Q and consider its sibling σ. If σ is not finished, we process E_α as a *watershed event* with time t'_α; otherwise we process it as a *basin event* with time t'_α.

Watershed event: A watershed event occurs when a basin α spills into a non-full basin α', thereby increasing the watershed of α'. To process a watershed event E_α with time t, we find the active basin α' that α spills into using a FIND($\lambda_r(\alpha)$) operation on U. We update the information for α' as $V^r_{\alpha'} := V^r_{\alpha'} - W_{\alpha'}(t - u_{\alpha'})$, $W_{\alpha'} := W_{\alpha'} + W_\alpha$, $u_{\alpha'} := t$, and $t'_{\alpha'} := t + V^r_{\alpha'}/W_{\alpha'}$, and then update the priority of α' in Q accordingly. If $\alpha \in \mathcal{R}_\beta$, this finishes the processing of E_α. If $\alpha \in \mathcal{M}_\beta$, we need to update U to reflect that water falling or flowing onto W_α after time t flows into α'. We do this by performing a UNION($\lambda_f(\alpha), \lambda_r(\alpha)$) operation on U and ensuring that the representative of the resulting set of elementary basins points to α'. We also label the node α in $\mathcal{M}_\beta$ as finished.

Basin event: A basin event occurs when the second of two sibling basins becomes full, leaving its parent basin in $\mathcal{M}_\beta$ to fill. When processing a basin event E_α with time t, for some $\alpha \in \mathcal{M}_\beta$, both α and its sibling σ in $\mathcal{M}_\beta$ are full at time t. Thus, we label α as finished in $\mathcal{M}_\beta$ and mark its parent γ as active. Water that flowed into α before time t now collects in γ. Thus, we set $W_\gamma := W_\alpha$ and ensure that the representative of α now points to γ. Since both α and σ are full at time t, we set $V^r_\gamma := V_\gamma - V_\alpha - V_\sigma$, $u_\gamma := t$, and $t'_\gamma := t + V^r_\gamma / W_\gamma$. Then we insert γ into Q with priority t'_γ.

The following lemma states the correctness and I/O complexity of the above procedure.

LEMMA 1. *Let β be a basin with at most M sub-basins, and let $X := |\mathcal{M}_\beta| + |\mathcal{R}_\beta|$. The spill times of all basins $\alpha \in \mathcal{M}_\beta$ can be computed using $O(\text{sort}(X))$ I/Os.*

PROOF. To bound the I/O complexity of the procedure, we observe that Q, U, and $\mathcal{M}_\beta$ fit in memory and that scanning the sorted list of tributaries $\mathcal{R}_\beta$ requires us to keep only one buffer block of size B in memory. Thus, apart from sorting the tributaries in $\mathcal{R}_\beta$ by their spill times using $O(\text{sort}(X))$ I/Os, the algorithm only loads $\mathcal{M}_\beta$ into memory and scans $\mathcal{R}_\beta$, which takes $O(X/B)$ I/Os. All other processing happens in memory.

To prove the correctness of the algorithm, we consider the sequence of events $E_1, E_2, \ldots, E_X$ affecting basin β and its sub-basins, sorted by their times $t_1, t_2, \ldots, t_X$. That is, every event E_i is an event E_α with $\alpha \in \mathcal{M}_\beta$ or such that $\alpha \notin \mathcal{M}_\beta$ and α is a tributary of a basin $\alpha' \in \mathcal{M}_\beta$, in which case α is also a tributary of β and belongs to $\mathcal{R}_\beta$.

We use t'_i to denote the "current" predicted time of the event E_i. Consider the basin α such that $E_i = E_\alpha$. Then we define $t'_i := t_i$ if α is a tributary of β and $t'_i := \infty$ if $\alpha \in \mathcal{M}_\beta$ and α is inactive; if $\alpha \in \mathcal{M}_\beta$ and α is active, we define t'_i to be its priority in Q. We use induction on i to prove that $t'_i = t_i$ when event E_i is processed. To do so, we prove that the following holds after processing event E_i:

(i) Events $E_1, E_2, \ldots, E_i$ have been processed. No other events have been processed.

(ii) $W_\alpha = W_\alpha^{t_i}$, for all active basins $\alpha \in \mathcal{M}_\beta$.

(iii) $t'_{i+1} = t_{i+1}$, while $t'_j \geq t_j$, for all $j > i+1$.

The base case is $i = 0$, setting $t_0 = 0$. Property (i) holds because no events have been processed yet. Property (ii) holds because initially $W_\alpha = W_\alpha^0$, for every elementary basin in $\mathcal{M}_\beta$, which is exactly the set of active basins at the beginning of the procedure. To see that (iii) holds, observe that $t'_j = t_j$ if $E_j = E_\tau$, for some tributary τ of β. If $E_j = E_\alpha$, for $\alpha \in \mathcal{M}_\beta$, and α is inactive, then $t'_j = \infty$; if α is active, then $t'_j = V_\alpha / W_\alpha^0 \geq t_j$. Moreover, if $E_1 = E_\alpha$, for some $\alpha \in \mathcal{M}_\beta$, then α has no tributaries and $t_1 = V_\alpha / W_\alpha^0 = t'_1$.

For the inductive step, consider $i > 0$ and assume the claim holds for all $j < i$. By part (i) of the inductive hypothesis, E_{i-1} is the $(i-1)$st event to be processed. By part (iii) of the inductive hypothesis, we have $t'_i = t_i$ and $t'_j \geq t_j > t_i$, for all $j > i$, after processing E_{i-1}. Hence, E_i is the ith event to be processed. This establishes (i).

To prove (ii), we consider the two possible types of event E_i separately. Let $E_i = E_\alpha$. If E_i is a watershed event, part (ii) of the inductive hypothesis implies that we identify the correct watershed $W_{\alpha'}$ into which α spills at time t_i and, hence, that we update $W_{\alpha'}$ to $W_{\alpha'}^{t_i}$; all other watersheds remain unchanged. If E_i is a basin event, α and its sibling are full at time t_i, while α's parent γ has to fill. Furthermore, all water flowing into γ immediately before time t_i collects in α because α's sibling is already full. Therefore, $W_\gamma^{t_i} = W_\alpha^{t_i}$, and we correctly set $W_\gamma := W_\alpha$.

Finally, consider (iii). We consider only events $E_j = E_\alpha$ with α an active basin in $\mathcal{M}_\beta$ because, by definition, $t'_j = t_j$, for every spill event E_j of a tributary of β, and $t'_j = \infty$, for every spill event E_j of an inactive basin in $\mathcal{M}_\beta$. It is easily verified that we update t'_α correctly whenever we increase W_α. By (ii), each event E_h with $h \leq i$ updates W_α if and only if $E_h = E_\tau$, for some tributary τ of α. Thus, $t'_j \geq t_j$, for all $j \geq i$. For $j = i+1$, the spill events of the tributaries of α are a subset of $E_1, E_2, \ldots, E_i$, as they have to happen before $E_\alpha = E_{i+1}$. Thus, we have $t'_{i+1} = t_{i+1}$ after E_i is processed. ☐

3.3 Basin Sets With Linear Merge Trees

Now consider a path $P = \langle \beta = \alpha_0, \alpha_1, \ldots, \alpha_k \rangle$ from a merge tree node β to a descendant leaf α_k, and let β_i be the sibling of α_i, for all $1 \leq i \leq k$. The basic step of our solution for the case $|\mathcal{M}_\beta| > M$ computes the spill times of $\alpha_1, \beta_1, \alpha_2, \beta_2, \ldots, \alpha_k, \beta_k$, as well as the lists of tributaries $\mathcal{R}_{\beta_1}, \mathcal{R}_{\beta_2}, \ldots, \mathcal{R}_{\beta_k}$ of the basins $\beta_1, \beta_2, \ldots, \beta_k$. Our algorithm for this problem operates on the flow tree $\mathcal{F} := \mathcal{F}(S)$ of the set S of basins in P. Note that every edge in $\mathcal{F}$ corresponds to the spill point connecting two basins α_i and β_i, for $1 \leq i \leq k$, and that $\lambda_f(\alpha_i) = \lambda_r(\beta_i)$ and $\lambda_f(\beta_i) = \lambda_r(\alpha_i)$ in this case. So the tree is easy to construct using a constant number of sorting and scanning steps of S. Details appear in the full paper.

We call a spill event E_{β_i} *confluent*, as the water spilling from β_i at time t_{β_i} spills towards α_k. Similarly, we call a spill event E_{α_i} *diffluent*, as the water spilling from α_i at time t_{α_i} spills away from α_k (α_k is a sub-basin of α_i). We define $\mathcal{F}_{\beta_i}$ to be the subtree of $\mathcal{F}$ rooted in β_i, assuming α_k is chosen as the root of $\mathcal{F}$. Our algorithm proceeds in two phases. The *confluent phase* computes times $t'_{\beta_1}, t'_{\beta_2}, \ldots, t'_{\beta_k}$. These times satisfy $t'_{\beta_i} = t_{\beta_i}$ if E_{β_i} is a watershed event and $t'_{\beta_i} \geq t_{\beta_i}$ if E_{β_i} is a basin event. In addition, this phase constructs a list L_{β_i}, for each $1 \leq i \leq k$, which is a superset of those tributaries of β_i that belong to $\mathcal{F}_{\beta_i}$ or spill into β across a saddle on the boundary of a basin $\beta_j \in \mathcal{F}_{\beta_i}$. The second, *diffluent phase* computes times $t''_{\alpha_1}, t''_{\alpha_2}, \ldots, t''_{\alpha_k}$ and $t''_{\beta_1}, t''_{\beta_2}, \ldots, t''_{\beta_k}$ from the times and potential tributary lists computed in the confluent phase, and we prove that $t''_{\alpha_i} = t_{\alpha_i}$ and $t''_{\beta_i} = t_{\beta_i}$, for all $1 \leq i \leq k$. In the process, the diffluent phase computes the list $\mathcal{R}_{\beta_i}$ of tributaries of β_i, for every $1 \leq i \leq k$.

Intuitively, this two-phase approach works because the confluent phase ensures that the spill times of all basins β_i that are tributaries of other basins are computed correctly (since β_i can be a tributary only if its spill event is a watershed event). A basin α_i can have only confluent tributaries, since basins $\alpha_1, \alpha_2, \ldots, \alpha_k$ are nested. A basin β_i can have only one diffluent tributary, namely α_i, because β_i is a sub-basin of α_j, for all $j < i$, and α_i is a super-basin of α_h, for all $h > i$. Thus, by processing the basins "outwards" from α_k—that is, by decreasing index i—in the diffluent phase, we can ensure that the spill times of all tributaries of a basin are known by the time the basin is processed.

3.3.1 From Tributaries to Spill Times

Both phases of our algorithm use the same elementary procedure to compute a predicted spill time for a basin. To avoid duplication, we describe this procedure here and refer to it as procedure FINDSPILLTIME later. The input of this procedure is a basin α, a time u_α, the residual volume V_α^r of α at time u_α, and the watershed $W_\alpha = W_\alpha^{u_\alpha}$ of α at time u_α. In addition, we are given a priority queue Q containing a set of potential tributaries of α; each entry $\tau \in Q$ satisfies $t'_\tau > u_\alpha$, where t'_τ denotes the priority of τ. The output of the procedure is a predicted spill time t'_α of α and a list L of entries removed from Q while computing t'_α.

Initially, we set $t'_\alpha := u_\alpha + V_\alpha^r / W_\alpha$. Then we repeat the following steps to update t'_α until either Q is empty or the minimum entry τ in Q satisfies $t'_\tau \geq t'_\alpha$. We remove the minimum entry τ (which satisfies $t'_\tau < t'_\alpha$) from Q and append it to L. Then we set $V_\alpha^r := V_\alpha^r - W_\alpha(t'_\tau - u_\alpha)$, $W_\alpha := W_\alpha + W_\tau$, $u_\alpha := t'_\tau$, and $t'_\alpha := u_\alpha + V_\alpha^r / W_\alpha$.

LEMMA 2. *Assume at the beginning of procedure* FIND-SPILLTIME, *W_α and V_α^r reflect the actual watershed and residual volume of α at time u_α, Q contains only entries τ with $t'_\tau \geq u_\alpha$, and $t'_\tau < t_\alpha$ if and only if τ is a tributary of α. Assume further that every tributary $\tau \in Q$ of α satisfies $t'_\tau = t_\tau$. Then $t'_\alpha \geq t_\alpha$ when the procedure terminates. If Q*

contains every tributary τ of α with $t_\tau \geq u_\alpha$, then $t'_\alpha = t_\alpha$, and $L = \{\tau \in \mathcal{R}_\alpha \mid t_\tau \geq u_\alpha\}$.

Proof. First assume for the sake of contradiction that $t'_\alpha < t_\alpha$ when the algorithm terminates. Then the last element $\tau \in Q$ processed by procedure FindSpillTime satisfies $t'_\tau < t'_\alpha$, as the update of t'_α when processing an entry τ does not decrease t'_α below t'_τ. Hence, every processed entry τ satisfies $t'_\tau < t_\alpha$. This implies that all processed elements are tributaries of α that satisfy $u_\alpha < t'_\tau = t_\tau < t_\alpha$, and we process them in order. Thus, after processing every tributary τ, we have $W_\alpha \leq W_\alpha^{t_\tau}$, which implies that $t'_\alpha \geq t_\alpha$, a contradiction.

Now assume Q contains all tributaries of α and $t'_\alpha > t_\alpha$ when procedure FindSpillTime finishes. This is possible only if we do not process all tributaries of α. An unprocessed tributary τ would have to remain in Q by the end of the procedure and, thus, satisfies $t'_\tau > t'_\alpha$. However, $t'_\tau = t_\tau < t_\alpha < t'_\alpha$, again a contradiction.

Finally, observe that, if $t'_\alpha = t_\alpha$, we process exactly the elements $\tau \in Q$ with $t'_\tau < t_\alpha$, and place them into L. These are exactly the tributaries of α that satisfy $t_\tau \geq u_\alpha$. □

3.3.2 Confluent Phase

To implement the confluent phase of the algorithm, we root the flow tree $\mathcal{F}$ in α_k and process its nodes in postorder. With every node $\alpha \in \mathcal{F}$ we associate a list $\mathcal{S}_\alpha \subseteq \mathcal{R}_\beta$ containing all tributaries τ of β that spill into β across a saddle on the boundary of W_α^0. These lists are easy to compute using O(sort(X)) I/Os from the preorder numbers of the elementary basins associated with the tributaries, assuming that every basin in $\mathcal{M}$ stores the largest preorder interval of all its elementary sub-basins, which is easily computed in a preprocessing step using a bottom-up traversal in $\mathcal{M}$. Details appear in the full paper.

During the traversal of $\mathcal{F}$, we ensure that visiting a node β_i produces a priority queue Q_{β_i} that contains all basins τ that satisfy (i) $\tau \in \{\beta_j\} \cup \mathcal{S}_{\beta_j}$, for some $\beta_j \in \mathcal{F}_{\beta_i}$, and (ii) $t'_\tau \geq t'_{\beta_h}$, for all β_h on the path from β_j to β_i in $\mathcal{F}$, inclusive. At any point during the postorder traversal, there is a set of *active* nodes, which are nodes that have been visited already but whose parents in $\mathcal{F}$ have not. We maintain the priority queues of all active nodes in a sequence sorted in the order these nodes are visited and represent this sequence of priority queues using a data structure that supports Insert and DeleteMin operations on the last priority queue in the sequence, the creation of a new priority queue at the end of the sequence, as well as a Meld operation, which replaces the last two priority queues in the sequence with their union. In Section 4, we show that the external heap of Fadel et al. [12] can be extended to process a sequence of N Insert, DeleteMin, Create, and Meld operations using O(sort(N)) I/Os.

The processing of a node β_i distinguishes two cases. If β_i is a leaf, we create a new priority queue Q_{β_i} at the end of the sequence of priority queues of active nodes. If β_i is an internal node with children $\beta_{j_1}, \beta_{j_2}, \ldots, \beta_{j_h}$, the corresponding priority queues $Q_{\beta_{j_1}}, Q_{\beta_{j_2}}, \ldots, Q_{\beta_{j_h}}$ are at the end of the current sequence of priority queues, and we construct Q_{β_i} by melding these priority queues. In both cases, we continue by inserting all elements $\tau \in \mathcal{S}_{\beta_i}$ into Q_{β_i}, with priority $t'_\tau = t_\tau$. Then we use procedure FindSpillTime to compute t'_{β_i} and L_{β_i}; the input to the procedure is β_i, Q_{β_i}, $u_{\beta_i} := 0$, $W_{\beta_i} := W_{\beta_i}^0$, and $V_{\beta_i}^r := V_{\beta_i}$. Once this procedure terminates, we insert β_i into Q_{β_i}, with priority t'_{β_i}.

The confluent phase terminates when the traversal reaches the root α_k of $\mathcal{F}$. Since E_{α_k} is a diffluent spill event, we do not compute its time in this phase of the algorithm. We only construct a list L_{α_k} by collecting all elements in $Q_{\beta_{j_1}}, Q_{\beta_{j_2}}, \ldots, Q_{\beta_{j_h}}$ and $\mathcal{S}_{\alpha_k}$, where $\beta_{j1}, \beta_{j2}, \ldots, \beta_{jh}$ are the children of α_k in $\mathcal{F}$.

To establish the correctness of the confluent phase, we require a number of technical lemmas. The first one characterizes the spill events of basins on the flow path between a basin and its tributary. For three basins $\beta_j, \beta_h \in \mathcal{F}$ and a basin $\alpha \in \{\alpha_i, \beta_i\}$, we say β_h is on the path from β_j to α in $\mathcal{F}$ if β_h is not a sub-basin of α but belongs to the path from β_j to every sub-basin $\alpha' \in \mathcal{F}$ of α.

Lemma 3. *Consider a tributary τ of a basin $\alpha \in \{\alpha_i, \beta_i\}$, and assume that $\tau \in \{\beta_j\} \cup \mathcal{S}_{\beta_j}$, for some j. Then E_{β_h} is a watershed event, for every basin β_h on the path from β_j to α in $\mathcal{F}$ that is not a sub-basin of α_i.*

Proof. For $j > i$, the lemma holds vacuously because β_j is a sub-basin of α_i in this case and $\alpha \in \{\alpha_i, \beta_i\}$; this implies that every basin β_h on the path from β_j to α is a sub-basin of α_i. For $j \leq i$, assume there exists a basin β_h on the path from β_j to α that is not a sub-basin of α_i and such that E_{β_h} is a basin event. Since β_h is not a sub-basin of α_i, we have $h \leq i$. If $\alpha = \alpha_i$, this implies that α is a sub-basin of α_h and $t_\alpha \leq t_{\alpha_h} \leq t_{\beta_h}$. If $\alpha = \beta_i$, then $h < i$ because $\beta_h \neq \alpha$. Thus, α is again a sub-basin of α_h; in particular, $t_\alpha \leq t_{\beta_h}$. However, since β_j is a tributary of α, we have $t_{\beta_j} < t_\alpha$ and, therefore, $t_{\beta_j} < t_{\beta_h}$ in both cases. For β_j to be a tributary of α, there has to exist a down-hill path from β_j to α at time t_{β_j}. By the choice of β_h, any path from β_j to α has to pass through a point interior to β_h first and then through p_{β_h}. Since β_h is not full at time t_{β_j}, no such path is down-hill at time t_{β_j}, a contradiction. □

Our next lemma shows that, if a basin $\tau \in \{\beta_j\} \cup \mathcal{R}_{\beta_j}$ is a tributary of a basin β_i with $\beta_j \in \mathcal{F}_{\beta_i}$, then $\tau \in L_{\beta_i}$, that is, τ is processed when computing t'_{β_i}; otherwise, if it is a tributary of $\alpha \in \{\alpha_i, \beta_i\}$, then it is in L_γ, for some sub-basin γ of α_i. The first part is used to prove in Lemma 5 below that the confluent phase computes the correct spill times for all confluent watershed events. The second part is used to establish the correctness of the diffluent phase, discussed in Section 3.3.3.

Lemma 4. *Consider a basin $\tau \in \{\beta_j\} \cup \mathcal{S}_{\beta_j}$ with $\tau \in L_\gamma$. Assume further that every basin β_h in $\mathcal{F}_\gamma$ satisfies $t'_{\beta_h} \geq t_{\beta_h}$, with equality if E_{β_h} is a watershed event. If τ is a tributary of β_i and $\beta_j \in \mathcal{F}_{\beta_i}$, then $\gamma = \beta_i$. Otherwise, if τ is a tributary of a basin $\alpha \in \{\alpha_i, \beta_i\}$, then γ is a sub-basin of α_i.*

Proof. First assume τ is a tributary of β_i and $\beta_j \in \mathcal{F}_{\beta_i}$. Then E_τ is a watershed event and either $\tau \in \mathcal{S}_{\beta_j}$ or $\tau = \beta_j$. In both cases, we have $t'_\tau = t_\tau$, in the latter case by the assumption that $t'_{\beta_h} = t_{\beta_h}$ for every watershed event on the path from β_j to γ. If γ belongs to the path from β_j to β_i and $\gamma \neq \beta_i$, then we have $t'_\gamma = t_\gamma < t_\tau$ because τ is a tributary of β_i and, hence, E_γ is a watershed event. However, $\gamma \neq \alpha_k$ in this case, and every element τ in L_γ is removed from Q_γ while computing t'_γ. Thus, $t'_\tau < t'_\gamma$, a contradiction. This shows that γ is an ancestor of β_i in $\mathcal{F}$. This, however, implies that $t'_{\beta_i} \geq t_{\beta_i} > t_\tau = t'_\tau$. Thus, the computation of t'_{β_i} removes τ from Q_{β_i}, and $\tau \in L_{\beta_i}$.

Now assume that τ is a tributary of a basin $\alpha \in \{\alpha_i, \beta_i\}$ and, if $\alpha = \beta_i$, that $\beta_j \notin \mathcal{F}_{\beta_i}$. Then, if γ belongs to the path from β_j to α_i, we obtain $t'_\gamma = t_\gamma < t_\tau = t'_\tau$ on the one hand, because τ is a tributary of α and, by Lemma 3, E_γ is a watershed event; on the other hand, $t'_\gamma > t'_\tau$ because otherwise $\tau \notin L_\gamma$. Thus, we obtain a contradiction and γ is a sub-basin of α_i. □

LEMMA 5. *For all $1 \le i \le k$, we have $t'_{\beta_i} \ge t_{\beta_i}$. If E_{β_i} is a watershed event, equality holds.*

PROOF. By induction on $|\mathcal{F}_{\beta_i}|$. The base case is $|\mathcal{F}_{\beta_i}| = 0$, in which case there is nothing to prove. So consider a node β_i and assume the claim holds for all its descendants. Then, by Lemma 4, every tributary $\tau \in \{\beta_j\} \cup \mathcal{S}_{\beta_j}$, for some descendant β_j of β_i, is inspected when computing t'_{β_i}, and each such tributary satisfies $t'_\tau = t_\tau$ by the inductive hypothesis. In particular, each such tributary belongs to Q_{β_i} when invoking procedure FINDSPILLTIME to compute t'_{β_i}. We prove that any other element $\alpha \in Q_{\beta_i}$ satisfies $t'_\alpha \ge t_{\beta_i}$. By Lemma 2, this implies that $t'_{\beta_i} \ge t_{\beta_i}$, with $t'_{\beta_i} = t_{\beta_i}$ if Q_{β_i} contains *all* tributaries of β_i, which is the case if E_{β_i} is a watershed event. Indeed if there was a tributary τ such that $\tau \in \{\beta_j\} \cup \mathcal{R}_{\beta_j}$, for some $\beta_j \notin \mathcal{F}_{\beta_i}$, the water spilling from τ into β_i would have to flow through a point interior to α_i and then through $p_{\alpha_i} = p_{\beta_i}$. Since $t_\tau < t_{\beta_i}$ and E_{β_i} is a watershed event, α_i is not full at time t_τ, that is, the path from τ to β_i cannot be down-hill at time t_τ, a contradiction.

So consider an element $\alpha \in Q_{\beta_i}$, and assume that $\alpha \in \{\beta_j\} \cup \mathcal{S}_{\beta_j}$, for some $\beta_j \in \mathcal{F}_{\beta_i}$, and $t'_\alpha < t_{\beta_i}$. We prove that α is a tributary of β_i. We have $t'_\alpha \ge t'_{\beta_h}$, for all β_h on the path from β_j to β_i, excluding β_i, because otherwise β_h would have removed α from Q_{β_h} when computing t'_{β_h}. Since, by the inductive hypothesis, $t_{\beta_h} \le t'_{\beta_h}$, this implies that $t_{\beta_h} < t_{\beta_i}$. Also by the inductive hypothesis, we have $t'_\alpha \ge t_\alpha$. If $t_\alpha \ge t_{\beta_h}$, for all β_h on the path from β_j to β_i, then α is a tributary of β_i. If $t_\alpha < t_{\beta_h} \le t'_\alpha$, for some β_h, then, by the inductive hypothesis, E_α is not a watershed event. In particular, $\alpha = \beta_j$, for some $j < i$, and $t_{\beta_i} < t_{\alpha_j} \le t_{\beta_j} = t_\alpha$ because β_i is a sub-basin of α_j. This contradicts our assumption that $t_\alpha \le t'_\alpha < t_{\beta_i}$. □

3.3.3 Diffluent Phase

In the diffluent phase, we process the basins in $\mathcal{M}_\beta$ in the order $\alpha_k, \beta_k, \alpha_{k-1}, \beta_{k-1}, \dots, \alpha_1, \beta_1$. We initialize a priority queue Q to contain all events in L_{α_k}. Then we repeat the following steps for $i = k, k-1, \dots, 1$:

First we compute t''_{α_i}. If $i = k$, we do this by invoking procedure FINDSPILLTIME with arguments α_k, Q, $u_{\alpha_k} := 0$, $W_{\alpha_k} := W^0_{\alpha_k}$, and $V^r_{\alpha_k} := V_{\alpha_k}$. If $i < k$, we invoke the procedure with arguments α_i, Q, $u_{\alpha_i} := \max(t''_{\alpha_{i+1}}, t''_{\beta_{i+1}})$, $W_{\alpha_i} := \max(W_{\alpha_{i+1}}, W_{\beta_{i+1}})$, and $V^r_{\alpha_i} := V_{\alpha_i} - V_{\alpha_{i+1}} - V_{\beta_{i+1}}$. We place the elements of Q processed by procedure FINDSPILLTIME into a list $\mathcal{R}''_{\alpha_i}$.

Then we compute t''_{β_i}. To do so, we insert α_i (with priority t''_{α_i}) and the events in L_{β_i} into Q and invoke procedure FINDSPILLTIME with arguments β_i, Q, $u_{\beta_i} := 0$, $W_{\beta_i} := W^0_{\beta_i}$, and $V^r_{\beta_i} := V_{\beta_i}$. We place the elements of Q processed by procedure FINDSPILLTIME into a list $\mathcal{R}''_{\beta_i}$.

The computation of t''_{α_i} and t''_{β_i} may not process all elements in Q, and some of these elements may be sub-basins of α_i. These elements should be ignored in subsequent computations, as they cannot be tributaries of any α_j or β_j with $j < i$. To ensure this, we augment the above procedure to ignore in iteration i all elements α_j or β_j in Q with $j > i$. (Note that we ignore only these basins, not the elements of $\mathcal{S}_{\alpha_k}$ or $\mathcal{S}_{\beta_j}$ with $j > i$.)

LEMMA 6. *For all $1 \le i \le k$, we have $t_{\alpha_i} = t''_{\alpha_i}$, $t_{\beta_i} = t''_{\beta_i}$, $\mathcal{R}_{\beta_i} = \mathcal{R}''_{\beta_i}$, and $\mathcal{R}_{\alpha_i} = \mathcal{R}''_{\alpha_k} \cup \bigcup_{j=i}^{k-1} \mathcal{R}''_{\beta_j}$.*

PROOF. By induction on i. For $i = k$, Lemmas 4 and 5 imply that every tributary τ of α_k belongs to L_{α_k} and satisfies $t'_\tau = t_\tau$. Any other basin $\alpha \in L_{\alpha_k}$ satisfies $t'_\alpha \ge t_\alpha$, and the same arguments as in the proof of Lemma 5 show that $t'_\alpha \ge t_{\alpha_k}$ in this case. Hence, by Lemma 2, the first iteration computes $t''_{\alpha_k} = t_{\alpha_k}$ and processes only tributaries of α_k, that is, $\mathcal{R}''_{\alpha_k} = \mathcal{R}_{\alpha_k}$.

Now consider β_k. By Lemmas 4 and 5, every tributary of β_k belongs to $\{\alpha_k\} \cup L_{\alpha_k} \cup L_{\beta_k}$, and we have just argued that the computation of α_k processes only tributaries of α_k. Hence, Q contains all tributaries of β_k. We have just argued that $t''_{\alpha_k} = t_{\alpha_k}$ and, by Lemma 5, any other tributary τ of β_k satisfies $t'_\tau = t_\tau$. For an element $\alpha \in Q$ that is not a tributary of β_k, the same arguments as in the proof of Lemma 5 show that $t'_\alpha \ge t_{\beta_k}$. (However, we have to distinguish the cases $\beta_j \in \mathcal{F}_{\beta_k}$ and $\beta_j \notin \mathcal{F}_{\beta_k}$, where $\alpha \in \{\beta_j\} \cup \mathcal{R}_{\beta_j}$.) Thus, by Lemma 2, we compute $t''_{\beta_k} = t_{\beta_k}$ and $\mathcal{R}''_{\beta_k} = \mathcal{R}_{\beta_k}$.

Now assume that $i < k$ and that the inductive hypothesis holds for all $j > i$. By Lemmas 4 and 5, every tributary τ of α_i is contained in $L := L_{\alpha_k} \cup \bigcup_{j=i+1}^{k} L_{\beta_j} = Q \cup \bigcup_{j=i+1}^{k} (\mathcal{R}''_{\alpha_j} \cup \mathcal{R}''_{\beta_j})$ and satisfies $t'_\tau = t_\tau$. Using the arguments from the proof of Lemma 5 again, every $\alpha \in L$ that is not a tributary of α_i satisfies $t'_\alpha \ge t_{\alpha_i}$. Moreover, the elements of $L \setminus Q$ are exactly the tributaries of α_{i+1} and β_{i+1}, that is, the tributaries τ of α_i that satisfy $t_\tau < u_{\alpha_i}$. Hence, by Lemma 2, we compute $t''_{\alpha_i} = t_{\alpha_i}$ and $\mathcal{R}''_{\alpha_i}$ to contain exactly the tributaries τ of α_i that satisfy $t_\tau \ge u_{\alpha_i}$. Thus, $\mathcal{R}_\alpha = \mathcal{R}''_{\alpha_i} \cup \bigcup_{j=i+1}^{k} (\mathcal{R}''_{\alpha_j} \cup \mathcal{R}''_{\beta_j})$. The correctness proof for the computation of t''_{β_i} and $\mathcal{R}''_{\beta_i}$ is identical to that for β_k. □

LEMMA 7. *The computation of the spill times t_{α_i} and t_{β_i} and of the tributary lists $\mathcal{R}_{\beta_i}$, for all $1 \le i \le k$, takes $O(\mathrm{sort}(X))$ I/Os.*

PROOF. The correctness of the algorithm is established by Lemma 6. Its I/O-complexity is established as follows: Both phases of the algorithm perform $O(X)$ priority queue operations, as every event is inserted and removed from a priority queue only once in each of the two phases and the confluent phase performs at most X MELD operations. By Theorem 3 in Section 4, these priority queue operations cost $O(\mathrm{sort}(X))$ I/Os. Apart from this, the algorithm traverses trees $\mathcal{F}$ and $\mathcal{M}(S)$ once each and scans lists associated with the tree nodes of total length $O(X)$. After arranging the tree nodes and list elements in the right order, using a sorting step, the scanning of these lists takes $O(X/B)$ I/Os. □

3.4 Computing the Flooding Times of All Terrain Vertices

The terrain vertices that are not spill points of basins can be seen as partitioning the basins of $\mathcal{T}$ into sub-basins as follows. For each terrain vertex v, let α_v be the smallest basin that contains v. For a basin β, let $V(\beta)$ be the set of terrain vertices with $\alpha_v = \beta$. Each vertex $v \in V(\beta)$ defines a sub-basin $\beta_{\mathcal{T}(v)}$ of β containing the portion of β below elevation $\mathcal{T}(v)$. Let $v_1, v_2, \dots, v_k$ be the vertices in $V(\beta)$ sorted by increasing elevation. Then the water from every tributary in $\mathcal{R}''_{\beta_i}$ first collects in $\beta_{\mathcal{T}(v_1)}$; once $\beta_{\mathcal{T}(v_1)}$ is full, the water collects in $\beta_{\mathcal{T}(v_2)}$, and so on. This is just a simplified version of the diffluent flow computation in Section 3.3.3, and computing the spill times of basins $\beta_{\mathcal{T}(v_1)}, \beta_{\mathcal{T}(v_2)}, \ldots, \beta_{\mathcal{T}(v_k)}$—that is, the flooding times of vertices $v_1, v_2, \ldots, v_k$—from the list $\mathcal{R}''_\beta$ takes $O(\text{sort}(N))$ I/Os in total for all basins of $\mathcal{T}$. The computation of the sets $V(\beta)$ can be incorporated in the computation of the basins of $\mathcal{T}$ without increasing the I/O complexity of that phase. Details appear in the full paper. Thus, we have the following result.

THEOREM 2. *The flooding times of all vertices of a terrain $\mathcal{T}$ with N vertices and X pits can be computed using $O(\text{sort}(X)\log(X/M) + \text{sort}(N))$ I/Os, given the watersheds and volumes of all basins of $\mathcal{T}$.*

4. A MELDABLE PRIORITY QUEUE

In this section, we discuss how to extend the external heap of Fadel et al. [12] to obtain a meldable priority queue that can be used in the procedure in Section 3.3.2. This structure maintains a sequence of priority queues $Q_1, Q_2, \ldots, Q_k$ under CREATE, INSERT, DELETEMIN, and MELD operations. Given the current sequence $Q_1, Q_2, \ldots, Q_k$, a CREATE operation creates a new, empty priority queue Q_{k+1} and appends it to the end of the sequence; an INSERT(x) operation inserts element x into Q_k; a DELETEMIN operation deletes and returns the minimum element in Q_k; a MELD operation replaces Q_{k-1} and Q_k with a new priority queue $Q'_{k-1} := Q_{k-1} \cup Q_k$ containing the elements from Q_{k-1} and Q_k. We prove the following result.

THEOREM 3. *There exists a linear-space data structure that uses $O(\text{sort}(N))$ I/Os to process a sequence of N CREATE, INSERT, DELETEMIN, and MELD operations.*

4.1 The Structure

Each priority queue Q_i is represented as an *external heap* similar to the one presented in [12]. The underlying structure is a rooted tree whose internal nodes have between $a = M/(4B)$ and $b = M/B$ children. There are two types of leaves: *regular* leaves are on the lowest level of the tree, which we call the *leaf level*; leaves above the leaf level are *special*.

Every node v has an associated buffer X_v. If v is an internal node, X_v has size M. If v is a leaf, there is no bound on the size of X_v. The elements in X_v are sorted, and the buffer contents of adjacent nodes satisfy the *heap property*: for every node v with parent u and every pair of elements $x \in X_u$ and $y \in X_v$, we have $x \leq y$.

To support INSERT and DELETEMIN operations efficiently, every priority queue Q_i is equipped with an *insert/delete buffer* or *I/D buffer* for short. This buffer is capable of holding up to M elements and stores the minimum elements in Q_i as well as newly inserted elements. To distinguish newly inserted elements in Q_i's I/D buffer from minimum elements, Q_i has an associated priority p_i, which is the minimum priority of the elements stored in the external part of Q_i.

The I/D buffers of priority queues $Q_1, Q_2, \ldots, Q_k$ are kept on a *buffer stack*, with the buffer of Q_1 at the bottom and the buffer of Q_k at the top. The I/D buffers of consecutive priority queues are separated by special *marker elements*. We always keep the topmost M elements of this stack in memory, which ensures in particular that the I/D buffer of Q_k is in memory.

4.2 Operations

Create. To create a new priority queue Q_{k+1}, a CREATE operation pushes a new marker element onto the buffer stack.

Insert. An INSERT operation on Q_k adds the inserted element x to Q_k's I/D buffer. If the buffer now contains M elements, we FLUSH the buffer as described below. Then we FILL the I/D buffer with the $M/2$ minimum elements in Q_k and update p_k accordingly.

DeleteMin. A DELETEMIN operation on Q_k returns the minimum element in Q_k's I/D buffer. Before doing so, however, it checks whether the I/D buffer of Q_k is empty or its minimum element is greater than p_k. If so, it FLUSHes the I/D buffer and then FILLs it with the $M/2$ minimum elements in Q_k.

Meld. A MELD operation behaves differently depending on the structure of the two involved priority queues, Q_{k-1} and Q_k. During different stages of its life time, a priority queue may have no external portion because all its elements fit in the I/D buffer. If at least one of the two priority queues, say Q_k, has no external portion, we destroy its I/D buffer, and INSERT its elements into Q_{k-1}. If both priority queues have external portions, we FLUSH and destroy their I/D buffers, MERGE their two trees as described below, and then FILL the I/D buffer of the merged priority queue $Q'_{k-1} := Q_{k-1} \cup Q_k$ with the $M/2$ minimum elements in Q'_{k-1}.

Flush. A FLUSH operation of an I/D buffer containing K elements creates a new leaf l at the leaf level and stores these K elements in l. Then it applies a HEAPIFY operation to the path from l to the root to restore the heap property. If the addition of l increased the degree of l's parent p to $M/B + 1$, we split p into two nodes p' and p'', each with half of p's children. We associate the buffer of p with p' and populate the buffer of p'' with the M smallest elements in its subtree using a FILL operation. If this split increases the degree of p's parent to $M/B + 1$, we apply this rebalancing procedure recursively until we reach the root. If the root has degree greater than M/B, we split it into two nodes with a new parent.

Fill. A FILL operation applied to a node v repeatedly takes the smallest element stored in the buffers of v's children, removes it from the corresponding child's buffer and stores it in v's buffer. This continues until M elements have been collected in v's buffer or there are no elements left in the buffers of v's children. Whenever a child buffer runs empty while filling v's buffer, its buffer is filled recursively before continuing to fill v's buffer. Once there are no more elements left in a node v's subtree, we mark v as *exhausted*, in order to avoid repeatedly trying to fill v with elements. More precisely, a node is marked as exhausted once its buffer becomes empty and all its children are exhausted. To fill the I/D buffer of a priority queue Q_k with the $M/2$ smallest elements in Q_k, we transfer the $M/2$ smallest elements from the root of Q_k into the I/D buffer, FILLing the root's buffer whenever it runs empty. If the root becomes exhausted in the process, we delete the entire external portion of the priority queue.

Merge. A MERGE operation between two trees T_1 and T_2 of heights $h_1 > h_2$ proceeds as follows. We locate a node v at height $h_2 + 1$ in T_1 and make the root r_2 of T_2 a child of v. We also create a new special leaf node l that is a child of v. Now let $v = v_0, v_1, \ldots, v_h$ be the ancestors of v, by increasing distance from v, let K_i be the number of elements in X_{v_i}, and let $K = \sum_{i=0}^{h} K_i$. First we collect the elements in $X_{v_0}, X_{v_1}, \ldots, X_{v_h}$ in sorted order and store them in l. Then we repeatedly remove the minimum element from X_{r_2} and X_l, refilling X_{r_2} as necessary, until we have collected the K smallest elements in the subtrees rooted at r_2 and l. We store these elements in buffers $X_{v_0}, X_{v_1}, \ldots, X_{v_h}$, sorted top-down and so that each node v_i receives K_i elements. We clear the "exhausted" labels of all nodes among $v_0, v_1, \ldots, v_h$. If v has degree greater than $M/2$ as a result of gaining two children, r_2 and l, we rebalance the tree using node splits starting at v similar to the rebalancing done after a FLUSH operation.

Heapify. The final operation to discuss is the HEAPIFY operation. Given a node v and its path $v = v_0, v_1, \ldots, v_h$ to the root, a HEAPIFY operation ensures that the elements stored on the path satisfy the heap property. It assumes that the elements in $v_1, v_2, \ldots, v_h$ already do so, but some elements in v_0 may be less than elements stored at higher nodes. To restore the heap property, we sort the elements in v_0 and collect the elements in $v_1, v_2, \ldots, v_h$ in sorted order. Then we merge the two sorted sequences to obtain a sorted sequence of the elements stored in $v_0, v_1, \ldots, v_h$ and distribute these elements over the buffers of nodes $v_0, v_1, \ldots, v_h$, assigning the same number of elements to each node as it had before the operation and storing the elements sorted top-down on the path. If some of the nodes on the path were marked as exhausted before this operation, we unmark them.

4.3 Analysis

To prove the correctness of all priority queue operations, we need to verify that the heap property is maintained at all times. This is little more than an exercise and is therefore omitted.

It is easy to see that every CREATE, INSERT, DELETEMIN, and MELD operation makes only O(1) changes to the buffer stack and thus has an amortized cost of $O(1/B)$ I/Os, excluding the manipulations performed by the FLUSH, FILL, MERGE, and HEAPIFY operations they trigger. The following two lemmas bound the cost of all FLUSH, FILL, MERGE, and HEAPIFY operations performed during a sequence of N priority queue operations. Due to lack of space, their proofs are omitted.

LEMMA 8. *During a sequence of N priority queue operations, at most* $O(N/M)$ FLUSH, FILL, MERGE, *and* HEAPIFY *operations are performed.*

LEMMA 9. *The amortized cost per* FLUSH, FILL, MERGE *or* HEAPIFY *operation is* $O((M/B)\log_{M/B}(N/M))$ *I/Os.*

5. REFERENCES

[1] P. Agarwal, L. Arge, and K. Yi. I/O-efficient batched union-find and its applications to terrain analysis. In *Proc. 22nd SCG*, pp. 167–176, 2006.

[2] A. Aggarwal and J. S. Vitter. The input/output complexity of sorting and related problems. *Comm. of the ACM*, 31(9):1116–1127, 1988.

[3] L. Arge. The buffer tree: A technique for designing batched external data structures. *Algorithmica*, 37(1):1–24, 2003.

[4] L. Arge, J. Chase, P. Halpin, L. Toma, D. Urban, J. S. Vitter, and R. W. and. Flow computation on massive grid terrains. In *Proc. 9th ACM GIS*, pp. 82–87, 2001.

[5] L. Arge and M. Revsbæk. I/O-efficient contour tree simplification. In *Proc. 20th ISAAC*, pp. 1155–1165, 2009.

[6] Y.-J. Chiang, M. T. Goodrich, E. F. Grove, R. Tamassia, D. E. Vengroff, and J. S. Vitter. External-memory graph algorithms. In *Proc. 6th SODA*, pp. 139–149, 1995.

[7] A. Danner. *I/O Efficient Algorithms and Applications in Geographic Information Systems.* PhD thesis, Dept. of Comp. Sci., Duke University, 2006.

[8] A. Danner, K. Yi, T. Mølhave, P. K. Agarwal, L. Arge, and H. Mitasova. TerraStream: From elevation data to watershed hierarchies. Manuscript, 2007.

[9] M. de Berg, O. Cheong, H. Haverkort, J.-G. Lim, and L. Toma. I/O-efficient flow modelling on fat terrains. In *Proc. 10th WADS*, pp. 239–250, 2007.

[10] H. Edelsbrunner, J. Harer, and A. Zomorodian. Hierarchical morse complexes for piecewise linear 2-manifolds. In *Proc. 17th SCG*, pp. 70–79, 2001.

[11] H. Edelsbrunner, D. Letscher, and A. Zomorodian. Topological persistence and simplification. In *Proc. 41st FOCS*, pp. 454–463, 2000.

[12] R. Fadel, K. V. Jakobsen, J. Katajainen, and J. Teuhola. Heaps and heapsort on secondary storage. *Theor. Comp. Sci.*, 220(2):345–362, 1999.

[13] S. Jenson and J. Domingue. Extracting topographic structure from digital elevation data for geographic information system analysis. *Photogrammetric Eng. and Remote Sensing*, 54(11):1593–1600, 1988.

[14] Y. Liu and J. Snoeyink. Flooding triangulated terrain. In *Proceedings of the 11th International Symposium on Spatial Data Handling*, pages 137–148, 2005.

[15] J. F. O'Callaghan and D. M. Mark. The extraction of drainage networks from digital elevation data. *Computer Vision, Graphics and Image Proc.*, 28(3):323–344, 1984.

[16] O. Palacios-Velez, W. Gandoy-Bernasconi, and B. Cuevas-Renaud. Geometric analysis of surface runoff and the computation order of unit elements in distributed hydrological models. *J. Hydrology*, 211:266–274, 1998.

[17] D. M. Theobald and M. F. Goodchild. Artifacts of TIN-based surface flow modeling. In *Proc. GIS/LIS'90*, pp. 955–964, 1990.

[18] G. Tucker, S. Lancaster, N. Gasparini, and S. Rybarczyk. An object-oriented framework for hydrology and geomorphic modeling using triangulated irregular networks. *Computers and Geosciences*, 27(8):959–973, 2001.

Incidences in Three Dimensions and Distinct Distances in the Plane*

[Extended Abstract]

György Elekes
Eötvös University

Micha Sharir
Tel Aviv University and
New York University

ABSTRACT

We first describe a reduction from the problem of lower-bounding the number of distinct distances determined by a set S of s points in the plane to an incidence problem between points and a certain class of helices (or parabolas) in three dimensions. We offer conjectures involving the new setup, but are still unable to fully resolve them.

Instead, we adapt the recent new algebraic analysis technique of Guth and Katz [9], as further developed by Elekes et al. [6], to obtain sharp bounds on the number of incidences between these helices or parabolas and points in $\mathbb{R}^3$. Applying these bounds, we obtain, among several other results, the upper bound $O(s^3)$ on the number of rotations (rigid motions) which map (at least) three points of S to three other points of S. In fact, we show that the number of such rotations which map at least $k \geq 3$ points of S to k other points of S is close to $O(s^3/k^{12/7})$.

One of our unresolved conjectures is that this number is $O(s^3/k^2)$, for $k \geq 2$. If true, it would imply the lower bound $\Omega(s/\log s)$ on the number of distinct distances in the plane.

Categories and Subject Descriptors

F.2.2 [**Analysis of algorithms and problem complexity**]: Nonnumerical algorithms and problems—*Geometrical problems and computations*; G.2.1 [**Discrete mathematics**]: Combinatorics—*Counting problems*

General Terms

Theory

Keywords

Distinct distances, Incidences, Algebraic Tecniques

*Work by Micha Sharir has been supported by NSF Grants CCF-05-14079 and CCF-08-30272, by grant 2006/194 from the U.S.-Israeli Binational Science Foundation, by grants 155/05 and 338/09 from the Israel Science Fund, and by the Hermann Minkowski–MINERVA Center for Geometry at Tel Aviv University.

SCG'10, June 13–16, 2010, Snowbird, Utah, USA.

1. THE INFRASTRUCTURE

The motivation for the study reported in this paper comes from the celebrated and long-standing problem, originally posed by Erdős [8] in 1946, of obtaining a sharp lower bound for the number of distinct distances guaranteed to exist in any set S of s points in the plane. Erdős has shown that a section of the integer lattice determines only $O(s/\sqrt{\log s})$ distinct distances, and conjectured this to be a lower bound for any planar point set. In spite of steady progress on this problem, reviewed next, Erdős's conjecture is still open.

L. Moser [12], Chung [4], and Chung *et al.* [5] proved that the number of distinct distances determined by s points in the plane is $\Omega(s^{2/3})$, $\Omega(s^{5/7})$, and $\Omega(s^{4/5}/\mathrm{polylog}(s))$, respectively. Székely [19] managed to get rid of the polylogarithmic factor, while Solymosi and Tóth [17] improved this bound to $\Omega(s^{6/7})$. This was a real breakthrough. Their analysis was subsequently refined by Tardos [21] and then by Katz and Tardos [11], who obtained the current record of $\Omega(s^{(48-14e)/(55-16e)-\varepsilon})$, for any $\varepsilon > 0$, which is $\Omega(s^{0.8641})$.

In this paper we transform the problem of distinct distances in the plane to an incidence problem between points and a certain kind of curves (helices or parabolas) in three dimensions. As we show, sharp upper bounds on the number of such incidences translate back to sharp lower bounds on the number of distinct distances. Incidence problems in three dimensions between points and curves have been studied in several recent works [2, 6, 16], and a major push in this direction has been made last year, with the breakthrough result of Guth and Katz [9], who have introduced methods from algebraic geometry for studying problems of this kind. This has been picked up by the authors [6], where worst-case tight bounds on the number of incidences between points and lines in three dimensions (under certain restrictions) have been obtained.

The present paper serves two purposes. First, it studies in detail the connection between the distinct distances problem and the corresponding 3-dimensional incidence problem. As it turns out, there is a lot of interesting geometric structure behind this reduction, and the paper (or rather its full version) develops it in detail. We offer several conjectures on the number of incidences, and show how, if true, they yield the almost worst-case tight lower bound $\Omega(s/\log s)$ on the number of distinct distances. Unfortunately, so far we have not succeeded in proving these conjectures. Nevertheless, we have made considerable progress on the incidence problem itself, which is the second purpose of the study in this paper. We show how to adapt the algebraic machinery of [6, 9, 10, 14] to derive sharp bounds for the incidence problem. These bounds are very similar to, and in fact even better than the bounds obtained in [6] for point-line incidences, where they have been shown to be worst-case tight. However, they are not (yet) good enough to yield significant lower bounds for distinct distances. We believe that there is additional geometric structure in the particular problem studied here, which should enable one to further improve the bounds, but so far this remains elusive.

The paper is organized as follows. We first describe the reduction from the planar distinct distances problem to the 3-dimensional incidence problem mentioned above. In doing so, we note and explore several additional geometric connections between the two problems (as manifested, e.g., in the analysis of *special surfaces* given below). We then present the tools from algebraic geometry that are needed to tackle the incidence problem; they are variants of the tools used in [6, 9], adapted to the specific curves that we need to handle. We then go on to bound the number of incidences. We first bound the number of rotations in terms of the number of parabolas, and then bound the number of incidences themselves. The latter task is achieved in two steps. We first use a "purely algebraic" analysis, akin to those in [6, 9], to obtain a weaker bound, which we then refine in the second step, using more traditional space decomposition techniques. The final bound is still not as good as we would like it to be, but it shows that the case studied in this paper "behaves better" than its counterpart involving lines.

Due to severe lack of space, many details are omitted in this version. They can be found in the full version [7].

Distinct distances and incidences with helices. We offer the following novel approach to the problem of distinct distances.

(H1) Notation. Let S be a set of s points in the plane with x distinct distances. Let K denote the set of all quadruples $(a, b, a', b') \in S^4$, such that the pairs (a, b) and (a', b') are distinct (although the points themselves need not be) and $|ab| = |a'b'| > 0$.

Let $\delta_1, \ldots, \delta_x$ denote the x distinct distances in S, and let $E_i = \{(a, b) \in S^2 \mid |ab| = \delta_i\}$. We have

$$|K| = 2\sum_{i=1}^{x}\binom{|E_i|}{2} \geq \sum_{i=1}^{x}(|E_i| - 1)^2$$
$$\geq \frac{1}{x}\left[\sum_{i=1}^{x}(|E_i| - 1)\right]^2 = \frac{[s(s-1) - x]^2}{x}.$$

(H2) Rotations. We associate each $(a, b, a', b') \in K$ with a (unique) *rotation* (or, rather, a rigid, orientation-preserving transformation of the plane) τ, which maps a to a' and b to b'. A rotation τ, in complex notation, can be written as the transformation $z \mapsto pz + q$, where $p, q \in \mathbb{C}$ and $|p| = 1$. Putting $p = e^{i\theta}$, $q = \xi + i\eta$, we can represent τ by the point $(\xi, \eta, \theta) \in \mathbb{R}^3$. In the planar context, θ is the counterclockwise angle of the rotation, and the center of rotation is $c = q/(1 - e^{i\theta})$, which is defined for $\theta \neq 0$; for $\theta = 0$, τ is a pure translation.

The *multiplicity* $\mu(\tau)$ of a rotation τ (with respect to S) is defined as $|\tau(S) \cap S|$ = the number of pairs $(a, b) \in S^2$ such that $\tau(a) = b$. Clearly, one always has $\mu(\tau) \leq s$, and we will mostly consider only rotations satisfying $\mu(\tau) \geq 2$. As a matter of fact, the bulk of the paper will only consider rotations with multiplicity at least 3. Rotations with multiplicity 2 are harder to analyze.

If $\mu(\tau) = k$ then S contains two congruent and equally oriented copies A, B of some k-element set, such that $\tau(A) = B$. Thus, studying multiplicities of rotations is closely related to analyzing repeated (congruent and equally oriented) patterns in a planar point set; see [3] for a review of many problems of this kind.

(H3) Bounding $|K|$. If $\mu(\tau) = k$ then τ contributes $\binom{k}{2}$ quadruples to K. Let N_k (resp., $N_{\geq k}$) denote the number of rotations with multiplicity exactly k (resp., at least k), for $k \geq 2$. Then

$$|K| = \sum_{k=2}^{s}\binom{k}{2}N_k = \sum_{k=2}^{s}\binom{k}{2}(N_{\geq k} - N_{\geq k+1})$$
$$= N_{\geq 2} + \sum_{k\geq 3}(k-1)N_{\geq k}.$$

(H4) The main conjecture.

CONJECTURE 1. *For any $2 \leq k \leq s$, we have*
$$N_{\geq k} = O\left(s^3/k^2\right).$$

Suppose that the conjecture were true. Then we would have

$$\frac{[s(s-1) - x]^2}{x} \leq |K| = O(s^3) \cdot \left[1 + \sum_{k\geq 3}\frac{1}{k}\right] = O(s^3 \log s),$$

which would have implied that $x = \Omega(s/\log s)$. This would have almost settled the problem of obtaining a tight bound for the minimum number of distinct distances guaranteed to exist in any set of s points in the plane, since, as mentioned above, the upper bound for this quantity is $O(s/\sqrt{\log s})$ [8].

We note that Conjecture 1 is rather deep; even the simple instance $k = 2$, asserting that there are only $O(s^3)$ rotations which map (at least) two points of S to two other points of S (at the same distance apart), seems quite difficult. In this paper we establish a variety of upper bounds on the number of rotations and on the sum of their multiplicities. In particular, these results provide a partial positive answer, showing that $N_{\geq 3} = O(s^3)$; that is, the number of rotations which map a (degenerate or non-degenerate) triangle determined by S to another congruent (and equally oriented) such triangle, is $O(s^3)$. Bounding N_2 by $O(s^3)$ is still an open problem. See Section 5 for a simple proof of the weaker bound $N_{\geq 2} = O(s^{10/3})$.

Lower bound. In the full version [7] we present a construction (suggested by Haim Kaplan) which shows:

LEMMA 2. *There exist sets S in the plane of arbitrarily large cardinality, which determine $\Theta(|S|^3)$ distinct rotations, each mapping a triple of points of S to another triple of points of S.*

A "weakness" of this construction is that all these rotations map a *collinear* triple of points of S to another collinear triple. (In the terminology to follow, these will be called *flat* rotations.) We do not know whether the number of rotations which map a *non-collinear* triple of points of S to another non-collinear triple can be $\Omega(|S|^3)$. We tend to conjecture that this is indeed the case.

We also do not know whether Conjecture 1 is worst-case tight (if true). That is, do there exist sets S, with $s = |S|$ arbitrarily large, so that there are $\Omega(s^3/k^2)$ distinct rotations, each mapping at least k points of S to k other points of S?

(H5) Helices. To estimate $N_{\geq k}$, we reduce the problem of analyzing rotations and their interaction with S to an incidence problem in three dimensions, as follows.

With each pair $(a, b) \in S^2$, we associate the curve $h_{a,b}$, in a 3-dimensional space parametrized by (ξ, η, θ), which is the locus of all rotations which map a to b. That is, the equation of $h_{a,b}$ is given by

$$h_{a,b} = \{(\xi, \eta, \theta) \mid b = ae^{i\theta} + (\xi, \eta)\}.$$

Putting $a = (a_1, a_2)$, $b = (b_1, b_2)$, this becomes

$$\begin{aligned} \xi &= b_1 - (a_1\cos\theta - a_2\sin\theta), \\ \eta &= b_2 - (a_1\sin\theta + a_2\cos\theta). \end{aligned} \qquad (1)$$

This is a *helix* in $\mathbb{R}^3$, having four degrees of freeedom, which we parametrize by (a_1, a_2, b_1, b_2). It extends from the plane $\theta = 0$ to the plane $\theta = 2\pi$; its two endpoints lie vertically above each other, and it completes exactly one revolution between them.

(H6) Helices, rotations, and incidences. Let P be a set of rotations, represented by points in $\mathbb{R}^3$, as above, and let H denote the set of all s^2 helices $h_{a,b}$, for $(a,b) \in S^2$ (note that $a = b$ is permitted). Let $I(P,H)$ denote the number of incidences between P and H. Then we have

$$I(P,H) = \sum_{\tau \in P} \mu(\tau).$$

Rotations τ with $\mu(\tau) = 1$ are not interesting, because each of them only contributes 1 to the count $I(P,H)$, and we will mostly ignore them. For the same reason, rotations with $\mu(\tau) = 2$ are also not interesting for estimating $I(P,H)$, but they need to be included in the analysis of $N_{\geq 2}$. Unfortunately, as already noted, we do not yet have a good upper bound (i.e., cubic in s) on the number of such rotations.

(H7) Incidences and the second conjecture.

CONJECTURE 3. *For any P and H as above, we have*

$$I(P,H) = O\left(|P|^{1/2}|H|^{3/4} + |P| + |H|\right).$$

Suppose that Conjecture 3 were true. Let $P_{\geq k}$ denote the set of all rotations with multiplicity at least k (with respect to S). We then have

$$kN_{\geq k} = k|P_{\geq k}| \leq I(P_{\geq k}, H) = O\left(N_{\geq k}^{1/2}|H|^{3/4} + N_{\geq k} + |H|\right),$$

from which we obtain

$$N_{\geq k} = O\left(\frac{s^3}{k^2} + \frac{s^2}{k}\right) = O\left(\frac{s^3}{k^2}\right),$$

thus establishing Conjecture 1, and therefore also the lower bound for x (the number of distinct distances) derived above from this conjecture.

Remark. Conjecture 3 can also be formulated for an *arbitrary* subset H of all possible helices.

Note that two helices $h_{a,b}$ and $h_{c,d}$ intersect in at most one point—this is the unique rotation which maps a to b and c to d (if it exists at all, namely if $|ac| = |bd|$). Hence, combining this fact with a standard cutting-based decomposition technique, similar to what has been noted in [16], say, yields the weaker bound

$$I(P,H) = O\left(|P|^{2/3}|H|^{2/3} + |P| + |H|\right), \qquad (2)$$

which, alas, only yields the much weaker bound $N_{\geq k} = O\left(s^4/k^3\right)$, which is completely useless for deriving any lower bound on x. (We will use this bound, though, in Section 6.)

(H8) From helices to parabolas. The helices $h_{a,b}$ are non-algebraic curves, because of the use of the angle θ as a parameter. This can be easily remedied, in the following standard manner. Assume that θ ranges from $-\pi$ to π, and substitute, in the equations (1), $Z = \tan(\theta/2)$, $X = \xi(1+Z^2)$, and $Y = \eta(1+Z^2)$, to obtain

$$\begin{aligned} X &= (a_1+b_1)Z^2 + 2a_2 Z + (b_1 - a_1) \qquad (3)\\ Y &= (a_2+b_2)Z^2 - 2a_1 Z + (b_2 - a_2), \end{aligned}$$

which are the equations of a *planar parabola* in the (X,Y,Z)-space. (The parabola degenerates to a line if $b = -a$, a situation that we will rule out by choosing an appropriate generic coordinate frame in the original xy-plane.) We denote the parabola corresponding to the helix $h_{a,b}$ as $h^*_{a,b}$, and refer to it as an *h-parabola*.

(H9) Joint and flat rotations. A rotation $\tau \in P$ is called a *joint* of H if τ is incident to at least three helices of H whose tangent lines at τ are non-coplanar. Otherwise, still assuming that τ is incident to at least three helices of H, τ is called *flat*.

Let $\tau = (\xi, \eta, \theta) \in P$ be a rotation, incident to three distinct helices $h_{a,b}$, $h_{c,d}$, $h_{e,f}$. From their equations, as given in (1), the directions of the tangents to these helices at τ are

$$\begin{gathered}(a_1 \sin\theta + a_2\cos\theta,\ -a_1\cos\theta + a_2\sin\theta,\ 1)\\ (c_1 \sin\theta + c_2\cos\theta,\ -c_1\cos\theta + c_2\sin\theta,\ 1)\\ (e_1 \sin\theta + e_2\cos\theta,\ -e_1\cos\theta + e_2\sin\theta,\ 1).\end{gathered}$$

Put $p = \cos\theta$ and $q = \sin\theta$. Then the three tangents are coplanar if and only if

$$\begin{vmatrix} a_1q + a_2p & -a_1p + a_2q & 1 \\ c_1q + c_2p & -c_1p + c_2q & 1 \\ e_1q + e_2p & -e_1p + e_2q & 1 \end{vmatrix} = 0.$$

Simplifying the determinant, and recalling that $p^2 + q^2 = 1$, the condition is equivalent to

$$\begin{vmatrix} a_1 & a_2 & 1 \\ c_1 & c_2 & 1 \\ e_1 & e_2 & 1 \end{vmatrix} = 0.$$

In other words, the three helices $h_{a,b}$, $h_{c,d}$, $h_{e,f}$ form a joint at τ if and only if the three points a, c, e (and thus also b, d, f) are non-collinear.

CLAIM 4. *A rotation τ is a joint of H if and only if τ maps a non-degenerate triangle determined by S to another (congruent and equally oriented) non-degenerate triangle determined by S. A rotation τ is a flat rotation if and only if τ maps at least three collinear points of S to another collinear triple of points of S, but does not map any point of S outside the line containing the triple to another point of S.*

The preceding analysis also shows that, for any fixed rotation τ, the directions of the tangents at τ to the helices incident to τ are all distinct. This will be important in the algebraic analysis given below.

(H10) Special surfaces. In preparation for the forthcoming algebraic analysis, we need the following property of our helices.

Let τ be a flat rotation, with multiplicity $k \geq 3$, and let ℓ and ℓ' be the corresponding lines in the plane, such that there exist k points $a_1, \ldots, a_k \in S \cap \ell$ and k points $b_1, \ldots, b_k \in S \cap \ell'$, such that τ maps a_i to b_i for each i (and in particular maps ℓ to ℓ'). By definition, τ is incident to the k helices h_{a_i,b_i}, for $i = 1, \ldots, k$.

Let u and v denote unit vectors in the direction of ℓ and ℓ', respectively. Clearly, there exist two reference points $a \in \ell$ and $b \in \ell'$, such that for each i there is a real number t_i such that $a_i = a + t_i u$ and $b_i = b + t_i v$. As a matter of fact, for each real t, τ maps $a + tu$ to $b + tv$, so it is incident to $h_{a+tu,b+tv}$. Note that a and b are not uniquely defined: we can take a to be any point on ℓ, and shift b accordingly along ℓ'.

Let $H(a,b;u,v)$ denote the set of these helices. Since a pair of helices can meet in at most one point, all the helices in $H(a,b;u,v)$ pass through τ but are otherwise pairwise disjoint. Using the reparametrization $(\xi,\eta,\theta) \mapsto (X,Y,Z)$, we denote by $\Sigma = \Sigma(a,b;u,v)$ the surface which is the union of all the h-parabolas that are the images of the helices in $H(a,b;u,v)$. We refer to such a surface Σ as a *special surface*.

An important comment is that most of the ongoing analysis also applies when only two helices are incident to τ; they suffice to determine the four parameters a, b, u, v that define the surface Σ.

We also remark that, although we started the definition of $\Sigma(a,b;u,v)$ with a flat rotation τ, the definition only depends on the parameters a, b, u, and v. If τ is not flat it may determine many special surfaces, one for each line that contains two or more points of S which τ maps to other (also collinear) points of S. Also, as we will shortly see, the same surface can be obtained from a different set (in fact, many such sets) of parameters a', b', u', and v' (or, alternatively, from different flat rotations τ'). An "intrinsic" definition of special surfaces will be given shortly.

The surface $\Sigma(a,b;u,v)$ is a cubic algebraic surface, whose equation, worked out in detail in the full version [7], is

$$E_2(Z)X - E_1(Z)Y + K(Z) = 0, \quad \text{where} \tag{4}$$

$$\begin{aligned} E_1(Z) &= (u_1+v_1)Z + (u_2+v_2) \\ E_2(Z) &= (u_2+v_2)Z - (u_1+v_1), \end{aligned} \tag{5}$$

and $K(Z)$ is the cubic polynomial

$$\Big((u_1+v_1)Z + (u_2+v_2)\Big)\Big((a_2+b_2)Z^2 - 2a_1Z + (b_2-a_2)\Big) -$$
$$\Big((u_2+v_2)Z - (u_1+v_1)\Big)\Big((a_1+b_1)Z^2 + 2a_2Z + (b_1-a_1)\Big).$$

We refer to the cubic polynomial in the left-hand side of (4) as a *special polynomial*. Thus a special surface is the zero set of a special polynomial.

(H11) The geometry of special surfaces. Special surfaces pose a technical challenge to the analysis. Specifically, each special surface Σ captures a certain underlying pattern in the ground set S, which may result in many incidences between rotations and h-parabolas, all contained in Σ. The next step of the analysis studies this pattern in detail.

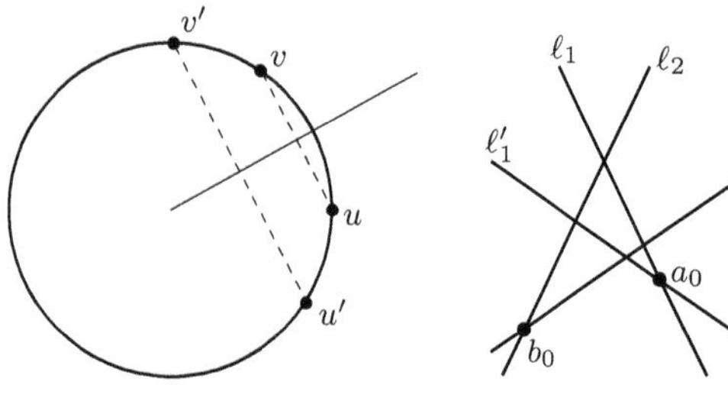

Figure 1: Left: The configuration of u, v, u', v'. Right: The structure of τ and τ' on a common special surface Σ.

Consider first a simple instance of this situation, in which two special surfaces Σ, Σ', generated by two distinct flat rotations τ, τ', coincide. More precisely, there exist four parameters a, b, u, v such that τ maps the line $\ell_1 = a + tu$ to the line $\ell_2 = b + tv$ (so that points with the same parameter t are mapped to one another), and four other parameters a', b', u', v' such that τ' maps (in a similar manner) the line $\ell_1' = a' + tu'$ to the line $\ell_2' = b' + tv'$, and $\Sigma(a,b;u,v) = \Sigma(a',b';u',v')$. Denote this common surface by Σ. Since the surfaces coincide, simple algebraic calculations, detailed in [7], show that the angle bisector between u and v must coincide with that between u' and v', as depicted in Figure 1(left). Moreover, as is easily checked, if we let a_0 be the intersection point of ℓ_1 and ℓ_1', and let b_0 be the intersection point of ℓ_2 and ℓ_2', then both τ and τ' map a_0 to b_0, and $h^*_{a_0,b_0}$ is contained in Σ. (See Figure 1(right) and [7] for details.)

Since the preceding analysis applies to any pair of distinct rotations on a common special surface Σ, it follows that we can associate with Σ a common direction w and a common shift δ, so that for each $\tau \in \Sigma$ there exist two lines ℓ, ℓ', where τ maps ℓ to ℓ', so that the angle bisector between these lines is in direction w, and τ is the unique rigid motion, obtained by rotating ℓ to ℓ' around their intersection point $\ell \cap \ell'$, and then shifting ℓ' along itself by a distance whose projection in direction w is δ. See Figure 1(right).

Let Σ be a special surface, generated by $H(a,b;u,v)$; that is, Σ is the union of all parabolas of the form $h^*_{a+tu,b+tv}$, for $t \in \mathbb{R}$. Let τ_0 be the common rotation to all these parabolas, so it maps the line $\ell_0 = \{a + tu \mid t \in \mathbb{R}\}$ to the line $\ell_0' = \{b + tv \mid t \in \mathbb{R}\}$, so that every point $a + tu$ is mapped to $b + tv$.

Let $h^*_{c,d}$ be a parabola contained in Σ but not passing through τ_0. Take any pair of distinct rotations τ_1, τ_2 on $h^*_{c,d}$. Then there exist two respective real numbers t_1, t_2, such that $\tau_i \in h^*_{a+t_iu,b+t_iv}$, for $i = 1, 2$. Thus τ_i is the unique rotation which maps c to d and $a_i = a + t_iu$ to $b_i = b + t_iv$. In particular, we have $|a + t_iu - c| = |b + t_iv - d|$. This in turn implies that the triangles a_1a_2c and b_1b_2d are congruent; see Figure 2.

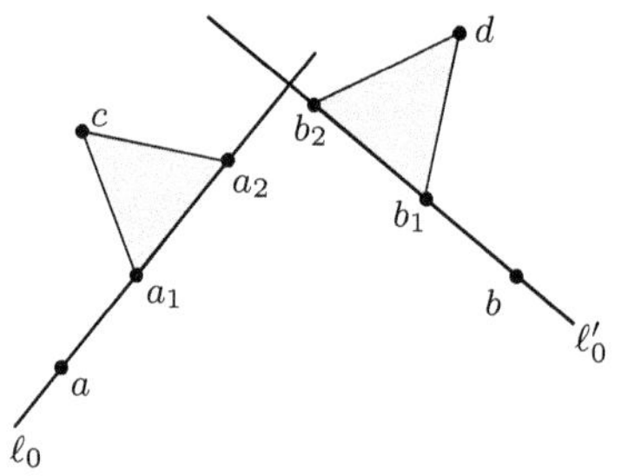

Figure 2: The geometric configuration corresponding to a parabola $h^*_{c,d}$ contained in Σ.

Given c, this determines d, up to a reflection about ℓ_0'. We claim that d has to be on the "other side" of ℓ_0', namely, be such that the triangles a_1a_2c and b_1b_2d are oppositely oriented. Indeed, if they were equally oriented, then τ_0 would have mapped c to d, and then $h^*_{c,d}$ would have passed through τ_0, contrary to assumption.

Now form the two sets

$$\begin{aligned} A &= \{p \in S \mid \text{there exists } q \in S \text{ such that } h^*_{p,q} \subset \Sigma\} \\ B &= \{q \in S \mid \text{there exists } p \in S \text{ such that } h^*_{p,q} \subset \Sigma\}. \end{aligned} \tag{6}$$

The preceding discussion implies that A and B are congruent and oppositely oriented.

To recap, each rotation $\tau \in \Sigma$, incident to $k \geq 2$ parabolas contained in Σ, corresponds to a pair of lines ℓ, ℓ' with the above properties, so that τ maps k points of $S \cap \ell$ (rather, of $A \cap \ell$) to k points of $S \cap \ell'$ (that is, of $B \cap \ell'$). If τ is flat, its entire multiplicity comes from points of S on ℓ (these are the points of $A \cap \ell$) which are mapped by τ to points of S on ℓ' (these are points of $B \cap \ell'$), and all the corresponding parabolas are contained in Σ. If τ is a joint then, for any other point $p \in S$ outside ℓ which is mapped by τ to a point $q \in S$ outside ℓ', the parabola $h^*_{p,q}$ is not contained in Σ, and crosses it transversally at the unique rotation τ.

Note also that any pair of parabolas $h^*_{c_1,d_1}$ and $h^*_{c_2,d_2}$ which are contained in Σ intersect, necessarily at the unique rotation which maps c_1 to d_1 and c_2 to d_2. This holds because $|c_1c_2| = |d_1d_2|$, as follows from the preceding discussion.

Special surfaces are anti-rotations. Let Σ be a special surface, and let A, B be the subsets of S associated with Σ, as in (6). Then there exists a single *anti-rotation* (a rigid, orientation-reversiong motion of the plane) which maps A to B. Conversely, any anti-rotation can be associated with a unique special surface in this manner. However, the number of incidences within a special surface may be larger than the incidence count of the anti-rotation with the appropriate variants of the h-parabolas: the former counts incidences between the points of A (or of B) and the lines that they determine, while the latter only counts the size of A (or of B).

Parabolas on special surfaces.

LEMMA 5. *A special surface can contain at most s h-parabolas.*

Proof: Let Ξ be the given special surface. We claim that for each $a \in S$ there can be at most one point $b \in S$ such that $h^*_{a,b} \subset \Xi$. Indeed, suppose that there exist two such points $b_1, b_2 \in S$. Since any pair of h-parabolas on Ξ intersect, h^*_{a,b_1} and h^*_{a,b_2} meet at a rotation τ, which maps a to both b_1 and b_2, an impossibility which completes the proof. □

2. TOOLS FROM ALGEBRAIC GEOMETRY

We review in this section (without proofs) the basic tools from algebraic geometry that have been used in [6, 9]. We state here the variants that arise in the context of incidences between points and our h-parabolas. The proofs can be found in the full version of the paper [7].

So let C be a set of $n \le s^2$ h-parabolas in $\mathbb{R}^3$. Recalling the definitions in (H9), we say that a point (rotation) a is a *joint* of C if it is incident to three parabolas of C whose tangents at a are non-coplanar. Let $J = J_C$ denote the set of joints of C. We will also consider points a that are incident to three or more parabolas of C, so that the tangents to all these parabolas are coplanar, and refer to such points as *flat* points of C. We recall (see (H9)) that any pair of distinct h-parabolas which meet at a point have there distinct tangents.

First, we note that, using a trivial application of Bézout's theorem [15], a trivariate polynomial p of degree d which vanishes at $2d+1$ points that lie on a common h-parabola $h^* \in C$ must vanish identically on h^*.

Critical points and parabolas. A point a is *critical* (or *singular*) for a trivariate polynomial p if $p(a) = 0$ and $\nabla p(a) = 0$; any other point a in the zero set of p is called *regular*. A parabola h^* is *critical* if all its points are critical.

Another application of Bézout's theorem implies the following.

PROPOSITION 6. *Let C be as above. Then any trivariate square-free polynomial p of degree d can have at most $d(d-1)$ critical parabolas in C.*

For regular points of p, we have the following easy observation.

PROPOSITION 7. *Let a be a regular point of p, so that $p \equiv 0$ on three parabolas of C passing through a. Then these parabolas must have coplanar tangents at a.*

Hence, a point a incident to three parabolas of C whose tangent lines at a are non-coplanar, so that $p \equiv 0$ on each of these parabolas, must be a critical point of p.

The main ingredient in the algebraic approach to incidence problems is the following, fairly easy (and rather well-known) result.

PROPOSITION 8. *Given a set S of m points in 3-space, there exists a nontrivial trivariate polynomial $p(x, y, z)$ which vanishes at all the points of S, of degree d, for any d satisfying $\binom{d+3}{3} > m$.*

Proof: (See [6, 7, 9].) A trivariate polynomial of degree d has $\binom{d+3}{3}$ monomials, and requiring it to vanish at m points yields these many homogeneous equations in the coefficients of these monomials. Such an underdetermined system always has a nontrivial solution. □

Flat points and parabolas. Call a regular point τ of a trivariate polynomial p *geometrically flat* if it is incident to three distinct parabolas of C (with necessarily coplanar tangent lines at τ, no pair of which are collinear) on which p vanishes identically.

Handling geometrically flat points in our analysis is somewhat trickier than handling critical points, and involves the second-order partial derivatives of p. The analysis, detailed in [7] (and similar to those in [6, 9]) leads to the following properties.

PROPOSITION 9. *Let p be a trivariate polynomial, and define*

$$\Pi(p) = p_Y^2 p_{XX} - 2p_X p_Y p_{XY} + p_X^2 p_{YY}.$$

Then, if τ is a regular geometrically flat point of p (with respect to three parabolas of C) then $\Pi(p)(\tau) = 0$.

Remarks. (1) $\Pi(p)$ is one of the polynomials that form the *second fundamental form* of p; see [6, 7, 9, 13] for details.

(2) Although most details are suppressed, it is important to note that for Proposition 9 to hold it is crucial that τ be incident to (at least) three parabolas of C. This is why we can only handle rotations of multiplicity at least 3.

In particular, if the degree of p is d then the degree of $\Pi(p)$ is at most $(d-1) + (d-1) + (d-2) = 3d - 4$.

In what follows, we call a point τ *flat* for p if $\Pi(p)(\tau) = 0$. Call an h-parabola $h^* \in C$ *flat* for p if all the points of h^* are flat points of p (with the possible exception of a discrete subset). Arguing as in the case of critical points, if h^* contains more than $2(3d-4)$ flat points then h^* is a flat parabola.

The next proposition shows that, in general, trivariate polynomials do not have too many flat parabolas. The proof is based on Bézout's theorem, as does the proof of Proposition 6.

PROPOSITION 10. *Let p be any trivariate square-free polynomial of degree d with no special polynomial factors. Then p can have at most $d(3d-4)$ flat h-parabolas in C.*

3. THE NUMBER OF ROTATIONS

In this section we extend the recent algebraic machinery of Guth and Katz [9], as further developed by Elekes et al. [6], using the algebraic tools set forth in the preceding section, to establish the bound $O(n^{3/2}) = O(s^3)$ on the number of rotations with multiplicity at least 3 in a collection of n h-parabolas.

THEOREM 11. *Let C be a set of at most n h-parabolas in $\mathbb{R}^3$, and let P be a set of m rotations, each of which is incident to at least three parabolas of C. Suppose further that no special surface contains more than q parabolas of C. Then $m = O(n^{3/2} + nq)$.*

Remarks. (1) The recent results of [10, 14] imply that the number of joints in a set of n h-parabolas is $O(n^{3/2})$. The proofs in [10, 14] are much simpler than the proof given below, but they do not apply to flat points (rotations) as does Theorem 11. Since flat rotations are an integral part of the setup considered in this paper, we need to count them too, using the stronger Theorem 11. Moreover, even if we were to consider only joint rotations, the analysis of their incidences with the h-parabolas will turn some of them into flat rotations (by pruning some of the parabolas), so we will need to face flat rotations, no matter what.

(2) By Lemma 5, we always have $q \le s$, and we also have $n^{1/2} \le s$, so the "worst-case" bound on m is $O(ns)$.

(3) Note that the parameter n in the statement of the theorem is arbitrary, not necessarily the maximum number s^2. When n attains its maximum possible value s^2, the bound becomes $m = O(n^{3/2}) = O(s^3)$.

The proof of Theorem 11 uses the proof technique of [6], properly adapted to the present, somewhat more involved context of h-parabolas and rotations.

Proof. We first prove the theorem under the additional assumption that $q = n^{1/2}$. The proof proceeds by induction on n, and shows that $m \le An^{3/2}$, where A is a sufficiently large constant whose choice will be dictated by the forthcoming analysis. The statement holds for all $n \le n_0$, for some constant n_0, if we choose A to be sufficiently large. Fix $n > n_0$, and suppose that the claim holds for all $n' < n$. Let C and P be as in the statement of the theorem, with $|C| = n$, and suppose to the contrary that $|P| > An^{3/2}$.

We first apply the following iterative pruning process to C. As long as there exists a parabola $h^* \in C$ incident to fewer than $cn^{1/2}$ rotations of P, for some constant $1 \le c \ll A$ that we will fix later, we remove h^* from C, remove its incident rotations from P, and repeat this step with respect to the reduced set of rotations. In this process we delete at most $cn^{3/2}$ rotations. We are thus left with a subset of at least $(A-c)n^{3/2}$ of the original parabolas, each incident to at least $cn^{1/2}$ surviving rotations, and each surviving rotation is incident to at least three surviving parabolas. For simplicity, continue to denote these sets as C and P.

Choose a random sample C^s of parabolas from C, by picking each parabola independently with probability t, where t is a small constant that we will fix later.

The expected number of parabolas that we choose is $tn_1 \le tn$, where n_1 is the number of parabolas remaining after the pruning. We have $n_1 = \Omega(n^{1/2})$, because each surviving parabola is incident to at least $cn^{1/2}$ surviving rotations, each incident to at least two other surviving parabolas; since all these parabolas are distinct (recall that a pair of parabolas can meet in at most one rotation point), we have $n_1 \ge 2cn^{1/2}$. Hence, using Chernoff's bound, as in [6] (see, e.g., [1]), we obtain that, with positive probability, (a) $|C^s| \le 2tn$. (b) Each parabola $h^* \in C$ contains at least $\frac{1}{2}ctn^{1/2}$ rotations that lie on parabolas of C^s. (To see (b), take a parabola $h^* \in C$ and a rotation $\tau \in P \cap h^*$. Note that τ will be incident to a parabola of C^s with probability at least t, so the expected number of rotations in $P \cap h^*$ which lie on parabolas of C^s is at least $ctn^{1/2}$. This, combined with Chernoff's bound, implies (b).)

We assume that C^s does indeed satisfy (a) and (b), and then (recalling that $c \ge 1$) choose $n^{1/2}$ arbitrary rotations on each parabola in C^s, to obtain a set S of at most $2tn^{3/2}$ rotations.

Applying Proposition 8, we obtain a nontrivial trivariate polynomial $p(X,Y,Z)$ which vanishes at all the rotations of S, whose degree is at most the smallest integer d satisfying $\binom{d+3}{3} \ge |S|+1$, so

$$d \le \lceil (6|S|)^{1/3} \rceil \le (12t)^{1/3} n^{1/2} + 1 \le 2(12t)^{1/3} n^{1/2},$$

for n (i.e., n_0) sufficiently large. Without loss of generality, we may assume that p is square-free—by removing repeated factors, we get a square-free polynomial which vanishes on the same set as the original p, with the same upper bound on its degree.

The polynomial p vanishes on $n^{1/2}$ points on each parabola in C^s. This number is larger than $2d$, if we choose t sufficiently small so as to satisfy $4(12t)^{1/3} < 1$. Hence p vanishes identically on all these parabolas. Any other parabola of C meets at least $\frac{1}{2}ctn^{1/2}$ parabolas of C^s, at distinct points, and we can make this number also larger than $2d$, with an appropriate choice of t and c (we need to ensure that $ct > 8(12t)^{1/3}$). Hence, p vanishes identically on each parabola of C.

We will also later need the property that each parabola of C contains at least $9d$ points of P; that is, we require that $cn^{1/2} > 9d$, which will hold if $c > 18(12t)^{1/3}$.

To recap, the preceding paragraphs impose several inequalities on c and t, and a couple of additional similar inequalities will be imposed later on. All these inequalities are easy to satisfy by choosing $t < 1$ to be a sufficiently small positive constant, and c a sufficiently large constant. (These choices will also affect the choice of A—see below.)

We note that p can have at most $d/3$ special polynomial factors (since each of them is a cubic polynomial); i.e., p can vanish identically on at most $d/3$ respective special surfaces $\Xi_1, \ldots, \Xi_k$, for $k \le d/3$. We factor out all these special polynomial factors from p, and let $\tilde{p}$ denote the resulting polynomial, which is a square-free polynomial without any special polynomial factors, of degree at most d.

Consider one of the special surfaces Ξ_i, and let t_i denote the number of parabolas contained in Ξ_i. Then any rotation on Ξ_i is either an intersection point of (at least) two of these parabolas, or it lies on at most one of them. The number of rotations of the first kind is $O(t_i^2)$. Any rotation τ of the second kind is incident to at least one parabola of C which crosses Ξ_i transversally at τ. We note that each h-parabola h^* can cross Ξ_i in at most three points. Indeed, substituting the equations of h^* into the equation $E_2(Z)X - E_1(Z)Y + K(Z) = 0$ of Ξ_i (see (4)) yields a cubic equation in Z, with at most three roots. Hence, the number of rotations of the second kind is $O(n)$, and the overall number of rotations on Ξ_i is $O(t_i^2 + n) = O(n)$, since we have assumed in the present version of the proof that $t_i \le n^{1/2}$.

Summing the bounds over all surfaces Ξ_i, we conclude that altogether they contain $O(nd)$ rotations, which we bound by $bn^{3/2}$, for some absolute constant b.

We remove all these vanishing special surfaces, together with the rotations and the parabolas which are fully contained in them, and let $C_1 \subseteq C$ and $P_1 \subseteq P$ denote, respectively, the set of those parabolas of C (rotations of P) which are not contained in any of the vanishing surfaces Ξ_i.

Note that there are still at least three parabolas of C_1 incident to any remaining rotation in P_1, since none of the rotations of P_1 lie in any surface Ξ_i, so all parabolas incident to such a rotation are still in C_1.

Clearly, $\tilde{p}$ vanishes identically on every $h^* \in C_1$. Furthermore, every $h^* \in C_1$ contains at most d points in the surfaces Ξ_i, because, as just argued, it crosses each surface Ξ_i in at most three points.

Hence, each $h^* \in C_1$ contains at least $8d$ rotations of P_1. Since each of these rotations is incident to at least three parabolas in C_1, each of these rotations is either critical or geometrically flat for $\tilde{p}$.

Consider a parabola $h^* \in C_1$. If h^* contains more than $2d$ critical rotations then h^* is a critical parabola for $\tilde{p}$. By Proposition 6, the number of such parabolas is at most $d(d-1)$. Any other parabola $h^* \in C_1$ contains more than $6d$ geometrically flat points and hence h^* must be a flat parabola for $\tilde{p}$. By Proposition 10, the number of such parabolas is at most $d(3d-4)$. Summing up we obtain

$$|C_1| \le d(d-1) + d(3d-4) < 4d^2.$$

We require that $4d^2 < n/2$; that is, $32(12t)^{2/3} < 1$, which can be guaranteed by choosing t sufficiently small.

We next want to apply the induction hypothesis to C_1, with the parameter $4d^2$ (which dominates the size of C_1). For this, we first need to argue that each special surface contains at most $(4d^2)^{1/2} = 2d$ parabolas of C_1. Indeed, let Ξ be a special surface. Using (4), eliminate, say, Y from the equation of Ξ and substitute the resulting expression into the equation of $\tilde{p}$, to obtain a bivariate polynomial $\tilde{p}_0(X,Z)$. Let h^* be a parabola of C_1 contained in Ξ. We represent h^* by its X-equation of the form $X = Q(Z)$, and observe that $\tilde{p}_0(X,Z)$ vanishes on the zero set of $X - Q(Z)$. Hence $\tilde{p}_0$ must be divisible by $X - Q(Z)$. Note that, in a generic coordinate frame in the xy-plane, two different parabolas cannot have the same equation $X = Q(Z)$, because this equation uniquely determines a_1, b_1, and a_2, and then, in a generic frame, b_2 is also uniquely determined. Note also that the degree of $\tilde{p}_0$ is at most $3d$, and that the degree of each factor $X - Q(Z)$ is 2, implying that Σ can contain at most $3d/2$ parabolas of C_1.

Hence, the maximum number of parabolas of C_1 contained in a special surface is at most $3d/2 \le (4d^2)^{1/2}$, so, by the induction hypothesis, the number of points in P_1 is at most

$$A(4d^2)^{3/2} \le \frac{A}{2^{3/2}} n^{3/2}.$$

Adding up the bounds on the number of points on parabolas removed during the pruning process and on the special surfaces Ξ_i (which correspond to the special polynomial factors of p), we obtain

$$|P| \le \frac{A}{2^{3/2}} n^{3/2} + (b+c)n^{3/2} \le An^{3/2},$$

with an appropriate, final choice of t, c, and A. This contradicts the assumption that $|P| > An^{3/2}$, and thus establishes the induction step for n, and, consequently, completes the proof of the restricted version of the theorem.

Proof of the general version: The proof proceeds almost exactly as the proof of the restricted version, except for the analysis of the number of rotations on the special surfaces Ξ_i, which, using the preceding notations, is bounded by

$$O\left(\sum_i (t_i^2 + n)\right) = O\left(q \cdot \sum_i t_i + nd\right) = O(n^{3/2} + nq).$$

See [7]. □

We summarize the remarks following Theorem 11, combined with Lemma 2, in the following corollary.

COROLLARY 12. *Let S be a set of s points in the plane. Then there are at most $O(s^3)$ rotations which map some (degenerate or non-degenerate) triangle spanned by S to another (congruent and equally oriented) such triangle. This bound is tight in the worst case.*

4. INCIDENCES BETWEEN PARABOLAS AND ROTATIONS

In this section we further adapt the machinery of [6] to derive an upper bound on the number of incidences between m rotations and n h-parabolas in $\mathbb{R}^3$, where each rotation is incident to at least three parabolas.

THEOREM 13. *For an underlying ground set S of s points in the plane, let C be a set of at most $n \le s^2$ h-parabolas defined on S, and let P be a set of m rotations with multiplicity at least 3 (with respect to S). Then*

$$I(P,C) = O\left(m^{1/3}n + m^{2/3}n^{1/3}s^{1/3}\right).$$

Remark. As easily checked, the first term dominates the second term when $m \le n^2/s$, and the second term dominates when $n^2/s < m \le ns$. In particular, the first term dominates when $n = s^2$, because we have $m = O(s^3) = O(n^2/s)$

Proof: The proof of Theorem 13 proceeds in two steps. We first establish a bound which is independent of m, and then apply it to obtain the m-dependent bound asserted in the theorem. Due to lack of space, we only sketch the proof for the first step, given in

THEOREM 14. *Let C be a set of at most $n \le s^2$ h-parabolas defined on S, and let P be a set of rotations with multiplicity at least 3 with respect to S, such that no special surface contains more than $n^{1/2}$ parabolas of C. Then the number of incidences between P and C is $O(n^{3/2})$.*

Proof. Write $I = I(P,C)$ for short, and put $m = |P|$. We will establish the upper bound $I \le Bn^{3/2}$, for some sufficiently large absolute constant B, whose specific choice will be dictated by the various steps of the proof. Suppose then to the contrary that $I > Bn^{3/2}$ for the given C and P.

For $h^* \in C$, let $\nu(h^*)$, the *multiplicity* of h^*, denote the number of rotations incident to h^*. We have $\sum_{h^* \in C} \nu(h^*) = I$; the average multiplicity of a parabola h^* is I/n.

We begin by applying the following pruning process. Put $\nu = I/(6n)$. As long as there exists a parabola $h^* \in C$ whose multiplicity is smaller than ν, we remove h^* from C, but do not remove any rotation incident to h^*. We keep repeating this step (without changing ν), until each of the surviving parabolas has multiplicity at least ν. Moreover, if, during the pruning process, some rotation τ loses $\lfloor \mu(\tau)/2 \rfloor$ incident parabolas, we remove τ from P. This decreases the multiplicity of some parabolas, and we use the new multiplicities in the test for pruning further parabolas, but we keep using the original threshold ν.

When we delete a parabola h^*, we lose at most ν incidences with surviving rotations. When a rotation τ is removed, the number of current incidences with τ is smaller than or equal to twice the number of incidences with τ that have already been removed. Hence, the total number of incidences that were lost during the pruning process is a most $3n\nu = I/2$. Thus, we are left with a subset P_1 of the rotations and with a subset C_1 of the parabolas, so that each $h^* \in C_1$ is incident to at least $\nu = I/(6n)$ rotations of P_1, and each rotation $\tau \in P_1$ is incident to at least three parabolas of C_1 (the latter is an immediate consequence of the rule for pruning a rotation). Moreover, we have $I(P_1, C_1) \ge I/2$. It therefore suffices to bound $I(P_1, C_1)$.

Let $n_1 = |C_1|$. Since at least three parabolas in C_1 are incident to each rotation in P_1, it follows that each parabola in C_1 is incident to at most $n_1/2$ rotations of P_1, and therefore $I(P_1, C_1) \le n_1^2/2$. Combining this with the fact that $I(P_1, C_1) \ge I/2$, we get that $n_1 \ge B^{1/2}n^{3/4}$.

We fix the following parameters

$$x = \frac{n_1}{n^{1/2}} \quad \text{and} \quad t = \delta \frac{n_1}{n},$$

for an appropriate absolute constant $\delta < 1$, whose value will be fixed shortly. Clearly, $t < 1$, and we can also ensure that $x < \nu$, i.e., that $I > 6n_1 n^{1/2}$, by choosing $B > 6$. Furthermore, since $n_1 \ge B^{1/2}n^{3/4}$ we have $x \ge B^{1/2}n^{1/4}$.

We construct a random sample C_1^s of parabolas of C_1 by choosing each parabola independently at random with probability t; the expected size of C_1^s is tn_1. Now take x (arbitrary) rotations of P_1 on each parabola of C_1^s (which can always be done since $x < \nu$), to form a sample S of rotations in P_1, of expected size at most txn_1.

For any parabola $h^* \in C_1$, the expected number of rotations of $P_1 \cap h^*$ which lie on parabolas of C_1^s is at least $t\nu$ (each of the at least ν rotations $a \in P_1 \cap h^*$ is incident to at least one other parabola of C_1, and the probability of this parabola to be chosen in C_1^s is t). We assume that B is large enough so that $t\nu = \delta \frac{n_1}{n} \frac{I}{6n} \geq \frac{\delta B}{6} \frac{n_1}{n^{1/2}}$ is larger than $2x$ (it suffices to choose $B > 12/\delta$). Since $t\nu > 2x = \Omega(n^{1/4})$, and the expected size of C_1^s is $tn_1 = \frac{\delta n_1^2}{n} \geq B\delta n^{1/2}$, we can use Chernoff's bound, to show that there exists a sample C_1^s such that (i) $|C_1^s| \leq 2tn_1$, and (ii) each parabola $h^* \in C_1$ contains at least $\frac{1}{2}t\nu > x$ rotations of P_1 which lie on parabolas of C_1^s. In what follows, we assume that C_1^s satisfies these properties. In this case, we have $|S| \leq 2txn_1$.

Now construct, using Proposition 8, a nontrivial suqare-free trivariate polynomial p which vanishes on S, of smallest degree d satisfying $\binom{d+3}{3} \geq |S| + 1$, so

$$d \leq \lceil (6|S|)^{1/3} \rceil \leq (12txn_1)^{1/3} + 1 = (12\delta)^{1/3} \frac{n_1}{n^{1/2}} + 1 \leq 2(12\delta)^{1/3} \frac{n_1}{n^{1/2}}$$

for n sufficiently large (for small values of n we ensure the bound by choosing B sufficiently large, as before).

We will choose $\delta < 1/6144$, so $x > 4d$.

As above, and without loss of generality, we may assume that p is square-free: factoring out repeated factors only lowers the degree of p and does not change its zero set.

The following properties hold: (a) Since $x > 2d$, p vanishes at more than $2d$ rotations on each parabola of C_1^s, and therefore, as already argued, it vanishes identically on each of these parabolas. (b) Each parabola $h^* \in C_1$ contains at least $\frac{1}{2}t\nu > x > 2d$ rotations which lie on parabolas of C_1^s. Since, as just argued, p vanishes at these rotations, it must vanish identically on h^*. Thus, $p \equiv 0$ on every parabola of C_1.

Before proceeding, we enforce the inequality $d^2 < \frac{1}{8}n_1$ which will hold if we choose δ so that $(12\delta)^{2/3} < 1/32$. Similarly, an appropriate choice of δ (or B) also ensures that $\nu > 9d$.

We next consider all the special polynomial factors of p, and factor them out, to obtain a square-free polynomial $\tilde{p}$, of degree at most d, with no special polynomial factors. As in the previous analysis, p can have at most $d/3$ special polynomial factors, so it can vanish identically on at most $d/3$ special surfaces $\Xi_1, \ldots, \Xi_k$, for $k \leq d/3$. Let $C_2 \subseteq C_1$ denote the set of those parabolas of C_1 which are not contained in any of the vanishing surfaces Ξ_i. For each parabola $h^* \in C_2$, $\tilde{p}$ vanishes identically on h^*, and (as argued above) at most d rotations in $P_1 \cap h^*$ lie in the surfaces Ξ_i. Hence, h^* contains at least $8d$ remaining rotations, each of which is either critical or flat for $\tilde{p}$, because each such point is incident to at least three parabolas (necessarily of C_2) on which $\tilde{p} \equiv 0$.

Hence, either at least $2d$ of these rotations are critical, and then h^* is a critical parabola for $\tilde{p}$, or at least $6d$ of these rotations are flat, and then h^* is a flat parabola for $\tilde{p}$. Applying Propositions 6 and 10, the overall number of parabolas in C_2 is therefore at most

$$d(d-1) + d(3d-4) < 4d^2 < \frac{1}{2}n_1.$$

On the other hand, by assumption, each vanishing special surface Ξ_i contains at most $n^{1/2}$ parabolas of C, so the number of parabolas contained in the special vanishing surfaces is at most $n^{1/2}d < \frac{1}{4}n^{1/2}x \leq \frac{1}{4}n_1$, with our choice of δ.

Hence, the overall number of parabolas in C_1 is smaller than $\frac{1}{2}n_1 + \frac{1}{4}n_1 < n_1$, a contradiction that completes the proof of Theorem 14. □

Proof of Theorem 13. Write $I = I(P, C)$ for short. Set $\nu = cm^{1/3}$ and $\mu = cn/m^{2/3}$, for some sufficiently large constant c whose value will be determined later, and apply the following pruning process. As long as there exists a parabola $h^* \in C$ whose multiplicity is smaller than ν, we remove h^* from C, but do not remove any rotation incident to h^*. Similarly, as long as there exists a rotation $\tau \in P$ whose multiplicity is smaller than μ, we remove τ from P. Of course, these removals may reduce the multiplicity of some surviving rotations or parabolas, making additional rotations and parabolas eligible for removal. We keep repeating this step (without changing the initial thresholds ν and μ), until each of the surviving parabolas has multiplicity at least ν and each of the surviving rotations has multiplicity at least μ. We may assume that $\mu \geq 3$, by choosing c suficiently large and using Theorem 11(i).

When we delete a parabola h^*, we lose at most ν incidences with surviving rotations. When a rotation τ is removed, we lose at most μ incidences with surviving parabolas. All in all, we lose at most $n\nu + m\mu = 2cm^{1/3}n$ incidences, and are left with a subset P_1 of P and with a subset C_1 of C, so that each parabola of C_1 is incident to at least ν rotations of P_1, and each rotation of P_1 is incident to at least μ parabolas of C_1 (these subsets might be empty). Put $n_1 = |C_1|$ and $m_1 = |P_1|$. We have $I \leq I(P_1, C_1) + 2cm^{1/3}n$, so it remains to bound $I(P_1, C_1)$, which we do as follows.

We fix some sufficiently small positive parameter $t < 1$, and construct a random sample $P_1^s \subset P_1$ by choosing each rotation of P_1 independently with probability t. The expected size of P_1^s is m_1t, and the expected number of points of P_1^s on any parabola of C_1 is at least $\nu t = ctm^{1/3}$. Chernoff's bound implies that, with positive probability, $|P_1^s| \leq 2m_1t$, and $|P_1^s \cap h^*| \geq \frac{1}{2}ctm^{1/3}$ for every $h^* \in C_1$, and we assume that P_1^s does satisfy all these inequalities. (For the bound to apply, m_1 (and m) must be at least some sufficiently large constant; if this is not the case, we turn the trivial bound m_1n (or mn) on I into the bound $O(m_1^{1/3}n)$ (or $O(m^{1/3}n)$) by choosing the constant of proportionality sufficiently large.)

Construct, using Proposition 8, a nontrivial square-free trivariate polynomial p which vanishes on P_1^s, whose degree is at most the smallest integer d satisfying $\binom{d+3}{3} \geq 2tm_1 + 1$, so

$$d \leq \lceil (12tm_1)^{1/3} \rceil \leq 3t^{1/3}m_1^{1/3},$$

assuming (as above) that m_1 is sufficiently large.

Choosing c to be large enough, we may assume that $\nu t > 18d$. (This will hold if we ensure that $ct > 54t^{1/3}$.) This implies that p vanishes at more than $9d$ points on each parabola $h^* \in C_1$, and therefore it vanishes identically on each of these parabolas.

As in the previous analysis, we factor out the special polynomial factors of p, obtaining a square-free polynomial $\tilde{p}$, of degree at most d, with no special polynomial factors. Let $\Xi_1, \ldots, \Xi_k$ denote the special surfaces on which p vanishes identically (the zero sets of the special polynomial factors of p), for some $k \leq d/3$.

Let $C_2 \subseteq C_1$ (resp., $P_2 \subseteq P_1$) denote the set of those parabolas of C_1 (resp., rotations of P_1) which are not contained in any of the vanishing surfaces Ξ_i. Put $C_2' = C_1 \setminus C_2$ and $P_2' = P_1 \setminus P_2$.

For each parabola $h^* \in C_2$, $\tilde{p}$ vanishes identically on h^*, and, as argued in the proof of Theorem 11, at most d rotations of $P_1 \cap h^*$ lie in the surfaces Ξ_i. Hence, h^* contains more than $8d$ rotations of P_2, and, arguing as in the preceding proof, each of these rotations is either critical or flat for $\tilde{p}$. Hence, either more than $2d$ of these rotations are critical, and then h^* is a critical parabola for $\tilde{p}$, or more than $6d$ of these rotations are flat, and then h^* is a flat parabola for $\tilde{p}$. Applying Propositions 6 and 10, the overall number of parabolas in C_2 is therefore at most

$$d(d-1) + d(3d-4) < 4d^2.$$

We now apply Theorem 14 to C_2 and P_2, with the bound $4d^2$ on the size of C_2. Arguing as before, the conditions of this theorem are easily seen to hold for these sets. Theorem 14 then implies that the number of incidences between P_2 and C_2, which is also equal to the number of incidences between P_2 and C_1, is

$$I(P_2, C_1) = I(P_2, C_2) = O((4d^2)^{3/2}) = O(d^3) = O(m) .$$

Moreover, since each parabola of C_2 contains at least eight times more rotations of P_2 than of P_2', this bound also applies to the number of incidences between P_2' and C_2.

It therefore remains to bound the number of incidences between P_2' and C_2', namely, between the rotations and parabolas contained in the vanishing special surfaces Ξ_i. To do so, we iterate over the surfaces, say, in the order $\Xi_1, \ldots, \Xi_k$. For each surface Ξ_i in turn, we process the rotations and parabolas contained in Ξ_i and then remove them from further processing on subsequent surfaces.

Let us then consider a special surface Ξ_i. Let m_i and n_i denote respectively the number of rotations and parabolas contained in Ξ_i, which were not yet removed when processing previous surfaces. The number of incidences between these rotations and parabolas can be bounded by the classical Szemerédi-Trotter incidence bound [20] (see also (2)), which is $O(m_i^{2/3}n_i^{2/3} + m_i + n_i)$. Summing these bounds over all the special surfaces Ξ_i, and using Hölder's inequality and the fact, established in Lemma 5, that $n_i \le s$, we get an overall bound of

$$O\left(s^{1/3}\sum_i m_i^{2/3}n_i^{1/3} + \sum_i (m_i + n_i)\right) =$$
$$O\left(m^{2/3}n^{1/3}s^{1/3} + m + n\right),$$

where we use the facts that $\sum_i m_i \le m$ and $\sum_i n_i \le n$, which follow since in this analysis each parabola and rotation is processed at most once. The two linear terms satisfy $n = O(m^{1/3}n)$ (the bound obtained in the pruning process), and $m = O(m^{2/3}n^{1/3}s^{1/3})$ since $m = O(ns)$; see Remark (2) following Theorem 11.

We are not done yet, because each rotation of P_2' is processed only once, within the first surface Ξ_i containing it. This, however, can be handled as in [6]. That is, let τ be a rotation which was processed within the first surface Ξ_i containing it. Suppose that τ also lies on some later surface Ξ_j, with $j > i$, and let h^* be a parabola contained in Ξ_j, which has not been removed yet; in particular, h^* is not contained in Ξ_i, and thus meets it transversally, so the incidence between h^* and τ can be regarded as one of the transversal incidences in Ξ_i, which we have been ignoring so far. To count them, we simply recall that each parabola, whether of C_2' or of C_2, has at most three transversal intersections with a surface Ξ_i, for a total of at most d crossings with all the vanishing surfaces. Since each of these parabolas contains at least $9d$ rotations of P_1, those "transversal incidences" are only a fraction of the total number of incidences, and we simply ignore them altogether.

To recap, we obtain the following bound on the number of incidences between P_1 and C_1:

$$I(P_1, C_1) = O\left(m^{1/3}n + m^{2/3}n^{1/3}s^{1/3}\right).$$

Adding the bound $2cm^{1/3}n$ on the incidences lost during the pruning process, we get the asserted bound. □

5. FURTHER IMPROVEMENTS

In this section we further improve the bound in Theorem 13 using more standard space decomposition techniques. We show:

THEOREM 15. *The number of incidences between m arbitrary rotations and n h-parabolas, defined for a planar ground set with s points, is*

$$O^*\left(m^{5/12}n^{5/6}s^{1/12} + m^{2/3}n^{1/3}s^{1/3} + n\right),$$

where the $O^*(\cdot)$ notation hides polylogarithmic factors. In particular, when all $n = s^2$ h-parabolas are considered, the bound is

$$O^*\left(m^{5/12}s^{7/4} + s^2\right).$$

Brief sketch of the proof: We dualize the problem, mapping each h-parabola into a point in parametric 4-space, so that each rotation becomes a 2-plane. We project the dual points and planes onto some generic 3-space, and bound the number of incidences between these n points and m planes. We do this using a $(1/r)$-cutting of the arrangement of these planes, for an appropriate parameter r, and use the bound of Theorem 13 within each cell of the cutting. We need to pay special attention to situations where many points lie on a line which is contained in many planes (which is always a problematic issue in analyzing point-plane incidences). Fortunately, the special geometric structure in our setup allows us to control this situation, and get the bound asserted in the theorem. See [7] for full details. □

COROLLARY 16. *Let C be a set of n h-parabolas and P a set of rotations, with respect to a planar ground set S of s points. Then, for any $k \ge 3$, the number $M_{\ge k}$ of rotations of P incident to at least k parabolas of C satisfies*

$$M_{\ge k} = O^*\left(\frac{n^{10/7}s^{1/7}}{k^{12/7}} + \frac{ns}{k^3} + \frac{n}{k}\right).$$

For $n = s^2$, the bound becomes

$$M_{\ge k} = O^*\left(\frac{s^3}{k^{12/7}}\right).$$

Proof: We have $I(P, C) \ge kM_{\ge k}$. Comparing this bound with the upper bounds in Theorem 15 yields the asserted bounds. □

6. CONCLUSION

In this paper we have reduced the problem of obtaining a near-linear lower bound for the number of distinct distances in the plane to a problem involving incidences between points and a special class of parabolas (or helices) in three dimensions. We have made significant progress in obtaining upper bounds for the number of such incidences, but we are still short of tightening these bounds to meet the conjectures on these bounds made in the introduction.

To see how far we still have to go, consider the bound in Corollary 16, for the case $n = s^2$, which then becomes $O^*(s^3/k^{12/7})$. (Here $M_{\ge k}$ coincides with $N_{\ge k}$ as defined in (H3).) Moreover, we also have the Szemerédi-Trotter bound $O(s^4/k^3)$, which is smaller than the previous bound for $k \ge s^{7/9}$. Substituting these bounds in the analysis of (H3) and (H4), we get

$$\frac{[s(s-1)-x]^2}{x} \le |K| =$$

$$N_{\ge 2} + \sum_{k\ge 3}(k-1)N_{\ge k} =$$

$$N_{\ge 2} + O(s^3)\cdot\left[1 + \sum_{k=3}^{s^{7/9}}\frac{1}{k^{5/7}} + \sum_{k>s^{7/9}}\frac{s}{k^2}\right] =$$

$$N_{\ge 2} + O(s^{29/9}).$$

It is fairly easy to show that $N_{\geq 2}$ is $O(s^{10/3})$, by noting that $N_{\geq 2}$ can be upper bounded by $O\left(\sum_i |E_i|^2\right)$, where E_i is as defined in (H1). Using the upper bound $|E_i| = O(s^{4/3})$ [18], we get

$$N_{\geq 2} = O\left(\sum_i |E_i|^2\right) = O(s^{4/3}) \cdot O\left(\sum_i |E_i|\right) = O(s^{10/3}).$$

Thus, at the moment, $N_{\geq 2}$ is the bottleneck in the above bound, and we only get the (weak) lower bound $\Omega(s^{2/3})$ on the number of distinct distances. Showing that $N_{\geq 2} = O(s^{29/9})$ too (hopefully, a rather modest goal) would improve the lower bound to $\Omega(s^{7/9})$, still a rather weak lower bound.

Nevertheless, we feel that the reduction to incidences in three dimensions is fruitful, because
(i) It sheds new light on the geometry of planar point sets, related to the distinct distances problem.
(ii) It gave us a new, and considerably more involved setup in which the new algebraic technique of Guth and Katz could be applied. As such, the analysis in this paper might prove useful for obtaining improved incidence bounds for points and other classes of curves in three dimensions. The case of points and circles is an immediate next challenge.

Another comment is in order. Our work can be regarded as a special variant of the complex version of the Szemerédi-Trotter theorem on point-line incidences [20]. In the complex plane, the equation of a line (in complex notation) is $w = pz + q$. Interpreting this equation as a transformation of the real plane, we get a *homothetic map*, i.e., a rigid motion followed by a scaling. We can therefore rephrase the complex version of the Szemerédi-Trotter theorem as follows. We are given a set P of m pairs of points in the (real) plane, and a set M of n homothetic maps, and we seek an upper bound on the number of times a map $\tau \in M$ and a pair $(a, b) \in P$ "coincide", in the sense that $\tau(a) = b$. In our work we only consider "complex lines" whose "slope" p has absolute value 1 (these are our rotations), and the set P is simply $S \times S$.

The main open problems raised by this work are:
(a) Obtain a cubic upper bound for the number of rotations which map only two points of the given ground planar set S to another pair of points of S. Any upper bound smaller than $O(s^{3.1358})$ would already be a significant step towards improving the current lower bound of $\Omega(s^{0.8641})$ on distinct distances [11].
(b) Improve further the upper bound on the number of incidences between rotations and h-parabolas. Ideally, establish Conjectures 1 and 2.

Homage and Acknowledgments

The bulk of the paper was written after the passing away of György Elekes in September 2008. However, the initial infrastructure, including the transformation of the distinct distances problem to an incidence problem in three dimensions, and many other steps, is due to him. As a matter of fact, it was already discovered by Elekes about 10 years ago, and lay dormant since then, mainly because of the lack of effective tools for tackling the incidence problem. These tools became available with the breakthrough result of Guth and Katz [9] in December 2008, and have made this paper possible. Thanks are due to Márton Elekes, who was a driving force in restarting the research on this problem.

Many thanks are due to Haim Kaplan, for many hours of helpful discussions concerning the work in this paper. As mentioned, the construction in Lemma 2 is due to him.

Finally, thanks are also due to Jozsef Solymosi for some helpful comments on the technique used in the paper.

7. REFERENCES

[1] N. Alon and J. Spencer, *The Probabilistic Method*, Wiley-Interscience, New York, 1992.

[2] B. Aronov, V. Koltun, and M. Sharir, Incidences between points and circles in three and higher dimensions, *Discrete Comput. Geom.* 33 (2005), 185–206.

[3] P. Brass, W. Moser, and J. Pach, *Research Problems in Discrete Geometry*, Springer Verlag, New York, 2005.

[4] F.R.K. Chung, The number of different distances determined by n points in the plane. *J. Combin. Theory Ser. A* 36 (1984), 342–354.

[5] F.R.K. Chung, E. Szemerédi, and W.T. Trotter, The number of different distances determined by a set of points in the Euclidean plane, *Discrete Comput. Geom.* 7 (1992), 1–11.

[6] Gy. Elekes, H. Kaplan, and M. Sharir, On lines, joints, and incidences in three dimensions, manuscript, March 2009; arXiv:0905.1583.

[7] Gy. Elekes and M. Sharir, Incidences in three dimensions and distinct distances in the plane, `http://www.cs.tau.ac.il/~michas/Distinct.pdf`.

[8] P. Erdős, On sets of distances of n points, *Amer. Math. Monthly* 53 (1946), 248–250.

[9] L. Guth and N. H. Katz, Algebraic methods in discrete analogs of the Kakeya problem, arXiv:0812.1043v1, 4 Dec 2008.

[10] H. Kaplan, M. Sharir, and E. Shustin, On lines and joints, *Discrete Comput. Geom.*, in press. Also in arXiv:0906.0558, posted June 2, 2009.

[11] N. H. Katz and G. Tardos, A new entropy inequality for the Erdős distance problem, in *Towards a Theory of Geometric Graphs*, J. Pach, Ed., *Contemporary Math.*, Vol. 342, Amer. Math. Soc. Press, Providence, RI, 2004, pp. 119–126.

[12] L. Moser, On the different distances determined by n points, *Amer. Math. Monthly* 59 (1952), 85–91.

[13] A. Pressley, *Elementary Differential Geometry*, Springer Undergraduate Mathematics Series, Springer Verlag, London, 2001.

[14] R. Quilodrán, The joints problem in $\mathbb{R}^n$, arXiv:0906.0555, posted June 2, 2009.

[15] I. R. Shafarevich, *Basic Algebraic Geometry*, Springer Verlag, Berlin, 1977.

[16] M. Sharir and E. Welzl, Point-line incidences in space, *Combinat. Probab. Comput.* 13 (2004), 203–220.

[17] J. Solymosi and Cs.D. Tóth, On a question of Bourgain about geometric incidences, *Combinat. Probab. Comput.* 17 (2008), 619–625.

[18] J. Spencer, E. Szemerédi, and W.T. Trotter, Unit distances in the Euclidean plane, in: *Graph Theory and Combinatorics* (B. Bollobás, ed.), Academic Press, New York, 1984, 293–303.

[19] L. Székely, Crossing numbers and hard Erdős problems in discrete geometry, *Combinatorics, Probability and Computing* 6 (1997), 353–358.

[20] E. Szemerédi and W.T. Trotter, Extremal problems in discrete geometry, *Combinatorica* 3 (1983), 381–392.

[21] G. Tardos, On distinct sums and distinct distances, *Advances in Mathematics* 180 (2003), 275–289.

Tangencies Between Families of Disjoint Regions in the Plane

János Pach*
City College, Courant Institute and EPFL
New York, NY and Lausanne, Switzerland
pach@cims.nyu.edu

Andrew Suk†
Department of Mathematics
Courant Institute, NYU
251 Mercer St., New York, NY 10012
suk@cims.nyu.edu

Miroslav Treml
University of Banja Luka
Bosnia and Herzegovina
mptreml@yahoo.com

ABSTRACT

Let $\mathcal{C}$ be a family of n convex bodies in the plane, which can be decomposed into k subfamilies of pairwise disjoint sets. It is shown that the number of tangencies between the members of $\mathcal{C}$ is at most $O(kn)$, and that this bound cannot be improved. If we only assume that our sets are connected and *vertically convex*, that is, their intersection with any vertical line is either a segment or the empty set, then the number of tangencies can be *superlinear* in n, but it cannot exceed $O(n \log^2 n)$. Our results imply a new upper bound on the number of regular intersection points on the boundary of $\cup\mathcal{C}$.

Categories and Subject Descriptors

G.2.1 [**Discrete Mathematics**]: Combinatorics

General Terms

Theory

Keywords

Convexity, Arrangements, Tangencies

1. INTRODUCTION

Analyzing the structure of the union of convex bodies or other geometric objects in the plane and in higher dimensions is a classical topic in discrete and computational geometry, with many applications in motion planning and computer graphics (see [AgPS08], for a survey). It was shown in [KLP86] that the number of arcs comprising the boundary of the union of n Jordan regions in the plane, any pair of which share at most two boundary points, is $O(n)$. This fact was applied for planning a collision-free translational motion of a convex robot amidst several polygonal obstacles in the plane. Similar results with algorithmic consequences have been established for "fat" objects [MPS94], [AgS00], [PSS03], [Ez08], [ES07] and "round" objects [ArEK06], [Ef05] in the plane and in higher dimensions. The aim of this paper is to derive a new upper bound on the number of tangencies in an arrangement of convex bodies in the plane.

Two nonoverlapping Jordan *regions* in the plane are said to *touch* each other or to be *tangent* to each other if their boundaries have precisely one point in common and their interiors are disjoint. Two Jordan *curves touch* if they intersect in precisely one point, at which they do not cross each other properly, that is, one curve does not pass from one side of the other curve to the other side.

Estimating the maximum number of tangencies between circles was initiated by de Rocquigny [Ro97] at the end of the 19th century. Erdős's famous unsolved question [Er46] on the maximum number of unit distance pairs among n points in the plane can also be formulated as a problem about tangencies: What is the maximum number tangencies among n (possibly overlapping) disks of unit diameter in the plane? The answer is superlinear in n.

It was first observed by Tamaki and Tokuyama [TT98] that in order to obtain an upper bound on the number of incidences between a family $\mathcal{C}$ of curves and a set of points in the plane, it is sufficient to estimate the minimum number of points needed to cut the curves in $\mathcal{C}$ into smaller pieces such that any pair of them are either disjoint or cross precisely once. Obviously, this number is at least as large as the number of tangencies between the members of $\mathcal{C}$, and in most cases these two quantities do not differ too much. For a number of applications, this approach leads to the best known upper bounds for the number of incidences between curves and points [AgNP04], [C05], [MT06].

Consider a family $\mathcal{R}$ of n closed Jordan regions in the plane such that any pair of them have *one* or *two* boundary points in common, but no three boundary curves pass through the same point. It was shown in [AgNP04] (see also [AlLP01]) that the number of tangencies between the members of $\mathcal{R}$ is $O(n)$. As is illustrated by Erdős's unit distance problem mentioned above, if we also allow two members of $\mathcal{R}$ to be *disjoint*, then the number of tangencies can be superlinear in n. However, if we count only those tangencies that do not belong to the interior of any member of $\mathcal{R}$, then again we can obtain a linear upper bound [KLP86]. In the last section, we show that our results imply a new

*Supported by Grants from NSF, NSA, PSC-CUNY, BSF, OTKA, and SNF.

†Supported by NSF grant CCF-0830272 and the Dean's Dissertation Fellowship at NYU.

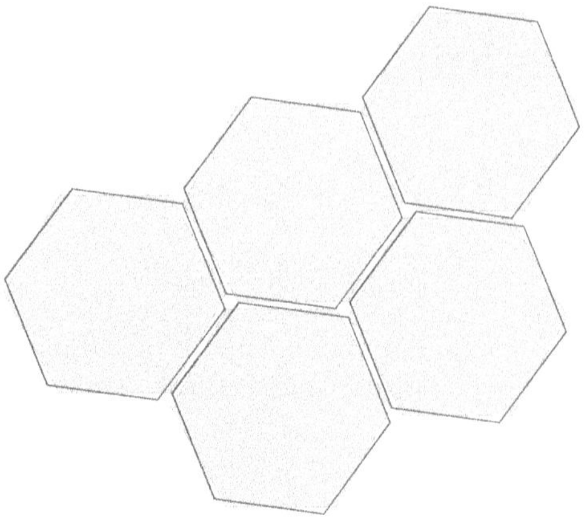

Figure 1: A construction on n pairwise disjoint red convex bodies and n pairwise disjoint blue convex bodies with $6n(1 + o(1))$ tangent pairs.

upper bound on the number of so called "regular" intersection points along the boundary of the union of all sets in $\mathcal{R}$, which is often better than the best known estimates. This quantity plays a role in analyzing the complexity of higher dimensional arrangements.

In this paper, we study the structure of tangencies between two families of closed Jordan regions, each consisting of n pairwise disjoint members. It was shown by Pinchasi and Ben-Dan [BP07], who independently from us arrived at the same question, that the maximum number of such tangencies is $O(n^{3/2} \log n)$. Their proof is based on a theorem of Marcus-Tardos [MT06] and Pinchasi-Radoičić [PiR04]. They suggested that the correct order of magnitude of the maximum may be linear in n. We start by proving this conjecture in the special case where both families consist of closed *convex* regions (convex *bodies*).

Theorem 1. *The number of tangencies between two families of convex bodies in the plane, each consisting of $n > 2$ pairwise disjoint members, cannot exceed $8n - 16$.*

This bound is not far from being optimal. Figure 1 shows two such families with $(6 - o(1))n$ tangencies. We can start with two slightly rotated hexagons of different colors. Taking n translates of each hexagon and arranging them in a lattice-like fashion as in Figure 1, we obtain two families such that all but $O(\sqrt{n})$ of their members are tangent to *six* hexagons of the opposite color.

Consider a family $\mathcal{C}$ of closed convex bodies in the plane. Assign a vertex to each member of $\mathcal{C}$, and connect two vertices by an edge if the corresponding bodies have a nonempty intersection. The resulting graph $G_{\mathcal{C}}$ is called the *intersection graph* of $\mathcal{C}$. Suppose that the chromatic number of this graph $\chi(G_{\mathcal{C}}) \leq k$, that is, $\mathcal{C}$ can be decomposed into k subfamilies consisting of pairwise disjoint bodies. By denoting n_i as the size of the ith pairwise disjoint subfamily and by Theorem 1, $\mathcal{C}$ has at most

$$\sum_{i=1}^{k-1} \sum_{j>i} O(n_i + n_j) = O(nk)$$

tangencies. Therefore we have the following corollary.

Corollary 2. *Let $\mathcal{C}$ be a family of n convex bodies in the plane, which can be decomposed into k subfamilies consisting of pairwise disjoint bodies. The total number of tangencies between members of $\mathcal{C}$ is $O(kn)$. This bound is tight up to a multiplicative constant.*

According to an old conjecture of Erdős, there exists a constant c with the property that any family of segments in the plane, no *two* of which share an endpoint and no *three* are pairwise crossing, can be decomposed into at most c subfamilies consisting of pairwise disjoint segments (see [Ko03], for a survey). More generally, it can be conjectured [FoP08] that there exists a function ϕ such that the chromatic number of the intersection graph of any family of convex bodies with no k pairwise intersecting members is bounded from above by $\phi(k)$. Combining this conjecture with Corollary 2, we would obtain the following statement, which we pose as a conjecture.

Conjecture 3. *For every fixed integer $k > 2$, the number of tangencies in any n-member family of convex bodies, no k of which are pairwise intersecting, is at most $O_k(n)$.*

In Section 3, we address the analogous problem for *vertically convex* sets in the plane, that is, for closed connected sets with the property that every vertical line either misses them or intersects them in a nonempty interval. A curve (connected arc) is *x-monotone* if every vertical line intersects it in at most one point, i.e., if it is vertically convex. Given a vertically convex set r with no vertical boundary interval, the set of upper (lower) endpoints of the segments $\ell \cap r$ for every vertical line ℓ which intersects r forms the *upper (lower) contour* of r. Clearly, the upper and lower contours of r are x-monotone curves. Every tangency between two Jordan regions occurs along their upper or lower contours. Thus, to obtain an upper bound on the number of tangencies between two families of pairwise disjoint vertically convex sets, it is sufficient to estimate the number of tangencies between two families of pairwise disjoint x-monotone curves.

Concerning this problem, we establish the following result in Section 3.

Theorem 4. *Let $f(n)$ denote the maximum number of tangencies between two n-member families of pairwise disjoint x-monotone curves in the plane. Then we have*

$$\Omega(n \log n) \leq f(n) \leq O(n \log^2 n).$$

Corollary 5. *The number of tangencies between two families of vertically convex sets in the plane, each consisting of $n > 2$ pairwise disjoint members, is at most $O(n \log^2 n)$.*

The key step in the proof of Theorem 4 is that we solve the same problem in the special case when one of the families form a "flag".

A family of pairwise disjoint x-monotone curves in the plane is called a *left-flag (right-flag)* if the left (right) endpoint of each of its members lies on a vertical line l, called the "pole" of the flag. We use the same terminology for families of pairwise disjoint vertically convex sets in the plane if their leftmost (rightmost) points lie on the same vertical line.

Theorem 6. (One flag theorem for curves) *Let $f_1(n)$ denote the maximum number of tangencies between n pairwise disjoint x-monotone curves that form a left-flag and a set of n pairwise disjoint x-monotone curves. Then we have* $f_1(n) = \Theta(n \log n)$.

2. CONVEX BODIES

We prove Theorem 3 in the following slightly stronger form.

Theorem 7. *Let $\mathcal{C} = \mathcal{R} \cup \mathcal{B}$ be a family of $n > 5$ convex bodies in the plane, where $\mathcal{R}$ and $\mathcal{B}$ are pairwise disjoint families, each consisting of pairwise disjoint bodies. Then the number of tangencies between the members of $\mathcal{R}$ and the members of $\mathcal{B}$ is at most $4n - 16$.*

Proof of Theorem 7. We will refer to the members of $\mathcal{R}$ and $\mathcal{B}$ as red and blue sets, respectively. We assume, for the sake of simplicity, that no three points of tangency along the boundary of any member of $\mathcal{C}$ are collinear.

The proof is by induction on n. In the base case $n = 6$, the statement readily follows from the fact that a planar graph cannot contain $K_{3,3}$ as a subgraph. Hence for $n - 6$ the maximum number of tangencies is at most 8 and the statement for holds. Suppose now that $n > 6$ and that the theorem has already been verified for all families of size smaller than n. Clearly, we can assume that every member $C \in \mathcal{C}$ is tangent to at least *five* other members. Otherwise, we can delete C and apply the induction hypothesis to the remaining family.

Let m denote the number of red-blue tangencies in $\mathcal{C}$. We start by replacing each member of $\mathcal{C}$ by the convex hull of all points of tangencies along its boundary. That is, we assume that each member of $\mathcal{C}$ is a convex polygon with at least *five* sides, and all tangencies occur at the vertices of these polygons. If we place a vertex at each point of tangency and at each intersection point between the sides of the polygons, then we obtain a *4-regular planar graph* $G = (V, E)$. We can also assume without loss of generality that G is *2-connected.* Let $F = F^{int} \cup F^{ext}$ denote the set of *faces* of G, where F^{int} is the set of *interior* faces that lie inside some convex region in $\mathcal{C}$, and F^{ext} is the set of *exterior* faces that do not lie inside any member of $\mathcal{C}$. Furthermore, let $F^{int-1} \subseteq F^{int}$ be the set of faces that lie inside exactly *one* member of $\mathcal{C}$. For any $C \in \mathcal{C}$, let $|C|$ denote the number of tangencies along the boundary of C, that is, the number of *sides* of the polygon replacing it. Analogously, for any face $f \in F$, let $|f|$ stand for the number of *sides (edges)* of f. Finally, let $F(C) \subseteq F^{int}$ stand for the set of faces that lie inside C.

We would like to use the following form of Euler's polyhedral formula for G.

$$\sum_{v \in V}(d(v) - 4) + \sum_{f \in F}(|f| - 4) = 4(|E| - |V| - |F|) = -8. \quad (1)$$

For any $C \in \mathcal{C}$, the interior of C contains a number of disjoint segments (edges of G) connecting pairs of interior points of the sides of C. Each such edge increases the number of faces within C by *one*, and each adds *four* to the total number of sides of these faces. Therefore, we have

$$\sum_{f \in F(C)} (|f| - 4) = |C| - 4.$$

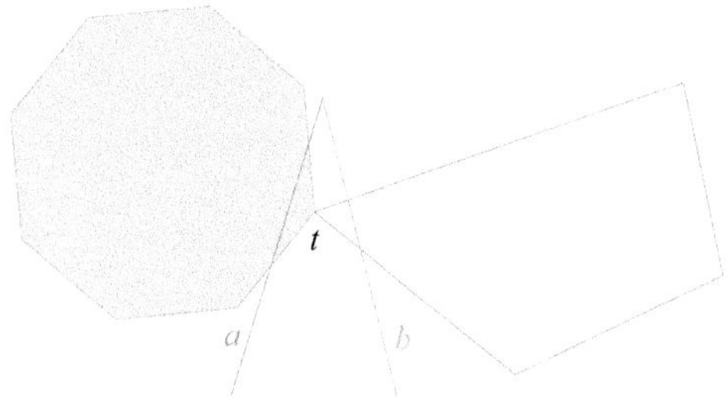

Figure 2: A point from T

This implies

$$\sum_{C \in \mathcal{C}} \sum_{f \in F(C)} (|f| - 4) = \sum_{C \in \mathcal{C}}(|C| - 4) = 2m - 4n. \quad (2)$$

Since each polygon $C \in \mathcal{C}$ has at least *five* sides, triangular interior faces can only occur near the vertices of the polygons C, where a side of some other polygon C' crosses two adjacent sides of C. Also notice that there are no triangular faces in the exterior since $\mathcal{R}$ and $\mathcal{B}$ are pairwise disjoint families. Let $F_3 = \{f \in F : |f| = 3\}$ and let $T \subset V$ be the set of vertices that belong to *two* members of F_3. Notice that each vertex $t \in T$ belongs to two triangular interior faces and to two exterior faces, because G is 2-connected.

Consider the two triangular faces meeting at a vertex $t \in T$, and let a and b denote the sides of the polygons in $\mathcal{C}$ containing the sides of these triangles opposite to t. See Figure 2. These two segments must belong to polygons of different colors. By convexity, a and b cannot have a common point in both exterior faces incident to t. Thus, at least one of the exterior faces incident to t has at least *six* sides. It is also clear that neither of the vertices next to t along this exterior face is a point of tangency between a red and a blue polygon. Therefore, each exterior face f contains at most $|f|/2$ vertices belonging to T. By defining $F^{ext}_{6+} = \{f \in F^{ext} : |f| \geq 6\}$, we have

$$|T| \leq \frac{1}{2} \sum_{f \in F^{ext}_{6+}} |f|,$$

which implies that

$$|F_3| \leq m + |T| \leq m + \frac{1}{2} \sum_{f \in F^{ext}_{6+}} |f|.$$

Therefore, we have

$$\sum_{f \in F^{int-1}} (|f| - 4) \geq \sum_{f \in F_3} (|f| - 4) = -|F_3| \geq -m - \frac{1}{2} \sum_{f \in F^{ext}_{6+}} |f|. \quad (3)$$

Combining (2) and (3), we obtain

$$\sum_{f \in F} (|f| - 4)$$

$$= \sum_{f\in F^{ext}} (|f|-4) + \frac{1}{2}\sum_{C\in \mathcal{C}}\sum_{f\in F(C)} (|f|-4) + \frac{1}{2}\sum_{f\in F^{int-1}} (|f|-4)$$

$$\geq \sum_{f\in F^{ext}_{6+}} (|f|-4) + \frac{1}{2}(2m-4n) - \frac{1}{2}\left(m + \frac{1}{2}\sum_{f\in F^{ext}_{6+}} |f|\right)$$

$$= \frac{1}{2}m - 2n + \sum_{f\in F^{ext}_{6+}} \left(\frac{3}{4}|f| - 4\right)$$

$$\geq \frac{1}{2}m - 2n.$$

On the other hand, using the fact that G is a 4-regular graph, Euler's formula (1) yields that

$$\sum_{f\in F}(|f|-4) = -8.$$

Comparing the last two relations, we obtain

$$\frac{1}{2}m - 2n \leq -8,$$

which implies that $m \leq 4n - 16$, as required. □

3. X-MONOTONE CURVES

In this section, we prove Theorems 4 and 6. We make no attempt here to optimize the constants hidden in the Ω- and O-notation. In the proofs, for simplicity, we omit all floor and ceiling signs whenever these are not crucial. All logarithms are of base 2.

We start with the proof of Theorem 6, for which we need two simple lemmas.

Lemma 8. *Let $\mathcal{R} = \{r_1, ..., r_n\}$ and $\mathcal{B} = \{b_1, ..., b_n\}$ be a family of n pairwise disjoint x-monotone red curves and a family n pairwise disjoint x-monotone blue curves in the plane such that all of them meet a vertical line l. Then the number of red-blue pairs of curves tangent to each other is at most $8n$.*

Proof. Suppose without loss of generality that no pair of curves (r_i, b_j) touch each other at a point on l. Consider first the right half-plane bounded by l and only the point of tangency for which a red curve touches a blue curve from *below*. Among these tangencies, the rightmost point of tangency along the curve r_i or b_i is called *extreme*. The number of pairs (r_i, b_j) for which r_i touches b_j from below is at most $2n$. Indeed, there are altogether at most $2n$ extreme tangencies, and there are no non-extreme point of tangency since the curves are x-monotone. See Figure 3. Analogously, the number of pairs (r_i, b_j) for which r_i touches b_j from *above* in the right half-plane is at most $2n$. A symmetric argument shows that the number of pairs (r_i, b_j) that touch each other in the left half-plane bounded by l is also at most $4n$. □

Lemma 9. *Let $\mathcal{R} = \{r_1, ..., r_n\}$ and $\mathcal{B} = \{b_1, ..., b_n\}$ be a family of pairwise disjoint x-monotone red curves and a family of pairwise disjoint x-monotone blue curves in the plane. Suppose that there are two vertical lines, l_1 and l_2, which intersect every $b_i \in \mathcal{B}$. Then the number of pairs (r_i, b_j) that touch each other in the strip between l_1 and l_2 is at most $2n$.*

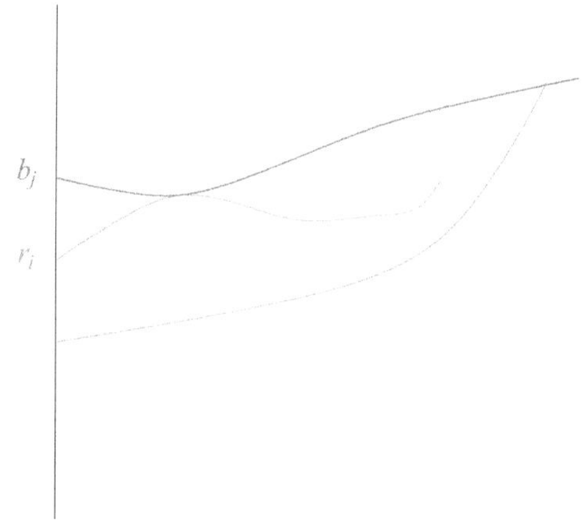

Figure 3: If the point where r_i touches b_j from below is not an extreme tangency, then b_j must touch some red curve below r_i, and r_i must touch some blue curve above b_j. However this is impossible since the curves are x-monotone.

Proof. Each red curve can be tangent to at most *two* blue curves. □

We are now ready to prove the upper bound of Theorem 6 in the following slightly stronger form.

Theorem 10. *Let $\mathcal{C} = \mathcal{R} \cup \mathcal{B}$ be a family of n x-monotone curves such that $\mathcal{R}$ consists of pairwise disjoint red curves with their left endpoints on a vertical line l (left-flag), and $\mathcal{B}$ is a family of pairwise disjoint blue curves lying entirely to the right of l. Then the number of red-blue tangencies between the curves is at most $30n \log n$.*

Proof. Without loss generality, we can assume that x-coordinate of the endpoints of each curve are distinct. We proceed by induction on n. The base case is trivial. For the inductive step, the proof falls into two cases.

Case 1. Assume $|\mathcal{B}| \geq n/2$. Then there exists a vertical line l', such that there are exactly $|\mathcal{B}|/2$ blue curves completely to the right of l'. Now let

$$\mathcal{R}_1 = \{r \in \mathcal{R} : r \text{ lies completely to the left of } l'\}$$

$$\mathcal{R}_2 = \{r \in \mathcal{R} : r \text{ intersects } l'\}$$

and

$$\mathcal{B}_1 = \{b \in \mathcal{B} : b \text{ lies completely to the left of } l' \text{ or intersects } l'\}$$

$$\mathcal{B}_2 = \{b \in \mathcal{B} : b \text{ lies completely to the right of } l'\}.$$

By Lemma 8 and 9, the number of tangent pairs between $\mathcal{R}_2$ and $\mathcal{B}_1$ is at most $10n$. Since $|\mathcal{R}_1 \cup \mathcal{B}_1|$ and $|\mathcal{R}_2 \cup \mathcal{B}_2|$ is at most $3n/4$, by the induction hypothesis, the number of tangent pairs is at most

$$\leq 10n + 30|\mathcal{R}_1 \cup \mathcal{B}_1| \log(3n/4) + 30|\mathcal{R}_2 \cup \mathcal{B}_2| \log(3n/4)$$

$$= 30n \log n + 10n - 30n \log(4/3)$$

$$\leq 30n \log n.$$

Case 2. If $|\mathcal{R}| \geq n/2$, then there exists a vertical line l' such that there are exactly $|\mathcal{R}|/2$ red curves completely to the left of l'. By following the exact same argument as in Case 1, the number of tangent pairs is at most $30n \log n$.

□

Proof of Theorem 6. The upper bound follows from Theorem 10. The lower bound follows from the following construction of n-member red left-flag and an n-member right-flag with $\Omega(n \log n)$ tangencies between them. The construction is recursive. Let $\{r_1, \ldots, r_{n/2}\}$ and $\{b_1, \ldots, b_{n/2}\}$ be a red left-flag and a blue right-flag with poles $x = 2$ and $x = 3$, respectively, with $f_1(n/2)$ tangencies between them. Let $\{r_{n/2+1}, \ldots, r_n\}$ and $\{b_{n/2+1}, \ldots, b_n\}$ be a red left-flag and a blue right-flag with poles $x = 0$ and $x = 1$, having $f_1(n/2)$ tangencies. It is easy to see that the curves r_i $(i \leq n/2)$ can be extended to the left and the curves b_j $(j > n/2)$ to the right until they hit the lines $x = 0$ and $x = 3$, respectively, so that r_i touches from above $b_{i+n/2}$, for every $i \leq n/2$, in the vertical strip $1 < x < 2$. See Fig. 4. Hence, the maximum number of tangencies between an n-member left-flag and n-member right-flag satisfies the recurrence

$$f_1(n) \geq 2f_1(n/2) + n/2,$$

which implies that $f_1(n) = \Omega(n \log n)$.

□

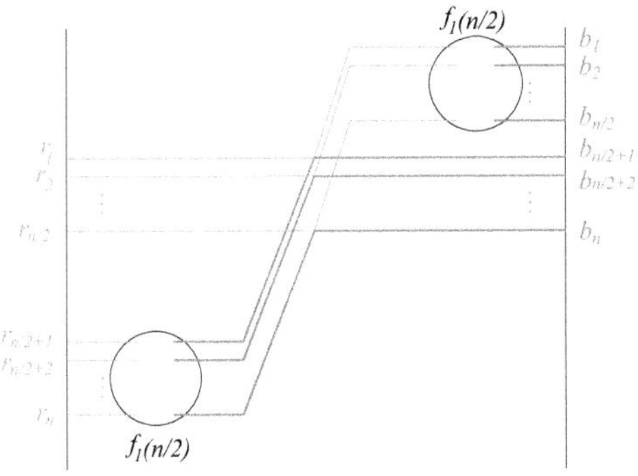

Figure 4: The construction.

The lower bound in Theorem 4 follows from Theorem 6. The upper bound immediately follows from the following lemma.

Lemma 11. *Let $\mathcal{C} = \mathcal{R} \cup \mathcal{B}$ be an n-member family of x-monotone curves such that both $\mathcal{R}$ and $\mathcal{B}$ consist of pairwise disjoint curves in the plane. Then the number of tangent pairs in $\mathcal{R} \cup \mathcal{B}$ is at most $100n \log^2 n$.*

Proof. Induction on n. The base cases $n = 1, 2, 3, 4$ are trivial. For the inductive step, we can assume the x-coordinate of the endpoints of all n curves are distinct. Hence, there exists a vertical line l, such that there are exactly $n/2$ curves completely to the left of l, and at most $n/2$ curves completely to the right of l. Let

$$\mathcal{R}_1 = \{r \in \mathcal{R} : r \text{ lies completely to the left of } l\}$$

$$\mathcal{R}_2 = \mathcal{R} \setminus \mathcal{R}_1$$

and likewise

$$\mathcal{B}_1 = \{b \in \mathcal{B} : b \text{ lies completely to the left of } l\}$$

$$\mathcal{B}_2 = \mathcal{B} \setminus \mathcal{B}_1.$$

By Theorem 10, the number of tangent pairs in $\mathcal{R}_1 \cup \mathcal{B}_2$ and in $\mathcal{R}_2 \cup \mathcal{B}_1$ is at most $30n \log n$. Since $|\mathcal{R}_1 \cup \mathcal{B}_1| = |\mathcal{R}_2 \cup \mathcal{B}_2| = n/2$ and $n \geq 5$, the maximum number of tangencies is at most

$$2 \cdot 30n \log n + 2 \cdot 100(n/2) \log^2(n/2)) \leq 100n \log^2 n.$$

□

4. CONCLUDING REMARKS

Given a family $\mathcal{C}$ of n convex bodies in the plane, no three of which share a boundary point, it was shown by Erdős and Grünbaum [ErG73] that the number of tangencies not contained in the interior of a third region can be as large as $\Omega(n^{4/3})$. It was proved in [EPS09] that this bound is not far from being optimal.

More generally, if the boundaries of two members of $\mathcal{C}$ intersect at most twice, then we call these intersection points *regular*. All other boundary intersections are called *irregular*. Let $R(\mathcal{C})$ and $I(\mathcal{C})$ denote the sets of regular and irregular intersection points that belong to the boundary of the union of all members of $\mathcal{C}$. It readily follows from the result in [EPS09], referred to in the last paragraph, that

$$|R(\mathcal{C})| = O(n^{4/3+\varepsilon}),$$

for every $\varepsilon > 0$. Pach and Sharir [PS99] established another upper bound on the number of regular intersection points on the boundary of $\cup\mathcal{C}$:

$$|R(\mathcal{C})| = O(|I(\mathcal{C})| + n). \quad (4)$$

Using, e.g., Lemma 1 in [ArEH01], it is easy to reformulate Corollary 2, as follows.

Theorem 12. *Let $\mathcal{C}$ be a family of n convex bodies in the plane, no three of which share a boundary point. Suppose that $\mathcal{C}$ can be decomposed into k subfamilies consisting of pairwise disjoint bodies. Then we have*

$$|R(\mathcal{C})| = O(kn).$$

Note that this bound is often better than the previous two estimates. For instance, for the family depicted on Fig. 5, $|I(\mathcal{C})| = \Theta(n^2)$, so that (4) implies a quadratic upper bound on $|R(\mathcal{C})|$. On the other hand, Theorem 12 gives a linear bound, as the condition is satisfied with $k = 2$.

Two families $\mathcal{R}$ and $\mathcal{B}$ of convex bodies are said to be *touching* if every member of $\mathcal{R}$ is tangent to all members of $\mathcal{B}$. It was shown in [KaP94] that there exists a constant $c > 0$ such that for any pair $\mathcal{R}, \mathcal{B}$ of touching n-member families of convex bodies in the plane, $\mathcal{R}$ or $\mathcal{B}$ must have at least cn members that share a point. If $\mathcal{R}$ and $\mathcal{B}$ are touching families with $|\mathcal{R}|, |\mathcal{B}| \geq 6$, then it is conjectured that at least one of them has *three* members that share a point.

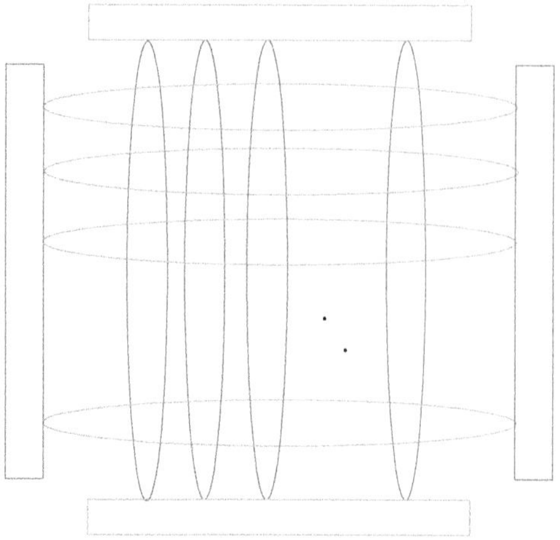

Figure 5: $n/2$ horizontal red ellipses crossing $n/2$ vertical blue ellipses such that each ellipse touches precisely two rectangles.

5. REFERENCES

[AgNP04] P.K. Agarwal, E. Nevo, J. Pach, R. Pinchasi, M. Sharir, and S. Smorodinsky, Lenses in arrangements of pseudo-circles and their applications, *J. ACM* **51** (2004), 139–186.

[AgPS08] P.K. Agarwal, J. Pach, and M. Sharir, State of the union (of geometric objects), in: *Surveys on Discrete and Computational Geometry, Contemp. Math.* **453**, Amer. Math. Soc., Providence, RI, 2008, 9–48.

[AgS00] P.K. Agarwal and M. Sharir, Pipes, cigars, and Kreplach: the union of Minkowski sums in three dimensions, *Discrete Comput. Geom.* **24** (2000), no. 4, 645–685.

[AlLP01] N. Alon, H. Last, R. Pinchasi, and M. Sharir, On the complexity of arrangements of circles in the plane, *Discrete Comput. Geom.* **26** (2001), 465–492.

[ArEH01] B. Aronov, A. Efrat, D. Halperin, and M. Sharir, On the number of regular vertices of the union of Jordan regions, *Discrete Comput. Geom.* **25** (2001), 203–220.

[ArEK06] B. Aronov, A. Efrat, V. Koltun, and M. Sharir, On the union of κ-round objects in three and four dimensions, *Discrete Comput. Geom.* **36** (2006), no. 4, 511–526.

[BP07] I. Ben-Dan and R. Pinchasi, personal communication, November 2007.

[C05] T.M. Chan, On levels in arrangements of curves. II. A simple inequality and its consequences, *Discrete Comput. Geom.* **34** (2005), no. 1, 11–24.

[Ef05] A. Efrat, The complexity of the union of (α, β)-covered objects, *SIAM J. Computing* **34** (2005), 775-787.

[Er46] P. Erdős, On sets of distances of n points, *Amer. Math. Monthly* **53** (1946), 248–250.

[ErG73] P. Erdős and B. Grünbaum, Osculation vertices in arrangements of curves, *Geometriae Dedicata* **1** (1973), 322–333.

[Ez08] E. Ezra, On the union of cylinders in three dimensions, in: *49th Annual IEEE Symp. on Foundations of Comp. Sci.* 2008, 179–188.

[EPS09] E. Ezra, J. Pach, and M. Sharir, On regular vertices of the union of planar convex objects, *Discrete Comput. Geom.* **41** (2009), 216–231.

[ES07] E. Ezra and M. Sharir, Almost tight bound for the union of fat tetrahedra in three dimensions. In: *Proc. 48nd Annu. IEEE Sympos. Found. Comput. Sci.*, 2007, 525-Ű535.

[FoP08] J. Fox and J. Pach: Coloring K_k-free intersection graphs of geometric objects in the plane, in: *Proc. of 24th Ann. Symp. on Computational Geometry*, ACM Press, New York, 2008, 346–354.

[KaP94] M. Katchalski and J. Pach, Touching convex sets in the plane, *Canad. Math. Bull.* **37** (1994), no. 4, 495–504.

[KLP86] K. Kedem, R. Livne, J. Pach, and M. Sharir, On the union of Jordan regions and collision-free translational motion amidst polygonal obstacles, *Discrete Comput. Geom.* **1** (1986), 59–71.

[Ko03] A. Kostochka, Coloring intersection graphs of geometric graphs, in: *Towards a Theory of Geometric Graphs, Contemporary Mathematics* (J. Pach, ed.), **342**, American Mathematical Society, Providence, RI, 2004, 127–138.

[MT06] A. Marcus and G. Tardos, Intersection reverse sequences and geometric applications, *J. Combin. Theory Ser. A* **113** (2006), 675–691.

[MPS94] J. Matoušek, J. Pach, M. Sharir, S. Sifrony, and E. Welzl, Fat triangles determine linearly many holes, *SIAM J. Comput.* **23** (1994), no. 1, 154–169.

[PSS03] J. Pach, I. Safruti, and M. Sharir, The union of congruent cubes in three dimensions, *Discrete Comput. Geom.* **30** (2003), no. 1, 133–160.

[PS99] J. Pach and M. Sharir, On the boundary of the union of planar convex sets, *Discrete Comput. Geom.* **21** (1999), no. 3, 321–328.

[PiR04] R. Pinchasi and R. Radoičić, On the number of edges in geometric graphs with no self-intersecting cycle of length 4, in: *Towards a Theory of Geometric Graphs, Contemporary Mathematics* (J. Pach, ed.), **342**, American Mathematical Society, Providence, RI, 2004.

[Ro97] G. de Rocquigny, Questions 1179 et 1180, *Intermed. Math.* **4** (1897), 267 and **15** (1908), 169.

[TT98] H. Tamaki, T. Tokuyama, How to cut pseudoparabolas into segments *Discrete Comput. Geom.* **19** (1998), no. 2, 265–290.

Steinitz Theorems for Orthogonal Polyhedra

David Eppstein
Computer Science Department
University of California, Irvine
eppstein@uci.edu

Elena Mumford
Department of Mathematics and Computer Science
Technische Universiteit Eindhoven
e.mumford@tue.nl

ABSTRACT

We define a *simple orthogonal polyhedron* to be a three-dimensional polyhedron with the topology of a sphere in which three mutually-perpendicular edges meet at each vertex. By analogy to Steinitz's theorem characterizing the graphs of convex polyhedra, we characterize the graphs of simple orthogonal polyhedra: they are exactly the 3-regular bipartite planar graphs in which the removal of any two vertices produces at most two connected components. We also characterize two subclasses of these polyhedra: *corner polyhedra*, which can be drawn by isometric projection in the plane with only one hidden vertex, and *xyz polyhedra*, in which each axis-parallel line through a vertex contains exactly one other vertex. Based on our characterizations we find efficient algorithms for constructing orthogonal polyhedra from their graphs.

Categories and Subject Descriptors:

G.2.2 [**Discrete Mathematics**]: Graph Theory—*Graph labeling*; F.2.2 [**Analysis of Algorithms and Problem Complexity**]: Nonnumerical Algorithms and Problems—*Geometrical problems and computations*

General Terms: Algorithms, Theory

Keywords: Steinitz theorem, orthogonal polyhedron, planar graph

1. INTRODUCTION

Steinitz's theorem [37,59,66] characterizes the skeletons of three-dimensional convex polyhedra in purely graph-theoretic terms: they are exactly the 3-vertex-connected planar graphs. In one direction, this is straightforward to prove: every convex polyhedron has a skeleton that is 3-connected and planar. The main content of Steinitz's theorem lies in the other direction, the statement that every 3-connected planar graph can be represented as a polyhedron. Steinitz's theorem, together with Balinski's theorem that every d-dimensional polytope has a d-connected skeleton [3], form the foundation stones of polyhedral combinatorics; Grünbaum writes [37] that Steinitz's theorem is "the most important and deepest known result on 3-polytopes."

However, analogous results characterizing the skeletons of other classes of polyhedra or higher dimensional polytopes have been elusive. As Ziegler [66] writes, "No similar theorem is known, and it seems that no similarly effective theorem is possible, in higher dimensions." Even in three dimensions, generalizations to higher genus surfaces are difficult: it was open for many years whether the toroidal embedding of K_7 as the Császár polyhedron [19] could be generalized to realize the complete graph K_{12} as the boundary of a (genus six) triangulated polyhedral surface, although this is now known to be impossible [10].

In this paper, we characterize another class of three-dimensional non-convex polyhedra, which we call *simple orthogonal polyhedra* (Fig. 1): polyhedra with the topology of a sphere, with simply-connected faces, and with exactly three mutually-perpendicular axis-parallel edges meeting at every vertex. We also consider two special cases of simple orthogonal polyhedra, which we call *corner polyhedra* and *xyz polyhedra*. A corner polyhedron (Fig. 1, left) is a simple orthogonal polyhedron in which all but three faces are oriented towards the vector $(1, 1, 1)$; it can be drawn in the plane by isometric projection with only one the vertex incident to the three back faces hidden. Although we use corner polyhedra primarily as a building block to our main results on simple polyhedra, they are closely related to the solid Young diagrams of plane partitions studied widely in mathematics [16]. An xyz polyhedron (Fig. 1, center) is a simple orthogonal polyhedron in which each axis-parallel line contains at most two vertices. We show:

- The graphs of simple orthogonal polyhedra are exactly the cubic (that is, 3-regular) bipartite planar graphs such that the removal of any two vertices leaves at most two connected components.
- The graphs of xyz polyhedra are exactly the cubic bipartite polyhedral (that is, planar 3-connected) graphs.
- The graphs of corner polyhedra are exactly the cubic bipartite polyhedral graphs such that every separating triangle of the planar dual graph has the same parity (we define the parity of a separating triangle later). A special case of this result, that we use as the building black for all our other constructions, is that every cubic bipartite polyhedral graph with a 4-connected planar dual is the graph of a corner polyhedron.

Based on our graph-theoretic characterizations of these classes of polyhedron, we find efficient algorithms for finding a poly-

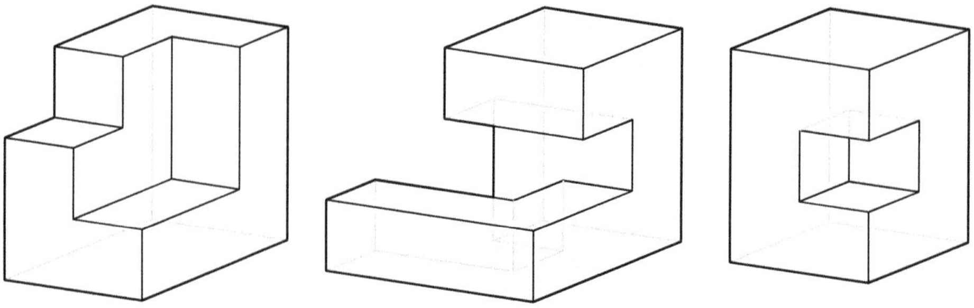

Figure 1: Three types of simple orthogonal polyhedron: Left, a corner polyhedron. Center, an *xyz* polyhedron that is not a corner polyhedron. Right, a simple orthogonal polyhedron that is not an *xyz* polyhedron.

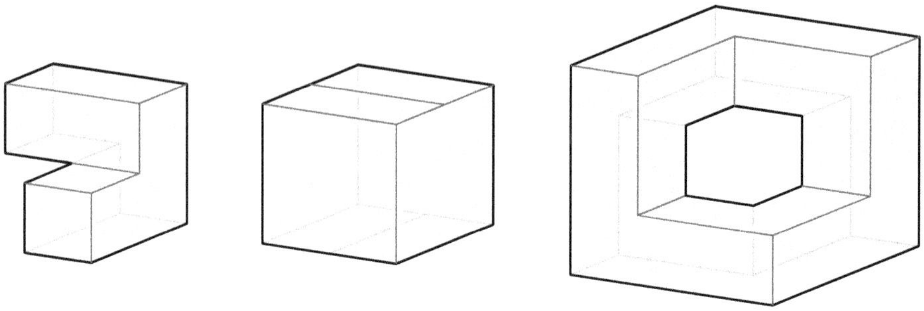

Figure 2: Three orthogonal polyhedra that are not simple: Left, more than three edges meet at a vertex. Center, the bidiakis cube, with edges and faces meeting non-perpendicularly. Right, an orthogonally convex orthogonal polyhedron (a polyhedron such that every axis parallel line intersects it in a single interval) that does not have the topology of a sphere.

hedral realization of the graph of any corner polyhedron, *xyz* polyhedron, or simple orthogonal polyhedron. Beyond the obvious applications of our results in graph drawing and architectural design, we believe that these results may have applications in image understanding, where an analysis of the structure of polyhedral and rectilinear objects has been an important subtopic [44, 48, 62].

Due to space considerations we defer the proofs of our results to the full version of the paper [32], and provide only a sketch of the main ideas of these proofs here.

2. RELATED WORK

Along with convex polyhedra, two other classes of polyhedra have previously-known graph-theoretic characterizations. They are the *inscribable polyhedra* (convex polyhedra with all vertices on a common sphere or, almost equivalently, graphs of Delaunay triangulations) [22, 40, 57] and a class of nonconvex polyhedra with star-shaped faces all but one of which are visible from a common viewpoint [41].

The most direct predecessor of the work described here is our previous paper on three-dimensional bendless orthogonal graph drawing [30]. We defined an *xyz graph* to be a cubic graph with axis-parallel edges such that the line through each edge does not pass through any other vertex. These graphs may also be defined in a coordinate-free way from their points, as there can be only one way of rotating a point set to form a connected *xyz* graph [50]. From every *xyz* graph one may define an abstract topological surface by forming a face for every coplanar cycle; these faces may be 3-colored by the orientations of their defining planes. Conversely, for every 3-face-colored cubic topological cell complex on a manifold, assigning arbitrary distinct numbers to the faces and using these numbers as the Cartesian coordinates of the incident vertices leads to a representation as an *xyz* graph. As we proved, the planar *xyz* graphs are exactly the bipartite cubic 3-connected planar graphs. Unlike polyhedra, an *xyz* graph may have crossing points where pairs of edges or even triples of edges intersect (Fig. 3, left), and its face cycles may be linked in three-dimensional space. However, in some cases, an *xyz* graph may be drawn as an orthogonal polyhedron, eliminating all edge crossings; for instance, we found an orthogonal polyhedron representation of the truncated octahedron (Fig. 3, right), and based on this example we posed as an open problem the algorithmic question of determining which *xyz* graphs have a crossing-free representation. In this paper we answer that question in the planar case: all of them do, and more strongly all planar *xyz* graphs have not just a crossing-free but a polyhedral representation.

Biedl and Genc [8, 9] investigated analogues for orthogonal polyhedra of a different result about convex polyhedra, Cauchy's theorem [13] that specifying the shape of each face of a convex polyhedron fixes the shape of a whole polyhedron. In contrast, for nonconvex polyhedra, specifying the shape of each face is enough to fix the volume of the whole polyhedron under continuous motions [18] but there exist flexible nonconvex polyhedra with fixed face shapes and an uncountably infinite number of global configurations [17]. Analogously to Cauchy's theorem, fixing the shape of each face is enough to determine the shape of an orthogonally convex polyhedron [8] or more generally of an orthogonal polyhedron with the topology of a sphere [9]. (Note that

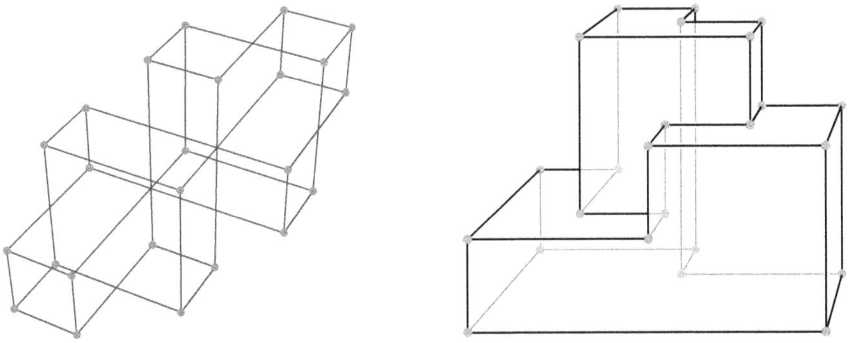

Figure 3: Two xyz graph representations of the truncated octahedron, from [30]. The first has many edge crossings, while the second forms an orthogonal polyhedron but not a corner poyhedron. The results of this paper provide a corner polyhedron representation of the same graph.

in these works a stronger definition of an orthogonally convex polyhedron than ours is used, namely, an orthogonally convex polyhedron in [8] is a polyhedron for which "every intersection with a plane perpendicular to a coordinate axis is a single orthogonally convex polygon.") Although these results concern a different problem, they suggest as do ours that orthogonal polyhedra may be closely analogous to convex polyhedra.

Rectangular layouts form an important two-dimensional analogue of orthogonal polyhedra. These are planar drawings of cubic graphs for which each edge is axis-parallel and has no bends, and in which every face (including the outer face) is a rectangle. Rectangular layouts have applications in the visualization of geographic data [55], floorplan layout in architectural design [26,56], VLSI design [65], treemap information visualization [12], and graph drawing [46]. A plane graph admits a rectangular layout, with a given partition of its outer faces into the sides of an outer rectangle, if and only if a variant of its dual graph (with one dual vertex for each side of the outer rectangle rather than a single vertex for the outer face) is a plane triangulated graph with an exterior quadrilateral and no separating triangles [49]; a closely related characterization also holds for the cubic graphs that can be drawn on a grid with no bends but without requiring that the faces be rectangles [54]. There is a combinatorial bijection between the rectangular layouts of a graph and its *regular edge labelings* or *transversal structures*, (improper) two-colorings of the edges of the dual graph together with an orientation for each edge satisfying certain constraints on the cyclic order in which the colored edges of each orientation meet each dual vertex [46]. The regular edge labelings of a graph form a distributive lattice [35,36] and this lattice structure has algorithmic applications in finding rectangular layouts with additional properties [31,33]. In our three-dimensional problem, as in the two-dimensional case, dual separating triangles form an obstacle to embedding. Additionally, our new results use a structure closely related to a regular edge labeling, with three edge colors rather than two, although the local constraints on colorings and orientations are different than in the two dimensional case.

Schnyder [58] developed algorithms for embedding planar graphs with the vertices on an integer grid, but with edges of arbitrary slopes, based on the concept now known as a *Schnyder wood*, a (non-proper) 3-coloring of the edges of a maximal planar graph together with an orientation on each edge, with constraints about how the colors and orientations must be arranged at each vertex. Felsner and Zickfeld [34] study geometric representations of Schnyder woods as orthogonal surfaces that are very similar to the corner polyhedra we study here. Their representation provides an embedding of the input graph onto the surface found by their representation, but the edges of the embedding do not in general follow the edges of the orthogonal surface. Our results on corner polyhedra also involve colorings and orientations of maximal planar graphs (the dual graphs of the graphs we wish to represent), and our impetus for considering this sort of combinatorial data on a graph came from these two papers as well as from the work on two-dimensional rectangular representations and regular edge labelings. However there seems to be no direct connection between our results and the results of Schnyder, Felsner, and Zickfeld: our colorings are proper and our orientations do not form Schnyder woods, our polyhedral representation is not of the colored and oriented graph but of its dual, and unlike Felsner and Zickfeld we develop a polyhedral representation of a graph in which the graph edges and the polyhedron edges coincide.

More generally there has been a large body of research on planar and spatial embeddings of graphs on low-dimensional grids, or otherwise having a small number of edge slopes. Much of this work allows the edges of the graph to bend in order to follow the edges of the grid, and seeks to minimize the number of bends [2,45,60,63,64]; as we show, for the graphs of corner polyhedra, isometrically projection leads to a hexagonal grid drawing with three slopes and only two bends, improving a bound of three bends by Kant [45] which however applies more generally to all 3-connected cubic planar graphs. Graph drawing researchers have also studied the *slope number* of a graph, the minimum number of distinct edge slopes needed to draw the graph in the plane with straight line edges and no bends [24, 25, 47, 52, 53]. Every graph of an orthogonal polyhedron, and every xyz graph, has slope number three, since a three-dimensional orthogonal representation may be transformed into a planar drawing with three slopes (allowing edge crossings) by axonometric projection. However, not every graph with slope number three comes from an orthogonal drawing in this way; for instance, K_3 has slope number 3 but has no orthogonal drawing, as does Fig. 6.

Both xyz graphs and our polyhedral representations can be viewed as embedding the given graph onto the three-dimensional integer grid, with axis-aligned edges that can have arbitrary lengths. Embedding a graph onto a grid with unit-length edges is NP-complete [6]. Embeddings with unit length edges that additionally preserve distances between vertices farther than one unit apart can be found in polynomial time, when they exist, for two- and three-dimensional integer lattices [27] and hexagonal and diamond lattices [29], but the graphs that have such embeddings (the *partial cubes*) form a restricted subclass of all graphs. The embeddings we consider in this paper only apply to cubic (3-regular) graphs, and of the infinitely many known cubic partial cubes all but one (the Desargues graph) are bipartite polyhedral graphs [28], and may therefore be represented as orthogonal polyhedra using the algorithms we describe here.

A hint that care is needed in defining orthogonal polyhedra is given by Donoso and O'Rourke [23]. As they show, spherical and toroidal polyhedra in which all faces are rectangles (even allowing adjacent faces to be coplanar) must also have all faces and edges axis-parallel for some orientation of the polyhedron, but there exist higher-genus polyhedra with rectangular faces that have more than three edge orientations. Biedl et al. [7] define two interesting subclasses of orthogonal polyhedra, which they call *orthostacks* and *orthotubes*; they also consider orthogonal polyhedra that are somewhat more general than ours, in that they allow the graph of the polyhedron to be disconnected (resulting in faces that are not simple polygons) while we do not.

Bipartite cubic polyhedral graphs and their dual graphs, the Eulerian triangulations, have also been studied independently of their geometric representations, in connection with Barnette's conjecture that all bipartite cubic polyhedral graphs are Hamiltonian [4]. Batagelj, Brinkmann and McKay [5,11] described a method for reducing any Eulerian triangulation to a simpler graph in the same class, based on which Brinkmann and McKay show how to efficiently generate all sufficiently small Eulerian triangulations; they also generate 4-connected Eulerian triangulations by filtering them from the larger set of all Eulerian triangulations. Our proof that 4-connected Eulerian triangulations are dual to corner polyhedra uses a different reduction scheme that remains within the class of 4-connected Eulerian triangulations.

3. CORNER POLYHEDRA AND ROOTED CYCLE COVERS

As stated in the introduction, we define a corner polyhedron to be a simple orthogonal polyhedron with the additional property that three faces (the *back faces*) are oriented towards the vector $(-1,-1,-1)$, and all remaining faces (the *front faces*) are oriented towards the vector $(1,1,1)$. The three back faces necessarily share a vertex, the *hidden vertex*. Parallel projection of a corner polyhedron onto a plane perpendicular to the vector $(1,1,1)$ gives rise to a drawing, the so-called *isometric projection*, in which the axis-parallel edges of the three-dimensional polyhedron are mapped to three sets of parallel lines that form angles of $\pi/3$ with respect to each other; see Fig. 4 (left) for an example. If the edges of the corner polyhedron have integer lengths, the resulting isometric projection is a drawing of all of the vertices of the polyhedron, except the hidden vertex, on the hexagonal lattice. It is possible to include the hidden vertex as well by connecting it to its three neighbors by lattice paths, one of which is straight and the other two have one bend each; the resulting drawing of the whole graph has two bends.

In an isometric drawing of a corner polyhedron, none of the faces can have an interior angle of $5\pi/3$, for any simple orthogonal polyhedron with such a projected angle would have more than three back faces. Additionally, each face (being the projection of a planar orthogonal polygon) has edges of only two of the three possible slopes. Therefore, each face of the drawing has the shape of a *double staircase*: there are two vertices at which the interior angle is $\pi/3$, and the two sequences of interior angles on the paths between these vertices alternate between interior angles of $2\pi/3$ and $4\pi/3$. (Conversely, it follows by Thurston's results on height functions [61] that a drawing in the hexagonal lattice for which all faces have this shape comes from a three-dimensional orthogonal surface.) Because a simple orthogonal polyhedron forms a planar graph in which all faces have an even number of edges, it must be bipartite; one of its two color classes consists of the vertices at which two edges meet at a sharp ($\pi/3$) angle in the isometric drawing, and the other color class contains all the other vertices.

The two-to-one correspondence between interior faces and vertices with sharp angles gives rise to an important structure on the graph of the polyhedron, which we find simpler to describe in terms of its dual graph. The dual graph of a corner polyhedron (as with a bipartite cubic polyhedral graph more generally) is an *Eulerian triangulation*, a maximal planar graph in which every vertex has even degree. It has a unique planar embedding, for which all the faces are triangles; the triangles may be two-colored so that the two triangles that share each edge have different colors. Within each interior face of the projected corner polyhedron, we connect the dual vertex to its two sharp corners. The result of forming these connections is a structure that we call a *rooted cycle cover*: a set of vertex-disjoint cycles in the dual Eulerian triangulation, that cover every dual vertex except for the three vertices of the *root triangle* dual to the hidden vertex, and that include exactly one edge from every triangle with the same color as the root triangle. Conversely, as we show, every rooted cycle cover of an Eulerian triangulation gives rise to a corner polyhedron representation of its dual graph. This equivalence between a combinatorial structure (a rooted cycle cover) and a geometric structure (a corner polyhedron) is a key component of our characterization of the graphs of corner polyhedra.

Specifically, we prove the following results:

THEOREM 1. *A graph $\mathcal{G}$ can be represented as a corner polyhedron, with a specified vertex v as the single hidden vertex, if and only if the dual graph of $\mathcal{G}$ has a cycle cover rooted at the triangle dual to v.*

THEOREM 2. *If $\mathcal{G}$ is a cubic bipartite polyhedral graph with a 4-connected dual, then it can be represented as a corner polyhedron.*

If Δ is an Eulerian triangulation (the dual to a cubic bipartite planar graph), with a chosen root triangle δ, then we may uniquely two-color the triangles of Δ so that any two adjacent triangles have distinct colors. For any separating triangle γ of Δ, this coloring will assign equal colors to the three triangles that are on the side of γ that does not contain δ and that are incident to one of the edges of γ. We say that γ has *even parity* if these three triangles have the same color as δ, and *odd parity* otherwise.

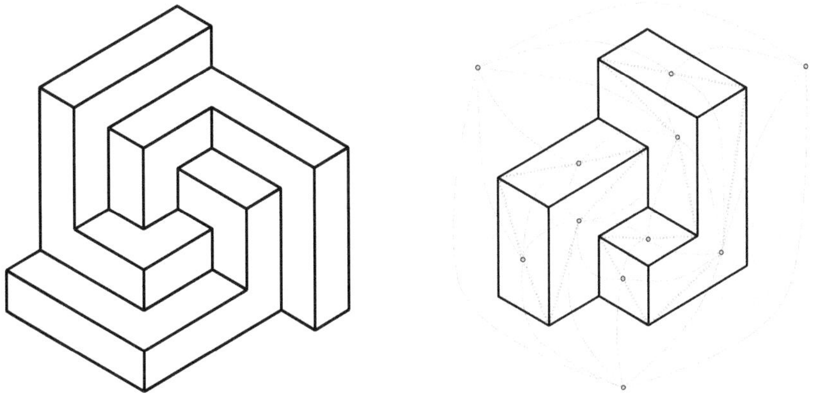

Figure 4: Left: isometric projection of a corner polyhedron for a truncated rhombic dodecahedron. Right: connecting each sharp corner of a visible face to the dual vertex of the face produces a rooted cycle cover.

THEOREM 3. *If $\mathcal{G}$ is a cubic bipartite graph with a non-4-connected dual, and v is any vertex of $\mathcal{G}$, then $\mathcal{G}$ has a corner representation for which v is the hidden vertex if and only if all separating triangles have odd parity with respect to the root triangle dual to v.*

In the rest of this section, we provide a rough sketch of our proofs of the claims stated above. The detailed proof of Theorem 1 comprises Appendices II, III, and IV, the proof of Theorem 2 is in Appendices V and VI, and the proof of Theorem 3 is in Appendix VII of the full version of the paper [32].

From a corner polyhedron representation of a graph $\mathcal{G}$, we can derive several associated combinatorial structures, the first of which is a rooted cycle cover of the dual of $\mathcal{G}$ as described above. The graph of the polyhedron also has a unique 3-edge-coloring given by the orientations of its edges. These colors may be carried over to the dual Eulerian triangulation Δ, but in Δ they do not form an edge coloring but rather a *rainbow partition*, a partition of the edges of Δ into three monochromatic subgraphs such that each triangle of Δ participates in each of these subgraphs. Each monochromatic subgraph must be biconnected, which implies that it can be oriented as an st-planar graph with the two terminals on the chosen root triangle. From the corner polyhedron representation we may also determine an orientation for each edge of Δ based on which of the two adjacent primal faces is on which side of the edge in the isometric drawing; this orientation can be shown to be simultaneously st-planar in each monochromatic subgraph, and the requirement that each face of the corner polyhedron is a double staircase may be translated via planar duality into local consistency conditions on the orientations of the edges incident to each dual vertex.

Conversely, given a rooted cycle cover of a graph, we can use it to construct a similar set of combinatorial structures. Because the graph is 3-connected, planar, and bipartite, a theorem of Heawood [39] states that it is 3-face-colorable; the face coloring gives rise to an edge coloring that dualizes to a rainbow partition. A local transformation rule allows us to derive from the cycle cover an orientation on the edges of the dual Eulerian triangulation, in which the orientations of the edges alternate around each vertex except within two triangles incident to the vertex, which both have the same color as the root triangle in the two-coloring of triangles dual to the bipartition of the input graph. We call a rainbow partition together with an orientation having this local alternation property a *regular edge labeling*. Based on the alternating edge orientations at each vertex, we can show that a regular edge labeling is simultaneously st-planar in each monochromatic subgraph, and that unions of two monochromatic subgraphs (with the orientation reversed in one of the two) are again st-planar. A regular edge labeling allows us to construct a polyhedral representation of the given graph by numbering the vertices of each of these bichromatic subgraphs consistently with the st-planar orientation, and using these numbers as the coordinates of the face planes of $\mathcal{G}$. As we show, the polyhedron constructed in this way must be a corner polyhedron. It follows from this construction that $\mathcal{G}$ is the graph of a corner polyhedron if and only if $\mathcal{G}$ has a rooted cycle cover.

To complete our characterization, we need to determine the graphs that have rooted cycle covers. To set up an inductive proof that all 4-connected Eulerian triangulations have rooted cycle covers, we develop a technique for decomposing every 4-connected Eulerian triangulation into smaller 4-connected Eulerian triangulations. The decomposition uses three operations: splitting the graph into two subgraphs along a 4-cycle (with two subcases depending on the parity of the number of vertices inside the cycle), removing a pair of adjacent degree-four vertices, and collapsing two opposite edges of a degree-four vertex. We prove that these decomposition steps always reduce any 4-connected Eulerian triangulation into smaller graphs, with two base cases: the 6-vertex octahedron and an 11-vertex graph shown as the shaded triangulation in Figure 4 (right). We use this decomposition to prove inductively that every 4-connected Eulerian triangulation has a rooted cycle cover, by showing how to transform cycle covers for the smaller graphs in the decomposition into a cycle cover for the whole graph. Therefore, by the above equivalence between cycle covers and corner polyhedron representations, every cubic bipartite graph with a 4-connected dual can be represented as a corner polyhedron.

If a bipartite cubic graph does not have a 4-connected dual, it may still have a rooted cycle cover. In one direction of the full characterization, if all separating triangles have odd parity, we may show that a rooted cycle cover exists by splitting the dual graph at all of its separating triangles,

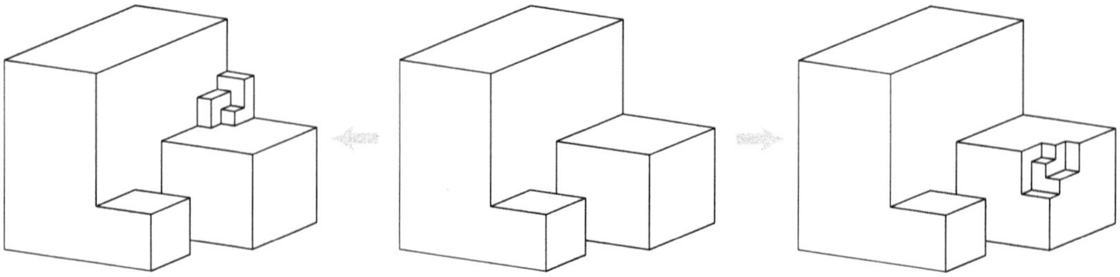

Figure 5: Gluing a corner polyhedron onto a convex or concave vertex of an orthogonal polyhedron (right) and onto a saddle vertex (left).

finding a cycle cover separately for each subgraph created by this splitting process, and forming a cycle cover of the original graph as the union of these separate cycle covers. In the converse direction, if there exists a separating triangle with the same parity as the chosen root vertex, we show by a simple counting argument that no cycle cover can exist.

4. *XYZ* POLYHEDRA

Our previous paper [30] defined an *xyz graph* to be cubic graphs embedded in three dimensional space, with axis parallel edges, such that the line through each edge passes through no other vertices. We can extend this definition to an *xyz polyhedron*, a simple orthogonal polyhedron whose skeleton forms an *xyz* graph. An alternative weaker definition is that a *singly-intersecting* orthogonal polyhedron is a simple orthogonal polyhedron with the property that, for any two faces with a nonempty intersection, their intersection is a single line segment. Geometrically, the intersection of two faces lies along the line of intersection of their planes, so a singly-intersecting polyhedron must be an *xyz* polyhedron, but not necessarily vice versa. However, the graphs of the two classes of polyhedra are the same: by perturbing the face planes of a singly-intersecting polyhedron, one may obtain an *xyz* polyhedron that represents the same graph.

As we showed in our previous paper, a planar *xyz* graph must be 3-connected and bipartite, and the same results hold for *xyz* polyhedra. Our main result is a converse to this:

THEOREM 4. *The following three classes of graphs are equivalent:*

- *Cubic 3-connected bipartite planar graphs,*
- *Graphs of xyz polyhedra, and*
- *Graphs of singly-intersecting orthogonal polyhedra.*

The idea of the proof is to use induction on the number of separating triangles in the dual Eulerian triangulation. If there are no separating triangles, the given graph has a corner polyhedron representation and we are done. Otherwise, we find a separating triangle that splits the dual graph into two smaller Eulerian triangulations, one of them four-connected. By induction, the other one has a polyhedral representation, and we can replace one vertex of this polyhedron by a very small copy of a corner polyhedron representing the other split component, forming a representation of the overall polyhedron. Fig. 5 demonstrates an example of the operations needed to glue small copies of split components into a larger polyhedron.

The repeated replacement of polyhedron vertices by small corner polyhedra may eventually lead to features of exponentially small size, but this issue can be sidestepped by replacing the coordinates of the faces by small integers, leading to a polyhedral representation in which all vertex coordinates are integers in the interval $[1, n/4]$.

The proof is in the full paper [32].

5. SIMPLE ORTHOGONAL POLYHEDRA

As can be seen in Fig. 1 (right), the graph of an arbitrary simple orthogonal polyhedra may not always be 3-connected, although it is always 2-connected: if any vertex v is deleted, any path through v connecting any two other vertices u and w may be replaced by detouring around the boundary of one of the faces incident to v. Pairs of faces of the polyhedron may meet in multiple edges, and the removal of any two of these edges (or the removal of endpoints from any two of these edges) leaves a disconnected graph. Therefore, there exist graphs of simple orthogonal polyhedra that are not graphs of *xyz* polyhedra, and we need to use a more general class of graphs to characterize the simple orthogonal polyhedra. Replacing the 3-connectivity condition in the characterization of *xyz* polyhedra by 2-connectivity would be too general, however. Not every 2-connected bipartite 3-regular graph is the graph of a simple orthogonal polyhedron; for instance, the graph depicted in Fig. 6 is not the graph of a simple orthogonal polyhedron, as the results in this section will show.

Instead, our characterization uses the SPQR tree, a standard tool for representing the planar embeddings of a graph in terms of its triconnected components [20, 21, 38, 42, 51]. The triconnected components of a graph may be multigraphs rather than simple graphs; for instance, the graph shown in Fig. 6 has seven triconnected components: three cubes (the R nodes of an SPQR tree), three 4-cycles (the S nodes of an SPQR tree), and a multigraph with two vertices and three edges (the P node of an SPQR tree).

THEOREM 5. *The following three classes of graphs are equivalent:*

- *Cubic 2-connected graphs in which every triconnected component is either a bipartite polyhedral graph or an even cycle,*
- *Bipartite cubic planar graphs in which the removal of any two vertices leaves at most two connected components (counting an edge between the two vertices as a component, if one exists), and*

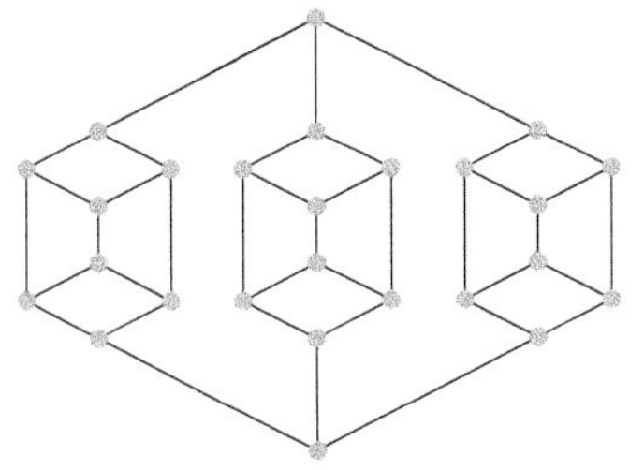

Figure 6: A 2-connected bipartite cubic planar graph that is not the graph of a simple orthogonal polyhedron.

- *Graphs of simple orthogonal polyhedra.*

For instance, the graph of Fig. 6 cannot be the graph of a simple orthogonal polyhedron, because removing its top and bottom vertex leaves three connected components, and because it has a multigraph as one of its triconnected components.

The main idea of the proof of Theorem 5 (for which see the full version of the paper [32]) is to follow the structure given by a decomposition of the graph into triconnected components. In one direction, we show that when any simple orthogonal polyhedron is decomposed into triconnected components, each non-cyclic component inherits a (nonpolyhedral) geometric embedding based on which we can rule out the possibility that any component forms a P node in the SPQR tree. In the converse direction, when we are given a graph in which each triconnected component has the stated form, we represent each bipartite polyhedral triconnected component as a simple orthogonal polyhedron using the results of the previous section, and use the even cycles in the SPQR tree to guide a sequence of gluing steps that combine each of these polyhedral pieces into a single polyhedron that represents the whole graph. Our proof technique leads to a stronger result: if $\mathcal{G}$ is the graph of a simple orthogonal polyhedron, then every planar embedding of $\mathcal{G}$ can be represented as a simple orthogonal polyhedron.

6. ALGORITHMS

Below we outline an algorithm that takes a 2-connected cubic planar graph as an input and embeds it as a simple orthogonal polyhedron, when such a representation exists. The algorithms for constructing xyz polyhedra and corner polyhedra are similar but with fewer steps.

1. Decompose the graph into its triconnected components, as represented by an SPQR tree, in linear time [38,42]. Check that the SPQR tree does not contain any P nodes (triconnected components that are multigraphs rather than simple graphs). If it does, report that no orthogonal polyhedral representation exists and abort the algorithm.

2. Transform each triconnected component that is not a cycle into its dual Eulerian triangulation, using a linear time planar embedding algorithm [43]. If any component is nonplanar or has a non-Eulerian dual, report that no orthogonal polyhedral representation exists and abort the algorithm.

3. Partition each Eulerian triangulation into 4-connected Eulerian triangulations by splitting it on its separating triangles. All separating triangles may be found in $O(n)$ time [14,15].

4. Recursively decompose each 4-connected Eulerian triangulation into simpler 4-connected Eulerian triangulations using separating 4-cycles, pairs of adjacent degree-4 vertices, and isolated degree-4 vertices. While returning from the recursion, undo the decomposition and build a cycle cover for the Eulerian triangulation.

5. Convert the cycle covers into regular edge labelings by a simple local pattern matching rule.

6. For each pair of colors x and y in the rainbow partition, construct the subgraph Δ_{xy} formed by edges with those two colors, oriented by reversing the orientations of one of the two colors from the orientation given by the regular edge labeling, and find an st-numbering of each such graph using breadth-first search.

7. For each graph dual to one of the 4-connected Eulerian triangulations, use the st-numbering to construct a representation of the graph as a corner polyhedron: the coordinates of each vertex of the corner polyhedron are triples of numbers from the st-numbering, one from each of the three bichromatic subgraphs of Δ.

8. Glue the corner polyhedra together to form orthogonal polyhedra dual to each non-4-connected Eulerian triangulation. In order to perform this step and the next one efficiently, we represent vertex coordinates implicitly throughout these steps, as positions within a doubly linked list, and after the gluing is completed convert these implicit positions back into numeric values.

9. Glue 3-connected polyhedra together to form arbitrary simple orthogonal polyhedra.

The algorithm needs $O(n)$ expected time when implemented using randomized hash tables; deterministically, it can be implemented to run in $O(n(\log\log n)^2/(\log\log\log n))$ time with linear space. The most complicated step, and the only step that uses more than $O(n)$ deterministic running time, is the one in which we decompose each 4-connected Eulerian triangulation into simpler 4-connected Eulerian triangulations; this step uses a data structure for testing adjacency of pairs of vertices in a dynamic plane graph. If the adjacency testing data structure is implemented using linear-space deterministic integer searching data structures [1], the total running time is $O(n(\log\log n)^2/(\log\log\log n))$, whereas if it is implemented using hash tables, the total expected running time is $O(n)$.

THEOREM 6. *We may construct a representation of a given graph as a corner polyhedron, xyz polyhedron, or simple orthogonal polyhedron, when such a representation exists, in $O(n)$ randomized expected time, or deterministically in $O(n(\log\log n)^2/(\log\log\log n))$ time with linear space.*

Detailed descriptions of each step together with the running time analyses are given in the full paper [32].

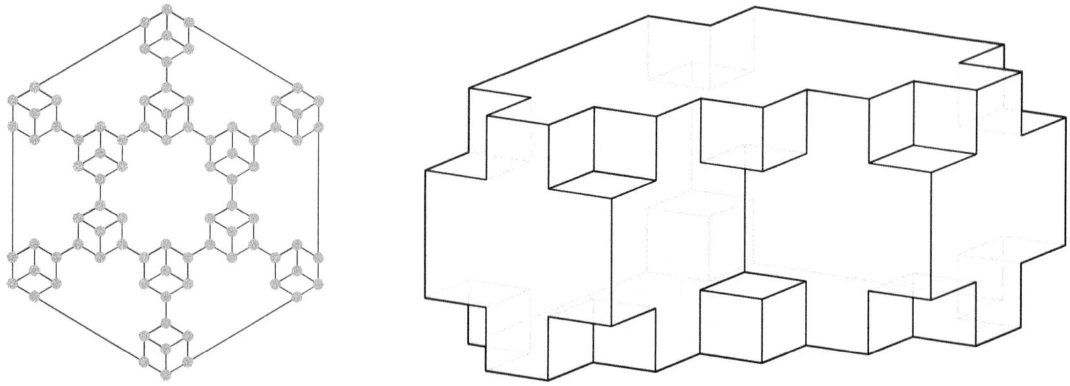

Figure 7: A bipartite cubic polyhedral graph (left) that has no orthogonally convex representation as a simple orthogonal polyhedron, and its representation as a nonconvex simple orthogonal polyhedron (right).

7. CONCLUSIONS

We have defined three interesting classes of orthogonal polyhedra, and provided exact graph-theoretic characterizations of the graphs that may be represented by these polyhedra. In particular, every bipartite cubic polyhedral graph has a representation as an orthogonal polyhedron. The following problems remain open for additional investigation:

- Corner polyhedra are orthogonally convex, and orthogonally convex simple polyhedra may be represented as xyz polyhedra, so the orthogonally convex simple polyhedra are sandwiched between two of the classes of polyhedron that we can precisely characterize and for which we provide polynomial time recognition algorithms. However, not every bipartite cubic polyhedral graph has an orthogonally convex representation: if enough dual separating triangles share edges with each other, they may interfere with each other and force any orthogonal polyhedral representation to be nonconvex (Fig. 7). Is there a simple condition on the position of the dual separating triangles that characterizes orthogonally convex simple orthogonal polyhedra, and can we test this condition in polynomial time?

- The *orthostacks* defined by Biedl et al. [7] are also intermediate between corner polyhedra and xyz polyhedra. Can we characterize their graphs?

- Our results hold only for orthogonal polyhedra with three perpendicular edges at each vertex. Can we relax this requirement, and either allow non-perpendicular edges (as in the bidiakis cube, Fig. 2, center) or more than three edges per vertex (Fig. 2, left)? In this case, as the figures show, the graph of the polyhedron does not need to be bipartite. Is there some way of replacing problematic vertices by small subgraphs in which all vertices have degree three and all edges are perpendicular, allowing the methods from this paper to apply?

- Since nonplanar xyz graph recognition is hard [30] it seems likely that it will also be difficult to determine whether a given graph is the graph of an orthogonal polyhedron with nonzero genus (Fig. 2, right), but what about graphs for which an xyz graph representation is already known? In that case, how difficult is it to detemine whether the faces of the xyz representation can be untangled to form a polyhedral representation?

Acknowledgements

Work of David Eppstein was supported in part by NSF grant 0830403 and by the Office of Naval Research under grant N00014-08-1-1015. We thank Patrizio Angelini, Mike Dillencourt, Fabrizio Frati, Mike Goodrich, Branko Grünbaum, Maarten Löffler, Brendan McKay, and the SoCG reviewers, for many helpful suggestions.

8. REFERENCES

[1] A. A. Andersson and M. Thorup. Tight(er) worst-case bounds on dynamic searching and priority queues. *Proc. 32nd ACM Symp. Theory of Computing (STOC 2000)*, pp. 335–342, 2000, doi:10.1145/335305.335344.

[2] S. Aziza and T. Biedl. Hexagonal grid drawings: algorithms and lower bounds. *Proc. 12th Int. Symp. Graph Drawing (GD 2004)*, 3383 edition, pp. 18–24. Springer-Verlag, Lecture Notes in Computer Science, 2005.

[3] M. L. Balinski. On the graph structure of convex polyhedra in n-space. *Pacific J. Math.* 11(2):431–434, 1961, `http://projecteuclid.org/euclid.pjm/1103037323`.

[4] D. W. Barnette. Conjecture 5. *Recent Progress in Combinatorics*, p. 343. Academic Press, 1969.

[5] V. Batagelj. An improved inductive definition of two restricted classes of triangulations of the plane. *Combinatorics and Graph Theory, Warsaw, 1987*, 25 edition, pp. 11–18. PWN, Banach Center Publ., 1989.

[6] S. Bhatt and S. Cosmodakis. The complexity of minimizing wire lengths in VLSI layouts. *Inform. Proc. Lett.* 25:263–267, 1987, doi:10.1016/0020-0190(87)90173-6.

[7] T. Biedl, E. Demaine, M. Demaine, A. Lubiw, M. Overmars, J. O'Rourke, S. Robbins, and S. Whitesides. Unfolding some classes of orthogonal polyhedra. *Proc. 10th Canadian Conference on Computational Geometry (CCCG'98)*, 1998, `http://erikdemaine.org/papers/CCCG98b/`.

[8] T. Biedl and B. Genc. When can a graph form an orthogonal polyhedron? *Proc. 16th Canadian Conf. Computational Geometry (CCCG 2004)*, pp. 53–56, 2004, `http://www.cccg.ca/proceedings/2004/15.pdf`.

[9] T. Biedl and B. Genc. Cauchy's theorem for orthogonal polyhedra of genus 0. *Proc. 17th European Symp. Algorithms (ESA 2009)*, 5757 edition, pp. 71–83. Springer-Verlag, Lecture Notes in Computer Science, 2009, doi:10.1007/978-3-642-04128-0_7.

[10] J. Bokowski and A. Guedes de Oliveira. On the generation of oriented matroids. *Discrete and Computational Geometry* 24(2–3):197–208, 2000, doi:10.1007/s004540010027.

[11] G. Brinkmann and B. D. McKay. Fast generation of planar graphs. *Communications in Mathematical and in Computer Chemistry* 58(2):323–357, 2007, `http://cs.anu.edu.au/people/bdm/papers/plantri-full.pdf`.

[12] M. Bruls, K. Huizing, and J. J. van Wijk. Squarified treemaps. *Data Visualization 2000: Proc. Joint Eurographics and IEEE TCVG Symp. on Visualization*, pp. 33–42. Springer-Verlag, 2000, `http://www.win.tue.nl/~vanwijk/stm.pdf`.

[13] A. L. Cauchy. Sur les polygones et polyèdres. *J. École Polytechnique* 19:87–98, 1813.

[14] N. Chiba and T. Nishizeki. Arboricity and subgraph listing algorithms. *SIAM J. Comput.* 14(1):210–223, 1985, doi:10.1137/0214017.

[15] M. Chrobak and D. Eppstein. Planar orientations with low out-degree and compaction of adjacency matrices. *Theoretical Computer Science* 86(2):243–266, September 1991, doi:10.1016/0304-3975(91)90020-3.

[16] H. Cohn, M. Larsen, and J. Propp. The shape of a typical boxed plane partition. *New York J. Math.* 4:137–165, 1998, arXiv:math.CO/9801059, `http://nyjm.albany.edu:8000/j/1998/4_137.html`.

[17] R. Connelly. A counterexample to the rigidity conjecture for polyhedra. *Pub. Math. de l'IHÉS* 47:333–338, 1977, doi:10.1007/BF02684342.

[18] R. Connelly, I. Sabitov, and A. Walz. The bellows conjecture. *Beiträge Algebra Geom.* 38:1–10, 1997, `http://www.emis.de/journals/BAG/vol.38/no.1/1.html`.

[19] A. Császár. A polyhedron without diagonals. *Acta Sci. Math. Szeged* 13:140–142, 1949.

[20] G. Di Battista and R. Tamassia. Incremental planarity testing. *Proc. 30th Symp. Foundations of Computer Science (FOCS 1989)*, pp. 436–441, 1989, doi:10.1109/SFCS.1989.63515.

[21] G. Di Battista and R. Tamassia. On-line graph algorithms with SPQR-trees. *Proc. 17th Internat. Colloq. Automata, Languages and Programming (ICALP 1990)*, 443 edition, pp. 598–611. Springer-Verlag, Lecture Notes in Computer Science, 1990, doi:10.1007/BFb0032061.

[22] M. B. Dillencourt and W. D. Smith. Graph-theoretical conditions for inscribability and Delaunay realizability. *Discrete Math.* 161(1–3):63–77, 1996, doi:10.1016/0012-365X(95)00276-3.

[23] M. Donoso and J. O'Rourke. Nonorthogonal polyhedra built from rectangles. *Proc. 14th Canadian Conference on Computational Geometry (CCCG'98)*, 2002, arXiv:cs/0110059.

[24] V. Dujmović, D. Eppstein, M. Suderman, and D. R. Wood. Drawings of planar graphs with few slopes and segments. *Computational Geometry Theory &Applications* 38(3):194–212, 2007, doi:10.1016/j.comgeo.2006.09.002, arXiv:math/0606450.

[25] V. Dujmović, M. Suderman, and D. R. Wood. Graph drawings with few slopes. *Computational Geometry Theory &Applications* 38(3):181–193, 2007, doi:10.1016/j.comgeo.2006.08.002, arXiv:math/0606446.

[26] C. F. Earl and L. J. March. Architectural applications of graph theory. *Applications of Graph Theory*, pp. 327–355. Academic Press, 1979.

[27] D. Eppstein. The lattice dimension of a graph. *Eur. J. Combinatorics* 26(5):585–592, July 2005, doi:10.1016/j.ejc.2004.05.001, arXiv:cs.DS/0402028.

[28] D. Eppstein. Cubic partial cubes from simplicial arrangements. *Electronic J. Combinatorics* 13(1, R79):1–14, September 2006, arXiv:math.CO/0510263, `http://www.combinatorics.org/Volume_13/Abstracts/v13i1r79.html`.

[29] D. Eppstein. Isometric diamond subgraphs. *Proc. 16th Int. Symp. Graph Drawing (GD 2008)*, 5417 edition, pp. 384–389. Springer-Verlag, Lecture Notes in Computer Science, 2008, doi:10.1007/978-3-642-00219-9_37, arXiv:0807.2218.

[30] D. Eppstein. The topology of bendless three-dimensional orthogonal graph drawing. *Proc. 16th Int. Symp. Graph Drawing (GD 2008)*, 5417 edition, pp. 78–89. Springer-Verlag, Lecture Notes in Computer Science, 2008, doi:10.1007/978-3-642-00219-9_9, arXiv:0709.4087.

[31] D. Eppstein and E. Mumford. Orientation-constrained rectangular layouts. *Proc. Algorithms and Data Structures Symposium (WADS 2009)*, 5664 edition, pp. 266–277. Springer-Verlag, Lecture Notes in Computer Science, 2009, arXiv:0904.4312.

[32] D. Eppstein and E. Mumford. Steinitz Theorems for Orthogonal Polyhedra, arXiv:arXiv:0912.0537v1. Electronic preprint, 2010.

[33] D. Eppstein, E. Mumford, B. Speckmann, and K. A. B. Verbeek. Area-universal rectangular layouts. *Proc. 25th ACM Symp. Comp. Geom.*, pp. 267–276, 2009, doi:10.1145/1542362.1542411, arXiv:0901.3924.

[34] S. Felsner and F. Zickfeld. Schnyder woods and orthogonal surfaces. *Discrete and Computational Geometry* 40(1):103–126, 2008, doi:10.1007/s00454-007-9027-9.

[35] É. Fusy. Transversal structures on triangulations, with application to straight-line drawing. *Proc. 13th Int. Symp. Graph Drawing (GD 2005)*, 3843 edition, pp. 177–188. Springer-Verlag, Lecture Notes in Computer Science, 2006, doi:10.1007/11618058_17, `http://algo.inria.fr/fusy/Articles/FusyGraphDrawing.pdf`.

[36] É. Fusy. Transversal structures on triangulations: A combinatorial study and straight-line drawings.

Discrete Mathematics 309(7):1870–1894, 2009, doi:10.1016/j.disc.2007.12.093, arXiv:math/0602163.

[37] B. Grünbaum. *Convex Polytopes*. Graduate Texts in Mathematics. Springer-Verlag, Berlin, Heidelberg, and New York, 2nd edition, 2003.

[38] C. Gutwenger and P. Mutzel. A linear time implementation of SPQR-trees. *Proc. 8th Int. Symp. Graph Drawing (GD 2000)*, 1984 edition, pp. 77–90. Springer-Verlag, Lecture Notes in Computer Science, 2001.

[39] P. J. Heawood. On the four-colour map theorem. *Quarterly J. Pure Appl. Math.* 29:270–285, 1898.

[40] C. D. Hodgson, I. Rivin, and W. D. Smith. A characterization of convex hyperbolic polyhedra and of convex polyhedra inscribed in the sphere. *Bull. Amer. Math. Soc.* 27:246–251, 1992, doi:10.1090/S0273-0979-1992-00303-8.

[41] S.-H. Hong and H. Nagamochi. Extending Steinitz' Theorem to Non-convex Polyhedra. Tech. Rep. 2008-012, Department of Applied Mathematics &Physics, Kyoto University, 2008, `http://www.amp.i.kyoto-u.ac.jp/tecrep/abst/2008/2008-012.html`.

[42] J. Hopcroft and R. Tarjan. Dividing a graph into triconnected components. *SIAM J. Comput.* 2(3):135–158, 1973, doi:10.1137/0202012.

[43] J. Hopcroft and R. Tarjan. Efficient Planarity Testing. *J. ACM* 21(4):549–568, 1974, doi:10.1145/321850.321852.

[44] D. A. Huffman. Impossible objects as nonsense sentences. *Machine Intelligence 6*, pp. 295–323. Edinburgh University Press, 1971.

[45] G. Kant. Hexagonal grid drawings. *Proc. Int. Worksh. Graph-Theoretic Concepts in Computer Science*, 657 edition, pp. 263–276. Springer-Verlag, Lecture Notes in Computer Science, 1993, doi:10.1007/3-540-56402-0_53.

[46] G. Kant and X. He. Regular edge labeling of 4-connected plane graphs and its applications in graph drawing problems. *Theoretical Computer Science* 172(1–2):175–193, 1997, doi:10.1016/S0304-3975(95)00257-X.

[47] B. Keszegh, J. Pach, D. Pálvölgyi, and G. Tóth. Drawing cubic graphs with at most five slopes. *Computational Geometry Theory &Applications* 40(2):138–147, 2008, doi:10.1016/j.comgeo.2007.05.003.

[48] L. M. Kirousis and C. H. Papadimitriou. The complexity of recognizing polyhedral scenes. *Journal of Computer and System Sciences* 37(1):14–38, 1988, doi:10.1016/0022-0000(88)90043-8, `http://lca.ceid.upatras.gr/~kirousis/publications/j29.pdf`.

[49] K. Koźmiński and E. Kinnen. Rectangular duals of planar graphs. *Networks* 5(2):145–157, 1985, doi:10.1002/net.3230150202.

[50] M. Löffler and E. Mumford. Connected rectilinear graphs on point sets. *Proc. 16th Int. Symp. Graph Drawing (GD 2008)*, 5417 edition, pp. 313–318. Springer-Verlag, Lecture Notes in Computer Science, 2008, doi:10.1007/978-3-642-00219-9_30, `http://www.cs.uu.nl/research/techreps/repo/CS-2008/2008-028.pdf`.

[51] S. Mac Lane. A structural characterization of planar combinatorial graphs. *Duke Math. J.* 3(3):460–472, 1937, doi:10.1215/S0012-7094-37-00336-3.

[52] P. Mukkamala and M. Szegedy. Geometric representation of cubic graphs with four directions. *Computational Geometry Theory &Applications* 42(9):842–851, 2009, doi:10.1016/j.comgeo.2009.01.005.

[53] J. Pach and D. Pálvölgyi. Bounded degree graphs can have arbitrarily large slope numbers. *Electronic Journal of Combinatorics* 13(1), 2006, `http://www.combinatorics.org/Volume_13/PDF/v13i1n1.pdf`.

[54] M. S. Rahman, T. Nishizeki, and M. Naznin. Orthogonal drawings of plane graphs without bends. *J. Graph Algorithms &Applications* 7(4):335–362, 2003, `http://jgaa.info/accepted/2003/Rahman+2003.7.4.pdf`.

[55] E. Raisz. The rectangular statistical cartogram. *Geographical Review* 24(2):292–296, 1934, doi:10.2307/208794.

[56] I. Rinsma. Rectangular and orthogonal floorplans with required rooms areas and tree adjacency. *Environment and Planning B: Planning and Design* 15:111–118, 1988.

[57] I. Rivin. A characterization of ideal polyhedra in hyperbolic 3-space. *Annals of Mathematics* 143(1):51–70, 1996, doi:10.2307/2118652.

[58] W. Schnyder. Embedding planar graphs on the grid. *Proc. 1st ACM-SIAM Symp. Discrete Algorithms*, pp. 138–148, 1990.

[59] E. Steinitz. Polyeder und Raumeinteilungen. *Encyclopädie der mathematischen Wissenschaften, Band 3 (Geometries)*, pp. 1–139, 1922.

[60] R. Tamassia. On embedding a graph in the grid with the minimum number of bends. *SIAM J. Comput.* 16(3):421–444, 1987, doi:10.1137/0216030.

[61] W. P. Thurston. Conway's tiling groups. *Amer. Mathematical Monthly* 97(8):757–773, 1990, doi:10.2307/2324578.

[62] D. Waltz. Understanding line drawings of scenes with shadows. *The Psychology of Computer Vision*, pp. 19–91. McGraw-Hill, 1975.

[63] D. R. Wood. Lower bounds for the number of bends in three-dimensional orthogonal graph drawings. *J. Graph Algorithms &Applications* 7(1):33–77, 2003, `http://jgaa.info/accepted/2003/Wood2003.7.1.pdf`.

[64] D. R. Wood. Optimal three-dimensional orthogonal graph drawing in the general position model. *Theoretical Computer Science* 299(1–3):151–178, 2003, doi:10.1016/S0304-3975(02)00044-0, `http://www.ms.unimelb.edu.au/~woodd/papers/Wood-TCS03.pdf`.

[65] G. K. H. Yeap and M. Sarrafzadeh. Sliceable floorplanning by graph dualization. *SIAM Journal of Discrete Mathematics* 8(2):258–280, 1995, doi:10.1137/S0895480191266700.

[66] G. M. Ziegler. *Lectures on Polytopes*. Graduate Texts in Mathematics. Springer-Verlag, Berlin, Heidelberg, and New York, 152 edition, 1995.

Author Index

www.ingramcontent.com/pod-product-compliance
Ingram Content Group UK Ltd.
Pitfield, Milton Keynes, MK11 3LW, UK
UKHW051412290926
15471UKWH00009B/1569

9 781450 300162